Blackstone's Statutes on
Intellectual Property

16th edition

edited by

Andrew Christie

BSc, LLB (Hons) (Melb), LLM (Lond), PhD (Cantab)

Chair of Intellectual Property, Melbourne Law School,
University of Melbourne

OXFORD
UNIVERSITY PRESS

Great Clarendon Street, Oxford, OX2 6DP,
United Kingdom

Oxford University Press is a department of the University of Oxford.
It furthers the University's objective of excellence in research, scholarship,
and education by publishing worldwide. Oxford is a registered trade mark of
Oxford University Press in the UK and in certain other countries

First published by Blackstone Press 1992

Thirteenth edition 2016
Fourteenth edition 2018
Fifteenth edition 2020
Sixteenth edition 2023

Public sector information reproduced under Open Government Licence v3.0
(http://www.nationalarchives.gov.uk/doc/open-government-licence/open-government-licence.htm)

Published in the United States of America by Oxford University Press
198 Madison Avenue, New York, NY 10016, United States of America

British Library Cataloguing in Publication Data
Data available

ISBN 978-0-19-285854-2

Printed in the UK by
Bell & Bain Ltd., Glasgow

Contents

Part A Copyright, Design and Related Rights   1

A1. United Kingdom   1

A2. United States   168

A3. European Union   188

Part C   Patents, Plant Varieties and Related Rights   464

Alphabetical contents

Editor's preface

Based on feedback from anonymous reviewers of the previous edition—whose input is gratefully acknowledged, and thanked—it seems clear that the United Kingdom's exit from the European Union hasn't lessened the significance of EU law to the teaching of intellectual property law subjects. Accordingly, this edition includes select provisions from the EU's new Digital Services Act, as well as from the UK's EU (Withdrawal) Act. Also new to this edition is the Convention for the Safeguarding of the Intangible Cultural Heritage, which reflects the increasing attention being given to this type of IP-like subject matter. This edition also incorporates amendments to material in the previous edition that were made by legislation in force as of 17 March 2023.

Andrew Christie
17 March 2023

Blackstone's Statutes
Unsurpassed in authority, reliability, and accuracy

The titles in the Blackstone's Statutes series are collections of carefully reviewed and selected unannotated legislative material and official documents.

We make every effort to ensure titles in the series meet the needs of their target market. They are reviewed by lecturers to match university courses closely and are expertly edited to be manageable in size, whilst retaining their comprehensive coverage.

The editors only include material from legislation that will be valuable to students and lecturers and it is therefore abridged where necessary.

Conventions used in *Blackstone's Statutes on Intellectual Property*
An ellipsis symbol . . . indicates text that has not been included in this edition.

The material in this book is reproduced in its most recent form. Supplementary notes and details of amending provisions are generally not included.

New to this edition

The sixteenth edition of *Blackstone's Statutes on Intellectual Property* has been fully revised and updated to take account of all relevant legislation through to 17 March 2023.

The following international treaty has been included in this edition:

- Convention for the Safeguarding of the Intangible Cultural Heritage 2003

This edition also includes the following new European Union Regulation:

- Digital Services Act Regulation 2022/2065

The UK legislation that has been added to this edition is:

- European Union (Withdrawal) Act 2018

Acknowledgements

We are grateful to the following organisations for consenting to the reproduction of extracts of their respective publications:

Organisation	Material
EPO Published with the permission of the European Patent Office.	European Patent Convention 1973 (2000 revision) Protocol on the Interpretation of Article 69 of the European Patent Convention
UN Environment Programme Published with the permission of the Secretariat to the Convention on Biological Diversity.	Rio Convention on Biological Diversity 1992
UNESCO Published under the Creative Commons—Attribution 3.0 IGO license	Convention for the Safeguarding of the Intangible Cultural Heritage 2003
UPOV Published with the permission of UPOV, the owner of copyright.	UPOV Convention for the Protection of New Varieties of Plants 1961 (1991 revision)
WIPO Material originally provided by the World Intellectual Property Organization (WIPO). The Secretariat of WIPO assumes no liability or responsibility with regard to the transformation of this data.	Paris Convention for the Protection of Industrial Property 1883 (1967 revision with 1979 amendments) Berne Convention for the Protection of Literary and Artistic Works 1886 (1971 revision with 1979 amendments) Lisbon Agreement for the Protection of Appellations of Origin 1958 (1967 revision with 1979 amendments) Rome Convention for the Protection of Performers, Producers of Phonograms and Broadcasting Organisations 1961 WIPO Copyright Treaty 1996 and Agreed Statements WIPO Performances and Phonograms Treaty 1996 and Agreed Statements Geneva Act of the Hague Agreement concerning the International Registration of Industrial Designs 1999 Marrakesh Treaty to Facilitate Access to Published Works for Persons Who Are Blind, Visually Impaired, or Otherwise Print Disabled 2013 Beijing Treaty on Audiovisual Performances 2012 Geneva Act of the Lisbon Agreement on Appellations of Origin and Geographical Indications 2015
WTO Published with the permission of the WTO.	TRIPS Agreement 1994 Doha Declaration on the TRIPS Agreement and Public Health 2001

UK legislation has been sourced from legislation.gov.uk, and is utilised under the Open Government Licence v3.0 at: http://www.nationalarchives.gov.uk/doc/open-government-licence/version/3/. European Union material has been sourced from eur-lex.europa.eu. Only European Union documents published in the *Official Journal of the European Union* are deemed authentic.

Part A

Copyright, Design and Related Rights

A1.   UNITED KINGDOM

Registered Designs Act 1949*

(1949, c. 88)

An Act to consolidate certain enactments relating to registered designs. Amended by Copyright, Designs and Patents Act 1988.   [16 December 1949]

Arrangement of Sections

---

* **Editor's Note:** Contains amendments effected by *Designs and International Trade Marks (Amendments etc.) (EU Exit) Regulations 2019*, and *Intellectual Property (Exhaustion of Rights) (EU Exit) Regulations 2019*. By virtue of the *European Union (Withdrawal Agreement) Act 2020*, these amendments take effect on 'IP completion day', which is defined to be 31 December 2020 at 11:00pm.

Registrable designs and proceedings for registration

1   Registration of designs

(1) A design may, subject to the following provisions of this Act, be registered under this Act on the making of an application for registration.

(2) In this Act 'design' means the appearance of the whole or a part of a product resulting from the features of, in particular, the lines, contours, colours, shape, texture or materials of the product or its ornamentation.

(3) In this Act—

'complex product' means a product which is composed of at least two replaceable component parts permitting disassembly and reassembly of the product; and

'product' means any industrial or handicraft item other than a computer program; and, in particular, includes packaging, get-up, graphic symbols, typographic type-faces and parts intended to be assembled into a complex product.

1B   Requirement of novelty and individual character

(1) A design shall be protected by a right in a registered design to the extent that the design is new and has individual character.

(2) For the purposes of subsection (1) above, a design is new if no identical design or no design whose features differ only in immaterial details has been made available to the public before the relevant date.

(3) For the purposes of subsection (1) above, a design has individual character if the overall impression it produces on the informed user differs from the overall impression produced on such a user by any design which has been made available to the public before the relevant date.

(4) In determining the extent to which a design has individual character, the degree of freedom of the author in creating the design shall be taken into consideration.

(5) For the purposes of this section, a design has been made available to the public before the relevant date if—

(a) it has been published (whether following registration or otherwise), exhibited, used in trade or otherwise disclosed before that date; and

(b) the disclosure does not fall within subsection (6) below.

(6) A disclosure falls within this subsection if—

(a) it could not reasonably have become known before the relevant date in the normal course of business to persons carrying on business in the geographical area comprising the United Kingdom and the European Economic Area and specialising in the sector concerned;

(b) it was made to a person other than the designer, or any successor in title of his, under conditions of confidentiality (whether express or implied);

(c) it was made by the designer, or any successor in title of his, during the period of 12 months immediately preceding the relevant date;

(d) it was made by a person other than the designer, or any successor in title of his, during the period of 12 months immediately preceding the relevant date in consequence of information provided or other action taken by the designer or any successor in title of his; or

(e) it was made during the period of 12 months immediately preceding the relevant date as a consequence of an abuse in relation to the designer or any successor in title of his.

(7) In subsections (2), (3), (5) and (6) above 'the relevant date' means the date on which the application for the registration of the design was made or is treated by virtue of section 3B(2), (3) or (5) or 14(2) of this Act as having been made.

(8) For the purposes of this section, a design applied to or incorporated in a product which constitutes a component part of a complex product shall only be considered to be new and to have individual character—

(a) if the component part, once it has been incorporated into the complex product, remains visible during normal use of the complex product; and

(b) to the extent that those visible features of the component part are in themselves new and have individual character.

(9) In subsection (8) above 'normal use' means use by the end user; but does not include any maintenance, servicing or repair work in relation to the product.

1C   Designs dictated by their technical function

(1) A right in a registered design shall not subsist in features of appearance of a product which are solely dictated by the product's technical function.

(2) A right in a registered design shall not subsist in features of appearance of a product which must necessarily be reproduced in their exact form and dimensions so as to permit the product in which the design is incorporated or to which it is applied to be mechanically connected to, or placed in, around or against, another product so that either product may perform its function.

(3) Subsection (2) above does not prevent a right in a registered design subsisting in a design serving the purpose of allowing multiple assembly or connection of mutually interchangeable products within a modular system.

1D   Designs contrary to public policy or morality

A right in a registered design shall not subsist in a design which is contrary to public policy or to accepted principles of morality.

2   Proprietorship of designs

(1) The author of a design shall be treated for the purposes of this Act as the original proprietor of the design, subject to the following provisions.

(1B) Where, in a case not falling within subsection (1A), a design is created by an employee in the course of his employment, his employer shall be treated as the original proprietor of the design.

(2) Where a design becomes vested, whether by assignment, transmission or operation of law, in any person other than the original proprietor, either alone or jointly with the original proprietor, that other person, or as the case may be the original proprietor and that other person, shall be treated for the purposes of this Act as the proprietor of the design.

(3) In this Act the 'author' of a design means the person who creates it.

(4) In the case of a design generated by computer in circumstances such that there is no human author, the person by whom the arrangements necessary for the creation of the design are made shall be taken to be the author.

3   Applications for registration

(1) An application for the registration of a design or designs shall be filed at the Patent Office in the prescribed manner.

(3) An application for the registration of a design or designs in which national unregistered design right subsists shall be made by the person claiming to be the design right owner.

...

(5) An application for the registration of a design which, owing to any default or neglect on the part of the applicant, has not been completed so as to enable registration to be effected within such time as may be prescribed shall be deemed to be abandoned.

3A   Determination of applications for registration

(1) Subject as follows, the registrar shall not refuse to register a design included in an application under this Act.

(2) If it appears to the registrar that an application for the registration of a design or designs has not been made in accordance with any rules made under this Act, he may refuse to register any design included in it.

(3) If it appears to the registrar that the applicant is not under section 3(2) or (3) or 14 entitled to apply for the registration of a design included in the application, he shall refuse to register that design.

(4) If it appears to the registrar that the application for registration includes—

(a) something which does not fulfil the requirements of section 1(2) of this Act;

(b) a design that does not fulfil the requirements of section 1C or 1D of this Act; or

(c) a design to which a ground of refusal mentioned in Schedule A1 to this Act applies,

he shall refuse to register that thing or that design.

...

3C   Date of registration of designs

(1) Subject as follows, a design, when registered, shall be registered as of the date on which the application was made or is treated as having been made.

...

5   Provisions for secrecy of certain designs

(1) Where, either before or after the commencement of this Act, an application for the registration of a design has been made, and it appears to the registrar that the design is one of a class notified to him by the Secretary of State as relevant for defence purposes, he may give directions for prohibiting or restricting the publication of information with respect to the design, or the communication of such information to any person or class of persons specified in the directions.

...

Effect of registration, &c.

7   Right given by registration

(1) The registration of a design under this Act gives the registered proprietor the exclusive right to use the design and any design which does not produce on the informed user a different overall impression.

(2) For the purposes of subsection (1) above and section 7A of this Act any reference to the use of a design includes a reference to—

(a) the making, offering, putting on the market, importing, exporting or using of a product in which the design is incorporated or to which it is applied; or

(b) stocking such a product for those purposes.

(3) In determining for the purposes of subsection (1) above whether a design produces a different overall impression on the informed user, the degree of freedom of the author in creating his design shall be taken into consideration.

(4) The right conferred by subsection (1) above is subject to any limitation attaching to the registration in question (including, in particular, any partial disclaimer or any declaration by the registrar or a court of partial invalidity).

7A   Infringements of rights in registered designs

(1) Subject as follows, the right in a registered design is infringed by a person who, without the consent of the registered proprietor, does anything which by virtue of section 7 of this Act is the exclusive right of the registered proprietor.

(2) The right in a registered design is not infringed by—

(a) an act which is done privately and for purposes which are not commercial;

(b) an act which is done for experimental purposes;

(c) an act of reproduction for teaching purposes or for the purpose of making citations provided that the conditions mentioned in subsection (3) below are satisfied;

(d) the use of equipment on ships or aircraft which are registered in another country but which are temporarily in the United Kingdom;

(e) the importation into the United Kingdom of spare parts or accessories for the purpose of repairing such ships or aircraft; or

(f) the carrying out of repairs on such ships or aircraft.

(3) The conditions mentioned in this subsection are—

(a) the act of reproduction is compatible with fair trade practice and does not unduly prejudice the normal exploitation of the design; and

(b) mention is made of the source.

(4) The right in a registered design is not infringed by an act which relates to a product in which any design protected by the registration is incorporated or to which it is applied if the product has been put on the market in the United Kingdom or the European Economic Area by the registered proprietor or with his consent.

(5) The right in a registered design of a component part which may be used for the purpose of the repair of a complex product so as to restore its original appearance is not infringed by the use for that purpose of any design protected by the registration.

(6) No proceedings shall be taken in respect of an infringement of the right in a registered design committed before the date on which the certificate of registration of the design under this Act is granted.

7B   Right of prior use

(1) A person who, before the application date, used a registered design in good faith or made serious and effective preparations to do so may continue to use the design for the purposes for which, before that date, the person had used it or made the preparations to use it.

(2) In subsection (1), the 'application date', in relation to a registered design, means—

(a) the date on which an application for the registration was made under section 3, or

(b) where an application for the registration was treated as having been made by virtue of section 14(2), the date on which it was treated as having been so made.

(3) Subsection (1) does not apply if the design which the person used, or made preparations to use, was copied from the design which was subsequently registered.

(4) The right conferred on a person by subsection (1) does not include a right to licence another person to use the design.

(5) Nor may the person on whom the right under subsection (1) is conferred assign the right, or transmit it on death (or in the case of a body corporate on its dissolution), unless—

(a) the design was used, or the preparations for its use were made, in the course of a business, and

(b) the right is assigned or transmitted with the part of the business in which the design was used or the preparations for its use were made.

8   Duration of right in registered design

(1) The right in a registered design subsists in the first instance for a period of five years from the date of the registration of the design.

(2) The period for which the right subsists may be extended for a second, third, fourth and fifth period of five years, by applying to the registrar for an extension and paying the prescribed renewal fee.

...

11 Cancellation of registration

The registrar may, upon a request made in the prescribed manner by the registered proprietor, cancel the registration of a design.

11ZA Grounds for invalidity of registration

(1) The registration of a design may be declared invalid

(a) on the ground that it does not fulfil the requirements of section 1(2) of this Act;

(b) on the ground that it does not fulfil the requirements of sections 1B to 1D of this Act; or

(c) where any ground of refusal mentioned in Schedule A1 to this Act applies.

(1A) The registration of a design ('the later design') may be declared invalid if it is not new or does not have individual character when compared to a design which—

(a) has been made available to the public on or after the relevant date; but

(b) is protected as from a date prior to the relevant date by virtue of registration under this Act or an application for such registration.

(1B) In subsection (1A) 'the relevant date' means the date on which the application for the registration of the later design was made or is treated by virtue of section 3B(2), (3) or (5) or 14(2) of this Act as having been made.

(2) The registration of a design may be declared invalid on the ground of the registered proprietor not being the proprietor of the design and the proprietor of the design objecting.

(3) The registration of a design involving the use of an earlier distinctive sign may be declared invalid on the ground of an objection by the holder of rights to the sign which include the right to prohibit in the United Kingdom such use of the sign.

(4) The registration of a design constituting an unauthorised use of a work protected by the law of copyright in the United Kingdom may be declared invalid on the ground of an objection by the owner of the copyright.

(5) In this section and sections 11ZB, 11ZC and 11ZE of this Act (other than section 11ZE(1)) references to the registration of a design include references to the former registration of a design; and these sections shall apply, with necessary modifications, in relation to such former registrations.

11ZB Applications for declaration of invalidity

(1) Any person interested may make an application to the registrar for a declaration of invalidity under section 11ZA(1)(a) or (b).

(2) Any person concerned by the use in question may make an application to the registrar for a declaration of invalidity under section 11ZA(1)(c).

(3) The relevant person may make an application to the registrar for a declaration of invalidity under section 11ZA(1A) of this Act.

(4) In subsection (3) above 'the relevant person' means, in relation to an earlier design protected by virtue of registration under this Act or an application for such registration, the registered proprietor of the design or (as the case may be) the applicant.

(5) The person able to make an objection under subsection (2), (3) or (4) of section 11ZA of this Act may make an application to the registrar for a declaration of invalidity under that subsection.

(6) An application may be made under this section in relation to a design at any time after the design has been registered.

…

11ZE Effect of cancellation or invalidation of registration

(1) A cancellation of registration under section 11 of this Act takes effect from the date of the registrar's decision or from such other date as the registrar may direct.

(2) Where the registrar declares the registration of a design invalid to any extent, the registration shall to that extent be treated as having been invalid from the date of registration or from such other date as the registrar may direct.

11ZF   Appeals in relation to cancellation or invalidation

An appeal lies from any decision of the registrar under section 11 to 11ZE of this Act.

11A   Powers exercisable for protection of the public interest

(1) Where a report of the Competition and Markets Authority has been laid before parliament containing conclusions to the effect—

...

    (c) on a competition reference, that a person was engaged in an anti-competitive practice which operated or may be expected to operate against the public interest, or

    (d) on a reference under section 11 of the Competition Act 1980 (reference of public bodies and certain other persons), that a person is pursuing a course of conduct which operates against the public interest,

the appropriate Minister or Ministers may apply to the registrar to take action under this section.

...

(3) If on an application under this section it appears to the registrar that the matters specified in the Competition and Markets Authority's report as being those which in the opinion of the Competition and Markets Authority operate or operated or may be expected to operate against the public interest include—

    (a) conditions in licences granted in respect of a registered design by its proprietor restricting the use of the design by the licensee or the right of the proprietor to grant other licences,

he may by order cancel or modify any such condition.

...

12   Use for services of the Crown

The provisions of the First Schedule to this Act shall have effect with respect to the use of registered designs for the services of the Crown and the rights of third parties in respect of such use.

International arrangements

...

Property in and dealing with registered designs and applications

15A   The nature of registered designs

A registered design or an application for a registered design is personal property (in Scotland, incorporeal moveable property).

15B   Assignment, &c. of registered designs and applications for registered designs

(1) A registered design or an application for a registered design is transmissible by assignment, testamentary disposition or operation of law in the same way as other personal or moveable property, subject to the following provisions of this section.

(2) Any transmission of a registered design or an application for a registered design is subject to any rights vested in any other person of which notice is entered in the register of designs, or in the case of applications, notice is given to the registrar.

(3) An assignment of, or an assent relating to, a registered design or application for a registered design is not effective unless it is in writing signed by or on behalf of the assignor or, as the case may be, a personal representative.

(4) Except in Scotland, the requirement in subsection (3) may be satisfied in a case where the assignor or personal representative is a body corporate by the affixing of its seal.

(5) Subsections (3) and (4) apply to assignment by way of security as in relation to any other assignment.

(6) A registered design or application for a registered design may be the subject of a charge (in Scotland, security) in the same way as other personal or moveable property.

(7) The proprietor of a registered design may grant a licence to use that registered design.

(8) Any equities (in Scotland, rights) in respect of a registered design or an application for a registered design may be enforced in like manner as in respect of any other personal or moveable property.

15C Exclusive licences

(1) In this Act an 'exclusive licence' means a licence in writing signed by or on behalf of the proprietor of the registered design authorising the licensee to the exclusion of all other persons, including the person granting the licence, to exercise a right which would otherwise be exercisable exclusively by the proprietor of the registered design.

(2) The licensee under an exclusive licence has the same rights against any successor in title who is bound by the licence as he has against the person granting the licence.

...

Register of designs, &c.

17 Register of designs, &c.

(1) The registrar shall maintain the register of designs, in which shall be entered—

    (a) the names and addresses of proprietors of registered designs;

    (b) notices of assignments and of transmissions of registered designs; and

    (c) such other matters as may be prescribed or as the registrar may think fit.

(2) No notice of any trust, whether express, implied or constructive, shall be entered in the register of designs, and the registrar shall not be affected by any such notice.

...

18 Certificate of registration

(1) The registrar shall grant a certificate of registration in the prescribed form to the registered proprietor of a design when the design is registered.

...

19 Registration of assignments, etc.

(1) Where any person becomes entitled by assignment, transmission or operation of law to a registered design or to a share in a registered design, or becomes entitled as mortgagee, licensee or otherwise to any other interest in a registered design, he shall apply to the registrar in the prescribed manner for the registration of his title as proprietor or co-proprietor or, as the case may be, of notice of his interests, in the register of designs.

...

(5) Except for the purposes of an application to rectify the register under the following provisions of this Act, a document in respect of which no entry has been made in the register of designs under subsection (3) of this section shall not be admitted in any court as evidence of the title of any person to a registered design or share of or interest in a registered design unless the court otherwise directs.

20 Rectification of register

(1) The court may, on the application of the relevant person, order the register of designs to be rectified by the making of any entry therein or the variation or deletion of any entry therein.

...

22 Inspection of registered designs

(1) Where a design has been registered under this Act, there shall be open to inspection at the Patent Office on and after the day on which the certificate of registration is granted—

    (a) the representation or specimen of the design.

This subsection has effect subject to subsection (4) and to any rules made under section 5(2) of this Act.

...

Legal proceedings: general

24A   Action for infringement

(1) An infringement of the right in a registered design is actionable by the registered proprietor.

(2) In an action for infringement all such relief by way of damages, injunctions, accounts or otherwise is available to him as is available in respect of the infringement of any other property right.

(3) This section has effect subject to section 24B of this Act (exemption of innocent infringer from liability).

24B   Exemption of innocent infringer from liability

(1) In proceedings for the infringement of the right in a registered design damages shall not be awarded against a defendant who proves that at the date of the infringement he was not aware, and had no reasonable ground for supposing, that the design was registered.

(2) For the purposes of subsection (1), a person shall not be deemed to have been aware or to have had reasonable grounds for supposing that the design was registered by reason only of the marking of a product with—

(a) the word 'registered' or any abbreviation thereof, or

(b) any word or words expressing or implying that the design applied to, or incorporated in, the product has been registered,

unless the number of the design or a relevant internet link accompanied the word or words or the abbreviation in question.

(2A) The reference in subsection (2) to a relevant internet link is a reference to an address of a posting on the internet—

(a) which is accessible to the public free of charge, and

(b) which clearly associates the product with the number of the design.

(3) Nothing in this section shall affect the power of the court to grant an injunction in any proceedings for infringement of the right in a registered design.

24C   Order for delivery up

(1) Where a person—

(a) has in his possession, custody or control for commercial purposes an infringing article, or

(b) has in his possession, custody or control anything specifically designed or adapted for making articles to a particular design which is a registered design, knowing or having reason to believe that it has been or is to be used to make an infringing article,

the registered proprietor in question may apply to the court for an order that the infringing article or other thing be delivered up to him or to such other person as the court may direct.

. . .

(7) The reference in subsection (1) to an act being done in relation to an article for 'commercial purposes' are to its being done with a view to the article in question being sold or hired in the course of a business.

. . .

24D   Order as to disposal of infringing articles, &c.

(1) An application may be made to the court for an order that an infringing article or other thing delivered up in pursuance of an order under section 24C of this Act shall be—

(a) forfeited to the registered proprietor, or

(b) destroyed or otherwise dealt with as the court may think fit,

or for a decision that no such order should be made.

(2) In considering what order (if any) should be made, the court shall consider whether other remedies available in an action for infringement of the right in a registered design would be adequate to compensate the registered proprietor and to protect his interests.

. . .

24F   Rights and remedies of exclusive licensee

(1) In relation to a registered design, an exclusive licensee has, except against the registered proprietor, the same rights and remedies in respect of matters occurring after the grant of the licence as if the licence had been an assignment.

(2) His rights and remedies are concurrent with those of the registered proprietor; and references to the registered proprietor in the provisions of this Act relating to infringement shall be construed accordingly.

(3) In an action brought by an exclusive licensee by virtue of this section a defendant may avail himself of any defence which would have been available to him if the action had been brought by the registered proprietor.

...

24G   Meaning of 'infringing article'

(1) In this Act 'infringing article', in relation to a design, shall be construed in accordance with this section.

(2) An article is an infringing article if its making to that design was an infringement of the right in a registered design.

(3) An article is also an infringing article if—

   (a) it has been or is proposed to be imported into the United Kingdom, and

   (b) its making to that design in the United Kingdom would have been an infringement of the right in a registered design or a breach of an exclusive licensing agreement relating to that registered design.

(4) Where it is shown that an article is made to a design which is or has been a registered design, it shall be presumed until the contrary is proved that the article was made at a time when the right in the registered design subsisted.

(5) Nothing in subsection (3) shall be construed as applying to an article which may be lawfully imported into the United Kingdom by virtue of anything which forms part of retained EU law as a result of section 3 or 4 of the European Union (Withdrawal) Act 2018.

25   Certificate of contested validity of registration

(1) If in any proceedings before the court the validity of the registration of a design is contested, and it is found by the court that the design is to any extent validly registered, the court may certify that the validity of the registration of the design was contested in those proceedings.

(2) Where any such certificate has been granted, then if in any subsequent proceedings before the court for infringement of the right in the registered design or for invalidation of the registration of the design, a final order or judgment is made or given in favour of the registered proprietor, he shall, unless the court otherwise directs, be entitled to his costs as between solicitor and client:

   Provided that this subsection shall not apply to the costs of any appeal in any such proceedings as aforesaid.

...

Unjustified threats

26   Threats of infringement proceedings

(1) A communication contains a 'threat of infringement proceedings' if a reasonable person in the position of a recipient would understand from the communication that—

   (a) a registered design exists, and

   (b) a person intends to bring proceedings (whether in a court in the United Kingdom or elsewhere) against another person for infringement of the right in the registered design by—

      (i)   an act done in the United Kingdom, or

      (ii) an act which, if done, would be done in the United Kingdom.

(2) References in this section and in section 26C to a 'recipient' include, in the case of a communication directed to the public or a section of the public, references to a person to whom the communication is directed.

26A   Actionable threats

(1) Subject to subsections (2) to (5), a threat of infringement proceedings made by any person is actionable by any person aggrieved by the threat.

(2) A threat of infringement proceedings is not actionable if the infringement is alleged to consist of—

    (a) making a product for disposal, or

    (b) importing a product for disposal.

(3) A threat of infringement proceedings is not actionable if the infringement is alleged to consist of an act which, if done, would constitute an infringement of a kind mentioned in subsection (2)(a) or (b).

(4) A threat of infringement proceedings is not actionable if the threat—

    (a) is made to a person who has done, or intends to do, an act mentioned in subsection (2)(a) or (b) in relation to a product, and

    (b) is a threat of proceedings for an infringement alleged to consist of doing anything else in relation to that product.

(5) A threat of infringement proceedings which is not an express threat is not actionable if it is contained in a permitted communication.

(6) In sections 26C and 26D an 'actionable threat' means a threat of infringement proceedings that is actionable in accordance with this section.

26B   Permitted communications

(1) For the purposes of section 26A(5), a communication containing a threat of infringement proceedings is a 'permitted communication' if—

    (a) the communication, so far as it contains information that relates to the threat, is made for a permitted purpose;

    (b) all of the information that relates to the threat is information that—

        (i)   is necessary for that purpose (see subsection (5)(a) to (c) for some examples of necessary information), and

        (ii) the person making the communication reasonably believes is true.

(2) Each of the following is a 'permitted purpose'—

    (a) giving notice that a registered design exists;

    (b) discovering whether, or by whom, the right in a registered design has been infringed by an act mentioned in section 26A(2)(a) or (b);

    (c) giving notice that a person has a right in or under a registered design, where another person's awareness of the right is relevant to any proceedings that may be brought in respect of the registered design.

(3) The court may, having regard to the nature of the purposes listed in subsection (2)(a) to (c), treat any other purpose as a 'permitted purpose' if it considers that it is in the interests of justice to do so.

(4) But the following may not be treated as a 'permitted purpose'—

    (a) requesting a person to cease doing, for commercial purposes, anything in relation to a product in which a design is incorporated or to which it is applied,

    (b) requesting a person to deliver up or destroy a product in which a design is incorporated or to which it is applied, or

    (c) requesting a person to give an undertaking relating to a product in which a design is incorporated or to which it is applied.

(5) If any of the following information is included in a communication made for a permitted purpose, it is information that is 'necessary for that purpose' (see subsection (1)(b)(i))—

    (a) a statement that a right in a registered design exists and is in force or that an application for registration of a design has been made;

    (b) details of the registered design, or of a right in or under the right in the registered design, which—

        (i)   are accurate in all material respects, and

        (ii) are not misleading in any material respect; and

    (c) information enabling the identification of the products in which the registered design is allegedly incorporated or to which the registered design is allegedly applied.

26C Remedies and defences

(1) Proceedings in respect of an actionable threat may be brought against the person who made the threat for—

    (a) a declaration that the threat is unjustified;

    (b) an injunction against the continuance of the threat;

    (c) damages in respect of any loss sustained by the aggrieved person by reason of the threat.

(2) It is a defence for the person who made the threat to show that the act in respect of which proceedings were threatened constitutes (or if done would constitute) an infringement of the right in the registered design.

(3) It is a defence for the person who made the threat to show—

    (a) that, despite having taken reasonable steps, the person has not identified anyone who has done an act mentioned in section 26A(2)(a) or (b) in relation to the product which is the subject of the threat, and

    (b) that the person notified the recipient, before or at the time of making the threat, of the steps taken.

26D Professional advisers

(1) Proceedings in respect of an actionable threat may not be brought against a professional adviser (or any person vicariously liable for the actions of that professional adviser) if the conditions in subsection (3) are met.

(2) In this section 'professional adviser' means a person who, in relation to the making of the communication containing the threat—

    (a) is acting in a professional capacity in providing legal services or the services of a trade mark attorney or a patent attorney, and

    (b) is regulated in the provision of legal services, or the services of a trade mark attorney or a patent attorney, by one or more regulatory bodies (whether through membership of a regulatory body, the issue of a licence to practise or any other means).

(3) The conditions are that—

    (a) in making the communication the professional adviser is acting on the instructions of another person, and

    (b) when the communication is made the professional adviser identifies the person on whose instructions the adviser is acting.

(4) This section does not affect any liability of the person on whose instructions the professional adviser is acting.

(5) It is for a person asserting that subsection (1) applies to prove (if required) that at the material time—

    (a) the person concerned was acting as a professional adviser, and

    (b) the conditions in subsection (3) were met.

26E Supplementary: pending registration

(1) In sections 26 and 26B references to a registered design include references to a design in respect of which an application for registration has been made under section 3.

(2) Where the threat of infringement proceedings is made after an application for registration has been made (but before registration) the reference in section 26C(2) to 'the registered design' is to be treated as a reference to the design registered in pursuance of that application.

26F Supplementary: proceedings for delivery up etc.

In section 26(1)(b) the reference to proceedings for infringement of the right in a registered design includes a reference to—

    (a) proceedings for an order under section 24C (order for delivery up), and

    (b) proceedings for an order under section 24D (order as to disposal of infringing articles).

    ...

Offences

...

35   Fine for falsely representing a design as registered

(1) If any person falsely represents that a design applied to, or incorporated in, any product sold by him is registered, he shall be liable on summary conviction to a fine not exceeding level 3 on the standard scale; and for the purposes of this provision a person who sells a product having stamped, engraved or impressed thereon or otherwise applied thereto the word 'registered', or any other word expressing or implying that the design applied to, or incorporated in, the product is registered, shall be deemed to represent that the design applied to, or incorporated in, the product is registered.

(2) If any person, after the right in a registered design has expired, marks any product to which the design has been applied or in which it has been incorporated with the word 'registered', or any word or words implying that there is a subsisting right in the design under this Act, or causes any such product to be so marked, he shall be liable on summary conviction to a fine not exceeding level 1 on the standard scale.

(3) For the purposes of this section, the use in the United Kingdom in relation to a design—

(a) of the word 'registered', or

(b) of any other word or symbol importing a reference (express or implied) to registration, shall be deemed to be a representation as to registration under this Act unless it is shown that the reference is to registration elsewhere than in the United Kingdom and that the design is in fact so registered.

35ZA   Offence of unauthorised copying etc. of design in course of business

(1) A person commits an offence if—

(a) in the course of a business, the person intentionally copies a registered design so as to make a product—

(i) exactly to that design, or

(ii) with features that differ only in immaterial details from that design, and

(b) the person does so—

(i) knowing, or having reason to believe, that the design is a registered design, and

(ii) without the consent of the registered proprietor of the design.

(2) Subsection (3) applies in relation to a product where a registered design has been intentionally copied so as to make the product—

(a) exactly to the design, or

(b) with features that differ only in immaterial details from the design.

(3) A person commits an offence if—

(a) in the course of a business, the person offers, puts on the market, imports, exports or uses the product, or stocks it for one or more of those purposes,

(b) the person does so without the consent of the registered proprietor of the design, and

(c) the person does so knowing, or having reason to believe, that—

(i) a design has been intentionally copied without the consent of the registered proprietor so as to make the product exactly to the design or with features that differ only in immaterial details from the design, and

(ii) the design is a registered design.

(4) It is a defence for a person charged with an offence under this section to show that the person reasonably believed that the registration of the design was invalid.

(5) It is also a defence for a person charged with an offence under this section to show that the person—

(a) did not infringe the right in the design, or

(b) reasonably believed that the person did not do so.

(6) The reference in subsection (3) to using a product in the course of a business does not include a reference to using it for a purpose which is merely incidental to the carrying on of the business.

...

Supplemental

...

43   Savings

(2) Nothing in this Act shall affect the right of the Crown or of any person deriving title directly or indirectly from the Crown to sell or use products forfeited under the laws relating to customs or excise.

44   Interpretation

(1) In this Act, except where the context otherwise requires, the following expressions have the meanings hereby respectively assigned by them, that is to say—

...

'assignee' includes the personal representative of a deceased assignee, and references to the assignee of any person include references to the assignee of the personal representative or assignee of that person;

'author', in relation to a design, has the meaning given by section 2(3) and (4);

'complex product' has the meaning assigned to it by section 1(3) of this Act;

'the court' shall be construed in accordance with section 27 of this Act;

'design' has the meaning assigned to it by section 1(2) of this Act;

'electronic communication' has the same meaning as in the Electronic Communications Act 2000;

'employee', 'employment' and 'employer' refer to employment under a contract of service or of apprenticeship;

'national unregistered design right' means design right within the meaning of Part III of the Copyright, Designs and Patents Act 1988;

'prescribed' means prescribed by rules made by the Secretary of State under this Act;

'product' has the meaning assigned to it by section 1(3) of this Act;

'proprietor' has the meaning assigned to it by section two of this Act;

'registered proprietor' means the person or persons for the time being entered in the register of designs as proprietor of the design;

'registrar' means the Comptroller-General of Patents Designs and Trade Marks;

(4) For the purposes of subsection (1) of section 14 of this Act, the expression 'personal representative', in relation to a deceased person, includes the legal representative of the deceased appointed in any country outside the United Kingdom.

45   Application to Scotland

(1) In the application of this Act to Scotland—

'account of profits' means accounting and payment of profits;

'accounts' means count, reckoning and payment;

'arbitrator' means arbiter;

'assignment' means assignation;

'claimant' means pursuer;

'costs' means expenses;

'defendant' means defender;

'delivery up' means delivery;

'injunction' means interdict;

'interlocutory relief' means interim remedy.

(1A) In the application of section 26C(1)(a) (remedy for unjustified threat of infringement proceedings) to Scotland, 'declaration' means 'declarator'.

(2) References to the Crown shall be construed as including references to the Crown in right of the Scottish Administration.

46   Application to Northern Ireland

In the application of this Act to Northern Ireland—

...

(3) References to enactments include enactments comprised in Northern Ireland legislation:

(3A) References to the Crown include the Crown in right of Her Majesty's Government in Northern Ireland:

(4) References to a government department shall be construed as including references to a Northern Ireland department, and in relation to a Northern Ireland department references to the Treasury shall be construed as references to the Department of Finance and Personnel.

(4A) Any reference to a claimant includes a reference to a plaintiff.

47   Application to Isle of Man

This Act extends to the Isle of Man, subject to any modifications contained in an Order made by Her Majesty in Council, and accordingly, subject to any such Order, references in this Act to the United Kingdom shall be construed as including the Isle of Man.

47A   Territorial waters and the continental shelf

(1) For the purposes of this Act the territorial waters of the United Kingdom shall be treated as part of the United Kingdom.

(2) This Act applies to things done in the United Kingdom sector of the continental shelf on a structure or vessel which is present there for purposes directly connected with the exploration of the sea bed or subsoil or the exploitation of their natural resources as it applies to things done in the United Kingdom.

(3) The United Kingdom sector of the continental shelf means the areas designated by order under section 1(7) of the Continental Shelf Act 1964.

...

SCHEDULE A1   GROUNDS FOR REFUSAL OF REGISTRATION IN RELATION TO EMBLEMS ETC.

Grounds for refusal in relation to certain emblems etc.

1.—(1) A design shall be refused registration under this Act if it involves the use of—

(a) the Royal arms, or any of the principal armorial bearings of the Royal arms, or any insignia or device so nearly resembling the Royal arms or any such armorial bearing as to be likely to be mistaken for them or it;

(b) a representation of the Royal crown or any of the Royal flags;

(c) a representation of Her Majesty or any member of the Royal family, or any colourable imitation thereof; or

(d) words, letters or devices likely to lead persons to think that the applicant either has or recently has had Royal patronage or authorisation;

unless it appears to the registrar that consent for such use has been given by or on behalf of Her Majesty or (as the case may be) the relevant member of the Royal family.

(2) A design shall be refused registration under this Act if it involves the use of—

(a) the national flag of the United Kingdom (commonly known as the Union Jack); or

(b) the flag of England, Wales, Scotland, Northern Ireland or the Isle of Man, and it appears to the registrar that the use would be misleading or grossly offensive.

(3) A design shall be refused registration under this Act if it involves the use of—

(a) arms to which a person is entitled by virtue of a grant of arms by the Crown; or

(b) insignia so nearly resembling such arms as to be likely to be mistaken for them;

unless it appears to the registrar that consent for such use has been given by or on behalf of the person concerned and the use is not in any way contrary to the law of arms.

(4) A design shall be refused registration under this Act if it involves the use of a controlled representation within the meaning of the Olympic Symbol etc. (Protection) Act 1995 unless it appears to the registrar that—

(a) the application is made by the person for the time being appointed under section 1(2) of the Olympic Symbol etc. (Protection) Act 1995 (power of Secretary of State to appoint a person as the proprietor of the Olympics association right); or

(b) consent for such use has been given by or on behalf of the person mentioned in paragraph (a) above.

Grounds for refusal in relation to emblems &c. of Paris Convention countries

2.—(1) A design shall be refused registration under this Act if it involves the use of the flag of a Paris Convention country unless—

(a) the authorisation of the competent authorities of that country has been given for the registration; or

(b) it appears to the registrar that the use of the flag in the manner proposed is permitted without such authorisation.

(2) A design shall be refused registration under this Act if it involves the use of the armorial bearings or any other state emblem of a Paris Convention country which is protected under the Paris Convention unless the authorisation of the competent authorities of that country has been given for the registration.

(3) A design shall be refused registration under this Act if—

(a) the design involves the use of an official sign or hallmark adopted by a Paris Convention country and indicating control and warranty;

(b) the sign or hallmark is protected under the Paris Convention; and

(c) the design could be applied to or incorporated in goods of the same, or a similar, kind as those in relation to which the sign or hallmark indicates control and warranty;

unless the authorisation of the competent authorities of that country has been given for the registration.

(4) The provisions of this paragraph as to national flags and other state emblems, and official signs or hallmarks, apply equally to anything which from a heraldic point of view imitates any such flag or other emblem, or sign or hallmark.

(5) Nothing in this paragraph prevents the registration of a design on the application of a national of a country who is authorised to make use of a state emblem, or official sign or hallmark, of that country, notwithstanding that it is similar to that of another country.

Grounds for refusal in relation to emblems &c. of certain international organisations

3.—(1) This paragraph applies to—

(a) the armorial bearings, flags or other emblems; and

(b) the abbreviations and names,

of international intergovernmental organisations of which one or more Paris Convention countries are members.

(2) A design shall be refused registration under this Act if it involves the use of any such emblem, abbreviation or name which is protected under the Paris Convention unless—

(a) the authorisation of the international organisation concerned has been given for the registration; or

(b) it appears to the registrar that the use of the emblem, abbreviation or name in the manner proposed—

(i) is not such as to suggest to the public that a connection exists between

(ii) the organisation and the design; or (ii) is not likely to mislead the public as to the existence of a connection between the user and the organisation.

(3) The provisions of this paragraph as to emblems of an international organisation apply equally to anything which from a heraldic point of view imitates any such emblem.

(4) Nothing in this paragraph affects the rights of a person whose *bona fide* use of the design in question began before 4th January 1962 (when the relevant provisions of the Paris Convention entered into force in relation to the United Kingdom).

Paragraphs 2 and 3: supplementary

4.—(1) For the purposes of paragraph 2 above state emblems of a Paris Convention country (other than the national flag), and official signs or hallmarks, shall be regarded as protected under the Paris Convention only if, or to the extent that—

(a) the country in question has notified the United Kingdom in accordance with Article 6*ter*(3) of the Convention that it desires to protect that emblem, sign or hallmark;

(b) the notification remains in force; and

(c) the United Kingdom has not objected to it in accordance with Article 6*ter*(4) or any such objection has been withdrawn.

(2) For the purposes of paragraph 3 above the emblems, abbreviations and names of an international organisation shall be regarded as protected under the Paris Convention only if, or to the extent that—

(a) the organisation in question has notified the United Kingdom in accordance with Article 6*ter*(3) of the Convention that it desires to protect that emblem, abbreviation or name;

(b) the notification remains in force; and

(c) the United Kingdom has not objected to it in accordance with Article 6*ter*(4) or any such objection has been withdrawn.

(3) Notification under Article 6*ter*(3) of the Paris Convention shall have effect only in relation to applications for the registration of designs made more than two months after the receipt of the notification.

Interpretation

5. In this Schedule—

'a Paris Convention country' means a country, other than the United Kingdom, which is a party to the Paris Convention; and

'the Paris Convention' means the Paris Convention for the Protection of Industrial Property of 20th March 1883.

SCHEDULE 1   PROVISIONS AS TO THE USE OF REGISTERED DESIGNS FOR THE SERVICES OF THE CROWN AND AS TO THE RIGHTS OF THIRD PARTIES IN RESPECT OF SUCH USE

Use of registered designs for services of the Crown

1.—(1) Notwithstanding anything in this Act, any Government department, and any person authorised in writing by a Government department, may use any registered design for the services of the Crown in accordance with the following provisions of this paragraph.

...

(6) For the purposes of this and the next following paragraph 'the services of the Crown' shall be deemed to include—

(a) the supply to the government of any country outside the United Kingdom, in pursuance of an agreement or arrangement between Her Majesty's Government in the United Kingdom and the government of that country, of products required—

(i) for the defence of that country; or

(ii) for the defence of any other country whose government is party to any agreement or arrangement with Her Majesty's said Government in respect of defence matters;

(b) the supply to the United Nations, or the government of any country belonging to that organisation, in pursuance of an agreement or arrangement between Her Majesty's Government and that organisation or government, of products required for any armed forces operating in pursuance of a resolution of that organisation or any organ of that organisation;

and the power of a Government department or a person authorised by a Government department under this paragraph to use a design shall include power to sell to any such government or to the said organisation any products the supply of which is authorised by this sub-paragraph, and to sell to any person any products made in the exercise of the powers conferred by this paragraph which are no longer required for the purpose for which they were made.

(7) The purchaser of any products sold in the exercise of powers conferred by this paragraph, and any person claiming through him, shall have power to deal with them in the same manner as if the rights in the registered design were held on behalf of His Majesty.

Rights of third parties in respect of Crown use

. . .

Compensation for loss of profit

2A.—(1) Where Crown use is made of a registered design, the government department concerned shall pay—

(a) to the registered proprietor, or

(b) if there is an exclusive licence in force in respect of the design, to the exclusive licensee,

compensation for any loss resulting from his not being awarded a contract to supply the products to which the design is applied or in which it is incorporated.

. . .

(6) In this paragraph—

'Crown use', in relation to a design, means the doing of anything by virtue of paragraph 1 which would otherwise be an infringement of the right in the design; and

'the government department concerned', in relation to such use, means the government department by whom or on whose authority the act was done.

. . .

Special provisions as to Crown use during emergency

4.—(1) During any period of emergency within the meaning of this paragraph, the powers exercisable in relation to a design by a Government department, or a person authorised by a Government department under paragraph 1 of this Schedule shall include power to use the design for any purpose which appears to the department necessary or expedient—

(a) for the efficient prosecution of any war in which His Majesty may be engaged;

(b) for the maintenance of supplies and services essential to the life of the community;

(c) for securing a sufficiency of supplies and services essential to the well-being of the community;

(d) for promoting the productivity of industry, commerce and agriculture;

(e) for fostering and directing exports and reducing imports, or imports of any classes, from all or any countries and for redressing the balance of trade;

(f) generally for ensuring that the whole resources of the community are available for use, and are used, in a manner best calculated to serve the interests of the community; or

(g) for assisting the relief of suffering and the restoration and distribution of essential supplies and services in any part of His Majesty's dominions or any foreign countries that are in grave of distress as the result war;

and any reference in this Schedule to the services of the Crown shall be construed as including a reference to the purposes aforesaid.

. . .

Copyright, Designs and Patents Act 1988*

(1988, c. 48)

An Act to restate the law of copyright, with amendments; to make fresh provision as to the rights of performers and others in performances; to confer a design right in original designs; to amend the Registered

---

*   **Editor's Note:** Contains amendments effected by *Broadcasting (Amendment etc.) (EU Exit) Regulations 2019*, *Competition (Amendment etc.) (EU Exit) (No. 2) Regulations 2019*, *Designs and International Trade Marks (Amendments etc.) (EU Exit) Regulations 2019*, *Intellectual Property (Copyright and Related Rights) (Amendment) (EU Exit) Regulations 2019*, and *Intellectual Property (Exhaustion of Rights) (EU Exit) Regulations 2019*. By virtue of the *European Union (Withdrawal Agreement) Act 2020*, these amendments take effect on 'IP completion day', which is defined to be 31 December 2020 at 11:00pm.

Designs Act 1949; to make provision with respect to patent agents and trade mark agents; to confer patents and designs jurisdiction on certain county courts; to amend the law of patents; to make provision with respect to devices designed to circumvent copy-protection of works in electronic form; to make fresh provision penalising the fraudulent application or use of a trade mark an offence; to make provision for the benefit of the Hospital for Sick Children, Great Ormond Street, London; to enable financial assistance to be given to certain international bodies; and for connected purposes. [15 November 1988]

. . .

Arrangement of Sections

PART I   COPYRIGHT

Chapter I   Subsistence, Ownership and Duration of Copyright

Introductory

1   Copyright and copyright works

(1) Copyright is a property right which subsists in accordance with this Part in the following descriptions of work—

(a) original literary, dramatic, musical or artistic works,

(b) sound recordings, films or broadcasts, and

(c) the typographical arrangement of published editions.

(2) In this Part 'copyright work' means a work of any of those descriptions in which copyright subsists.

(3) Copyright does not subsist in a work unless the requirements of this Part with respect to qualification for copyright protection are met (see section 153 and the provisions referred to there).

2 Rights subsisting in copyright works

(1) The owner of the copyright in a work of any description has the exclusive right to do the acts specified in Chapter II as the acts restricted by the copyright in a work of that description.

(2) In relation to certain descriptions of copyright work the following rights conferred by Chapter IV (moral rights) subsist in favour of the author, director or commissioner of the work, whether or not he is the owner of the copyright—

(a) section 77 (right to be identified as author or director),

(b) section 80 (right to object to derogatory treatment of work), and

(c) section 85 (right to privacy of certain photographs and films).

Descriptions of work and related provisions

3 Literary, dramatic and musical works

(1) In this Part—

'literary work' means any work, other than a dramatic or musical work, which is written, spoken or sung, and accordingly includes—

(a) a table or compilation other than a database,

(b) a computer program,

(c) preparatory design material for a computer program, and

(d) a database;

'dramatic work' includes a work of dance or mime; and

'musical work' means a work consisting of music, exclusive of any words or action intended to be sung, spoken or performed with the music.

(2) Copyright does not subsist in a literary, dramatic or musical work unless and until it is recorded, in writing or otherwise; and references in this Part to the time at which such a work is made are to the time at which it is so recorded.

(3) It is immaterial for the purposes of subsection (2) whether the work is recorded by or with the permission of the author; and where it is not recorded by the author, nothing in that subsection affects the question whether copyright subsists in the record as distinct from the work recorded.

3A Databases

(1) In this Part 'database' means a collection of independent works, data or other materials which—

(a) are arranged in a systematic or methodical way, and

(b) are individually accessible by electronic or other means.

(2) For the purposes of this Part a literary work consisting of a database is original if, and only if, by reason of the selection or arrangement of the contents of the database the database constitutes the author's own intellectual creation.

4 Artistic works

(1) In this Part 'artistic work' means—

(a) a graphic work, photograph, sculpture or collage, irrespective of artistic quality,

(b) a work of architecture being a building or a model for a building, or

(c) a work of artistic craftsmanship.

(2) In this Part—

'building' includes any fixed structure, and a part of a building or fixed structure;

'graphic work' includes—

(a) any painting, drawing, diagram, map, chart or plan, and

(b) any engraving, etching, lithograph, woodcut or similar work;

'photograph' means a recording of light or other radiation on any medium on which an image is produced or from which an image may by any means be produced, and which is not part of a film;

'sculpture' includes a cast or model made for purposes of sculpture.

5A Sound recordings

(1) In this Part 'sound recording' means—

(a) a recording of sounds, from which the sounds may be reproduced, or

(b) a recording of the whole or any part of a literary, dramatic or musical work, from which sounds reproducing the work or part may be produced,

regardless of the medium on which the recording is made or the method by which the sounds are reproduced or produced.

(2) Copyright does not subsist in a sound recording which is, or to the extent that it is, a copy taken from a previous sound recording.

5B Films

(1) In this Part 'film' means a recording on any medium from which a moving image may by any means be produced.

(2) The sound track accompanying a film shall be treated as part of the film for the purposes of this Part.

(3) Without prejudice to the generality of subsection (2), where that subsection applies—

(a) references in this Part to showing a film include playing the film sound track to accompany the film,

(b) references in this Part to playing a sound recording, or to communicating a sound recording to the public, do not include playing or communicating the film sound track to accompany the film,

(c) references in this Part to copying a work, so far as they apply to a sound recording, do not include copying the film sound track to accompany the film, and

(d) references in this Part to the issuing, rental or lending of copies of a work, so far as they apply to a sound recording, do not include the issuing, rental or lending of copies of the sound track to accompany the film.

(4) Copyright does not subsist in a film which is, or to the extent that it is, a copy taken from a previous film.

(5) Nothing in this section affects any copyright subsisting in a film sound track as a sound recording.

6 Broadcasts

(1) In this Part a 'broadcast' means an electronic transmission of visual images, sounds or other information which—

(a) is transmitted for simultaneous reception by members of the public and is capable of being lawfully received by them, or

(b) is transmitted at a time determined solely by the person making the transmission for presentation to members of the public,

and which is not excepted by subsection (1A); and references to broadcasting shall be construed accordingly.

(1A) Excepted from the definition of 'broadcast' is any Internet transmission unless it is—

(a) a transmission taking place simultaneously on the Internet and by other means,

(b) a concurrent transmission of a live event, or

(c) a transmission of recorded moving images or sounds forming part of a programme service offered by the person responsible for making the transmission, being a service in which programmes are transmitted at scheduled times determined by that person.

(2) An encrypted transmission shall be regarded as capable of being lawfully received by members of the public only if decoding equipment has been made available to members of the public by or with the authority of the person making the transmission or the person providing the contents of the transmission.

(3) References in this Part to the person making a broadcast or a transmission which is a broadcast are—

    (a) to the person transmitting the programme, if he has responsibility to any extent for its contents, and

    (b) to any person providing the programme who makes with the person transmitting it the arrangements necessary for its transmission;

and references in this Part to a programme, in the context of broadcasting, are to any item included in a broadcast.

(4) For the purposes of this Part, the place from which a wireless broadcast is made is the place where, under the control and responsibility of the person making the broadcast, the programme-carrying signals are introduced into an uninterrupted chain of communication (including, in the case of a satellite transmission, the chain leading to the satellite and down towards the earth).

(4A) Subsections (3) and (4) have effect subject to section 6A (safeguards in case of certain satellite broadcasts).

(5) References in this Part to the reception of a broadcast include reception of a broadcast relayed by means of a telecommunications system.

(5A) The relaying of a broadcast by reception and immediate re-transmission shall be regarded for the purposes of this Part as a separate act of broadcasting from the making of the broadcast which is so re-transmitted.

(6) Copyright does not subsist in a broadcast which infringes, or to the extent that it infringes, the copyright in another broadcast.

6A Safeguards in case of certain satellite broadcasts

(1) This section applies where the place from which a broadcast by way of satellite transmission is made is located in a country other than the United Kingdom and the law of that country fails to provide at least the following level of protection—

    (a) exclusive rights in relation to wireless broadcasting equivalent to those conferred by section 20 (infringement by communication to the public) on the authors of literary, dramatic, musical and artistic works, films and broadcasts;

    (b) a right in relation to live wireless broadcasting equivalent to that conferred on a performer by section 182(1)(b) (consent required for live broadcast of performance); and

    (c) a right for authors of sound recordings and performers to share in a single equitable remuneration in respect of the wireless broadcasting of sound recordings.

(2) Where the place from which the programme-carrying signals are transmitted to the satellite ('the uplink station') is located in the United Kingdom—

    (a) the United Kingdom shall be treated as the place from which the broadcast is made, and

    (b) the person operating the uplink station shall be treated as the person making the broadcast.

(3) Where the uplink station is not located in the United Kingdom but a person who is established in the United Kingdom has commissioned the making of the broadcast—

    (a) that person shall be treated as the person making the broadcast, and

    (b) the United Kingdom shall be treated as the place from which the broadcast is made.

8 Published editions

(1) In this Part 'published edition', in the context of copyright in the typographical arrangement of a published edition, means a published edition of the whole or any part of one or more literary, dramatic or musical works.

(2) Copyright does not subsist in the typographical arrangement of a published edition if, or to the extent that, it reproduces the typographical arrangement of a previous edition.

Authorship and ownership of copyright

9 Authorship of work

(1) In this Part 'author', in relation to a work, means the person who creates it.

(2) That person shall be taken to be—

(aa) in the case of a sound recording, the producer;

(ab) in the case of a film, the producer and the principal director;

(b) in the case of a broadcast, the person making the broadcast (see section 6(3)) or, in the case of a broadcast which relays another broadcast by reception and immediate re-transmission, the person making that other broadcast;

(c) (repealed);

(d) in the case of the typographical arrangement of a published edition, the publisher.

(3) In the case of a literary, dramatic, musical or artistic work which is computer-generated, the author shall be taken to be the person by whom the arrangements necessary for the creation of the work are undertaken.

(4) For the purposes of this Part a work is of 'unknown authorship' if the identity of the author is unknown or, in the case of a work of joint authorship, if the identity of none of the authors is known.

(5) For the purposes of this Part the identity of an author shall be regarded as unknown if it is not possible for a person to ascertain his identity by reasonable inquiry; but if his identity is once known it shall not subsequently be regarded as unknown.

10 Works of joint authorship

(1) In this Part a 'work of joint authorship' means a work produced by the collaboration of two or more authors in which the contribution of each author is not distinct from that of the other author or authors.

(1A) A film shall be treated as a work of joint authorship unless the producer and the principal director are the same person.

(2) A broadcast shall be treated as a work of joint authorship in any case where more than one person is to be taken as making the broadcast (see section 6(3)).

(3) References in this Part to the author of a work shall, except as otherwise provided; be construed in relation to a work of joint authorship as references to all the authors of the work.

10A Works of co-authorship

(1) In this part a 'work of co-authorship' means a work produced by the collaboration of the author of a musical work and the author of a literary work where the two works are created in order to be used together.

(2) References in this Part to a work or the author of a work shall, except as otherwise provided, be construed in relation to a work of co-authorship as references to each of the separate musical and literary works comprised in the work of co-authorship and to each of the authors of such works.

11 First ownership of copyright

(1) The author of a work is the first owner of any copyright in it, subject to the following provisions.

(2) Where a literary, dramatic, musical or artistic work, or a film, is made by an employee in the course of his employment, his employer is the first owner of any copyright in the work subject to any agreement to the contrary.

(3) This section does not apply to Crown copyright or Parliamentary copyright (see sections 163 and 165) or to copyright which subsists by virtue of section 168 (copyright of certain international organisations).

Duration of copyright

12 Duration of copyright in literary, dramatic, musical or artistic works

(1) The following provisions have effect with respect to the duration of copyright in a literary, dramatic, musical or artistic work.

(2) Copyright expires at the end of the period of 70 years from the end of the calendar year in which the author dies, subject as follows.

(3) If the work is of unknown authorship, copyright expires—

(a) at the end of the period of 70 years from the end of the calendar year in which the work was made, or

(b) if during that period the work is made available to the public, at the end of the period of 70 years from the end of the calendar year in which it is first so made available, subject as follows.

(4) Subsection (2) applies if the identity of the author becomes known before the end of the period specified in paragraph (a) or (b) of subsection (3).

(5) For the purposes of subsection (3) making available to the public includes—

(a) in the case of a literary, dramatic or musical work—

    (i) performance in public, or

    (ii) communication to the public;

(b) in the case of an artistic work—

    (i) exhibition in public,

    (ii) a film including the work being shown in public, or

    (iii) communication to the public;

but in determining generally for the purposes of that subsection whether a work has been made available to the public no account shall be taken of any unauthorised act.

(6) Where the country of origin of the work is not the United Kingdom and the author of the work is not a national of the United Kingdom, the duration of copyright is that to which the work is entitled in the country of origin, provided that does not exceed the period which would apply under subsections (2) to (5).

(7) If the work is computer-generated the above provisions do not apply and copyright expires at the end of the period of 50 years from the end of the calendar year in which the work was made.

(8) The provisions of this section are adapted as follows in relation to a work of joint authorship or a work of co-authorship—

(a) the reference in subsection (2) to the death of the author shall be construed—

    (i) if the identity of all the authors is known, as a reference to the death of the last of them to die, and

    (ii) if the identity of one or more of the authors is known and the identity of one or more others is not, as a reference to the death of the last whose identity is known;

(b) the reference in subsection (4) to the identity of the author becoming known shall be construed as a reference to the identity of any of the authors becoming known;

(c) the reference in subsection (6) to the author not being a national of the United Kingdom shall be construed as a reference to none of the authors being a national of the United Kingdom.

(9) This section does not apply to Crown copyright or Parliamentary copyright (see sections 163 to 166D) or to copyright which subsists by virtue of section 168 (copyright of certain international organisations).

13A   Duration of copyright in sound recordings

(1) The following provisions have effect with respect to the duration of copyright in a sound recording.

(2) Subject to subsections (4) and (5) and section 191HA(4), copyright expires—

(a) at the end of the period of 50 years from the end of the calendar year in which the recording is made, or

(b) if during that period the recording is published, 70 years from the end of the calendar year in which it is first published, or

(c) if during that period the recording is not published but is made available to the public by being played in public or communicated to the public, 70 years from the end of the calendar year in which it is first so made available,

but in determining whether a sound recording has been published, played in public or communicated to the public, no account shall be taken of any unauthorised act.

(3) (repealed).

(4) Where the author of a sound recording is not a national of the United Kingdom, the duration of copyright is that to which the sound recording is entitled in the country of which the author is a national, provided that does not exceed the period which would apply under subsection (2).

(5) If or to the extent that the application of subsection (4) would be at variance with an international obligation to which the United Kingdom became subject prior to 29th October 1993, the duration of copyright shall be as specified in subsection (2).

13B   Duration of copyright in films

(1) The following provisions have effect with respect to the duration of copyright in a film.

(2) Copyright expires at the end of the period of 70 years from the end of the calendar year in which the death occurs of the last to die of the following persons—

  (a) the principal director,

  (b) the author of the screenplay,

  (c) the author of the dialogue, or

  (d) the composer of music specially created for and used in the film; subject as follows.

(3) If the identity of one or more of the persons referred to in subsection (2)(a) to (d) is known and the identity of one or more others is not, the reference in that subsection to the death of the last of them to die shall be construed as a reference to the death of the last whose identity is known.

(4) If the identity of the persons referred to in subsection (2)(a) to (d) is unknown, copyright expires at—

  (a) the end of the period of 70 years from the end of the calendar year in which the film was made, or

  (b) if during that period the film is made available to the public, at the end of the period of 70 years from the end of the calendar year in which it is first so made available.

(5) Subsections (2) and (3) apply if the identity of any of those persons becomes known before the end of the period specified in paragraph (a) or (b) of subsection (4).

(6) For the purposes of subsection (4) making available to the public includes—

  (a) showing in public, or

  (b) communicating to the public;

but in determining generally for the purposes of that subsection whether a film has been made available to the public no account shall be taken of any unauthorised act.

(7) Where the country of origin is not the United Kingdom and the author of the film is not a national of the United Kingdom, the duration of copyright is that to which the work is entitled in the country of origin, provided that does not exceed the period which would apply under subsections (2) to (6).

(8) In relation to a film of which there are joint authors, the reference in subsection (7) to the author not being a national of the United Kingdom shall be construed as a reference to none of the authors being a national of the United Kingdom.

(9) If in any case there is no person falling within paragraphs (a) to (d) of subsection (2), the above provisions do not apply and copyright expires at the end of the period of 50 years from the end of the calendar year in which the film was made.

(10) For the purposes of this section the identity of any of the persons referred to in subsection (2)(a) to (d) shall be regarded as unknown if it is not possible for a person to ascertain his identity by reasonable inquiry; but if the identity of any such person is once known it shall not subsequently be regarded as unknown.

14   Duration of copyright in broadcasts

(1) The following provisions have effect with respect to the duration of copyright in a broadcast.

(2) Copyright in a broadcast expires at the end of the period of 50 years from the end of the calendar year in which the broadcast was made, subject as follows.

(3) Where the author of the broadcast is not a national of the United Kingdom, the duration of copyright in the broadcast is that to which it is entitled in the country of which the author is a national, provided that does not exceed the period which would apply under subsection (2).

(4) If or to the extent that the application of subsection (3) would be at variance with an international obligation to which the United Kingdom became subject prior to 29th October 1993, the duration of copyright shall be as specified in subsection (2).

(5) Copyright in a repeat broadcast expires at the same time as the copyright in the original broadcast; and accordingly no copyright arises in respect of a repeat broadcast which is broadcast after the expiry of the copyright in the original broadcast.

(6) A repeat broadcast means one which is a repeat of a broadcast previously made.

15   Duration of copyright in typographical arrangement of published editions

Copyright in the typographical arrangement of a published edition expires at the end of the period of 25 years from the end of the calendar year in which the edition was first published.

15A   Meaning of country of origin

(1) For the purposes of the provisions of this Part relating to the duration of copyright the country of origin of a work shall be determined as follows.

(2) If the work is first published in a Berne Convention country and is not simultaneously published elsewhere, the country of origin is that country.

(3) If the work is first published simultaneously in two or more countries only one of which is a Berne Convention country, the country of origin is that country.

(4) If the work is first published simultaneously in two or more countries of which two or more are Berne Convention countries, then—

(a) if the United Kingdom is one of those countries, the country of origin is the United Kingdom; and

(b) if the United Kingdom is not one of those countries, the country of origin is the Berne Convention country which grants the shorter or shortest period of copyright protection.

(5) If the work is unpublished or is first published in a country which is not a Berne Convention country (and is not simultaneously published in a Berne Convention country), the country of origin is—

(a) if the work is a film and the maker of the film has his headquarters in, or is domiciled or resident in a Berne Convention country, that country;

(b) if the work is—

(i) a work of architecture constructed in a Berne Convention country, or

(ii) an artistic work incorporated in a building or other structure situated in a Berne Convention country,

that country;

(c) in any other case, the country of which the author of the work is a national.

(6) In this section—

(a) a 'Berne Convention country' means a country which is a party to any Act of the International Convention for the Protection of Literary and Artistic Works signed at Berne on 9th September 1886; and

(b) references to simultaneous publication are to publication within 30 days of first publication.

Chapter II   Rights of Copyright Owner

The acts restricted by copyright

16   The acts restricted by copyright in a work

(1) The owner of the copyright in a work has, in accordance with the following provisions of this Chapter, the exclusive right to do the following acts in the United Kingdom—

(a) to copy the work (see section 17);

(b) to issue copies of the work to the public (see section 18);

(ba) to rent or lend the work to the public (see section 18A);

(c) to perform, show or play the work in public (see section 19);

(d) to communicate the work to the public (see section 20);

(e) to make an adaptation of the work or do any of the above in relation to an adaptation (see section 21);

and those acts are referred to in this Part as the 'act restricted by the copyright'.

(2) Copyright in a work is infringed by a person who without the licence of the copyright owner does, or authorises another to do, any of the acts restricted by the copyright.

(3) References in this Part to the doing of an act restricted by the copyright in a work are to the doing of it—

(a) in relation to the work as a whole or any substantial part of it, and

(b) either directly or indirectly;

and it is immaterial whether any intervening acts themselves infringe copyright.

(4) This Chapter has effect subject to—

(a) the provisions of Chapter III (acts permitted in relation to copyright works), and

(b) the provisions of Chapter VII (provisions with respect to copyright licensing).

17   Infringement of copyright by copying

(1) The copying of the work is an act restricted by the copyright in every description of copyright work; and references in this Part to copying and copies shall be construed as follows.

(2) Copying in relation to a literary, dramatic, musical or artistic work means reproducing the work in any material form. This includes storing the work in any medium by electronic means.

(3) In relation to an artistic work copying includes the making of a copy in three dimensions of a two-dimensional work and the making of a copy in two dimensions of a three-dimensional work.

(4) Copying in relation to a film or broadcast includes making a photograph of the whole or any substantial part of any image forming part of the film or broadcast.

(5) Copying in relation to the typographical arrangement of a published edition means making a facsimile copy of the arrangement.

(6) Copying in relation to any description of work includes the making of copies which are transient or are incidental to some other use of the work.

18   Infringement by issue of copies to the public

(1) The issue to the public of copies of the work is an act restricted by the copyright in every description of copyright work.

(2) References in this Part to the issue to the public of copies of a work are to the act of putting into circulation in the United Kingdom copies not previously put into circulation in the United Kingdom or the EEA by or with the consent of the copyright owner.

(3) References in this Part to the issue to the public of copies of a work do not include—

(a) any subsequent distribution, sale, hiring or loan of those copies previously put into circulation (but see section 18A: infringement by rental or lending).

(4) References in this Part to the issue of copies of a work include the issue of the original.

18A   Infringement by rental or lending of work to the public

(1) The rental or lending of copies of the work to the public is an act restricted by the copyright in—

(a) a literary, dramatic or musical work,

(b) an artistic work, other than—

(i)   a work of architecture in the form of a building or a model for a building, or

(ii) a work of applied art, or

(c) a film or a sound recording.

(2) In this Part, subject to the following provisions of this section—

(a) 'rental' means making a copy of the work available for use, on terms that it will or may be returned, for direct or indirect economic or commercial advantage, and

(b) 'lending' means making a copy of the work available for use, on terms that it will or may be returned, otherwise than for direct or indirect economic or commercial advantage, through an establishment which is accessible to the public.

(3) The expressions 'rental' and 'lending' do not include—

(a) making available for the purpose of public performance, playing or showing in public or communication to the public;

(b) making available for the purpose of exhibition in public; or

(c) making available for on-the-spot reference use.

(4) The expression 'lending' does not include making available between establishments which are accessible to the public.

(5) Where lending by an establishment accessible to the public gives rise to a payment the amount of which does not go beyond what is necessary to cover the operating costs of the establishment, there is no direct or indirect economic or commercial advantage for the purposes of this section.

(6) References in this Part to the rental or lending of copies of a work include the rental or lending of the original.

19 Infringement by performance, showing or playing of work in public

(1) The performance of the work in public is an act restricted by the copyright in a literary, dramatic or musical work.

(2) In this Part 'performance', in relation to a work—

(a) includes delivery in the case of lectures, addresses, speeches and sermons, and

(b) in general, includes any mode of visual or acoustic presentation, including presentation by means of a sound recording, film or broadcast of the work.

(3) The playing or showing of the work in public is an act restricted by the copyright in a sound recording, film or broadcast.

(4) Where copyright in a work is infringed by its being performed, played or shown in public by means of apparatus for receiving visual images or sounds conveyed by electronic means, the person by whom the visual images or sounds are sent, and in the case of a performance the performers, shall not be regarded as responsible for the infringement.

20 Infringement by communication to the public

(1) The communication to the public of the work is an act restricted by the copyright in—

(a) a literary, dramatic, musical or artistic work,

(b) a sound recording or film, or

(c) a broadcast.

(2) References in this Part to communication to the public are to communication to the public by electronic transmission, and in relation to a work include—

(a) the broadcasting of the work;

(b) the making available to the public of the work by electronic transmission in such a way that members of the public may access it from a place and at a time individually chosen by them.

21 Infringement by making adaptation or act done
in relation to adaptation

(1) The making of an adaptation of the work is an act restricted by the copyright in a literary, dramatic or musical work.

For this purpose an adaptation is made when it is recorded, in writing or otherwise.

(2) The doing of any of the acts specified in sections 17 to 20, or subsection (1) above, in relation to an adaptation of the work is also an act restricted by the copyright in a literary, dramatic or musical work.

For this purpose it is immaterial whether the adaptation has been recorded, in writing or otherwise, at the time the act is done.

(3) In this Part 'adaptation'—

(a) in relation to a literary work, other than a computer program or a database, or in relation to a dramatic work, means—

(i) a translation of the work;

(ii) a version of a dramatic work in which it is converted into a non-dramatic work or, as the case may be, of a non-dramatic work in which it is converted into a dramatic work;

(iii) a version of the work in which the story or action is conveyed wholly or mainly by means of pictures in a form suitable for reproduction in a book, or in a newspaper, magazine or similar periodical;

(ab) in relation to a computer program, means an arrangement or altered version of the program or a translation of it;

(ac) in relation to a database, means an arrangement or altered version of the database or a translation of it;

(b) in relation to a musical work, means an arrangement or transcription of the work.

(4) In relation to a computer program a 'translation' includes a version of the program in which it is converted into or out of a computer language or code or into a different computer language or code.

(5) No inference shall be drawn from this section as to what does or does not amount to copying a work.

Secondary infringement of copyright

22 Secondary infringement: importing infringing copy

The copyright in a work is infringed by a person who, without the licence of the copyright owner, imports into the United Kingdom, otherwise than for his private and domestic use, an article which is, and which he knows or has reason to believe is, an infringing copy of the work.

23 Secondary infringement: possessing or dealing with infringing copy

The copyright in a work is infringed by a person who, without the licence of the copyright owner—

(a) possesses in the course of a business,

(b) sells or lets for hire, or offers or exposes for sale or hire,

(c) in the course of a business exhibits in public or distributes, or

(d) distributes otherwise than in the course of a business to such an extent as to affect prejudicially the owner of the copyright,

an article which is, and which he knows or has reason to believe is, an infringing copy of the work.

24 Secondary infringement: providing means for making infringing copies

(1) Copyright in a work is infringed by a person who, without the licence of the copyright owner—

(a) makes,

(b) imports into the United Kingdom,

(c) possesses in the course of a business, or

(d) sells or lets for hire, or offers or exposes for sale or hire,

an article specifically designed or adapted for making copies of that work, knowing or having reason to believe that it is to be used to make infringing copies.

(2) Copyright in a work is infringed by a person who without the licence of the copyright owner transmits the work by means of a telecommunications system (otherwise than by communication to the public), knowing or having reason to believe that infringing copies of the work will be made by means of the reception of the transmission in the United Kingdom or elsewhere.

25 Secondary infringement: permitting use of premises for infringing performance

(1) Where the copyright in a literary, dramatic or musical work is infringed by a performance at a place of public entertainment, any person who gave permission for that place to be used for the performance is also liable for the infringement unless when he gave permission he believed on reasonable grounds that the performance would not infringe copyright.

(2) In this section 'place of public entertainment' includes premises which are occupied mainly for other purposes but are from time to time made available for hire for the purposes of public entertainment.

26 Secondary infringement: provision of apparatus for infringing performance, &c.

(1) Where copyright in a work is infringed by a public performance of the work, or by the playing or showing of the work in public, by means of apparatus for—

(a) playing sound recordings,

(b) showing films, or

(c) receiving visual images or sounds conveyed by electronic means,

the following persons are also liable for the infringement.

(2) A person who supplied the apparatus, or any substantial part of it, is liable for the infringement if when he supplied the apparatus or part—

(a) he knew or had reason to believe that the apparatus was likely to be so used as to infringe copyright, or

(b) in the case of apparatus whose normal use involves a public performance, playing or showing, he did not believe on reasonable grounds that it would not be so used as to infringe copyright.

(3) An occupier of premises who gave permission for the apparatus to be brought onto the premises is liable for the infringement if when he gave permission he knew or had reason to believe that the apparatus was likely to be so used as to infringe copyright.

(4) A person who supplied a copy of a sound recording or film used to infringe copyright is liable for the infringement if when he supplied it he knew or had reason to believe that what he supplied, or a copy made directly or indirectly from it, was likely to be so used as to infringe copyright.

Infringing copies

27 Meaning of 'infringing copy'

(1) In this Part 'infringing copy', in relation to a copyright work, shall be construed in accordance with this section.

(2) An article is an infringing copy if its making constituted an infringement of the copyright in the work in question.

(3) An article is also an infringing copy if—

(a) it has been or is proposed to be imported into the United Kingdom, and

(b) its making in the United Kingdom would have constituted an infringement of the copyright in the work in question, or a breach of an exclusive licence agreement relating to that work.

(4) Where in any proceedings the question arises whether an article is an infringing copy and it is shown—

(a) that the article is a copy of the work, and

(b) that copyright subsists in the work or has subsisted at any time,

it shall be presumed until the contrary is proved that the article was made at a time when copyright subsisted in the work.

(5) Nothing in subsection (3) shall be construed as applying to an article which may lawfully be imported into the United Kingdom by virtue of anything which forms part of retained EU law as a result of section 3 or 4 of the European Union (Withdrawal) Act 2018.

(6) In this Part 'infringing copy' includes a copy falling to be treated as an infringing copy by virtue of any of the following provisions—

section 29A(3) (copies for text and data analysis for non-commercial research),

section 31A(5) and (6) (disabled persons: copies of works for personal use),

section 31B(11) (making and supply of accessible copies by authorised bodies),

section 35(5) (recording by educational establishments of broadcasts),

section 36(8) (copying and use of extracts of works by educational establishments),

section 42A(5)(b) (copying by librarians: single copies of published works),

section 43(5)(b) (copying by librarians or archivists: single copies of unpublished works),

section 56(2) (further copies, adaptations, &c. of work in electronic form retained on transfer of principal copy), section 61(6)(b) (recordings of folksongs),

section 63(2) (copies made for purpose of advertising artistic work for sale),

section 68(4) (copies made for purpose of broadcast),

section 70(2) (recording for the purposes of time-shifting),

section 71(2) (photographs of broadcasts), or

any provision of an order under section 141 (statutory licence for certain reprographic copying by educational establishments).

Chapter III   Acts Permitted in Relation to Copyright Works

Introductory

28 Introductory provisions

(1) The provisions of this Chapter specify acts which may be done in relation to copyright works notwithstanding the subsistence of copyright; they relate only to the question of infringement of copyright and do not affect any other right or obligation restricting the doing of any of the specified acts.

(2) Where it is provided by this Chapter that an act does not infringe copyright, or may be done without infringing copyright, and no particular description of copyright work is mentioned, the act in question does not infringe the copyright in a work of any description.

(3) No inference shall be drawn from the description of any act which may by virtue of this Chapter be done without infringing copyright as to the scope of the acts restricted by the copyright in any description of work.

(4) The provisions of this Chapter are to be construed independently of each other, so that the fact that an act does not fall within one provision does not mean that it is not covered by another provision.

General

28A Making of temporary copies

Copyright in a literary work, other than a computer program or a database, or in a dramatic, musical or artistic work, the typographical arrangement of a published edition, a sound recording or a film, is not infringed by the making of a temporary copy which is transient or incidental, which is an integral and essential part of a technological process and the sole purpose of which is to enable—

(a) a transmission of the work in a network between third parties by an intermediary; or

(b) a lawful use of the work;

and which has no independent economic significance.

29 Research and private study

(1) Fair dealing with a work for the purposes of research for a non-commercial purpose does not infringe any copyright in the work provided that it is accompanied by a sufficient acknowledgement.

(1B) No acknowledgement is required in connection with fair dealing for the purposes mentioned in subsection (1) where this would be impossible for reasons of practicality or otherwise.

(1C) Fair dealing with a work for the purposes of private study does not infringe any copyright in the work.

(3) Copying by a person other than the researcher or student himself is not fair dealing if—

(a) in the case of a librarian, or a person acting on behalf of a librarian, that person does anything which is not permitted under section 42A (copying by librarians: single copies of published works), or

(b) in any other case, the person doing the copying knows or has reason to believe that it will result in copies of substantially the same material being provided to more than one person at substantially the same time and for substantially the same purpose.

(4) It is not fair dealing—

(a) to convert a computer program expressed in a low level language into a version expressed in a higher level language, or

(b) incidentally in the course of so converting the program to copy it,

(these acts being permitted if done in accordance with section 50B (decompilation)).

(4A) It is not fair dealing to observe, study or test the functioning of a computer program in order to determine the ideas and principles which underlie any element of the program (these acts being permitted if done in accordance with section 50BA (observing, studying and testing)).

(4B) To the extent that a term of a contract purports to prevent or restrict the doing of any act which, by virtue of this section, would not infringe copyright, that term is unenforceable.

29A   Copies for text and data analysis for non-commercial research

(1) The making of a copy of a work by a person who has lawful access to the work does not infringe copyright in the work provided that—

    (a) the copy is made in order that a person who has lawful access to the work may carry out a computational analysis of anything recorded in the work for the sole purpose of research for a non-commercial purpose, and

    (b) the copy is accompanied by a sufficient acknowledgement (unless this would be impossible for reasons of practicality or otherwise).

(2) Where a copy of a work has been made under this section, copyright in the work is infringed if—

    (a) the copy is transferred to any other person, except where the transfer is authorised by the copyright owner, or

    (b) the copy is used for any purpose other than that mentioned in subsection (1)(a), except where the use is authorised by the copyright owner.

(3) If a copy made under this section is subsequently dealt with—

    (a) it is to be treated as an infringing copy for the purposes of that dealing, and

    (b) if that dealing infringes copyright, it is to be treated as an infringing copy for all subsequent purposes.

(4) In subsection (3) 'dealt with' means sold or let for hire, or offered or exposed for sale or hire.

(5) To the extent that a term of a contract purports to prevent or restrict the making of a copy which, by virtue of this section, would not infringe copyright, that term is unenforceable.

30   Criticism, review, quotation and news reporting

(1) Fair dealing with a work for the purpose of criticism or review, of that or another work or of a performance of a work, does not infringe any copyright in the work provided that it is accompanied by a sufficient acknowledgement (unless this would be impossible for reasons of practicality or otherwise) and provided that the work has been made available to the public.

(1ZA) Copyright in a work is not infringed by the use of a quotation from the work (whether for criticism or review or otherwise) provided that—

    (a) the work has been made available to the public,

    (b) the use of the quotation is fair dealing with the work,

    (c) the extent of the quotation is no more than is required by the specific purpose for which it is used, and

    (d) the quotation is accompanied by a sufficient acknowledgement (unless this would be impossible for reasons of practicality or otherwise).

(1A) For the purposes of subsections (1) and (1ZA) a work has been made available to the public if it has been made available by any means, including—

    (a) the issue of copies to the public;

    (b) making the work available by means of an electronic retrieval system;

    (c) the rental or lending of copies of the work to the public;

    (d) the performance, exhibition, playing or showing of the work in public;

    (e) the communication to the public of the work,

but in determining generally for the purposes of those subsections whether a work has been made available to the public no account shall be taken of any unauthorised act.

(2) Fair dealing with a work (other than a photograph) for the purpose of reporting current events does not infringe any copyright in the work provided that (subject to subsection (3)) it is accompanied by a sufficient acknowledgement.

(3) No acknowledgement is required in connection with the reporting of current events by means of a sound recording, film or broadcast where this would be impossible for reasons of practicality or otherwise.

(4) To the extent that a term of a contract purports to prevent or restrict the doing of any act which, by virtue of subsection (1ZA), would not infringe copyright, that term is unenforceable.

30A   Caricature, parody or pastiche

(1) Fair dealing with a work for the purposes of caricature, parody or pastiche does not infringe copyright in the work.

(2) To the extent that a term of a contract purports to prevent or restrict the doing of any act which, by virtue of this section, would not infringe copyright, that term is unenforceable.

31   Incidental inclusion of copyright material

(1) Copyright in a work is not infringed by its incidental inclusion in an artistic work, sound recording, film or broadcast.

(2) Nor is the copyright infringed by the issue to the public of copies, or the playing, showing or communication to the public, of anything whose making was, by virtue of subsection (1), not an infringement of the copyright.

(3) A musical work, words spoken or sung with music, or so much of a sound recording or broadcast as includes a musical work or such words, shall not be regarded as incidentally included in another work if it is deliberately included.

Disability

31A   Disabled persons: copies of works for personal use

(1) This section applies if—
    (a) a disabled person has lawful access to a copy of the whole or part of a work, and
    (b) the person's disability prevents the person from enjoying the work to substantially the same degree as a person who does not have that disability.

(2) The making of an accessible copy of the copy of the work referred to in subsection (1)(a) does not infringe copyright if—
    (a) the copy is made by the disabled person or by a person acting on behalf of the disabled person, and
    (b) the copy is made for the disabled person's personal use.

(4) Copyright is infringed by the transfer of an accessible copy of a work made under this section to any person other than—
    (a) a person by or for whom an accessible copy of the work may be made under this section, or
    (b) a person who intends to transfer the copy to a person falling within paragraph (a),
except where the transfer is authorised by the copyright owner.

(5) An accessible copy of a work made under this section is to be treated for all purposes as an infringing copy if it is held by a person at a time when the person does not fall within subsection (4)(a) or (b).

(6) If an accessible copy made under this section is subsequently dealt with—
    (a) it is to be treated as an infringing copy for the purposes of that dealing, and
    (b) if that dealing infringes copyright, it is to be treated as an infringing copy for all subsequent purposes.

(7) In this section 'dealt with' means sold or let for hire or offered or exposed for sale or hire.

31B   Making, communicating, making available, distributing or lending of accessible copies by authorised bodies

(1) If

(a) an authorised body has lawful access to the whole or part of a work which has been published or otherwise made available, and

(b) the body complies with subsection (1A),

the body may, without infringing copyright, make, communicate, make available, distribute or lend accessible copies of the work on a non-profit basis for the personal use of disabled persons in the United Kingdom or another member State of the European Union.

(1A) An authorised body complies with this subsection if it—

(a) distributes, communicates, makes available or lends accessible copies only to disabled persons or other authorised bodies,

(b) takes appropriate steps to discourage the unauthorised reproduction, distribution, communication to the public or making available to the public of accessible copies,

(c) demonstrates due care in, and maintains records of, its handling of works and accessible copies, and

(d) publishes and updates, on its website if appropriate, or through other online or offline channels, information on how it complies with the obligations in paragraphs (a), (b) and (c).

(5) For the purposes of subsection (1), to communicate, make available, distribute or lend 'for the personal use of disabled persons' includes to communicate, make available, distribute or lend to a person acting on behalf of a disabled person.

(9) An authorised body which has made an accessible copy of a work under this section may communicate, make available, distribute or lend it to another authorised body established in the United Kingdom which is entitled to make accessible copies of the work under this section for the purposes of enabling that other body to make accessible copies of the work.

(11) If an accessible copy made under this section is subsequently dealt with—

(a) it is to be treated as an infringing copy for the purposes of that dealing, and

(b) if that dealing infringes copyright, it is to be treated as an infringing copy for all subsequent purposes.

(12) In this section 'dealt with' means sold or let for hire or offered or exposed for sale or hire.

31BA   Making, communicating, making available, distributing or lending of intermediate copies by authorised bodies

(1) An authorised body which is entitled to make an accessible copy of a work under section 31B may, without infringing copyright, make a copy of the work ('an intermediate copy') if this is necessary in order to make the accessible copy.

(2) An authorised body which has made an intermediate copy of a work under this section may communicate, make available, distribute or lend it on a non-profit basis to another authorised body which is entitled to make accessible copies of the work under section 31B for the purposes of enabling that other body to make accessible copies of the work.

(3) Copyright is infringed by the transfer of an intermediate copy made under this section to a person other than another authorised body as permitted by subsection (2), except where the transfer is authorised by the copyright owner.

. . .

31F   Sections 31A to 31BB: interpretation and general

(1) This section supplements sections 31A to 31BB and includes definitions.

(2) 'Disabled person' means a person who has a physical or mental impairment which prevents the person from enjoying a copyright work to substantially the same degree as a person who does not have that impairment, and 'disability' is to be construed accordingly.

(3) But a person is not to be regarded as disabled by reason only of an impairment of visual function which can be improved, for example by the use of corrective lenses, to a level that is normally acceptable for reading without a special level or kind of light.

(4) An 'accessible copy' of a copyright work means a version of the work which enables the disabled persons to access the work, including accessing it as feasibly and comfortably as a person who is not a disabled person,

(5) An accessible copy—

(a) may include facilities for navigating around the version of the work, but

(b) must not include any changes to the work which are not necessary to overcome the problems suffered by the disabled persons for whom the accessible copy is intended.

(6) 'Authorised body' means—

(a) an educational establishment, or

(b) a body that is not conducted for profit.

(8) To the extent that a term of a contract purports to prevent or restrict the doing of any act which, by virtue of section 27, 31A, 31B or 31BA, would not infringe copyright, that term is unenforceable.

Education

32   Illustration for instruction

(1) Fair dealing with a work for the sole purpose of illustration for instruction does not infringe copyright in the work provided that the dealing is—

(a) for a non-commercial purpose,

(b) by a person giving or receiving instruction (or preparing for giving or receiving instruction), and

(c) accompanied by a sufficient acknowledgement (unless this would be impossible for reasons of practicality or otherwise).

(2) For the purposes of subsection (1), 'giving or receiving instruction' includes setting examination questions, communicating the questions to pupils and answering the questions.

(3) To the extent that a term of a contract purports to prevent or restrict the doing of any act which, by virtue of this section, would not infringe copyright, that term is unenforceable.

33   Anthologies for educational use

(1) The inclusion of a short passage from a published literary or dramatic work in a collection which—

(a) is intended for use in educational establishments and is so described in its title, and in any advertisements issued by or on behalf of the publisher, and

(b) consists mainly of material in which no copyright subsists,

does not infringe the copyright in the work if the work itself is not intended for use in such establishments and the inclusion is accompanied by a sufficient acknowledgement.

(2) Subsection (1) does not authorise the inclusion of more than two excerpts from copyright works by the same author in collections published by the same publisher over any period of five years.

(3) In relation to any given passage the reference in subsection (2) to excerpts from works by the same author—

(a) shall be taken to include excerpts from works by him in collaboration with another, and

(b) if the passage in question is from such a work, shall be taken to include excerpts from works by any of the authors, whether alone or in collaboration with another.

(4) References in this section to the use of a work in an educational establishment are to any use for the educational purposes of such an establishment.

34   Performing, playing or showing work in course of activities of educational establishment

(1) The performance of a literary, dramatic or musical work before an audience consisting of teachers and pupils at an educational establishment and other persons directly connected with the activities of the establishment—

    (a) by a teacher or pupil in the course of the activities of the establishment, or

    (b) at the establishment by any person for the purposes of instruction,

is not a public performance for the purposes of infringement of copyright.

(2) The playing or showing of a sound recording, film or broadcast before such an audience at an educational establishment for the purposes of instruction is not a playing or showing of the work in public for the purposes of infringement of copyright.

(3) A person is not for this purpose directly connected with the activities of the educational establishment simply because he is the parent of a pupil at the establishment.

35   Recording by educational establishments of broadcasts

(1) A recording of a broadcast, or a copy of such a recording, may be made by or on behalf of an educational establishment for the educational purposes of that establishment without infringing copyright in the broadcast, or in any work included in it, provided that—

    (a) the educational purposes are non-commercial, and

    (b) the recording or copy is accompanied by a sufficient acknowledgement (unless this would be impossible for reasons of practicality or otherwise).

(2) Copyright is not infringed where a recording of a broadcast or a copy of such a recording, made under subsection (1), is communicated by or on behalf of the educational establishment to its pupils or staff for the non-commercial educational purposes of that establishment.

(3) Subsection (2) only applies to a communication received outside the premises of the establishment if that communication is made by means of a secure electronic network accessible only by the establishment's pupils and staff.

(4) Acts which would otherwise be permitted by this section are not permitted if, or to the extent that, licences are available authorising the acts in question and the educational establishment responsible for those acts knew or ought to have been aware of that fact.

(5) If a copy made under this section is subsequently dealt with—

    (a) it is to be treated as an infringing copy for the purposes of that dealing, and

    (b) if that dealing infringes copyright, it is to be treated as an infringing copy for all subsequent purposes.

(6) In this section 'dealt with' means—

    (a) sold or let for hire,

    (b) offered or exposed for sale or hire, or

    (c) communicated otherwise than as permitted by subsection (2).

36   Copying and use of extracts of works by educational establishments

(1) The copying of extracts of a relevant work by or on behalf of an educational establishment does not infringe copyright in the work, provided that—

    (a) the copy is made for the purposes of instruction for a non-commercial purpose, and

    (b) the copy is accompanied by a sufficient acknowledgement (unless this would be impossible for reasons of practicality or otherwise).

(2) Copyright is not infringed where a copy of an extract made under subsection (1) is communicated by or on behalf of the educational establishment to its pupils or staff for the purposes of instruction for a non-commercial purpose.

(3) Subsection (2) only applies to a communication received outside the premises of the establishment if that communication is made by means of a secure electronic network accessible only by the establishment's pupils and staff.

(4) In this section 'relevant work' means a copyright work other than—

(a) a broadcast, or

(b) an artistic work which is not incorporated into another work.

(5) Not more than 5% of a work may be copied under this section by or on behalf of an educational establishment in any period of 12 months, and for these purposes a work which incorporates another work is to be treated as a single work.

(6) Acts which would otherwise be permitted by this section are not permitted if, or to the extent that, licences are available authorising the acts in question and the educational establishment responsible for those acts knew or ought to have been aware of that fact.

(7) The terms of a licence granted to an educational establishment authorising acts permitted by this section are of no effect so far as they purport to restrict the proportion of a work which may be copied (whether on payment or free of charge) to less than that which would be permitted by this section.

(8) If a copy made under this section is subsequently dealt with—

(a) it is to be treated as an infringing copy for the purposes of that dealing, and

(b) if that dealing infringes copyright, it is to be treated as an infringing copy for all subsequent purposes.

(9) In this section 'dealt with' means—

(a) sold or let for hire,

(b) offered or exposed for sale or hire, or

(c) communicated otherwise than as permitted by subsection (2).

36A Lending of copies by educational establishments

Copyright in a work is not infringed by the lending of copies of the work by an educational establishment.

Libraries and archives

40A Lending of copies by libraries or archives

(1) Copyright in a work of any description is not infringed by the following acts by a public library in relation to a book within the public lending right scheme—

(a) lending the book;

(b) in relation to an audio-book or e-book, copying or issuing a copy of the book as an act incidental to lending it.

(1A) In subsection (1)—

(a) 'book', 'audio-book' and 'e-book' have the meanings given in section 5 of the Public Lending Right Act 1979,

(b) 'the public lending right scheme' means the scheme in force under section 1 of that Act,

(c) a book is within the public lending right scheme if it is a book within the meaning of the provisions of the scheme relating to eligibility, whether or not it is in fact eligible, and

(d) 'lending' is to be read in accordance with the definition of 'lent out' in section 5 of that Act (and section 18A of this Act does not apply).

(2) Copyright in a work is not infringed by the lending of copies of the work by a library or archive (other than a public library) which is not conducted for profit.

40B Libraries and educational establishments etc.: making works available through dedicated terminals

(1) Copyright in a work is not infringed by an institution specified in subsection (2) communicating the work to the public or making it available to the public by means of a dedicated terminal on its premises, if the conditions in subsection (3) are met.

(2) The institutions are—

(a) a library,

(b) an archive,

    (c) a museum, and

    (d) an educational establishment.

  (3) The conditions are that the work or a copy of the work—

    (a) has been lawfully acquired by the institution,

    (b) is communicated or made available to individual members of the public for the purposes of research or private study, and

    (c) is communicated or made available in compliance with any purchase or licensing terms to which the work is subject.

41 Copying by librarians: supply of single copies to other libraries

  (1) A librarian may, if the conditions in subsection (2) are met, make a single copy of the whole or part of a published work and supply it to another library, without infringing copyright in the work.

  (2) The conditions are—

    (a) the copy is supplied in response to a request from a library which is not conducted for profit, and

    (b) at the time of making the copy the librarian does not know, or could not reasonably find out, the name and address of a person entitled to authorise the making of a copy of the work.

  (3) The condition in subsection (2)(b) does not apply where the request is for a copy of an article in a periodical.

  (4) Where a library makes a charge for supplying a copy under this section, the sum charged must be calculated by reference to the costs attributable to the production of the copy.

  (5) To the extent that a term of a contract purports to prevent or restrict the doing of any act which, by virtue of this section, would not infringe copyright, that term is unenforceable.

42 Copying by librarians etc: replacement copies of works

  (1) A librarian, archivist or curator of a library, archive or museum may, without infringing copyright, make a copy of an item in that institution's permanent collection—

    (a) in order to preserve or replace that item in that collection, or

    (b) where an item in the permanent collection of another library, archive or museum has been lost, destroyed or damaged, in order to replace the item in the collection of that other library, archive or museum,

provided that the conditions in subsections (2) and (3) are met.

  (2) The first condition is that the item is—

    (a) included in the part of the collection kept wholly or mainly for the purposes of reference on the institution's premises,

    (b) included in a part of the collection not accessible to the public, or

    (c) available on loan only to other libraries, archives or museums.

  (3) The second condition is that it is not reasonably practicable to purchase a copy of the item to achieve either of the purposes mentioned in subsection (1).

  (4) The reference in subsection (1)(b) to a library, archive or museum is to a library, archive or museum which is not conducted for profit.

  (5) Where an institution makes a charge for supplying a copy to another library, archive or museum under subsection (1)(b), the sum charged must be calculated by reference to the costs attributable to the production of the copy.

  (6) In this section 'item' means a work or a copy of a work.

  (7) To the extent that a term of a contract purports to prevent or restrict the doing of any act which, by virtue of this section, would not infringe copyright, that term is unenforceable.

42A Copying by librarians: single copies of published works

  (1) A librarian of a library which is not conducted for profit may, if the conditions in subsection (2) are met, make and supply a single copy of—

    (a) one article in any one issue of a periodical, or

(b) a reasonable proportion of any other published work,
without infringing copyright in the work.

(2) The conditions are—

(a) the copy is supplied in response to a request from a person who has provided the librarian with a declaration in writing which includes the information set out in subsection (3), and

(b) the librarian is not aware that the declaration is false in a material particular.

(3) The information which must be included in the declaration is—

(a) the name of the person who requires the copy and the material which that person requires,

(b) a statement that the person has not previously been supplied with a copy of that material by any library,

(c) a statement that the person requires the copy for the purposes of research for a non-commercial purpose or private study, will use it only for those purposes and will not supply the copy to any other person, and

(d) a statement that to the best of the person's knowledge, no other person with whom the person works or studies has made, or intends to make, at or about the same time as the person's request, a request for substantially the same material for substantially the same purpose.

(4) Where a library makes a charge for supplying a copy under this section, the sum charged must be calculated by reference to the costs attributable to the production of the copy.

(5) Where a person ('P') makes a declaration under this section that is false in a material particular and is supplied with a copy which would have been an infringing copy if made by P—

(a) P is liable for infringement of copyright as if P had made the copy, and

(b) the copy supplied to P is to be treated as an infringing copy for all purposes.

(6) To the extent that a term of a contract purports to prevent or restrict the doing of any act which, by virtue of this section, would not infringe copyright, that term is unenforceable.

43   Copying by librarians or archivists: single copies of unpublished works

(1) A librarian or archivist may make and supply a single copy of the whole or part of a work without infringing copyright in the work, provided that—

(a) the copy is supplied in response to a request from a person who has provided the librarian or archivist with a declaration in writing which includes the information set out in subsection (2), and

(b) the librarian or archivist is not aware that the declaration is false in a material particular.

(2) The information which must be included in the declaration is—

(a) the name of the person who requires the copy and the material which that person requires,

(b) a statement that the person has not previously been supplied with a copy of that material by any library or archive, and

(c) a statement that the person requires the copy for the purposes of research for a non-commercial purpose or private study, will use it only for those purposes and will not supply the copy to any other person.

(3) But copyright is infringed if—

(a) the work had been published or communicated to the public before the date it was deposited in the library or archive, or

(b) the copyright owner has prohibited the copying of the work,
and at the time of making the copy the librarian or archivist is, or ought to be, aware of that fact.

(4) Where a library or archive makes a charge for supplying a copy under this section, the sum charged must be calculated by reference to the costs attributable to the production of the copy.

(5) Where a person ('P') makes a declaration under this section that is false in a material particular and is supplied with a copy which would have been an infringing copy if made by P—

(a) P is liable for infringement of copyright as if P had made the copy, and

(b) the copy supplied to P is to be treated as an infringing copy for all purposes.

43A   Sections 40A to 43: interpretation

(1) The following definitions have effect for the purposes of sections 40A to 43.

(2) 'Library' means—

    (a) a library which is publicly accessible, or

    (b) a library of an educational establishment.

(3) 'Museum' includes a gallery.

(4) 'Conducted for profit', in relation to a library, archive or museum, means a body of that kind which is established or conducted for profit or which forms part of, or is administered by, a body established or conducted for profit.

(5) References to a librarian, archivist or curator include a person acting on behalf of a librarian, archivist or curator.

44   Copy of work required to be made as condition of export

If an article of cultural or historical importance or interest cannot lawfully be exported from the United Kingdom unless a copy of it is made and deposited in an appropriate library or archive, it is not an infringement of copyright to make that copy.

44A   Legal deposit libraries

(1) Copyright is not infringed by the copying of a work from the Internet by a deposit library or person acting on its behalf if—

    (a) the work is of a description prescribed by regulations under section 10(5) of the 2003 Act,

    (b) its publication on the Internet, or a person publishing it there, is connected with the United Kingdom in a manner so prescribed, and

    (c) the copying is done in accordance with any conditions so prescribed.

(2) Copyright is not infringed by the doing of anything in relation to relevant material permitted to be done under regulations under section 7 of the 2003 Act.

(3) The Secretary of State may by regulations make provision excluding, in relation to prescribed activities done in relation to relevant material, the application of such of the provisions of this Chapter as are prescribed.

(4) Regulations under subsection (3) may in particular make provision prescribing activities—

    (a) done for a prescribed purpose,

    (b) done by prescribed descriptions of reader,

    (c) done in relation to prescribed descriptions of relevant material,

    (d) done other than in accordance with prescribed conditions.

(5) Regulations under this section may make different provision for different purposes.

(6) Regulations under this section shall be made by statutory instrument which shall be subject to annulment in pursuance of a resolution of either House of Parliament.

(7) In this section—

    (a) 'the 2003 Act' means the Legal Deposit Libraries Act 2003;

    (b) 'deposit library', 'reader' and 'relevant material' have the same meaning as in section 7 of the 2003 Act;

    (c) 'prescribed' means prescribed by regulations made by the Secretary of State.

Orphan Works

Public administration

45   Parliamentary and judicial proceedings

(1) Copyright is not infringed by anything done for the purposes of parliamentary or judicial proceedings.

(2) Copyright is not infringed by anything done for the purposes of reporting such proceedings; but this shall not be construed as authorising the copying of a work which is itself a published report of the proceedings.

46   Royal Commissions and statutory inquiries

(1) Copyright is not infringed by anything done for the purposes of the proceedings of a Royal Commission or statutory inquiry.

(2) Copyright is not infringed by anything done for the purpose of reporting any such proceedings held in public; but this shall not be construed as authorising the copying of a work which is itself a published report of the proceedings.

(3) Copyright in a work is not infringed by the issue to the public of copies of the report of a Royal Commission or statutory inquiry containing the work or material from it.

(4) In this section—

'Royal Commission' includes a Commission appointed for Northern Ireland by the Secretary of State in pursuance of the prerogative powers of Her Majesty delegated to him under section 7(2) of the Northern Ireland Constitution Act 1973; and

'statutory inquiry' means an inquiry held or investigation conducted in pursuance of a duty imposed or power conferred by or under an enactment.

47   Material open to public inspection or on official register

(1) Where material is open to public inspection pursuant to a statutory requirement, or is on a statutory register, any copyright in the material as a literary work is not infringed by the copying of so much of the material as contains factual information of any description, by or with the authority of the appropriate person, for a purpose which does not involve the issuing of copies to the public.

(2) Where material is open to public inspection pursuant to a statutory requirement, copyright in the material is not infringed by an act to which subsection (3A) applies provided that—

(a) the act is done by or with the authority of the appropriate person,

(b) the purpose of the act is—

   (i)   to enable the material to be inspected at a more convenient time or place, or

   (ii) to otherwise facilitate the exercise of any right for the purpose of which the statutory requirement is imposed, and

(c) in the case of the act specified in subsection (3A)(c), the material is not commercially available to the public by or with the authority of the copyright owner.

(3) Where material which contains information about matters of general scientific, technical, commercial or economic interest is on a statutory register or is open to public inspection pursuant to a statutory requirement, copyright in the material is not infringed by an act to which subsection (3A) applies provided that—

(a) the act is done by or with the authority of the appropriate person,

(b) the purpose of the act is to disseminate that information, and

(c) in the case of the act specified in subsection (3A)(c), the material is not commercially available to the public by or with the authority of the copyright owner.

(3A) This subsection applies to any of the following acts—

(a) copying the material,

(b) issuing copies of the material to the public, and

(c) making the material (or a copy of it) available to the public by electronic transmission in such a way that members of the public may access it from a place and at a time individually chosen by them.

(4) The Secretary of State may by order provide that subsection (1), (2) or (3) shall, in such cases as may be specified in the order, apply only to copies marked in such manner as may be so specified.

(5) The Secretary of State may by order provide that subsections (1) to (3) apply, to such extent and with such modifications as may be specified in the order—

(a) to material made open to public inspection by—

   (i)   an international organisation specified in the order, or

(ii) a person so specified who has functions in the United Kingdom under an international agreement to which the United Kingdom is party, or

(b) to a register maintained by an international organisation specified in the order,

as they apply in relation to material open to public inspection pursuant to a statutory requirement or to a statutory register.

(6) In this section—

'appropriate person' means the person required to make the material open to public inspection or, as the case may be, the person maintaining the register;

'statutory register' means a register maintained in pursuance of a statutory requirement; and

'statutory requirement' means a requirement imposed by provision made by or under an enactment.

(7) An order under this section shall be made by statutory instrument which shall be subject to annulment in pursuance of a resolution of either House of Parliament.

48　Material communicated to the Crown in the course of public business

(1) This section applies where a literary, dramatic, musical or artistic work has in the course of public business been communicated to the Crown for any purpose, by or with the licence of the copyright owner and a document or other material thing recording or embodying the work is owned by or in the custody or control of the Crown.

(2) The Crown may, without infringing copyright in the work, do an act specified in subsection (3) provided that—

(a) the act is done for the purpose for which the work was communicated to the Crown, or any related purpose which could reasonably have been anticipated by the copyright owner, and

(b) the work has not been previously published otherwise than by virtue of this section.

(3) The acts referred to in subsection (2) are—

(a) copying the work,

(b) issuing copies of the work to the public, and

(c) making the work (or a copy of it) available to the public by electronic transmission in such a way that members of the public may access it from a place and at a time individually chosen by them.

(4) In subsection (1) 'public business' includes any activity carried on by the Crown.

(5) This section has effect subject to any agreement to the contrary between the Crown and the copyright owner.

(6) In this section 'the Crown' includes a health service body, as defined in section 60(7) of the National Health Service and Community Care Act 1990, NHS England, an integrated care board established under section 14Z25 of the National Health Service Act 2006, the Care Quality Commission, Health Education England, the Health Research Authority and a National Health Service trust established under section 25 of the National Health Service Act 2006, section 18 of the National Health Service (Wales) Act 2006 or the National Health Service (Scotland) Act 1978 and an NHS foundation trust and also includes a health and social services body, as defined in Article 7(6) of the Health and Personal Social Services (Northern Ireland) Order 1991, and a Health and Social Services trust established under that Order; and the reference in subsection (1) above to public business shall be construed accordingly.

49　Public records

Material which is comprised in public records within the meaning of the Public Records Act 1958, the Public Records (Scotland) Act 1937 or the Public Records Act (Northern Ireland) 1923, or in Welsh public records (as defined in the Government of Wales Act 2006), which are open to public inspection in pursuance of that Act, may be copied, and a copy may be supplied to any person, by or with the authority of any officer appointed under that Act, without infringement of copyright.

50   Acts done under statutory authority

(1) Where the doing of a particular act is specifically authorised by an Act of Parliament, whenever passed, then, unless the Act provides otherwise, the doing of that act does not infringe copyright.

(2) Subsection (1) applies in relation to an enactment contained in Northern Ireland legislation as it applies in relation to an Act of Parliament.

(3) Nothing in this section shall be construed as excluding any defence of statutory authority otherwise available under or by virtue of any enactment.

Computer programs: lawful users

50A   Back up copies

(1) It is not an infringement of copyright for a lawful user of a copy of a computer program to make any back up copy of it which it is necessary for him to have for the purposes of his lawful use.

(2) For the purposes of this section and sections 50B, 50BA and 50C a person is a lawful user of a computer program if (whether under a licence to do any acts restricted by the copyright in the program or otherwise), he has a right to use the program.

(3) Where an act is permitted under this section, it is irrelevant whether or not there exists any term or condition in an agreement which purports to prohibit or restrict the act (such terms being, by virtue of section 296A, void).

50B   Decompilation

(1) It is not an infringement of copyright for a lawful user of a copy of a computer program expressed in a low level language—

    (a) to convert it into a version expressed in a higher level language, or

    (b) incidentally in the course of so converting the program, to copy it,

(that is, to 'decompile' it), provided that the conditions in subsection (2) are met.

(2) The conditions are that—

    (a) it is necessary to decompile the program to obtain the information necessary to create an independent program which can be operated with the program decompiled or with another program ('the permitted objective'); and

    (b) the information so obtained is not used for any purpose other than the permitted objective.

(3) In particular, the conditions in subsection (2) are not met if the lawful user—

    (a) has readily available to him the information necessary to achieve the permitted objective;

    (b) does not confine the decompiling to such acts as are necessary to achieve the permitted objective;

    (c) supplies the information obtained by the decompiling to any person to whom it is not necessary to supply it in order to achieve the permitted objective; or

    (d) uses the information to create a program which is substantially similar in its expression to the program decompiled or to do any act restricted by copyright.

(4) Where an act is permitted under the section, it is irrelevant whether or not there exists any term or condition in an agreement which purports to prohibit or restrict the act (such terms being, by virtue of section 296A, void).

50BA   Observing, studying and testing of computer programs

(1) It is not an infringement of copyright for a lawful user of a copy of a computer program to observe, study or test the functioning of the program in order to determine the ideas and principles which underlie any element of the program if he does so while performing any of the acts of loading, displaying, running, transmitting or storing the program which he is entitled to do.

(2) Where an act is permitted under this section, it is irrelevant whether or not there exists any term or condition in an agreement which purports to prohibit or restrict the act (such terms being, by virtue of section 296A, void).

50C Other acts permitted to lawful users

(1) It is not an infringement of copyright for a lawful user of a copy of a computer program to copy or adapt it, provided that the copying or adapting—

(a) is necessary for his lawful use; and

(b) is not prohibited under any term or condition of an agreement regulating the circumstances in which his use is lawful.

(2) It may, in particular, be necessary for the lawful use of a computer program to copy it or adapt it for the purpose of correcting errors in it.

(3) This section does not apply to any copying or adapting permitted under section 50A, 50B or 50BA.

Databases: permitted acts

50D Acts permitted in relation to databases

(1) It is not an infringement of copyright in database for a person who has a right to use the database or any part of the database, (whether under a licence to do any of the acts restricted by the copyright in the database or otherwise) to do, in the exercise of that right, anything which is necessary for the purposes of access to and use of the contents of the database or of that part of the database.

(2) Where an act which would otherwise infringe copyright in a database is permitted under this section, it is irrelevant whether or not there exists any term or condition in any agreement which purports to prohibit or restrict the act (such terms being, by virtue of section 296B, void).

Designs

51 Design documents and models

(1) It is not an infringement of any copyright in a design document or model recording or embodying a design for anything other than an artistic work or a typeface to make an article to the design or to copy an article made to the design.

(2) Nor is it an infringement of the copyright to issue to the public, or include in a film or communicate to the public, anything the making of which was, by virtue of subsection (1), not an infringement of that copyright.

(3) In this section—

'design' means the design of the shape or configuration (whether internal or external) of the whole or part of an article, other than surface decoration; and

'design document' means any record of a design, whether in the form of a drawing, a written description, a photograph, data stored in a computer or otherwise.

...

53 Things done in reliance on registration of design

(1) The copyright in an artistic work is not infringed by anything done—

(a) in pursuance of an assignment or licence made or granted by a person registered—

(i) under the Registered Designs Act 1949 as the proprietor of a corresponding design, or

(ii) under the Community Design Regulation as the right holder of a corresponding registered Community design, and

(b) in good faith in reliance on the registration and without notice of any proceedings for the cancellation or invalidation of the registration or, in the case of registration under the 1949 Act, for rectifying the relevant entry into the register of designs;

and this is so notwithstanding that the person registered as the proprietor was not the proprietor of the design for the purposes of the 1949 Act or, in a case of registration under the Community Design Regulation, that the person registered as the right holder was not the right holder of the design for the purposes of the Regulation.

(2) In subsection (1) a 'corresponding design', in relation to an artistic work, means a design within the meaning of the 1949 Act which if applied to an article would produce something which would be treated for the purposes of this Part as a copy of the artistic work.

(3) In subsection (1), a 'corresponding registered Community design', in relation to an artistic work, means a design within the meaning of the Community Design Regulation which if applied to an article would produce something which would be treated for the purposes of this Part as a copy of the artistic work.

(4) In this section, 'the Community Design Regulation' means Council Regulation (EC) No 6/2002 of 12 December 2001 on Community designs.

Typefaces

54 Use of typeface in ordinary course of printing

(1) It is not an infringement of copyright in an artistic work consisting of the design of a typeface—

(a) to use the typeface in the ordinary course of typing, composing text, typesetting or printing,

(b) to possess an article for the purpose of such use, or

(c) to do anything in relation to material produced by such use;

and this is so notwithstanding that an article is used which is an infringing copy of the work.

(2) However, the following provisions of this Part apply in relation to persons making, importing or dealing with articles specifically designed or adapted for producing material in a particular typeface, or possessing such articles for the purpose of dealing with them, as if the production of material as mentioned in subsection (1) did infringe copyright in the artistic work consisting of the design of the typeface—

section 24 (secondary infringement: making, importing, possessing or dealing with article for making infringing copy),

sections 99 and 100 (order for delivery up and right of seizure),

section 107(2) (offence of making or possessing such an article), and

section 108 (order for delivery up in criminal proceedings).

(3) The references in subsection (2) to 'dealing with' an article are to selling, letting for hire, or offering or exposing for sale or hire, exhibiting in public, or distributing.

55 Articles for producing material in particular typeface

(1) This section applies to the copyright in an artistic work consisting of the design of a typeface where articles specifically designed or adapted for producing material in that typeface have been marketed by or with the licence of the copyright owner.

(2) After the period of 25 years from the end of the calendar year in which the first such articles are marketed, the work may be copied by making further such articles, or doing anything for the purpose of making such articles, and anything may be done in relation to articles so made, without infringing copyright in the work.

(3) In subsection (1) 'marketed' means sold, let for hire or offered or exposed for sale or hire, in the United Kingdom or elsewhere.

Works in electronic form

56   Transfers of copies of works in electronic form

(1) This section applies where a copy of a work in electronic form has been purchased on terms which, expressly or impliedly or by virtue of any rule of law, allow the purchaser to copy the work, or to adapt it or make copies of an adaptation, in connection with his use of it.

(2) If there are no express terms—

    (a) prohibiting the transfer of the copy by the purchaser, imposing obligations which continue after a transfer, prohibiting the assignment of any licence or terminating any licence on a transfer, or

    (b) providing for the terms on which a transferee may do the things which the purchaser was permitted to do,

anything which the purchaser was allowed to do may also be done without infringement of copyright by a transferee; but any copy, adaptation or copy of an adaptation made by the purchaser which is not also transferred shall be treated as an infringing copy for all purposes after the transfer.

(3) The same applies where the original purchased copy is no longer usable and what is transferred is a further copy used in its place.

(4) The above provisions also apply on a subsequent transfer, with the substitution for references in subsection (2) to the purchaser of references to the subsequent transferor.

Miscellaneous: literary, dramatic, musical and artistic works

57   Anonymous or pseudonymous works: acts permitted on assumptions as to expiry of copyright or death of author

(1) Copyright in a literary, dramatic, musical or artistic work is not infringed by an act done at a time when, or in pursuance of arrangements made at a time when—

    (a) it is not possible by reasonable inquiry to ascertain the identity of the author, and

    (b) it is reasonable to assume—

        (i)   that copyright has expired, or

        (ii) that the author died 70 years or more before the beginning of the calendar year in which the act is done or the arrangements are made.

(2) Subsection (1)(b)(ii) does not apply in relation to—

    (a) a work in which Crown copyright subsists, or

    (b) a work in which copyright originally vested in an international organisation by virtue of section 168 and in respect of which an Order under that section specifies a copyright period longer than 70 years.

(3) In relation to a work of joint authorship—

    (a) the reference in subsection (1) to its being possible to ascertain the identity of the author shall be construed as a reference to its being possible to ascertain the identity of any of the authors, and

    (b) the reference in subsection (1)(b)(ii) to the author having died shall be construed as a reference to all the authors having died.

58   Use of notes or recordings of spoken words in certain cases

(1) Where a record of spoken words is made, in writing or otherwise, for the purpose—

    (a) of reporting current events, or

    (b) of communicating to the public the whole or part of the work,

it is not an infringement of any copyright in the words as a literary work to use the record or material taken from it (or to copy the record, or any such material, and use the copy) for that purpose, provided the following conditions are met.

(2) The conditions are that—

(a) the record is a direct record of the spoken words and is not taken from a previous record or from a broadcast;

(b) the making of the record was not prohibited by the speaker and, where copyright already subsisted in the work, did not infringe copyright;

(c) the use made of the record or material taken from it is not of a kind prohibited by or on behalf of the speaker or copyright owner before the record was made; and

(d) the use is by or with the authority of a person who is lawfully in possession of the record.

59   Public reading or recitation

(1) The reading or recitation in public by one person of a reasonable extract from a published literary or dramatic work does not infringe any copyright in the work if it is accompanied by a sufficient acknowledgement.

(2) Copyright in a work is not infringed by the making of a sound recording, or the communication to the public, of a reading or recitation which by virtue of subsection (1) does not infringe copyright in the work, provided that the recording or communication to the public consists mainly of material in relation to which it is not necessary to rely on that subsection.

60   Abstracts of scientific or technical articles

(1) Where an article on a scientific or technical subject is published in a periodical accompanied by an abstract indicating the contents of the article, it is not an infringement of copyright in the abstract, or in the article, to copy the abstract or issue copies of it to the public.

(2) This section does not apply if or to the extent that there is a licensing scheme certified for the purposes of this section under section 143 providing for the grant of licences.

61   Recordings of folksongs

(1) A sound recording of a performance of a song may be made for the purpose of including it in an archive maintained by a body not established or conducted for profit without infringing any copyright in the words as a literary work or in the accompanying musical work, provided the conditions in subsection (2) below are met.

(2) The conditions are that—

(a) the words are unpublished and of unknown authorship at the time the recording is made,

(b) the making of the recording does not infringe any other copyright, and

(c) its making is not prohibited by any performer.

(3) A single copy of a sound recording made in reliance on subsection (1) and included in an archive referred to in that subsection may be made and supplied by the archivist without infringing copyright in the recording or the works included in it, provided that—

(a) the copy is supplied in response to a request from a person who has provided the archivist with a declaration in writing which includes the information set out in subsection (4), and

(b) the archivist is not aware that the declaration is false in a material particular.

(4) The information which must be included in the declaration is—

(a) the name of the person who requires the copy and the sound recording which is the subject of the request,

(b) a statement that the person has not previously been supplied with a copy of that sound recording by any archivist, and

(c) a statement that the person requires the copy for the purposes of research for a non-commercial purpose or private study, will use it only for those purposes and will not supply the copy to any other person.

(5) Where an archive makes a charge for supplying a copy under this section, the sum charged must be calculated by reference to the costs attributable to the production of the copy.

(6) Where a person ('P') makes a declaration under this section that is false in a material particular and is supplied with a copy which would have been an infringing copy if made by P—

    (a) P is liable for infringement of copyright as if P had made the copy, and

    (b) the copy supplied to P is to be treated as an infringing copy for all purposes.

(7) In this section references to an archivist include a person acting on behalf of an archivist.

62 Representation of certain artistic works on public display

(1) This section applies to—

    (a) buildings, and

    (b) sculptures, models for buildings and works of artistic craftsmanship, if permanently situated in a public place or in premises open to the public.

(2) The copyright in such a work is not infringed by—

    (a) making a graphic work representing it,

    (b) making a photograph or film of it, or

    (c) making a broadcast of a visual image of it.

(3) Nor is the copyright infringed by the issue to the public of copies, or the communication to the public, of anything whose making was, by virtue of this section, not an infringement of the copyright.

63 Advertisement of sale of artistic work

(1) It is not an infringement of copyright in an artistic work to copy it, or to issue copies to the public, for the purpose of advertising the sale of the work.

(2) Where a copy which would otherwise be an infringing copy is made in accordance with this section but is subsequently dealt with for any other purpose, it shall be treated as an infringing copy for the purposes of that dealing, and if that dealing infringes copyright for all subsequent purposes.

For this purpose 'dealt with' means sold or let for hire, offered or exposed for sale or hire, exhibited in public, distributed or communicated to the public.

64 Making of subsequent works by same artist

Where the author of an artistic work is not the copyright owner, he does not infringe the copyright by copying the work in making another artistic work, provided he does not repeat or imitate the main design of the earlier work.

65 Reconstruction of buildings

Anything done for the purposes of reconstructing a building does not infringe any copyright—

    (a) in the building, or

    (b) in any drawings or plans in accordance with which the building was, by or with the licence of the copyright owner, constructed.

Miscellaneous: lending of works and playing of sound recordings

66 Lending to public of copies of certain works

(1) The Secretary of State may by order provide that in such cases as may be specified in the order the lending to the public of copies of literary, dramatic, musical or artistic works, sound recordings or films shall be treated as licensed by the copyright owner subject only to the payment of such reasonable royalty or other payment as may be agreed or determined in default of agreement by the Copyright Tribunal.

(2) No such order shall apply if, or to the extent that, there is a licensing scheme certified for the purposes of this section under section 143 providing for the grant of licences.

(3) An order may make different provision for different cases and may specify cases by reference to any factor relating to the work, the copies lent, the lender or the circumstances of the lending.

(4) An order shall be made by statutory instrument; and no order shall be made unless a draft of it has been laid before and approved by a resolution of each House of Parliament.

(5) Nothing in this section affects any liability under section 23 (secondary infringement: possessing or dealing with infringing copy) in respect of the lending of infringing copies.

Miscellaneous: films and sound recordings

66A   Films: acts permitted on assumptions as to expiry of copyright, &c.

(1) Copyright in a film is not infringed by an act done at a time when, or in pursuance of arrangements made at a time when—

    (a) it is not possible by reasonable inquiry to ascertain the identity of any of the persons referred to in section 13B(2)(a) to (d) (persons by reference to whose life the copyright period is ascertained), and

    (b) it is reasonable to assume—

        (i) that copyright has expired, or

        (ii) that the last to die of those persons died 70 years or more before the beginning of the calendar year in which the act is done or the arrangements are made.

(2) Subsection (1)(b)(ii) does not apply in relation to—

    (a) a film in which Crown copyright subsists, or

    (b) a film in which copyright originally vested in an international organisation by virtue of section 168 and in respect of which an Order under that section specifies a copyright period longer than 70 years.

Miscellaneous: broadcasts

68   Incidental recording for purposes of broadcast

(1) This section applies where by virtue of a licence or assignment of copyright a person is authorised to broadcast—

    (a) a literary, dramatic or musical work, or an adaptation of such a work,

    (b) an artistic work, or

    (c) a sound recording or film.

(2) He shall by virtue of this section be treated as licensed by the owner of the copyright in the work to do or authorise any of the following for the purposes of the broadcast—

    (a) in the case of a literary, dramatic or musical work, or an adaptation of such a work, to make a sound recording or film of the work or adaptation;

    (b) in the case of an artistic work, to take a photograph or make a film of the work;

    (c) in the case of a sound recording or film, to make a copy of it.

(3) That licence is subject to the condition that the recording, film, photograph or copy in question—

    (a) shall not be used for any other purpose, and

    (b) shall be destroyed within 28 days of being first used for broadcasting the work.

(4) A recording, film, photograph or copy made in accordance with this section shall be treated as an infringing copy—

    (a) for the purposes of any use in breach of the condition mentioned in subsection (3)(a), and

    (b) for all purposes after that condition or the condition mentioned in subsection (3)(b) is broken.

69   Recording for purposes of supervision and control of broadcasts and other services

(1) Copyright is not infringed by the making or use by the British Broadcasting Corporation, for the purpose of maintaining supervision and control over programmes broadcast by them or included in any on-demand programme service provided by them, of recordings of those programmes.

(2) Copyright is not infringed by anything done in pursuance of—

    (a) section 167(1) of the Broadcasting Act 1990, section 115(4) or (6) or 117 of the Broadcasting Act 1996 or paragraph 20 of Schedule 12 to the Communications Act 2003;

    (b) a condition which, by virtue of section 334(1) of the Communications Act 2003, is included in a licence granted under Part I or III of that Act or Part I or II of the Broadcasting Act 1996; or

    (c) a direction given under section 109(2) of the Broadcasting Act 1990 (power of OFCOM to require production of recordings etc.).

    (d) section 334(3), 368O(1) or (3) of the Communications Act 2003.

(3) Copyright is not infringed by the use by OFCOM in connection with the performance of any of their functions under the Broadcasting Act 1990, the Broadcasting Act 1996 or the Communications Act 2003 of—

    (a) any recording, script or transcript which is provided to them under or by virtue of any provision of those Acts; or

    (b) any existing material which is transferred to them by a scheme made under section 30 of the Communications Act 2003.

(4) In subsection (3), 'existing material' means—

    (a) any recording, script or transcript which was provided to the Independent Television Commission or the Radio Authority under or by virtue of any provision of the Broadcasting Act 1990 or the Broadcasting Act 1996; and

    (b) any recording or transcript which was provided to the Broadcasting Standards Commission under section 115(4) or (6) or 116(5) of the Broadcasting Act 1996.

(5) Copyright is not infringed by the use by an appropriate regulatory authority designated under section 368B of the Communications Act 2003, in connection with the performance of any of their functions under that Act, of any recording, script or transcript which is provided to them under or by virtue of any provision of that Act.

(6) In this section 'on-demand programme service' has the same meaning as in the Communications Act 2003 (see section 368A of that Act).

70 Recording for purposes of time-shifting

(1) The making in domestic premises for private and domestic use of a recording of a broadcast solely for the purpose of enabling it to be viewed or listened to at a more convenient time does not infringe any copyright in the broadcast or in any work included in it.

(2) Where a copy which would otherwise be an infringing copy is made in accordance with this section but is subsequently dealt with—

    (a) it shall be treated as an infringing copy for the purposes of that dealing; and

    (b) if that dealing infringes copyright, it shall be treated as an infringing copy for all subsequent purposes.

(3) In subsection (2), 'dealt with' means sold or let for hire, offered or exposed for sale or hire or communicated to the public.

71 Photographs of broadcasts

(1) The making in domestic premises for private and domestic use of a photograph of the whole or any part of an image forming part of a broadcast, or a copy of such a photograph, does not infringe any copyright in the broadcast or in any film included in it.

(2) Where a copy which would otherwise be an infringing copy is made in accordance with this section but is subsequently dealt with—

    (a) it shall be treated as an infringing copy for the purposes of that dealing; and

    (b) if that dealing infringes copyright, it shall be treated as an infringing copy for all subsequent purposes.

(3) In subsection (2), 'dealt with' means sold or let for hire, offered or exposed for sale or hire or communicated to the public.

72 Free public showing or playing of broadcast

(1) The showing or playing in public of a broadcast to an audience who have not paid for admission to the place where the broadcast is to be seen or heard does not infringe any copyright in—

    (a) the broadcast; or

    (b) any sound recording (except so far as it is an excepted sound recording) included in it.

(1A) For the purposes of this Part an 'excepted sound recording' is a sound recording—

(a) whose author is not the author of the broadcast in which it is included; and

(b) which is a recording of music with or without words spoken or sung.

(1B) Where by virtue of subsection (1) the copyright in a broadcast shown or played in public is not infringed, copyright in any film or excepted sound recording included in it is not infringed if the playing or showing of that broadcast in public—

(b) is necessary for the purposes of—

(i)   repairing equipment for the reception of broadcasts;

(ii) demonstrating that a repair to such equipment has been carried out; or

(iii) demonstrating such equipment which is being sold or let for hire or offered or exposed for sale or hire.

(2) The audience shall be treated as having paid for admission to a place—

(a) if they have paid for admission to a place of which that place forms part; or

(b) if goods or services are supplied at that place (or a place of which it forms part)—

(i)   at prices which are substantially attributable to the facilities afforded for seeing or hearing the broadcast, or

(ii) at prices exceeding those usually charged there and which are partly attributable to those facilities.

(3) The following shall not be regarded as having paid for admission to a place—

(a) persons admitted as residents or inmates of the place;

(b) persons admitted as members of a club or society where the payment is only for membership of the club or society and the provision of facilities for seeing or hearing broadcasts is only incidental to the main purposes of the club or society.

(4) Where the making of the broadcast was an infringement of the copyright in a sound recording or film, the fact that it was heard or seen in public by the reception of the broadcast shall be taken into account in assessing the damages for that infringement.

…

75   Recording of broadcast for archival purposes

(1) A recording of a broadcast or a copy of such a recording may be made for the purpose of being placed in an archive maintained by a body which is not established or conducted for profit without infringing any copyright in the broadcast or in any work included in it.

(2) To the extent that a term of a contract purports to prevent or restrict the doing of any act which, by virtue of this section, would not infringe copyright, that term is unenforceable.

Adaptations

76   Adaptations

An act which by virtue of this Chapter may be done without infringing copyright in a literary, dramatic or musical work does not, where that work is an adaptation, infringe any copyright in the work from which the adaptation was made.

CHAPTER 3A   CERTAIN PERMITTED USES OF ORPHAN WORKS

Chapter IV   Moral Rights

Right to be identified as author or director

77   Right to be identified as author or director

(1) The author of a copyright literary, dramatic, musical or artistic work, and the director of a copyright film, has the right to be identified as the author or director of the work in the circumstances

mentioned in this section; but the right is not infringed unless it has been asserted in accordance with section 78.

(2) The author of a literary work (other than words intended to be sung or spoken with music) or a dramatic work has the right to be identified whenever—

(a) the work is published commercially, performed in public or communicated to the public; or

(b) copies of a film or sound recording including the work are issued to the public;

and that right includes the right to be identified whenever any of those events occur in relation to an adaptation of the work as the author of the work from which the adaptation was made.

(3) The author of a musical work, or a literary work consisting of words intended to be sung or spoken with music, has the right to be identified whenever—

(a) the work is published commercially;

(b) copies of a sound recording of the work are issued to the public; or

(c) a film of which the sound-track includes the work is shown in public or copies of such a film are issued to the public;

and that right includes the right to be identified whenever any of those events occur in relation to an adaptation of the work as the author of the work from which the adaptation was made.

(4) The author of an artistic work has the right to be identified whenever—

(a) the work is published commercially or exhibited in public, or a visual image of it is communicated to the public;

(b) a film including a visual image of the work is shown in public or copies of such a film are issued to the public; or

(c) in the case of a work of architecture in the form of a building or a model for a building, a sculpture or a work of artistic craftsmanship, copies of a graphic work representing it, or of a photograph of it, are issued to the public.

(5) The author of a work of architecture in the form of a building also has the right to be identified on the building as constructed or, where more than one building is constructed to the design, on the first to be constructed.

(6) The director of a film has the right to be identified whenever the film is shown in public or communicated to the public or copies of the film are issued to the public.

(7) The right of the author or director under this section is—

(a) in the case of commercial publication or the issue to the public of copies of a film or sound recording, to be identified in or on each copy or, if that is not appropriate, in some other manner likely to bring his identity to the notice of a person acquiring a copy,

(b) in the case of identification on a building, to be identified by appropriate means visible to persons entering or approaching the building, and

(c) in any other case, to be identified in a manner likely to bring his identity to the attention of a person seeing or hearing the performance, exhibition, showing or communication to the public in question;

and the identification must in each case be clear and reasonably prominent.

(8) If the author or director in asserting his right to be identified specifies a pseudonym, initials or some other particular form of identification, that form shall be used; otherwise any reasonable form of identification may be used.

(9) This section has effect subject to section 79 (exceptions to right).

78 Requirement that right be asserted

(1) A person does not infringe the right conferred by section 77 (right to be identified as author or director) by doing any of the acts mentioned in that section unless the right has been asserted in accordance with the following provisions so as to bind him in relation to that act.

(2) The right may be asserted generally, or in relation to any specified act or description of acts—

(a) on an assignment of copyright in the work, by including in the instrument effecting the assignment a statement that the author or director asserts in relation to that work his right to be identified, or

(b) by instrument in writing signed by the author or director.

(3) The right may also be asserted in relation to the public exhibition of an artistic work—

(a) by securing that when the author or other first owner of copyright parts with possession of the original, or of a copy made by him or under his direction or control, the author is identified on the original or copy, or on a frame, mount or other thing to which it is attached, or

(b) by including in a licence by which the author or other first owner of copyright authorises the making of copies of the work a statement signed by or on behalf of the person granting the licence that the author asserts his right to be identified in the event of the public exhibition of a copy made in pursuance of the licence.

(4) The persons bound by an assertion of the right under subsection (2) or (3) are—

(a) in the case of an assertion under subsection (2)(a), the assignee and anyone claiming through him, whether or not he has notice of the assertion;

(b) in the case of an assertion under subsection (2)(b), anyone to whose notice the assertion is brought;

(c) in the case of an assertion under subsection (3)(a), anyone into whose hands that original or copy comes, whether or not the identification is still present or visible;

(d) in the case of an assertion under subsection (3)(b), the licensee and anyone into whose hands a copy made in pursuance of the licence comes, whether or not he has notice of the assertion.

(5) In an action for infringement of the right the court shall, in considering remedies, take into account any delay in asserting the right.

79   Exceptions to right

(1) The right conferred by section 77 (right to be identified as author or director) is subject to the following exceptions.

(2) The right does not apply in relation to the following descriptions of work—

(a) a computer program;

(b) the design of a typeface;

(c) any computer-generated work.

(3) The right does not apply to anything done by or with the authority of the copyright owner where copyright in the work originally vested in the author's or director's employer by virtue of section 11(2) (works produced in the course of employment).

(4) The right is not infringed by an act which by virtue of any of the following provisions would not infringe copyright in the work—

(a) section 30 (fair dealing for certain purposes), so far as it relates to the reporting of current events by means of a sound recording, film or broadcast;

(b) section 31 (incidental inclusion of work in an artistic work, sound recording, film or broadcast);

(d) section 45 (parliamentary and judicial proceedings);

(e) section 46(1) or (2) (Royal Commissions and statutory inquiries);

(f) section 51 (use of design documents and models);

(g) section 52 (effect of exploitation of design derived from artistic work);

(h) section 57 or 66A (acts permitted on assumptions as to expiry of copyright, etc.).

(4A) The right is also not infringed by any act done for the purposes of an examination which by virtue of any provision of Chapter 3 of Part 1 would not infringe copyright.

(5) The right does not apply in relation to any work made for the purpose of reporting current events.

(6) The right does not apply in relation to the publication in—

(a) a newspaper, magazine or similar periodical, or

(b) an encyclopaedia, dictionary, yearbook or other collective work of reference,

of a literary, dramatic, musical or artistic work made for the purposes of such publication or made available with the consent of the author for the purposes of such publication.

(7) The right does not apply in relation to—

(a) a work in which Crown copyright or Parliamentary copyright subsists, or

(b) a work in which copyright originally vested in an international organisation by virtue of section 168,

unless the author or director has previously been identified as such in or on published copies of the work.

Right to object to derogatory treatment of work

80   Right to object to derogatory treatment of work

(1) The author of a copyright literary, dramatic, musical or artistic work, and the director of a copyright film, has the right in the circumstances mentioned in this section not to have his work subjected to derogatory treatment.

(2) For the purposes of this section—

(a) 'treatment' of a work means any addition to, deletion from or alteration to or adaptation of the work, other than—

(i) a translation of a literary or dramatic work, or

(ii) an arrangement or transcription of a musical work involving no more than a change of key or register; and

(b) the treatment of a work is derogatory if it amounts to distortion or mutilation of the work or is otherwise prejudicial to the honour or reputation of the author or director;

and in the following provisions of this section references to a derogatory treatment of a work shall be construed accordingly.

(3) In the case of a literary, dramatic or musical work the right is infringed by a person who—

(a) publishes commercially, performs in public or communicates to the public a derogatory treatment of the work; or

(b) issues to the public copies of a film or sound recording of, or including, a derogatory treatment of the work.

(4) In the case of an artistic work the right is infringed by a person who—

(a) publishes commercially or exhibits in public a derogatory treatment of the work, or communicates to the public a visual image of a derogatory treatment of the work,

(b) shows in public a film including a visual image of a derogatory treatment of the work or issues to the public copies of such a film, or

(c) in the case of—

(i) a work of architecture in the form of a model for a building,

(ii) a sculpture, or

(iii) a work of artistic craftsmanship,

issues to the public copies of a graphic work representing, or of a photograph of, a derogatory treatment of the work.

(5) Subsection (4) does not apply to a work of architecture in the form of a building; but where the author of such a work is identified on the building and it is the subject of derogatory treatment he has the right to require the identification to be removed.

(6) In the case of a film, the right is infringed by a person who—

(a) shows in public or communicates to the public a derogatory treatment of the film; or

(b) issues to the public copies of a derogatory treatment of the film.

(7) The right conferred by this section extends to the treatment of parts of a work resulting from a previous treatment by a person other than the author or director, if those parts are attributed to, or are likely to be regarded as the work of, the author or director.

(8) This section has effect subject to sections 81 and 82 (exceptions to and qualifications of right).

81   Exceptions to right

(1) The right conferred by section 80 (right to object to derogatory treatment of work) is subject to the following exceptions.

(2) The right does not apply to a computer program or to any computer-generated work.

(3) The right does not apply in relation to any work made for the purpose of reporting current events.

(4) The right does not apply in relation to the publication in—

(a) a newspaper, magazine or similar periodical, or

(b) an encyclopaedia, dictionary, yearbook or other collective work of reference,

of a literary, dramatic, musical or artistic work made for the purposes of such publication or made available with the consent of the author for the purposes of such publication. Nor does the right apply in relation to any subsequent exploitation elsewhere of such a work without any modification of the published version.

(5) The right is not infringed by an act which by virtue of section 57 or 66A (acts permitted on assumptions as to expiry of copyright, etc.) would not infringe copyright.

(6) The right is not infringed by anything done for the purpose of—

(a) avoiding the commission of an offence,

(b) complying with a duty imposed by or under an enactment, or

(c) in the case of the British Broadcasting Corporation, avoiding the inclusion in a programme broadcast by them of anything which offends against good taste or decency or which is likely to encourage or incite to crime or to lead to disorder or to be offensive to public feeling,

provided, where the author or director is identified at the time of the relevant act or has previously been identified in or on published copies of the work, that there is a sufficient disclaimer.

82   Qualification of right in certain cases

(1) This section applies to—

(a) works in which copyright originally vested in the author's or director's employer by virtue of section 11(2) (works produced in course of employment),

(b) works in which Crown copyright or Parliamentary copyright subsists, and

(c) works in which copyright originally vested in an international organisation by virtue of section 168.

(2) The right conferred by section 80 (right to object to derogatory treatment of work) does not apply to anything done in relation to such a work by or with the authority of the copyright owner unless the author or director—

(a) is identified at the time of the relevant act, or

(b) has previously been identified in or on published copies of the work;

and where in such a case the right does apply, it is not infringed if there is a sufficient disclaimer.

83   Infringement of right by possessing or dealing with infringing article

(1) The right conferred by section 80 (right to object to derogatory treatment of work) is also infringed by a person who—

(a) possesses in the course of a business, or

(b) sells or lets for hire, or offers or exposes for sale or hire, or

(c) in the course of a business exhibits in public or distributes, or

(d) distributes otherwise than in the course of a business so as to affect prejudicially the honour or reputation of the author or director,

an article which is, and which he knows or has reason to believe is, an infringing article.

(2) An 'infringing article' means a work or a copy of a work which—

(a) has been subjected to derogatory treatment within the meaning of section 80, and

(b) has been or is likely to be the subject of any of the acts mentioned in that section in circumstances infringing that right.

False attribution of work

84   False attribution of work

(1) A person has the right in the circumstances mentioned in this section—

(a) not to have a literary, dramatic, musical or artistic work falsely attributed to him as author, and

(b) not to have a film falsely attributed to him as director;

and in this section an 'attribution', in relation to such a work, means a statement (express or implied) as to who is the author or director.

(2) The right is infringed by a person who—

(a) issues to the public copies of a work of any of those descriptions in or on which there is a false attribution, or

(b) exhibits in public an artistic work, or a copy of an artistic work, in or on which there is a false attribution.

(3) The right is also infringed by a person who—

(a) in the case of a literary, dramatic or musical work, performs the work in public or communicates it to the public as being the work of a person, or

(b) in the case of a film, shows it in public or communicates it to the public as being directed by a person,

knowing or having reason to believe that the attribution is false.

(4) The right is also infringed by the issue to the public or public display of material containing a false attribution in connection with any of the acts mentioned in subsection (2) or (3).

(5) The right is also infringed by a person who in the course of a business—

(a) possesses or deals with a copy of a work of any of the descriptions mentioned in subsection (1) in or on which there is a false attribution, or

(b) in the case of an artistic work, possesses or deals with the work itself when there is a false attribution in or on it,

knowing or having reason to believe that there is such an attribution and that it is false.

(6) In the case of an artistic work the right is also infringed by a person who in the course of a business—

(a) deals with a work which has been altered after the author parted with possession of it as being the unaltered work of the author, or

(b) deals with a copy of such a work as being a copy of the unaltered work of the author,

knowing or having reason to believe that that is not the case.

(7) References in this section to dealing are to selling or letting for hire, offering or exposing for sale or hire, exhibiting in public, or distributing.

(8) This section applies where, contrary to the fact—

(a) a literary, dramatic or musical work is falsely represented as being an adaptation of the work of a person, or

(b) a copy of an artistic work is falsely represented as being a copy made by the author of the artistic work,

as it applies where the work is falsely attributed to a person as author.

Right to privacy of certain photographs and films

85   Right to privacy of certain photographs and films

(1) A person who for private and domestic purposes commissions the taking of a photograph or the making of a film has, where copyright subsists in the resulting work, the right not to have—

(a) copies of the work issued to the public,

(b) the work exhibited or shown in public, or

(c) the work communicated to the public;

and, except as mentioned in subsection (2), a person who does or authorises the doing of any of those acts infringes that right.

(2) The right is not infringed by an act which by virtue of any of the following provisions would not infringe copyright in the work—

(a) section 31 (incidental inclusion of work in an artistic work, film or broadcast);

(b) section 45 (parliamentary and judicial proceedings);

(c) section 46 (Royal Commissions and statutory inquiries);

(d) section 50 (acts done under statutory authority);

(e) section 57 or 66A (acts permitted on assumptions as to expiry of copyright, etc.).

Supplementary

86   Duration of rights

(1) The rights conferred by section 77 (right to be identified as author or director), section 80 (right to object to derogatory treatment of work) and section 85 (right to privacy of certain photographs and films) continue to subsist so long as copyright subsists in the work.

(2) The right conferred by section 84 (false attribution) continues to subsist until 20 years after a person's death.

87   Consent and waiver of rights

(1) It is not an infringement of any of the rights conferred by this Chapter to do any act to which the person entitled to the right has consented.

(2) Any of those rights may be waived by instrument in writing signed by the person giving up the right.

(3) A waiver—

(a) may relate to a specific work, to works of a specified description or to works generally, and may relate to existing or future works, and

(b) may be conditional or unconditional and may be expressed to be subject to revocation;

and if made in favour of the owner or prospective owner of the copyright in the work or works to which it relates, it shall be presumed to extend to his licensees and successors in title unless a contrary intention is expressed.

(4) Nothing in this Chapter shall be construed as excluding the operation of the general law of contract or estoppel in relation to an informal waiver or other transaction in relation to any of the rights mentioned in subsection (1).

88   Application of provisions to joint works

(1) The right conferred by section 77 (right to be identified as author or director) is, in the case of a work of joint authorship, a right of each joint author to be identified as a joint author and must be asserted in accordance with section 78 by each joint author in relation to himself.

(2) The right conferred by section 80 (right to object to derogatory treatment of work) is, in the case of a work of joint authorship, a right of each joint author and his right is satisfied if he consents to the treatment in question.

(3) A waiver under section 87 of those rights by one joint author does not affect the rights of the other joint authors.

(4) The right conferred by section 84 (false attribution) is infringed, in the circumstances mentioned in that section—

(a) by any false statement as to the authorship of a work of joint authorship, and

(b) by the false attribution of joint authorship in relation to a work of sole authorship;

and such a false attribution infringes the right of every person to whom authorship of any description is, whether rightly or wrongly, attributed.

(5) The above provisions also apply (with any necessary adaptations) in relation to a film which was, or is alleged to have been, jointly directed, as they apply to a work which is, or is alleged to be, a work of joint authorship.

A film is 'jointly directed' if it is made by the collaboration of two or more directors and the contribution of each director is not distinct from that of the other director or directors.

(6) The right conferred by section 85 (right to privacy of certain photographs and films) is, in the case of a work made in pursuance of a joint commission, a right of each person who commissioned the making of the work, so that—

(a) the right of each is satisfied if he consents to the act in question, and

(b) a waiver under section 87 by one of them does not affect the rights of the others.

89   Application of provisions to parts of works

(1) The rights conferred by section 77 (right to be identified as author or director) and section 85 (right to privacy of certain photographs and films) apply in relation to the whole or any substantial part of a work.

(2) The rights conferred by section 80 (right to object to derogatory treatment of work) and section 84 (false attribution) apply in relation to the whole or any part of a work.

Chapter V   Dealings with Rights in Copyright Works

Copyright

90   Assignment and licences

(1) Copyright is transmissible by assignment, by testamentary disposition or by operation of law, as personal or moveable property.

(2) An assignment or other transmission of copyright may be partial, that is, limited so as to apply—

(a) to one or more, but not all, of the things the copyright owner has the exclusive right to do;

(b) to part, but not the whole, of the period for which the copyright is to subsist.

(3) An assignment of copyright is not effective unless it is in writing signed by or on behalf of the assignor.

(4) A licence granted by a copyright owner is binding on every successor in title to his interest in the copyright, except a purchaser in good faith for valuable consideration and without notice (actual or constructive) of the licence or a person deriving title from such a purchaser; and references in this Part to doing anything with, or without, the licence of the copyright owner shall be construed accordingly.

91   Prospective ownership of copyright

(1) Where by an agreement made in relation to future copyright, and signed by or on behalf of the prospective owner of the copyright, the prospective owner purports to assign the future copyright (wholly or partially) to another person, then if, on the copyright coming into existence, the assignee or another person claiming under him would be entitled as against all other persons to require the copyright to be vested in him, the copyright shall vest in the assignee or his successor in title by virtue of this subsection.

(2) In this Part—

'future copyright' means copyright which will or may come into existence in respect of a future work or class or works or on the occurrence of a future event; and 'prospective owner' shall be construed accordingly, and includes a person who is prospectively entitled to copyright by virtue of such an agreement as is mentioned in subsection (1).

(3) A licence granted by a prospective owner of copyright is binding on every successor in title to his interest (or prospective interest) in the right, except a purchaser in good faith for valuable consideration and without notice (actual or constructive) of the licence or a person deriving title from such a purchaser; and references in this Part to doing anything with, or without the licence of the copyright owner shall be construed accordingly.

92   Exclusive licences

(1) In this Part an 'exclusive licence' means a licence in writing signed by or on behalf of the copyright owner authorising the licensee to the exclusion of all other persons, including the person granting the licence, to exercise a right which would otherwise be exercisable exclusively by the copyright owner.

(2) The licensee under an exclusive licence has the same rights against a successor in title who is bound by the licence as he has against the person granting the licence.

93   Copyright to pass under will with unpublished work

Where under a bequest (whether specific or general) a person entitled, beneficially or otherwise, to—

(a) an original document or other material thing recording or embodying a literary, dramatic, musical or artistic work which was not published before the death of the testator, or

(b) an original material thing containing a sound recording or film which was not published before the death of the testator,

the bequest shall, unless a contrary intention is indicated in the testator's will or a codicil to it, be construed as including the copyright in the work in so far as the testator was the owner of the copyright immediately before his death.

93A   Presumption of transfer of rental right in case of film production agreement

(1) Where an agreement concerning film production is concluded between an author and a film producer, the author shall be presumed, unless the agreement provides to the contrary, to have transferred to the film producer any rental right in relation to the film arising by virtue of the inclusion of a copy of the author's work in the film.

(2) In this section 'author' means an author, or prospective author, of a literary, dramatic, musical or artistic work.

(3) Subsection (1) does not apply to any rental right in relation to the film arising by virtue of the inclusion in the film of the screenplay, the dialogue or music specifically created for and used in the film.

(4) Where this section applies, the absence of signature by or on behalf of the author does not exclude the operation of section 91(1) (effect of purported assignment of future copyright).

(5) The reference in subsection (1) to an agreement concluded between an author and a film producer includes any agreement having effect between those persons, whether made by them directly or through intermediaries.

(6) Section 93B (right to equitable remuneration on transfer of rental right) applies where there is a presumed transfer by virtue of this section as in the case of an actual transfer.

Right to equitable remuneration where rental right transferred

93B   Right to equitable remuneration where rental right transferred

(1) Where an author to whom this section applies has transferred his rental right concerning a sound recording or a film to the producer of the sound recording or film, he retains the right to equitable remuneration for the rental.

The authors to whom this section applies are—

(a) the author of a literary, dramatic, musical or artistic work, and

(b) the principal director of a film.

(2) The right to equitable remuneration under this section may not be assigned by the author except to a collecting society for the purpose of enabling it to enforce the right on his behalf.

The right is, however, transmissible by testamentary disposition or by operation of law as personal or moveable property; and it may be assigned or further transmitted by any person into whose hands it passes.

(3) Equitable remuneration under this section is payable by the person for the time being entitled to the rental right, that is, the person to whom the right was transferred or any successor in title of his.

(4) The amount payable by way of equitable remuneration is as agreed by or on behalf of the persons by and to whom it is payable, subject to section 93C (reference of amount to Copyright Tribunal).

(5) An agreement is of no effect in so far as it purports to exclude or restrict the right to equitable remuneration under this section.

(6) References in this section to the transfer of rental right by one person to another include any arrangement having that effect, whether made by them directly or through intermediaries.

(7) In this section a 'collecting society' means a society or other organisation which has as its main object, or one of its main objects, the exercise of the right to equitable remuneration under this section on behalf of more than one author.

93C Equitable remuneration: reference of amount to Copyright Tribunal

(1) In default of agreement as to the amount payable by way of equitable remuneration under section 93B, the person by or to whom it is payable may...

(4) Remuneration shall not be considered inequitable merely because it was paid by way of a single payment or at the time of the transfer of the rental right.

(5) An agreement is of no effect in so far as it purports to prevent a person questioning the amount of equitable remuneration or to restrict the powers of the Copyright Tribunal under this section.

Moral rights

94 Moral rights not assignable

The rights conferred by Chapter IV (moral rights) are not assignable.

95 Transmission of moral rights on death

(1) On the death of a person entitled to the right conferred by section 77 (right to identification of author or director), section 80 (right to object to derogatory treatment of work) or section 85 (right to privacy of certain photographs and films)—

    (a) the right passes to such person as he may by testamentary disposition specifically direct,

    (b) if there is no such direction but the copyright in the work in question forms part of his estate, the right passes to the person to whom the copyright passes, and

    (c) if or to the extent that the right does not pass under paragraph (a) or (b) it is exercisable by his personal representatives.

(2) Where copyright forming part of a person's estate passes in part to one person and in part to another, as for example where a bequest is limited so as to apply—

    (a) to one or more, but not all, of the things the copyright owner has the exclusive right to do or authorise, or

    (b) to part, but not the whole, of the period for which the copyright is to subsist,

any right which passes with the copyright by virtue of subsection (1) is correspondingly divided.

(3) Where by virtue of subsection (1)(a) or (b) a right becomes exercisable by more than one person—

    (a) it may, in the case of the right conferred by section 77 (right to identification of author or director), be asserted by any of them;

    (b) it is, in the case of the right conferred by section 80 (right to object to derogatory treatment of work) or section 85 (right to privacy of certain photographs and films), a right exercisable by each of them and is satisfied in relation to any of them if he consents to the treatment or act in question; and

(c) any waiver of the right in accordance with section 87 by one of them does not affect the rights of the others.

(4) A consent or waiver previously given or made binds any person to whom a right passes by virtue of subsection (1).

(5) Any infringement after a person's death of the right conferred by section 84 (false attribution) is actionable by his personal representatives.

(6) Any damages recovered by personal representatives by virtue of this section in respect of an infringement after a person's death shall devolve as part of his estate as if the right of action had subsisted and been vested in him immediately before his death.

Chapter VI   Remedies for Infringement

Rights and remedies of copyright owner

96   Infringement actionable by copyright owner

(1) An infringement of copyright is actionable by the copyright owner.

(2) In an action for infringement of copyright all such relief by way of damages, injunctions, accounts or otherwise is available to the plaintiff as is available in respect of the infringement of any other property right.

(3) This section has effect subject to the following provisions of this Chapter.

97   Provisions as to damages in infringement action

(1) Where in an action for infringement of copyright it is shown that at the time of the infringement the defendant did not know, and had no reason to believe, that copyright subsisted in the work to which the action relates, the plaintiff is not entitled to damages against him, but without prejudice to any other remedy.

(2) The court may in an action for infringement of copyright having regard to all the circumstances, and in particular to—

(a) the flagrancy of the infringement, and

(b) any benefit accruing to the defendant by reason of the infringement,

award such additional damages as the justice of the case may require.

97A   Injunctions against service providers

(1) The High Court (in Scotland, the Court of Session) shall have power to grant an injunction against a service provider, where that service provider has actual knowledge of another person using their service to infringe copyright.

(2) In determining whether a service provider has actual knowledge for the purpose of this section, a court shall take into account all matters which appear to it in the particular circumstances to be relevant and, amongst other things, shall have regard to—

(a) whether a service provider has received a notice through a means of contact made available in accordance with regulation 6(1)(c) of the Electronic Commerce (EC Directive) Regulations 2002 (SI 2002/2013); and

(b) the extent to which any notice includes—

(i)   the full name and address of the sender of the notice;

(ii) details of the infringement in question.

(3) In this section 'service provider' has the meaning given to it by regulation 2 of the Electronic Commerce (EC Directive) Regulations 2002.

98   Undertaking to take licence of right in infringement proceedings

(1) If in proceedings for infringement of copyright in respect of which a licence is available as of right under section 144 (powers exercisable in consequence of report of Competition and Markets

Authority) the defendant undertakes to take a licence on such terms as may be agreed or, in default of agreement, settled by the Copyright Tribunal under that section—

(a) no injunction shall be granted against him,

(b) no order for delivery up shall be made under section 99, and

(c) the amount recoverable against him by way of damages or on an account of profits shall not exceed double the amount which would have been payable by him as licensee if such a licence on those terms had been granted before the earliest infringement.

(2) An undertaking may be given at any time before final order in the proceedings, without any admission of liability.

(3) Nothing in this section affects the remedies available in respect of an infringement committed before licences of right were available.

99   Order for delivery up

(1) Where a person—

(a) has an infringing copy of a work in his possession, custody or control in the course of a business, or

(b) has in his possession, custody or control an article specifically designed or adapted from making copies of a particular copyright work, knowing or having reason to believe that it has been or is to be used to make infringing copies,

the owner of the copyright in the work may apply to the court for an order that the infringing copy or article be delivered up to him or to such other person as the court may direct.

...

100   Right to seize infringing copies and other articles

(1) An infringing copy of a work which is found exposed or otherwise immediately available for sale or hire, and in respect of which the copyright owner would be entitled to apply for an order under section 99, may be seized and detained by him or a person authorised by him.

The right to seize and detain is exercisable subject to the following conditions and is subject to any decision of the court under section 114.

...

Rights and remedies of exclusive licensee

101   Rights and remedies of exclusive licensee

(1) An exclusive licensee has, except against the copyright owner, the same rights and remedies in respect of matters occurring after the grant of the licence as if the licence had been an assignment.

(2) His rights and remedies are concurrent with those of the copyright owner; and references in the relevant provisions of this Part to the copyright owner shall be construed accordingly.

(3) In an action brought by an exclusive licensee by virtue of this section a defendant may avail himself of any defence which would have been available to him if the action had been brought by the copyright owner.

101A   Certain infringements actionable by a non-exclusive licensee

(1) A non-exclusive licensee may bring an action for infringement of copyright if—

(a) the infringing act was directly connected to a prior licensed act of the licensee; and

(b) the licence—

(i) is in writing and is signed by or on behalf of the copyright owner; and

(ii) expressly grants the non-exclusive licensee a right of action under this section.

(2) In an action brought under this section, the non-exclusive licensee shall have the same rights and remedies available to him as the copyright owner would have had if he had brought the action.

(3) The rights granted under this section are concurrent with those of the copyright owner and references in the relevant provisions of this Part to the copyright owner shall be construed accordingly.

(4) In an action brought by a non-exclusive licensee by virtue of this section a defendant may avail himself of any defence which would have been available to him if the action had been brought by the copyright owner.

(5) Subsections (1) to (4) of section 102 shall apply to a non-exclusive licensee who has a right of action by virtue of this section as it applies to an exclusive licensee.

(6) In this section a 'non-exclusive licensee' means the holder of a licence authorising the licensee to exercise a right which remains exercisable by the copyright owner.

102   Exercise of concurrent rights

(1) Where an action for infringement of copyright brought by the copyright owner or an exclusive licensee relates (wholly or partly) to an infringement in respect of which they have concurrent rights of action, the copyright owner or, as the case may be, the exclusive licensee may not, without the leave of the court, proceed with the action unless the other is either joined as a plaintiff or added as a defendant.

. . .

(3) The above provisions do not affect the granting of interlocutory relief on an application by a copyright owner or exclusive licensee alone.

. . .

Remedies for infringement of moral rights

103   Remedies for infringement of moral rights

(1) An infringement of a right conferred by Chapter IV (moral rights) is actionable as a breach of statutory duty owed to the person entitled to the right.

(2) In proceedings for infringement of the right conferred by section 80 (right to object to derogatory treatment of work) the court may, if it thinks it is an adequate remedy in the circumstances, grant an injunction on terms prohibiting the doing of any act unless a disclaimer is made, in such terms and in such manner as may be approved by the court, dissociating the author or director from the treatment of the work.

Presumptions

104   Presumptions relevant to literary, dramatic, musical and artistic works

(1) The following presumptions apply in proceedings brought by virtue of this Chapter with respect to a literary, dramatic, musical or artistic work.

(2) Where a name purporting to be that of the author appeared on copies of the work as published or on the work when it was made, the person whose name appeared shall be presumed, until the contrary is proved—

    (a) to be the author of the work;

    (b) to have made it in circumstances not falling within section 11(2), 163, 165 or 168 (works produced in course of employment, Crown copyright, Parliamentary copyright or copyright of certain international organisations).

(3) In the case of a work alleged to be a work of joint authorship, subsection (2) applies in relation to each person alleged to be one of the authors.

(4) Where no name purporting to be that of the author appeared as mentioned in subsection (2) but—

    (a) the work qualifies for copyright protection by virtue of section 155 (qualification by reference to country of first publication), and

    (b) a name purporting to be that of the publisher appeared on copies of the work as first published,

the person whose name appeared shall be presumed, until the contrary is proved, to have been the owner of the copyright at the time of publication.

(5) If the author of the work is dead or the identity of the author cannot be ascertained by reasonable inquiry, it shall be presumed, in the absence of evidence to the contrary—

(a) that the work is an original work, and

(b) that the plaintiff's allegations as to what was the first publication of the work and as to the country of first publication are correct.

105 Presumptions relevant to sound recordings and films

(1) In proceedings brought by virtue of this Chapter with respect to a sound recording, where copies of the recording as issued to the public bear a label or other mark stating—

(a) that a named person was the owner of copyright in the recording at the date of issue of the copies, or

(aa) that a named person was the principal director, the author of the screenplay, the author of the dialogue or the composer of music specifically created for and used in the film,

(b) that the recording was first published in a specified year or in a specified country,

the label or mark shall be admissible as evidence of the fact stated and shall be presumed to be correct until the contrary is proved.

(2) In proceedings brought by virtue of this Chapter with respect to a film, where copies of the film as issued to the public bear a statement—

(a) that a named person was the director or producer of the film,

(b) that a named person was the owner of copyright in the film at the date of issue of the copies, or

(c) that the film was first published in a specified year or in a specified country,

the statement shall be admissible as evidence of the facts stated and shall be presumed to be correct until the contrary is proved.

(3) In proceedings brought by virtue of this Chapter with respect to a computer program, where copies of the program are issued to the public in electronic form bearing a statement—

(a) that a named person was the owner of copyright in the program at the date of issue of the copies, or

(b) that the program was first published in a specified country or that copies of it were first issued to the public in electronic form in a specified year,

the statement shall be admissible as evidence of the facts stated and shall be presumed to be correct until the contrary is proved.

(4) The above presumptions apply equally in proceedings relating to an infringement alleged to have occurred before the date on which the copies were issued to the public.

(5) In proceedings brought by virtue of this Chapter with respect to a film, where the film as shown in public or communicated to the public bears a statement—

(a) that a named person was the director or producer of the film, or

(aa) that a named person was the principal director of the film, the author of the screenplay, the author of the dialogue or the composer of music specifically created for and used in the film, or,

(b) that a named person was the owner of copyright in the film immediately after it was made,

the statement shall be admissible as evidence of the facts stated and shall be presumed to be correct until the contrary is proved.

This presumption applies equally in proceedings relating to an infringement alleged to have occurred before the date on which the film was shown in public or communicated to the public.

(6) For the purposes of this section, a statement that a person was the director of a film shall be taken, unless a contrary indication appears, as meaning that he was the principal director of the film.

106 Presumptions relevant to works subject to Crown copyright

In proceedings brought by virtue of this Chapter with respect to a literary, dramatic or musical work in which Crown copyright subsists, where there appears on printed copies of the work a statement of the year in which the work was first published commercially, that statement shall be admissible as evidence of the fact stated and shall be presumed to be correct in the absence of evidence to the contrary.

Offences

107   Criminal liability for making or dealing with infringing articles, &c.

(1)   A person commits an offence who, without the licence of the copyright owner—

    (a) makes for sale or hire, or

    (b) imports into the United Kingdom otherwise than for his private and domestic use, or

    (c) possesses in the course of a business with a view to committing any act infringing the copyright, or

    (d) in the course of a business—

       (i)   sells or lets for hire, or

       (ii)   offers or exposes for sale or hire, or

       (iii) exhibits in public, or

       (iv)   distributes, or

    (e) distributes otherwise than in the course of a business to such an extent as to affect prejudicially the owner of the copyright,

an article which is, and which he knows or has reason to believe is, an infringing copy of a copyright work.

(2)   A person commits an offence who—

    (a) makes an article specifically designed or adapted for making copies of a particular copyright work, or

    (b) has such an article in his possession,

knowing or having reason to believe that it is to be used to make infringing copies for sale or hire or for use in the course of a business.

(2A)   A person ('P') who infringes copyright in a work by communicating the work to the public commits an offence if P—

    (a) knows or has reason to believe that P is infringing copyright in the work, and

    (b) either—

       (i)   intends to make a gain for P or another person, or

       (ii) knows or has reason to believe that communicating the work to the public will cause loss to the owner of the copyright, or will expose the owner of the copyright to a risk of loss.

(2B)   For the purposes of subsection (2A)—

    (a) 'gain' and 'loss'—

       (i)   extend only to gain or loss in money, and

       (ii) include any such gain or loss whether temporary or permanent, and

    (b) 'loss' includes a loss by not getting what one might.

(3)   Where copyright is infringed (otherwise than by reception of a communication to the public)—

    (a) by the public performance of a literary, dramatic or musical work, or

    (b) by the playing or showing in public of a sound recording or film,

any person who caused the work to be so performed, played or shown is guilty of an offence if he knew or had reason to believe that copyright would be infringed.

   …

108   Order for delivery up in criminal proceedings

(1)   The court before which proceedings are brought against a person for an offence under section 107 may, if satisfied that at the time of his arrest or charge—

    (a) he had in his possession, custody or control in the course of a business an infringing copy of a copyright work, or

    (b) he had in his possession, custody or control an article specifically designed or adapted for making copies of a particular copyright work, knowing or having reason to believe that it had been or was to be used to make infringing copies,

order that the infringing copy or article be delivered up to the copyright owner or to such other person as the court may direct.

   …

109   Search warrants

(1) Where a justice of the peace (in Scotland, a sheriff or justice of the peace) is satisfied by information on oath given by a constable (in Scotland, by evidence on oath) that there are reasonable grounds for believing—

    (a) that an offence under section 107(1), (2) or (2A) has been or is about to be committed in any premises, and

    (b) that evidence that such an offence has been or is about to be committed is in those premises,

he may issue a warrant authorising a constable to enter and search the premises, using such reasonable force as is necessary.

...

(4) In executing a warrant issued under this section a constable may seize an article if he reasonably believes that it is evidence that any offence under section 107(1), (2) or (2A) has been or is about to be committed.

(5) In this section 'premises' includes land, buildings, fixed or moveable structures, vehicles, vessels, aircraft and hovercraft.

110   Offence by body corporate: liability of officers

(1) Where an offence under section 107 committed by a body corporate is proved to have been committed with the consent or connivance of a director, manager, secretary or other similar officer of the body, or a person purporting to act in any such capacity, he as well as the body corporate is guilty of the offence and liable to be proceeded against and punished accordingly.

(2) In relation to a body corporate whose affairs are managed by its members 'director' means a member of the body corporate.

Provision for preventing importation of infringing copies

111   Infringing copies may be treated as prohibited goods

(1) The owner of the copyright in a published literary, dramatic or musical work may give notice in writing to the Commissioners of Customs and Excise—

    (a) that he is the owner of the copyright in the work, and

    (b) that he requests the Commissioners, for a period specified in the notice, to treat as prohibited goods printed copies of the work which are infringing copies.

(2) The period specified in a notice under subsection (1) shall not exceed five years and shall not extend beyond the period for which copyright is to subsist.

(3) The owner of the copyright in a sound recording or film may give notice in writing to the Commissioners of Customs and Excise—

    (a) that he is the owner of the copyright in the work,

    (b) that infringing copies of the work are expected to arrive in the United Kingdom at a time and a place specified in the notice, and

    (c) that he requests the Commissioners to treat the copies as prohibited goods.

(3A) The Commissioners may treat as prohibited goods only infringing copies of works which arrive in the United Kingdom—

    (a) from outside the European Economic Area, or

    (b) from within that Area but not having been entered for free circulation.

(3B) This section does not apply to goods placed in, or expected to be placed in, one of the situations referred to in Article 1(1), in respect of which an application may be made under Article 3 of Regulation (EU) No 608/2013 of the European Parliament and of the Council of 12 June 2013 concerning customs enforcement of intellectual property rights.

(4) When a notice is in force under this section the importation of goods to which the notice relates, otherwise than by a person for his private and domestic use, subject to subsections (3A) and (3B), is prohibited; but a person is not by reason of the prohibition liable to any penalty other than forfeiture of the goods.

...

Supplementary

...

114 Order as to disposal of infringing copy or other article

(1) An application may be made to the court for an order that an infringing copy or other article delivered up in pursuance of an order under section 99 or 108, or seized and detained in pursuance of the right conferred by section 100, shall be—

    (a) forfeited to the copyright owner, or

    (b) destroyed or otherwise dealt with as the court may think fit,

or for a decision that no such order should be made.

...

114A Forfeiture of infringing copies, etc.: England and Wales or Northern Ireland

(1) In England and Wales or Northern Ireland where there have come into the possession of any person in connection with the investigation or prosecution of a relevant offence—

    (a) infringing copies of a copyright work, or

    (b) articles specifically designed or adapted for making copies of a particular copyright work,

that person may apply under this section for an order for the forfeiture of the infringing copies or articles.

(2) For the purposes of this section 'relevant offence' means—

    (a) an offence under section 107(1), (2) or (2A) (criminal liability for making or dealing with infringing articles, etc.),

    (b) an offence under the Trade Descriptions Act 1968, or

    (ba) an offence under the Business Protection from Misleading Marketing Regulations 2008,

    (bb) an offence under the Consumer Protection from Unfair Trading Regulations 2008, or

    (c) an offence involving dishonesty or deception.

...

114B Forfeiture of infringing copies, etc.: Scotland

(1) In Scotland the court may make an order under this section for the forfeiture of any—

    (a) infringing copies of a copyright work, or

    (b) articles specifically designed or adapted for making copies of a particular copyright work.

(2) An order under this section may be made—

    (a) on an application by the procurator-fiscal made in the manner specified in section 134 of the Criminal Procedure (Scotland) Act 1995, or

    (b) where a person is convicted of a relevant offence, in addition to any other penalty which the court may impose.

...

Chapter VII   Copyright Licensing

Licensing schemes and licensing bodies

116 Licensing schemes and licensing bodies

(1) In this Part a 'licensing scheme' means a scheme setting out—

    (a) the classes of case in which the operator of the scheme, or the person on whose behalf he acts, is willing to grant copyright licences, and

    (b) the terms on which licences would be granted in those classes of case;

and for this purpose a 'scheme' includes anything in the nature of a scheme, whether described as a scheme or as a tariff or by any other name.

(2) In this Chapter a 'licensing body' means

    (a) a society or other organisation which has as its main object, or one of its main objects, the negotiation or granting, either as owner or prospective owner of copyright or as agent for him, of copyright licences, and whose objects include the granting of licences covering works of more than one author, or

(b) any other organisation which is a collective management organisation as defined by regulation 2 of the Collective Management of Copyright (EU Directive) Regulations 2016.

(3) In this section 'copyright licences' means licences to do, or authorise the doing of, any of the acts restricted by copyright.

(4) References in this Chapter to licences or licensing schemes covering works of more than one author do not include licences or schemes covering only—

(a) a single collective work or collective works of which the authors are the same, or

(b) works made by, or by employees of or commissioned by, a single individual, firm, company or group of companies.

For this purpose a group of companies means a holding company and its subsidiaries, within the meaning of section 1159 of the Companies Act 2006.

Orphan works licensing and extended collective licensing

116A   Power to provide for licensing of orphan works

(1) The Secretary of State may by regulations provide for the grant of licences in respect of works that qualify as orphan works under the regulations.

(2) The regulations may—

(a) specify a person or a description of persons authorised to grant licences, or

(b) provide for a person designated in the regulations to specify a person or a description of persons authorised to grant licences.

(3) The regulations must provide that, for a work to qualify as an orphan work, it is a requirement that the owner of copyright in it has not been found after a diligent search made in accordance with the regulations.

(4) The regulations may provide for the granting of licences to do, or authorise the doing of, any act restricted by copyright that would otherwise require the consent of the missing owner.

(5) The regulations must provide for any licence—

(a) to have effect as if granted by the missing owner;

(b) not to give exclusive rights;

(c) not to be granted to a person authorised to grant licences.

(6) The regulations may apply to a work although it is not known whether copyright subsists in it, and references to a missing owner and a right or interest of a missing owner are to be read as including references to a supposed owner and a supposed right or interest.

116B   Extended collective licensing

(1) The Secretary of State may by regulations provide for a licensing body that applies to the Secretary of State under the regulations to be authorised to grant copyright licences in respect of works in which copyright is not owned by the body or a person on whose behalf the body acts.

(2) An authorisation must specify—

(a) the types of work to which it applies, and

(b) the acts restricted by copyright that the licensing body is authorised to license.

(3) The regulations must provide for the copyright owner to have a right to limit or exclude the grant of licences by virtue of the regulations.

(4) The regulations must provide for any licence not to give exclusive rights.

(5) In this section 'copyright licences' has the same meaning as in section 116.

(6) Nothing in this section applies in relation to Crown copyright or Parliamentary copyright.

116C   General provision about licensing under sections 116A and 116B

(1) This section and section 116D apply to regulations under sections 116A and 116B.

(2) The regulations may provide for a body to be or remain authorised to grant licences only if specified requirements are met, and for a question whether they are met to be determined by a person, and in a manner, specified in the regulations.

(3) The regulations may specify other matters to be taken into account in any decision to be made under the regulations as to whether to authorise a person to grant licences.

(4) The regulations must provide for the treatment of any royalties or other sums paid in respect of a licence, including—

(a) the deduction of administrative costs;

(b) the period for which sums must be held;

(c) the treatment of sums after that period (as bona vacantia or otherwise).

(5) The regulations must provide for circumstances in which an authorisation to grant licences may be withdrawn, and for determining the rights and obligations of any person if an authorisation is withdrawn.

(6) The regulations may include other provision for the purposes of authorisation and licensing, including in particular provision—

(a) for determining the rights and obligations of any person if a work ceases to qualify as an orphan work (or ceases to qualify by reference to any copyright owner), or if a rights owner exercises the right referred to in section 116B(3), while a licence is in force;

(b) about maintenance of registers and access to them;

(c) permitting the use of a work for incidental purposes including an application or search;

(d) for a right conferred by section 77 to be treated as having been asserted in accordance with section 78;

(e) for the payment of fees to cover administrative expenses.

116D   Regulations under sections 116A and 116B

(1) The power to make regulations includes power—

(a) to make incidental, supplementary or consequential provision, including provision extending or restricting the jurisdiction of the Copyright Tribunal or conferring powers on it;

(b) to make transitional, transitory or saving provision;

(c) to make different provision for different purposes.

(2) Regulations under any provision may amend this Part, or any other enactment or subordinate legislation passed or made before that provision comes into force, for the purpose of making consequential provision or extending or restricting the jurisdiction of the Copyright Tribunal or conferring powers on it.

(3) Regulations may make provision by reference to guidance issued from time to time by any person.

(4) The power to make regulations is exercisable by statutory instrument.

(5) A statutory instrument containing regulations may not be made unless a draft of the instrument has been laid before and approved by a resolution of each House of Parliament.

. . .

Chapter IX   Qualification for and Extent of Copyright Protection

Qualification for copyright protection

153   Qualification for copyright protection

(1) Copyright does not subsist in a work unless the qualification requirements of this Chapter are satisfied as regards—

(a) the author (see section 154), or

(b) the country in which the work was first published (see section 155), or

(c) in the case of a broadcast, the country from which the broadcast was made (see section 156).

(2) Subsection (1) does not apply in relation to Crown copyright or Parliamentary copyright (see sections 163 to 166D) or to copyright subsisting by virtue of section 168 (copyright of certain international organisations).

(3) If the qualification requirements of this Chapter, or section 163, 165 or 168, are once satisfied in respect of a work, copyright does not cease to subsist by reason of any subsequent event.

154   Qualification by reference to author

(1) A work qualifies for copyright protection if the author was at the material time a qualifying person, that is—

   (a) a British citizen, a British overseas territories citizen, a British National (Overseas), a British Overseas citizen, a British subject or a British protected person within the meaning of the British Nationality Act 1981, or

   (b) an individual domiciled or resident in the United Kingdom or another country to which the relevant provisions of this Part extend, or

   (c) a body incorporated under the law of a part of the United Kingdom or of another country to which the relevant provisions of this Part extend.

(2) Where, or so far as, provision is made by Order under section 159 (application of this Part to countries to which it does not extend), a work also qualifies for copyright protection if at the material time the author was a citizen or subject of, an individual domiciled or resident in, or a body incorporated under the law of, a country to which the Order relates.

(3) A work of joint authorship qualifies for copyright protection if at the material time any of the authors satisfies the requirements of subsection (1) or (2); but where a work qualifies for copyright protection only under this section, only those authors who satisfy those requirements shall be taken into account for the purposes of—

   section 11(1) and (2) (first ownership of copyright; entitlement of author or author's employer),

   section 12 (duration of copyright), and section 9(4) (meaning of 'unknown authorship') so far as it applies for the purposes of section 12, and

   section 57 (anonymous or pseudonymous works: acts permitted on assumptions as to expiry of copyright or death of author).

(4) The material time in relation to a literary, dramatic, musical or artistic work is—

   (a) in the case of an unpublished work, when the work was made or, if the making of the work extended over a period, a substantial part of that period;

   (b) in the case of a published work, when the work was first published or, if the author had died before that time, immediately before his death.

(5) The material time in relation to other descriptions of work is as follows—

   (a) in the case of a sound recording or film, when it was made;

   (b) in the case of a broadcast, when the broadcast was made;

   (c) (repealed);

   (d) in the case of the typographical arrangement of a published edition, when the edition was first published.

155   Qualification by reference to country of first publication

(1) A literary, dramatic, musical or artistic work, a sound recording or film, or the typographical arrangement of a published edition, qualifies for copyright protection if it is first published—

   (a) in the United Kingdom, or

   (b) in another country to which the relevant provisions of this Part extend.

(2) Where, or so far as, provision is made by Order under section 159 (application of this Part to countries to which it does not extend), such a work also qualifies for copyright protection if it is first published in a country to which the Order relates.

(3) For the purposes of this section, publication in one country shall not be regarded as other than the first publication by reason of simultaneous publication elsewhere; and for this purpose publication elsewhere within the previous 30 days shall be treated as simultaneous.

156   Qualification by reference to place of transmission

(1) A broadcast qualifies for copyright protection if it is made from a place in—

   (a) the United Kingdom, or

   (b) another country to which the relevant provisions of this Part extend.

(2) Where, or so far as, provision is made by Order under section 159 (application of this Part to countries to which it does not extend), a broadcast also qualifies for copyright protection if it is made from a place in a country to which the Order relates.

Extent and application of this Part

157   Countries to which this Part extends

(1) This Part extends to England and Wales, Scotland and Northern Ireland.

(2) Her Majesty may by Order in Council direct that this Part shall extend, subject to such exceptions and modifications as may be specified in the Order to—

(a) any of the Channel Islands,

(b) the Isle of Man, or

(c) any colony.

(3) That power includes power to extend, subject to such exceptions and modifications as may be specified in the Order, any Order in Council made under the following provisions of this Chapter.

(4) The legislature of a country to which this Part has been extended may modify or add to the provisions of this Part, in their operation as part of the law of that country, as the legislature may consider necessary to adapt the provisions to the circumstances of that country—

(a) as regards procedure and remedies, or

(b) as regards works qualifying for copyright protection by virtue of a connection with that country.

(5) Nothing in this section shall be construed as restricting the extent of paragraph 36 of Schedule 1 (transitional provisions: dependent territories where the Copyright Act 1956 or the Copyright Act 1911 remains in force) in relation to the law of a dependent territory to which this Part does not extend.

...

159   Application of this Part to countries to which it does not extend

(1) Where a country is a party to the Berne Convention or a member of the World Trade Organisation, this Part, so far as it relates to literary, dramatic, musical and artistic works, films and typographical arrangements of published editions—

(a) applies in relation to a citizen or subject of that country or a person domiciled or resident there as it applies in relation to a person who is a British citizen or is domiciled or resident in the United Kingdom,

(b) applies in relation to a body incorporated under the law of that country as it applies in relation to a body incorporated under the law of a part of the United Kingdom, and

(c) applies in relation to a work first published in that country as it applies in relation to a work first published in the United Kingdom.

(2) Where a country is a party to the Rome Convention, this Part, so far as it relates to sound recordings and broadcasts —

(a) applies in relation to that country as mentioned in paragraphs (a), (b) and (c) of subsection (1), and

(b) applies in relation to a broadcast made from that country as it applies to a broadcast made from the United Kingdom.

(3) Where a country is a party to the WPPT, this Part, so far as relating to sound recordings, applies in relation to that country as mentioned in paragraphs (a), (b) and (c) of subsection (1).

(4) Her Majesty may by Order in Council—

(a) make provision for the application of this Part to a country by subsection (1), (2) or (3) to be subject to specified restrictions;

(b) make provision for applying this Part, or any of its provisions, to a specified country;

(c) make provision for applying this Part, or any of its provisions, to any country of a specified description;

(d) make provision for the application of legislation to a country under paragraph (b) or (c) to be subject to specified restrictions.

(5) Provision made under subsection (4) may apply generally or in relation to such classes of works, or other classes of case, as are specified.

(6) Her Majesty may not make an Order in Council containing provision under subsection (4)(b) or (c) unless satisfied that provision has been or will be made under the law of the country or countries in question, in respect of the classes to which the provision under subsection (4)(b) or (c) relates, giving adequate protection to the owners of copyright under this Part.

160   Denial of copyright protection to citizens of countries not giving adequate protection to British works

(1) If it appears to Her Majesty that the law of a country fails to give adequate protection to British works to which this section applies, or to one or more classes of such works, Her Majesty may make provision by Order in Council in accordance with this section restricting the rights conferred by this Part in relation to works of authors connected with that country.

(2) An Order in Council under this section shall designate the country concerned and provide that, for the purposes specified in the Order, works first published after a date specified in the Order shall not be treated as qualifying for copyright protection by virtue of such publication if at that time the authors are—

(a) citizens or subjects of that country (not domiciled or resident in the United Kingdom or another country to which the relevant provisions of this Part extend), or

(b) bodies incorporated under the law of that country;

and the Order may make such provision for all the purposes of this Part or for such purposes as are specified in the Order, and either generally or in relation to such class of cases as are specified in the Order, having regard to the nature and extent of that failure referred to in subsection (1).

(3) This section applies to literary, dramatic, musical and artistic works, sound recordings and films; and 'British works' means works of which the author was a qualifying person at the material time within the meaning of section 154.

(4) A statutory instrument containing an Order in Council under this section shall be subject to annulment in pursuance of a resolution of either House of Parliament.

Supplementary

161   Territorial waters and the continental shelf

(1) For the purposes of this Part the territorial waters of the United Kingdom shall be treated as part of the United Kingdom.

(2) This Part applies to things done in the United Kingdom sector of the continental shelf on a structure or vessel which is present there for purposes directly connected with the exploration of the sea bed or subsoil or the exploitation of their natural resources as it applies to things done in the United Kingdom.

(3) The United Kingdom sector of the continental shelf means the areas designated by order under section 1(7) of the Continental Shelf Act 1964.

162   British ships, aircraft and hovercraft

(1) This Part applies to things done on a British ship, aircraft or hovercraft as it applies to things done in the United Kingdom.

(2) In this section—

'British ship' means a ship which is a British ship for the purposes of the Merchant Shipping Act 1995 otherwise than by virtue of registration in a country outside the United Kingdom; and

'British aircraft' and 'British hovercraft' mean an aircraft or hovercraft registered in the United Kingdom.

Chapter X   Miscellaneous and General

Crown and Parliamentary copyright

163   Crown copyright

(1) Where a work is made by Her Majesty or by an officer or servant of the Crown in the course of his duties—

(a) the work qualifies for copyright protection notwithstanding section 153(1) (ordinary requirement as to qualification for copyright protection), and

(b) Her Majesty is the first owner of any copyright in the work.

(2) Copyright in such a work is referred to in this Part as 'Crown copyright', notwithstanding that it may be, or have been, assigned to another person.

(3) Crown copyright in a literary, dramatic, musical or artistic work continues to subsist—

(a) until the end of the period of 125 years from the end of the calendar year in which the work was made, or

(b) if the work is published commercially before the end of the period of 75 years from the end of the calendar year in which it was made, until the end of the period of 50 years from the end of the calendar year in which it was first so published.

(4) In the case of a work of joint authorship where one or more but not all of the authors are persons falling within subsection (1), this section applies only in relation to those authors and the copyright subsisting by virtue of their contribution to the work.

(5) Except as mentioned above, and subject to any express exclusion elsewhere in this Part, the provisions of this Part apply in relation to Crown copyright as to other copyright.

(6) This section does not apply to a work if, or to the extent that, Parliamentary copyright subsists in the work (see sections 165 to 166D).

164 Copyright in Acts and Measures

(1) Her Majesty is entitled to copyright in every Act of Parliament, Act of the Scottish Parliament, Measure of the National Assembly for Wales, Act of the National Assembly for Wales, Act of the Northern Ireland Assembly or Measure of the General Synod of the Church of England.

(2) The copyright subsists

(a) in the case of an Act or a Measure of the General Synod of the Church of England, until the end of the period of 50 years from the end of the calendar year in which Royal Assent was given, and

(b) in the case of a Measure of the National Assembly for Wales, until the end of the period of 50 years from the end of the calendar year in which the Measure was approved by Her Majesty in Council.

(3) References in this Part to Crown copyright (except in section 163) include copyright under this section; and, except as mentioned above, the provisions of this Part apply in relation to copyright under this section as to other Crown copyright.

(4) No other copyright, or right in the nature of copyright, subsists in an Act or Measure.

165 Parliamentary copyright

(1) Where a work is made by or under the direction or control of the House of Commons or the House of Lords—

(a) the work qualifies for copyright protection notwithstanding section 153(1) (ordinary requirement as to qualification for copyright protection), and

(b) the House by whom, or under whose direction or control, the work is made is the first owner of any copyright in the work, and if the work is made by or under the direction or control of both Houses, the two Houses are joint first owners of copyright.

(2) Copyright in such a work is referred to in this Part as 'Parliamentary copyright', notwithstanding that it may be, or have been, assigned to another person.

(3) Parliamentary copyright in a literary, dramatic, musical or artistic work continues to subsist until the end of the period of 50 years from the end of the calendar year in which the work was made.

(4) For the purposes of this section, works made by or under the direction or control of the House of Commons or the House of Lords include—

(a) any work made by an officer or employee of that House in the course of his duties, and

(b) any sound recording, film or live broadcast of the proceedings of that House;

but a work shall not be regarded as made by or under the direction or control of either House by reason only of its being commissioned by or on behalf of that House.

(5) In the case of a work of joint authorship where one or more but not all of the authors are acting on behalf of, or under the direction or control of, the House of Commons or the House of Lords, this section applies only in relation to those authors and the copyright subsisting by virtue of their contribution to the work.

(6) Except as mentioned above, and subject to any express exclusion elsewhere in this Part, the provisions of this Part apply in relation to Parliamentary copyright as to other copyright.

(7) The provisions of this section also apply, subject to any exceptions or modifications specified by Order in Council, to works made by or under the direction or control of any other legislative body of a country to which this Part extends; and references in this Part to 'Parliamentary copyright' shall be construed accordingly.

(8) A statutory instrument containing an Order in Council under subsection (7) shall be subject to annulment in pursuance of a resolution of either House of Parliament.

166   Copyright in Parliamentary Bills

(1) Copyright in every Bill introduced into Parliament belongs, in accordance with the following provisions, to one or both of the Houses of Parliament.

(2) Copyright in a public Bill belongs in the first instance to the House into which the Bill is introduced, and after the Bill has been carried to the second House to both Houses jointly, and subsists from the time when the text of the Bill is handed in to the House in which it is introduced.

(3) Copyright in a private Bill belongs to both Houses jointly and subsists from the time when a copy of the Bill is first deposited in either House.

(4) Copyright in a personal Bill belongs in the first instance to the House of Lords, and after the Bill has been carried to the House of Commons to both Houses jointly, and subsists from the time when it is given a First Reading in the House of Lords.

(5) Copyright under this section ceases—

    (a) on Royal Assent, or

    (b) if the Bill does not receive Royal Assent, on the withdrawal or rejection of the Bill or the end of the Session:

provided that, copyright in a Bill continues to subsist notwithstanding its rejection in any Session by the House of Lords if, by virtue of the Parliament Acts 1911 and 1949, it remains possible for it to be presented for Royal Assent in that Session.

(6) References in this Part to Parliamentary copyright (except in section 165) include copyright under this section; and, except as mentioned above, the provisions of this Part apply in relation to copyright under this section as to other Parliamentary copyright.

(7) No other copyright, or right in the nature of copyright, subsists in a Bill after copyright has once subsisted under this section; but without prejudice to the subsequent operation of this section in relation to a Bill which, not having passed in one Session, is reintroduced in a subsequent Session.

166A   Copyright in Bills of the Scottish Parliament

(1) Copyright in every Bill introduced into the Scottish Parliament belongs to the Scottish Parliamentary Corporate Body.

(2) Copyright under this section subsists from the time when the text of the Bill is handed in to the Parliament for introduction—

    (a) until the Bill receives Royal Assent, or

    (b) if the Bill does not receive Royal Assent, until it is withdrawn or rejected or no further parliamentary proceedings may be taken in respect of it.

(3) References in this Part to Parliamentary copyright (except in section 165) include copyright under this section; and, except as mentioned above, the provisions of this Part apply in relation to copyright under this section as to other Parliamentary copyright.

(4) No other copyright, or right in the nature of copyright, subsists in a Bill after copyright has once subsisted under this section; but without prejudice to the subsequent operation of this section in relation to a Bill which, not having received Royal Assent, is later reintroduced into the Parliament.

166B   Copyright in Bills of the Northern Ireland Assembly

(1) Copyright in every Bill introduced into the Northern Ireland Assembly belongs to the Northern Ireland Assembly Commission.

(2) Copyright under this section subsists from the time when the text of the Bill is handed in to the Assembly for introduction—

(a) until the Bill receives Royal Assent, or

(b) if the Bill does not receive Royal Assent, until it is withdrawn or rejected or no further proceedings of the Assembly may be taken in respect of it.

(3) References in this Part to Parliamentary copyright (except in section 165) include copyright under this section; and, except as mentioned above, the provisions of this Part apply in relation to copyright under this section as to other Parliamentary copyright.

(4) No other copyright, or right in the nature of copyright, subsists in a Bill after copyright has once subsisted under this section; but without prejudice to the subsequent operation of this section in relation to a Bill which, not having received Royal Assent, is later reintroduced into the Assembly.

166C   Copyright in proposed Measures of the National Assembly for Wales

(1) Copyright in every proposed Assembly Measure introduced into the National Assembly for Wales belongs to the National Assembly for Wales Commission.

(2) Copyright under this section subsists from the time when the text of the proposed Assembly Measure is handed in to the Assembly for introduction—

(a) until the proposed Assembly Measure is approved by Her Majesty in Council, or

(b) if the proposed Assembly Measure is not approved by Her Majesty in Council, until it is withdrawn or rejected or no further proceedings of the Assembly may be taken in respect of it.

(3) References in this Part to Parliamentary copyright (except in section 165) include copyright under this section; and, except as mentioned above, the provisions of this Part apply in relation to copyright under this section as to other Parliamentary copyright.

(4) No other copyright, or right in the nature of copyright, subsists in a proposed Assembly Measure after copyright has once subsisted under this section; but without prejudice to the subsequent operation of this section in relation to a proposed Assembly Measure which, not having been approved by Her Majesty in Council, is later reintroduced into the Assembly.

166D   Copyright in Bills of the National Assembly for Wales

(1) Copyright in every Bill introduced into the National Assembly for Wales belongs to the National Assembly for Wales Commission.

(2) Copyright under this section subsists from the time when the text of the Bill is handed in to the Assembly for introduction—

(a) until the Bill receives Royal Assent, or

(b) if the Bill does not receive Royal Assent, until it is withdrawn or rejected or no further proceedings of the Assembly may be taken in respect of it.

(3) References in this Part to Parliamentary copyright (except in section 165) include copyright under this section; and, except as mentioned above, the provisions of this Part apply in relation to copyright under this section as to other Parliamentary copyright.

(4) No other copyright, or right in the nature of copyright, subsists in a Bill after copyright has once subsisted under this section; but without prejudice to the subsequent operation of this section in relation to a Bill which, not having received Royal Assent, is later reintroduced into the Assembly.

167   Houses of Parliament: supplementary provisions with respect to copyright

(1) For the purposes of holding, dealing with and enforcing copyright, and in connection with all legal proceedings relating to copyright, each House of Parliament shall be treated as having the legal capacities of a body corporate, which shall not be affected by a prorogation or dissolution.

(2) The functions of the House of Commons as owner of copyright shall be exercised by the Speaker on behalf of the House; and if so authorised by the Speaker, or in case of a vacancy in the office of Speaker, those functions may be discharged by the Chairman of Ways and Means or a Deputy Chairman.

(3) For this purpose a person who on the dissolution of Parliament was Speaker of the House of Commons, Chairman of Ways and Means or a Deputy Chairman may continue to act until the corresponding appointment is made in the next Session of Parliament.

(4) The functions of the House of Lords as owner of copyright shall be exercised by the Clerk of the Parliaments on behalf of the House; and if so authorised by him, or in case of a vacancy in the office of Clerk of the Parliaments, those functions may be discharged by the Clerk Assistant or the Reading Clerk.

(5) Legal proceedings relating to copyright—

    (a) shall be brought by or against the House of Commons in the name of 'The Speaker of the House of Commons'; and

    (b) shall be brought by or against the House of Lords in the name of 'The Clerk of the Parliaments'.

Other miscellaneous provisions

168 **Copyright vesting in certain international organisations**

(1) Where an original literary, dramatic, musical or artistic work—

    (a) is made by an officer or employee of, or is published by, an international organisation to which this section applies, and

    (b) does not qualify for copyright protection under section 154 (qualification by reference to author) or section 155 (qualification by reference to country of first publication),

copyright nevertheless subsists in the work by virtue of this section and the organisation is first owner of that copyright.

(2) The international organisations to which this section applies are those as to which Her Majesty has by Order in Council declared that it is expedient that this section should apply.

(3) Copyright of which an international organisation is first owner by virtue of this section continues to subsist until the end of the period of 50 years from the end of the calendar year in which the work was made or such longer period as may be specified by Her Majesty by Order in Council for the purpose of complying with the international obligations of the United Kingdom.

(4) An international organisation to which this section applies shall be deemed to have, and to have had at all material times, the legal capacities of a body corporate for the purpose of holding, dealing with and enforcing copyright and in connection with all legal proceedings relating to copyright.

(5) A statutory instrument containing an Order in Council under this section shall be subject to annulment in pursuance of a resolution of either House of Parliament.

169 **Folklore, &c.: anonymous unpublished works**

(1) Where in the case of an unpublished literary, dramatic, musical or artistic work of unknown authorship there is evidence that the author (or, in the case of a joint work, any of the authors) was a qualifying individual by connection with a country outside the United Kingdom, it shall be presumed until the contrary is proved that he was such a qualifying individual and that copyright accordingly subsists in the work, subject to the provisions of this Part.

(2) If under the law of that country a body is appointed to protect and enforce copyright in such works, Her Majesty may by Order in Council designate that body for the purposes of this section.

(3) A body so designated shall be recognised in the United Kingdom as having authority to do in place of the copyright owner anything, other than assign copyright, which it is empowered to do under the law of that country; and it may, in particular, bring proceedings in its own name.

(4) A statutory instrument containing an Order in Council under this section shall be subject to annulment in pursuance of a resolution of either House of Parliament.

(5) In subsection (1) a 'qualifying individual' means an individual who at the material time (within the meaning of section 154) was a person whose works qualified under that section for copyright protection.

(6) This section does not apply if there has been an assignment of copyright in the work by the author of which notice has been given to the designated body; and nothing in this section affects the validity of an assignment of copyright made, or licence granted, by the author or a person lawfully claiming under him.

Transitional provisions and savings

170   Transitional provisions and savings

(1) Schedule 1 contains transitional provisions and savings relating to works made, and acts or events occurring, before the commencement of this Part, and otherwise with respect to the operation of the provisions of this Part.

(2) The Secretary of State may by regulations amend Schedule 1 to reduce the duration of copyright in existing works which are unpublished, other than photographs or films.

(4) 'Existing works' has the same meaning as in Schedule 1.

(5) Regulations under subsection (2) may—

    (a) make different provisions for different purposes;

    (b) make supplementary or transitional provision;

    (c) make consequential provision, including provision amending any enactment or subordinate legislation passed or made before that subsection comes into force.

(6) The power to make regulations under subsection (2) is exercisable by statutory instrument.

(7) A statutory instrument containing regulations under subsection (2) may not be made unless a draft of the instrument has been laid before and approved by resolution of each House of Parliament.

171   Rights and privileges under other enactments or the common law

(1) Nothing in this Part affects—

    (a) any right or privilege of any person under any enactment (except where the enactment is expressly repealed, amended or modified by this Act);

    (b) any right or privilege of the Crown subsisting otherwise than under an enactment;

    (c) any right or privilege of either House of Parliament;

    (d) the right of the Crown or any person deriving title from the Crown to sell, use or otherwise deal with articles forfeited under the laws relating to customs and excise;

    (e) the operation of any rule of equity relating to breaches of trust or confidence.

(2) Subject to those savings, no copyright or right in the nature of copyright shall subsist otherwise than by virtue of this Part or some other enactment in that behalf.

(3) Nothing in this Part affects any rule of law preventing or restricting the enforcement of copyright, on grounds of public interest or otherwise.

(4) Nothing in this Part affects any right of action or other remedy, whether civil or criminal, available otherwise than under this Part in respect of acts infringing any of the rights conferred by Chapter IV (moral rights).

(5) The savings in subsection (1) have effect subject to section 164(4) and section 166(7) (copyright in Acts, Measures and Bills: exclusion of other rights in the nature of copyright).

Interpretation

172   General provisions as to construction

(1) This Part restates and amends the law of copyright, that is, the provisions of the Copyright Act 1956, as amended.

(2) A provision of this Part which corresponds to a provision of the previous law shall not be construed as departing from the previous law merely because of a change of expression.

(3) Decisions under the previous law may be referred to for the purpose of establishing whether a provision of this Part departs from the previous law, or otherwise for establishing the true construction of this Part.

172A Meaning of EEA and related expressions

(1) In this Part—

'the EEA' means the European Economic Area; and

'EEA state' means a member State, Iceland, Liechtenstein or Norway.

173 Construction of references to copyright owner

(1) Where different persons are (whether in consequence of a partial assignment or otherwise) entitled to different aspects of copyright in a work, the copyright owner for any purpose of this Part is the person who is entitled to the aspect of copyright relevant for that purpose.

(2) Where copyright (or any aspect of copyright) is owned by more than one person jointly, references in this Part to the copyright owner are to all the owners, so that, in particular, any requirement of the licence of the copyright owner requires the licence of all of them.

174 Meaning of 'educational establishment' and related expressions

(1) The expression 'educational establishment' in a provision of this Part means—

    (a) any school, and

    (b) any other description of educational establishment specified for the purposes of this Part, or that provision, by order of the Secretary of State.

(2) The Secretary of State may by order provide that the provisions of this Part relating to educational establishments shall apply, with such modifications and adaptations as may be specified in the order, in relation to teachers who are employed by a local authority (as defined in section 579(1) of the Education Act 1996) or (in Northern Ireland) a local education authority, to give instruction elsewhere to pupils who are unable to attend an educational establishment.

(3) In subsection (1)(a) 'school'—

    (a) in relation to England and Wales, has the same meaning as in the Education Act 1996;

    (b) in relation to Scotland, has the same meaning as in the Education (Scotland) Act 1962, except that it includes an approved school within the meaning of the Social Work (Scotland) Act 1968; and

    (c) in relation to Northern Ireland, has the same meaning as in the Education and Libraries (Northern Ireland) Order 1986.

(4) An order under subsection (1)(b) may specify a description of educational establishment by reference to the instruments from time to time in force under any enactment specified in the order.

(5) In relation to an educational establishment the expressions 'teacher' and 'pupil' in this Part include, respectively, any person who gives and any person who receives instruction.

(6) References in this Part to anything being done 'on behalf of' an educational establishment are to its being done for the purposes of that establishment by any person.

(7) An order under this section shall be made by statutory instrument which shall be subject to annulment in pursuance of a resolution of either House of Parliament.

175 Meaning of publication and commercial publication

(1) In this Part 'publication', in relation to a work—

    (a) means the issue of copies to the public, and

    (b) includes, in the case of a literary, dramatic, musical or artistic work, making it available to the public by means of an electronic retrieval system;

and related expressions shall be construed accordingly.

(2) In this Part 'commercial publication', in relation to a literary, dramatic, musical or artistic work means—

    (a) issuing copies of the work to the public at a time when copies made in advance of the receipt of orders are generally available to the public, or

    (b) making the work available to the public by means of an electronic retrieval system;

and related expressions shall be construed accordingly.

(3) In the case of a work of architecture in the form of a building, or an artistic work incorporated in a building, construction of the building shall be treated as equivalent to publication of the work.

(4) The following do not constitute publication for the purposes of this Part and references to commercial publication shall be construed accordingly—

    (a) in the case of a literary, dramatic or musical work—

        (i) the performance of the work, or

        (ii) the communication to the public of the work (otherwise than for the purposes of an electronic retrieval system);

    (b) in the case of an artistic work—

        (i) the exhibition of the work,

        (ii) the issue to the public of copies of a graphic work representing, or of photographs of, a work of architecture in the form of a building or a model for a building, a sculpture or a work of artistic craftsmanship,

        (iii) the issue to the public of copies of a film including the work, or

        (iv) the communication to the public of the work (otherwise than for the purposes of an electronic retrieval system);

    (c) in the case of a sound recording or film—

        (i) the work being played or shown in public, or

        (ii) the communication to the public of the work.

(5) References in this Part to publication or commercial publication do not include publication which is merely colourable and not intended to satisfy the reasonable requirements of the public.

(6) No account shall be taken for the purposes of this section of any unauthorised act.

176   Requirement of signature: application in relation to body corporate

(1) The requirement in the following provisions that an instrument be signed by or on behalf of a person is also satisfied in the case of a body corporate by the affixing of its seal—

section 78(3)(b) (assertion by licensor of right to identification of author in case of public exhibition of copy made in pursuance of the licence),

section 90(3) (assignment of copyright),

section 91(1) (assignment of future copyright),

section 92(1) (grant of exclusive licence).

(2) The requirement in the following provisions that an instrument be signed by a person is satisfied in the case of a body corporate by signature on behalf of the body or by the affixing of its seal—

section 78(2)(b) (assertion by instrument in writing of right to have author identified),

section 87(2) (waiver of moral rights).

177   Adaptation of expressions for Scotland

In the application of this Part to Scotland—

'account of profits' means accounting and payment of profits;

'accounts' means count, reckoning and payment;

'assignment' means assignation;

'costs' means expenses;

'defendant' means defender;

'delivery up' means delivery;

'estoppel' means personal bar;

'injunction' means interdict;

'interlocutory relief' means interim remedy; and

'plaintiff' means pursuer.

178   Minor definitions

In this Part—

'article', in the context of an article in a periodical, includes an item of any description;

'business' includes a trade or profession;

'collective work' means—

    (a) a work of joint authorship, or

    (b) a work in which there are distinct contributions by different authors or in which works or parts of works of different authors are incorporated;

'computer-generated', in relation to a work, means that the work is generated by computer in circumstances such that there is no human author of the work;

'country' includes any territory;

'the Crown' includes the Crown in right of the Scottish Administration, of the Welsh Assembly Government or of Her Majesty's Government in Northern Ireland or in any country outside the United Kingdom to which this Part extends;

'electronic' means actuated by electric, magnetic, electro-magnetic, electro-chemical or electro-mechanical energy, and 'in electronic form' means in a form usable only by electronic means;

'employed', 'employee', 'employer' and 'employment' refer to employment under a contract of service or of apprenticeship;

'facsimile copy' includes a copy which is reduced or enlarged in scale;

'international organisation' means an organisation the members of which include one or more states;

'judicial proceedings' includes proceedings before any court, tribunal or person having authority to decide any matter affecting a person's legal rights or liabilities;

'national of the United Kingdom' means—

(a) a British citizen, a British overseas territories citizen, a British National (Overseas) or a British Overseas Citizen,

(b) a person who under the British Nationality Act 1981 is a British subject,

(c) a British protected person within the meaning of that Act, or

(d) a body incorporated under the law of any part of the United Kingdom.

'parliamentary proceedings' includes proceedings of the Northern Ireland Assembly, of the Scottish Parliament or of the European Parliament and Assembly proceedings within the meaning of section 1(5) of the Government of Wales Act 2006;

'private study' does not include any study which is directly or indirectly for a commercial purpose;

'producer', in relation to a sound recording or a film, means the person by whom the arrangements necessary for the making of the sound recording or film are undertaken;

'public library' means a library administered by or on behalf of—

(a) in England and Wales, a library authority within the meaning of the Public Libraries and Museums Act 1964;

(b) in Scotland, a statutory library authority within the meaning of the Public Libraries (Scotland) Act 1955;

(c) in Northern Ireland, an Education and Library Board within the meaning of the Education and Libraries (Northern Ireland) Order 1986;

'rental right' means the right of a copyright owner to authorise or prohibit the rental of copies of the work (see section 18A);

'reprographic copy' and 'reprographic copying' refer to copying by means of a reprographic process;

'reprographic process' means a process—

(a) for making facsimile copies, or

(b) involving the use of an appliance for making multiple copies,

and includes, in relation to a work held in electronic form, any copying by electronic means, but does not include the making of a film or sound recording;

'sufficient acknowledgement' means an acknowledgement identifying the work in question by its title or other description, and identifying the author unless—

(a) in the case of a published work, it is published anonymously;

(b) in the case of an unpublished work, it is not possible for a person to ascertain the identity of the author by reasonable inquiry;

'sufficient disclaimer', in relation to an act capable of infringing the right conferred by section 80 (right to object to derogatory treatment of work), means a clear and reasonably prominent indication—

(a) given at the time of the act, and

(b) if the author or director is then identified, appearing along with the identification,

that the work has been subjected to treatment to which the author or director has not consented;

'telecommunications system' means a system for conveying visual images, sounds or other information by electronic means;

'typeface' includes an ornamental motif used in printing;

'unauthorised', as regards anything done in relation to a work, means done otherwise than—

(a) by or with the licence of the copyright owner, or

(b) if copyright does not subsist in the work, by or with the licence of the author or, in a case where section 11 (2) would have applied, the author's employer or, in either case, persons lawfully claiming under him, or

(c) in pursuance of section 48 (copying, &c. of certain material by the Crown);

'wireless telegraphy' means the sending of electro-magnetic energy over paths not provided by a material substance constructed or arranged for that purpose but does not include the transmission of microwave energy between terrestrial fixed points;

'wireless broadcast' means a broadcast by means of wireless telegraphy;

'writing' includes any form of notation or code, whether by hand or otherwise and regardless of the method by which, or medium in or on which, it is recorded, and

'written' shall be construed accordingly.

179   Index of defined expressions

The following Table shows provisions defining or otherwise explaining expressions used in this Part (other than provisions defining or explaining an expression used only in the same section)—

accessible copy (in sections 31A to section 31F)	section 31F(4)
account of profits and accounts (in Scotland)	section 177
acts restricted by copyright	section 16(1)
adaptation	section 21(3)
archivist (in sections 40A to 43)	section 43A(5)
article (in a periodical)	section 178
artistic work	section 4(1)
assignment (in Scotland)	section 177
author	sections 9 and 10(3)
authorised body (in sections 31B to 31BB)	section 31F(6)
broadcast (and related expressions)	section 6
building	section 4(2)
business	section 178
...	
collective work	section 178
commencement (in Schedule 1)	paragraph 1(2) of that Schedule
commercial publication	section 175
communication to the public	section 20
computer-generated	section 178
conducted for profit (in sections 40A to 43)	section 43A(4)
copy and copying	section 17
copyright (generally)	section 1
copyright (in Schedule 1)	paragraph 2(2) of that Schedule
copyright owner	sections 101(2) and 173
Copyright Tribunal	section 145
copyright work	section 1(2)
costs (in Scotland)	section 177
country	section 178
country of origin	section 15A
the Crown	section 178
Crown copyright	sections 163(2) and 164(3)
curator (in sections 40A to 43)	section 43A(5)
database	section 3A(1)
defendant (in Scotland)	section 177
delivery up (in Scotland)	section 177
disabled person (in sections 31A to 31F)	section 31F(2) and 3
dramatic work	section 3(1)

educational establishment	sections 174(1) to (4)
the EEA and EEA state	section 172A
electronic and electronic form	section 178
employed, employee, employer and employment	section 178
excepted sound recording	section 72(1A)
exclusive licence	section 92(1)
existing works (in Schedule 1)	paragraph 1(3) of that Schedule
facsimile copy	section 178
film	section 5B
future copyright	section 91(2)
general licence (in sections 140 and 141)	section 140(7)
graphic work	section 4(2)
infringing copy	section 27
injunction (in Scotland)	section 177
interlocutory relief (in Scotland)	section 177
international organisation	section 178
issue of copies to the public	section 18
joint authorship (work of)	sections 10(1) and (2)
judicial proceedings	section 178
lawful user (in sections 50A to 50C)	section 50A(2)
lending	section 18A(2) to (6)
librarian (in sections 40A to 43)	section 43A(5)
library (in sections 40A to 43)	section 43A(2)
licence (in sections 125 to 128)	section 124
licence of copyright owner	sections 90(4), 91(3) and 173
licensing body (in Chapter VII)	section 116(2)
licensing scheme (generally)	section 116(1)
licensing scheme (in sections 118 to 121)	section 117
literary work	section 3(1)
made (in relation to a literary, dramatic or musical work)	section 3(2)
museum (in sections 40A to 43)	section 43A(3)
musical work	section 3(1)
national of the United Kingdom	section 178
needletime	section 135A
the new copyright provisions (in Schedule 1)	paragraph 1(1) of that Schedule
the 1911 Act (in Schedule 1)	paragraph 1(1) of that Schedule
the 1956 Act (in Schedule 1)	paragraph 1(1) of that Schedule
on behalf of (in relation to an educational establishment)	section 174(5)
original (in relation to a database)	section 3A(2)
Parliamentary copyright	sections 165(2) and (7), 166(6), 166A(3), 166B(3), 166C(3) and 166D(3)
parliamentary proceedings	section 178
performance	section 19(2)
photograph	section 4(2)
plaintiff (in Scotland)	section 177
private study	section 178
producer (in relation to a sound recording or film)	section 178
programme (in the context of broadcasting)	section 6(3)
prospective owner (of copyright)	section 91(2)
publication and related expressions	section 175
public library	section 178

published edition (in the context of copyright in the typographical arrangement)	section 8
pupil	section 174(5)
rental	section 18A(2) to (6)
rental right	section 178
reprographic copies and reprographic copying	section 178
reprographic process	section 178
sculpture	section 4(2)
signed	section 176
sound recording	sections 5A and 135A
sufficient acknowledgement	section 178
sufficient disclaimer	section 178
supply (in sections 31B to 31BB)	section 31F(7)
teacher	section 174(5)
telecommunications system	section 178
terms of payment	section 135A
typeface	section 178
unauthorised (as regards things done in relation to a work)	section 178
unknown (in relation to the author of a work)	section 9(5)
unknown authorship (work of)	section 9(4)
wireless broadcast	section 178
wireless telegraphy	section 178
work (in Schedule 1)	paragraph 2(1) of that Schedule
work of more than one author (in Chapter VII)	section 116(4)
writing and written	section 178

PART II   RIGHTS IN PERFORMANCES

Chapter 1   Introductory

180   Rights conferred on performers and persons having recording rights

(1) Chapter 2 of this Part (economic rights) confers rights—

(a) on a performer, by requiring his consent to the exploitation of his performances (see sections 181 to 184), and

(b) on a person having recording rights in relation to a performance, in relation to recordings made without his consent or that of the performer (see sections 185 to 188),

and creates offences in relation to dealing with or using illicit recordings and certain other related acts (see sections 198 and 201).

(1A) Rights are also conferred on a performer by the following provisions of Chapter 3 of this Part (moral rights)—

(a) section 205 C (right to be identified);

(b) section 205F (right to object to derogatory treatment of performance).

(2) In this Part—

'performance' means—

(a) a dramatic performance (which includes dance and mime),

(b) a musical performance,

(c) a reading or recitation of a literary work, or

(d) a performance of a variety act or any similar presentation,

which is, or so far as it is, a live performance given by one or more individuals; and

'recording', in relation to a performance, means a film or sound recording—

(a) made directly from the live performance,

(b) made from a broadcast of the performance, or

(c) made, directly or indirectly, from another recording of the performance.

(3) The rights conferred by this Part apply in relation to performances taking place before the commencement of this Part; but no act done before commencement, or in pursuance of arrangements made before commencement, shall be regarded as infringing those rights.

(4) The rights conferred by this Part are independent of—

(a) any copyright in, or moral rights relating to, any work performed or any film or sound recording of, or broadcast including, the performance, and

(b) any other right or obligation arising otherwise than under this Part.

181 Qualifying performances

A performance is a qualifying performance for the purposes of the provisions of this Part relating to performers' rights if it is given by a qualifying individual (as defined in section 206) or takes place in a qualifying country (as so defined).

Chapter 2   Economic Rights

Performers' rights

182 Consent required for recording, &c. of live performance

(1) A performer's rights are infringed by a person who, without his consent—

(a) makes a recording of the whole or any substantial part of a qualifying performance directly from the live performance,

(b) broadcasts live the whole or any substantial part of a qualifying performance,

(c) makes a recording of the whole or any substantial part of a qualifying performance directly from a broadcast of the live performance.

(3) In an action for infringement of a performer's rights brought by virtue of this section damages shall not be awarded against a defendant who shows that at the time of the infringement he believed on reasonable grounds that consent had been given.

182A Consent required for copying of recording

(1) A performer's rights are infringed by a person who, without his consent, makes a copy of a recording of the whole or any substantial part of a qualifying performance.

(1A) In subsection (1), making a copy of a recording includes making a copy which is transient or is incidental to some other use of the original recording.

(2) It is immaterial whether the copy is made directly or indirectly.

(3) The right of a performer under this section to authorise or prohibit the making of such copies is referred to in this Chapter as 'reproduction right'.

182B Consent required for issue of copies to public

(1) A performer's rights are infringed by a person who, without his consent, issues to the public copies of a recording of the whole or any substantial part of a qualifying performance.

. . .

(5) The right of a performer under this section to authorise or prohibit the issue of copies to the public is referred to in this Chapter as 'distribution right'.

182C Consent required for rental or lending of copies to public

(1) A performer's rights are infringed by a person who, without his consent, rents or lends to the public copies of a recording of the whole or any substantial part of a qualifying performance.

(2) In this Chapter, subject to the following provisions of this section—

(a) 'rental' means making a copy of a recording available for use, on terms that it will or may be returned, for direct or indirect economic or commercial advantage, and

(b) 'lending' means making a copy of a recording available for use, on terms that it will or may be returned, otherwise than for direct or indirect economic or commercial advantage, through an establishment which is accessible to the public.

(3) The expressions 'rental' and 'lending' do not include—

(a) making available for the purpose of public performance, playing or showing in public or communication to the public;

(b) making available for the purpose of exhibition in public; or

(c) making available for on-the-spot reference use.

(4) The expression 'lending' does not include making available between establishments which are accessible to the public.

(5) Where lending by an establishment accessible to the public gives rise to a payment the amount of which does not go beyond what is necessary to cover the operating costs of the establishment, there is no direct or indirect economic or commercial advantage for the purposes of this section.

(6) References in this Chapter to the rental or lending of copies of a recording of a performance include the rental or lending of the original recording of the live performance.

(7) In this Chapter—

'rental right' means the right of a performer under this section to authorise or prohibit the rental of copies to the public, and

'lending right' means the right of a performer under this section to authorise or prohibit the lending of copies to the public.

182CA   Consent required for making available to the public

(1) A performer's rights are infringed by a person who, without his consent, makes available to the public a recording of the whole or any substantial part of a qualifying performance by electronic transmission in such a way that members of the public may access the recording from a place and at a time individually chosen by them.

(2) The right of a performer under this section to authorise or prohibit the making available to the public of a recording is referred to in this Chapter as 'making available right'.

182D   Right to equitable remuneration for exploitation of sound recording

(1) Where a commercially published sound recording of the whole or any substantial part of a qualifying performance—

(a) is played in public, or

(b) is communicated to the public otherwise than by its being made available to the public in the way mentioned in section 182CA(1),

the performer is entitled to equitable remuneration from the owner of the copyright in the sound recording or, where copyright in the sound recording has expired pursuant to section 191HA(4), from a person who plays the sound recording in public or communicates the sound recording to the public.

(1A) In subsection (1), the reference to publication of a sound recording includes making it available to the public by electronic transmission in such a way that members of the public may access it from a place and at a time individually chosen by them.

(2) The right to equitable remuneration under this section may not be assigned by the performer except to a collecting society for the purpose of enabling it to enforce the right on his behalf.

The right is, however, transmissible by testamentary disposition or by operation of law as personal or moveable property; and it may be assigned or further transmitted by any person into whose hands it passes.

. . .

(7) An agreement is of no effect in so far as it purports—

(a) to exclude or restrict the right to equitable remuneration under this section, or

(b) to prevent a person questioning the amount of equitable remuneration or to restrict the powers of the Copyright Tribunal under this section.

. . .

183   Infringement of performer's rights by use of recording made without consent

A performer's rights are infringed by a person who, without his consent—

(a) shows or plays in public the whole or any substantial part of a qualifying performance, or

(b) communicates to the public the whole or any substantial part of a qualifying performance,

by means of a recording which was, and which that person knows or has reason to believe was, made without the performer's consent.

184   Infringement of performer's rights by importing, possessing or dealing with illicit recording

(1) A performer's rights are infringed by a person who, without his consent—

(a) imports into the United Kingdom otherwise than for his private and domestic use, or

(b) in the course of a business possesses, sells or lets for hire, offers or exposes for sale or hire, or distributes,

a recording of a qualifying performance which is, and which that person knows or has reason to believe is, an illicit recording.

(2) Where in an action for infringement of a performer's rights brought by virtue of this section a defendant shows that the illicit recording was innocently acquired by him or a predecessor in title of his, the only remedy available against him in respect of the infringement is damages not exceeding a reasonable payment in respect of the act complained of.

(3) In subsection (2) 'innocently acquired' means that the person acquiring the recording did not know and had no reason to believe that it was an illicit recording.

Rights of person having recording rights

185   Exclusive recording contracts and persons having recording rights

(1) In this Chapter an 'exclusive recording contract' means a contract between a performer and another person under which that person is entitled to the exclusion of all other persons (including the performer) to make recordings of one or more of his performances with a view to their commercial exploitation.

(2) References in this Chapter to a 'person having recording rights', in relation to a performance, are (subject to subsection (3)) to a person—

(a) who is party to and has the benefit of an exclusive recording contract to which the performance is subject, or

(b) to whom the benefit of such a contract has been assigned,

and who is a qualifying person.

(3) If a performance is subject to an exclusive recording contract but the person mentioned in subsection (2) is not a qualifying person, references in this Chapter to a 'person having recording rights' in relation to the performance are to any person—

(a) who is licensed by such a person to make recordings of the performance with a view to their commercial exploitation, or

(b) to whom the benefit of such a licence has been assigned,

and who is a qualifying person.

(4) In this section 'with a view to commercial exploitation' means with a view to the recordings being sold or let for hire, or shown or played in public.

186   Consent required for recording of performance subject to exclusive contract

(1) A person infringes the rights of a person having recording rights in relation to a performance who, without his consent or that of the performer, makes a recording of the whole or any substantial part of the performance.

(2) In an action for infringement of those rights brought by virtue of this section damages shall not be awarded against a defendant who shows that at the time of the infringement he believed on reasonable grounds that consent had been given.

187   Infringement of recording rights by use of recording made without consent

(1) A person infringes the rights of a person having recording rights in relation to a performance who, without his consent or, in the case of a qualifying performance, that of the performer—

(a) shows or plays in public the whole or any substantial part of the performance, or

(b) communicates to the public the whole or any substantial part of the performance,

by means of a recording which was, and which that person knows or has reason to believe was, made without the appropriate consent.

(2) The reference in subsection (1) to 'the appropriate consent' is to the consent of—

(a) the performer, or

(b) the person who at the time the consent was given had recording rights in relation to the performance (or, if there was more than one such person, of all of them).

188 Infringement of recording rights by importing, possessing or dealing with illicit recording

(1) A person infringes the rights of a person having recording rights in relation to a performance who, without his consent or, in the case of a qualifying performance, that of the performer—

(a) imports into the United Kingdom otherwise than for his private and domestic use, or

(b) in the course of a business possesses, sells or lets for hire, offers or exposes for sale or hire, or distributes,

a recording of the performance which is, and which that person knows or has reason to believe is, an illicit recording.

(2) Where in an action for infringement of those rights brought by virtue of this section a defendant shows that the illicit recording was innocently acquired by him or a predecessor in title of his, the only remedy available against him in respect of the infringement is damages not exceeding a reasonable payment in respect of the act complained of.

(3) In subsection (2) 'innocently acquired' means that the person acquiring the recording did not know and had no reason to believe that it was an illicit recording.

Exceptions to rights conferred

189 Acts permitted notwithstanding rights conferred by this Chapter

The provisions of Schedule 2 specify acts which may be done notwithstanding the rights conferred by this Chapter, being acts which correspond broadly to certain of those specified in Chapter III of Part I (acts permitted notwithstanding copyright).

190 Power of Tribunal to give consent on behalf of performer in certain cases

(1) The Copyright Tribunal may, on the application of a person wishing to make a copy of a recording of a performance, give consent in a case where the identity or whereabouts of the person entitled to the reproduction right cannot be ascertained by reasonable inquiry.

...

(5) In any case the Tribunal shall take into account the following factors—

(a) whether the original recording was made with the performer's consent and is lawfully in the possession or control of the person proposing to make the further recording;

(b) whether the making of the further recording is consistent with the obligations of the parties to the arrangements under which, or is otherwise consistent with the purposes for which, the original recording was made.

(6) Where the Tribunal gives consent under this section it shall, in default of agreement between the applicant and the person entitled to the reproduction right, make such order as it thinks fit as to the payment to be made to that person in consideration of consent being given.

Duration of rights

191 Duration of rights

(1) The following provisions have effect with respect to the duration of the rights conferred by this Chapter.

(2) The rights conferred by this Chapter in relation to a performance expire—

(a) at the end of the period of 50 years from the end of the calendar year in which the performance takes place, or

(b) if during that period a recording of the performance other than a sound recording, is released, 50 years from the end of the calendar year in which it is released, or

(c) if during that period a sound recording of the performance is released, 70 years from the end of the calendar year in which it is released,

subject as follows.

(3) For the purposes of subsection (2) a recording is 'released' when it is first published, played or shown in public or communicated to the public; but in determining whether a recording has been released no account shall be taken of any unauthorised act.

(4) Where a performer is not a national of the United Kingdom, the duration of the rights conferred by this Chapter in relation to his performance is that to which the performance is entitled in the country of which he is a national, provided that does not exceed the period which would apply under subsections (2) and (3).

(5) If or to the extent that the application of subsection (4) would be at variance with an international obligation to which the United Kingdom became subject prior to 29th October 1993, the duration of the rights conferred by this Chapter shall be as specified in subsections (2) and (3).

Performers' property rights

191A   Performers' property rights

(1) The following rights conferred by this Chapter on a performer—

reproduction right (section 182A),

distribution right (section 182B),

rental right and lending right (section 182C),

making available right (section 182CA),

are property rights ('performer's property rights').

(2) References in this Chapter to the consent of the performer shall be construed in relation to a performer's property rights as references to the consent of the rights owner.

(3) Where different persons are (whether in consequence of a partial assignment or otherwise) entitled to different aspects of a performer's property rights in relation to a performance, the rights owner for any purpose of this Chapter is the person who is entitled to the aspect of those rights relevant for that purpose.

(4) Where a performer's property rights (or any aspect of them) is owned by more than one person jointly, references in this Chapter to the rights owner are to all the owners, so that, in particular, any requirement of the licence of the rights owner requires the licence of all of them.

191B   Assignment and licences

(1) A performer's property rights are transmissible by assignment, by testamentary disposition or by operation of law, as personal or moveable property.

(2) An assignment or other transmission of a performer's property rights maybe partial, that is, limited so as to apply—

(a) to one or more, but not all, of the things requiring the consent of the rights owner;

(b) to part, but not the whole, of the period for which the rights are to subsist.

(3) An assignment of a performer's property rights is not effective unless it is in writing signed by or on behalf of the assignor.

(4) A licence granted by the owner of a performer's property rights is binding on every successor in title to his interest in the rights, except a purchaser in good faith for valuable consideration and without notice (actual or constructive) of the licence or a person deriving title from such a purchaser; and references in this Chapter to doing anything with, or without, the licence of the rights owner shall be construed accordingly.

191C   Prospective ownership of a performer's property rights

(1) This section applies where by an agreement made in relation to a future recording of a performance, and signed by or on behalf of the performer, the performer purports to assign his performer's property rights (wholly or partially) to another person.

(2) If on the rights coming into existence the assignee or another person claiming under him would be entitled as against all other persons to require the rights to be vested in him, they shall vest in the assignee or his successor in title by virtue of this subsection.

(3) A licence granted by a prospective owner of a performer's property rights is binding on every successor in title to his interest (or prospective interest) in the rights, except a purchaser in good faith for valuable consideration and without notice (actual or constructive) of the licence or a person deriving title from such a purchaser.

References in this Chapter to doing anything with, or without, the licence of the rights owner shall be construed accordingly.

(4) In subsection (3) 'prospective owner' in relation to a performer's property rights means a person who is prospectively entitled to those rights by virtue of such an agreement as is mentioned in subsection (1).

191D   Exclusive licences

(1) In this Chapter an 'exclusive licence' means a licence in writing signed by or on behalf of the owner of a performer's property rights authorising the licensee to the exclusion of all other persons, including the person granting the licence, to do anything requiring the consent of the rights owner.

(2) The licensee under an exclusive licence has the same rights against a successor in title who is bound by the licence as he has against the person granting the licence.

191E   Performer's property right to pass under will with unpublished original recording

Where under a bequest (whether general or specific) a person is entitled beneficially or otherwise to any material thing containing an original recording of a performance which was not published before the death of the testator, the bequest shall, unless a contrary intention is indicated in the testator's will or a codicil to it, be construed as including any performer's rights in relation to the recording to which the testator was entitled immediately before his death.

191F   Presumption of transfer of rental right in case of film production agreement

(1) Where an agreement concerning film production is concluded between a performer and a film producer, the performer shall be presumed, unless the agreement provides to the contrary, to have transferred to the film producer any rental right in relation to the film arising from the inclusion of a recording of his performance in the film.

...

(4) Section 191G (right to equitable remuneration on transfer of rental right) applies where there is a presumed transfer by virtue of this section as in the case of an actual transfer.

191G   Right to equitable remuneration where rental right transferred

(1) Where a performer has transferred his rental right concerning a sound recording or a film to the producer of the sound recording or film, he retains the right to equitable remuneration for the rental.

The reference above to the transfer of rental right by one person to another includes any arrangement having that effect, whether made by them directly or through intermediaries.

(2) The right to equitable remuneration under this section may not be assigned by the performer except to a collecting society for the purpose of enabling it to enforce the right on his behalf.

The right is, however, transmissible by testamentary disposition or by operation of law as personal or moveable property; and it may be assigned or further transmitted by any person into whose hands it passes.

...

(5) An agreement is of no effect in so far as it purports to exclude or restrict the right to equitable remuneration under this section.

...

191H   Equitable remuneration: reference of amount to Copyright Tribunal

(1) In default of agreement as to the amount payable by way of equitable remuneration under section 191G, the person by or to whom it is payable may apply to the Copyright Tribunal to determine the amount payable.

...

(4) Remuneration shall not be considered inequitable merely because it was paid by way of a single payment or at the time of the transfer of the rental right.

(5) An agreement is of no effect in so far as it purports to prevent a person questioning the amount of equitable remuneration or to restrict the powers of the Copyright Tribunal under this section.

191HA   Assignment of performer's property rights in a sound recording

(1) This section applies where a performer has by an agreement assigned the following rights concerning a sound recording to the producer of the sound recording—
    (a) reproduction, distribution and making available rights, or
    (b) performer's property rights.

(2) If, at the end of the 50-year period, the producer has failed to meet one or both of the following conditions, the performer may give a notice in writing to the producer of the performer's intention to terminate the agreement—
    (a) condition 1 is to issue to the public copies of the sound recording in sufficient quantities;
    (b) condition 2 is to make the sound recording available to the public by electronic transmission in such a way that a member of the public may access the recording from a place and at a time chosen by him or her.

(3) If, at any time after the end of the 50-year period, the producer, having met one or both of the conditions referred to in subsection (2), fails to do so, the performer may give a notice in writing to the producer of the performer's intention to terminate the agreement.

(4) If at the end of the period of 12 months beginning with the date of the date notice, the producer has not met the conditions referred to in subsection (2), the agreement terminates and the copyright in the sound recording expires with immediate effect.

(5) An agreement is of no effect in so far as it purports to exclude or restrict the right to give notice under subsection (2) or (3).

(6) A reference to this section to the assignment of rights includes any arrangement having that effect, whether made directly between the parties or through intermediaries.

(7) In this section—
'50-year period' means
    (a) where the sound recording is published during the initial period, the period of 50 years from the end of the calendar year in which the sound recording is first published, or
    (b) where during the initial period the sound recording is not published but is made available to the public by being played in public or communicated to the public, the period of 50 years from the end of the calendar year in which it was first made available to the public,
but in determining whether a sound recording has been published, played in public or communicated to the public, no account shall be taken of any unauthorised act,
'initial period' means the period beginning on the date the recording is made and ending 50 years from the end of the calendar year in which the sound recording is made,
'producer' means the person for the time being entitled to the copyright in the sound recording,
'sufficient quantities' means such quantity as to satisfy the reasonable requirements of the public for copies of the sound recording,
'unauthorised act' has the same meaning as in section 178.

191HB   Payment in consideration of assignment

(1) A performer who, under agreement relating to the assignment of rights referred to in section 191HA(1) (an 'assignment agreement'), is entitled to a non-recurring payment in consideration of the assignment, is entitled to an annual payment for each relevant period from—
    (a) the producer, or

(b) where the producer has granted an exclusive licence of the copyright in the sound recording, the licensee under the exclusive licence (the 'exclusive licensee').

(2) In this section, 'relevant period' means—

(a) the period of 12 months beginning at the end of the 50-year period, and

(b) each subsequent period of 12 months beginning with the end of the previous period, until the date on which the copyright in the sound recording expires.

(3) The producer or, where relevant, the exclusive licensee gives effect to the entitlement under subsection (1) by remitting to a collecting society for distribution to the performer in accordance with its rules an amount for each relevant period equal to 20% of the gross revenue received during that period in respect of—

(a) the reproduction and issue to the public of copies of the sound recording, and

(b) the making available to the public of the sound recording by electronic transmission in such a way that members of the public may access it from a place and at a time individually chosen by them.

(4) The amount required to be remitted under subsection (3) is payable within 6 months of the end of each relevant period and is recoverable by the collecting society as a debt.

(5) Subsection (6) applies where—

(a) the performer makes a written request to the producer or, where relevant, the exclusive licensee for information in that person's possession or under that person's control to enable the performer—

(i) to ascertain the amount of the annual payment to which the performer is entitled under subsection (1), or

(ii) to secure its distribution by the collecting society, and

(b) the producer or, where relevant, the exclusive licensee does not supply the information within the period of 90 days beginning with the date of the request.

(6) The performer may apply to the county court, or in Scotland to the sheriff, for an order requiring the producer or, where relevant, the exclusive licensee to supply the information.

(7) An agreement is of no effect in so far as it purports to exclude or restrict the entitlement under subsection (1).

(8) In the event of any dispute as to the amount required to be remitted under subsection (3), the performer may apply to the Copyright Tribunal to determine the amount payable.

(9) Where a performer is entitled under an assignment agreement to recurring payments in consideration of the assignment, the payments must, from the end of the 50-year period, be made in full, regardless of any provision in the agreement which entitles the producer to withhold or deduct sums from the amounts payable.

(10) In this section—

'producer' and '50-year period' each has the same meaning as in section 191HA,

'exclusive licence' has the same meaning as in section 92, and

'collecting society' has the same meaning as in section 191G.

191I   Infringement actionable by rights owner

(1) An infringement of a performer's property rights is actionable by the rights owner.

(2) In an action for infringement of a performer's property rights all such relief by way of damages, injunctions, accounts or otherwise is available to the plaintiff as is available in respect of the infringement of any other property right.

(3) This section has effect subject to the following provisions of this Chapter.

191J   Provisions as to damages in infringement action

(1) Where in an action for infringement of a performer's property rights it is shown that at the time of the infringement the defendant did not know, and had no reason to believe, that the rights subsisted in the recording to which the action relates, the plaintiff is not entitled to damages against him, but without prejudice to any other remedy.

(2) The court may in an action for infringement of a performer's property rights having regard to all the circumstances, and in particular to—

> (a) the flagrancy of the infringement, and
>
> (b) any benefit accruing to the defendant by reason of the infringement, award such additional damages as the justice of the case may require.

191JA   Injunctions against service providers

(1) The High Court (in Scotland, the Court of Session) shall have power to grant an injunction against a service provider, where that service provider has actual knowledge of another person using their service to infringe a performer's property right.

(2) In determining whether a service provider has actual knowledge for the purpose of this section, a court shall take into account all matters which appear to it in the particular circumstances to be relevant and, amongst other things, shall have regard to—

> (a) whether a service provider has received a notice through a means of contact made available in accordance with regulation 6(1)(c) of the Electronic Commerce (EC Directive) Regulations 2002 (SI 2002/2013); and
>
> (b) the extent to which any notice includes—
>> (i)   the full name and address of the sender of the notice;
>> (ii)   details of the infringement in question.

(3) In this section 'service provider' has the meaning given to it by regulation 2 of the Electronic Commerce (EC Directive) Regulations 2002.

(4) Section 177 applies in respect of this section as it applies in respect of Part 1.

...

191L   Rights and remedies for exclusive licensee

(1) An exclusive licensee has, except against the owner of a performer's property rights, the same rights and remedies in respect of matters occurring after the grant of the licence as if the licence had been an assignment.

...

Non-property rights

192A   Performers' non-property rights

(1) The rights conferred on a performer by—

section 182 (consent required for recording, &c. of live performance),

section 183 (infringement of performer's rights by use of recording made without consent),

section 184 (infringement of performer's rights importing, possessing or dealing with illicit recording),

section 191HA (assignment of performer's property rights in a sound recording),

and section 191HB (payment in consideration of assignment),

are not assignable or transmissible, except to the following extent.

They are referred to in this Chapter as 'performer's non-property rights'.

(2) On the death of a person entitled to any such right—

> (a) the right passes to such person as he may by testamentary disposition specifically direct, and
>
> (b) if or to the extent that there is no such direction, the right is exercisable by his personal representatives.

...

192B   Transmissibility of rights of person having recording rights

(1) The rights conferred by this Chapter on a person having recording rights are not assignable or transmissible.

(2) This does not affect section 185(2)(b) or (3)(b), so far as those provisions confer rights under this Chapter on a person to whom the benefit of a contract or licence is assigned.

193   Consent

(1) Consent for the purposes of this Chapter by a person having a performer's non-property rights, or by a person having recording rights, may be given in relation to a specific performance, a specified description of performances or performances generally, and may relate to past or future performances.

(2) A person having recording rights in a performance is bound by any consent given by a person through whom he derives his rights under the exclusive recording contract or licence in question, in the same way as if the consent had been given by him.

(3) Where a performer's non-property right passes to another person, any consent binding on the person previously entitled binds the person to whom the right passes in the same way as if the consent had been given by him.

194   Infringement actionable as breach of statutory duty

An infringement of—

(a) a performer's non-property rights, or

(b) any right conferred by this Chapter on a person having recording rights, is actionable by the person entitled to the right as a breach of statutory duty.

Delivery up or seizure of illicit recordings

195   Order for delivery up

(1) Where a person has in his possession, custody or control in the course of a business an illicit recording of a performance, a person having performer's rights or recording rights in relation to the performance under this Chapter may apply to the court for an order that the recording be delivered up to him or to such other person as the court may direct.

. . .

196   Right to seize illicit recordings

(1) An illicit recording of a performance which is found exposed or otherwise immediately available for sale or hire, and in respect of which a person would be entitled to apply for an order under section 195, may be seized and detained by him or a person authorised by him.

The right to seize and detain is exercisable subject to the following conditions and is subject to any decision of the court under section 204 (order as to disposal of illicit recording).

. . .

197   Meaning of 'illicit recording'

(1) In this Chapter 'illicit recording', in relation to a performance, shall be construed in accordance with this section.

(2) For the purposes of a performer's rights, a recording of the whole or any substantial part of a performance of his is an illicit recording if it is made, otherwise than for private purposes, without his consent.

(3) For the purposes of the rights of a person having recording rights, a recording of the whole or any substantial part of a performance subject to the exclusive recording contract is an illicit recording if it is made, otherwise than for private purposes, without his consent or that of the performer.

(4) For the purposes of sections 198 and 199 (offences and orders for delivery up in criminal proceedings), a recording is an illicit recording if it is an illicit recording for the purposes mentioned in subsection (2) or subsection (3).

(5) In this Chapter 'illicit recording' includes a recording falling to be treated as an illicit recording by virtue of any of the following provisions of Schedule 2—

paragraph 1B(5) and (7) (personal copies of recordings for private use),

paragraph 1D(3) (copies for text and analysis for non-commercial research),

paragraph 3A(5) or (6) or 3B(10) (accessible copies of recordings made for disabled persons),

paragraph 6(5) (recording by educational establishments of broadcasts), paragraph 6ZA(7) (copying and use of extracts of recordings by educational establishments),

paragraph 6F(5)(b) (copying by librarians: single copies of published recordings),

paragraph 6G(5)(b) (copying by librarians or archivists: single copies of unpublished recordings),

paragraph 12(2) (recordings of performance in electronic form retained on transfer of principal recording),

paragraph 14(6)(b) (recordings of folksongs),

paragraph 16(3) (recordings made for purposes of broadcast),

paragraph 17A(2) (recording for the purposes of time-shifting), or

paragraph 17B(2) (photographs of broadcasts),but otherwise does not include a recording made in accordance with any of the provisions of that Schedule.

(6) It is immaterial for the purposes of this section where the recording was made.

197A   Presumptions relevant to recordings of performances

(1) In proceedings brought by virtue of this Part with respect to the rights in a performance, where copies of a recording of the performance as issued to the public bear a statement that a named person was the performer, the statement shall be admissible as evidence of the fact stated and shall be presumed to be correct until the contrary is proved.

(2) Subsection (1) does not apply to proceedings for an offence under section 198 (criminal liability for making etc. illicit recordings); but without prejudice to its application in proceedings for an order under section 199 (order for delivery up in criminal proceedings).

Offences

198   Criminal liability for making, dealing with or using illicit recordings

(1) A person commits an offence who without sufficient consent—

(a) makes for sale or hire, or

(b) imports into the United Kingdom otherwise than for his private and domestic use, or

(c) possesses in the course of a business with a view to committing any act infringing the rights conferred by this Chapter, or

(d) in the course of a business—

(i)   sells or lets for hire, or

(ii)   offers or exposes for sale or hire, or

(iii) distributes,

a recording which is, and which he knows or has reason to believe is, an illicit recording.

(1A) A person ('P') who infringes a performer's making available right in a recording commits an offence if P—

(a) knows or has reason to believe that P is infringing the right, and

(b) either—

(i)   intends to make a gain for P or another person, or

(ii)   knows or has reason to believe that infringing the right will cause loss to the owner of the right, or expose the owner of the right to a risk of loss.

(1B) For the purposes of subsection (1A)—

(a) 'gain' and 'loss'—

(i)   extend only to gain or loss in money, and

(ii)   include any such gain or loss whether temporary or permanent, and

(b) 'loss' includes a loss by not getting what one might get.

(2) A person commits an offence who causes a recording of a performance made without sufficient consent to be—

(a) shown or played in public, or

(b) communicated to the public,

thereby infringing any of the rights conferred by this Chapter, if he knows or has reason to believe that those rights are thereby infringed.

(3) In subsections (1) and (2) 'sufficient consent' means—

(a) in the case of a qualifying performance, the consent of the performer, and

    (b) in the case of a non-qualifying performance subject to an exclusive recording contract—

        (i) for the purposes of subsection (1)(a) (making of recording), the consent of the performer or the person having recording rights, and

        (ii) for the purposes of subsection (1)(b), (c) and (d) and subsection (2) (dealing with or using recording), the consent of the person having recording rights.

The references in this subsection to the person having recording rights are to the person having those rights at the time the consent is given or, if there is more than one such person, to all of them.

    (4) No offence is committed under subsection (1) or (2) by the commission of an act which by virtue of any provision of Schedule 2 may be done without infringing the rights conferred by this Chapter.

. . .

199 Order for delivery up in criminal proceedings

    (1) The court before which proceedings are brought against a person for an offence under section 198 may, if satisfied that at the time of his arrest or charge he had in his possession, custody or control in the course of a business an illicit recording of a performance, order that it be delivered up to a person having performers' rights or recording rights in relation to the performance or to such other person as the court may direct.

. . .

201 False representation of authority to give consent

    (1) It is an offence for a person to represent falsely that he is authorised by any person to give consent for the purposes of this Chapter in relation to a performance, unless he believes on reasonable grounds that he is so authorised.

    (2) A person guilty of an offence under this section is liable on summary conviction to imprisonment for a term not exceeding six months or a fine not exceeding level 5 on the standard scale or both.

202 Offence by body corporate: liability of officers

    (1) Where an offence under this Chapter committed by a body corporate is proved to have been committed with the consent or connivance of a director, manager, secretary or other similar officer of the body, or a person purporting to act in any such capacity, he as well as the body corporate is guilty of the offence and liable to be proceeded against and punished accordingly.

    (2) In relation to a body corporate whose affairs are managed by its members 'director' means a member of the body corporate.

. . .

204A Forfeiture of illicit recordings: England and Wales or Northern Ireland

    (1) In England and Wales or Northern Ireland where illicit recordings of a performance have come into the possession of any person in connection with the investigation or prosecution of a relevant offence, that person may apply under this section for an order for the forfeiture of the illicit recordings.

    (2) For the purposes of this section 'relevant offence' means—

        (a) an offence under section 198(1) or (1A) (criminal liability for making or dealing with illicit recordings),

        (b) an offence under the Trade Descriptions Act 1968, or

        (ba) an offence under the Business Protection from Misleading Marketing Regulations 2008,

        (bb) an offence under the Consumer Protection from Unfair Trading Regulations 2008, or

        (c) an offence involving dishonesty or deception.

. . .

204B Forfeiture: Scotland

    (1) In Scotland the court may make an order under this section for the forfeiture of any illicit recordings.

(2) An order under this section may be made—

(a) on an application by the procurator-fiscal made in the manner specified in section 134 of the Criminal Procedure (Scotland) Act 1995, or

(b) where a person is convicted of a relevant offence, in addition to any other penalty which the court may impose.

…

(15) For the purposes of this section—

'relevant offence' means—

(a) an offence under section 198(1) or (1A) (criminal liability for making or dealing with illicit recordings),

(b) an offence under the Trade Descriptions Act 1968,

(c) an offence under the Business Protection from Misleading Marketing Regulations 2008,

(d) an offence under the Consumer Protection from Unfair Trading Regulations 2008, or

(e) any offence involving dishonesty or deception;

'the court' means—

(a) in relation to an order made on an application under subsection (2)(a), the sheriff, and

(b) in relation to an order made under subsection (2)(b), the court which imposed the penalty.

…

Licensing of performers' rights

205A   Licensing of performers' property rights

The provisions of Schedule 2A have effect with respect to the licensing of performers' property rights.

Jurisdiction of Copyright Tribunal

205B   Jurisdiction of Copyright Tribunal

(1) The Copyright Tribunal has jurisdiction under this Chapter to hear and determine proceedings under—

(a) section 182D (amount of equitable remuneration for exploitation of commercial sound recording);

(b) section 190 (application to give consent on behalf of owner of reproduction right);

(c) section 191H (amount of equitable remuneration on transfer of rental right);

(d) paragraph 3, 4 or 5 of Schedule 2A (reference of licensing scheme);

(e) paragraph 6 or 7 of that Schedule (application with respect to licence under licensing scheme);

(f) paragraph 10, 11 or 12 of that Schedule (reference or application with respect to licensing by licensing body);

(g) paragraph 15 of that Schedule (application to settle royalty for certain lending);

(h) paragraph 17 of that Schedule (application to settle terms of licence available as of right).

(2) The provisions of Chapter VIII of Part I (general provisions relating to the Copyright Tribunal) apply in relation to the Tribunal when exercising any jurisdiction under this Chapter.

(3) Provision shall be made by rules under section 150 prohibiting the Tribunal from entertaining a reference under paragraph 3, 4 or 5 of Schedule 2A (reference of licensing scheme) by a representative organisation unless the Tribunal is satisfied that the organisation is reasonably representative of the class of persons which it claims to represent.

Chapter 3   Moral Rights

Right to be identified as performer

205C   Right to be identified as performer

(1) Whenever a person—

(a) produces or puts on a qualifying performance that is given in public,

(b) broadcasts live a qualifying performance,

(c) communicates to the public a sound recording of a qualifying performance, or

(d) issues to the public copies of such a recording,

the performer has the right to be identified as such.

(2) The right of the performer under this section is—

(a) in the case of a performance that is given in public, to be identified in any programme accompanying the performance or in some other manner likely to bring his identity to the notice of a person seeing or hearing the performance,

(b) in the case of a performance that is broadcast, to be identified in a manner likely to bring his identity to the notice of a person seeing or hearing the broadcast,

(c) in the case of a sound recording that is communicated to the public, to be identified in a manner likely to bring his identity to the notice of a person hearing the communication,

(d) in the case of a sound recording that is issued to the public, to be identified in or on each copy or, if that is not appropriate, in some other manner likely to bring his identity to the notice of a person acquiring a copy,

or (in any of the above cases) to be identified in such other manner as may be agreed between the performer and the person mentioned in subsection (1).

(3) The right conferred by this section in relation to a performance given by a group (or so much of a performance as is given by a group) is not infringed—

(a) in a case falling within paragraph (a), (b) or (c) of subsection (2), or

(b) in a case falling within paragraph (d) of that subsection in which it is not reasonably practicable for each member of the group to be identified,

if the group itself is identified as specified in subsection (2).

(4) In this section 'group' means two or more performers who have a particular name by which they may be identified collectively.

(5) If the assertion under section 205D specifies a pseudonym, initials or some other particular form of identification, that form shall be used; otherwise any reasonable form of identification may be used.

(6) This section has effect subject to section 205E (exceptions to right).

205D   Requirement that right be asserted

(1) A person does not infringe the right conferred by section 205C (right to be identified as performer) by doing any of the acts mentioned in that section unless the right has been asserted in accordance with the following provisions so as to bind him in relation to that act.

...

205E   Exceptions to right

(1) The right conferred by section 205C (right to be identified as performer) is subject to the following exceptions.

(2) The right does not apply where it is not reasonably practicable to identify the performer (or, where identification of a group is permitted by virtue of section 205C(3), the group).

(3) The right does not apply in relation to any performance given for the purposes of reporting current events.

(4) The right does not apply in relation to any performance given for the purposes of advertising any goods or services.

(5) The right is not infringed by an act which by virtue of any of the following provisions of Schedule 2 would not infringe any of the rights conferred by Chapter 2—

(a) paragraph 2(1A) (news reporting);

(b) paragraph 3 (incidental inclusion of a performance or recording);

(c) paragraph 4(2) (things done for the purposes of examination);

(d) paragraph 8 (parliamentary and judicial proceedings);

(e) paragraph 9 (Royal Commissions and statutory inquiries).

Right to object to derogatory treatment

205F   Right to object to derogatory treatment of performance

(1) The performer of a qualifying performance has a right which is infringed if—

(a) the performance is broadcast live, or

(b) by means of a sound recording the performance is played in public or communicated to the public,

with any distortion, mutilation or other modification that is prejudicial to the reputation of the performer.

(2) This section has effect subject to section 205G (exceptions to right).

205G   Exceptions to right

(1) The right conferred by section 205F (right to object to derogatory treatment of performance) is subject to the following exceptions.

(2) The right does not apply in relation to any performance given for the purposes of reporting current events.

(3) The right is not infringed by modifications made to a performance which are consistent with normal editorial or production practice.

(4) Subject to subsection (5), the right is not infringed by anything done for the purpose of—

(a) avoiding the commission of an offence,

(b) complying with a duty imposed by or under an enactment, or

(c) in the case of the British Broadcasting Corporation, avoiding the inclusion in a programme broadcast by them of anything which offends against good taste or decency or which is likely to encourage or incite crime or lead to disorder or to be offensive to public feeling.

(5) Where—

(a) the performer is identified in a manner likely to bring his identity to the notice of a person seeing or hearing the performance as modified by the act in question; or

(b) he has previously been identified in or on copies of a sound recording issued to the public,

subsection (4) applies only if there is sufficient disclaimer.

(6) In subsection (5) 'sufficient disclaimer', in relation to an act capable of infringing the right, means a clear and reasonably prominent indication—

(a) given in a manner likely to bring it to the notice of a person seeing or hearing the performance as modified by the act in question, and

(b) if the performer is identified at the time of the act, appearing along with the identification, that the modifications were made without the performer's consent.

205H   Infringement of right by possessing or dealing with infringing article

(1) The right conferred by section 205F (right to object to derogatory treatment of performance) is also infringed by a person who—

(a) possesses in the course of business, or

(b) sells or lets for hire, or offers or exposes for sale or hire, or

(c) distributes,

an article which is, and which he knows or has reason to believe is, an infringing article.

(2) An 'infringing article' means a sound recording of a qualifying performance with any distortion, mutilation or other modification that is prejudicial to the reputation of the performer.

Supplementary

205I   Duration of rights

(1) A performer's rights under this Chapter in relation to a performance subsist so long as that performer's rights under Chapter 2 subsist in relation to the performance.

(2) In subsection (1) 'performer's rights' includes rights of a performer that are vested in a successor of his.

205J   Consent and waiver of rights

(1) It is not an infringement of the rights conferred by this Chapter to do any act to which consent has been given by or on behalf of the person entitled to the right.

. . .

205K   Application of provisions to parts of performances

(1) The right conferred by section 205C (right to be identified as performer) applies in relation to the whole or any substantial part of a performance.

(2) The right conferred by section 205F (right to object to derogatory treatment of performance) applies in relation to the whole or any part of a performance.

205L   Moral rights not assignable

The rights conferred by this Chapter are not assignable.

205M   Transmission of moral rights on death

(1) On the death of a person entitled to a right conferred by this Chapter—

(a) the right passes to such person as he may by testamentary disposition specifically direct,

(b) if there is no such direction but the performer's property rights in respect of the performance in question form part of his estate, the right passes to the person to whom the property rights pass,

(c) if or to the extent that the right does not pass under paragraph (a) or (b) it is exercisable by his personal representatives.

(2) Where a performer's property rights pass in part to one person and in part to another, as for example where a bequest is limited so as to apply—

(a) to one or more, but not all, of the things to which the owner has the right to consent, or

(b) to part, but not the whole, of the period for which the rights subsist,

any right which by virtue of subsection (1) passes with the performer's property rights is correspondingly divided.

. . .

(4) A consent or waiver previously given or made binds any person to whom a right passes by virtue of subsection (1).

. . .

205N   Remedies for infringement of moral rights

(1) An infringement of a right conferred by this Chapter is actionable as a breach of statutory duty owed to the person entitled to the right.

(2) Where—

(a) there is an infringement of a right conferred by this Chapter,

(b) a person falsely claiming to act on behalf of a performer consented to the relevant conduct or purported to waive the right, and

(c) there would have been no infringement if he had been so acting,

that person shall be liable, jointly and severally with any person liable in respect of the infringement by virtue of subsection (1), as if he himself had infringed the right.

(3) Where proceedings for infringement of the right conferred on a performer by this Chapter, it shall be a defence to prove—

(a) that a person claiming to act on behalf of the performer consented to the defendant's conduct or purported to waive the right, and

(b) that the defendant reasonably believed that the person was acting on behalf of the performer.

(4) In proceedings for infringement of the right conferred by section 205F the court may, if it thinks it an adequate remedy in the circumstances, grant an injunction on terms prohibiting the doing

of any act unless a disclaimer is made, in such terms and in such manner as may be approved by the court, dissociating the performer from the broadcast or sound recording of the performance.

Chapter 4   Qualification for Protection, Extent and Interpretation

Qualification for protection and extent

206   Qualifying countries, individuals and persons

(1) In this Part—

'qualifying country' means—

(a) the United Kingdom,

(c) to the extent that an Order under section 208 so provides, a country designated under that section as enjoying reciprocal protection;

'qualifying individual' means a citizen or subject of, or an individual resident in, a qualifying country; and

'qualifying person' means a qualifying individual or a body corporate or other body having legal personality which—

(a) is formed under the law of a part of the United Kingdom or another qualifying country, and

(b) has in any qualifying country a place of business at which substantial business activity is carried on.

(2) The reference in the definition of 'qualifying individual' to a person's being a citizen or subject of a qualifying country shall be construed—

(a) in relation to the United Kingdom, as a reference to his being a British citizen, and

(b) in relation to a colony of the United Kingdom, as a reference to his being a British overseas territories citizen by connection with that colony.

(3) In determining for the purpose of the definition of 'qualifying person' whether substantial business activity is carried on at a place of business in any country, no account shall be taken of dealings in goods which are at all material times outside that country.

207   Countries to which this Part extends

This Part extends to England and Wales, Scotland and Northern Ireland.

208   Countries enjoying reciprocal protection

(1) Her Majesty may by Order in Council designate as enjoying reciprocal protection under this Part—

(a) a Convention country, or

(b) a country as to which Her Majesty is satisfied that provision has been or will be made under its law giving adequate protection for British performances.

(2) A 'Convention country' means a country which is a party to a Convention relating to performers' rights to which the United Kingdom is also a party.

(3) A 'British performance' means a performance—

(a) given by an individual who is a British citizen or resident in the United Kingdom, or

(b) taking place in the United Kingdom.

(4) If the law of that country provides adequate protection only for certain descriptions of performance, an Order under subsection (1)(b) designating that country shall contain provision limiting to a corresponding extent the protection afforded by this Part in relation to performances connected with that country.

(5) The power conferred by subsection (1)(b) is exercisable in relation to any of the Channel Islands, the Isle of Man or any colony of the United Kingdom, as in relation to a foreign country.

(6) A statutory instrument containing an Order in Council under this section shall be subject to annulment in pursuance of a resolution of either House of Parliament.

209   Territorial waters and the continental shelf

(1) For the purposes of this Part the territorial waters of the United Kingdom shall be treated as part of the United Kingdom.

(2) This Part applies to things done in the United Kingdom sector of the continental shelf on a structure or vessel which is present there for purposes directly connected with the exploration of the sea bed or subsoil or the exploitation of their natural resources as it applies to things done in the United Kingdom.

(3) The United Kingdom sector of the continental shelf means the areas designated by order under section 1(7) of the Continental Shelf Act 1964.

210   British ships, aircraft and hovercraft

(1) This Part applies to things done on a British ship, aircraft or hovercraft as it applies to things done in the United Kingdom.

(2) In this section—

'British ship' means a ship which is a British ship for the purposes of the Merchant Shipping Act 1995 otherwise than by virtue of registration in a country outside the United Kingdom; and

'British aircraft' and 'British hovercraft' mean an aircraft or hovercraft registered in the United Kingdom.

210A   Requirement of signature: application in relation to body corporate

(1) The requirement in the following provisions that an instrument be signed by or on behalf of a person is also satisfied in the case of a body corporate by the affixing of its seal—

section 191B(3) (assignment of performer's property rights);

section 191C(1) (assignment of future performer's property rights);

section 191D(1) (grant of exclusive licence).

(2) The requirement in the following provisions that an instrument be signed by a person is also satisfied in the case of a body corporate by signature on behalf of the body or by the affixing of its seal—

section 205D(2)(a) (assertion of performer's moral rights);

section 205J(2) (waiver of performer's moral rights).

Interpretation

211   Expressions having same meaning as in copyright provisions

(1) The following expressions have the same meaning in this Part as in Part I (copyright)—

assignment (in Scotland),

broadcast,

business,

communication to the public,

country,

defendant (in Scotland),

delivery up (in Scotland),

the EEA,

EEA state,

film,

injunction (in Scotland),

literary work,

published,

signed,

sound recording, and

wireless broadcast.

(2) The provisions of—

(a) section 5B(2) and (3) (supplementary provisions relating to films), and

(b) section 6(3) to (5A) and section 19(4) (supplementary provisions relating to broadcasting),

apply for the purposes of this Part, and in relation to an infringement of the rights conferred by this Part, as they apply for the purposes of Part I and in relation to an infringement of copyright.

212 Index of defined expressions

The following Table shows provisions defining or otherwise explaining expressions used in this Part (other than provision defining or explaining an expression used only in the same section)—

accessible copy (in paragraphs 3A to 3E in Schedule 2)	paragraph 3E(4) of Schedule 2
assignment (in Scotland)	section 211(1) (and section 177)
broadcast (and related expressions)	section 211 (and section 6)
business	section 211(1) (and section 178)
communication to the public	section 211(1) (and section 20)
consent of performer (in relation to performer's property rights)	section 191A(2)
country	section 211(1) (and section 178)
defendant (in Scotland)	section 211(1) (and section 177)
delivery up (in Scotland)	section 211(1) (and section 177)
disabled person (in paragraphs 3A to 3E of Schedule 2)	paragraph 3E(2) and (3) of Schedule 2
distribution right	section 182B(5)
the EEA and EEA state	section 211(1) (and section 172A)
exclusive recording contract	section 185(1)
film	section 211(1) (and section 5B)
group	section 205C(4)
illicit recording	section 197
injunction (in Scotland)	section 211(1) (and section 177)
issue to the public	section 182B
lending right	section 182C(7)
literary work	section 211(1) (and section 3(1))
making available right	section 182CA
performance	section 180(2)
performer's non-property rights	section 192A(1)
performer's property rights	section 191A(1)
published	section 211(1) (and section 175)
qualifying country	section 206(1)
qualifying individual	section 206(1) and (2)
qualifying performance	section 181
qualifying person	section 206(1) and (3)
recording (of a performance)	section 180(2)
recording rights (person having)	section 185(2) and (3)
rental right	section 182C(7)
reproduction right	section 182A(3)
rights owner (in relation to performer's property rights)	section 191A(3) and (4)
signed	section 211(1) (and section 176)
sound recording	section 211(1) (and section 5A)
wireless broadcast	section 211(1) (and section 178).

PART III   DESIGN RIGHT

Chapter I   Design Right in Original Designs

Introductory

213   Design right

(1) Design right is a property right which subsists in accordance with this Part in an original design.

(2) In this Part 'design' means the design of the shape or configuration (whether internal or external) of the whole or part of an article.

(3) Design right does not subsist in—

(a) a method or principle of construction,

(b) features of shape or configuration of an article which—

    (i) enable the article to be connected to, or placed in, around or against, another article so that either article may perform its function, or

    (ii) are dependent upon the appearance of another article of which the article is intended by the designer to form an integral part, or

(c) surface decoration.

(4) A design is not 'original' for the purposes of this Part if it is commonplace in a qualifying country in the design field in question at the time of its creation; and 'qualifying country' has the meaning given in section 217(3).

(5) Design right subsists in a design only if the design qualifies for design right protection by reference to—

(a) the designer or the person by whom the designer was employed (see sections 218 and 219), or

(b) the person by whom and country in which articles made to the design were first marketed (see section 220),

or in accordance with any Order under section 221 (power to make further provision with respect to qualification).

(5A) Design right does not subsist in a design which consists of or contains a controlled representation within the meaning of the Olympic Symbol etc. (Protection) Act 1995.

(6) Design right does not subsist unless and until the design has been recorded in a design document or an article has been made to the design.

(7) Design right does not subsist in a design which was so recorded, or to which an article was made, before the commencement of this Part.

214   The designer

(1) In this Part the 'designer', in relation to a design, means the person who creates it.

(2) In the case of a computer-generated design the person by whom the arrangements necessary for the creation of the design are undertaken shall be taken to be the designer.

215   Ownership of design right

(1) The designer is the first owner of any design right in a design which is not created in the course of employment.

(3) Where a design is created by an employee in the course of his employment, his employer is the first owner of any design right in the design.

(4) If a design qualifies for design right protection by virtue of section 220 (qualification by reference to first marketing of articles made to the design), the above rules do not apply and the person by whom the articles in question are marketed is the first owner of the design right.

216   Duration of design right

(1) Design right expires—

    (a) fifteen years from the end of the calendar year in which the design was first recorded in a design document or an article was first made to the design, whichever first occurred, or

    (b) if articles made to the design are made available for sale or hire within five years from the end of that calendar year, ten years from the end of the calendar year in which that first occurred.

(2) The reference in subsection (1) to articles being made available for sale or hire is to their being made so available anywhere in the world by or with the licence of the design right owner.

Qualification for design right protection

217   Qualifying individuals and qualifying persons

(1) In this Part—

'qualifying person' means—

    (a) an individual habitually resident in a qualifying country, or

    (b) a body corporate or other body having legal personality which—

        (i) is formed under the law of a part of the United Kingdom or another qualifying country, and

        (ii) has in any qualifying country a place of business at which substantial business activity is carried on.

(2) References in this Part to a qualifying person include the Crown and the government of any other qualifying country.

(3) In this section 'qualifying country' means—

    (a) the United Kingdom,

    (b) a country to which this Part extends by virtue of an Order under section 255, or

    (d) to the extent that an Order under section 256 so provides, a country designated under that section as enjoying reciprocal protection.

(5) In determining for the purpose of the definition of 'qualifying person' whether substantial business activity is carried on at a place of business in any country, no account shall be taken of dealings in goods which are at all material times outside that country.

218   Qualification by reference to designer

(1) This section applies to a design which is not created in the course of employment.

(2) A design to which this section applies qualifies for design right protection if the designer is a qualifying person.

(3) A joint design to which this section applies qualifies for design right protection if any of the designers is a qualifying person.

(4) Where a joint design qualifies for design right protection under this section, only those designers who are qualifying persons are entitled to design right under section 215(1) (first ownership of design right: entitlement of designer).

219   Qualification by reference to employer

(1) A design qualifies for design right protection if it is created in the course of employment with a qualifying person.

(2) In the case of joint employment a design qualifies for design right protection if any of the employers is a qualifying person.

(3) Where a design which is created in the course of joint employment qualifies for design right protection under this section, only those employers who are qualifying persons are entitled to design right under section 215 (3) (first ownership of design right: entitlement of employer).

220   Qualification by reference to first marketing

(1) A design which does not qualify for design right protection under section 218 or 219 (qualification by reference to designer, or employer) qualifies for design right protection if the first marketing of articles made to the design—

(a) is by a qualifying person, and

(b) takes place in the United Kingdom, or another country to which this Part extends by virtue of an Order under section 255.

(2) If the first marketing of articles made to the design is done jointly by two or more persons, the design qualifies for design right protection if any of those persons meets the requirement specified in subsection (1)(a).

(3) In such a case only the persons who meet that requirement are entitled to design right under section 215(4) (first ownership of design right: entitlement of first marketer of articles made to the design).

221   Power to make further provision as to qualification

(1) Her Majesty may, with a view to fulfilling an international obligation of the United Kingdom, by Order in Council provide that a design qualifies for design right protection if such requirements as are specified in the Order are met.

(2) An Order may make different provision for different descriptions of design or article; and may make such consequential modifications of the operation of sections 215 (ownership of design right) and sections 218 to 220 (other means of qualification) as appear to Her Majesty to be appropriate.

(3) A statutory instrument containing an Order in Council under this section shall be subject to annulment in pursuance of a resolution of either House of Parliament.

Dealings with design right

222   Assignment and licences

(1) Design right is transmissible by assignment, by testamentary disposition or by operation of law, as personal or moveable property.

(2) An assignment or other transmission of design right may be partial, that is, limited so as to apply—

(a) to one or more, but not all, of the things the design right owner has the exclusive right to do;

(b) to part, but not the whole, of the period for which the right is to subsist.

(3) An assignment of design right is not effective unless it is in writing signed by or on behalf of the assignor.

(4) A licence granted by the owner of design right is binding on every successor in title to his interest in the right, except a purchaser in good faith for valuable consideration and without notice (actual or constructive) of the licence or a person deriving title from such a purchaser; and references in this Part to doing anything with, or without, the licence of the design right owner shall be construed accordingly.

223   Prospective ownership of design right

(1) Where by an agreement made in relation to future design right, and signed by or on behalf of the prospective owner of the design right, the prospective owner purports to assign the future design right (wholly or partially) to another person, then if, on the right coming into existence, the assignee or another person claiming under him would be entitled as against all other persons to require the right to be vested in him, the right shall vest in him by virtue of this section.

(2) In this section—

'future design right' means design right which will or may come into existence in respect of a future design or class of designs or on the occurrence of a future event; and

'prospective owner' shall be construed accordingly, and includes a person who is prospectively entitled to design right by virtue of such an agreement as is mentioned in subsection (1).

(3) A licence granted by a prospective owner of design right is binding on every successor in title to his interest (or prospective interest) in the right, except a purchaser in good faith for valuable consideration and without notice (actual or constructive) or the licence or a person deriving title from such a purchaser; and references in this Part to doing anything with, or without, the licence of the design right owner shall be construed accordingly.

224 Assignment of right in registered design presumed to carry with it design right

Where a design consisting of a design in which design right subsists is registered under the Registered Designs Act 1949 and the proprietor of the registered design is also the design right owner, an assignment of the right in the registered design shall be taken to be also an assignment of the design right, unless a contrary intention appears.

225 Exclusive licences

(1) In this Part an 'exclusive licence' means a licence in writing signed by or on behalf of the design right owner authorising the licensee to the exclusion of all other persons, including the person granting the licence, to exercise a right which would otherwise be exercisable exclusively by the design right owner.

(2) The licensee under an exclusive licence has the same rights against any successor in title who is bound by the licence as he has against the person granting the licence.

Chapter II   Rights of Design Right Owner and Remedies

Infringement of design right

226 Primary infringement of design right

(1) The owner of design right in a design has the exclusive right to reproduce the design for commercial purposes—
  (a) by making articles to that design, or
  (b) by making a design document recording the design for the purpose of enabling such articles to be made.

(2) Reproduction of a design by making articles to the design means copying the design so as to produce articles exactly or substantially to that design, and references in this Part to making articles to a design shall be construed accordingly.

(3) Design right is infringed by a person who without the licence of the design right owner does, or authorises another to do, anything which by virtue of this section is the exclusive right of the design right owner.

(4) For the purposes of this section reproduction may be direct or indirect, and it is immaterial whether any intervening acts themselves infringe the design right.

(5) This section has effect subject to the provisions of Chapter III (exceptions to rights of design right owner).

227 Secondary infringement: importing or dealing with infringing article

(1) Design right is infringed by a person who, without the licence of the design right owner—
  (a) imports into the United Kingdom for commercial purposes, or
  (b) has in his possession for commercial purposes, or
  (c) sells, lets for hire, or offers or exposes for sale or hire, in the course of a business, an article
      which is, and which he knows or has reason to believe is, an infringing article.

(2) This section has effect subject to the provisions of Chapter III (exceptions to rights of design right owner).

228 Meaning of 'infringing article'

(1) In this Part 'infringing article', in relation to a design, shall be construed in accordance with this section.

(2) An article is an infringing article if its making to that design was an infringement of design right in the design.

(3) An article is also an infringing article if—

    (a) it has been or is proposed to be imported into the United Kingdom, and

    (b) its making to that design in the United Kingdom would have been an infringement of design right in the design or a breach of an exclusive licence agreement relating to the design.

(4) Where it is shown that an article is made to a design in which design right subsists or has subsisted at any time, it shall be presumed until the contrary is proved that the article was made at a time when design right subsisted.

(5) Nothing in subsection (3) shall be construed as applying to an article which may lawfully be imported into the United Kingdom by virtue of anything which forms part of retained EU law as a result of section 3 or 4 of the European Union (Withdrawal) Act 2018.

(6) The expression 'infringing article' does not include a design document, notwithstanding that its making was or would have been an infringement of design right.

Remedies for infringement

229   Rights and remedies of design right owner

(1) An infringement of design right is actionable by the design right owner.

(2) In an action for infringement of design right all such relief by way of damages, injunctions, accounts or otherwise is available to the plaintiff as is available in respect of the infringement of any other property right.

(3) The court may in an action for infringement of design right, having regard to all the circumstances and in particular to—

    (a) the flagrancy of the infringement, and

    (b) any benefit accruing to the defendant by reason of the infringement,

award such additional damages as the justice of the case may require.

(4) This section has effect subject to section 233 (innocent infringement).

230   Order for delivery up

(1) Where a person—

    (a) has in his possession, custody or control for commercial purposes an infringing article, or

    (b) has in his possession, custody or control anything specifically designed or adapted for making articles to a particular design, knowing or having reason to believe that it has been or is to be used to make an infringing article,

the owner of the design right in the design in question may apply to the court for an order that the infringing article or other thing be delivered up to him or to such other person as the court may direct.

. . .

231   Order as to disposal of infringing articles &c.

(1) An application may be made to the court for an order that an infringing article or other thing delivered up in pursuance of an order under section 230 shall be—

    (a) forfeited to the design right owner, or

    (b) destroyed or otherwise dealt with as the court may think fit, or for a decision that no such order should be made.

(2) In considering what order (if any) should be made, the court shall consider whether other remedies available in an action for infringement of design right would be adequate to compensate the design right owner and to protect his interests.

. . .

233   Innocent infringement

(1) Where in an action for infringement of design right brought by virtue of section 226 (primary infringement) it is shown that at the time of the infringement the defendant did not know, and had no

reason to believe, that design right subsisted in the design to which the action relates, the plaintiff is not entitled to damages against him, but without prejudice to any other remedy.

(2) Where in an action for infringement of design right brought by virtue of section 227 (secondary infringement) a defendant shows that the infringing article was innocently acquired by him or a predecessor in title of his, the only remedy available against him in respect of the infringement is damages not exceeding a reasonable royalty in respect of the act complained of.

(3) In subsection (2) 'innocently acquired' means that the person acquiring the article did not know and had no reason to believe that it was an infringing article.

234　Rights and remedies of exclusive licensee

(1) An exclusive licensee has, except against the design right owner, the same rights and remedies in respect of matters occurring after the grant of the licence as if the licence had been an assignment.

. . .

Chapter III　Exceptions to Rights of Design Right Owners

Infringement of copyright

236　Infringement of copyright

Where copyright subsists in a work which consists of or includes a design in which design right subsists, it is not an infringement of design right in the design to do anything which is an infringement of the copyright in that work.

Availability of licences of right

237　Licences available in last five years of design right

(1) Any person is entitled as of right to a licence to do in the last five years of the design right term anything which would otherwise infringe the design right.

(2) The terms of the licence shall, in default of agreement, be settled by the comptroller.

(3) The Secretary of State may if it appears to him necessary in order to—

    (a) comply with an international obligation of the United Kingdom, or

    (b) secure or maintain reciprocal protection for British designs in other countries,

by order exclude from the operation of subsection (1) designs of a description specified in the order or designs applied to articles of a description so specified.

(4) An order shall be made by statutory instrument; and no order shall be made unless a draft of it has been laid before and approved by a resolution of each House of Parliament.

238　Powers exercisable for protection of the public interest

(1) Subsection (1A) applies where whatever needs to be remedied, mitigated or prevented by the Secretary of State or (as the case may be) the Competition and Markets Authority under section 12(5) of the Competition Act 1980 or section 41(2), 55(2), 66(6), 75(2), 83(2), 84C(2), 138(2), 147(2), 147A(2) or 160(2) of, or paragraph 5(2) or 10(2) of Schedule 7 to, the Enterprise Act 2002 (powers to take remedial action following references to the Competition and Markets Authority in connection with public bodies and certain other persons, mergers or market investigations etc, or in respect of retained EU merger commitments) consists of or includes—

    (a) conditions in licences granted by a design right owner restricting the use of the design by the licensee or the right of the design right owner to grant other licences, or

    (b) a refusal of a design right owner to grant licences on reasonable terms.

(1A) The powers conferred by Schedule 8 to the Enterprise Act 2002 include power to cancel or modify those conditions and, instead or in addition, to provide that licences in respect of the design right shall be available as of right.

. . .

(3) The terms of a licence available by virtue of this section shall, in default of agreement, be settled by the comptroller.

. . .

Crown use of designs

240   Crown use of designs

(1) A government department, or a person authorised in writing by a government department, may without the licence of the design right owner—

(a) do anything for the purpose of supplying articles for the services of the Crown, or

(b) dispose of articles no longer required for the services of the Crown; and nothing done by virtue of this section infringes the design right.

(2) References in this Part to 'the services of the Crown' are to—

(a) the defence of the realm,

(b) foreign defence purposes, and

(c) health service purposes.

. . .

243   Crown use: compensation for loss of profit

(1) Where Crown use is made of a design, the government department concerned shall pay—

(a) to the design right owner, or

(b) if there is an exclusive licence in force in respect of the design, to the exclusive licensee,

compensation for any loss resulting from his not being awarded a contract to supply the articles made to the design.

. . .

General

. . .

Chapter IV   Jurisdiction of the Comptroller and the Court

Jurisdiction of the comptroller

246   Jurisdiction to decide matters relating to design right

(1) A party to a dispute as to any of the following matters may refer the dispute to the comptroller for his decision—

(a) the subsistence of design right,

(b) the term of design right, or

(c) the identity of the person in whom design right first vested;

and the comptroller's decision on the reference is binding on the parties to the dispute.

(2) No other court or tribunal shall decide any such matter except—

(a) on a reference or appeal from the comptroller,

(b) in infringement or other proceedings in which the issue arises incidentally, or

(c) in proceedings brought with the agreement of the parties or the leave of the comptroller.

(3) The comptroller has jurisdiction to decide any incidental question of fact or law arising in the course of a reference under this section.

247   Application to settle terms of licence of right

(1) A person requiring a licence which is available as of right by virtue of—

(a) section 237 (licences available in last few years of design right), or

(b) an order under section 238 (licences made available in the public interest),

may apply to the comptroller to settle the terms of the licence.

(2) No application for the settlement of the terms of a licence available by virtue of section 237 may be made earlier than one year before the earliest date on which the licence may take effect under that section.

(3) The terms of a licence settled by the comptroller shall authorise the licensee to do—

(a) in the case of licence available by virtue of section 237, everything which would be an infringement of the design right in the absence of a licence;

(b) in the case of a licence available by virtue of section 238, everything in respect of which a licence is so available.

...

Chapter V   Miscellaneous and General

Unjustified Threats

253   Threats of infringement proceedings

(1) A communication contains a 'threat of infringement proceedings' if a reasonable person in the position of a recipient would understand from the communication that—

(a) design right subsists in a design, and

(b) a person intends to bring proceedings (whether in a court in the United Kingdom or elsewhere) against another person for infringement of the design right by—

(i) an act done in the United Kingdom, or

(ii) an act which, if done, would be done in the United Kingdom.

(2) References in this section and in section 253C to a 'recipient' include, in the case of a communication directed to the public or a section of the public, references to a person to whom the communication is directed.

253A   Actionable threats

(1) Subject to subsections (2) to (5), a threat of infringement proceedings made by any person is actionable by any person aggrieved by the threat.

(2) A threat of infringement proceedings is not actionable if the infringement is alleged to consist of—

(a) making an article for disposal, or

(b) importing an article for disposal.

(3) A threat of infringement proceedings is not actionable if the infringement is alleged to consist of an act which, if done, would constitute an infringement of a kind mentioned in subsection (2) (a) or (b).

(4) A threat of infringement proceedings is not actionable if the threat—

(a) is made to a person who has done, or intends to do, an act mentioned in subsection (2)(a) or (b) in relation to an article, and

(b) is a threat of proceedings for an infringement alleged to consist of doing anything else in relation to that article.

(5) A threat of infringement proceedings which is not an express threat is not actionable if it is contained in a permitted communication.

(6) In sections 253C and 253D an 'actionable threat' means a threat of infringement proceedings that is actionable in accordance with this section.

253B   Permitted communications

(1) For the purposes of section 253A(5), a communication containing a threat of infringement proceedings is a 'permitted communication' if—

(a) the communication, so far as it contains information that relates to the threat, is made for a permitted purpose;

(b) all of the information that relates to the threat is information that—

(i) is necessary for that purpose (see subsection (5)(a) to (c) for some examples of necessary information), and

(ii) the person making the communication reasonably believes is true.

(2) Each of the following is a 'permitted purpose'—

(a) giving notice that design right subsists in a design;

(b) discovering whether, or by whom, design right in a design has been infringed by an act mentioned in section 253A(2)(a) or (b);

    (c) giving notice that a person has a right in or under the design right in a design, where another person's awareness of the right is relevant to any proceedings that may be brought in respect of the design right in the design.

(3) The court may, having regard to the nature of the purposes listed in subsection (2)(a) to (c), treat any other purpose as a 'permitted purpose' if it considers that it is in the interests of justice to do so.

    (4) But the following may not be treated as a 'permitted purpose'—

    (a) requesting a person to cease doing, for commercial purposes, anything in relation to an article made to a design,

    (b) requesting a person to deliver up or destroy an article made to a design, or

    (c) requesting a person to give an undertaking relating to an article made to a design.

    (5) If any of the following information is included in a communication made for a permitted purpose, it is information that is 'necessary for that purpose' (see subsection (1)(b)(i))—

    (a) a statement that design right subsists in a design;

    (b) details of the design, or of a right in or under the design right in the design, which—

      (i) are accurate in all material respects, and

      (ii) are not misleading in any material respect; and

    (c) information enabling the identification of articles that are alleged to be infringing articles in relation to the design.

253C   Remedies and defences

(1) Proceedings in respect of an actionable threat may be brought against the person who made the threat for—

    (a) a declaration that the threat is unjustified;

    (b) an injunction against the continuance of the threat;

    (c) damages in respect of any loss sustained by the aggrieved person by reason of the threat.

(2) It is a defence for the person who made the threat to show that the act in respect of which proceedings were threatened constitutes (or if done would constitute) an infringement of design right.

(3) It is a defence for the person who made the threat to show—

    (a) that, despite having taken reasonable steps, the person has not identified anyone who has done an act mentioned in section 253A(2)(a) or (b) in relation to the article which is the subject of the threat, and

    (b) that the person notified the recipient, before or at the time of making the threat, of the steps taken.

253D   Professional advisers

(1) Proceedings in respect of an actionable threat may not be brought against a professional adviser (or any person vicariously liable for the actions of that professional adviser) if the conditions in subsection (3) are met.

(2) In this section 'professional adviser' means a person who, in relation to the making of the communication containing the threat—

    (a) is acting in a professional capacity in providing legal services or the services of a trade mark attorney or a patent attorney, and

    (b) is regulated in the provision of legal services, or the services of a trade mark attorney or a patent attorney, by one or more regulatory bodies (whether through membership of a regulatory body, the issue of a licence to practise or any other means).

(3) The conditions are that—

    (a) in making the communication the professional adviser is acting on the instructions of another person, and

    (b) when the communication is made the professional adviser identifies the person on whose instructions the adviser is acting.

(4) This section does not affect any liability of the person on whose instructions the professional adviser is acting.

(5) It is for a person asserting that subsection (1) applies to prove (if required) that at the material time—

(a) the person concerned was acting as a professional adviser, and

(b) the conditions in subsection (3) were met.

253E　Supplementary: proceedings for delivery up etc.

In section 253(1)(b) the reference to proceedings for infringement of design right includes a reference to—

(a) proceedings for an order under section 230 (order for delivery up), and

(b) proceedings for an order under section 231 (order as to disposal of infringing articles).

. . .

Extent of operation of this Part

255　Countries to which this Part extends

(1) This Part extends to England and Wales, Scotland and Northern Ireland.

(2) Her Majesty may by Order in Council direct that this Part shall extend, subject to such exceptions and modifications as may be specified in the Order, to—

(a) any of the Channel Islands,

(b) the Isle of Man, or

(c) any colony.

(3) That power includes power to extend, subject to such exceptions and modifications as may be specified in the Order, any Order in Council made under section 221 (further provision as to qualification for design right protection) or section 256 (countries enjoying reciprocal protection).

. . .

256　Countries enjoying reciprocal protection

(1) Her Majesty may, if it appears to Her that the law of a country provides adequate protection for British design, by Order in Council designate that country as one enjoying reciprocal protection under this Part.

(2) If the law of a country provides adequate protection only for certain classes of British designs, or only for designs applied to certain classes of article, any Order designating that country shall contain provision limiting, to a corresponding extent, the protection afforded by this Part in relation to designs connected with that country.

. . .

Interpretation

258　Construction of references to design right owner

(1) Where different persons are (whether in consequence of a partial assignment or otherwise) entitled to different aspects of design right in a work, the design right owner for any purpose of this Part is the person who is entitled to the right in the respect relevant for that purpose.

(2) Where design right (or any aspect of design right) is owned by more than one person jointly, references in this Part to the design right owner are to all the owners, so that, in particular, any requirement of the licence of the design right owner requires the licence of all of them.

259　Joint designs

(1) In this Part a 'joint design' means a design produced by the collaboration of two or more designers in which the contribution of each is not distinct from that of the other or others.

(2) References in this Part to the designer of a design shall, except as otherwise provided, be construed in relation to a joint design as references to all the designers of the design.

260   Application of provisions to articles in kit form

(1) The provisions of this Part apply in relation to a kit, that is, a complete or substantially complete set of components intended to be assembled into an article, as they apply in relation to the assembled article.

(2) Subsection (1) does not affect the question whether design right subsists in any aspect of the design of the components of a kit as opposed to the design of the assembled article.

...

262   Adaptation of expressions in relation to Scotland

In the application of this Part to Scotland—

'account of profits' means accounting and payment of profits;

'accounts' means count, reckoning and payment;

'assignment' means assignation;

'costs' means expenses;

'declaration' means 'declarator'

'defendant' means defender;

'delivery up' means delivery;

'injunction' means interdict;

'interlocutory relief' means interim remedy; and

'plaintiff' means pursuer.

263   Minor definitions

(1) In this Part—

'British design' means a design which qualifies for design right protection by reason of a connection with the United Kingdom of the designer or the person by whom the designer is employed;

'business' includes a trade or profession;

'the comptroller' means the Comptroller-General of Patents, Designs and Trade Marks;

'computer-generated', in relation to a design, means that the design is generated by computer in circumstances such that there is no human designer,

'country' includes any territory;

'the Crown' includes the Crown in right of Her Majesty's Government in Northern Ireland and the Crown in right of the Welsh Assembly Government;

'design document' means any record of a design, whether in the form of a drawing, a written description, a photograph, data stored in a computer or otherwise;

'employee', 'employment' and 'employer' refer to employment under a contract of service or of apprenticeship;

'government department' includes a Northern Ireland department and any part of the Welsh Assembly Government.

(2) References in this Part to 'marketing', in relation to an article, are to its being sold or let for hire, or offered or exposed for sale or hire, in the course of a business, and related expressions shall be construed accordingly; but no account shall be taken for the purposes of this Part of marketing which is merely colourable and not intended to satisfy the reasonable requirements of the public.

(3) References in this Part to an act being done in relation to an article for 'commercial purposes' are to its being done with a view to the article in question being sold or hired in the course of a business.

264   Index of defined expressions

The following Table shows provisions defining or otherwise explaining expressions used in this Part (other than provisions defining or explaining an expression used only in the same section)—

account of profits and accounts (in Scotland)	section 262
assignment (in Scotland)	section 262
British designs	section 263(1)
business	section 263(1)
commercial purposes	section 263(3)
the comptroller	section 263(1)
computer-generated	section 263(1)
costs (in Scotland)	section 262
country	section 263(1)
the Crown	section 263(1)
Crown use	sections 240(5) and 244(2)
defendant (in Scotland)	section 262
delivery up (in Scotland)	section 262
design	section 213(2)
design document	section 263(1)
designer	sections 214 and 259(2)
design right	section 213(1)
design right owner	sections 234(2) and 258
employee, employment and employer	section 263(1)
exclusive licence	section 225(1)
government department	section 263(1)
government department concerned (in relation to Crown use)	section 240(5)
infringing article	section 228
injunction (in Scotland)	section 262
interlocutory relief (in Scotland)	section 262
joint design	section 259(1)
licence (of the design right owner)	sections 222(4), 222(3) and 258
making articles to a design	section 226(2)
marketing (and related expressions)	section 263(2)
original	section 213(4)
plaintiff (in Scotland)	section 262
qualifying person	sections 217(1) and (2)
signed	section 261

...

PART VII   MISCELLANEOUS AND GENERAL

296   Circumvention of technical devices applied to computer programs

(1) This section applies where—

   (a) a technical device has been applied to a computer program; and

   (b) a person (A) knowing or having reason to believe that it will be used to make infringing copies—

      (i) manufactures for sale or hire, imports, distributes, sells or lets for hire, offers or exposes for sale or hire, advertises for sale or hire or has in his possession for commercial purposes any means the sole intended purpose of which is to facilitate the unauthorised removal or circumvention of the technical device; or

(ii) publishes information intended to enable or assist persons to remove or circumvent the technical device.

(2) The following persons have the same rights against A as a copyright owner has in respect of an infringement of copyright—

(a) a person—

(i) issuing to the public copies of, or

(ii) communicating to the public,

the computer program to which the technical device has been applied;

(b) the copyright owner or his exclusive licensee, if he is not the person specified in paragraph (a);

(c) the owner or exclusive licensee of any intellectual property right in the technical device applied to the computer program.

(3) The rights conferred by subsection (2) are concurrent, and sections 101(3) and 102(1) to (4) apply, in proceedings under this section, in relation to persons with concurrent rights as they apply, in proceedings mentioned in those provisions, in relation to a copyright owner and exclusive licensee with concurrent rights.

(4) Further, the persons in subsection (2) have the same rights under section 99 or 100 (delivery up or seizure of certain articles) in relation to any such means as is referred to in subsection (1) which a person has in his possession, custody or control with the intention that it should be used to facilitate the unauthorised removal or circumvention of any technical device which has been applied to a computer program, as a copyright owner has in relation to an infringing copy.

(5) The rights conferred by subsection (4) are concurrent, and section 102(5) shall apply, as respects anything done under section 99 or 100 by virtue of subsection (4), in relation to persons with concurrent rights as it applies, as respects anything done under section 99 or 100, in relation to a copyright owner and exclusive licensee with concurrent rights.

(6) In this section references to a technical device in relation to a computer program are to any device intended to prevent or restrict acts that are not authorised by the copyright owner of that computer program and are restricted by copyright.

(7) The following provisions apply in relation to proceedings under this section as in relation to proceedings under Part 1 (copyright)—

(a) sections 104 to 106 of this Act (presumptions as to certain matters relating to copyright); and

(b) section 72 of the Supreme Court Act 1981, section 15 of the Law Reform (Miscellaneous Provisions) (Scotland) Act 1985 and section 94A of the Judicature (Northern Ireland) Act 1978 (withdrawal of privilege against self-incrimination in certain proceedings relating to intellectual property);

and section 114 of this Act applies, with the necessary modifications, in relation to the disposal of anything delivered up or seized by virtue of subsection (4).

(8) Expressions used in this section which are defined for the purposes of Part 1 of this Act (copyright) have the same meaning as in that Part.

296ZA   Circumvention of technological measures

(1) This section applies where—

(a) effective technological measures have been applied to a copyright work other than a computer program; and

(b) a person (B) does anything which circumvents those measures knowing, or with reasonable grounds to know, that he is pursuing that objective.

(2) This section does not apply where a person, for the purposes of research into cryptography, does anything which circumvents effective technological measures unless in so doing, or in issuing information derived from that research, he affects prejudicially the rights of the copyright owner.

(3) The following persons have the same rights against B as a copyright owner has in respect of an infringement of copyright—

    (a) a person—

        (i)   issuing to the public copies of, or

        (ii) communicating to the public,

        the work to which effective technological measures have been applied; and

    (b) the copyright owner or his exclusive licensee, if he is not the person specified in paragraph (a).

(4) The rights conferred by subsection (3) are concurrent, and sections 101(3) and 102(1) to (4) apply, in proceedings under this section, in relation to persons with concurrent rights as they apply, in proceedings mentioned in those provisions, in relation to a copyright owner and exclusive licensee with concurrent rights.

(5) The following provisions apply in relation to proceedings under this section as in relation to proceedings under Part 1 (copyright)—

    (a) sections 104 to 106 of this Act (presumptions as to certain matters relating to copyright); and

    (b) section 72 of the Supreme Court Act 1981, section 15 of the Law Reform (Miscellaneous Provisions) (Scotland) Act 1985 and section 94A of the Judicature (Northern Ireland) Act 1978 (withdrawal of privilege against self-incrimination in certain proceedings relating to intellectual property).

(6) Subsections (1) to (4) and (5)(b) and any other provision of this Act as it has effect for the purposes of those subsections apply, with any necessary adaptations, to rights in performances, publication right and database right.

(7) The provisions of regulation 22 (presumptions relevant to database right) of the Copyright and Rights in Databases Regulations 1997 (SI 1997/3032) apply in proceedings brought by virtue of this section in relation to database right.

296ZB   Devices and services designed to circumvent technological measures

    (1) A person commits an offence if he—

    (a) manufactures for sale or hire, or

    (b) imports otherwise than for his private and domestic use, or

    (c) in the course of a business—

        (i)   sells or lets for hire, or

        (ii)   offers or exposes for sale or hire, or

        (iii) advertises for sale or hire, or

        (iv) possesses, or

        (v)   distributes, or

    (d) distributes otherwise than in the course of a business to such an extent as to affect prejudicially the copyright owner,

any device, product or component which is primarily designed, produced, or adapted for the purpose of enabling or facilitating the circumvention of effective technological measures.

    (2) A person commits an offence if he provides, promotes, advertises or markets—

    (a) in the course of a business, or

    (b) otherwise than in the course of a business to such an extent as to affect prejudicially the copyright owner,

a service the purpose of which is to enable or facilitate the circumvention of effective technological measures.

    (3) Subsections (1) and (2) do not make unlawful anything done by, or on behalf of, law enforcement agencies or any of the intelligence services—

    (a) in the interests of national security; or

    (b) for the purpose of the prevention or detection of crime, the investigation of an offence, or the conduct of a prosecution, and in this subsection 'intelligence services' has the meaning given in section 81 of the Regulation of Investigatory Powers Act 2000.

(4) A person guilty of an offence under subsection (1) or (2) is liable—

(a) on summary conviction, to imprisonment for a term not exceeding three months, or to a fine not exceeding the statutory maximum, or both;

(b) on conviction on indictment to a fine or imprisonment for a term not exceeding two years, or both.

(5) It is a defence to any prosecution for an offence under this section for the defendant to prove that he did not know, and had no reasonable ground for believing, that—

(a) the device, product or component; or

(b) the service,

enabled or facilitated the circumvention of effective technological measures.

296ZC Devices and services designed to circumvent technological measures: search warrants and forfeiture

(1) The provisions of sections 297B (search warrants), 297C (forfeiture of unauthorised decoders: England and Wales or Northern Ireland) and 297D (forfeiture of unauthorised decoders: Scotland) apply to offences under section 296ZB with the following modifications.

(2) In section 297B the reference to an offence under section 297A(1) shall be construed as a reference to an offence under section 296ZB(1) or (2).

(3) In sections 297C(2)(a) and 297D(15) the references to an offence under section 297A(1) shall be construed as a reference to an offence under section 296ZB(1).

(4) In sections 297C and 297D references to unauthorised decoders shall be construed as references to devices, products or components for the purpose of circumventing effective technological measures.

296ZD Rights and remedies in respect of devices and services designed to circumvent technological measures

(1) This section applies where—

(a) effective technological measures have been applied to a copyright work other than a computer program; and

(b) a person (C) manufactures, imports, distributes, sells or lets for hire, offers or exposes for sale or hire, advertises for sale or hire, or has in his possession for commercial purposes any device, product or component, or provides services which—

(i)   are promoted, advertised or marketed for the purpose of the circumvention of, or

(ii) have only a limited commercially significant purpose or use other than to circumvent, or

(iii) are primarily designed, produced, adapted or performed for the purpose of enabling or facilitating the circumvention of,

those measures.

(2) The following persons have the same rights against C as a copyright owner has in respect of an infringement of copyright—

(a) a person—

(i)   issuing to the public copies of, or

(ii) communicating to the public,

the work to which effective technological measures have been applied;

(b) the copyright owner or his exclusive licensee, if he is not the person specified in paragraph (a); and

(c) the owner or exclusive licensee of any intellectual property right in the effective technological measures applied to the work.

(3) The rights conferred by subsection (2) are concurrent, and sections 101(3) and 102(1) to (4) apply, in proceedings under this section, in relation to persons with concurrent rights as they apply, in proceedings mentioned in those provisions, in relation to a copyright owner and exclusive licensee with concurrent rights.

(4) Further, the persons in subsection (2) have the same rights under section 99 or 100 (delivery up or seizure of certain articles) in relation to any such device, product or component which a person has in his possession, custody or control with the intention that it should be used to circumvent effective technological measures, as a copyright owner has in relation to any infringing copy.

(5) The rights conferred by subsection (4) are concurrent, and section 102(5) shall apply, as respects anything done under section 99 or 100 by virtue of subsection (4), in relation to persons with concurrent rights as it applies, as respects anything done under section 99 or 100, in relation to a copyright owner and exclusive licensee with concurrent rights.

(6) The following provisions apply in relation to proceedings under this section as in relation to proceedings under Part 1 (copyright)—

    (a) sections 104 to 106 of this Act (presumptions as to certain matters relating to copyright); and

    (b) section 72 of the Supreme Court Act 1981, section 15 of the Law Reform (Miscellaneous Provisions) (Scotland) Act 1985 and section 94A of the Judicature (Northern Ireland) Act 1978 (withdrawal of privilege against self-incrimination in certain proceedings relating to intellectual property);

and section 114 of this Act applies, with the necessary modifications, in relation to the disposal of anything delivered up or seized by virtue of subsection (4).

(7) In section 97(1) (innocent infringement of copyright) as it applies to proceedings for infringement of the rights conferred by this section, the reference to the defendant not knowing or having reason to believe that copyright subsisted in the work shall be construed as a reference to his not knowing or having reason to believe that his acts enabled or facilitated an infringement of copyright.

(8) Subsections (1) to (5), (6)(b) and (7) and any other provision of this Act as it has effect for the purposes of those subsections apply, with any necessary adaptations, to rights in performances, publication right and database right.

(9) The provisions of regulation 22 (presumptions relevant to database right) of the Copyright and Rights in Databases Regulations 1997 (SI 1997/3032) apply in proceedings brought by virtue of this section in relation to database right.

296ZE Remedy where effective technological measures prevent permitted acts

(1) In this section—

'Marrakesh beneficiary' means a person who—

    (a) is blind,

    (b) has a visual impairment which cannot be improved so as to give the person visual function substantially equivalent to that of a person who has no such impairment, and who is, as a result, unable to read printed works to substantially the same degree as a person without such an impairment,

    (c) has a perceptual or reading disability and is, as a result, unable to read printed works to substantially the same degree as a person without such disability, or

    (d) is otherwise unable, due to a physical disability, to hold or manipulate a book or to focus or move their eyes to the extent that would normally be acceptable for reading;

'Marrakesh work' means a work in the form of a book, journal, newspaper, magazine or other kind of writing, notation, including sheet music, and related illustrations, in any media, including in audio form such as audiobooks and in digital format, which is protected by copyright, related rights or database rights and which is published or otherwise lawfully made publicly available;

'permitted act' means an act which may be done in relation to copyright works, notwithstanding the subsistence of copyright, by virtue of a provision of this Act listed in Part 1 of Schedule 5A;

'voluntary measure or agreement' means—

    (a) any measure taken voluntarily by a copyright owner, his exclusive licensee or a person issuing copies of, or communicating to the public, a work other than a computer program, or

    (b) any agreement between a copyright owner, his exclusive licensee or a person issuing copies of, or communicating to the public, a work other than a computer program and another party, the effect of which is to enable a person to carry out a permitted act.

(2) Where the application of any effective technological measure to a copyright work other than a computer program prevents a person from carrying out a permitted act in relation to that work then that person or a person being a representative of a class of persons prevented from carrying out a permitted act may issue a notice of complaint to the Secretary of State.

(3) Following receipt of a notice of complaint, the Secretary of State may give to the owner of that copyright work or an exclusive licensee such directions as appear to the Secretary of State to be requisite or expedient for the purpose of—

   (a) establishing whether any voluntary measure or agreement relevant to the copyright work the subject of the complaint subsists; or

   (b) (where it is established there is no subsisting voluntary measure or agreement) ensuring that the owner or exclusive licensee of that copyright work makes available to the complainant the means of carrying out the permitted act the subject of the complaint to the extent necessary to so benefit from that permitted act.

(4) The Secretary of State may also give directions—

   (a) as to the form and manner in which a notice of complaint in subsection (2) may be delivered to him;

   (b) as to the form and manner in which evidence of any voluntary measure or agreement may be delivered to him; and

   (c) generally as to the procedure to be followed in relation to a complaint made under this section;

and shall publish directions given under this subsection in such manner as in his opinion will secure adequate publicity for them.

(5) It shall be the duty of any person to whom a direction is given under subsection (3)(a) or (b) to give effect to that direction.

(6) The obligation to comply with a direction given under subsection (3)(b) is a duty owed to the complainant or, where the complaint is made by a representative of a class of persons, to that representative and to each person in the class represented; and a breach of the duty is actionable accordingly (subject to the defences and other incidents applying to actions for breach of statutory duty).

(7) Any direction under this section may be varied or revoked by a subsequent direction under this section.

(8) Any direction given under this section shall be in writing.

(9) Subject to subsection (9A), this section does not apply to copyright works made available to the public on agreed contractual terms in such a way that members of the public may access them from a place and at a time individually chosen by them.

(9A) But this section does apply where the application of any effective technological measure to a Marrakesh work prevents the making of an accessible copy of that work under sections 31A, 31B or 31BA, or paragraphs 3A, 3B or 3C of Schedule 2, for the benefit of a Marrakesh beneficiary.

(10) This section applies only where a complainant has lawful access to the protected copyright work, or where the complainant is a representative of a class of persons, where the class of persons have lawful access to the work.

(11) Subsections (1) to (10) apply with any necessary adaptations to—

   (a) rights in performances, and in this context the expression 'permitted act' refers to an act that may be done by virtue of a provision of this Act listed in Part 2 of Schedule 5A;

   (b) database right, and in this context the expression 'permitted act' refers to an act that may be done by virtue of a provision of this Act listed in Part 3 of Schedule 5A; and

   (c) publication right.

296ZF Interpretation of sections 296ZA to 296ZE

(1) In sections 296ZA to 296ZE, 'technological measures' are any technology, device or component which is designed, in the normal course of its operation, to protect a copyright work other than a computer program.

(2) Such measures are 'effective' if the use of the work is controlled by the copyright owner through—

(a) an access control or protection process such as encryption, scrambling or other transformation of the work, or

(b) a copy control mechanism,

which achieves the intended protection.

(3) In this section, the reference to—

(a) protection of a work is to the prevention or restriction of acts that are not authorised by the copyright owner of that work and are restricted by copyright; and

(b) use of a work does not extend to any use of the work that is outside the scope of the acts restricted by copyright.

(4) Expressions used in sections 296ZA to 296ZE which are defined for the purposes of Part 1 of this Act (copyright) have the same meaning as in that Part.

Rights management information

296ZG   Electronic rights management information

(1) This section applies where a person (D), knowingly and without authority, removes or alters electronic rights management information which—

(a) is associated with a copy of a copyright work, or

(b) appears in connection with the communication to the public of a copyright work,

and where D knows, or has reason to believe, that by so doing he is inducing, enabling, facilitating or concealing an infringement of copyright.

(2) This section also applies where a person (E), knowingly and without authority, distributes, imports for distribution or communicates to the public copies of a copyright work from which electronic rights management information—

(a) associated with the copies, or

(b) appearing in connection with the communication to the public of the work,

has been removed or altered without authority and where E knows, or has reason to believe, that by so doing he is inducing, enabling, facilitating or concealing an infringement of copyright.

(3) A person issuing to the public copies of, or communicating, the work to the public, has the same rights against D and E as a copyright owner has in respect of an infringement of copyright.

(4) The copyright owner or his exclusive licensee, if he is not the person issuing to the public copies of, or communicating, the work to the public, also has the same rights against D and E as he has in respect of an infringement of copyright.

(5) The rights conferred by subsections (3) and (4) are concurrent, and sections 101(3) and 102(1) to (4) apply, in proceedings under this section, in relation to persons with concurrent rights as they apply, in proceedings mentioned in those provisions, in relation to a copyright owner and exclusive licensee with concurrent rights.

(6) The following provisions apply in relation to proceedings under this section as in relation to proceedings under Part I (copyright)—

(a) sections 104 to 106 of this Act (presumptions as to certain matters relating to copyright); and

(b) section 72 of the Supreme Court Act 1981, section 15 of the Law Reform (Miscellaneous Provisions) (Scotland) Act 1985 and section 94A of the Judicature (Northern Ireland) Act 1978 (withdrawal of privilege against self-incrimination in certain proceedings relating to intellectual property).

(7) In this section—

(a) expressions which are defined for the purposes of Part I of this Act (copyright) have the same meaning as in that Part; and

(b) 'rights management information' means any information provided by the copyright owner or the holder of any right under copyright which identifies the work, the author, the copyright owner or the holder of any intellectual property rights, or information about the terms and conditions of use of the work, and any numbers or codes that represent such information.

(8) Subsections (1) to (5) and (6)(b), and any other provision of this Act as it has effect for the purposes of those subsections, apply, with any necessary adaptations, to rights in performances, publication right and database right.

(9) The provisions of regulation 22 (presumptions relevant to database right) of the Copyright and Rights in Databases Regulations 1997 (SI 1997/3032) apply in proceedings brought by virtue of this section in relation to database right.

Computer programs

296A   Avoidance of certain terms

(1) Where a person has the use of a computer program under an agreement, any term or condition in the agreement shall be void in so far as it purports to prohibit or restrict—

(a) the making of any back up copy of the program which it is necessary for him to have for the purposes of the agreed use;

(b) where the conditions in section 50B(2) are met, the decompiling of the program; or

(c) the observing, studying or testing of the functioning of the program in accordance with section 50BA.

(2) In this section, decompile, in relation to a computer program, has the same meaning as in section 50B.

Databases

296B   Avoidance of certain terms relating to databases

Where under an agreement a person has a right to use a database or part of a database, any term or condition in the agreement shall be void in so far as it purports to prohibit or restrict the performance of any act which would but for section 50D infringe the copyright in the database.

Fraudulent reception of transmissions

297   Offence of fraudulently receiving programmes

(1) A person who dishonestly receives a programme included in a broadcasting service provided from a place in the United Kingdom with intent to avoid payment of any charge applicable to the reception of the programme commits an offence and is liable on summary conviction to a fine not exceeding level 5 on the standard scale.

(2) Where an offence under this section committed by a body corporate is proved to have been committed with the consent or connivance of a director, manager, secretary or other similar officer of the body, or a person purporting to act in any such capacity, he as well as the body corporate is guilty of the offence and liable to be proceeded against and punished accordingly.

In relation to a body corporate whose affairs are managed by its members 'director' means a member of the body corporate.

297A   Unauthorised decoders

(1) A person commits an offence if he—

(a) makes, imports, distributes, sells or lets for hire or offers or exposes for sale or hire any unauthorised decoder;

(b) has in his possession for commercial purposes any unauthorised decoder;

(c) instals, maintains or replaces for commercial purposes any unauthorised decoder; or

(d) advertises any unauthorised decoder for sale or hire or otherwise promotes any unauthorised decoder by means of commercial communications.

(2) A person guilty of an offence under subsection (1) is liable—

(a) on summary conviction, to imprisonment for a term not exceeding six months, or to a fine not exceeding the statutory maximum, or to both;

(b) on conviction on indictment, to imprisonment for a term not exceeding ten years, or to a fine, or to both.

(3) It is a defence to any prosecution for an offence under this section for the defendant to prove that he did not know, and had no reasonable ground for believing, that the decoder was an unauthorised decoder.

(4) In this section—

'apparatus' includes any device, component or electronic data (including software);

'conditional access technology' means any technical measure or arrangement whereby access to encrypted transmissions in an intelligible form is made conditional on prior individual authorisation;

'decoder' means any apparatus which is designed or adapted to enable (whether on its own or with any other apparatus) an encrypted transmission to be decoded;

'encrypted' includes subjected to scrambling or the operation of cryptographic envelopes, electronic locks, passwords or any other analogous application;

'transmission' means—

  (a) any programme included in a broadcasting service which is provided from a place in the United Kingdom; or

  (b) an information society service (within the meaning of Directive 98/34/EC of the European Parliament and of the Council of 22nd June 1998, as amended by Directive 98/48/EC of the European Parliament and of the Council of 20th July 1998) which is provided from a place in the United Kingdom or any other member State; and

'unauthorised', in relation to a decoder, means that the decoder is designed or adapted to enable an encrypted transmission, or any service of which it forms part, to be accessed in an intelligible form without payment of the fee (however imposed) which the person making the transmission, or on whose behalf it is made, charges for accessing the transmission or service (whether by the circumvention of any conditional access technology related to the transmission or service or by any other means).

297B Search warrants

(1) Where a justice of the peace (in Scotland, a sheriff or justice of the peace) is satisfied by information on oath given by a constable (in Scotland, by evidence on oath) that there are reasonable grounds for believing—

  (a) that an offence under section 297A(1) has been or is about to be committed in any premises, and

  (b) that evidence that such an offence has been or is about to be committed is in those premises,

he may issue a warrant authorising a constable to enter and search the premises, using such reasonable force as is necessary.

  . . .

(4) In executing a warrant issued under subsection (1) a constable may seize an article if he reasonably believes that it is evidence that any offence under section 297A(1) has been or is about to be committed.

(5) In this section 'premises' includes land, buildings, fixed or moveable structures, vehicles, vessels, aircraft and hovercraft.

297C Forfeiture of unauthorised decoders: England and Wales or Northern Ireland

(1) In England and Wales or Northern Ireland where unauthorised decoders have come into the possession of any person in connection with the investigation or prosecution of a relevant offence, that person may apply under this section for an order for the forfeiture of the unauthorised decoders.

(2) For the purposes of this section 'relevant offence' means—

  (a) an offence under section 297A(1) (criminal liability for making, importing, etc. unauthorised decoders),

  (b) an offence under the Trade Descriptions Act 1968, or

  (ba) an offence under the Business Protection from Misleading Marketing Regulations 2008,

  (bb) an offence under the Consumer Protection from Unfair Trading Regulations 2008, or

  (c) an offence involving dishonesty or deception.

  . . .

297D   Forfeiture of unauthorised decoders: Scotland

(1) In Scotland the court may make an order under this section for the forfeiture of unauthorised decoders.

(2) An order under this section may be made—

(a) on an application by the procurator-fiscal made in the manner specified in section 134 of the Criminal Procedure (Scotland) Act 1995, or

(b) where a person is convicted of a relevant offence, in addition to any other penalty which the court may impose.

(3) On an application under subsection (2)(a), the court shall make an order for the forfeiture of any unauthorised decoders only if it is satisfied that a relevant offence has been committed in relation to the unauthorised decoders.

...

(15) For the purposes of this section—

'relevant offence' means—

(a) an offence under section 297A(1) (criminal liability for making, importing, etc unauthorised decoders),

(b) an offence under the Trade Descriptions Act 1968,

(c) an offence under the Business Protection from Misleading Marketing Regulations 2008,

(d) an offence under the Consumer Protection from Unfair Trading Regulations 2008, or

(e) any offence involving dishonesty or deception;

'the court' means—

(a) in relation to an order made on an application under subsection (2)(a), the sheriff, and

(b) in relation to an order made under subsection (2)(b), the court which imposed the penalty.

298   Rights and remedies in respect of apparatus, &c. for unauthorised reception of transmissions

(1) A person who—

(a) makes charges for the reception of programmes included in a broadcasting service provided from a place in the United Kingdom,

(b) sends encrypted transmissions of any other description from a place in the United Kingdom, or

(c) provides conditional access services from a place in the United Kingdom or,

is entitled to the following rights and remedies.

(2) He has the same rights and remedies against a person—

(a) who—

(i)   makes, imports, distributes, sells or lets for hire, offers or exposes for sale or hire, or advertises for sale or hire,

(ii) has in his possession for commercial purposes, or

(iii) instals, maintains or replaces for commercial purposes,

any apparatus designed or adapted to enable or assist persons to access the programmes or other transmissions or circumvent conditional access technology related to the programmes or other transmissions when they are not entitled to do so, or

(b) who publishes or otherwise promotes by means of commercial communications any information which is calculated to enable or assist persons to access the programmes or other transmissions or circumvent conditional access technology related to the programmes or other transmissions when they are not entitled to do so,

as a copyright owner has in respect of an infringement of copyright.

(3) Further, he has the same rights under section 99 or 100 (delivery up or seizure of certain articles) in relation to any such apparatus as a copyright owner has in relation to an infringing copy.

(4) Section 72 of the Supreme Court Act 1981, section 15 of the Law Reform (Miscellaneous Provisions) (Scotland) Act 1985 and section 94A of the Judicature (Northern Ireland) Act 1978 (withdrawal of privilege against self-incrimination in certain proceedings relating to intellectual property) apply to proceedings under this section as to proceedings under Part 1 of this Act (copyright).

(5) In section 97(1) (innocent infringement of copyright) as it applies to proceedings for infringement of the rights conferred by this section, the reference to the defendant not knowing or having reason to believe that copyright subsisted in the work shall be construed as a reference to his not knowing or having reason to believe that his acts infringed the rights conferred by this section.

(6) Section 114 applies, with the necessary modifications, in relation to the disposal of anything delivered up or seized by virtue of subsection (3) above.

(7) In this section 'apparatus', 'conditional access technology' and 'encrypted' have the same meanings as in section 297A, 'transmission' includes transmissions as defined in that section and 'conditional access services' means services comprising the provision of conditional access technology.

299   Supplementary provisions as to fraudulent reception

(1) Her Majesty may by Order in Council—
- (a) provide that section 297 applies in relation to programmes included in services provided from a country or territory outside the United Kingdom, and
- (b) provide that section 298 applies in relation to such programmes and to encrypted transmissions sent from such a country or territory.

(3) A statutory instrument containing an Order in Council under subsection (1) shall be subject to annulment in pursuance of a resolution of either House of Parliament.

(4) Where sections 297, 297A and 298 apply in relation to a broadcasting service, they also apply to any service run for the person providing that service, or a person providing programmes for that service, which consists wholly or mainly in the sending by means of a telecommunications system of sounds or visual images, or both.

(5) In sections 297, 297A and 298, and this section, 'programme' and 'broadcasting', and related expressions, have the same meaning as in Part I (copyright).

Provisions for the benefit of Great Ormond Street Hospital for Children

301   Provisions for the benefit of Great Ormond Street Hospital for Children

The provisions of Schedule 6 have effect for conferring on GOSH Children's Charity for the benefit of Great Ormond Street Hospital for Children a right to a royalty in respect of the public performance, commercial publication or communication to the public of the play 'Peter Pan' by Sir James Matthew Barrie, or of any adaptation of that work, notwithstanding that copyright in the work expired on 31 December 1987.

...

General

304   Extent

(1) Provision as to the extent of Part I (copyright), Part II (rights in performances) and Part III (design right) is to be found in sections 157, 207 and 255 respectively; the extent of the other provisions of this Act is as follows.

...

SCHEDULES

...

SCHEDULE 2

RIGHTS IN PERFORMANCES: PERMITTED ACTS

Introductory

1.—(1) The provisions of this Schedule specify acts which may be done in relation to a performance or recording notwithstanding the rights conferred by this Chapter; they relate only to the question of infringement of those rights and do not affect any other right or obligation restricting the doing of any of the specified acts.

(2) No inference shall be drawn from the description of any act which may by virtue of this Schedule be done without infringing the rights conferred by this Chapter as to the scope of those rights.

(3) The provisions of this Schedule are to be construed independently of each other, so that the fact that an act does not fall within one provision does not mean that it is not covered by another provision.

Making of temporary copies

1A. The rights conferred by this Chapter are not infringed by the making of a temporary copy of a recording of a performance which is transient or incidental, which is an integral and essential part of a technological process and the sole purpose of which is to enable—

(a) a transmission of the recording in a network between third parties by an intermediary; or

(b) a lawful use of the recording;

and which has no independent economic significance.

Research and private study

1C.—(1) Fair dealing with a performance or a recording of a performance for the purposes of research for a non-commercial purpose does not infringe the rights conferred by this Chapter.

(2) Fair dealing with a performance or recording of a performance for the purposes of private study does not infringe the rights conferred by this Chapter.

(3) Copying of a recording by a person other than the researcher or student is not fair dealing if—

(a) in the case of a librarian, or a person acting on behalf of a librarian, that person does anything which is not permitted under paragraph 6F (copying by librarians: single copies of published recordings), or

(b) in any other case, the person doing the copying knows or has reason to believe that it will result in copies of substantially the same material being provided to more than one person at substantially the same time and for substantially the same purpose.

(4) To the extent that a term of a contract purports to prevent or restrict the doing of any act which, by virtue of this paragraph, would not infringe any right conferred by this Chapter, that term is unenforceable.

(5) Expressions used in this paragraph have the same meaning as in section 29.

Copies for text and data analysis for non-commercial research

1D.—(1) The making of a copy of a recording of a performance by a person who has lawful access to the recording does not infringe any rights conferred by this Chapter provided that the copy is made in order that a person who has lawful access to the recording may carry out a computational analysis of anything recorded in the recording for the sole purpose of research for a non-commercial purpose.

(2) Where a copy of a recording has been made under this paragraph, the rights conferred by this Chapter are infringed if—

(a) the copy is transferred to any other person, except where the transfer is authorised by the rights owner, or

(b) the copy is used for any purpose other than that mentioned in sub-paragraph (1), except where the use is authorised by the rights owner.

(3) If a copy of a recording made under this paragraph is subsequently dealt with—

(a) it is to be treated as an illicit recording for the purposes of that dealing, and

(b) if that dealing infringes any right conferred by this Chapter, it is to be treated as an illicit recording for all subsequent purposes.

(4) To the extent that a term of a contract purports to prevent or restrict the making of a copy which, by virtue of this paragraph, would not infringe any right conferred by this Chapter, that term is unenforceable.

(5) Expressions used in this paragraph have the same meaning as in section 29A.

Criticism, reviews, quotation and news reporting

2.—(1) Fair dealing with a performance or recording for the purpose of criticism or review, of that or another performance or recording, or of a work, does not infringe any of the rights conferred by this Chapter provided that the performance or recording has been made available to the public.

(1ZA) The rights conferred by this Chapter in a performance or a recording of a performance are not infringed by the use of a quotation from the performance or recording (whether for criticism or review or otherwise) provided that—

(a) the performance or recording has been made available to the public,

(b) the use of the quotation is fair dealing with the performance or recording, and

(c) the extent of the quotation is no more than is required by the specific purpose for which it is used.

(1A) Fair dealing with a performance or recording for the purpose of reporting current events does not infringe any of the rights conferred by this Chapter.

(1B) To the extent that a term of a contract purports to prevent or restrict the doing of any act which, by virtue of sub-paragraph (1ZA), would not infringe any right conferred by this Chapter, that term is unenforceable.

(2) Expressions used in this paragraph have the same meaning as in section 30.

Caricature, parody or pastiche

2A.—(1) Fair dealing with a performance or a recording of a performance for the purposes of caricature, parody or pastiche does not infringe the rights conferred by this Chapter in the performance or recording.

(2) To the extent that a term of a contract purports to prevent or restrict the doing of any act which, by virtue of this paragraph, would not infringe any right conferred by this Chapter, that term is unenforceable.

(3) Expressions used in this paragraph have the same meaning as in section 30A.

Incidental inclusion of performance or recording

3.—(1) The rights conferred by this Chapter are not infringed by the incidental inclusion of a performance or recording in a sound recording, film or broadcast.

(2) Nor are those rights infringed by anything done in relation to copies of, or the playing, showing or communication to the public of, anything whose making was, by virtue of sub-paragraph (1), not an infringement of those rights.

(3) A performance or recording so far as it consists of music, or words spoken or sung with music, shall not be regarded as incidentally included in a sound recording or broadcast if it is deliberately included.

(4) Expressions used in this paragraph have the same meaning as in section 31.

Disabled persons: copies of recordings for personal use

3A.—(1) This paragraph applies if—

(a) a disabled person has lawful access to a copy of the whole or part of a recording of a performance, and

(b) the person's disability prevents the person from enjoying the recording to substantially the same degree as a person who does not have that disability.

(2) The making of an accessible copy of the copy of the recording referred to in sub-paragraph (1)(a) does not infringe the rights conferred by this Chapter if—

(a) the copy is made by the disabled person or by a person acting on behalf of the disabled person, and

(b) the copy is made for the disabled person's personal use,

(4) The rights conferred by this Chapter are infringed by the transfer of an accessible copy of a recording made under this paragraph to any person other than—

(a) a person by or for whom an accessible copy of the recording may be made under this paragraph, or

(b) a person who intends to transfer the copy to a person falling within paragraph (a),

except where the transfer is authorised by the rights owner.

(5) An accessible copy of a recording made under this paragraph is to be treated for all purposes as an illicit recording if it is held by a person at a time when the person does not fall within sub-paragraph (4)(a) or (b).

(6) If an accessible copy of a recording made under this paragraph is subsequently dealt with—

(a) it is to be treated as an illicit recording for the purposes of that dealing, and

(b) if that dealing infringes any right conferred by this Chapter, it is to be treated as an illicit recording for all subsequent purposes.

Making, communicating, making available, distributing or lending of accessible copies by authorised bodies

3B.—(1) If—

(a) an authorised body has lawful access to the whole or part of a work which has been published or otherwise made available, and

(b) the body complies with sub-paragraph (1A),

the body may, without infringing the rights conferred by this Chapter, make, communicate, make available, distribute or lend accessible copies of the work on a non-profit basis for the personal use of disabled persons in the United Kingdom.

(1A) An authorised body complies with this sub-paragraph if it—

(a) distributes, communicates, makes available or lends accessible copies only to disabled persons or other authorised bodies,

(b) takes appropriate steps to discourage the unauthorised reproduction, distribution, communication to the public or making available to the public of accessible copies,

(c) demonstrates due care in, and maintains records of, its handling of works and accessible copies, and

(d) publishes and updates, on its website if appropriate, or through other online or offline channels, information on how it complies with the obligations in paragraphs (a), (b) and (c).

(4) For the purposes of sub-paragraph (1), communicate, make available, distribute or lend 'for the personal use of disabled persons' includes to communicate, make available, distribute or lend to a person acting on behalf of a disabled person.

(8) An authorised body which has made an accessible copy of a recording under this paragraph may communicate, make available, distribute or lend it to another authorised body established in the United Kingdom which is entitled to make accessible copies of the recording under this paragraph for the purposes of enabling that other body to make accessible copies of the recording.

(10) If an accessible copy of a recording made under this paragraph is subsequently dealt with—

(a) it is to be treated as an illicit recording for the purposes of that dealing, and

(b) if that dealing infringes any right conferred by this Chapter, it is to be treated as an illicit recording for all subsequent purposes.

(11) In this paragraph 'dealt with' means sold or let for hire or offered or exposed for sale or hire.

Making communicating, making available, distributing or lending of intermediate copies by authorised bodies

3C.—(1) An authorised body which is entitled to make an accessible copy of a recording of a performance under paragraph 3B may, without infringing the rights conferred by this Chapter, make a copy of the recording ('an intermediate copy') if this is necessary in order to make the accessible copy.

(2) An authorised body which has made an intermediate copy of a recording under this paragraph may communicate, make available, distribute or lend it on a non-profit basis to another authorised body which is entitled to make accessible copies of the recording under paragraph 3B for the purposes of enabling that other body to make accessible copies of the recording.

(3) The rights conferred by this Chapter are infringed by the transfer of an intermediate copy made under this paragraph to a person other than another authorised body as permitted by subparagraph (2), except where the transfer is authorised by the rights owner.

Accessible and intermediate copies: records

...

Paragraphs 3A to 3D: interpretation and general

3E.—(1) This paragraph supplements paragraphs 3A to 3D and includes definitions.

(2) 'Disabled person' means a person who has a physical or mental impairment which prevents the person from enjoying a recording of a performance to substantially the same degree as a person who does not have that impairment, and 'disability' is to be construed accordingly.

(3) But a person is not to be regarded as disabled by reason only of an impairment of visual function which can be improved, for example by the use of corrective lenses, to a level that is normally acceptable for reading without a special level or kind of light.

(4) An 'accessible copy' of a recording of a performance means a version of the recording which enables disabled persons to access that version, including accessing it as feasibly and comfortably as a person who is not a disabled person.

(5) An accessible copy—

(a) may include facilities for navigating around the version of the recording, but

(b) must not include any changes to the recording which are not necessary to overcome the problems suffered by the disabled persons for whom the accessible copy is intended.

(6) To the extent that a term of a contract purports to prevent or restrict the doing of any act which, by virtue of paragraph 3A, 3B or 3C, would not infringe any right conferred by this Chapter, that term is unenforceable.

(7) 'Authorised body' has the meaning given in section 31F, and other expressions used in paragraphs 3A to 3D but not defined in this paragraph have the same meaning as in sections 31A to 31BB.

Illustration for instruction

4.—(1) Fair dealing with a performance or a recording of a performance for the sole purpose of illustration for instruction does not infringe the rights conferred by this Chapter provided that the dealing is—

    (a) for a non-commercial purpose, and

    (b) by a person giving or receiving instruction (or preparing for giving or receiving instruction).

(2) To the extent that a term of a contract purports to prevent or restrict the doing of any act which, by virtue of this paragraph, would not infringe any right conferred by this Chapter, that term is unenforceable.

(3) Expressions used in this paragraph have the same meaning as in section 32.

Playing or showing sound recording, film or broadcast at educational establishment

5.—(1) The playing or showing of a sound recording, film or broadcast at an educational establishment for the purposes of instruction before an audience consisting of teachers and pupils at the establishment and other persons directly connected with the activities of the establishment is not a playing or showing of a performance in public for the purposes of infringement of the rights conferred by this Chapter.

(2) A person is not for this purpose directly connected with the activities of the educational establishment simply because he is the parent of a pupil at the establishment.

(3) Expressions used in this paragraph have the same meaning as in section 34 and any provision made under section 174(2) with respect to the application of that section also applies for the purposes of this paragraph.

Recording by educational establishments of broadcasts

6.—(1) A recording of a broadcast, or a copy of such a recording, may be made by or on behalf of an educational establishment for the educational purposes of that establishment without infringing any of the rights conferred by this Chapter in relation to any performance or recording included in it, provided that the educational purposes are non-commercial.

(2) The rights conferred by this Chapter are not infringed where a recording of a broadcast or a copy of such a recording, made under sub-paragraph (1), is communicated by or on behalf of the educational establishment to its pupils or staff for the non-commercial educational purposes of that establishment.

(3) Sub-paragraph (2) only applies to a communication received outside the premises of the establishment if that communication is made by means of a secure electronic network accessible only by the establishment's pupils and staff.

(4) Acts which would otherwise be permitted by this paragraph are not permitted if, or to the extent that, licences are available authorising the acts in question and the educational establishment responsible for those acts knew or ought to have been aware of that fact.

(5) If a recording made under this paragraph is subsequently dealt with—

    (a) it is to be treated as an illicit recording for the purposes of that dealing, and

    (b) if that dealing infringes any right conferred by this Chapter, it is to be treated as an illicit recording for all subsequent purposes.

(6) In this paragraph 'dealt with' means—

    (a) sold or let for hire,

    (b) offered or exposed for sale or hire, or

    (c) communicated otherwise than as permitted by sub-paragraph (2).

(7) Expressions used in this paragraph (other than 'dealt with') have the same meaning as in section 35 and any provision made under section 174(2) with respect to the application of that section also applies for the purposes of this paragraph.

Copying and use of extracts of recordings by educational establishments

6ZA.—(1) The copying of extracts of a recording of a performance by or on behalf of an educational establishment does not infringe any of the rights conferred by this Chapter in the recording provided that the copy is made for the purposes of instruction for a non-commercial purpose.

(2) The rights conferred by this Chapter are not infringed where an extract of a recording of a performance, made under sub-paragraph (1), is communicated by or on behalf of the educational establishment to its pupils or staff for the purposes of instruction for a non-commercial purpose.

(3) Sub-paragraph (2) only applies to a communication received outside the premises of the establishment if that communication is made by means of a secure electronic network accessible only by the establishment's pupils and staff.

(4) Not more than 5% of a recording may be copied under this paragraph by or on behalf of an educational establishment in any period of 12 months.

(5) Acts which would otherwise be permitted by this paragraph are not permitted if, or to the extent that, licences are available authorising the acts in question and the educational establishment responsible for those acts knew or ought to have been aware of that fact.

(6) The terms of a licence granted to an educational establishment authorising acts permitted by this paragraph are of no effect so far as they purport to restrict the proportion of a recording which may be copied (whether on payment or free of charge) to less than that which would be permitted by this paragraph.

(7) If a recording made under this paragraph is subsequently dealt with—

(a) it is to be treated as an illicit recording for the purposes of that dealing, and

(b) if that dealing infringes any right conferred by this Chapter, it is to be treated as an illicit recording for all subsequent purposes.

(8) In this paragraph 'dealt with' means—

(a) sold or let for hire,

(b) offered or exposed for sale or hire, or

(c) communicated otherwise than as permitted by sub-paragraph (2).

(9) Expressions used in this paragraph (other than 'dealt with') have the same meaning as in section 36 and any provision made under section 174(2) with respect to the application of that section also applies for the purposes of this paragraph.

Lending of copies by educational establishments

6A.—(1) The rights conferred by this Chapter are not infringed by the lending of copies of a recording of a performance by an educational establishment.

(2) Expressions used in this paragraph have the same meaning as in section 36A; and any provision with respect to the application of that section made under section 174(2) (instruction given elsewhere than an educational establishment) applies also for the purposes of this paragraph.

Lending of copies by libraries or archives

6B.—(A1) The rights conferred by this Chapter are not infringed by the following acts by a public library in relation to a book within the public lending right scheme—

(a) lending the book;

(b) in relation to an audio-book or e-book, copying or issuing a copy of the book as an act incidental to lending it.

(A2) Expressions used in sub-paragraph (A1) have the same meaning as in section 40A(1).

(1) The rights conferred by this Chapter are not infringed by the lending of copies of a recording of a performance by a library or archive (other than a public library) which is not conducted for profit.

Libraries and educational establishments etc: making recordings of performances available through dedicated terminals

6C.—(1) The rights conferred by this Chapter in a recording of a performance are not infringed by an institution specified in sub-paragraph (2) communicating the recording to the public or making it available to the public by means of a dedicated terminal on its premises, if the conditions in sub-paragraph (3) are met.

(2) The institutions are—

(a) a library,

(b) an archive,

(c) a museum, and

(d) an educational establishment.

(3) The conditions are that the recording or a copy of the recording—

(a) has been lawfully acquired by the institution,

(b) is communicated or made available to individual members of the public for the purposes of research or private study, and

(c) is communicated or made available in compliance with any purchase or licensing terms to which the recording is subject.

Copying by librarians: supply of single copies to other libraries

6D.—(1) A librarian may, if the conditions in sub-paragraph (2) are met, make a single copy of the whole or part of a published recording of a performance and supply it to another library, without infringing any rights conferred by this Chapter in the recording.

(2) The conditions are—

(a) the copy is supplied in response to a request from a library which is not conducted for profit, and

(b) at the time of making the copy the librarian does not know, or could not reasonably find out, the name and address of a person entitled to authorise the making of a copy of the recording.

(3) Where a library makes a charge for supplying a copy under this paragraph, the sum charged must be calculated by reference to the costs attributable to the production of the copy.

(4) To the extent that a term of a contract purports to prevent or restrict the doing of any act which, by virtue of this paragraph, would not infringe any right conferred by this Chapter, that term is unenforceable.

Copying by librarians etc: replacement copies of recordings

6E.—(1) A librarian, archivist or curator of a library, archive or museum may, without infringing any rights conferred by this Chapter, make a copy of a recording of a performance in that institution's permanent collection—

(a) in order to preserve or replace that recording in that collection, or

(b) where a recording in the permanent collection of another library, archive or museum has been lost, destroyed or damaged, in order to replace the recording in the collection of that other library, archive or museum,

provided that the conditions in sub-paragraphs (2) and (3) are met.

(2) The first condition is that the recording is—

(a) included in the part of the collection kept wholly or mainly for the purposes of reference on the institution's premises,

(b) included in a part of the collection not accessible to the public, or

(c) available on loan only to other libraries, archives or museums.

(3) The second condition is that it is not reasonably practicable to purchase a copy of the recording to achieve either of the purposes mentioned in sub-paragraph (1).

(4) The reference in sub-paragraph (1)(b) to a library, archive or museum is to a library, archive or museum which is not conducted for profit.

(5) Where an institution makes a charge for supplying a copy to another library, archive or museum under sub-paragraph (1)(b), the sum charged must be calculated by reference to the costs attributable to the production of the copy.

(6) To the extent that a term of a contract purports to prevent or restrict the doing of any act which, by virtue of this paragraph, would not infringe any right conferred by this Chapter, that term is unenforceable.

Copying by librarians: single copies of published recordings

6F.—(1) A librarian of a library which is not conducted for profit may, if the conditions in sub-paragraph (2) are met, make and supply a single copy of a reasonable proportion of a published recording without infringing any of the rights in the recording conferred by this Chapter.

(2) The conditions are—

(a) the copy is supplied in response to a request from a person who has provided the librarian with a declaration in writing which includes the information set out in sub-paragraph (3), and

(b) the librarian is not aware that the declaration is false in a material particular.

(3) The information which must be included in the declaration is—

(a) the name of the person who requires the copy and the material which that person requires,

(b) a statement that the person has not previously been supplied with a copy of that material by any library,

(c) a statement that the person requires the copy for the purposes of research for a non-commercial purpose or private study, will use it only for those purposes and will not supply the copy to any other person, and

(d) a statement that to the best of the person's knowledge, no other person with whom the person works or studies has made, or intends to make, at or about the same time as the person's request, a request for substantially the same material for substantially the same purpose.

(4) Where a library makes a charge for supplying a copy under this paragraph, the sum charged must be calculated by reference to the costs attributable to the production of the copy.

(5) Where a person ('P') makes a declaration under this paragraph that is false in a material particular and is supplied with a copy of a recording which would have been an illicit recording if made by P—

(a) P is liable for infringement of the rights conferred by this Chapter as if P had made the copy, and

(b) the copy supplied to P is to be treated as an illicit recording for all purposes.

(6) To the extent that a term of a contract purports to prevent or restrict the doing of any act which, by virtue of this paragraph, would not infringe any right conferred by this Chapter, that term is unenforceable.

Copying by librarians or archivists: single copies of unpublished recordings

6G.—(1) A librarian or archivist may make and supply a single copy of the whole or part of a recording without infringing any of the rights conferred by this Chapter in the recording, provided that—

(a) the copy is supplied in response to a request from a person who has provided the librarian or archivist with a declaration in writing which includes the information set out in sub-paragraph (2), and

(b) the librarian or archivist is not aware that the declaration is false in a material particular.

(2) The information which must be included in the declaration is—

(a) the name of the person who requires the copy and the material which that person requires,

(b) a statement that the person has not previously been supplied with a copy of that material by any library or archive, and

(c) a statement that the person requires the copy for the purposes of research for a non-commercial purpose or private study, will use it only for those purposes and will not supply the copy to any other person.

(3) But the rights conferred by this Chapter are infringed if—

    (a) the recording had been published or communicated to the public before the date it was deposited in the library or archive, or

    (b) the rights owner has prohibited the copying of the recording,

and at the time of making the copy the librarian or archivist is, or ought to be, aware of that fact.

(4) Where a library or archive makes a charge for supplying a copy under this paragraph, the sum charged must be calculated by reference to the costs attributable to the production of the copy.

(5) Where a person ('P') makes a declaration under this paragraph that is false in a material particular and is supplied with a copy of a recording which would have been an illicit recording if made by P—

    (a) P is liable for infringement of the rights conferred by this Chapter as if P had made the copy, and

    (b) the copy supplied to P is to be treated as an illicit recording for all purposes.

Paragraphs 6B to 6G: interpretation

6H. Expressions used in paragraphs 6B to 6G have the same meaning as in sections 40A to 43.

Certain permitted uses of orphan works

6I.—(1) The rights conferred by this Chapter are not infringed by a relevant body in the circumstances set out in paragraph 1(2) of Schedule ZA1 (subject to paragraph 6 of that Schedule).

(2) 'Relevant body' has the meaning given by that Schedule.

Copy of work required to be made as condition of export

7.—(1) If an article of cultural or historical importance or interest cannot lawfully be exported from the United Kingdom unless a copy of it is made and deposited in an appropriate library or archive, it is not an infringement of any right conferred by this Chapter to make that copy.

(2) Expressions used in this paragraph have the same meaning as in section 44.

Parliamentary and judicial proceedings

8.—(1) The rights conferred by this Chapter are not infringed by anything done for the purposes of parliamentary or judicial proceedings or for the purpose of reporting such proceedings.

(2) Expressions used in this paragraph have the same meaning as in section 45.

Royal Commissions and statutory inquiries

9.—(1) The rights conferred by this Chapter are not infringed by anything done for the purposes of the proceedings of a Royal Commission or statutory inquiry or for the purpose of reporting any such proceedings held in public.

(2) Expressions used in this paragraph have the same meaning as in section 46.

Public records

10.—(1) Material which is comprised in public records within the meaning of the Public Records Act 1958, the Public Records (Scotland) Act 1937 or the Public Records Act (Northern Ireland) 1923, or in Welsh public records (as defined in the Government of Wales Act 2006), which are open to public inspection in pursuance of that Act, may be copied, and a copy may be supplied to any person, by or with the authority of any officer appointed under that Act, without infringing any right conferred by this Chapter.

(2) Expressions used in this paragraph have the same meaning as in section 49.

Acts done under statutory authority

11.—(1) Where the doing of a particular act is specifically authorised by an Act of Parliament, whenever passed, then, unless the Act provides otherwise, the doing of that act does not infringe the rights conferred by this Chapter.

(2) Sub-paragraph (1) applies in relation to an enactment contained in Northern Ireland legislation as it applies to an Act of Parliament.

(3) Nothing in this paragraph shall be construed as excluding any defence of statutory authority otherwise available under or by virtue of any enactment.

(4) Expressions used in this paragraph have the same meaning as in section 50.

Transfer of copies of works in electronic form

12.—(1) This paragraph applies where a recording of a performance in electronic form has been purchased on terms which, expressly or impliedly or by virtue of any rule of law, allow the purchaser to make further recordings in connection with his use of the recording.

(2) If there are no express terms—

(a) prohibiting the transfer of the recording by the purchaser, imposing obligations which continue after a transfer, prohibiting the assignment of any consent or terminating any consent on a transfer, or

(b) providing for the terms on which a transferee may do the things which the purchaser was permitted to do,

anything which the purchaser was allowed to do may also be done by a transferee without infringement of the rights conferred by this Chapter, but any recording made by the purchaser which is not also transferred shall be treated as an illicit recording for all purposes after the transfer.

(3) The same applies where the original purchased recording is no longer usable and what is transferred is a further copy used in its place.

(4) The above provisions also apply on a subsequent transfer, with the substitution for references in sub-paragraph (2) to the purchaser of references to the subsequent transferor.

(5) This paragraph does not apply in relation to a recording purchased before the commencement of this Chapter.

(6) Expressions used in this paragraph have the same meaning as in section 56.

Use of recordings of spoken works in certain cases

13.—(1) Where a recording of the reading or recitation of a literary work is made for the purpose—

(a) of reporting current events, or

(b) of communicating to the public the whole or part of the reading or recitation,

it is not an infringement of the rights conferred by this Chapter to use the recording (or to copy the recording and use the copy) for that purpose, provided the following conditions are met.

(2) The conditions are that—

(a) the recording is a direct recording of the reading or recitation and is not taken from a previous recording or from a broadcast;

(b) the making of the recording was not prohibited by or on behalf of the person giving the reading or recitation;

(c) the use made of the recording is not of a kind prohibited by or on behalf of that person before the recording was made; and

(d) the use is by or with the authority of a person who is lawfully in possession of the recording.

(3) Expressions used in this paragraph have the same meaning as in section 58.

Recordings of folksongs

14.—(1) A recording of a performance of a song may be made for the purpose of including it in an archive maintained by a body not established or conducted for profit without infringing any of the rights conferred by this Chapter, provided the conditions in sub-paragraph (2) below are met.

(2) The conditions are that—

(a) the words are unpublished and of unknown authorship at the time the recording is made,

(b) the making of the recording does not infringe any copyright, and

(c) its making is not prohibited by any performer.

(3) A single copy of a recording made in reliance on sub-paragraph (1) and included in an archive referred to in that sub-paragraph may be made and supplied by the archivist without infringing any right conferred by this Chapter, provided that—

   (a) the copy is supplied in response to a request from a person who has provided the archivist with a declaration in writing which includes the information set out in sub-paragraph (4), and

   (b) the archivist is not aware that the declaration is false in a material particular.

(4) The information which must be included in the declaration is—

   (a) the name of the person who requires the copy and the recording which is the subject of the request,

   (b) a statement that the person has not previously been supplied with a copy of that recording by any archivist, and

   (c) a statement that the person requires the copy for the purposes of research for a non-commercial purpose or private study, will use it only for those purposes and will not supply the copy to any other person.

(5) Where an archive makes a charge for supplying a copy under this paragraph, the sum charged must be calculated by reference to the costs attributable to the production of the copy.

(6) Where a person ('P') makes a declaration under this paragraph that is false in a material particular and is supplied with a copy of a recording which would have been an illicit recording if made by P—

   (a) P is liable for infringement of the rights conferred by this Chapter as if P had made the copy, and

   (b) the copy supplied to P is to be treated as an illicit recording for all purposes.

(7) In this paragraph references to an archivist include a person acting on behalf of an archivist.

(8) Expressions used in this paragraph have the same meaning as in section 61.

Lending of certain recordings

14A.—(1) The Secretary of State may by order provide that in such cases as may be specified in the order the lending to the public of copies of films or sound recordings shall be treated as licensed by the performer subject only to the payment of such reasonable royalty or other payment as may be agreed or determined in default of agreement by the Copyright Tribunal.

(2) No such order shall apply if, or to the extent that, there is a licensing scheme certified by the purposes of this paragraph under paragraph 16 of Schedule 2A providing for the grant of licences.

(3) An order may make different provision for different cases and may specify cases by reference to any factor relating to the work, the copies lent, the lender or the circumstances of the lending.

(4) An order shall be made by statutory instrument; and no order shall be made unless a draft of it has been laid before and approved by a resolution of each House of Parliament.

(5) Nothing in this section affects any liability under section 184(1)(b) (secondary infringement: possessing or dealing with illicit recording) in respect of the lending of illicit recordings.

(6) Expressions used in this paragraph have the same meaning as in section 66.

Playing of sound recordings for purposes of club, society, &c.

Incidental recording for purposes of broadcast

16.—(1) A person who proposes to broadcast a recording of a performance in circumstances not infringing the rights conferred by this Chapter shall be treated as having consent for the purposes of this Chapter for the making of a further recording for the purposes of the broadcast.

(2) That consent is subject to the condition that the further recording—

   (a) shall not be used for any other purpose, and

   (b) shall be destroyed within 28 days of being first used for broadcasting the performance.

(3) A recording made in accordance with this paragraph shall be treated as an illicit recording—

   (a) for the purposes of any use in breach of the condition mentioned in sub-paragraph (2) (a), and

(b) for all purposes after that condition or the condition mentioned in sub-paragraph (2)(b) is broken.

(4) Expressions used in this paragraph have the same meaning as in section 68.

...

Recording for the purposes of time-shifting

17A.—(1) The making in domestic premises for private and domestic use of a recording of a broadcast solely for the purpose of enabling it to be viewed or listened to at a more convenient time does not infringe any right conferred by this Chapter in relation to a performance or recording included in the broadcast.

(2) Where a recording which would otherwise be an illicit recording is made in accordance with this paragraph but is subsequently dealt with—

(a) it shall be treated as an illicit recording for the purposes of that dealing; and

(b) if that dealing infringes any right conferred by this Chapter, it shall be treated as an illicit recording for all subsequent purposes.

(3) In sub-paragraph (2), 'dealt with' means sold or let for hire, offered or exposed for sale or hire or communicated to the public.

(4) Expressions used in this paragraph have the same meaning as in section 70.

Photographs of broadcasts

17B.—(1) The making in domestic premises for private and domestic use of a photograph of the whole or any part of an image forming part of a broadcast, or a copy of such a photograph, does not infringe any right conferred by this Chapter in relation to a performance or recording included in the broadcast.

(2) Where a recording which would otherwise be an illicit recording is made in accordance with this paragraph but is subsequently dealt with—

(a) it shall be treated as an illicit recording for the purposes of that dealing; and

(b) if that dealing infringes any right conferred by this Chapter, it shall be treated as an illicit recording for all subsequent purposes.

(3) In sub-paragraph (2), 'dealt with' means sold or let for hire, offered or exposed for sale or hire or communicated to the public.

(4) Expressions used in this paragraph have the same meaning as in section 71.

Free public showing or playing of broadcast

18.—(1) The showing or playing in public of a broadcast to an audience who have not paid for admission to the place where the broadcast is to be seen or heard does not infringe any right conferred by this Chapter in relation to a performance or recording included in—

(a) the broadcast, or

(b) any sound recording (except so far as it is an excepted sound recording) or film which is played or shown in public by reception of the broadcast.

(1A) The showing or playing in public of a broadcast to an audience who have not paid for admission to the place where the broadcast is to be seen or heard does not infringe any right conferred by this Chapter in relation to a performance or recording included in any excepted sound recording which is played in public by reception of the broadcast, if the playing or showing of that broadcast in public—

(b) is necessary for the purposes of—

(i) repairing equipment for the reception of broadcasts;

(ii) demonstrating that a repair to such equipment has been carried out; or

(iii) demonstrating such equipment which is being sold or let for hire or offered or exposed for sale or hire.

(2) The audience shall be treated as having paid for admission to a place—

(a) if they have paid for admission to a place of which that place forms part; or

(b) if goods or services are supplied at that place (or a place of which it forms part)—

(i) at prices which are substantially attributable to the facilities afforded for seeing or hearing the broadcast, or

(ii) at prices exceeding those usually charged there and which are partly attributable to those facilities.

(3) The following shall not be regarded as having paid for admission to a place—

(a) persons admitted as residents or inmates of the place;

(b) persons admitted as members of a club or society where the payment is only for membership of the club or society and the provision of facilities for seeing or hearing broadcasts is only incidental to the main purposes of the club or society.

(4) Where the making of the broadcast was an infringement of the rights conferred by this Chapter in relation to a performance or recording, the fact that it was heard or seen in public by the reception of the broadcast shall be taken into account in assessing the damages for that infringement.

(5) Expressions used in this paragraph have the same meaning as in section 72.

Reception and re-transmission of wireless broadcast by cable

21.—(1) A recording of a broadcast or a copy of such a recording may be made for the purpose of being placed in an archive maintained by a body which is not established or conducted for profit without infringing any right conferred by this Chapter in relation to a performance or recording included in the broadcast.

(2) To the extent that a term of a contract purports to prevent or restrict the doing of any act which, by virtue of this paragraph, would not infringe any right conferred by this Chapter, that term is unenforceable.

(3) Expressions used in this paragraph have the same meaning as in section 75.

. . .

Section 296ZE   # SCHEDULE 5A

PERMITTED ACTS TO WHICH SECTION 296ZE APPLIES

PART I   COPYRIGHT EXCEPTIONS

section 29 (research and private study)

section 29A (copies for text and data analysis for non-commercial research)

section 31A (disabled persons: copies of works for personal use)

section 31B (making and supply of accessible copies for authorised bodies)

section 31BA (making and supply of intermediate copies for authorised bodies)

section 32 (illustration for instruction)

section 35 (recording by educational establishments of broadcasts)

section 36 (copying and use of extracts of works by educational establishments)

section 41 (copying by librarians: supply of single copies to other libraries)

section 42 (copying by librarians, etc: replacement copies of works)

section 42A (copying by librarians: single copies of published works)

section 43 (copying by librarians or archivists: single copies of unpublished works)

section 44 (copy of work required to be made as condition of export)

section 45 (Parliamentary and judicial proceedings)

section 46 (Royal Commissions and statutory inquiries)

section 47 (material open to public inspection or on official register)

section 48 (material communicated to the Crown in the course of public business)

section 49 (public records)

section 50 (acts done under statutory authority)

section 61 (recordings of folksongs)

section 68 (incidental recording for purposes of broadcast)

section 69 (recording for purposes of supervision and control of broadcasts)

section 70 (recording for purposes of time-shifting)

section 71 (photographs of broadcasts)

section 75 (recording of broadcast for archival purposes)

PART 2   RIGHTS IN PERFORMANCES EXCEPTIONS

paragraph 1C of Schedule 2 (research and private study)

paragraph 1D of Schedule 2 (copies for text and data analysis for non-commercial research)

paragraph 3A of Schedule 2 (disabled persons: copies of recordings for personal use)

paragraph 3B of Schedule 2 (making and supply of accessible copies by authorised bodies)

paragraph 3C of Schedule 2 (making and supply of intermediate copies by authorised bodies)

paragraph 4 of Schedule 2 (illustration for instruction)

paragraph 6 of Schedule 2 (recording by educational establishments of broadcasts)

paragraph 6ZA of schedule 2 (copying and use of extracts of recordings by educational establishments)

paragraph 6D of Schedule 2 (copying by librarians: supply of single copies to other libraries)

paragraph 6E of Schedule 2 (copying by librarians etc: replacement copies of recordings)

paragraph 6F of Schedule 2 (copying by librarians: single copies of published recordings)

paragraph 6G of Schedule 2 (copying by librarian or archivists: single copies of unpublished recordings)

paragraph 7 of Schedule 2 (copy of work required to be made as condition of export)

paragraph 8 of Schedule 2 (Parliamentary and judicial proceedings)

paragraph 9 of Schedule 2 (Royal Commissions and statutory inquiries)

paragraph 10 of Schedule 2 (public records)

paragraph 11 of Schedule 2 (acts done under statutory authority)

paragraph 14 of Schedule 2 (recordings of folksongs)

paragraph 16 of Schedule 2 (incidental recording for purposes of broadcast)

paragraph 17 of Schedule 2 (recordings for purposes of supervision and control of broadcasts)

paragraph 17A of Schedule 2 (recording for the purpose of time-shifting)

paragraph 17B of Schedule 2 (photographs of broadcasts)

paragraph 21 of Schedule 2 (recording of broadcast for archival purposes)

PART 3   DATABASE RIGHT EXCEPTIONS

regulation 20 of and Schedule 1 to the Copyright and Rights in Databases Regulations 1997 (SI 1997/3032)

...

Copyright and Related Rights Regulations 1996*

(SI 1996/2967)

PART I   INTRODUCTORY PROVISIONS

1   Citation, commencement and extent

(1) These Regulations may be cited as the Copyright and Related Rights Regulations 1996.

(2) These Regulations come into force on 1st December 1996.

(3) These Regulations extend to the whole of the United Kingdom.

2   Interpretation

In these Regulations—

'EEA Agreement' means the Agreement on the European Economic Area signed at Oporto on 2nd May 1992, as adjusted by the Protocol signed at Brussels on 17th March 1993; and

'EEA state' means a member State, Iceland, Liechtenstein or Norway.

'national of the United Kingdom' has the meaning given by section 178 of the Copyright, Designs and Patents Act 1988.

---

* **Editor's Note:** Contains amendments effected by *Intellectual Property (Copyright and Related Rights) (Amendment) (EU Exit) Regulations 2019*. By virtue of the *European Union (Withdrawal Agreement) Act 2020*, these amendments take effect on 'IP completion day', which is defined to be 31 December 2020 at 11:00pm.

3   Implementation of Directives, &c.

These Regulations make provision for the purpose of implementing—

    (a) Council Directive No. 92/100/EEC of 19 November 1992 on rental right and lending right and on certain rights related to copyright in the field of intellectual property;

    (b) Council Directive No. 93/83/EEC of 27 September 1993 on the coordination of certain rules concerning copyright and rights related to copyright applicable to satellite broadcasting and cable retransmission;

    (c) the provisions of Council Directive No. 93/98/EEC of 29 October 1993 harmonising the term of protection of copyright and certain related rights, so far as not implemented by the Duration of Copyright and Rights in Performances Regulations 1995; and

    (d) certain obligations of the United Kingdom created by or arising under the EEA Agreement so far as relevant to the implementation of those Directives.

4   Scheme of the Regulations

The Copyright, Designs, and Patents Act 1988 is amended in accordance with the provisions of Part II of these Regulations, subject to the savings and transitional provisions in Part III of these Regulations.

PART II   AMENDMENTS OF THE COPYRIGHT, DESIGNS AND PATENTS ACT 1988

...

Publication right

16   Publication right

    (1) A person who after the expiry of copyright protection, publishes for the first time a previously unpublished work has, in accordance with the following provisions, a property right ('publication right') equivalent to copyright.

    (2) For this purpose publication includes any making available to the public, in particular—

    (a) the issue of copies to the public;

    (b) making the work available by means of an electronic retrieval system;

    (c) the rental or lending of copies of the work to the public;

    (d) the performance, exhibition or showing of the work in public; or

    (e) communicating the work to the public.

    (3) No account shall be taken for this purpose of any unauthorised act. In relation to a time when there is no copyright in the work, an unauthorised act means an act done without the consent of the owner of the physical medium in which the work is embodied or on which it is recorded.

    (4) A work qualifies for publication right protection only if—

    (a) first publication is in the European Economic Area or in the United Kingdom, and

    (b) the publisher of the work is at the time of first publication a national of an EEA state or a national of the United Kingdom.

Where two or more persons jointly publish the work, it is sufficient for the purposes of paragraph (b) if any of them is a national of an EEA state or a national of the United Kingdom.

    (5) No publication right arises from the publication of a work in which Crown copyright or Parliamentary copyright subsisted.

    (6) Publication right expires at the end of the period of 25 years from the end of the calendar year in which the work was first published.

    (7) In this regulation and regulation 17A a 'work' means a literary, dramatic, musical or artistic work or a film.

    (8) Expressions used in this regulation (other than 'publication') have the same meaning as in Part I.

17 Application of copyright provisions to publication right

(1) The substantive provisions of Part I relating to copyright (but not moral rights in copyright works), that is, the relevant provisions of—

Chapter II (rights of copyright owner),

Chapter III (acts permitted in relation to copyright works),

Chapter V (dealings with rights in copyright works),

Chapter VI (remedies for infringement), and

Chapter VII (copyright licensing),

apply in relation to publication right as in relation to copyright, subject to the following exceptions and modifications.

(2) The following provisions do not apply—

(a) in Chapter III (acts permitted in relation to copyright works), sections 57, 64, 66A and 67;

(b) in Chapter VI (remedies for infringement), sections 104 to 106;

(c) in Chapter VII (copyright licensing), section 116(4).

(3) The following provisions have effect with the modifications indicated—

(a) in section 107(4) and (5) (offences of making or dealing in infringing articles, &c.), the maximum punishment on summary conviction is imprisonment for a term not exceeding three months or a fine not exceeding level 5 on the standard scale, or both;

(b) in sections 116(2), 117 and 124 for 'works of more than one author' substitute 'works of more than one publisher'.

(4) The other relevant provisions of Part I, that is—

in Chapter I, provisions defining expressions used generally in Part I, Chapter VIII (the Copyright Tribunal),

in Chapter IX—

section 161 (territorial waters and the continental shelf), and

section 162 (British ships, aircraft and hovercraft), and

in Chapter X—

section 171(1) and (3) (savings for other rules of law, &c.), and

sections 172 to 179 (general interpretation provisions),

apply, with any necessary adaptations, for the purposes of supplementing the substantive provisions of that Part as applied by this regulation.

(5) Except where the context otherwise requires, any other enactment relating to copyright (whether passed or made before or after these regulations) applies in relation to publication right as in relation to copyright.

In this paragraph 'enactment' includes an enactment contained in subordinate legislation within the meaning of the Interpretation Act 1978.

17A Presumptions relevant to works subject to publication right

In proceedings brought by virtue of Chapter 6 of Part 1 of the Copyright, Designs and Patents Act 1988, as applied to publication right by regulation 17, with respect to a work, where copies of the work as issued to the public bear a statement that a named person was the owner of publication right in the work at the date of issue of the copies, the statement shall be admissible as evidence of the fact stated and shall be presumed to be correct until the contrary is proved.

17B Application of presumptions in relation to an order
for delivery up in criminal proceedings

Regulation 17A does not apply to proceedings for an offence under section 107 of the Copyright, Designs and Patents Act 1988 as applied and modified by regulation 17 in relation to publication right; but without prejudice to its application in proceedings for an order under section 108 of the Copyright, Designs and Patents Act 1988 as that section applies to publication right by virtue of regulation 17.

Copyright and Rights in Databases Regulations 1997

(SI 1997/3032)

PART I   INTRODUCTORY PROVISIONS

1   Citation, commencement and extent

(1) These Regulations may be cited as the Copyright and Rights in Databases Regulations 1997.

(2) These Regulations come into force on 1 January 1998.

(3) These Regulations extend to the whole of the United Kingdom.

2   Implementation of Directive

(1) These Regulations make provision for the purposes of implementing—

    (a) Council Directive No. 96/9/EC of 11 March 1996 on the legal protection of databases,

    (b) certain obligations of the United Kingdom created by or arising under the EEA Agreement so far as relating to the implementation of that Directive, and

    (c) an Agreement in the form of an exchange of letters between the United Kingdom of Great Britain and Northern Ireland on behalf of the Isle of Man and the European Union extending to the Isle of Man the legal protection of databases as provided for in Chapter III of that Directive.

(2) In this Regulation 'the EEA Agreement' means the Agreement on the European Economic Area signed at Oporto on 2 May 1992, as adjusted by the Protocol signed at Brussels on 17 March 1993.

3   Interpretation

In these Regulations 'the 1998 Act' means the Copyright, Designs and Patents Act 1988.

4   Scheme of the Regulations

(1) The 1988 Act is amended in accordance with the provisions of Part II of these Regulations, subject to the savings and transitional provisions in Part IV of these Regulations.

(2) Part III of these Regulations has effect subject to those savings and transitional provisions.

. . .

PART III   DATABASE RIGHT

12   Interpretation

(1) In this Part—

'database' has the meaning given by section 3A(1) of the 1988 Act (as inserted by Regulation 6);

'extraction', in relation to any contents of a database, means the permanent or temporary transfer of those contents to another medium by any means or in any form;

'insubstantial', in relation to part of the contents of a database, shall be construed subject to Regulation 16(2);

'investment' includes any investment, whether of financial, human or technical resources;

'jointly', in relation to the making of a database, shall be construed in accordance with Regulation 14(6);

'lawful user', in relation to a database, means any person who (whether under a licence to do any of the acts restricted by any database right in the database or otherwise) has a right to use the database;

'maker', in relation to a database, shall be construed in accordance with Regulation 14;

'Marrakesh beneficiary' has the meaning given by section 296ZE(1) of the 1988 Act;

'national of the United Kingdom' has the meaning given by section 178 of the 1988 Act;

're-utilisation', in relation to any contents of a database, means making those contents available to the public by any means;

'substantial', in relation to any investment, extraction or re-utilisation, means substantial in terms of quantity or quality or a combination of both.

(2) The making of a copy of a database available for use, on terms that it will or may be returned, otherwise than for direct or indirect economic or commercial advantage, through an establishment which is accessible to the public shall not be taken for the purposes of this Part to constitute extraction or re-utilisation of the contents of the database.

(3) Where the making of a copy of a database available through an establishment which is accessible to the public gives rise to a payment the amount of which does not go beyond what is necessary to cover the costs of the establishment, there is no direct or indirect economic or commercial advantage for the purposes of paragraph (2).

(4) Paragraph (2) does not apply to the making of a copy of a database available for on-the-spot reference use.

(5) Where a copy of a database has been sold within the EEA, the United Kingdom or the Isle of Man by, or with the consent of, the owner of the database right in the database, the further sale within the EEA, the United Kingdom or the Isle of Man of that copy shall not be taken for the purposes of this Part to constitute extraction or reutilisation of the contents of the database.

13   Database right

(1) A property right ('database right') subsists, in accordance with this Part, in a database if there has been a substantial investment in obtaining, verifying or presenting the contents of the database.

(2) For the purposes of paragraph (1) it is immaterial whether or not the database or any of its contents is a copyright work, within the meaning of Part I of the 1988 Act.

(3) This Regulation has effect subject to Regulation 18.

14   The maker of a database

(1) Subject to paragraphs (2) to (4), the person who takes the initiative in obtaining, verifying or presenting the contents of a database and assumes the risk of investing in that obtaining, verification or presentation shall be regarded as the maker of, and as having made, the database.

(2) Where a database is made by an employee in the course of his employment, his employer shall be regarded as the maker of the database, subject to any agreement to the contrary.

(3) Subject to paragraph (4), where a database is made by Her Majesty or by an officer or servant of the Crown in the course of his duties, Her Majesty shall be regarded as the maker of the database.

(4) Where a database is made by or under the direction or control of the House of Commons or the House of Lords—

  (a) the House by whom, or under whose direction or control, the database is made shall be regarded as the maker of the database, and

  (b) if the database is made by or under the direction or control of both Houses, the two Houses shall be regarded as the joint makers of the database.

(4A) Where a database is made by or under the direction or control of the Scottish Parliament, the Scottish Parliamentary Corporate Body shall be regarded as the maker of the database.

(5) For the purposes of this Part a database is made jointly if two or more persons acting together in collaboration take the initiative in obtaining, verifying or presenting the contents of the database and assume the risk of investing in that obtaining, verification or presentation.

(6) References in this Part to the maker of a database shall, except as otherwise provided, be construed, in relation to a database which is made jointly, as references to all the makers of the database.

15   First ownership of database right

The maker of a database is the first owner of database right in it.

16   Acts infringing database right

(1) Subject to the provisions of this Part, a person infringes database right in a database if, without the consent of the owner of the right, he extracts or re-utilises all or a substantial part of the contents of the database.

(2) For the purposes of this Part, the repeated and systematic extraction or re-utilisation of in-substantial parts of the contents of a database may amount to the extraction or re-utilisation of a substantial part of those contents.

17 Term of protection

(1) Database right in a database expires at the end of the period of fifteen years from the end of the calendar year in which the making of the database was completed.

(2) Where a database is made available to the public before the end of the period referred to in paragraph (1), database right in the database shall expire fifteen years from the end of the calendar year in which the database was first made available to the public.

(3) Any substantial change to the contents of a database, including a substantial change resulting from the accumulation of successive additions, deletions or alterations, which would result in the database being considered to be a substantial new investment shall qualify the database resulting from that investment for its own term of protection.

(4) This Regulation has effect subject to Regulation 30.

18 Qualification for database right

(1) Database right does not subsist in a database unless, at the material time, its maker, or if it was made jointly, one or more of its makers, was—

  (a) an individual who was a national of the United Kingdom or habitually resident within the United Kingdom,

  (b) a body which was incorporated under the law of any part of the United Kingdom and which, at that time, satisfied one of the conditions in paragraph (2),

  (c) a partnership or other unincorporated body which was formed under the law of any part of the United Kingdom and which, at that time, satisfied the condition in paragraph (2)(a).

  (d) an individual who was habitually resident within the Isle of Man,

  (e) a body which was incorporated under the law of the Isle of Man and which, at that time, satisfied one of the conditions in paragraph (2A), or

  (f) a partnership or other unincorporated body which was formed under the law of the Isle of Man and which, at that time, satisfied the condition in paragraph (2A)(a).

(2) The conditions mentioned in paragraphs (1)(b) and (c) are—

  (a) that the body has its central administration or principal place of business within the United Kingdom, or

  (b) that the body has its registered office within the United Kingdom and the body's operations are linked on an ongoing basis with the economy of the United Kingdom.

(2A) The conditions mentioned in paragraphs (1)(e) and (f) are—

  (a) that the body has its central administration or principal place of business within the Isle of Man, or

  (b) that the body has its registered office within the Isle of Man and the body's operations are linked on an ongoing basis with the economy of the Isle of Man.

(3) Paragraph (1) does not apply in any case falling within Regulation 14(4).

(4) In this Regulation—

  (b) 'the material time' means the time when the database was made, or if the making extended over period, a substantial part of that period.

19 Avoidance of certain terms affecting lawful users

(1) A lawful user of a database which has been made available to the public in any manner shall be entitled to extract or re-utilise insubstantial parts of the contents of the database for any purpose.

(2) Where under an agreement a person has a right to use a database, or part of a database, which has been made available to the public in any manner, any term or condition in the agreement shall be void in so far as it purports to prevent that person from extracting or re-utilising insubstantial parts of the contents of the database, or of that part of the database, for any purpose.

20 Exceptions to database right

(1) Database right in a database which has been made available to the public in any manner is not infringed by fair dealing with a substantial part of its contents if—

(a) that part is extracted from the database by a person who is apart from this paragraph a lawful user of the database,

(b) it is extracted for the purpose of illustration for teaching or research and not for any commercial purpose, and

(c) the source is indicated.

(2) The provisions of Schedule 1 specify other acts which may be done in relation to a database notwithstanding the existence of database right.

20A Exceptions to database right: deposit libraries

(1) Database right in a database is not infringed by the copying of a work from the Internet by a deposit library or person acting on its behalf if—

(a) the work is of a description prescribed by regulations under section 10(5) of the 2003 Act,

(b) its publication on the Internet, or a person publishing it there, is connected with the United Kingdom in a manner so prescribed, and

(c) the copying is done in accordance with any conditions so prescribed.

(2) Database right in a database is not infringed by the doing of anything in relation to relevant material permitted to be done under regulations under section 7 of the 2003 Act.

(3) Regulations under section 44A(3) of the 1988 Act exclude the application of paragraph (2) in relation to prescribed activities in relation to relevant material as (and to the extent that) they exclude the application of section 44A(2) of that Act in relation to those activities.

(4) In this Regulation—

(a) 'the 2003 Act' means the Legal Deposit Libraries Act 2003;

(b) 'deposit library' and 'relevant material' have the same meaning as in section 7 of the 2003 Act.

20B Exceptions to database right: Marrakesh beneficiaries

Database right in a database is not infringed by the making of an accessible copy of a work under sections 31A, 31B or 31BA of, or paragraphs 3A, 3B or 3C of Schedule 2 to, the 1988 Act for the benefit of a Marrakesh beneficiary.

21 Acts permitted on assumption as to expiry of database right

(1) Database right in a database is not infringed by the extraction or re-utilisation of a substantial part of the contents of the database at a time when, or in pursuance of arrangements made at a time when—

(a) it is not possible by reasonable inquiry to ascertain the identity of the maker, and

(b) it is reasonable to assume that database right has expired.

(2) In the case of a database alleged to have been made jointly, paragraph (1) applies in relation to each person alleged to be one of the makers.

22 Presumptions relevant to database right

(1) The following presumptions apply in proceedings brought by virtue of this Part of these Regulations with respect to a database.

(2) Where a name purporting to be that of the maker appeared on copies of the database as published, or on the database when it was made, the person whose name appeared shall be presumed, until the contrary is proved—

(a) to be the maker of the database, and

(b) to have made it in circumstances not falling within Regulation 14(2) to (4).

(3) Where copies of the database as published bear a label or a mark stating—

(a) that a named person was the maker of the database, or

(b) that the database was first published in a specified year,

the label or mark shall be admissible as evidence of the facts stated and shall be presumed to be correct until the contrary is proved.

(4) In the case of a database alleged to have been made jointly, paragraphs (2) and (3), so far as is applicable, apply in relation to each person alleged to be one of the makers.

23 Application of copyright provisions to database right

The following provisions of the 1988 Act apply in relation to database right and databases in which that right subsists as they apply in relation to copyright and copyright works—

sections 90 to 93 (dealing with rights in copyright works)

sections 96 to 102 (rights and remedies of copyright owner and exclusive licensee)

sections 113 and 114 (supplementary provisions relating to delivery up)

section 115 (jurisdiction of county court and sheriff court).

24 Licensing of database right

The provisions of Schedule 2 have effect with respect to the licensing of database right.

25 Database right: jurisdiction of Copyright Tribunal

(1) The Copyright Tribunal has jurisdiction under this Part to hear and determine proceedings under the following provisions of Schedule 2—

(a) paragraph 3, 4 or 5 (reference of licensing scheme);

(b) paragraph 6 or 7 (application with respect to licence under licensing scheme);

(c) paragraph 10, 11 or 12 (reference or application with respect to licence by licensing body).

(2) The provisions of Chapter VIII of Part I of the 1988 Act (general provisions relating to the Copyright Tribunal) apply in relation to the Tribunal when exercising any jurisdiction under this Part.

(3) Provision shall be made by rules under section 150 of the 1988 Act prohibiting the Tribunal from entertaining a reference under paragraph 3, 4 or 5 of Schedule 2 (reference of licensing scheme) by a representative organisation unless the Tribunal is satisfied that the organisation is reasonably representative of the class of persons which it claims to represent.

PART IV SAVINGS AND TRANSITIONAL PROVISIONS

26 Introductory

Expressions used in this Part which are defined for the purposes of Part I of the 1988 Act have the same meaning as in that Part.

27 General rule

Subject to Regulations 28 and 29, these Regulations apply to databases made before or after 1st January 1998.

28 General savings

(1) Nothing in these Regulations affects any agreement made before 1st January 1998.

(2) Nothing in these Regulations affects any agreement made after 31st December 1997 and before 1st November 2003 in so far as the effect would only arise as a result of the amendment of these Regulations by the Copyright and Rights in Databases (Amendment) Regulations 2003.

(3) No act done in respect of any database, in which database right subsists by virtue of the maker of the database (or one or more of its makers) falling within one of the provisions contained in Regulations 14(4) and 18(1)(a), (b) and (c),—

(a) before 1st January 1998, or

(b) after 31st December 1997, in pursuance of an agreement made before 1st January 1998,

shall be regarded as an infringement of database right in the database.

(4) No act done in respect of any database, in which database right subsists by virtue of its maker (or one or more of its makers) falling within one of the provisions contained in Regulation 18(1)(d), (e) and (f),—

(a) before 1st November 2003, or

(b) after 31st October 2003, in pursuance of an agreement made before 1st November 2003,

shall be regarded as an infringement of database right in the database.

29   Saving for copyright in certain existing databases

(1) Where a database—

(a) was created on or before 27 March 1996, and

(b) is a copyright work immediately before 1st January 1998,

copyright shall continue to subsist in the database for the remainder of its copyright term.

(2) In this Regulation 'copyright term' means the period of the duration of copyright under section 12 of the 1988 Act (duration of copyright in literary, dramatic, musical or artistic works).

30   Database right: term applicable to certain existing databases

Where—

(a) the making of any database is completed on or after 1st January 1983, and before 1st January 1998, and

(b) either—

(i) the database is a database in which database right subsists by virtue of the maker of the database (or one or more of its makers) falling within one of the provisions contained in Regulations 14(4) and 18(1)(a), (b) and (c) and database right begins to subsist in the database on 1st January 1998, or

(ii) the database is a database in which database right subsists by virtue of its maker (or one or more of its makers) falling within one of the provisions contained in Regulation 18(1)(d), (e) and (f) and database right begins to subsist in the database on 1st November 2003,

then database right shall subsist in the database for a period of fifteen years beginning with 1st January 1998.

Regulation 20(2)   # SCHEDULE 1

EXCEPTIONS TO DATABASE RIGHT FOR PUBLIC ADMINISTRATION

Parliamentary and judicial proceedings

1. Database right in a database is not infringed by anything done for the purposes of parliamentary or judicial proceedings or for the purposes of reporting such proceedings.

Royal Commissions and statutory inquiries

2.—(1) Database right in a database is not infringed by anything done for—

(a) the purposes of the proceedings of a Royal Commission or statutory inquiry, or

(b) the purpose of reporting any such proceedings held in public.

(2) Database right in a database is not infringed by the issue to the public of copies of the report of a Royal Commission or statutory inquiry containing the contents of the database.

(3) In this paragraph 'Royal Commission' and 'statutory inquiry' have the same meaning as in section 46 of the 1988 Act.

Material open to public inspection or on official register

3.—(1) Where the contents of a database are open to public inspection pursuant to a statutory requirement, or are on a statutory register, database right in the database is not infringed by the extraction of all or a substantial part of the contents containing factual information of any description, by or with the authority of the appropriate person, for a purpose which does not involve re-utilisation of all or a substantial part of the contents.

(2) Where the contents of a database are open to public inspection pursuant to a statutory requirement, database right in the database is not infringed by the extraction or re-utilisation of all or a substantial part of the contents, by or with the authority of the appropriate person, for the purpose of enabling the contents to be inspected at a more convenient time or place or otherwise facilitating the exercise of any right for the purpose of which the requirement is imposed.

(3) Where the contents of a database which is open to public inspection pursuant to a statutory requirement, or which is on a statutory register, contain information about matters of general scientific, technical, commercial or economic interest, database right in the database is not infringed by the extraction or re-utilisation of all or a substantial part of the contents, by or with the authority of the appropriate person, for the purpose of disseminating that information.

(4) In this paragraph—

'appropriate person' means the person required to make the contents of the database open to public inspection or, as the case may be, the person maintaining the register;

'statutory register' means a register maintained in pursuance of a statutory requirement; and

'statutory requirement' means a requirement imposed by provision made by or under an enactment.

(5) In sub-paragraph (4) the reference to an enactment includes any enactment contained in Part 3 of the Regulatory Reform (Scotland) Act 2014.

Material communicated to the Crown in the course of public business

4.—(1) This paragraph applies where the contents of a database have in the course of public business been communicated to the Crown for any purpose, by or with the licence of the owner of the database right and a document or other material thing recording or embodying the contents of the database is owned by or in the custody or control of the Crown.

(2) The Crown may, for the purpose for which the contents of the database were communicated to it, or any related purpose which could reasonably have been anticipated by the owner of the database right in the database, extract or re-utilise all or a substantial part of the contents without infringing database right in the database.

(3) The Crown may not re-utilise the contents of a database by virtue of this paragraph if the contents have previously been published otherwise than by virtue of this paragraph.

(4) In sub-paragraph (1) 'public business' includes any activity carried on by the Crown.

(5) This paragraph has effect subject to any agreement to the contrary between the Crown and the owner of the database right in the database.

Public records

5. The contents of a database which are comprised in public records within the meaning of the Public Records Act 1958, the Public Records (Scotland) Act 1937 or the Public Records Act (Northern Ireland) 1923 which are open to public inspection in pursuance of that Act, maybe re-utilised by or with the authority of any officer appointed under that Act, without infringement of database right in the database.

Acts done under statutory authority

6.—(1) Where the doing of a particular act is specifically authorised by an Act of Parliament, whenever passed, then, unless the Act provides otherwise, the doing of that act does not infringe database right in a database.

(2) Sub-paragraph (1) applies in relation to an enactment contained in Northern Ireland legislation as it applies in relation to an Act of Parliament.

(2A) Sub-paragraph (1) applies in relation to an enactment contained in Part 3 of the Regulatory Reform (Scotland) Act 2014 as it applies in relation to an Act of Parliament.

(3) Nothing in this paragraph shall be construed as excluding any defence of statutory authority otherwise available under or by virtue of any enactment or other statutory provision.

Regulation 24

SCHEDULE 2

LICENSING OF DATABASE RIGHT

Licensing scheme and licensing bodies

1.—(1) In this Schedule a 'licensing scheme' means a scheme setting out—

    (a) the classes of case in which the operator of the scheme, or the person on whose behalf he acts, is willing to grant database right licences, and

    (b) the term on which licences would be granted in those classes of case;

and for this purpose a 'scheme' includes anything in the nature of a scheme, whether described as a scheme or as a tariff or by any other name.

    (2) In this Schedule a 'licensing body' means a society or other organisation which has as its main object, or one of its main objects, the negotiating or granting, whether as owner or prospective owner of a database right or as agent for him, of database right licences, and whose objects include the granting of licences covering the databases of more than one maker.

    (3) In this paragraph 'database right licences' means licences to do, or authorise the doing of, any of the things for which consent is required under Regulation 16.

2. Paragraphs 3 to 8 apply to licensing schemes which are operated by licensing bodies and cover databases of more than one maker so far as they relate to licences for extracting or re-utilising all or a substantial part of the contents of a database; and references in those paragraphs to a licensing scheme shall be construed accordingly.

Reference of proposed licensing scheme to Tribunal

3.—(1) The terms of a licensing scheme proposed to be operated by a licensing body may be referred to the Copyright Tribunal by an organisation claiming to be representative of persons claiming that they require licences in cases of a description to which the scheme would apply, either generally or in relation to any description of case.

...

Effect of order of Tribunal as to licensing scheme

8.—(1) A licensing scheme which has been confirmed or varied by the Copyright Tribunal—

    (a) under paragraph 3 (reference of terms of proposed scheme), or

    (b) under paragraph 4 or 5 (reference of existing scheme to Tribunal),

shall be in force or, as the case maybe, remain in operation, so far as it relates to the description of case in respect of which the order was made, so long as the order remains in force.

    (2) While the order is in force a person who in a case of a class to which the order applies—

    (a) pays to the operator of the scheme any charges payable under the scheme in respect of a licence covering the case in question or, if the amount cannot be ascertained, gives an undertaking to the operator to pay them when ascertained, and

    (b) complies with the other terms applicable to such a licence under the scheme,

shall be in the same position as regards infringement of database right as if he had at all material times been the holder of a licence granted by the owner of the database right in question in accordance with the scheme.

    ...

    (4) Where the Tribunal has made an order under paragraph 6 (order as to entitlement to licence under licensing scheme) and the order remains in force, the person in whose favour the order is made shall if he—

    (a) pays to the operator of the scheme any charges payable in accordance with the order or, if the amount cannot be ascertained, gives an undertaking to pay the charges when ascertained, and

(b) complies with the other terms specified in the order,

be in the same position as regards infringement of database right as if he had at all material times been the holder of a licence granted by the owner of the database right in question on the terms specified in the order.

References and applications with respect to licences by licensing bodies

9. Paragraphs 10 to 13 (references and applications with respect to licensing by licensing bodies) apply to licences relating to database right which cover databases of more than one maker granted by a licensing body otherwise than in pursuance of a licensing scheme, so far as the licences authorise extracting or re-utilising all or a substantial part of the contents of a database; and references in those paragraphs to a licence shall be construed accordingly.

Reference to Tribunal of proposed licence

10.—(1) The terms on which a licensing body proposes to grant a licence may be referred to the Copyright Tribunal by the prospective licensee.

...

Effect of order of Tribunal as to licence

13.—(1) Where the Copyright Tribunal has made an order under paragraph 10 or 11 and the order remains in force, the person entitled to the benefit of the order shall if he—

    (a) pays to the licensing body any charges payable in accordance with the order or, if the amount cannot be ascertained, gives an undertaking to pay the charges when ascertained, and

    (b) complies with the other terms specified in the order,

be in the same position as regards infringement of database right as if he had at all material times been the holder of a licence granted by the owner of the database right in question on the terms specified in the order.

  (2) The benefit of the order may be assigned—

    (a) in the case of an order under paragraph 10, if assignment is not prohibited under the terms of the Tribunal's order; and

    (b) in the case of an order under paragraph 11, if assignment was not prohibited under the terms of the original licence.

...

General considerations: unreasonable discrimination

14. In determining what is reasonable on a reference or application under this Schedule relating to a licensing scheme or licence, the Copyright Tribunal shall have regard to—

    (a) the availability of other schemes, or the granting of other licences, to other persons in similar circumstances, and

    (b) the terms of those schemes or licences,

and shall exercise its powers so as to secure that there is no unreasonable discrimination between licensees, or prospective licensees, under the scheme or licence to which the reference or application relates and licensees under other schemes operated by, or other licences granted by, the same person.

...

Electronic Commerce (EC Directive) Regulations 2002

(SI 2002/2013)

...

2 Interpretation

  (1) In these Regulations and in the Schedule—

...

'information society services' (which is summarised in recital 17 of the Directive as covering 'any service normally provided for remuneration, at a distance, by means of electronic equipment for the processing (including digital compression) and storage of data, and at the individual request of a recipient of a service') has the meaning set out in Article 2(a) of the Directive, (which refers to Article 1(2) of Directive 98/34/EC of the European Parliament and of the Council of 22 June 1998 laying down a procedure for the provision of information in the field of technical standards and regulations, as amended by Directive 98/48/EC of 20 July 1998);

...

'recipient of the service' means any person who, for professional ends or otherwise, uses an information society service, in particular for the purposes of seeking information or making it accessible;

...

'service provider' means any person providing an information society service;

...

(2) In regulations 4 and 5, 'requirement' means any legal requirement under the law of the United Kingdom, or any part of it, imposed by or under any enactment or otherwise.

(3) Terms used in the Directive other than those in paragraph (1) above shall have the same meaning as in the Directive.

...

17   Mere conduit

(1) Where an information society service is provided which consists of the transmission in a communication network of information provided by a recipient of the service or the provision of access to a communication network, the service provider (if he otherwise would) shall not be liable for damages or for any other pecuniary remedy or for any criminal sanction as a result of that transmission where the service provider—

    (a) did not initiate the transmission;

    (b) did not select the receiver of the transmission; and

    (c) did not select or modify the information contained in the transmission.

(2) The acts of transmission and of provision of access referred to in paragraph (1) include the automatic, intermediate and transient storage of the information transmitted where:

    (a) this takes place for the sole purpose of carrying out the transmission in the communication network, and

    (b) the information is not stored for any period longer than is reasonably necessary for the transmission.

18   Caching

Where an information society service is provided which consists of the transmission in a communication network of information provided by a recipient of the service, the service provider (if he otherwise would) shall not be liable for damages or for any other pecuniary remedy or for any criminal sanction as a result of that transmission where—

    (a) the information is the subject of automatic, intermediate and temporary storage where that storage is for the sole purpose of making more efficient onward transmission of the information to other recipients of the service upon their request, and

    (b) the service provider—

        (i)   does not modify the information;

        (ii) complies with conditions on access to the information;

        (iii) complies with any rules regarding the updating of the information, specified in a manner widely recognised and used by industry;

        (iv) does not interfere with the lawful use of technology, widely recognised and used by industry, to obtain data on the use of the information; and

        (v)   acts expeditiously to remove or to disable access to the information he has stored upon obtaining actual knowledge of the fact that the information at the initial source of the transmission has been removed from the network, or access to it has been disabled, or that a court or an administrative authority has ordered such removal or disablement.

19   Hosting

Where an information society service is provided which consists of the storage of information provided by a recipient of the service, the service provider (if he otherwise would) shall not be liable for damages or for any other pecuniary remedy or for any criminal sanction as a result of that storage where—

(a) the service provider—

(i) does not have actual knowledge of unlawful activity or information and, where a claim for damages is made, is not aware of facts or circumstances from which it would have been apparent to the service provider that the activity or information was unlawful; or

(ii) upon obtaining such knowledge or awareness, acts expeditiously to remove or to disable access to the information, and

(b) the recipient of the service was not acting under the authority or the control of the service provider.

20   Protection of rights

(1) Nothing in regulations 17, 18 and 19 shall—

(a) prevent a person agreeing different contractual terms; or

(b) affect the rights of any party to apply to a court for relief to prevent or stop infringement of any rights.

(2) Any power of an administrative authority to prevent or stop infringement of any rights shall continue to apply notwithstanding regulations 17, 18 and 19.

21   Defence in criminal proceedings: burden of proof

(1) This regulation applies where a service provider charged with an offence in criminal proceedings arising out of any transmission, provision of access or storage falling within regulation 17, 18 or 19 relies on a defence under any of regulations 17, 18 and 19.

(2) Where evidence is adduced which is sufficient to raise an issue with respect to that defence, the court or jury shall assume that the defence is satisfied unless the prosecution proves beyond reasonable doubt that it is not.

22   Notice for the purposes of actual knowledge

In determining whether a service provider has actual knowledge for the purposes of regulations 18(b)(v) and 19(a)(i), a court shall take into account all matters which appear to it in the particular circumstances to be relevant and, among other things, shall have regard to—

(a) whether a service provider has received a notice through a means of contact made available in accordance with regulation 6(1)(c), and

(b) the extent to which any notice includes—

(i)   the full name and address of the sender of the notice;

(ii) details of the location of the information in question; and

(iii) details of the unlawful nature of the activity or information in question.

. . .

Communications Act 2003

(2003, c. 21)

An Act to confer functions on the Office of Communications; to make provision about the regulation of the provision of electronic communications networks and services and of the use of the electro-magnetic spectrum; to make provision about the regulation of broadcasting and of the provision of television and radio services; to make provision about mergers involving newspaper and other media enterprises and, in that connection, to amend the Enterprise Act 2002; and for connected purposes.   [17 July 2003]

. . .

PART 2   NETWORKS, SERVICES AND THE RADIO SPECTRUM

Chapter 1   Electronic Communications Networks and Services

...

Online infringement of copyright: obligations of internet service providers

124A   Obligation to notify subscribers of copyright infringement reports

(1)   This section applies if it appears to a copyright owner that—

    (a)   a subscriber to an internet access service has infringed the owner's copyright by means of the service; or

    (b)   a subscriber to an internet access service has allowed another person to use the service, and that other person has infringed the owner's copyright by means of the service.

(2)   The owner may make a copyright infringement report to the internet service provider who provided the internet access service if a code in force under section 124C or 124D (an 'initial obligations code') allows the owner to do so.

(3)   A 'copyright infringement report' is a report that—

    (a)   states that there appears to have been an infringement of the owner's copyright;

    (b)   includes a description of the apparent infringement;

    (c)   includes evidence of the apparent infringement that shows the subscriber's IP address and the time at which the evidence was gathered;

    (d)   is sent to the internet service provider within the period of 1 month beginning with the day on which the evidence was gathered; and

    (e)   complies with any other requirement of the initial obligations code.

(4)   An internet service provider who receives a copyright infringement report must notify the subscriber of the report if the initial obligations code requires the provider to do so.

(5)   A notification under subsection (4) must be sent to the subscriber within the period of 1 month beginning with the day on which the provider receives the report.

(6)   A notification under subsection (4) must include—

    (a)   a statement that the notification is sent under this section in response to a copyright infringement report;

    (b)   the name of the copyright owner who made the report;

    (c)   a description of the apparent infringement;

    (d)   evidence of the apparent infringement that shows the subscriber's IP address and the time at which the evidence was gathered;

    (e)   information about subscriber appeals and the grounds on which they may be made;

    (f)   information about copyright and its purpose;

    (g)   advice, or information enabling the subscriber to obtain advice, about how to obtain lawful access to copyright works;

    (h)   advice, or information enabling the subscriber to obtain advice, about steps that a subscriber can take to protect an internet access service from unauthorised use; and

    (i)   anything else that the initial obligations code requires the notification to include.

(7)   For the purposes of subsection (6)(h) the internet service provider must take into account the suitability of different protection for subscribers in different circumstances.

(8)   The things that may be required under subsection (6)(i), whether in general or in a particular case, include in particular—

    (a)   a statement that information about the apparent infringement may be kept by the internet service provider;

    (b)   a statement that the copyright owner may require the provider to disclose which copyright infringement reports made by the owner to the provider relate to the subscriber;

(c) a statement that, following such a disclosure, the copyright owner may apply to a court to learn the subscriber's identity and may bring proceedings against the subscriber for copyright infringement; and

(d) where the requirement for the provider to send the notification arises partly because of a report that has already been the subject of a notification under subsection (4), a statement that the number of copyright infringement reports relating to the subscriber may be taken into account for the purposes of any technical measures.

(9) In this section 'notify', in relation to a subscriber, means send a notification to the electronic or postal address held by the internet service provider for the subscriber (and sections 394 to 396 do not apply).

124B   Obligation to provide copyright infringement lists to copyright owners

(1) An internet service provider must provide a copyright owner with a copyright infringement list for a period if—

(a) the owner requests the list for that period; and

(b) an initial obligations code requires the internet service provider to provide it.

(2) A 'copyright infringement list' is a list that—

(a) sets out, in relation to each relevant subscriber, which of the copyright infringement reports made by the owner to the provider relate to the subscriber, but

(b) does not enable any subscriber to be identified.

(3) A subscriber is a 'relevant subscriber' in relation to a copyright owner and an internet service provider if copyright infringement reports made by the owner to the provider in relation to the subscriber have reached the threshold set in the initial obligations code.

...

124G   Obligations to limit internet access: assessment and preparation

...

(2) A 'technical obligation', in relation to an internet service provider, is an obligation for the provider to take a technical measure against some or all relevant subscribers to its service for the purpose of preventing or reducing infringement of copyright by means of the internet.

(3) A 'technical measure' is a measure that—

(a) limits the speed or other capacity of the service provided to a subscriber;

(b) prevents a subscriber from using the service to gain access to particular material, or limits such use;

(c) suspends the service provided to a subscriber; or

(d) limits the service provided to a subscriber in another way.

(4) A subscriber to an internet access service is 'relevant' if the subscriber is a relevant subscriber, within the meaning of section 124B(3), in relation to the provider of the service and one or more copyright owners.

...

124H   Obligations to limit internet access

(1) The Secretary of State may by order impose a technical obligation on internet service providers if—

(a) OFCOM have assessed whether one or more technical obligations should be imposed on internet service providers; and

(b) taking into account that assessment, reports prepared by OFCOM under section 124F, and any other matter that appears to the Secretary of State to be relevant, the Secretary of State considers it appropriate to make the order.

(2) No order may be made under this section within the period of 12 months beginning with the first day on which there is an initial obligations code in force.

(3) An order under this section must specify the date from which the technical obligation is to have effect, or provide for it to be specified.

(4) The order may also specify—

(a) the criteria for taking the technical measure concerned against a subscriber;

    (b) the steps to be taken as part of the measure and when they are to be taken.

...

124N   Interpretation

...

'internet access service' means an electronic communications service that—

    (a) is provided to a subscriber;

    (b) consists entirely or mainly of the provision of access to the internet; and

    (c) includes the allocation of an IP address or IP addresses to the subscriber to enable that access;

'internet service provider' means a person who provides an internet access service;

'IP address' means an internet protocol address;

'subscriber', in relation to an internet access service, means a person who—

    (a) receives the service under an agreement between the person and the provider of the service; and

    (b) does not receive it as a communications provider;

...

Community Design Regulations 2005*

(SI 2005/2339)

1 Introductory and interpretation

    (1) These Regulations may be cited as the Community Design Regulations 2005 and shall come into force on 1st October 2005.

    (2) In these Regulations—

'design court has the meaning given by Article 81 of the Design Regulation;

'Design Regulation' means Council Regulation (EC) No 6/2002 of 12th December 2001 on Community Designs as amended by regulation 4(1) of, and Part 1 of Schedule 1 to, the Designs and International Trade Marks (Amendment etc.) (EU Exit) Regulations 2018; and

'supplementary unregistered design' has the meaning given by Article 1 of the Design Regulation.

1A Infringement proceedings

    (1) This regulation and regulations 1B to 1D are without prejudice to the duties of the design court under the provisions of Article 89(1)(a) to (c) of the Design Regulation.

    (2) Subject to paragraph (5), in an action for infringement of a supplementary unregistered design all such relief by way of damages, injunctions, accounts or otherwise is available to the holder of the supplementary unregistered design as is available in respect of the infringement of any other property right.

    (5) In an action for the infringement of a supplementary unregistered Community design, damages shall not be awarded against a person who proves that at the date of the infringement that they were not aware, and had no reason to believe, that the design to which the action relates was protected as a supplementary unregistered Community design.

1B Order for delivery up

    (1) Where a person—

        (a) has in his possession, custody or control for commercial purposes an infringing article, or

        (b) has in his possession, custody or control anything specifically designed or adapted for making articles to a particular design which is a supplementary unregistered design, knowing or having reason to believe that it has been or is to be used to make an infringing article,

---

* **Editor's Note:** Contains amendments effected by *Designs and International Trade Marks (Amendments etc.) (EU Exit) Regulations 2019*. By virtue of the *European Union (Withdrawal Agreement) Act 2020*, these amendments take effect on 'IP completion day', which is defined to be 31 December 2020 at 11:00pm.

the holder of the supplementary unregistered design in question may apply to the design court for an order that the infringing article or other thing be delivered up to him or to such other person as the design court may direct.

...

1C   Order as to disposal of infringing articles, &c

(1) An application may be made to the design court for an order that an infringing article or other thing delivered up in pursuance of an order under regulation 1B shall be—
  (a) forfeited to the holder of the supplementary unregistered design, or
  (b) destroyed or otherwise dealt with as the design court may think fit, or for a decision that no such order should be made.

...

1D   Meaning of 'infringing article'

(1) In these Regulations 'infringing article', in relation to a design, shall be construed in accordance with this regulation.

(2) An article is an infringing article if its making to that design was an infringement of a supplementary unregistered design.

(3) An article is also an infringing article if—
  (a) it has been or is proposed to be imported into the United Kingdom, and
  (b) its making to that design in the United Kingdom would have been an infringement of a supplementary unregistered design or a breach of an exclusive licensing agreement relating to that supplementary unregistered design.

(4) Where it is shown that an article is made to a design which is or has been a supplementary unregistered design, it shall be presumed until the contrary is proved that the article was made at a time when the right in the supplementary unregistered design subsisted.

(5) Nothing in paragraph (3) shall be construed as applying to an article which may be lawfully imported into the United Kingdom by virtue of anything which forms part of retained EU law as a result of section 3 or 4 of the European Union (Withdrawal) Act 2018.

2   Unjustified threats: threats of infringement proceedings

(1) A communication contains a 'threat of infringement proceedings' if a reasonable person in the position of a recipient would understand from the communication that—
  (a) a supplementary unregistered design exists, and
  (b) a person intends to bring proceedings (whether in a court in the United Kingdom or elsewhere) against another person for infringement of the supplementary unregistered design by—
    (i) an act done in the United Kingdom, or
    (ii) an act which, if done, would be done in the United Kingdom.

(2) References in this regulation and in regulation 2C to a 'recipient' include, in the case of a communication directed to the public or a section of the public, references to a person to whom the communication is directed.

2A   Unjustified threats: actionable threats

(1) Subject to paragraphs (2) to (5), a threat of infringement proceedings made by any person is actionable by any person aggrieved by the threat.

(2) A threat of infringement proceedings is not actionable if the infringement is alleged to consist of—
  (a) making an article for disposal, or
  (b) importing an article for disposal.

(3) A threat of infringement proceedings is not actionable if the infringement is alleged to consist of an act which, if done, would constitute an infringement of a kind mentioned in paragraph (2)(a) or (b).

(4) A threat of infringement proceedings is not actionable if the threat—

    (a) is made to a person who has done, or intends to do, an act mentioned in paragraph (2)(a) or (b) in relation to an article, and

    (b) is a threat of proceedings for an infringement alleged to consist of doing anything else in relation to that article.

(5) A threat of infringement proceedings which is not an express threat is not actionable if it is contained in a permitted communication.

(6) In regulations 2C and 2D an 'actionable threat' means a threat of infringement proceedings that is actionable in accordance with this regulation.

2B   Unjustified threats: permitted communications

(1) For the purposes of regulation 2A(5), a communication containing a threat of infringement proceedings is a 'permitted communication' if—

    (a) the communication, so far as it contains information that relates to the threat, is made for a permitted purpose;

    (b) all of the information that relates to the threat is information that—

        (i) is necessary for that purpose (see paragraph (5)(a) to (c) for some examples of necessary information), and

        (ii) the person making the communication reasonably believes is true.

(2) Each of the following is a 'permitted purpose'—

    (a) giving notice that a supplementary unregistered design exists;

    (b) discovering whether, or by whom, a supplementary unregistered design has been infringed by an act mentioned in regulation 2A(2)(a) or (b);

    (c) giving notice that a person has a right in or under a supplementary unregistered design, where another person's awareness of the right is relevant to any proceedings that may be brought in respect of the supplementary unregistered design.

(3) The design court may, having regard to the nature of the purposes listed in paragraph (2)(a) to (c), treat any other purpose as a 'permitted purpose' if it considers that it is in the interests of justice to do so.

(4) But the following may not be treated as a 'permitted purpose'—

    (a) requesting a person to cease doing, for commercial purposes, anything in relation to an article made to a design, in which a design is incorporated or to which it is applied,

    (b) requesting a person to deliver up or destroy an article made to a design, in which a design is incorporated or to which it is applied, or

    (c) requesting a person to give an undertaking relating to an article made to a design, in which a design is incorporated or to which it is applied.

(5) If any of the following information is included in a communication made for a permitted purpose, it is information that is 'necessary for that purpose' (see paragraph (1)(b)(i))—

    (a) a statement—

        (iii) that a design is protected as a supplementary unregistered design;

    (b) details of the supplementary unregistered design, or of a right in or under the supplementary unregistered design, which—

        (i) are accurate in all material respects, and

        (ii) are not misleading in any material respect; and

    (c) information enabling the identification of the article that is alleged to be infringing an article in relation to the design.

2C Unjustified threats: remedies and defences

(1) Proceedings in respect of an actionable threat may be brought against the person who made the threat for—

(a) a declaration that the threat is unjustified;

(b) an injunction against the continuance of the threat;

(c) damages in respect of any loss sustained by the aggrieved person by reason of the threat.

(2) It is a defence for the person who made the threat to show that the act in respect of which proceedings were threatened constitutes (or if done would constitute) an infringement of the supplementary unregistered design.

(3) It is a defence for the person who made the threat to show—

(a) that, despite having taken reasonable steps, the person has not identified anyone who has done an act mentioned in regulation 2A(2)(a) or (b) in relation to the article which is the subject of the threat, and

(b) that the person notified the recipient, before or at the time of making the threat, of the steps taken.

2D Unjustified threats: professional advisers

(1) Proceedings in respect of an actionable threat may not be brought against a professional adviser (or any person vicariously liable for the actions of that professional adviser) if the conditions in paragraph (3) are met.

(2) In this section 'professional adviser' means a person who, in relation to the making of the communication containing the threat—

(a) is acting in a professional capacity in providing legal services or the services of a trade mark attorney or a patent attorney, and

(b) is regulated in the provision of legal services, or the services of a trade mark attorney or a patent attorney, by one or more regulatory bodies (whether through membership of a regulatory body, the issue of a licence to practise or any other means).

(3) The conditions are that—

(a) in making the communication the professional adviser is acting on the instructions of another person, and

(b) when the communication is made the professional adviser identifies the person on whose instructions the adviser is acting.

(4) This section does not affect any liability of the person on whose instructions the professional adviser is acting.

(5) It is for a person asserting that paragraph (1) applies to prove (if required) that at the material time—

(a) the person concerned was acting as a professional adviser, and

(b) the conditions in paragraph (3) were met.

2F Unjustified threats: supplementary: proceedings for delivery up etc.

In regulation 2(1)(b) the reference to proceedings for infringement of the supplementary unregistered design includes a reference to—

(a) proceedings for an order under regulation 1B (order for delivery up), and

(b) proceedings for an order under regulation 1C (order as to disposal of infringing articles).

. . .

5 Use of supplementary unregistered design for services of the Crown

The provisions of the Schedule to these Regulations shall have effect with respect to the use of supplementary unregistered designs for the services of the Crown and the rights of third parties in respect of such use.

. . .

Regulation 5   **SCHEDULE**

USE OF SUPPLEMENTARY UNREGISTERED
DESIGNS FOR SERVICES OF THE CROWN

Use of supplementary unregistered design for services of the Crown

1.—(1) A government department, or a person authorised in writing by a government department, may without the consent of the holder of a supplementary unregistered design—

(a) do anything for the purpose of supplying products for the services of the Crown, or

(b) dispose of products no longer required for the services of the Crown;

and nothing done by virtue of this paragraph infringes the supplementary unregistered design.

(2) References in this Schedule to 'the services of the Crown' are limited to those which are necessary for essential defence or security needs.

. . .

2.—(1)   Where Crown use is made of a supplementary unregistered design, the government department concerned shall—

(a) notify the holder of the supplementary unregistered design as soon as practicable, and

(b) give him such information as to the extent of the use as he may from time to time require, unless it appears to the department that it would be contrary to the public interest to do so or the identity of the holder of the supplementary unregistered design cannot be ascertained on reasonable inquiry.

(2) Crown use of a supplementary unregistered design shall be on such terms as, either before or after the use, are agreed between the government department concerned and the holder of the supplementary unregistered design with the approval of the Treasury or, in default of agreement, are determined by the design court.

. . .

Crown use: compensation for loss of profit

4.—(1)   Where Crown use is made of a supplementary unregistered design, the government department concerned shall pay—

(a) to the holder of the supplementary unregistered design, or

(b) if there is an exclusive licence in force in respect of the supplementary unregistered design, to the exclusive licensee,

compensation for any loss resulting from his not being awarded a contract to supply the products to which the supplementary unregistered design is applied or in which it is incorporated.

. . .

Artist's Resale Right Regulations 2006*

(SI 2006/346)

1 Citation, commencement and extent

(1) These Regulations may be cited as the Artist's Resale Right Regulations 2006 and shall come into force on the day after the day on which they are made.

(2) These Regulations extend to the whole of the United Kingdom.

---

* **Editor's Note:** Contains amendments effected by *Intellectual Property (Copyright and Related Rights) (Amendment) (EU Exit) Regulations 2019*. By virtue of the *European Union (Withdrawal Agreement) Act 2020*, these amendments take effect on 'IP completion day', which is defined to be 31 December 2020 at 11:00pm.

2 Interpretation

In these Regulations—

'author', in relation to a work, means the person who creates it;

'collecting society' has the meaning given in regulation 14(5);

'contract date', in relation to a sale, means the time at which the contract of sale was made (and 'contract of sale' has the meaning given in section 2 of the Sale of Goods Act 1979);

'copyright' has the meaning given in section 1 of the Copyright, Designs and Patents Act 1988;

'national of the United Kingdom' has the meaning given by section 178 of the Copyright, Designs and Patents Act 1988

'qualifying body' has the meaning given in regulation 7(4);

'resale' is to be construed in accordance with regulation 12;

'resale right' has the meaning given in regulation 3 (and, unless the context otherwise requires, includes a share in resale right);

'resale royalty' has the meaning given in regulation 3;

'sale' has the meaning given in section 2 of the Sale of Goods Act 1979;

'sale price' has the meaning given in regulation 3(4);

'trustee in bankruptcy' means, in relation to Scotland, an interim or permanent trustee appointed under the Bankruptcy (Scotland) Act 1985;

'work' has the meaning given in regulation 4;

'work of joint authorship' has the meaning given in regulation 5(4).

3 Artist's resale right

(1) The author of a work in which copyright subsists shall, in accordance with these Regulations, have a right ('resale right') to a royalty on any sale of the work which is a resale subsequent to the first transfer of ownership by the author ('resale royalty').

(2) Resale right in a work shall continue to subsist so long as copyright subsists in the work.

(3) The royalty shall be an amount based on the sale price which is calculated in accordance with Schedule 1.

(4) The sale price is the price obtained for the sale, net of the tax payable on the sale, and converted into euro at the European Central Bank reference rate prevailing at the contract date.

(5) For the purposes of paragraph (1), 'transfer of ownership by the author' includes in particular—

    (a) transmission of the work from the author by testamentary disposition, or in accordance with the rules of intestate succession;

    (b) disposal of the work by the author's personal representatives for the purposes of the administration of his estate; and

    (c) disposal of the work by an official receiver (or, in Northern Ireland, the Official Receiver for Northern Ireland) or a trustee in bankruptcy, for the purposes of the realisation of the author's estate.

4 Works covered

(1) For the purposes of these Regulations, 'work' means any work of graphic or plastic art such as a picture, a collage, a painting, a drawing, an engraving, a print, a lithograph, a sculpture, a tapestry, a ceramic, an item of glassware or a photograph.

(2) However, a copy of a work is not to be regarded as a work unless the copy is one of a limited number which have been made by the author or under his authority.

5 Joint authorship

(1) In the case of a work of joint authorship, the resale right shall belong to the authors as owners in common.

(2) The right shall be held in equal shares or in such other shares as may be agreed.

(3) Such an agreement must be in writing signed by or on behalf of each party to the agreement.

(4) 'Work of joint authorship' means a work created by two or more authors.

6   Proof of authorship

(1) Where a name purporting to be that of the author appeared on the work when it was made, the person whose name appeared shall, unless the contrary is proved, be presumed to be the author of the work.

(2) In the case of a work alleged to be a work of joint authorship, paragraph (1) applies in relation to each person alleged to be one of the authors.

7   Assignment etc.

(1) Resale right is not assignable.

(2) Any charge on a resale right is void.

(3) Paragraph (1) does not prevent the transfer of a resale right which was transmitted to a qualifying body under regulation 9 (or is deemed to have been so transmitted under regulation 16), provided that the transfer is to another qualifying body.

(4) A qualifying body is a body which—

    (a) is a charity within the meaning of section 96(1) of the Charities Act 1993 or section 35 of the Charities Act (Northern Ireland) 1964;

    (b) is a Scottish charity; or

    (c) is a foreign charity.

(5) In paragraph (4)—

    (a) 'Scottish charity' means—

        (i) a body entered in the Scottish Charity Register under section 3 of the Charities and Trustee Investment (Scotland) Act 2005; or

        (ii) a 'recognised body' within the meaning of section 1(7) of the Law Reform (Miscellaneous Provisions) (Scotland) Act 1990; and

    (b) 'foreign charity' means a body which is established outside the United Kingdom for purposes similar to those for which a body within paragraph (4)(a) or (b) may be established, and which is subject to similar rules regarding the distribution and application of its assets.

8   Waiver etc.

(1) A waiver of a resale right shall have no effect.

(2) An agreement to share or repay resale royalties shall be void.

(3) Paragraph (2) does not affect any agreement made for the purposes of the management of resale right in accordance with regulation 14.

9   Transmission and vesting of resale right

(1) Where by virtue of this regulation resale right is transmitted to, or vests in, any person, it may be exercised by that person.

(2) Resale right—

    (a) is transmissible as personal or moveable property by testamentary disposition or in accordance with the rules of intestate succession but only to a natural person or a qualifying body; and

    (b) may vest by operation of law in the personal representative of a deceased person.

(3) Resale right may be further transmitted to a natural person or a qualifying body by any person to whom it passes under paragraph (2)(a).

(4) Resale right may be transmitted as bona vacantia.

(5) Resale right may vest by operation of law in an official receiver (or in Northern Ireland, the Official Receiver for Northern Ireland) or a trustee in bankruptcy.

(6) Where resale right is transmitted to more than one person it belongs to them as owners in common.

10   Requirements as to nationality

Resale right may only be exercised in respect of the sale of a work where its author is—

    (a) living at the date of the sale and is at that date a national of—

        (i) the United Kingdom; or

        (ii) a state the legislation of which permits resale right protection for authors from the United Kingdom and their successors in title; or

(b) deceased at the date of the sale and, at the date of the author's death, the author was a national of a state falling within paragraph (a)(i) or (ii).

11 Trusts

Nothing in regulations 7, 9 or 10 prevents a resale right from being—

(a) held, and exercised in respect of a sale, by any person acting as trustee for the person who would otherwise be entitled to exercise the right ('the beneficiary'); or

(b) transferred to such a trustee, or from the trustee to the beneficiary.

12 'Resale'

(1) The sale of a work may be regarded as a resale notwithstanding that the first transfer of ownership was not made for a money (or any) consideration.

(2) The sale of a work may regarded as a resale only if the conditions mentioned in paragraph (3) are satisfied in respect of that sale.

(3) The conditions are that—

(a) the buyer or the seller, or (where the sale takes place through an agent) the agent of the buyer or the seller, is acting in the course of a business of dealing in works of art; and

(b) the sale price is not less than 1,000 euro.

(4) The sale of a work is not to be regarded as a resale if—

(a) the seller previously acquired the work directly from the author less than three years before the sale; and

(b) the sale price does not exceed 10,000 euro.

13 Liability to pay resale royalty

(1) The following shall be jointly and severally liable to pay the resale royalty due in respect of a sale—

(a) the seller; and

(b) the relevant person (within the meaning of paragraph (2)).

(2) The relevant person is a person who satisfies the condition mentioned in regulation 12(3)(a) and who is—

(a) the agent of the seller; or

(b) where there is no such agent, the agent of the buyer; or

(c) where there are no such agents, the buyer.

(3) Liability shall arise on the completion of the sale; however, a person who is liable may withhold payment until evidence of entitlement to be paid the royalty is produced.

(4) Any liability to pay resale royalty in respect of a resale right which belongs to two or more persons as owners in common is discharged by a payment of the total amount of royalty to one of those persons.

14 Collective management

(1) Resale right may be exercised only through a collecting society.

...

15 Right to information

(1) A holder of resale right in respect of a sale, or a person acting on his behalf, shall have the right to obtain information by making a request under this regulation.

(2) Such a request—

(a) may be made to any person who (in relation to that sale) satisfies the condition mentioned in regulation 12(3)(a); but

(b) must be made within three years of the sale to which it relates.

(3) The information that may be so requested is any that may be necessary in order to secure payment of the resale royalty, and in particular to ascertain—

(a) the amount of royalty that is due; and

(b) where the royalty is not paid by the person to whom the request is made, the name and address of any person who is liable.

(4) The person to whom the request is made shall do everything within his power to supply the information requested within 90 days of the receipt of the request.

(5) If that information is not supplied within the period mentioned in paragraph (4), the person making the request may, in accordance with rules of court, apply to the county court for an order requiring the person to whom the request is made to supply the information.

(6) In Scotland, such an application shall be by way of summary application to the sheriff, and the procedure for breach of an order shall proceed in like manner as for a contempt of court.

(7) Information obtained under this regulation shall be treated as confidential.

16 Transitional provisions

(1) These Regulations—
  (a) do not apply to sales where the contract date preceded the commencement of the Regulations; but
  (b) apply notwithstanding that the work sold was made before that commencement.

(2) Where the author of a work (or a person to whom the resale right in that work is deemed to have been transmitted under this regulation) died before the commencement of these Regulations, and was at the time of his death a qualifying individual within the meaning of regulation 10(3) as originally enacted—
  (a) if he was the owner of the copyright in the work immediately before his death, and on his death a qualifying person became beneficially entitled to that copyright (or to part of it), the resale right in the work shall be deemed to have been transmitted to that person;
  (b) if he was the owner of the work (but not the copyright in it) immediately before his death, and on his death a qualifying person became beneficially entitled to the work, the resale right shall be deemed to have been transmitted to that person;
  (c) otherwise, the resale right shall be deemed to have been transmitted to the qualifying persons who were beneficially entitled to the residue of his personal estate.

(3) Where the author of the work was one of a number of joint authors, the right deemed to have been transmitted by the author under this regulation is one of that number of equal shares in the resale right.

(4) Where a resale right is deemed to have been transmitted to more than one person under paragraph (2)(a), (b) or (c), the resale right shall be deemed to have been transmitted to them in equal shares as owners in common.

(5) In this regulation, 'qualifying person' means a person to whom a resale right maybe transmitted under regulation 9(2) and (3) as originally enacted.

Regulation 3(3) **SCHEDULE 1**

CALCULATION OF RESALE ROYALTY

1. The resale royalty payable on the sale of a work shall be the sum of the following amounts, being percentage amounts of consecutive portions of the sale price—

Portion of the sale price	Percentage amount
From 0 to 50,000 euro	4%
From 50,000.01 to 200,000 euro	3%
From 200,000.01 to 350,000 euro	1%
From 350,000.01 to 500,000 euro	0.5%
Exceeding 500,000 euro	0.25%

2. However, the total amount of royalty payable on the sale shall not in any event exceed 12,500 euro.

...

A2.   UNITED STATES

Copyright Act of 1976

(United States Code Title 17 – Copyrights)

Chapter 1.   Subject Matter and
Scope of Copyright

§ 101.   Definitions

Except as otherwise provided in this title, as used in this title, the following terms and their variant forms mean the following:

...

An 'architectural work' is the design of a building as embodied in any tangible medium of expression, including a building, architectural plans, or drawings. The work includes the overall form as well as the arrangement and composition of spaces and elements in the design, but does not include individual standard features.

'Audiovisual works' are works that consist of a series of related images which are intrinsically intended to be shown by the use of machines or devices such as projectors, viewers, or electronic equipment, together with accompanying sounds, if any, regardless of the nature of the material objects, such as films or tapes, in which the works are embodied.

...

A 'collective work' is a work, such as a periodical issue, anthology, or encyclopedia, in which a number of contributions, constituting separate and independent works in themselves, are assembled into a collective whole.

A 'compilation' is a work formed by the collection and assembling of preexisting materials or of data that are selected, coordinated, or arranged in such a way that the resulting work as a whole constitutes an original work of authorship. The term 'compilation' includes collective works.

A 'computer program' is a set of statements or instructions to be used directly or indirectly in a computer in order to bring about a certain result.

'Copies' are material objects, other than phonorecords, in which a work is fixed by any method now known or later developed, and from which the work can be perceived, reproduced, or otherwise communicated, either directly or with the aid of a machine or device. The term 'copies' includes the material object, other than a phonorecord, in which the work is first fixed.

'Copyright owner', with respect to any one of the exclusive rights comprised in a copyright, refers to the owner of that particular right.

...

A work is 'created' when it is fixed in a copy or phonorecord for the first time; where a work is prepared over a period of time, the portion of it that has been fixed at any particular time constitutes the work as of that time, and where the work has been prepared in different versions, each version constitutes a separate work.

A 'derivative work' is a work based upon one or more preexisting works, such as a translation, musical arrangement, dramatization, fictionalization, motion picture version, sound recording, art reproduction, abridgment, condensation, or any other form in which a work may be recast, transformed, or adapted. A work consisting of editorial revisions, annotations, elaborations, or other modifications, which, as a whole, represent an original work of authorship, is a 'derivative work'.

A 'device', 'machine', or 'process' is one now known or later developed.

A 'digital transmission' is a transmission in whole or in part in a digital or other nonanalog format.

To 'display' a work means to show a copy of it, either directly or by means of a film, slide, television image, or any other device or process or, in the case of a motion picture or other audiovisual work, to show individual images nonsequentially.

. . .

A work is 'fixed' in a tangible medium of expression when its embodiment in a copy or phono-record, by or under the authority of the author, is sufficiently permanent or stable to permit it to be perceived, reproduced, or otherwise communicated for a period of more than transitory duration. A work consisting of sounds, images, or both, that are being transmitted, is 'fixed' for purposes of this title if a fixation of the work is being made simultaneously with its transmission.

. . .

The terms 'including' and 'such as' are illustrative and not limitative.

. . .

A 'joint work' is a work prepared by two or more authors with the intention that their contributions be merged into inseparable or interdependent parts of a unitary whole.

'Literary works' are works, other than audiovisual works, expressed in words, numbers, or other verbal or numerical symbols or indicia, regardless of the nature of the material objects, such as books, periodicals, manuscripts, phonorecords, film, tapes, disks, or cards, in which they are embodied.

. . .

To 'perform' a work means to recite, render, play, dance, or act it, either directly or by means of any device or process or, in the case of a motion picture or other audiovisual work, to show its images in any sequence or to make the sounds accompanying it audible.

. . .

'Phonorecords' are material objects in which sounds, other than those accompanying a motion picture or other audiovisual work, are fixed by any method now known or later developed, and from which the sounds can be perceived, reproduced, or otherwise communicated, either directly or with the aid of a machine or device. The term 'phonorecords' includes the material object in which the sounds are first fixed.

'Pictorial, graphic, and sculptural works' include two-dimensional and three-dimensional works of fine, graphic, and applied art, photographs, prints and art reproductions, maps, globes, charts, diagrams, models, and technical drawings, including architectural plans. Such works shall include works of artistic craftsmanship insofar as their form but not their mechanical or utilitarian aspects are concerned; the design of a useful article, as defined in this section, shall be considered a pictorial, graphic, or sculptural work only if, and only to the extent that, such design incorporates pictorial, graphic, or sculptural features that can be identified separately from, and are capable of existing independently of, the utilitarian aspects of the article.

. . .

'Publication' is the distribution of copies or phonorecords of a work to the public by sale or other transfer of ownership, or by rental, lease, or lending. The offering to distribute copies or phonorecords to a group of persons for purposes of further distribution, public performance, or public display, constitutes publication. A public performance or display of a work does not of itself constitute publication.

To perform or display a work 'publicly' means—

(1) to perform or display it at a place open to the public or at any place where a substantial number of persons outside of a normal circle of a family and its social acquaintances is gathered; or

(2) to transmit or otherwise communicate a performance or display of the work to a place specified by clause (1) or to the public, by means of any device or process, whether the members of the public capable of receiving the performance or display receive it in the same place or in separate places and at the same time or at different times.

. . .

'Sound recordings' are works that result from the fixation of a series of musical, spoken, or other sounds, but not including the sounds accompanying a motion picture or other audiovisual work, regardless of the nature of the material objects, such as disks, tapes, or other phonorecords, in which they are embodied.

. . .

A 'transmission program' is a body of material that, as an aggregate, has been produced for the sole purpose of transmission to the public in sequence and as a unit.

To 'transmit' a performance or display is to communicate it by any device or process whereby images or sounds are received beyond the place from which they are sent.

…

A 'useful article' is an article having an intrinsic utilitarian function that is not merely to portray the appearance of the article or to convey information. An article that is normally a part of a useful article is considered a 'useful article'.

…

A 'work of visual art' is—

(1) a painting, drawing, print or sculpture, existing in a single copy, in a limited edition of 200 copies or fewer that are signed and consecutively numbered by the author, or, in the case of a sculpture, in multiple cast, carved, or fabricated sculptures of 200 or fewer that are consecutively numbered by the author and bear the signature or other identifying mark of the author; or

(2) a still photographic image produced for exhibition purposes only, existing in a single copy that is signed by the author, or in a limited edition of 200 copies or fewer that are signed and consecutively numbered by the author.

A work of visual art does not include—

(A) (i) any poster, map, globe, chart, technical drawing, diagram, model, applied art, motion picture or other audiovisual work, book, magazine, newspaper, periodical, data base, electronic information service, electronic publication, or similar publication;

(ii) any merchandising item or advertising, promotional, descriptive, covering, or packaging material or container;

(iii) any portion or part of any item described in clause (i) or (ii);

(B) any work made for hire; or

(C) any work not subject to copyright protection under this title.

A 'work of the United States Government' is a work prepared by an officer or employee of the United States Government as part of that person's official duties.

A 'work made for hire' is—

(1) a work prepared by an employee within the scope of his or her employment; or

(2) a work specially ordered or commissioned for use as a contribution to a collective work, as a part of a motion picture or other audiovisual work, as a translation, as a supplementary work, as a compilation, as an instructional text, as a test, as answer material for a test, or as an atlas, if the parties expressly agree in a written instrument signed by them that the work shall be considered a work made for hire. For the purpose of the foregoing sentence, a 'supplementary work' is a work prepared for publication as a secondary adjunct to a work by another author for the purpose of introducing, concluding, illustrating, explaining, revising, commenting upon, or assisting in the use of the other work, such as forewords, afterwords, pictorial illustrations, maps, charts, tables, editorial notes, musical arrangements, answer material for tests, bibliographies, appendixes, and indexes, and an 'instructional text' is a literary, pictorial, or graphic work prepared for publication and with the purpose of use in systematic instructional activities.

…

§ 102. Subject matter of copyright: In general

(a) Copyright protection subsists, in accordance with this title, in original works of authorship fixed in any tangible medium of expression, now known or later developed, from which they can be perceived, reproduced, or otherwise communicated, either directly or with the aid of a machine or device. Works of authorship include the following categories:

(1) literary works;

(2) musical works, including any accompanying words;

    (3) dramatic works, including any accompanying music;

    (4) pantomimes and choreographic works;

    (5) pictorial, graphic, and sculptural works;

    (6) motion pictures and other audiovisual works;

    (7) sound recordings; and

    (8) architectural works.

  (b) In no case does copyright protection for an original work of authorship extend to any idea, procedure, process, system, method of operation, concept, principle, or discovery, regardless of the form in which it is described, explained, illustrated, or embodied in such work.

§ 103. Subject matter of copyright: Compilations and derivative works

  (a) The subject matter of copyright as specified by section 102 includes compilations and derivative works, but protection for a work employing preexisting material in which copyright subsists does not extend to any part of the work in which such material has been used unlawfully.

  (b) The copyright in a compilation or derivative work extends only to the material contributed by the author of such work, as distinguished from the preexisting material employed in the work, and does not imply any exclusive right in the preexisting material. The copyright in such work is independent of, and does not affect or enlarge the scope, duration, ownership, or subsistence of, any copyright protection in the preexisting material.

. . .

§ 105. Subject matter of copyright: United States Government works

  (a) In general, copyright protection under this title is not available for any work of the United States Government, but the United States Government is not precluded from receiving and holding copyrights transferred to it by assignment, bequest, or otherwise.

. . .

§ 106. Exclusive rights in copyrighted works

Subject to sections 107 through 122, the owner of copyright under this title has the exclusive rights to do and to authorize any of the following:

    (1) to reproduce the copyrighted work in copies or phonorecords;

    (2) to prepare derivative works based upon the copyrighted work;

    (3) to distribute copies or phonorecords of the copyrighted work to the public by sale or other transfer of ownership, or by rental, lease, or lending;

    (4) in the case of literary, musical, dramatic, and choreographic works, pantomimes, and motion pictures and other audiovisual works, to perform the copyrighted work publicly;

    (5) in the case of literary, musical, dramatic, and choreographic works, pantomimes, and pictorial, graphic, or sculptural works, including the individual images of a motion picture or other audiovisual work, to display the copyrighted work publicly; and

    (6) in the case of sound recordings, to perform the copyrighted work publicly by means of a digital audio transmission.

§ 106A. Rights of certain authors to attribution and integrity

  (a) Rights of Attribution and Integrity.—Subject to section 107 and independent of the exclusive rights provided in section 106, the author of a work of visual art—

    (1) shall have the right—

        (A) to claim authorship of that work, and

        (B) to prevent the use of his or her name as the author of any work of visual art which he or she did not create;

    (2) shall have the right to prevent the use of his or her name as the author of the work of visual art in the event of a distortion, mutilation, or other modification of the work which would be prejudicial to his or her honor or reputation; and

(3) subject to the limitations set forth in section 113(d), shall have the right—

    (A) to prevent any intentional distortion, mutilation, or other modification of that work which would be prejudicial to his or her honor or reputation, and any intentional distortion, mutilation, or modification of that work is a violation of that right, and

    (B) to prevent any destruction of a work of recognized stature, and any intentional or grossly negligent destruction of that work is a violation of that right.

(b) Scope and Exercise of Rights.—Only the author of a work of visual art has the rights conferred by subsection (a) in that work, whether or not the author is the copyright owner. The authors of a joint work of visual art are coowners of the rights conferred by subsection (a) in that work.

(c) Exceptions.—

(1) The modification of a work of visual art which is the result of the passage of time or the inherent nature of the materials is not a distortion, mutilation, or other modification described in subsection (a)(3)(A).

(2) The modification of a work of visual art which is the result of conservation, or of the public presentation, including lighting and placement, of the work is not a destruction, distortion, mutilation, or other modification described in subsection (a)(3) unless the modification is caused by gross negligence.

(3) The rights described in paragraphs (1) and (2) of subsection (a) shall not apply to any reproduction, depiction, portrayal, or other use of a work in, upon, or in any connection with any item described in subparagraph (A) or (B) of the definition of 'work of visual art' in section 101, and any such reproduction, depiction, portrayal, or other use of a work is not a destruction, distortion, mutilation, or other modification described in paragraph (3) of subsection (a).

(d) Duration of Rights.—

(1) With respect to works of visual art created on or after the effective date set forth in section 610(a) of the Visual Artists Rights Act of 1990, the rights conferred by subsection (a) shall endure for a term consisting of the life of the author.

(2) With respect to works of visual art created before the effective date set forth in section 610(a) of the Visual Artists Rights Act of 1990, but title to which has not, as of such effective date, been transferred from the author, the rights conferred by subsection (a) shall be coextensive with, and shall expire at the same time as, the rights conferred by section 106.

(3) In the case of a joint work prepared by two or more authors, the rights conferred by subsection (a) shall endure for a term consisting of the life of the last surviving author.

(4) All terms of the rights conferred by subsection (a) run to the end of the calendar year in which they would otherwise expire.

(e) Transfer and Waiver.—

(1) The rights conferred by subsection (a) may not be transferred, but those rights may be waived if the author expressly agrees to such waiver in a written instrument signed by the author. Such instrument shall specifically identify the work, and uses of that work, to which the waiver applies, and the waiver shall apply only to the work and uses so identified. In the case of a joint work prepared by two or more authors, a waiver of rights under this paragraph made by one such author waives such rights for all such authors.

(2) Ownership of the rights conferred by subsection (a) with respect to a work of visual art is distinct from ownership of any copy of that work, or of a copyright or any exclusive right under a copyright in that work. Transfer of ownership of any copy of a work of visual art, or of a copyright or any exclusive right under a copyright, shall not constitute a waiver of the rights conferred by subsection (a). Except as may otherwise be agreed by the author in a written instrument signed by the author, a waiver of the rights conferred by subsection (a) with respect to a work of visual art shall not constitute a transfer of ownership of any copy of that work, or of ownership of a copyright or of any exclusive right under a copyright in that work.

§ 107. Limitations on exclusive rights: Fair use

Notwithstanding the provisions of sections 106 and 106A, the fair use of a copyrighted work, including such use by reproduction in copies or phonorecords or by any other means specified by that section, for purposes such as criticism, comment, news reporting, teaching (including multiple copies for classroom use), scholarship, or research, is not an infringement of copyright. In determining whether the use made of a work in any particular case is a fair use the factors to be considered shall include—

> (1) the purpose and character of the use, including whether such use is of a commercial nature or is for nonprofit educational purposes;
>
> (2) the nature of the copyrighted work;
>
> (3) the amount and substantiality of the portion used in relation to the copyrighted work as a whole; and
>
> (4) the effect of the use upon the potential market for or value of the copyrighted work.

The fact that a work is unpublished shall not itself bar a finding of fair use if such finding is made upon consideration of all the above factors.

...

§ 109. Limitations on exclusive rights: Effect of transfer of particular copy or phonorecord

(a) Notwithstanding the provisions of section 106(3), the owner of a particular copy or phonorecord lawfully made under this title, or any person authorized by such owner, is entitled, without the authority of the copyright owner, to sell or otherwise dispose of the possession of that copy or phonorecord...

(c) Notwithstanding the provisions of section 106(5), the owner of a particular copy lawfully made under this title, or any person authorized by such owner, is entitled, without the authority of the copyright owner, to display that copy publicly, either directly or by the projection of no more than one image at a time, to viewers present at the place where the copy is located.

(d) The privileges prescribed by subsections (a) and (c) do not, unless authorized by the copyright owner, extend to any person who has acquired possession of the copy or phonorecord from the copyright owner, by rental, lease, loan, or otherwise, without acquiring ownership of it.

...

§ 114. Scope of exclusive rights in sound recordings

(a) The exclusive rights of the owner of copyright in a sound recording are limited to the rights specified by clauses (1), (2), (3) and (6) of section 106, and do not include any right of performance under section 106(4).

(b) The exclusive right of the owner of copyright in a sound recording under clause (1) of section 106 is limited to the right to duplicate the sound recording in the form of phonorecords or copies that directly or indirectly recapture the actual sounds fixed in the recording. The exclusive right of the owner of copyright in a sound recording under clause (2) of section 106 is limited to the right to prepare a derivative work in which the actual sounds fixed in the sound recording are rearranged, remixed, or otherwise altered in sequence or quality. The exclusive rights of the owner of copyright in a sound recording under clauses (1) and (2) of section 106 do not extend to the making or duplication of another sound recording that consists entirely of an independent fixation of other sounds, even though such sounds imitate or simulate those in the copyrighted sound recording. The exclusive rights of the owner of copyright in a sound recording under clauses (1), (2), and (3) of section 106 do not apply to sound recordings included in educational television and radio programs (as defined in section 397 of title 47) distributed or transmitted by or through public broadcasting entities (as defined by section 118(f)): Provided, That copies or phonorecords of said programs are not commercially distributed by or through public broadcasting entities to the general public.

(c) This section does not limit or impair the exclusive right to perform publicly, by means of a phonorecord, any of the works specified by section 106(4).

...

§ 117.   Limitations on exclusive rights: Computer programs

(a) Making of Additional Copy or Adaptation by Owner of Copy.—Notwithstanding the provisions of section 106, it is not an infringement for the owner of a copy of a computer program to make or authorize the making of another copy or adaptation of that computer program provided:

    (1) that such a new copy or adaptation is created as an essential step in the utilization of the computer program in conjunction with a machine and that it is used in no other manner, or

    (2) that such new copy or adaptation is for archival purposes only and that all archival copies are destroyed in the event that continued possession of the computer program should cease to be rightful.

...

Chapter 2.   Copyright Ownership and Transfer

§ 201.   Ownership of copyright

(a) Initial Ownership.—Copyright in a work protected under this title vests initially in the author or authors of the work. The authors of a joint work are coowners of copyright in the work.

(b) Works Made for Hire.—In the case of a work made for hire, the employer or other person for whom the work was prepared is considered the author for purposes of this title, and, unless the parties have expressly agreed otherwise in a written instrument signed by them, owns all of the rights comprised in the copyright.

(c) Contributions to Collective Works.—Copyright in each separate contribution to a collective work is distinct from copyright in the collective work as a whole, and vests initially in the author of the contribution. In the absence of an express transfer of the copyright or of any rights under it, the owner of copyright in the collective work is presumed to have acquired only the privilege of reproducing and distributing the contribution as part of that particular collective work, any revision of that collective work, and any later collective work in the same series.

(d) Transfer of Ownership.—

    (1) The ownership of a copyright may be transferred in whole or in part by any means of conveyance or by operation of law, and may be bequeathed by will or pass as personal property by the applicable laws of intestate succession.

    (2) Any of the exclusive rights comprised in a copyright, including any subdivision of any of the rights specified by section 106, may be transferred as provided by clause (1) and owned separately. The owner of any particular exclusive right is entitled, to the extent of that right, to all of the protection and remedies accorded to the copyright owner by this title.

(e) Involuntary Transfer.—When an individual author's ownership of a copyright, or of any of the exclusive rights under a copyright, has not previously been transferred voluntarily by that individual author, no action by any governmental body or other official or organization purporting to seize, expropriate, transfer, or exercise rights of ownership with respect to the copyright, or any of the exclusive rights under a copyright, shall be given effect under this title, except as provided under title 11.

§ 202.   Ownership of copyright as distinct from ownership of material object

Ownership of a copyright, or of any of the exclusive rights under a copyright, is distinct from ownership of any material object in which the work is embodied. Transfer of ownership of any material object, including the copy or phonorecord in which the work is first fixed, does not of itself convey any rights in the copyrighted work embodied in the object; nor, in the absence of an agreement, does transfer of ownership of a copyright or of any exclusive rights under a copyright convey property rights in any material object.

...

Chapter 5.   Copyright Infringement and Remedies

§ 501.   Infringement of copyright

(a) Anyone who violates any of the exclusive rights of the copyright owner as provided by sections 106 through 122 or of the author as provided in section 106A(a), or who imports copies or phonorecords into the United States in violation of section 602, is an infringer of the copyright or right of the author, as the case may be. For purposes of this chapter (other than section 506), any reference to copyright shall be deemed to include the rights conferred by section 106A(a). As used in this subsection, the term 'anyone' includes any State, any instrumentality of a State, and any officer or employee of a State or instrumentality of a State acting in his or her official capacity. Any State, and any such instrumentality, officer, or employee, shall be subject to the provisions of this title in the same manner and to the same extent as any nongovernmental entity.

(b) The legal or beneficial owner of an exclusive right under a copyright is entitled, subject to the requirements of section 411, to institute an action for any infringement of that particular right committed while he or she is the owner of it. The court may require such owner to serve written notice of the action with a copy of the complaint upon any person shown, by the records of the Copyright Office or otherwise, to have or claim an interest in the copyright, and shall require that such notice be served upon any person whose interest is likely to be affected by a decision in the case. The court may require the joinder, and shall permit the intervention, of any person having or claiming an interest in the copyright.

...

§ 512.   Limitations on liability relating to material online

(a) Transitory Digital Network Communications.—A service provider shall not be liable for monetary relief, or, except as provided in subsection (j), for injunctive or other equitable relief, for infringement of copyright by reason of the provider's transmitting, routing, or providing connections for, material through a system or network controlled or operated by or for the service provider, or by reason of the intermediate and transient storage of that material in the course of such transmitting, routing, or providing connections, if—

(1) the transmission of the material was initiated by or at the direction of a person other than the service provider;

(2) the transmission, routing, provision of connections, or storage is carried out through an automatic technical process without selection of the material by the service provider;

(3) the service provider does not select the recipients of the material except as an automatic response to the request of another person;

(4) no copy of the material made by the service provider in the course of such intermediate or transient storage is maintained on the system or network in a manner ordinarily accessible to anyone other than anticipated recipients, and no such copy is maintained on the system or network in a manner ordinarily accessible to such anticipated recipients for a longer period than is reasonably necessary for the transmission, routing, or provision of connections; and

(5) the material is transmitted through the system or network without modification of its content.

(b) System Caching.—

(1) Limitation on liability.—A service provider shall not be liable for monetary relief, or, except as provided in subsection (j), for injunctive or other equitable relief, for infringement of copyright by reason of the intermediate and temporary storage of material on a system or network controlled or operated by or for the service provider in a case in which—

(A) the material is made available online by a person other than the service provider;

(B) the material is transmitted from the person described in subparagraph (A) through the system or network to a person other than the person described in subparagraph (A) at the direction of that other person; and

(C) the storage is carried out through an automatic technical process for the purpose of making the material available to users of the system or network who, after the material is transmitted as described in subparagraph (B), request access to the material from the person described in subparagraph (A), if the conditions set forth in paragraph (2) are met.

(2) Conditions.—The conditions referred to in paragraph (1) are that—

(A) the material described in paragraph (1) is transmitted to the subsequent users described in paragraph (1)(C) without modification to its content from the manner in which the material was transmitted from the person described in paragraph (1)(A);

(B) the service provider described in paragraph (1) complies with rules concerning the refreshing, reloading, or other updating of the material when specified by the person making the material available online in accordance with a generally accepted industry standard data communications protocol for the system or network through which that person makes the material available, except that this subparagraph applies only if those rules are not used by the person described in paragraph (1)(A) to prevent or unreasonably impair the intermediate storage to which this subsection applies;

(C) the service provider does not interfere with the ability of technology associated with the material to return to the person described in paragraph (1)(A) the information that would have been available to that person if the material had been obtained by the subsequent users described in paragraph (1)(C) directly from that person, except that this subparagraph applies only if that technology—

(i)   does not significantly interfere with the performance of the provider's system or network or with the intermediate storage of the material;

(ii) is consistent with generally accepted industry standard communications protocols; and

(iii) does not extract information from the provider's system or network other than the information that would have been available to the person described in paragraph (1)(A) if the subsequent users had gained access to the material directly from that person;

(D) if the person described in paragraph (1)(A) has in effect a condition that a person must meet prior to having access to the material, such as a condition based on payment of a fee or provision of a password or other information, the service provider permits access to the stored material in significant part only to users of its system or network that have met those conditions and only in accordance with those conditions; and

(E) if the person described in paragraph (1)(A) makes that material available online without the authorization of the copyright owner of the material, the service provider responds expeditiously to remove, or disable access to, the material that is claimed to be infringing upon notification of claimed infringement as described in subsection (c)(3), except that this subparagraph applies only if—

(i)   the material has previously been removed from the originating site or access to it has been disabled, or a court has ordered that the material be removed from the originating site or that access to the material on the originating site be disabled; and

      (ii) the party giving the notification includes in the notification a statement confirming that the material has been removed from the originating site or access to it has been disabled or that a court has ordered that the material be removed from the originating site or that access to the material on the originating site be disabled.

(c) Information Residing on Systems or Networks at Direction of Users.—

  (1) In general.—A service provider shall not be liable for monetary relief, or, except as provided in subsection (j), for injunctive or other equitable relief, for infringement of copyright by reason of the storage at the direction of a user of material that resides on a system or network controlled or operated by or for the service provider, if the service provider—

    (A) (i) does not have actual knowledge that the material or an activity using the material on the system or network is infringing;

        (ii) in the absence of such actual knowledge, is not aware of facts or circumstances from which infringing activity is apparent; or

        (iii) upon obtaining such knowledge or awareness, acts expeditiously to remove, or disable access to, the material;

    (B) does not receive a financial benefit directly attributable to the infringing activity, in a case in which the service provider has the right and ability to control such activity; and

    (C) upon notification of claimed infringement as described in paragraph (3), responds expeditiously to remove, or disable access to, the material that is claimed to be infringing or to be the subject of infringing activity.

  (2) Designated agent.—The limitations on liability established in this subsection apply to a service provider only if the service provider has designated an agent to receive notifications of claimed infringement described in paragraph (3), by making available through its service, including on its website in a location accessible to the public, and by providing to the Copyright Office, substantially the following information:

    (A) the name, address, phone number, and electronic mail address of the agent;

    (B) other contact information which the Register of Copyrights may deem appropriate.

The Register of Copyrights shall maintain a current directory of agents available to the public for inspection, including through the Internet, and may require payment of a fee by service providers to cover the costs of maintaining the directory.

  (3) Elements of notification.—

    (A) To be effective under this subsection, a notification of claimed infringement must be a written communication provided to the designated agent of a service provider that includes substantially the following:

      (i) A physical or electronic signature of a person authorized to act on behalf of the owner of an exclusive right that is allegedly infringed.

      (ii) Identification of the copyrighted work claimed to have been infringed, or, if multiple copyrighted works at a single online site are covered by a single notification, a representative list of such works at that site.

      (iii) Identification of the material that is claimed to be infringing or to be the subject of infringing activity and that is to be removed or access to which is to be disabled, and information reasonably sufficient to permit the service provider to locate the material.

      (iv) Information reasonably sufficient to permit the service provider to contact the complaining party, such as an address, telephone number, and, if available, an electronic mail address at which the complaining party may be contacted.

      (v) A statement that the complaining party has a good faith belief that use of the material in the manner complained of is not authorized by the copyright owner, its agent, or the law.

      (vi) A statement that the information in the notification is accurate, and under penalty of perjury, that the complaining party is authorized to act on behalf of the owner of an exclusive right that is allegedly infringed.

(B) (i) Subject to clause (ii), a notification from a copyright owner or from a person authorized to act on behalf of the copyright owner that fails to comply substantially with the provisions of subparagraph (A) shall not be considered under paragraph (1)(A) in determining whether a service provider has actual knowledge or is aware of facts or circumstances from which infringing activity is apparent.

(ii) In a case in which the notification that is provided to the service provider's designated agent fails to comply substantially with all the provisions of subparagraph (A) but substantially complies with clauses (ii), (iii), and (iv) of subparagraph (A), clause (i) of this subparagraph applies only if the service provider promptly attempts to contact the person making the notification or takes other reasonable steps to assist in the receipt of notification that substantially complies with all the provisions of subparagraph (A).

(d) Information Location Tools.—A service provider shall not be liable for monetary relief, or, except as provided in subsection (j), for injunctive or other equitable relief, for infringement of copyright by reason of the provider referring or linking users to an online location containing infringing material or infringing activity, by using information location tools, including a directory, index, reference, pointer, or hypertext link, if the service provider—

(1) (A) does not have actual knowledge that the material or activity is infringing;

(B) in the absence of such actual knowledge, is not aware of facts or circumstances from which infringing activity is apparent; or

(C) upon obtaining such knowledge or awareness, acts expeditiously to remove, or disable access to, the material;

(2) does not receive a financial benefit directly attributable to the infringing activity, in a case in which the service provider has the right and ability to control such activity; and

(3) upon notification of claimed infringement as described in subsection (c)(3), responds expeditiously to remove, or disable access to, the material that is claimed to be infringing or to be the subject of infringing activity, except that, for purposes of this paragraph, the information described in subsection (c)(3)(A)(iii) shall be identification of the reference or link, to material or activity claimed to be infringing, that is to be removed or access to which is to be disabled, and information reasonably sufficient to permit the service provider to locate that reference or link.

(e) Limitation on Liability of Nonprofit Educational Institutions.—

(1) When a public or other nonprofit institution of higher education is a service provider, and when a faculty member or graduate student who is an employee of such institution is performing a teaching or research function, for the purposes of subsections (a) and (b) such faculty member or graduate student shall be considered to be a person other than the institution, and for the purposes of subsections (c) and (d) such faculty member's or graduate student's knowledge or awareness of his or her infringing activities shall not be attributed to the institution, if—

(A) such faculty member's or graduate student's infringing activities do not involve the provision of online access to instructional materials that are or were required or recommended, within the preceding 3-year period, for a course taught at the institution by such faculty member or graduate student;

(B) the institution has not, within the preceding 3-year period, received more than 2 notifications described in subsection (c)(3) of claimed infringement by such faculty member or graduate student, and such notifications of claimed infringement were not actionable under subsection (f); and

(C) the institution provides to all users of its system or network informational materials that accurately describe, and promote compliance with, the laws of the United States relating to copyright.

(2) For the purposes of this subsection, the limitations on injunctive relief contained in subsections (j)(2) and (j)(3), but not those in (j)(1), shall apply.

(f) Misrepresentations.—Any person who knowingly materially misrepresents under this section—

    (1) that material or activity is infringing, or

    (2) that material or activity was removed or disabled by mistake or misidentification,

shall be liable for any damages, including costs and attorneys' fees, incurred by the alleged infringer, by any copyright owner or copyright owner's authorized licensee, or by a service provider, who is injured by such misrepresentation, as the result of the service provider relying upon such misrepresentation in removing or disabling access to the material or activity claimed to be infringing, or in replacing the removed material or ceasing to disable access to it.

(g) Replacement of Removed or Disabled Material and Limitation on Other Liability.—

    (1) No liability for taking down generally.—Subject to paragraph (2), a service provider shall not be liable to any person for any claim based on the service provider's good faith disabling of access to, or removal of, material or activity claimed to be infringing or based on facts or circumstances from which infringing activity is apparent, regardless of whether the material or activity is ultimately determined to be infringing.

    (2) Exception.—Paragraph (1) shall not apply with respect to material residing at the direction of a subscriber of the service provider on a system or network controlled or operated by or for the service provider that is removed, or to which access is disabled by the service provider, pursuant to a notice provided under subsection (c)(1)(C), unless the service provider—

        (A) takes reasonable steps promptly to notify the subscriber that it has removed or disabled access to the material;

        (B) upon receipt of a counter notification described in paragraph (3), promptly provides the person who provided the notification under subsection (c)(1)(C) with a copy of the counter notification, and informs that person that it will replace the removed material or cease disabling access to it in 10 business days; and

        (C) replaces the removed material and ceases disabling access to it not less than 10, nor more than 14, business days following receipt of the counter notice, unless its designated agent first receives notice from the person who submitted the notification under subsection (c)(1)(C) that such person has filed an action seeking a court order to restrain the subscriber from engaging in infringing activity relating to the material on the service provider's system or network.

    (3) Contents of counter notification.—To be effective under this subsection, a counter notification must be a written communication provided to the service provider's designated agent that includes substantially the following:

        (A) A physical or electronic signature of the subscriber.

        (B) Identification of the material that has been removed or to which access has been disabled and the location at which the material appeared before it was removed or access to it was disabled.

        (C) A statement under penalty of perjury that the subscriber has a good faith belief that the material was removed or disabled as a result of mistake or misidentification of the material to be removed or disabled.

        (D) The subscriber's name, address, and telephone number, and a statement that the subscriber consents to the jurisdiction of Federal District Court for the judicial district in which the address is located, or if the subscriber's address is outside of the United States, for any judicial district in which the service provider may be found, and that the subscriber will accept service of process from the person who provided notification under subsection (c)(1)(C) or an agent of such person.

    (4) Limitation on other liability.—A service provider's compliance with paragraph (2) shall not subject the service provider to liability for copyright infringement with respect to the material identified in the notice provided under subsection (c)(1)(C).

(h) Subpoena to Identify Infringer.—

    (1) Request.—A copyright owner or a person authorized to act on the owner's behalf may request the clerk of any United States district court to issue a subpoena to a service provider for identification of an alleged infringer in accordance with this subsection.

(2) Contents of request.—The request may be made by filing with the clerk—

    (A) a copy of a notification described in subsection (c)(3)(A);

    (B) a proposed subpoena; and

    (C) a sworn declaration to the effect that the purpose for which the subpoena is sought is to obtain the identity of an alleged infringer and that such information will only be used for the purpose of protecting rights under this title.

(3) Contents of subpoena.—The subpoena shall authorize and order the service provider receiving the notification and the subpoena to expeditiously disclose to the copyright owner or person authorized by the copyright owner information sufficient to identify the alleged infringer of the material described in the notification to the extent such information is available to the service provider.

(4) Basis for granting subpoena.—If the notification filed satisfies the provisions of subsection (c)(3)(A), the proposed subpoena is in proper form, and the accompanying declaration is properly executed, the clerk shall expeditiously issue and sign the proposed subpoena and return it to the requester for delivery to the service provider.

(5) Actions of service provider receiving subpoena.—Upon receipt of the issued subpoena, either accompanying or subsequent to the receipt of a notification described in subsection (c)(3)(A), the service provider shall expeditiously disclose to the copyright owner or person authorized by the copyright owner the information required by the subpoena, notwithstanding any other provision of law and regardless of whether the service provider responds to the notification.

(6) Rules applicable to subpoena.—Unless otherwise provided by this section or by applicable rules of the court, the procedure for issuance and delivery of the subpoena, and the remedies for noncompliance with the subpoena, shall be governed to the greatest extent practicable by those provisions of the Federal Rules of Civil Procedure governing the issuance, service, and enforcement of a subpoena *duces tecum*.

(i) Conditions for Eligibility.—

(1) Accommodation of technology.—The limitations on liability established by this section shall apply to a service provider only if the service provider—

    (A) has adopted and reasonably implemented, and informs subscribers and account holders of the service provider's system or network of, a policy that provides for the termination in appropriate circumstances of subscribers and account holders of the service provider's system or network who are repeat infringers; and

    (B) accommodates and does not interfere with standard technical measures.

(2) Definition.—As used in this subsection, the term 'standard technical measures' means technical measures that are used by copyright owners to identify or protect copyrighted works and—

    (A) have been developed pursuant to a broad consensus of copyright owners and service providers in an open, fair, voluntary, multi-industry standards process;

    (B) are available to any person on reasonable and nondiscriminatory terms; and

    (C) do not impose substantial costs on service providers or substantial burdens on their systems or networks.

(j) Injunctions.—The following rules shall apply in the case of any application for an injunction under section 502 against a service provider that is not subject to monetary remedies under this section:

(1) Scope of relief.—

    (A) With respect to conduct other than that which qualifies for the limitation on remedies set forth in subsection (a), the court may grant injunctive relief with respect to a service provider only in one or more of the following forms:

        (i) An order restraining the service provider from providing access to infringing material or activity residing at a particular online site on the provider's system or network.

        (ii) An order restraining the service provider from providing access to a subscriber or account holder of the service provider's system or network who is engaging in infringing activity and is identified in the order, by terminating the accounts of the subscriber or account holder that are specified in the order.

    (iii) Such other injunctive relief as the court may consider necessary to prevent or restrain infringement of copyrighted material specified in the order of the court at a particular online location, if such relief is the least burdensome to the service provider among the forms of relief comparably effective for that purpose.

  (B) If the service provider qualifies for the limitation on remedies described in subsection (a), the court may only grant injunctive relief in one or both of the following forms:

    (i) An order restraining the service provider from providing access to a subscriber or account holder of the service provider's system or network who is using the provider's service to engage in infringing activity and is identified in the order, by terminating the accounts of the subscriber or account holder that are specified in the order.

    (ii) An order restraining the service provider from providing access, by taking reasonable steps specified in the order to block access, to a specific, identified, online location outside the United States.

  (2) Considerations.—The court, in considering the relevant criteria for injunctive relief under applicable law, shall consider—

    (A) whether such an injunction, either alone or in combination with other such injunctions issued against the same service provider under this subsection, would significantly burden either the provider or the operation of the provider's system or network;

    (B) the magnitude of the harm likely to be suffered by the copyright owner in the digital network environment if steps are not taken to prevent or restrain the infringement;

    (C) whether implementation of such an injunction would be technically feasible and effective, and would not interfere with access to noninfringing material at other online locations; and

    (D) whether other less burdensome and comparably effective means of preventing or restraining access to the infringing material are available.

  (3) Notice and ex parte orders.—Injunctive relief under this subsection shall be available only after notice to the service provider and an opportunity for the service provider to appear are provided, except for orders ensuring the preservation of evidence or other orders having no material adverse effect on the operation of the service provider's communications network.

(k) Definitions.—

  (1) Service provider.—

    (A) As used in subsection (a), the term 'service provider' means an entity offering the transmission, routing, or providing of connections for digital online communications, between or among points specified by a user, of material of the user's choosing, without modification to the content of the material as sent or received.

    (B) As used in this section, other than subsection (a), the term 'service provider' means a provider of online services or network access, or the operator of facilities therefor, and includes an entity described in subparagraph (A).

  (2) Monetary relief.—As used in this section, the term 'monetary relief' means damages, costs, attorneys' fees, and any other form of monetary payment.

(l) Other Defenses Not Affected.—The failure of a service provider's conduct to qualify for limitation of liability under this section shall not bear adversely upon the consideration of a defense by the service provider that the service provider's conduct is not infringing under this title or any other defense.

(m) Protection of Privacy.—Nothing in this section shall be construed to condition the applicability of subsections (a) through (d) on—

  (1) a service provider monitoring its service or affirmatively seeking facts indicating infringing activity, except to the extent consistent with a standard technical measure complying with the provisions of subsection (i); or

  (2) a service provider gaining access to, removing, or disabling access to material in cases in which such conduct is prohibited by law.

(n) Construction.—Subsections (a), (b), (c), and (d) describe separate and distinct functions for purposes of applying this section. Whether a service provider qualifies for the limitation on liability in any one of those subsections shall be based solely on the criteria in that subsection, and shall not affect a determination of whether that service provider qualifies for the limitations on liability under any other such subsection.

...

Chapter 11.   Sound Recordings and Music Videos

§ 1101.   Unauthorized fixation and trafficking in sound recordings and music videos

(a) Unauthorized Acts.—Anyone who, without the consent of the performer or performers involved—

(1) fixes the sounds or sounds and images of a live musical performance in a copy or phonorecord, or reproduces copies or phonorecords of such a performance from an unauthorized fixation,

(2) transmits or otherwise communicates to the public the sounds or sounds and images of a live musical performance, or

(3) distributes or offers to distribute, sells or offers to sell, rents or offers to rent, or traffics in any copy or phonorecord fixed as described in paragraph (1), regardless of whether the fixations occurred in the United States,

shall be subject to the remedies provided in sections 502 through 505, to the same extent as an infringer of copyright.

(b) Definition.—As used in this section, the term 'traffic in' means transport, transfer, or otherwise dispose of, to another, as consideration for anything of value, or make or obtain control of with intent to transport, transfer, or dispose of.

(c) Applicability.—This section shall apply to any act or acts that occur on or after the date of the enactment of the Uruguay Round Agreements Act.

(d) State Law Not Preempted.—Nothing in this section may be construed to annul or limit any rights or remedies under the common law or statutes of any State.

Chapter 12.   Copyright Protection and Management Systems

§ 1201.   Circumvention of copyright protection systems

(a) Violations Regarding Circumvention of Technological Measures.—

(1) (A) No person shall circumvent a technological measure that effectively controls access to a work protected under this title. The prohibition contained in the preceding sentence shall take effect at the end of the 2-year period beginning on the date of the enactment of this chapter.

(B) The prohibition contained in subparagraph (A) shall not apply to persons who are users of a copyrighted work which is in a particular class of works, if such persons are, or are likely to be in the succeeding 3-year period, adversely affected by virtue of such prohibition in their ability to make noninfringing uses of that particular class of works under this title, as determined under subparagraph (C).

(C) During the 2-year period described in subparagraph (A), and during each succeeding 3-year period, the Librarian of Congress, upon the recommendation of the Register of Copyrights, who shall consult with the Assistant Secretary for Communications and Information of the Department of Commerce and report and comment on his or her views in making such recommendation, shall make the determination in a rulemaking proceeding for purposes of subparagraph (B) of whether persons who are users of a copyrighted work are, or are likely to be in the succeeding 3-year period, adversely affected by the prohibition under subparagraph (A) in their ability to make noninfringing uses under this title of a particular class of copyrighted works. In conducting such rulemaking, the Librarian shall examine—

  (i) the availability for use of copyrighted works;

  (ii) the availability for use of works for nonprofit archival, preservation, and educational purposes;

  (iii) the impact that the prohibition on the circumvention of technological measures applied to copyrighted works has on criticism, comment, news reporting, teaching, scholarship, or research;

  (iv) the effect of circumvention of technological measures on the market for or value of copyrighted works; and

  (v) such other factors as the Librarian considers appropriate.

(D) The Librarian shall publish any class of copyrighted works for which the Librarian has determined, pursuant to the rulemaking conducted under subparagraph (C), that noninfringing uses by persons who are users of a copyrighted work are, or are likely to be, adversely affected, and the prohibition contained in subparagraph (A) shall not apply to such users with respect to such class of works for the ensuing 3-year period.

(E) Neither the exception under subparagraph (B) from the applicability of the prohibition contained in subparagraph (A), nor any determination made in a rulemaking conducted under subparagraph (C), may be used as a defense in any action to enforce any provision of this title other than this paragraph.

(2) No person shall manufacture, import, offer to the public, provide, or otherwise traffic in any technology, product, service, device, component, or part thereof, that—

(A) is primarily designed or produced for the purpose of circumventing a technological measure that effectively controls access to a work protected under this title;

(B) has only limited commercially significant purpose or use other than to circumvent a technological measure that effectively controls access to a work protected under this title; or

(C) is marketed by that person or another acting in concert with that person with that person's knowledge for use in circumventing a technological measure that effectively controls access to a work protected under this title.

(3) As used in this subsection—

(A) to 'circumvent a technological measure' means to descramble a scrambled work, to decrypt an encrypted work, or otherwise to avoid, bypass, remove, deactivate, or impair a technological measure, without the authority of the copyright owner; and

(B) a technological measure 'effectively controls access to a work' if the measure, in the ordinary course of its operation, requires the application of information, or a process or a treatment, with the authority of the copyright owner, to gain access to the work.

(b) Additional Violations.—

(1) No person shall manufacture, import, offer to the public, provide, or otherwise traffic in any technology, product, service, device, component, or part thereof, that—

(A) is primarily designed or produced for the purpose of circumventing protection afforded by a technological measure that effectively protects a right of a copyright owner under this title in a work or a portion thereof;

(B) has only limited commercially significant purpose or use other than to circumvent protection afforded by a technological measure that effectively protects a right of a copyright owner under this title in a work or a portion thereof; or

(C) is marketed by that person or another acting in concert with that person with that person's knowledge for use in circumventing protection afforded by a technological measure that effectively protects a right of a copyright owner under this title in a work or a portion thereof.

(2) As used in this subsection—

(A) to 'circumvent protection afforded by a technological measure' means avoiding, bypassing, removing, deactivating, or otherwise impairing a technological measure; and

(B) a technological measure 'effectively protects a right of a copyright owner under this title' if the measure, in the ordinary course of its operation, prevents, restricts, or otherwise limits the exercise of a right of a copyright owner under this title.

(c) Other Rights, Etc., Not Affected.—

(1) Nothing in this section shall affect rights, remedies, limitations, or defenses to copyright infringement, including fair use, under this title.

(2) Nothing in this section shall enlarge or diminish vicarious or contributory liability for copyright infringement in connection with any technology, product, service, device, component, or part thereof.

(3) Nothing in this section shall require that the design of, or design and selection of parts and components for, a consumer electronics, telecommunications, or computing product provide for a response to any particular technological measure, so long as such part or component, or the product in which such part or component is integrated, does not otherwise fall within the prohibitions of subsection (a)(2) or (b)(1).

(4) Nothing in this section shall enlarge or diminish any rights of free speech or the press for activities using consumer electronics, telecommunications, or computing products.

(d) Exemption for Nonprofit Libraries, Archives, and Educational Institutions.—
    …

(e) Law Enforcement, Intelligence, and Other Government Activities.—This section does not prohibit any lawfully authorized investigative, protective, information security, or intelligence activity of an officer, agent, or employee of the United States, a State, or a political subdivision of a State, or a person acting pursuant to a contract with the United States, a State, or a political subdivision of a State. For purposes of this subsection, the term 'information security' means activities carried out in order to identify and address the vulnerabilities of a government computer, computer system, or computer network.

(f) Reverse Engineering.—
    …

(g) Encryption Research.—
    …

(h) Exceptions Regarding Minors.—In applying subsection (a) to a component or part, the court may consider the necessity for its intended and actual incorporation in a technology, product, service, or device, which—

(1) does not itself violate the provisions of this title; and

(2) has the sole purpose to prevent the access of minors to material on the Internet.

(i) Protection of Personally Identifying Information.—
    …

(j) Security Testing.—
    …

(k) Certain Analog Devices and Certain Technological Measures.—
    …

(5) Violations.—Any violation of paragraph (1) of this subsection shall be treated as a violation of subsection (b)(1) of this section. Any violation of paragraph (2) of this subsection shall be deemed an 'act of circumvention' for the purposes of section 1203(c)(3)(A) of this chapter.

§ 1202. Integrity of copyright management information

(a) False Copyright Management Information.—No person shall knowingly and with the intent to induce, enable, facilitate, or conceal infringement—

(1) provide copyright management information that is false, or

(2) distribute or import for distribution copyright management information that is false.

(b) Removal or Alteration of Copyright Management Information.—No person shall, without the authority of the copyright owner or the law—

(1) intentionally remove or alter any copyright management information,

(2) distribute or import for distribution copyright management information knowing that the copyright management information has been removed or altered without authority of the copyright owner or the law, or

(3) distribute, import for distribution, or publicly perform works, copies of works, or phonorecords, knowing that copyright management information has been removed or altered without authority of the copyright owner or the law,

knowing, or, with respect to civil remedies under section 1203, having reasonable grounds to know, that it will induce, enable, facilitate, or conceal an infringement of any right under this title.

(c) Definition.—As used in this section, the term 'copyright management information' means any of the following information conveyed in connection with copies or phonorecords of a work or performances or displays of a work, including in digital form, except that such term does not include any personally identifying information about a user of a work or of a copy, phonorecord, performance, or display of a work:

(1) The title and other information identifying the work, including the information set forth on a notice of copyright.

(2) The name of, and other identifying information about, the author of a work.

(3) The name of, and other identifying information about, the copyright owner of the work, including the information set forth in a notice of copyright.

(4) With the exception of public performances of works by radio and television broadcast stations, the name of, and other identifying information about, a performer whose performance is fixed in a work other than an audiovisual work.

(5) With the exception of public performances of works by radio and television broadcast stations, in the case of an audiovisual work, the name of, and other identifying information about, a writer, performer, or director who is credited in the audiovisual work.

(6) Terms and conditions for use of the work.

(7) Identifying numbers or symbols referring to such information or links to such information.

(8) Such other information as the Register of Copyrights may prescribe by regulation, except that the Register of Copyrights may not require the provision of any information concerning the user of a copyrighted work.

. . .

§ 1203. Civil remedies

(a) Civil Actions.—Any person injured by a violation of section 1201 or 1202 may bring a civil action in an appropriate United States district court for such violation.

. . .

§ 1204. Criminal offenses and penalties

(a) In General.—Any person who violates section 1201 or 1202 willfully and for purposes of commercial advantage or private financial gain—

(1) shall be fined not more than $500,000 or imprisoned for not more than 5 years, or both, for the first offense; and

(2) shall be fined not more than $1,000,000 or imprisoned for not more than 10 years, or both, for any subsequent offense.

(b) Limitation for Nonprofit Library, Archives, Educational Institution, or Public Broadcasting Entity.—Subsection (a) shall not apply to a nonprofit library, archives, educational institution, or public broadcasting entity (as defined under section 118(f)).

. . .

Chapter 13.   Protection of Original Designs

§ 1301. Designs protected

(a) Designs protected.—

(1) In general.—The designer or other owner of an original design of a useful article which makes the article attractive or distinctive in appearance to the purchasing or using public may secure the protection provided by this chapter upon complying with and subject to this chapter.

(2) Vessel features.—The design of a vessel hull, deck, or combination of a hull and deck, including a plug or mold, is subject to protection under this chapter, notwithstanding section 1302(4).

(3) Exceptions.—Department of Defense rights in a registered design under this chapter, including the right to build to such registered design, shall be determined solely by operation of section 2320 of title 10 or by the instrument under which the design was developed for the United States Government.

(b) Definitions.—For the purpose of this chapter, the following terms have the following meanings:

(1) A design is 'original' if it is the result of the designer's creative endeavor that provides a distinguishable variation over prior work pertaining to similar articles which is more than merely trivial and has not been copied from another source.

(2) A 'useful article' is a vessel hull or deck, including a plug or mold, which in normal use has an intrinsic utilitarian function that is not merely to portray the appearance of the article or to convey information. An article which normally is part of a useful article shall be deemed to be a useful article.

(3) A 'vessel' is a craft—

(A) that is designed and capable of independently steering a course on or through water through its own means of propulsion; and

(B) that is designed and capable of carrying and transporting one or more passengers.

(4) A 'hull' is the exterior frame or body of a vessel, exclusive of the deck, superstructure, masts, sails, yards, rigging, hardware, fixtures, and other attachments.

(5) A 'plug' means a device or model used to make a mold for the purpose of exact duplication, regardless of whether the device or model has an intrinsic utilitarian function that is not only to portray the appearance of the product or to convey information.

(6) A 'mold' means a matrix or form in which a substance for material is used, regardless of whether the matrix or form has an intrinsic utilitarian function that is not only to portray the appearance of the product or to convey information.

(7) A 'deck' is the horizontal surface of a vessel that covers the hull, including exterior cabin and cockpit surfaces, and exclusive of masts, sails, yards, rigging, hardware, fixtures, and other attachments.

§ 1302.   Designs not subject to protection

Protection under this chapter shall not be available for a design that is—

(1) not original;

(2) staple or commonplace, such as a standard geometric figure, a familiar symbol, an emblem, or a motif, or another shape, pattern, or configuration which has become standard, common, prevalent, or ordinary;

(3) different from a design excluded by paragraph (2) only in insignificant details or in elements which are variants commonly used in the relevant trades;

(4) dictated solely by a utilitarian function of the article that embodies it; or

(5) embodied in a useful article that was made public by the designer or owner in the United States or a foreign country more than 2 years before the date of the application for registration under this chapter.

...

§ 1308.   Exclusive rights

The owner of a design protected under this chapter has the exclusive right to—

(1) make, have made, or import, for sale or for use in trade, any useful article embodying that design; and

(2) sell or distribute for sale or for use in trade any useful article embodying that design.

§ 1309. Infringement

(a) Acts of Infringement.—Except as provided in subsection (b), it shall be infringement of the exclusive rights in a design protected under this chapter for any person, without the consent of the owner of the design, within the United States and during the term of such protection, to—

> (1) make, have made, or import, for sale or for use in trade, any infringing article as defined in subsection (e); or
>
> (2) sell or distribute for sale or for use in trade any such infringing article.

(b) Acts of Sellers and Distributors.—A seller or distributor of an infringing article who did not make or import the article shall be deemed to have infringed on a design protected under this chapter only if that person—

> (1) induced or acted in collusion with a manufacturer to make, or an importer to import such article, except that merely purchasing or giving an order to purchase such article in the ordinary course of business shall not of itself constitute such inducement or collusion; or
>
> (2) refused or failed, upon the request of the owner of the design, to make a prompt and full disclosure of that person's source of such article, and that person orders or reorders such article after receiving notice by registered or certified mail of the protection subsisting in the design.

(c) Acts without Knowledge.—It shall not be infringement under this section to make, have made, import, sell, or distribute, any article embodying a design which was created without knowledge that a design was protected under this chapter and was copied from such protected design.

(d) Acts in Ordinary Course of Business.—A person who incorporates into that person's product of manufacture an infringing article acquired from others in the ordinary course of business, or who, without knowledge of the protected design embodied in an infringing article, makes or processes the infringing article for the account of another person in the ordinary course of business, shall not be deemed to have infringed the rights in that design under this chapter except under a condition contained in paragraph (1) or (2) of subsection (b). Accepting an order or reorder from the source of the infringing article shall be deemed ordering or reordering within the meaning of subsection (b)(2).

(e) Infringing Article Defined.—As used in this section, an 'infringing article' is any article the design of which has been copied from a design protected under this chapter, without the consent of the owner of the protected design. An infringing article is not an illustration or picture of a protected design in an advertisement, book, periodical, newspaper, photograph, broadcast, motion picture, or similar medium. A design shall not be deemed to have been copied from a protected design if it is original and not substantially similar in appearance to a protected design.

(f) Establishing Originality.—The party to any action or proceeding under this chapter who alleges rights under this chapter in a design shall have the burden of establishing the design's originality whenever the opposing party introduces an earlier work which is identical to such design, or so similar as to make prima facie showing that such design was copied from such work.

(g) Reproduction for Teaching or Analysis.—It is not an infringement of the exclusive rights of a design owner for a person to reproduce the design in a useful article or in any other form solely for the purpose of teaching, analyzing, or evaluating the appearance, concepts, or techniques embodied in the design, or the function of the useful article embodying the design.

§ 1310. Application for registration

(a) Time Limit for Application for Registration.—Protection under this chapter shall be lost if application for registration of the design is not made within 2 years after the date on which the design is first made public.

(b) When Design Is Made Public.—A design is made public when an existing useful article embodying the design is anywhere publicly exhibited, publicly distributed, or offered for sale or sold to the public by the owner of the design or with the owner's consent.

(c) Application by Owner of Design.—Application for registration may be made by the owner of the design.

. . .

A3.   EUROPEAN UNION

Council Directive 93/83/EEC

of 27 September 1993 on the coordination of certain rules concerning copyright and rights related to copyright applicable to satellite broadcasting and cable retransmission

THE COUNCIL OF THE EUROPEAN COMMUNITIES,

Having regard to the Treaty establishing the European Economic Community, and in particular Articles 57(2) and 66 thereof,

Having regard to the proposal from the Commission,

In cooperation with the European Parliament,

Having regard to the opinion of the Economic and Social Committee,

(1) Whereas the objectives of the Community as laid down in the Treaty include establishing an ever closer union among the peoples of Europe, fostering closer relations between the States belonging to the Community and ensuring the economic and social progress of the Community countries by common action to eliminate the barriers which divide Europe;

(2) Whereas, to that end, the Treaty provides for the establishment of a common market and an area without internal frontiers; whereas measures to achieve this include the abolition of obstacles to the free movement of services and the institution of a system ensuring that competition in the common market is not distorted; whereas, to that end, the Council may adopt directives for the coordination of the provisions laid down by law, regulation or administrative action in Member States concerning the taking up and pursuit of activities as self-employed persons;

(3) Whereas broadcasts transmitted across frontiers within the Community, in particular by satellite and cable, are one of the most important ways of pursuing these Community objectives, which are at the same time political, economic, social, cultural and legal;

(4) Whereas the Council has already adopted Directive 89/552/EEC of 3 October 1989 on the coordination of certain provisions laid down by law, regulation or administrative action in Member States concerning the pursuit of television broadcasting activities which makes provision for the promotion of the distribution and production of European television programmes and for advertising and sponsorship, the protection of minors and the right of reply;

(5) Whereas, however, the achievement of these objectives in respect of crossborder satellite broadcasting and the cable retransmission of programmes from other Member States is currently still obstructed by a series of differences between national rules of copyright and some degree of legal uncertainty; whereas this means that holders of rights are exposed to the threat of seeing their works exploited without payment of remuneration or that the individual holders of exclusive rights in various Member States block the exploitation of their rights; whereas the legal uncertainty in particular constitutes a direct obstacle in the free circulation of programmes within the Community;

(6) Whereas a distinction is currently drawn for copyright purposes between communication to the public by direct satellite and communication to the public by communications satellite; whereas, since individual reception is possible and affordable nowadays with both types of satellite, there is no longer any justification for this differing legal treatment;

(7) Whereas the free broadcasting of programmes is further impeded by the current legal uncertainty over whether broadcasting by a satellite whose signals can be received directly affects the rights in the country of transmission only or in all countries of reception together; whereas, since communications satellites and direct satellites are treated alike for copyright purposes, this legal uncertainty now affects almost all programmes broadcast in the Community by satellite;

(8) Whereas, furthermore, legal certainty, which is a prerequisite for the free movement of broadcasts within the Community, is missing where programmes transmitted across frontiers are fed into and retransmitted through cable networks;

(9) Whereas the development of the acquisition of rights on a contractual basis by authorisation is already making a vigorous contribution to the creation of the desired European audiovisual area; whereas the continuation of such contractual agreements should be ensured and their smooth application in practice should be promoted wherever possible;

(10) Whereas at present cable operators in particular cannot be sure that they have actually acquired all the programme rights covered by such an agreement;

(11) Whereas, lastly, parties in different Member States are not all similarly bound by obligations which prevent them from refusing without valid reasons to negotiate on the acquisition of the rights necessary for cable distribution or allowing such negotiations to fail;

(12) Whereas the legal framework for the creation of a single audiovisual area laid down in Directive 89/552/EEC must, therefore, be supplemented with reference to copyright;

(13) Whereas, therefore, an end should be put to the differences of treatment of the transmission of programmes by communications satellite which exist in the Member States, so that the vital distinction throughout the Community becomes whether works and other protected subject matter are communicated to the public; whereas this will also ensure equal treatment of the suppliers of cross-border broadcasts, regardless of whether they use a direct broadcasting satellite or a communications satellite;

(14) Whereas the legal uncertainty regarding the rights to be acquired which impedes cross-border satellite broadcasting should be overcome by defining the notion of communication to the public by satellite at a Community level; whereas this definition should at the same time specify where the act of communication takes place; whereas such a definition is necessary to avoid the cumulative application of several national laws to one single act of broadcasting; whereas communication to the public by satellite occurs only when, and in the Member State where, the programme-carrying signals are introduced under the control and responsibility of the broadcasting organisation into an uninterrupted chain of communication leading to the satellite and down towards the earth; whereas normal technical procedures relating to the programme-carrying signals should not be considered as interruptions to the chain of broadcasting;

(15) Whereas the acquisition on a contractual basis of exclusive broadcasting rights should comply with any legislation on copyright and rights related to copyright in the Member State in which communication to the public by satellite occurs;

(16) Whereas the principle of contractual freedom on which the Directive is based will make it possible to continue limiting the exploitation of these rights, especially as far as certain technical means of transmission or certain language versions are concerned;

(17) Whereas, in arriving at the amount of the payment to be made for the rights acquired, the parties should take account of all aspects of the broadcast, such as the actual audience, the potential audience and the language version;

(18) Whereas the application of the country-of-origin principle contained in this Directive could pose a problem with regard to existing contracts; whereas this Directive should provide for a period of five years for existing contracts to be adapted, where necessary, in the light of the Directive; whereas the said country-of-origin principle should not, therefore, apply to existing contracts which expire before 1 January 2000; whereas if by that date parties still have an interest in the contract, the same parties should be entitled to renegotiate the conditions of the contract;

(19) Whereas existing international co-production agreements must be interpreted in the light of the economic purpose and scope envisaged by the parties upon signature; whereas in the past international co-production agreements have often not expressly and specifically addressed communication to the public by satellite within the meaning of this Directive a particular form

of exploitation; whereas the underlying philosophy of many existing international co-production agreements is that the rights in the co-production are exercised separately and independently by each co-producer, by dividing the exploitation rights between them along territorial lines; whereas, as a general rule, in the situation where a communication to the public by satellite authorised by one co-producer would prejudice the value of the exploitation rights of another co-producer, the interpretation of such an existing agreement would normally suggest that the latter co-producer would have to give his consent to the authorisation, by the former co-producer, of the communication to the public by satellite; whereas the language exclusivity of the latter co-producer will be prejudiced where the language version or versions of the communication to the public, including where the version is dubbed or subtitled, coincide(s) with the language or the languages widely understood in the territory allotted by the agreement to the latter co-producer; whereas the notion of exclusivity should be understood in a wider sense where the communication to the public by satellite concerns a work which consists merely of images and contains no dialogue or subtitles; whereas a clear rule is necessary in cases where the international co-production agreement does not expressly regulate the division of rights in the specific case of communication to the public by satellite within the meaning of this Directive;

(20) Whereas communications to the public by satellite from non-member countries will under certain conditions be deemed to occur within a Member State of the Community;

(21) Whereas it is necessary to ensure that protection for authors, performers, producers of phonograms and broadcasting organisations is accorded in all Member States and that this protection is not subject to a statutory licence system; whereas only in this way is it possible to ensure that any difference in the level of protection within the common market will not create distortions of competition;

(22) Whereas the advent of new technologies is likely to have an impact on both the quality and the quantity of the exploitation of works and other subject matter;

(23) Whereas in the light of these developments the level of protection granted pursuant to this Directive to all rightholders in the areas covered by this Directive should remain under consideration;

(24) Whereas the harmonisation of legislation envisaged in this Directive entails the harmonisation of the provisions ensuring a high level of protection of authors, performers, phonogram producers and broadcasting organisations; whereas this harmonisation should not allow a broadcasting organisation to take advantage of differences in levels of protection by relocating activities, to the detriment of audiovisual productions;

(25) Whereas the protection provided for rights related to copyright should be aligned on that contained in Council Directive 92/100/EEC of 19 November 1992 on rental right and lending right and on certain rights related to copyright in the field of intellectual property for the purposes of communication to the public by satellite; whereas, in particular, this will ensure that performers and phonogram producers are guaranteed an appropriate remuneration for the communication to the public by satellite of their performances or phonograms;

(26) Whereas the provisions of Article 4 do not prevent Member States from extending the presumption set out in Article 2(5) of Directive 92/100/EEC to the exclusive rights referred to in Article 4; whereas, furthermore, the provisions of Article 4 do not prevent Member States from providing for a rebuttable presumption of the authorisation of exploitation in respect of the exclusive rights of performers referred to in that Article, in so far as such presumption is compatible with the International Convention for the Protection of Performers, Producers of Phonograms and Broadcasting Organisations;

(27) Whereas the cable retransmission of programmes from other Member States in an act subject to copyright and, as the case may be, rights related to copyright; whereas the cable operator must, therefore, obtain the authorisation from every holder of rights in each part of the programme retransmitted; whereas, pursuant to this Directive, the authorisations should be

granted contractually unless a temporary exception is provided for in the case of existing legal licence schemes;

(28) Whereas, in order to ensure that the smooth operation of contractual arrangements is not called into question by the intervention of outsiders holding rights in individual parts of the programme, provision should be made, through the obligation to have recourse to a collecting society, for the exclusive collective exercise of the authorisation right to the extent that this is required by the special features of cable retransmission; whereas the authorisation right as such remains intact and only the exercise of this right is regulated to some extent, so that the right to authorise a cable retransmission can still be assigned; whereas this Directive does not affect the exercise of moral rights;

(29) Whereas the exemption provided for in Article 10 should not limit the choice of holders of rights to transfer their rights to a collecting society and thereby have a direct share in the remuneration paid by the cable distributor for cable retransmission;

(30) Whereas contractual arrangements regarding the authorisation of cable retransmission should be promoted by additional measures; whereas a party seeking the conclusion of a general contract should, for its part, be obliged to submit collective proposals for an agreement; whereas, furthermore, any party shall be entitled, at any moment, to call upon the assistance of impartial mediators whose task is to assist negotiations and who may submit proposals; whereas any such proposals and any opposition thereto should be served on the parties concerned in accordance with the applicable rules concerning the service of legal documents, in particular as set out in existing international conventions; whereas, finally, it is necessary to ensure that the negotiations are not blocked without valid justification or that individual holders are not prevented without valid justification from taking part in the negotiations; whereas none of these measures for the promotion of the acquisition of rights calls into question the contractual nature of the acquisition of cable retransmission rights;

(31) Whereas for a transitional period Member States should be allowed to retain existing bodies with jurisdiction in their territory over cases where the right to retransmit a programme by cable to the public has been unreasonably refused or offered on unreasonable terms by a broadcasting organisation; whereas it is understood that the right of parties concerned to be heard by the body should be guaranteed and that the existence of the body should not prevent the parties concerned from having normal access to the courts;

(32) Whereas, however, Community rules are not needed to deal with all of those matters, the effects of which perhaps with some commercially insignificant expectations, are felt only inside the borders of a single Member State;

(33) Whereas minimum rules should be laid down in order to establish and guarantee free and uninterrupted cross-border broadcasting by satellite and simultaneous, unaltered cable retransmission of programmes broadcast from other Member States, on an essentially contractual basis;

(34) Whereas this Directive should not prejudice further harmonisation in the field of copyright and rights related to copyright and the collective administration of such rights; whereas the possibility for Member States to regulate the activities of collecting societies should not prejudice the freedom of contractual negotiation of the rights provided for in this Directive, on the understanding that such negotiation takes place within the framework of general or specific national rules with regard to competition law or the prevention of abuse of monopolies;

(35) Whereas it should, therefore, be for the Member States to supplement the general provisions needed to achieve the objectives of this Directive by taking legislative and administrative measures in their domestic law, provided that these do not run counter to the objectives of this Directive and are compatible with Community law;

(36) Whereas this Directive does not affect the applicability of the competition rules in Articles 85 and 86 of the Treaty,

HAS ADOPTED THIS DIRECTIVE:

Chapter I Definitions

Article 1 Definitions

1. For the purpose of this Directive, 'satellite' means any satellite operating on frequency bands which, under telecommunications law, are reserved for the broadcast of signals for reception by the public or which are reserved for closed, point-to-point communication. In the latter case, however, the circumstances in which individual reception of the signals takes place must be comparable to those which apply in the first case.

2. (a) For the purpose of this Directive, 'communication to the public by satellite' means the act of introducing, under the control and responsibility of the broadcasting organisation, the programme-carrying signals intended for reception by the public into an uninterrupted chain of communication leading to the satellite and down towards the earth.

   (b) The act of communication to the public by satellite occurs solely in the Member State where, under the control and responsibility of the broadcasting organisation, the programme-carrying signals are introduced into an uninterrupted chain of communication leading to the satellite and down towards the earth.

   (c) If the programme-carrying signals are encrypted, then there is communication to the public by satellite on condition that the means for decrypting the broadcast are provided to the public by the broadcasting organisation or with its consent.

   (d) Where an act of communication to the public by satellite occurs in a non-Community State which does not provide the level of protection provided for under Chapter II,

     (i) if the programme-carrying signals are transmitted to the satellite from an uplink situation situated in a Member State, that act of communication to the public by satellite shall be deemed to have occurred in that Member State and the rights provided for under Chapter II shall be exercisable against the person operating the uplink station; or

     (ii) if there is no use of an uplink station situated in a Member State but a broadcasting organisation established in a Member State has commissioned the act of communication to the public by satellite, that act shall be deemed to have occurred in the Member State in which the broadcasting organisation has its principal establishment in the Community and the rights provided for under Chapter II shall be exercisable against the broadcasting organisation.

3. For the purposes of this Directive, 'cable retransmission' means the simultaneous, unaltered and unabridged retransmission by a cable or microwave system for reception by the public of an initial transmission from another Member State, by wire or over the air, including that by satellite, of television or radio programmes intended for reception by the public, regardless of how the operator of a cable retransmission service obtains the programme-carrying signals from the broadcasting organisation for the purpose of retransmission.

4. For the purposes of this Directive 'collecting society' means any organisation which manages or administers copyright or rights related to copyright as its sole purpose or as one of its main purposes.

5. For the purposes of this Directive, the principal director of a cinematographic or audiovisual work shall be considered as its author or one of its authors. Member States may provide for others to be considered as its co-authors.

Chapter II Broadcasting of Programmes by Satellite

Article 2 Broadcasting right

Member States shall provide an exclusive right for the author to authorise the communication to the public by satellite of copyright works, subject to the provisions set out in this chapter.

Article 3 Acquisition of broadcasting rights

1. Member States shall ensure that the authorisation referred to in Article 2 may be acquired only by agreement.

2. A Member State may provide that a collective agreement between a collecting society and a broadcasting organisation concerning a given category of works may be extended to rightholders of the same category who are not represented by the collecting society, provided that:

— the communication to the public by satellite simulcasts a terrestrial broadcast by the same broadcaster, and

— the unrepresented rightholder shall, at any time, have the possibility of excluding the extension of the collective agreement to his works and of exercising his rights either individually or collectively.

3. Paragraph 2 shall not apply to cinematographic works, including works created by a process analogous to cinematography.

4. Where the law of a Member State provides for the extension of a collective agreement in accordance with the provisions of paragraph 2, that Member States shall inform the Commission which broadcasting organisations are entitled to avail themselves of that law. The Commission shall publish this information in the *Official Journal of the European Communities* (C series).

Article 4   Rights of performers, phonogram producers and broadcasting organisations

1. For the purposes of communication to the public by satellite, the rights of performers, phonogram producers and broadcasting organisations shall be protected in accordance with the provisions of Articles 6, 7, 8 and 10 of Directive 92/100/EEC.

2. For the purposes of paragraph 1, 'broadcasting by wireless means' in Directive 92/100/EEC shall be understood as including communication to the public by satellite.

3. With regard to the exercise of the rights referred to in paragraph 1, Articles 2(7) and 12 of Directive 92/100/EC shall apply.

Article 5   Relation between copyright and related rights

Protection of copyright-related rights under this Directive shall leave intact and shall in no way affect the protection of copyright.

Article 6   Minimum protection

1. Member States may provide for more far-reaching protection for holders of rights related to copyright than that required by Article 8 of Directive 92/100/EEC.

2. In applying paragraph 1 Member States shall observe the definitions contained in Article 1(1) and (2).

Article 7   Transitional provisions

1. With regard to the application in time of the rights referred to in Article 4(1) of this Directive, Article 13(1), (2), (6) and (7) of Directive 92/100/EEC shall apply. Article 13(4) and (5) of Directive 92/100/EEC shall apply *mutatis mutandis*.

2. Agreements concerning the exploitation of works and other protected subject matter which are in force on the date mentioned in Article 14(1) shall be subject to the provisions of Articles 1(2), 2 and 3 as from 1 January 2000 if they expire after that date.

3. When an international co-production agreement concluded before the date mentioned in Article 14(1) between a co-producer from a Member State and one or more co-producers from other Member States or third countries expressly provides for a system of division of exploitation rights between the co-producers by geographical areas for all means of communication to the public, without distinguishing the arrangement applicable to communication to the public by satellite from the provisions applicable to the other means of communication, and where communication to the public by satellite of the co-production would prejudice the exclusivity, in particular the language exclusivity, of one of the co-producers or his assignees in a given territory, the authorisation by one of the co-producers or his assignees for a communication to the public by satellite shall require the prior consent of the holder of that exclusivity, whether co-producer or assignee.

Chapter III   Cable Retransmission

Article 8   Cable retransmission right

1. Member States shall ensure that when programmes from other Member States are retransmitted by cable in their territory the applicable copyright and related rights are observed and that such retransmission takes place on the basis of individual or collective contractual agreements between copyright owners, holders or related rights and cable operators.

2. Notwithstanding paragraph 1, Member States may retain until 31 December 1997 such statutory licence systems which are in operation or expressly provided for by national law on 31 July 1991.

Article 9   Exercise of the cable retransmission right

1. Member States shall ensure that the right of copyright owners and holders or related rights to grant or refuse authorisation to a cable operator for a cable retransmission may be exercised only through a collecting society.

2. Where a rightholder has not transferred the management of his rights to a collecting society, the collecting society which manages rights of the same category shall be deemed to be mandated to manage his rights. Where more than one collecting society manages rights of that category, the rightholder shall be free to choose which of those collecting societies is deemed to be mandated to manage his rights. A rightholder referred to in this paragraph shall have the same rights and obligations resulting from the agreement between the cable operator and the collecting society which is deemed to be mandated to manage his rights as the rightholders who have mandated that collecting society and he shall be able to claim those rights within a period, to be fixed by the Member State concerned, which shall not be shorter than three years from the date of the cable retransmission which includes his work or other protected subject matter.

3. A Member State may provide that, when a rightholder authorises the initial transmission within its territory of a work or other protected subject matter, he shall be deemed to have agreed not to exercise his cable retransmission rights on an individual basis but to exercise them in accordance with the provisions of this Directive.

Article 10   Exercise of the cable retransmission right
by broadcasting organisations

Member States shall ensure that Article 9 does not apply to the rights exercised by a broadcasting organisation in respect of its own transmission, irrespective of whether the rights concerned are its own or have been transferred to it by other copyright owners and/or holders of related rights.

Article 11   Mediators

1. Where no agreement is concluded regarding authorisation of the cable retransmission of a broadcast. Member States shall ensure that either party may call upon the assistance of one or more mediators.

2. The task of the mediators shall be to provide assistance with negotiation. They may also submit proposals to the parties.

3. It shall be assumed that all the parties accept a proposal as referred to in paragraph 2 if none of them expresses its opposition within a period of three months. Notice of the proposal and of any opposition thereto shall be served on the parties concerned in accordance with the applicable rules concerning the service of legal documents.

4. The mediators shall be so selected that their independence and impartiality are beyond reasonable doubt.

Article 12   Prevention of the abuse of negotiating positions

1. Member States shall ensure by means of civil or administrative law, as appropriate, that the parties enter and conduct negotiations regarding authorisation for cable retransmission in good faith and do not prevent or hinder negotiation without valid justification.

2. A Member State which, on the date mentioned in Article 14(1), has a body with jurisdiction in its territory over cases where the right to retransmit a programme by cable to the public in the Member State has been unreasonably refused or offered on unreasonable terms by a broadcasting organisation may retain that body.

3. Paragraph 2 shall apply for a transitional period of eight years from the date mentioned in Article 14(1).

Chapter IV General Provisions

Article 13 Collective administration of rights
This Directive shall be without prejudice to the regulation of the activities of collecting societies by the Member States.

Article 14 Final provisions
1. Member States shall bring into force the laws, regulations and administrative provisions necessary to comply with this Directive before 1 January 1995. They shall immediately inform the Commission thereof.

When Member States adopt these measures, the latter shall contain a reference to this Directive or shall be accompanied by such reference at the time of their official publication. The methods of making such a reference shall be laid down by the Member States.

2. Member States shall communicate to the Commission the provisions of national law which they adopt in the field covered by this Directive.

3. Not later than 1 January 2000, the Commission shall submit to the European Parliament, the Council and the Economic and Social Committee a report on the application of this Directive and, if necessary, make further proposals to adapt it to developments in the audio and audiovisual sector.

Article 15
This Directive is addressed to the Member States.

Directive 96/9/EC of the European Parliament and of the Council

of 11 March 1996 on the legal protection of databases

THE EUROPEAN PARLIAMENT AND THE COUNCIL OF THE EUROPEAN UNION,

Having regard to the Treaty establishing the European Community, and in particular Article 57(2), 66 and 100a thereof, Having regard to the proposal from the Commission,

Having regard to the opinion of the Economic and Social Committee,

Acting in accordance with the procedure laid down in Article 189b of the Treaty,

(1) Whereas databases are at present not sufficiently protected in all Member States by existing legislation; whereas such protection, where it exists, has different attributes;

(2) Whereas such differences in the legal protection of databases offered by the legislation of the Member States have direct negative effects on the functioning of the internal market as regards databases and in particular on the freedom of natural and legal persons to provide on-line database goods and services on the basis of harmonised legal arrangements throughout the Community; whereas such differences could well become more pronounced as Member States introduce new legislation in this field, which is now taking on an increasingly international dimension;

(3) Whereas existing differences distorting the functioning of the internal market need to be removed and new ones prevented from arising, while differences not adversely affecting the functioning of the internal market or the development of an information market within the Community need not be removed or prevented from arising;

(4) Whereas copyright protection for databases exists in varying forms in the Member States according to legislation or case-law, and whereas, if differences in legislation in the scope and conditions of protection remain between the Member States, such unharmonised intellectual property rights can have the effect of preventing the free movement of goods or services within the Community;

(5) Whereas copyright remains an appropriate form of exclusive right for authors who have created databases;

(6) Whereas, nevertheless, in the absence of a harmonised system of unfair-competition legislation or of case-law, other measures are required in addition to prevent the unauthorised extraction and/or re-utilisation of the contents of a database;

(7) Whereas the making of databases requires the investment of considerable human, technical and financial resources while such databases can be copied or accessed at a fraction of the cost needed to design them independently;

(8) Whereas the unauthorised extraction and/or re-utilisation of the contents of a database constitute acts which can have serious economic and technical consequences;

(9) Whereas databases are a vital tool in the development of an information market within the Community; whereas this tool will also be of use in many other fields;

(10) Whereas the exponential growth, in the Community and worldwide, in the amount of information generated and processed annually in all sectors of commerce and industry calls for investment in all the Member States in advanced information processing systems;

(11) Whereas there is at present a very great imbalance in the level of investment in the database sector both as between the Member States and between the Community and the world's largest database-producing third countries;

(12) Whereas such an investment in modern information storage and processing systems will not take place within the Community unless a stable and uniform legal protection regime is introduced for the protection of the rights of makers of databases;

(13) Whereas this Directive protects collections, sometimes called 'compilations', of works, data or other materials which are arranged, stored and accessed by means which include electronic, electromagnetic or electro-optical processes or analogous processes;

(14) Whereas protection under this Directive should be extended to cover non-electronic databases;

(15) Whereas the criteria used to determine whether a database should be protected by copyright should be defined to the fact that the selection or the arrangement of the contents of the database is the author's own intellectual creation; whereas such protection should cover the structure of the database;

(16) Whereas no criterion other than originality in the sense of the author's intellectual creation should be applied to determine the eligibility of the database for copyright protection, and in particular no aesthetic or qualitative criteria should be applied;

(17) Whereas the term 'database' should be understood to include literary, artistic, musical or other collections of works or collections of other material such as texts, sound, images, numbers, facts, and data; whereas it should cover collections of independent works, data or other materials which are systematically or methodically arranged and can be individually accessed; whereas this means that a recording or an audiovisual, cinematographic, literary or musical work as such does not fall within the scope of this Directive;

(18) Whereas this Directive is without prejudice to the freedom of authors to decide whether, or in what manner, they will allow their works to be included in a database, in particular whether or not the authorisation given is exclusive; whereas the protection of databases by the *sui generis* right is without prejudice to existing rights over their contents, and whereas in particular where an author or the holder of a related right permits some of his works or subject matter to be included in a database pursuant to a non-exclusive agreement, a third party may make use of those works or subject matter subject to the required consent of the author or of the holder of the related right without the *sui generis* right of the maker of the database being invoked to prevent him doing so, on condition that those works or subject matter are neither extracted from the database nor re-utilised on the basis thereof;

(19) Whereas, as a rule, the compilation of several recordings of musical performances on a CD does not come within the scope of this Directive, both because, as a compilation, it does not meet the conditions for copyright protection and because it does not represent a substantial enough investment to be eligible under the *sui generis* right;

(20) Whereas protection under this Directive may also apply to the materials necessary for the operation or consultation of certain databases such as thesaurus and indexation systems;

(21) Whereas the protection provided for in this Directive relates to databases in which works, data or other materials have been arranged systematically or methodically; whereas it is not necessary for those materials to have been physically stored in an organised manner;

(22) Whereas electronic databases within the meaning of this Directive may also include devices such as CD-ROM and CD-i;

(23) Whereas the term 'database' should not be taken to extend to computer programs used in the making or operation of a database, which are protected by Council Directive 91/250/EEC of 14 May 1991 on the legal protection of computer programs;

(24) Whereas the rental and lending of databases in the field of copyright and related rights are governed exclusively by Council Directive 92/100/EEC of 19 November 1992 on rental right and lending right and on certain rights related to copyright in the field of intellectual property;

(25) Whereas the term of copyright is already governed by Council Directive 93/98/EEC of 29 October 1993 harmonising the term of protection of copyright and certain related rights;

(26) Whereas works protected by copyright and subject matter protected by related rights, which are incorporated into a database, remain nevertheless protected by the respective exclusive rights and may not be incorporated into, or extracted from, the database without the permission of the rightholder or his successors in title;

(27) Whereas copyright in such works and related rights in subject matter thus incorporated into a database are in no way affected by the existence of a separate right in the selection or arrangement of these works and subject matter in a database;

(28) Whereas the moral rights of the natural person who created the database belong to the author and should be exercised according to the legislation of the Member States and the provisions of the Berne Convention for the Protection of Literary and Artistic Works; whereas such moral rights remain outside the scope of this Directive;

(29) Whereas the arrangements applicable to databases created by employees are left to the discretion of the Member States; whereas, therefore nothing in this Directive prevents Member States from stipulating in their legislation that where a database is created by an employee in the execution of his duties or following the instructions given by his employer, the employer exclusively shall be entitled to exercise all economic rights in the database so created, unless otherwise provided by contract;

(30) Whereas the author's exclusive rights should include the right to determine the way in which his work is exploited and by whom, and in particular to control the distribution of his work to unauthorised persons;

(31) Whereas the copyright protection of databases includes making databases available by means other than the distribution of copies;

(32) Whereas Member States are required to ensure that their national provisions are at least materially equivalent in the case of such acts subject to restrictions as are provided for by this Directive;

(33) Whereas the question of exhaustion of the right of distribution does not arise in the case of on-line databases, which come within the field of provision of services; whereas this also applies with regard to a material copy of such a database made by the user of such a service with the consent of the rightholder; whereas, unlike CD-ROM or CD-i, where the intellectual property is incorporated in a material medium, namely an item of goods, every on-line service is in fact an act which will have to be subject to authorisation where the copyright so provides;

(34) Whereas, nevertheless, once the rightholder has chosen to make available a copy of the database to a user, whether by an on-line service or by other means of distribution, that lawful user must be able to access and use the database for the purposes and in the way set out in the

agreement with the rightholder, even if such access and use necessitate performance of otherwise restricted acts;

(35) Whereas a list should be drawn up of exceptions to restricted acts, taking into account the fact that copyright as covered by this Directive applies only to the selection or arrangements of the contents of a database; whereas Member States should be given the option of providing for such exceptions in certain cases; whereas, however, this option should be exercised in accordance with the Berne Convention and to the extent that the exceptions relate to the structure of the database; whereas a distinction should be drawn between exceptions for private use and exceptions for reproduction for private purposes, which concerns provisions under national legislation of some Member States on levies on blank media or recording equipment;

(36) Whereas the term 'scientific research' within the meaning of this Directive covers both the natural sciences and the human sciences;

(37) Whereas Article 10(1) of the Berne Convention is not affected by this Directive;

(38) Whereas the increasing use of digital recording technology exposes the database maker to the risk that the contents of his database may be copied and rearranged electronically, without his authorisation, to produce a database of identical content which, however, does not infringe any copyright in the arrangement of his database;

(39) Whereas, in addition to aiming to protect the copyright in the original selection or arrangement of the contents of a database, this Directive seeks to safeguard the position of makers of databases against misappropriation of the results of the financial and professional investment made in obtaining and collection the contents by protecting the whole or substantial parts of a database against certain acts by a user or competitor;

(40) Whereas the object of this *sui generis* right is to ensure protection of any investment in obtaining, verifying or presenting the contents of a database for the limited duration of the right; whereas such investment may consist in the deployment of financial resources and/or the expending of time, effort and energy;

(41) Whereas the objective of the *sui generis* right is to give the maker of a database the option of preventing the unauthorised extraction and/or re-utilisation of all or a substantial part of the contents of that database; whereas the maker of a database is the person who takes the initiative and the risk of investing; whereas this excludes subcontractors in particular from the definition of maker;

(42) Whereas the special right to prevent unauthorised extraction and/or reutilisation relates to acts by the user which go beyond his legitimate rights and thereby harm the investment; whereas the right to prohibit extraction and/or re-utilisation of all or a substantial part of the contents relates not only to the manufacture of a parasitical competing product but also to any user who, through his acts, causes significant detriment, evaluated qualitatively or quantitatively, to the investment;

(43) Whereas, in the case of on-line transmission, the right to prohibit re-utilisation is not exhausted either as regards the database or as regards a material copy of the database or of part thereof made by the addressee of the transmission with the consent of the rightholder;

(44) Whereas, when on-screen display of the contents of a database necessitates the permanent or temporary transfer of all or a substantial part of such contents to another medium, that act should be subject to authorisation by the rightholder;

(45) Whereas the right to prevent unauthorised extraction and/or re-utilisation does not in any way constitute an extension of copyright protection to mere facts or data;

(46) Whereas the existence of a right to prevent the unauthorised extraction and/or re-utilisation of the whole or a substantial part of works, data or materials from a database should not give rise to the creation of a new right in the works, data or materials themselves;

(47) Whereas, in the interests of competition between suppliers of information products and services, protection by the *sui generis* right must not be afforded in such a way as to facilitate abuses of a dominant position, in particular, as regards the creation and distribution of new products and services which have an intellectual, documentary, technical, economic or commercial added value; whereas, therefore, the provisions of this Directive are without prejudice to the application of Community or national competition rules;

(48) Whereas the objective of this Directive, which is to afford an appropriate and uniform level of protection of databases as a means to secure the remuneration of the maker of the database, is different from the aim of Directive 95/46/EC of the European Parliament and of the Council of 24 October 1995 on the protection of individuals with regard to the processing of personal data and on the free movement of such data, which is to guarantee free circulation of personal data on the basis of harmonised rules designed to protect fundamental rights, notably the right to privacy which is recognised in Article 8 of the European Convention for the Protection of Human Rights and Fundamental Freedoms; whereas the provisions of this Directive are without prejudice to data protection legislation;

(49) Whereas, notwithstanding the right to prevent extraction and/or re-utilisation of all or a substantial part of a database, it should be laid down that the maker of a database or rightholder may not prevent a lawful user of the database from extracting and re-utilising insubstantial parts; whereas, however, that user may not unreasonably prejudice either the legitimate interests of the holder of the *sui generis* right or the holder of copyright or a related right in respect of the works or subject matter contained in the database;

(50) Whereas the Member States should be given the option of providing for exceptions to the right to prevent the unauthorised extraction and/or re-utilisation of a substantial part of the contents of a database in the case of extraction for private purposes, for the purposes of illustration for teaching or scientific research, or where extraction and/or re-utilisation are/is carried out in the interests of public security or for the purposes of an administrative or judicial procedure; whereas such operations must not prejudice the exclusive rights of the maker to exploit the database and their purpose must not be commercial;

(51) Whereas the Member States, where they avail themselves of the option to permit a lawful user of a database to extract a substantial part of the contents for the purposes of illustration for teaching or scientific research, may limit that permission to certain categories of teaching or scientific research institution;

(52) Whereas those Member States which have specific rules providing for a right comparable to the *sui generis* right provided for in this Directive should be permitted to retain, as far as the new right is concerned, the expectations traditionally specified by such rules;

(53) Whereas the burden of proof regarding the date of completion of the making of a database lies with the maker of the database;

(54) Whereas the burden of proof that the criteria exist for concluding that a substantial modification of the contents of a database is to be regarded as a substantial new investment lies with the maker of the database resulting from such investment;

(55) Whereas a substantial new investment involving a new term of protection may include a substantial verification of the contents of the database;

(56) Whereas the right to prevent unauthorised extraction and/or re-utilisation in respect of a database should apply to databases whose makers are nationals or habitual residents of third countries or to those produced by legal persons not established in a Member State, within the meaning of the Treaty, only if such third countries offer comparable protection to databases produced by nationals of a Member State or persons who have their habitual residence in the territory of the Community;

(57) Whereas, in addition to remedies provided under the legislation of the Member States for infringements of copyright or other rights, Member States should provide for appropriate remedies against unauthorised extraction and/or re-utilisation of the contents of a database;

(58) Whereas, in addition to the protection given under this Directive to the structure of the database by copyright, and to its contents against unauthorised extraction and/or re-utilisation under the *sui generis* right, other legal provisions in the Member States relevant to the supply of database goods and services continue to apply;

(59) Whereas this Directive is without prejudice to the application to databases composed of audiovisual works of any rules recognised by a Member State's legislation concerning the broadcasting of audiovisual programmes;

(60) Whereas some Member States currently protect under copyright arrangements databases which do not meet the criteria for eligibility for copyright protection laid down in this Directive; whereas,

even if the databases concerned are eligible for protection under the right laid down in this Directive to prevent unauthorised extraction and/or re-utilisation of their contents, the term of protection under that right is considerably shorter than that which they enjoy under the national arrangements currently in force; whereas harmonisation of the criteria for determining whether a database is to be protected by copyright may not have the effect of reducing the term of protection currently enjoyed by the rightholders concerned; whereas a derogation should be laid down to that effect; whereas the effects of such derogation must be confined to the territories of the Member States concerned,

HAVE ADOPTED THIS DIRECTIVE:

Chapter I   Scope

Article 1   Scope

1. This Directive concerns the legal protection of databases in any form.

2. For the purposes of this Directive, 'database' shall mean a collection of independent works, data or other materials arranged in a systematic or methodical way and individually accessible by electronic or other means.

3. Protection under this Directive shall not apply to computer programs used in the making or operation of databases accessible by electronic means.

Article 2   Limitations on the scope

This Directive shall apply without prejudice to Community provisions relating to:

    (a) the legal protection of computer programs;

    (b) rental right, lending right and certain rights related to copyright in the field of intellectual property;

    (c) the term of protection of copyright and certain related rights.

Chapter II   Copyright

Article 3   Object of protection

1. In accordance with this Directive, databases which, by reason of the selection or arrangement of their contents, constitute the author's own intellectual creation shall be protected as such by copyright. No other criteria shall be applied to determine their eligibility for that protection.

2. The copyright protection of databases provided for by this Directive shall not extend to their contents and shall be without prejudice to any rights subsisting in those contents themselves.

Article 4   Database authorship

1. The author of a database shall be the natural person or group of natural persons who created the base or, where the legislation of the Member States so permits, the legal person designated as the rightholder by the legislation.

2. Where collective works are recognised by the legislation of a Member State, the economic rights shall be owned by the person holding the copyright.

3. In respect of a database created by a group of natural persons jointly, the exclusive rights shall be owned jointly.

Article 5   Restricted acts

In respect of the expression of the database which is protectable by copyright, the author of a database shall have the exclusive right to carry out or to authorise:

    (a) temporary or permanent reproduction by any means and in any form, in whole or in part;

    (b) translation, adaptation, arrangement and any other alteration;

    (c) any form of distribution to the public of the database or of copies thereof. The first sale in the Community of a copy of the database by the rightholder or with his consent shall exhaust the right to control resale of that copy within the Community;

(d) any communication, display or performance to the public;

(e) any reproduction, distribution, communication, display or performance to the public of the results of the acts referred to in (b).

Article 6   Exceptions to restricted acts

1. The performance by the lawful user of a database or of a copy thereof of any of the acts listed in Article 5 which is necessary for the purposes of access to the contents of the databases and normal use of the contents by the lawful user shall not require the authorisation of the author of the database. Where the lawful user is authorised to use only part of the database, this provision shall apply only to that part.

2. Member States shall have the option of providing for limitations on the rights set out in Article 5 in the following cases:

(a) in the case of reproduction for private purposes of a non-electronic database;

(b) where there is use for the sole purpose of illustration for teaching or scientific research, as long as the source is indicated and to the extent justified by the non-commercial purpose to be achieved, without prejudice to the exceptions and limitations provided for in Directive (EU) 2019/790 of the European Parliament and of the Council;

(c) where there is use for the purposes of public security or for the purposes of an administrative or judicial procedure;

(d) where other exceptions to copyright which are traditionally authorised under national law are involved, without prejudice to points (a), (b) and (c).

3. In accordance with the Berne Convention for the protection of Literary and Artistic Works, this Article may not be interpreted in such a way as to allow its application to be used in a manner which unreasonably prejudices the rightholder's legitimate interests or conflicts with normal exploitation of the database.

Chapter III   *Sui Generis* Right

Article 7   Object of protection

1. Member States shall provide for a right for the maker of a database which shows that there has been qualitatively and/or quantitatively a substantial investment in either the obtaining, verification or presentation of the contents to prevent extraction and/or re-utilisation of the whole or of a substantial part, evaluated qualitatively and/or quantitatively, of the contents of that database.

2. For the purposes of this Chapter:

(a) 'extraction' shall mean the permanent or temporary transfer of all or a substantial part of the contents of a database to another medium by any means or in any form;

(b) 're-utilisation' shall mean any form of making available to the public all or a substantial part of the contents of a database by the distribution of copies, by renting, by on-line or other forms of transmission. The first sale of a copy of a database within the Community be the rightholder or with his consent shall exhaust the right to control resale of that copy within the Community;

Public lending is not an act of extraction or re-utilisation.

3. The right referred to in paragraph 1 may be transferred, assigned or granted under contractual licence.

4. The right provided for in paragraph 1 shall apply irrespective of the eligibility of that database for protection by copyright or by other rights. Moreover, it shall apply irrespective of eligibility of the contents of that database for protection by copyright or by other rights. Protection of databases under the right provided for in paragraph 1 shall be without prejudice to rights existing in respect of their contents.

5. The repeated and systematic extraction and/or re-utilisation of insubstantial parts of the contents of the database implying acts which conflict with a normal exploitation of that database or which unreasonably prejudice the legitimate interests of the maker of the database shall not be permitted.

Article 8   Rights and obligations of lawful users

1. The maker of a database which is made available to the public in whatever manner may not prevent a lawful user of the database from extracting and/or re-utilising insubstantial parts of its contents, evaluated qualitatively and/or quantitatively, for any purposes whatsoever. Where the lawful user is authorised to extract and/or re-utilise only part of the database, this paragraph shall apply only to that part.

2. A lawful user of a database which is made available to the public in whatever manner may not perform acts which conflict with normal exploitation of the database or unreasonably prejudice the legitimate interests of the maker of the database.

3. A lawful user of a database which is made available to the public in any manner may not cause prejudice to the holder of a copyright or related right in respect of the works or subject matter contained in the database.

Article 9   Exception to the *sui generis* right

Member States may stipulate that lawful users of a database which is made available to the public in whatever manner may, without the authorisation of its maker, extract or re-utilise a substantial part of its contents:

(a) in the case of extraction for private purposes of the contents of a non-electronic database;

(b) in the case of extraction for the purposes of illustration for teaching or scientific research, as long as the source is indicated and to the extent justified by the non-commercial purpose to be achieved, without prejudice to the exceptions and limitations provided for in Directive (EU) 2019/790;

(c) in the case of extraction and/or re-utilisation for the purposes of public security or an administrative or judicial procedure.

Article 10   Term of protection

1. The right provided for in Article 7 shall run from the date of completion of the making of the database. It shall expire fifteen years from the first of January of the year following the date of completion.

2. In the case of a database which is made available to the public in whatever manner before expiry of the period provided for in paragraph 1, the term of protection by that right shall expire fifteen years from the first of January of the year following the date when the database was first made available to the public.

3. Any substantial change, evaluated qualitatively or quantitatively, to the contents of a database, including any substantial change resulting from the accumulation of successive additions, deletions or alterations, which would result in the database being considered to be a substantial new investment, evaluated qualitatively or quantitatively, shall qualify the database resulting from that investment for its own term of protection.

Article 11   Beneficiaries of protection under the *sui generis* right

1. The right provided for in Article 7 shall apply to database whose makers or right-holders are nationals of a Member State or who have their habitual residence in the territory of the Community.

2. Paragraph 1 shall also apply to companies and firms formed in accordance with the law of a Member State and having their registered office, central administration or principal place of business within the Community; however, where such a company or firm has only its registered office in the territory of the Community, its operations must be genuinely linked on an ongoing basis with the economy of a Member State.

3. Agreements extending the right provided for in Article 7 to databases made in third countries and falling outside the provisions of paragraphs 1 and 2 shall be concluded by the Council acting on a proposal from the Commission. The term of any protection extended to databases by virtue of that procedure shall not exceed that available pursuant to Article 10.

Chapter IV   Common Provisions

Article 12   Remedies
Member States shall provide appropriate remedies in respect of infringements of the rights provided for in this Directive.

Article 13   Continued application of other legal provisions
This Directive shall be without prejudice to provisions concerning in particular copyright, rights related to copyright or any other rights or obligations subsisting in the data, works or other materials incorporated into a database, patent rights, trade marks, design rights, the protection of national treasures, laws on restrictive practices and unfair competition, trade secrets, security, confidentiality, data protection and privacy, access to public documents, and the law of contract.

Article 14   Application over time
1. Protection pursuant to this Directive as regards copyright shall also be available in respect of databases created prior to the date referred to in Article 16(1) which on that date fulfil the requirements laid down in this Directive as regards copyright protection of databases.

2. Notwithstanding paragraph 1, where a database protected under copyright arrangements in a Member State on the date of publication of this Directive does not fulfil the eligibility criteria for copyright protection laid down in Article 3(1), this Directive shall not result in any curtailing in that Member State of the remaining term of protection afforded under those arrangements.

3. Protection pursuant to the provisions of this Directive as regards the right provided for in Article 7 shall also be available in respect of databases the making of which was completed not more than fifteen years prior to the date referred to in Article 16(1) and which on that date fulfil the requirements laid down in Article 7.

4. The protection provided for in paragraphs 1 and 3 shall be without prejudice to any acts concluded and rights acquired before the date referred to in those paragraphs.

5. In the case of a database the making of which was completed not more than fifteen years prior to the date referred to in Article 16(1), the term of protection by the right provided for in Article 7 shall expire fifteen years from the first of January following that date.

Article 15   Binding nature of certain provisions
Any contractual provision contrary to Articles 6(1) and 8 shall be null and void.

Article 16   Final provisions
1. Member States shall bring into force the laws, regulations and administrative provisions necessary to comply with this Directive before 1 January 1998.

When Member States adopt these provisions, they shall contain a reference to this Directive or shall be accompanied by such reference on the occasion of their official publication. The methods of making such reference shall be laid down by Member States.

2. Member States shall communicate to the Commission the text of the provisions of domestic law which they adopt in the field governed by this Directive.

3. Not later than at the end of the third year after the date referred to in paragraph 1, and every three years thereafter, the Commission shall submit to the European Parliament, the Council and the Economic and Social Committee a report on the application of this Directive, in which, *inter alia*, on the basis of specific information supplied by the Member States, it shall examine in particular the application of the *sui generis* right, including Articles 8 and 9, and shall verify especially whether the application of this right has led to abuse of a dominant position or other interference with free competition which would justify appropriate measures being taken, including the establishment of non-voluntary licensing arrangements. Where necessary, it shall submit proposals for adjustment of this Directive in line with developments in the area of databases.

Article 17
This Directive is addressed to the Member States.

Directive 98/71/EC of the European Parliament and of the Council

of 13 October 1998 on the legal protection of designs

THE EUROPEAN PARLIAMENT AND THE COUNCIL OF THE EUROPEAN UNION,

Having regard to the Treaty establishing the European Community and in particular Article 100a thereof,

Having regard to the proposal by the Commission, Having regard to the opinion of the Economic and Social Committee,

Acting in accordance with the procedure laid down in Article 189b of the Treaty, in the light of the joint text approved by the Conciliation Committee on 29 July 1998,

(1) Whereas the objectives of the Community, as laid down in the Treaty, include laying the foundations of an ever closer union among the peoples of Europe, fostering closer relations between Member States of the Community, and ensuring the economic and social progress of the Community countries by common action to eliminate the barriers which divide Europe; whereas to that end the Treaty provides for the establishment of an internal market characterised by the abolition of obstacles to the free movement of goods and also for the institution of a system ensuring that competition in the internal market is not distorted; whereas an approximation of the laws of the Member States on the legal protection of designs would further those objectives;

(2) Whereas the differences in the legal protection of designs offered by the legislation of the Member States directly affect the establishment and functioning of the internal market as regards goods embodying designs; whereas such differences can distort competition within the internal market;

(3) Whereas it is therefore necessary for the smooth functioning of the internal market to approximate the design protection laws of the Member States;

(4) Whereas, in doing so, it is important to take into consideration the solutions and the advantages with which the Community design system will provide undertakings wishing to acquire design rights;

(5) Whereas it is unnecessary to undertake a full-scale approximation of the design laws of the Member States, and it will be sufficient if approximation is limited to those national provisions of law which most directly affect the functioning of the internal market; whereas provisions on sanctions, remedies and enforcement should be left to national law; whereas the objectives of this limited approximation cannot be sufficiently achieved by the Member States acting alone;

(6) Whereas Member States should accordingly remain free to fix the procedural provisions concerning registration, renewal and invalidation of design rights and provisions concerning the effects of such invalidity;

(7) Whereas this Directive does not exclude the application to designs of national or Community legislation providing for protection other than that conferred by registration or publication as design, such as legislation relating to unregistered design rights, trade marks, patents and utility models, unfair competition or civil liability;

(8) Whereas, in the absence of harmonisation of copyright law, it is important to establish the principle of cumulation of protection under specific registered design protection law and under copyright law, whilst leaving Member States free to establish the extent of copyright protection and the conditions under which such protection is conferred;

(9) Whereas the attainment of the objectives of the internal market requires that the conditions for obtaining a registered design right be identical in all the Member States; whereas to that end it is necessary to give a unitary definition of the notion of design and of the requirements as to novelty and individual character with which registered design rights must comply;

(10) Whereas it is essential, in order to facilitate the free movement of goods, to ensure in principle that registered design rights confer upon the right holder equivalent protection in all Member States;

(11) Whereas protection is conferred by way of registration upon the right holder for those design features of a product, in whole or in part, which are shown visibly in an application and made available to the public by way of publication or consultation of the relevant file;

(12) Whereas protection should not be extended to those component parts which are not visible during normal use of a product, or to those features of such part which are not visible when the part is mounted, or which would not, in themselves, fulfil the requirements as to novelty and individual character; whereas features of design which are excluded from protection for these reasons should not be taken into consideration for the purpose of assessing whether other features of the design fulfil the requirements for protection;

(13) Whereas the assessment as to whether a design has individual character should be based on whether the overall impression produced on an informed user viewing the design clearly differs from that produced on him by the existing design corpus, taking into consideration the nature of the product to which the design is applied or in which it is incorporated, and in particular the industrial sector to which it belongs and the degree of freedom of the designer in developing the design;

(14) Whereas technological innovation should not be hampered by granting design protection to features dictated solely by a technical function; whereas it is understood that this does not entail that a design must have an aesthetic quality; whereas, likewise, the interoperability of products of different makes should not be hindered by extending protection to the design of mechanical fittings; whereas features of a design which are excluded from protection for these reasons should not be taken into consideration for the purpose of assessing whether other features of the design fulfil the requirements for protection;

(15) Whereas the mechanical fittings of modular products may nevertheless constitute an important element of the innovative characteristics of modular products and present a major marketing asset and therefore should be eligible for protection;

(16) Whereas a design right shall not subsist in a design which is contrary to public policy or to accepted principles of morality; whereas this Directive does not constitute a harmonisation of national concepts of public policy or accepted principles of morality;

(17) Whereas it is fundamental for the smooth functioning of the internal market to unify the term of protection afforded by registered design rights;

(18) Whereas the provisions of this Directive are without prejudice to the application of the competition rules under Articles 85 and 86 of the Treaty;

(19) Whereas the rapid adoption of this Directive has become a matter of urgency for a number of industrial sectors; whereas full-scale approximation of the laws of the Member States on the use of protected designs for the purpose of permitting the repair of a complex product so as to restore its original appearance, where the product incorporating the design or to which the design is applied constitutes a component part of a complex product upon whose appearance the protected design is dependent, cannot be introduced at the present stage; whereas the lack of full-scale approximation of the laws of the Member States on the use of protected designs for such repair of a complex product should not constitute an obstacle to the approximation of those other national provisions of design law which most directly affect the functioning of the internal market; whereas for this reason Member States should in the meantime maintain in force any provisions in conformity with the Treaty relating to the use of the design of a component part used for the purpose of the repair of a complex product so as to restore its original appearance, or, if they introduce any new provisions relating to such use, the purpose of these provisions should be only to liberalise the market in such parts; whereas those Member States which, on the date of entry into force of this Directive, do not provide for protection for designs of component parts are not required to introduce registration of designs for such parts; whereas three years after the implementation date the Commission should submit an analysis of the consequences of the provisions of this Directive for Community industry, for consumers, for competition and for the functioning of the internal market; whereas, in respect of component parts of complex products, the analysis should, in particular, consider harmonisation on the basis of possible options, including a remuneration system and a limited term of exclusivity; whereas, at the latest one year

after the submission of its analysis, the Commission should, after consultation with the parties most affected, propose to the European Parliament and the Council any changes to this Directive needed to complete the internal market in respect of component parts of complex products, and any other changes which it considers necessary;

(20) Whereas the transitional provision in Article 14 concerning the design of a component part used for the purpose of the repair of a complex product so as to restore its original appearance is in no case to be construed as constituting an obstacle to the free movement of a product which constitutes such a component part;

(21) Whereas the substantive grounds for refusal of registration in those Member States which provide for substantive examination of applications prior to registration, and the substantive grounds for the invalidation of registered design rights in all the Member States, must be exhaustively enumerated,

HAVE ADOPTED THIS DIRECTIVE:

Article 1   Definitions

For the purpose of this Directive:
- (a) 'design' means the appearance of the whole or a part of a product resulting from the features of, in particular, the lines, contours, colours, shape, texture and/or materials of the product itself and/or its ornamentation;
- (b) 'product' means any industrial or handicraft item, including inter alia parts intended to be assembled into a complex product, packaging, get-up, graphic symbols and typographic typefaces, but excluding computer programs;
- (c) 'complex product' means a product which is composed of multiple components which can be replaced permitting disassembly and reassembly of the product.

Article 2   Scope of application

1. This Directive shall apply to:
   - (a) design rights registered with the central industrial property offices of the Member States;
   - (b) design rights registered at the Benelux Design Office;
   - (c) design rights registered under international arrangements which have effect in a Member State;
   - (d) applications for design rights referred to under (a), (b) and (c).

2. For the purpose of this Directive, design registration shall also comprise the publication following filing of the design with the industrial property office of a Member State in which such publication has the effect of bringing a design right into existence.

Article 3   Protection requirements

1. Member States shall protect designs by registration, and shall confer exclusive rights upon their holders in accordance with the provisions of this Directive.

2. A design shall be protected by a design right to the extent that it is new and has individual character.

3. A design applied to or incorporated in a product which constitutes a component part of a complex product shall only be considered to be new and to have individual character:
   - (a) if the component part, once it has been incorporated into the complex product, remains visible during normal use of the latter, and
   - (b) to the extent that those visible features of the component part fulfil in themselves the requirements as to novelty and individual character.

4. 'Normal use' within the meaning of paragraph (3)(a) shall mean use by the end user, excluding maintenance, servicing or repair work.

Article 4   Novelty

A design shall be considered new if no identical design has been made available to the public before the date of filing of the application for registration or, if priority is claimed, the date of priority. Designs shall be deemed to be identical if their features differ only in immaterial details.

Article 5   Individual character

1. A design shall be considered to have individual character if the overall impression it produces on the informed user differs from the overall impression produced on such a user by any design which has been made available to the public before the date of filing of the application for registration or, if priority is claimed, the date of priority.

2. In assessing individual character, the degree of freedom of the designer in developing the design shall be taken into consideration.

Article 6   Disclosure

1. For the purpose of applying Articles 4 and 5, a design shall be deemed to have been made available to the public if it has been published following registration or otherwise, or exhibited, used in trade or otherwise disclosed, except where these events could not reasonably have become known in the normal course of business to the circles specialised in the sector concerned, operating within the Community, before the date of filing of the application for registration or, if priority is claimed, the date of priority. The design shall not, however, be deemed to have been made available to the public for the sole reason that it has been disclosed to a third person under explicit or implicit conditions of confidentiality.

2. A disclosure shall not be taken into consideration for the purpose of applying Articles 4 and 5 if a design for which protection is claimed under a registered design right of a Member State has been made available to the public:

    (a) by the designer, his successor in title, or a third person as a result of information provided or action taken by the designer, or his successor in title; and

    (b) during the 12-month period preceding the date of filing of the application or, if priority is claimed, the date of priority.

3. Paragraph 2 shall also apply if the design has been made available to the public as a consequence of an abuse in relation to the designer or his successor in title.

Article 7   Designs dictated by their technical function and designs of interconnections

1. A design right shall not subsist in features of appearance of a product which are solely dictated by its technical function.

2. A design right shall not subsist in features of appearance of a product which must necessarily be reproduced in their exact form and dimensions in order to permit the product in which the design is incorporated or to which it is applied to be mechanically connected to or placed in, around or against another product so that either product may perform its function.

3. Notwithstanding paragraph 2, a design right shall, under the conditions set out in Articles 4 and 5, subsist in a design serving the purpose of allowing multiple assembly or connection of mutually interchangeable products within a modular system.

Article 8   Designs contrary to public policy or morality

A design right shall not subsist in a design which is contrary to public policy or to accepted principles of morality.

Article 9   Scope of protection

1. The scope of the protection conferred by a design right shall include any design which does not produce on the informed user a different overall impression.

2. In assessing the scope of protection, the degree of freedom of the designer in developing his design shall be taken into consideration.

Article 10   Term of protection

Upon registration, a design which meets the requirements of Article 3(2) shall be protected by a design right for one or more periods of five years from the date of filing of the application. The right holder may have the term of protection renewed for one or more periods of five years each, up to a total term of 25 years from the date of filing.

Article 11   Invalidity or refusal of registration

1. A design shall be refused registration, or, if the design has been registered, the design right shall be declared invalid:

    (a) if the design is not a design within the meaning of Article 1(a); or

    (b) if it does not fulfil the requirements of Articles 3 to 8; or

    (c) if the applicant for or the holder of the design right is not entitled to it under the law of the Member State concerned; or

    (d) if the design is in conflict with a prior design which has been made available to the public after the date of filing of the application or, if priority is claimed, the date of priority, and which is protected from a date prior to the said date by a registered Community design or an application for a registered Community design or by a design right of the Member State concerned, or by an application for such a right.

2. Any Member State may provide that a design shall be refused registration, or, if the design has been registered, that the design right shall be declared invalid:

    (a) if a distinctive sign is used in a subsequent design, and Community law or the law of the Member State concerned governing that sign confers on the right holder of the sign the right to prohibit such use; or

    (b) if the design constitutes an unauthorised use of a work protected under the copyright law of the Member State concerned; or

    (c) if the design constitutes an improper use of any of the items listed in Article 6b of the Paris Convention for the Protection of Industrial Property, or of badges, emblems and escutcheons other than those covered by Article 6b of the said Convention which are of particular public interest in the Member State concerned.

3. The ground provided for in paragraph 1(c) may be invoked solely by the person who is entitled to the design right under the law of the Member State concerned.

4. The grounds provided for in paragraph 1(d) and in paragraph 2(a) and (b) may be invoked solely by the applicant for or the holder of the conflicting right.

5. The ground provided for in paragraph 2(c) may be invoked solely by the person or entity concerned by the use.

6. Paragraphs 4 and 5 shall be without prejudice to the freedom of Member States to provide that the grounds provided for in paragraphs 1(d) and 2(c) may also be invoked by the appropriate authority of the Member State in question on its own initiative.

7. When a design has been refused registration or a design right has been declared invalid pursuant to paragraph 1(b) or to paragraph 2, the design may be registered or the design right maintained in an amended form, if in that form it complies with the requirements for protection and the identity of the design is retained. Registration or maintenance in an amended form may include registration accompanied by a partial disclaimer by the holder of the design right or entry in the design Register of a court decision declaring the partial invalidity of the design right.

8. Any Member State may provide that, by way of derogation from paragraphs 1 to 7, the grounds for refusal of registration or for invalidation in force in that State prior to the date on which the provisions necessary to comply with this Directive enter into force shall apply to design applications which have been made prior to that date and to resulting registrations.

9. A design right may be declared invalid even after it has lapsed or has been surrendered.

Article 12   Rights conferred by the design right

1. The registration of a design shall confer on its holder the exclusive right to use it and to prevent any third party not having his consent from using it. The aforementioned use shall cover, in particular, the making, offering, putting on the market, importing, exporting or using of a product in which the design is incorporated or to which it is applied, or stocking such a product for those purposes.

2. Where, under the law of a Member State, acts referred to in paragraph 1 could not be prevented before the date on which the provisions necessary to comply with this Directive entered into force, the rights conferred by the design right may not be invoked to prevent continuation of such acts by any person who had begun such acts prior to that date.

Article 13 Limitation of the rights conferred by the design right

1. The rights conferred by a design right upon registration shall not be exercised in respect of:
   (a) acts done privately and for non-commercial purposes;
   (b) acts done for experimental purposes;
   (c) acts of reproduction for the purposes of making citations or of teaching, provided that such acts are compatible with fair trade practice and do not unduly prejudice the normal exploitation of the design, and that mention is made of the source.

2. In addition, the rights conferred by a design right upon registration shall not be exercised in respect of:
   (a) the equipment on ships and aircraft registered in another country when these temporarily enter the territory of the Member State concerned;
   (b) the importation in the Member State concerned of spare parts and accessories for the purpose of repairing such craft;
   (c) the execution of repairs on such craft.

Article 14 Transitional provision

Until such time as amendments to this Directive are adopted on a proposal from the Commission in accordance with the provisions of Article 18, Member States shall maintain in force their existing legal provisions relating to the use of the design of a component part used for the purpose of the repair of a complex product so as to restore its original appearance and shall introduce changes to those provisions only if the purpose is to liberalise the market for such parts.

Article 15 Exhaustion of rights

The rights conferred by a design right upon registration shall not extend to acts relating to a product in which a design included within the scope of protection of the design right is incorporated or to which it is applied, when the product has been put on the market in the Community by the holder of the design right or with his consent.

Article 16 Relationship to other forms of protection

The provisions of this Directive shall be without prejudice to any provisions of Community law or of the law of the Member State concerned relating to unregistered design rights, trade marks or other distinctive signs, patents and utility models, typefaces, civil liability or unfair competition.

Article 17 Relationship to copyright

A design protected by a design right registered in or in respect of a Member State in accordance with this Directive shall also be eligible for protection under the law of copyright of that State as from the date on which the design was created or fixed in any form. The extent to which, and the conditions under which, such a protection is conferred, including the level of originality required, shall be determined by each Member State.

Article 18 Revision

Three years after the implementation date specified in Article 19, the Commission shall submit an analysis of the consequences of the provisions of this Directive for Community industry, in particular the industrial sectors which are most affected, particularly manufacturers of complex products and component parts, for consumers, for competition and for the functioning of the internal market. At the latest one year later the Commission shall propose to the European Parliament and the Council any changes to this Directive needed to complete the internal market in respect of component parts of complex products and any other changes which it considers necessary in light of its consultations with the parties most affected.

Article 19   Implementation

1. Member States shall bring into force the laws, regulations or administrative provisions necessary to comply with this Directive not later than 28 October 2001.

When Member States adopt these provisions, they shall contain a reference to this Directive or shall be accompanied by such reference on the occasion of their official publication. The methods of making such reference shall be laid down by Member States.

2. Member States shall communicate to the Commission the provisions of national law which they adopt in the field governed by this Directive.

...

Directive 98/84/EC of the European Parliament and of the Council

of 20 November 1998 on the legal protection of services based on, or consisting of, conditional access

THE EUROPEAN PARLIAMENT AND THE COUNCIL OF THE EUROPEAN UNION,

Having regard to the Treaty establishing the European Community, and in particular Articles 57(2), 66 and 100a thereof,

Having regard to the proposal from the Commission,

Having regard to the opinion of the Economic and Social Committee,

Acting in accordance with the procedure laid down in Article 189b of the Treaty,

(1) Whereas the objectives of the Community as laid down in the Treaty include creating an ever closer union among the peoples of Europe and ensuring economic and social progress, by eliminating the barriers which divide them;

(2) Whereas the cross-border provision of broadcasting and information society services may contribute, from the individual point of view, to the full effectiveness of freedom of expression as a fundamental right and, from the collective point of view, to the achievement of the objectives laid down in the Treaty;

(3) Whereas the Treaty provides for the free movement of all services which are normally provided for remuneration; whereas this right, as applied to broadcasting and information society services, is also a specific manifestation in Community law of a more general principle, namely freedom of expression as enshrined in Article 10 of the European Convention for the Protection of Human Rights and Fundamental Freedoms; whereas that Article explicitly recognizes the right of citizens to receive and impart information regardless of frontiers and whereas any restriction of that right must be based on due consideration of other legitimate interests deserving of legal protection;

(4) Whereas the Commission undertook a wide-ranging consultation based on the Green Paper 'Legal Protection of Encrypted Services in the Internal Market'; whereas the results of that consultation confirmed the need for a Community legal instrument ensuring the legal protection of all those services whose remuneration relies on conditional access;

(5) Whereas the European Parliament, in its Resolution of 13 May 1997 on the Green Paper, called on the Commission to present a proposal for a Directive covering all encoded services in respect of which encoding is used to ensure payment of a fee, and agreed that this should include information society services provided at a distance by electronic means and at the individual request of a service receiver, as well as broadcasting services;

(6) Whereas the opportunities offered by digital technologies provide the potential for increasing consumer choice and contributing to cultural pluralism, by developing an even wider range of services within the meaning of Articles 59 and 60 of the Treaty; whereas the viability of those services will often depend on the use of conditional access in order to obtain the remuneration of the service provider; whereas, accordingly, the legal protection of service providers against illicit devices

which allow access to these services free of charge seems necessary in order to ensure the economic viability of the services;

(7) Whereas the importance of this issue was recognized by the Commission Communication on 'A European Initiative in Electronic Commerce';

(8) Whereas, in accordance with Article 7a of the Treaty, the internal market is to comprise an area without internal frontiers in which the free movement of services and goods is ensured; whereas Article 128(4) of the Treaty requires the Community to take cultural aspects into account in its action under other provisions of the Treaty; whereas by virtue of Article 130(3) of the Treaty, the Community must, through the policies and activities it pursues, contribute to creating the conditions necessary for the competitiveness of its industry;

(9) Whereas this Directive is without prejudice to possible future Community or national provisions meant to ensure that a number of broadcasting services, recognized as being of public interest, are not based on conditional access;

(10) Whereas this Directive is without prejudice to the cultural aspects of any further Community action concerning new services;

(11) Whereas the disparity between national rules concerning the legal protection of services based on, or consisting of, conditional access is liable to create obstacles to the free movement of services and goods;

(12) Whereas the application of the Treaty is not sufficient to remove these internal market obstacles; whereas those obstacles should therefore be removed by providing for an equivalent level of protection between Member States; whereas this implies an approximation of the national rules relating to the commercial activities which concern illicit devices;

(13) Whereas it seems necessary to ensure that Member States provide appropriate legal protection against the placing on the market, for direct or indirect financial gain, of an illicit device which enables or facilitates without authority the circumvention of any technological measures designed to protect the remuneration of a legally provided service;

(14) Whereas those commercial activities which concern illicit devices include commercial communications covering all forms of advertising, direct marketing, sponsorship, sales promotion and public relations promoting such products and services;

(15) Whereas those commercial activities are detrimental to consumers who are misled about the origin of illicit devices; whereas a high level of consumer protection is needed in order to fight against this kind of consumer fraud; whereas Article 129a(1) of the Treaty provides that the Community should contribute to the achievement of a high level of consumer protection by the measures it adopts pursuant to Article 100a thereof;

(16) Whereas, therefore, the legal framework for the creation of a single audiovisual area laid down in Council Directive 89/552/EEC of 3 October 1989 on the coordination of certain provisions laid down by law, regulation or administrative action in Member States concerning the pursuit of television broadcasting activities should be supplemented with reference to conditional access techniques as laid down in this Directive, in order, not least, to ensure equal treatment of the suppliers of cross-border broadcasts, regardless of their place of establishment;

(17) Whereas, in accordance with the Council Resolution of 29 June 1995 on the effective uniform application of Community law and on the penalties applicable for breaches of Community law in the internal market, Member States are required to take action to ensure that Community law is duly applied with the same effectiveness and thoroughness as national law;

(18) Whereas, in accordance with Article 5 of the Treaty, Member States are required to take all appropriate measures to guarantee the application and effectiveness of Community law, in particular by ensuring that the sanctions chosen are effective, dissuasive and proportionate and the remedies appropriate;

(19) Whereas the approximation of the laws, regulations and administrative provisions of the Member States should be limited to what is needed in order to achieve the objectives of the internal market, in accordance with the principle of proportionality as set out in the third paragraph of Article 3b of the Treaty;

(20) Whereas the distribution of illicit devices includes transfer by any means and putting such devices on the market for circulation inside or outside the Community;

(21) Whereas this Directive is without prejudice to the application of any national provisions which may prohibit the private possession of illicit devices, to the application of Community competition rules and to the application of Community rules concerning intellectual property rights;

(22) Whereas national law concerning sanctions and remedies for infringing commercial activities may provide that the activities have to be carried out in the knowledge or with reasonable grounds for knowing that the devices in question were illicit;

(23) Whereas the sanctions and remedies provided for under this Directive are without prejudice to any other sanction or remedy for which provision may be made under national law, such as preventive measures in general or seizure of illicit devices; whereas Member States are not obliged to provide criminal sanctions for infringing activities covered by this Directive; whereas Member States' provisions for actions for damages are to be in conformity with their national legislative and judicial systems;

(24) Whereas this Directive is without prejudice to the application of national rules which do not fall within the field herein coordinated, such as those adopted for the protection of minors, including those in compliance with Directive 89/552/EEC, or national provisions concerned with public policy or public security,

HAVE ADOPTED THIS DIRECTIVE:

Article 1 Scope

The objective of this Directive is to approximate provisions in the Member States concerning measures against illicit devices which give unauthorised access to protected services.

Article 2 Definitions

For the purposes of this Directive:

(a) *protected service* shall mean any of the following services, where provided against remuneration and on the basis of conditional access:
  — television broadcasting, as defined in Article 1(a) of Directive 89/552/EEC,
  — radio broadcasting, meaning any transmission by wire or over the air, including by satellite, of radio programmes intended for reception by the public,
  — information society services within the meaning of Article 1(2) of Directive 98/34/EC of the European Parliament and of the Council of 22 June 1998 laying down a procedure for the provision of information in the field of technical standards and regulations and of rules on information society services,
  or the provision of conditional access to the above services considered as a service in its own right;

(b) *conditional access* shall mean any technical measure and/or arrangement whereby access to the protected service in an intelligible form is made conditional upon prior individual authorisation;

(c) *conditional access device* shall mean any equipment or software designed or adapted to give access to a protected service in an intelligible form;

(d) *associated service* shall mean the installation, maintenance or replacement of conditional access devices, as well as the provision of commercial communication services in relation to them or to protected services;

(e) *illicit device* shall mean any equipment or software designed or adapted to give access to a protected service in an intelligible form without the authorisation of the service provider;

(f) *field coordinated by this Directive* shall mean any provision relating to the infringing activities specified in Article 4.

Article 3   Internal market principles

1. Each Member State shall take the measures necessary to prohibit on its territory the activities listed in Article 4, and to provide for the sanctions and remedies laid down in Article 5.

2. Without prejudice to paragraph 1, Member States may not:

(a) restrict the provision of protected services, or associated services, which originate in another Member State; or

(b) restrict the free movement of conditional access devices; for reasons falling within the field coordinated by this Directive.

Article 4   Infringing activities

Member States shall prohibit on their territory all of the following activities:

(a) the manufacture, import, distribution, sale, rental or possession for commercial purposes of illicit devices;

(b) the installation, maintenance or replacement for commercial purposes of an illicit device;

(c) the use of commercial communications to promote illicit devices.

Article 5   Sanctions and remedies

1. The sanctions shall be effective, dissuasive and proportionate to the potential impact of the infringing activity.

2. Member States shall take the necessary measures to ensure that providers of protected services whose interests are affected by an infringing activity as specified in Article 4, carried out on their territory, have access to appropriate remedies, including bringing an action for damages and obtaining an injunction or other preventive measure, and where appropriate, applying for disposal outside commercial channels of illicit devices.

Article 6   Implementation

1. Member States shall bring into force the laws, regulations and administrative provisions necessary to comply with this Directive by 28 May 2000. They shall notify them to the Commission forthwith.

When Member States adopt such measures, they shall contain a reference to this Directive or shall be accompanied by such reference at the time of their official publication. The methods of making such reference shall be laid down by Member States.

2. Member States shall communicate to the Commission the text of the provisions of national law which they adopt in the field coordinated by this Directive.

...

Directive 2001/29/EC of the European Parliament and of the Council

of 22 May 2001 on the harmonisation of certain aspects of copyright and related rights in the information society

THE EUROPEAN PARLIAMENT AND THE COUNCIL OF THE EUROPEAN UNION,

Having regard to the Treaty establishing the European Community, and in particular Articles 47(2), 55 and 95 thereof,

Having regard to the proposal from the Commission,

Having regard to the opinion of the Economic and Social Committee,

Acting in accordance with the procedure laid down in Article 251 of the Treaty,

Whereas:

(1) The Treaty provides for the establishment of an internal market and the institution of a system ensuring that competition in the internal market is not distorted. Harmonisation of the laws of the Member States on copyright and related rights contributes to the achievement of these objectives.

(2) The European Council, meeting at Corfu on 24 and 25 June 1994, stressed the need to create a general and flexible legal framework at Community level in order to foster the development of the information society in Europe. This requires, *inter alia,* the existence of an internal market for new products and services. Important Community legislation to ensure such a regulatory framework is already in place or its adoption is well under way. Copyright and related rights play an important role in this context as they protect and stimulate the development and marketing of new products and services and the creation and exploitation of their creative content.

(3) The proposed harmonisation will help to implement the four freedoms of the internal market and relates to compliance with the fundamental principles of law and especially of property, including intellectual property, and freedom of expression and the public interest.

(4) A harmonised legal framework on copyright and related rights, through increased legal certainty and while providing for a high level of protection of intellectual property, will foster substantial investment in creativity and innovation, including network infrastructure, and lead in turn to growth and increased competitiveness of European industry, both in the area of content provision and information technology and more generally across a wide range of industrial and cultural sectors. This will safeguard employment and encourage new job creation.

(5) Technological development has multiplied and diversified the vectors for creation, production and exploitation. While no new concepts for the protection of intellectual property are needed, the current law on copyright and related rights should be adapted and supplemented to respond adequately to economic realities such as new forms of exploitation.

(6) Without harmonisation at Community level, legislative activities at national level which have already been initiated in a number of Member States in order to respond to the technological challenges might result in significant differences in protection and thereby in restrictions on the free movement of services and products incorporating, or based on, intellectual property, leading to a refragmentation of the internal market and legislative inconsistency. The impact of such legislative differences and uncertainties will become more significant with the further development of the information society, which has already greatly increased transborder exploitation of intellectual property. This development will and should further increase. Significant legal differences and uncertainties in protection may hinder economies of scale for new products and services containing copyright and related rights.

(7) The Community legal framework for the protection of copyright and related rights must, therefore, also be adapted and supplemented as far as is necessary for the smooth functioning of the internal market. To that end, those national provisions on copyright and related rights which vary considerably from one Member State to another or which cause legal uncertainties hindering the smooth functioning of the internal market and the proper development of the information society in Europe should be adjusted, and inconsistent national responses to the technological developments should be avoided, whilst differences not adversely affecting the functioning of the internal market need not be removed or prevented.

(8) The various social, societal and cultural implications of the information society require that account be taken of the specific features of the content of products and services.

(9) Any harmonisation of copyright and related rights must take as a basis a high level of protection, since such rights are crucial to intellectual creation. Their protection helps to ensure the maintenance and development of creativity in the interests of authors, performers, producers, consumers, culture, industry and the public at large. Intellectual property has therefore been recognised as an integral part of property.

(10) If authors or performers are to continue their creative and artistic work, they have to receive an appropriate reward for the use of their work, as must producers in order to be able to finance this work. The investment required to produce products such as phonograms, films or multimedia products, and services such as 'on-demand' services, is considerable. Adequate legal protection of intellectual property rights is necessary in order to guarantee the availability of such a reward and provide the opportunity for satisfactory returns on this investment.

(11) A rigorous, effective system for the protection of copyright and related rights is one of the main ways of ensuring that European cultural creativity and production receive the necessary resources and of safeguarding the independence and dignity of artistic creators and performers.

(12) Adequate protection of copyright works and subject-matter of related rights is also of great importance from a cultural standpoint. Article 151 of the Treaty requires the Community to take cultural aspects into account in its action.

(13) A common search for, and consistent application at European level of, technical measures to protect works and other subject-matter and to provide the necessary information on rights are essential insofar as the ultimate aim of these measures is to give effect to the principles and guarantees laid down in law.

(14) This Directive should seek to promote learning and culture by protecting works and other subject-matter while permitting exceptions or limitations in the public interest for the purpose of education and teaching.

(15) The Diplomatic Conference held under the auspices of the World Intellectual Property Organisation (WIPO) in December 1996 led to the adoption of two new Treaties, the 'WIPO Copyright Treaty' and the 'WIPO Performances and Phonograms Treaty', dealing respectively with the protection of authors and the protection of performers and phonogram producers. Those Treaties update the international protection for copyright and related rights significantly, not least with regard to the so-called 'digital agenda', and improve the means to fight piracy world-wide. The Community and a majority of Member States have already signed the Treaties and the process of making arrangements for the ratification of the Treaties by the Community and the Member States is under way. This Directive also serves to implement a number of the new international obligations.

(16) Liability for activities in the network environment concerns not only copyright and related rights but also other areas, such as defamation, misleading advertising, or infringement of trademarks, and is addressed horizontally in Directive 2000/31/EC of the European Parliament and of the Council of 8 June 2000 on certain legal aspects of information society services, in particular electronic commerce, in the internal market ('Directive on electronic commerce'), which clarifies and harmonises various legal issues relating to information society services including electronic commerce. This Directive should be implemented within a timescale similar to that for the implementation of the Directive on electronic commerce, since that Directive provides a harmonised framework of principles and provisions relevant *inter alia* to important parts of this Directive. This Directive is without prejudice to provisions relating to liability in that Directive.

(17) It is necessary, especially in the light of the requirements arising out of the digital environment, to ensure that collecting societies achieve a higher level of rationalisation and transparency with regard to compliance with competition rules.

(18) This Directive is without prejudice to the arrangements in the Member States concerning the management of rights such as extended collective licences.

(19) The moral rights of rightholders should be exercised according to the legislation of the Member States and the provisions of the Berne Convention for the Protection of Literary and Artistic Works, of the WIPO Copyright Treaty and of the WIPO Performances and Phonograms Treaty. Such moral rights remain outside the scope of this Directive.

(20) This Directive is based on principles and rules already laid down in the Directives currently in force in this area, in particular Directives 91/250/EEC, 92/100/EEC, 93/83/EEC, 93/98/EEC and 96/9/EC and it develops those principles and places them in the context of the information society. The provisions of this Directive should be without prejudice to the provisions of those Directives, unless otherwise provided in this Directive.

(21) This Directive should define the scope of the acts covered by the reproduction right with regard to the different beneficiaries. This should be done in conformity with the acquis communautaire. A broad definition of these acts is needed to ensure legal certainty within the internal market.

(22) The objective of proper support for the dissemination of culture must not be achieved by sacrificing strict protection of rights or by tolerating illegal forms of distribution of counterfeited or pirated works.

(23) This Directive should harmonise further the author's right of communication to the public. This right should be understood in a broad sense covering all communication to the public not present

at the place where the communication originates. This right should cover any such transmission or retransmission of a work to the public by wire or wireless means, including broadcasting. This right should not cover any other acts.

(24) The right to make available to the public subject-matter referred to in Article 3(2) should be understood as covering all acts of making available such subject-matter to members of the public not present at the place where the act of making available originates, and as not covering any other acts.

(25) The legal uncertainty regarding the nature and the level of protection of acts of on-demand transmission of copyright works and subject-matter protected by related rights over networks should be overcome by providing for harmonised protection at Community level. It should be made clear that all rightholders recognised by this Directive should have an exclusive right to make available to the public copyright works or any other subject-matter by way of interactive on-demand transmissions. Such interactive on-demand transmissions are characterised by the fact that members of the public may access them from a place and at a time individually chosen by them.

(26) With regard to the making available in on-demand services by broadcasters of their radio or television productions incorporating music from commercial phonograms as an integral part thereof, collective licensing arrangements are to be encouraged in order to facilitate the clearance of the rights concerned.

(27) The mere provision of physical facilities for enabling or making a communication does not in itself amount to communication within the meaning of this Directive.

(28) Copyright protection under this Directive includes the exclusive right to control distribution of the work incorporated in a tangible article. The first sale in the Community of the original of a work or copies thereof by the rightholder or with his consent exhausts the right to control resale of that object in the Community. This right should not be exhausted in respect of the original or of copies thereof sold by the rightholder or with his consent outside the Community. Rental and lending rights for authors have been established in Directive 92/100/EEC. The distribution right provided for in this Directive is without prejudice to the provisions relating to the rental and lending rights contained in Chapter I of that Directive.

(29) The question of exhaustion does not arise in the case of services and on-line services in particular. This also applies with regard to a material copy of a work or other subject-matter made by a user of such a service with the consent of the rightholder. Therefore, the same applies to rental and lending of the original and copies of works or other subject-matter which are services by nature. Unlike CD-ROM or CD-I, where the intellectual property is incorporated in a material medium, namely an item of goods, every on-line service is in fact an act which should be subject to authorisation where the copyright or related right so provides.

(30) The rights referred to in this Directive maybe transferred, assigned or subject to the granting of contractual licences, without prejudice to the relevant national legislation on copyright and related rights.

(31) A fair balance of rights and interests between the different categories of right-holders, as well as between the different categories of rightholders and users of protected subject-matter must be safeguarded. The existing exceptions and limitations to the rights as set out by the Member States have to be reassessed in the light of the new electronic environment. Existing differences in the exceptions and limitations to certain restricted acts have direct negative effects on the functioning of the internal market of copyright and related rights. Such differences could well become more pronounced in view of the further development of transborder exploitation of works and cross-border activities. In order to ensure the proper functioning of the internal market, such exceptions and limitations should be defined more harmoniously. The degree of their harmonisation should be based on their impact on the smooth functioning of the internal market.

(32) This Directive provides for an exhaustive enumeration of exceptions and limitations to the reproduction right and the right of communication to the public. Some exceptions or limitations only apply to the reproduction right, where appropriate. This list takes due account of the different legal traditions in Member States, while, at the same time, aiming to ensure a functioning internal market. Member States should arrive at a coherent application of these exceptions and limitations, which will be assessed when reviewing implementing legislation in the future.

(33) The exclusive right of reproduction should be subject to an exception to allow certain acts of temporary reproduction, which are transient or incidental reproductions, forming an integral and essential part of a technological process and carried out for the sole purpose of enabling either efficient transmission in a network between third parties by an intermediary, or a lawful use of a work or other subject-matter to be made. The acts of reproduction concerned should have no separate economic value on their own. To the extent that they meet these conditions, this exception should include acts which enable browsing as well as acts of caching to take place, including those which enable transmission systems to function efficiently, provided that the intermediary does not modify the information and does not interfere with the lawful use of technology, widely recognised and used by industry, to obtain data on the use of the information. A use should be considered lawful where it is authorised by the rightholder or not restricted by law.

(34) Member States should be given the option of providing for certain exceptions or limitations for cases such as educational and scientific purposes, for the benefit of public institutions such as libraries and archives, for purposes of news reporting, for quotations, for use by people with disabilities, for public security uses and for uses in administrative and judicial proceedings.

(35) In certain cases of exceptions or limitations, rightholders should receive fair compensation to compensate them adequately for the use made of their protected works or other subject-matter. When determining the form, detailed arrangements and possible level of such fair compensation, account should be taken of the particular circumstances of each case. When evaluating these circumstances, a valuable criterion would be the possible harm to the right-holders resulting from the act in question. In cases where rightholders have already received payment in some other form, for instance as part of a licence fee, no specific or separate payment maybe due. The level of fair compensation should take full account of the degree of use of technological protection measures referred to in this Directive. In certain situations where the prejudice to the rightholder would be minimal, no obligation for payment may arise.

(36) The Member States may provide for fair compensation for rightholders also when applying the optional provisions on exceptions or limitations which do not require such compensation.

(37) Existing national schemes on reprography, where they exist, do not create major barriers to the internal market. Member States should be allowed to provide for an exception or limitation in respect of reprography.

(38) Member States should be allowed to provide for an exception or limitation to the reproduction right for certain types of reproduction of audio, visual and audio-visual material for private use, accompanied by fair compensation. This may include the introduction or continuation of remuneration schemes to compensate for the prejudice to rightholders. Although differences between those remuneration schemes affect the functioning of the internal market, those differences, with respect to analogue private reproduction, should not have a significant impact on the development of the information society. Digital private copying is likely to be more widespread and have a greater economic impact. Due account should therefore be taken of the differences between digital and analogue private copying and a distinction should be made in certain respects between them.

(39) When applying the exception or limitation on private copying, Member States should take due account of technological and economic developments, in particular with respect to digital private copying and remuneration schemes, when effective technological protection measures are available. Such exceptions or limitations should not inhibit the use of technological measures or their enforcement against circumvention.

(40) Member States may provide for an exception or limitation for the benefit of certain non-profit making establishments, such as publicly accessible libraries and equivalent institutions, as well as archives. However, this should be limited to certain special cases covered by the reproduction right. Such an exception or limitation should not cover uses made in the context of on-line delivery of protected works or other subject-matter. This Directive should be without prejudice to the Member States' option to derogate from the exclusive public lending right in accordance with Article 5 of Directive 92/100/EEC. Therefore, specific contracts or licences should be promoted which, without creating imbalances, favour such establishments and the disseminative purposes they serve.

(41) When applying the exception or limitation in respect of ephemeral recordings made by broadcasting organisations, it is understood that a broadcaster's own facilities include those of a person acting on behalf of and under the responsibility of the broadcasting organisation.

(42) When applying the exception or limitation for non-commercial educational and scientific research purposes, including distance learning, the non-commercial nature of the activity in question should be determined by that activity as such. The organisational structure and the means of funding of the establishment concerned are not the decisive factors in this respect.

(43) It is in any case important for the Member States to adopt all necessary measures to facilitate access to works by persons suffering from a disability which constitutes an obstacle to the use of the works themselves, and to pay particular attention to accessible formats.

(44) When applying the exceptions and limitations provided for in this Directive, they should be exercised in accordance with international obligations. Such exceptions and limitations may not be applied in a way which prejudices the legitimate interests of the rightholder or which conflicts with the normal exploitation of his work or other subject-matter. The provision of such exceptions or limitations by Member States should, in particular, duly reflect the increased economic impact that such exceptions or limitations may have in the context of the new electronic environment. Therefore, the scope of certain exceptions or limitations may have to be even more limited when it comes to certain new uses of copyright works and other subject-matter.

(45) The exceptions and limitations referred to in Article 5(2), (3) and (4) should not, however, prevent the definition of contractual relations designed to ensure fair compensation for the rightholders insofar as permitted by national law.

(46) Recourse to mediation could help users and rightholders to settle disputes. The Commission, in cooperation with the Member States within the Contact Committee, should undertake a study to consider new legal ways of settling disputes concerning copyright and related rights.

(47) Technological development will allow rightholders to make use of technological measures designed to prevent or restrict acts not authorised by the rightholders of any copyright, rights related to copyright or the *sui generis* right in databases. The danger, however, exists that illegal activities might be carried out in order to enable or facilitate the circumvention of the technical protection provided by these measures. In order to avoid fragmented legal approaches that could potentially hinder the functioning of the internal market, there is a need to provide for harmonised legal protection against circumvention of effective technological measures and against provision of devices and products or services to this effect.

(48) Such legal protection should be provided in respect of technological measures that effectively restrict acts not authorised by the rightholders of any copyright, rights related to copyright or the *sui generis* right in databases without, however, preventing the normal operation of electronic equipment and its technological development. Such legal protection implies no obligation to design devices, products, components or services to correspond to technological measures, so long as such device, product, component or service does not otherwise fall under the prohibition of Article 6. Such legal protection should respect proportionality and should not prohibit those devices or activities which have a commercially significant purpose or use other than to circumvent the technical protection. In particular, this protection should not hinder research into cryptography.

(49) The legal protection of technological measures is without prejudice to the application of any national provisions which may prohibit the private possession of devices, products or components for the circumvention of technological measures.

(50) Such a harmonised legal protection does not affect the specific provisions on protection provided for by Directive 91/250/EEC. In particular, it should not apply to the protection of technological measures used in connection with computer programs, which is exclusively addressed in that Directive. It should neither inhibit nor prevent the development or use of any means of circumventing a technological measure that is necessary to enable acts to be undertaken in accordance with the terms of Article 5(3) or Article 6 of Directive 91/250/EEC. Articles 5 and 6 of that Directive exclusively determine exceptions to the exclusive rights applicable to computer programs.

(51) The legal protection of technological measures applies without prejudice to public policy, as reflected in Article 5, or public security. Member States should promote voluntary measures taken by rightholders, including the conclusion and implementation of agreements between rightholders and other parties concerned, to accommodate achieving the objectives of certain exceptions or limitations provided for in national law in accordance with this Directive. In the absence of such voluntary measures or agreements within a reasonable period of time, Member States should take appropriate measures to ensure that rightholders provide beneficiaries of such exceptions or limitations with appropriate means of benefiting from them, by modifying an implemented technological measure or by other means. However, in order to prevent abuse of such measures taken by rightholders, including within the framework of agreements, or taken by a Member State, any technological measures applied in implementation of such measures should enjoy legal protection.

(52) When implementing an exception or limitation for private copying in accordance with Article 5(2)(b), Member States should likewise promote the use of voluntary measures to accommodate achieving the objectives of such exception or limitation. If, within a reasonable period of time, no such voluntary measures to make reproduction for private use possible have been taken, Member States may take measures to enable beneficiaries of the exception or limitation concerned to benefit from it. Voluntary measures taken by right-holders, including agreements between rightholders and other parties concerned, as well as measures taken by Member States, do not prevent rightholders from using technological measures which are consistent with the exceptions or limitations on private copying in national law in accordance with Article 5(2)(b), taking account of the condition of fair compensation under that provision and the possible differentiation between various conditions of use in accordance with Article 5(5), such as controlling the number of reproductions. In order to prevent abuse of such measures, any technological measures applied in their implementation should enjoy legal protection.

(53) The protection of technological measures should ensure a secure environment for the provision of interactive on-demand services, in such a way that members of the public may access works or other subject-matter from a place and at a time individually chosen by them. Where such services are governed by contractual arrangements, the first and second subparagraphs of Article 6(4) should not apply. Non-interactive forms of online use should remain subject to those provisions.

(54) Important progress has been made in the international standardisation of technical systems of identification of works and protected subject matter in digital format. In an increasingly networked environment, differences between technological measures could lead to an incompatibility of systems within the Community. Compatibility and interoperability of the different systems should be encouraged. It would be highly desirable to encourage the development of global systems.

(55) Technological development will facilitate the distribution of works, notably on networks, and this will entail the need for rightholders to identify better the work or other subject-matter, the author or any other rightholder, and to provide information about the terms and conditions of use of the work or other subject-matter in order to render easier the management of rights attached to them. Rightholders should be encouraged to use markings indicating, in addition to the information referred to above, *inter alia* their authorisation when putting works or other subject-matter on networks.

(56) There is, however, the danger that illegal activities might be carried out in order to remove or alter the electronic copyright-management information attached to it, or otherwise to distribute, import for distribution, broadcast, communicate to the public or make available to the public works or other protected subject-matter from which such information has been removed without authority. In order to avoid fragmented legal approaches that could potentially hinder the functioning of the internal market, there is a need to provide for harmonised legal protection against any of these activities.

(57) Any such rights-management information systems referred to above may, depending on their design, at the same time process personal data about the consumption patterns of protected subject-matter by individuals and allow for tracing of on-line behaviour. These technical means, in their technical functions, should incorporate privacy safeguards in accordance with Directive 95/46/EC of the European Parliament and of the Council of 24 October 1995 on the protection of individuals with regard to the processing of personal data and the free movement of such data.

(58) Member States should provide for effective sanctions and remedies for infringements of rights and obligations as set out in this Directive. They should take all the measures necessary to ensure that those sanctions and remedies are applied. The sanctions thus provided for should be effective, proportionate and dissuasive and should include the possibility of seeking damages and/or injunctive relief and, where appropriate, of applying for seizure of infringing material.

(59) In the digital environment, in particular, the services of intermediaries may increasingly be used by third parties for infringing activities. In many cases such intermediaries are best placed to bring such infringing activities to an end. Therefore, without prejudice to any other sanctions and remedies available, rightholders should have the possibility of applying for an injunction against an intermediary who carries a third party's infringement of a protected work or other subject-matter in a network. This possibility should be available even where the acts carried out by the intermediary are exempted under Article 5. The conditions and modalities relating to such injunctions should be left to the national law of the Member States.

(60) The protection provided under this Directive should be without prejudice to national or Community legal provisions in other areas, such as industrial property, data protection, conditional access, access to public documents, and the rule of media exploitation chronology, which may affect the protection of copyright or related rights.

(61) In order to comply with the WIPO Performances and Phonograms Treaty, Directives 92/100/EEC and 93/98/EEC should be amended,

HAVE ADOPTED THIS DIRECTIVE:

Chapter I   Objective and Scope

Article 1   Scope

1. This Directive concerns the legal protection of copyright and related rights in the framework of the internal market, with particular emphasis on the information society.

2. Except in the cases referred to in Article 11, this Directive shall leave intact and shall in no way affect existing Community provisions relating to:
   (a) the legal protection of computer programs;
   (b) rental right, lending right and certain rights related to copyright in the field of intellectual property;
   (c) copyright and related rights applicable to broadcasting of programmes by satellite and cable retransmission;
   (d) the term of protection of copyright and certain related rights;
   (e) the legal protection of databases.

Chapter II   Rights and Exceptions

Article 2   Reproduction right

Member States shall provide for the exclusive right to authorise or prohibit direct or indirect, temporary or permanent reproduction by any means and in any form, in whole or in part:
   (a) for authors, of their works;
   (b) for performers, of fixations of their performances;
   (c) for phonogram producers, of their phonograms;
   (d) for the producers of the first fixations of films, in respect of the original and copies of their films;
   (e) for broadcasting organisations, of fixations of their broadcasts, whether those broadcasts are transmitted by wire or over the air, including by cable or satellite.

Article 3   Right of communication to the public of works and right of making available to the public other subject-matter

1. Member States shall provide authors with the exclusive right to authorise or prohibit any communication to the public of their works, by wire or wireless means, including the making available to the public of their works in such a way that members of the public may access them from a place and at a time individually chosen by them.

2. Member States shall provide for the exclusive right to authorise or prohibit the making available to the public, by wire or wireless means, in such a way that members of the public may access them from a place and at a time individually chosen by them:

(a) for performers, of fixations of their performances;

(b) for phonogram producers, of their phonograms;

(c) for the producers of the first fixations of films, of the original and copies of their films;

(d) for broadcasting organisations, of fixations of their broadcasts, whether these broadcasts are transmitted by wire or over the air, including by cable or satellite.

3. The rights referred to in paragraphs 1 and 2 shall not be exhausted by any act of communication to the public or making available to the public as set out in this Article.

Article 4   Distribution right

1. Member States shall provide for authors, in respect of the original of their works or of copies thereof, the exclusive right to authorise or prohibit any form of distribution to the public by sale or otherwise.

2. The distribution right shall not be exhausted within the Community in respect of the original or copies of the work, except where the first sale or other transfer of ownership in the Community of that object is made by the rightholder or with his consent.

Article 5   Exceptions and limitations

1. Temporary acts of reproduction referred to in Article 2, which are transient or incidental, which are an integral and essential part of a technological process and the sole purpose of which is to enable:

(a) a transmission in a network between third parties by an intermediary, or

(b) a lawful use

of a work or other subject-matter to be made, and which have no independent economic significance, shall be exempted from the reproduction right provided for in Article 2.

2. Member States may provide for exceptions or limitations to the reproduction right provided for in Article 2 in the following cases:

(a) in respect of reproductions on paper or any similar medium, effected by the use of any kind of photographic technique or by some other process having similar effects, with the exception of sheet music, provided that the rightholders receive fair compensation;

(b) in respect of reproductions on any medium made by a natural person for private use and for ends that are neither directly nor indirectly commercial, on condition that the rightholders receive fair compensation, which takes account of the application or non-application of technological measures referred to in Article 6 to the work or subject-matter concerned;

(c) in respect of specific acts of reproduction made by publicly accessible libraries, educational establishments or museums, or by archives, which are not for direct or indirect economic or commercial advantage, without prejudice to the exceptions and limitations provided for in Directive (EU) 2019/790 of the European Parliament and of the Council;

(d) in respect of ephemeral recordings of works made by broadcasting organisations by means of their own facilities and for their own broadcasts; the preservation of these recordings in official archives may, on the grounds of their exceptional documentary character, be permitted;

(e) in respect of reproductions of broadcasts made by social institutions pursuing non-commercial purposes, such as hospitals or prisons, on condition that the rightholders receive fair compensation.

3. Member States may provide for exceptions or limitations to the rights provided for in Articles 2 and 3 in the following cases:

(a) use for the sole purpose of illustration for teaching or scientific research, as long as the source, including the author's name, is indicated, unless this turns out to be impossible and to the extent justified by the non-commercial purpose to be achieved, without prejudice to the exceptions and limitations provided for in Directive (EU) 2019/790;

(b) uses, for the benefit of people with a disability, which are directly related to the disability and of a non-commercial nature, to the extent required by the specific disability, without prejudice to the obligations of Member States under Directive (EU) 2017/1564 of the European Parliament and of the Council;

(c) reproduction by the press, communication to the public or making available of published articles on current economic, political or religious topics or of broadcast works or other subject-matter of the same character, in cases where such use is not expressly reserved, and as long as the source, including the author's name, is indicated, or use of works or other subject-matter in connection with the reporting of current events, to the extent justified by the informatory purpose and as long as the source, including the author's name, is indicated, unless this turns out to be impossible;

(d) quotations for purposes such as criticism or review, provided that they relate to a work or other subject-matter which has already been lawfully made available to the public, that, unless this turns out to be impossible, the source, including the author's name, is indicated, and that their use is in accordance with fair practice, and to the extent required by the specific purpose;

(e) use for the purposes of public security or to ensure the proper performance or reporting of administrative, parliamentary or judicial proceedings;

(f) use of political speeches as well as extracts of public lectures or similar works or subject-matter to the extent justified by the informatory purpose and provided that the source, including the author's name, is indicated, except where this turns out to be impossible;

(g) use during religious celebrations or official celebrations organised by a public authority;

(h) use of works, such as works of architecture or sculpture, made to be located permanently in public places;

(i) incidental inclusion of a work or other subject-matter in other material;

(j) use for the purpose of advertising the public exhibition or sale of artistic works, to the extent necessary to promote the event, excluding any other commercial use;

(k) use for the purpose of caricature, parody or pastiche;

(l) use in connection with the demonstration or repair of equipment;

(m) use of an artistic work in the form of a building or a drawing or plan of a building for the purposes of reconstructing the building;

(n) use by communication or making available, for the purpose of research or private study, to individual members of the public by dedicated terminals on the premises of establishments referred to in paragraph 2(c) of works and other subject-matter not subject to purchase or licensing terms which are contained in their collections;

(o) use in certain other cases of minor importance where exceptions or limitations already exist under national law, provided that they only concern analogue uses and do not affect the free circulation of goods and services within the Community, without prejudice to the other exceptions and limitations contained in this Article.

4. Where the Member States may provide for an exception or limitation to the right of reproduction pursuant to paragraphs 2 and 3, they may provide similarly for an exception or limitation to the right of distribution as referred to in Article 4 to the extent justified by the purpose of the authorised act of reproduction.

5. The exceptions and limitations provided for in paragraphs 1, 2, 3 and 4 shall only be applied in certain special cases which do not conflict with a normal exploitation of the work or other subject-matter and do not unreasonably prejudice the legitimate interests of the rightholder.

Chapter III   Protection of Technological Measures and Rights-Management Information

Article 6   Obligations as to technological measures

1. Member States shall provide adequate legal protection against the circumvention of any effective technological measures, which the person concerned carries out in the knowledge, or with reasonable grounds to know, that he or she is pursuing that objective.

2. Member States shall provide adequate legal protection against the manufacture, import, distribution, sale, rental, advertisement for sale or rental, or possession for commercial purposes of devices, products or components or the provision of services which:

    (a) are promoted, advertised or marketed for the purpose of circumvention of, or

    (b) have only a limited commercially significant purpose or use other than to circumvent, or

    (c) are primarily designed, produced, adapted or performed for the purpose of enabling or facilitating the circumvention of,

any effective technological measures.

3. For the purposes of this Directive, the expression 'technological measures' means any technology, device or component that, in the normal course of its operation, is designed to prevent or restrict acts, in respect of works or other subject-matter, which are not authorised by the rightholder of any copyright or any right related to copyright as provided for by law or the *sui generis* right provided for in Chapter III of Directive 96/9/EC. Technological measures shall be deemed 'effective' where the use of a protected work or other subject-matter is controlled by the rightholders through application of an access control or protection process, such as encryption, scrambling or other transformation of the work or other subject-matter or a copy control mechanism, which achieves the protection objective.

4. Notwithstanding the legal protection provided for in paragraph 1, in the absence of voluntary measures taken by rightholders, including agreements between right-holders and other parties concerned, Member States shall take appropriate measures to ensure that right-holders make available to the beneficiary of an exception or limitation provided for in national law in accordance with Article 5(2)(a), (2)(c), (2)(d), (2)(e), (3)(a), (3)(b) or (3)(e) the means of benefiting from that exception or limitation, to the extent necessary to benefit from that exception or limitation and where that beneficiary has legal access to the protected work or subject-matter concerned.

A Member State may also take such measures in respect of a beneficiary of an exception or limitation provided for in accordance with Article 5(2)(b), unless reproduction for private use has already been made possible by rightholders to the extent necessary to benefit from the exception or limitation concerned and in accordance with the provisions of Article 5(2)(b) and (5), without preventing rightholders from adopting adequate measures regarding the number of reproductions in accordance with these provisions.

The technological measures applied voluntarily by rightholders, including those applied in implementation of voluntary agreements, and technological measures applied in implementation of the measures taken by Member States, shall enjoy the legal protection provided for in paragraph 1.

The provisions of the first and second subparagraphs shall not apply to works or other subject-matter made available to the public on agreed contractual terms in such a way that members of the public may access them from a place and at a time individually chosen by them.

When this Article is applied in the context of Directives 92/100/EEC and 96/9/EC, this paragraph shall apply *mutatis mutandis*.

Article 7   Obligations concerning rights-management information

1. Member States shall provide for adequate legal protection against any person knowingly performing without authority any of the following acts:

    (a) the removal or alteration of any electronic rights-management information;

    (b) the distribution, importation for distribution, broadcasting, communication or making available to the public of works or other subject-matter protected under this Directive or under Chapter III of Directive 96/9/EC from which electronic rights-management information has been removed or altered without authority,

if such person knows, or has reasonable grounds to know, that by so doing he is inducing, enabling, facilitating or concealing an infringement of any copyright or any rights related to copyright as provided by law, or of the *sui generis* right provided for in Chapter III of Directive 96/9/EC.

    2. For the purposes of this Directive, the expression 'rights-management information' means any information provided by rightholders which identifies the work or other subject-matter referred to in this Directive or covered by the *sui generis* right provided for in Chapter III of Directive 96/9/EC, the author or any other rightholder, or information about the terms and conditions of use of the work or other subject-matter, and any numbers or codes that represent such information.

    The first subparagraph shall apply when any of these items of information is associated with a copy of, or appears in connection with the communication to the public of, a work or other subject-matter referred to in this Directive or covered by the *sui generis* right provided for in Chapter III of Directive 96/9/EC.

Chapter IV   Common Provisions

Article 8   Sanctions and remedies

    1. Member States shall provide appropriate sanctions and remedies in respect of infringements of the rights and obligations set out in this Directive and shall take all the measures necessary to ensure that those sanctions and remedies are applied. The sanctions thus provided for shall be effective, proportionate and dissuasive.

    2. Each Member State shall take the measures necessary to ensure that rightholders whose interests are affected by an infringing activity carried out on its territory can bring an action for damages and/or apply for an injunction and, where appropriate, for the seizure of infringing material as well as of devices, products or components referred to in Article 6(2).

    3. Member States shall ensure that rightholders are in a position to apply for an injunction against intermediaries whose services are used by a third party to infringe a copyright or related right.

Article 9   Continued application of other legal provisions

This Directive shall be without prejudice to provisions concerning in particular patent rights, trade marks, design rights, utility models, topographies of semi-conductor products, type faces, conditional access, access to cable of broadcasting services, protection of national treasures, legal deposit requirements, laws on restrictive practices and unfair competition, trade secrets, security, confidentiality, data protection and privacy, access to public documents, the law of contract.

Article 10   Application over time

    1. The provisions of this Directive shall apply in respect of all works and other subject-matter referred to in this Directive which are, on 22 December 2002, protected by the Member States' legislation in the field of copyright and related rights, or which meet the criteria for protection under the provisions of this Directive or the provisions referred to in Article 1(2).

    2. This Directive shall apply without prejudice to any acts concluded and rights acquired before 22 December 2002.

. . .

Done at Brussels, 22 May 2001.

Directive 2001/84/EC of the European Parliament and of the Council

of 27 September 2001 on the resale right for the benefit of the author of an original work of art

THE EUROPEAN PARLIAMENT AND THE COUNCIL OF THE EUROPEAN UNION,

Having regard to the Treaty establishing the European Community, and in particular Article 95 thereof,

Having regard to the proposal from the Commission,

Having regard to the opinion of the Economic and Social Committee,

Acting in accordance with the procedure laid down in Article 251 of the Treaty, and in the light of the joint text approved by the Conciliation Committee on 6 June 2001.

Whereas:

(1) In the field of copyright, the resale right is an unassignable and inalienable right, enjoyed by the author of an original work of graphic or plastic art, to an economic interest in successive sales of the work concerned.

(2) The resale right is a right of a productive character which enables the author/artist to receive consideration for successive transfers of the work. The subject-matter of the resale right is the physical work, namely the medium in which the protected work is incorporated.

(3) The resale right is intended to ensure that authors of graphic and plastic works of art share in the economic success of their original works of art. It helps to redress the balance between the economic situation of authors of graphic and plastic works of art and that of other creators who benefit from successive exploitations of their works.

(4) The resale right forms an integral part of copyright and is an essential prerogative for authors. The imposition of such a right in all Member States meets the need for providing creators with an adequate and standard level of protection.

(5) Under Article 151(4) of the Treaty the Community is to take cultural aspects into account in its action under other provisions of the Treaty.

(6) The Berne Convention for the Protection of Literary and Artistic Works provides that the resale right is available only if legislation in the country to which the author belongs so permits. The right is therefore optional and subject to the rule of reciprocity. It follows from the case-law of the Court of Justice of the European Communities on the application of the principle of non-discrimination laid down in Article 12 of the Treaty, as shown in the judgment of 20 October 1993 in Joined Cases C-92/92 and C-326/92 Phil Collins and Others, that domestic provisions containing reciprocity clauses cannot be relied upon in order to deny nationals of other Member States rights conferred on national authors. The application of such clauses in the Community context runs counter to the principle of equal treatment resulting from the prohibition of any discrimination on grounds of nationality.

(7) The process of internationalisation of the Community market in modern and contemporary art, which is now being speeded up by the effects of the new economy, in a regulatory context in which few States outside the EU recognise the resale right, makes it essential for the European Community, in the external sphere, to open negotiations with a view to making Article 14b of the Berne Convention compulsory.

(8) The fact that this international market exists, combined with the lack of a resale right in several Member States and the current disparity as regards national systems which recognise that right, make it essential to lay down transitional provisions as regards both entry into force and the substantive regulation of the right, which will preserve the competitiveness of the European market.

(9) The resale right is currently provided for by the domestic legislation of a majority of Member States. Such laws, where they exist, display certain differences, notably as regards the works covered, those entitled to receive royalties, the rate applied, the transactions subject to payment of a royalty, and the basis on which these are calculated. The application or non-application of such a right has a significant impact on the competitive environment within the internal market, since the existence or absence

of an obligation to pay on the basis of the resale right is an element which must be taken into account by each individual wishing to sell a work of art. This right is therefore a factor which contributes to the creation of distortions of competition as well as displacement of sales within the Community.

(10) Such disparities with regard to the existence of the resale right and its application by the Member States have a direct negative impact on the proper functioning of the internal market in works of art as provided for by Article 14 of the Treaty. In such a situation Article 95 of the Treaty constitutes the appropriate legal basis.

(11) The objectives of the Community as set out in the Treaty include laying the foundations of an ever closer union among the peoples of Europe, promoting closer relations between the Member States belonging to the Community, and ensuring their economic and social progress by common action to eliminate the barriers which divide Europe. To that end the Treaty provides for the establishment of an internal market which presupposes the abolition of obstacles to the free movement of goods, freedom to provide services and freedom of establishment, and for the introduction of a system ensuring that competition in the common market is not distorted. Harmonisation of Member States' laws on the resale right contributes to the attainment of these objectives.

(12) The Sixth Council Directive (77/388/EEC) of 17 May 1977 on the harmonisation of the laws of the Member States relating to turnover taxes—common system of value added tax: uniform basis of assessment, progressively introduces a Community system of taxation applicable *inter alia* to works of art. Measures confined to the tax field are not sufficient to guarantee the harmonious functioning of the art market. This objective cannot be attained without harmonisation in the field of the resale right.

(13) Existing differences between laws should be eliminated where they have a distorting effect on the functioning of the internal market, and the emergence of any new differences of that kind should be prevented. There is no need to eliminate, or prevent the emergence of, differences which cannot be expected to affect the functioning of the internal market.

(14) A precondition of the proper functioning of the internal market is the existence of conditions of competition which are not distorted. The existence of differences between national provisions on the resale right creates distortions of competition and displacement of sales within the Community and leads to unequal treatment between artists depending on where their works are sold. The issue under consideration has therefore transnational aspects which cannot be satisfactorily regulated by action by Member States. A lack of Community action would conflict with the requirement of the Treaty to correct distortions of competition and unequal treatment.

(15) In view of the scale of divergences between national provisions it is therefore necessary to adopt harmonising measures to deal with disparities between the laws of the Member States in areas where such disparities are liable to create or maintain distorted conditions of competition. It is not however necessary to harmonise every provision of the Member States' laws on the resale right and, in order to leave as much scope for national decision as possible, it is sufficient to limit the harmonisation exercise to those domestic provisions that have the most direct impact on the functioning of the internal market.

(16) This Directive complies therefore, in its entirety, with the principles of subsidiarity and proportionality as laid down in Article 5 of the Treaty.

(17) Pursuant to Council Directive 93/98/EEC of 29 October 1993 harmonising the term of protection of copyright and certain related rights, the term of copyright runs for 70 years after the author's death. The same period should be laid down for the resale right. Consequently, only the originals of works of modern and contemporary art may fall within the scope of the resale right. However, in order to allow the legal systems of Member States which do not, at the time of the adoption of this Directive, apply a resale right for the benefit of artists to incorporate this right into their respective legal systems and, moreover, to enable the economic operators in those Member States to adapt gradually to the aforementioned right whilst maintaining their economic viability, the Member States concerned should be allowed a limited transitional period during which they may choose not to apply the resale right for the benefit of those entitled under the artist after his death.

(18) The scope of the resale right should be extended to all acts of resale, with the exception of those effected directly between persons acting in their private capacity without the participation of an art market professional. This right should not extend to acts of resale by persons acting in their private capacity to museums which are not for profit and which are open to the public. With regard to the particular situation of art galleries which acquire works directly from the author, Member States should be allowed the option of exempting from the resale right acts of resale of those works which take place within three years of that acquisition. The interests of the artist should also be taken into account by limiting this exemption to such acts of resale where the resale price does not exceed EUR 10 000.

(19) It should be made clear that the harmonisation brought about by this Directive does not apply to original manuscripts of writers and composers.

(20) Effective rules should be laid down based on experience already gained at national level with the resale right. It is appropriate to calculate the royalty as a percentage of the sale price and not of the increase in value of works whose original value has increased.

(21) The categories of works of art subject to the resale right should be harmonised.

(22) The non-application of royalties below the minimum threshold may help to avoid disproportionately high collection and administration costs compared with the profit for the artist. However, in accordance with the principle of subsidiarity, the Member States should be allowed to establish national thresholds lower than the Community threshold, so as to promote the interests of new artists. Given the small amounts involved, this derogation is not likely to have a significant effect on the proper functioning of the internal market.

(23) The rates set by the different Member States for the application of the resale right vary considerably at present. The effective functioning of the internal market in works of modern and contemporary art requires the fixing of uniform rates to the widest possible extent.

(24) It is desirable to establish, with the intention of reconciling the various interests involved in the market for original works of art, a system consisting of a tapering scale of rates for several price bands. It is important to reduce the risk of sales relocating and of the circumvention of the Community rules on the resale right.

(25) The person by whom the royalty is payable should, in principle, be the seller. Member States should be given the option to provide for derogations from this principle in respect of liability for payment. The seller is the person or undertaking on whose behalf the sale is concluded.

(26) Provision should be made for the possibility of periodic adjustment of the threshold and rates. To this end, it is appropriate to entrust to the Commission the task of drawing up periodic reports on the actual application of the resale right in the Member States and on the impact on the art market in the Community and, where appropriate, of making proposals relating to the amendment of this Directive.

(27) The persons entitled to receive royalties must be specified, due regard being had to the principle of subsidiarity. It is not appropriate to take action through this Directive in relation to Member States' laws of succession. However, those entitled under the author must be able to benefit fully from the resale right after his death, at least following the expiry of the transitional period referred to above.

(28) The Member States are responsible for regulating the exercise of the resale right, particularly with regard to the way this is managed. In this respect management by a collecting society is one possibility. Member States should ensure that collecting societies operate in a transparent and efficient manner. Member States must also ensure that amounts intended for authors who are nationals of other Member States are in fact collected and distributed. This Directive is without prejudice to arrangements in Member States for collection and distribution.

(29) Enjoyment of the resale right should be restricted to Community nationals as well as to foreign authors whose countries afford such protection to authors who are nationals of Member States. A Member State should have the option of extending enjoyment of this right to foreign authors who have their habitual residence in that Member State.

(30) Appropriate procedures for monitoring transactions should be introduced so as to ensure by practical means that the resale right is effectively applied by Member States. This implies also a right on the part of the author or his authorised representative to obtain any necessary information from

the natural or legal person liable for payment of royalties. Member States which provide for collective management of the resale right may also provide that the bodies responsible for that collective management should alone be entitled to obtain information,

HAVE ADOPTED THIS DIRECTIVE:

Chapter I   Scope

Article 1   Subject matter of the resale right

1. Member States shall provide, for the benefit of the author of an original work of art, a resale right, to be defined as an inalienable right, which cannot be waived, even in advance, to receive a royalty based on the sale price obtained for any resale of the work, subsequent to the first transfer of the work by the author.

2. The right referred to in paragraph 1 shall apply to all acts of resale involving as sellers, buyers or intermediaries art market professionals, such as salesrooms, art galleries and, in general, any dealers in works of art.

3. Member States may provide that the right referred to in paragraph 1 shall not apply to acts of resale where the seller has acquired the work directly from the author less than three years before that resale and where the resale price does not exceed EUR 10 000.

4. The royalty shall be payable by the seller. Member States may provide that one of the natural or legal persons referred to in paragraph 2 other than the seller shall alone be liable or shall share liability with the seller for payment of the royalty.

Article 2   Works of art to which the resale right relates

1. For the purposes of this Directive, 'original work of art' means works of graphic or plastic art such as pictures, collages, paintings, drawings, engravings, prints, lithographs, sculptures, tapestries, ceramics, glassware and photographs, provided they are made by the artist himself or are copies considered to be original works of art.

2. Copies of works of art covered by this Directive, which have been made in limited numbers by the artist himself or under his authority, shall be considered to be original works of art for the purposes of this Directive. Such copies will normally have been numbered, signed or otherwise duly authorised by the artist.

Chapter II   Particular Provisions

Article 3   Threshold

1. It shall be for the Member States to set a minimum sale price from which the sales referred to in Article 1 shall be subject to resale right.

2. This minimum sale price may not under any circumstances exceed EUR 3 000.

Article 4   Rates

1. The royalty provided for in Article 1 shall be set at the following rates:
    (a) 4% for the portion of the sale price up to EUR 50 000;
    (b) 3% for the portion of the sale price from EUR 50 000,01 to EUR 200 000;
    (c) 1% for the portion of the sale price from EUR 200 000,01 to EUR 350 000;
    (d) 0,5% for the portion of the sale price from EUR 350 000,01 to EUR 500 000;
    (e) 0,25% for the portion of the sale price exceeding EUR 500 000.
However, the total amount of the royalty may not exceed EUR 12 500.

2. By way of derogation from paragraph 1, Member States may apply a rate of 5% for the portion of the sale price referred to in paragraph 1(a).

3. If the minimum sale price set should be lower than EUR 3 000, the Member State shall also determine the rate applicable to the portion of the sale price up to EUR 3 000; this rate may not be lower than 4%.

Article 5   Calculation basis
The sale prices referred to in Articles 3 and 4 are net of tax.

Article 6   Persons entitled to receive royalties
1. The royalty provided for under Article 1 shall be payable to the author of the work and, subject to Article 8(2), after his death to those entitled under him/her.

2. Member States may provide for compulsory or optional collective management of the royalty provided for under Article 1.

Article 7   Third-country nationals entitled to receive royalties
1. Member States shall provide that authors who are nationals of third countries and, subject to Article 8(2), their successors in title shall enjoy the resale right in accordance with this Directive and the legislation of the Member State concerned only if legislation in the country of which the author or his/her successor in title is a national permits resale right protection in that country for authors from the Member States and their successors in title.

...

3. Any Member State may treat authors who are not nationals of a Member State but who have their habitual residence in that Member State in the same way as its own nationals for the purpose of resale right protection.

Article 8   Term of protection of the resale right
1. The term of protection of the resale right shall correspond to that laid down in Article 1 of Directive 93/98/EEC.

2. By way of derogation from paragraph 1, those Member States which do not apply the resale right on (the entry into force date referred to in Article 13), shall not be required, for a period expiring not later than 1 January 2010, to apply the resale right for the benefit of those entitled under the artist after his/her death.

...

Article 9   Right to obtain information
The Member States shall provide that for a period of three years after the resale, the persons entitled under Article 6 may require from any art market professional mentioned in Article 1(2) to furnish any information that may be necessary in order to secure payment of royalties in respect of the resale.

Chapter III   Final Provisions

Article 10   Application in time
This Directive shall apply in respect of all original works of art as defined in Article 2 which, on 1 January 2006, are still protected by the legislation of the Member States in the field of copyright or meet the criteria for protection under the provisions of this Directive at that date.

...

Article 12   Implementation
1. Member States shall bring into force the laws, regulations and administrative provisions necessary to comply with this Directive before 1 January 2006. They shall forthwith inform the Commission thereof.

When Member States adopt these measures, they shall contain a reference to this Directive or shall be accompanied by such reference on the occasion of their official publication. The methods of making such a reference shall be laid down by the Member States.

...

Council Regulation (EC) No. 6/2002

of 12 December 2001 on Community designs

THE COUNCIL OF THE EUROPEAN UNION,

Having regard to the Treaty establishing the European Community, and in particular Article 308 thereof,

Having regard to the proposal from the Commission,

Having regard to the opinion of the European Parliament,

Having regard to the opinion of the Economic and Social Committee,

Whereas:

(1) A unified system for obtaining a Community design to which uniform protection is given with uniform effect throughout the entire territory of the Community would further the objectives of the Community as laid down in the Treaty.

(2) Only the Benelux countries have introduced a uniform design protection law. In all the other Member States the protection of designs is a matter for the relevant national law and is confined to the territory of the Member State concerned. Identical designs may be therefore protected differently in different Member States and for the benefit of different owners. This inevitably leads to conflicts in the course of trade between Member States.

(3) The substantial differences between Member States' design laws prevent and distort Community-wide competition. In comparison with domestic trade in, and competition between, products incorporating a design, trade and competition within the Community are prevented and distorted by the large number of applications, offices, procedures, laws, nationally circumscribed exclusive rights and the combined administrative expense with correspondingly high costs and fees for the applicant. Directive 98/71/EC of the European Parliament and of the Council of 13 October 1998 on the legal protection of designs contributes to remedying this situation.

(4) The effect of design protection being limited to the territory of the individual Member States, whether or not their laws are approximated, leads to a possible division of the internal market with respect to products incorporating a design which is the subject of national rights held by different individuals, and hence constitutes an obstacle to the free movement of goods.

(5) This calls for the creation of a Community design which is directly applicable in each Member State, because only in this way will it be possible to obtain, through one application made to the Office for Harmonisation in the Internal Market (Trade Marks and Design) in accordance with a single procedure under one law, one design right for one area encompassing all Member States.

(6) Since the objectives of the proposed action, namely, the protection of one design right for one area encompassing all the Member States, cannot be sufficiently achieved by the Member States by reason of the scale and the effects of the creation of a Community design and a Community design authority and can therefore be better achieved at Community level, the Community may adopt measures, in accordance with the principle of subsidiarity as set out in Article 5 of the Treaty. In accordance with the principle of proportionality, as set out in that Article, this Regulation does not go beyond what is necessary in order to achieve those objectives.

(7) Enhanced protection for industrial design not only promotes the contribution of individual designers to the sum of Community excellence in the field, but also encourages innovation and development of new products and investment in their production.

(8) Consequently, a more accessible design-protection system adapted to the needs of the internal market is essential for Community industries.

(9) The substantive provisions of this Regulation on design law should be aligned with the respective provisions in Directive 98/71/EC.

(10) Technological innovation should not be hampered by granting design protection to features dictated solely by a technical function. It is understood that this does not entail that a design must have an aesthetic quality. Likewise, the interoperability of products of different makes should not be hindered by extending protection to the design of mechanical fittings. Consequently, those features of a design which are excluded from protection for those reasons should not be taken into consideration for the purpose of assessing whether other features of the design fulfil the requirements for protection.

(11) The mechanical fittings of modular products may nevertheless constitute an important element of the innovative characteristics of modular products and present a major marketing asset, and therefore should be eligible for protection.

(12) Protection should not be extended to those component parts which are not visible during normal use of a product, nor to those features of such part which are not visible when the part is mounted, or which would not, in themselves, fulfil the requirements as to novelty and individual character. Therefore, those features of design which are excluded from protection for these reasons should not be taken into consideration for the purpose of assessing whether other features of the design fulfil the requirements for protection.

(13) Full-scale approximation of the laws of the Member States on the use of protected designs for the purpose of permitting the repair of a complex product so as to restore its original appearance, where the design is applied to or incorporated in a product which constitutes a component part of a complex product upon whose appearance the protected design is dependent, could not be achieved through Directive 98/71/EC. Within the framework of the conciliation procedure on the said Directive, the Commission undertook to review the consequences of the provisions of that Directive three years after the deadline for transposition of the Directive, in particular for the industrial sectors which are most affected. Under these circumstances, it is appropriate not to confer any protection as a Community design for a design which is applied to or incorporated in a product which constitutes a component part of a complex product upon whose appearance the design is dependent and which is used for the purpose of the repair of a complex product so as to restore its original appearance, until the Council has decided its policy on this issue on the basis of a Commission proposal.

(14) The assessment as to whether a design has individual character should be based on whether the overall impression produced on an informed user viewing the design clearly differs from that produced on him by the existing design corpus, taking into consideration the nature of the product to which the design is applied or in which it is incorporated, and in particular the industrial sector to which it belongs and the degree of freedom of the designer in developing the design.

(15) A Community design should, as far as possible, serve the needs of all sectors of industry in the Community.

(16) Some of those sectors produce large numbers of designs for products frequently having a short market life where protection without the burden of registration formalities is an advantage and the duration of protection is of lesser significance. On the other hand, there are sectors of industry which value the advantages of registration for the greater legal certainty it provides and which require the possibility of a longer term of protection corresponding to the foreseeable market life of their products.

(17) This calls for two forms of protection, one being a short-term unregistered design and the other being a longer term registered design.

(18) A registered Community design requires the creation and maintenance of a register in which will be registered all those applications which comply with formal conditions and which have been accorded a date of filing. This registration system should in principle not be based upon substantive examination as to compliance with requirements for protection prior to registration, thereby keeping to a minimum the registration and other procedural burdens on applicants.

(19) A Community design should not be upheld unless the design is new and unless it also possesses an individual character in comparison with other designs.

(20) It is also necessary to allow the designer or his successor in title to test the products embodying the design in the market place before deciding whether the protection resulting from a registered Community design is desirable. To this end it is necessary to provide that disclosures of the design by the designer or his successor in title, or abusive disclosures during a period of 12 months prior to the date of the filing of the application for a registered Community design should not be prejudicial in assessing the novelty or the individual character of the design in question.

(21) The exclusive nature of the right conferred by the registered Community design is consistent with its greater legal certainty. It is appropriate that the unregistered Community design should, however, constitute a right only to prevent copying. Protection could not therefore extend to design products which are the result of a design arrived at independently by a second designer. This right should also extend to trade in products embodying infringing designs.

(22) The enforcement of these rights is to be left to national laws. It is necessary therefore to provide for some basic uniform sanctions in all Member States. These should make it possible, irrespective of the jurisdiction under which enforcement is sought, to stop the infringing acts.

(23) Any third person who can establish that he has in good faith commenced use even for commercial purposes within the Community, or has made serious and effective preparations to that end, of a design included within the scope of protection of a registered Community design, which has not been copied from the latter, may be entitled to a limited exploitation of that design.

(24) It is a fundamental objective of this Regulation that the procedure for obtaining a registered Community design should present the minimum cost and difficulty to applicants, so as to make it readily available to small and medium-sized enterprises as well as to individual designers.

(25) Those sectors of industry producing large numbers of possibly short-lived designs over short periods of time of which only some may be eventually commercialised will find advantage in the unregistered Community design. Furthermore, there is also a need for these sectors to have easier recourse to the registered Community design. Therefore, the option of combining a number of designs in one multiple application would satisfy that need. However, the designs contained in a multiple application may be dealt with independently of each other for the purposes of enforcement of rights, licensing, rights in rem, levy of execution, insolvency proceedings, surrender, renewal, assignment, deferred publication or declaration of invalidity.

(26) The normal publication following registration of a Community design could in some cases destroy or jeopardise the success of a commercial operation involving the design. The facility of a deferment of publication for a reasonable period affords a solution in such cases.

(27) A procedure for hearing actions concerning validity of a registered Community design in a single place would bring savings in costs and time compared with procedures involving different national courts.

(28) It is therefore necessary to provide safeguards including a right of appeal to a Board of Appeal, and ultimately to the Court of Justice. Such a procedure would assist the development of uniform interpretation of the requirements governing the validity of Community designs.

(29) It is essential that the rights conferred by a Community design can be enforced in an efficient manner throughout the territory of the Community.

(30) The litigation system should avoid as far as possible 'forum shopping'. It is therefore necessary to establish clear rules of international jurisdiction.

(31) This Regulation does not preclude the application to designs protected by Community designs of the industrial property laws or other relevant laws of the Member States, such as those relating to design protection acquired by registration or those relating to unregistered designs, trade marks, patents and utility models, unfair competition or civil liability.

(32) In the absence of the complete harmonisation of copyright law, it is important to establish the principle of cumulation of protection under the Community design and under copyright law, whilst leaving Member States free to establish the extent of copyright protection and the conditions under which such protection is conferred.

(33) The measures necessary for the implementation of this Regulation should be adopted in accordance with Council Decision 1999/468/EC of 28 June 1999 laying down the procedures for the exercise of implementing powers conferred on the Commission,

HAS ADOPTED THIS REGULATION:

Title I   General Provisions

Article 1   Community design

1. A design which complies with the conditions contained in this Regulation is hereinafter referred to as a 'Community design'.

2. A design shall be protected:

(a) by an 'unregistered Community design', if made available to the public in the manner provided for in this Regulation;

(b) by a 'registered Community design', if registered in the manner provided for in this Regulation.

3. A Community design shall have a unitary character. It shall have equal effect throughout the Community. It shall not be registered, transferred or surrendered or be the subject of a decision declaring it invalid, nor shall its use be prohibited, save in respect of the whole Community. This principle and its implications shall apply unless otherwise provided in this Regulation.

Article 2   Office

The Office for Harmonisation in the Internal Market (Trade Marks and Designs), hereinafter referred to as 'the Office', instituted by Council Regulation (EC) No 40/94 of 20 December 1993 on the Community trade mark(6), hereinafter referred to as the 'Regulation on the Community trade mark', shall carry out the tasks entrusted to it by this Regulation.

Title II   The Law Relating to Designs

Section 1   Requirements for Protection

Article 3   Definitions

For the purposes of this Regulation:

(a) 'design' means the appearance of the whole or a part of a product resulting from the features of, in particular, the lines, contours, colours, shape, texture and/or materials of the product itself and/or its ornamentation;

(b) 'product' means any industrial or handicraft item, including inter alia parts intended to be assembled into a complex product, packaging, get-up, graphic symbols and typographic typefaces, but excluding computer programs;

(c) 'complex product' means a product which is composed of multiple components which can be replaced permitting disassembly and re-assembly of the product.

Article 4   Requirements for protection

1. A design shall be protected by a Community design to the extent that it is new and has individual character.

2. A design applied to or incorporated in a product which constitutes a component part of a complex product shall only be considered to be new and to have individual character:

(a) if the component part, once it has been incorporated into the complex product, remains visible during normal use of the latter; and

(b) to the extent that those visible features of the component part fulfil in themselves the requirements as to novelty and individual character.

3. 'Normal use' within the meaning of paragraph (2)(a) shall mean use by the end user, excluding maintenance, servicing or repair work.

Article 5   Novelty

1. A design shall be considered to be new if no identical design has been made available to the public:

    (a) in the case of an unregistered Community design, before the date on which the design for which protection is claimed has first been made available to the public;

    (b) in the case of a registered Community design, before the date of filing of the application for registration of the design for which protection is claimed, or, if priority is claimed, the date of priority.

2. Designs shall be deemed to be identical if their features differ only in immaterial details.

Article 6   Individual character

1. A design shall be considered to have individual character if the overall impression it produces on the informed user differs from the overall impression produced on such a user by any design which has been made available to the public:

    (a) in the case of an unregistered Community design, before the date on which the design for which protection is claimed has first been made available to the public;

    (b) in the case of a registered Community design, before the date of filing the application for registration or, if a priority is claimed, the date of priority.

2. In assessing individual character, the degree of freedom of the designer in developing the design shall be taken into consideration.

Article 7   Disclosure

1. For the purpose of applying Articles 5 and 6, a design shall be deemed to have been made available to the public if it has been published following registration or otherwise, or exhibited, used in trade or otherwise disclosed, before the date referred to in Articles 5(1)(a) and 6(1)(a) or in Articles 5(1)(b) and 6(1)(b), as the case may be, except where these events could not reasonably have become known in the normal course of business to the circles specialised in the sector concerned, operating within the Community. The design shall not, however, be deemed to have been made available to the public for the sole reason that it has been disclosed to a third person under explicit or implicit conditions of confidentiality.

2. A disclosure shall not be taken into consideration for the purpose of applying Articles 5 and 6 and if a design for which protection is claimed under a registered Community design has been made available to the public:

    (a) by the designer, his successor in title, or a third person as a result of information provided or action taken by the designer or his successor in title; and

    (b) during the 12-month period preceding the date of filing of the application or, if a priority is claimed, the date of priority.

3. Paragraph 2 shall also apply if the design has been made available to the public as a consequence of an abuse in relation to the designer or his successor in title.

Article 8   Designs dictated by their technical function and designs of interconnections

1. A Community design shall not subsist in features of appearance of a product which are solely dictated by its technical function.

2. A Community design shall not subsist in features of appearance of a product which must necessarily be reproduced in their exact form and dimensions in order to permit the product in which the design is incorporated or to which it is applied to be mechanically connected to or placed in, around or against another product so that either product may perform its function.

3. Notwithstanding paragraph 2, a Community design shall under the conditions set out in Articles 5 and 6 subsist in a design serving the purpose of allowing the multiple assembly or connection of mutually interchangeable products within a modular system.

Article 9 Designs contrary to public policy or morality

A Community design shall not subsist in a design which is contrary to public policy or to accepted principles of morality.

Section 2 Scope and Term of Protection

Article 10 Scope of protection

1. The scope of the protection conferred by a Community design shall include any design which does not produce on the informed user a different overall impression.

2. In assessing the scope of protection, the degree of freedom of the designer in developing his design shall be taken into consideration.

Article 11 Commencement and term of protection of the unregistered Community design

1. A design which meets the requirements under Section 1 shall be protected by an unregistered Community design for a period of three years as from the date on which the design was first made available to the public within the Community.

2. For the purpose of paragraph 1, a design shall be deemed to have been made available to the public within the Community if it has been published, exhibited, used in trade or otherwise disclosed in such a way that, in the normal course of business, these events could reasonably have become known to the circles specialised in the sector concerned, operating within the Community. The design shall not, however, be deemed to have been made available to the public for the sole reason that it has been disclosed to a third person under explicit or implicit conditions of confidentiality.

Article 12 Commencement and term of protection of the registered Community design

Upon registration by the Office, a design which meets the requirements under Section 1 shall be protected by a registered Community design for a period of five years as from the date of the filing of the application. The right holder may have the term of protection renewed for one or more periods of five years each, up to a total term of 25 years from the date of filing.

…

Section 3 Right to the Community Design

Article 14 Right to the Community design

1. The right to the Community design shall vest in the designer or his successor in title.

2. If two or more persons have jointly developed a design, the right to the Community design shall vest in them jointly.

3. However, where a design is developed by an employee in the execution of his duties or following the instructions given by his employer, the right to the Community design shall vest in the employer, unless otherwise agreed or specified under national law.

Article 15 Claims relating to the entitlement to a Community design

1. If an unregistered Community design is disclosed or claimed by, or a registered Community design has been applied for or registered in the name of, a person who is not entitled to it under Article 14, the person entitled to it under that provision may, without prejudice to any other remedy which may be open to him, claim to become recognised as the legitimate holder of the Community design.

2. Where a person is jointly entitled to a Community design, that person may, in accordance with paragraph 1, claim to become recognised as joint holder.

3. Legal proceedings under paragraphs 1 or 2 shall be barred three years after the date of publication of a registered Community design or the date of disclosure of an unregistered Community design. This provision shall not apply if the person who is not entitled to the Community design was acting in bad faith at the time when such design was applied for or disclosed or was assigned to him.

4. In the case of a registered Community design, the following shall be entered in the register:
   (a) the mention that legal proceedings under paragraph 1 have been instituted;
   (b) the final decision or any other termination of the proceedings;
   (c) any change in the ownership of the registered Community design resulting from the final decision.

. . .

Article 17   Presumption in favour of the registered holder of the design

The person in whose name the registered Community design is registered or, prior to registration, the person in whose name the application is filed, shall be deemed to be the person entitled in any proceedings before the Office as well as in any other proceedings.

Article 18   Right of the designer to be cited

The designer shall have the right, in the same way as the applicant for or the holder of a registered Community design, to be cited as such before the Office and in the register. If the design is the result of teamwork, the citation of the team may replace the citation of the individual designers.

Section 4   Effects of the Community Design

Article 19   Rights conferred by the Community design

1. A registered Community design shall confer on its holder the exclusive right to use it and to prevent any third party not having his consent from using it. The aforementioned use shall cover, in particular, the making, offering, putting on the market, importing, exporting or using of a product in which the design is incorporated or to which it is applied, or stocking such a product for those purposes.

2. An unregistered Community design shall, however, confer on its holder the right to prevent the acts referred to in paragraph 1 only if the contested use results from copying the protected design.

The contested use shall not be deemed to result from copying the protected design if it results from an independent work of creation by a designer who may be reasonably thought not to be familiar with the design made available to the public by the holder.

3. Paragraph 2 shall also apply to a registered Community design subject to deferment of publication as long as the relevant entries in the register and the file have not been made available to the public in accordance with Article 50(4).

Article 20   Limitation of the rights conferred by a Community design

1. The rights conferred by a Community design shall not be exercised in respect of:
   (a) acts done privately and for non-commercial purposes;
   (b) acts done for experimental purposes;
   (c) acts of reproduction for the purpose of making citations or of teaching, provided that such acts are compatible with fair trade practice and do not unduly prejudice the normal exploitation of the design, and that mention is made of the source.
2. In addition, the rights conferred by a Community design shall not be exercised in respect of:
   (a) the equipment on ships and aircraft registered in a third country when these temporarily enter the territory of the Community;
   (b) the importation in the Community of spare parts and accessories for the purpose of repairing such craft;
   (c) the execution of repairs on such craft.

Article 21   Exhaustion of rights

The rights conferred by a Community design shall not extend to acts relating to a product in which a design included within the scope of protection of the Community design is incorporated or to which it is applied, when the product has been put on the market in the Community by the holder of the Community design or with his consent.

Article 22   Rights of prior use in respect of a registered Community design

1. A right of prior use shall exist for any third person who can establish that before the date of filing of the application, or, if a priority is claimed, before the date of priority, he has in good faith commenced use within the Community, or has made serious and effective preparations to that end, of a design included within the scope of protection of a registered Community design, which has not been copied from the latter.

2. The right of prior use shall entitle the third person to exploit the design for the purposes for which its use had been effected, or for which serious and effective preparations had been made, before the filing or priority date of the registered Community design.

3. The right of prior use shall not extend to granting a licence to another person to exploit the design.

4. The right of prior use cannot be transferred except, where the third person is a business, along with that part of the business in the course of which the act was done or the preparations were made.

Article 23   Government use

Any provision in the law of a Member State allowing use of national designs by or for the government may be applied to Community designs, but only to the extent that the use is necessary for essential defence or security needs.

Section 5   Invalidity

Article 24   Declaration of invalidity

1. A registered Community design shall be declared invalid on application to the Office in accordance with the procedure in Titles VI and VII or by a Community design court on the basis of a counterclaim in infringement proceedings.

2. A Community design may be declared invalid even after the Community design has lapsed or has been surrendered.

3. An unregistered Community design shall be declared invalid by a Community design court on application to such a court or on the basis of a counterclaim in infringement proceedings.

Article 25   Grounds for invalidity

1. A Community design may be declared invalid only in the following cases:
   (a) if the design does not correspond to the definition under Article 3(a);
   (b) if it does not fulfil the requirements of Articles 4 to 9;
   (c) if, by virtue of a court decision, the right holder is not entitled to the Community design under Article 14;
   (d) if the Community design is in conflict with a prior design which has been made available to the public after the date of filing of the application or, if priority is claimed, the date of priority of the Community design, and which is protected from a date prior to the said date
      (i)   by a registered Community design or an application for such a design, or
      (ii) by a registered design right of a Member State, or by an application for such a right, or
      (iii) by a design right registered under the Geneva Act of the Hague Agreement concerning the international registration of industrial designs, adopted in Geneva on 2 July 1999, hereinafter referred to as 'the Geneva Act', which was approved by Council Decision 954/2006 and which has effect in the Community, or by an application for such a right;
   (e) if a distinctive sign is used in a subsequent design, and Community law or the law of the Member State governing that sign confers on the right holder of the sign the right to prohibit such use;

(f) if the design constitutes an unauthorised use of a work protected under the copyright law of a Member State;

(g) if the design constitutes an improper use of any of the items listed in Article 6*ter* of the 'Paris Convention', or of badges, emblems and escutcheons other than those covered by the said Article 6*ter* and which are of particular public interest in a Member State.

2. The ground provided for in paragraph (1)(c) may be invoked solely by the person who is entitled to the Community design under Article 14.

3. The grounds provided for in paragraph (1)(d), (e) and (f) may be invoked solely by the applicant for or holder of the earlier right.

4. The ground provided for in paragraph (1)(g) may be invoked solely by the person or entity concerned by the use.

5. Paragraphs 3 and 4 shall be without prejudice to the freedom of Member States to provide that the grounds provided for in paragraphs 1(d) and (g) may also be invoked by the appropriate authority of the Member State in question on its own initiative.

6. A registered Community design which has been declared invalid pursuant to paragraph (1)(b), (e), (f) or (g) may be maintained in an amended form, if in that form it complies with the requirements for protection and the identity of the design is retained. 'Maintenance' in an amended form may include registration accompanied by a partial disclaimer by the holder of the registered Community design or entry in the register of a court decision or a decision by the Office declaring the partial invalidity of the registered Community design.

Article 26   Consequences of invalidity

1. A Community design shall be deemed not to have had, as from the outset, the effects specified in this Regulation, to the extent that it has been declared invalid.

2. Subject to the national provisions relating either to claims for compensation for damage caused by negligence or lack of good faith on the part of the holder of the Community design, or to unjust enrichment, the retroactive effect of invalidity of the Community design shall not affect:

(a) any decision on infringement which has acquired the authority of a final decision and been enforced prior to the invalidity decision;

(b) any contract concluded prior to the invalidity decision, in so far as it has been performed before the decision; however, repayment, to an extent justified by the circumstances, of sums paid under the relevant contract may be claimed on grounds of equity.

Title III   Community Designs as Objects of Property

Article 27   Dealing with Community designs as national design rights

1. Unless Articles 28, 29, 30, 31 and 32 provide otherwise, a Community design as an object of property shall be dealt with in its entirety, and for the whole area of the Community, as a national design right of the Member State in which:

(a) the holder has his seat or his domicile on the relevant date; or

(b) where point (a) does not apply, the holder has an establishment on the relevant date.

...

Article 28   Transfer of the registered Community design

The transfer of a registered Community design shall be subject to the following provisions:

(a) at the request of one of the parties, a transfer shall be entered in the register and published;

(b) until such time as the transfer has been entered in the register, the successor in title may not invoke the rights arising from the registration of the Community design;

(c) where there are time limits to be observed in dealings with the Office, the successor in title may make the corresponding statements to the Office once the request for registration of the transfer has been received by the Office;

(d) all documents which by virtue of Article 66 require notification to the holder of the registered Community design shall be addressed by the Office to the person registered as holder or his representative, if one has been appointed.

Article 29   Rights in rem on a registered Community design

1. A registered Community design may be given as security or be the subject of rights in rem.

2. On request of one of the parties, the rights mentioned in paragraph 1 shall be entered in the register and published.

...

Article 32   Licensing

1. A Community design may be licensed for the whole or part of the Community. A licence may be exclusive or non-exclusive.

2. Without prejudice to any legal proceedings based on the law of contract, the holder may invoke the rights conferred by the Community design against a licensee who contravenes any provision in his licensing contract with regard to its duration, the form in which the design may be used, the range of products for which the licence is granted and the quality of products manufactured by the licensee.

3. Without prejudice to the provisions of the licensing contract, the licensee may bring proceedings for infringement of a Community design only if the right holder consents thereto. However, the holder of an exclusive licence may bring such proceedings if the right holder in the Community design, having been given notice to do so, does not himself bring infringement proceedings within an appropriate period.

4. A licensee shall, for the purpose of obtaining compensation for damage suffered by him, be entitled to intervene in an infringement action brought by the right holder in a Community design.

5. In the case of a registered Community design, the grant or transfer of a licence in respect of such right shall, at the request of one of the parties, be entered in the register and published.

...

Title IV   Application for a Registered Community Design

Section 1   Filing of Applications and the Conditions which Govern Them

Article 35   Filing and forwarding of applications

1. An application for a registered Community design shall be filed, at the option of the applicant:
   (a) at the Office; or
   (b) at the central industrial property office of a Member State; or
   (c) in the Benelux countries, at the Benelux Design Office.

...

Article 36   Conditions with which applications must comply

1. An application for a registered Community design shall contain:
   (a) a request for registration;
   (b) information identifying the applicant;

(c) a representation of the design suitable for reproduction. However, if the object of the application is a two-dimensional design and the application contains a request for deferment of publication in accordance with Article 50, the representation of the design may be replaced by a specimen.

2. The application shall further contain an indication of the products in which the design is intended to be incorporated or to which it is intended to be applied.

3. In addition, the application may contain:

(a) a description explaining the representation or the specimen;

(b) a request for deferment of publication of the registration in accordance with Article 50;

(c) information identifying the representative if the applicant has appointed one;

(d) the classification of the products in which the design is intended to be incorporated or to which it is intended to be applied according to class;

(e) the citation of the designer or of the team of designers or a statement under the applicant's responsibility that the designer or the team of designers has waived the right to be cited.

...

6. The information contained in the elements mentioned in paragraph 2 and in paragraph 3(a) and (d) shall not affect the scope of protection of the design as such.

...

Article 38   Date of filing

1. The date of filing of an application for a registered Community design shall be the date on which documents containing the information specified in Article 36(1) are filed with the Office by the applicant, or, if the application has been filed with the central industrial property office of a Member State or with the Benelux Design Office, with that office.

2. By derogation from paragraph 1, the date of filing of an application filed with the central industrial property office of a Member State or with the Benelux Design Office and reaching the Office more than two months after the date on which documents containing the information specified in Article 36(1) have been filed shall be the date of receipt of such documents by the Office.

Article 39   Equivalence of Community filing with national filing

An application for a registered Community design which has been accorded a date of filing shall, in the Member States, be equivalent to a regular national filing, including where appropriate the priority claimed for the said application.

Article 40   Classification

For the purpose of this Regulation, use shall be made of the Annex to the Agreement establishing an International Classification for Industrial Designs, signed at Locarno on 8 October 1968.

Section 2   Priority

Article 41   Right of priority

1. A person who has duly filed an application for a design right or for a utility model in or for any State party to the Paris Convention for the Protection of Industrial Property, or to the Agreement establishing the World Trade Organisation, or his successors in title, shall enjoy, for the purpose of filing an application for a registered Community design in respect of the same design or utility model, a right of priority of six months from the date of filing of the first application.

2. Every filing that is equivalent to a regular national filing under the national law of the State where it was made or under bilateral or multilateral agreements shall be recognised as giving rise to a right of priority.

3. 'Regular national filing' means any filing that is sufficient to establish the date on which the application was filed, whatever may be the outcome of the application.

4. A subsequent application for a design which was the subject of a previous first application, and which is filed in or in respect of the same State, shall be considered as the first application for the purpose of determining priority, provided that, at the date of the filing of the subsequent application, the previous application has been withdrawn, abandoned or refused without being open to public inspection and without leaving any rights outstanding, and has not served as a basis for claiming priority. The previous application may not thereafter serve as a basis for claiming a right of priority.

5. If the first filing has been made in a State which is not a party to the Paris Convention, or to the Agreement establishing the World Trade Organisation, paragraphs 1 to 4 shall apply only in so far as that State, according to published findings, grants, on the basis of a filing made at the Office and subject to conditions equivalent to those laid down in this Regulation, a right of priority having equivalent effect.

...

Article 43   Effect of priority right

The effect of the right of priority shall be that the date of priority shall count as the date of the filing of the application for a registered Community design for the purpose of Articles 5, 6, 7, 22, 25(1)(d) and 50(1).

Article 44   Exhibition priority

1. If an applicant for a registered Community design has disclosed products in which the design is incorporated, or to which it is applied, at an official or officially recognised international exhibition falling within the terms of the Convention on International Exhibitions signed in Paris on 22 November 1928 and last revised on 30 November 1972, he may, if he files the application within a period of six months from the date of the first disclosure of such products, claim a right of priority from that date within the meaning of Article 43.

...

3. An exhibition priority granted in a Member State or in a third country does not extend the period of priority laid down in Article 41.

Title V   Registration Procedure

Article 45   Examination as to formal requirements for filing

1. The Office shall examine whether the application complies with the requirements laid down in Article 36(1) for the accordance of a date of filing.

2. The Office shall examine whether:
   (a) the application complies with the other requirements laid down in Article 36(2), (3), (4) and (5) and, in the case of a multiple application, Article 37(1) and (2);
   (b) the application meets the formal requirements laid down in the implementing regulation for the implementation of Articles 36 and 37;
   (c) the requirements of Article 77(2) are satisfied;
   (d) the requirements concerning the claim to priority are satisfied, if a priority is claimed.

3. The conditions for the examination as to the formal requirements for filing shall be laid down in the implementing regulation.

...

Article 47   Grounds for non-registrability

1. If the Office, in carrying out the examination pursuant to Article 45, notices that the design for which protection is sought:
   (a) does not correspond to the definition under Article 3(a); or
   (b) is contrary to public policy or to accepted principles of morality, it shall refuse the application.

2. The application shall not be refused before the applicant has been allowed the opportunity of withdrawing or amending the application or of submitting his observations.

Article 48   Registration

If the requirements that an application for a registered Community design must satisfy have been fulfilled and to the extent that the application has not been refused by virtue of Article 47, the Office shall register the application in the Community design Register as a registered Community design. The registration shall bear the date of filing of the application referred to in Article 38.

...

Title VI   Surrender and Invalidity of the Registered Community Design

...

Article 52   Application for a declaration of invalidity

1. Subject to Article 25(2), (3), (4) and (5), any natural or legal person, as well as a public authority empowered to do so, may submit to the Office an application for a declaration of invalidity of a registered Community design.

...

Title VII   Appeals

Article 55   Decisions subject to appeal

1. An appeal shall lie from decisions of the examiners, the Administration of Trade Marks and Designs and Legal Division and Invalidity Divisions. It shall have suspensive effect.

2. A decision which does not terminate proceedings as regards one of the parties can only be appealed together with the final decision, unless the decision allows separate appeal.

Article 56   Persons entitled to appeal and to be parties to appeal proceedings

Any party to proceedings adversely affected by a decision may appeal. Any other parties to the proceedings shall be parties to the appeal proceedings as of right.

...

Article 61   Actions before the Court of Justice

1. Actions may be brought before the Court of Justice against decisions of the Boards of Appeal on appeals.

...

Title IX   Jurisdiction and Procedure in Legal Actions Relating to Community Designs

...

Section 2   Disputes Concerning the Infringement and Validity of Community Designs

...

Article 81   Jurisdiction over infringement and validity

The Community design courts shall have exclusive jurisdiction:
  (a) for infringement actions and—if they are permitted under national law—actions in respect of threatened infringement of Community designs;
  (b) for actions for declaration of non-infringement of Community designs, if they are permitted under national law;
  (c) for actions for a declaration of invalidity of an unregistered Community design;

(d) for counterclaims for a declaration of invalidity of a Community design raised in connection with actions under (a).

...

Article 87   Effects of the judgement on invalidity

When it has become final, a judgment of a Community design court declaring a Community design invalid shall have in all the Member States the effects specified in Article 26.

Article 88   Applicable law

1. The Community design courts shall apply the provisions of this Regulation.

2. On all matters not covered by this Regulation, a Community design court shall apply its national law, including its private international law.

3. Unless otherwise provided in this Regulation, a Community design court shall apply the rules of procedure governing the same type of action relating to a national design right in the Member State where it is situated.

...

Article 92   Jurisdiction of Community design courts of second instance—further appeal

1. An appeal to the Community design courts of second instance shall lie from judgments of the Community design courts of first instance in respect of proceedings arising from the actions and claims referred to in Article 81.

2. The conditions under which an appeal may be lodged with a Community design court of second instance shall be determined by the national law of the Member State in which that court is located.

3. The national rules concerning further appeal shall be applicable in respect of judgments of Community design courts of second instance.

...

Title X   Effects on the Laws of the Member States

...

Article 96   Relationship to other forms of protection under national law

1. The provisions of this Regulation shall be without prejudice to any provisions of Community law or of the law of the Member States concerned relating to unregistered designs, trade marks or other distinctive signs, patents and utility models, typefaces, civil liability and unfair competition.

2. A design protected by a Community design shall also be eligible for protection under the law of copyright of Member States as from the date on which the design was created or fixed in any form. The extent to which, and the conditions under which, such a protection is conferred, including the level of originality required, shall be determined by each Member State.

...

Title XII   Final Provisions

...

Article 110   Transitional provision

1. Until such time as amendments to this Regulation enter into force on a proposal from the Commission on this subject, protection as a Community design shall not exist for a design which constitutes a component part of a complex product used within the meaning of Article 19(1) for the purpose of the repair of that complex product so as to restore its original appearance.

2. The proposal from the Commission referred to in paragraph 1 shall be submitted together with, and take into consideration, any changes which the Commission shall propose on the same subject pursuant to Article 18 of Directive 98/71/EC.

...

Directive 2006/115/EC of the European Parliament and of the Council

of 12 December 2006 on rental right and lending right and on certain rights related to copyright in the field of intellectual property (codified version)

THE EUROPEAN PARLIAMENT AND THE COUNCIL OF THE EUROPEAN UNION,

Having regard to the Treaty establishing the European Community, and in particular Articles 47(2), 55 and 95 thereof,

Having regard to the proposal from the Commission,

Having regard to the opinion of the European Economic and Social Committee,

Acting in accordance with the procedure laid down in Article 251 of the Treaty,

Whereas:

(1) Council Directive 92/100/EEC of 19 November 1992 on rental right and lending right and on certain rights related to copyright in the field of intellectual property has been substantially amended several times. In the interests of clarity and rationality the said Directive should be codified.

(2) Rental and lending of copyright works and the subject matter of related rights protection is playing an increasingly important role in particular for authors, performers and producers of phonograms and films. Piracy is becoming an increasing threat.

(3) The adequate protection of copyright works and subject matter of related rights protection by rental and lending rights as well as the protection of the subject matter of related rights protection by the fixation right, distribution right, right to broadcast and communication to the public can accordingly be considered as being of fundamental importance for the economic and cultural development of the Community.

(4) Copyright and related rights protection must adapt to new economic developments such as new forms of exploitation.

(5) The creative and artistic work of authors and performers necessitates an adequate income as a basis for further creative and artistic work, and the investments required particularly for the production of phonograms and films are especially high and risky. The possibility of securing that income and recouping that investment can be effectively guaranteed only through adequate legal protection of the rightholders concerned.

(6) These creative, artistic and entrepreneurial activities are, to a large extent, activities of self-employed persons. The pursuit of such activities should be made easier by providing a harmonised legal protection within the Community. To the extent that these activities principally constitute services, their provision should equally be facilitated by a harmonised legal framework in the Community.

(7) The legislation of the Member States should be approximated in such a way as not to conflict with the international conventions on which the copyright and related rights laws of many Member States are based.

(8) The legal framework of the Community on the rental right and lending right and on certain rights related to copyright can be limited to establishing that Member States provide rights with respect to rental and lending for certain groups of rightholders and further to establishing the rights of fixation, distribution, broadcasting and communication to the public for certain groups of rightholders in the field of related rights protection.

(9) It is necessary to define the concepts of rental and lending for the purposes of this Directive.

(10) It is desirable, with a view to clarity, to exclude from rental and lending within the meaning of this Directive certain forms of making available, as for instance making available phonograms or

films for the purpose of public performance or broadcasting, making available for the purpose of exhibition, or making available for on-the-spot reference use. Lending within the meaning of this Directive should not include making available between establishments which are accessible to the public.

(11) Where lending by an establishment accessible to the public gives rise to a payment the amount of which does not go beyond what is necessary to cover the operating costs of the establishment, there is no direct or indirect economic or commercial advantage within the meaning of this Directive.

(12) It is necessary to introduce arrangements ensuring that an unwaivable equitable remuneration is obtained by authors and performers who must remain able to entrust the administration of this right to collecting societies representing them.

(13) The equitable remuneration may be paid on the basis of one or several payments at any time on or after the conclusion of the contract. It should take account of the importance of the contribution of the authors and performers concerned to the phonogram or film.

(14) It is also necessary to protect the rights at least of authors as regards public lending by providing for specific arrangements. However, any measures taken by way of derogation from the exclusive public lending right should comply in particular with Article 12 of the Treaty.

(15) The provisions laid down in this Directive as to rights related to copyright should not prevent Member States from extending to those exclusive rights the presumption provided for in this Directive with regard to contracts concerning film production concluded individually or collectively by performers with a film producer. Furthermore, those provisions should not prevent Member States from providing for a rebuttable presumption of the authorisation of exploitation in respect of the exclusive rights of performers provided for in the relevant provisions of this Directive, in so far as such presumption is compatible with the International Convention for the Protection of Performers, Producers of Phonograms and Broadcasting Organisations (hereinafter referred to as the Rome Convention).

(16) Member States should be able to provide for more far-reaching protection for owners of rights related to copyright than that required by the provisions laid down in this Directive in respect of broadcasting and communication to the public.

(17) The harmonised rental and lending rights and the harmonised protection in the field of rights related to copyright should not be exercised in a way which constitutes a disguised restriction on trade between Member States or in a way which is contrary to the rule of media exploitation chronology, as recognised in the judgment handed down in Société Cinéthèque v. FNCF.

(18) This Directive should be without prejudice to the obligations of the Member States relating to the time-limits for transposition into national law of the Directives as set out in Part B of Annex I,

HAVE ADOPTED THIS DIRECTIVE:

Chapter I   Rental and Lending Right

Article 1   Object of harmonisation

1. In accordance with the provisions of this Chapter, Member States shall provide, subject to Article 6, a right to authorise or prohibit the rental and lending of originals and copies of copyright works, and other subject matter as set out in Article 3(1).

2. The rights referred to in paragraph 1 shall not be exhausted by any sale or other act of distribution of originals and copies of copyright works and other subject matter as set out in Article 3(1).

Article 2   Definitions

1. For the purposes of this Directive the following definitions shall apply:
    (a) 'rental' means making available for use, for a limited period of time and for direct or indirect economic or commercial advantage;
    (b) 'lending' means making available for use, for a limited period of time and not for direct or indirect economic or commercial advantage, when it is made through establishments which are accessible to the public;

(c) 'film' means a cinematographic or audiovisual work or moving images, whether or not accompanied by sound.

2. The principal director of a cinematographic or audiovisual work shall be considered as its author or one of its authors. Member States may provide for others to be considered as its co-authors.

Article 3   Rightholders and subject matter of rental and lending right

1. The exclusive right to authorise or prohibit rental and lending shall belong to the following:

(a) the author in respect of the original and copies of his work;

(b) the performer in respect of fixations of his performance;

(c) the phonogram producer in respect of his phonograms;

(d) the producer of the first fixation of a film in respect of the original and copies of his film.

2. This Directive shall not cover rental and lending rights in relation to buildings and to works of applied art.

3. The rights referred to in paragraph 1 may be transferred, assigned or subject to the granting of contractual licences.

4. Without prejudice to paragraph 6, when a contract concerning film production is concluded, individually or collectively, by performers with a film producer, the performer covered by this contract shall be presumed, subject to contractual clauses to the contrary, to have transferred his rental right, subject to Article 5.

5. Member States may provide for a similar presumption as set out in paragraph 4 with respect to authors.

6. Member States may provide that the signing of a contract concluded between a performer and a film producer concerning the production of a film has the effect of authorising rental, provided that such contract provides for an equitable remuneration within the meaning of Article 5. Member States may also provide that this paragraph shall apply *mutatis mutandis* to the rights included in Chapter II.

Article 4   Rental of computer programs

This Directive shall be without prejudice to Article 4(c) of Council Directive 91/250/EEC of 14 May 1991 on the legal protection of computer programs.

Article 5   Unwaivable right to equitable remuneration

1. Where an author or performer has transferred or assigned his rental right concerning a phonogram or an original or copy of a film to a phonogram or film producer, that author or performer shall retain the right to obtain an equitable remuneration for the rental.

2. The right to obtain an equitable remuneration for rental cannot be waived by authors or performers.

3. The administration of this right to obtain an equitable remuneration may be entrusted to collecting societies representing authors or performers.

4. Member States may regulate whether and to what extent administration by collecting societies of the right to obtain an equitable remuneration may be imposed, as well as the question from whom this remuneration may be claimed or collected.

Article 6   Derogation from the exclusive public lending right

1. Member States may derogate from the exclusive right provided for in Article 1 in respect of public lending, provided that at least authors obtain a remuneration for such lending. Member States shall be free to determine this remuneration taking account of their cultural promotion objectives.

2. Where Member States do not apply the exclusive lending right provided for in Article 1 as regards phonograms, films and computer programs, they shall introduce, at least for authors, a remuneration.

3. Member States may exempt certain categories of establishments from the payment of the remuneration referred to in paragraphs 1 and 2.

Chapter II   Rights Related to Copyright

Article 7   Fixation right

1. Member States shall provide for performers the exclusive right to authorise or prohibit the fixation of their performances.

2. Member States shall provide for broadcasting organisations the exclusive right to authorise or prohibit the fixation of their broadcasts, whether these broadcasts are transmitted by wire or over the air, including by cable or satellite.

3. A cable distributor shall not have the right provided for in paragraph 2 where it merely retransmits by cable the broadcasts of broadcasting organisations.

Article 8   Broadcasting and communication to the public

1. Member States shall provide for performers the exclusive right to authorise or prohibit the broadcasting by wireless means and the communication to the public of their performances, except where the performance is itself already a broadcast performance or is made from a fixation.

2. Member States shall provide a right in order to ensure that a single equitable remuneration is paid by the user if a phonogram published for commercial purposes, or a reproduction of such phonogram, is used for broadcasting by wireless means or for any communication to the public, and to ensure that this remuneration is shared between the relevant performers and phonogram producers. Member States may, in the absence of agreement between the performers and phonogram producers, lay down the conditions as to the sharing of this remuneration between them.

3. Member States shall provide for broadcasting organisations the exclusive right to authorise or prohibit the rebroadcasting of their broadcasts by wireless means, as well as the communication to the public of their broadcasts if such communication is made in places accessible to the public against payment of an entrance fee.

Article 9   Distribution right

1. Member States shall provide the exclusive right to make available to the public, by sale or otherwise, the objects indicated in points (a) to (d), including copies thereof, hereinafter 'the distribution right':

(a) for performers, in respect of fixations of their performances;

(b) for phonogram producers, in respect of their phonograms;

(c) for producers of the first fixations of films, in respect of the original and copies of their films;

(d) for broadcasting organisations, in respect of fixations of their broadcasts as set out in Article 7(2).

2. The distribution right shall not be exhausted within the Community in respect of an object as referred to in paragraph 1, except where the first sale in the Community of that object is made by the rightholder or with his consent.

3. The distribution right shall be without prejudice to the specific provisions of Chapter I, in particular Article 1(2).

4. The distribution right may be transferred, assigned or subject to the granting of contractual licences.

Article 10   Limitations to rights

1. Member States may provide for limitations to the rights referred to in this Chapter in respect of:

(a) private use;

(b) use of short excerpts in connection with the reporting of current events;

(c) ephemeral fixation by a broadcasting organisation by means of its own facilities and for its own broadcasts;

(d) use solely for the purposes of teaching or scientific research.

2. Irrespective of paragraph 1, any Member State may provide for the same kinds of limitations with regard to the protection of performers, producers of phonograms, broadcasting organisations and of producers of the first fixations of films, as it provides for in connection with the protection of copyright in literary and artistic works.

However, compulsory licences may be provided for only to the extent to which they are compatible with the Rome Convention.

3. The limitations referred to in paragraphs 1 and 2 shall be applied only in certain special cases which do not conflict with a normal exploitation of the subject matter and do not unreasonably prejudice the legitimate interests of the rightholder.

Chapter III Common Provisions

Article 11 Application in time

1. This Directive shall apply in respect of all copyright works, performances, phonograms, broadcasts and first fixations of films referred to in this Directive which were, on 1 July 1994, still protected by the legislation of the Member States in the field of copyright and related rights or which met the criteria for protection under this Directive on that date.

2. This Directive shall apply without prejudice to any acts of exploitation performed before 1 July 1994.

3. Member States may provide that the rightholders are deemed to have given their authorisation to the rental or lending of an object referred to in points (a) to (d) of Article 3(1) which is proven to have been made available to third parties for this purpose or to have been acquired before 1 July 1994.

However, in particular where such an object is a digital recording, Member States may provide that rightholders shall have a right to obtain an adequate remuneration for the rental or lending of that object.

4. Member States need not apply the provisions of Article 2(2) to cinematographic or audiovisual works created before 1 July 1994.

5. This Directive shall, without prejudice to paragraph 3 and subject to paragraph 7, not affect any contracts concluded before 19 November 1992.

6. Member States may provide, subject to the provisions of paragraph 7, that when rightholders who acquire new rights under the national provisions adopted in implementation of this Directive have, before 1 July 1994, given their consent for exploitation, they shall be presumed to have transferred the new exclusive rights.

7. For contracts concluded before 1 July 1994, the unwaivable right to an equitable remuneration provided for in Article 5 shall apply only where authors or performers or those representing them have submitted a request to that effect before 1 January 1997. In the absence of agreement between rightholders concerning the level of remuneration, Member States may fix the level of equitable remuneration.

Article 12 Relation between copyright and related rights

Protection of copyright-related rights under this Directive shall leave intact and shall in no way affect the protection of copyright.

Article 13 Communication

Member States shall communicate to the Commission the main provisions of national law adopted in the field covered by this Directive.

...

Directive 2006/116/EC of the European Parliament and of the Council

of 12 December 2006 on the term of protection of copyright and certain related rights (codified version)

THE EUROPEAN PARLIAMENT AND THE COUNCIL OF THE EUROPEAN UNION,

Having regard to the Treaty establishing the European Community, and in particular Articles 47(2), 55 and 95 thereof,

Having regard to the proposal from the Commission,

Having regard to the opinion of the European Economic and Social Committee,

Acting in accordance with the procedure laid down in Article 251 of the Treaty,

Whereas:

(1) Council Directive 93/98/EEC of 29 October 1993 harmonising the term of protection of copyright and certain related rights has been substantially amended. In the interests of clarity and rationality the said Directive should be codified.

(2) The Berne Convention for the protection of literary and artistic works and the International Convention for the protection of performers, producers of phonograms and broadcasting organisations (Rome Convention) lay down only minimum terms of protection of the rights they refer to, leaving the Contracting States free to grant longer terms. Certain Member States have exercised this entitlement. In addition, some Member States have not yet become party to the Rome Convention.

(3) There are consequently differences between the national laws governing the terms of protection of copyright and related rights, which are liable to impede the free movement of goods and freedom to provide services and to distort competition in the common market. Therefore, with a view to the smooth operation of the internal market, the laws of the Member States should be harmonised so as to make terms of protection identical throughout the Community.

(4) It is important to lay down not only the terms of protection as such, but also certain implementing arrangements, such as the date from which each term of protection is calculated.

(5) The provisions of this Directive should not affect the application by the Member States of the provisions of Article 14 bis (2)(b), (c) and (d) and (3) of the Berne Convention.

(6) The minimum term of protection laid down by the Berne Convention, namely the life of the author and 50 years after his death, was intended to provide protection for the author and the first two generations of his descendants. The average lifespan in the Community has grown longer, to the point where this term is no longer sufficient to cover two generations.

(7) Certain Member States have granted a term longer than 50 years after the death of the author in order to offset the effects of the world wars on the exploitation of authors' works.

(8) For the protection of related rights certain Member States have introduced a term of 50 years after lawful publication or lawful communication to the public.

(9) The Diplomatic Conference held in December 1996, under the auspices of the World Intellectual Property Organization (WIPO), led to the adoption of the WIPO Performances and Phonograms Treaty, which deals with the protection of performers and producers of phonograms. This Treaty took the form of a substantial up-date of the international protection of related rights.

(10) Due regard for established rights is one of the general principles of law protected by the Community legal order. Therefore, the terms of protection of copyright and related rights established by Community law cannot have the effect of reducing the protection enjoyed by rightholders in the Community before the entry into force of Directive 93/98/EEC. In order to keep the effects of transitional measures to a minimum and to allow the internal market to function smoothly, those terms of protection should be applied for long periods.

(11) The level of protection of copyright and related rights should be high, since those rights are fundamental to intellectual creation. Their protection ensures the maintenance and development of creativity in the interest of authors, cultural industries, consumers and society as a whole.

(12) In order to establish a high level of protection which at the same time meets the requirements of the internal market and the need to establish a legal environment conducive to the harmonious development of literary and artistic creation in the Community, the term of protection for copyright should be harmonised at 70 years after the death of the author or 70 years after the work is lawfully made available to the public, and for related rights at 50 years after the event which sets the term running.

(13) Collections are protected according to Article 2(5) of the Berne Convention when, by reason of the selection and arrangement of their content, they constitute intellectual creations. Those works are protected as such, without prejudice to the copyright in each of the works forming part of such collections. Consequently, specific terms of protection may apply to works included in collections.

(14) In all cases where one or more physical persons are identified as authors, the term of protection should be calculated after their death. The question of authorship of the whole or a part of a work is a question of fact which the national courts may have to decide.

(15) Terms of protection should be calculated from the first day of January of the year following the relevant event, as they are in the Berne and Rome Conventions.

(16) The protection of photographs in the Member States is the subject of varying regimes. A photographic work within the meaning of the Berne Convention is to be considered original if it is the author's own intellectual creation reflecting his personality, no other criteria such as merit or purpose being taken into account. The protection of other photographs should be left to national law.

(17) In order to avoid differences in the term of protection as regards related rights it is necessary to provide the same starting point for the calculation of the term throughout the Community. The performance, fixation, transmission, lawful publication, and lawful communication to the public, that is to say the means of making a subject of a related right perceptible in all appropriate ways to persons in general, should be taken into account for the calculation of the term of protection regardless of the country where this performance, fixation, transmission, lawful publication, or lawful communication to the public takes place.

(18) The rights of broadcasting organisations in their broadcasts, whether these broadcasts are transmitted by wire or over the air, including by cable or satellite, should not be perpetual. It is therefore necessary to have the term of protection running from the first transmission of a particular broadcast only. This provision is understood to avoid a new term running in cases where a broadcast is identical to a previous one.

(19) The Member States should remain free to maintain or introduce other rights related to copyright in particular in relation to the protection of critical and scientific publications. In order to ensure transparency at Community level, it is, however, necessary for Member States which introduce new related rights to notify the Commission.

(20) It should be made clear that this Directive does not apply to moral rights.

(21) For works whose country of origin within the meaning of the Berne Convention is a third country and whose author is not a Community national, comparison of terms of protection should be applied, provided that the term accorded in the Community does not exceed the term laid down in this Directive.

(22) Where a rightholder who is not a Community national qualifies for protection under an international agreement, the term of protection of related rights should be the same as that laid down in this Directive. However, this term should not exceed that fixed in the third country of which the rightholder is a national.

(23) Comparison of terms should not result in Member States being brought into conflict with their international obligations.

(24) Member States should remain free to adopt provisions on the interpretation, adaptation and further execution of contracts on the exploitation of protected works and other subject matter which were concluded before the extension of the term of protection resulting from this Directive.

(25) Respect of acquired rights and legitimate expectations is part of the Community legal order. Member States may provide in particular that in certain circumstances the copyright and related rights which are revived pursuant to this Directive may not give rise to payments by persons who

undertook in good faith the exploitation of the works at the time when such works lay within the public domain.

(26) This Directive should be without prejudice to the obligations of the Member States relating to the time-limits for transposition into national law and application of the Directives, as set out in Part B of Annex I,

HAVE ADOPTED THIS DIRECTIVE:

Article 1   Duration of authors' rights

1. The rights of an author of a literary or artistic work within the meaning of Article 2 of the Berne Convention shall run for the life of the author and for 70 years after his death, irrespective of the date when the work is lawfully made available to the public.

2. In the case of a work of joint authorship, the term referred to in paragraph 1 shall be calculated from the death of the last surviving author.

3. In the case of anonymous or pseudonymous works, the term of protection shall run for 70 years after the work is lawfully made available to the public. However, when the pseudonym adopted by the author leaves no doubt as to his identity, or if the author discloses his identity during the period referred to in the first sentence, the term of protection applicable shall be that laid down in paragraph 1.

4. Where a Member State provides for particular provisions on copyright in respect of collective works or for a legal person to be designated as the rightholder, the term of protection shall be calculated according to the provisions of paragraph 3, except if the natural persons who have created the work are identified as such in the versions of the work which are made available to the public. This paragraph is without prejudice to the rights of identified authors whose identifiable contributions are included in such works, to which contributions paragraph 1 or 2 shall apply.

5. Where a work is published in volumes, parts, instalments, issues or episodes and the term of protection runs from the time when the work was lawfully made available to the public, the term of protection shall run for each such item separately.

6. In the case of works for which the term of protection is not calculated from the death of the author or authors and which have not been lawfully made available to the public within 70 years from their creation, the protection shall terminate.

7. The term of protection of a musical composition with words shall expire 70 years after the death of the last of the following persons to survive, whether or not those persons are designated as co-authors: the author of the lyrics and the composer of the musical composition, provided that both contributions were specifically created for the respective musical composition with words.

Article 2   Cinematographic or audiovisual works

1. The principal director of a cinematographic or audiovisual work shall be considered as its author or one of its authors. Member States shall be free to designate other co-authors.

2. The term of protection of cinematographic or audiovisual works shall expire 70 years after the death of the last of the following persons to survive, whether or not these persons are designated as co-authors: the principal director, the author of the screenplay, the author of the dialogue and the composer of music specifically created for use in the cinematographic or audiovisual work.

Article 3   Duration of related rights

1. The rights of performers shall expire 50 years after the date of the performance. However,
   - if a fixation of the performance otherwise than in a phonogram is lawfully published or lawfully communicated to the public within this period, the rights shall expire 50 years from the date of the first such publication or the first such communication to the public, whichever is the earlier,
   - if a fixation of the performance in a phonogram is lawfully published or lawfully communicated to the public within this period, the rights shall expire 70 years from the date of the first such publication or the first such communication to the public, whichever is the earlier.

2. The rights of producers of phonograms shall expire 50 years after the fixation is made. However, if the phonogram has been lawfully published within this period, the said rights shall expire 70 years from the date of the first lawful publication. If no lawful publication has taken place within the period mentioned in the first sentence, and if the phonogram has been lawfully communicated to the public within this period, the said rights shall expire 70 years from the date of the first lawful communication to the public.

However, this paragraph shall not have the effect of protecting anew the rights of producers of phonograms where, through the expiry of the term of protection granted them pursuant to Article 3(2) of Directive 93/98/EEC in its version before amendment by Directive 2001/29/EEC, they were no longer protected on 22 December 2002.

2a. If, 50 years after the phonogram was lawfully published or, failing such publication, 50 years after it was lawfully communicated to the public, the phonogram producer does not offer copies of the phonogram for sale in sufficient quantity or does not make it available to the public, by wire or wireless means, in such a way that members of the public may access it from a place and at a time individually chosen by them, the performer may terminate the contract by which the performer has transferred or assigned his rights in the fixation of his performance to a phonogram producer (herein-after a 'contract on transfer or assignment'). The right to terminate the contract on transfer or assign-ment may be exercised if the producer, within a year from the notification by the performer of his intention to terminate the contract on transfer or assignment pursuant to the previous sentence, fails to carry out both of the acts of exploitation referred to in that sentence. This right to terminate may not be waived by the performer. Where a phonogram contains the fixation of the performances of a plurality of performers, they may terminate their contracts on transfer or assignment in accordance with applicable national law. If the contract on transfer or assignment is terminated pursuant to this paragraph, the rights of the phonogram producer in the phonogram shall expire.

2b. Where a contract on transfer or assignment gives the performer a right to claim a non-recur-ring remuneration, the performer shall have the right to obtain an annual supplementary remuner-ation from the phonogram producer for each full year immediately following the 50th year after the phonogram was lawfully published or, failing such publication, the 50th year after it was lawfully communicated to the public. The right to obtain such annual supplementary remuneration may not be waived by the performer.

2c. The overall amount to be set aside by a phonogram producer for payment of the annual sup-plementary remuneration referred to in paragraph 2b shall correspond to 20% of the revenue which the phonogram producer has derived, during the year preceding that for which the said remuneration is paid, from the reproduction, distribution and making available of the phonogram in question, fol-lowing the 50th year after it was lawfully published or, failing such publication, the 50th year after it was lawfully communicated to the public.

Member States shall ensure that phonogram producers are required on request to provide to performers who are entitled to the annual supplementary remuneration referred to in paragraph 2b any information which may be necessary in order to secure payment of that remuneration.

2d. Member States shall ensure that the right to obtain an annual supplementary remuneration as referred to in paragraph 2b is administered by collecting societies.

2e. Where a performer is entitled to recurring payments, neither advance payments nor any con-tractually defined deductions shall be deducted from the payments made to the performer following the 50th year after the phonogram was lawfully published or, failing such publication, the 50th year after it was lawfully communicated to the public.

3. The rights of producers of the first fixation of a film shall expire 50 years after the fixation is made. However, if the film is lawfully published or lawfully communicated to the public during this period, the rights shall expire 50 years from the date of the first such publication or the first such com-munication to the public, whichever is the earlier. The term 'film' shall designate a cinematographic or audiovisual work or moving images, whether or not accompanied by sound.

4. The rights of broadcasting organisations shall expire 50 years after the first transmission of a broadcast, whether this broadcast is transmitted by wire or over the air, including by cable or satellite.

Article 4   Protection of previously unpublished works

Any person who, after the expiry of copyright protection, for the first time lawfully publishes or lawfully communicates to the public a previously unpublished work, shall benefit from a protection equivalent to the economic rights of the author. The term of protection of such rights shall be 25 years from the time when the work was first lawfully published or lawfully communicated to the public.

Article 5   Critical and scientific publications

Member States may protect critical and scientific publications of works which have come into the public domain. The maximum term of protection of such rights shall be 30 years from the time when the publication was first lawfully published.

Article 6   Protection of photographs

Photographs which are original in the sense that they are the author's own intellectual creation shall be protected in accordance with Article 1. No other criteria shall be applied to determine their eligibility for protection. Member States may provide for the protection of other photographs.

Article 7   Protection vis-à-vis third countries

1. Where the country of origin of a work, within the meaning of the Berne Convention, is a third country, and the author of the work is not a Community national, the term of protection granted by the Member States shall expire on the date of expiry of the protection granted in the country of origin of the work, but may not exceed the term laid down in Article 1.

2. The terms of protection laid down in Article 3 shall also apply in the case of rightholders who are not Community nationals, provided Member States grant them protection. However, without prejudice to the international obligations of the Member States, the term of protection granted by Member States shall expire no later than the date of expiry of the protection granted in the country of which the rightholder is a national and may not exceed the term laid down in Article 3.

3. Member States which, on 29 October 1993 in particular, pursuant to their international obligations, granted a longer term of protection than that which would result from the provisions of paragraphs 1 and 2 may maintain this protection until the conclusion of international agreements on the term of protection of copyright or related rights.

Article 8   Calculation of terms

The terms laid down in this Directive shall be calculated from the first day of January of the year following the event which gives rise to them.

Article 9   Moral rights

This Directive shall be without prejudice to the provisions of the Member States regulating moral rights.

Article 10   Application in time

1. Where a term of protection which is longer than the corresponding term provided for by this Directive was already running in a Member State on 1 July 1995, this Directive shall not have the effect of shortening that term of protection in that Member State.

2. The terms of protection provided for in this Directive shall apply to all works and subject matter which were protected in at least one Member State on the date referred to in paragraph 1, pursuant to national provisions on copyright or related rights, or which meet the criteria for protection under [Council Directive 92/100/EEC of 19 November 1992 on rental right and lending right and on certain rights related to copyright in the field of intellectual property].

3. This Directive shall be without prejudice to any acts of exploitation performed before the date referred to in paragraph 1. Member States shall adopt the necessary provisions to protect in particular acquired rights of third parties.

4. Member States need not apply the provisions of Article 2(1) to cinematographic or audiovisual works created before 1 July 1994.

5. Article 3(1) to (2e) in the version thereof in force on 31 October 2011 shall apply to fixations of performances and phonograms in regard to which the performer and the phonogram producer are still protected, by virtue of those provisions in the version thereof in force on 30 October 2011, as at 1 November 2013 and to fixations of performances and phonograms which come into being after that date.

6. Article 1(7) shall apply to musical compositions with words of which at least the musical composition or the lyrics are protected in at least one Member State on 1 November 2013, and to musical compositions with words which come into being after that date.

The first subparagraph of this paragraph shall be without prejudice to any acts of exploitation performed before 1 November 2013. Member States shall adopt the necessary provisions to protect, in particular, acquired rights of third parties.

Article 10a   Transitional measures

1. In the absence of clear contractual indications to the contrary, a contract on transfer or assignment concluded before 1 November 2013 shall be deemed to continue to produce its effects beyond the moment at which, by virtue of Article 3(1) in the version thereof in force on 30 October 2011, the performer would no longer be protected.

2. Member States may provide that contracts on transfer or assignment which entitle a performer to recurring payments and which are concluded before 1 November 2013 can be modified following the 50th year after the phonogram was lawfully published or, failing such publication, the 50th year after it was lawfully communicated to the public.

Article 11   Notification and communication

1. Member States shall immediately notify the Commission of any governmental plan to grant new related rights, including the basic reasons for their introduction and the term of protection envisaged.

2. Member States shall communicate to the Commission the texts of the provisions of internal law which they adopt in the field governed by this Directive.

...

Directive 2009/24/EC of the European Parliament and of the Council

of 23 April 2009 on the legal protection of computer programs (codified version) (Text with EEA relevance)

THE EUROPEAN PARLIAMENT AND THE COUNCIL OF THE EUROPEAN UNION,

Having regard to the Treaty establishing the European Community and in particular Article 95 thereof,

Having regard to the proposal from the Commission,

Having regard to the opinion of the European Economic and Social Committee,

Acting in accordance with the procedure laid down in Article 251 of the Treaty,

Whereas:

(1) The content of Council Directive 91/250/EEC of 14 May 1991 on the legal protection of computer programs has been amended. In the interests of clarity and rationality the said Directive should be codified.

(2) The development of computer programs requires the investment of considerable human, technical and financial resources while computer programs can be copied at a fraction of the cost needed to develop them independently.

(3) Computer programs are playing an increasingly important role in a broad range of industries and computer program technology can accordingly be considered as being of fundamental importance for the Community's industrial development.

(4) Certain differences in the legal protection of computer programs offered by the laws of the Member States have direct and negative effects on the functioning of the internal market as regards computer programs.

(5) Existing differences having such effects need to be removed and new ones prevented from arising, while differences not adversely affecting the functioning of the internal market to a substantial degree need not be removed or prevented from arising.

(6) The Community's legal framework on the protection of computer programs can accordingly in the first instance be limited to establishing that Member States should accord protection to computer programs under copyright law as literary works and, further, to establishing who and what should be protected, the exclusive rights on which protected persons should be able to rely in order to authorise or prohibit certain acts and for how long the protection should apply.

(7) For the purpose of this Directive, the term 'computer program' shall include programs in any form, including those which are incorporated into hardware. This term also includes preparatory design work leading to the development of a computer program provided that the nature of the preparatory work is such that a computer program can result from it at a later stage.

(8) In respect of the criteria to be applied in determining whether or not a computer program is an original work, no tests as to the qualitative or aesthetic merits of the program should be applied.

(9) The Community is fully committed to the promotion of international standardisation.

(10) The function of a computer program is to communicate and work together with other components of a computer system and with users and, for this purpose, a logical and, where appropriate, physical interconnection and interaction is required to permit all elements of software and hardware to work with other software and hardware and with users in all the ways in which they are intended to function. The parts of the program which provide for such interconnection and interaction between elements of software and hardware are generally known as 'interfaces'. This functional interconnection and interaction is generally known as 'interoperability'; such interoperability can be defined as the ability to exchange information and mutually to use the information which has been exchanged.

(11) For the avoidance of doubt, it has to be made clear that only the expression of a computer program is protected and that ideas and principles which underlie any element of a program, including those which underlie its interfaces, are not protected by copyright under this Directive. In accordance with this principle of copyright, to the extent that logic, algorithms and programming languages comprise ideas and principles, those ideas and principles are not protected under this Directive. In accordance with the legislation and case-law of the Member States and the international copyright conventions, the expression of those ideas and principles is to be protected by copyright.

(12) For the purposes of this Directive, the term 'rental' means the making available for use, for a limited period of time and for profit-making purposes, of a computer program or a copy thereof. This term does not include public lending, which, accordingly, remains outside the scope of this Directive.

(13) The exclusive rights of the author to prevent the unauthorised reproduction of his work should be subject to a limited exception in the case of a computer program to allow the reproduction technically necessary for the use of that program by the lawful acquirer. This means that the acts of loading and running necessary for the use of a copy of a program which has been lawfully acquired, and the act of correction of its errors, may not be prohibited by contract. In the absence of specific contractual provisions, including when a copy of the program has been sold, any other act necessary for the use of the copy of a program may be performed in accordance with its intended purpose by a lawful acquirer of that copy.

(14) A person having a right to use a computer program should not be prevented from performing acts necessary to observe, study or test the functioning of the program, provided that those acts do not infringe the copyright in the program.

(15) The unauthorised reproduction, translation, adaptation or transformation of the form of the code in which a copy of a computer program has been made available constitutes an infringement

of the exclusive rights of the author. Nevertheless, circumstances may exist when such a reproduction of the code and translation of its form are indispensable to obtain the necessary information to achieve the interoperability of an independently created program with other programs. It has therefore to be considered that, in these limited circumstances only, performance of the acts of reproduction and translation by or on behalf of a person having a right to use a copy of the program is legitimate and compatible with fair practice and must therefore be deemed not to require the authorisation of the rightholder. An objective of this exception is to make it possible to connect all components of a computer system, including those of different manufacturers, so that they can work together. Such an exception to the author's exclusive rights may not be used in a way which prejudices the legitimate interests of the rightholder or which conflicts with a normal exploitation of the program.

(16) Protection of computer programs under copyright laws should be without prejudice to the application, in appropriate cases, of other forms of protection. However, any contractual provisions contrary to the provisions of this Directive laid down in respect of decompilation or to the exceptions provided for by this Directive with regard to the making of a back-up copy or to observation, study or testing of the functioning of a program should be null and void.

(17) The provisions of this Directive are without prejudice to the application of the competition rules under Articles 81 and 82 of the Treaty if a dominant supplier refuses to make information available which is necessary for interoperability as defined in this Directive.

(18) The provisions of this Directive should be without prejudice to specific requirements of Community law already enacted in respect of the publication of interfaces in the telecommunications sector or Council Decisions relating to standardisation in the field of information technology and telecommunication.

(19) This Directive does not affect derogations provided for under national legislation in accordance with the Berne Convention on points not covered by this Directive.

(20) This Directive should be without prejudice to the obligations of the Member States relating to the time-limits for transposition into national law of the Directives set out in Annex I, Part B,

HAVE ADOPTED THIS DIRECTIVE:

Article 1   Object of protection

1. In accordance with the provisions of this Directive, Member States shall protect computer programs, by copyright, as literary works within the meaning of the Berne Convention for the Protection of Literary and Artistic Works. For the purposes of this Directive, the term 'computer programs' shall include their preparatory design material.

2. Protection in accordance with this Directive shall apply to the expression in any form of a computer program. Ideas and principles which underlie any element of a computer program, including those which underlie its interfaces, are not protected by copyright under this Directive.

3. A computer program shall be protected if it is original in the sense that it is the author's own intellectual creation. No other criteria shall be applied to determine its eligibility for protection.

4. The provisions of this Directive shall apply also to programs created before 1 January 1993, without prejudice to any acts concluded and rights acquired before that date.

Article 2   Authorship of computer programs

1. The author of a computer program shall be the natural person or group of natural persons who has created the program or, where the legislation of the Member State permits, the legal person designated as the rightholder by that legislation.

Where collective works are recognised by the legislation of a Member State, the person considered by the legislation of the Member State to have created the work shall be deemed to be its author.

2. In respect of a computer program created by a group of natural persons jointly, the exclusive rights shall be owned jointly.

3. Where a computer program is created by an employee in the execution of his duties or following the instructions given by his employer, the employer exclusively shall be entitled to exercise all economic rights in the program so created, unless otherwise provided by contract.

Article 3   Beneficiaries of protection

Protection shall be granted to all natural or legal persons eligible under national copyright legislation as applied to literary works.

Article 4   Restricted acts

1. Subject to the provisions of Articles 5 and 6, the exclusive rights of the rightholder within the meaning of Article 2 shall include the right to do or to authorise:

(a) the permanent or temporary reproduction of a computer program by any means and in any form, in part or in whole; in so far as loading, displaying, running, transmission or storage of the computer program necessitate such reproduction, such acts shall be subject to authorisation by the rightholder;

(b) the translation, adaptation, arrangement and any other alteration of a computer program and the reproduction of the results thereof, without prejudice to the rights of the person who alters the program;

(c) any form of distribution to the public, including the rental, of the original computer program or of copies thereof.

2. The first sale in the Community of a copy of a program by the rightholder or with his consent shall exhaust the distribution right within the Community of that copy, with the exception of the right to control further rental of the program or a copy thereof.

Article 5   Exceptions to the restricted acts

1. In the absence of specific contractual provisions, the acts referred to in points (a) and (b) of Article 4(1) shall not require authorisation by the rightholder where they are necessary for the use of the computer program by the lawful acquirer in accordance with its intended purpose, including for error correction.

2. The making of a back-up copy by a person having a right to use the computer program may not be prevented by contract in so far as it is necessary for that use.

3. The person having a right to use a copy of a computer program shall be entitled, without the authorisation of the rightholder, to observe, study or test the functioning of the program in order to determine the ideas and principles which underlie any element of the program if he does so while performing any of the acts of loading, displaying, running, transmitting or storing the program which he is entitled to do.

Article 6   Decompilation

1. The authorisation of the rightholder shall not be required where reproduction of the code and translation of its form within the meaning of points (a) and (b) of Article 4(1) are indispensable to obtain the information necessary to achieve the interoperability of an independently created computer program with other programs, provided that the following conditions are met:

(a) those acts are performed by the licensee or by another person having a right to use a copy of a program, or on their behalf by a person authorised to do so;

(b) the information necessary to achieve interoperability has not previously been readily available to the persons referred to in point (a); and

(c) those acts are confined to the parts of the original program which are necessary in order to achieve interoperability.

2. The provisions of paragraph 1 shall not permit the information obtained through its application:

(a) to be used for goals other than to achieve the interoperability of the independently created computer program;

(b) to be given to others, except when necessary for the interoperability of the independently created computer program; or

(c) to be used for the development, production or marketing of a computer program substantially similar in its expression, or for any other act which infringes copyright.

3. In accordance with the provisions of the Berne Convention for the protection of Literary and Artistic Works, the provisions of this Article may not be interpreted in such a way as to allow its application to be used in a manner which unreasonably prejudices the rightholder's legitimate interests or conflicts with a normal exploitation of the computer program.

Article 7   Special measures of protection

1. Without prejudice to the provisions of Articles 4, 5 and 6, Member States shall provide, in accordance with their national legislation, appropriate remedies against a person committing any of the following acts:

(a) any act of putting into circulation a copy of a computer program knowing, or having reason to believe, that it is an infringing copy;

(b) the possession, for commercial purposes, of a copy of a computer program knowing, or having reason to believe, that it is an infringing copy;

(c) any act of putting into circulation, or the possession for commercial purposes of, any means the sole intended purpose of which is to facilitate the unauthorised removal or circumvention of any technical device which may have been applied to protect a computer program.

2. Any infringing copy of a computer program shall be liable to seizure in accordance with the legislation of the Member State concerned.

3. Member States may provide for the seizure of any means referred to in point (c) of paragraph 1.

Article 8   Continued application of other legal provisions

The provisions of this Directive shall be without prejudice to any other legal provisions such as those concerning patent rights, trademarks, unfair competition, trade secrets, protection of semi-conductor products or the law of contract.

Any contractual provisions contrary to Article 6 or to the exceptions provided for in Article 5(2) and (3) shall be null and void.

Article 9   Communication

Member States shall communicate to the Commission the provisions of national law adopted in the field governed by this Directive.

Article 10   Repeal

Directive 91/250/EEC, as amended by the Directive indicated in Annex I, Part A, is repealed, without prejudice to the obligations of the Member States relating to the time-limits for transposition into national law of the Directives set out in Annex I, Part B.

References to the repealed Directive shall be construed as references to this Directive and shall be read in accordance with the correlation table in Annex II.

Article 11   Entry into force

This Directive shall enter into force on the 20th day following its publication in the *Official Journal of the European Union*.

Article 12   Addressees

This Directive is addressed to the Member States.

...

Directive 2012/28/EU of the European Parliament and of the Council

of 25 October 2012 on certain permitted uses of orphan works (Text with EEA relevance)

THE EUROPEAN PARLIAMENT AND THE COUNCIL OF THE EUROPEAN UNION,

Having regard to the Treaty on the Functioning of the European Union, and in particular Articles 53(1), 62 and 114 thereof,

Having regard to the proposal from the European Commission,

After transmission of the draft legislative act to the national parliaments,

Having regard to the opinion of the European Economic and Social Committee,

Acting in accordance with the ordinary legislative procedure,

Whereas:

(1) Publicly accessible libraries, educational establishments and museums, as well as archives, film or audio heritage institutions and public-service broadcasting organisations, established in the Member States, are engaged in large-scale digitisation of their collections or archives in order to create European Digital Libraries. They contribute to the preservation and dissemination of European cultural heritage, which is also important for the creation of European Digital Libraries, such as Europeana. Technologies for mass digitisation of print materials and for search and indexing enhance the research value of the libraries' collections. Creating large online libraries facilitates electronic search and discovery tools which open up new sources of discovery for researchers and academics who would otherwise have to content themselves with more traditional and analogue search methods.

(2) The need to promote free movement of knowledge and innovation in the internal market is an important component of the Europe 2020 Strategy, as set out in the Communication from the Commission entitled 'Europe 2020: A strategy for smart, sustainable and inclusive growth', which includes as one of its flagship initiatives the development of a Digital Agenda for Europe.

(3) Creating a legal framework to facilitate the digitisation and dissemination of works and other subject-matter which are protected by copyright or related rights and for which no rightholder is identified or for which the rightholder, even if identified, is not located—so-called orphan works—is a key action of the Digital Agenda for Europe, as set out in the Communication from the Commission entitled 'A Digital Agenda for Europe'. This Directive targets the specific problem of the legal determination of orphan work status and its consequences in terms of the permitted users and permitted uses of works or phonograms considered to be orphan works.

(4) This Directive is without prejudice to specific solutions being developed in the Member States to address larger mass digitisation issues, such as in the case of so-called 'out-of-commerce' works. Such solutions take into account the specificities of different types of content and different users and build upon the consensus of the relevant stakeholders. This approach has also been followed in the Memorandum of Understanding on key principles on the digitisation and making available of out-of-commerce works, signed on 20 September 2011 by representatives of European libraries, authors, publishers and collecting societies and witnessed by the Commission. This Directive is without prejudice to that Memorandum of Understanding, which calls on Member States and the Commission to ensure that voluntary agreements concluded between users, rightholders and collective rights management organisations to licence the use of out-of-commerce works on the basis of the principles contained therein benefit from the requisite legal certainty in a national and cross-border context.

(5) Copyright is the economic foundation for the creative industry, since it stimulates innovation, creation, investment and production. Mass digitisation and dissemination of works is therefore a means of protecting Europe's cultural heritage. Copyright is an important tool for ensuring that the creative sector is rewarded for its work.

(6) The rightholders' exclusive rights of reproduction of their works and other protected subject-matter and of making them available to the public, as harmonised under Directive 2001/29/EC of the European Parliament and of the Council of 22 May 2001 on the harmonisation of certain aspects of copyright and related rights in the information society, necessitate the prior consent of rightholders to the digitisation and the making available to the public of a work or other protected subject-matter.

(7) In the case of orphan works, it is not possible to obtain such prior consent to the carrying-out of acts of reproduction or of making available to the public.

(8) Different approaches in the Member States to the recognition of orphan work status can present obstacles to the functioning of the internal market and the use of, and cross-border access to, orphan works. Such different approaches can also result in restrictions on the free movement of goods and services which incorporate cultural content. Therefore, ensuring the mutual recognition of such status is appropriate, since it will allow access to orphan works in all Member States.

(9) In particular, a common approach to determining the orphan work status and the permitted uses of orphan works is necessary in order to ensure legal certainty in the internal market with respect to the use of orphan works by publicly accessible libraries, educational establishments and museums, as well as by archives, film or audio heritage institutions and public-service broadcasting organisations.

(10) Cinematographic or audiovisual works and phonograms in the archives of public-service broadcasting organisations and produced by them include orphan works. Taking into account the special position of broadcasters as producers of phonograms and audiovisual material and the need to adopt measures to limit the phenomenon of orphan works in the future, it is appropriate to set a cut-off date for the application of this Directive to works and phonograms in the archives of broadcasting organisations.

(11) Cinematographic and audiovisual works and phonograms contained in the archives of public-service broadcasting organisations and produced by them, should for the purposes of this Directive be regarded as including cinematographic and audiovisual works and phonograms which are commissioned by such organisations for the exclusive exploitation by them or other co-producing public-service broadcasting organisations. Cinematographic and audiovisual works and phonograms contained in the archives of public-service broadcasting organisations which have not been produced or commissioned by such organisations, but which those organisations have been authorised to use under a licensing agreement, should not fall within the scope of this Directive.

(12) For reasons of international comity, this Directive should apply only to works and phonograms that are first published in the territory of a Member State or, in the absence of publication, first broadcast in the territory of a Member State or, in the absence of publication or broadcast, made publicly accessible by the beneficiaries of this Directive with the consent of the rightholders. In the latter case, this Directive should only apply provided that it is reasonable to assume that the rightholders would not oppose the use allowed by this Directive.

(13) Before a work or phonogram can be considered an orphan work, a diligent search for the rightholders in the work or phonogram, including rightholders in works and other protected subject-matter that are embedded or incorporated in the work or phonogram, should be carried out in good faith. Member States should be permitted to provide that such diligent search may be carried out by the organisations referred to in this Directive or by other organisations. Such other organisations may charge for the service of carrying out a diligent search.

(14) It is appropriate to provide for a harmonised approach concerning such diligent search in order to ensure a high level of protection of copyright and related rights in the Union. A diligent search should involve the consultation of sources that supply information on the works and other protected subject-matter as determined, in accordance with this Directive, by the Member State where the diligent search has to be carried out. In so doing, Member States could refer to the diligent search guidelines agreed in the context of the High Level Working Group on Digital Libraries established as part of the i2010 digital library initiative.

(15) In order to avoid duplication of search efforts, a diligent search should be carried out in the Member State where the work or phonogram was first published or, in cases where no publication has taken place, where it was first broadcast. The diligent search in respect of cinematographic or audiovisual works the producer of which has his headquarters or habitual residence in a Member State should be carried out in that Member State. In the case of cinematographic or audiovisual works which are co-produced by producers established in different Member States, the diligent search should be carried out in each of those Member States. With regard to works and phonograms which have neither been published nor broadcast but which have been made publicly accessible by the beneficiaries of this Directive with the consent of the rightholders, the diligent search should be carried out in the Member State where the organisation that made the work or phonogram publicly accessible with the consent

of the rightholder is established. Diligent searches for the rightholders in works and other protected subject-matter that are embedded or incorporated in a work or phonogram should be carried out in the Member State where the diligent search for the work or phonogram containing the embedded or incorporated work or other protected subject-matter is carried out. Sources of information available in other countries should also be consulted if there is evidence to suggest that relevant information on rightholders is to be found in those other countries. The carrying-out of diligent searches may generate various kinds of information, such as a search record and the result of the search. The search record should be kept on file in order for the relevant organisation to be able to substantiate that the search was diligent.

(16) Member States should ensure that the organisations concerned keep records of their diligent searches and that the results of such searches, consisting in particular of any finding that a work or phonogram is to be considered an orphan work within the meaning of this Directive, as well as information on the change of status and on the use which those organisations make of orphan works, are collected and made available to the public at large, in particular through the recording of the relevant information in an online database. Considering in particular the pan-European dimension, and in order to avoid duplication of efforts, it is appropriate to make provision for the creation of a single online database for the Union containing such information and for making it available to the public at large in a transparent manner. This can enable both the organisations which are carrying out diligent searches and the rightholders easily to access such information. The database could also play an important role in preventing and bringing to an end possible copyright infringements, particularly in the case of changes to the orphan work status of the works and phonograms under Regulation (EU) No 386/2012, the Office for Harmonization in the Internal Market ('the Office') is entrusted with certain tasks and activities, financed by making use of its own budgetary means, aimed at facilitating and supporting the activities of national authorities, the private sector and the Union institutions in the fight against, including the prevention of, infringement of intellectual property rights.

In particular, pursuant to point (g) of Article 2(1) of that Regulation, those tasks include providing mechanisms which help to improve the online exchange of relevant information between the Member States' authorities concerned and fostering cooperation between those authorities. It is therefore appropriate to rely on the Office to establish and manage the European database containing information related to orphan works referred to in this Directive.

(17) There can be several rightholders in respect of a particular work or phonogram, and works and phonograms can themselves include other works or protected subject-matter. This Directive should not affect the rights of identified and located rightholders. If at least one rightholder has been identified and located, a work or phonogram should not be considered an orphan work. The beneficiaries of this Directive should only be permitted to use a work or phonogram one or more of the rightholders in which are not identified or not located, if they are authorised to carry out the acts of reproduction and of making available to the public covered by Articles 2 and 3 respectively of Directive 2001/29/EC by those rightholders that have been identified and located, including the rightholders of works and other protected subject-matter which are embedded or incorporated in the works or phonograms. Rightholders that have been identified and located can give this authorisation only in relation to the rights that they themselves hold, either because the rights are their own rights or because the rights were transferred to them, and should not be able to authorise under this Directive any use on behalf of rightholders that have not been identified and located. Correspondingly, when previously non-identified or non-located rightholders come forward in order to claim their rights in the work or phonogram, the lawful use of the work or phonogram by the beneficiaries can continue only if those rightholders give their authorisation to do so under Directive 2001/29/EC in relation to the rights that they hold.

(18) Rightholders should be entitled to put an end to the orphan work status in the event that they come forward to claim their rights in the work or other protected subject-matter. Rightholders that put an end to the orphan work status of a work or other protected subject-matter should receive fair compensation for the use that has been made of their works or other protected subject-matter under this Directive, to be determined by the Member State where the organisation that uses an orphan work is established. Member States should be free to determine the circumstances under which the payment of such compensation may be organised, including the point in time at which the payment is due. For the purposes of determining the possible level of fair compensation, due account should be taken, inter alia, of Member States' cultural promotion objectives, of the non-commercial nature of the use made by

the organisations in question in order to achieve aims related to their public-interest missions, such as promoting learning and disseminating culture, and of the possible harm to rightholders.

(19) If a work or phonogram has been wrongly found to be an orphan work, following a search which was not diligent, the remedies for copyright infringement in Member States' legislation, provided for in accordance with the relevant national provisions and Union law, remain available.

(20) In order to promote learning and the dissemination of culture, Member States should provide for an exception or limitation in addition to those provided for in Article 5 of Directive 2001/29/EC. That exception or limitation should permit certain organisations, as referred to in point (c) of Article 5(2) of Directive 2001/29/EC and film or audio heritage institutions which operate on a non-profit making basis, as well as public-service broadcasting organisations, to reproduce and make available to the public, within the meaning of that Directive, orphan works, provided that such use fulfils their public interest missions, in particular the preservation of, the restoration of, and the provision of cultural and educational access to, their collections, including their digital collections. Film or audio heritage institutions should, for the purposes of this Directive, cover organisations designated by Member States to collect, catalogue, preserve and restore films and other audiovisual works or phonograms forming part of their cultural heritage. Public-service broadcasters should, for the purposes of this Directive, cover broadcasters with a public-service remit as conferred, defined and organised by each Member State. The exception or limitation established by this Directive to permit the use of orphan works is without prejudice to the exceptions and limitations provided for in Article 5 of Directive 2001/29/EC. It can be applied only in certain special cases which do not conflict with the normal exploitation of the work or other protected subject-matter and do not unreasonably prejudice the legitimate interests of the rightholder.

(21) In order to incentivise digitisation, the beneficiaries of this Directive should be allowed to generate revenues in relation to their use of orphan works under this Directive in order to achieve aims related to their public-interest missions, including in the context of public-private partnership agreements.

(22) Contractual arrangements may play a role in fostering the digitisation of European cultural heritage, it being understood that publicly accessible libraries, educational establishments and museums, as well as archives, film or audio heritage institutions and public-service broadcasting organisations, should be allowed, with a view to undertaking the uses permitted under this Directive, to conclude agreements with commercial partners for the digitisation and making available to the public of orphan works. Those agreements may include financial contributions by such partners. Such agreements should not impose any restrictions on the beneficiaries of this Directive as to their use of orphan works and should not grant the commercial partner any rights to use, or control the use of, the orphan works.

(23) In order to foster access by the Union's citizens to Europe's cultural heritage, it is also necessary to ensure that orphan works which have been digitised and made available to the public in one Member State may also be made available to the public in other Member States. Publicly accessible libraries, educational establishments and museums, as well as archives, film or audio heritage institutions and public-service broadcasting organisations that use an orphan work in order to achieve their public-interest missions should be able to make the orphan work available to the public in other Member States.

(24) This Directive is without prejudice to the arrangements in the Member States concerning the management of rights such as extended collective licences, legal presumptions of representation or transfer, collective management or similar arrangements or a combination of them, including for mass digitisation.

(25) Since the objective of this Directive, namely ensuring legal certainty with respect to the use of orphan works, cannot be sufficiently achieved by the Member States and can therefore, by reason of the need for uniformity of the rules governing the use of orphan works, be better achieved at Union level, the Union may adopt measures, in accordance with the principle of subsidiarity as set out in Article 5 of the Treaty on European Union. In accordance with the principle of proportionality, as set out in that Article, this Directive does not go beyond what is necessary in order to achieve that objective,

HAVE ADOPTED THIS DIRECTIVE:

Article 1   Subject-matter and scope

1. This Directive concerns certain uses made of orphan works by publicly accessible libraries, educational establishments and museums, as well as by archives, film or audio heritage institutions

and public-service broadcasting organisations, established in the Member States, in order to achieve aims related to their public-interest missions.

2. This Directive applies to:

(a) works published in the form of books, journals, newspapers, magazines or other writings contained in the collections of publicly accessible libraries, educational establishments or museums as well as in the collections of archives or of film or audio heritage institutions;

(b) cinematographic or audiovisual works and phonograms contained in the collections of publicly accessible libraries, educational establishments or museums as well as in the collections of archives or of film or audio heritage institutions; and

(c) cinematographic or audiovisual works and phonograms produced by public-service broadcasting organisations up to and including 31 December 2002 and contained in their archives;

which are protected by copyright or related rights and which are first published in a Member State or, in the absence of publication, first broadcast in a Member State.

3. This Directive also applies to works and phonograms referred to in paragraph 2 which have never been published or broadcast but which have been made publicly accessible by the organisations referred to in paragraph 1 with the consent of the rightholders, provided that it is reasonable to assume that the rightholders would not oppose the uses referred to in Article 6. Member States may limit the application of this paragraph to works and phonograms which have been deposited with those organisations before 29 October 2014.

4. This Directive shall also apply to works and other protected subject-matter that are embedded or incorporated in, or constitute an integral part of, the works or phonograms referred to in paragraphs 2 and 3.

5. This Directive does not interfere with any arrangements concerning the management of rights at national level.

Article 2   Orphan works

1. A work or a phonogram shall be considered an orphan work if none of the rightholders in that work or phonogram is identified or, even if one or more of them is identified, none is located despite a diligent search for the rightholders having been carried out and recorded in accordance with Article 3.

2. Where there is more than one right holder in a work or phonogram, and not all of them have been identified or, even if identified, located after a diligent search has been carried out and recorded in accordance with Article 3, the work or phonogram may be used in accordance with this Directive provided that the rightholders that have been identified and located have, in relation to the rights they hold, authorised the organisations referred to in Article 1(1) to carry out the acts of reproduction and making available to the public covered respectively by Articles 2 and 3 of Directive 2001/29/EC.

3. Paragraph 2 shall be without prejudice to the rights in the work or phonogram of rightholders that have been identified and located.

4. Article 5 shall apply *mutatis mutandis* to the rightholders that have not been identified and located in the works referred to in paragraph 2.

5. This Directive shall be without prejudice to national provisions on anonymous or pseudonymous works.

Article 3   Diligent search

1. For the purposes of establishing whether a work or phonogram is an orphan work, the organisations referred to in Article 1(1) shall ensure that a diligent search is carried out in good faith in respect of each work or other protected subject-matter, by consulting the appropriate sources for the category of works and other protected subject-matter in question. The diligent search shall be carried out prior to the use of the work or phonogram.

2. The sources that are appropriate for each category of works or phonogram in question shall be determined by each Member State, in consultation with rightholders and users, and shall include at least the relevant sources listed in the Annex.

3. A diligent search shall be carried out in the Member State of first publication or, in the absence of publication, first broadcast, except in the case of cinematographic or audiovisual works the

producer of which has his headquarters or habitual residence in a Member State, in which case the diligent search shall be carried out in the Member State of his headquarters or habitual residence.

In the case referred to in Article 1(3), the diligent search shall be carried out in the Member State where the organisation that made the work or phonogram publicly accessible with the consent of the rightholder is established.

4. If there is evidence to suggest that relevant information on rightholders is to be found in other countries, sources of information available in those other countries shall also be consulted.

5. Member States shall ensure that the organisations referred to in Article 1(1) maintain records of their diligent searches and that those organisations provide the following information to the competent national authorities:

    (a) the results of the diligent searches that the organisations have carried out and which have led to the conclusion that a work or a phonogram is considered an orphan work;

    (b) the use that the organisations make of orphan works in accordance with this Directive;

    (c) any change, pursuant to Article 5, of the orphan work status of works and phonograms that the organisations use;

    (d) the relevant contact information of the organisation concerned.

6. Member States shall take the necessary measures to ensure that the information referred to in paragraph 5 is recorded in a single publicly accessible online database established and managed by the Office for Harmonization in the Internal Market ('the Office') in accordance with Regulation (EU) No 386/2012. To that end, they shall forward that information to the Office without delay upon receiving it from the organisations referred to in Article 1(1).

Article 4   Mutual recognition of orphan work status

A work or phonogram which is considered an orphan work according to Article 2 in a Member State shall be considered an orphan work in all Member States. That work or phonogram may be used and accessed in accordance with this Directive in all Member States. This also applies to works and phonograms referred to in Article 2(2) in so far as the rights of the non-identified or non-located rightholders are concerned.

Article 5   End of orphan work status

Member States shall ensure that a rightholder in a work or phonogram considered to be an orphan work has, at any time, the possibility of putting an end to the orphan work status in so far as his rights are concerned.

Article 6   Permitted uses of orphan works

1. Member States shall provide for an exception or limitation to the right of reproduction and the right of making available to the public provided for respectively in Articles 2 and 3 of Directive 2001/29/EC to ensure that the organisations referred to in Article 1(1) are permitted to use orphan works contained in their collections in the following ways:

    (a) by making the orphan work available to the public, within the meaning of Article 3 of Directive 2001/29/EC;

    (b) by acts of reproduction, within the meaning of Article 2 of Directive 2001/29/EC, for the purposes of digitisation, making available, indexing, cataloguing, preservation or restoration.

2. The organisations referred to in Article (1) shall use an orphan work in accordance with paragraph 1 of this Article only in order to achieve aims related to their public-interest missions, in particular the preservation of, the restoration of, and the provision of cultural and educational access to, works and phonograms contained in their collection. The organisations may generate revenues in the course of such uses, for the exclusive purpose of covering their costs of digitising orphan works and making them available to the public.

3. Member States shall ensure that the organisations referred to in Article 1(1) indicate the name of identified authors and other rightholders in any use of an orphan work.

4. This Directive is without prejudice to the freedom of contract of such organisations in the pursuit of their public-interest missions, particularly in respect of public-private partnership agreements.

5. Member States shall provide that a fair compensation is due to rightholders that put an end to the orphan work status of their works or other protected subject-matter for the use that has been made by the organisations referred to in Article 1(1) of such works and other protected subject-matter in accordance with paragraph 1 of this Article. Member States shall be free to determine the circumstances under which the payment of such compensation may be organised. The level of the compensation shall be determined, within the limits imposed by Union law, by the law of the Member State in which the organisation which uses the orphan work in question is established.

Article 7   Continued application of other legal provisions

This Directive shall be without prejudice to provisions concerning, in particular, patent rights, trade marks, design rights, utility models, the topographies of semi-conductor products, type faces, conditional access, access to cable of broadcasting services, the protection of national treasures, legal deposit requirements, laws on restrictive practices and unfair competition, trade secrets, security, confidentiality, data protection and privacy, access to public documents, the law of contract, and rules on the freedom of the press and freedom of expression in the media.

Article 8   Application in time

1. This Directive shall apply in respect of all works and phonograms referred to in Article 1 which are protected by the Member States' legislation in the field of copyright on or after 29 October 2014.

2. This Directive shall apply without prejudice to any acts concluded and rights acquired before 29 October 2014.

Article 9   Transposition

1. Member States shall bring into force the laws, regulations and administrative provisions necessary to comply with this Directive by 29 October 2014. They shall forthwith communicate to the Commission the text of those provisions.

When Member States adopt those provisions, they shall contain a reference to this Directive or shall be accompanied by such a reference on the occasion of their official publication. The methods of making such reference shall be laid down by Member States.

2. Member States shall communicate to the Commission the text of the main provisions of national law which they adopt in the field covered by this Directive.

Article 10   Review clause

The Commission shall keep under constant review the development of rights information sources and shall by 29 October 2015, and at annual intervals thereafter, submit a report concerning the possible inclusion in the scope of application of this Directive of publishers and of works or other protected subject-matter not currently included in its scope, and in particular stand-alone photographs and other images.

By 29 October 2015, the Commission shall submit to the European Parliament, the Council and the European Economic and Social Committee a report on the application of this Directive, in the light of the development of digital libraries.

When necessary, in particular to ensure the functioning of the internal market, the Commission shall submit proposals for amendment of this Directive.

A Member State that has valid reasons to consider that the implementation of this Directive hinders one of the national arrangements concerning the management of rights referred to in Article 1(5) may bring the matter to the attention of the Commission together with all relevant evidence. The Commission shall take such evidence into account when drawing up the report referred to in the second paragraph of this Article and when assessing whether it is necessary to submit proposals for amendment of this Directive.

Article 11   Entry into force

This Directive shall enter into force on the day following that of its publication in the *Official Journal of the European Union*.

Article 12   Addressees

This Directive is addressed to the Member States.

Directive (EU) 2017/1564 of the European Parliament and of the Council

of 13 September 2017 on certain permitted uses of certain works and other subject matter protected by copyright and related rights for the benefit of persons who are blind, visually impaired or otherwise print-disabled and amending Directive 2001/29/EC on the harmonisation of certain aspects of copyright and related rights in the information society

THE EUROPEAN PARLIAMENT AND THE COUNCIL OF THE EUROPEAN UNION,

Having regard to the Treaty on the Functioning of the European Union, and in particular Article 114 thereof, Having regard to the proposal from the European Commission,

After transmission of the draft legislative act to the national parliaments,

Having regard to the opinion of the European Economic and Social Committee,

Acting in accordance with the ordinary legislative procedure,

Whereas:

(1) Union legal acts in the area of copyright and related rights provide legal certainty and a high level of protection for rightholders, and constitute a harmonised legal framework. That framework contributes to the proper functioning of the internal market and stimulates innovation, creation, investment and the production of new content, including in the digital environment. It also aims to promote access to knowledge and culture by protecting works and other subject matter and by permitting exceptions or limitations that are in the public interest. A fair balance of rights and interests between rightholders and users should be safeguarded.

(2) Directives 96/9/EC, 2001/29/EC, 2006/115/EC and 2009/24/EC of the European Parliament and of the Council harmonise the rights of rightholders in the area of copyright and related rights. Those Directives, together with Directive 2012/28/EU of the European Parliament and of the Council, provide for an exhaustive list of exceptions and limitations to those rights, which allow the use of content without the rightholders' authorisation under certain conditions in order to achieve certain policy objectives.

(3) Persons who are blind, visually impaired or otherwise print-disabled continue to face many barriers to accessing books and other printed material which are protected by copyright and related rights. Taking into consideration the rights of blind, visually impaired or otherwise print-disabled persons as recognised in the Charter of Fundamental Rights of the European Union (the 'Charter') and the United Nations Convention on the Rights of Persons with Disabilities (the 'UNCRPD'), measures should be taken to increase the availability of books and other printed material in accessible formats, and to improve their circulation in the internal market.

(4) The Marrakesh Treaty to Facilitate Access to Published Works for Persons Who Are Blind, Visually Impaired, or Otherwise Print Disabled (the 'Marrakesh Treaty') was signed on behalf of the Union on 30 April 2014. Its aim is to improve the availability and cross-border exchange of certain works and other protected subject matter in accessible formats for persons who are blind, visually impaired or otherwise print-disabled. The Marrakesh Treaty requires contracting parties to provide for exceptions or limitations to copyright and related rights for the making and dissemination of copies, in accessible formats, of certain works and other protected subject matter, and for the cross-border exchange of those copies. The conclusion of the Marrakesh Treaty by the Union requires the adaptation of Union law by establishing a mandatory and harmonised exception for uses, works and beneficiary persons covered by that treaty.

(5) According to Opinion 3/15 of the Court of Justice of the European Union, the exceptions or limitations to copyright and related rights for the making and dissemination of copies, in accessible formats, of certain works and other subject matter, provided for by the Marrakesh Treaty, have to be implemented within the field harmonised by Directive 2001/29/EC.

(6) This Directive implements the obligations that the Union has to meet under the Marrakesh Treaty in a harmonised manner, with a view to ensuring that the corresponding measures are applied consistently throughout the internal market. This Directive should therefore provide for a mandatory

exception to the rights that are harmonised by Union law and are relevant for the uses and works covered by the Marrakesh Treaty. Such rights include, in particular, the rights of reproduction, communication to the public, making available to the public, distribution and lending, as provided for in Directives 2001/29/EC, 2006/115/EC and 2009/24/EC, as well as the corresponding rights provided for in Directive 96/9/EC. As the scope of the exceptions or limitations required by the Marrakesh Treaty also includes works in audio form, like audiobooks, the mandatory exception provided for under this Directive should also apply to related rights.

(7) This Directive concerns persons who are blind, persons who have a visual impairment which cannot be improved so as to give them visual function substantially equivalent to that of a person who has no such impairment, persons who have a perceptual or reading disability, including dyslexia or any other learning disability preventing them from reading printed works to substantially the same degree as persons without such disability, and persons who are unable, due to a physical disability, to hold or manipulate a book or to focus or move the eyes to the extent that would be normally acceptable for reading, insofar as, as a result of such impairments or disabilities, those persons are unable to read printed works to substantially the same degree as persons without such impairments or disabilities. This Directive therefore aims to improve the availability of books, including e-books, journals, newspapers, magazines and other kinds of writing, notation, including sheet music, and other printed material, including in audio form, whether digital or analogue, online or offline, in formats that make those works and other subject matter accessible to those persons to substantially the same degree as to persons without such impairment or disability. Accessible formats include, for example, Braille, large print, adapted e-books, audio books and radio broadcasts.

(8) The mandatory exception provided for in this Directive should limit the right of reproduction so as to allow for any act that is necessary in order to make changes to or convert or adapt a work or other subject matter in such a way as to produce an accessible format copy that makes it possible for beneficiary persons to access that work or other subject matter. This includes providing the necessary means to navigate information in an accessible format copy. It also includes changes that might be required in cases in which the format of a work or of other subject matter is already accessible to certain beneficiary persons while it might not be accessible to other beneficiary persons, due to different impairments or disabilities, or the different degree of such impairments or disabilities.

(9) The permitted uses laid down in this Directive should include the making of accessible format copies by either beneficiary persons or authorised entities serving their needs, whether those authorised entities be public or private organisations, in particular libraries, educational establishments and other non-profit organisations, that serve persons with a print disability as one of their primary activities, institutional obligations or as part of their public interest missions. The uses laid down in this Directive should also include the making of accessible format copies, for the exclusive use of beneficiary persons, by a natural person who does so on behalf of a beneficiary person or who assists the beneficiary person making such copies. Accessible format copies should only be made of works or other subject matter to which beneficiary persons or authorised entities have lawful access. Member States should ensure that any contractual provision which seeks to prevent or limit the application of the exception in any way is void of legal effect.

(10) The exception provided for in this Directive should allow authorised entities to make and disseminate, online and offline within the Union, accessible format copies of works or other subject matter covered by this Directive. This Directive should not impose an obligation on authorised entities to make and disseminate such copies.

(11) It should be possible for accessible format copies made in one Member State to be available in all Member States, in order to ensure their greater availability across the internal market. This would reduce the demand for duplication of work in producing accessible format copies of one and the same work or other subject matter across the Union, thus generating savings and efficiency gains. This Directive should therefore ensure that accessible format copies made by authorised entities in any Member State can be circulated and accessed by beneficiary persons and authorised entities

throughout the Union. In order to foster such cross-border exchange and to facilitate authorised entities' mutual identification and cooperation, the voluntary sharing of information regarding the names and contact details of authorised entities established in the Union, including websites if available, should be encouraged. Member States should therefore provide the information received from authorised entities to the Commission. This should not imply an obligation for Member States to check the completeness and accuracy of such information or its compliance with their national law transposing this Directive. Such information should be made available online by the Commission on a central information access point at Union level. This would also assist authorised entities, as well as beneficiary persons and rightholders in contacting authorised entities to receive further information, in line with the provisions set out in this Directive and in Regulation (EU) 2017/1563 of the European Parliament and of the Council. The aforementioned central information access point should be complementary to the information access point to be established by the International Bureau of the World Intellectual Property Organisation (WIPO), as provided for in the Marrakesh Treaty, aiming to facilitate the identification of, and cooperation among, authorised entities at international level.

(12) In order to improve the availability of accessible format copies and to prevent the unauthorised dissemination of works or other subject matter, authorised entities which engage in the distribution, communication to the public or making available to the public of accessible format copies should comply with certain obligations.

(13) Authorisation or recognition requirements that Member States may apply to authorised entities, such as those relating to the provision of services of a general nature to beneficiary persons, should not have the effect of preventing entities that are covered by the definition of authorised entity under this Directive from undertaking the uses allowed under this Directive.

(14) In view of the specific nature of the exception provided for under this Directive, its specific scope and the need for legal certainty for its beneficiaries, Member States should not be allowed to impose additional requirements for the application of the exception, such as the prior verification of the commercial availability of works in accessible formats, other than those laid down in this Directive. Member States should only be allowed to provide for compensation schemes regarding the permitted uses of works or other subject matter by authorised entities. In order to avoid burdens for beneficiary persons, prevent barriers to the cross-border dissemination of accessible format copies and excessive requirements on authorised entities, it is important that the possibility for Member States to provide for such compensation schemes be limited. Consequently, compensation schemes should not require payments by beneficiary persons. They should only apply to uses by authorised entities established in the territory of the Member State providing for such a scheme, and they should not require payments by authorised entities established in other Member States or third countries that are parties to the Marrakesh Treaty. Member States should ensure that there are not more burdensome requirements for the cross-border exchange of accessible format copies under such compensation schemes than for non-cross border situations, including with regard to the form and possible level of compensation. When determining the level of compensation, due account should be taken of the non-profit nature of the activities of authorised entities, of the public interest objectives pursued by this Directive, of the interests of beneficiaries of the exception, of the possible harm to rightholders and of the need to ensure cross-border dissemination of accessible format copies. Account should also be taken of the particular circumstances of each case, resulting from the making of a particular accessible format copy. Where the harm to a rightholder is minimal, no obligation for payment of compensation should arise.

(15) It is essential that any processing of personal data under this Directive respect fundamental rights, including the right to respect for private and family life and the right to protection of personal data under Articles 7 and 8 of the Charter, and it is imperative that any such processing also be in compliance with Directives 95/46/EC and 2002/58/EC of the European Parliament and of the Council, which govern the processing of personal data, as may be carried out by authorised entities within the

framework of this Directive and under the supervision of the Member States' competent authorities, in particular the public independent authorities designated by the Member States.

(16) The UNCRPD, to which the Union is a party, guarantees persons with disabilities the right of access to information and education and the right to participate in cultural, economic and social life, on an equal basis with others. The UNCRPD requires parties to the Convention to take all appropriate steps, in accordance with international law, to ensure that laws protecting intellectual property rights do not constitute an unreasonable or discriminatory barrier to access by persons with disabilities to cultural materials.

(17) Under the Charter, all forms of discrimination, including on grounds of disability, are prohibited and the right of persons with disabilities to benefit from measures designed to ensure their independence, social and occupational integration and participation in the life of the community is recognised and respected by the Union.

(18) With the adoption of this Directive, the Union aims to ensure that beneficiary persons have access to books and other printed material in accessible formats across the internal market. Accordingly, this Directive is an essential first step in improving access to works for persons with disabilities.

(19) The Commission should assess the situation regarding the availability in accessible formats of works and other subject matter other than those covered by this Directive, as well as the availability of works and other subject matter in accessible formats for persons with other disabilities. It is important that the Commission review the situation in that regard closely. Changes to the scope of this Directive could be considered, if necessary, on the basis of a report presented by the Commission.

(20) Member States should be allowed to continue to provide for an exception or limitation for the benefit of persons with a disability in cases which are not covered by this Directive, in particular as regards works and other subject matter and disabilities other than those covered by this Directive, pursuant to point (b) of Article 5(3) of Directive 2001/29/EC. This Directive does not prevent Member States from providing for exceptions or limitations to rights that are not harmonised in the copyright framework of the Union.

(21) This Directive respects the fundamental rights and observes the principles recognised in particular by the Charter and the UNCRPD. This Directive should be interpreted and applied in accordance with those rights and principles.

(22) The Marrakesh Treaty imposes certain obligations regarding the exchange of accessible format copies between the Union and third countries that are parties to that Treaty. The measures taken by the Union to fulfil those obligations are contained in Regulation (EU) 2017/1563 which should be read in conjunction with this Directive.

(23) Since the objective of this Directive, namely to improve access in the Union to works and other subject matter protected by copyright and related rights for persons who are blind, visually impaired or otherwise print-disabled, cannot be sufficiently achieved by the Member States but can rather, by reason of its scale and effects, be better achieved at Union level, the Union may adopt measures in accordance with the principle of subsidiarity as set out in Article 5 of the Treaty on European Union. In accordance with the principle of proportionality as set out in that Article, this Directive does not go beyond what is necessary in order to achieve that objective.

(24) In accordance with the Joint Political Declaration of 28 September 2011 of Member States and the Commission on explanatory documents (1), Member States have undertaken to accompany, in justified cases, the notification of their transposition measures with one or more documents explaining the relationship between the components of a directive and the corresponding parts of national transposition instruments. With regard to this Directive, the legislator considers the transmission of such documents to be justified,

HAVE ADOPTED THIS DIRECTIVE:

Article 1   Subject matter and scope

This Directive aims to further harmonise Union law applicable to copyright and related rights in the framework of the internal market, by establishing rules on the use of certain works and other subject matter without the authorisation of the rightholder, for the benefit of persons who are blind, visually impaired or otherwise print-disabled.

Article 2   Definitions

For the purposes of this Directive the following definitions apply:

(1) 'work or other subject matter' means a work in the form of a book, journal, newspaper, magazine or other kind of writing, notation, including sheet music, and related illustrations, in any media, including in audio form such as audiobooks and in digital format, which is protected by copyright or related rights and which is published or otherwise lawfully made publicly available;

(2) 'beneficiary person' means, regardless of any other disabilities, a person who:

(a) is blind;

(b) has a visual impairment which cannot be improved so as to give the person visual function substantially equivalent to that of a person who has no such impairment, and who is, as a result, unable to read printed works to substantially the same degree as a person without such an impairment;

(c) has a perceptual or reading disability and is, as a result, unable to read printed works to substantially the same degree as a person without such disability; or

(d) is otherwise unable, due to a physical disability, to hold or manipulate a book or to focus or move their eyes to the extent that would be normally acceptable for reading.

(3) 'accessible format copy' means a copy of a work or other subject matter in an alternative manner or form that gives a beneficiary person access to the work or other subject matter, including allowing such person to have access as feasibly and comfortably as a person without any of the impairments or disabilities referred to in point 2;

(4) 'authorised entity' means an entity that is authorised or recognised by a Member State to provide education, instructional training, adaptive reading or information access to beneficiary persons on a non-profit basis. It also includes a public institution or non-profit organisation that provides the same services to beneficiary persons as one of its primary activities, institutional obligations or as part of its public-interest missions.

Article 3   Permitted uses

1. Member States shall provide for an exception to the effect that no authorisation of the rightholder of any copyright or related right in a work or other subject matter is required pursuant to Articles 5 and 7 of Directive 96/9/EC, Articles 2, 3 and 4 of Directive 2001/29/EC, Article 1(1), Article 8(2) and (3) and Article 9 of Directive 2006/115/EC and Article 4 of Directive 2009/24/EC for any act necessary for:

(a) a beneficiary person, or a person acting on their behalf, to make an accessible format copy of a work or other subject matter to which the beneficiary person has lawful access for the exclusive use of the beneficiary person; and

(b) an authorised entity to make an accessible format copy of a work or other subject matter to which it has lawful access, or to communicate, make available, distribute or lend an accessible format copy to a beneficiary person or another authorised entity on a non-profit basis for the purpose of exclusive use by a beneficiary person.

2. Member States shall ensure that each accessible format copy respects the integrity of the work or other subject matter, with due consideration given to the changes required to make the work or other subject matter accessible in the alternative format.

3. The exception provided for in paragraph 1 shall only be applied in certain special cases which do not conflict with a normal exploitation of the work or other subject matter and do not unreasonably prejudice the legitimate interests of the rightholder.

4. The first, third and fifth subparagraphs of Article 6(4) of Directive 2001/29/EC shall apply to the exception provided for in paragraph 1 of this Article.

5. Member States shall ensure that the exception provided for in paragraph 1 cannot be overridden by contract.

6. Member States may provide that uses permitted under this Directive, if undertaken by authorised entities established in their territory, be subject to compensation schemes within the limits provided for in this Directive.

Article 4   Accessible format copies in the internal market

Member States shall ensure that an authorised entity established in their territory may carry out the acts referred to in point (b) of Article 3(1) for a beneficiary person or another authorised entity established in any Member State. Member States shall also ensure that a beneficiary person or an authorised entity established in their territory may obtain or may have access to an accessible format copy from an authorised entity established in any Member State.

Article 5   Obligations of authorised entities

1. Member States shall provide that an authorised entity established in their territory carrying out the acts referred to in Article 4 establishes and follows its own practices to ensure that it:
   - (a) distributes, communicates and makes available accessible format copies only to beneficiary persons or other authorised entities;
   - (b) takes appropriate steps to discourage the unauthorised reproduction, distribution, communication to the public or making available to the public of accessible format copies;
   - (c) demonstrates due care in, and maintains records of, its handling of works or other subject matter and of accessible format copies thereof; and
   - (d) publishes and updates, on its website if appropriate, or through other online or offline channels, information on how it complies with the obligations laid down in points (a) to (c).

Member States shall ensure that the practices referred to in the first subparagraph are established and followed in full respect of the rules applicable to the processing of personal data of beneficiary persons referred to in Article 7.

2. Member States shall ensure that an authorised entity established in their territory carrying out the acts referred to in Article 4 provides the following information in an accessible way, on request, to beneficiary persons, other authorised entities or rightholders:
   - (a) the list of works or other subject matter for which it has accessible format copies and the available formats; and
   - (b) the name and contact details of the authorised entities with which it has engaged in the exchange of accessible format copies pursuant to Article 4.

Article 6   Transparency and exchange of information

1. Member States shall encourage authorised entities established in their territory carrying out the acts referred to in Article 4 of this Directive and Articles 3 and 4 of Regulation (EU) 2017/1563 to communicate to them, on a voluntary basis, their names and contact details.

2. Member States shall provide the information they have received pursuant to paragraph 1 to the Commission. The Commission shall make such information publicly available online on a central information access point and keep it up to date.

Article 7   Protection of personal data

The processing of personal data carried out within the framework of this Directive shall be carried out in compliance with Directives 95/46/EC and 2002/58/EC.

Article 8   Amendment to Directive 2001/29/EC

In Article 5(3) of Directive 2001/29/EC, point (b) is replaced by the following:

'(b) uses, for the benefit of people with a disability, which are directly related to the disability and of a non-commercial nature, to the extent required by the specific disability, without prejudice to the obligations of Member States under Directive (EU) 2017/1564 of the European Parliament and of the Council . . .'.

Article 9   Report

By 11 October 2020, the Commission shall present a report to the European Parliament, the Council and the European Economic and Social Committee on the availability, in accessible formats, of works and other subject matter other than those defined in point 1 of Article 2 for beneficiary persons, and of works and other subject matter for persons with disabilities other than those referred to in point 2 of Article 2, in the internal market. The report shall take into account developments concerning relevant technology and shall contain an assessment of the appropriateness of broadening the scope of this Directive in order to improve access to other types of works and other subject matter and to improve access for persons with disabilities other than those covered by this Directive.

Article 10   Review

1. By 11 October 2023, the Commission shall carry out an evaluation of this Directive and present the main findings in a report to the European Parliament, the Council and the European Economic and Social Committee, accompanied, where appropriate, by proposals for amending this Directive. Such evaluation shall include an assessment of the impact of compensation schemes, provided for by Member States pursuant to Article 3(6), on the availability of accessible format copies for beneficiary persons and on their cross-border exchange. The Commission's report shall take into account the views of relevant civil society actors and of non-governmental organisations, including organisations representing persons with disabilities and those representing older persons.

2. Member States shall provide the Commission with the necessary information for the preparation of the report referred to in paragraph 1 of this Article and the preparation of the report referred to in Article 9.

3. A Member State that has valid reasons to consider that the implementation of this Directive has had a significant negative impact on the commercial availability of works or other subject matter in accessible formats for beneficiary persons may bring the matter to the attention of the Commission providing all relevant evidence. The Commission shall take that evidence into account when drawing up the report referred to in paragraph 1.

Article 11   Transposition

1. Member States shall bring into force the laws, regulations and administrative provisions necessary to comply with this Directive by 11 October 2018. They shall immediately inform the Commission thereof.

When Member States adopt those measures, they shall contain a reference to this Directive or be accompanied by such a reference on the occasion of their official publication. The methods of making such reference shall be laid down by Member States.

2. Member States shall communicate to the Commission the text of the main measures of national law which they adopt in the field covered by this Directive.

Article 12   Entry into force

This Directive shall enter into force on the twentieth day following that of its publication in the *Official Journal of the European Union*.

Article 13   Addressees

This Directive is addressed to the Member States.

Done at Strasbourg, 13 September 2017.

Directive (EU) 2019/790 of the European Parliament and of the Council

of 17 April 2019 on copyright and related rights in the Digital Single Market and amending Directives 96/9/EC and 2001/29/EC

THE EUROPEAN PARLIAMENT AND THE COUNCIL OF THE EUROPEAN UNION,

. . .

HAVE ADOPTED THIS DIRECTIVE:

Title I   General Provisions

Article 1   Subject matter and scope

1. This Directive lays down rules which aim to harmonise further Union law applicable to copyright and related rights in the framework of the internal market, taking into account, in particular, digital and cross-border uses of protected content. It also lays down rules on exceptions and limitations to copyright and related rights, on the facilitation of licences, as well as rules which aim to ensure a well-functioning marketplace for the exploitation of works and other subject matter.

2. Except in the cases referred to in Article 24, this Directive shall leave intact and shall in no way affect existing rules laid down in the directives currently in force in this area, in particular Directives 96/9/EC, 2000/31/EC, 2001/29/EC, 2006/115/EC, 2009/24/EC, 2012/28/EU and 2014/26/EU.

Article 2   Definitions

For the purposes of this Directive, the following definitions apply:

(1) 'research organisation' means a university, including its libraries, a research institute or any other entity, the primary goal of which is to conduct scientific research or to carry out educational activities involving also the conduct of scientific research:

    (a) on a not-for-profit basis or by reinvesting all the profits in its scientific research; or

    (b) pursuant to a public interest mission recognised by a Member State;

in such a way that the access to the results generated by such scientific research cannot be enjoyed on a preferential basis by an undertaking that exercises a decisive influence upon such organisation;

(2) 'text and data mining' means any automated analytical technique aimed at analysing text and data in digital form in order to generate information which includes but is not limited to patterns, trends and correlations;

(3) 'cultural heritage institution' means a publicly accessible library or museum, an archive or a film or audio heritage institution;

(4) 'press publication' means a collection composed mainly of literary works of a journalistic nature, but which can also include other works or other subject matter, and which:

    (a) constitutes an individual item within a periodical or regularly updated publication under a single title, such as a newspaper or a general or special interest magazine;

    (b) has the purpose of providing the general public with information related to news or other topics; and

    (c) is published in any media under the initiative, editorial responsibility and control of a service provider.

Periodicals that are published for scientific or academic purposes, such as scientific journals, are not press publications for the purposes of this Directive;

(5) 'information society service' means a service within the meaning of point (b) of Article 1(1) of Directive (EU) 2015/1535;

(6) 'online content-sharing service provider' means a provider of an information society service of which the main or one of the main purposes is to store and give the public access to a large amount of copyright-protected works or other protected subject matter uploaded by its users, which it organises and promotes for profit-making purposes.

Providers of services, such as not-for-profit online encyclopedias, not-for-profit educational and scientific repositories, open source software-developing and-sharing platforms, providers of electronic communications services as defined in Directive (EU) 2018/1972, online marketplaces, business-to-business cloud services and cloud services that allow users to upload content for their own use, are not 'online content-sharing service providers' within the meaning of this Directive.

Title II   Measures to Adapt Exceptions and Limitations to the Digital and Cross-Border Environment

Article 3   Text and data mining for the purposes of scientific research

1. Member States shall provide for an exception to the rights provided for in Article 5(a) and Article 7(1) of Directive 96/9/EC, Article 2 of Directive 2001/29/EC, and Article 15(1) of this Directive for reproductions and extractions made by research organisations and cultural heritage institutions in order to carry out, for the purposes of scientific research, text and data mining of works or other subject matter to which they have lawful access.

2. Copies of works or other subject matter made in compliance with paragraph 1 shall be stored with an appropriate level of security and may be retained for the purposes of scientific research, including for the verification of research results.

3. Rightholders shall be allowed to apply measures to ensure the security and integrity of the networks and databases where the works or other subject matter are hosted. Such measures shall not go beyond what is necessary to achieve that objective.

4. Member States shall encourage rightholders, research organisations and cultural heritage institutions to define commonly agreed best practices concerning the application of the obligation and of the measures referred to in paragraphs 2 and 3 respectively.

Article 4   Exception or limitation for text and data mining

1. Member States shall provide for an exception or limitation to the rights provided for in Article 5(a) and Article 7(1) of Directive 96/9/EC, Article 2 of Directive 2001/29/EC, Article 4(1)(a) and (b) of Directive 2009/24/EC and Article 15(1) of this Directive for reproductions and extractions of lawfully accessible works and other subject matter for the purposes of text and data mining.

2. Reproductions and extractions made pursuant to paragraph 1 may be retained for as long as is necessary for the purposes of text and data mining.

3. The exception or limitation provided for in paragraph 1 shall apply on condition that the use of works and other subject matter referred to in that paragraph has not been expressly reserved by their rightholders in an appropriate manner, such as machine-readable means in the case of content made publicly available online.

4. This Article shall not affect the application of Article 3 of this Directive.

Article 5   Use of works and other subject matter in digital and cross-border teaching activities

1. Member States shall provide for an exception or limitation to the rights provided for in Article 5(a), (b), (d) and (e) and Article 7(1) of Directive 96/9/EC, Articles 2 and 3 of Directive 2001/29/EC, Article 4(1) of Directive 2009/24/EC and Article 15(1) of this Directive in order to allow the digital use of works and other subject matter for the sole purpose of illustration for teaching, to the extent justified by the non-commercial purpose to be achieved, on condition that such use:

(a) takes place under the responsibility of an educational establishment, on its premises or at other venues, or through a secure electronic environment accessible only by the educational establishment's pupils or students and teaching staff; and

(b) is accompanied by the indication of the source, including the author's name, unless this turns out to be impossible.

2. Notwithstanding Article 7(1), Member States may provide that the exception or limitation adopted pursuant to paragraph 1 does not apply or does not apply as regards specific uses or types of works or other subject matter, such as material that is primarily intended for the educational market

or sheet music, to the extent that suitable licences authorising the acts referred to in paragraph 1 of this Article and covering the needs and specificities of educational establishments are easily available on the market.

Member States that decide to avail of the first subparagraph of this paragraph shall take the necessary measures to ensure that the licences authorising the acts referred to in paragraph 1 of this Article are available and visible in an appropriate manner for educational establishments.

3. The use of works and other subject matter for the sole purpose of illustration for teaching through secure electronic environments undertaken in compliance with the provisions of national law adopted pursuant to this Article shall be deemed to occur solely in the Member State where the educational establishment is established.

4. Member States may provide for fair compensation for rightholders for the use of their works or other subject matter pursuant to paragraph 1.

Article 6   Preservation of cultural heritage

Member States shall provide for an exception to the rights provided for in Article 5(a) and Article 7(1) of Directive 96/9/EC, Article 2 of Directive 2001/29/EC, Article 4(1)(a) of Directive 2009/24/EC and Article 15(1) of this Directive, in order to allow cultural heritage institutions to make copies of any works or other subject matter that are permanently in their collections, in any format or medium, for purposes of preservation of such works or other subject matter and to the extent necessary for such preservation.

Article 7   Common provisions

1. Any contractual provision contrary to the exceptions provided for in Articles 3, 5 and 6 shall be unenforceable.

2. Article 5(5) of Directive 2001/29/EC shall apply to the exceptions and limitations provided for under this Title. The first, third and fifth subparagraphs of Article 6(4) of Directive 2001/29/EC shall apply to Articles 3 to 6 of this Directive.

Title III   Measures to Improve Licensing Practices and Ensure Wider Access to Content

Chapter 1   Out-of-commerce works and other subject matter

Article 8   Use of out-of-commerce works and other subject matter by cultural heritage institutions

1. Member States shall provide that a collective management organisation, in accordance with its mandates from rightholders, may conclude a non-exclusive licence for non-commercial purposes with a cultural heritage institution for the reproduction, distribution, communication to the public or making available to the public of out-of-commerce works or other subject matter that are permanently in the collection of the institution, irrespective of whether all rightholders covered by the licence have mandated the collective management organisation, on condition that:

    (a) the collective management organisation is, on the basis of its mandates, sufficiently representative of rightholders in the relevant type of works or other subject matter and of the rights that are the subject of the licence; and

    (b) all rightholders are guaranteed equal treatment in relation to the terms of the licence.

2. Member States shall provide for an exception or limitation to the rights provided for in Article 5(a), (b), (d) and (e) and Article 7(1) of Directive 96/9/EC, Articles 2 and 3 of Directive 2001/29/EC, Article 4(1) of Directive 2009/24/EC, and Article 15(1) of this Directive, in order to allow cultural heritage institutions to make available, for non-commercial purposes, out-of-commerce works or other subject matter that are permanently in their collections, on condition that:

    (a) the name of the author or any other identifiable rightholder is indicated, unless this turns out to be impossible; and

(b) such works or other subject matter are made available on non-commercial websites.

3. Member States shall provide that the exception or limitation provided for in paragraph 2 only applies to types of works or other subject matter for which no collective management organisation that fulfils the condition set out in point (a) of paragraph 1 exists.

4. Member States shall provide that all rightholders may, at any time, easily and effectively, exclude their works or other subject matter from the licensing mechanism set out in paragraph 1 or from the application of the exception or limitation provided for in paragraph 2, either in general or in specific cases, including after the conclusion of a licence or after the beginning of the use concerned.

5. A work or other subject matter shall be deemed to be out of commerce when it can be presumed in good faith that the whole work or other subject matter is not available to the public through customary channels of commerce, after a reasonable effort has been made to determine whether it is available to the public.

Member States may provide for specific requirements, such as a cut-off date, to determine whether works and other subject matter can be licensed in accordance with paragraph 1 or used under the exception or limitation provided for in paragraph 2. Such requirements shall not extend beyond what is necessary and reasonable, and shall not preclude being able to determine that a set of works or other subject matter as a whole is out of commerce, when it is reasonable to presume that all works or other subject matter are out of commerce.

6. Member States shall provide that the licences referred to in paragraph 1 are to be sought from a collective management organisation that is representative for the Member State where the cultural heritage institution is established.

7. This Article shall not apply to sets of out-of-commerce works or other subject matter if, on the basis of the reasonable effort referred to in paragraph 5, there is evidence that such sets predominantly consist of:

(a) works or other subject matter, other than cinematographic or audiovisual works, first published or, in the absence of publication, first broadcast in a third country;

(b) cinematographic or audiovisual works, of which the producers have their headquarters or habitual residence in a third country; or

(c) works or other subject matter of third country nationals, where after a reasonable effort no Member State or third country could be determined pursuant to points (a) and (b).

By way of derogation from the first subparagraph, this Article shall apply where the collective management organisation is sufficiently representative, within the meaning of point (a) of paragraph 1, of rightholders of the relevant third country.

Article 9   Cross-border uses

1. Member States shall ensure that licences granted in accordance with Article 8 may allow the use of out-of-commerce works or other subject matter by cultural heritage institutions in any Member State.

2. The uses of works and other subject matter under the exception or limitation provided for in Article 8(2) shall be deemed to occur solely in the Member State where the cultural heritage institution undertaking that use is established.

Article 10   Publicity measures

1. Member States shall ensure that information from cultural heritage institutions, collective management organisations or relevant public authorities, for the purposes of the identification of the out-of-commerce works or other subject matter, covered by a licence granted in accordance with Article 8(1), or used under the exception or limitation provided for in Article 8(2), as well as information about the options available to rightholders as referred to in Article 8(4), and, as soon as it is available and where relevant, information on the parties to the licence, the territories covered and the uses, is made permanently, easily and effectively accessible on a public single online portal from at

least six months before the works or other subject matter are distributed, communicated to the public or made available to the public in accordance with the licence or under the exception or limitation.

The portal shall be established and managed by the European Union Intellectual Property Office in accordance with Regulation (EU) No 386/2012.

2. Member States shall provide that, if necessary for the general awareness of rightholders, additional appropriate publicity measures are taken regarding the ability of collective management organisations to license works or other subject matter in accordance with Article 8, the licences granted, the uses under the exception or limitation provided for in Article 8(2) and the options available to rightholders as referred to in Article 8(4).

The appropriate publicity measures referred to in the first subparagraph of this paragraph shall be taken in the Member State where the licence is sought in accordance with Article 8(1) or, for uses under the exception or limitation provided for in Article 8(2), in the Member State where the cultural heritage institution is established. If there is evidence, such as the origin of the works or other subject matter, to suggest that the awareness of rightholders could be more efficiently raised in other Member States or third countries, such publicity measures shall also cover those Member States and third countries.

Article 11 Stakeholder dialogue

Member States shall consult rightholders, collective management organisations and cultural heritage institutions in each sector before establishing specific requirements pursuant to Article 8(5), and shall encourage regular dialogue between representative users' and rightholders' organisations, including collective management organisations, and any other relevant stakeholder organisations, on a sector-specific basis, to foster the relevance and usability of the licensing mechanisms set out in Article 8(1) and to ensure that the safeguards for rightholders referred to in this Chapter are effective.

Chapter 2 Measures to facilitate collective licensing

Article 12 Collective licensing with an extended effect

1. Member States may provide, as far as the use on their territory is concerned and subject to the safeguards provided for in this Article, that where a collective management organisation that is subject to the national rules implementing Directive 2014/26/EU, in accordance with its mandates from rightholders, enters into a licensing agreement for the exploitation of works or other subject matter:

(a) such an agreement can be extended to apply to the rights of rightholders who have not authorised that collective management organisation to represent them by way of assignment, licence or any other contractual arrangement; or

(b) with respect to such an agreement, the organisation has a legal mandate or is presumed to represent rightholders who have not authorised the organisation accordingly.

2. Member States shall ensure that the licensing mechanism referred to in paragraph 1 is only applied within well-defined areas of use, where obtaining authorisations from rightholders on an individual basis is typically onerous and impractical to a degree that makes the required licensing transaction unlikely, due to the nature of the use or of the types of works or other subject matter concerned, and shall ensure that such licensing mechanism safeguards the legitimate interests of rightholders.

3. For the purposes of paragraph 1, Member States shall provide for the following safeguards:

(a) the collective management organisation is, on the basis of its mandates, sufficiently representative of rightholders in the relevant type of works or other subject matter and of the rights which are the subject of the licence, for the relevant Member State;

(b) all rightholders are guaranteed equal treatment, including in relation to the terms of the licence;

(c) rightholders who have not authorised the organisation granting the licence may at any time easily and effectively exclude their works or other subject matter from the licensing mechanism established in accordance with this Article; and

(d) appropriate publicity measures are taken, starting from a reasonable period before the works or other subject matter are used under the licence, to inform rightholders about the ability of the collective management organisation to license works or other subject matter, about the licensing taking place in accordance with this Article and about the options available to rightholders as referred to in point (c). Publicity measures shall be effective without the need to inform each rightholder individually.

4. This Article does not affect the application of collective licensing mechanisms with an extended effect in accordance with other provisions of Union law, including provisions that allow exceptions or limitations.

This Article shall not apply to mandatory collective management of rights.

Article 7 of Directive 2014/26/EU shall apply to the licensing mechanism provided for in this Article.

5. Where a Member State provides in its national law for a licensing mechanism in accordance with this Article, that Member State shall inform the Commission about the scope of the corresponding national provisions, about the purposes and types of licences that may be introduced under those provisions, about the contact details of organisations issuing licences in accordance with that licensing mechanism, and about the means by which information on the licensing and on the options available to rightholders as referred to in point (c) of paragraph 3 can be obtained. The Commission shall publish that information.

6. Based on the information received pursuant to paragraph 5 of this Article and on the discussions within the contact committee established in Article 12(3) of Directive 2001/29/EC, the Commission shall, by 10 April 2021, submit to the European Parliament and to the Council a report on the use in the Union of the licensing mechanisms referred to in paragraph 1 of this Article, their impact on licensing and rightholders, including rightholders who are not members of the organisation granting the licences or who are nationals of, or resident in, another Member State, their effectiveness in facilitating the dissemination of cultural content, and their impact on the internal market, including the cross-border provision of services and competition. That report shall be accompanied, if appropriate, by a legislative proposal, including as regards the cross-border effect of such national mechanisms.

Chapter 3   Access to and availability of audiovisual works on video-on-demand platforms

Article 13   Negotiation mechanism

Member States shall ensure that parties facing difficulties related to the licensing of rights when seeking to conclude an agreement for the purpose of making available audiovisual works on video-on-demand services may rely on the assistance of an impartial body or of mediators. The impartial body established or designated by a Member State for the purpose of this Article and mediators shall provide assistance to the parties with their negotiations and help the parties reach agreements, including, where appropriate, by submitting proposals to them.

Member States shall notify the Commission of the body or mediators referred to in the first paragraph no later than 7 June 2021. Where Member States have chosen to rely on mediation, the notification to the Commission shall at least include, when available, the source where relevant information on the mediators entrusted can be found.

Chapter 4   Works of visual art in the public domain

Article 14   Works of visual art in the public domain

Member States shall provide that, when the term of protection of a work of visual art has expired, any material resulting from an act of reproduction of that work is not subject to copyright or related rights, unless the material resulting from that act of reproduction is original in the sense that it is the author's own intellectual creation.

Title IV   Measures to Achieve a Well-Functioning Marketplace for Copyright

Chapter 1   Rights in publications

Article 15   Protection of press publications concerning online uses

1. Member States shall provide publishers of press publications established in a Member State with the rights provided for in Article 2 and Article 3(2) of Directive 2001/29/EC for the online use of their press publications by information society service providers.

The rights provided for in the first subparagraph shall not apply to private or non-commercial uses of press publications by individual users.

The protection granted under the first subparagraph shall not apply to acts of hyperlinking.

The rights provided for in the first subparagraph shall not apply in respect of the use of individual words or very short extracts of a press publication.

2. The rights provided for in paragraph 1 shall leave intact and shall in no way affect any rights provided for in Union law to authors and other rightholders, in respect of the works and other subject matter incorporated in a press publication. The rights provided for in paragraph 1 shall not be invoked against those authors and other rightholders and, in particular, shall not deprive them of their right to exploit their works and other subject matter independently from the press publication in which they are incorporated.

When a work or other subject matter is incorporated in a press publication on the basis of a non-exclusive licence, the rights provided for in paragraph 1 shall not be invoked to prohibit the use by other authorised users. The rights provided for in paragraph 1 shall not be invoked to prohibit the use of works or other subject matter for which protection has expired.

3. Articles 5 to 8 of Directive 2001/29/EC, Directive 2012/28/EU and Directive (EU) 2017/1564 of the European Parliament of the Council shall apply mutatis mutandis in respect of the rights provided for in paragraph 1 of this Article.

4. The rights provided for in paragraph 1 shall expire two years after the press publication is published. That term shall be calculated from 1 January of the year following the date on which that press publication is published.

Paragraph 1 shall not apply to press publications first published before 6 June 2019.

5. Member States shall provide that authors of works incorporated in a press publication receive an appropriate share of the revenues that press publishers receive for the use of their press publications by information society service providers.

Article 16   Claims to fair compensation

Member States may provide that where an author has transferred or licensed a right to a publisher, such a transfer or licence constitutes a sufficient legal basis for the publisher to be entitled to a share of the compensation for the use of the work made under an exception or limitation to the transferred or licensed right.

The first paragraph shall be without prejudice to existing and future arrangements in Member States concerning public lending rights.

Chapter 2   Certain uses of protected content by online services

Article 17   Use of protected content by online content-sharing service providers

1. Member States shall provide that an online content-sharing service provider performs an act of communication to the public or an act of making available to the public for the purposes of this Directive when it gives the public access to copyright-protected works or other protected subject matter uploaded by its users.

An online content-sharing service provider shall therefore obtain an authorisation from the rightholders referred to in Article 3(1) and (2) of Directive 2001/29/EC, for instance by concluding a licensing agreement, in order to communicate to the public or make available to the public works or other subject matter.

2. Member States shall provide that, where an online content-sharing service provider obtains an authorisation, for instance by concluding a licensing agreement, that authorisation shall also cover acts carried out by users of the services falling within the scope of Article 3 of Directive 2001/29/EC when they are not acting on a commercial basis or where their activity does not generate significant revenues.

3. When an online content-sharing service provider performs an act of communication to the public or an act of making available to the public under the conditions laid down in this Directive, the limitation of liability established in Article 14(1) of Directive 2000/31/EC shall not apply to the situations covered by this Article.

The first subparagraph of this paragraph shall not affect the possible application of Article 14(1) of Directive 2000/31/EC to those service providers for purposes falling outside the scope of this Directive.

4. If no authorisation is granted, online content-sharing service providers shall be liable for unauthorised acts of communication to the public, including making available to the public, of copyright-protected works and other subject matter, unless the service providers demonstrate that they have:

(a) made best efforts to obtain an authorisation, and

(b) made, in accordance with high industry standards of professional diligence, best efforts to ensure the unavailability of specific works and other subject matter for which the rightholders have provided the service providers with the relevant and necessary information; and in any event

(c) acted expeditiously, upon receiving a sufficiently substantiated notice from the rightholders, to disable access to, or to remove from their websites, the notified works or other subject matter, and made best efforts to prevent their future uploads in accordance with point (b).

5. In determining whether the service provider has complied with its obligations under paragraph 4, and in light of the principle of proportionality, the following elements, among others, shall be taken into account:

(a) the type, the audience and the size of the service and the type of works or other subject matter uploaded by the users of the service; and

(b) the availability of suitable and effective means and their cost for service providers.

6. Member States shall provide that, in respect of new online content-sharing service providers the services of which have been available to the public in the Union for less than three years and which have an annual turnover below EUR 10 million, calculated in accordance with Commission Recommendation 2003/361/EC, the conditions under the liability regime set out in paragraph 4 are limited to compliance with point (a) of paragraph 4 and to acting expeditiously, upon receiving a sufficiently substantiated notice, to disable access to the notified works or other subject matter or to remove those works or other subject matter from their websites.

Where the average number of monthly unique visitors of such service providers exceeds 5 million, calculated on the basis of the previous calendar year, they shall also demonstrate that they have made best efforts to prevent further uploads of the notified works and other subject matter for which the rightholders have provided relevant and necessary information.

7. The cooperation between online content-sharing service providers and rightholders shall not result in the prevention of the availability of works or other subject matter uploaded by users, which do not infringe copyright and related rights, including where such works or other subject matter are covered by an exception or limitation.

Member States shall ensure that users in each Member State are able to rely on any of the following existing exceptions or limitations when uploading and making available content generated by users on online content-sharing services:

(a) quotation, criticism, review;

(b) use for the purpose of caricature, parody or pastiche.

8. The application of this Article shall not lead to any general monitoring obligation.

Member States shall provide that online content-sharing service providers provide rightholders, at their request, with adequate information on the functioning of their practices with regard to the cooperation referred to in paragraph 4 and, where licensing agreements are concluded between service providers and rightholders, information on the use of content covered by the agreements.

9. Member States shall provide that online content-sharing service providers put in place an effective and expeditious complaint and redress mechanism that is available to users of their services in the event of disputes over the disabling of access to, or the removal of, works or other subject matter uploaded by them.

Where rightholders request to have access to their specific works or other subject matter disabled or to have those works or other subject matter removed, they shall duly justify the reasons for their requests. Complaints submitted under the mechanism provided for in the first subparagraph shall be processed without undue delay, and decisions to disable access to or remove uploaded content shall be subject to human review. Member States shall also ensure that out-of-court redress mechanisms are available for the settlement of disputes. Such mechanisms shall enable disputes to be settled impartially and shall not deprive the user of the legal protection afforded by national law, without prejudice to the rights of users to have recourse to efficient judicial remedies. In particular, Member States shall ensure that users have access to a court or another relevant judicial authority to assert the use of an exception or limitation to copyright and related rights.

This Directive shall in no way affect legitimate uses, such as uses under exceptions or limitations provided for in Union law, and shall not lead to any identification of individual users nor to the processing of personal data, except in accordance with Directive 2002/58/EC and Regulation (EU) 2016/679.

Online content-sharing service providers shall inform their users in their terms and conditions that they can use works and other subject matter under exceptions or limitations to copyright and related rights provided for in Union law.

10. As of 6 June 2019 the Commission, in cooperation with the Member States, shall organise stakeholder dialogues to discuss best practices for cooperation between online content-sharing service providers and rightholders. The Commission shall, in consultation with online content-sharing service providers, rightholders, users' organisations and other relevant stakeholders, and taking into account the results of the stakeholder dialogues, issue guidance on the application of this Article, in particular regarding the cooperation referred to in paragraph 4. When discussing best practices, special account shall be taken, among other things, of the need to balance fundamental rights and of the use of exceptions and limitations. For the purpose of the stakeholder dialogues, users' organisations shall have access to adequate information from online content-sharing service providers on the functioning of their practices with regard to paragraph 4.

Chapter 3   Fair remuneration in exploitation contracts of authors and performers

Article 18   Principle of appropriate and proportionate remuneration

1. Member States shall ensure that where authors and performers license or transfer their exclusive rights for the exploitation of their works or other subject matter, they are entitled to receive appropriate and proportionate remuneration.

2. In the implementation in national law of the principle set out in paragraph 1, Member States shall be free to use different mechanisms and take into account the principle of contractual freedom and a fair balance of rights and interests.

Article 19   Transparency obligation

1. Member States shall ensure that authors and performers receive on a regular basis, at least once a year, and taking into account the specificities of each sector, up to date, relevant and comprehensive information on the exploitation of their works and performances from the parties to whom they have licensed or transferred their rights, or their successors in title, in particular as regards modes of exploitation, all revenues generated and remuneration due.

2. Member States shall ensure that, where the rights referred to in paragraph 1 have subsequently been licensed, authors and performers or their representatives shall, at their request, receive from sub-licensees additional information, in the event that their first contractual counterpart does not hold all the information that would be necessary for the purposes of paragraph 1.

Where that additional information is requested, the first contractual counterpart of authors and performers shall provide information on the identity of those sub-licensees.

Member States may provide that any request to sub-licensees pursuant to the first subparagraph is made directly or indirectly through the contractual counterpart of the author or the performer.

3. The obligation set out in paragraph 1 shall be proportionate and effective in ensuring a high level of transparency in every sector. Member States may provide that in duly justified cases where the administrative burden resulting from the obligation set out in paragraph 1 would become disproportionate in the light of the revenues generated by the exploitation of the work or performance, the obligation is limited to the types and level of information that can reasonably be expected in such cases.

4. Member States may decide that the obligation set out in paragraph 1 of this Article does not apply when the contribution of the author or performer is not significant having regard to the overall work or performance, unless the author or performer demonstrates that he or she requires the information for the exercise of his or her rights under Article 20(1) and requests the information for that purpose.

5. Member States may provide that, for agreements subject to or based on collective bargaining agreements, the transparency rules of the relevant collective bargaining agreement are applicable, on condition that those rules meet the criteria provided for in paragraphs 1 to 4.

6. Where Article 18 of Directive 2014/26/EU is applicable, the obligation laid down in paragraph 1 of this Article shall not apply in respect of agreements concluded by entities defined in Article 3(a) and (b) of that Directive or by other entities subject to the national rules implementing that Directive.

Article 20   Contract adjustment mechanism

1. Member States shall ensure that, in the absence of an applicable collective bargaining agreement providing for a mechanism comparable to that set out in this Article, authors and performers or their representatives are entitled to claim additional, appropriate and fair remuneration from the party with whom they entered into a contract for the exploitation of their rights, or from the successors in title of such party, when the remuneration originally agreed turns out to be disproportionately low compared to all the subsequent relevant revenues derived from the exploitation of the works or performances.

2. Paragraph 1 of this Article shall not apply to agreements concluded by entities defined in Article 3(a) and (b) of Directive 2014/26/EU or by other entities that are already subject to the national rules implementing that Directive.

Article 21   Alternative dispute resolution procedure

Member States shall provide that disputes concerning the transparency obligation under Article 19 and the contract adjustment mechanism under Article 20 may be submitted to a voluntary, alternative dispute resolution procedure. Member States shall ensure that representative organisations of authors and performers may initiate such procedures at the specific request of one or more authors or performers.

Article 22   Right of revocation

1. Member States shall ensure that where an author or a performer has licensed or transferred his or her rights in a work or other protected subject matter on an exclusive basis, the author or performer may revoke in whole or in part the licence or the transfer of rights where there is a lack of exploitation of that work or other protected subject matter.

2. Specific provisions for the revocation mechanism provided for in paragraph 1 may be provided for in national law, taking into account the following:

(a) the specificities of the different sectors and the different types of works and performances; and

(b) where a work or other subject matter contains the contribution of more than one author or performer, the relative importance of the individual contributions, and the legitimate interests of all authors and performers affected by the application of the revocation mechanism by an individual author or performer.

Member States may exclude works or other subject matter from the application of the revocation mechanism if such works or other subject matter usually contain contributions of a plurality of authors or performers.

Member States may provide that the revocation mechanism can only apply within a specific time frame, where such restriction is duly justified by the specificities of the sector or of the type of work or other subject matter concerned.

Member States may provide that authors or performers can choose to terminate the exclusivity of the contract instead of revoking the licence or transfer of the rights.

3. Member States shall provide that the revocation provided for in paragraph 1 may only be exercised after a reasonable time following the conclusion of the licence or the transfer of the rights. The author or performer shall notify the person to whom the rights have been licensed or transferred and set an appropriate deadline by which the exploitation of the licensed or transferred rights is to take place. After the expiry of that deadline, the author or performer may choose to terminate the exclusivity of the contract instead of revoking the licence or the transfer of the rights.

4. Paragraph 1 shall not apply if the lack of exploitation is predominantly due to circumstances that the author or the performer can reasonably be expected to remedy.

5. Member States may provide that any contractual provision derogating from the revocation mechanism provided for in paragraph 1 is enforceable only if it is based on a collective bargaining agreement.

Article 23 Common provisions

1. Member States shall ensure that any contractual provision that prevents compliance with Articles 19, 20 and 21 shall be unenforceable in relation to authors and performers.

2. Members States shall provide that Articles 18 to 22 of this Directive do not apply to authors of a computer program within the meaning of Article 2 of Directive 2009/24/EC.

Title V Final Provisions

...

Article 25 Relationship with exceptions and limitations provided for in other directives

Member States may adopt or maintain in force broader provisions, compatible with the exceptions and limitations provided for in Directives 96/9/EC and 2001/29/EC, for uses or fields covered by the exceptions or limitations provided for in this Directive.

Article 26 Application in time

1. This Directive shall apply in respect of all works and other subject matter that are protected by national law in the field of copyright on or after 7 June 2021.

2. This Directive shall apply without prejudice to any acts concluded and rights acquired before 7 June 2021.

Article 27 Transitional provision

Agreements for the licence or transfer of rights of authors and performers shall be subject to the transparency obligation set out in Article 19 as from 7 June 2022.

...

Article 30 Review

1. No sooner than 7 June 2026, the Commission shall carry out a review of this Directive and present a report on the main findings to the European Parliament, the Council and the European Economic and Social Committee.

The Commission shall, by 7 June 2024, assess the impact of the specific liability regime set out in Article 17 applicable to online content-sharing service providers that have an annual turnover of less than EUR 10 million and the services of which have been available to the public in the Union for less than three years under Article 17(6) and, if appropriate, take action in accordance with the conclusions of its assessment.

2. Member States shall provide the Commission with the necessary information for the preparation of the report referred to in paragraph 1.

...

A4. INTERNATIONAL

Berne Convention for the Protection of Literary and Artistic Works

of September 9, 1886, completed at PARIS on May 4, 1896, revised at BERLIN on November 13, 1908, completed at BERNE on March 20, 1914, revised at ROME on June 2, 1928, at BRUSSELS on June 26, 1948, at STOCKHOLM on July 14, 1967, and at PARIS on July 24, 1971, and amended on September 28, 1979

The countries of the Union, being equally animated by the desire to protect, in as effective and uniform a manner as possible, the rights of authors in their literary and artistic works,

Recognising the importance of the work of the Revision Conference held at Stockholm in 1967,

Have resolved to revise the Act adopted by the Stockholm Conference, while maintaining without change Articles 1 to 20 and 22 to 26 of that Act.

Consequently, the undersigned Plenipotentiaries, having presented their full powers, recognised as in good and due form, have agreed as follows:

Article 1 Establishment of a Union
The countries to which this Convention applies constitute a Union for the protection of the rights of authors in their literary and artistic works.

Article 2 Protected works: 1. 'Literary and artistic works'; 2. Possible requirement of fixation; 3. Derivative works; 4. Official texts; 5. Collections; 6. Obligation to protect; beneficiaries of protection; 7. Works of applied art and industrial designs; 8. News

(1) The expression 'literary and artistic works' shall include every production in the literary, scientific and artistic domain, whatever may be the mode or form of its expression, such as books, pamphlets and other writings; lectures, addresses, sermons and other works of the same nature; dramatic or dramatico-musical works; choreographic works and entertainments in dumb show; musical compositions with or without words; cinematographic works to which are assimilated works expressed by a process analogous to cinematography; works of drawing, painting, architecture, sculpture, engraving and lithography; photographic works to which are assimilated works expressed by a process analogous to photography; works of applied art; illustrations, maps, plans, sketches and three-dimensional works relative to geography, topography, architecture or science.

(2) It shall, however, be a matter for legislation in the countries of the Union to prescribe that works in general or any specified categories of works shall not be protected unless they have been fixed in some material form.

(3) Translations, adaptations, arrangements of music and other alterations of a literary or artistic work shall be protected as original works without prejudice to the copyright in the original work.

(4) It shall be a matter for legislation in the countries of the Union to determine the protection to be granted to official texts of a legislative, administrative and legal nature, and to official translations of such texts.

(5) Collections of literary or artistic works such as encyclopaedias and anthologies which, by reason of the selection and arrangement of their contents, constitute intellectual creations shall be protected as such, without prejudice to the copyright in each of the works forming part of such collections.

(6) The works mentioned in this Article shall enjoy protection in all countries of the Union. This protection shall operate for the benefit of the author and his successors in title.

(7) Subject to the provisions of Article 7(4) of this Convention, it shall be a matter for legislation in the countries of the Union to determine the extent of the application of their laws to works of applied art and industrial designs and models, as well as the conditions under which such works, designs and models shall be protected. Works protected in the country of origin solely as designs and models shall be entitled in another country of the Union only to such special protection as is granted in that country to designs and models; however, if no such special protection is granted in that country, such works shall be protected as artistic works.

(8) The protection of this Convention shall not apply to news of the day or to miscellaneous facts having the character of mere items of press information.

Article 2bis   Possible limitation of protection of certain works:
1. Certain speeches; 2. Certain uses of lectures and addresses;
3. Right to make collections of such works

(1) It shall be a matter for legislation in the countries of the Union to exclude, wholly or in part, from the protection provided by the preceding Article political speeches and speeches delivered in the course of legal proceedings.

(2) It shall also be a matter for legislation in the countries of the Union to determine the conditions under which lectures, addresses and other works of the same nature which are delivered in public may be reproduced by the press, broadcast, communicated to the public by wire and made the subject of public communication as envisaged in Article 11bis(1) of this Convention, when such use is justified by the informatory purpose.

(3) Nevertheless, the author shall enjoy the exclusive right of making a collection of his works mentioned in the preceding paragraphs.

Article 3   Criteria of eligibility for protection: 1. Nationality of author;
place of publication of work; 2. Residence of author; 3. 'Published' works;
4. 'Simultaneously published' works

(1) The protection of this Convention shall apply to:
  (a) authors who are nationals of one of the countries of the Union, for their works, whether published or not;
  (b) authors who are not nationals of one of the countries of the Union, for their works first published in one of those countries, or simultaneously in a country outside the Union and in a country of the Union.

(2) Authors who are not nationals of one of the countries of the Union but who have their habitual residence in one of them shall, for the purposes of this Convention, be assimilated to nationals of that country.

(3) The expression 'published works' means works published with the consent of their authors, whatever may be the means of manufacture of the copies, provided that the availability of such copies has been such as to satisfy the reasonable requirements of the public, having regard to the nature of the work. The performance of a dramatic, dramatico-musical, cinematographic or musical work, the public recitation of a literary work, the communication by wire or the broadcasting of literary or artistic works, the exhibition of a work of art and the construction of a work of architecture shall not constitute publication.

(4) A work shall be considered as having been published simultaneously in several countries if it has been published in two or more countries within thirty days of its first publication.

Article 4   Criteria of eligibility for protection of cinematographic
works, works of architecture and certain artistic works

The protection of this Convention shall apply, even if the conditions of Article 3 are not fulfilled, to:
  (a) authors of cinematographic works the maker of which has his headquarters or habitual residence in one of the countries of the Union;

(b) authors of works of architecture erected in a country of the Union or of other artistic works incorporated in a building or other structure located in a country of the Union.

Article 5   Rights guaranteed: 1. and 2. outside the country of origin; 3. In the country of origin; 4. 'Country of origin'

(1) Authors shall enjoy, in respect of works for which they are protected under this Convention, in countries of the Union other than the country of origin, the rights which their respective laws do now or may hereafter grant to their nationals, as well as the rights specially granted by this Convention.

(2) The enjoyment and the exercise of these rights shall not be subject to any formality; such enjoyment and such exercise shall be independent of the existence of protection in the country of origin of the work. Consequently, apart from the provisions of this Convention, the extent of protection, as well as the means of redress afforded to the author to protect his rights, shall be governed exclusively by the laws of the country where protection is claimed.

(3) Protection in the country of origin is governed by domestic law. However, when the author is not a national of the country of origin of the work for which he is protected under this Convention, he shall enjoy in that country the same rights as national authors.

(4) The country of origin shall be considered to be:
(a) in the case of works first published in a country of the Union, that country; in the case of works published simultaneously in several countries of the Union which grant different terms of protection, the country whose legislation grants the shortest term of protection;
(b) in the case of works published simultaneously in a country outside the Union and in a country of the Union, the latter country;
(c) in the case of unpublished works or of works first published in a country outside the Union, without simultaneous publication in a country of the Union, the country of the Union of which the author is a national, provided that:
   (i) When these are cinematographic works the maker of which has his headquarters or his habitual residence in a country of the Union, the country of origin shall be that country, and
   (ii) when these are works of architecture created in a country of the Union or other artistic works incorporated in a building or other structure located in a country of the Union, the country of origin shall be that country.

Article 6   Possible restrictions of protection in respect of certain works of nationals of certain countries outside the Union: 1. In the country of the first publication and in other countries; 2. No retroactivity; 3. Notice

(1) Where any country outside the Union fails to protect in an adequate manner the works of authors who are nationals of one of the countries of the Union, the latter country may restrict the protection given to the works of authors who are, at the date of the first publication thereof, nationals of the other country and are not habitually resident in one of the countries of the Union. If the country of first publication avails itself of this right, the other countries of the Union shall not be required to grant to works thus subjected to special treatment a wider protection than that granted to them in the country of first publication.

(2) No restrictions introduced by virtue of the preceding paragraph shall affect the rights which an author may have acquired in respect of a work published in a country of the Union before such restrictions were put into force.

(3) The countries of the Union which restrict the grant of copyright in accordance with this Article shall give notice thereof to the Director General of the World Intellectual Property Organisation (hereinafter designated as 'the Director General') by a written declaration specifying the countries in regard to which protection is restricted, and the restrictions to which rights of authors who are nationals of those countries are subjected. The Director General shall immediately communicate this declaration to all the countries of the Union.

Article 6bis Moral rights: 1. To claim authorship; to object to certain modifications and other derogatory actions; 2. After the author's death; 3. Means of redress

(1) Independently of the author's economic rights, and even after the transfer of the said rights, the author shall have the right to claim authorship of the work and to object to any distortion, mutilation or other modification of, or other derogatory action in relation to, the said work, which would be prejudicial to his honour or reputation.

(2) The rights granted to the author in accordance with the preceding paragraph shall, after his death, be maintained, at least until the expiry of the economic rights, and shall be exercisable by the persons or institutions authorised by the legislation of the country where protection is claimed. However, those countries whose legislation, at the moment of their ratification of or accession to this Act, does not provide for the protection after the death of the author of all the rights set out in the preceding paragraph may provide that some of these rights may, after his death, cease to be maintained.

(3) The means of redress for safeguarding the rights granted by this Article shall be governed by the legislation of the country where protection is claimed.

Article 7   Term of protection: 1. Generally; 2. For cinematographic works; 3. For anonymous and pseudonymous works; 4. For photographic works and works of applied art; 5. Starting date of computation; 6. Longer terms; 7. Shorter terms; 8. Applicable law; 'comparison' of terms

(1) The term of protection granted by this Convention shall be the life of the author and fifty years after his death.

(2) However, in the case of cinematographic works, the countries of the Union may provide that the term of protection shall expire fifty years after the work has been made available to the public with the consent of the author, or, failing such an event within fifty years from the making of such a work, fifty years after the making.

(3) In the case of anonymous or pseudonymous works, the term of protection granted by this Convention shall expire fifty years after the work has been lawfully made available to the public. However, when the pseudonym adopted by the author leaves no doubt as to his identity, the term of protection shall be that provided in paragraph (1). If the author of an anonymous or pseudonymous work discloses his identity during the above-mentioned period, the term of protection applicable shall be that provided in paragraph (1). The countries of the Union shall not be required to protect anonymous or pseudonymous works in respect of which it is reasonable to presume that their author has been dead for fifty years.

(4) It shall be a matter for legislation in the countries of the Union to determine the term of protection of photographic works and that of works of applied art in so far as they are protected as artistic works; however, this term shall last at least until the end of a period of twenty-five years from the making of such a work.

(5) The term of protection subsequent to the death of the author and the terms provided by paragraphs (2), (3) and (4) shall run from the date of death or of the event referred to in those paragraphs, but such terms shall always be deemed to begin on the first of January of the year following the death or such event.

(6) The countries of the Union may grant a term of protection in excess of those provided by the preceding paragraphs.

(7) Those countries of the Union bound by the Rome Act of this Convention which grant, in their national legislation in force at the time of signature of the present act, shorter terms of protection than those provided for in the preceding paragraphs shall have the right to maintain such terms when ratifying or acceding to the present Act.

(8) In any case, the term shall be governed by the legislation of the country where protection is claimed; however, unless the legislation of that country otherwise provides, the term shall not exceed the term fixed in the country of origin of the work.

Article 7bis   Term of protection for works of joint authorship

The provisions of the preceding Article shall also apply in the case of a work of joint authorship, provided that the terms measured from the death of the author shall be calculated from the death of the last surviving author.

Article 8   Right of translation

Authors of literary and artistic works protected by this Convention shall enjoy the exclusive right of making and of authorising the translation of their works throughout the term of protection of their rights in the original works.

Article 9   Right of reproduction: 1. Generally; 2. Possible exceptions; 3. Sound and visual recordings

(1) Authors of literary and artistic works protected by this Convention shall have the exclusive right of authorising the reproduction of these works, in any manner or form.

(2) It shall be a matter for legislation in the countries of the Union to permit the reproduction of such works in certain special cases, provided that such reproduction does not conflict with a normal exploitation of the work and does not unreasonably prejudice the legitimate interests of the author.

(3) Any sound or visual recording shall be considered as a reproduction for the purposes of this Convention.

Article 10   Certain free uses of works: 1. Quotations; 2. Illustrations for teaching; 3. Indication of source and author

(1) It shall be permissible to make quotations from a work which has already been lawfully made available to the public, provided that their making is compatible with fair practice, and their extent does not exceed that justified by the purpose, including quotations from newspaper articles and periodicals in the form of press summaries.

(2) It shall be a matter for legislation in the countries of the Union, and for special agreements existing or to be concluded between them, to permit the utilisation, to the extent justified by the purpose, of literary or artistic works by way of illustration in publications, broadcasts or sound or visual recordings for teaching, provided such utilisation is compatible with fair practice.

(3) Where use is made of works in accordance with the preceding paragraphs of this Article, mention shall be made of the source, and of the name of the author if it appears thereon.

Article 10bis   Further possible free uses of works: 1. Of certain articles and broadcast works; 2. Of works seen or heard in connection with current events

(1) It shall be a matter for legislation in the countries of the Union to permit the reproduction by the press, the broadcasting or the communication to the public by wire of articles published in newspapers or periodicals on current economic, political or religious topics, and of broadcast works of the same character, in cases in which the reproduction, broadcasting or such communication thereof is not expressly reserved. Nevertheless, the source must always be clearly indicated; the legal consequences of a breach of this obligation shall be determined by the legislation of the country where protection is claimed.

(2) It shall also be a matter for legislation in the countries of the Union to determine the conditions under which, for the purpose of reporting current events by means of photography, cinematography, broadcasting or communication to the public by wire, literary or artistic works seen or heard in the course of the event may, to the extent justified by the informatory purpose, be reproduced and made available to the public.

Article 11   Certain rights in dramatic and musical works: 1. Right of public performance and of communication to the public of a performance; 2. In respect of translations

(1) Author of dramatic, dramatico-musical and musical works shall enjoy the exclusive right of authorising:

    (i)   the public performance of their works, including such public performance by any means or process;

    (ii) any communication to the public of the performance of their works.

(2) Authors of dramatic or dramatico-musical works shall enjoy, during the full term of their rights in the original works, the same rights with respect to translations thereof.

Article 11bis Broadcasting and related rights: 1. Broadcasting and other wireless communications, public communications of broadcast by wire or rebroadcast, public communication of broadcast by loudspeaker or analogous instruments; 2. Compulsory licences; 3. Recording; ephemeral recordings

(1) Authors of literary and artistic works shall enjoy the exclusive right of authorising:

    (i)   the broadcasting of their works or the communication thereof to the public by any other means of wireless diffusion of signs, sounds or images;

    (ii) any communication to the public by wire or by rebroadcasting of the broadcast of the work, when this communication is made by an organisation other than the original one;

    (iii) the public communication by loudspeaker or any other analogous instrument transmitting, by signs, sounds or images, the broadcast of the work.

(2) It shall be a matter for legislation in the countries of the Union to determine the conditions under which the rights mentioned in the preceding paragraph may be exercised, but these conditions shall apply only in the countries where they have been prescribed. They shall not in any circumstances be prejudicial to the moral rights of the author, nor to his right to obtain equitable remuneration which, in the absence of agreement, shall be fixed by component authority.

(3) In the absence of any contrary stipulation, permission granted in accordance with paragraph (1) of this Article shall not imply permission to record, by means of instruments recording sounds or images, the work broadcast. It shall, however, be a matter for legislation in the countries of the Union to determine the regulations for ephemeral recordings made by a broadcasting organisation by means of its own facilities and used for its own broadcasts. The preservation of these recordings in official archives may, on the ground of their exceptional documentary character, be authorised by such legislation.

Article 11ter Certain rights in literary works: 1. Right of public recitation and of communication to the public of a recitation; 2. In respect of translations

(1) Authors of literary works shall enjoy the exclusive right of authorising:

    (i)   the public recitation of their works, including such public recitation by any means or process;

    (ii) any communication to the public of the recitation of their works.

(2) Authors of literary works shall enjoy, during the full term of their rights in the original works, the same rights with respect to translations thereof.

Article 12   Right of adaptation, arrangement and other alteration

Authors of literary or artistic works shall enjoy the exclusive right of authorising adaptations, arrangements and other alterations of their works.

Article 13   Possible limitation of the right of recording of musical works and any words pertaining thereto: 1. Compulsory licences; 2. Transitory measures; 3. Seizure on importation of copies made without the author's permission

(1) Each country of the Union may impose for itself reservations and conditions on the exclusive right granted to the author of a musical work and to the author of any words, the recording of which together with the musical work has already been authorised by the latter, to authorise the sound recording of that musical work, together with such words, if any; but all such reservations and conditions shall apply only in the countries which have imposed them and shall not, in any circumstances, be prejudicial to the rights of these authors to obtain equitable remuneration which, in the absence of agreement, shall be fixed by competent authority.

(2) Recordings of musical works made in a country of the Union in accordance with Article 13(3) of the Conventions signed at Rome on 2 June 1928, and at Brussels on 26 June 1948, may be reproduced in that country without the permission of the author of the musical work until a date two years after that country becomes bound by this Act.

(3) Recordings made in accordance with paragraphs (1) and (2) of this Article and imported without permission from the parties concerned into a country where they are treated as infringing recordings shall be liable to seizure.

Article 14   Cinematographic and related rights: 1. Cinematographic adaptation and reproduction; distribution; public performance and public communication by wire of works thus adapted or reproduced; 2. Adaptation of cinematographic productions; 3. No compulsory licences

(1) Authors of literary or artistic works shall have the exclusive right of authorising:
- (i) the cinematographic adaptation and reproduction of these works, and the distribution of the works thus adapted or reproduced;
- (ii) the public performance and communication to the public by wire of the works thus adapted or reproduced.

(2) The adaptation into any other artistic form of a cinematographic production derived from literary or artistic works shall, without prejudice to the authorisation of the author of the cinematographic production, remain subject to the authorisation of the authors of the original works.

(3) The provisions of Article 13(1) shall not apply.

Article 14bis   Special provisions concerning cinematographic works: 1. Assimilation to 'original' works; 2. Ownership; limitation of certain rights of certain contributors; 3. Certain other contributors

(1) Without prejudice to the copyright in any work which may have been adapted or reproduced, a cinematographic work shall be protected as an original work. The owner of copyright in a cinematographic work shall enjoy the same rights as the author of an original work, including the rights referred to in the preceding Article.

(2) (a) Ownership of copyright in a cinematographic work shall be a matter for legislation in the country where protection is claimed.

(b) However, in the countries of the Union which, by legislation, include among the owners of copyright in a cinematographic work authors who have brought contributions to the making of the work, such authors, if they have undertaken to bring such contributions, may not, in the absence of any contrary or special stipulation, object to the reproduction, distribution, public performance, communication to the public by wire, broadcasting or any other communication to the public, or to the subtitling or dubbing of texts, of the work.

(c) The question whether or not the form of the undertaking referred to above should, for the application of the preceding subparagraph (b), be in a written agreement or a written act of the same effect shall be a matter for the legislation of the country where the maker of the cinematographic work has his headquarters or habitual residence. However, it shall be a matter for the legislation of the country of the Union where protection is claimed to provide that the said undertaking shall be in a written agreement or a written act of the same effect. The countries whose legislation so provides shall notify the Director General by means of a written declaration, which will be immediately communicated by him to all the other countries of the Union.

(d) By 'contrary or special stipulation' is meant any restrictive condition which is relevant to the aforesaid undertaking.

(3) Unless the national legislation provides to the contrary, the provisions of paragraph (2)(b) above shall not be applicable to authors of scenarios, dialogues and musical works created for the making of the cinematographic work, or to the principal director thereof. However, those countries of the Union whose legislation does not contain rules providing for the application of the said paragraph (2)(b) to such director shall notify the Director General by means of a written declaration, which will be immediately communicated by him to all the other countries of the Union.

Article 14ter 'Droit de suite' in works of art and manuscripts: 1. Right to an interest in resales; 2. Applicable law; 3. Procedure

(1) The author, or after his death the persons or institutions authorised by national legislation, shall, with respect to original works of art and original manuscripts of writers and composers, enjoy the inalienable right to an interest in any sale of the work subsequent to the first transfer by the author of the work.

(2) The protection provided by the preceding paragraph may be claimed in a country of the Union only if legislation in the country to which the author belongs so permits, and to the extent permitted by the country where this protection is claimed.

(3) The procedure for collection and the amounts shall be matters for determination by national legislation.

Article 15   Right to enforce protected rights: 1. Where author's name is indicated or where pseudonym leaves no doubt as to author's identity; 2. In the case of cinematographic works; 3. In the case of anonymous and pseudonymous works; 4. In the case of certain unpublished works of unknown authorship

(1) In order that the author of a literary or artistic work protected by this Convention shall, in the absence of proof to the contrary, be regarded as such, and consequently be entitled to institute infringement proceedings in the countries of the Union, it shall be sufficient for his name to appear on the work in the usual manner. This paragraph shall be applicable even if this name is a pseudonym, where the pseudonym adopted by the author leaves no doubt as to his identity.

(2) The person or body corporate whose name appears on a cinematographic work in the usual manner shall, in the absence of proof to the contrary, be presumed to be the maker of the said work.

(3) In the case of anonymous and pseudonymous works, other than those referred to in paragraph (1) above, the publisher whose name appears on the work shall, in the absence of proof to the contrary, be deemed to represent the author, and in this capacity he shall be entitled to protect and enforce the author's rights. The provisions of this paragraph shall cease to apply when the author reveals his identity and establishes his claim to authorship of the work.

(4) (a) In a case of unpublished works where the identity of the author is unknown, but where there is every ground to presume that he is a national of a country of the Union, it shall be a matter for legislation in that country to designate the competent authority which shall represent the author and shall be entitled to protect and enforce his rights in the countries of the Union.

(b) Countries of the Union which make such designation under the terms of this provision shall notify the Director General by means of a written declaration giving full information concerning the authority thus designated. The Director General shall at once communicate this declaration to all other countries of the Union.

Article 16   Infringing copies: 1. Seizure; 2. Seizure on importation; 3. Applicable law

(1) Infringing copies of a work shall be liable to seizure in any country of the Union where the work enjoys legal protection.

(2) The provisions of the preceding paragraph shall also apply to reproductions coming from a country where the work is not protected, or has ceased to be protected.

(3) The seizure shall take place in accordance with the legislation of each country.

Article 17   Possibility of control of circulation, presentation and exhibition of works

The provisions of this Convention cannot in any way affect the right of the Government of each country of the Union to permit, to control, or to prohibit, by legislation or regulation, the circulation, presentation, or exhibition of any work or production in regard to which the competent authority may find it necessary to exercise that right.

Article 18   Works existing on convention's entry into force: 1. Protectable where protection not yet expired in country of origin; 2. Non-protectable where protection already expired in country where it is claimed; 3. Application of these principles; 4. Special cases

(1) This Convention shall apply to all works which, at the moment of its coming into force, have not yet fallen into the public domain in the country of origin through the expiry of the term of protection.

(2) If, however, through the expiry of the term of protection which was previously granted, a work has fallen into the public domain of the country where protection is claimed, that work shall not be protected anew.

(3) The application of this principle shall be subject to any provisions contained in special conventions to that effect existing or to be concluded between countries of the Union. In the absence of such provisions, the respective countries shall determine, each in so far as it is concerned, the conditions of application of this principle.

(4) The preceding provisions shall also apply in the case of new accessions to the Union and to cases in which protection is extended by the application of Article 7 or by the abandonment of reservations.

Article 19   Protection greater than resulting from Convention

The provisions of this Convention shall not preclude the making of a claim to the benefit of any greater protection which may be granted by legislation in a country of the Union.

Article 20   Special agreements among countries of the Union

The Governments of the countries of the Union reserve the right to enter into special agreements among themselves, in so far as such agreements grant to authors more extensive rights than those granted by the Convention, or contain other provisions not contrary to this Convention. The provisions of existing agreements which satisfy these conditions shall remain applicable.

Article 21   Special provisions regarding developing countries:
1. Reference to Appendix; 2. Appendix part of act

(1) Special provisions regarding developing countries are included in the Appendix.

...

International Convention for the Protection of Performers, Producers of Phonograms and Broadcasting Organisations (Rome Convention)

Done at Rome, on 26 October 1961

The Contracting States, moved by the desire to protect the rights of performers, producers of phonograms, and broadcasting organisations,

Have agreed as follows:

Article 1

Protection granted under this Convention shall leave intact and shall in no way affect the protection of copyright in literary and artistic works. Consequently, no provision of this Convention may be interpreted as prejudicing such protection.

Article 2

1. For the purposes of this Convention, national treatment shall mean the treatment accorded by the domestic law of the Contracting State in which protection is claimed:

(a) to performers who are its nationals, as regards performances taking place, broadcast, or first fixed, on its territory;

(b) to producers of phonograms who are its nationals, as regards phonograms first fixed or first published on its territory;

(c) to broadcasting organisations which have their headquarters on its territory, as regards broadcasts transmitted from transmitters situated on its territory.

2. National treatment shall be subject to the protection specifically guaranteed, and the limitations specifically provided for, in this Convention.

Article 3

For the purposes of this Convention:

(a) 'performers' means actors, singers, musicians, dancers, and other persons who act, sing, deliver, declaim, play in, or otherwise perform literary or artistic works;

(b) 'phonogram' means any exclusively aural fixation of sounds of a performance or of other sounds;

(c) 'producer of phonograms' means the person who, or the legal entity which, first fixes the sounds of a performance or other sounds;

(d) 'publication' means the offering of copies of a phonogram to the public in reasonable quantity;

(e) 'reproduction' means the making of a copy or copies of a fixation;

(f) 'broadcasting' means the transmission by wireless means for public reception of sounds or of images and sounds;

(g) 'rebroadcasting' means the simultaneous broadcasting by one broadcasting organisation of the broadcast of another broadcasting organisation.

Article 4

Each Contracting State shall grant national treatment to performers if any of the following conditions is met:

(a) the performance takes place in another Contracting State;

(b) the performance is incorporated in a phonogram which is protected under Article 5 of the Convention;

(c) the performance, not being fixed on a phonogram, is carried by a broadcast which is protected by Article 6 of this Convention.

Article 5

1. Each Contracting State shall grant national treatment to producers of phonograms if any of the following conditions is met:

(a) the producer of the phonogram is a national of another Contracting State (criterion of nationality);

(b) the first fixation of the sound was made in another Contracting State (criterion of fixation);

(c) the phonogram was first published in another Contracting State (criterion of publication).

2. If a phonogram was first published in a non-contracting State but if it was also published, within thirty days of its first publication, in a Contracting State (simultaneous publication), it shall be considered as first published in the Contracting State.

3. By means of a notification deposited with the Secretary-General of the United Nations, any Contracting State may declare that it will not apply the criterion of publication or, alternatively, the criterion of fixation. Such notification may be deposited at the time of ratification, acceptance or accession, or at any time thereafter; in the last case, it shall become effective six months after it has been deposited.

Article 6

1. Each Contracting State shall grant national treatment to broadcasting organisations if either of the following conditions is met:

(a) the headquarters of the broadcasting organisation is situated in another Contracting State;

(b) the broadcast was transmitted from a transmitter situated in another Contracting State.

2. By means of a notification deposited with the Secretary-General of the United Nations, any Contracting State may declare that it will protect broadcasts only if the headquarters of the broadcasting organisation is situated in another Contracting State and the broadcast was transmitted from a transmitter situated in the same Contracting State. Such notification may be deposited at the time of ratification, acceptance or accession, or at any time thereafter; in the last case, it shall become effective six months after it has been deposited.

Article 7

1. The protection provided for performers by this Convention shall include the possibility of preventing:

(a) the broadcasting and the communication to the public, without their consent, of their performance, except where the performance used in the broadcasting or the public communication is itself already a broadcast performance or is made from a fixation;

(b) the fixation, without their consent, of their unfixed performance;

(c) the reproduction, without their consent, of a fixation of their performance:

(i) if the original fixation itself was made without their consent;

(ii) if the reproduction is made for purposes different from those for which the performers gave their consent;

(iii) if the original fixation was made in accordance with the provisions of Article 15, and the reproduction is made for purposes different from those referred to in those provisions.

2. (1) If broadcasting was consented to by the performers, it shall be a matter for the domestic law of the Contracting State where protection is claimed to regulate the protection against rebroadcasting, fixation for broadcasting purposes, and the reproduction of such fixation for broadcasting purposes.

(2) The terms and conditions governing the use by broadcasting organisations of fixations made for broadcasting purposes shall be determined in accordance with the domestic law of the Contracting State where protection is claimed.

(3) However, the domestic law referred to in sub-paragraphs (1) and (2) of this paragraph shall not operate to deprive performers of the ability to control, by contract, their relations with broadcasting organisations.

Article 8

Any Contracting State may, by its domestic laws and regulations, specify the manner in which performers will be represented in connexion with the exercise of their rights if several of them participate in the same performance.

Article 9

Any Contracting State may, by its domestic laws and regulations, extend the protection provided for in this Convention to artists who do not perform literary or artistic works.

Article 10

Producers of phonograms shall enjoy the right to authorise or prohibit the direct or indirect reproduction of their phonograms.

Article 11

If, as a condition of protecting the rights of producers of phonograms, or of performers, or both, in relation to phonograms, a Contracting State, under its domestic law, requires compliance with formalities, these shall be considered as fulfilled if all the copies in commerce of the published phonogram or their containers bear a notice consisting of the symbol (P), accompanied by the year date of the first publication, placed in such a manner as to give reasonable notice of claim of protection; and if the copies or their containers do not identify the producer or the licensee of the producer (by carrying his name, trade mark or other appropriate designation), the notice shall also include the name of the owner of the rights of the producer; and, furthermore, if the copies or their containers do not identify the principal performers, the notice shall also include the name of the person who, in the country in which the fixation was effected, owns the rights of such performers.

Article 12

If a phonogram published for commercial purposes, or a reproduction of such phonogram, is used directly for broadcasting or for any communication to the public, a single equitable remuneration shall be paid by the user to the performers, or to the producers of the phonograms, or to both. Domestic law may, in the absence of agreement between these parties, lay down the conditions as to the sharing of this remuneration.

Article 13

Broadcasting organisations shall enjoy the right to authorise or prohibit:

    (a) the rebroadcasting of their broadcasts;

    (b) the fixation of their broadcasts;

    (c) the reproduction:

        (i) of fixations, made without their consent, of their broadcasts;

        (ii) of fixations, made in accordance with the provisions of Article 15, of their broadcasts, if the reproduction is made for purposes different from those referred to in those provisions;

    (d) the communication to the public of their television broadcasts if such communication is made in places accessible to the public against payment of an entrance fee; it shall be a matter for the domestic law of the State where protection of this right is claimed to determine the conditions under which it may be exercised.

Article 14

The term of protection to be granted under this Convention shall last at least until the end of a period of twenty years computed from the end of the year in which:

    (a) the fixation was made—for phonograms and for performances incorporated therein;

    (b) the performance took place—for performances not incorporated in phonograms;

    (c) the broadcast took place—for broadcasts.

Article 15

1. Any Contracting State may, in its domestic laws and regulations, provide for exceptions to the protection guaranteed by this Convention as regards:

    (a) private use;

    (b) use of short excerpts in connexion with the reporting of current events;

    (c) ephemeral fixation by a broadcasting organisation by means of its own facilities and for its own broadcasts;

    (d) use solely for the purposes of teaching or scientific research.

2. Irrespective of paragraph 1 of this Article, any Contracting State may, in its domestic laws and regulations, provide for the same kinds of limitations with regard to the protection of performers, producers of phonograms and broadcasting organisations, as it provides for, in its domestic laws and regulations, in connexion with the protection of copyright in literary and artistic works. However, compulsory licences may be provided for only to the extent to which they are compatible with this Convention.

Article 16

1. Any State, upon becoming party to this Convention, shall be bound by all the obligations and shall enjoy all the benefits thereof. However, a State may at any time, in a notification deposited with the Secretary-General of the United Nations, declare that:

    (a) as regards Article 12:

        (i)   it will not apply the provisions of that Article;

        (ii) it will not apply the provisions of that Article in respect of certain uses;

        (iii) as regard phonograms the producer of which is not a national of another Contracting State, it will not apply that Article;

        (iv) as regards phonograms the producer of which is a national of another Contracting State, it will limit the protection provided for by that Article to the extent to which, and to the term for which, the latter State grants protection to phonograms first fixed by a national of the State making the declaration; however, the fact that the Contracting State of which the producer is a national does not grant the protection to the same beneficiary or beneficiaries as the State making the declaration shall not be considered as a difference in the extent of the protection;

    (b) as regards Article 13, it will not apply item (d) of that Article; if a Contracting State makes such a declaration, the other Contracting States shall not be obliged to grant the right referred to in Article 13, item (d), to broadcasting organisations whose headquarters are in that State.

2. If the notification referred to in paragraph 1 of this Article is made after the date of the deposit of the instrument of ratification, acceptance or accession, the declaration will become effective six months after it has been deposited.

Article 17

Any State which, on October 26, 1961, grants protection to producers of phonograms solely on the basis of the criterion of fixation may, by a notification deposited with the Secretary-General of the

United Nations at the time of ratification, acceptance or accession, declare that it will apply, for the purposes of Article 5, the criterion of fixation alone and, for the purposes of paragraph 1(a)(iii) and (iv) of Article 16, the criterion of fixation instead of the criterion of nationality.

Article 18
Any State which has deposited a notification under paragraph 3 of Article 5, paragraph 2 of Article 6, paragraph 1 of Article 16 or Article 17, may, by a further notification deposited with the Secretary-General of the United Nations, reduce its scope or withdraw it.

Article 19
Notwithstanding anything in this Convention, once a performer has consented to the incorporation of his performance in a visual or audio-visual fixation, Article 7 shall have no further application.

Article 20
1. This Convention shall not prejudice rights acquired in any Contracting State before the date of coming into force of this Convention for that State.

2. No Contracting State shall be bound to apply the provisions of this Convention to performances or broadcasts which took place, or to phonograms which were fixed, before the date of coming into force of this Convention for that State.

Article 21
The protection provided for in this Convention shall not prejudice any protection otherwise secured to performers, producers of phonograms and broadcasting organisations.

Article 22
Contracting States reserve the right to enter into special agreements among themselves in so far as such agreements grant to performers, producers of phonograms or broadcasting organisations more extensive rights than those granted by this Convention or contain other provisions not contrary to this Convention.

...

Article 31
Without prejudice to the provisions of paragraph 3 of Article 5, paragraph 2 of Article 6, paragraph 1 of Article 16 and Article 17, no reservation may be made to this Convention.

...

WIPO Copyright Treaty

adopted by the Diplomatic Conference on 20 December 1996; declared to be a Community Treaty by European Communities (Definition of Treaties) (WIPO Copyright Treaty and WIPO Performances and Phonograms Treaty) Order 2005 (SI 2005/3431)

Preamble
The Contracting Parties,

Desiring to develop and maintain the protection of the rights of authors in their literary and artistic works in a manner as effective and uniform as possible,

Recognising the need to introduce new international rules and clarify the interpretation of certain existing rules in order to provide adequate solutions to the questions raised by new economic, social, cultural and technological developments,

Recognising the profound impact of the development and convergence of information and communication technologies on the creation and use of literary and artistic works,

Emphasising the outstanding significance of copyright protection as an incentive for literary and artistic creation,

Recognising the need to maintain a balance between the rights of authors and the large public interest, particularly education, research and access to information, as reflected in the Berne Convention,

Have agreed as follows:

Article 1   Relation to the Berne Convention

(1) This Treaty is a special agreement within the meaning of Article 20 of the Berne Convention for the Protection of Literary and Artistic Works, as regards Contracting Parties that are countries of the Union established by that Convention. This Treaty shall not have any connection with treaties other than the Berne Convention, nor shall it prejudice any rights and obligations under any other treaties.

(2) Nothing in this Treaty shall derogate from existing obligations that Contracting Parties have to each other under the Berne Convention for the Protection of Literary and Artistic Works.

(3) Hereinafter 'Berne Convention' shall refer to the Paris Act of July 24, 1971 of the Berne Convention for the Protection of Literary and Artistic Works.

(4) Contracting Parties shall comply with Articles 1 to 21 and the Appendix of the Berne Convention.

Article 2   Scope of copyright protection

Copyright protection extends to expressions and not to ideas, procedures, methods of operation or mathematical concepts as such.

Article 3   Application of Articles 2 to 6 of the Berne Convention

Contracting Parties shall apply *mutatis mutandis* the provisions of Articles 2 to 6 of the Berne Convention in respect of the protection provided for in this Treaty.

Article 4   Computer programs

Computer programs are protected as literary works within the meaning of Article 2 of the Berne Convention. Such protection applies to computer programs, whatever may be the mode or form of their expression.

Article 5   Compilations of data (databases)

Compilations of data or other material, in any form, which by reason of the selection or arrangement of their contents constitute intellectual creations, are protected as such. This protection does not extend to the data or the material itself and is without prejudice to any copyright subsisting in the data or material contained in the compilation.

Article 6   Right of distribution

(1) Authors of literary and artistic works shall enjoy the exclusive right of authorising the making available to the public of the original and copies of their works through sale or other transfer of ownership.

(2) Nothing in this Treaty shall affect the freedom of Contracting Parties to determine the conditions, if any, under which the exhaustion of the right in paragraph (1) applies after the first sale or other transfer of ownership of the original or a copy of the work with the authorisation of the author.

Article 7   Right of rental

(1) Authors of:
  (i)   computer programs;
  (ii) cinematographic works; and
  (iii) works embodied in phonograms as determined in the national law of Contracting Parties,
shall enjoy the exclusive right of authorising commercial rental to the public of the originals or copies of their works.

(2) Paragraph (1) shall not apply:
  (i)   in the case of computer programs where the program itself is not the essential object of the rental; and
  (ii) in the case of cinematographic works, unless such commercial rental has led to widespread copying of such works materially impairing the exclusive right of reproduction.

(3) Notwithstanding the provisions of paragraph (1), a Contracting Party that, on April 15, 1994, had and continues to have in force a system of equitable remuneration of authors for the rental of copies of their works embodied in phonograms may maintain that system provided that the commercial rental of works embodied in phonograms is not giving rise to the material impairment of the exclusive rights of reproduction of authors.

Article 8   Right of communication to the public
Without prejudice to the provisions of Articles 11(1)(ii), 11*bis*(1)(i) and (ii), 11*ter*(1)(ii), 14(1)(ii) and 14*bis*(1) of the Berne Convention, authors of literary and artistic works shall enjoy the exclusive right of authorising any communication to the public of their works, by wire or wireless means, including the making available to the public of their works in such a way that members of the public may access these works from a place and at a time individually chosen by them.

Article 9   Duration of the protection of photographic works
In respect of photographic works, the Contracting Parties shall not apply the provision of Article 7(4) of the Berne Convention.

Article 10   Limitations and exceptions
(1) Contracting Parties may, in their national legislation, provide for limitations of or exceptions to the rights granted to authors of literary and artistic works under this Treaty in certain special cases that do not conflict with a normal exploitation of the work and do not unreasonably prejudice the legitimate interests of the author.

(2) Contracting Parties shall, when applying the Berne Convention, confine any limitations of or exceptions to rights provided for therein to certain special cases that do not conflict with a normal exploitation of the work and do not unreasonably prejudice the legitimate interests of the author.

Article 11   Obligations concerning technological measures
Contracting Parties shall provide adequate legal protection and effective legal remedies against the circumvention of effective technological measures that are used by authors in connection with the exercise of their rights under this Treaty or the Berne Convention and that restrict acts, in respect of their works, which are not authorised by the authors concerned or permitted by law.

Article 12   Obligations concerning rights management information
(1) Contracting Parties shall provide adequate and effective legal remedies against any person knowingly performing any of the following acts knowing or, with respect to civil remedies having reasonable grounds to know, that it will induce, enable, facilitate or conceal an infringement of any right covered by this Treaty or the Berne Convention:
  (i) to remove or alter any electronic rights management information without authority;
  (ii) to distribute, import for distribution, broadcast or communicate to the public, without authority, works or copies of works knowing that electronic rights management information has been removed or altered without authority.

(2) As used in this Article, 'rights management information' means information which identifies the work, the author of the work, the owner of any right in the work, or information about the terms and conditions of use of the work, and any number or codes that represent such information, when any of these items of information is attached to a copy of a work or appears in connection with the communication of a work to the public.

Article 13   Application in time
Contracting Parties shall apply the provisions of Article 18 of the Berne Convention to all protection provided for in this Treaty.

Article 14   Provisions on enforcement of rights
(1) Contracting Parties undertake to adopt, in accordance with their legal systems, the measures necessary to ensure the application of this Treaty.

(2) Contracting Parties shall ensure that enforcement procedures are available under their law so as to permit effective action against any act of infringement of rights covered by this Treaty,

including expeditious remedies to prevent infringements and remedies which constitute a deterrent to further infringements.

...

Article 22   No reservations to the Treaty

No reservation to this Treaty shall be admitted.

...

Agreed Statements concerning the WIPO Copyright Treaty

adopted by the Diplomatic Conference on 20 December 1996

Concerning Article 1(4)

The reproduction right, as set out in Article 9 of the Berne Convention, and the exceptions permitted thereunder, fully apply in the digital environment, in particular to the use of works in digital form. It is understood that the storage of a protected work in digital form in an electronic medium constitutes a reproduction within the meaning of Article 9 of the Berne Convention.

Concerning Article 3

It is understood that in applying Article 3 of this Treaty, the expression 'country of the Union' in Articles 2 to 6 of the Berne Convention will be read as if it were a reference to a Contracting Party to this Treaty, in the application of those Berne Articles in respect of protection provided for in this Treaty. It is also understood that the expression 'country outside the Union' in those Articles in the Berne Convention will, in the same circumstances, be read as if it were a reference to a country that is not a Contracting Party to this Treaty, and that 'this Convention' in Articles 2(8), *2bis* (2), 3, 4 and 5 of the Berne Convention will be read as if it were a reference to the Berne Convention and this Treaty. Finally, it is understood that a reference in Articles 3 to 6 of the Berne Convention to a 'national of one of the countries of the Union' will, when these Articles are applied to this Treaty, mean, in regard to an intergovernmental organisation that is a Contracting Party to this Treaty, a national of one of the countries that is member of that organisation.

Concerning Article 4

The scope of protection for computer programs under Article 4 of this Treaty, read with Article 2, is consistent with Article 2 of the Berne Convention and on a par with the relevant provisions of the TRIPS Agreement.

Concerning Article 5

The scope of protection for compilations of data (databases) under Article 5 of this Treaty, read with Article 2, is consistent with Article 2 of the Berne Convention and on a par with the relevant provisions of the TRIPS Agreement.

Concerning Articles 6 and 7

As used in these Articles, the expressions 'copies' and 'original and copies', being subject to the right of distribution and the right of rental under the said Articles, refer exclusively to fixed copies that can be put into circulation as tangible objects.

Concerning Article 7

It is understood that the obligation under Article 7(1) does not require a Contracting Party to provide an exclusive right of commercial rental to authors who, under that Contracting Party's law, are not granted rights in respect of phonograms. It is understood that this obligation is consistent with Article 14(4) of the TRIPS Agreement.

Concerning Article 8

It is understood that the mere provision of physical facilities for enabling or making a communication does not in itself amount to communication within the meaning of this Treaty or the Berne Convention. It is further understood that nothing in Article 8 precludes a Contracting Party from applying Article 11*bis*(2).

Concerning Article 10

It is understood that the provisions of Article 10 permit Contracting Parties to carry forward and appropriately extend into the digital environment limitations and exceptions in their national laws which have been considered acceptable under the Berne Convention. Similarly, these provisions should be understood to permit Contracting Parties to devise new exceptions and limitations that are appropriate in the digital network environment.

It is also understood that Article 10(2) neither reduces nor extends the scope of applicability of the limitations and exceptions permitted by the Berne Convention.

Concerning Article 12

It is understood that the reference to 'infringement of any right covered by this Treaty or the Berne Convention' includes both exclusive rights and rights of remuneration.

It is further understood that Contracting Parties will not rely on this Article to devise or implement rights management systems that would have the effect of imposing formalities which are not permitted under the Berne Convention or this Treaty, prohibiting the free movement of goods or impeding the enjoyment of rights under this Treaty.

WIPO Performances and Phonograms Treaty

adopted by the Diplomatic Conference on 20 December 1996; declared to be a Community Treaty by European Communities (Definition of Treaties) (WIPO Copyright Treaty and WIPO Performances and Phonograms Treaty) Order 2005 (SI 2005/3431)

Preamble

The Contracting Parties,

Desiring to develop and maintain the protection of the rights of performers and producers of phonograms in a manner as effective and uniform as possible,

Recognising the need to introduce new international rules in order to provide adequate solutions to the questions raised by economic, social, cultural and technological developments,

Recognising the profound impact of the development and convergence of information and communication technologies on the production and use of performances and phonograms,

Recognising the need to maintain a balance between the rights of the performers and producers of phonograms and the larger public interest, particularly education, research and access to information,

Have agreed as follows:

Chapter I   General Provisions

Article 1   Relation to other Conventions

(1) Nothing in this Treaty shall derogate from existing obligations that Contracting Parties have to each other under the International Convention for the Protection of Performers, Producers of Phonograms and Broadcasting Organisations done in Rome, October 26, 1961 (hereinafter the 'Rome Convention').

(2) Protection granted under this Treaty shall leave intact and shall in no way affect the protection of copyright in literary and artistic works. Consequently, no provision of this Treaty may be interpreted as prejudicing such protection.

(3) This Treaty shall not have any connection with, nor shall it prejudice any rights and obligations under, any other treaties.

Article 2   Definitions

For the purposes of this Treaty:

    (a) 'performers' are actors, singers, musicians, dancers, and other persons who act, sing, deliver, declaim, play in, interpret, or otherwise perform literary or artistic works or expressions of folklore;

    (b) 'phonogram' means the fixation of the sounds of a performance or of other sounds, or of a representation of sounds other than in the form of a fixation incorporated in a cinematographic or other audiovisual work;

    (c) 'fixation' means the embodiment of sounds, or of the representations thereof, from which they can be perceived, reproduced or communicated through a device;

    (d) 'producer of a phonogram' means the person, or the legal entity, who or which takes the initiative and has the responsibility for the first fixation of the sounds of a performance or other sounds, or the representations of sounds;

    (e) 'publication' of a fixed performance or a phonogram means the offering of copies of the fixed performance or the phonogram to the public, with the consent of the rightholder, and provided that copies are offered to the public in reasonable quantity.

    (f) 'broadcasting' means the transmission by wireless means for public reception of sounds or of images and sounds or of the representations thereof; such transmission by satellite is also 'broadcasting'; transmission of encrypted signals is 'broadcasting' where the means for decrypting are provided to the public by the broadcasting organisation or with its consent;

    (g) 'communication to the public' of a performance or a phonogram means the transmission to the public by any medium, otherwise than by broadcasting, of sounds of a performance or the sounds or the representations of sounds fixed in a phonogram. For the purposes of Article 15, 'communication to the public' includes making the sounds or representations of sounds fixed in a phonogram audible to the public.

Article 3   Beneficiaries of protection under this Treaty

(1) Contracting Parties shall accord the protection provided under this Treaty to the performers and producers of phonograms who are nationals of other Contracting Parties.

(2) The nationals of other Contracting Parties shall be understood to be those performers or producers of phonograms who would meet the criteria for eligibility for protection provided under the Rome Convention, were all the Contracting Parties to this Treaty Contracting States of that Convention. In respect of these criteria of eligibility, Contracting Parties shall apply the relevant definitions in Article 2 of this Treaty.

(3) Any Contracting Party availing itself of the possibilities provided in Article 5(3) of the Rome Conventions or, for the purposes of Article 5 of the same Convention, Article thereof 17 shall make a notification as foreseen in those provisions to the Director General of the World Intellectual Property Organisation (WIPO).

Article 4   National treatment

(1) Each Contracting Party shall accord to nationals of other Contracting Parties, as defined in Article 3(2), the treatment it accords to its own nationals with regard to the exclusive rights specifically granted in this Treaty and to the right to equitable remuneration provided for in Article 15 of this Treaty.

(2) The obligation provided for in paragraph (1) does not apply to the extent that another Contracting Party makes use of the reservations permitted by Article 15(3) of this Treaty.

Chapter II   Rights of Performers

Article 5   Moral rights of performers

(1) Independently of a performer's economic rights, and even after the transfer of those rights, the performer shall, as regards his live aural performances or performances fixed in phonograms have the right to claim to be identified as the performer of his performances, except

where omission is dictated by the manner of the use of the performance, and to object to any distortion, mutilation or other modification of his performances that would be prejudicial to his reputation.

(2) The rights granted to a performer in accordance with paragraph (1) shall, after his death, be maintained, at least until the expiry of the economic rights, and shall be exercisable by the persons or institutions authorised by the legislation of the Contracting Party where protection is claimed. However, those Contracting Parties whose legislation, at the moment of their ratification of or accession to this Treaty, does not provide for protection after the death of the performer of all rights set out in the preceding paragraph may provide that some of these rights will, after his death, cease to be maintained.

(3) The means of redress for safeguarding the rights granted under this Article shall be governed by the legislation of the Contracting Party where protection is claimed.

Article 6   Economic rights of performers in their unfixed performances

Performers shall enjoy the exclusive right of authorising, as regards their performances:

(i) the broadcasting and communication to the public of their unfixed performances except where the performance is already a broadcast performance; and

(ii) the fixation of their unfixed performances.

Article 7   Right of reproduction

Performers shall enjoy the exclusive right of authorising the direct or indirect reproduction of their performances fixed in phonograms, in any manner or form.

Article 8   Right of distribution

(1) Performers shall enjoy the exclusive right of authorising the making available to the public of the original and copies of their performances fixed in phonograms through sale or other transfer of ownership.

(2) Nothing in this Treaty shall affect the freedom of Contracting Parties to determine the conditions, if any, under which the exhaustion of the right in paragraph (1) applies after the first sale or other transfer of ownership of the original or a copy of the fixed performance with the authorisation of the performer.

Article 9   Right of rental

(1) Performers shall enjoy the exclusive right of authorising the commercial rental to the public of the original and copies of their performances fixed in phonograms as determined in the national law of Contracting Parties, even after distribution of them by, or pursuant to, authorisation by the performer.

(2) Notwithstanding the provisions of paragraph (1), a Contracting Party that, on April 15, 1994, had and continues to have in force a system of equitable remuneration of performers for the rental of copies of their performances fixed in phonograms, may maintain that system provided that the commercial rental of phonograms is not giving rise to the material impairment of the exclusive rights of reproduction of performers.

Article 10   Right of making available of fixed performances

Performers shall enjoy the exclusive right of authorising the making available to the public of their performances fixed in phonograms, by wire or wireless means, in such a way that members of the public may access them from a place and at a time individually chosen by them.

Chapter III   Rights of Producers of Phonograms

Article 11   Right of reproduction

Producers of phonograms shall enjoy the exclusive right of authorising the direct or indirect reproduction of their phonograms, in any manner or form.

Article 12   Right of distribution

(1) Producers of phonograms shall enjoy the exclusive right of authorising the making available to the public of the original and copies of their phonograms through sale or other transfer of ownership.

(2) Nothing in this Treaty shall affect the freedom of Contracting Parties to determine the conditions, if any, under which the exhaustion of the right in paragraph (1) applies after the first sale or transfer of ownership of the original or a copy of the phonogram with the authorisation of the producer of phonograms.

Article 13   Right of rental

(1) Producers of phonograms shall enjoy the exclusive right of authorising the commercial rental to the public of the original and copies of their phonograms, even after distribution of them by or pursuant to authorisation by the producer.

(2) Notwithstanding the provisions of paragraph (1), a Contracting Party that, on April 15, 1994, had and continues to have in force a system of equitable remuneration of producers of phonograms for the rental of copies of their phonograms, may maintain that system provided that the commercial rental of phonograms is not giving rise to the material impairment of the exclusive rights of reproduction of producers of phonograms.

Article 14   Right of making available of phonograms

Producers of phonograms shall enjoy the exclusive right of authorising the making available to the public of their phonograms, by wire or wireless means, in such a way that members of the public may access them from a place and at a time individually chosen by them.

Chapter IV   Common Provisions

Article 15   Right to remuneration for broadcasting and communication to the public

(1) Performers and producers of phonograms shall enjoy the right to a single equitable remuneration for the direct or indirect use of phonograms published for commercial purposes for broadcasting or for any communication to the public.

(2) Contracting Parties may establish in their national legislation that the single equitable remuneration shall be claimed from the user by the performer or by the producer of a phonogram or by both. Contracting Parties may enact national legislation that, in the absence of an agreement between the performer and the producer of a phonogram, sets the terms according to which performers and producers of phonograms shall share the single equitable remuneration.

(3) Any Contracting Party may in a notification deposited with the Director General of WIPO, declare that it will apply the provisions of paragraph (1) only in respect of certain uses, or that it will limit their application in some other way, or that it will not apply these provisions at all.

(4) For the purposes of this Article, phonograms made available to the public by wire or wireless means in such a way that members of the public may access them from a place and at a time individually chosen by them shall be considered as if they had been published for commercial purposes.

Article 16   Limitations and exceptions

(1) Contracting Parties may, in their national legislation, provide for the same kinds of limitations or exceptions with regard to the protection of performers and producers of phonograms as they provide for, in their national legislation, in connection with the protection of copyright in literary and artistic works.

(2) Contracting Parties shall confine any limitations of or exceptions to rights provided for in this Treaty to certain special cases which do not conflict with a normal exploitation of the performance or phonogram and do not unreasonably prejudice the legitimate interests of the performer or of the producer of phonograms.

Article 17   Term of protection

(1) The term of protection to be granted to performers under this Treaty shall last, as least, until the end of a period of 50 years computed from the end of the year in which the performance was fixed in a phonogram.

(2) The term of protection to be granted to producers of phonograms under this Treaty shall last, at least, until the end of a period of 50 years computed from the end of the year in which the phonogram was published, or failing such publication within 50 years from fixation of the phonogram, 50 years from the end of the year in which the fixation was made.

Article 18   Obligations concerning technological measures

Contracting Parties shall provide adequate legal protection and effective legal remedies against the circumvention of effective technological measures that are used by performers or producers of phonograms in connection with the exercise of their right under this Treaty and that restrict acts, in respect of their performances or phonograms, which are not authorised by the performers or the producers of phonograms concerned or permitted by law.

Article 19   Obligations concerning rights management information

(1) Contracting Parties shall provide adequate and effective legal remedies against any person knowingly performing any of the following acts knowing or, with respect to civil remedies, having reasonable grounds to know that it will induce, enable, facilitate or conceal on infringement of any right covered by this Treaty:

   (i) to remove or alter any electronic rights management information without authority;

   (ii) to distribute, import for distribution, broadcast, communicate or make available to the public, without authority, performances, copies of fixed performances or phonograms knowing that electronic rights management information has been removed or altered without authority.

(2) As used in this Article, 'rights management information' means information which identifies the performer, the performance of the performer, the producer of the phonogram, the phonogram, the owner of any right in the performance or phonogram, or information about the terms and conditions of use of the performance or phonogram, and any numbers or codes that represent such information, when any of those items of information is attached to a copy of a fixed performance or a phonogram or appears in connection with the communication or making available of a fixed performance or a phonogram to the public.

Article 20   Formalities

The enjoyment and exercise of the rights provided for in this Treaty shall not be subject to any formality.

Article 21   Reservations

Subject to the provisions of Article 15(3), no reservations to this Treaty shall be permitted.

Article 22   Application in time

(1) Contracting Parties shall apply the provisions of Article 18 of the Berne Convention, *mutatis mutandis*, to the rights of performers and producers of phonograms provided for in this Treaty for that Party.

Article 23   Provisions on enforcement of rights

(1) Contracting Parties undertake to adopt, in accordance with their legal systems, the measures necessary to ensure the application of this Treaty.

(2) Contracting Parties shall ensure that enforcement procedures are available under their law so as to permit effective action against any act of infringement of rights covered by this Treaty, including expeditious remedies to prevent infringements and remedies which constitute a deterrent to further infringements.

   ...

Agreed Statements concerning the WIPO Performances and Phonograms Treaty

adopted by the Diplomatic Conference on 20 December 1996

Concerning Article 1

It is understood that Article 1(2) clarifies the relationship between rights in phonograms under this Treaty and copyright in works embodied in the phonograms. In cases where authorisation is needed from both the author of a work embodied in the phonogram and a performer or producer owning rights in the phonogram, the need for the authorisation of the author does not cease to exist because the authorisation of the performer or producer is also required, and vice versa.

It is further understood that nothing in Article 1(2) precludes a Contracting Party from providing exclusive rights to a performer or producer of phonograms beyond those required to be provided under this Treaty.

Concerning Article 2(b)

It is understood that the definition of phonogram provided in Article 2(b) does not suggest that rights in the phonogram are in any way affected through their incorporation into a cinematographic or other audiovisual work.

Concerning Articles 2(e), 8, 9, 12, and 13

As used in these Articles, the expressions 'copies' and 'original and copies', being subject to the right of distribution and the right of rental under the said Articles, refer exclusively to fixed copies that can be put into circulation as tangible objects.

Concerning Article 3

It is understood that the reference in Articles 5(a) and 16(a)(iv) of the Rome Convention to 'national of another Contracting State' will, when applied to this Treaty, mean, in regard to an intergovernmental organisation that is a Contracting Party to this Treaty, a national of one of the countries that is a member of that organisation.

Concerning Article 3(2)

For the application of Article 3(2), it is understood that fixation means the finalisation of the master tape ('bande-mere').

Concerning Articles 7, 11 and 16

The reproduction right, as set out in Articles 7 and 11, and the exceptions permitted thereunder through Article 16, fully apply in the digital environment, in particular to the use of performances and phonograms in digital form. It is understood that the storage of a protected performance or phonogram in digital form in an electronic medium constitutes a reproduction within the meaning of these Articles.

Concerning Article 15

It is understood that Article 15 does not represent a complete resolution of the level of rights of broadcasting and communication to the public that should be enjoyed by performers and phonogram producers in the digital age. Delegations were unable to achieve consensus on differing proposals for aspects of exclusivity to be provided in certain circumstances or for rights to be provided without the possibility of reservations, and have therefore left the issue to future resolution.

Concerning Article 15

It is understood that Article 15 does not prevent the granting of the right conferred by this Article to performers of folklore and producers of phonograms recording folklore where such phonograms have not been published for commercial gain.

Concerning Article 16

The agreed statement concerning Article 10 (on Limitations and Exceptions) of the WIPO Copyright Treaty is applicable *mutatis mutandis* also to Article 16 (on Limitations and Exceptions) of the WIPO Performances and Phonograms Treaty.

Concerning Article 19
The agreed statement concerning Article 12 (on Obligations concerning Rights Management Information) of the WIPO Copyright Treaty is applicable *mutatis mutandis* also to Article 19 (on Obligations concerning Rights Management Information) of the WIPO Performances and Phonograms Treaty.

Geneva Act of the Hague Agreement concerning the International Registration of Industrial Designs

adopted by the Diplomatic Conference on 2 July 1999

INTRODUCTORY PROVISIONS

Article 1   Abbreviated Expressions

For the purposes of this Act:

(i)   'the Hague Agreement' means the Hague Agreement Concerning the International Deposit of Industrial Designs, henceforth renamed the Hague Agreement Concerning the International Registration of Industrial Designs;

(ii)   'this Act' means the Hague Agreement as established by the present Act;

(iii)   'Regulations' means the Regulations under this Act;

(iv)   'prescribed' means prescribed in the Regulations;

(v)   'Paris Convention' means the Paris Convention for the Protection of Industrial Property, signed at Paris on March 20, 1883, as revised and amended;

(vi)   'international registration' means the international registration of an industrial design effected according to this Act;

(vii)   'international application' means an application for international registration;

(viii) 'International Register' means the official collection of data concerning international registrations maintained by the International Bureau, which data this Act or the Regulations require or permit to be recorded, regardless of the medium in which such data are stored;

(ix)   'person' means a natural person or a legal entity;

(x)   'applicant' means the person in whose name an international application is filed;

(xi)   'holder' means the person in whose name an international registration is recorded in the International Register;

(xii)   'intergovernmental organization' means an intergovernmental organization eligible to become party to this Act in accordance with Article 27(1)(ii);

(xiii) 'Contracting Party' means any State or intergovernmental organization party to this Act;

(xiv)   'applicant's Contracting Party' means the Contracting Party or one of the Contracting Parties from which the applicant derives its entitlement to file an international application by virtue of satisfying, in relation to that Contracting Party, at least one of the conditions specified in Article 3; where there are two or more Contracting Parties from which the applicant may, under Article 3, derive its entitlement to file an international application, 'applicant's Contracting Party' means the one which, among those Contracting Parties, is indicated as such in the international application;

(xv)   'territory of a Contracting Party' means, where the Contracting Party is a State, the territory of that State and, where the Contracting Party is an intergovernmental organization, the territory in which the constituent treaty of that intergovernmental organization applies;

(xvi)   'Office' means the agency entrusted by a Contracting Party with the grant of protection for industrial designs with effect in the territory of that Contracting Party;

(xvii)   'Examining Office' means an Office which *ex officio* examines applications filed with it for the protection of industrial designs at least to determine whether the industrial designs satisfy the condition of novelty;

(xviii) 'designation' means a request that an international registration have effect in a Contracting Party; it also means the recording, in the International Register, of that request;

(xix)   'designated Contracting Party' and 'designated Office' means the Contracting Party and the Office of the Contracting Party, respectively, to which a designation applies;

(xx)   '1934 Act' means the Act signed at London on June 2, 1934, of the Hague Agreement;

(xxi)   '1960 Act' means the Act signed at The Hague on November 28, 1960, of the Hague Agreement;

(xxii)   '1961 Additional Act' means the Act signed at Monaco on November 18, 1961, additional to the 1934 Act;

(xxiii) 'Complementary Act of 1967' means the Complementary Act signed at Stockholm on July 14, 1967, as amended, of the Hague Agreement;

(xxiv)   'Union' means the Hague Union established by the Hague Agreement of November 6, 1925, and maintained by the 1934 and 1960 Acts, the 1961 Additional Act, the Complementary Act of 1967 and this Act;

(xxv)   'Assembly' means the Assembly referred to in Article 21(1)(a) or any body replacing that Assembly;

(xxvi)   'Organization' means the World Intellectual Property Organization;

(xxvii) 'Director General' means the Director General of the Organization;

(xxviii) 'International Bureau' means the International Bureau of the Organization;

(xxix)   'instrument of ratification' shall be construed as including instruments of acceptance or approval.

Article 2   Applicability of Other Protection Accorded by Laws of Contracting Parties and by Certain International Treaties

(1) [*Laws of Contracting Parties and Certain International Treaties*] The provisions of this Act shall not affect the application of any greater protection which may be accorded by the law of a Contracting Party, nor shall they affect in any way the protection accorded to works of art and works of applied art by international copyright treaties and conventions, or the protection accorded to industrial designs under the Agreement on Trade-Related Aspects of Intellectual Property Rights annexed to the Agreement Establishing the World Trade Organization.

(2) [*Obligation to Comply with the Paris Convention*] Each Contracting Party shall comply with the provisions of the Paris Convention which concern industrial designs.

Chapter I   International Application and International Registration

Article 3   Entitlement to File an International Application

Any person that is a national of a State that is a Contracting Party or of a State member of an intergovernmental organization that is a Contracting Party, or that has a domicile, a habitual residence or a real and effective industrial or commercial establishment in the territory of a Contracting Party, shall be entitled to file an international application.

Article 4   Procedure for Filing the International Application

(1) [*Direct or Indirect Filing*]

(a) The international application may be filed, at the option of the applicant, either directly with the International Bureau or through the Office of the applicant's Contracting Party.

(b) Notwithstanding subparagraph (a), any Contracting Party may, in a declaration, notify the Director General that international applications may not be filed through its Office.

(2) [*Transmittal Fee in Case of Indirect Filing*] The Office of any Contracting Party may require that the applicant pay a transmittal fee to it, for its own benefit, in respect of any international application filed through it.

. . .

Article 6   Priority

(1) [*Claiming of Priority*]

    (a) The international application may contain a declaration claiming, under Article 4 of the Paris Convention, the priority of one or more earlier applications filed in or for any country party to that Convention or any Member of the World Trade Organization.

    (b) The Regulations may provide that the declaration referred to in subparagraph (a) may be made after the filing of the international application. In such case, the Regulations shall prescribe the latest time by which such declaration may be made.

(2) [*International Application Serving as a Basis for Claiming Priority*] The international application shall, as from its filing date and whatever may be its subsequent fate, be equivalent to a regular filing within the meaning of Article 4 of the Paris Convention.

. . .

Article 10[2]   International Registration, Date of the International Registration, Publication and Confidential Copies of the International Registration

(1) [*International Registration*] The International Bureau shall register each industrial design that is the subject of an international application immediately upon receipt by it of the international application or, where corrections are invited under Article 8, immediately upon receipt of the required corrections. The registration shall be effected whether or not publication is deferred under Article 11.

(2) [*Date of the International Registration*]

    (a) Subject to subparagraph (b), the date of the international registration shall be the filing date of the international application.

    (b) Where the international application has, on the date on which it is received by the International Bureau, an irregularity which relates to Article 5(2), the date of the international registration shall be the date on which the correction of such irregularity is received by the International Bureau or the filing date of the international application, whichever is the later.

(3) [*Publication*]

    (a) The international registration shall be published by the International Bureau. Such publication shall be deemed in all Contracting Parties to be sufficient publicity, and no other publicity may be required of the holder.

    (b) The International Bureau shall send a copy of the publication of the international registration to each designated Office.

. . .

Article 12   Refusal

(1) [*Right to Refuse*] The Office of any designated Contracting Party may, where the conditions for the grant of protection under the law of that Contracting Party are not met in respect of any or all of the industrial designs that are the subject of an international registration, refuse the effects, in part or in whole, of the international registration in the territory of the said Contracting Party, provided that no Office may refuse the effects, in part or in whole, of any international registration on the ground that requirements relating to the form or contents of the international application that are provided for in this Act or the Regulations or are additional to, or different from, those requirements have not been satisfied under the law of the Contracting Party concerned.

---

[2] When adopting Article 10, the Diplomatic Conference understood that nothing in this Article precludes access to the international application or the international registration by the applicant or the holder or a person having the consent of the applicant or the holder.

(2) [*Notification of Refusal*]

    (a) The refusal of the effects of an international registration shall be communicated by the Office to the International Bureau in a notification of refusal within the prescribed period.

    (b) Any notification of refusal shall state all the grounds on which the refusal is based.

(3) [*Transmission of Notification of Refusal; Remedies*]

    (a) The International Bureau shall, without delay, transmit a copy of the notification of refusal to the holder.

    (b) The holder shall enjoy the same remedies as if any industrial design that is the subject of the international registration had been the subject of an application for the grant of protection under the law applicable to the Office that communicated the refusal. Such remedies shall at least consist of the possibility of a re-examination or a review of the refusal or an appeal against the refusal.

(4)[3] [*Withdrawal of Refusal*] Any refusal may be withdrawn, in part or in whole, at any time by the Office that communicated it.

. . .

Article 14   Effects of the International Registration

(1) [*Effect as Application Under Applicable Law*] The international registration shall, from the date of the international registration, have at least the same effect in each designated Contracting Party as a regularly-filed application for the grant of protection of the industrial design under the law of that Contracting Party.

(2) [*Effect as Grant of Protection Under Applicable Law*]

    (a) In each designated Contracting Party the Office of which has not communicated a refusal in accordance with Article 12, the international registration shall have the same effect as a grant of protection for the industrial design under the law of that Contracting Party at the latest from the date of expiration of the period allowed for it to communicate a refusal or, where a Contracting Party has made a corresponding declaration under the Regulations, at the latest at the time specified in that declaration.

    (b)* Where the Office of a designated Contracting Party has communicated a refusal and has subsequently withdrawn, in part or in whole, that refusal, the international registration shall, to the extent that the refusal is withdrawn, have the same effect in that Contracting Party as a grant of protection for the industrial design under the law of the said Contracting Party at the latest from the date on which the refusal was withdrawn.

    (c) The effect given to the international registration under this paragraph shall apply to the industrial design or designs that are the subject of that registration as received from the International Bureau by the designated Office or, where applicable, as amended in the procedure before that Office.

(3) [*Declaration Concerning Effect of Designation of Applicant's Contracting Party*]

    (a) Any Contracting Party whose Office is an Examining Office may, in a declaration, notify the Director General that, where it is the applicant's Contracting Party, the designation of that Contracting Party in an international registration shall have no effect.

    (b) Where a Contracting Party having made the declaration referred to in subparagraph (a) is indicated in an international application both as the applicant's Contracting Party and as a designated Contracting Party, the International Bureau shall disregard the designation of that Contracting Party.

---

[3] When adopting Article 12(4), Article 14(2)(b) and Rule 18(4), the Diplomatic Conference understood that a withdrawal of refusal by an Office that has communicated a notification of refusal may take the form of a statement to the effect that the Office concerned has decided to accept the effects of the international registration in respect of the industrial designs, or some of the industrial designs, to which the notification of refusal related. It was also understood that an Office may, within the period allowed for communicating a notification of refusal, send a statement to the effect that it has decided to accept the effects of the international registration even where it has not communicated such a notification of refusal.

* **Editor's Note:** See footnote to Article 12(4).

Article 15   Invalidation

(1) [*Requirement of Opportunity of Defense*] Invalidation, by the competent authorities of a designated Contracting Party, of the effects, in part or in whole, in the territory of that Contracting Party, of the international registration may not be pronounced without the holder having, in good time, been afforded the opportunity of defending his rights.

(2) [*Notification of Invalidation*] The Office of the Contracting Party in whose territory the effects of the international registration have been invalidated shall, where it is aware of the invalidation, notify it to the International Bureau.

...

Article 17   Initial Term and Renewal of the International Registration and Duration of Protection

(1) [*Initial Term of the International Registration*] The international registration shall be effected for an initial term of five years counted from the date of the international registration.

(2) [*Renewal of the International Registration*] The international registration may be renewed for additional terms of five years, in accordance with the prescribed procedure and subject to the payment of the prescribed fees.

(3) [*Duration of Protection in Designated Contracting Parties*]

   (a) Provided that the international registration is renewed, and subject to sub-paragraph (b), the duration of protection shall, in each of the designated Contracting Parties, be 15 years counted from the date of the international registration.

   (b) Where the law of a designated Contracting Party provides for a duration of protection of more than 15 years for an industrial design for which protection has been granted under that law, the duration of protection shall, provided that the international registration is renewed, be the same as that provided for by the law of that Contracting Party.

   (c) Each Contracting Party shall, in a declaration, notify the Director General of the maximum duration of protection provided for by its law.

(4) [*Possibility of Limited Renewal*] The renewal of the international registration may be effected for any or all of the designated Contracting Parties and for any or all of the industrial designs that are the subject of the international registration.

(5) [*Recording and Publication of Renewal*] The International Bureau shall record renewals in the International Register and publish a notice to that effect. It shall send a copy of the publication of the notice to the Office of each of the Contracting Parties concerned.

...

Marrakesh Treaty to Facilitate Access to Published Works for Persons Who Are Blind, Visually Impaired, or Otherwise Print Disabled*

CONTENTS

Preamble

---

* This Treaty was adopted by the Diplomatic Conference to Conclude a Treaty to Facilitate Access to Published Works by Visually Impaired Persons and Persons with Print Disabilities on June 27, 2013.

Preamble

The Contracting Parties,

Recalling the principles of non-discrimination, equal opportunity, accessibility and full and effective participation and inclusion in society, proclaimed in the Universal Declaration of Human Rights and the United Nations Convention on the Rights of Persons with Disabilities,

Mindful of the challenges that are prejudicial to the complete development of persons with visual impairments or with other print disabilities, which limit their freedom of expression, including the freedom to seek, receive and impart information and ideas of all kinds on an equal basis with others, including through all forms of communication of their choice, their enjoyment of the right to education, and the opportunity to conduct research,

Emphasizing the importance of copyright protection as an incentive and reward for literary and artistic creations and of enhancing opportunities for everyone, including persons with visual impairments or with other print disabilities, to participate in the cultural life of the community, to enjoy the arts and to share scientific progress and its benefits,

Aware of the barriers of persons with visual impairments or with other print disabilities to access published works in achieving equal opportunities in society, and the need to both expand the number of works in accessible formats and to improve the circulation of such works,

Taking into account that the majority of persons with visual impairments or with other print disabilities live in developing and least-developed countries,

Recognizing that, despite the differences in national copyright laws, the positive impact of new information and communication technologies on the lives of persons with visual impairments or with other print disabilities may be reinforced by an enhanced legal framework at the international level,

Recognizing that many Member States have established limitations and exceptions in their national copyright laws for persons with visual impairments or with other print disabilities, yet there is a continuing shortage of available works in accessible format copies for such persons, and that considerable resources are required for their effort of making works accessible to these persons, and that the lack of possibilities of cross-border exchange of accessible format copies has necessitated duplication of these efforts,

Recognizing both the importance of rightholders' role in making their works accessible to persons with visual impairments or with other print disabilities and the importance of appropriate limitations and exceptions to make works accessible to these persons, particularly when the market is unable to provide such access,

Recognizing the need to maintain a balance between the effective protection of the rights of authors and the larger public interest, particularly education, research and access to information, and that such a balance must facilitate effective and timely access to works for the benefit of persons with visual impairments or with other print disabilities,

Reaffirming the obligations of Contracting Parties under the existing international treaties on the protection of copyright and the importance and flexibility of the three-step test for limitations and exceptions established in Article 9(2) of the Berne Convention for the Protection of Literary and Artistic Works and other international instruments,

Recalling the importance of the Development Agenda recommendations, adopted in 2007 by the General Assembly of the World Intellectual Property Organization (WIPO), which aim to ensure that development considerations form an integral part of the Organization's work,

Recognizing the importance of the international copyright system and desiring to harmonize limitations and exceptions with a view to facilitating access to and use of works by persons with visual impairments or with other print disabilities,

Have agreed as follows:

Article 1   Relation to Other Conventions and Treaties

Nothing in this Treaty shall derogate from any obligations that Contracting Parties have to each other under any other treaties, nor shall it prejudice any rights that a Contracting Party has under any other treaties.

Article 2   Definitions

For the purposes of this Treaty:

(a) 'works' means literary and artistic works within the meaning of Article 2(1) of the Berne Convention for the Protection of Literary and Artistic Works, in the form of text, notation and/or related illustrations, whether published or otherwise made publicly available in any media[1];

(b) 'accessible format copy' means a copy of a work in an alternative manner or form which gives a beneficiary person access to the work, including to permit the person to have access as feasibly and comfortably as a person without visual impairment or other print disability. The accessible format copy is used exclusively by beneficiary persons and it must respect the integrity of the original work, taking due consideration of the changes needed to make the work accessible in the alternative format and of the accessibility needs of the beneficiary persons;

(c) 'authorized entity' means an entity that is authorized or recognized by the government to provide education, instructional training, adaptive reading or information access to beneficiary persons on a non-profit basis. It also includes a government institution or non-profit organization that provides the same services to beneficiary persons as one of its primary activities or institutional obligations[2].

An authorized entity establishes and follows its own practices:

(i) to establish that the persons it serves are beneficiary persons;

(ii) to limit to beneficiary persons and/or authorized entities its distribution and making available of accessible format copies;

(iii) to discourage the reproduction, distribution and making available of unauthorized copies; and

(iv) to maintain due care in, and records of, its handling of copies of works, while respecting the privacy of beneficiary persons in accordance with Article 8.

---

[1] Agreed statement concerning Article 2(a): For the purposes of this Treaty, it is understood that this definition includes such works in audio form, such as audiobooks.

[2] Agreed statement concerning Article 2(c): For the purposes of this Treaty, it is understood that 'entities recognized by the government' may include entities receiving financial support from the government to provide education, instructional training, adaptive reading or information access to beneficiary persons on a non-profit basis.

Article 3   Beneficiary Persons

A beneficiary person is a person who:

(a) is blind;

(b) has a visual impairment or a perceptual or reading disability which cannot be improved to give visual function substantially equivalent to that of a person who has no such impairment or disability and so is unable to read printed works to substantially the same degree as a person without an impairment or disability; or[3]

(c) is otherwise unable, through physical disability, to hold or manipulate a book or to focus or move the eyes to the extent that would be normally acceptable for reading;

regardless of any other disabilities.

Article 4   National Law Limitations and Exceptions Regarding Accessible Format Copies

1. (a) Contracting Parties shall provide in their national copyright laws for a limitation or exception to the right of reproduction, the right of distribution, and the right of making available to the public as provided by the WIPO Copyright Treaty (WCT), to facilitate the availability of works in accessible format copies for beneficiary persons. The limitation or exception provided in national law should permit changes needed to make the work accessible in the alternative format.

   (b) Contracting Parties may also provide a limitation or exception to the right of public performance to facilitate access to works for beneficiary persons.

2. A Contracting Party may fulfill Article 4(1) for all rights identified therein by providing a limitation or exception in its national copyright law such that:

   (a) Authorized entities shall be permitted, without the authorization of the copyright rightholder, to make an accessible format copy of a work, obtain from another authorized entity an accessible format copy, and supply those copies to beneficiary persons by any means, including by non-commercial lending or by electronic communication by wire or wireless means, and undertake any intermediate steps to achieve those objectives, when all of the following conditions are met:

      (i) the authorized entity wishing to undertake said activity has lawful access to that work or a copy of that work;

      (ii) the work is converted to an accessible format copy, which may include any means needed to navigate information in the accessible format, but does not introduce changes other than those needed to make the work accessible to the beneficiary person;

      (iii) such accessible format copies are supplied exclusively to be used by beneficiary persons; and

      (iv) the activity is undertaken on a non-profit basis; and

   (b) A beneficiary person, or someone acting on his or her behalf including a primary caretaker or caregiver, may make an accessible format copy of a work for the personal use of the beneficiary person or otherwise may assist the beneficiary person to make and use accessible format copies where the beneficiary person has lawful access to that work or a copy of that work.

3. A Contracting Party may fulfill Article 4(1) by providing other limitations or exceptions in its national copyright law pursuant to Articles 10 and 11[4].

---

[3] Agreed statement concerning Article 3(b): Nothing in this language implies that 'cannot be improved' requires the use of all possible medical diagnostic procedures and treatments.

[4] Agreed statement concerning Article 4(3): It is understood that this paragraph neither reduces nor extends the scope of applicability of limitations and exceptions permitted under the Berne Convention, as regards the right of translation, with respect to persons with visual impairments or with other print disabilities.

4. A Contracting Party may confine limitations or exceptions under this Article to works which, in the particular accessible format, cannot be obtained commercially under reasonable terms for beneficiary persons in that market. Any Contracting Party availing itself of this possibility shall so declare in a notification deposited with the Director General of WIPO at the time of ratification of, acceptance of or accession to this Treaty or at any time thereafter[5].

5. It shall be a matter for national law to determine whether limitations or exceptions under this Article are subject to remuneration.

Article 5   Cross-Border Exchange of Accessible Format Copies

1. Contracting Parties shall provide that if an accessible format copy is made under a limitation or exception or pursuant to operation of law, that accessible format copy may be distributed or made available by an authorized entity to a beneficiary person or an authorized entity in another Contracting Party[6].

2. A Contracting Party may fulfill Article 5(1) by providing a limitation or exception in its national copyright law such that:

(a) authorized entities shall be permitted, without the authorization of the rightholder, to distribute or make available for the exclusive use of beneficiary persons accessible format copies to an authorized entity in another Contracting Party; and

(b) authorized entities shall be permitted, without the authorization of the rightholder and pursuant to Article 2(c), to distribute or make available accessible format copies to a beneficiary person in another Contracting Party;

provided that prior to the distribution or making available the originating authorized entity did not know or have reasonable grounds to know that the accessible format copy would be used for other than beneficiary persons[7].

3. A Contracting Party may fulfill Article 5(1) by providing other limitations or exceptions in its national copyright law pursuant to Articles 5(4), 10 and 11.

4. (a) When an authorized entity in a Contracting Party receives accessible format copies pursuant to Article 5(1) and that Contracting Party does not have obligations under Article 9 of the Berne Convention, it will ensure, consistent with its own legal system and practices, that the accessible format copies are only reproduced, distributed or made available for the benefit of beneficiary persons in that Contracting Party's jurisdiction.

(b) The distribution and making available of accessible format copies by an authorized entity pursuant to Article 5(1) shall be limited to that jurisdiction unless the Contracting Party is a Party to the WIPO Copyright Treaty or otherwise limits limitations and exceptions implementing this Treaty to the right of distribution and the right of making available to the public to certain special cases which do not conflict with a normal exploitation of the work and do not unreasonably prejudice the legitimate interests of the rightholder[8,9].

(c) Nothing in this Article affects the determination of what constitutes an act of distribution or an act of making available to the public.

5. Nothing in this Treaty shall be used to address the issue of exhaustion of rights.

---

[5] Agreed statement concerning Article 4(4): It is understood that a commercial availability requirement does not prejudge whether or not a limitation or exception under this Article is consistent with the three-step test.

[6] Agreed statement concerning Article 5(1): It is further understood that nothing in this Treaty reduces or extends the scope of exclusive rights under any other treaty.

[7] Agreed statement concerning Article 5(2): It is understood that, to distribute or make available accessible format copies directly to a beneficiary person in another Contracting Party, it may be appropriate for an authorized entity to apply further measures to confirm that the person it is serving is a beneficiary person and to follow its own practices as described in Article 2(c).

[8] Agreed statement concerning Article 5(4)(b): It is understood that nothing in this Treaty requires or implies that a Contracting Party adopt or apply the three-step test beyond its obligations under this instrument or under other international treaties.

[9] Agreed statement concerning Article 5(4)(b): It is understood that nothing in this Treaty creates any obligations for a Contracting Party to ratify or accede to the WCT or to comply with any of its provisions and nothing in this Treaty prejudices any rights, limitations and exceptions contained in the WCT.

Article 6   Importation of Accessible Format Copies

To the extent that the national law of a Contracting Party would permit a beneficiary person, someone acting on his or her behalf, or an authorized entity, to make an accessible format copy of a work, the national law of that Contracting Party shall also permit them to import an accessible format copy for the benefit of beneficiary persons, without the authorization of the rightholder[10].

Article 7   Obligations Concerning Technological Measures

Contracting Parties shall take appropriate measures, as necessary, to ensure that when they provide adequate legal protection and effective legal remedies against the circumvention of effective technological measures, this legal protection does not prevent beneficiary persons from enjoying the limitations and exceptions provided for in this Treaty[11].

Article 8   Respect for Privacy

In the implementation of the limitations and exceptions provided for in this Treaty, Contracting Parties shall endeavor to protect the privacy of beneficiary persons on an equal basis with others.

Article 9   Cooperation to Facilitate Cross-Border Exchange

1. Contracting Parties shall endeavor to foster the cross-border exchange of accessible format copies by encouraging the voluntary sharing of information to assist authorized entities in identifying one another. The International Bureau of WIPO shall establish an information access point for this purpose.

2. Contracting Parties undertake to assist their authorized entities engaged in activities under Article 5 to make information available regarding their practices pursuant to Article 2(c), both through the sharing of information among authorized entities, and through making available information on their policies and practices, including related to cross-border exchange of accessible format copies, to interested parties and members of the public as appropriate.

3. The International Bureau of WIPO is invited to share information, where available, about the functioning of this Treaty.

4. Contracting Parties recognize the importance of international cooperation and its promotion, in support of national efforts for realization of the purpose and objectives of this Treaty[12].

Article 10   General Principles on Implementation

1. Contracting Parties undertake to adopt the measures necessary to ensure the application of this Treaty.

2. Nothing shall prevent Contracting Parties from determining the appropriate method of implementing the provisions of this Treaty within their own legal system and practice[13].

3. Contracting Parties may fulfill their rights and obligations under this Treaty through limitations or exceptions specifically for the benefit of beneficiary persons, other limitations or exceptions, or a combination thereof, within their national legal system and practice. These may include judicial, administrative or regulatory determinations for the benefit of beneficiary persons as to fair practices, dealings or uses to meet their needs consistent with the Contracting Parties' rights and obligations under the Berne Convention, other international treaties, and Article 11.

---

[10] Agreed statement concerning Article 6: It is understood that the Contracting Parties have the same flexibilities set out in Article 4 when implementing their obligations under Article 6.

[11] Agreed statement concerning Article 7: It is understood that authorized entities, in various circumstances, choose to apply technological measures in the making, distribution and making available of accessible format copies and nothing herein disturbs such practices when in accordance with national law.

[12] Agreed statement concerning Article 9: It is understood that Article 9 does not imply mandatory registration for authorized entities nor does it constitute a precondition for authorized entities to engage in activities recognized under this Treaty; but it provides for a possibility for sharing information to facilitate the cross-border exchange of accessible format copies.

[13] Agreed statement concerning Article 10(2): It is understood that when a work qualifies as a work under Article 2(a), including such works in audio form, the limitations and exceptions provided for by this Treaty apply *mutatis mutandis* to related rights as necessary to make the accessible format copy, to distribute it and to make it available to beneficiary persons.

Article 11 General Obligations on Limitations and Exceptions

In adopting measures necessary to ensure the application of this Treaty, a Contracting Party may exercise the rights and shall comply with the obligations that that Contracting Party has under the Berne Convention, the Agreement on Trade-Related Aspects of Intellectual Property Rights and the WIPO Copyright Treaty, including their interpretative agreements so that:

(a) in accordance with Article 9(2) of the Berne Convention, a Contracting Party may permit the reproduction of works in certain special cases provided that such reproduction does not conflict with a normal exploitation of the work and does not unreasonably prejudice the legitimate interests of the author;

(b) in accordance with Article 13 of the Agreement on Trade-Related Aspects of Intellectual Property Rights, a Contracting Party shall confine limitations or exceptions to exclusive rights to certain special cases which do not conflict with a normal exploitation of the work and do not unreasonably prejudice the legitimate interests of the rightholder;

(c) in accordance with Article 10(1) of the WIPO Copyright Treaty, a Contracting Party may provide for limitations of or exceptions to the rights granted to authors under the WCT in certain special cases, that do not conflict with a normal exploitation of the work and do not unreasonably prejudice the legitimate interests of the author;

(d) in accordance with Article 10(2) of the WIPO Copyright Treaty, a Contracting Party shall confine, when applying the Berne Convention, any limitations of or exceptions to rights to certain special cases that do not conflict with a normal exploitation of the work and do not unreasonably prejudice the legitimate interests of the author.

Article 12 Other Limitations and Exceptions

1. Contracting Parties recognize that a Contracting Party may implement in its national law other copyright limitations and exceptions for the benefit of beneficiary persons than are provided by this Treaty having regard to that Contracting Party's economic situation, and its social and cultural needs, in conformity with that Contracting Party's international rights and obligations, and in the case of a least-developed country taking into account its special needs and its particular international rights and obligations and flexibilities thereof.

2. This Treaty is without prejudice to other limitations and exceptions for persons with disabilities provided by national law.

. . .

Done in Marrakesh on the 27th day of June, 2013.

Beijing Treaty on Audiovisual Performances

adopted by the Diplomatic Conference on the Protection of Audiovisual Performances in Beijing, on June 24, 2012

Preamble

The Contracting Parties,

Desiring to develop and maintain the protection of the rights of performers in their audiovisual performances in a manner as effective and uniform as possible,

Recalling the importance of the Development Agenda recommendations, adopted in 2007 by the General Assembly of the Convention Establishing the World Intellectual Property Organization (WIPO), which aim to ensure that development considerations form an integral part of the Organization's work,

Recognizing the need to introduce new international rules in order to provide adequate solutions to the questions raised by economic, social, cultural and technological developments,

Recognizing the profound impact of the development and convergence of information and communication technologies on the production and use of audiovisual performances,

Recognizing the need to maintain a balance between the rights of performers in their audiovisual performances and the larger public interest, particularly education, research and access to information,

Recognizing that the WIPO Performances and Phonograms Treaty (WPPT) done in Geneva on December 20, 1996, does not extend protection to performers in respect of their performances fixed in audiovisual fixations,

Referring to the Resolution concerning Audiovisual Performances adopted by the Diplomatic Conference on Certain Copyright and Neighboring Rights Questions on December 20, 1996,

Have agreed as follows:

Article 1   Relation to Other Conventions and Treaties

(1) Nothing in this Treaty shall derogate from existing obligations that Contracting Parties have to each other under the WPPT or the International Convention for the Protection of Performers, Producers of Phonograms and Broadcasting Organizations done in Rome on October 26, 1961.

(2) Protection granted under this Treaty shall leave intact and shall in no way affect the protection of copyright in literary and artistic works. Consequently, no provision of this Treaty may be interpreted as prejudicing such protection.

(3) This Treaty shall not have any connection with treaties other than the WPPT, nor shall it prejudice any rights and obligations under any other treaties.

Article 2   Definitions

For the purposes of this Treaty:

(a) 'performers' are actors, singers, musicians, dancers, and other persons who act, sing, deliver, declaim, play in, interpret, or otherwise perform literary or artistic works or expressions of folklore;

(b) 'audiovisual fixation' means the embodiment of moving images, whether or not accompanied by sounds or by the representations thereof, from which they can be perceived, reproduced or communicated through a device;

(c) 'broadcasting' means the transmission by wireless means for public reception of sounds or of images or of images and sounds or of the representations thereof; such transmission by satellite is also 'broadcasting'; transmission of encrypted signals is 'broadcasting' where the means for decrypting are provided to the public by the broadcasting organization or with its consent;

(d) 'communication to the public' of a performance means the transmission to the public by any medium, otherwise than by broadcasting, of an unfixed performance, or of a performance fixed in an audiovisual fixation. For the purposes of Article 11, 'communication to the public' includes making a performance fixed in an audiovisual fixation audible or visible or audible and visible to the public.

Article 3   Beneficiaries of Protection

(1) Contracting Parties shall accord the protection granted under this Treaty to performers who are nationals of other Contracting Parties.

(2) Performers who are not nationals of one of the Contracting Parties but who have their habitual residence in one of them shall, for the purposes of this Treaty, be assimilated to nationals of that Contracting Party.

Article 4   National Treatment

(1) Each Contracting Party shall accord to nationals of other Contracting Parties the treatment it accords to its own nationals with regard to the exclusive rights specifically granted in this Treaty and the right to equitable remuneration provided for in Article 11 of this Treaty.

(2) A Contracting Party shall be entitled to limit the extent and term of the protection accorded to nationals of another Contracting Party under paragraph (1), with respect to the rights granted

in Article 11(1) and 11(2) of this Treaty, to those rights that its own nationals enjoy in that other Contracting Party.

(3) The obligation provided for in paragraph (1) does not apply to a Contracting Party to the extent that another Contracting Party makes use of the reservations permitted by Article 11(3) of this Treaty, nor does it apply to a Contracting Party, to the extent that it has made such reservation.

Article 5   Moral Rights

(1) Independently of a performer's economic rights, and even after the transfer of those rights, the performer shall, as regards his live performances or performances fixed in audiovisual fixations, have the right:

    (i)   to claim to be identified as the performer of his performances, except where omission is dictated by the manner of the use of the performance; and

    (ii)   to object to any distortion, mutilation or other modification of his performances that would be prejudicial to his reputation, taking due account of the nature of audiovisual fixations.

(2) The rights granted to a performer in accordance with paragraph (1) shall, after his death, be maintained, at least until the expiry of the economic rights, and shall be exercisable by the persons or institutions authorized by the legislation of the Contracting Party where protection is claimed. However, those Contracting Parties whose legislation, at the moment of their ratification of or accession to this Treaty, does not provide for protection after the death of the performer of all rights set out in the preceding paragraph may provide that some of these rights will, after his death, cease to be maintained.

(3) The means of redress for safeguarding the rights granted under this Article shall be governed by the legislation of the Contracting Party where protection is claimed.

Article 6   Economic Rights of Performers in their Unfixed Performances

Performers shall enjoy the exclusive right of authorizing, as regards their performances:

    (i)   the broadcasting and communication to the public of their unfixed performances except where the performance is already a broadcast performance; and

    (ii)   the fixation of their unfixed performances.

Article 7   Right of Reproduction

Performers shall enjoy the exclusive right of authorizing the direct or indirect reproduction of their performances fixed in audiovisual fixations, in any manner or form.

Article 8   Right of Distribution

(1) Performers shall enjoy the exclusive right of authorizing the making available to the public of the original and copies of their performances fixed in audiovisual fixations through sale or other transfer of ownership.

(2) Nothing in this Treaty shall affect the freedom of Contracting Parties to determine the conditions, if any, under which the exhaustion of the right in paragraph (1) applies after the first sale or other transfer of ownership of the original or a copy of the fixed performance with the authorization of the performer.

Article 9   Right of Rental

(1) Performers shall enjoy the exclusive right of authorizing the commercial rental to the public of the original and copies of their performances fixed in audiovisual fixations as determined in the national law of Contracting Parties, even after distribution of them by, or pursuant to, authorization by the performer.

(2) Contracting Parties are exempt from the obligation of paragraph (1) unless the commercial rental has led to widespread copying of such fixations materially impairing the exclusive right of reproduction of performers.

Article 10 Right of Making Available of Fixed Performances

Performers shall enjoy the exclusive right of authorizing the making available to the public of their performances fixed in audiovisual fixations, by wire or wireless means, in such a way that members of the public may access them from a place and at a time individually chosen by them.

Article 11 Right of Broadcasting and Communication to the Public

(1) Performers shall enjoy the exclusive right of authorizing the broadcasting and communication to the public of their performances fixed in audiovisual fixations.

(2) Contracting Parties may in a notification deposited with the Director General of WIPO declare that, instead of the right of authorization provided for in paragraph (1), they will establish a right to equitable remuneration for the direct or indirect use of performances fixed in audiovisual fixations for broadcasting or for communication to the public. Contracting Parties may also declare that they will set conditions in their legislation for the exercise of the right to equitable remuneration.

(3) Any Contracting Party may declare that it will apply the provisions of paragraphs (1) or (2) only in respect of certain uses, or that it will limit their application in some other way, or that it will not apply the provisions of paragraphs (1) and (2) at all.

Article 12 Transfer of Rights

(1) A Contracting Party may provide in its national law that once a performer has consented to fixation of his or her performance in an audiovisual fixation, the exclusive rights of authorization provided for in Articles 7 to 11 of this Treaty shall be owned or exercised by or transferred to the producer of such audiovisual fixation subject to any contract to the contrary between the performer and the producer of the audiovisual fixation as determined by the national law.

(2) A Contracting Party may require with respect to audiovisual fixations produced under its national law that such consent or contract be in writing and signed by both parties to the contract or by their duly authorized representatives.

(3) Independent of the transfer of exclusive rights described above, national laws or individual, collective or other agreements may provide the performer with the right to receive royalties or equitable remuneration for any use of the performance, as provided for under this Treaty including as regards Articles 10 and 11.

Article 13 Limitations and Exceptions

(1) Contracting Parties may, in their national legislation, provide for the same kinds of limitations or exceptions with regard to the protection of performers as they provide for, in their national legislation, in connection with the protection of copyright in literary and artistic works.

(2) Contracting Parties shall confine any limitations of or exceptions to rights provided for in this Treaty to certain special cases which do not conflict with a normal exploitation of the performance and do not unreasonably prejudice the legitimate interests of the performer.

Article 14 Term of Protection

The term of protection to be granted to performers under this Treaty shall last, at least, until the end of a period of 50 years computed from the end of the year in which the performance was fixed.

Article 15 Obligations concerning Technological Measures

Contracting Parties shall provide adequate legal protection and effective legal remedies against the circumvention of effective technological measures that are used by performers in connection with the exercise of their rights under this Treaty and that restrict acts, in respect of their performances, which are not authorized by the performers concerned or permitted by law.

Article 16 Obligations concerning Rights Management Information

(1) Contracting Parties shall provide adequate and effective legal remedies against any person knowingly performing any of the following acts knowing, or with respect to civil remedies having reasonable grounds to know, that it will induce, enable, facilitate, or conceal an infringement of any right covered by this Treaty:

(i) to remove or alter any electronic rights management information without authority;

(ii) to distribute, import for distribution, broadcast, communicate or make available to the public, without authority, performances or copies of performances fixed in audiovisual fixations knowing that electronic rights management information has been removed or altered without authority.

(2) As used in this Article, 'rights management information' means information which identifies the performer, the performance of the performer, or the owner of any right in the performance, or information about the terms and conditions of use of the performance, and any numbers or codes that represent such information, when any of these items of information is attached to a performance fixed in an audiovisual fixation.

Article 17   Formalities

The enjoyment and exercise of the rights provided for in this Treaty shall not be subject to any formality.

Article 18   Reservations and Notifications

(1) Subject to provisions of Article 11(3), no reservations to this Treaty shall be permitted.

(2) Any notification under Article 11(2) or 19(2) may be made in instruments of ratification or accession, and the effective date of the notification shall be the same as the date of entry into force of this Treaty with respect to the Contracting Party having made the notification. Any such notification may also be made later, in which case the notification shall have effect three months after its receipt by the Director General of WIPO or at any later date indicated in the notification.

Article 19   Application in Time

(1) Contracting Parties shall accord the protection granted under this Treaty to fixed performances that exist at the moment of the entry into force of this Treaty and to all performances that occur after the entry into force of this Treaty for each Contracting Party.

(2) Notwithstanding the provisions of paragraph (1), a Contracting Party may declare in a notification deposited with the Director General of WIPO that it will not apply the provisions of Articles 7 to 11 of this Treaty, or any one or more of those, to fixed performances that existed at the moment of the entry into force of this Treaty for each Contracting Party. In respect of such Contracting Party, other Contracting Parties may limit the application of the said Articles to performances that occurred after the entry into force of this Treaty for that Contracting Party.

(3) The protection provided for in this Treaty shall be without prejudice to any acts committed, agreements concluded or rights acquired before the entry into force of this Treaty for each Contracting Party.

(4) Contracting Parties may in their legislation establish transitional provisions under which any person who, prior to the entry into force of this Treaty, engaged in lawful acts with respect to a performance, may undertake with respect to the same performance acts within the scope of the rights provided for in Articles 5 and 7 to 11 after the entry into force of this Treaty for the respective Contracting Parties.

Article 20   Provisions on Enforcement of Rights

(1) Contracting Parties undertake to adopt, in accordance with their legal systems, the measures necessary to ensure the application of this Treaty.

(2) Contracting Parties shall ensure that enforcement procedures are available under their law so as to permit effective action against any act of infringement of rights covered by this Treaty, including expeditious remedies to prevent infringements and remedies which constitute a deterrent to further infringements.

. . .

Agreed Statements Concerning the Beijing Treaty on Audiovisual Performances

adopted by the Diplomatic Conference on the Protection of Audiovisual Performances in Beijing, on June 24, 2012

Agreed statement concerning Article 1: It is understood that nothing in this Treaty affects any rights or obligations under the WIPO Performances and Phonograms Treaty (WPPT) or their interpretation and it is further understood that paragraph 3 does not create any obligations for a Contracting Party to this Treaty to ratify or accede to the WPPT or to comply with any of its provisions.

Agreed statement concerning Article 1(3): It is understood that Contracting Parties who are members of the World Trade Organization (WTO) acknowledge all the principles and objectives of the Agreement on Trade-Related Aspects of Intellectual Property Rights (TRIPS Agreement) and understand that nothing in this Treaty affects the provisions of the TRIPS Agreement, including, but not limited to, the provisions relating to anti-competitive practices.

Agreed statement concerning Article 2(a): It is understood that the definition of 'performers' includes those who perform a literary or artistic work that is created or first fixed in the course of a performance.

Agreed statement concerning Article 2(b): It is hereby confirmed that the definition of 'audiovisual fixation' contained in Article 2(b) is without prejudice to Article 2(c) of the WPPT.

Agreed statement concerning Article 5: For the purposes of this Treaty and without prejudice to any other treaty, it is understood that, considering the nature of audiovisual fixations and their production and distribution, modifications of a performance that are made in the normal course of exploitation of the performance, such as editing, compression, dubbing, or formatting, in existing or new media or formats, and that are made in the course of a use authorized by the performer, would not in themselves amount to modifications within the meaning of Article 5(1)(ii). Rights under Article 5(1)(ii) are concerned only with changes that are objectively prejudicial to the performer's reputation in a substantial way. It is also understood that the mere use of new or changed technology or media, as such, does not amount to modification within the meaning of Article 5(1)(ii).

Agreed statement concerning Article 7: The reproduction right, as set out in Article 7, and the exceptions permitted thereunder through Article 13, fully apply in the digital environment, in particular to the use of performances in digital form. It is understood that the storage of a protected performance in digital form in an electronic medium constitutes a reproduction within the meaning of this Article.

Agreed statement concerning Articles 8 and 9: As used in these Articles, the expression 'original and copies,' being subject to the right of distribution and the right of rental under the said Articles, refers exclusively to fixed copies that can be put into circulation as tangible objects.

Agreed statement concerning Article 13: The Agreed statement concerning Article 10 (on Limitations and Exceptions) of the WIPO Copyright Treaty (WCT) is applicable *mutatis mutandis* also to Article 13 (on Limitations and Exceptions) of the Treaty.

Agreed statement concerning Article 15 as it relates to Article 13: It is understood that nothing in this Article prevents a Contracting Party from adopting effective and necessary measures to ensure that a beneficiary may enjoy limitations and exceptions provided in that Contracting Party's national law, in accordance with Article 13, where technological measures have been applied to an audiovisual performance and the beneficiary has legal access to that performance, in circumstances such as where appropriate and effective measures have not been taken by rights holders in relation to that performance to enable the beneficiary to enjoy the limitations and exceptions under that Contracting Party's national law. Without prejudice to the legal protection of an audiovisual work in which a performance is fixed, it is further understood that the obligations under Article 15 are not applicable to performances unprotected or no longer protected under the national law giving effect to this Treaty.

Agreed statement concerning Article 15: The expression 'technological measures used by performers' should, as this is the case regarding the WPPT, be construed broadly, referring also to those acting on behalf of performers, including their representatives, licensees or assignees, including producers, service providers, and persons engaged in communication or broadcasting using performances on the basis of due authorization.

Agreed statement concerning Article 16: The Agreed statement concerning Article 12 (on Obligations concerning Rights Management Information) of the WCT is applicable *mutatis mutandis* also to Article 16 (on Obligations concerning Rights Management Information) of the Treaty.

Part B

Trade Marks and Related Rights

B1. UNITED KINGDOM

Trade Marks Act 1994*

(1994, c. 26)

An Act to make new provision for registered trade marks, implementing Council Directive No. 89/104/EEC of 21st December 1988 to approximate the laws of the Member States relating to trade marks; to make provision in connection with Council Regulation (EC) No. 40/94 of 20th December 1993 on the Community trade mark; to give effect to the Madrid Protocol Relating to the International Registration of Marks of 27th June 1989, and to certain provisions of the Paris Convention for the Protection of Industrial Property of 20th March 1883, as revised and amended; and for connected purposes.   [21 July 1994]

Arrangement of Sections

* **Editor's Note:** Contains amendments effected by *Designs and International Trade Marks (Amendments etc.) (EU Exit) Regulations 2019*, *Intellectual Property (Exhaustion of Rights) (EU Exit) Regulations* 2019, and *Trade Marks (Amendment etc.) (EU Exit) Regulations 2019*. By virtue of the *European Union (Withdrawal Agreement) Act 2020*, these amendments take effect on 'IP completion day', which is defined to be 31 December 2020 at 11:00pm.

PART I REGISTERED TRADE MARKS

Introductory

1 Trade marks

(1) In this Act 'trade mark' means any sign which is capable—

(a) of being represented in the register in a manner which enables the registrar and other competent authorities and the public to determine the clear and precise subject matter of the protection afforded to the proprietor, and

(b) of distinguishing goods or services of one undertaking from those of other undertakings.

A trade mark may, in particular, consist of words (including personal names), designs, letters, numerals, colours, sounds or the shape of goods or their packaging.

(2) References in this Act to a trade mark include, unless the context otherwise requires, references to a collective mark (see section 49) or certification mark (see section 50).

2 Registered trade marks

(1) A registered trade mark is a property right obtained by the registration of the trade mark under this Act and the proprietor of a registered trade mark has the rights and remedies provided by this Act.

(2) No proceedings lie to prevent or recover damages for the infringement of an unregistered trade mark as such; but nothing in this Act affects the law relating to passing off.

Grounds for refusal of registration

3 Absolute grounds for refusal of registration

(1) The following shall not be registered—

(a) signs which do not satisfy the requirements of section 1(1),

(b) trade marks which are devoid of any distinctive character,

(c) trade marks which consist exclusively of signs or indications which may serve, in trade, to designate the kind, quality, quantity, intended purpose, value, geographical origin, the time of production of goods or of rendering of services, or other characteristics of goods or services,

(d) trade marks which consist exclusively of signs or indications which have become customary in the current language or in the *bona fide* and established practices of the trade:

Provided that, a trade mark shall not be refused registration by virtue of paragraph (b), (c) or (d) above if, before the date of application for registration, it has in fact acquired a distinctive character as a result of the use made of it.

(2) A sign shall not be registered as a trade mark if it consists exclusively of—

(a) the shape, or another characteristic, which results from the nature of the goods themselves,

(b) the shape, or another characteristic, of goods which is necessary to obtain a technical result, or

(c) the shape, or another characteristic, which gives substantial value to the goods.

(3) A trade mark shall not be registered if it is—

(a) contrary to public policy or to accepted principles of morality, or

(b) of such a nature as to deceive the public (for instance as to the nature, quality or geographical origin of the goods or service).

(4) A trade mark shall not be registered if or to the extent that its use is prohibited in the United Kingdom by any enactment or rule of law other than law relating to trade marks.

(4A) A trade mark is not to be registered if its registration is prohibited by or under—

(a) any enactment or rule of law, or

(c) any international agreement to which the United Kingdom is a party, providing for the protection of designations of origin or geographical indications.

(4C) A trade mark is not to be registered if it—

(a) consists of, or reproduces in its essential elements, an earlier plant variety denomination registered as mentioned in subsection (4D), and

(b) is in respect of plant varieties of the same or closely related species.

(4D) Subsection (4C)(a) refers to registration in accordance with any—

(a) enactment or rule of law, or

(c) international agreement to which the United Kingdom is a party,

providing for the protection of plant variety rights.

(5) A trade mark shall not be registered in the cases specified, or referred to, in section 4 (specially protected emblems).

(6) A trade mark shall not be registered if or to the extent that the application is made in bad faith.

4   Specially protected emblems

(1) A trade mark which consists of or contains—

(a) the Royal arms, or any of the principal armorial bearings of the Royal arms, or any insignia or device so nearly resembling the Royal arms or any such armorial bearing as to be likely to be mistaken for them or it,

(b) a representation of the Royal crown or any of the Royal flags,

(c) a representation of Her Majesty or any member of the Royal family, or any colourable imitation thereof, or

(d) words, letters or devices likely to lead persons to think that the applicant either has or recently has had Royal patronage or authorisation,

shall not be registered unless it appears to the registrar that consent has been given by or on behalf of Her Majesty or, as the case may be, the relevant member of the Royal family.

(2) A trade mark which consists of or contains a representation of—

(a) the national flag of the United Kingdom (commonly known as the Union Jack), or

(b) the flag of England, Wales, Scotland, Northern Ireland or the Isle of Man,

shall not be registered if it appears to the registrar that the use of the trade mark would be misleading or grossly offensive.

Provision may be made by rules identifying the flags to which paragraph (b) applies.

(3) A trade mark shall not be registered in the cases specified in—section 57 (national emblems, &c. of Convention countries), or section 58 (emblems, &c. of certain international organisations).

(4) Provision may be made by rules prohibiting in such cases as may be prescribed the registration of a trade mark which consists of or contains—

(a) arms to which a person is entitled by virtue of a grant of arms by the Crown, or

(b) insignia so nearly resembling such arms as to be likely to be mistaken for them,

unless it appears to the registrar that consent has been given by or on behalf of that person.

Where such a mark is registered, nothing in this Act shall be construed as authorising its use in any way contrary to the laws of arms.

(5) A trade mark which consists of or contains a controlled representation within the meaning of the Olympic Symbol etc. (Protection) Act 1995 shall not be registered unless it appears to the registrar—

(a) that the application is made by the person for the time being appointed under section 1(2) of the Olympic Symbol etc. (Protection) Act 1995 (power of Secretary of State to appoint a person as the proprietor of the Olympics association right), or

(b) that consent has been given by or on behalf of the person mentioned in paragraph (a) above.

5   Relative grounds for refusal of registration

(1) A trade mark shall not be registered if it is identical with an earlier trade mark and the goods or services for which the trade mark is applied for are identical with the goods or services for which the earlier trade mark is protected.

(2) A trade mark shall not be registered if—

(a) it is identical with an earlier trade mark and is to be registered for goods or services similar to those for which the earlier trade mark is protected, or

(b) it is similar to an earlier trade mark and is to be registered for goods or services identical with or similar to those for which the earlier trade mark is protected,

there exists a likelihood of confusion on the part of the public, which includes the likelihood of association with the earlier trade mark.

(3) A trade mark which—

    (a) is identical with or similar to an earlier trade mark

shall not be registered if, or to the extent that, the earlier trade mark has a reputation in the United Kingdom and the use of the later mark without due cause would take unfair advantage of, or be detrimental to, the distinctive character or the repute of the earlier trade mark.

(3A) Subsection (3) applies irrespective of whether the goods and services for which the trade mark is to be registered are identical with, similar to or not similar to those for which the earlier trade mark is protected.

(4) A trade mark shall not be registered if, or to the extent that, its use in the United Kingdom is liable to be prevented—

    (a) by virtue of any rule of law (in particular, the law of passing off) protecting an unregistered trade mark or other sign used in the course of trade, where the condition in subsection (4A) is met,

    (aa) by virtue of any enactment or rule of law, providing for protection of designations of origin or geographical indications, where the condition in subsection (4B) is met, or

    (b) by virtue of an earlier right other than those referred to in subsections (1) to (3) or paragraph (a) or (aa) above, in particular by virtue of the law of copyright, or the law relating to industrial property rights.

A person thus entitled to prevent the use of a trade mark is referred to in this Act as the proprietor of an 'earlier right' in relation to the trade mark.

(4A) The condition mentioned in subsection (4)(a) is that the rights to the unregistered trade mark or other sign were acquired prior to the date of application for registration of the trade mark or date of the priority claimed for that application.

(4B) The condition mentioned in subsection 4(aa) is that—

    (a) an application for a designation of origin or a geographical indication has been submitted prior to the date of application for registration of the trade mark or the date of the priority claimed for that application, and

    (b) the designation of origin or (as the case may be) geographical indication is subsequently registered.

(5) Nothing in this section prevents the registration of a trade mark where the proprietor of the earlier trade mark or other earlier right consents to the registration.

(6) Where an agent or representative ('R') of the proprietor of a trade mark applies, without the proprietor's consent, for the registration of the trade mark in R's own name, the application is to be refused unless R justifies that action.

5A   Grounds for refusal relating to only some of the goods or services

Where grounds for refusal of an application for registration of a trade mark exist in respect of only some of the goods or services in respect of which the trade mark is applied for, the application is to be refused in relation to those goods and services only.

6   Meaning of 'earlier trade mark'

(1) In this Act an 'earlier trade mark' means—

    (a) a registered trade mark or international trade mark (UK), which has a date of application for registration earlier than that of the trade mark in question, taking account (where appropriate) of the priorities claimed in respect of the trade marks,

    (aa) a comparable trade mark (EU) or a trade mark registered pursuant to an application made under paragraph 25 of Schedule 2A which has a valid claim to seniority of an earlier registered trade mark or protected international trade mark (UK) even where the earlier trade mark has been surrendered or its registration has expired,

    (ab) a comparable trade mark (IR) or a trade mark registered pursuant to an application made under paragraph 28, 29 or 33 of Schedule 2B which has a valid claim to seniority of an earlier registered trade mark or protected international trade mark (UK) even where the earlier trade mark has been surrendered or its registration has expired,

    (ba) a registered trade mark or international trade mark (UK) which—

  (i) prior to exit day has been converted from a European Union trade mark or international trade mark (EC) which itself had a valid claim to seniority of an earlier registered trade mark or protected international trade mark (UK) even where the earlier trade mark has been surrendered or its registration has expired, and

  (ii) accordingly has the same claim to seniority, or

 (c) a trade mark which, at the date of application for registration of the trade mark in question or (where appropriate) of the priority claimed in respect of the application, was entitled to protection under the Paris Convention or the WTO agreement as a well known trade mark.

(1A) In subsection (1), 'protected international trade mark (UK)' has the same meaning as in the Trade Marks (International Registration) Order 2008.

(2) References in this Act to an earlier trade mark include a trade mark in respect of which an application for registration has been made and which, if registered, would be an earlier trade mark by virtue of subsection (1)(a), subject to its being so registered (taking account of subsection (2C)).

(2A) References in this Act to an earlier trade mark include a trade mark in respect of which an application for registration has been made pursuant to paragraph 25 of Schedule 2A and which if registered would be an earlier trade mark by virtue of subsection (1)(aa), subject to its being so registered.

(2B) References in this Act to an earlier trade mark include a trade mark in respect of which an application for registration has been made pursuant to paragraph 28, 29 or 33 of Schedule 2B and which if registered would be an earlier trade mark by virtue of subsection (1)(ab), subject to its being so registered.

(2C) Where an application for registration of a trade mark has been made pursuant to paragraph 25 of Schedule 2A or paragraph 28, 29 or 33 of Schedule 2B, subsection (1)(a) is to apply as if the date of application for registration of the trade mark were—

 (a) in the case of an application made pursuant to paragraph 25 of Schedule 2A, the relevant date referred to in paragraph 25(2) in respect of that application;

 (b) in the case of an application made pursuant to paragraph 28 of Schedule 2B, the relevant date referred to in paragraph 28(2) in respect of that application (taking account of paragraph 28(5));

 (c) in the case of an application made pursuant to paragraph 29 of Schedule 2B, the relevant date referred to in paragraph 29(2) in respect of that application (taking account of paragraph 29(4));

 (d) in the case of an application made pursuant to paragraph 33 of Schedule 2B, the relevant date referred to in paragraph 33(2) or (3) (as the case may be) in respect of that application (taking account of paragraph 33(4)).

6A Raising of relative grounds in opposition proceedings in case of non-use

(1) This section applies where—

 (a) an application for registration of a trade mark has been published,

 (b) there is an earlier trade mark of a kind falling within section 6(1)(a), (aa) or (ba) in relation to which the conditions set out in section 5(1), (2) or (3) obtain, and

 (c) the registration procedure for the earlier trade mark was completed before the start of the relevant period.

(1A) In this section 'the relevant period' means the period of 5 years ending with the date of the application for registration mentioned in subsection (1)(a) or (where applicable) the date of the priority claimed for that application.

(2) In opposition proceedings, the registrar shall not refuse to register the trade mark by reason of the earlier trade mark unless the use conditions are met.

(3) The use conditions are met if—

 (a) within the relevant period the earlier trade mark has been put to genuine use in the United Kingdom by the proprietor or with his consent in relation to the goods or services for which it is registered, or

 (b) the earlier trade mark has not been so used, but there are proper reasons for non-use.

(4) For these purposes—

    (a) use of a trade mark includes use in a form (the 'variant form') differing in elements which do not alter the distinctive character of the mark in the form in which it was registered (regardless of whether or not the trade mark in the variant form is also registered in the name of the proprietor), and

    (b) use in the United Kingdom includes affixing the trade mark to goods or to the packaging of goods in the United Kingdom solely for export purposes.

(6) Where an earlier trade mark satisfies the use conditions in respect of some only of the goods or services for which it is registered, it shall be treated for the purposes of this section as if it were registered only in respect of those goods or services.

(7) Nothing in this section affects—

    (a) the refusal of registration on the grounds mentioned in section 3 (absolute grounds for refusal) or section 5(4) (relative grounds of refusal on the basis of an earlier right), or

    (b) the making of an application for a declaration of invalidity under section 47(2) (application on relative grounds where no consent to registration).

7 Raising of relative grounds in case of honest concurrent use

(1) This section applies where on an application for the registration of a trade mark it appears to the registrar—

    (a) that there is an earlier trade mark in relation to which the conditions set out in section 5(1), (2) or (3) obtain, or

    (b) that there is an earlier right in relation to which the condition set out in section 5(4) is satisfied,

but the applicant shows to the satisfaction of the registrar that there has been honest concurrent use of the trade mark for which registration is sought.

(2) In that case the registrar shall not refuse the application by reason of the earlier trade mark or other earlier right unless objection on that ground is raised in opposition proceedings by the proprietor of that earlier trade mark or other earlier right.

(3) For the purposes of this section 'honest concurrent use' means such use in the United Kingdom, by the applicant or with his consent, as would formerly have amounted to honest concurrent use for the purposes of section 12(2) of the Trade Marks Act 1938.

(4) Nothing in this section affects—

    (a) the refusal of registration on the grounds mentioned in section 3 (absolute grounds for refusal), or

    (b) the making of an application for a declaration of invalidity under section 47(2) (application on relative grounds, where no consent to registration).

(5) This section does not apply when there is an order in force under section 8 below.

   . . .

Effects of registered trade mark

9 Rights conferred by registered trade mark

(1) The proprietor of a registered trade mark has exclusive rights in the trade mark which are infringed by use of the trade mark in the United Kingdom without his consent.

   The acts amounting to infringement, if done without the consent of the proprietor, are specified in subsections (1) to (3) of section 10.

(1A) See subsection (3B) of section 10 for provision about certain other acts amounting to infringement of a registered trade mark.

(1B) Subsection (1) is without prejudice to the rights of proprietors acquired before the date of filing of the application for registration or (where applicable) the date of the priority claimed in respect of that application.

(2) References in this Act to the infringement of a registered trade mark are to any infringement of the rights of the proprietor such as is mentioned in subsection (1) or (1A).

(3) The rights of the proprietor have effect from the date of registration (which in accordance with section 40(3) is the date of filing of the application for registration): Provided that—

    (a) no infringement proceedings may be begun before the date on which the trade mark is in fact registered; and

    (b) no offence under section 92 (unauthorised use of trade mark, &c. in relation to goods) is committed by anything done before the date of publication of the registration.

10 Infringement of registered trade mark

(1) A person infringes a registered trade mark if he uses in the course of trade a sign which is identical with the trade mark in relation to goods or services which are identical with those for which it is registered.

(2) A person infringes a registered trade mark if he uses in the course of trade a sign where because—

    (a) the sign is identical with the trade mark and is used in relation to goods or services similar to those for which the trade mark is registered, or

    (b) the sign is similar to the trade mark and is used in relation to goods or services identical with or similar to those for which the trade mark is registered,

there exists a likelihood of confusion on the part of the public, which includes the likelihood of association with the trade mark.

(3) A person infringes a registered trade mark if he uses in the course of trade, in relation to goods or services, a sign which—

    (a) is identical with or similar to the trade mark,

where the trade mark has a reputation in the United Kingdom and the use of the sign, being without due cause, takes unfair advantage of, or is detrimental to, the distinctive character or the repute of the trade mark.

(3A) Subsection (3) applies irrespective of whether the goods and services in relation to which the sign is used are identical with, similar to or not similar to those for which the trade mark is registered.

(3B) Where the risk exists that the packaging, labels, tags, security or authenticity features or devices, or any other means to which the trade mark is affixed could be used in relation to goods or services and that use would constitute an infringement of the rights of the proprietor of the trade mark, a person infringes a registered trade mark if the person carries out in the course of trade any of the following acts—

    (a) affixing a sign identical with, or similar to, the trade mark on packaging, labels, tags, security or authenticity features or devices, or any other means to which the mark may be affixed; or

    (b) offering or placing on the market, or stocking for those purposes, or importing or exporting, packaging, labels, tags, security or authenticity features or devices, or any other means to which the mark is affixed.

(4) For the purposes of this section a person uses a sign if, in particular, he—

    (a) affixes it to goods or the packaging thereof,

    (b) offers or exposes goods for sale, puts them on the market or stocks them for those purposes under the sign, or offers or supplies services under the sign;

    (c) imports or exports goods under the sign;

    (ca) uses the sign as a trade or company name or part of a trade or company name;

    (d) uses the sign on business papers and in advertising; or

    (e) uses the sign in comparative advertising in a manner that is contrary to the Business Protection from Misleading Marketing Regulations 2008.

10A Right to prevent goods entering the UK without being released for free circulation

(1) The proprietor of a registered trade mark is entitled to prevent third parties from bringing goods into the United Kingdom in the course of trade without being released for free circulation if they are goods for which the trade mark is registered which—

    (a) come from outside the customs territory of the United Kingdom; and

    (b) bear without authorisation a sign which is identical with the trade mark or cannot be distinguished in its essential aspects from the trade mark.

(2) In subsection (1) the reference to goods for which the trade mark is registered includes a reference to the packaging of goods for which the trade mark is registered.

(3) Subsection (1) is without prejudice to the rights of proprietors acquired before the date of application for registration of the trade mark, or (where applicable) the date of the priority claimed in respect of that application.

(4) The entitlement of the proprietor under subsection (1) is to lapse if—

(a) proceedings are initiated in accordance with the European Customs Enforcement Regulation to determine whether the trade mark has been infringed; and

(b) during those proceedings evidence is provided by the declarant or the holder of the goods that the proprietor of the trade mark is not entitled to prohibit the placing of the goods on the market in the country of final destination.

(5) References in this Act to the 'European Customs Enforcement Regulation' are references to Regulation (EU) No 608/2013 of the European Parliament and of the Council of 12 June 2013 concerning customs enforcement of intellectual property rights as amended from time to time.

10B Prohibition on the use of a trade mark registered in the name of an agent or representative

(1) Subsection (2) applies where a trade mark is registered in the name of an agent or representative of a person ('P') who is the proprietor of the trade mark, without P's consent.

(2) Unless the agent or representative justifies the action mentioned in subsection (1), P may do either or both of the following—

(a) prevent the use of the trade mark by the agent or representative (notwithstanding the rights conferred by this Act in relation to a registered trade mark);

(b) apply for the rectification of the register so as to substitute P's name as the proprietor of the registered trade mark.

11 Limits on effect of registered trade mark

(1) A registered trade mark is not infringed by the use of a later registered trade mark where that later registered trade mark would not be declared invalid pursuant to section 47(2A) or (2G) or section 48(1).

(1B) Where subsection (1) applies, the later registered trade mark is not infringed by the use of the earlier trade mark even though the earlier trade mark may no longer be invoked against the later registered trade mark.

(2) A registered trade mark is not infringed by—

(a) the use by an individual of his own name or address,

(b) the use of signs or indications which are not distinctive or which concern the kind, quality, quantity, intended purpose, value, geographical origin, the time of production of goods or of rendering of services, or other characteristics of goods or services, or

(c) the use of the trade mark for the purpose of identifying or referring to goods or services as those of the proprietor of that trade mark, in particular where that use is necessary to indicate the intended purpose of a product or service (in particular, as accessories or spare parts),

provided the use is in accordance with honest practices in industrial or commercial matters.

(3) A registered trade mark is not infringed by the use in the course of trade in a particular locality of an earlier right which applies only in that locality.

For this purpose an 'earlier right' means an unregistered trade mark or other sign continuously used in relation to goods or services by a person or a predecessor in title of his from a date prior to whichever is the earlier of—

(a) the use of the first-mentioned trade mark in relation to those goods or services by the proprietor or a predecessor in title of his, or

(b) the registration of the first-mentioned trade mark in respect of those goods or services in the name of the proprietor or a predecessor in title of his;

and an earlier right shall be regarded as applying in a locality if, or to the extent that, its use in that locality is protected by virtue of any rule of law (in particular, the law of passing off).

11A   Non-use as defence in infringement proceedings

(1) The proprietor of a trade mark is entitled to prohibit the use of a sign only to the extent that the registration of the trade mark is not liable to be revoked pursuant to section 46(1)(a) or (b) (revocation on basis of non-use) at the date the action for infringement is brought.

(2) Subsection (3) applies in relation to an action for infringement of a registered trade mark where the registration procedure for the trade mark was completed before the start of the period of five years ending with the date the action is brought.

(3) If the defendant so requests, the proprietor of the trade mark must furnish proof—

    (a) that during the five-year period preceding the date the action for infringement is brought, the trade mark has been put to genuine use in the United Kingdom by or with the consent of the proprietor in relation to the goods and services for which it is registered and which are cited as justification for the action, or

    (b) that there are proper reasons for non-use.

(4) Nothing in subsections (2) and (3) overrides any provision of section 46, as applied by subsection (1) (including the words from 'Provided that' to the end of subsection (3)).

12   Exhaustion of rights conferred by registered trade mark

(1) A registered trade mark is not infringed by the use of the trade mark in relation to goods which have been put on the market in the United Kingdom or the European Economic Area under that trade mark by the proprietor or with his consent.

(2) Subsection (1) does not apply where there exist legitimate reasons for the proprietor to oppose further dealings in the goods (in particular, where the condition of the goods has been changed or impaired after they have been put on the market).

13   Registration subject to disclaimer or limitation

(1) An applicant for registration of a trade mark, or the proprietor of a registered trade mark, may—

    (a) disclaim any right to the exclusive use of any specified element of the trade mark, or

    (b) agree that the rights conferred by the registration shall be subject to a specified territorial or other limitation;

and where the registration of a trade mark is subject to a disclaimer or limitation, the rights conferred by section 9 (rights conferred by registered trade mark) are restricted accordingly.

(2) Provision shall be made by rules as to the publication and entry in the register of a disclaimer or limitation.

Infringement proceedings

14   Action for infringement

(1) An infringement of a registered trade mark is actionable by the proprietor of the trade mark.

(2) In an action for infringement all such relief by way of damages, injunctions, accounts or otherwise is available to him as is available in respect of the infringement of any other property right.

15   Order for erasure, &c. of offending sign

(1) Where a person is found to have infringed a registered trade mark, the court may make an order requiring him—

    (a) to cause the offending sign to be erased, removed or obliterated from any infringing goods, material or articles in his possession, custody or control, or

    (b) if it is not reasonably practicable for the offending sign to be erased, removed or obliterated, to secure the destruction of the infringing goods, material or articles in question.

(2) If an order under subsection (1) is not complied with, or it appears to the court likely that such an order would not be complied with, the court may order that the infringing goods, material or articles be delivered to such person as the court may direct for erasure, removal or obliteration of the sign, or for destruction, as the case may be.

16　Order for delivery up of infringing goods, material or articles

(1)　The proprietor of a registered trade mark may apply to the court for an order for the delivery up to him, or such other person as the court may direct, of any infringing goods, material or articles which a person has in his possession, custody or control in the course of a business.

(2)　An application shall not be made after the end of the period specified in section 18 (period after which remedy of delivery up not available); and no order shall be made unless the court also makes, or it appears to the court that there are grounds for making, an order under section 19 (order as to disposal of infringing goods, &c.).

(3)　A person to whom any infringing goods, material or articles are delivered up in pursuance of an order under this section shall, if an order under section 19 is not made, retain them pending the making of an order, or the decision not to make an order, under that section.

(4)　Nothing in this section affects any other power of the court.

17　Meaning of 'infringing goods, material or articles'

(1)　In this Act the expressions 'infringing goods', 'infringing material' and 'infringing articles' shall be construed as follows.

(2)　Goods are 'infringing goods', in relation to a registered trade mark, if they or their packaging bear a sign identical or similar to that mark and—

(a)　the application of the sign to the goods or their packaging was an infringement of the registered trade mark, or

(b)　the goods are proposed to be imported into the United Kingdom and the application of the sign in the United Kingdom to them or their packaging would be an infringement of the registered trade mark, or

(c)　the sign has otherwise been used in relation to the goods in such a way as to infringe the registered trade mark.

(3)　Nothing in subsection (2) shall be construed as affecting the importation of goods which may lawfully be imported into the United Kingdom by virtue of anything which forms part of retained EU law as a result of section 3 or 4 of the European Union (Withdrawal) Act 2018.

(4)　Material is 'infringing material', in relation to a registered trade mark if it bears a sign identical or similar to that mark and either—

(a)　it is used for labelling or packaging goods, as a business paper, or for advertising goods or services, in such a way as to infringe the registered trade mark, or

(b)　it is intended to be so used and such use would infringe the registered trade mark.

(5)　'Infringing articles', in relation to a registered trade mark, means articles—

(a)　which are specifically designed or adapted for making copies of a sign identical or similar to that mark, and

(b)　which a person has in his possession, custody or control, knowing or having reason to believe that they have been or are to be used to produce infringing goods or material.

18　Period after which remedy of delivery up not available

(1)　An application for an order under section 16 (order for delivery up of infringing goods, material or articles) may not be made after the end of the period of six years from—

(a)　in the case of infringing goods, the date on which the trade mark was applied to the goods or their packaging,

(b)　in the case of infringing material, the date on which the trade mark was applied to the material, or

(c)　in the case of infringing articles, the date on which they were made, except as mentioned in the following provisions.

(2)　If during the whole or part of that period the proprietor of the registered trade mark—

(a)　is under a disability, or

(b)　is prevented by fraud or concealment from discovering the facts entitling him to apply for an order, an application may be made at any time before the end of the period of six years from the date on which he ceased to be under a disability or, as the case may be, could with reasonable diligence have discovered those facts.

    (3) In subsection (2) 'disability'—

        (a) in England and Wales, has the same meaning as in the Limitation Act 1980;

        (b) in Scotland, means legal disability within the meaning of the Prescription and Limitation (Scotland) Act 1973;

        (c) in Northern Ireland, has the same meaning as in the Limitation (Northern Ireland) Order 1989.

. . .

Unjustified Threats

21   Threats of infringement proceedings

    (1) A communication contains a 'threat of infringement proceedings' if a reasonable person in the position of a recipient would understand from the communication that—

        (a) a registered trade mark exists, and

        (b) a person intends to bring proceedings (whether in a court in the United Kingdom or elsewhere) against another person for infringement of the registered trade mark by—

           (i) an act done in the United Kingdom, or

           (ii) an act which, if done, would be done in the United Kingdom.

    (2) References in this section and in section 21C to a 'recipient' include, in the case of a communication directed to the public or a section of the public, references to a person to whom the communication is directed.

21A   Actionable threats

    (1) Subject to subsections (2) to (6), a threat of infringement proceedings made by any person is actionable by any person aggrieved by the threat.

    (2) A threat of infringement proceedings is not actionable if the infringement is alleged to consist of—

        (a) applying, or causing another person to apply, a sign to goods or their packaging,

        (b) importing, for disposal, goods to which, or to the packaging of which, a sign has been applied, or

        (c) supplying services under a sign.

    (3) A threat of infringement proceedings is not actionable if the infringement is alleged to consist of an act which, if done, would constitute an infringement of a kind mentioned in subsection (2)(a), (b) or (c).

    (4) A threat of infringement proceedings is not actionable if the threat—

        (a) is made to a person who has done, or intends to do, an act mentioned in subsection (2)(a) or (b) in relation to goods or their packaging, and

        (b) is a threat of proceedings for an infringement alleged to consist of doing anything else in relation to those goods or their packaging.

    (5) A threat of infringement proceedings is not actionable if the threat—

        (a) is made to a person who has done, or intends to do, an act mentioned in subsection (2)(c) in relation to services, and

        (b) is a threat of proceedings for an infringement alleged to consist of doing anything else in relation to those services.

    (6) A threat of infringement proceedings which is not an express threat is not actionable if it is contained in a permitted communication.

    (7) In sections 21C and 21D 'an actionable threat' means a threat of infringement proceedings that is actionable in accordance with this section.

21B   Permitted communications

    (1) For the purposes of section 21A(6), a communication containing a threat of infringement proceedings is a 'permitted communication' if—

(a) the communication, so far as it contains information that relates to the threat, is made for a permitted purpose;

(b) all of the information that relates to the threat is information that—

    (i)   is necessary for that purpose (see subsection (5)(a) to (c) for some examples of necessary information), and

    (ii) the person making the communication reasonably believes is true.

(2) Each of the following is a 'permitted purpose'—

(a) giving notice that a registered trade mark exists;

(b) discovering whether, or by whom, a registered trade mark has been infringed by an act mentioned in section 21A(2)(a), (b) or (c);

(c) giving notice that a person has a right in or under a registered trade mark, where another person's awareness of the right is relevant to any proceedings that may be brought in respect of the registered trade mark.

(3) The court may, having regard to the nature of the purposes listed in subsection (2)(a) to (c), treat any other purpose as a 'permitted purpose' if it considers that it is in the interests of justice to do so.

(4) But the following may not be treated as a 'permitted purpose'—

(a) requesting a person to cease using, in the course of trade, a sign in relation to goods or services,

(b) requesting a person to deliver up or destroy goods, or

(c) requesting a person to give an undertaking relating to the use of a sign in relation to goods or services.

(5) If any of the following information is included in a communication made for a permitted purpose, it is information that is 'necessary for that purpose' (see subsection (1)(b)(i))—

(a) a statement that a registered trade mark exists and is in force or that an application for the registration of a trade mark has been made;

(b) details of the registered trade mark, or of a right in or under the registered trade mark, which—

    (i)   are accurate in all material respects, and

    (ii) are not misleading in any material respect; and

(c) information enabling the identification of the goods or their packaging, or the services, in relation to which it is alleged that the use of a sign constitutes an infringement of the registered trade mark.

21C   Remedies and defences

(1) Proceedings in respect of an actionable threat may be brought against the person who made the threat for—

(a) a declaration that the threat is unjustified;

(b) an injunction against the continuance of the threat;

(c) damages in respect of any loss sustained by the aggrieved person by reason of the threat.

(2) It is a defence for the person who made the threat to show that the act in respect of which proceedings were threatened constitutes (or if done would constitute) an infringement of the registered trade mark.

(3) It is a defence for the person who made the threat to show—

(a) that, despite having taken reasonable steps, the person has not identified anyone who has done an act mentioned in section 21A(2)(a), (b) or (c) in relation to the goods or their packaging or the services which are the subject of the threat, and

(b) that the person notified the recipient, before or at the time of making the threat, of the steps taken.

21D   Professional advisers

(1) Proceedings in respect of an actionable threat may not be brought against a professional adviser (or any person vicariously liable for the actions of that professional adviser) if the conditions in subsection (3) are met.

(2) In this section 'professional adviser' means a person who, in relation to the making of the communication containing the threat—

    (a) is acting in a professional capacity in providing legal services or the services of a trade mark attorney or a patent attorney, and

    (b) is regulated in the provision of legal services, or the services of a trade mark attorney or a patent attorney, by one or more regulatory bodies (whether through membership of a regulatory body, the issue of a licence to practise or any other means).

(3) The conditions are that—

    (a) in making the communication the professional adviser is acting on the instructions of another person, and

    (b) when the communication is made the professional adviser identifies the person on whose instructions the adviser is acting.

(4) This section does not affect any liability of the person on whose instructions the professional adviser is acting.

(5) It is for a person asserting that subsection (1) applies to prove (if required) that at the material time—

    (a) the person concerned was acting as a professional adviser, and

    (b) the conditions in subsection (3) were met.

21E Supplementary: pending registration

(1) In sections 21 and 21B references to a registered trade mark include references to a trade mark in respect of which an application for registration has been published under section 38.

(2) Where the threat of infringement proceedings is made after an application for registration has been published (but before registration) the reference in section 21C(2) to 'the registered trade mark' is to be treated as a reference to the trade mark registered in pursuance of that application.

21F Supplementary: proceedings for delivery up etc.

In section 21(1)(b) the reference to proceedings for infringement of a registered trade mark includes a reference to—

    (a) proceedings for an order under section 16 (order for delivery up of infringing goods, material or articles), and

    (b) proceedings for an order under section 19 (order as to disposal of infringing goods, material or articles).

Registered trade mark as object of property

22 Nature of registered trade mark

A registered trade mark is personal property (in Scotland, incorporeal moveable property).

23 Co-ownership of registered trade mark

(1) Where a registered trade mark is granted to two or more persons jointly, each of them is entitled, subject to any agreement to the contrary, to an equal undivided share in the registered trade mark.

(2) The following provisions apply where two or more persons are co-proprietors of a registered trade mark, by virtue of subsection (1) or otherwise.

(3) Subject to any agreement to the contrary, each co-proprietor is entitled, by himself or his agents, to do for his own benefit and without the consent of or the need to account to the other or others, any act which would otherwise amount to an infringement of the registered trade mark.

(4) One co-proprietor may not without the consent of the other or others—

    (a) grant a licence to use the registered trade mark, or

    (b) assign or charge his share in the registered trade mark (or, in Scotland, cause or permit security to be granted over it).

(5) Infringement proceedings may be brought by any co-proprietor, but he may not, without the leave of the court, proceed with the action unless the other, or each of the others, is either joined as a plaintiff or added as a defendant.

A co-proprietor who is thus added as a defendant shall not be made liable for any costs in the action unless he takes part in the proceedings.

Nothing in this subsection affects the granting of interlocutory relief on the application of a single co-proprietor.

(6) Nothing in this section affects the mutual rights and obligations of trustees or personal representatives, or their rights and obligations as such.

24 Assignment, &c. of registered trade mark

(1) A registered trade mark is transmissible by assignment, testamentary disposition or operation of law in the same way as other personal or moveable property.

It is so transmissible either in connection with the goodwill of a business or independently.

(1A) A contractual obligation to transfer a business is to be taken to include an obligation to transfer any registered trade mark, except where there is agreement to the contrary or it is clear in all the circumstances that this presumption should not apply.

(2) An assignment or other transmission of a registered trade mark may be partial, that is, limited so as to apply—

    (a) in relation to some but not all of the goods or services for which the trade mark is registered, or

    (b) in relation to use of the trade mark in a particular manner or a particular locality.

(3) An assignment of a registered trade mark, or an assent relating to a registered trade mark, is not effective unless it is in writing signed by or on behalf of the assignor or, as the case may be, a personal representative.

Except in Scotland, this requirement may be satisfied in a case where the assignor or personal representative is a body corporate by the affixing of its seal.

(4) The above provisions apply to assignment by way of security as in relation to any other assignment.

(5) A registered trade mark may be the subject of a charge (in Scotland, security) in the same way as other personal or moveable property.

(6) Nothing in this Act shall be construed as affecting the assignment or other transmission of an unregistered trade mark as part of the goodwill of a business.

25 Registration of transactions affecting registered trade mark

(1) On application being made to the registrar by—

    (a) a person claiming to be entitled to an interest in or under a registered trade mark by virtue of a registrable transaction, or

    (b) any other person claiming to be affected by such a transaction,

the prescribed particulars of the transaction shall be entered in the register.

(2) The following are registrable transactions—

    (a) an assignment of a registered trade mark or any right in it;

    (b) the grant of a licence under a registered trade mark;

    (c) the granting of any security interest (whether fixed or floating) over a registered trade mark or any right in or under it;

    (d) the making by personal representatives of an assent in relation to a registered trade mark or any right in or under it;

    (e) an order of a court or other competent authority transferring a registered trade mark or any right in or under it.

(3) Until an application has been made for registration of the prescribed particulars of a registrable transaction—

    (a) the transaction is ineffective as against a person acquiring a conflicting interest in or under the registered trade mark in ignorance of it, and

    (b) a person claiming to be a licensee by virtue of the transaction does not have the protection of section 30 or 31 (rights and remedies of licensee in relation to infringement).

(4) Where a person becomes the proprietor or a licensee of a registered trade mark by virtue of a registrable transaction, and the mark is infringed before the prescribed particulars of the transaction are registered, in proceedings for such an infringement, the court shall not award him costs unless—

     (a) an application for registration of the prescribed particulars of the transaction is made before the end of the period of six months beginning with its date, or

     (b) the court is satisfied that it was not practicable for such an application to be made before the end of that period and that an application was made as soon as practicable thereafter.

  (5) Provision may be made by rules as to—

     (a) the amendment of registered particulars relating to a licence so as to reflect any alteration of the terms of the licence, and

     (b) the removal of such particulars from the register—

        (i) where it appears from the registered particulars that the licence was granted for a fixed period and that period has expired, or

        (ii) where no such period is indicated and, after such period as may be prescribed, the registrar has notified the parties of his intention to remove the particulars from the register.

  (6) Provision may also be made by rules as to the amendment or removal from the register of particulars relating to a security interest on the application of, or with the consent of, the person entitled to the benefit of that interest.

26 Trusts and equities

  (1) No notice of any trust (express, implied or constructive) shall be entered in the register; and the registrar shall not be affected by any such notice.

  (2) Subject to the provisions of this Act, equities (in Scotland, rights) in respect of a registered trade mark may be enforced in like manner as in respect of other personal or moveable property.

27 Application for registration of trade mark as an object of property

  (1) The provisions of sections 22 to 26 (which relate to a registered trade mark as an object of property) and sections 28 to 31 (which relate to licensing) apply, with the necessary modifications, in relation to an application for the registration of a trade mark as in relation to a registered trade mark.

  (2) In section 23 (co-ownership of registered trade mark) as it applies in relation to an application for registration the reference in subsection (1) to the granting of the registration shall be construed as a reference to the making of the application.

  (3) In section 25 (registration of transactions affecting registered trade marks) as it applies in relation to a transaction affecting an application for the registration of a trade mark, the references to the entry of particulars in the register, and to the making of an application to register particulars, shall be construed as references to the giving of notice to the registrar of those particulars.

Licensing

28 Licensing of registered trade mark

  (1) A licence to use a registered trade mark may be general or limited. A limited licence may, in particular, apply—

     (a) in relation to some but not all of the goods or services for which the trade mark is registered, or

     (b) in relation to use of the trade mark in a particular manner or a particular locality.

  (2) A licence is not effective unless it is in writing signed by or on behalf of the grantor. Except in Scotland, this requirement may be satisfied in a case where the grantor is a body corporate by the affixing of its seal.

  (3) Unless the licence provides otherwise, it is binding on a successor in title to the grantor's interest. References in this Act to doing anything with, or without, the consent of the proprietor of a registered trade mark shall be construed accordingly.

  (4) Where the licence so provides, a sub-licence may be granted by the licensee; and references in this Act to a licence or licensee include a sub-licence or sub-licensee.

  (5) The proprietor of a registered trade mark may invoke the rights conferred by that trade mark against a licensee who contravenes any provision in the licence with regard to—

     (a) its duration,

     (b) the form covered by the registration in which the trade mark may be used,

     (c) the scope of the goods or services for which the licence is granted,

     (d) the territory in which the trade mark may be affixed, or

     (e) the quality of the goods manufactured or of the services provided by the licensee.

29   Exclusive licences

(1) In this Act an 'exclusive licence' means a licence (whether general or limited) authorising the licensee to the exclusion of all other persons, including the person granting the licence, to use a registered trade mark in the manner authorised by the licence.

The expression 'exclusive licensee' shall be construed accordingly.

(2) An exclusive licensee has the same rights against a successor in title who is bound by the licence as he has against the person granting the licence.

30   General provisions as to rights of licensees in case of infringement

(1) This section has effect with respect to the rights of a licensee in relation to infringement of a registered trade mark.

The provisions of this section do not apply where or to the extent that, by virtue of section 31(1) below (exclusive licensee having rights and remedies of assignee), the licensee has a right to bring proceedings in his own name.

(1A) Except so far as the licence provides otherwise a licensee may only bring proceedings for infringement of the registered trade mark with the consent of the proprietor (but see subsections (2) and (3)).

(2) An exclusive licensee may call on the proprietor of the registered trade mark to take infringement proceedings in respect of any matter which affects his interests.

(3) If the proprietor mentioned in subsection (2)—

  (a) refuses to do so, or

  (b) fails to do so within two months after being called upon,

the exclusive licensee may bring the proceedings in his own name as if he were the proprietor.

(4) Where infringement proceedings are brought by a licensee by virtue of this section or with the consent of the proprietor or pursuant to the licence, the licensee may not, without the leave of the court, proceed with the action unless the proprietor is either joined as a plaintiff or added as a defendant.

This does not affect the granting of interlocutory relief on an application by a licensee alone.

(5) A proprietor who is added as a defendant as mentioned in subsection (4) shall not be made liable for any costs in the action unless he takes part in the proceedings.

(6) In infringement proceedings brought by the proprietor of a registered trade mark any loss suffered or likely to be suffered by licensees shall be taken into account; and the court may give such directions as it thinks fit as to the extent to which the plaintiff is to hold the proceeds of any pecuniary remedy on behalf of licensees.

(6A) Where the proprietor of a registered trade mark brings infringement proceedings, a licensee who has suffered loss is entitled to intervene in the proceedings for the purpose of obtaining compensation for that loss.

(7) The provisions of this section apply in relation to an exclusive licensee if or to the extent that he has, by virtue of section 31(1), the rights and remedies of an assignee as if he were the proprietor of the registered trade mark.

31   Exclusive licensee having rights and remedies of assignee

(1) An exclusive licence may provide that the licensee shall have, to such extent as may be provided by the licence, the same rights and remedies in respect of matters occurring after the grant of the licence as if the licence had been an assignment.

Where or to the extent that such provision is made, the licensee is entitled, subject to the provisions of the licence and to the following provisions of this section, to bring infringement proceedings, against any person other than the proprietor, in his own name.

(2) Any such rights and remedies of an exclusive licensee are concurrent with those of the proprietor of the registered trade mark; and references to the proprietor of a registered trade mark in the provisions of this Act relating to infringement shall be construed accordingly.

(3) In an action brought by an exclusive licensee by virtue of this section a defendant may avail himself of any defence which would have been available to him if the action had been brought by the proprietor of the registered trade mark.

(4) Where proceedings for infringement of a registered trade mark brought by the proprietor or an exclusive licensee relate wholly or partly to an infringement in respect of which they have

concurrent rights of action, the proprietor or, as the case may be, the exclusive licensee may not, without the leave of the court, proceed with the action unless the other is either joined as a plaintiff or added as a defendant.

This does not affect the granting of interlocutory relief on an application by a proprietor or exclusive licensee alone.

(5) A person who is added as a defendant as mentioned in subsection (4) shall not be made liable for any costs in the action unless he takes part in the proceedings.

(6) Where an action for infringement of a registered trade mark is brought which relates wholly or partly to an infringement in respect of which the proprietor and an exclusive licensee have or had concurrent rights of action—

    (a) the court shall in assessing damages take into account—

        (i) the terms of the licence, and

        (ii) any pecuniary remedy already awarded or available to either of them in respect of the infringement;

    (b) no account of profits shall be directed if an award of damages has been made, or an account of profits has been directed, in favour of the other of them in respect of the infringement; and

    (c) the court shall if an account of profits is directed apportion the profits between them as the court considers just, subject to any agreement between them.

The provisions of this subsection apply whether or not the proprietor and the exclusive licensee are both parties to the action; and if they are not both parties the court may give such directions as it thinks fit as to the extent to which the party to the proceedings is to hold the proceeds of any pecuniary remedy on behalf of the other.

(7) The proprietor of a registered trade mark shall notify any exclusive licensee who has a concurrent right of action before applying for an order under section 16 (order for delivery up); and the court may on the application of the licensee make such order under that section as it thinks fit having regard to the terms of the licence.

(8) The provisions of subsections (4) to (7) above have effect subject to any agreement to the contrary between the exclusive licensee and the proprietor.

Application for registered trade mark

32   Application for registration

(1) An application for registration of a trade mark shall be made to the registrar.

(2) The application shall contain—

    (a) a request for registration of a trade mark,

    (b) the name and address of the applicant,

    (c) a statement of the goods or services in relation to which it is sought to register the trade mark, and

    (d) a representation of the trade mark, which is capable of being represented in the register in a manner which enables the registrar and other competent authorities and the public to determine the clear and precise subject matter of the protection afforded to the proprietor.

(2A) Where a notice of opposition is filed on the basis of one or more earlier trade marks or other earlier rights—

    (a) the rights (if plural) must all belong to the same proprietor;

    (b) the notice may be filed on the basis of part, or the totality, of the goods or services in respect of which the earlier right is protected or applied for.

(2B) A notice of opposition may be directed against part or the totality of the goods or services in respect of which the contested mark is applied for.

(3) The application shall state that the trade mark is being used, by the applicant or with his consent, in relation to those goods or services, or that he has a *bona fide* intention that it should be so used.

(4) The application shall be subject to the payment of the application fee and such class fees as may be appropriate.

33 Date of filing

(1) The date of filing of an application for registration of a trade mark is the date on which documents containing everything required by section 32(2) are furnished to the registrar by the applicant.

If the documents are furnished on different days, the date of filing is the last of those days.

(2) References in this Act to the date of application for registration are to the date of filing of the application.

34 Classification of trade marks

(1) Goods and services shall be classified for the purposes of the registration of trade marks according to a prescribed system of classification.

(2) Any question arising as to the class within which any goods or services fall shall be determined by the registrar, whose decision shall be final.

Priority

35 Claim to priority of Convention application

(1) A person who has duly filed an application for protection of a trade mark in a Convention country (a 'Convention application'), or his successor in title, has a right to priority, for the purposes of registering the same trade mark under this Act for some or all of the same goods or services, for a period of six months from the date of filing of the first such application.

(2) If the application for registration under this Act is made within that six-month period—

 (a) the relevant date for the purposes of establishing which rights take precedence shall be the date of filing of the first Convention application, and

 (b) the registrability of the trade mark shall not be affected by any use of the mark in the United Kingdom in the period between that date and the date of the application under this Act.

(3) Any filing which in a Convention country is equivalent to a regular national filing, under its domestic legislation or an international agreement, shall be treated as giving rise to the right of priority.

A 'regular national filing' means a filing which is adequate to establish the date on which the application was filed in that country, whatever may be the subsequent fate of the application.

(4) A subsequent application concerning the same subject as the first Convention application, filed in the same Convention country, shall be considered the first Convention application (of which the filing date is the starting date of the period of priority), if at the time of the subsequent application—

 (a) the previous application has been withdrawn, abandoned or refused, without having been laid open to public inspection and without leaving any rights outstanding, and

 (b) it has not yet served as a basis for claiming a right of priority.

The previous application may not thereafter serve as a basis for claiming a right of priority.

. . .

(6) A right to priority arising as a result of a Convention application may be assigned or otherwise transmitted, either with the application or independently.

The reference in subsection (1) to the applicant's 'successor in title' shall be construed accordingly.

36 Claim to priority from other relevant overseas application

(1) Her Majesty may by Order in Council make provision for conferring on a person who has duly filed an application for protection of a trade mark in—

 (a) any of the Channel Islands or a colony, or

 (b) a country or territory in relation to which Her Majesty's Government in the United Kingdom have entered into a treaty, convention, arrangement or engagement for the reciprocal protection of trade marks,

a right to priority, for the purpose of registering the same trade mark under this Act for some or all of the same goods or services, for a specified period from the date of filing of that application.

. . .

Registration procedure

37   Examination of application

(1) The registrar shall examine whether an application for registration of a trade mark satisfies the requirements of this Act (including any requirements imposed by rules).

(3) If it appears to the registrar that the requirements for registration are not met, he shall inform the applicant and give him an opportunity, within such period as the registrar may specify, to make representations or to amend the application.

(4) If the applicant fails to satisfy the registrar that those requirements are met, or to amend the application so as to meet them, or fails to respond before the end of the specified period, the registrar shall refuse to accept the application.

(5) If it appears to the registrar that the requirements for registration are met, he shall accept the application.

38   Publication, opposition proceedings and observations

(1) When an application for registration has been accepted, the registrar shall cause the application to be published in the prescribed manner.

(2) Any person may, within the prescribed time from the date of the publication of the application, give notice to the registrar of opposition to the registration.

The notice shall be given in writing in the prescribed manner, and shall include a statement of the grounds of opposition.

(3) Where an application has been published, any person may, at any time before the registration of the trade mark, make observations in writing to the registrar as to whether the trade mark should be registered; and the registrar shall inform the applicant of any such observations.

A person who makes observations does not thereby become a party to the proceedings on the application.

39   Withdrawal, restriction or amendment of application

(1) The applicant may at any time withdraw his application or restrict the goods or services covered by the application.

If the application has been published, the withdrawal or restriction shall also be published.

(2) In other respects, an application may be amended, at the request of the applicant, only by correcting—

    (a) the name or address of the applicant,

    (b) errors of wording or of copying, or

    (c) obvious mistakes,

and then only where the correction does not substantially affect the identity of the trade mark or extend the goods or services covered by the application.

40   Registration

(1) Where an application has been accepted and—

    (a) no notice of opposition is given within the period referred to in section 38(2), or

    (b) all opposition proceedings are withdrawn or decided in favour of the applicant,

the registrar shall register the trade mark, unless it appears to him having regard to matters coming to his notice since the application was accepted that the registration requirements (other than those mentioned in section 5(1), (2) or (3)) were not met at that time.

(2) A trade mark shall not be registered unless any fee prescribed for the registration is paid within the prescribed period.

If the fee is not paid within that period, the application shall be deemed to be withdrawn.

(3) A trade mark when registered shall be registered as of the date of filing of the application for registration; and that date shall be deemed for the purposes of this Act to be the date of registration.

(4) On the registration of a trade mark the registrar shall publish the registration in the prescribed manner and issue to the applicant a certificate of registration.

. . .

Duration, renewal and alteration of registered trade mark

42 Duration of registration

(1) A trade mark shall be registered for a period of ten years from the date of registration.

(2) Registration may be renewed in accordance with section 43 for further periods of ten years.

43 Renewal of registration

(1) The registration of a trade mark may be renewed at the request of the proprietor, subject to payment of a renewal fee.

(2) Provision shall be made by rules for the registrar to inform the proprietor of a registered trade mark, before the expiry of the registration, of the date of expiry and the manner in which the registration may be renewed.

(3) A request for renewal must be made, and the renewal fee paid, before the expiry of the registration.

Failing this, the request may be made and the fee paid within such further period (of not less than six months) as may be prescribed, in which case an additional renewal fee must also be paid within that period.

(3A) If a request for renewal is made or the renewal fee is paid in respect of only some of the goods or services for which the trade mark is registered, the registration is to be renewed for those goods or services only.

(4) Renewal shall take effect from the expiry of the previous registration.

(5) If the registration is not renewed in accordance with the above provisions, the registrar shall remove the trade mark from the register.

Provision may be made by rules for the restoration of the registration of a trade mark which has been removed from the register, subject to such conditions (if any) as may be prescribed.

(6) The renewal or restoration of the registration of a trade mark shall be published in the prescribed manner.

44 Alteration of registered trade mark

(1) A registered trade mark shall not be altered in the register, during the period of registration or on renewal.

(2) Nevertheless, the registrar may, at the request of the proprietor, allow the alteration of a registered trade mark where the mark includes the proprietor's name or address and the alteration is limited to alteration of that name or address and does not substantially affect the identity of the mark.

(3) Provision shall be made by rules for the publication of any such alteration and the making of objections by any person claiming to be affected by it.

Surrender, revocation and invalidity

45 Surrender of registered trade mark

(1) A registered trade mark may be surrendered by the proprietor in respect of some or all of the goods or services for which it is registered.

. . .

46 Revocation of registration

(1) The registration of a trade mark may be revoked on any of the following grounds—

  (a) that within the period of five years following the date of completion of the registration procedure it has not been put to genuine use in the United Kingdom, by the proprietor or with his consent, in relation to the goods or services for which it is registered, and there are no proper reasons for non-use;

  (b) that such use has been suspended for an uninterrupted period of five years, and there are no proper reasons for non-use;

  (c) that, in consequence of acts or inactivity of the proprietor, it has become the common name in the trade for a product or service for which it is registered;

(d) that in consequence of the use made of it by the proprietor or with his consent in relation to the goods or services for which it is registered, it is liable to mislead the public, particularly as to the nature, quality or geographical origin of those goods or services.

(2) For the purposes of subsection (1) use of a trade mark includes use in a form (the 'variant form') differing in elements which do not alter the distinctive character of the mark in the form in which it was registered (regardless of whether or not the trade mark in the variant form is also registered in the name of the proprietor), and use in the United Kingdom includes affixing the trade mark to goods or to the packaging of goods in the United Kingdom solely for export purposes.

(3) The registration of a trade mark shall not be revoked on the ground mentioned in subsection (1)(a) or (b) if such use as is referred to in that paragraph is commenced or resumed after the expiry of the five year period and before the application for revocation is made:

Provided that, any such commencement or resumption of use after the expiry of the five year period but within the period of three months before the making of the application shall be disregarded unless preparations for the commencement or resumption began before the proprietor became aware that the application might be made.

(4) An application for revocation may be made by any person, and may be made either to the registrar or to the court, except that—

(a) if proceedings concerning the trade mark in question are pending in the court, the application must be made to the court; and

(b) if in any other case the application is made to the registrar, he may at any stage of the proceedings refer the application to the court.

(5) Where grounds for revocation exist in respect of only some of the goods or services for which the trade mark is registered, revocation shall relate to those goods or services only.

(6) Where the registration of a trade mark is revoked to any extent, the rights of the proprietor shall be deemed to have ceased to that extent as from—

(a) the date of the application for revocation, or

(b) if the registrar or court is satisfied that the grounds for revocation existed at an earlier date, that date.

47   Grounds for invalidity of registration

(1) The registration of a trade mark may be declared invalid on the ground that the trade mark was registered in breach of section 3 or any of the provisions referred to in that section (absolute grounds for refusal of registration).

Where the trade mark was registered in breach of subsection (1)(b), (c) or (d) of that section, it shall not be declared invalid if, in consequence of the use which has been made of it, it has after registration acquired a distinctive character in relation to the goods or services for which it is registered.

(2) Subject to subsections (2A) and (2G), the registration of a trade mark may be declared invalid on the ground—

(a) that there is an earlier trade mark in relation to which the conditions set out in section 5(1), (2) or (3) obtain, or

(b) that there is an earlier right in relation to which the condition set out in section 5(4) is satisfied,

unless the proprietor of that earlier trade mark or other earlier right has consented to the registration.

(2ZA) The registration of a trade mark may be declared invalid on the ground that the trade mark was registered in breach of section 5(6).

(2A) The registration of a trade mark may not be declared invalid on the ground that there is an earlier trade mark unless—

(a) the registration procedure for the earlier trade mark was completed within the period of five years ending with the date of the application for the declaration,

(b) the registration procedure for the earlier trade mark was not completed before that date, or

(c) the use conditions are met.

(2B) The use conditions are met if—
  (a) the earlier trade mark has been put to genuine use in the United Kingdom by the proprietor or with their consent in relation to the goods or services for which it is registered—
    (i) within the period of 5 years ending with the date of application for the declaration, and
    (ii) within the period of 5 years ending with the date of filing of the application for registration of the later trade mark or (where applicable) the date of the priority claimed in respect of that application where, at that date, the five year period within which the earlier trade mark should have been put to genuine use as provided in section 46(1)(a) has expired, or
  (b) it has not been so used, but there are proper reasons for non-use.
(2C) For these purposes—
  (a) use of a trade mark includes use in a form (the 'variant form') differing in elements which do not alter the distinctive character of the mark in the form in which it was registered (regardless of whether or not the trade mark in the variant form is also registered in the name of the proprietor), and
  (b) use in the United Kingdom includes affixing the trade mark to goods or to the packaging of goods in the United Kingdom solely for export purposes.
(2E) Where an earlier trade mark satisfies the use conditions in respect of some only of the goods or services for which it is registered, it shall be treated for the purposes of this section as if it were registered only in respect of those goods or services.
(2F) Subsection (2A) does not apply where the earlier trade mark is a trade mark within section 6(1)(c).
(2G) An application for a declaration of invalidity on the basis of an earlier trade mark must be refused if it would have been refused, for any of the reasons set out in subsection (2H), had the application for the declaration been made on the date of filing of the application for registration of the later trade mark or (where applicable) the date of the priority claimed in respect of that application.
(2H) The reasons referred to in subsection (2G) are—
  (a) that on the date in question the earlier trade mark was liable to be declared invalid by virtue of section 3(1)(b), (c) or (d), (and had not yet acquired a distinctive character as mentioned in the words after paragraph (d) in section 3(1));
  (b) that the application for a declaration of invalidity is based on section 5(2) and the earlier trade mark had not yet become sufficiently distinctive to support a finding of likelihood of confusion within the meaning of section 5(2);
  (c) that the application for a declaration of invalidity is based on section 5(3)(a) and the earlier trade mark had not yet acquired a reputation within the meaning of section 5(3).
(3) An application for a declaration of invalidity may be made by any person, and may be made either to the registrar or to the court, except that—
  (a) if proceedings concerning the trade mark in question are pending in the court, the application must be made to the court; and
  (b) if in any other case the application is made to the registrar, he may at any stage of the proceedings refer the application to the court.
(4) In the case of bad faith in the registration of a trade mark, the registrar himself may apply to the court for a declaration of the invalidity of the registration.
(5) Where the grounds of invalidity exist in respect of only some of the goods or services for which the trade mark is registered, the trade mark shall be declared invalid as regards those goods or services only.
(5A) An application for a declaration of invalidity may be filed on the basis of one or more earlier trade marks or other earlier rights provided they all belong to the same proprietor.
(6) Where the registration of a trade mark is declared invalid to any extent, the registration shall to that extent be deemed never to have been made:
  Provided that this shall not affect transactions past and closed.

48   Effect of acquiescence

(1) Where the proprietor of an earlier trade mark or other earlier right has acquiesced for a continuous period of five years in the use of a registered trade mark in the United Kingdom, being aware of that use, there shall cease to be any entitlement on the basis of that earlier trade mark or other right—

   (a) to apply for a declaration that the registration of the later trade mark is invalid, or

   (b) to oppose the use of the later trade mark in relation to the goods or services in relation to which it has been so used,

unless the registration of the later trade mark was applied for in bad faith.

(2) Where subsection (1) applies, the proprietor of the later trade mark is not entitled to oppose the use of the earlier trade mark or, as the case may be, the exploitation of the earlier right, notwithstanding that the earlier trade mark or right may no longer be invoked against his later trade mark.

Collective marks

49   Collective marks

(1) A collective mark is a mark which is described as such when it is applied for and is capable of distinguishing the goods and services of members of the association which is the proprietor of the mark from those of other undertakings.

(1A) The following may be registered as the proprietor of a collective mark—

   (a) an association of manufacturers, producers, suppliers of services or traders which has the capacity in its own name to enter into contracts and to sue or be sued; and

   (b) a legal person governed by public law.

(2) The provisions of this Act apply to collective marks subject to the provisions of Schedule 1.

Certification marks

50   Certification marks

(1) A certification mark is a mark which is described as such when the mark is applied for and indicates that the goods or services in connection with which it is used are certified by the proprietor of the mark in respect of origin, material, mode of manufacture of goods or performance of services, quality, accuracy or other characteristics.

(2) The provisions of this Act apply to certification marks subject to the provisions of Schedule 2.

PART II   EUROPEAN UNION TRADE MARKS AND INTERNATIONAL MATTERS

European Union trade marks

51   Meaning of 'European Union trade mark'

In this Act—

   'European Union trade mark' has the meaning given by Article 1(1) of the European Union Trade Mark Regulation ; and

   'the European Union Trade Mark Regulation' means Regulation (EU) 2017/1001 of the European Parliament and of the Council of 14 June 2017 on the European Union Trade Mark (as it had effect immediately before exit day).

52A   Certain trade marks registered as European Union trade marks to be treated as registered trade marks

Schedule 2A makes provision for European Union trade marks (including certain expired and removed marks) to be treated as registered trade marks with effect from exit day and about certain applications for a European Union trade mark made before exit day.

The Madrid Protocol: international registration

53   The Madrid Protocol
In this Act—

'the Madrid Protocol' means the Protocol relating to the Madrid Agreement concerning the International Registration of Marks, adopted at Madrid on 27th June 1989;

'the International Bureau' has the meaning given by Article 2(1) of that Protocol;

'international 'trade mark (UK)' means a trade mark which is entitled to protection in the United Kingdom under that Protocol.

54   Power to make provision giving effect to Madrid Protocol
(1) The Secretary of State may by order make such provision as he thinks fit for giving effect in the United Kingdom to the provisions of the Madrid Protocol.

(2) Provision may, in particular, be made with respect to—

    (a) the making of applications for international registrations by way of the Patent Office as office of origin;

    (b) the procedures to be followed where the basic United Kingdom application or registration fails or ceases to be in force;

    (c) the procedures to be followed where the Patent Office receives from the International Bureau a request for extension of protection to the United Kingdom;

    (d) the effects of a successful request for extension of protection to the United Kingdom;

    (e) the transformation of an application for an international registration, or an international registration, into a national application for registration;

    (f) the communication of information to the International Bureau;

    (g) the payment of fees and amounts prescribed in respect of applications for international registrations, extensions of protection and renewals.

(3) Without prejudice to the generality of subsection (1), provision may be made by regulations under this section applying in relation to an international trade mark (UK) the provisions of—

    (a) sections 21 to 21F (unjustified threats);

    (b) sections 89 to 91 (importation of infringing goods, material or articles); and

    (c) sections 92, 93, 95 and 96 (offences). . . .

54A   Certain international trade marks protected in the European Union to be treated as registered trade marks
Schedule 2B makes provision for international trade marks protected in the European Union (including certain expired marks) to be treated as registered trade marks with effect from exit day and about certain applications for the protection of an international trade mark in the European Union and transformation applications made before exit day.

The Paris Convention: supplementary provisions

55   The Paris Convention
(1) In this Act—

    (a) 'the Paris Convention' means the Paris Convention for the Protection of Industrial Property of March 20th 1883, as revised or amended from time to time, and

    (aa) 'the WTO agreement' means the Agreement establishing the World Trade Organisation signed at Marrakesh on 15 April 1994, and

    (b) a 'Convention country' means a country, other than the United Kingdom, which is a party to that Convention or to that Agreement.

(2) The Secretary of State may by order make such amendments of this Act, and rules made under this Act, as appear to him appropriate in consequence of any revision or amendment of the Paris Convention or the WTO agreement after the passing of this Act.

    . . .

56 Protection of well-known trade marks: Article 6*bis*

(1) References in this Act to a trade mark which is entitled to protection under the Paris Convention or the WTO agreement as a well known trade mark are to a mark which is well-known in the United Kingdom as being the mark of a person who—

(a) is a national of the United Kingdom or a Convention country, or

(b) is domiciled in, or has a real and effective industrial or commercial establishment in, the United Kingdom or a Convention country,

whether or not that person carries on business, or has any goodwill, in the United Kingdom.

References to the proprietor of such a mark shall be construed accordingly.

(2) The proprietor of a trade mark which is entitled to protection under the Paris Convention or the WTO agreement as a well known trade mark is entitled to restrain by injunction the use in the United Kingdom of a trade mark which, or the essential part of which, is identical or similar to the well known trade mark—

(a) in relation to identical or similar goods or services, where the use is likely to cause confusion, or

(b) where the well known trade mark has a reputation in the United Kingdom and the use of the other trade mark—

(i) is without due cause, and

(ii) takes unfair advantage of, or is detrimental to, the distinctive character or the repute of the well known trade mark.

This right is subject to section 48 (effect of acquiescence by proprietor of earlier trade mark).

(2A) Subsection (2)(b) applies irrespective of whether the goods or services in relation to which the other trade mark is used are identical with, similar to or not similar to those for which the well known trade mark is entitled to protection.

(3) Nothing in subsection (2) affects the continuation of any bona fide use of a trade mark begun before the commencement of this section.

57 National emblems, &c. of convention countries: Article 6*ter*

(1) A trade mark which consists of or contains the flag of a Convention country shall not be registered without the authorisation of the competent authorities of that country, unless it appears to the registrar that use of the flag in the manner proposed is permitted without such authorisation.

(2) A trade mark which consists of or contains the armorial bearings or any other state emblem of a Convention country which is protected under the Paris Convention or the WTO agreement shall not be registered without the authorisation of the competent authorities of that country.

(3) A trade mark which consists of or contains an official sign or hallmark adopted by a Convention country and indicating control and warranty shall not, where the sign or hallmark is protected under the Paris Convention or the WTO agreement, be registered in relation to goods or services of the same, or a similar kind, as those in relation to which it indicates control and warranty, without the authorisation of the competent authorities of the country concerned.

(4) The provisions of this section as to national flags and other state emblems, and official signs or hallmarks, apply equally to anything which from a heraldic point of view imitates any such flag or other emblem, or sign or hallmark.

(5) Nothing in this section prevents the registration of a trade mark on the application of a national of a country who is authorised to make use of a state emblem, or official sign or hallmark, of that country, notwithstanding that it is similar to that of another country.

(6) Where by virtue of this section the authorisation of the competent authorities of a Convention country is or would be required for the registration of a trade mark, those authorities are entitled to restrain by injunction any use of the mark in the United Kingdom without their authorisation.

58 Emblems, &c. of certain international organisations: Article 6*ter*

(1) This section applies to—

(a) the armorial bearings, flags or other emblems, and

(b) the abbreviations and names,

of international intergovernmental organisations of which one or more Convention countries are members.

(2) A trade mark which consists of or contains any such emblem, abbreviation or name which is protected under the Paris Convention or the WTO agreement shall not be registered without the authorisation of the international organisation concerned, unless it appears to the registrar that the use of the emblem, abbreviation or name in the manner proposed—

(a) is not such as to suggest to the public that a connection exists between the organisation and the trade mark, or

(b) is not likely to mislead the public as to the existence of a connection between the user and the organisation.

(3) The provisions of this section as to emblems of an international organisation apply equally to anything which from a heraldic point of view imitates any such emblem.

(4) Where by virtue of this section the authorisation of an international organisation is or would be required for the registration of a trade mark, that organisation is entitled to restrain by injunction any use of the mark in the United Kingdom without its authorisation.

(5) Nothing in this section affects the rights of a person whose *bona fide* use of the trade mark in question began before 4th January 1962 (when the relevant provisions of the Paris Convention entered into force in relation to the United Kingdom).

59 Notification under Article 6*ter* of the Convention

(1) For the purposes of section 57, state emblems of a Convention country (other than the national flag), and official signs or hallmarks, shall be regarded as protected under the Paris Convention only if, or to the extent that—

(a) the country in question has notified the United Kingdom in accordance with Article 6*ter*(3) of the Convention that it desires to protect that emblem, sign or hallmark,

(b) the notification remains in force, and

(c) the United Kingdom has not objected to it in accordance with Article 6*ter*(4) or any such objection has been withdrawn.

(2) For the purposes of section 58 the emblems, abbreviations and names of an international organisation shall be regarded as protected under the Paris Convention only if, or to the extent that—

(a) the organisation in question has notified the United Kingdom in accordance with Article 6*ter*(3) of the Convention that it desires to protect that emblem, abbreviation or name,

(b) the notification remains in force, and

(c) the United Kingdom has not objected to it in accordance with Article 6*ter*(4) or any such objection has been withdrawn.

(3) Notification under Article 6*ter*(3) of the Paris Convention shall have effect only in relation to applications for registration made more than two months after the receipt of the notification.

(4) The registrar shall keep and make available for public inspection by any person, at all reasonable hours and free of charge, a list of—

(a) the state emblems and official signs or hallmarks, and

(b) the emblems, abbreviations and names of international organisations,

which are for the time being protected under the Paris Convention by virtue of notification under Article 6*ter*(3).

(5) Any reference in this section to Article 6*ter* of the Paris Convention shall be construed as including a reference to that Article as applied by the WTO agreement.

. . .

PART III   ADMINISTRATIVE AND OTHER SUPPLEMENTARY PROVISIONS

The registrar

62 The registrar

In this Act 'the registrar' means the Comptroller-General of Patents, Designs and Trade Marks.

The register

63   The register

(1) The registrar shall maintain a register of trade marks.

References in this Act to 'the register' are to that register; and references to registration (in particular, in the expression 'registered trade mark') are, unless the context otherwise requires, to registration in that register.

(2) There shall be entered in the register in accordance with this Act—

(a) registered trade marks,

(b) such particulars as may be prescribed of registrable transactions affecting a registered trade mark, and

(c) such other matters relating to registered trade marks as may be prescribed.

(3) The register shall be kept in such manner as may be prescribed, and provision shall in particular be made for—

(a) public inspection of the register, and

(b) the supply of certified or uncertified copies, or extracts, of entries in the register.

64   Rectification or correction of the register

(1) Any person having a sufficient interest may apply for the rectification of an error or omission in the register:

Provided that an application for rectification may not be made in respect of a matter affecting the validity of the registration of a trade mark.

. . .

(3) Except where the registrar or the court directs otherwise, the effect of rectification of the register is that the error or omission in question shall be deemed never to have been made.

. . .

70   Exclusion of liability in respect of official acts

(1) The registrar shall not be taken to warrant the validity of the registration of a trade mark under this Act or under any treaty, convention, arrangement or engagement to which the United Kingdom is a party.

(2) The registrar is not subject to any liability by reason of, or in connection with, any examination required or authorised by this Act, or any such treaty, convention, arrangement or engagement, or any report or other proceedings consequent on such examination.

(3) No proceedings lie against an officer of the registrar in respect of any matter for which, by virtue of this section, the registrar is not liable.

. . .

Legal proceedings and appeals

72   Registration to be *prima facie* evidence of validity

In all legal proceedings relating to a registered trade mark (including proceedings for rectification of the register) the registration of a person as proprietor of a trade mark shall be prima facie evidence of the validity of the original registration and of any subsequent assignment or other transmission of it.

73   Certificate of validity of contested registration

(1) If in proceedings before the court the validity of the registration of a trade mark is contested and it is found by the court that the trade mark is validly registered, the court may give a certificate to that effect.

(2) If the court gives such a certificate and in subsequent proceedings—

(a) the validity of the registration is again questioned, and

(b) the proprietor obtains a final order or judgment in his favour,

he is entitled to his costs as between solicitor and client unless the court directs otherwise.

This subsection does not extend to the costs of an appeal in any such proceedings.

74   Registrar's appearance in proceedings involving the register

(1) In proceedings before the court involving an application for—

(a) the revocation of the registration of a trade mark,

(b) a declaration of the invalidity of the registration of a trade mark, or

(c) the rectification of the register, the registrar is entitled to appear and be heard, and shall appear if so directed by the court.

. . .

75   The court

In this Act, unless the context otherwise requires, 'the court' means—

(a) in England and Wales, the High Court or the county court where it has jurisdiction by virtue of an order made under section 1 of the Courts and Legal Services Act 1990,

(aa) in Northern Ireland, the High Court, and

(b) in Scotland, the Court of Session.

76   Appeals from the registrar

(1) An appeal lies from any decision of the registrar under this Act, except as otherwise expressly provided by rules.

For this purpose 'decision' includes any act of the registrar in exercise of a discretion vested in him by or under this Act.

(2) Any such appeal may be brought either to an appointed person or to the court.

(3) Where an appeal is made to an appointed person, he may refer the appeal to the court if—

(a) it appears to him that a point of general legal importance is involved,

(b) the registrar requests that it be so referred, or

(c) such a request is made by any party to the proceedings before the registrar in which the decision appealed against was made.

Before doing so the appointed person shall give the appellant and any other party to the appeal an opportunity to make representations as to whether the appeal should be referred to the court.

(4) Where an appeal is made to an appointed person and he does not refer it to the court, he shall hear and determine the appeal and his decision shall be final.

(5) The provisions of sections 68 and 69 (costs and security for costs; evidence) apply in relation to proceedings before an appointed person as in relation to proceedings before the registrar.

(6) In the application of this section to England and Wales, 'the court' means the High Court.

77   Persons appointed to hear and determine appeals

(1) For the purposes of section 76 an 'appointed person' means a person appointed by the Lord Chancellor to hear and decide appeals under this Act.

. . .

81   The trade marks journal

Provision shall be made by rules for the publication by the registrar of a journal containing particulars of any application for the registration of a trade mark (including a representation of the mark) and such other information relating to trade marks as the registrar thinks fit.

. . .

Importation of infringing goods, material or articles

89   Infringing goods, material or articles may be treated as prohibited goods

(1) The proprietor of a registered trade mark, or a licensee, may give notice in writing to the Commissioners of Customs and Excise—

(a) that he is the proprietor or, as the case may be, a licensee of the registered trade mark

(b) that, at a time and place specified in the notice, goods which are, in relation to that registered trade mark, infringing goods, material or articles are expected to arrive in the United Kingdom—

(i) from outside the European Economic Area, or

(ii) from within that Area but not having been entered for free circulation, and

(c) that he requests the Commissioners to treat them as prohibited goods.

(2) When a notice is in force under this section the importation of the goods to which the notice relates, otherwise than by a person for his private and domestic use, is prohibited; but a person is not by reason of the prohibition liable to any penalty other than forfeiture of the goods.

(3) This section does not apply to goods placed in, or expected to be placed in, one of the situations referred to in Article 3 of the European Customs Enforcement Regulation.

. . .

91 Power of Commissioners for Revenue and Customs to disclose information

Where information relating to infringing goods, material or articles has been obtained or is held by the Commissioners for Her Majesty's Revenue and Customs for the purposes of, or in connection with, the exercise of functions of Her Majesty's Revenue and Customs in relation to imported goods, the Commissioners may authorise the disclosure of that information for the purpose of facilitating the exercise by any person of any function in connection with the investigation or prosecution of an offence under—

(a) section 92 below (unauthorised use of trade mark, &c in relation to goods),

(b) the Trade Descriptions Act 1968,

(c) the Business Protection from Misleading Marketing Regulations 2008, or

(d) the Consumer Protection from Unfair Trading Regulations 2008.

Offences

92 Unauthorised use of trade mark, &c. in relation to goods

(1) A person commits an offence who, with a view to gain for himself or another, or with intent to cause loss to another, and without the consent of the proprietor—

(a) applies to goods or their packaging a sign identical to, or likely to be mistaken for, a registered trade mark, or

(b) sells or lets for hire, offers or exposes for sale or hire or distributes goods which bear, or the packaging of which bears, such a sign, or

(c) has in his possession, custody or control in the course of a business any such goods with a view to the doing of anything, by himself or another, which would be an offence under paragraph (b).

(2) A person commits an offence who with a view to gain for himself or another, or with intent to cause loss to another, and without the consent of the proprietor—

(a) applies a sign identical to, or likely to be mistaken for, a registered trade mark to material intended to be used—

(i) for labelling or packaging goods,

(ii) as a business paper in relation to goods, or

(iii) for advertising goods, or

(b) uses in the course of a business material bearing such a sign for labelling or packaging goods, as a business paper in relation to goods, or for advertising goods, or

(c) has in his possession, custody or control in the course of a business any such material with a view to the doing of anything, by himself or another, which would be an offence under paragraph (b).

(3) A person commits an offence who with a view to gain for himself or another, or with intent to cause loss to another, and without the consent of the proprietor—

(a) makes an article specifically designed or adapted for making copies of a sign identical to, or likely to be mistaken for, a registered trade mark, or

(b) has such an article in his possession, custody or control in the course of a business,

knowing or having reason to believe that it has been, or is to be, used to produce goods, or material for labelling or packaging goods, as a business paper in relation to goods, or for advertising goods.

(4) A person does not commit an offence under this section unless—

(a) the goods are goods in respect of which the trade mark is registered, or

(b) the trade mark has a reputation in the United Kingdom and the use of the sign takes or would take unfair advantage of, or is or would be detrimental to, the distinctive character or the repute of the trade mark.

(5) It is a defence for a person charged with an offence under this section to show that he believed on reasonable grounds that the use of the sign in the manner in which it was used, or was to be used, was not an infringement of the registered trade mark.

(6) A person guilty of an offence under this section is liable—

    (a) on summary conviction to imprisonment for a term not exceeding six months or a fine not exceeding the statutory maximum, or both;

    (b) on conviction on indictment to a fine or imprisonment for a term not exceeding ten years, or both.

. . .

93 Enforcement function of local weights and measures authority

(1) It is the duty of every local weights and measures authority to enforce within their area the provisions of section 92 (unauthorised use of trade mark, &c. in relation to goods).

  . . .

94 Falsification of register, &c.

(1) It is an offence for a person to make, or cause to be made, a false entry in the register of trade marks, knowing or having reason to believe that it is false.

(2) It is an offence for a person—

    (a) to make or cause to be made anything falsely purporting to be a copy of an entry in the register, or

    (b) to produce or tender or cause to be produced or tendered in evidence any such thing,

knowing or having reason to believe that it is false.

(3) A person guilty of an offence under this section is liable—

    (a) on conviction on indictment, to imprisonment for a term not exceeding two years or a fine, or both;

    (b) on summary conviction, to imprisonment for a term not exceeding six months or a fine not exceeding the statutory maximum, or both.

95 Falsely representing trade mark as registered

(1) It is an offence for a person—

    (a) falsely to represent that a mark is a registered trade mark, or

    (b) to make a false representation as to the goods or services for which a trade mark is registered knowing or having reason to believe that the representation is false.

(2) For the purposes of this section, the use in the United Kingdom in relation to a trade mark—

    (a) of the word 'registered', or

    (b) of any other word or symbol importing a reference (express or implied) to registration,

shall be deemed to be a representation as to registration under this Act unless it is shown that the reference is to registration elsewhere than in the United Kingdom and that the trade mark is in fact so registered for the goods or services in question.

(3) A person guilty of an offence under this section is liable on summary conviction to a fine not exceeding level 3 on the standard scale.

. . .

Forfeiture of counterfeit goods, &c.

97 Forfeiture: England and Wales or Northern Ireland

(1) In England and Wales or Northern Ireland where there has come into the possession of any person in connection with the investigation or prosecution of a relevant offence—

    (a) goods which, or the packaging of which, bears a sign identical to or likely to be mistaken for a registered trade mark,

    (b) material bearing such a sign and intended to be used for labelling or packaging goods, as a business paper in relation to goods, or for advertising goods, or

    (c) articles specifically designed or adapted for making copies of such a sign, that person may apply under this section for an order for the forfeiture of the goods, material or articles.

...

(8) For the purposes of this section a 'relevant offence' means an offence under—

    (a) an offence under section 92 above (unauthorised use of trade mark, &c in relation to goods),

    (b) an offence under the Trade Descriptions Act 1968,

    (c) an offence under the Business Protection from Misleading Marketing Regulations 2008,

    (d) an offence under the Consumer Protection from Unfair Trading Regulations 2008, or

    (e) any offence involving dishonesty or deception.

98 Forfeiture: Scotland

(1) In Scotland the court may make an order for the forfeiture of any—

    (a) goods which bear, or the packaging of which bears, a sign identical to or likely to be mistaken for a registered trade mark,

    (b) material bearing such a sign and intended to be used for labelling or packaging goods, as a business paper in relation to goods, or for advertising goods, or

    (c) articles specifically designed or adapted for making copies of such a sign.

...

(14) For the purposes of this section—

'relevant offence' means an offence under—

    (a) an offence under section 92 above (unauthorised use of trade mark, &c in relation to goods),

    (b) an offence under the Trade Descriptions Act 1968,

    (c) an offence under the Business Protection from Misleading Marketing Regulations 2008,

    (d) an offence under the Consumer Protection from Unfair Trading Regulations 2008, or

    (e) any offence involving dishonesty or deception;

'the court' means—

    (a) in relation to an order made on an application under subsection (2)(a), the sheriff, and

    (b) in relation to an order made under subsection (2)(b), the court which imposed the penalty.

PART IV   MISCELLANEOUS AND GENERAL PROVISIONS

Miscellaneous

99 Unauthorised use of Royal arms, &c.

(1) A person shall not, without the authority of Her Majesty, use in connection with any business the Royal arms (or arms so closely resembling the Royal arms as to be calculated to deceive) in such manner as to be calculated to lead to the belief that he is duly authorised to use the Royal arms.

(2) A person shall not, without the authority of Her Majesty or of a member of the Royal family, use in connection with any business any device, emblem or title in such a manner as to be calculated to lead to the belief that he is employed by, or supplies goods or services to, Her Majesty or that member of the Royal family.

(3) A person who contravenes subsection (1) commits an offence and is liable on summary conviction to a fine not exceeding level 2 on the standard scale.

(4) Contravention of subsection (1) or (2) may be restrained by injunction in proceedings brought by—

(a) any person who is authorised to use the arms, device, emblem or title in question, or

(b) any person authorised by the Lord Chamberlain to take such proceedings.

(5) Nothing in this section affects any right of the proprietor of a trade mark containing any such arms, device, emblem or title to use that trade mark.

99A   Reproduction of trade marks in dictionaries, encyclopaedias etc.

(1) Subsection (2) applies if the reproduction of a trade mark in a dictionary, encyclopaedia or similar reference work, in print or electronic form, gives the impression that it constitutes the generic name of the goods or services for which the trade mark is registered.

(2) The publisher of the work must, at the request in writing of the proprietor of the trade mark, ensure that the reproduction of the trade mark is accompanied by an indication that it is a registered trade mark.

(3) The action required by subsection (2) must be taken—

(a) without delay, and

(b) in the case of works in printed form, at the latest in the next edition of the publication.

(4) If the publisher fails to take any action required by subsection (2) the court may, on an application by the proprietor—

(a) order the publisher to take the action concerned;

(b) if the work is in printed form, order the publisher to erase or amend the reproduction of the trade mark or secure the destruction of copies of the work in the publisher's possession, custody or control; or

(c) grant such other order as the court in the circumstances considers appropriate.

100   Burden of proving use of trade mark

If in any civil proceedings under this Act a question arises as to the use to which a registered trade mark has been put, it is for the proprietor to show what use has been made of it.

101   Offences committed by partnerships and bodies corporate

(1) Proceedings for an offence under this Act alleged to have been committed by a partnership shall be brought against the partnership in the name of the firm and not in that of the partners; but without prejudice to any liability of the partners under subsection (4) below.

. . .

(4) Where a partnership is guilty of an offence under this Act, every partner, other than a partner who is proved to have been ignorant of or to have attempted to prevent the commission of the offence, is also guilty of the offence and liable to be proceeded against and punished accordingly.

(5) Where an offence under this Act committed by a body corporate is proved to have been committed with the consent or connivance of a director, manager, secretary or other similar officer of the body, or a person purporting to act in any such capacity, he as well as the body corporate is guilty of the offence and liable to be proceeded against and punished accordingly.

Interpretation

102   Adaptation of expressions for Scotland

In the application of this Act to Scotland—

'account of profits' means accounting and payment of profits;

'accounts' means count, reckoning and payment;

'assignment' means assignation;

'costs' means expenses;

'declaration' means declarator;

'defendant' means defender;

'delivery up' means delivery;

'injunction' means interdict;

'interlocutory relief' means interim remedy; and

'plaintiff' means pursuer.

103   Minor definitions

(1) In this Act—

'business' includes a trade or profession;

'director', in relation to a body corporate whose affairs are managed by its members, means any member of the body;

'infringement proceedings', in relation to a registered trade mark, includes proceedings under section 16 (order for delivery up of infringing goods, &c.);

'publish' means make available to the public, and references to publication—

(a) in relation to an application for registration, are to publication under section 38(1), and

(b) in relation to registration, are to publication under section 40(4);

'statutory provisions' includes provisions of subordinate legislation within the meaning of the Interpretation Act 1978;

'trade' includes any business or profession.

(2) References in this Act to use (or any particular description of use) of a trade mark, or of a sign identical with, similar to, or likely to be mistaken for a trade mark, include use (or that description of use) otherwise than by means of a graphic representation.

104   Index of defined expressions

In this Act the expressions listed below are defined by or otherwise fall to be construed in accordance with the provisions indicated—

account of profits and accounts (in Scotland)	section 102
appointed person (for purposes of section 76)	section 77
assignment (in Scotland)	section 102
business	section 103(1)
certification mark	section 50(1)
collective mark	section 49(1)
commencement (of this Act)	section 109(2)
comparable trade mark (EU)	Schedule 2A, paragraph 1(2)
comparable trade mark (IR)	Schedule 2B, paragraph 1(4)
Convention country	section 55(1)(b)
costs (in Scotland)	section 102
the court	section 75
date of application	section 33(2)
date of application (comparable trade mark (EU))	Schedule 2A, paragraph 1(8)(b)
date of application (comparable trade mark (IR))	Schedule 2B, paragraph 1(10)(b)
date of filing	section 33(1)
date of filing (comparable trade mark (EU))	Schedule 2A, paragraph 1(8)(a)
date of filing (comparable trade mark (IR))	Schedule 2B, paragraph 1(10)(a)
date of registration	section 40(3)
date of registration (comparable trade mark (EU))	Schedule 2A, paragraph 1(4)
date of registration (comparable trade mark (IR))	Schedule 2B, paragraph 1(6)
defendant (in Scotland)	section 102
delivery up (in Scotland)	section 102
director	section 103(1)
earlier right	section 5(4)
earlier trade mark	section 6
European Customs Enforcement Regulation	section 10A
European Union trade mark	section 51
European Union Trade Mark Regulation	section 51
exclusive licence and licensee	section 29(1)

infringement (of registered trade mark)	sections 9(1) and (2) and 10
infringement proceedings	section 103(1)
infringing articles	section 17
infringing goods	section 17
infringing material	section 17
injunction (in Scotland)	section 102
interlocutory relief (in Scotland)	section 102
the International Bureau	section 53
international trade mark (UK)	section 53
Madrid Protocol	section 53
Paris Convention	section 55(1)(a)
plaintiff (in Scotland)	section 102
prescribed	section 78(1)(b)
protected under the Paris Convention	
— well-known trade marks	section 56(1)
— state emblems and official signs or hallmarks	section 57(1)
— emblems, &c. of international organisations	section 58(2)
publish and references to publication	section 103(1)
register, registered (and related expressions)	section 63(1)
registered trade mark attorney	section 83(2)
registrable transaction	section 25(2)
the registrar	section 62
rules	section 78
statutory provisions	section 103(1)
trade/	section 103(1)
trade mark	
— generally	section 1(1)
— includes collective mark or certification mark	section 1(2)
United Kingdom (references include Isle of Man)	section 108(2)
use (of trade mark or sign)	section 103(2)
well-known trade mark (under Paris Convention)	section 56(1)

Other general provisions

105 Transitional provisions

The provisions of Schedule 3 have effect with respect to transitional matters, including the treatment of marks registered under the Trade Marks Act 1938, and applications for registration and other proceedings pending under that Act, on the commencement of this Act.

106 Consequential amendments and repeals

(1) The enactments specified in Schedule 4 are amended in accordance with that Schedule, the amendments being consequential on the provisions of this Act.

(2) The enactments specified in Schedule 5 are repealed to the extent specified.

107 Territorial waters and the continental shelf

(1) For the purposes of this Act the territorial waters of the United Kingdom shall be treated as part of the United Kingdom.

(2) This Act applies to things done in the United Kingdom sector of the continental shelf on a structure or vessel which is present there for purposes directly connected with the exploration of the sea bed or subsoil or the exploitation of their natural resources as it applies to things done in the United Kingdom.

(3) The United Kingdom sector of the continental shelf means the areas designated by order under section 1(7) of the Continental Shelf Act 1964.

108   Extent

(1) This Act extends to England and Wales, Scotland and Northern Ireland.

(2) This Act also extends to the Isle of Man, subject to such exceptions and modifications as Her Majesty may specify by Order in Council; and subject to any such Order references in this Act to the United Kingdom shall be construed as including the Isle of Man.

. . .

Section 49   **SCHEDULE 1   COLLECTIVE MARKS**

General

1. The provisions of this Act apply to collective marks subject to the following provisions.

Signs of which a collective mark may consist

2. In relation to a collective mark the reference in section 1(1) (signs of which a trade mark may consist) to distinguishing goods or services of one undertaking from those of other undertakings shall be construed as a reference to distinguishing goods or services of members of the association which is the proprietor of the mark from those of other undertakings.

Indication of geographical origin

3.—(1) Notwithstanding section 3(1)(c), a collective mark may be registered which consists of signs or indications which may serve, in trade, to designate the geographical origin of the goods or services.

(2) However, the proprietor of such a mark is not entitled to prohibit the use of the signs or indications in accordance with honest practices in industrial or commercial matters (in particular, by a person who is entitled to use a geographical name).

Mark not to be misleading as to character or significance

4.—(1) A collective mark shall not be registered if the public is liable to be misled as regards the character or significance of the mark, in particular if it is likely to be taken to be something other than a collective mark.

(2) The registrar may accordingly require that a mark in respect of which application is made for registration include some indication that it is a collective mark.

Notwithstanding section 39(2), an application may be amended so as to comply with any such requirement.

Regulations governing use of collective mark

5.—(1) An applicant for registration of a collective mark must file with the registrar regulations governing the use of the mark.

(2) The regulations must specify the persons authorised to use the mark, the conditions of membership of the association and the conditions of use of the mark, including any sanctions against misuse.

(3) Where the regulations govern use of a mark referred to in paragraph 3(1), they must authorise any person whose goods or services originate in the geographical area concerned to become a member of the association which is the proprietor of the mark, provided that the person fulfils all the other conditions of the regulations.

(4) Further requirements with which the regulations have to comply may be imposed by rules.

Approval of regulations by registrar

6.—(1) A collective mark shall not be registered unless the regulations governing the use of the mark—

    (a) comply with paragraph 5(2) and (3) and any further requirements imposed by rules, and

    (b) are not contrary to public policy or to accepted principles of morality.

(2) Before the end of the prescribed period after the date of the application for registration of a collective mark, the applicant must file the regulations with the registrar and pay the prescribed fee.

If he does not do so, the application shall be deemed to be withdrawn.

7.—(1) The registrar shall consider whether the requirements mentioned in paragraph 6(1) are met.

(2) If it appears to the registrar that those requirements are not met, he shall inform the applicant and give him an opportunity, within such period as the registrar may specify, to make representations or to file amended regulations.

(3) If the applicant fails to satisfy the registrar that those requirements are met, or to file regulations amended so as to meet them, or fails to respond before the end of the specified period, the registrar shall refuse the application.

(4) If it appears to the registrar that those requirements, and the other requirements for registration, are met, he shall accept the application and shall proceed in accordance with section 38 (publication, opposition proceedings and observations).

8. The regulations shall be published and notice of opposition may be given, and observations may be made, relating to the matters mentioned in paragraph 6(1).

This is in addition to any other grounds on which the application may be opposed or observations made.

Regulations to be open to inspection

9. The regulations governing the use of a registered collective mark shall be open to public inspection in the same way as the register.

Amendment of regulations

10.—(1) An amendment of the regulations governing the use of a registered collective mark is not effective unless and until the amended regulations are filed with the registrar and accepted by him.

(2) Before accepting any amended regulations the registrar may in any case where it appears to him expedient to do so cause them to be published.

(3) If he does so, notice of opposition may be given, and observations may be made, relating to the matters mentioned in paragraph 6(1).

Infringement: rights of authorised users

11. The following provisions apply in relation to an authorised user of a registered collective mark as in relation to a licensee of a trade mark—

    (a) section 10(5) (definition of infringement: unauthorised application of mark to certain material);

    (b) section 19(2) (order as to disposal of infringing goods, material or articles: adequacy of other remedies);

    (c) section 89 (prohibition of importation of infringing goods, material or articles: request to Commissioners of Customs and Excise).

12.—(1) The following provisions (which correspond to the provisions of section 30 (general provisions as to rights of licensees in case of infringement)) have effect as regards the rights of an authorised user in relation to infringement of a registered collective mark.

(2) Subject to any agreement to the contrary between the authorised user and the proprietor, an authorised user may only bring proceedings for infringement of a registered collective mark with the consent of the proprietor.

(4) Where proceedings are brought by an authorised user for infringement of a registered collective mark (with the consent of the proprietor or pursuant to any agreement referred to in sub-paragraph (2)), the authorised user may not, without the leave of the court, proceed with the action unless the proprietor is either joined as a plaintiff or added as a defendant.

This does not affect the granting of interlocutory relief on an application by an authorised user alone.

(5) A proprietor who is added as a defendant as mentioned in sub-paragraph (4) shall not be made liable for any costs in the action unless he takes part in the proceedings.

(6) In infringement proceedings brought by the proprietor of a registered collective mark any loss suffered or likely to be suffered by authorised users shall be taken into account; and the court may give such directions as it thinks fit as to the extent to which the plaintiff is to hold the proceeds of any pecuniary remedy on behalf of such users.

(7) Where the proprietor of a registered collective mark brings infringement proceedings, an authorised user who has suffered loss is entitled to intervene in the proceedings for the purpose of obtaining compensation for that loss.

Grounds for revocation of registration

13. Apart from the grounds of revocation provided for in section 46, the registration of a collective mark may be revoked on the ground—

(a) that the manner in which the mark has been used by the persons authorised to use it has caused it to become liable to mislead the public in the manner referred to in paragraph 4(1), or

(b) that the proprietor has not taken reasonable steps to prevent the mark being used in a manner that is incompatible with the conditions of use laid down in the regulations governing the use of the mark (as amended from time to time), or

(c) that an amendment of the regulations has been made so that the regulations—

(i) no longer comply with paragraph 5(2) and (3) and any further conditions imposed by rules, or

(ii) are contrary to public policy or to accepted principles of morality.

Grounds for invalidity of registration

14. Apart from the grounds of invalidity provided for in section 47, the registration of a collective mark shall be declared invalid on the ground that the mark was registered in breach of the provisions of section 49(1A) (definition of who may be registered as the proprietor of a certification mark) or paragraph 4(1) or 6(1) unless the breach was only of paragraph 6(1) and the proprietor of the mark, by amending the regulations governing use, complies with the requirements of paragraph 6(1).

Section 50   SCHEDULE 2   CERTIFICATION MARKS

General

1. The provisions of this Act apply to certification marks subject to the following provisions.

Signs of which a certification mark may consist

2. In relation to a certification mark the reference in section 1(1) (signs of which a trade mark may consist) to distinguishing goods or services of one undertaking from those of other undertakings shall be construed as a reference to distinguishing goods or services which are certified from those which are not.

Indication of geographical origin

3.—(1) Notwithstanding section 3(1)(c), a certification mark may be registered which consists of signs or indications which may serve, in trade, to designate the geographical origin of the goods or services.

(2) However, the proprietor of such a mark is not entitled to prohibit the use of the signs or indications in accordance with honest practices in industrial or commercial matters (in particular, by a person who is entitled to use a geographical name).

Nature of proprietor's business

4. A certification mark shall not be registered if the proprietor carries on a business involving the supply of goods or services of the kind certified.

Mark not to be misleading as to character or significance

5.—(1) A certification mark shall not be registered if the public is liable to be misled as regards the character or significance of the mark, in particular if it is likely to be taken to be something other than a certification mark.

(2) The registrar may accordingly require that a mark in respect of which application is made for registration include some indication that it is a certification mark.

Notwithstanding section 39(2), an application may be amended so as to comply with any such requirement.

Regulations governing use of certification mark

6.—(1) An applicant for registration of a certification mark must file with the registrar regulations governing the use of the mark.

(2) The regulations must indicate who is authorised to use the mark, the characteristics to be certified by the mark, how the certifying body is to test those characteristics and to supervise the use of the mark, the fees (if any) to be paid in connection with the operation of the mark and the procedures for resolving disputes.

Further requirements with which the regulations have to comply may be imposed by rules.

Approval of regulations, &c.

7.—(1) A certification mark shall not be registered unless—
   (a) the regulations governing the use of the mark—
      (i)   comply with paragraph 6(2) and any further requirements imposed by rules, and
      (ii) are not contrary to public policy or to accepted principles of morality, and
   (b) the applicant is competent to certify the goods or services for which the mark is to be registered.

(2) Before the end of the prescribed period after the date of the application for registration of a certification mark, the applicant must file the regulations with the registrar and pay the prescribed fee.

If he does not do so, the application shall be deemed to be withdrawn.

8.—(1) The registrar shall consider whether the requirements mentioned in paragraph 7(1) are met.

(2) If it appears to the registrar that those requirements are not met, he shall inform the applicant and give him an opportunity, within such period as the registrar may specify, to make representations or to file amended regulations.

(3) If the applicant fails to satisfy the registrar that those requirements are met, or to file regulations amended so as to meet them, or fails to respond before the end of the specified period, the registrar shall refuse the application.

(4) If it appears to the registrar that those requirements, and the other requirements for registration, are met, he shall accept the application and shall proceed in accordance with section 38 (publication, opposition proceedings and observations).

9. The regulations shall be published and notice of opposition may be given, and observations may be made, relating to the matters mentioned in paragraph 7(1).

This is in addition to any other grounds on which the application may be opposed or observations made.

Regulations to be open to inspection

10. The regulations governing the use of a registered certification mark shall be open to public inspection in the same way as the register.

Amendment of regulations

11.—(1) An amendment of the regulations governing the use of a registered certification mark is not effective unless and until the amended regulations are filed with the registrar and accepted by him.

(2) Before accepting any amended regulations the registrar may in any case where it appears to him expedient to do so cause them to be published.

(3) If he does so, notice of opposition may be given, and observations may be made, relating to the matters mentioned in paragraph 7(1).

Consent to assignment of registered certification mark

12. The assignment or other transmission of a registered certification mark is not effective without the consent of the registrar.

Infringement: rights of authorised users

13. The following provisions apply in relation to an authorised user of a registered certification mark as in relation to a licensee of a trade mark—

(a) section 10(5) (definition of infringement: unauthorised application of mark to certain material);

(b) section 19(2) (order as to disposal of infringing goods, material or articles: adequacy of other remedies);

(c) section 89 (prohibition of importation of infringing goods, material or articles: request to Commissioners of Customs and Excise).

14. In infringement proceedings brought by the proprietor of a registered certification mark any loss suffered or likely to be suffered by authorised users shall be taken into account; and the court may give such directions as it thinks fit as to the extent to which the plaintiff is to hold the proceeds of any pecuniary remedy on behalf of such users.

Grounds for revocation of registration

15. Apart from the grounds of revocation provided for in section 46, the registration of a certification mark may be revoked on the ground—

(a) that the proprietor has begun to carry on such a business as is mentioned in paragraph 4,

(b) that the manner in which the mark has been used by the proprietor has caused it to become liable to mislead the public in the manner referred to in paragraph 5(1),

(c) that the proprietor has failed to observe, or to secure the observance of, the regulations governing the use of the mark,

(d) that an amendment of the regulations has been made so that the regulations—

(i) no longer comply with paragraph 6(2) and any further conditions imposed by rules, or

(ii) are contrary to public policy or to accepted principles of morality, or

(e) that the proprietor is no longer competent to certify the goods or services for which the mark is registered.

Grounds for invalidity of registration

16. Apart from the grounds of invalidity provided for in section 47, the registration of a certification mark may be declared invalid on the ground that the mark was registered in breach of the provisions of paragraph 4, 5(1) or 7(1).

. . .

Section 52A # SCHEDULE 2A   EUROPEAN UNION TRADE MARKS

PART 1   Existing European Union trade marks

A trade mark registered as an existing EUTM to be treated as registered under this Act

1.—(1) A trade mark which is registered in the EUTM Register immediately before exit day (an 'existing EUTM') is to be treated on and after exit day as if an application had been made, and the trade mark had been registered, under this Act in respect of the same goods or services as the existing EUTM is registered in the EUTM Register.

(2) A registered trade mark which comes into being by virtue of sub-paragraph (1) is referred to in this Act as a comparable trade mark (EU).

(3) This Act applies to a comparable trade mark (EU) as it applies to other registered trade marks except as otherwise provided in this Schedule.

(4) A comparable trade mark (EU) is deemed for the purposes of this Act to be registered as of the filing date accorded pursuant to Article 32 to the application which resulted in the registration of the corresponding EUTM and that date is deemed for the purposes of this Act to be the date of registration.

(5) Section 40(3) and (4) does not apply to the registration of a comparable trade mark (EU) under this Part.

. . .

(8) For the purposes of this Act—
- (a) the date of filing of an application for registration of a comparable trade mark (EU) is the filing date accorded pursuant to Article 32 to the application which resulted in the registration of the corresponding EUTM;
- (b) references to the date of application for registration of a comparable trade mark (EU) are to the date of filing of the application;
- (c) where an earlier trade mark is a comparable trade mark (EU), references to the completion of the registration procedure for the earlier trade mark are to the completion of the registration procedure in respect of the corresponding EUTM.

(9) In this Schedule—
- (a) 'corresponding EUTM', in relation to a comparable trade mark (EU), means the existing EUTM from which the comparable trade mark (EU) derives;
- (b) 'the EUTM Register' means the register of European Union trade marks maintained by the European Union Intellectual Property Office.

Opt out

2.—(1) Subject to sub-paragraph (2), the proprietor of an existing EUTM may, at any time on or after exit day, serve notice on the registrar that the trade mark is not to be treated as if the trade mark had been registered under this Act (an 'opt out notice').

(2) An opt out notice may not be served where on or after exit day—
- (a) the comparable trade mark (EU) has been put to use in the United Kingdom by the proprietor or with the proprietor's consent (which use includes affixing the trade mark to goods or to the packaging of goods in the United Kingdom solely for export purposes);
- (b) the comparable trade mark (EU) (or any right in or under it) has been made the subject of an assignment, licence, security interest or any other agreement or document except for an assent by personal representatives in relation to the comparable trade mark (EU); or
- (c) proceedings based on the comparable trade mark (EU) have been initiated by the proprietor or with the proprietor's consent.

(3) An opt out notice must—
- (a) identify the existing EUTM; and
- (b) include the name and address of any person having an interest in the existing EUTM which had effect before exit day in the United Kingdom, and in respect of which an entry was recorded in the EUTM Register.

(4) An opt out notice is of no effect unless the proprietor in that notice certifies that any such person—
- (a) has been given not less than three months' notice of the proprietor's intention to serve an opt out notice; or
- (b) is not affected or if affected, consents to the opt out.

(5) Where a notice has been served in accordance with this paragraph—
- (a) the comparable trade mark (EU) which derives from the existing EUTM ceases with effect from exit day to be treated as if it had been registered under this Act; and
- (b) the registrar must, where particulars of the comparable trade mark (EU) have been entered in the register, remove the comparable trade mark (EU) from the register.

Entries to be made in the register in relation to a comparable trade mark (EU)

3.—(1) The registrar must as soon as reasonably practicable after exit day enter a comparable trade mark (EU) in the register.

(2) The particulars of the goods or services in respect of which the comparable trade mark (EU) is treated as if it had been registered must be taken from the English language version of the entry for the corresponding EUTM in the EUTM Register.

(3) Where—

    (a) the application for registration of the corresponding EUTM was not filed in English; or

    (b) the second language indicated by the applicant pursuant to Article 146(3) was a language other than English,

a person having a sufficient interest who considers that the English language version is inaccurate may apply to the registrar for rectification of the register by the substitution of an English translation of the relevant authentic text (as determined in accordance with Article 147(3)) verified to the satisfaction of the registrar as corresponding to the authentic text.

Comparable trade mark (EU) which derives from an EU Collective Mark or EU Certification Mark

4.—(1) This paragraph applies where the European Union trade mark from which a comparable trade mark (EU) derives is an EU collective mark or an EU certification mark.

(2) The comparable trade mark (EU) is to be treated as either a collective mark or a certification mark, as the case may be.

(3) The proprietor of the comparable trade mark (EU) must, following notice from the registrar, file with the registrar regulations governing the use of the European Union trade mark, submitted pursuant to the European Union Trade Mark Regulation, which had effect immediately before exit day.

(4) Where the regulations referred to in sub-paragraph (3) are in a language other than English they must be filed together with a translation into English verified to the satisfaction of the registrar as corresponding to the original text.

(5) Paragraph 9 of Schedule 1 and paragraph 10 of Schedule 2 apply in relation to the translation referred to in sub-paragraph (4) as they apply in relation to the regulations referred to in sub-paragraph (3).

(6) Where the regulations or any translation are not filed in accordance with the above provisions—

    (a) the registrar must remove the comparable trade mark (EU) from the register; and

    (b) the rights of the proprietor shall be deemed to have ceased as from the date of removal.

. . .

Reputation of a comparable trade mark (EU)

10.—(1) Sections 5 and 10 apply in relation to a comparable trade mark (EU), subject to the modifications set out below.

(2) Where the reputation of a comparable trade mark (EU) falls to be considered in respect of any time before exit day, references in sections 5(3) and 10(3) to—

    (a) the reputation of the mark are to be treated as references to the reputation of the corresponding EUTM; and

    (b) the United Kingdom include the European Union.

Rights conferred by registered trade mark

11. Section 9 applies in relation to a comparable trade mark (EU) but as if—

    (a) the words in brackets in subsection (3) referring to section 40(3) were replaced with a reference to paragraph 1(4) of this Schedule; and

    (b) the proviso in subsection (3) were omitted.

. . .

Assignment of an existing EUTM not registered on exit day

16.—(1) This paragraph applies where before exit day an existing EUTM (or any right in it) is the subject of an assignment (a 'relevant assignment') which immediately before exit day is not recorded in the EUTM Register.

(2) Section 25 applies in relation to a relevant assignment as if it were a registrable transaction affecting a comparable trade mark (EU), subject to the modification set out below.

(3) An application under section 25(1) may only be made by—

(a) a person claiming to be entitled to an interest in or under a comparable trade mark (EU) by virtue of a relevant assignment of the corresponding EUTM; or

(b) the proprietor of the comparable trade mark (EU).

Effect of a licence of an existing EUTM

17.—(1) This paragraph applies where immediately before exit day an existing EUTM is the subject of a licence (a 'relevant licence') which—

(a) authorises the doing of acts in the United Kingdom which would otherwise infringe the European Union trade mark; and

(b) does not expire on exit day.

(2) Subject to any agreement to the contrary between the licensee and the licensor, a relevant licence continues to authorise the doing of acts in the United Kingdom which would otherwise infringe the comparable trade mark (EU) which derives from the existing EUTM.

(3) Sub-paragraph (2) is subject to—

(a) the terms on which the relevant licence was granted; and

(b) such modifications to the terms referred to in paragraph (a) as are necessary for their application in the United Kingdom.

(4) Section 25 applies in relation to a relevant licence as if it were a registrable transaction affecting a comparable trade mark (EU), subject to the modifications set out below.

(5) An application under section 25(1) may only be made by—

(a) a person claiming to be a licensee by virtue of the relevant licence; or

(b) the proprietor of the comparable trade mark (EU).

(6) Where immediately before exit day there is an entry in the EUTM Register relating to a relevant licence—

(a) section 25(3) and (4) does not apply until after the expiry of the relevant period; and

(b) section 25(4)(a) applies after the expiry of the relevant period but as if the reference to six months beginning with the date of the transaction were a reference to eighteen months beginning with exit day.

(7) In paragraph (6)(a), the 'relevant period' means the period of twelve months beginning with the day after that on which exit day falls.

...

Continuity of rights in relation to a comparable trade mark (EU)

19.—(1) References to an existing EUTM or the registration of an existing EUTM in any document made before exit day shall, unless there is evidence that the document was not intended to have effect in the United Kingdom, be read on and after exit day as including references to the comparable trade mark (EU) or the registration of the comparable trade mark (EU) which derives from the existing EUTM.

(2) Subject to any agreement to the contrary, a consent granted before exit day by the proprietor of an existing EUTM to the doing on or after exit day of an act in the United Kingdom which would otherwise infringe the comparable trade mark (EU) which derives from the existing EUTM is to be treated for the purposes of section 9 as a consent to the doing of that act.

...

PART 5   Interpretation

Interpretation

30.—(1) In this Schedule—

'comparable trade mark (EU)' has the meaning given by paragraph 1(2);

'the Continuing EUTM Regulation' has the meaning given by paragraph 23(5);

'corresponding EUTM' has the meaning given by paragraph 1(9)(a);

'the EUTM Register' has the meaning given by paragraph 1(9)(b);

'existing EUTM' has the meaning given by paragraph 1(1);

'existing EUTM application' has the meaning given by paragraph 24(1);

'expired EUTM' has the meaning given by paragraph 22(1);

'the previous EUTM Regulations' means Council Regulation (EC) No 207/2009 of 26th February 2009 on the European Union trade mark and Council Regulation (EC) No 40/94 of 20th December 1993 on the Community trade mark;

'protected international trade mark (UK)' has the same meaning as in the Trade Marks (International Registration) Order 2008.

(2) References in this Schedule to—

(a) an 'Article' are to an Article of the European Union Trade Mark Regulation and include references to any equivalent Article contained in the previous EUTM Regulations;

(b) the European Union Trade Mark Regulation include references to the previous EUTM Regulations;

(c) a European Union trade mark include references to an EU collective mark and an EU certification mark as defined in Articles 74 and 83.

Section 54A   SCHEDULE 2B   INTERNATIONAL TRADE MARKS PROTECTED IN THE EUROPEAN UNION

PART 1   Existing international trade marks protected in the European Union trade marks

An international trade mark protected in the European Union to be treated as registered under this Act

1.—(1) A trade mark which, immediately before exit day, is an international trade mark which is protected in the European Union in accordance with Article 189(2) of the European Union Trade Mark Regulation (an 'existing IR(EU)') is to be treated on and after exit day as if an application had been made, and the trade mark had been registered, under this Act in respect of the same goods or services in respect of which the international trade mark is protected in the European Union.

. . .

(4) A registered trade mark which comes into being by virtue of sub-paragraph (1) is referred to in this Act as a comparable trade mark (IR).

(5) This Act applies to a comparable trade mark (IR) as it applies to other registered trade marks except as otherwise provided in this Schedule.

. . .

PART 5   Interpretation

Interpretation

34.—(1) In this Schedule—

'comparable trade mark (IR)' has the meaning given by paragraph 1(4);

'the Common Regulations' means the Common Regulations under the Madrid Agreement concerning the international registration of marks and the Madrid Protocol in force on 1st November 2017;

'corresponding (IR)' has the meaning given by paragraph 3(4);

'existing IR(EU)' has the meaning given by paragraph 1(1);

'expired IR(EU)' has the meaning given by paragraph 23(1);

'international application' has the meaning given by paragraph 27(1)(c);

'the International Register' has the meaning given by paragraph 1(11)(a);

'international registration' has the meaning given by paragraph 1(11)(b);

'international trade mark' has the meaning given by paragraph 1(11)(c);

'Office of origin' has the meaning given by Article 2(2);

'the previous EUTM Regulations' means Council Regulation (EC) No 207/2009 of 26th February 2009 on the European Union trade mark and Council Regulation (EC) No 40/94 of 20th December 1993 on the Community trade mark;

'protected international trade mark (UK)' has the same meaning as in the Trade Marks (International Registration) Order 2008;

(2) References in this Schedule to—

    (a) an 'Article' are to an Article of the Madrid Protocol;

    (b) an Article of the European Union Trade mark Regulation include references to any equivalent Article contained in the previous EUTM Regulations;

    (c) the European Union Trade Mark Regulation include references to the previous EUTM Regulations;

    (d) an international trade mark include references to an international trade mark which is dealt with for the purposes of the European Union Trade Mark Regulation as an EU collective mark or an EU certification mark;

    (e) a 'Rule' are to a Rule of the Common Regulations.

(3) In this Schedule, references to a request for territorial extension, in relation to an existing IR(EU) which is the subject of a separate international registration within the meaning of paragraph 1(3), are to the request made before the separate international registration was created.

Community Trade Mark Regulations 2006

(SI 2006/1027)

1 Citation, commencement, extent and revocations

(1) These Regulations may be cited as the Community Trade Mark Regulations 2006 and shall come into force on 29th April 2006.

(2) These Regulations extend to England and Wales, Scotland and Northern Ireland.

. . .

2 Interpretation

. . .

(3) In these Regulations 'the Act' means the Trade Marks Act 1994, and any reference to a section is, unless the context otherwise requires, a reference to a section of that Act.

. . .

5 Remedies in infringement proceedings

(1) This regulation is without prejudice to the duties of the European Union trade mark court under Article 130(1) of the European Union Trade Mark Regulation.

(2) In an action for infringement of a European Union trade mark all such relief by way of damages, injunctions, accounts or otherwise is available to the proprietor of the European Union trade mark as is available in respect of the infringement of any other property right.

(3) The provisions of sections 15 to 19 apply in relation to a European Union trade mark as they apply to a registered trade mark; and any reference to the court shall be construed as meaning the European Union trade mark court.

6 Groundless threats of infringement proceedings

(1) The provisions of sections 21 to 21D and section 21F apply in relation to a European Union trade mark as they apply to a registered trade mark.

...

7 Importation of infringing goods, material or articles

(1) The provisions of—

(a) section 89 (infringing goods, material or articles may be treated as prohibited goods);

(b) section 90 and section 91 (power of Commissioners of Customs and Excise to disclose information),

apply in relation to a European Union trade mark as they apply in relation to a registered trade mark.

...

8 Offences and forfeiture

(1) The provisions of—

(a) section 92 (unauthorised use of trade mark, etc, in relation to goods);

(b) section 92A (search warrants);

(c) section 93 (enforcement function of local weights and measures authority);

(d) section 97 (forfeiture: England and Wales or Northern Ireland); and

(e) section 98 (forfeiture: Scotland),

apply in relation to a European Union trade mark as they apply in relation to a registered trade mark.

(2) For the purposes of those provisions, references to goods in respect of which a trade mark is registered shall include goods in respect of which an international trade mark (EC) confers protection in the European Union.

9 Falsely representing trade mark as a European Union trade mark

(1) It is an offence for a person—

(a) falsely to represent that a mark is a European Union trade mark, or

(b) to make a false representation as to the goods or services for which a European Union trade mark is registered,

knowing or having reason to believe that the representation is false.

(2) A person guilty of an offence under this regulation is liable on summary conviction to a fine not exceeding level 3 on the standard scale.

...

Trade Marks (Relative Grounds) Order 2007

(SI 2007/1976)

...

Refusing to register a mark on a ground mentioned in section 5 of the Trade Marks Act 1994

2. The registrar shall not refuse to register a trade mark on a ground mentioned in section 5 of the Trade Marks Act 1994 (relative grounds for refusal) unless objection on that ground is raised in opposition proceedings by the proprietor of the earlier trade mark or other earlier right.

3. Section 37(2) of the Trade Marks Act 1994 (search of earlier trade marks) shall cease to have effect.

4. The registrar may, in connection with an examination under section 37(1) of the Trade Marks Act 1994, carry out a search of earlier trade marks for the purpose of notifying the applicant and other persons about the existence of earlier trade marks that might be relevant to the proposed registration.

5.—(1) Only the persons specified in paragraph (2) may make an application for a declaration of invalidity on the grounds in section 47(2) of the Trade Marks Act 1994 (relative grounds).

(2) Those persons are—

(a) in the case of an application on the ground in section 47(2)(a) of that Act, the proprietor or a licensee of the earlier trade mark or, in the case of an earlier collective mark or certification mark, the proprietor or an authorised user of such collective mark or certification mark; and

(b) in the case of an application on the ground in section 47(2)(b) of that Act, the proprietor of the earlier right.

(3) So much of section 47(3) of that Act as provides that any person may make an application for a declaration of invalidity shall have effect subject to this article.

. . .

Business Protection from Misleading Marketing Regulations 2008

(SI 2008/1276)

PART 1   DEFINITIONS AND PROHIBITIONS

Citation and Commencement

1. These Regulations may be cited as the Business Protection from Misleading Marketing Regulations 2008 and shall come into force on 26th May 2008.

Interpretation

2.—(1) In these Regulations—

'advertising' means any form of representation which is made in connection with a trade, business, craft or profession in order to promote the supply or transfer of a product and 'advertiser' shall be construed accordingly;

. . .

'CMA' means the Competition and Markets Authority;

. . .

'comparative advertising' means advertising which in any way, either explicitly or by implication, identifies a competitor or a product offered by a competitor;

'court', in relation to England and Wales and Northern Ireland, means a county court or the High Court, and, in relation to Scotland, the sheriff or the Court of Session;

'DETINI' means the Department of Enterprise, Trade and Investment in Northern Ireland;

'enforcement authority' means the CMA, every local weights and measures authority, DETINI and GEMA;

'GEMA' means the Gas and Electricity Markets Authority;

'goods' includes ships, aircraft, animals, things attached to land and growing crops;

'local weights and measures authority' means a local weights and measures authority in Great Britain (within the meaning of section 69 of the Weights and Measures Act 1985);

. . .

'product' means any goods or services and includes immovable property, rights and obligations;

'ship' includes any boat and any other description of vessel used in navigation; and

'trader' means any person who is acting for purposes relating to his trade, craft, business or profession and anyone acting in the name of or on behalf of a trader.

. . .

Prohibition of advertising which misleads traders

3.—(1) Advertising which is misleading is prohibited.

(2) Advertising is misleading which—

(a) in any way, including its presentation, deceives or is likely to deceive the traders to whom it is addressed or whom it reaches; and by reason of its deceptive nature, is likely to affect their economic behaviour; or

(b) for those reasons, injures or is likely to injure a competitor.

(3) In determining whether advertising is misleading, account shall be taken of all its features, and in particular of any information it contains concerning—

(a) the characteristics of the product (as defined in paragraph (4));

(b) the price or manner in which the price is calculated;

(c) the conditions on which the product is supplied or provided; and

(d) the nature, attributes and rights of the advertiser (as defined in paragraph (5)).

(4) In paragraph (3)(a) the 'characteristics of the product' include—

. . .

(k) geographical or commercial origin of the product;

. . .

(5) In paragraph (3)(d) the 'nature, attributes and rights' of the advertiser include the advertiser's—

(a) identity;

(b) assets;

(c) qualifications;

(d) ownership of industrial, commercial or intellectual property rights; or

(e) awards and distinctions.

Comparative advertising

4. Comparative advertising shall, as far as the comparison is concerned, be permitted only when the following conditions are met—

(a) it is not misleading under regulation 3;

(b) it is not a misleading action under regulation 5 of the Consumer Protection from Unfair Trading Regulations 2008 or a misleading omission under regulation 6 of those Regulations;

(c) it compares products meeting the same needs or intended for the same purpose;

(d) it objectively compares one or more material, relevant, verifiable and representative features of those products, which may include price;

(e) it does not create confusion among traders—

(i) between the advertiser and a competitor, or

(ii) between the trade marks, trade names, other distinguishing marks or products of the advertiser and those of a competitor;

(f) it does not discredit or denigrate the trade marks, trade names, other distinguishing marks products, activities, or circumstances of a competitor;

(g) for products with designation of origin, it relates in each case to products with the same designation;

(h) it does not take unfair advantage of the reputation of a trade mark, trade name or other distinguishing marks of a competitor or of the designation of origin of competing products;

(i) it does not present products as imitations or replicas of products bearing a protected trade mark or trade name.

. . .

PART 2   OFFENCES

Misleading advertising

6. A trader is guilty of an offence if he engages in advertising which is misleading under regulation 3.

. . .

Due diligence defence

11.—(1) In any proceedings against a person for an offence under regulation 6 it is a defence for that person to prove—

    (a) that the commission of the offence was due to—

        (i) a mistake;

        (ii) reliance on information supplied to him by another person;

        (iii) the act or default of another person;

        (iv) an accident; or

        (v) another cause beyond his control;

and

    (b) that he took all reasonable precautions and exercised all due diligence to avoid the commission of such an offence by himself or any person under his control.

. . .

Innocent publication defence

12. In any proceedings against a person for an offence under regulation 6 committed by the publication of advertising it is a defence for that person to prove that—

    (a) he is a person whose business it is to publish or to arrange for the publication of advertising;

    (b) he received the advertising for publication in the ordinary course of business; and

    (c) he did not know and had no reason to suspect that its publication would amount to an offence under regulation 6.

PART 3   ENFORCEMENT

. . .

Powers of the court

18.—(1) The court on an application by an enforcement authority may grant an injunction on such terms as it may think fit to secure compliance with regulation 3, 4 or 5.

    (2) Before granting an injunction the court shall have regard to all the interests involved and in particular the public interest.

    (3) An injunction may relate not only to particular advertising but to any advertising in similar terms or likely to convey a similar impression.

    (4) The court may also require any person against whom an injunction (other than an interim injunction) is granted to publish in such form and manner and to such extent as the court thinks appropriate for the purpose of eliminating any continuing effects of the advertising—

    (a) the injunction; and

    (b) a corrective statement.

    (5) In considering an application for an injunction the court may require the person named in the application to provide evidence as to the accuracy of any factual claim made as part of the advertising of that person if, taking into account the legitimate interests of that person and any other party to the proceedings, it appears appropriate in the circumstances.

. . .

Consumer Protection from Unfair Trading Regulations 2008

(SI 2008/1277)

PART 1   GENERAL

Citation and commencement

1. These Regulations may be cited as the Consumer Protection from Unfair Trading Regulations 2008 and shall come into force on 26th May 2008.

Interpretation

2.—(1) In these Regulations—

'average consumer' shall be construed in accordance with paragraphs (2) to (6);

'business' includes—

    (a) a trade, craft or profession, and

    (b) the activities of any government department or local authority;

'CMA' means the Competition and Markets Authority;

'code of conduct' means an agreement or set of rules (which is not imposed by legal or administrative requirements), which defines the behaviour of traders who undertake to be bound by it in relation to one or more commercial practices or business sectors;

. . .

'commercial practice' means any act, omission, course of conduct, representation or commercial communication (including advertising and marketing) by a trader, which is directly connected with the promotion, sale or supply of a product to or from consumers, whether occurring before, during or after a commercial transaction (if any) in relation to a product;

'consumer' means an individual acting for purposes that are wholly or mainly outside that individual's business;

'digital content' means data which are produced and supplied in digital form;

'DETINI' means the Department of Enterprise, Trade and Investment in Northern Ireland;

'enforcement authority' means the CMA, every local weights and measures authority and DETINI;

'goods' means any tangible moveable items, but that includes water, gas and electricity if and only if they are put up for sale in a limited volume or set quantity;

'invitation to purchase' means a commercial communication which indicates characteristics of the product and the price in a way appropriate to the means of that commercial communication and thereby enables the consumer to make a purchase;

'local weights and measures authority' means a local weights and measures authority in Great Britain (within the meaning of section 69 of the Weights and Measures Act 1985);

'materially distort the economic behaviour' means in relation to an average consumer, appreciably to impair the average consumer's ability to make an informed decision thereby causing him to take a transactional decision that he would not have taken otherwise;

. . .

'product' means—

    (a) goods,

    (b) a service,

    (c) digital content,

    (d) immoveable property,

    (e) rights or obligations, or

    (f) a product of the kind mentioned in paragraphs (1A) and (1B),

but the application of this definition to Part 4A is subject to regulations 27C and 27D;

. . .

'ship' includes any boat and any other description of vessel used in navigation;

'trader'—

    (a) means a person acting for purposes relating to that person's business, whether acting personally or through another person acting in the trader's name or on the trader's behalf, and

    (b) except in Part 4A, includes a person acting in the name of or on behalf of a trader;

'transactional decision' means any decision taken by a consumer, whether it is to act or to refrain from acting, concerning—

    (a) whether, how and on what terms to purchase, make payment in whole or in part for, retain or dispose of a product; or

    (b) whether, how and on what terms to exercise a contractual right in relation to a product (but the application of this definition to regulations 5 and 7 as they apply for the purposes of Part 4A is subject to regulation 27B(2)).

(1A) A trader ('T') who demands payment from a consumer ('C') in full or partial settlement of C's liabilities or purported liabilities to T is to be treated for the purposes of these Regulations as offering to supply a product to C.

(1B) In such a case the product that T offers to supply comprises the full or partial settlement of those liabilities or purported liabilities.

(2) In determining the effect of a commercial practice on the average consumer where the practice reaches or is addressed to a consumer or consumers account shall be taken of the material characteristics of such an average consumer including his being reasonably well informed, reasonably observant and circumspect.

(3) Paragraphs (4) and (5) set out the circumstances in which a reference to the average consumer shall be read as in addition referring to the average member of a particular group of consumers.

(4) In determining the effect of a commercial practice on the average consumer where the practice is directed to a particular group of consumers, a reference to the average consumer shall be read as referring to the average member of that group.

(5) In determining the effect of a commercial practice on the average consumer—

    (a) where a clearly identifiable group of consumers is particularly vulnerable to the practice or the underlying product because of their mental or physical infirmity, age or credulity in a way which the trader could reasonably be expected to foresee, and

    (b) where the practice is likely to materially distort the economic behaviour only of that group, a reference to the average consumer shall be read as referring to the average member of that group.

(6) Paragraph (5) is without prejudice to the common and legitimate advertising practice of making exaggerated statements which are not meant to be taken literally.

PART 2   PROHIBITIONS

Prohibition of unfair commercial practices

3.—(1) Unfair commercial practices are prohibited.

. . .

    (4) A commercial practice is unfair if—

        (a) it is a misleading action under the provisions of regulation 5;

        (b) it is a misleading omission under the provisions of regulation 6;

        (c) it is aggressive under the provisions of regulation 7; or

        (d) it is listed in Schedule 1.

. . .

Misleading actions

5.—(1) A commercial practice is a misleading action if it satisfies the conditions in either paragraph (2) or paragraph (3).

    (2) A commercial practice satisfies the conditions of this paragraph—

        (a) if it contains false information and is therefore untruthful in relation to any of the matters in paragraph (4) or if it or its overall presentation in any way deceives or is likely to deceive the average consumer in relation to any of the matters in that paragraph, even if the information is factually correct; and

        (b) it causes or is likely to cause the average consumer to take a transactional decision he would not have taken otherwise.

    (3) A commercial practice satisfies the conditions of this paragraph if—

        (a) it concerns any marketing of a product (including comparative advertising) which creates confusion with any products, trade marks, trade names or other distinguishing marks of a competitor; or

        (b) it concerns any failure by a trader to comply with a commitment contained in a code of conduct which the trader has undertaken to comply with, if—

       (i) the trader indicates in a commercial practice that he is bound by that code of conduct, and

      (ii) the commitment is firm and capable of being verified and is not aspirational, and it causes or is likely to cause the average consumer to take a transactional decision he would not have taken otherwise, taking account of its factual context and of all its features and circumstances.

  (4) The matters referred to in paragraph (2)(a) are—

    (a) the existence or nature of the product;

    (b) the main characteristics of the product (as defined in paragraph 5);

    . . .

    (f) any statement or symbol relating to direct or indirect sponsorship or approval of the trader or the product;

    . . .

    (j) the nature, attributes and rights of the trader (as defined in paragraph 6);

    . . .

  (5) In paragraph (4)(b), the 'main characteristics of the product' include—

    . . .

    (p) geographical or commercial origin of the product;

    . . .

  (6) In paragraph (4)(j), the 'nature, attributes and rights' as far as concern the trader include the trader's—

    (a) identity;

    (b) assets;

    (c) qualifications;

    (d) status;

    (e) approval;

    (f) affiliations or connections;

    (g) ownership of industrial, commercial or intellectual property rights; and

    (h) awards and distinctions.

  . . .

PART 3   OFFENCES

Offences relating to unfair commercial practices

. . .

9. A trader is guilty of an offence if he engages in a commercial practice which is a misleading action under regulation 5 otherwise than by reason of the commercial practice satisfying the condition in regulation 5(3)(b).

  . . .

12. A trader is guilty of an offence if he engages in a commercial practice set out in any of paragraphs 1 to 10, 12 to 27 and 29 to 31 of Schedule 1.

  . . .

Due diligence defence

17.—(1) In any proceedings against a person for an offence under regulation 9, 10, 11 or 12 it is a defence for that person to prove—

    (a) that the commission of the offence was due to—

       (i)   a mistake;

      (ii)   reliance on information supplied to him by another person;

     (iii)   the act or default of another person;

      (iv)   an accident; or

      (v)   another cause beyond his control; and

    (b) that he took all reasonable precautions and exercised all due diligence to avoid the commission of such an offence by himself or any person under his control.

  . . .

Innocent publication of advertisement defence

18.—(1) In any proceedings against a person for an offence under regulation 9, 10, 11 or 12 committed by the publication of an advertisement it shall be a defence for a person to prove that—

(a) he is a person whose business it is to publish or to arrange for the publication of advertisements;

(b) he received the advertisement for publication in the ordinary course of business; and

(c) he did not know and had no reason to suspect that its publication would amount to an offence under the regulation to which the proceedings relate.

(2) In paragraph (1) 'advertisement' includes a catalogue, a circular and a price list.

. . .

Regulation 3(4)(d)   **SCHEDULE 1**

COMMERCIAL PRACTICES WHICH ARE IN ALL CIRCUMSTANCES CONSIDERED UNFAIR

. . .

13. Promoting a product similar to a product made by a particular manufacturer in such a manner as deliberately to mislead the consumer into believing that the product is made by that same manufacturer when it is not.

. . .

B2. UNITED STATES

Trademark Act of 1946

(United States Code Title 15 Chapter 22 – Trademarks)

Subchapter I – The Principal Register

§ 1051. Application for registration; verification

(a) Application for use of trademark

(1) The owner of a trademark used in commerce may request registration of its trademark on the principal register hereby established by paying the prescribed fee and filing in the Patent and Trademark Office an application and a verified statement, in such form as may be prescribed by the Director, and such number of specimens or facsimiles of the mark as used as may be required by the Director.

(2) The application shall include specification of the applicant's domicile and citizenship, the date of the applicant's first use of the mark, the date of the applicant's first use of the mark in commerce, the goods in connection with which the mark is used, and a drawing of the mark.

. . .

(b) Application for bona fide intention to use trademark

(1) A person who has a bona fide intention, under circumstances showing the good faith of such person, to use a trademark in commerce may request registration of its trademark on the principal register hereby established by paying the prescribed fee and filing in the Patent and Trademark Office an application and a verified statement, in such form as may be prescribed by the Director.

(2) The application shall include specification of the applicant's domicile and citizenship, the goods in connection with which the applicant has a bona fide intention to use the mark, and a drawing of the mark.

. . .

(c) Amendment of application under subsection (b) to conform to requirements of subsection (a)

At any time during examination of an application filed under subsection (b) of this section, an applicant who has made use of the mark in commerce may claim the benefits of such use for purposes of this chapter, by amending his or her application to bring it into conformity with the requirements of subsection (a) of this section.

. . .

§ 1052. Trademarks registrable on principal register; concurrent registration

No trademark by which the goods of the applicant may be distinguished from the goods of others shall be refused registration on the principal register on account of its nature unless it—

(a) Consists of or comprises immoral, deceptive, or scandalous matter; or matter which may disparage or falsely suggest a connection with persons, living or dead, institutions, beliefs, or national symbols, or bring them into contempt, or disrepute; or a geographical indication which, when used on or in connection with wines or spirits, identifies a place other than the origin of the goods and is first used on or in connection with wines or spirits by the applicant on or after one year after the date on which the WTO Agreement (as defined in section 3501 (9) of title 19) enters into force with respect to the United States.

(b) Consists of or comprises the flag or coat of arms or other insignia of the United States, or of any State or municipality, or of any foreign nation, or any simulation thereof.

(c) Consists of or comprises a name, portrait, or signature identifying a particular living individual except by his written consent, or the name, signature, or portrait of a deceased President of the United States during the life of his widow, if any, except by the written consent of the widow.

(d) Consists of or comprises a mark which so resembles a mark registered in the Patent and Trademark Office, or a mark or trade name previously used in the United States by another and not abandoned, as to be likely, when used on or in connection with the goods of the applicant, to cause confusion, or to cause mistake, or to deceive: Provided, That if the Director determines that confusion, mistake, or deception is not likely to result from the continued use by more than one person of the same or similar marks under conditions and limitations as to the mode or place of use of the marks or the goods on or in connection with which such marks are used, concurrent registrations may be issued to such persons when they have become entitled to use such marks as a result of their concurrent lawful use in commerce prior to

  (1) the earliest of the filing dates of the applications pending or of any registration issued under this chapter;

  . . .

(e) Consists of a mark which—

  (1) when used on or in connection with the goods of the applicant is merely descriptive or deceptively misdescriptive of them,

  (2) when used on or in connection with the goods of the applicant is primarily geographically descriptive of them, except as indications of regional origin may be registrable under section 1054 of this title,

  (3) when used on or in connection with the goods of the applicant is primarily geographically deceptively misdescriptive of them,

  (4) is primarily merely a surname, or

  (5) comprises any matter that, as a whole, is functional.

(f) Except as expressly excluded in subsections (a), (b), (c), (d), (e)(3), and (e)(5) of this section, nothing in this chapter shall prevent the registration of a mark used by the applicant which has become distinctive of the applicant's goods in commerce. The Director may accept as prima facie evidence that the mark has become distinctive, as used on or in connection with the applicant's goods in commerce, proof of substantially exclusive and continuous use thereof as a mark by the applicant in commerce for the five years before the date on which the claim of distinctiveness is made. Nothing in this section shall prevent the registration of a mark which, when used on or in connection with the goods of the applicant, is primarily geographically deceptively misdescriptive of them, and which became distinctive of the applicant's goods in commerce before December 8, 1993.

A mark which would be likely to cause dilution by blurring or dilution by tarnishment under section 1125 (c) of this title, may be refused registration only pursuant to a proceeding brought under section 1063 of this title. A registration for a mark which would be likely to cause dilution by blurring or dilution by tarnishment under section 1125 (c) of this title may be canceled pursuant to a proceeding brought under either section 1064 of this title or section 1092 of this title.

. . .

Subchapter III – General Provisions

§ 1111.   Notice of registration; display with mark; recovery of profits and damages in infringement suit

Notwithstanding the provisions of section 1072 of this title, a registrant of a mark registered in the Patent and Trademark Office, may give notice that his mark is registered by displaying with the mark the words 'Registered in U.S. Patent and Trademark Office' or 'Reg. U.S. Pat. & Tm. Off.' or the letter R enclosed within a circle, thus ®; and in any suit for infringement under this chapter by such a registrant failing to give such notice of registration, no profits and no damages shall be recovered under the provisions of this chapter unless the defendant had actual notice of the registration.

. . .

§ 1114.   Remedies; infringement; innocent infringement by printers and publishers

(1) Any person who shall, without the consent of the registrant—

    (a) use in commerce any reproduction, counterfeit, copy, or colorable imitation of a registered mark in connection with the sale, offering for sale, distribution, or advertising of any goods or services on or in connection with which such use is likely to cause confusion, or to cause mistake, or to deceive; or

    (b) reproduce, counterfeit, copy, or colorably imitate a registered mark and apply such reproduction, counterfeit, copy, or colorable imitation to labels, signs, prints, packages, wrappers, receptacles or advertisements intended to be used in commerce upon or in connection with the sale, offering for sale, distribution, or advertising of goods or services on or in connection with which such use is likely to cause confusion, or to cause mistake, or to deceive,

shall be liable in a civil action by the registrant for the remedies hereinafter provided. Under subsection (b) hereof, the registrant shall not be entitled to recover profits or damages unless the acts have been committed with knowledge that such imitation is intended to be used to cause confusion, or to cause mistake, or to deceive.

. . . .

§ 1125.   False designations of origin, false descriptions, and dilution forbidden

(a) Civil action

    (1) Any person who, on or in connection with any goods or services, or any container for goods, uses in commerce any word, term, name, symbol, or device, or any combination thereof, or any false designation of origin, false or misleading description of fact, or false or misleading representation of fact, which—

        (A) is likely to cause confusion, or to cause mistake, or to deceive as to the affiliation, connection, or association of such person with another person, or as to the origin, sponsorship, or approval of his or her goods, services, or commercial activities by another person, or

(B) in commercial advertising or promotion, misrepresents the nature, characteristics, qualities, or geographic origin of his or her or another person's goods, services, or commercial activities,

shall be liable in a civil action by any person who believes that he or she is or is likely to be damaged by such act.

. . .

(c) Dilution by blurring; dilution by tarnishment

(1) Injunctive relief

Subject to the principles of equity, the owner of a famous mark that is distinctive, inherently or through acquired distinctiveness, shall be entitled to an injunction against another person who, at any time after the owner's mark has become famous, commences use of a mark or trade name in commerce that is likely to cause dilution by blurring or dilution by tarnishment of the famous mark, regardless of the presence or absence of actual or likely confusion, of competition, or of actual economic injury.

(2) Definitions

(A) For purposes of paragraph (1), a mark is famous if it is widely recognized by the general consuming public of the United States as a designation of source of the goods or services of the mark's owner. In determining whether a mark possesses the requisite degree of recognition, the court may consider all relevant factors, including the following:

(i) The duration, extent, and geographic reach of advertising and publicity of the mark, whether advertised or publicized by the owner or third parties.

(ii) The amount, volume, and geographic extent of sales of goods or services offered under the mark.

(iii) The extent of actual recognition of the mark.

(iv) Whether the mark was registered under the Act of March 3, 1881, or the Act of February 20, 1905, or on the principal register.

(B) For purposes of paragraph (1), 'dilution by blurring' is association arising from the similarity between a mark or trade name and a famous mark that impairs the distinctiveness of the famous mark. In determining whether a mark or trade name is likely to cause dilution by blurring, the court may consider all relevant factors, including the following:

(i) The degree of similarity between the mark or trade name and the famous mark.

(ii) The degree of inherent or acquired distinctiveness of the famous mark.

(iii) The extent to which the owner of the famous mark is engaging in substantially exclusive use of the mark.

(iv) The degree of recognition of the famous mark.

(v) Whether the user of the mark or trade name intended to create an association with the famous mark.

(vi) Any actual association between the mark or trade name and the famous mark.

(C) For purposes of paragraph (1), 'dilution by tarnishment' is association arising from the similarity between a mark or trade name and a famous mark that harms the reputation of the famous mark.

(3) Exclusions

The following shall not be actionable as dilution by blurring or dilution by tarnishment under this subsection:

(A) Any fair use, including a nominative or descriptive fair use, or facilitation of such fair use, of a famous mark by another person other than as a designation of source for the person's own goods or services, including use in connection with—

(i)   advertising or promotion that permits consumers to compare goods or services; or

(ii) identifying and parodying, criticizing, or commenting upon the famous mark owner or the goods or services of the famous mark owner.

(B) All forms of news reporting and news commentary.

(C) Any noncommercial use of a mark.

(4) Burden of proof

In a civil action for trade dress dilution under this chapter for trade dress not registered on the principal register, the person who asserts trade dress protection has the burden of proving that—

(A) the claimed trade dress, taken as a whole, is not functional and is famous; and

(B) if the claimed trade dress includes any mark or marks registered on the principal register, the unregistered matter, taken as a whole, is famous separate and apart from any fame of such registered marks.

. . .

(6) Ownership of valid registration a complete bar to action

The ownership by a person of a valid registration under the Act of March 3, 1881, or the Act of February 20, 1905, or on the principal register under this chapter shall be a complete bar to an action against that person, with respect to that mark, that—

(A) is brought by another person under the common law or a statute of a State; and

(B)

(i)   seeks to prevent dilution by blurring or dilution by tarnishment; or

(ii) asserts any claim of actual or likely damage or harm to the distinctiveness or reputation of a mark, label, or form of advertisement.

(7) Savings clause

Nothing in this subsection shall be construed to impair, modify, or supersede the applicability of the patent laws of the United States.

(d) Cyberpiracy prevention

(1)

(A) A person shall be liable in a civil action by the owner of a mark, including a personal name which is protected as a mark under this section, if, without regard to the goods or services of the parties, that person—

(i)   has a bad faith intent to profit from that mark, including a personal name which is protected as a mark under this section; and

(ii) registers, traffics in, or uses a domain name that—

(I)   in the case of a mark that is distinctive at the time of registration of the domain name, is identical or confusingly similar to that mark;

(II)   in the case of a famous mark that is famous at the time of registration of the domain name, is identical or confusingly similar to or dilutive of that mark; or

(III) is a trademark, word, or name protected by reason of section 706 of title 18 or section 220506 of title 36.

(B)

(i)   In determining whether a person has a bad faith intent described under subparagraph (A), a court may consider factors such as, but not limited to—

(I)   the trademark or other intellectual property rights of the person, if any, in the domain name;

(II)   the extent to which the domain name consists of the legal name of the person or a name that is otherwise commonly used to identify that person;

(III) the person's prior use, if any, of the domain name in connection with the bona fide offering of any goods or services;

(IV)   the person's bona fide noncommercial or fair use of the mark in a site accessible under the domain name;

(V)   the person's intent to divert consumers from the mark owner's online location to a site accessible under the domain name that could harm the goodwill represented by the mark, either for commercial gain or with the intent to tarnish or disparage the mark, by creating a likelihood of confusion as to the source, sponsorship, affiliation, or endorsement of the site;

(VI)   the person's offer to transfer, sell, or otherwise assign the domain name to the mark owner or any third party for financial gain without having used, or having an intent to use, the domain name in the bona fide offering of any goods or services, or the person's prior conduct indicating a pattern of such conduct;

(VII)   the person's provision of material and misleading false contact information when applying for the registration of the domain name, the person's intentional failure to maintain accurate contact information, or the person's prior conduct indicating a pattern of such conduct;

(VIII)   the person's registration or acquisition of multiple domain names which the person knows are identical or confusingly similar to marks of others that are distinctive at the time of registration of such domain names, or dilutive of famous marks of others that are famous at the time of registration of such domain names, without regard to the goods or services of the parties; and

(IX)   the extent to which the mark incorporated in the person's domain name registration is or is not distinctive and famous within the meaning of subsection (c).

(ii)   Bad faith intent described under subparagraph (A) shall not be found in any case in which the court determines that the person believed and had reasonable grounds to believe that the use of the domain name was a fair use or otherwise lawful.

(C)   In any civil action involving the registration, trafficking, or use of a domain name under this paragraph, a court may order the forfeiture or cancellation of the domain name or the transfer of the domain name to the owner of the mark.

(D)   A person shall be liable for using a domain name under subparagraph (A) only if that person is the domain name registrant or that registrant's authorized licensee.

(E)   As used in this paragraph, the term 'traffics in' refers to transactions that include, but are not limited to, sales, purchases, loans, pledges, licenses, exchanges of currency, and any other transfer for consideration or receipt in exchange for consideration.

(2)

(A)   The owner of a mark may file an in rem civil action against a domain name in the judicial district in which the domain name registrar, domain name registry, or other domain name authority that registered or assigned the domain name is located if—

(i)   the domain name violates any right of the owner of a mark registered in the Patent and Trademark Office, or protected under subsection (a) or (c) of this section; and

(ii)   the court finds that the owner—

(I)   is not able to obtain in personam jurisdiction over a person who would have been a defendant in a civil action under paragraph (1); or

(II)   through due diligence was not able to find a person who would have been a defendant in a civil action under paragraph (1) by—

(aa)   sending a notice of the alleged violation and intent to proceed under this paragraph to the registrant of the domain name at the postal and e-mail address provided by the registrant to the registrar; and

(bb)   publishing notice of the action as the court may direct promptly after filing the action.

(B)   The actions under subparagraph (A)(ii) shall constitute service of process.

(C)   In an in rem action under this paragraph, a domain name shall be deemed to have its situs in the judicial district in which—

(i) the domain name registrar, registry, or other domain name authority that registered or assigned the domain name is located; or

(ii) documents sufficient to establish control and authority regarding the disposition of the registration and use of the domain name are deposited with the court.

(D)

(i) The remedies in an in rem action under this paragraph shall be limited to a court order for the forfeiture or cancellation of the domain name or the transfer of the domain name to the owner of the mark. Upon receipt of written notification of a filed, stamped copy of a complaint filed by the owner of a mark in a United States district court under this paragraph, the domain name registrar, domain name registry, or other domain name authority shall—

(I) expeditiously deposit with the court documents sufficient to establish the court's control and authority regarding the disposition of the registration and use of the domain name to the court; and

(II) not transfer, suspend, or otherwise modify the domain name during the pendency of the action, except upon order of the court.

(ii) The domain name registrar or registry or other domain name authority shall not be liable for injunctive or monetary relief under this paragraph except in the case of bad faith or reckless disregard, which includes a willful failure to comply with any such court order.

(3) The civil action established under paragraph (1) and the in rem action established under paragraph (2), and any remedy available under either such action, shall be in addition to any other civil action or remedy otherwise applicable.

(4) The in rem jurisdiction established under paragraph (2) shall be in addition to any other jurisdiction that otherwise exists, whether in rem or in personam.

. . .

§ 1127. Construction and definitions; intent of chapter

In the construction of this chapter, unless the contrary is plainly apparent from the context—

. . .

The terms 'trade name' and 'commercial name' mean any name used by a person to identify his or her business or vocation.

The term 'trademark' includes any word, name, symbol, or device, or any combination thereof—

(1) used by a person, or

(2) which a person has a bona fide intention to use in commerce and applies to register on the principal register established by this chapter,

to identify and distinguish his or her goods, including a unique product, from those manufactured or sold by others and to indicate the source of the goods, even if that source is unknown.

The term 'service mark' means any word, name, symbol, or device, or any combination thereof—

(1) used by a person, or

(2) which a person has a bona fide intention to use in commerce and applies to register on the principal register established by this chapter,

to identify and distinguish the services of one person, including a unique service, from the services of others and to indicate the source of the services, even if that source is unknown. Titles, character names, and other distinctive features of radio or television programs may be registered as service marks notwithstanding that they, or the programs, may advertise the goods of the sponsor.

. . .

The term 'mark' includes any trademark, service mark, collective mark, or certification mark.

The term 'use in commerce' means the bona fide use of a mark in the ordinary course of trade, and not made merely to reserve a right in a mark. For purposes of this chapter, a mark shall be deemed to be in use in commerce—

    (1) on goods when—

        (A) it is placed in any manner on the goods or their containers or the displays associated therewith or on the tags or labels affixed thereto, or if the nature of the goods makes such placement impracticable, then on documents associated with the goods or their sale, and

        (B) the goods are sold or transported in commerce, and

    (2) on services when it is used or displayed in the sale or advertising of services and the services are rendered in commerce, or the services are rendered in more than one State or in the United States and a foreign country and the person rendering the services is engaged in commerce in connection with the services.

. . .

The term 'colorable imitation' includes any mark which so resembles a registered mark as to be likely to cause confusion or mistake or to deceive.

. . .

A 'counterfeit' is a spurious mark which is identical with, or substantially indistinguishable from, a registered mark.

The term 'domain name' means any alphanumeric designation which is registered with or assigned by any domain name registrar, domain name registry, or other domain name registration authority as part of an electronic address on the Internet.

The term 'Internet' has the meaning given that term in section 230 (f)(1) of title 47.

. . .

B3. EUROPEAN UNION

Directive 2006/114/EC of the European Parliament and of the Council

of 12 December 2006 concerning misleading and comparative advertising (codified version)
(Text with EEA relevance)

THE EUROPEAN PARLIAMENT AND THE COUNCIL OF THE EUROPEAN UNION,

Having regard to the Treaty establishing the European Community, and in particular Article 95 thereof,

Having regard to the proposal from the Commission,

Having regard to the opinion of the European Economic and Social Committee,

Acting in accordance with the procedure laid down in Article 251 of the Treaty,

Whereas:

(1) Council Directive 84/450/EEC of 10 September 1984 concerning misleading and comparative advertising has been substantially amended several times. In the interests of clarity and rationality the said Directive should be codified.

(2) The laws against misleading advertising in force in the Member States differ widely. Since advertising reaches beyond the frontiers of individual Member States, it has a direct effect on the smooth functioning of the internal market.

(3) Misleading and unlawful comparative advertising can lead to distortion of competition within the internal market.

(4) Advertising, whether or not it induces a contract, affects the economic welfare of consumers and traders.

(5) The differences between the laws of the Member States on advertising which misleads business hinder the execution of advertising campaigns beyond national boundaries and thus affect the free circulation of goods and provision of services.

(6) The completion of the internal market means a wide range of choice. Given that consumers and traders can and must make the best possible use of the internal market, and that advertising is a very important means of creating genuine outlets for all goods and services throughout the Community, the basic provisions governing the form and content of comparative advertising should be uniform and the conditions of the use of comparative advertising in the Member States should be harmonised. If these conditions are met, this will help demonstrate objectively the merits of the various comparable products. Comparative advertising can also stimulate competition between suppliers of goods and services to the consumer's advantage.

(7) Minimum and objective criteria for determining whether advertising is misleading should be established.

(8) Comparative advertising, when it compares material, relevant, verifiable and representative features and is not misleading, may be a legitimate means of informing consumers of their advantage. It is desirable to provide a broad concept of comparative advertising to cover all modes of comparative advertising.

(9) Conditions of permitted comparative advertising, as far as the comparison is concerned, should be established in order to determine which practices relating to comparative advertising may distort competition, be detrimental to competitors and have an adverse effect on consumer choice. Such conditions of permitted advertising should include criteria of objective comparison of the features of goods and services.

(10) The international conventions on copyright as well as the national provisions on contractual and non-contractual liability should apply when the results of comparative tests carried out by third parties are referred to or reproduced in comparative advertising.

(11) The conditions of comparative advertising should be cumulative and respected in their entirety. In accordance with the Treaty, the choice of forms and methods for the implementation of these conditions should be left to the Member States, insofar as those forms and methods are not already determined by this Directive.

(12) These conditions should include, in particular, consideration of the provisions resulting from Council Regulation (EC) No 510/2006 of 20 March 2006 on the protection of geographical indications and designations of origin for agricultural products and foodstuffs, and in particular Article 13 thereof, and of the other Community provisions adopted in the agricultural sphere.

(13) Article 5 of First Council Directive 89/104/EEC of 21 December 1988 to approximate the laws of the Member States relating to trade marks confers exclusive rights on the proprietor of a registered trade mark, including the right to prevent all third parties from using, in the course of trade, any sign which is identical to, or similar to, the trade mark in relation to identical goods or services or even, where appropriate, other goods.

(14) It may, however, be indispensable, in order to make comparative advertising effective, to identify the goods or services of a competitor, making reference to a trade mark or trade name of which the latter is the proprietor.

(15) Such use of another's trade mark, trade name or other distinguishing marks does not breach this exclusive right in cases where it complies with the conditions laid down by this Directive, the intended target being solely to distinguish between them and thus to highlight differences objectively.

(16) Persons or organisations regarded under national law as having a legitimate interest in the matter should have facilities for initiating proceedings against misleading and unlawful comparative advertising, either before a court or before an administrative authority which is competent to decide upon complaints or to initiate appropriate legal proceedings.

(17) The courts or administrative authorities should have powers enabling them to order or obtain the cessation of misleading and unlawful comparative advertising. In certain cases it may be desirable to prohibit misleading and unlawful comparative advertising even before it is published. However, this in no way implies that Member States are under an obligation to introduce rules requiring the systematic prior vetting of advertising.

(18) The voluntary control exercised by self-regulatory bodies to eliminate misleading or unlawful comparative advertising may avoid recourse to administrative or judicial action and ought therefore to be encouraged.

(19) While it is for national law to determine the burden of proof, it is appropriate to enable courts and administrative authorities to require traders to produce evidence as to the accuracy of factual claims they have made.

(20) Regulating comparative advertising is necessary for the smooth functioning of the internal market. Action at Community level is therefore required. The adoption of a Directive is the appropriate instrument because it lays down uniform general principles while allowing the Member States to choose the form and appropriate method by which to attain these objectives. It is in accordance with the principle of subsidiarity.

(21) This Directive should be without prejudice to the obligations of the Member States relating to the time limits for transposition into national law and application of the Directives as set out in Part B of Annex I,

HAVE ADOPTED THIS DIRECTIVE:

Article 1

The purpose of this Directive is to protect traders against misleading advertising and the unfair consequences thereof and to lay down the conditions under which comparative advertising is permitted.

Article 2

For the purposes of this Directive:
  (a) 'advertising' means the making of a representation in any form in connection with a trade, business, craft or profession in order to promote the supply of goods or services, including immovable property, rights and obligations;
  (b) 'misleading advertising' means any advertising which in any way, including its presentation, deceives or is likely to deceive the persons to whom it is addressed or whom it reaches and which, by reason of its deceptive nature, is likely to affect their economic behaviour or which, for those reasons, injures or is likely to injure a competitor;
  (c) 'comparative advertising' means any advertising which explicitly or by implication identifies a competitor or goods or services offered by a competitor;
  (d) 'trader' means any natural or legal person who is acting for purposes relating to his trade, craft, business or profession and anyone acting in the name of or on behalf of a trader;
  (e) 'code owner' means any entity, including a trader or group of traders, which is responsible for the formulation and revision of a code of conduct and/or for monitoring compliance with the code by those who have undertaken to be bound by it.

Article 3

In determining whether advertising is misleading, account shall be taken of all its features, and in particular of any information it contains concerning:
  (a) the characteristics of goods or services, such as their availability, nature, execution, composition, method and date of manufacture or provision, fitness for purpose, uses, quantity, specification, geographical or commercial origin or the results to be expected from their use, or the results and material features of tests or checks carried out on the goods or services;
  (b) the price or the manner in which the price is calculated, and the conditions on which the goods are supplied or the services provided;
  (c) the nature, attributes and rights of the advertiser, such as his identity and assets, his qualifications and ownership of industrial, commercial or intellectual property rights or his awards and distinctions.

Article 4

Comparative advertising shall, as far as the comparison is concerned, be permitted when the following conditions are met:

(a) it is not misleading within the meaning of Articles 2(b), 3 and 8(1) of this Directive or Articles 6 and 7 of Directive 2005/29/EC of the European Parliament and of the Council of 11 May 2005 concerning unfair business-to-consumer commercial practices in the internal market ('Unfair Commercial Practices Directive');

(b) it compares goods or services meeting the same needs or intended for the same purpose;

(c) it objectively compares one or more material, relevant, verifiable and representative features of those goods and services, which may include price;

(d) it does not discredit or denigrate the trade marks, trade names, other distinguishing marks, goods, services, activities or circumstances of a competitor;

(e) for products with designation of origin, it relates in each case to products with the same designation;

(f) it does not take unfair advantage of the reputation of a trade mark, trade name or other distinguishing marks of a competitor or of the designation of origin of competing products;

(g) it does not present goods or services as imitations or replicas of goods or services bearing a protected trade mark or trade name;

(h) it does not create confusion among traders, between the advertiser and a competitor or between the advertiser's trade marks, trade names, other distinguishing marks, goods or services and those of a competitor.

Article 5

1. Member States shall ensure that adequate and effective means exist to combat misleading advertising and enforce compliance with the provisions on comparative advertising in the interests of traders and competitors.

Such means shall include legal provisions under which persons or organisations regarded under national law as having a legitimate interest in combating misleading advertising or regulating comparative advertising may:

(a) take legal action against such advertising; or

(b) bring such advertising before an administrative authority competent either to decide on complaints or to initiate appropriate legal proceedings.

2. It shall be for each Member State to decide which of the facilities referred to in the second subparagraph of paragraph 1 shall be available and whether to enable the courts or administrative authorities to require prior recourse to other established means of dealing with complaints, including those referred to in Article 6.

It shall be for each Member State to decide:

(a) whether these legal facilities may be directed separately or jointly against a number of traders from the same economic sector; and

(b) whether these legal facilities may be directed against a code owner where the relevant code promotes non-compliance with legal requirements.

3. Under the provisions referred to in paragraphs 1 and 2, Member States shall confer upon the courts or administrative authorities powers enabling them, in cases where they deem such measures to be necessary taking into account all the interests involved and in particular the public interest:

(a) to order the cessation of, or to institute appropriate legal proceedings for an order for the cessation of, misleading advertising or unlawful comparative advertising; or

(b) if the misleading advertising or unlawful comparative advertising has not yet been published but publication is imminent, to order the prohibition of, or to institute appropriate legal proceedings for an order for the prohibition of, such publication.

The first subparagraph shall apply even where there is no proof of actual loss or damage or of intention or negligence on the part of the advertiser.

Member States shall make provision for the measures referred to in the first subparagraph to be taken under an accelerated procedure either with interim effect or with definitive effect, at the Member States' discretion.

4. Member States may confer upon the courts or administrative authorities powers enabling them, with a view to eliminating the continuing effects of misleading advertising or unlawful comparative advertising, the cessation of which has been ordered by a final decision:

(a) to require publication of that decision in full or in part and in such form as they deem adequate;

(b) to require in addition the publication of a corrective statement.

5. The administrative authorities referred to in point (b) of the second subparagraph of paragraph 1 must:

(a) be composed so as not to cast doubt on their impartiality;

(b) have adequate powers, where they decide on complaints, to monitor and enforce the observance of their decisions effectively;

(c) normally give reasons for their decisions.

6. Where the powers referred to in paragraphs 3 and 4 are exercised exclusively by an administrative authority, reasons for its decisions shall always be given. In this case, provision must be made for procedures whereby improper or unreasonable exercise of its powers by the administrative authority or improper or unreasonable failure to exercise the said powers can be the subject of judicial review.

Article 6

This Directive does not exclude the voluntary control, which Member States may encourage, of misleading or comparative advertising by self-regulatory bodies and recourse to such bodies by the persons or organisations referred to in the second subparagraph of Article 5(1) on condition that proceedings before such bodies are additional to the court or administrative proceedings referred to in that Article.

Article 7

Member States shall confer upon the courts or administrative authorities powers enabling them in the civil or administrative proceedings referred to in Article 5:

(a) to require the advertiser to furnish evidence as to the accuracy of factual claims in advertising if, taking into account the legitimate interest of the advertiser and any other party to the proceedings, such a requirement appears appropriate on the basis of the circumstances of the particular case and in the case of comparative advertising to require the advertiser to furnish such evidence in a short period of time; and

(b) to consider factual claims as inaccurate if the evidence demanded in accordance with point (a) is not furnished or is deemed insufficient by the court or administrative authority.

Article 8

1. This Directive shall not preclude Member States from retaining or adopting provisions with a view to ensuring more extensive protection, with regard to misleading advertising, for traders and competitors.

The first subparagraph shall not apply to comparative advertising as far as the comparison is concerned.

2. The provisions of this Directive shall apply without prejudice to Community provisions on advertising for specific products and/or services or to restrictions or prohibitions on advertising in particular media.

3. The provisions of this Directive concerning comparative advertising shall not oblige Member States which, in compliance with the provisions of the Treaty, maintain or introduce advertising bans regarding certain goods or services, whether imposed directly or by a body or organisation responsible, under the law of the Member States, for regulating the exercise of a commercial, industrial, craft or professional activity, to permit comparative advertising regarding those goods or services. Where these bans are limited to particular media, this Directive shall apply to the media not covered by these bans.

4. Nothing in this Directive shall prevent Member States, in compliance with the provisions of the Treaty, from maintaining or introducing bans or limitations on the use of comparisons in

the advertising of professional services, whether imposed directly or by a body or organisation responsible, under the law of the Member States, for regulating the exercise of a professional activity.

Article 9
Member States shall communicate to the Commission the text of the main provisions of national law which they adopt in the field covered by this Directive.

. . .

Regulation (EU) No. 1151/2012 of the European Parliament and of the Council

of 21 November 2012 on quality schemes for agricultural products and foodstuffs

THE EUROPEAN PARLIAMENT AND THE COUNCIL OF THE EUROPEAN UNION,

Having regard to the Treaty on the Functioning of the European Union, and in particular Article 43(2) and the first paragraph of Article 118 thereof,

Having regard to the proposal from the European Commission,

After transmission of the draft legislative act to the national parliaments,

Having regard to the opinion of the European Economic and Social Committee,

Having regard to the opinion of the Committee of the Regions,

Acting in accordance with the ordinary legislative procedure,

Whereas:

(1) The quality and diversity of the Union's agricultural, fisheries and aquaculture production is one of its important strengths, giving a competitive advantage to the Union's producers and making a major contribution to its living cultural and gastronomic heritage. This is due to the skills and determination of Union farmers and producers who have kept traditions alive while taking into account the developments of new production methods and material.

(2) Citizens and consumers in the Union increasingly demand quality as well as traditional products. They are also concerned to maintain the diversity of the agricultural production in the Union. This generates a demand for agricultural products or foodstuffs with identifiable specific characteristics, in particular those linked to their geographical origin.

(3) Producers can only continue to produce a diverse range of quality products if they are rewarded fairly for their effort. This requires that they are able to communicate to buyers and consumers the characteristics of their product under conditions of fair competition. It also requires them to be able to correctly identify their products on the marketplace.

(4) Operating quality schemes for producers which reward them for their efforts to produce a diverse range of quality products can benefit the rural economy. This is particularly the case in less favoured areas, in mountain areas and in the most remote regions, where the farming sector accounts for a significant part of the economy and production costs are high. In this way quality schemes are able to contribute to and complement rural development policy as well as market and income support policies of the common agricultural policy (CAP). In particular, they may contribute to areas in which the farming sector is of greater economic importance and, especially, to disadvantaged areas.

(5) The Europe 2020 policy priorities as set out in the Commission Communication entitled 'Europe 2020: A strategy for smart, sustainable and inclusive growth', include the aims of achieving a competitive economy based on knowledge and innovation and fostering a high-employment economy delivering social and territorial cohesion. Agricultural product quality policy should therefore provide producers with the right tools to better identify and promote those of their products that have specific characteristics while protecting those producers against unfair practices.

(6) The set of complementary measures envisaged should respect the principles of subsidiarity and proportionality.

(7) Agricultural product quality policy measures are laid down in Council Regulation (EEC) No 1601/91 of 10 June 1991 laying down general rules on the definition, description and presentation of aromatized wines, aromatized wine-based drinks and aromatized wine-product cocktails; Council Directive 2001/110/EC of 20 December 2001 relating to honey and in particular in Article 2 thereof, Council Regulation (EC) No 247/2006 of 30 January 2006 laying down specific measures for agriculture in the outermost regions of the Union and in particular in Article 14 thereof; Council Regulation (EC) No 509/2006 of 20 March 2006 on agricultural products and foodstuffs as traditional specialities guaranteed; Council Regulation (EC) No 510/2006 of 20 March 2006 on the protection of geographical indications and designations of origin for agricultural products and foodstuffs; Council Regulation (EC) No 1234/2007 of 22 October 2007 establishing a common organisation of agricultural markets and on specific provisions for certain agricultural products (Single CMO Regulation) and in particular in Part II, Title II, Chapter I, Section I and in Section Ia, Subsection I thereof; Council Regulation (EC) No 834/2007 of 28 June 2007 on organic production and labelling of organic products; and Regulation (EC) No 110/2008 of the European Parliament and of the Council of 15 January 2008 on the definition, description, presentation, labelling and the protection of geographical indications of spirit drinks.

(8) The labelling of agricultural products and foodstuffs should be subject to the general rules laid down in Directive 2000/13/EC of the European Parliament and of the Council of 20 March 2000 on the approximation of the laws of the Member States relating to the labelling, presentation and advertising of foodstuffs, and in particular the provisions aimed at preventing labelling that may confuse or mislead consumers.

(9) The Communication from the Commission to the European Parliament, the Council, the European Economic and Social Committee and the Committee of the Regions on agricultural product quality policy identified the achievement of a greater overall coherence and consistency of agricultural product quality policy as a priority.

(10) The geographical indications scheme for agricultural products and foodstuffs and the traditional specialities guaranteed scheme have certain common objectives and provisions.

(11) The Union has for some time been pursuing an approach that aims to simplify the regulatory framework of the CAP. This approach should also be applied to regulations in the field of agricultural product quality policy, without, in so doing, calling into question the specific characteristics of those products.

(12) Some regulations that form part of the agricultural product quality policy have been reviewed recently but are not yet fully implemented. As a result, they should not be included in this Regulation. However, they may be incorporated at a later stage, once the legislation has been fully implemented.

(13) In the light of the aforementioned considerations, the following provisions should be amalgamated into a single legal framework comprising the new or updated provisions of Regulations (EC) No 509/2006 and (EC) No 510/2006 and those provisions of Regulations (EC) No 509/2006 and (EC) No 510/2006 that are maintained.

(14) In the interests of clarity and transparency, Regulations (EC) No 509/2006 and (EC) No 510/2006 should therefore be repealed and replaced by this Regulation.

(15) The scope of this Regulation should be limited to the agricultural products intended for human consumption listed in Annex I to the Treaty and to a list of products outside the scope of that Annex that are closely linked to agricultural production or to the rural economy.

(16) The rules provided for in this Regulation should apply without affecting existing Union legislation on wines, aromatised wines, spirit drinks, product of organic farming, or outermost regions.

(17) The scope for designations of origin and geographical indications should be limited to products for which an intrinsic link exists between product or foodstuff characteristics and geographical origin. The inclusion in the current scheme of only certain types of chocolate as confectionery products is an anomaly that should be corrected.

(18) The specific objectives of protecting designations of origin and geographical indications are securing a fair return for farmers and producers for the qualities and characteristics of a given product,

or of its mode of production, and providing clear information on products with specific characteristics linked to geographical origin, thereby enabling consumers to make more informed purchasing choices.

(19) Ensuring uniform respect throughout the Union for the intellectual property rights related to names protected in the Union is a priority that can be achieved more effectively at Union level.

(20) A Union framework that protects designations of origin and geographical indications by providing for their inclusion on a register facilitates the development of those instruments, since the resulting, more uniform, approach ensures fair competition between the producers of products bearing such indications and enhances the credibility of the products in the consumers' eyes. Provision should be made for the development of designations of origin and geographical indications at Union level and for promoting the creation of mechanisms for their protection in third countries in the framework of the World Trade Organisation (WTO) or multilateral and bilateral agreements, thereby contributing to the recognition of the quality of products and of their model of production as a factor that adds value.

(21) In the light of the experience gained from the implementation of Council Regulation (EEC) No 2081/92 of 14 July 1992 on the protection of geographical indications and designations of origin for agricultural products and foodstuffs and Regulation (EC) No 510/2006, there is a need to address certain issues, to clarify and simplify some rules and to streamline the procedures of this scheme.

(22) In the light of existing practice, the two different instruments for identifying the link between the product and its geographical origin, namely the protected designation of origin and the protected geographical indication, should be further defined and maintained. Without changing the concept of those instruments, some modifications to the definitions should be adopted in order to better take into account the definition of geographical indications laid down in the Agreement on Trade-Related Aspects of Intellectual Property Rights and to make them simpler and clearer for operators to understand.

(23) An agricultural product or foodstuff bearing such a geographical description should meet certain conditions set out in a specification, such as specific requirements aimed at protecting the natural resources or landscape of the production area or improving the welfare of farm animals.

(24) To qualify for protection in the territories of Member States, designations of origin and geographical indications should be registered only at Union level. With effect from the date of application for such registration at Union level, Member States should be able to grant transitional protection at national level without affecting intra-Union or international trade. The protection afforded by this Regulation upon registration, should be equally available to designations of origin and geographical indications of third countries that meet the corresponding criteria and that are protected in their country of origin.

(25) The registration procedure at Union level should enable any natural or legal person with a legitimate interest from a Member State, other than the Member State of the application, or from a third country, to exercise their rights by notifying their opposition.

(26) Entry in the register of protected designations of origin and protected geographical indications should also provide information to consumers and to those involved in trade.

(27) The Union negotiates international agreements, including those concerning the protection of designations of origin and geographical indications, with its trade partners. In order to facilitate the provision to the public of information about the names so protected, and in particular to ensure protection and control of the use to which those names are put, the names may be entered in the register of protected designations of origin and protected geographical indications. Unless specifically identified as designations of origin in such international agreements, the names should be entered in the register as protected geographical indications.

(28) In view of their specific nature, special provisions concerning labelling should be adopted in respect of protected designations of origin and protected geographical indications that require producers to use the appropriate Union symbols or indications on packaging. In the case of Union names, the use of such symbols or indications should be made obligatory in order to make this category of products, and the guarantees attached to them, better known to consumers and in order to permit easier identification of these products on the market, thereby facilitating checks. Taking into account

the requirements of the WTO, the use of such symbols or indications should be made voluntary for third-country geographical indications and designations of origin.

(29) Protection should be granted to names included in the register with the aim of ensuring that they are used fairly and in order to prevent practices liable to mislead consumers. In addition, the means of ensuring that geographical indications and designations of origin are protected should be clarified, particularly as regards the role of producer groups and competent authorities of Member States.

(30) Provision should be made for specific derogations that permit, for transitional periods, the use of a registered name alongside other names. Those derogations should be simplified and clari-fied. In certain cases, in order to overcome temporary difficulties and with the long-term objective of ensuring that all producers comply with the specifications, those derogations may be granted for a period of up to 10 years.

(31) The scope of the protection granted under this Regulation should be clarified, in particular with regard to those limitations on registration of new trade marks set out in Directive 2008/95/EC of the European Parliament and of the Council of 22 October 2008 to approximate the laws of the Member States relating to trade marks that conflict with the registration of protected designations of origin and protected geographical indications as is already the case for the registration of new trade marks at Union level. Such clarification is also necessary with regard to the holders of prior rights in intellectual property, in particular those concerning trade marks and homonymous names registered as protected designations of origin or as protected geographical indications.

(32) Protection of designations of origin and geographical indications should be extended to the misuse, imitation and evocation of the registered names on goods as well as on services in order to en-sure a high level of protection and to align that protection with that which applies to the wine sector. When protected designations of origin or protected geographical indications are used as ingredients, the Commission Communication entitled 'Guidelines on the labelling of foodstuffs using protected designations of origin (PDOs) or protected geographical indications (PGIs) as ingredients' should be taken into account.

(33) The names already registered under Regulation (EC) No 510/2006 on 3 January 2013 should continue to be protected under this Regulation and they should be automatically included in the register.

(34) The specific objective of the scheme for traditional specialities guaranteed is to help the producers of traditional products to communicate to consumers the value-adding attributes of their product. However, as only a few names have been registered, the current scheme for traditional speci-alities guaranteed has failed to realise its potential. Current provisions should therefore be improved, clarified and sharpened in order to make the scheme more understandable, operational and attractive to potential applicants.

(35) The current scheme provides the option to register a name for identification purposes without reservation of the name in the Union. As this option has not been well understood by stake-holders and since the function of identifying traditional products can be better achieved at Member State or regional level in application of the principle of subsidiarity, this option should be discontin-ued. In the light of experience, the scheme should only deal with the reservation of names across the Union.

(36) To ensure that names of genuine traditional products are registered under the scheme, the criteria and conditions for registration of a name should be adapted, in particular those concerning the definition of 'traditional', which should cover products that have been produced for a significant period of time.

(37) To ensure that traditional specialities guaranteed comply with their specification and are con-sistent, producers organised into groups should themselves define the product in a specification. The option of registering a name as a traditional speciality guaranteed should be open to third-country producers.

(38) To qualify for reservation, traditional specialities guaranteed should be registered at Union level. The entry in the register should also provide information to consumers and to those involved in the trade.

(39) In order to avoid creating unfair conditions of competition, any producer, including a third-country producer, should be able to use a registered name of a traditional speciality guaranteed, provided that the product concerned complies with the requirements of the relevant specification and the producer is covered by a system of controls. For traditional specialities guaranteed produced within the Union, the Union symbol should be indicated on the labelling and it should be possible to associate it with the indication 'traditional speciality guaranteed'.

(40) In order to protect registered names from misuse, or from practices that might mislead consumers, their use should be reserved.

(41) For those names already registered under Regulation (EC) No 509/2006 that, on 3 January 2013, would otherwise not be covered by the scope of this Regulation, the terms of use laid down in Regulation (EC) No 509/2006 should continue to apply for a transitional period.

(42) A procedure should be introduced for registering names that are registered without reservation of name pursuant to Regulation (EC) No 509/2006, enabling them to be registered with reservation of name.

(43) Provision should also be made for transitional measures applicable to registration applications received by the Commission before 3 January 2013.

(44) A second tier of quality systems, based on quality terms which add value, which can be communicated on the internal market and which are to be applied voluntarily, should be introduced. Those optional quality terms should refer to specific horizontal characteristics, with regard to one or more categories of products, farming methods or processing attributes which apply in specific areas. The optional quality term 'mountain product' has met the conditions up to now and will add value to the product on the market. In order to facilitate the application of Directive 2000/13/EC where the labelling of foodstuffs may give rise to consumer confusion in relation to optional quality terms, including in particular 'mountain products', the Commission may adopt guidelines.

(45) In order to provide mountain producers with an effective tool to better market their product and to reduce the actual risks of consumer confusion as to the mountain provenance of products in the market place, provision should be made for the definition at Union level of an optional quality term for mountain products. The definition of mountain areas should build on the general classification criteria employed to identify a mountain area in Council Regulation (EC) No 1257/1999 of 17 May 1999 on support for rural development from the European Agricultural Guidance and Guarantee Fund (EAGGF).

(46) The added value of the geographical indications and traditional specialities guaranteed is based on consumer trust. It is only credible if accompanied by effective verification and controls. Those quality schemes should be subject to a monitoring system of official controls, in line with the principles set out in Regulation (EC) No 882/2004 of the European Parliament and of the Council of 29 April 2004 on official controls performed to ensure the verification of compliance with feed and food law, animal health and animal welfare rules, and should include a system of checks at all stages of production, processing and distribution. In order to help Member States to better apply provisions of Regulation (EC) No 882/2004 for the controls of geographical indications and traditional specialities guaranteed, references to the most relevant articles should be mentioned in this Regulation.

(47) To guarantee to the consumer the specific characteristics of geographical indications and traditional specialities guaranteed, operators should be subject to a system that verifies compliance with the product specification.

(48) In order to ensure that they are impartial and effective, the competent authorities should meet a number of operational criteria. Provisions on delegating some competences of performing specific control tasks to control bodies should be envisaged.

(49) European standards (EN standards) developed by the European Committee for Standardisation (CEN) and international standards developed by the International Organisation for Standardisation (ISO) should be used for the accreditation of the control bodies as well as by those bodies for their operations. The accreditation of those bodies should take place in accordance with Regulation (EC) No 765/2008 of the European Parliament and of the Council of 9 July 2008 setting out the requirements for accreditation and market surveillance relating to the marketing of products.

(50) Information on control activities for geographical indications and traditional specialities guaranteed should be included in the multiannual national control plans and annual report prepared by the Member States in accordance with Regulation (EC) No 882/2004.

(51) Member States should be authorised to charge a fee to cover the costs incurred.

(52) Existing rules concerning the continued use of names that are generic should be clarified so that generic terms that are similar to or form part of a name or term that is protected or reserved should retain their generic status.

(53) The date for establishing the seniority of a trade mark and of a designation of origin or a geographical indication should be that of the date of application of the trade mark for registration in the Union or in the Member States and the date of application for protection of a designation of origin or a geographical indication to the Commission.

(54) The provisions dealing with the refusal or coexistence of a designation of origin or a geographical indication on the ground of conflict with a prior trade mark should continue to apply.

(55) The criteria by which subsequent trade marks should be refused or, if registered, invalidated on the ground that they conflict with a prior designation of origin or geographical indication should correspond to the scope of protection of designation of origin or a geographical indication laid down.

(56) The provisions of systems establishing intellectual property rights, and particularly of those established by the quality scheme for designations of origin and geographical indications or those established under trade mark law, should not be affected by the reservation of names and the establishment of indications and symbols pursuant to the quality schemes for traditional specialities guaranteed and for optional quality terms.

(57) The role of groups should be clarified and recognised. Groups play an essential role in the application process for the registration of names of designations of origin and geographical indications and traditional specialities guaranteed, as well as in the amendment of specifications and cancellation requests. The group can also develop activities related to the surveillance of the enforcement of the protection of the registered names, the compliance of the production with the product specification, the information and promotion of the registered name as well as, in general, any activity aimed at improving the value of the registered names and effectiveness of the quality schemes. Moreover, it should monitor the position of the products on the market. Nevertheless, these activities should not facilitate nor lead to anti-competitive conduct incompatible with Articles 101 and 102 of the Treaty.

(58) To ensure that registered names of designations of origin and geographical indications and traditional specialities guaranteed meet the conditions laid down by this Regulation, applications should be examined by the national authorities of the Member State concerned, in compliance with minimum common provisions, including a national opposition procedure. The Commission should subsequently scrutinise applications to ensure that there are no manifest errors and that Union law and the interests of stakeholders outside the Member State of application have been taken into account.

(59) Registration as designations of origin, geographical indications and traditional specialities guaranteed should be open to names that relate to products originating in third countries and that satisfy the conditions laid down by this Regulation.

(60) The symbols, indications and abbreviations identifying participation in a quality scheme, and the rights therein pertaining to the Union, should be protected in the Union as well as in third countries with the aim of ensuring that they are used on genuine products and that consumers are not misled as to the qualities of products. Furthermore, in order for the protection to be effective, the Commission should have recourse to reasonable budget resources on a centralised basis within the framework of Council Regulation (EC) No 1698/2005 of 20 September 2005 on support for rural development by the European Agricultural Fund for Rural Development (EAFRD) and in accordance with Article 5 of Council Regulation (EC) No 1290/2005 of 21 June 2005 on the financing of the common agricultural policy.

(61) The registration procedure for protected designations of origin, protected geographical indications and traditional specialities guaranteed, including the scrutiny and the opposition periods, should be shortened and improved, in particular as regards decision making. The Commission, in certain circumstances acting with the assistance of Member States, should be responsible for decision-making on registration. Procedures should be laid down to allow the amendment of product specifications after registration and the cancellation of registered names, in particular if the product no longer complies with the corresponding product specification or if a name is no longer used in the market place.

(62) In order to facilitate cross-border applications for joint registration of protected designations of origin, protected geographical indications or traditional specialities guaranteed, provision should be made for appropriate procedures.

. . .

HAVE ADOPTED THIS REGULATION:

Title I   General Provisions

Article 1   Objectives

1. This Regulation aims to help producers of agricultural products and foodstuffs to communicate the product characteristics and farming attributes of those products and foodstuffs to buyers and consumers, thereby ensuring:

(a) fair competition for farmers and producers of agricultural products and foodstuffs having value-adding characteristics and attributes;

(b) the availability to consumers of reliable information pertaining to such products;

(c) respect for intellectual property rights; and

(d) the integrity of the internal market.

The measures set out in this Regulation are intended to support agricultural and processing activities and the farming systems associated with high quality products, thereby contributing to the achievement of rural development policy objectives.

2. This Regulation establishes quality schemes which provide the basis for the identification and, where appropriate, protection of names and terms that, in particular, indicate or describe agricultural products with:

(a) value-adding characteristics; or

(b) value-adding attributes resulting from the farming or processing methods used in their production, or from the place of their production or marketing, or from their possible contribution to sustainable development.

Article 2   Scope

1. This Regulation covers agricultural products intended for human consumption listed in Annex I to the Treaty and other agricultural products and foodstuffs listed in Annex I to this Regulation.

In order to take into account international commitments or new production methods or material, the Commission shall be empowered to adopt delegated acts, in accordance with Article 56, supplementing the list of products set out in Annex I to this Regulation. Such products shall be closely linked to agricultural products or to the rural economy.

2. This Regulation shall not apply to spirit drinks or grapevine products as defined in Annex VII, Part II, to Regulation (EU) No 1308/2013, with the exception of wine-vinegars.

3. Registrations made pursuant to Article 52 are without prejudice to the obligation of producers to comply with other Union rules, in particular those relating to the placing of products on the market and to food labelling.

4. Directive 98/34/EC of the European Parliament and of the Council of 22 June 1998 laying down a procedure for the provision of information in the field of technical standards and regulations and of rules on Information Society services shall not apply to the quality schemes established by this Regulation.

Article 3   Definitions

For the purposes of this Regulation the following definitions shall apply:

(1) 'quality schemes' means the schemes established under Titles II, III and IV;

(2) 'group' means any association, irrespective of its legal form, mainly composed of producers or processors working with the same product;

(3) 'traditional' means proven usage on the domestic market for a period that allows transmission between generations; this period is to be at least 30 years;

(4) 'labelling' means any words, particulars, trade marks, brand name, pictorial matter or symbol relating to a foodstuff and placed on any packaging, document, notice, label, ring or collar accompanying or referring to such foodstuff;

(5) 'specific character' in relation to a product means the characteristic production attributes which distinguish a product clearly from other similar products of the same category;

(6) 'generic terms' means the names of products which, although relating to the place, region or country where the product was originally produced or marketed, have become the common name of a product in the Union;

(7) 'production step' means production, processing or preparation;

(8) 'processed products' means foodstuffs resulting from the processing of unprocessed products. Processed products may contain ingredients that are necessary for their manufacture or to give them specific characteristics.

Title II   Protected Designations of Origin and Protected Geographical Indications

Article 4   Objective

A scheme for protected designations of origin and protected geographical indications is established in order to help producers of products linked to a geographical area by:

(a) securing fair returns for the qualities of their products;

(b) ensuring uniform protection of the names as an intellectual property right in the territory of the Union;

(c) providing clear information on the value-adding attributes of the product to consumers.

Article 5   Requirements for designations of origin and geographical indications

1. For the purpose of this Regulation, 'designation of origin' is a name, which may be a traditionally used name, which identifies a product:

(a) originating in a specific place, region or, in exceptional cases, a country;

(b) whose quality or characteristics are essentially or exclusively due to a particular geographical environment with its inherent natural and human factors; and

(c) the production steps of which all take place in the defined geographical area.

2. For the purpose of this Regulation, 'geographical indication' is a name, including a traditionally used name, which identifies a product:

(a) originating in a specific place, region or country;

(b) whose given quality, reputation or other characteristic is essentially attributable to its geographical origin; and

(c) at least one of the production steps of which takes place in the defined geographical area.

3. Notwithstanding paragraph 1, certain names shall be treated as designations of origin even though the raw materials for the products concerned come from a geographical area larger than, or different from, the defined geographical area, provided that:

(a) the production area of the raw materials is defined;

(b) special conditions for the production of the raw materials exist;

(c) there are control arrangements to ensure that the conditions referred to in point (b) are adhered to; and

(d) the designations of origin in question were recognised as designations of origin in the country of origin before 1 May 2004.

Only live animals, meat and milk may be considered as raw materials for the purposes of this paragraph.

4. In order to take into account the specific character of production of products of animal origin, the Commission shall be empowered to adopt delegated acts, in accordance with Article 56, concerning restrictions and derogations with regard to the sourcing of feed in the case of a designation of origin.

In addition, in order to take into account the specific character of certain products or areas, the Commission shall be empowered to adopt delegated acts in accordance with Article 56, concerning restrictions and derogations with regard to the slaughtering of live animals or with regard to the sourcing of raw materials.

These restrictions and derogations shall, based on objective criteria, take into account quality or usage and recognised know-how or natural factors.

Article 6 Generic nature, conflicts with names of plant varieties and animal breeds, with homonyms and trade marks

1. Generic terms shall not be registered as protected designations of origin or protected geographical indications.

2. A name may not be registered as a designation of origin or geographical indication where it conflicts with a name of a plant variety or an animal breed and is likely to mislead the consumer as to the true origin of the product or to cause confusion between products with the registered designation and the variety or breed in question.

The conditions referred to in the first subparagraph shall be assessed in relation to the actual use of the names in conflict, including the use of the name of the plant variety or animal breed outside its area of origin and the use of the name of a plant variety protected by another intellectual property right.

3. A name proposed for registration that is wholly or partially homonymous with a name already entered in the register established under Article 11 may not be registered unless there is sufficient distinction in practice between the conditions of local and traditional usage and presentation of the homonym registered subsequently and the name already entered in the register, taking into account the need to ensure equitable treatment of the producers concerned and that consumers are not misled.

A homonymous name which misleads the consumer into believing that products come from another territory shall not be registered even if the name is accurate as far as the actual territory, region or place of origin of the products in question is concerned.

4. A name proposed for registration as a designation of origin or geographical indication shall not be registered where, in the light of a trade mark's reputation and renown and the length of time it has been used, registration of the name proposed as the designation of origin or geographical indication would be liable to mislead the consumer as to the true identity of the product.

Article 7 Product specification

1. A protected designation of origin or a protected geographical indication shall comply with a specification which shall include at least:

(a) the name to be protected as a designation of origin or geographical indication, as it is used, whether in trade or in common language, and only in the languages which are or were historically used to describe the specific product in the defined geographical area;

(b) a description of the product, including the raw materials, if appropriate, as well as the principal physical, chemical, microbiological or organoleptic characteristics of the product;

(c) the definition of the geographical area delimited with regard to the link referred to in point (f)(i) or (ii) of this paragraph, and, where appropriate, details indicating compliance with the requirements of Article 5(3);

(d) evidence that the product originates in the defined geographical area referred to in Article 5(1) or (2);

(e) a description of the method of obtaining the product and, where appropriate, the authentic and unvarying local methods as well as information concerning packaging, if the applicant group so determines and gives sufficient product-specific justification as to why the packaging must take place in the defined geographical area to safeguard quality, to ensure the origin or to ensure control, taking into account Union law, in particular that on the free movement of goods and the free provision of services;

(f) details establishing the following:

(i) as regards a protected designation of origin, the link between the quality or characteristics of the product and the geographical environment referred to in Article 5(1); the details concerning human factors of that geographical environment may, where relevant, be limited to a description of the soil and landscape management, cultivation practices or any other relevant human contribution to the maintenance of the natural factors of the geographical environment referred to in that paragraph;

(ii) as regards a protected geographical indication, the link between a given quality, the reputation or other characteristic of the product and the geographical origin referred to in Article 5(2);

(g) the name and address of the authorities or, if available, the name and address of bodies verifying compliance with the provisions of the product specification pursuant to Article 37 and their specific tasks;

(h) any specific labelling rule for the product in question.

The product specification may contain a description of the contribution of the designation of origin or geographical indication to sustainable development.

. . .

Article 8   Content of application for registration

1. An application for registration of a designation of origin or geographical indication pursuant to Article 49(2) or (5) shall include at least:

(a) the name and address of the applicant group and of the authorities or, if available, bodies verifying compliance with the provisions of the product specification;

(b) the product specification provided for in Article 7;

(c) a single document setting out the following:

(i) the main points of the product specification: the name, a description of the product, including, where appropriate, specific rules concerning packaging and labelling, and a concise definition of the geographical area;

(ii) a description of the link between the product and the geographical environment or geographical origin referred to in Article 5(1) or (2), as the case may be, including, where appropriate, the specific elements of the product description or production method justifying the link.

An application as referred to in Article 49(5) shall, in addition, include proof that the name of the product is protected in its country of origin.

2. An application dossier referred to in Article 49(4) shall comprise:

(a) the name and address of the applicant group;

(b) the single document referred to in point (c) of paragraph 1 of this Article;

(c) a declaration by the Member State that it considers that the application lodged by the applicant group and qualifying for the favourable decision meets the conditions of this Regulation and the provisions adopted pursuant thereto;

(d) the publication reference of the product specification.

Article 9   Transitional national protection

A Member State may, on a transitional basis only, grant protection to a name under this Regulation at national level, with effect from the date on which an application is lodged with the Commission.

Such national protection shall cease on the date on which either a decision on registration under this Regulation is taken or the application is withdrawn.

Where a name is not registered under this Regulation, the consequences of such national protection shall be the sole responsibility of the Member State concerned.

The measures taken by Member States under the first paragraph shall produce effects at national level only, and they shall have no effect on intra-Union or international trade.

Article 10   Grounds for opposition

1. A reasoned statement of opposition as referred to in Article 51(1) shall be admissible only if it is received by the Commission within the time limit set out in that paragraph and if it:

(a) shows that the conditions referred to in Article 5 and Article 7(1) are not complied with;

(b) shows that the registration of the name proposed would be contrary to Article 6(2), (3) or (4);

(c) shows that the registration of the name proposed would jeopardise the existence of an entirely or partly identical name or of a trade mark or the existence of products which have been legally on the market for at least five years preceding the date of the publication provided for in point (a) of Article 50(2); or

(d) gives details from which it can be concluded that the name for which registration is requested is a generic term.

2. The grounds for opposition shall be assessed in relation to the territory of the Union.

Article 11   Register of protected designations of origin and protected geographical indications

1. The Commission shall adopt implementing acts, without applying the procedure referred to in Article 57(2), establishing and maintaining a publicly accessible updated register of protected designations of origin and protected geographical indications recognised under this scheme.

2. Geographical indications pertaining to products of third countries that are protected in the Union under an international agreement to which the Union is a contracting party may be entered in the register. Unless specifically identified in the said agreement as protected designations of origin under this Regulation, such names shall be entered in the register as protected geographical indications.

3. The Commission may adopt implementing acts laying down detailed rules on the form and content of the register. Those implementing acts shall be adopted in accordance with the examination procedure referred to in Article 57(2).

4. The Commission shall make public and regularly update the list of the international agreements referred to in paragraph 2 as well as the list of geographical indications protected under those agreements.

Article 12   Names, symbols and indications

1. Protected designations of origin and protected geographical indications may be used by any operator marketing a product conforming to the corresponding specification.

2. Union symbols designed to publicise protected designations of origin and protected geographical indications shall be established.

3. In the case of products originating in the Union that are marketed under a protected designation of origin or protected geographical indication registered in accordance with the procedures laid down in this Regulation, the Union symbols associated with them shall appear on the labelling and advertising materials. The labelling requirements set out in Article 13(1) of Regulation (EU) No 1169/2011 for the presentation of mandatory particulars shall apply to the registered name of the product. The indications 'protected designation of origin' or 'protected geographical indication' or the corresponding abbreviations 'PDO' or 'PGI' may appear on the labelling.

4. In addition, the following may also appear on the labelling: depictions of the geographical area of origin, as referred to in Article 5, and text, graphics or symbols referring to the Member State and/or region in which that geographical area of origin is located.

5. Without prejudice to Directive 2000/13/EC, the collective geographical marks referred to in Article 15 of Directive 2008/95/EC may be used on labels, together with the protected designation of origin or protected geographical indication.

6. In the case of products originating in third countries marketed under a name entered in the register, the indications referred to in paragraph 3 or the Union symbols associated with them may appear on the labelling.

...

Article 13   Protection

1. Registered names shall be protected against:
    (a) any direct or indirect commercial use of a registered name in respect of products not covered by the registration where those products are comparable to the products registered under that name or where using the name exploits, weakens or dilutes the reputation of the protected name, including when those products are used as an ingredient;
    (b) any misuse, imitation or evocation, even if the true origin of the products or services is indicated or if the protected name is translated or accompanied by an expression such as 'style', 'type', 'method', 'as produced in', 'imitation' or similar, including when those products are used as an ingredient;
    (c) any other false or misleading indication as to the provenance, origin, nature or essential qualities of the product that is used on the inner or outer packaging, advertising material or

documents relating to the product concerned, and the packing of the product in a container liable to convey a false impression as to its origin;

(d) any other practice liable to mislead the consumer as to the true origin of the product.

Where a protected designation of origin or a protected geographical indication contains within it the name of a product which is considered to be generic, the use of that generic name shall not be considered to be contrary to points (a) or (b) of the first subparagraph.

2. Protected designations of origin and protected geographical indications shall not become generic.

3. Member States shall take appropriate administrative and judicial steps to prevent or stop the unlawful use of protected designations of origin and protected geographical indications, as referred to in paragraph 1, that are produced or marketed in that Member State.

To that end Member States shall designate the authorities that are responsible for taking these steps in accordance with procedures determined by each individual Member State.

These authorities shall offer adequate guarantees of objectivity and impartiality, and shall have at their disposal the qualified staff and resources necessary to carry out their functions.

. . .

Article 14   Relations between trade marks, designations of origin and geographical indications

1. Where a designation of origin or a geographical indication is registered under this Regulation, the registration of a trade mark the use of which would contravene Article 13(1) and which relates to a product of the same type shall be refused if the application for registration of the trade mark is submitted after the date of submission of the registration application in respect of the designation of origin or the geographical indication to the Commission.

Trade marks registered in breach of the first subparagraph shall be invalidated.

The provisions of this paragraph shall apply notwithstanding the provisions of Directive 2008/95/EC.

2. Without prejudice to Article 6(4), a trade mark the use of which contravenes Article 13(1) which has been applied for, registered, or established by use if that possibility is provided for by the legislation concerned, in good faith within the territory of the Union, before the date on which the application for protection of the designation of origin or geographical indication is submitted to the Commission, may continue to be used and renewed for that product notwithstanding the registration of a designation of origin or geographical indication, provided that no grounds for its invalidity or revocation exist under Council Regulation (EC) No 207/2009 of 26 February 2009 on the Community trade mark or under Directive 2008/95/EC. In such cases, the use of the protected designation of origin or protected geographical indication shall be permitted as well as use of the relevant trade marks.

Article 15   Transitional periods for use of protected designations of origin and protected geographical indications

1. Without prejudice to Article 14, the Commission may adopt implementing acts granting a transitional period of up to five years to enable products originating in a Member State or a third country the designation of which consists of or contains a name that contravenes Article 13(1) to continue to use the designation under which it was marketed on condition that an admissible statement of opposition under Article 49(3) or Article 51 shows that:

(a) the registration of the name would jeopardise the existence of an entirely or partly identical name; or

(b) such products have been legally marketed with that name in the territory concerned for at least five years preceding the date of the publication provided for point (a) of Article 50(2).

Those implementing acts shall be adopted in accordance with the examination procedure referred to in Article 57(2) except where an admissible statement of opposition is lodged under Article 49(3).

2. Without prejudice to Article 14, the Commission may adopt implementing acts extending the transitional period mentioned in paragraph 1 of this Article to up to 15 years in duly justified cases where it is shown that:

    (a) the designation referred to in paragraph 1 of this Article has been in legal use consistently and fairly for at least 25 years before the application for registration was submitted to the Commission;

    (b) the purpose of using the designation referred to in paragraph 1 of this Article has not, at any time, been to profit from the reputation of the registered name and it is shown that the consumer has not been nor could have been misled as to the true origin of the product.

Those implementing acts shall be adopted in accordance with the examination procedure referred to in Article 57(2).

3. When using a designation referred to in paragraphs 1 and 2, the indication of country of origin shall clearly and visibly appear on the labelling.

4. To overcome temporary difficulties with the long-term objective of ensuring that all producers in the area concerned comply with the specification, a Member State may grant a transitional period of up to 10 years, with effect from the date on which the application is lodged with the Commission, on condition that the operators concerned have legally marketed the products in question, using the names concerned continuously for at least the five years prior to the lodging of the application to the authorities of the Member State and have made that point in the national opposition procedure referred to in Article 49(3).

The first subparagraph shall apply *mutatis mutandis* to a protected geographical indication or protected designation of origin referring to a geographical area situated in a third country, with the exception of the opposition procedure.

Such transitional periods shall be indicated in the application dossier referred to in Article 8(2).

Article 16   Transitional provisions

1. Names entered in the register provided for in Article 7(6) of Regulation (EC) No 510/2006 shall automatically be entered in the register referred to in Article 11 of this Regulation. The corresponding specifications shall be deemed to be the specifications referred to in Article 7 of this Regulation. Any specific transitional provisions associated with such registrations shall continue to apply.

2. In order to protect the rights and legitimate interests of producers or stakeholders concerned, the Commission shall be empowered to adopt delegated acts, in accordance with Article 56, concerning additional transitional rules.

3. This Regulation shall apply without prejudice to any right of coexistence recognised under Regulation (EC) No 510/2006 in respect of designations of origin and geographical indications, on the one hand, and trade marks, on the other.

. . .

Title III   Traditional Specialities Guaranteed

Article 17   Objective

A scheme for traditional specialities guaranteed is established to safeguard traditional methods of production and recipes by helping producers of traditional product in marketing and communicating the value-adding attributes of their traditional recipes and products to consumers.

Article 18   Criteria

1. A name shall be eligible for registration as a traditional speciality guaranteed where it describes a specific product or foodstuff that:

    (a) results from a mode of production, processing or composition corresponding to traditional practice for that product or foodstuff; or

    (b) is produced from raw materials or ingredients that are those traditionally used.

2. For a name to be registered as a traditional speciality guaranteed, it shall:
   (a) have been traditionally used to refer to the specific product; or
   (b) identify the traditional character or specific character of the product.

3. If it is demonstrated in the opposition procedure under Article 51 that the name is also used in another Member State or in a third country, in order to distinguish comparable products or products that share an identical or similar name, the decision on registration taken in accordance with Article 52(3) may provide that the name of the traditional speciality guaranteed is to be accompanied by the claim 'made following the tradition of' immediately followed by the name of a country or a region thereof.

4. A name may not be registered if it refers only to claims of a general nature used for a set of products, or to claims provided for by particular Union legislation.

5. In order to ensure the smooth functioning of the scheme, the Commission shall be empowered to adopt delegated acts, in accordance with Article 56, concerning further details of the eligibility criteria laid down in this Article.

Article 19   Product specification

1. A traditional speciality guaranteed shall comply with a specification which shall comprise:
   (a) the name proposed for registration, in the appropriate language versions;
   (b) a description of the product including its main physical, chemical, microbiological or organoleptic characteristics, showing the product's specific character;
   (c) a description of the production method that the producers must follow, including, where appropriate, the nature and characteristics of the raw materials or ingredients used, and the method by which the product is prepared; and
   (d) the key elements establishing the product's traditional character.

2. In order to ensure that product specifications provide relevant and succinct information, the Commission shall be empowered to adopt delegated acts, in accordance with Article 56, laying down rules which limit the information contained in the specification referred to in paragraph 1 of this Article, where such a limitation is necessary to avoid excessively voluminous applications for registration.

The Commission may adopt implementing acts laying down rules on the form of the specification. Those implementing acts shall be adopted in accordance with the examination procedure referred to in Article 57(2).

Article 20   Content of application for registration

1. An application for registration of a name as a traditional speciality guaranteed referred to in Article 49(2) or (5) shall comprise:
   (a) the name and address of the applicant group;
   (b) the product specification as provided for in Article 19.

2. An application dossier referred to in Article 49(4) shall comprise:
   (a) the elements referred to in paragraph 1 of this Article; and
   (b) a declaration by the Member State that it considers that the application lodged by the group and qualifying for the favourable decision meets the conditions of this Regulation and the provisions adopted pursuant thereto.

Article 21   Grounds for opposition

1. A reasoned statement of opposition as referred to in Article 51(1) shall be admissible only if it is received by the Commission before expiry of the time limit and if it:
   (a) gives duly substantiated reasons why the proposed registration is incompatible with the terms of this Regulation; or
   (b) shows that use of the name is lawful, renowned and economically significant for similar agricultural products or foodstuffs.

2. The criteria referred to in point (b) of paragraph 1 shall be assessed in relation to the territory of the Union.

Article 22   Register of traditional specialities guaranteed

1. The Commission shall adopt implementing acts, without applying the procedure referred to in Article 57(2), establishing and maintaining a publicly accessible updated register of traditional specialties guaranteed recognised under this scheme.

2. The Commission may adopt implementing acts laying down detailed rules on the form and content of the register. Those implementing acts shall be adopted in accordance with the examination procedure referred to in Article 57(2).

Article 23   Names, symbol and indication

1. A name registered as a traditional speciality guaranteed may be used by any operator marketing a product that conforms to the corresponding specification.

2. A Union symbol shall be established in order to publicise the traditional specialities guaranteed.

3. In the case of products originating in the Union that are marketed under a traditional speciality guaranteed registered in accordance with this Regulation, the symbol referred to in paragraph 2 of this Article shall, without prejudice to paragraph 4 of this Article, appear on the labelling and advertising materials. The labelling requirements set out in Article 13(1) of Regulation (EU) No 1169/2011 for the presentation of mandatory particulars shall apply to the registered name of the product. The indication 'traditional speciality guaranteed' or the corresponding abbreviation 'TSG' may appear on the labelling.

The symbol shall be optional on the labelling of traditional specialities guaranteed which are produced outside the Union.

4. In order to ensure that the appropriate information is communicated to the consumer, the Commission shall be empowered to adopt delegated acts, in accordance with Article 56, establishing the Union symbol.

The Commission may adopt implementing acts defining the technical characteristics of the Union symbol and indication, as well as the rules of their use on the products bearing the name of a traditional speciality guaranteed, including as to the appropriate linguistic versions to be used. Those implementing acts shall be adopted in accordance with the examination procedure referred to in Article 57(2).

Article 24   Restriction on use of registered names

1. Registered names shall be protected against any misuse, imitation or evocation, including as regards products used as ingredients, or against any other practice liable to mislead the consumer.

2. Member States shall ensure that sales descriptions used at national level do not give rise to confusion with names that are registered.

3. The Commission may adopt implementing acts laying down rules for the protection of traditional specialities guaranteed. Those implementing acts shall be adopted in accordance with the examination procedure referred to in Article 57(2).

4. The protection referred to in paragraph 1 shall also apply with regard to goods sold through means of distance selling, such as electronic commerce.

. . .

Article 25   Transitional provisions

1. Names registered in accordance with Article 13(2) of Regulation (EC) No 509/2006 shall be automatically entered in the register referred to in Article 22 of this Regulation. The corresponding specifications shall be deemed to be the specifications referred to in Article 19 of this Regulation. Any specific transitional provisions associated with such registrations shall continue to apply.

2. Names registered in accordance with the requirements laid down in Article 13(1) of Regulation (EC) No 509/2006, including those registered pursuant to applications referred to in the second subparagraph of Article 58(1) of this Regulation, may continue to be used under the conditions provided for in Regulation (EC) No 509/2006 until 4 January 2023 unless Member States use the procedure set out in Article 26 of this Regulation.

3. In order to protect the rights and legitimate interests of producers or stakeholders concerned, the Commission shall be empowered to adopt delegated acts, in accordance with Article 56, laying down additional transitional rules.

Article 26   Simplified procedure

1. At the request of a group, a Member State may submit, no later than 4 January 2016, to the Commission names of traditional specialities guaranteed that are registered in accordance with Article 13(1) of Regulation (EC) No 509/2006 and that comply with this Regulation.

Before submitting a name, the Member State shall initiate an opposition procedure as defined in Article 49(3) and (4).

If it is demonstrated in the course of this procedure that the name is also used in reference to comparable products or products that share an identical or similar name, the name may be complemented by a term identifying its traditional or specific character.

A group from a third country may submit such names to the Commission, either directly or through the authorities of the third country.

2. The Commission shall publish the names referred to in paragraph 1 together with the specifications for each such name in the Official Journal of the European Union within two months from reception.

3. Articles 51 and 52 shall apply.

4. Once the opposition procedure has finished, the Commission shall, where appropriate, adjust the entries in the register set out in Article 22. The corresponding specifications shall be deemed to be the specifications referred to in Article 19.

Title IV   Optional Quality Terms

Article 27   Objective

A scheme for optional quality terms is established in order to facilitate the communication within the internal market of the value-adding characteristics or attributes of agricultural products by the producers thereof.

Article 28   National Rules

Member States may maintain national rules on optional quality terms which are not covered by this Regulation, provided that such rules comply with Union law.

Article 29   Optional quality terms

1. Optional quality terms shall satisfy the following criteria:
   (a) the term relates to a characteristic of one or more categories of products, or to a farming or processing attribute which applies in specific areas;
   (b) the use of the term adds value to the product as compared to products of a similar type; and
   (c) the term has a European dimension.

2. Optional quality terms that describe technical product qualities with the purpose of putting into effect compulsory marketing standards and are not intended to inform consumers about those product qualities shall be excluded from this scheme.

3. Optional quality terms shall exclude optional reserved terms which support and complement specific marketing standards determined on a sectoral or product category basis.

4. In order to take into account the specific character of certain sectors as well as consumer expectations, the Commission shall be empowered to adopt delegated acts, in accordance with Article 56, laying down detailed rules relating to the criteria referred to in paragraph 1 of this Article.

5. The Commission may adopt implementing acts laying down all measures related to forms, procedures or other technical details, necessary for the application of this Title. Those implementing acts shall be adopted in accordance with the examination procedure referred to in Article 57(2).

6. When adopting delegated and implementing acts in accordance with paragraphs 4 and 5 of this Article, the Commission shall take account of any relevant international standards.

Article 30   Reservation and amendment

1. In order to take account of the expectations of consumers, developments in scientific and technical knowledge, the market situation, and developments in marketing standards and in

international standards, the Commission shall be empowered to adopt delegated acts, in accordance with Article 56, reserving an additional optional quality term and laying down its conditions of use.

2. In duly justified cases and in order to take into account the appropriate use of the additional optional quality term, the Commission shall be empowered to adopt delegated acts, in accordance with Article 56, laying down amendments to the conditions of use referred to in paragraph 1 of this Article.

Article 31   Mountain product

1.   The term 'mountain product' is established as an optional quality term.

This term shall only be used to describe products intended for human consumption listed in Annex I to the Treaty in respect of which:

    (a) both the raw materials and the feedstuffs for farm animals come essentially from mountain areas;

    (b) in the case of processed products, the processing also takes place in mountain areas.

2. For the purposes of this Article, mountain areas within the Union are those delimited pursuant to Article 18(1) of Regulation (EC) No 1257/1999. For third-country products, mountain areas include areas officially designated as mountain areas by the third country or that meet criteria equivalent to those set out in Article 18(1) of Regulation (EC) No 1257/1999.

3. In duly justified cases and in order to take into account natural constraints affecting agricultural production in mountain areas, the Commission shall be empowered to adopt delegated acts, in accordance with Article 56, laying down derogations from the conditions of use referred to in paragraph 1 of this Article. In particular, the Commission shall be empowered to adopt a delegated act laying down the conditions under which raw materials or feedstuffs are permitted to come from outside the mountain areas, the conditions under which the processing of products is permitted to take place outside of the mountain areas in a geographical area to be defined, and the definition of that geographical area.

4. In order to take into account natural constraints affecting agricultural production in mountain areas, the Commission shall be empowered to adopt delegated acts, in accordance with Article 56, concerning the establishment of the methods of production, and other criteria relevant for the application of the optional quality term established in paragraph 1 of this Article.

Article 32   Product of island farming

No later than 4 January 2014 the Commission shall present a report to the European Parliament and to the Council on the case for a new term, 'product of island farming'. The term may only be used to describe the products intended for human consumption that are listed in Annex I to the Treaty the raw materials of which come from islands. In addition, for the term to be applied to processed products, processing must also take place on islands in cases where this substantially affects the particular characteristics of the final product.

That report shall, if necessary, be accompanied by appropriate legislative proposals to reserve an optional quality term 'product of island farming'.

Article 33   Restrictions on use

1. An optional quality term may only be used to describe products that comply with the corresponding conditions of use.

2. The Commission may adopt implementing acts laying down rules for the use of optional quality terms. Those implementing acts shall be adopted in accordance with the examination procedure referred to in Article 57(2).

Article 34   Monitoring

Member States shall undertake checks, based on a risk analysis, to ensure compliance with the requirements of this Title and, in the event of breach, shall apply appropriate administrative penalties.

Title V   Common Provisions

Chapter I   Official controls of protected designations of origin, protected geographical indications and traditional specialities guaranteed

. . .

Chapter II   Exceptions for certain prior uses

Article 41   Generic terms

1. Without prejudice to Article 13, this Regulation shall not affect the use of terms that are generic in the Union, even if the generic term is part of a name that is protected under a quality scheme.

2. To establish whether or not a term has become generic, account shall be taken of all relevant factors, in particular:

    (a) the existing situation in areas of consumption;

    (b) the relevant national or Union legal acts.

3. In order to fully protect the rights of interested parties, the Commission shall be empowered to adopt delegated acts, in accordance with Article 56, laying down additional rules for determining the generic status of terms referred to in paragraph 1 of this Article.

Article 42   Plant varieties and animal breeds

1. This Regulation shall not prevent the placing on the market of products the labelling of which includes a name or term protected or reserved under a quality scheme described in Title II, Title III, or Title IV that contains or comprises the name of a plant variety or animal breed, provided that the following conditions are met:

    (a) the product in question comprises or is derived from the variety or breed indicated;

    (b) consumers are not misled;

    (c) the usage of the name of the variety or breed name constitutes fair competition;

    (d) the usage does not exploit the reputation of the protected term; and

    (e) in the case of the quality scheme described in Title II, production and marketing of the product had spread beyond its area of origin prior to the date of application for registration of the geographical indication.

2. In order to further clarify the extent of rights and freedoms of food business operators to use the name of a plant variety or of an animal breed referred to in paragraph 1 of this Article, the Commission shall be empowered to adopt delegated acts, in accordance with Article 56, concerning rules for determining the use of such names.

Article 43   Relation to intellectual property

The quality schemes described in Titles III and IV shall apply without prejudice to Union rules or to those of Member States governing intellectual property, and in particular to those concerning designations of origin and geographical indications and trade marks, and rights granted under those rules.

Chapter III   Quality scheme indications and symbols and role of producers

Article 44   Protection of indications and symbols

1. Indications, abbreviations and symbols referring to the quality schemes may only be used in connection with products produced in conformity with the rules of the quality scheme to which they apply. This applies in particular to the following indications, abbreviations and symbols:

    (a) 'protected designation of origin', 'protected geographical indication', 'geographical indication', 'PDO', 'PGI', and the associated symbols, as provided for in Title II;

    (b) 'traditional speciality guaranteed', 'TSG', and the associated symbol, as provided for in Title III;

    (c) 'mountain product', as provided for in Title IV.

. . .

Chapter IV   Application and registration processes for designations of origin, geographical indications, and traditional specialities guaranteed

Article 48   Scope of application processes

The provisions of this Chapter shall apply in respect of the quality schemes set out in Title II and Title III.

Article 49   Application for registration of names

1. Applications for registration of names under the quality schemes referred to in Article 48 may only be submitted by groups who work with the products with the name to be registered. In the case of a 'protected designations of origin' or 'protected geographical indications' name that designates a trans-border geographical area or in the case of a 'traditional specialities guaranteed' name, several groups from different Member States or third countries may lodge a joint application for registration.

A single natural or legal person may be treated as a group where it is shown that both of the following conditions are fulfilled:

    (a) the person concerned is the only producer willing to submit an application;

    (b) with regard to protected designations of origin and protected geographical indications, the defined geographical area possesses characteristics which differ appreciably from those of neighbouring areas or the characteristics of the product are different from those produced in neighbouring areas.

2. Where the application under the scheme set out in Title II relates to a geographical area in a Member State, or where an application under the scheme set out in Title III is prepared by a group established in a Member State, the application shall be addressed to the authorities of that Member State.

The Member State shall scrutinise the application by appropriate means in order to check that it is justified and meets the conditions of the respective scheme.

. . .

5. Where the application under the scheme set out in Title II relates to a geographical area in a third country, or where an application under the scheme set out in Title III is prepared by a group established in a third country, the application shall be lodged with the Commission, either directly or via the authorities of the third country concerned.

. . .

Article 52   Decision on registration

1. Where, on the basis of the information available to the Commission from the scrutiny carried out pursuant to the first subparagraph of Article 50(1), the Commission considers that the conditions laid down in Articles 5 and 6, as regards the quality schemes set out in Title II, or in Article 18, as regards the quality schemes set out in Title III, are not fulfilled, it shall adopt implementing acts rejecting the application. Those implementing acts shall be adopted in accordance with the examination procedure referred to in Article 57(2).

2. If the Commission receives no admissible reasoned statement of opposition under Article 51, it shall adopt implementing acts, without applying the procedure referred to in Article 57(2), registering the name.

3. If the Commission receives an admissible reasoned statement of opposition, it shall, following the appropriate consultations referred to in Article 51(3), and taking into account the results thereof, either:

    (a) if an agreement has been reached, register the name by means of implementing acts adopted without applying the procedure referred to in Article 57(2), and, if necessary, amend the information published pursuant to Article 50(2) provided such amendments are not substantial; or

    (b) if an agreement has not been reached, adopt implementing acts deciding on the registration. Those implementing acts shall be adopted in accordance with the examination procedure referred to in Article 57(2).

4. Acts of registration and decisions on rejection shall be published in the Official Journal of the European Union.

Article 53   Amendment to product specifications

1. A group having a legitimate interest may apply for approval of an amendment to a product specification.

Applications shall describe and give reasons for the amendments requested.

. . .

Article 54   Cancellation

1. The Commission may, on its own initiative or at the request of any natural or legal person having a legitimate interest, adopt implementing acts to cancel the registration of a protected designation of origin or of a protected geographical indication or of a traditional speciality guaranteed in the following cases:

    (a) where compliance with the conditions of the specification is not ensured;

    (b) where no product is placed on the market under the traditional speciality guaranteed, the protected designation of origin or the protected geographical indication for at least seven years.

The Commission may, at the request of the producers of product marketed under the registered name, cancel the corresponding registration.

Those implementing acts shall be adopted in accordance with the examination procedure referred to in Article 57(2).

. . .

Title VI   Procedural and Final Provisions

. . .

Chapter III   Repeal and final provisions

. . .

Article 59   Entry into force

This Regulation shall enter into force on the twentieth day following that of its publication in the Official Journal of the European Union.

However, Article 12(3) and Article 23(3) shall apply from 4 January 2016, without prejudice to products already placed on the market before that date.

This Regulation shall be binding in its entirety and directly applicable in all Member States.

Annex I   Agricultural Products and Foodstuffs Referred to in Article 2(1)

I. Designations of Origin and Geographical indications
- beer,
- chocolate and derived products,
- bread, pastry, cakes, confectionery, biscuits and other baker's wares,
- beverages made from plant extracts,
- pasta,
- salt,
- natural gums and resins,
- mustard paste,
- hay,
- essential oils,
- cork,

- cochineal,
- flowers and ornamental plants,
- cotton,
- wool,
- wicker,
- scutched flax,
- leather,
- fur,
- feather.
- aromatised wines as defined in Article 3(2) of Regulation (EU) No 251/2014,
- other alcoholic beverages, except for spirit drinks and grapevine products as defined in Annex VII, Part II, to Regulation (EU) No 1308/2013,
- beeswax.

II. Traditional specialities guaranteed
- prepared meals,
- beer,
- chocolate and derived products,
- bread, pastry, cakes, confectionery, biscuits and other baker's wares,
- beverages made from plant extracts,
- pasta,
- salt.

. . .

Directive (EU) 2015/2436 of the European Parliament and of the Council

of 16 December 2015 to approximate the laws of the Member States relating to trade marks (Recast)
(Text with EEA relevance)

THE EUROPEAN PARLIAMENT AND THE COUNCIL OF THE EUROPEAN UNION,

Having regard to the Treaty on the Functioning of the European Union, and in particular Article 114(1) thereof,

Having regard to the proposal from the European Commission,

After transmission of the draft legislative act to the national parliaments,

Having regard to the opinion of the European Economic and Social Committee,

Acting in accordance with the ordinary legislative procedure,

Whereas:

(1) A number of amendments should be made to Directive 2008/95/EC of the European Parliament and of the Council. In the interests of clarity, that Directive should be recast.

(2) Directive 2008/95/EC has harmonised central provisions of substantive trade mark law which at the time of adoption were considered as most directly affecting the functioning of the internal market by impeding the free movement of goods and the freedom to provide services in the Union.

(3) Trade mark protection in the Member States coexists with protection available at Union level through European Union trade marks ('EU trade marks') which are unitary in character and valid throughout the Union as laid down in Council Regulation (EC) No 207/2009. The coexistence and balance of trade mark systems at national and Union level in fact constitutes a cornerstone of the Union's approach to intellectual property protection.

(4) Further to the Commission's communication of 16 July 2008 on an industrial property rights strategy for Europe, the Commission carried out a comprehensive evaluation of the overall functioning of the trade mark system in Europe as a whole, covering Union and national levels and the interrelation between the two.

(5) In its conclusions of 25 May 2010 on the future revision of the trade mark system in the European Union, the Council called on the Commission to present proposals for the revision of Regulation (EC) No 207/2009 and Directive 2008/95/EC. The revision of that Directive should include measures to make it more consistent with Regulation (EC) No 207/2009, which would thus reduce the areas of divergence within the trade mark system in Europe as a whole, while maintaining national trade mark protection as an attractive option for applicants. In this context, the complementary relationship between the EU trade mark system and national trade mark systems should be ensured.

(6) The Commission concluded in its communication of 24 May 2011 entitled 'A single market for intellectual property rights' that in order to meet increased demands from stakeholders for faster, higher quality, more streamlined trade mark registration systems, which are also more consistent, user friendly, publicly accessible and technologically up to date, there is a necessity to modernise the trade mark system in the Union as a whole and adapt it to the internet era.

(7) Consultation and evaluation for the purpose of this Directive has revealed that, in spite of the previous partial harmonisation of national laws, there remain areas where further harmonisation could have a positive impact on competitiveness and growth.

(8) In order to serve the objective of fostering and creating a well-functioning internal market and to facilitate acquiring and protecting trade marks in the Union, to the benefit of the growth and the competitiveness of European businesses, in particular small and medium-sized enterprises, it is necessary to go beyond the limited scope of approximation achieved by Directive 2008/95/EC and extend approximation to other aspects of substantive trade mark law governing trade marks protected through registration pursuant to Regulation (EC) No 207/2009.

(9) For the purpose of making trade mark registrations throughout the Union easier to obtain and administer, it is essential to approximate not only provisions of substantive law but also procedural rules. Therefore, the principal procedural rules in the area of trade mark registration in the Member States and in the EU trade mark system should be aligned. As regards procedures under national law, it is sufficient to lay down general principles, leaving the Member States free to establish more specific rules.

(10) It is essential to ensure that registered trade marks enjoy the same protection under the legal systems of all the Member States. In line with the extensive protection granted to EU trade marks which have a reputation in the Union, extensive protection should also be granted at national level to all registered trade marks which have a reputation in the Member State concerned.

(11) This Directive should not deprive the Member States of the right to continue to protect trade marks acquired through use but should take them into account only with regard to their relationship with trade marks acquired by registration.

(12) Attainment of the objectives of this approximation of laws requires that the conditions for obtaining and continuing to hold a registered trade mark be, in general, identical in all Member States.

(13) To this end, it is necessary to list examples of signs which are capable of constituting a trade mark, provided that such signs are capable of distinguishing the goods or services of one undertaking from those of other undertakings. In order to fulfil the objectives of the registration system for trade marks, namely to ensure legal certainty and sound administration, it is also essential to require that the sign is capable of being represented in a manner which is clear, precise, self-contained, easily accessible, intelligible, durable and objective. A sign should therefore be permitted to be represented in any appropriate form using generally available technology, and thus not necessarily by graphic means, as long as the representation offers satisfactory guarantees to that effect.

(14) Furthermore, the grounds for refusal or invalidity concerning the trade mark itself, including the absence of any distinctive character, or concerning conflicts between the trade mark and earlier rights, should be listed in an exhaustive manner, even if some of those grounds are listed as an option for the Member States which should therefore be able to maintain or introduce them in their legislation.

(15) In order to ensure that the levels of protection afforded to geographical indications by Union legislation and national law are applied in a uniform and exhaustive manner in the examination of

absolute and relative grounds for refusal throughout the Union, this Directive should include the same provisions in relation to geographical indications as contained in Regulation (EC) No 207/2009. Furthermore, it is appropriate to ensure that the scope of absolute grounds is extended to also cover protected traditional terms for wine and traditional specialties guaranteed.

(16) The protection afforded by the registered trade mark, the function of which is in particular to guarantee the trade mark as an indication of origin, should be absolute in the event of there being identity between the mark and the corresponding sign and the goods or services. The protection should apply also in the case of similarity between the mark and the sign and the goods or services. It is indispensable to give an interpretation of the concept of similarity in relation to the likelihood of confusion. The likelihood of confusion, the appreciation of which depends on numerous elements and, in particular, on the recognition of the trade mark on the market, the association which can be made with the used or registered sign, the degree of similarity between the trade mark and the sign and between the goods or services identified, should constitute the specific condition for such protection. The ways in which a likelihood of confusion can be established, and in particular the onus of proof in that regard, should be a matter for national procedural rules which should not be prejudiced by this Directive.

(17) In order to ensure legal certainty and full consistency with the principle of priority, under which a registered earlier trade mark takes precedence over later registered trade marks, it is necessary to provide that the enforcement of rights which are conferred by a trade mark should be without prejudice to the rights of proprietors acquired prior to the filing or priority date of the trade mark. Such an approach is in conformity with Article 16(1) of the Agreement on trade-related aspects of intellectual property rights of 15 April 1994 ('TRIPS Agreement').

(18) It is appropriate to provide that an infringement of a trade mark can only be established if there is a finding that the infringing mark or sign is used in the course of trade for the purposes of distinguishing goods or services. Use of the sign for purposes other than for distinguishing goods or services should be subject to the provisions of national law.

(19) The concept of infringement of a trade mark should also comprise the use of the sign as a trade name or similar designation, as long as such use is made for the purposes of distinguishing goods or services.

(20) In order to ensure legal certainty and full consistency with specific Union legislation, it is appropriate to provide that the proprietor of a trade mark should be entitled to prohibit a third party from using a sign in comparative advertising where such comparative advertising is contrary to Directive 2006/114/EC of the European Parliament and of the Council.

(21) In order to strengthen trade mark protection and combat counterfeiting more effectively, and in line with international obligations of the Member States under the World Trade Organisation (WTO) framework, in particular Article V of the General Agreement on Tariffs and Trade on freedom of transit and, as regards generic medicines, the 'Declaration on the TRIPS Agreement and public health' adopted by the Doha WTO Ministerial Conference on 14 November 2001, the proprietor of a trade mark should be entitled to prevent third parties from bringing goods, in the course of trade, into the Member State where the trade mark is registered without being released for free circulation there, where such goods come from third countries and bear without authorisation a trade mark which is identical or essentially identical with the trade mark registered in respect of such goods.

(22) To this effect, it should be permissible for trade mark proprietors to prevent the entry of infringing goods and their placement in all customs situations, including, in particular transit, transhipment, warehousing, free zones, temporary storage, inward processing or temporary admission, also when such goods are not intended to be placed on the market of the Member State concerned. In performing customs controls, the customs authorities should make use of the powers and procedures laid down in Regulation (EU) No 608/2013 of the European Parliament and of the Council, also at the request of the right holders. In particular, the customs authorities should carry out the relevant controls on the basis of risk analysis criteria.

(23) In order to reconcile the need to ensure the effective enforcement of trade mark rights with the necessity to avoid hampering the free flow of trade in legitimate goods, the entitlement of the

proprietor of the trade mark should lapse where, during the subsequent proceedings initiated before the judicial or other authority competent to take a substantive decision on whether the registered trade mark has been infringed, the declarant or the holder of the goods is able to prove that the proprietor of the registered trade mark is not entitled to prohibit the placing of the goods on the market in the country of final destination.

(24) Article 28 of Regulation (EU) No 608/2013 provides that a right holder is to be liable for damages towards the holder of the goods where, inter alia, the goods in question are subsequently found not to infringe an intellectual property right.

(25) Appropriate measures should be taken with a view to ensuring the smooth transit of generic medicines. With respect to international non-proprietary names (INN) as globally recognised generic names for active substances in pharmaceutical preparations, it is vital to take due account of the existing limitations on the effect of trade mark rights. Consequently, the proprietor of a trade mark should not have the right to prevent a third party from bringing goods into a Member State where the trade mark is registered without being released for free circulation there based upon similarities between the INN for the active ingredient in the medicines and the trade mark.

(26) In order to enable proprietors of registered trade marks to combat counterfeiting more effectively, they should be entitled to prohibit the affixing of an infringing trade mark to goods, and certain preparatory acts carried out prior to such affixing.

(27) The exclusive rights conferred by a trade mark should not entitle the proprietor to prohibit the use of signs or indications by third parties which are used fairly and thus in accordance with honest practices in industrial and commercial matters. In order to create equal conditions for trade names and trade marks against the background that trade names are regularly granted unrestricted protection against later trade marks, such use should only be considered to include the use of the personal name of the third party. Such use should further permit the use of descriptive or non-distinctive signs or indications in general. Furthermore, the proprietor should not be entitled to prevent the fair and honest use of the mark for the purpose of identifying or referring to the goods or services as those of the proprietor. Use of a trade mark by third parties to draw the consumer's attention to the resale of genuine goods that were originally sold by, or with the consent of, the proprietor of the trade mark in the Union should be considered as being fair as long as it is at the same time in accordance with honest practices in industrial and commercial matters. Use of a trade mark by third parties for the purpose of artistic expression should be considered as being fair as long as it is at the same time in accordance with honest practices in industrial and commercial matters. Furthermore, this Directive should be applied in a way that ensures full respect for fundamental rights and freedoms, and in particular the freedom of expression.

(28) It follows from the principle of free movement of goods that the proprietor of a trade mark should not be entitled to prohibit its use by a third party in relation to goods which have been put into circulation in the Union, under the trade mark, by him or with his consent, unless the proprietor has legitimate reasons to oppose further commercialisation of the goods.

(29) It is important, for reasons of legal certainty to provide that, without prejudice to his interests as a proprietor of an earlier trade mark, the latter may no longer request a declaration of invalidity or oppose the use of a trade mark subsequent to his own trade mark, of which he has knowingly tolerated the use for a substantial length of time, unless the application for the subsequent trade mark was made in bad faith.

(30) In order to ensure legal certainty and safeguard legitimately acquired trade mark rights, it is appropriate and necessary to provide that, without prejudice to the principle that the later trade mark cannot be enforced against the earlier trade mark, proprietors of earlier trade marks should not be entitled to obtain refusal or invalidation or to oppose the use of a later trade mark if the later trade mark was acquired at a time when the earlier trade mark was liable to be declared invalid or revoked, for example because it had not yet acquired distinctiveness through use, or if the earlier trade mark could not be enforced against the later trade mark because the necessary conditions were not applicable, for example when the earlier mark had not yet obtained a reputation.

(31) Trade marks fulfil their purpose of distinguishing goods or services and allowing consumers to make informed choices only when they are actually used on the market. A requirement of use is also

necessary in order to reduce the total number of trade marks registered and protected in the Union and, consequently, the number of conflicts which arise between them. It is therefore essential to require that registered trade marks actually be used in connection with the goods or services for which they are registered, or, if not used in that connection within five years of the date of the completion of the registration procedure, be liable to be revoked.

(32) Consequently, a registered trade mark should only be protected in so far as it is actually used and a registered earlier trade mark should not enable its proprietor to oppose or invalidate a later trade mark if that proprietor has not put his trade mark to genuine use. Furthermore, Member States should provide that a trade mark may not be successfully invoked in infringement proceedings if it is established, as a result of a plea, that the trade mark could be revoked or, when the action is brought against a later right, could have been revoked at the time when the later right was acquired.

(33) It is appropriate to provide that, where the seniority of a national mark or a trade mark registered under international arrangements having effect in the Member State has been claimed for an EU trade mark and the mark providing the basis for the seniority claim has thereafter been surrendered or allowed to lapse, the validity of that mark can still be challenged. Such a challenge should be limited to situations where the mark could have been declared invalid or revoked at the time it was removed from the register.

(34) For reasons of coherence and in order to facilitate the commercial exploitation of trade marks in the Union, the rules applicable to trade marks as objects of property should be aligned to the extent appropriate with those already in place for EU trade marks, and should include rules on assignment and transfer, licensing, rights *in rem* and levy of execution.

(35) Collective trade marks have proven a useful instrument for promoting goods or services with specific common properties. It is therefore appropriate to subject national collective trade marks to rules similar to the rules applicable to European Union collective marks.

(36) In order to improve and facilitate access to trade mark protection and to increase legal certainty and predictability, the procedure for the registration of trade marks in the Member States should be efficient and transparent and should follow rules similar to those applicable to EU trade marks.

(37) In order to ensure legal certainty with regard to the scope of trade mark rights and to facilitate access to trade mark protection, the designation and classification of goods and services covered by a trade mark application should follow the same rules in all Member States and should be aligned to those applicable to EU trade marks. In order to enable the competent authorities and economic operators to determine the extent of the trade mark protection sought on the basis of the application alone, the designation of goods and services should be sufficiently clear and precise. The use of general terms should be interpreted as including only goods and services clearly covered by the literal meaning of a term. In the interest of clarity and legal certainty, the Member States' central industrial property offices and the Benelux Office for Intellectual Property should, in cooperation with each other, endeavour to compile a list reflecting their respective administrative practices with regard to the classification of goods and services.

(38) For the purpose of ensuring effective trade mark protection, Member States should make available an efficient administrative opposition procedure, allowing at least the proprietor of earlier trade mark rights and any person authorised under the relevant law to exercise the rights arising from a protected designation of origin or a geographical indication to oppose the registration of a trade mark application. Furthermore, in order to offer efficient means of revoking trademarks or declaring them invalid, Member States should provide for an administrative procedure for revocation or declaration of invalidity within the longer transposition period of seven years, after the entry into force of this Directive.

(39) It is desirable that Member States' central industrial property offices and the Benelux Office for Intellectual Property cooperate with each other and with the European Union Intellectual Property Office in all fields of trade mark registration and administration in order to promote convergence of practices and tools, such as the creation and updating of common or connected databases and portals for consultation and search purposes. The Member States should further ensure that their offices cooperate with each other and with the European Union Intellectual Property Office in all other areas of their activities which are relevant for the protection of trade marks in the Union.

(40) This Directive should not exclude the application to trade marks of provisions of law of the Member States other than trade mark law, such as provisions relating to unfair competition, civil liability or consumer protection.

(41) Member States are bound by the Paris Convention for the Protection of Industrial Property ('the Paris Convention') and the TRIPS Agreement. It is necessary that this Directive be entirely consistent with that Convention and that Agreement. The obligations of the Member States resulting from that Convention and that Agreement should not be affected by this Directive. Where appropriate, the second paragraph of Article 351 of the Treaty on the Functioning of the European Union should apply.

(42) Since the objectives of this Directive, namely to foster and create a well-functioning internal market and to facilitate the registration, administration and protection of trade marks in the Union to the benefit of growth and competitiveness, cannot be sufficiently achieved by the Member States but can rather, by reason of its scale and effects, be better achieved at Union level, the Union may adopt measures, in accordance with the principle of subsidiarity as set out in Article 5 of the Treaty on European Union. In accordance with the principle of proportionality as set out in that Article, this Directive does not go beyond what is necessary in order to achieve those objectives.

(43) Directive 95/46/EC of the European Parliament and of the Council governs the processing of personal data carried out in the Member States in the context of this Directive.

(44) The European Data Protection Supervisor was consulted in accordance with Article 28(2) of Regulation (EC) No 45/2001 of the European Parliament and of the Council and delivered an opinion on 11 July 2013.

(45) The obligation to transpose this Directive into national law should be confined to those provisions which represent a substantive amendment as compared with the earlier Directive. The obligation to transpose the provisions which are unchanged arises under the earlier Directive.

(46) This Directive should be without prejudice to the obligations of the Member States under Directive 2008/95/EC relating to the time limit for transposition of Council Directive 89/104/EEC into national law as set out in Part B of Annex I to Directive 2008/95/EC,

HAVE ADOPTED THIS DIRECTIVE:

Chapter 1   General Provisions

Article 1   Scope
This Directive applies to every trade mark in respect of goods or services which is the subject of registration or of an application for registration in a Member State as an individual trade mark, a guarantee or certification mark or a collective mark, or which is the subject of a registration or an application for registration in the Benelux Office for Intellectual Property or of an international registration having effect in a Member State.

Article 2   Definitions
For the purpose of this Directive, the following definitions apply:
- (a) 'office' means the central industrial property office of the Member State or the Benelux Office for Intellectual Property, entrusted with the registration of trade marks;
- (b) 'register' means the register of trade marks kept by an office.

Chapter 2   Substantive Law on Trade Marks

Section 1   Signs of Which a Trade Mark May Consist

Article 3   Signs of which a trade mark may consist
A trade mark may consist of any signs, in particular words, including personal names, or designs, letters, numerals, colours, the shape of goods or of the packaging of goods, or sounds, provided that such signs are capable of:
- (a) distinguishing the goods or services of one undertaking from those of other undertakings; and

(b) being represented on the register in a manner which enables the competent authorities and the public to determine the clear and precise subject matter of the protection afforded to its proprietor.

Section 2   Grounds for Refusal or Invalidity

Article 4   Absolute grounds for refusal or invalidity

1. The following shall not be registered or, if registered, shall be liable to be declared invalid:
    (a) signs which cannot constitute a trade mark;
    (b) trade marks which are devoid of any distinctive character;
    (c) trade marks which consist exclusively of signs or indications which may serve, in trade, to designate the kind, quality, quantity, intended purpose, value, geographical origin, or the time of production of the goods or of rendering of the service, or other characteristics of the goods or services;
    (d) trade marks which consist exclusively of signs or indications which have become customary in the current language or in the bona fide and established practices of the trade;
    (e) signs which consist exclusively of:
        (i)   the shape, or another characteristic, which results from the nature of the goods themselves;
        (ii) the shape, or another characteristic, of goods which is necessary to obtain a technical result;
        (iii) the shape, or another characteristic, which gives substantial value to the goods;
    (f) trade marks which are contrary to public policy or to accepted principles of morality;
    (g) trade marks which are of such a nature as to deceive the public, for instance, as to the nature, quality or geographical origin of the goods or service;
    (h) trade marks which have not been authorised by the competent authorities and are to be refused or invalidated pursuant to Article 6*ter* of the Paris Convention;
    (i) trade marks which are excluded from registration pursuant to Union legislation or the national law of the Member State concerned, or to international agreements to which the Union or the Member State concerned is party, providing for protection of designations of origin and geographical indications;
    (j) trade marks which are excluded from registration pursuant to Union legislation or international agreements to which the Union is party, providing for protection of traditional terms for wine;
    (k) trade marks which are excluded from registration pursuant to Union legislation or international agreements to which the Union is party, providing for protection of traditional specialities guaranteed;
    (l) trade marks which consist of, or reproduce in their essential elements, an earlier plant variety denomination registered in accordance with Union legislation or the national law of the Member State concerned, or international agreements to which the Union or the Member State concerned is party, providing protection for plant variety rights, and which are in respect of plant varieties of the same or closely related species.

2. A trade mark shall be liable to be declared invalid where the application for registration of the trade mark was made in bad faith by the applicant. Any Member State may also provide that such a trade mark is not to be registered.

3. Any Member State may provide that a trade mark is not to be registered or, if registered, is liable to be declared invalid where and to the extent that:
    (a) the use of that trade mark may be prohibited pursuant to provisions of law other than trade mark law of the Member State concerned or of the Union;
    (b) the trade mark includes a sign of high symbolic value, in particular a religious symbol;
    (c) the trade mark includes badges, emblems and escutcheons other than those covered by Article 6*ter* of the Paris Convention and which are of public interest, unless the consent of the competent authority to their registration has been given in conformity with the law of the Member State.

4. A trade mark shall not be refused registration in accordance with paragraph 1(b), (c) or (d) if, before the date of application for registration, following the use which has been made of it, it has acquired a distinctive character. A trade mark shall not be declared invalid for the same reasons if, before the date of application for a declaration of invalidity, following the use which has been made of it, it has acquired a distinctive character.

5. Any Member State may provide that paragraph 4 is also to apply where the distinctive character was acquired after the date of application for registration but before the date of registration.

Article 5   Relative grounds for refusal or invalidity

1. A trade mark shall not be registered or, if registered, shall be liable to be declared invalid where:

    (a) it is identical with an earlier trade mark, and the goods or services for which the trade mark is applied for or is registered are identical with the goods or services for which the earlier trade mark is protected;

    (b) because of its identity with, or similarity to, the earlier trade mark and the identity or similarity of the goods or services covered by the trade marks, there exists a likelihood of confusion on the part of the public; the likelihood of confusion includes the likelihood of association with the earlier trade mark.

2. 'Earlier trade marks' within the meaning of paragraph 1 means:

    (a) trade marks of the following kinds with a date of application for registration which is earlier than the date of application for registration of the trade mark, taking account, where appropriate, of the priorities claimed in respect of those trade marks:

        (i)   EU trade marks;

        (ii) trade marks registered in the Member State concerned or, in the case of Belgium, Luxembourg or the Netherlands, at the Benelux Office for Intellectual Property;

        (iii) trade marks registered under international arrangements which have effect in the Member State concerned;

    (b) EU trade marks which validly claim seniority, in accordance with Regulation (EC) No 207/2009, of a trade mark referred to in points (a)(ii) and (iii), even when the latter trade mark has been surrendered or allowed to lapse;

    (c) applications for the trade marks referred to in points (a) and (b), subject to their registration;

    (d) trade marks which, on the date of application for registration of the trade mark, or, where appropriate, of the priority claimed in respect of the application for registration of the trade mark, are well known in the Member State concerned, in the sense in which the words 'well-known' are used in Article 6bis of the Paris Convention.

3. Furthermore, a trade mark shall not be registered or, if registered, shall be liable to be declared invalid where:

    (a) it is identical with, or similar to, an earlier trade mark irrespective of whether the goods or services for which it is applied or registered are identical with, similar to or not similar to those for which the earlier trade mark is registered, where the earlier trade mark has a reputation in the Member State in respect of which registration is applied for or in which the trade mark is registered or, in the case of an EU trade mark, has a reputation in the Union and the use of the later trade mark without due cause would take unfair advantage of, or be detrimental to, the distinctive character or the repute of the earlier trade mark;

    (b) an agent or representative of the proprietor of the trade mark applies for registration thereof in his own name without the proprietor's authorisation, unless the agent or representative justifies his action;

    (c) and to the extent that, pursuant to Union legislation or the law of the Member State concerned providing for protection of designations of origin and geographical indications:

(i) an application for a designation of origin or a geographical indication had already been submitted in accordance with Union legislation or the law of the Member State concerned prior to the date of application for registration of the trade mark or the date of the priority claimed for the application, subject to its subsequent registration;

(ii) that designation of origin or geographical indication confers on the person authorised under the relevant law to exercise the rights arising therefrom the right to prohibit the use of a subsequent trade mark.

4. Any Member State may provide that a trade mark is not to be registered or, if registered, is liable to be declared invalid where, and to the extent that:

(a) rights to a non-registered trade mark or to another sign used in the course of trade were acquired prior to the date of application for registration of the subsequent trade mark, or the date of the priority claimed for the application for registration of the subsequent trade mark, and that non-registered trade mark or other sign confers on its proprietor the right to prohibit the use of a subsequent trade mark;

(b) the use of the trade mark may be prohibited by virtue of an earlier right, other than the rights referred to in paragraph 2 and point (a) of this paragraph, and in particular:

(i) a right to a name;

(ii) a right of personal portrayal;

(iii) a copyright;

(iv) an industrial property right;

(c) the trade mark is liable to be confused with an earlier trade mark protected abroad, provided that, at the date of the application, the applicant was acting in bad faith.

5. The Member States shall ensure that in appropriate circumstances there is no obligation to refuse registration or to declare a trade mark invalid where the proprietor of the earlier trade mark or other earlier right consents to the registration of the later trade mark.

6. Any Member State may provide that, by way of derogation from paragraphs 1 to 5, the grounds for refusal of registration or invalidity in force in that Member State prior to the date of the entry into force of the provisions necessary to comply with Directive 89/104/EEC are to apply to trade marks for which an application has been made prior to that date.

Article 6 Establishment a posteriori of invalidity or revocation of a trade mark

Where the seniority of a national trade mark or of a trade mark registered under international arrangements having effect in the Member State, which has been surrendered or allowed to lapse, is claimed for an EU trade mark, the invalidity or revocation of the trade mark providing the basis for the seniority claim may be established a posteriori, provided that the invalidity or revocation could have been declared at the time the mark was surrendered or allowed to lapse. In such a case, the seniority shall cease to produce its effects.

Article 7 Grounds for refusal or invalidity relating to only some of the goods or services

Where grounds for refusal of registration or for invalidity of a trade mark exist in respect of only some of the goods or services for which that trade mark has been applied or registered, refusal of registration or invalidity shall cover those goods or services only.

Article 8 Lack of distinctive character or of reputation of an earlier trade mark precluding a declaration of invalidity of a registered trade mark

An application for a declaration of invalidity on the basis of an earlier trade mark shall not succeed at the date of application for invalidation if it would not have been successful at the filing date or the priority date of the later trade mark for any of the following reasons:

(a) the earlier trade mark, liable to be declared invalid pursuant to Article 4(1)(b), (c) or (d), had not yet acquired a distinctive character as referred to in Article 4(4);

(b) the application for a declaration of invalidity is based on Article 5(1)(b) and the earlier trade mark had not yet become sufficiently distinctive to support a finding of likelihood of confusion within the meaning of Article 5(1)(b);

(c) the application for a declaration of invalidity is based on Article 5(3)(a) and the earlier trade mark had not yet acquired a reputation within the meaning of Article 5(3)(a).

Article 9   Preclusion of a declaration of invalidity due to acquiescence

1. Where, in a Member State, the proprietor of an earlier trade mark as referred to in Article 5(2) or Article 5(3)(a) has acquiesced, for a period of five successive years, in the use of a later trade mark registered in that Member State while being aware of such use, that proprietor shall no longer be entitled on the basis of the earlier trade mark to apply for a declaration that the later trade mark is invalid in respect of the goods or services for which the later trade mark has been used, unless registration of the later trade mark was applied for in bad faith.

2. Member States may provide that paragraph 1 of this Article is to apply to the proprietor of any other earlier right referred to in Article 5(4)(a) or (b).

3. In the cases referred to in paragraphs 1 and 2, the proprietor of a later registered trade mark shall not be entitled to oppose the use of the earlier right, even though that right may no longer be invoked against the later trade mark.

Section 3   Rights Conferred and Limitations

Article 10   Rights conferred by a trade mark

1. The registration of a trade mark shall confer on the proprietor exclusive rights therein.

2. Without prejudice to the rights of proprietors acquired before the filing date or the priority date of the registered trade mark, the proprietor of that registered trade mark shall be entitled to prevent all third parties not having his consent from using in the course of trade, in relation to goods or services, any sign where:

(a) the sign is identical with the trade mark and is used in relation to goods or services which are identical with those for which the trade mark is registered;

(b) the sign is identical with, or similar to, the trade mark and is used in relation to goods or services which are identical with, or similar to, the goods or services for which the trade mark is registered, if there exists a likelihood of confusion on the part of the public; the likelihood of confusion includes the likelihood of association between the sign and the trade mark;

(c) the sign is identical with, or similar to, the trade mark irrespective of whether it is used in relation to goods or services which are identical with, similar to, or not similar to, those for which the trade mark is registered, where the latter has a reputation in the Member State and where use of that sign without due cause takes unfair advantage of, or is detrimental to, the distinctive character or the repute of the trade mark.

3. The following, in particular, may be prohibited under paragraph 2:

(a) affixing the sign to the goods or to the packaging thereof;

(b) offering the goods or putting them on the market, or stocking them for those purposes, under the sign, or offering or supplying services thereunder;

(c) importing or exporting the goods under the sign;

(d) using the sign as a trade or company name or part of a trade or company name;

(e) using the sign on business papers and in advertising;

(f) using the sign in comparative advertising in a manner that is contrary to Directive 2006/114/EC.

4. Without prejudice to the rights of proprietors acquired before the filing date or the priority date of the registered trade mark, the proprietor of that registered trade mark shall also be entitled to prevent all third parties from bringing goods, in the course of trade, into the Member State where the trade mark is registered, without being released for free circulation there, where such goods, including the packaging thereof, come from third countries and bear without authorisation a trade

mark which is identical with the trade mark registered in respect of such goods, or which cannot be distinguished in its essential aspects from that trade mark.

The entitlement of the trade mark proprietor pursuant to the first subparagraph shall lapse if, during the proceedings to determine whether the registered trade mark has been infringed, initiated in accordance with Regulation (EU) No 608/2013, evidence is provided by the declarant or the holder of the goods that the proprietor of the registered trade mark is not entitled to prohibit the placing of the goods on the market in the country of final destination.

5. Where, under the law of a Member State, the use of a sign under the conditions referred to in paragraph 2 (b) or (c) could not be prohibited before the date of entry into force of the provisions necessary to comply with Directive 89/104/EEC in the Member State concerned, the rights conferred by the trade mark may not be relied on to prevent the continued use of the sign.

6. Paragraphs 1, 2, 3 and 5 shall not affect provisions in any Member State relating to the protection against the use of a sign other than use for the purposes of distinguishing goods or services, where use of that sign without due cause takes unfair advantage of, or is detrimental to, the distinctive character or the repute of the trade mark.

Article 11   The right to prohibit preparatory acts in relation to the use of packaging or other means

Where the risk exists that the packaging, labels, tags, security or authenticity features or devices, or any other means to which the trade mark is affixed, could be used in relation to goods or services and that use would constitute an infringement of the rights of the proprietor of a trade mark under Article 10(2) and (3), the proprietor of that trade mark shall have the right to prohibit the following acts if carried out in the course of trade:

(a) affixing a sign identical with, or similar to, the trade mark on packaging, labels, tags, security or authenticity features or devices, or any other means to which the mark may be affixed;

(b) offering or placing on the market, or stocking for those purposes, or importing or exporting, packaging, labels, tags, security or authenticity features or devices, or any other means to which the mark is affixed.

Article 12   Reproduction of trade marks in dictionaries

If the reproduction of a trade mark in a dictionary, encyclopaedia or similar reference work, in print or electronic form, gives the impression that it constitutes the generic name of the goods or services for which the trade mark is registered, the publisher of the work shall, at the request of the proprietor of the trade mark, ensure that the reproduction of the trade mark is, without delay, and in the case of works in printed form at the latest in the next edition of the publication, accompanied by an indication that it is a registered trade mark.

Article 13   Prohibition of the use of a trade mark registered in the name of an agent or representative

1. Where a trade mark is registered in the name of the agent or representative of a person who is the proprietor of that trade mark, without the proprietor's consent, the latter shall be entitled to do either or both of the following:

(a) oppose the use of the trade mark by his agent or representative;

(b) demand the assignment of the trade mark in his favour.

2. Paragraph 1 shall not apply where the agent or representative justifies his action.

Article 14   Limitation of the effects of a trade mark

1. A trade mark shall not entitle the proprietor to prohibit a third party from using, in the course of trade:

(a) the name or address of the third party, where that third party is a natural person;

(b) signs or indications which are not distinctive or which concern the kind, quality, quantity, intended purpose, value, geographical origin, the time of production of goods or of rendering of the service, or other characteristics of goods or services;

(c) the trade mark for the purpose of identifying or referring to goods or services as those of the proprietor of that trade mark, in particular, where the use of the trade mark is necessary to indicate the intended purpose of a product or service, in particular as accessories or spare parts.

2. Paragraph 1 shall only apply where the use made by the third party is in accordance with honest practices in industrial or commercial matters.

3. A trade mark shall not entitle the proprietor to prohibit a third party from using, in the course of trade, an earlier right which only applies in a particular locality, if that right is recognised by the law of the Member State in question and the use of that right is within the limits of the territory in which it is recognised.

Article 15   Exhaustion of the rights conferred by a trade mark

1. A trade mark shall not entitle the proprietor to prohibit its use in relation to goods which have been put on the market in the Union under that trade mark by the proprietor or with the proprietor's consent.

2. Paragraph 1 shall not apply where there exist legitimate reasons for the proprietor to oppose further commercialisation of the goods, especially where the condition of the goods is changed or impaired after they have been put on the market.

Article 16   Use of trade marks

1. If, within a period of five years following the date of the completion of the registration procedure, the proprietor has not put the trade mark to genuine use in the Member State in connection with the goods or services in respect of which it is registered, or if such use has been suspended during a continuous five-year period, the trade mark shall be subject to the limits and sanctions provided for in Article 17, Article 19(1), Article 44(1) and (2), and Article 46(3) and (4), unless there are proper reasons for non-use.

2. Where a Member State provides for opposition proceedings following registration, the five-year period referred to in paragraph 1 shall be calculated from the date when the mark can no longer be opposed or, in the event that an opposition has been lodged, from the date when a decision terminating the opposition proceedings became final or the opposition was withdrawn.

3. With regard to trade marks registered under international arrangements and having effect in the Member State, the five-year period referred to in paragraph 1 shall be calculated from the date when the mark can no longer be rejected or opposed. Where an opposition has been lodged or when an objection on absolute or relative grounds has been notified, the period shall be calculated from the date when a decision terminating the opposition proceedings or a ruling on absolute or relative grounds for refusal became final or the opposition was withdrawn.

4. The date of commencement of the five-year period, as referred to in paragraphs 1 and 2, shall be entered in the register.

5. The following shall also constitute use within the meaning of paragraph 1:

(a) use of the trade mark in a form differing in elements which do not alter the distinctive character of the mark in the form in which it was registered, regardless of whether or not the trade mark in the form as used is also registered in the name of the proprietor;

(b) affixing of the trade mark to goods or to the packaging thereof in the Member State concerned solely for export purposes.

6. Use of the trade mark with the consent of the proprietor shall be deemed to constitute use by the proprietor.

Article 17   Non-use as defence in infringement proceedings

The proprietor of a trade mark shall be entitled to prohibit the use of a sign only to the extent that the proprietor's rights are not liable to be revoked pursuant to Article 19 at the time the infringement action is brought. If the defendant so requests, the proprietor of the trade mark shall furnish proof that, during the five-year period preceding the date of bringing the action, the trade mark has been put to genuine use as provided in Article 16 in connection with the goods or services in respect of which it is registered and which are cited as justification for the action, or that there are proper reasons for non-use, provided that the registration procedure of the trade mark has at the date of bringing the action been completed for not less than five years.

Article 18   Intervening right of the proprietor of a later registered trade mark as defence in infringement proceedings

1. In infringement proceedings, the proprietor of a trade mark shall not be entitled to prohibit the use of a later registered mark where that later trade mark would not be declared invalid pursuant to Article 8, Article 9(1) or (2) or Article 46(3).

2. In infringement proceedings, the proprietor of a trade mark shall not be entitled to prohibit the use of a later registered EU trade mark where that later trade mark would not be declared invalid pursuant to Article 53(1), (3) or (4), 54(1) or (2) or 57(2) of Regulation (EC) No 207/2009.

3. Where the proprietor of a trade mark is not entitled to prohibit the use of a later registered trade mark pursuant to paragraph 1 or 2, the proprietor of that later registered trade mark shall not be entitled to prohibit the use of the earlier trade mark in infringement proceedings, even though that earlier right may no longer be invoked against the later trade mark.

Section 4   Revocation of Trade Mark Rights

Article 19   Absence of genuine use as ground for revocation

1. A trade mark shall be liable to revocation if, within a continuous five-year period, it has not been put to genuine use in the Member State in connection with the goods or services in respect of which it is registered, and there are no proper reasons for non-use.

2. No person may claim that the proprietor's rights in a trade mark should be revoked where, during the interval between expiry of the five-year period and filing of the application for revocation, genuine use of the trade mark has been started or resumed.

3. The commencement or resumption of use within the three-month period preceding the filing of the application for revocation which began at the earliest on expiry of the continuous five-year period of non-use shall be disregarded where preparations for the commencement or resumption occur only after the proprietor becomes aware that the application for revocation may be filed.

Article 20   Trade mark having become generic or misleading indication as grounds for revocation

A trade mark shall be liable to revocation if, after the date on which it was registered:

(a) as a result of acts or inactivity of the proprietor, it has become the common name in the trade for a product or service in respect of which it is registered;

(b) as a result of the use made of it by the proprietor of the trade mark or with the proprietor's consent in respect of the goods or services for which it is registered, it is liable to mislead the public, particularly as to the nature, quality or geographical origin of those goods or services.

Article 21   Revocation relating to only some of the goods or services

Where grounds for revocation of a trade mark exist in respect of only some of the goods or services for which that trade mark has been registered, revocation shall cover those goods or services only.

Section 5   Trade Marks as Objects of Property

Article 22   Transfer of registered trade marks

1. A trade mark may be transferred, separately from any transfer of the undertaking, in respect of some or all of the goods or services for which it is registered.

2. A transfer of the whole of the undertaking shall include the transfer of the trade mark except where there is agreement to the contrary or circumstances clearly dictate otherwise. This provision shall apply to the contractual obligation to transfer the undertaking.

3. Member States shall have procedures in place to allow for the recordal of transfers in their registers.

Article 23   Rights *in rem*

1. A trade mark may, independently of the undertaking, be given as security or be the subject of rights *in rem*.

2. Member States shall have procedures in place to allow for the recordal of rights *in rem* in their registers.

Article 24   Levy of execution

1. A trade mark may be levied in execution.

2. Member States shall have procedures in place to allow for the recordal of levy of execution in their registers.

Article 25   Licensing

1. A trade mark may be licensed for some or all of the goods or services for which it is registered and for the whole or part of the Member State concerned. A licence may be exclusive or non-exclusive.

2. The proprietor of a trade mark may invoke the rights conferred by that trade mark against a licensee who contravenes any provision in his licensing contract with regard to:

(a) its duration;

(b) the form covered by the registration in which the trade mark may be used;

(c) the scope of the goods or services for which the licence is granted;

(d) the territory in which the trade mark may be affixed; or

(e) the quality of the goods manufactured or of the services provided by the licensee.

3. Without prejudice to the provisions of the licensing contract, the licensee may bring proceedings for infringement of a trade mark only if its proprietor consents thereto. However, the holder of an exclusive licence may bring such proceedings if the proprietor of the trade mark, after formal notice, does not himself bring infringement proceedings within an appropriate period.

4. A licensee shall, for the purpose of obtaining compensation for damage suffered by him, be entitled to intervene in infringement proceedings brought by the proprietor of the trade mark.

5. Member States shall have procedures in place to allow for the recordal of licences in their registers.

Article 26   Applications for a trade mark as an object of property

Articles 22 to 25 shall apply to applications for trade marks.

Section 6   Guarantee or Certification Marks and Collective Marks

Article 27   Definitions

For the purposes of this Directive, the following definitions apply:

(a) 'guarantee or certification mark' means a trade mark which is described as such when the mark is applied for and is capable of distinguishing goods or services which are certified by the proprietor of the mark in respect of material, mode of manufacture of goods or performance of services, quality, accuracy or other characteristics, from goods and services which are not so certified;

(b) 'collective mark' means a trade mark which is described as such when the mark is applied for and is capable of distinguishing the goods or services of the members of an association which is the proprietor of the mark from the goods or services of other undertakings.

Article 28   Guarantee or certification marks

1. Member States may provide for the registration of guarantee or certification marks.

2. Any natural or legal person, including institutions, authorities and bodies governed by public law, may apply for guarantee or certification marks provided that such person does not carry on a business involving the supply of goods or services of the kind certified.

Member States may provide that a guarantee or certification mark is not to be registered unless the applicant is competent to certify the goods or services for which the mark is to be registered.

3. Member States may provide that guarantee or certification marks are not to be registered, or are to be revoked or declared invalid, on grounds other than those specified in Articles 4, 19 and 20, where the function of those marks so requires.

4. By way of derogation from Article 4(1)(c), Member States may provide that signs or indications which may serve, in trade, to designate the geographical origin of the goods or services may constitute guarantee or certification marks. Such a guarantee or certification mark shall not entitle the proprietor to prohibit a third party from using in the course of trade such signs or indications, provided that third party uses them in accordance with honest practices in industrial or commercial matters. In particular, such a mark may not be invoked against a third party who is entitled to use a geographical name.

5. The requirements laid down in Article 16 shall be satisfied where genuine use of a guarantee or certification mark in accordance with Article 16 is made by any person who has the authority to use it.

Article 29   Collective marks

1. Member States shall provide for the registration of collective marks.

2. Associations of manufacturers, producers, suppliers of services or traders, which, under the terms of the law governing them, have the capacity in their own name to have rights and obligations, to make contracts or accomplish other legal acts, and to sue and be sued, as well as legal persons governed by public law, may apply for collective marks.

3. By way of derogation from Article 4(1)(c), Member States may provide that signs or indications which may serve, in trade, to designate the geographical origin of the goods or services may constitute collective marks. Such a collective mark shall not entitle the proprietor to prohibit a third party from using, in the course of trade, such signs or indications, provided that third party uses them in accordance with honest practices in industrial or commercial matters. In particular, such a mark may not be invoked against a third party who is entitled to use a geographical name.

Article 30   Regulations governing use of a collective mark

1. An applicant for a collective mark shall submit the regulations governing its use to the office.

2. The regulations governing use shall specify at least the persons authorised to use the mark, the conditions of membership of the association and the conditions of use of the mark, including sanctions. The regulations governing use of a mark referred to in Article 29(3) shall authorise any person whose goods or services originate in the geographical area concerned to become a member of the association which is the proprietor of the mark, provided that the person fulfils all the other conditions of the regulations.

Article 31   Refusal of an application

1. In addition to the grounds for refusal of a trade mark application provided for in Article 4, where appropriate with the exception of Article 4(1)(c) concerning signs or indications which may serve, in trade, to designate the geographical origin of the goods or services, and Article 5, and without prejudice to the right of an office not to undertake examination *ex officio* of relative grounds, an application for a collective mark shall be refused where the provisions of point (b) of Article 27, Article 29 or Article 30 are not satisfied, or where the regulations governing use of that collective mark are contrary to public policy or to accepted principles of morality.

2. An application for a collective mark shall also be refused if the public is liable to be misled as regards the character or the significance of the mark, in particular if it is likely to be taken to be something other than a collective mark.

3. An application shall not be refused if the applicant, as a result of amendment of the regulations governing use of the collective mark, meets the requirements referred to in paragraphs 1 and 2.

Article 32   Use of collective marks

The requirements of Article 16 shall be satisfied where genuine use of a collective mark in accordance with that Article is made by any person who has authority to use it.

Article 33   Amendments to the regulations governing use of a collective mark

1. The proprietor of a collective mark shall submit to the office any amended regulations governing use.

2. Amendments to the regulations governing use shall be mentioned in the register unless the amended regulations do not satisfy the requirements of Article 30 or involve one of the grounds for refusal referred to in Article 31.

3. For the purposes of this Directive, amendments to the regulations governing use shall take effect only from the date of entry of the mention of those amendments in the register.

Article 34   Persons entitled to bring an action for infringement

1. Article 25(3) and (4) shall apply to every person who has the authority to use a collective mark.

2. The proprietor of a collective mark shall be entitled to claim compensation on behalf of persons who have authority to use the mark where those persons have sustained damage as a result of unauthorised use of the mark.

Article 35   Additional grounds for revocation

In addition to the grounds for revocation provided for in Articles 19 and 20, the rights of the proprietor of a collective mark shall be revoked on the following grounds:

    (a) the proprietor does not take reasonable steps to prevent the mark being used in a manner that is incompatible with the conditions of use laid down in the regulations governing use, including any amendments thereto mentioned in the register;

    (b) the manner in which the mark has been used by authorised persons has caused it to become liable to mislead the public in the manner referred to in Article 31(2);

    (c) an amendment to the regulations governing use of the mark has been mentioned in the register in breach of Article 33(2), unless the proprietor of the mark, by further amending the regulations governing use, complies with the requirements of that Article.

Article 36   Additional grounds for invalidity

In addition to the grounds for invalidity provided for in Article 4, where appropriate with the exception of Article 4(1)(c) concerning signs or indications which may serve, in trade, to designate the geographical origin of the goods or services, and Article 5, a collective mark which is registered in breach of Article 31 shall be declared invalid unless the proprietor of the mark, by amending the regulations governing use, complies with the requirements of Article 31.

Chapter 3   Procedures

Section 1   Application and Registration

Article 37   Application requirements

1. An application for registration of a trade mark shall contain at least all of the following:

    (a) a request for registration;

    (b) information identifying the applicant;

    (c) a list of the goods or services in respect of which the registration is requested;

    (d) a representation of the trade mark, which satisfies the requirements set out in point (b) of Article 3.

    . . .

Article 39   Designation and classification of goods and services

1. The goods and services in respect of which trade mark registration is applied for shall be classified in conformity with the system of classification established by the Nice Agreement Concerning the International Classification of Goods and Services for the Purposes of the Registration of Marks of 15 June 1957 ('the Nice Classification').

    . . .

Section 2   Procedures for Opposition, Revocation and Invalidity

Article 43   Opposition procedure

1. Member States shall provide for an efficient and expeditious administrative procedure before their offices for opposing the registration of a trade mark application on the grounds provided for in Article 5.

...

Article 45   Procedure for revocation or declaration of invalidity

1. Without prejudice to the right of the parties to appeal to the courts, Member States shall provide for an efficient and expeditious administrative procedure before their offices for the revocation or declaration of invalidity of a trade mark.

2. The administrative procedure for revocation shall provide that the trade mark is to be revoked on the grounds provided for in Articles 19 and 20.

3. The administrative procedure for invalidity shall provide that the trade mark is to be declared invalid at least on the following grounds:

    (a) the trade mark should not have been registered because it does not comply with the requirements provided for in Article 4;

    (b) the trade mark should not have been registered because of the existence of an earlier right within the meaning of Article 5(1) to (3).

4. The administrative procedure shall provide that at least the following are to be entitled to file an application for revocation or for a declaration of invalidity:

    (a) in the case of paragraph 2 and paragraph 3(a), any natural or legal person and any group or body set up for the purpose of representing the interests of manufacturers, producers, suppliers of services, traders or consumers, and which, under the terms of the law governing it, has the capacity to sue in its own name and to be sued;

    (b) in the case of paragraph 3(b) of this Article, the proprietor of an earlier trade mark as referred to in Article 5(2) and Article 5(3)(a), and the person authorised under the relevant law to exercise the rights arising from a protected designation of origin or geographical indication as referred to in Article 5(3)(c).

...

Article 47   Consequences of revocation and invalidity

1. A registered trade mark shall be deemed not to have had, as from the date of the application for revocation, the effects specified in this Directive, to the extent that the rights of the proprietor have been revoked. An earlier date, on which one of the grounds for revocation occurred, may be fixed in the decision on the application for revocation, at the request of one of the parties.

2. A registered trade mark shall be deemed not to have had, as from the outset, the effects specified in this Directive, to the extent that the trade mark has been declared invalid.

Section 3   Duration and Renewal of Registration

Article 48   Duration of registration

1. Trade marks shall be registered for a period of 10 years from the date of filing of the application.

2. Registration may be renewed in accordance with Article 49 for further 10-year periods.

...

Chapter 5   Final Provisions

...

Article 54   Transposition

1. Member States shall bring into force the laws, regulations and administrative provisions necessary to comply with Articles 3 to 6, Articles 8 to 14, Articles 16, 17 and 18, Articles 22 to 39, Article 41, Articles 43 and 44 and Articles 46 to 50 by 14 January 2019. Member States shall

bring into force the laws, regulations and administrative provisions to comply with Article 45 by 14 January 2023. They shall immediately communicate the text of those measures to the Commission.

. . .

Article 55   Repeal

Directive 2008/95/EC is repealed with effect from 15 January 2019, without prejudice to the obligations of the Member States relating to the time limit for the transposition into national law of Directive 89/104/EEC set out in Part B of Annex I to Directive 2008/95/EC.

References to the repealed Directive shall be construed as references to this Directive and shall be read in accordance with the correlation table in the Annex.

Article 56   Entry into Force

This Directive shall enter into force on the twentieth day following that of its publication in the Official Journal of the European Union.

Articles 1, 7, 15, 19, 20 and 21 shall apply from 15 January 2019.

. . .

Regulation (EU) 2017/1001 of the European Parliament and of the Council

of 14 June 2017 on the European Union trade mark (codification) (Text with EEA relevance)

THE EUROPEAN PARLIAMENT AND THE COUNCIL OF THE EUROPEAN UNION,

Having regard to the Treaty on the Functioning of the European Union, and in particular the first paragraph of Article 118 thereof,

Having regard to the proposal from the European Commission,

After transmission of the draft legislative act to the national parliaments, Acting in accordance with the ordinary legislative procedure,

Whereas:

(1) Council Regulation (EC) No 207/2009 has been substantially amended several times. In the interests of clarity and rationality, that Regulation should be codified.

(2) Council Regulation (EC) No 40/94, which was codified in 2009 as Regulation (EC) No 207/2009, created a system of trade mark protection specific to the Union which provided for the protection of trade marks at the level of the Union, in parallel to the protection of trade marks available at the level of the Member States in accordance with the national trade mark systems, harmonised by Council Directive 89/104/EEC, which was codified as Directive 2008/95/EC of the European Parliament and of the Council.

(3) It is desirable to promote throughout the Union a harmonious development of economic activities and a continuous and balanced expansion by completing an internal market which functions properly and offers conditions which are similar to those obtaining in a national market. In order to establish a market of this kind and make it increasingly a single market, not only should barriers to free movement of goods and services be removed and arrangements be instituted which ensure that competition is not distorted, but, in addition, legal conditions should be laid down which enable undertakings to adapt their activities to the scale of the Union, whether in manufacturing and distributing goods or in providing services. For those purposes, trade marks enabling the products and services of undertakings to be distinguished by identical means throughout the entire Union, regardless of frontiers, should feature amongst the legal instruments which undertakings have at their disposal.

(4) For the purpose of pursuing the Union's said objectives it would appear necessary to provide for Union arrangements for trade marks whereby undertakings can by means of one procedural system obtain EU trade marks to which uniform protection is given and which produce their effects throughout the entire area of the Union. The principle of the unitary character of the EU trade mark thus stated should apply unless otherwise provided for in this Regulation.

(5) The barrier of territoriality of the rights conferred on proprietors of trade marks by the laws of the Member States cannot be removed by approximation of laws. In order to open up unrestricted economic activity in the whole of the internal market for the benefit of undertakings, it should be possible to register trade marks which are governed by a uniform Union law directly applicable in all Member States.

(6) The experience acquired since the establishment of the Community trade mark system has shown that undertakings from within the Union and from third countries have accepted the system which has become a successful and viable complement and alternative to the protection of trade marks at the level of the Member States.

(7) The Union law relating to trade marks nevertheless does not replace the laws of the Member States on trade marks. It would not in fact appear to be justified to require undertakings to apply for registration of their trade marks as EU trade marks.

(8) National trade marks continue to be necessary for those undertakings which do not want protection of their trade marks at Union level, or which are unable to obtain Union-wide protection while national protection does not face any obstacles. It should be left to each person seeking trade mark protection to decide whether the protection is sought only as a national trade mark in one or more Member States, or only as an EU trade mark, or both.

(9) The rights in an EU trade mark should not be obtained otherwise than by registration, and registration should be refused in particular if the trade mark is not distinctive, if it is unlawful or if it conflicts with earlier rights.

(10) A sign should be permitted to be represented in any appropriate form using generally available technology, and thus not necessarily by graphic means, as long as the representation is clear, precise, self-contained, easily accessible, intelligible, durable and objective.

(11) The protection afforded by an EU trade mark, the function of which is in particular to guarantee the trade mark as an indication of origin, should be absolute in the case of identity between the mark and the sign and the goods or services. The protection should apply also in cases of similarity between the mark and the sign and the goods or services. An interpretation should be given for the concept of similarity in relation to the likelihood of confusion. The likelihood of confusion, the appreciation of which depends on numerous elements and, in particular, on the recognition of the trade mark on the market, the association which can be made with the used or registered sign, the degree of similarity between the trade mark and the sign and between the goods or services identified, should constitute the specific condition for such protection.

(12) In order to ensure legal certainty and full consistency with the principle of priority, under which a registered earlier trade mark takes precedence over later registered trade marks, it is necessary to provide that the enforcement of rights conferred by an EU trade mark should be without prejudice to the rights of proprietors acquired prior to the filing or priority date of the EU trade mark. This is in conformity with Article 16(1) of the Agreement on trade-related aspects of intellectual property rights of 15 April 1994.

(13) Confusion as to the commercial source from which the goods or services emanate may occur when a company uses the same or a similar sign as a trade name in such a way that a link is established between the company bearing the name and the goods or services coming from that company. Infringement of an EU trade mark should therefore also comprise the use of the sign as a trade name or similar designation as long as the use is made for the purposes of distinguishing goods or services.

(14) In order to ensure legal certainty and full consistency with specific Union legislation, it is appropriate to provide that the proprietor of an EU trade mark should be entitled to prohibit a third party from using a sign in comparative advertising where such comparative advertising is contrary to Directive 2006/114/EC of the European Parliament and of the Council.

(15) In order to ensure trade mark protection and combat counterfeiting effectively, and in line with international obligations of the Union under the framework of the World Trade Organisation (WTO), in particular Article V of the General Agreement on Tariffs and Trade (GATT) on freedom of transit and, as regards generic medicines, the 'Declaration on the TRIPS Agreement and public

health' adopted by the Doha WTO Ministerial Conference on 14 November 2001, the proprietor of an EU trade mark should be entitled to prevent third parties from bringing goods, in the course of trade, into the Union without being released for free circulation there, where such goods come from third countries and bear without authorisation a trade mark which is identical or essentially identical with the EU trade mark registered in respect of such goods.

(16) To this effect, it should be permissible for EU trade mark proprietors to prevent the entry of infringing goods and their placement in all customs situations, including transit, transhipment, warehousing, free zones, temporary storage, inward processing or temporary admission, also when such goods are not intended to be placed on the market of the Union. In performing customs controls, the customs authorities should make use of the powers and procedures laid down in Regulation (EU) No 608/2013 of the European Parliament and the Council, also at the request of the right holders. In particular, the customs authorities should carry out the relevant controls on the basis of risk analysis criteria.

(17) In order to reconcile the need to ensure the effective enforcement of trade mark rights with the necessity to avoid hampering the free flow of trade in legitimate goods, the entitlement of the proprietor of the EU trade mark should lapse where, during the subsequent proceedings initiated before the European Union trade mark court ('EU trade mark court') competent to take a substantive decision on whether the EU trade mark has been infringed, the declarant or the holder of the goods is able to prove that the proprietor of the EU trade mark is not entitled to prohibit the placing of the goods on the market in the country of final destination.

(18) Article 28 of Regulation (EU) No 608/2013 provides that a right holder is to be liable for damages towards the holder of the goods where, inter alia, the goods in question are subsequently found not to infringe an intellectual property right.

(19) Appropriate measures should be taken with a view to ensuring the smooth transit of generic medicines. With respect to international non-proprietary names (INN) as globally recognised generic names for active substances in pharmaceutical preparations, it is vital to take due account of the existing limitations on the effect of EU trade mark rights. Consequently, the proprietor of an EU trade mark should not have the right to prevent a third party from bringing goods into the Union without being released for free circulation there, based upon similarities between the INN for the active ingredient in the medicines and the trade mark.

(20) In order to enable proprietors of EU trade marks to combat counterfeiting effectively, they should be entitled to prohibit the affixing of an infringing mark to goods and preparatory acts carried out prior to the affixing.

(21) The exclusive rights conferred by an EU trade mark should not entitle the proprietor to prohibit the use of signs or indications by third parties which are used fairly and thus in accordance with honest practices in industrial and commercial matters. In order to ensure equal conditions for trade names and EU trade marks in the event of conflicts, given that trade names are regularly granted unrestricted protection against later trade marks, such use should be only considered to include the use of the personal name of the third party. It should further permit the use of descriptive or non-distinctive signs or indications in general. Furthermore, the proprietor should not be entitled to prevent the fair and honest use of the EU trade mark for the purpose of identifying or referring to the goods or services as those of the proprietor. Use of a trade mark by third parties to draw the consumer's attention to the resale of genuine goods that were originally sold by or with the consent of the proprietor of the EU trade mark in the Union should be considered as being fair as long as it is at the same time in accordance with honest practices in industrial and commercial matters. Use of a trade mark by third parties for the purpose of artistic expression should be considered as being fair as long as it is at the same time in accordance with honest practices in industrial and commercial matters. Furthermore, this Regulation should be applied in a way that ensures full respect for fundamental rights and freedoms, and in particular the freedom of expression.

(22) It follows from the principle of free movement of goods that it is essential that the proprietor of an EU trade mark not be entitled to prohibit its use by a third party in relation to goods which have been put into circulation in the European Economic Area, under the trade mark, by him or with his

consent, save where there exist legitimate reasons for the proprietor to oppose further commercialisation of the goods.

(23) In order to ensure legal certainty and safeguard legitimately acquired trade mark rights, it is appropriate and necessary to lay down, without prejudice to the principle that the later trade mark cannot be enforced against the earlier trade mark, that proprietors of EU trade marks should not be entitled to oppose the use of a later trade mark if the later trade mark was acquired at a time when the earlier trade mark could not be enforced against the later trade mark.

(24) There is no justification for protecting EU trade marks or, as against them, any trade mark which has been registered before them, except where the trade marks are actually used.

(25) For reasons of equity and legal certainty, the use of an EU trade mark in a form that differs in elements which do not alter the distinctive character of that mark in the form in which it is registered should be sufficient to preserve the rights conferred regardless of whether the trade mark in the form as used is also registered.

(26) An EU trade mark is to be regarded as an object of property which exists separately from the undertakings whose goods or services are designated by it. Accordingly, it should be capable of being transferred, of being charged as security in favour of a third party and of being the subject matter of licences.

(27) Administrative measures are necessary at Union level for implementing in relation to every trade mark the trade mark law laid down by this Regulation. It is therefore essential, while retaining the Union's existing institutional structure and balance of powers, to provide for a European Union Intellectual Property Office ('the Office') which is independent in relation to technical matters and has legal, administrative and financial autonomy. To this end it is necessary and appropriate that the Office should be a body of the Union having legal personality and exercising the powers which are conferred on it by this Regulation, and that it should operate within the framework of Union law without detracting from the competences exercised by the Union institutions.

(28) EU trade mark protection is granted in relation to specific goods or services whose nature and number determine the extent of protection afforded to the trade mark proprietor. It is therefore essential to lay down rules for the designation and classification of goods and services in this Regulation and to ensure legal certainty and sound administration by requiring that the goods and services for which trade mark protection is sought are identified by the applicant with sufficient clarity and precision to enable the competent authorities and economic operators, on the basis of the application alone, to determine the extent of the protection applied for. The use of general terms should be interpreted as only including all goods and services clearly covered by the literal meaning of the term. Proprietors of EU trade marks, which because of the practice of the Office prior to 22 June 2012 were registered in respect of the entire heading of a class of the system of classification established by the Nice Agreement Concerning the International Classification of Goods and Services for the Purposes of the Registration of Marks of 15 June 1957, should be given the possibility to adapt their lists of goods and services in order to ensure that the content of the Register meets the requisite standard of clarity and precision in accordance with the case law of the Court of Justice of the European Union.

(29) In order to avoid unnecessary delays in registering an EU trade mark, it is appropriate to lay down a regime of optional EU and national trade mark searches that should be flexible in terms of user needs and preferences. The optional EU and national trade mark searches should be complemented by the making available of all-encompassing, fast and powerful search engines for the use of the public free of charge within the context of cooperation between the Office and the central industrial property offices of the Member States, including the Benelux Office for Intellectual Property.

(30) It is necessary to ensure that parties who are affected by decisions made by the Office are protected by the law in a manner which is suited to the special character of trade mark law. To that end, provision should be made for an appeal to lie from decisions of the various decision-making instances of the Office. A Board of Appeal of the Office should decide on the appeal. Decisions of the Boards of Appeal should, in turn, be amenable to actions before the General Court, which has jurisdiction to annul or to alter the contested decision.

(31) In order to ensure the protection of EU trade marks the Member States should designate, having regard to their own national system, as limited a number as possible of national courts of first and second instance having jurisdiction in matters of infringement and validity of EU trade marks.

(32) It is essential that decisions regarding the validity and infringement of EU trade marks have effect and cover the entire area of the Union, as this is the only way of preventing inconsistent decisions on the part of the courts and the Office and of ensuring that the unitary character of EU trade marks is not undermined. The provisions of Regulation (EU) No 1215/2012 of the European Parliament and of the Council (1) should apply to all actions at law relating to EU trade marks, save where this Regulation derogates from those rules.

(33) Contradictory judgments should be avoided in actions which involve the same acts and the same parties and which are brought on the basis of an EU trade mark and parallel national trade marks. For this purpose, when the actions are brought in the same Member State, the way in which this is to be achieved is a matter for national procedural rules, which are not prejudiced by this Regulation, whilst when the actions are brought in different Member States, provisions modelled on the rules on *lis pendens* and related actions of Regulation (EU) No 1215/2012 appear appropriate.

(34) With the aim of promoting convergence of practices and of developing common tools, it is necessary to establish an appropriate framework for cooperation between the Office and the industrial property offices of the Member States, including the Benelux Office for Intellectual Property, defining key areas of cooperation and enabling the Office to coordinate relevant common projects of interest to the Union and the Member States and to finance, up to a maximum amount, those projects. Those co-operation activities should be beneficial for undertakings using trade mark systems in Europe. For users of the Union regime laid down in this Regulation, the projects, particularly the databases for search and consultation purposes, should provide additional, inclusive, efficient tools that are free of charge to comply with the specific requirements arising from the unitary character of the EU trade mark.

(35) It is desirable to facilitate friendly, expeditious and efficient dispute resolution by entrusting the Office with the establishment of a mediation centre the services of which could be used by any person with the aim of achieving a friendly settlement of disputes relating to EU trade marks and Community designs by mutual agreement.

. . .

HAVE ADOPTED THIS REGULATION:

Chapter I   General Provisions

Article 1   EU trade mark

1. A trade mark for goods or services which is registered in accordance with the conditions contained in this Regulation and in the manner herein provided is hereinafter referred to as a 'European Union trade mark ('EU trade mark')'.

2. An EU trade mark shall have a unitary character. It shall have equal effect throughout the Union: it shall not be registered, transferred or surrendered or be the subject of a decision revoking the rights of the proprietor or declaring it invalid, nor shall its use be prohibited, save in respect of the whole Union. This principle shall apply unless otherwise provided for in this Regulation.

Article 2   Office

1. A European Union Intellectual Property Office ('the Office') is established.

2. All references in Union law to the Office for Harmonization in the Internal Market (Trade Marks and Designs) shall be read as references to the Office.

Article 3   Capacity to act

For the purpose of implementing this Regulation, companies or firms and other legal bodies shall be regarded as legal persons if, under the terms of the law governing them, they have the capacity in their own name to have rights and obligations of all kinds, to make contracts or accomplish other legal acts, and to sue and be sued.

Chapter II   The Law Relating to Trade Marks

Section 1   Definition of an EU trade mark and obtaining an EU trade mark

Article 4   Signs of which an EU trade mark may consist

An EU trade mark may consist of any signs, in particular words, including personal names, or designs, letters, numerals, colours, the shape of goods or of the packaging of goods, or sounds, provided that such signs are capable of:

(a) distinguishing the goods or services of one undertaking from those of other undertakings; and

(b) being represented on the Register of European Union trade marks ('the Register'), in a manner which enables the competent authorities and the public to determine the clear and precise subject matter of the protection afforded to its proprietor.

Article 5   Persons who can be proprietors of EU trade marks

Any natural or legal person, including authorities established under public law, may be the proprietor of an EU trade mark.

Article 6   Means whereby an EU trade mark is obtained

An EU trade mark shall be obtained by registration.

Article 7   Absolute grounds for refusal

1. The following shall not be registered:

   (a) signs which do not conform to the requirements of Article 4;

   (b) trade marks which are devoid of any distinctive character;

   (c) trade marks which consist exclusively of signs or indications which may serve, in trade, to designate the kind, quality, quantity, intended purpose, value, geographical origin or the time of production of the goods or of rendering of the service, or other characteristics of the goods or service;

   (d) trade marks which consist exclusively of signs or indications which have become customary in the current language or in the bona fide and established practices of the trade;

   (e) signs which consist exclusively of:

   (i) the shape, or another characteristic, which results from the nature of the goods themselves;

   (ii) the shape, or another characteristic, of goods which is necessary to obtain a technical result;

   (iii) the shape, or another characteristic, which gives substantial value to the goods;

   (f) trade marks which are contrary to public policy or to accepted principles of morality;

   (g) trade marks which are of such a nature as to deceive the public, for instance as to the nature, quality or geographical origin of the goods or service;

   (h) trade marks which have not been authorised by the competent authorities and are to be refused pursuant to Article 6*ter* of the Paris Convention for the Protection of Industrial Property ('Paris Convention');

   (i) trade marks which include badges, emblems or escutcheons other than those covered by Article 6*ter* of the Paris Convention and which are of particular public interest, unless the consent of the competent authority to their registration has been given;

   (j) trade marks which are excluded from registration, pursuant to Union legislation or national law or to international agreements to which the Union or the Member State concerned is party, providing for protection of designations of origin and geographical indications;

   (k) trade marks which are excluded from registration pursuant to Union legislation or international agreements to which the Union is party, providing for protection of traditional terms for wine;

    (l) trade marks which are excluded from registration pursuant to Union legislation or international agreements to which the Union is party, providing for protection of traditional specialities guaranteed;

    (m) trade marks which consist of, or reproduce in their essential elements, an earlier plant variety denomination registered in accordance with Union legislation or national law, or international agreements to which the Union or the Member State concerned is a party, providing for protection of plant variety rights, and which are in respect of plant varieties of the same or closely related species.

2. Paragraph 1 shall apply notwithstanding that the grounds of non-registrability obtain in only part of the Union.

3. Paragraph 1(b), (c) and (d) shall not apply if the trade mark has become distinctive in relation to the goods or services for which registration is requested as a consequence of the use which has been made of it.

Article 8   Relative grounds for refusal

1. Upon opposition by the proprietor of an earlier trade mark, the trade mark applied for shall not be registered:

    (a) if it is identical with the earlier trade mark and the goods or services for which registration is applied for are identical with the goods or services for which the earlier trade mark is protected;

    (b) if, because of its identity with, or similarity to, the earlier trade mark and the identity or similarity of the goods or services covered by the trade marks there exists a likelihood of confusion on the part of the public in the territory in which the earlier trade mark is protected; the likelihood of confusion includes the likelihood of association with the earlier trade mark.

2. For the purposes of paragraph 1, 'earlier trade mark' means:

    (a) trade marks of the following kinds with a date of application for registration which is earlier than the date of application for registration of the EU trade mark, taking account, where appropriate, of the priorities claimed in respect of those trade marks:

       (i)   EU trade marks;

      (ii) trade marks registered in a Member State, or, in the case of Belgium, the Netherlands or Luxembourg, at the Benelux Office for Intellectual Property;

     (iii) trade marks registered under international arrangements which have effect in a Member State;

     (iv) trade marks registered under international arrangements which have effect in the Union;

    (b) applications for the trade marks referred to in point (a), subject to their registration;

    (c) trade marks which, on the date of application for registration of the EU trade mark, or, where appropriate, of the priority claimed in respect of the application for registration of the EU trade mark, are well known in a Member State, in the sense in which the words 'well known' are used in Article 6*bis* of the Paris Convention.

3. Upon opposition by the proprietor of the trade mark, a trade mark shall not be registered where an agent or representative of the proprietor of the trade mark applies for registration thereof in his own name without the proprietor's consent, unless the agent or representative justifies his action.

4. Upon opposition by the proprietor of a non-registered trade mark or of another sign used in the course of trade of more than mere local significance, the trade mark applied for shall not be registered where and to the extent that, pursuant to Union legislation or the law of the Member State governing that sign:

    (a) rights to that sign were acquired prior to the date of application for registration of the EU trade mark, or the date of the priority claimed for the application for registration of the EU trade mark;

    (b) that sign confers on its proprietor the right to prohibit the use of a subsequent trade mark.

5. Upon opposition by the proprietor of a registered earlier trade mark within the meaning of paragraph 2, the trade mark applied for shall not be registered where it is identical with, or similar to,

an earlier trade mark, irrespective of whether the goods or services for which it is applied are identical with, similar to or not similar to those for which the earlier trade mark is registered, where, in the case of an earlier EU trade mark, the trade mark has a reputation in the Union or, in the case of an earlier national trade mark, the trade mark has a reputation in the Member State concerned, and where the use without due cause of the trade mark applied for would take unfair advantage of, or be detrimental to, the distinctive character or the repute of the earlier trade mark.

6. Upon opposition by any person authorised under the relevant law to exercise the rights arising from a designation of origin or a geographical indication, the trade mark applied for shall not be registered where and to the extent that, pursuant to the Union legislation or national law providing for the protection of designations of origin or geographical indications:

    (i) an application for a designation of origin or a geographical indication had already been submitted, in accordance with Union legislation or national law, prior to the date of application for registration of the EU trade mark or the date of the priority claimed for the application, subject to its subsequent registration;

    (ii) that designation of origin or geographical indication confers the right to prohibit the use of a subsequent trade mark.

Section 2   Effects of an EU trade mark

Article 9   Rights conferred by an EU trade mark

1. The registration of an EU trade mark shall confer on the proprietor exclusive rights therein.

2. Without prejudice to the rights of proprietors acquired before the filing date or the priority date of the EU trade mark, the proprietor of that EU trade mark shall be entitled to prevent all third parties not having his consent from using in the course of trade, in relation to goods or services, any sign where:

    (a) the sign is identical with the EU trade mark and is used in relation to goods or services which are identical with those for which the EU trade mark is registered;

    (b) the sign is identical with, or similar to, the EU trade mark and is used in relation to goods or services which are identical with, or similar to, the goods or services for which the EU trade mark is registered, if there exists a likelihood of confusion on the part of the public; the likelihood of confusion includes the likelihood of association between the sign and the trade mark;

    (c) the sign is identical with, or similar to, the EU trade mark irrespective of whether it is used in relation to goods or services which are identical with, similar to or not similar to those for which the EU trade mark is registered, where the latter has a reputation in the Union and where use of that sign without due cause takes unfair advantage of, or is detrimental to, the distinctive character or the repute of the EU trade mark.

3. The following, in particular, may be prohibited under paragraph 2:

    (a) affixing the sign to the goods or to the packaging of those goods;

    (b) offering the goods, putting them on the market, or stocking them for those purposes under the sign, or offering or supplying services thereunder;

    (c) importing or exporting the goods under the sign;

    (d) using the sign as a trade or company name or part of a trade or company name;

    (e) using the sign on business papers and in advertising;

    (f) using the sign in comparative advertising in a manner that is contrary to Directive 2006/114/EC.

4. Without prejudice to the rights of proprietors acquired before the filing date or the priority date of the EU trade mark, the proprietor of that EU trade mark shall also be entitled to prevent all third parties from bringing goods, in the course of trade, into the Union without being released for free circulation there, where such goods, including packaging, come from third countries and bear without authorisation a trade mark which is identical with the EU trade mark registered in respect of such goods, or which cannot be distinguished in its essential aspects from that trade mark.

The entitlement of the proprietor of an EU trade mark pursuant to the first subparagraph shall lapse if, during the proceedings to determine whether the EU trade mark has been infringed, initiated in accordance with Regulation (EU) No 608/2013, evidence is provided by the declarant or the holder of the goods that the proprietor of the EU trade mark is not entitled to prohibit the placing of the goods on the market in the country of final destination.

Article 10 Right to prohibit preparatory acts in relation to the use of packaging or other means

Where the risk exists that the packaging, labels, tags, security or authenticity features or devices or any other means to which the mark is affixed could be used in relation to goods or services and such use would constitute an infringement of the rights of the proprietor of an EU trade mark under Article 9(2) and (3), the proprietor of that trade mark shall have the right to prohibit the following acts if carried out in the course of trade:

   (a) affixing a sign identical with, or similar to, the EU trade mark on packaging, labels, tags, security or authenticity features or devices or any other means to which the mark may be affixed;
   (b) offering or placing on the market, or stocking for those purposes, or importing or exporting, packaging, labels, tags, security or authenticity features or devices or any other means to which the mark is affixed.

Article 11 Date from which rights against third parties prevail

1. The rights conferred by an EU trade mark shall prevail against third parties from the date of publication of the registration of the trade mark.

2. Reasonable compensation may be claimed in respect of acts occurring after the date of publication of an EU trade mark application, where those acts would, after publication of the registration of the trade mark, be prohibited by virtue of that publication.

3. A court seised of a case shall not decide upon the merits of that case until the registration has been published.

Article 12 Reproduction of an EU trade mark in a dictionary

If the reproduction of an EU trade mark in a dictionary, encyclopaedia or similar reference work gives the impression that it constitutes the generic name of the goods or services for which the trade mark is registered, the publisher of the work shall, at the request of the proprietor of the EU trade mark, ensure that the reproduction of the trade mark at the latest in the next edition of the publication is accompanied by an indication that it is a registered trade mark.

. . .

Article 14 Limitation of the effects of an EU trade mark

1. An EU trade mark shall not entitle the proprietor to prohibit a third party from using, in the course of trade:

   (a) the name or address of the third party, where that third party is a natural person;
   (b) signs or indications which are not distinctive or which concern the kind, quality, quantity, intended purpose, value, geographical origin, the time of production of goods or of rendering of the service, or other characteristics of the goods or services;
   (c) the EU trade mark for the purpose of identifying or referring to goods or services as those of the proprietor of that trade mark, in particular, where the use of that trade mark is necessary to indicate the intended purpose of a product or service, in particular as accessories or spare parts.

2. Paragraph 1 shall only apply where the use made by the third party is in accordance with honest practices in industrial or commercial matters.

Article 15 Exhaustion of the rights conferred by an EU trade mark

1. An EU trade mark shall not entitle the proprietor to prohibit its use in relation to goods which have been put on the market in the European Economic Area under that trade mark by the proprietor or with his consent.

2. Paragraph 1 shall not apply where there exist legitimate reasons for the proprietor to oppose further commercialisation of the goods, especially where the condition of the goods is changed or impaired after they have been put on the market.

Article 16 Intervening right of the proprietor of a later registered trade mark as a defence in infringement proceedings

1. In infringement proceedings, the proprietor of an EU trade mark shall not be entitled to prohibit the use of a later registered EU trade mark where that later trade mark would not be declared invalid pursuant to Article 60(1), (3) or (4), Article 61(1) or (2), or Article 64(2) of this Regulation.

2. In infringement proceedings, the proprietor of an EU trade mark shall not be entitled to prohibit the use of a later registered national trade mark where that later registered national trade mark would not be declared invalid pursuant to Article 8 or Article 9(1) or (2), or Article 46(3) of Directive (EU) 2015/2436 of the European Parliament and of the Council (1).

3. Where the proprietor of an EU trade mark is not entitled to prohibit the use of a later registered trade mark pursuant to paragraph 1 or 2, the proprietor of that later registered trade mark shall not be entitled to prohibit the use of that earlier EU trade mark in infringement proceedings.

Article 17 Complementary application of national law relating to infringement

1. The effects of EU trade marks shall be governed solely by the provisions of this Regulation. In other respects, infringement of an EU trade mark shall be governed by the national law relating to infringement of a national trade mark in accordance with the provisions of Chapter X.

2. This Regulation shall not prevent actions concerning an EU trade mark being brought under the law of Member States relating in particular to civil liability and unfair competition.

3. The rules of procedure to be applied shall be determined in accordance with the provisions of Chapter X.

Section 3   Use of an EU trade mark

Article 18   Use of an EU trade mark

1. If, within a period of five years following registration, the proprietor has not put the EU trade mark to genuine use in the Union in connection with the goods or services in respect of which it is registered, or if such use has been suspended during an uninterrupted period of five years, the EU trade mark shall be subject to the sanctions provided for in this Regulation, unless there are proper reasons for non-use.

The following shall also constitute use within the meaning of the first subparagraph:

    (a) use of the EU trade mark in a form differing in elements which do not alter the distinctive character of the mark in the form in which it was registered, regardless of whether or not the trade mark in the form as used is also registered in the name of the proprietor;

    (b) affixing of the EU trade mark to goods or to the packaging thereof in the Union solely for export purposes.

2. Use of the EU trade mark with the consent of the proprietor shall be deemed to constitute use by the proprietor.

Section 4   EU trade marks as objects of property

Article 19   Dealing with EU trade marks as national trade marks

1. Unless Articles 20 to 28 provide otherwise, an EU trade mark as an object of property shall be dealt with in its entirety, and for the whole area of the Union, as a national trade mark registered in the Member State in which, according to the Register:

    (a) the proprietor has his seat or his domicile on the relevant date;

    (b) where point (a) does not apply, the proprietor has an establishment on the relevant date.

2. In cases which are not provided for by paragraph 1, the Member State referred to in that paragraph shall be the Member State in which the seat of the Office is situated.

3. If two or more persons are mentioned in the Register as joint proprietors, paragraph 1 shall apply to the joint proprietor first mentioned; failing this, it shall apply to the subsequent joint proprietors in the order in which they are mentioned. Where paragraph 1 does not apply to any of the joint proprietors, paragraph 2 shall apply.

Article 20   Transfer

1. An EU trade mark may be transferred, separately from any transfer of the undertaking, in respect of some or all of the goods or services for which it is registered.

2. A transfer of the whole of the undertaking shall include the transfer of the EU trade mark except where, in accordance with the law governing the transfer, there is agreement to the contrary or circumstances clearly dictate otherwise. This provision shall apply to the contractual obligation to transfer the undertaking.

3. Without prejudice to paragraph 2, an assignment of the EU trade mark shall be made in writing and shall require the signature of the parties to the contract, except when it is a result of a judgment; otherwise it shall be void.

4. On request of one of the parties a transfer shall be entered in the Register and published.

5. An application for registration of a transfer shall contain information to identify the EU trade mark, the new proprietor, the goods and services to which the transfer relates, as well as documents duly establishing the transfer in accordance with paragraphs 2 and 3. The application may further contain, where applicable, information to identify the representative of the new proprietor.

. . .

11. As long as the transfer has not been entered in the Register, the successor in title may not invoke the rights arising from the registration of the EU trade mark.

. . .

Article 22   Rights *in rem*

1. An EU trade mark may, independently of the undertaking, be given as security or be the subject of rights *in rem*.

2. At the request of one of the parties, the rights referred to in paragraph 1 or the transfer of those rights shall be entered in the Register and published.

3. An entry in the Register effected pursuant to paragraph 2 shall be cancelled or modified at the request of one of the parties.

Article 23   Levy of execution

1. An EU trade mark may be levied in execution.

. . .

Article 24   Insolvency proceedings

1. The only insolvency proceedings in which an EU trade mark may be involved are those opened in the Member State in the territory of which the debtor has his centre of main interests.

. . .

Article 25   Licensing

1. An EU trade mark may be licensed for some or all of the goods or services for which it is registered and for the whole or part of the Union. A licence may be exclusive or non-exclusive.

2. The proprietor of an EU trade mark may invoke the rights conferred by that trade mark against a licensee who contravenes any provision in his licensing contract with regard to:

    (a) its duration;

    (b) the form covered by the registration in which the trade mark may be used;

    (c) the scope of the goods or services for which the licence is granted;

    (d) the territory in which the trade mark may be affixed; or

    (e) the quality of the goods manufactured or of the services provided by the licensee.

3. Without prejudice to the provisions of the licensing contract, the licensee may bring proceedings for infringement of an EU trade mark only if its proprietor consents thereto. However, the holder of an exclusive licence may bring such proceedings if the proprietor of the trade mark, after formal notice, does not himself bring infringement proceedings within an appropriate period.

4. A licensee shall, for the purpose of obtaining compensation for damage suffered by him, be entitled to intervene in infringement proceedings brought by the proprietor of the EU trade mark.

5. On request of one of the parties the grant or transfer of a licence in respect of an EU trade mark shall be entered in the Register and published.

6. An entry in the Register effected pursuant to paragraph 5 shall be cancelled or modified at the request of one of the parties.

. . .

Article 27 Effects vis-à-vis third parties

1. Legal acts referred to in Articles 20, 22 and 25 concerning an EU trade mark shall have effects vis-à-vis third parties in all the Member States only after entry in the Register. Nevertheless, such an act, before it is so entered, shall have effect vis-à-vis third parties who have acquired rights in the trade mark after the date of that act but who knew of the act at the date on which the rights were acquired.

2. Paragraph 1 shall not apply in the case of a person who acquires the EU trade mark or a right concerning the EU trade mark by way of transfer of the whole of the undertaking or by any other universal succession.

. . .

Article 28 The application for an EU trade mark as an object of property

Articles 19 to 27 shall apply to applications for EU trade marks.

Article 29 Procedure for cancelling or modifying the entry in the Register of licences and other rights

1. A registration effected under Article 26(1) shall be cancelled or modified at the request of one of the persons concerned.

. . .

Chapter III Application for EU Trade Marks

Section 1 Filing of applications and the conditions which govern them

Article 30 Filing of applications

1. An application for an EU trade mark shall be filed at the Office.

2. The Office shall issue to the applicant, without delay, a receipt which shall include at least the file number, a representation, description or other identification of the mark, the nature and the number of the documents and the date of their receipt. That receipt may be issued by electronic means.

Article 31 Conditions with which applications must comply

1. An application for an EU trade mark shall contain:
   (a) a request for the registration of an EU trade mark;
   (b) information identifying the applicant;
   (c) a list of the goods or services in respect of which the registration is requested;
   (d) a representation of the mark, which satisfies the requirements set out in Article 4(b).

2. The application for an EU trade mark shall be subject to the payment of the application fee covering one class of goods or services and, where appropriate, of one or more class fees for each class of goods and services exceeding the first class and, where applicable, the search fee.

. . .

Article 32 Date of filing

The date of filing of an EU trade mark application shall be the date on which the documents containing the information specified in Article 31(1) are filed with the Office by the applicant, subject to payment of the application fee within one month of filing those documents.

Article 33 Designation and classification of goods and services

1. Goods and services in respect of which trade mark registration is applied for shall be classified in conformity with the system of classification established by the Nice Agreement Concerning the

International Classification of Goods and Services for the Purposes of the Registration of Marks of 15 June 1957 ('the Nice Classification').

...

7. Goods and services shall not be regarded as being similar to each other on the ground that they appear in the same class under the Nice Classification. Goods and services shall not be regarded as being dissimilar from each other on the ground that they appear in different classes under the Nice Classification.

Section 2   Priority

Article 34   Right of priority

1. A person who has duly filed an application for a trade mark in or in respect of any State party to the Paris Convention or to the Agreement establishing the World Trade Organisation, or his successors in title, shall enjoy, for the purpose of filing an EU trade mark application for the same trade mark in respect of goods or services which are identical with or contained within those for which the application has been filed, a right of priority during a period of six months from the date of filing of the first application.

...

Article 35   Claiming priority

1. Priority claims shall be filed together with the EU trade mark application and shall include the date, number and country of the previous application. The documentation in support of priority claims shall be filed within three months of the filing date.

...

Article 36   Effect of priority right

The right of priority shall have the effect that the date of priority shall count as the date of filing of the EU trade mark application for the purposes of establishing which rights take precedence.

Article 37   Equivalence of Union filing with national filing

An EU trade mark application which has been accorded a date of filing shall, in the Member States, be equivalent to a regular national filing, where appropriate with the priority claimed for the EU trade mark application.

Section 3   Exhibition priority

Article 38   Exhibition priority

1. If an applicant for an EU trade mark has displayed goods or services under the mark applied for, at an official or officially recognised international exhibition falling within the terms of the Convention relating to international exhibitions signed at Paris on 22 November 1928 and last revised on 30 November 1972, he may, if he files the application within a period of six months of the date of the first display of the goods or services under the mark applied for, claim a right of priority from that date within the meaning of Article 36. The priority claim shall be filed together with the EU trade mark application.

...

Section 4   Seniority of a national trade mark

Article 39   Claiming seniority of a national trade mark in an application for an EU trade mark or subsequent to the filing of the application

1. The proprietor of an earlier trade mark registered in a Member State, including a trade mark registered in the Benelux countries, or registered under international arrangements having effect in a Member State, who applies for an identical trade mark for registration as an EU trade mark for goods or services which are identical with or contained within those for which the earlier trade mark has been registered, may claim for the EU trade mark the seniority of the earlier trade mark in respect of the Member State in or for which it is registered.

2. Seniority claims shall either be filed together with the EU trade mark application or within two months of the filing date of the application, and shall include the Member State or Member States in or for which the mark is registered, the number and the filing date of the relevant registration, and

the goods and services for which the mark is registered. Where the seniority of one or more registered earlier trade marks is claimed in the application, the documentation in support of the seniority claim shall be filed within three months of the filing date. Where the applicant wishes to claim the seniority subsequent to the filing of the application, the documentation in support of the seniority claim shall be submitted to the Office within three months of receipt of the seniority claim.

. . .

Article 40   Claiming seniority of a national trade mark after registration of an EU trade mark

1. The proprietor of an EU trade mark who is the proprietor of an earlier identical trade mark registered in a Member State, including a trade mark registered in the Benelux countries or of an earlier identical trade mark, with an international registration effective in a Member State, for goods or services which are identical to those for which the earlier trade mark has been registered, or contained within them, may claim the seniority of the earlier trade mark in respect of the Member State in or for which it was registered.

. . .

Chapter IV   Registration Procedure

Section 1   Examination of applications

Article 41   Examination of the conditions of filing

1. The Office shall examine whether:
   (a) the EU trade mark application satisfies the requirements for the accordance of a date of filing in accordance with Article 32;
   (b) the EU trade mark application complies with the conditions and requirements referred to in Article 31(3);
   (c) where appropriate, the class fees have been paid within the prescribed period.

2. Where the EU trade mark application does not satisfy the requirements referred to in paragraph 1, the Office shall request the applicant to remedy the deficiencies or the default on payment within two months of the receipt of the notification.

3. If the deficiencies or the default on payment established pursuant to paragraph 1(a) are not remedied within this period, the application shall not be dealt with as an EU trade mark application. If the applicant complies with the Office's request, the Office shall accord as the date of filing of the application the date on which the deficiencies or the default on payment established are remedied.

. . .

Article 42   Examination as to absolute grounds for refusal

1. Where, under Article 7, a trade mark is ineligible for registration in respect of some or all of the goods or services covered by the EU trade mark application, the application shall be refused as regards those goods or services.

2. The application shall not be refused before the applicant has been allowed the opportunity to withdraw or amend the application or to submit his observations. To this effect, the Office shall notify the applicant of the grounds for refusing registration and shall specify a period within which he may withdraw or amend the application or submit his observations. Where the applicant fails to overcome the grounds for refusing registration, the Office shall refuse registration in whole or in part.

Section 2   Search

Article 43   Search report

1. The Office shall, at the request of the applicant for the EU trade mark when filing the application, draw up a European Union search report ('EU search report') citing those earlier EU trade marks or EU trade mark applications discovered which may be invoked under Article 8 against the registration of the EU trade mark applied for.

. . .

Section 3   Publication of the application

Article 44   Publication of the application

1. If the conditions which the application for an EU trade mark is required to satisfy have been fulfilled, the application shall be published for the purposes of Article 46 to the extent that it has not been refused pursuant to Article 42. The publication of the application shall be without prejudice to information already made available to the public otherwise in accordance with this Regulation or acts adopted pursuant to this Regulation.

2. Where, after publication, the application is refused pursuant to Article 42, the decision that it has been refused shall be published upon becoming final.

. . .

Section 4   Observations by third parties and opposition

Article 45   Observations by third parties

1. Any natural or legal person and any group or body representing manufacturers, producers, suppliers of services, traders or consumers may submit to the Office written observations, explaining on which grounds, under Articles 5 and 7, the trade mark should not be registered ex officio.

Persons and groups or bodies as referred to in the first subparagraph shall not be parties to the proceedings before the Office.

2. Third party observations shall be submitted before the end of the opposition period or, where an opposition against the trade mark has been filed, before the final decision on the opposition is taken.

. . .

Article 46   Opposition

1. Within a period of three months following the publication of an EU trade mark application, notice of opposition to registration of the trade mark may be given on the grounds that it may not be registered under Article 8:

    (a) by the proprietors of earlier trade marks referred to in Article 8(2) as well as licensees authorised by the proprietors of those trade marks, in respect of Article 8(1) and (5);

    (b) by the proprietors of trade marks referred to in Article 8(3);

    (c) by the proprietors of earlier marks or signs referred to in Article 8(4) and by persons authorised under the relevant national law to exercise these rights;

    (d) by the persons authorised under the relevant Union legislation or national law to exercise the rights referred to in Article 8(6).

. . .

Article 47   Examination of opposition

1. In the examination of the opposition the Office shall invite the parties, as often as necessary, to file observations, within a period set by the Office, on communications from the other parties or issued by itself.

2. If the applicant so requests, the proprietor of an earlier EU trade mark who has given notice of opposition shall furnish proof that, during the five-year period preceding the date of filing or the date of priority of the EU trade mark application, the earlier EU trade mark has been put to genuine use in the Union in connection with the goods or services in respect of which it is registered and which he cites as justification for his opposition, or that there are proper reasons for non-use, provided that the earlier EU trade mark has at that date been registered for not less than five years. In the absence of proof to this effect, the opposition shall be rejected. If the earlier EU trade mark has been used in relation to only part of the goods or services for which it is registered it shall, for the purposes of the examination of the opposition, be deemed to be registered in respect only of that part of the goods or services.

. . .

Section 5   Withdrawal, restriction, amendment and division of the application

. . .

Section 6 Registration

Article 51 Registration

1. Where an application meets the requirements set out in this Regulation and where no notice of opposition has been given within the period referred to in Article 46(1) or where any opposition entered has been finally disposed of by withdrawal, rejection or other disposition, the trade mark and the particulars referred to in Article 111(2) shall be recorded in the Register. The registration shall be published.

. . .

Chapter V Duration, Renewal, Alteration and Division of EU Trade Marks

Article 52 Duration of registration

EU trade marks shall be registered for a period of 10 years from the date of filing of the application. Registration may be renewed in accordance with Article 53 for further periods of 10 years.

Article 53 Renewal

1. Registration of the EU trade mark shall be renewed at the request of the proprietor of the EU trade mark or any person expressly authorised by him, provided that the fees have been paid.

. . .

Chapter VI Surrender, Revocation and Invalidity

Section 1 Surrender

Article 57 Surrender

1. An EU trade mark may be surrendered in respect of some or all of the goods or services for which it is registered.

. . .

Section 2 Grounds for revocation

Article 58 Grounds for revocation

1. The rights of the proprietor of the EU trade mark shall be declared to be revoked on application to the Office or on the basis of a counterclaim in infringement proceedings:

(a) if, within a continuous period of five years, the trade mark has not been put to genuine use in the Union in connection with the goods or services in respect of which it is registered, and there are no proper reasons for non-use; however, no person may claim that the proprietor's rights in an EU trade mark should be revoked where, during the interval between expiry of the five-year period and filing of the application or counterclaim, genuine use of the trade mark has been started or resumed; the commencement or resumption of use within a period of three months preceding the filing of the application or counterclaim which began at the earliest on expiry of the continuous period of five years of non-use shall, however, be disregarded where preparations for the commencement or resumption occur only after the proprietor becomes aware that the application or counterclaim may be filed;

(b) if, in consequence of acts or inactivity of the proprietor, the trade mark has become the common name in the trade for a product or service in respect of which it is registered;

(c) if, in consequence of the use made of the trade mark by the proprietor of the trade mark or with his consent in respect of the goods or services for which it is registered, the trade mark is liable to mislead the public, particularly as to the nature, quality or geographical origin of those goods or services.

2. Where the grounds for revocation of rights exist in respect of only some of the goods or services for which the EU trade mark is registered, the rights of the proprietor shall be declared to be revoked in respect of those goods or services only.

Section 3   Grounds for invalidity

Article 59   Absolute grounds for invalidity

1. An EU trade mark shall be declared invalid on application to the Office or on the basis of a counterclaim in infringement proceedings:

    (a) where the EU trade mark has been registered contrary to the provisions of Article 7;

    (b) where the applicant was acting in bad faith when he filed the application for the trade mark.

2. Where the EU trade mark has been registered in breach of the provisions of Article 7(1)(b), (c) or (d), it may nevertheless not be declared invalid if, in consequence of the use which has been made of it, it has after registration acquired a distinctive character in relation to the goods or services for which it is registered.

3. Where the ground for invalidity exists in respect of only some of the goods or services for which the EU trade mark is registered, the trade mark shall be declared invalid as regards those goods or services only.

Article 60   Relative grounds for invalidity

1. An EU trade mark shall be declared invalid on application to the Office or on the basis of a counterclaim in infringement proceedings:

    (a) where there is an earlier trade mark as referred to in Article 8(2) and the conditions set out in paragraph 1 or 5 of that Article are fulfilled;

    (b) where there is a trade mark as referred to in Article 8(3) and the conditions set out in that paragraph are fulfilled;

    (c) where there is an earlier right as referred to in Article 8(4) and the conditions set out in that paragraph are fulfilled;

    (d) where there is an earlier designation of origin or geographical indication as referred to in Article 8(6) and the conditions set out in that paragraph are fulfilled.

All the conditions referred to in the first subparagraph shall be fulfilled at the filing date or the priority date of the EU trade mark.

2. An EU trade mark shall also be declared invalid on application to the Office or on the basis of a counterclaim in infringement proceedings where the use of such trade mark may be prohibited pursuant to another earlier right under the Union legislation or national law governing its protection, and in particular:

    (a) a right to a name;

    (b) a right of personal portrayal;

    (c) a copyright;

    (d) an industrial property right.

3. An EU trade mark may not be declared invalid where the proprietor of a right referred to in paragraph 1 or 2 consents expressly to the registration of the EU trade mark before submission of the application for a declaration of invalidity or the counterclaim.

4. Where the proprietor of one of the rights referred to in paragraph 1 or 2 has previously applied for a declaration that an EU trade mark is invalid or made a counterclaim in infringement proceedings, he may not submit a new application for a declaration of invalidity or lodge a counterclaim on the basis of another of the said rights which he could have invoked in support of his first application or counterclaim.

5. Article 59(3) shall apply.

Article 61   Limitation in consequence of acquiescence

1. Where the proprietor of an EU trade mark has acquiesced, for a period of five successive years, in the use of a later EU trade mark in the Union while being aware of such use, he shall no longer be entitled on the basis of the earlier trade mark to apply for a declaration that the later trade mark is

invalid in respect of the goods or services for which the later trade mark has been used, unless registration of the later EU trade mark was applied for in bad faith.

2. Where the proprietor of an earlier national trade mark as referred to in Article 8(2) or of another earlier sign referred to in Article 8(4) has acquiesced, for a period of five successive years, in the use of a later EU trade mark in the Member State in which the earlier trade mark or the other earlier sign is protected while being aware of such use, he shall no longer be entitled on the basis of the earlier trade mark or of the other earlier sign to apply for a declaration that the later trade mark is invalid in respect of the goods or services for which the later trade mark has been used, unless registration of the later EU trade mark was applied for in bad faith.

3. In the cases referred to in paragraphs 1 and 2, the proprietor of a later EU trade mark shall not be entitled to oppose the use of the earlier right, even though that right may no longer be invoked against the later EU trade mark.

Section 4   Consequences of revocation and invalidity

Article 62   Consequences of revocation and invalidity

1. The EU trade mark shall be deemed not to have had, as from the date of the application for revocation or of the counterclaim, the effects specified in this Regulation, to the extent that the rights of the proprietor have been revoked. An earlier date, on which one of the grounds for revocation occurred, may be fixed in the decision at the request of one of the parties.

2. The EU trade mark shall be deemed not to have had, as from the outset, the effects specified in this Regulation, to the extent that the trade mark has been declared invalid.

3. Subject to the national provisions relating either to claims for compensation for damage caused by negligence or lack of good faith on the part of the proprietor of the trade mark, or to unjust enrichment, the retroactive effect of revocation or invalidity of the trade mark shall not affect:

(a) any decision on infringement which has acquired the authority of a final decision and been enforced prior to the revocation or invalidity decision;

(b) any contract concluded prior to the revocation or invalidity decision, in so far as it has been performed before that decision; however, repayment, to an extent justified by the circumstances, of sums paid under the relevant contract may be claimed on grounds of equity.

Section 5   Proceedings in the office in relation to revocation or invalidity

Article 63   Application for revocation or for a declaration of invalidity

1. An application for revocation of the rights of the proprietor of an EU trade mark or for a declaration that the trade mark is invalid may be submitted to the Office:

(a) where Articles 58 and 59 apply, by any natural or legal person and any group or body set up for the purpose of representing the interests of manufacturers, producers, suppliers of services, traders or consumers, which, under the terms of the law governing it, has the capacity in its own name to sue and be sued;

(b) where Article 60(1) applies, by the persons referred to in Article 46(1);

(c) where Article 60(2) applies, by the owners of the earlier rights referred to in that provision or by the persons who are entitled under Union legislation or the law of the Member State concerned to exercise the rights in question.

. . .

Article 64   Examination of the application

1. On the examination of the application for revocation of rights or for a declaration of invalidity, the Office shall invite the parties, as often as necessary, to file observations, within a period to be fixed by the Office, on communications from the other parties or issued by itself.

2. If the proprietor of the EU trade mark so requests, the proprietor of an earlier EU trade mark, being a party to the invalidity proceedings, shall furnish proof that, during the period of five years preceding the date of the application for a declaration of invalidity, the earlier EU trade mark has been put to genuine use in the Union in connection with the goods or services in respect of which it is

registered and which the proprietor of that earlier trade mark cites as justification for his application, or that there are proper reasons for non-use, provided that the earlier EU trade mark has at that date been registered for not less than five years. If, at the date on which the EU trade mark application was filed or at the priority date of the EU trade mark application, the earlier EU trade mark had been registered for not less than five years, the proprietor of the earlier EU trade mark shall furnish proof that, in addition, the conditions set out in Article 47(2) were satisfied at that date. In the absence of proof to this effect, the application for a declaration of invalidity shall be rejected. If the earlier EU trade mark has been used only in relation to part of the goods or services for which it is registered, it shall, for the purpose of the examination of the application for a declaration of invalidity, be deemed to be registered in respect of that part of the goods or services only.

3. Paragraph 2 shall apply to earlier national trade marks referred to in Article 8(2)(a), by substituting use in the Member State in which the earlier national trade mark is protected for use in the Union.

4. The Office may, if it thinks fit, invite the parties to make a friendly settlement.

5. If the examination of the application for revocation of rights or for a declaration of invalidity reveals that the trade mark should not have been registered in respect of some or all of the goods or services for which it is registered, the rights of the proprietor of the EU trade mark shall be revoked or it shall be declared invalid in respect of those goods or services. Otherwise the application for revocation of rights or for a declaration of invalidity shall be rejected.

6. A record of the Office's decision on the application for revocation of rights or for a declaration of invalidity shall be entered in the Register once it has become final.

. . .

Chapter VII   Appeals

Article 66   Decisions subject to appeal

1. An appeal shall lie from decisions of any of the decision-making instances of the Office listed in points (a) to (d) of Article 159, and, where appropriate, point (f) of that Article. Those decisions shall take effect only as from the date of expiration of the appeal period referred to in Article 68. The filing of the appeal shall have suspensive effect.

2. A decision which does not terminate proceedings as regards one of the parties can only be appealed together with the final decision, unless the decision allows separate appeal.

Article 67   Persons entitled to appeal and to be parties to appeal proceedings

Any party to proceedings adversely affected by a decision may appeal. Any other parties to the proceedings shall be parties to the appeal proceedings as of right.

Article 68   Time limit and form of appeal

1. Notice of appeal shall be filed in writing at the Office within two months of the date of notification of the decision. The notice shall be deemed to have been filed only when the fee for appeal has been paid. It shall be filed in the language of the proceedings in which the decision subject to appeal was taken. Within four months of the date of notification of the decision, a written statement setting out the grounds of appeal shall be filed.

2. In *inter partes* proceedings, the defendant may, in his response, seek a decision annulling or altering the contested decision on a point not raised in the appeal. Such submissions shall cease to have effect should the appellant discontinue the proceedings.

Article 69   Revision of decisions in ex parte cases

1. If the party which has lodged the appeal is the sole party to the procedure, and if the department whose decision is contested considers the appeal to be admissible and well founded, the department shall rectify its decision.

2 If the decision is not rectified within one month of receipt of the statement of grounds, the appeal shall be remitted to the Board of Appeal without delay, and without comment as to its merit.

Article 70   Examination of appeals

1. If the appeal is admissible, the Board of Appeal shall examine whether the appeal is allowable.

2. In the examination of the appeal, the Board of Appeal shall invite the parties, as often as necessary, to file observations, within a period to be fixed by the Board of Appeal, on communications from the other parties or issued by itself.

Article 71   Decisions in respect of appeals

1. Following the examination as to the allowability of the appeal, the Board of Appeal shall decide on the appeal. The Board of Appeal may either exercise any power within the competence of the department which was responsible for the decision appealed or remit the case to that department for further prosecution.

2. If the Board of Appeal remits the case for further prosecution to the department whose decision was appealed, that department shall be bound by the *ratio decidendi* of the Board of Appeal, in so far as the facts are the same.

3. The decisions of the Board of Appeal shall take effect only as from the date of expiry of the period referred to in Article 72(5) or, if an action has been brought before the General Court within that period, as from the date of dismissal of such action or of any appeal filed with the Court of Justice against the decision of the General Court.

Article 72   Actions before the Court of Justice

1. Actions may be brought before the General Court against decisions of the Boards of Appeal in relation to appeals.

2. The action may be brought on grounds of lack of competence, infringement of an essential procedural requirement, infringement of the TFEU, infringement of this Regulation or of any rule of law relating to their application or misuse of power.

3. The General Court shall have jurisdiction to annul or to alter the contested decision.

4 The action shall be open to any party to proceedings before the Board of Appeal adversely affected by its decision.

5. The action shall be brought before the General Court within two months of the date of notification of the decision of the Board of Appeal.

6. The Office shall take the necessary measures to comply with the judgment of the General Court or, in the event of an appeal against that judgment, the Court of Justice.

. . .

Chapter VIII   Specific Provisions on European Union Collective Marks and Certification Marks

Section 1   EU collective marks

Article 74   EU collective marks

1. A European Union collective mark ('EU collective mark') shall be an EU trade mark which is described as such when the mark is applied for and is capable of distinguishing the goods or services of the members of the association which is the proprietor of the mark from those of other undertakings. Associations of manufacturers, producers, suppliers of services, or traders which, under the terms of the law governing them, have the capacity in their own name to have rights and obligations of all kinds, to make contracts or accomplish other legal acts, and to sue and be sued, as well as legal persons governed by public law, may apply for EU collective marks.

2. By way of derogation from Article 7(1)(c), signs or indications which may serve, in trade, to designate the geographical origin of the goods or services may constitute EU collective marks within the meaning of paragraph 1. An EU collective mark shall not entitle the proprietor to prohibit a third party from using in the course of trade such signs or indications, provided that he uses them in accordance with honest practices in industrial or commercial matters; in particular, such a mark shall not be invoked against a third party who is entitled to use a geographical name.

3. Chapters I to VII and IX to XIV shall apply to EU collective marks to the extent that this section does not provide otherwise.

Article 75   Regulations governing use of an EU collective mark

1. An applicant for an EU collective mark shall submit regulations governing use within two months of the date of filing.

2. The regulations governing use shall specify the persons authorised to use the mark, the conditions of membership of the association and, where they exist, the conditions of use of the mark, including sanctions. The regulations governing use of a mark referred to in Article 74(2) shall authorise any person whose goods or services originate in the geographical area concerned to become a member of the association which is the proprietor of the mark.

. . .

Article 76   Refusal of the application

1. In addition to the grounds for refusal of an EU trade mark application provided for in Articles 41 and 42, an application for an EU collective mark shall be refused where the provisions of Articles 74 or 75 are not satisfied, or where the regulations governing use are contrary to public policy or to accepted principles of morality.

2. An application for an EU collective mark shall also be refused if the public is liable to be misled as regards the character or the significance of the mark, in particular if it is likely to be taken to be something other than a collective mark.

3. An application shall not be refused if the applicant, as a result of amendment of the regulations governing use, meets the requirements of paragraphs 1 and 2.

Article 77   Observations by third parties

Where written observations on an EU collective mark are submitted to the Office pursuant to Article 45, those observations may also be based on the particular grounds on which the application for an EU collective mark should be refused pursuant to Article 76.

Article 78   Use of marks

Use of an EU collective mark by any person who has authority to use it shall satisfy the requirements of this Regulation, provided that the other conditions which this Regulation imposes with regard to the use of EU trade marks are fulfilled.

. . .

Article 80   Persons who are entitled to bring an action for infringement

1. The provisions of Article 25(3) and (4) concerning the rights of licensees shall apply to every person who has authority to use an EU collective mark.

2. The proprietor of an EU collective mark shall be entitled to claim compensation on behalf of persons who have authority to use the mark where they have sustained damage in consequence of unauthorised use of the mark.

Article 81   Grounds for revocation

Apart from the grounds for revocation provided for in Article 58, the rights of the proprietor of an EU collective mark shall be revoked on application to the Office or on the basis of a counterclaim in infringement proceedings, if:

(a) the proprietor does not take reasonable steps to prevent the mark being used in a manner incompatible with the conditions of use, where these exist, laid down in the regulations governing use, amendments to which have, where appropriate, been mentioned in the Register;

(b) the manner in which the mark has been used by the proprietor has caused it to become liable to mislead the public in the manner referred to in Article 76(2);

(c) an amendment to the regulations governing use of the mark has been mentioned in the Register in breach of the provisions of Article 79(2), unless the proprietor of the mark, by further amending the regulations governing use, complies with the requirements of those provisions.

Article 82   Grounds for invalidity

Apart from the grounds for invalidity provided for in Articles 59 and 60, an EU collective mark which is registered in breach of the provisions of Article 76 shall be declared invalid on application to the Office or on the basis of a counterclaim in infringement proceedings, unless the proprietor of the mark, by amending the regulations governing use, complies with the requirements of those provisions.

Section 2   EU certification marks

Article 83   EU certification marks

1. An EU certification mark shall be an EU trade mark which is described as such when the mark is applied for and is capable of distinguishing goods or services which are certified by the proprietor of the mark in respect of material, mode of manufacture of goods or performance of services, quality, accuracy or other characteristics, with the exception of geographical origin, from goods and services which are not so certified.

2. Any natural or legal person, including institutions, authorities and bodies governed by public law, may apply for EU certification marks provided that such person does not carry on a business involving the supply of goods or services of the kind certified.

3. Chapters I to VII and IX to XIV shall apply to EU certification marks to the extent that this Section does not provide otherwise.

Article 84   Regulations governing use of an EU certification mark

1. An applicant for an EU certification mark shall submit regulations governing the use of the EU certification mark within two months of the date of filing.

2. The regulations governing use shall specify the persons authorised to use the mark, the characteristics to be certified by the mark, how the certifying body is to test those characteristics and to supervise the use of the mark. Those regulations shall also specify the conditions of use of the mark, including sanctions.

. . .

Article 85   Refusal of the application

1. In addition to the grounds for refusal of an EU trade mark application provided for in Articles 41 and 42, an application for an EU certification mark shall be refused where the conditions set out in Articles 83 and 84 are not satisfied, or where the regulations governing use are contrary to public policy or to accepted principles of morality.

2. An application for an EU certification mark shall also be refused if the public is liable to be misled as regards the character or the significance of the mark, in particular if it is likely to be taken to be something other than a certification mark.

3. An application shall not be refused if the applicant, as a result of an amendment of the regulations governing use, meets the requirements of paragraphs 1 and 2.

Article 86   Observations by third parties

Where written observations on an EU certification mark are submitted to the Office pursuant to Article 45, those observations may also be based on the particular grounds on which the application for an EU certification mark should be refused pursuant to Article 85.

Article 87   Use of the EU certification mark

Use of an EU certification mark by any person who has authority to use it pursuant to the regulations governing use referred to in Article 84 shall satisfy the requirements of this Regulation, provided that the other conditions laid down in this Regulation with regard to the use of EU trade marks are fulfilled.

. . .

Article 89   Transfer

By way of derogation from Article 20(1), an EU certification mark may only be transferred to a person who meets the requirements of Article 83(2).

Article 90   Persons who are entitled to bring an action for infringement

1. Only the proprietor of an EU certification mark, or any person specifically authorised by him to that effect, shall be entitled to bring an action for infringement.

2. The proprietor of an EU certification mark shall be entitled to claim compensation on behalf of persons who have authority to use the mark where they have sustained damage as a consequence of unauthorised use of the mark.

Article 91   Grounds for revocation

In addition to the grounds for revocation provided for in Article 58, the rights of the proprietor of an EU certification mark shall be revoked on application to the Office or on the basis of a counterclaim in infringement proceedings, where any of the following conditions is fulfilled:

    (a) the proprietor no longer complies with the requirements set out in Article 83(2);

    (b) the proprietor does not take reasonable steps to prevent the EU certification mark being used in a manner that is incompatible with the conditions of use laid down in the regulations governing use, amendments to which have, where appropriate, been mentioned in the Register;

    (c) the manner in which the EU certification mark has been used by the proprietor has caused it to become liable to mislead the public in the manner referred to in Article 85(2);

    (d) an amendment to the regulations governing use of the EU certification mark has been mentioned in the Register in breach of Article 88(2), unless the proprietor of the mark, by further amending the regulations governing use, complies with the requirements of that Article.

Article 92   Grounds for invalidity

In addition to the grounds for invalidity provided for in Articles 59 and 60, an EU certification mark which is registered in breach of Article 85 shall be declared invalid on application to the Office or on the basis of a counterclaim in infringement proceedings, unless the proprietor of the EU certification mark, by amending the regulations governing use, complies with the requirements of Article 85.

Article 93   Conversion

Without prejudice to Article 139(2), conversion of an application for an EU certification mark or of a registered EU certification mark shall not take place where the national law of the Member State concerned does not provide for the registration of guarantee or certification marks pursuant to Article 28 of Directive (EU) 2015/2436.

Chapter IX   Procedure

. . .

Chapter X   Jurisdiction and Procedure in Legal Actions Relating to EU Trade Marks

Section 1   Application of Union rules on jurisdiction and the recognition and enforcement of judgments in civil and commercial matters

Article 122   Application of Union rules on jurisdiction and the recognition and enforcement of judgments in civil and commercial matters

1. Unless otherwise specified in this Regulation, the Union rules on jurisdiction and the recognition and enforcement of judgments in civil and commercial matters shall apply to proceedings

relating to EU trade marks and applications for EU trade marks, as well as to proceedings relating to simultaneous and successive actions on the basis of EU trade marks and national trade marks.

2. In the case of proceedings in respect of the actions and claims referred to in Article 124:

(a) Articles 4 and 6, points 1, 2, 3 and 5 of Article 7 and Article 35 of Regulation (EU) No 1215/2012 shall not apply;

(b) Articles 25 and 26 of Regulation (EU) No 1215/2012 shall apply subject to the limitations in Article 125(4) of this Regulation;

(c) the provisions of Chapter II of Regulation (EU) No 1215/2012 which are applicable to persons domiciled in a Member State shall also be applicable to persons who do not have a domicile in any Member State but have an establishment therein.

3. References in this Regulation to Regulation (EU) No 1215/2012 shall include, where appropriate, the Agreement between the European Community and the Kingdom of Denmark on jurisdiction and the recognition and enforcement of judgments in civil and commercial matters done on 19 October 2005.

Section 2 Disputes concerning the infringement and validity of EU trade marks

Article 123 EU trade mark courts

1. The Member States shall designate in their territories as limited a number as possible of national courts and tribunals of first and second instance, which shall perform the functions assigned to them by this Regulation.

2. Any change made in the number, names or territorial jurisdiction of the courts included in the list of EU trade mark courts communicated by a Member State to the Commission in accordance with Article 95(2) of Regulation (EC) No 207/2009 shall be notified without delay by the Member State concerned to the Commission.

3. The information referred to in paragraph 2 shall be notified by the Commission to the Member States and published in the *Official Journal of the European Union*.

Article 124 Jurisdiction over infringement and validity

The EU trade mark courts shall have exclusive jurisdiction:

(a) for all infringement actions and—if they are permitted under national law—actions in respect of threatened infringement relating to EU trade marks;

(b) for actions for declaration of non-infringement, if they are permitted under national law;

(c) for all actions brought as a result of acts referred to in Article 11(2);

(d) for counterclaims for revocation or for a declaration of invalidity of the EU trade mark pursuant to Article 128.

Article 125 International jurisdiction

1. Subject to the provisions of this Regulation as well as to any provisions of Regulation (EU) No 1215/2012 applicable by virtue of Article 122, proceedings in respect of the actions and claims referred to in Article 124 shall be brought in the courts of the Member State in which the defendant is domiciled or, if he is not domiciled in any of the Member States, in which he has an establishment.

2. If the defendant is neither domiciled nor has an establishment in any of the Member States, such proceedings shall be brought in the courts of the Member State in which the plaintiff is domiciled or, if he is not domiciled in any of the Member States, in which he has an establishment.

3. If neither the defendant nor the plaintiff is so domiciled or has such an establishment, such proceedings shall be brought in the courts of the Member State where the Office has its seat.

4. Notwithstanding the provisions of paragraphs 1, 2 and 3:

(a) Article 25 of Regulation (EU) No 1215/2012 shall apply if the parties agree that a different EU trade mark court shall have jurisdiction;

(b) Article 26 of Regulation (EU) No 1215/2012 shall apply if the defendant enters an appearance before a different EU trade mark court.

5. Proceedings in respect of the actions and claims referred to in Article 124, with the exception of actions for a declaration of non-infringement of an EU trade mark, may also be brought in the courts of the Member State in which the act of infringement has been committed or threatened, or in which an act referred to in Article 11(2) has been committed.

Article 126   Extent of jurisdiction

1. An EU trade mark court whose jurisdiction is based on Article 125(1) to (4) shall have jurisdiction in respect of:

  (a) acts of infringement committed or threatened within the territory of any of the Member States;

  (b) acts referred to in Article 11(2) committed within the territory of any of the Member States.

2. An EU trade mark court whose jurisdiction is based on Article 125(5) shall have jurisdiction only in respect of acts committed or threatened within the territory of the Member State in which that court is situated.

Article 127   Presumption of validity—Defence as to the merits

1. The EU trade mark courts shall treat the EU trade mark as valid unless its validity is put in issue by the defendant with a counterclaim for revocation or for a declaration of invalidity.

2. The validity of an EU trade mark may not be put in issue in an action for a declaration of non-infringement.

3. In the actions referred to in points (a) and (c) of Article 124, a plea relating to revocation of the EU trade mark submitted otherwise than by way of a counterclaim shall be admissible where the defendant claims that the EU trade mark could be revoked for lack of genuine use at the time the infringement action was brought.

Article 128   Counterclaims

1. A counterclaim for revocation or for a declaration of invalidity may only be based on the grounds for revocation or invalidity mentioned in this Regulation.

2. An EU trade mark court shall reject a counterclaim for revocation or for a declaration of invalidity if a decision taken by the Office relating to the same subject matter and cause of action and involving the same parties has already become final.

3. If the counterclaim is brought in a legal action to which the proprietor of the trade mark is not already a party, he shall be informed thereof and may be joined as a party to the action in accordance with the conditions set out in national law.

  . . .

Article 129   Applicable law

1. The EU trade mark courts shall apply the provisions of this Regulation.

2. On all trade mark matters not covered by this Regulation, the relevant EU trade mark court shall apply the applicable national law.

3. Unless otherwise provided for in this Regulation, an EU trade mark court shall apply the rules of procedure governing the same type of action relating to a national trade mark in the Member State in which the court is located.

Article 130   Sanctions

1. Where an EU trade mark court finds that the defendant has infringed or threatened to infringe an EU trade mark, it shall, unless there are special reasons for not doing so, issue an order prohibiting the defendant from proceeding with the acts which infringed or would infringe the EU trade mark. It shall also take such measures in accordance with its national law as are aimed at ensuring that this prohibition is complied with.

2. The EU trade mark court may also apply measures or orders available under the applicable law which it deems appropriate in the circumstances of the case.

Article 131   Provisional and protective measures

1. Application may be made to the courts of a Member State, including EU trade mark courts, for such provisional, including protective, measures in respect of an EU trade mark or EU trade mark

application as may be available under the law of that State in respect of a national trade mark, even if, under this Regulation, an EU trade mark court of another Member State has jurisdiction as to the substance of the matter.

2. An EU trade mark court whose jurisdiction is based on Article 125(1), (2), (3) or (4) shall have jurisdiction to grant provisional and protective measures which, subject to any necessary procedure for recognition and enforcement pursuant to Chapter III of Regulation (EU) No 1215/2012, are applicable in the territory of any Member State. No other court shall have such jurisdiction.

Article 132   Specific rules on related actions

1. An EU trade mark court hearing an action referred to in Article 124 other than an action for a declaration of non-infringement shall, unless there are special grounds for continuing the hearing, of its own motion after hearing the parties or at the request of one of the parties and after hearing the other parties, stay the proceedings where the validity of the EU trade mark is already in issue before another EU trade mark court on account of a counterclaim or where an application for revocation or for a declaration of invalidity has already been filed at the Office.

2. The Office, when hearing an application for revocation or for a declaration of invalidity shall, unless there are special grounds for continuing the hearing, of its own motion after hearing the parties or at the request of one of the parties and after hearing the other parties, stay the proceedings where the validity of the EU trade mark is already in issue on account of a counterclaim before an EU trade mark court. However, if one of the parties to the proceedings before the EU trade mark court so requests, the court may, after hearing the other parties to these proceedings, stay the proceedings. The Office shall in this instance continue the proceedings pending before it.

3. Where the EU trade mark court stays the proceedings it may order provisional and protective measures for the duration of the stay.

Article 133   Jurisdiction of EU trade mark courts of second instance—Further appeal

1. An appeal to the EU trade mark courts of second instance shall lie from judgments of the EU trade mark courts of first instance in respect of proceedings arising from the actions and claims referred to in Article 124.

2. The conditions under which an appeal may be lodged with an EU trade mark court of second instance shall be determined by the national law of the Member State in which that court is located.

3. The national rules concerning further appeal shall be applicable in respect of judgments of EU trade mark courts of second instance.

Section 3   Other disputes concerning EU trade marks

Article 134   Supplementary provisions on the jurisdiction of national courts other than EU trade mark courts

1. Within the Member State whose courts have jurisdiction under Article 122(1) those courts shall have jurisdiction for actions other than those referred to in Article 124, which would have jurisdiction *ratione loci* and *ratione materiae* in the case of actions relating to a national trade mark registered in that State.

2. Actions relating to an EU trade mark, other than those referred to in Article 124, for which no court has jurisdiction under Article 122(1) and paragraph 1 of this Article may be heard before the courts of the Member State in which the Office has its seat.

Article 135   Obligation of the national court

A national court which is dealing with an action relating to an EU trade mark, other than the action referred to in Article 124, shall treat the EU trade mark as valid.

Chapter XI   Effects on the Laws of the Member States

Section 1   Civil actions on the basis of more than one trade mark

Article 136   Simultaneous and successive civil actions on the basis of EU trade marks and national trade marks

1. Where actions for infringement involving the same cause of action and between the same parties are brought in the courts of different Member States, one seised on the basis of an EU trade mark and the other seised on the basis of a national trade mark:

    (a) the court other than the court first seised shall of its own motion decline jurisdiction in favour of that court where the trade marks concerned are identical and valid for identical goods or services. The court which would be required to decline jurisdiction may stay its proceedings if the jurisdiction of the other court is contested;

    (b) the court other than the court first seised may stay its proceedings where the trade marks concerned are identical and valid for similar goods or services and where the trade marks concerned are similar and valid for identical or similar goods or services.

2. The court hearing an action for infringement on the basis of an EU trade mark shall reject the action if a final judgment on the merits has been given on the same cause of action and between the same parties on the basis of an identical national trade mark valid for identical goods or services.

3. The court hearing an action for infringement on the basis of a national trade mark shall reject the action if a final judgment on the merits has been given on the same cause of action and between the same parties on the basis of an identical EU trade mark valid for identical goods or services.

4. Paragraphs 1, 2 and 3 shall not apply in respect of provisional, including protective, measures.

Section 2   Application of national laws for the purpose of prohibiting the use of EU trade marks

Article 137   Prohibition of use of EU trade marks

1. This Regulation shall, unless otherwise provided for, not affect the right existing under the laws of the Member States to invoke claims for infringement of earlier rights within the meaning of Article 8 or Article 60(2) in relation to the use of a later EU trade mark. Claims for infringement of earlier rights within the meaning of Article 8(2) and (4) may, however, no longer be invoked if the proprietor of the earlier right may no longer apply for a declaration that the EU trade mark is invalid in accordance with Article 61(2).

2. This Regulation shall, unless otherwise provided for, not affect the right to bring proceedings under the civil, administrative or criminal law of a Member State or under provisions of Union law for the purpose of prohibiting the use of an EU trade mark to the extent that the use of a national trade mark may be prohibited under the law of that Member State or under Union law.

. . .

Chapter XII   The Office

. . .

Chapter XIII   International Registration of Marks

Section I   General provisions

Article 182   Application of provisions

Unless otherwise specified in this chapter, this Regulation and the acts adopted pursuant to this Regulation shall apply to applications for international registrations under the Madrid Protocol ('international applications'), based on an application for an EU trade mark or on an EU trade mark and to registrations of marks in the international register maintained by the International Bureau of the World Intellectual Property Organisation ('international registrations' and 'the International Bureau', respectively) designating the Union.

Section 2   International registration on the basis of applications for an EU trade mark and of EU trade marks

Article 183   Filing of an international application

1. International applications pursuant to Article 3 of the Madrid Protocol based on an application for an EU trade mark or on an EU trade mark shall be filed at the Office.

2. Where an international application is filed before the mark on which the international registration is to be based has been registered as an EU trade mark, the applicant for the international registration shall indicate whether the international registration is to be based on an EU trade mark application or registration. Where the international registration is to be based on an EU trade mark once it is registered, the international application shall be deemed to have been received at the Office on the date of registration of the EU trade mark.

. . .

B4.   INTERNATIONAL

Lisbon Agreement for the Protection of Appellations of Origin and their International Registration

of 31 October 1958, as revised at Stockholm on 14 July 1967, and as amended on 28 September 1979

Article 1   Establishment of a Special Union; Protection of appellations of origin registered at the International Bureau

(1) The countries to which this Agreement applies constitute a Special Union within the framework of the Union for the Protection of Industrial Property.

(2) They undertake to protect on their territories, in accordance with the terms of this Agreement, the appellations of origin of products of the other countries of the Special Union, recognised and protected as such in the country of origin and registered at the International Bureau of Intellectual Property (hereinafter designated as 'the International Bureau' or 'the Bureau') referred to in the Convention establishing the World Intellectual Property Organisation (hereinafter designated as 'the Organisation').

Article 2   Definition of notions of appellation of origin and country of origin

(1) In this Agreement, 'appellation of origin' means the geographical name of a country, region, or locality, which serves to designate a product originating therein, the quality and characteristics of which are due exclusively or essentially to the geographical environment, including natural and human factors.

(2) The country of origin is the country whose name, or the country in which is situated the region or locality whose name, constitutes the appellation of origin which has given the product its reputation.

Article 3   Content of protection

Protection shall be ensured against any usurpation or imitation, even if the true origin of the product is indicated or if the appellation is used in translated form or accompanied by terms such as 'kind', 'type', 'make', 'imitation', or the like.

Article 4   Protection by virtue of other Texts

The provisions of this Agreement shall in no way exclude the protection already granted to appellations of origin in each of the countries of the Special Union by virtue of other international instruments, such as the Paris Convention of 20 March 1883, for the Protection of Industrial Property and its subsequent revisions, and the Madrid Agreement of 14 April 1891, for the Repression of False or Deceptive Indications of Source on Goods and its subsequent revisions, or by virtue of national legislation or court decisions.

Article 5   International registration; refusal and opposition to refusal; notifications; use tolerated for a fixed period

(1) The registration of appellations of origin shall be effected at the International Bureau, at the request of the Offices of the countries of the Special Union, in the name of any natural persons or legal entities, public or private, having, according to their national legislation, a right to use such appellations.

(2) The International Bureau shall, without delay, notify the Offices of the various countries of the Special Union of such registrations, and shall publish them in a periodical.

(3) The Office of any country may declare that it cannot ensure the protection of an appellation of origin whose registration has been notified to it, but only in so far as its declaration is notified to the International Bureau, together with an indication of the grounds therefor, within a period of one year from the receipt of the notification of registration, and provided that such declaration is not detrimental, in the country concerned, to the other forms of protection of the appellation which the owner thereof may be entitled to claim under Article 4, above.

(4) Such declaration may not be opposed by the Offices of the countries of the Union after the expiration of the period of one year provided for in the foregoing paragraph.

(5) The International Bureau shall, as soon as possible, notify the Office of the country of origin of any declaration made under the terms of paragraph (3) by the Office of another country. The interested party, when informed by his national Office of the declaration made by another country, may resort, in that other country, to all the judicial and administrative remedies open to the nationals of that country.

(6) If an appellation which has been granted protection in a given country pursuant to notification of its international registration has already been used by third parties in that country from a date prior to such notification, the competent Office of the said country shall have the right to grant to such third parties a period not exceeding two years to terminate such use, on condition that it advise the International Bureau accordingly during the three months following the expiration of the period of one year provided for in paragraph (3), above.

Article 6   Generic appellations

An appellation which has been granted protection in one of the countries of the Special Union pursuant to the procedure under Article 5 cannot, in that country, be deemed to have become generic, as long as it is protected as an appellation of origin in the country of origin.

Article 7   Period of validity of registration; fee

(1) Registration effected at the International Bureau in conformity with Article 5 shall ensure, without renewal, protection for the whole of the period referred to in the foregoing Article.

(2) A single fee shall be paid for the registration of each appellation of origin.

Article 8   Legal proceedings

Legal action required for ensuring the protection of appellations of origin may be taken in each of the countries of the Special Union under the provisions of the national legislation:

1. at the instance of the competent Office or at the request of the public prosecutor;
2. by any interested party, whether a natural person or a legal entity, whether public or private.

    . . .

Article 16   Application of the original Act of 1958

(1)(a) This Act shall, as regards the relations between the countries of the Special Union by which it has been ratified or acceded to, replace the original Act of 31 October 1958.

(b) However, any country of the Special Union which has ratified or acceded to this Act shall be bound by the original Act of 31 October 1958, as regards its relations with countries of the Special Union which have not ratified or acceded to this Act.

(2) Countries outside the Special Union which become party to this Act shall apply it to international registrations of appellations of origin effected at the International Bureau at the request of the Office of any country of the Special Union not party to this Act, provided that such registrations satisfy, with respect to the said countries, the requirements of this Act. With regard to international registrations effected at the International Bureau at the request of the Offices of the said countries outside the Special Union which become party to this Act, such countries recognise that the aforesaid country of the Special Union may demand compliance with the requirements of the original Act of 31 October 1958.

. . .

Geneva Act of the Lisbon Agreement on Appellations of Origin and Geographical Indications

adopted by the Diplomatic Conference on May 20, 2015

Chapter I   Introductory and General Provisions

Article 1   Abbreviated Expressions

For the purposes of this Act, unless expressly stated otherwise:

(i)   'Lisbon Agreement' means the Lisbon Agreement for the Protection of Appellations of Origin and their International Registration of October 31, 1958;

(ii)   '1967 Act' means the Lisbon Agreement as revised at Stockholm on July 14, 1967, and amended on September 28, 1979;

(iii)   'this Act' means the Lisbon Agreement on Appellations of Origin and Geographical Indications, as established by the present Act;

(iv)   'Regulations' means the Regulations as referred to in Article 25;

(v)   'Paris Convention' means the Paris Convention for the Protection of Industrial Property of March 20, 1883, as revised and amended;

(vi)   'appellation of origin' means a denomination as referred to in Article 2(1)(i);

(vii) 'geographical indication' means an indication as referred to in Article 2(1)(ii);

(viii) 'International Register' means the International Register maintained by the International Bureau in accordance with Article 4 as the official collection of data concerning international registrations of appellations of origin and geographical indications, regardless of the medium in which such data are maintained;

(ix)   'international registration' means an international registration recorded in the International Register;

(x)   'application' means an application for international registration;

(xi)   'registered' means entered in the International Register in accordance with this Act;

(xii) 'geographical area of origin' means a geographical area as referred to in Article 2(2);

(xiii) 'trans-border geographical area' means a geographical area situated in, or covering, adjacent Contracting Parties;

(xiv) 'Contracting Party' means any State or intergovernmental organization party to this Act;

(xv) 'Contracting Party of Origin' means the Contracting Party where the geographical area of origin is situated or the Contracting Parties where the trans-border geographical area of origin is situated;

(xvi)   'Competent Authority' means an entity designated in accordance with Article 3;

(xvii)   'beneficiaries' means the natural persons or legal entities entitled under the law of the Contracting Party of Origin to use an appellation of origin or a geographical indication;

(xviii) 'intergovernmental organization' means an intergovernmental organization eligible to become party to this Act in accordance with Article 28(1)(iii);

(xix)   'Organization' means the World Intellectual Property Organization;

(xx)   'Director General' means the Director General of the Organization;

(xxi)   'International Bureau' means the International Bureau of the Organization.

Article 2   Subject-Matter

(1) *[Appellations of Origin and Geographical Indications]* This Act applies in respect of:

   (i)   any denomination protected in the Contracting Party of Origin consisting of or containing the name of a geographical area, or another denomination known as referring to such area, which serves to designate a good as originating in that geographical area, where the quality or characteristics of the good are due exclusively or essentially to the geographical environment, including natural and human factors, and which has given the good its reputation; as well as

   (ii)   any indication protected in the Contracting Party of Origin consisting of or containing the name of a geographical area, or another indication known as referring to such area, which identifies a good as originating in that geographical area, where a given quality, reputation or other characteristic of the good is essentially attributable to its geographical origin.

(2) *[Possible Geographical Areas of Origin]* A geographical area of origin as described in paragraph (1) may consist of the entire territory of the Contracting Party of Origin or a region, locality or place in the Contracting Party of Origin. This does not exclude the application of this Act in respect of a geographical area of origin, as described in paragraph (1), consisting of a trans-border geographical area, or a part thereof.

Article 3   Competent Authority

Each Contracting Party shall designate an entity which shall be responsible for the administration of this Act in its territory and for communications with the International Bureau under this Act and the Regulations. The Contracting Party shall notify the name and contact details of such Competent Authority to the International Bureau, as specified in the Regulations.

Article 4   International Register

The International Bureau shall maintain an International Register recording international registrations effected under this Act, under the Lisbon Agreement and the 1967 Act, or under both, and data relating to such international registrations.

Chapter II   Application and International Registration

Article 5   Application

(1) *[Place of Filing]* Applications shall be filed with the International Bureau.

(2) *[Application Filed by Competent Authority]* Subject to paragraph (3), the application for the international registration of an appellation of origin or a geographical indication shall be filed by the Competent Authority in the name of:

   (i)   the beneficiaries; or

   (ii)   a natural person or legal entity having legal standing under the law of the Contracting Party of Origin to assert the rights of the beneficiaries or other rights in the appellation of origin or geographical indication.

(3) *[Application Filed Directly]*

   (a)   Without prejudice to paragraph (4), if the legislation of the Contracting Party of Origin so permits, the application may be filed by the beneficiaries or by a natural person or legal entity referred to in paragraph (2)(ii).

(b) Subparagraph (a) applies subject to a declaration from the Contracting Party that its legislation so permits. Such declaration may be made by the Contracting Party at the time of deposit of its instrument of ratification or accession or at any later time. Where the declaration is made at the time of the deposit of its instrument of ratification or accession, it shall take effect upon the entry into force of this Act with respect to that Contracting Party. Where the declaration is made after the entry into force of this Act with respect to the Contracting Party, it shall take effect three months after the date on which the Director General has received the declaration.

(4) *[Possible Joint Application in the Case of a Trans-border Geographical Area]* In case of a geographical area of origin consisting of a trans-border geographical area, the adjacent Contracting Parties may, in accordance with their agreement, file an application jointly through a commonly designated Competent Authority.

(5) *[Mandatory Contents]* The Regulations shall specify the mandatory particulars that must be included in the application, in addition to those specified in Article 6(3).

(6) *[Optional Contents]* The Regulations may specify the optional particulars that may be included in the application.

Article 6   International Registration

(1) *[Formal Examination by the International Bureau]* Upon receipt of an application for the international registration of an appellation of origin or a geographical indication in due form, as specified in the Regulations, the International Bureau shall register the appellation of origin, or the geographical indication, in the International Register.

(2) *[Date of International Registration]* Subject to paragraph (3), the date of the international registration shall be the date on which the application was received by the International Bureau.

(3) *[Date of International Registration Where Particulars Missing]* Where the application does not contain all the following particulars:

(i)   the identification of the Competent Authority or, in the case of Article 5(3), the applicant or applicants;

(ii)   the details identifying the beneficiaries and, where applicable, the natural person or legal entity referred to in Article 5(2)(ii);

(iii)   the appellation of origin, or the geographical indication, for which international registration is sought;

(iv)   the good or goods to which the appellation of origin, or the geographical indication, applies;

the date of the international registration shall be the date on which the last of the missing particulars is received by the International Bureau.

(4) *[Publication and Notification of International Registrations]* The International Bureau shall, without delay, publish each international registration and notify the Competent Authority of each Contracting Party of the international registration.

(5) *[Date of Effect of International Registration]*

(a) Subject to subparagraph (b), a registered appellation of origin or geographical indication shall, in each Contracting Party that has not refused protection in accordance with Article 15, or that has sent to the International Bureau a notification of grant of protection in accordance with Article 18, be protected from the date of the international registration.

(b) A Contracting Party may, in a declaration, notify the Director General that, in accordance with its national or regional legislation, a registered appellation of origin or geographical indication is protected from a date that is mentioned in the declaration, which date shall however not be later than the date of expiry of the time limit for refusal specified in the Regulations in accordance with Article 15(1)(a).

Article 7   Fees

(1) *[International Registration Fee]* International registration of each appellation of origin, and each geographical indication, shall be subject to payment of the fee specified in the Regulations.

(2) *[Fees for Other Entries in the International Register]* The Regulations shall specify the fees to be paid in respect of other entries in the International Register and for the supply of extracts, attestations, or other information concerning the contents of the international registration.

(3) *[Fee Reductions]* Reduced fees shall be established by the Assembly in respect of certain international registrations of appellations of origin, and in respect of certain international registrations of geographical indications, in particular those in respect of which the Contracting Party of Origin is a developing country or a least-developed country.

(4) *[Individual Fee]*

    (a) Any Contracting Party may, in a declaration, notify the Director General that the protection resulting from international registration shall extend to it only if a fee is paid to cover its cost of substantive examination of the international registration. The amount of such individual fee shall be indicated in the declaration and can be changed in further declarations. The said amount may not be higher than the equivalent of the amount required under the national or regional legislation of the Contracting Party diminished by the savings resulting from the international procedure. Additionally, the Contracting Party may, in a declaration, notify the Director General that it requires an administrative fee relating to the use by the beneficiaries of the appellation of origin or the geographical indication in that Contracting Party.

    (b) Non-payment of an individual fee shall, in accordance with the Regulations, have the effect that protection is renounced in respect of the Contracting Party requiring the fee.

Article 8   Period of Validity of International Registrations

(1) *[Dependency]* International registrations shall be valid indefinitely, on the understanding that the protection of a registered appellation of origin or geographical indication shall no longer be required if the denomination constituting the appellation of origin, or the indication constituting the geographical indication, is no longer protected in the Contracting Party of Origin.

(2) *[Cancellation]*

    (a) The Competent Authority of the Contracting Party of Origin, or, in the case of Article 5(3), the beneficiaries or the natural person or legal entity referred to in Article 5(2)(ii) or the Competent Authority of the Contracting Party of Origin, may at any time request the International Bureau to cancel the international registration concerned.

    (b) In case the denomination constituting a registered appellation of origin, or the indication constituting a registered geographical indication, is no longer protected in the Contracting Party of Origin, the Competent Authority of the Contracting Party of Origin shall request cancellation of the international registration.

Chapter III   Protection

Article 9   Commitment to Protect

Each Contracting Party shall protect registered appellations of origin and geographical indications on its territory, within its own legal system and practice but in accordance with the terms of this Act, subject to any refusal, renunciation, invalidation or cancellation that may become effective with respect to its territory, and on the understanding that Contracting Parties that do not distinguish in their national or regional legislation as between appellations of origin and geographical indications shall not be required to introduce such a distinction into their national or regional legislation.

Article 10   Protection Under Laws of Contracting Parties or Other Instruments

(1) *[Form of Legal Protection]* Each Contracting Party shall be free to choose the type of legislation under which it establishes the protection stipulated in this Act, provided that such legislation meets the substantive requirements of this Act.

(2) *[Protection Under Other Instruments]* The provisions of this Act shall not in any way affect any other protection a Contracting Party may accord in respect of registered appellations of origin or registered geographical indications under its national or regional legislation, or under other international instruments.

(3) *[Relation to Other Instruments]* Nothing in this Act shall derogate from any obligations that Contracting Parties have to each other under any other international instruments, nor shall it prejudice any rights that a Contracting Party has under any other international instruments.

Article 11 Protection in Respect of Registered Appellations of Origin and Geographical Indications

(1) *[Content of Protection]* Subject to the provisions of this Act, in respect of a registered appellation of origin or a registered geographical indication, each Contracting Party shall provide the legal means to prevent:

    (a) use of the appellation of origin or the geographical indication

        (i) in respect of goods of the same kind as those to which the appellation of origin or the geographical indication applies, not originating in the geographical area of origin or not complying with any other applicable requirements for using the appellation of origin or the geographical indication;

        (ii) in respect of goods that are not of the same kind as those to which the appellation of origin or geographical indication applies or services, if such use would indicate or suggest a connection between those goods or services and the beneficiaries of the appellation of origin or the geographical indication, and would be likely to damage their interests, or, where applicable, because of the reputation of the appellation of origin or geographical indication in the Contracting Party concerned, such use would be likely to impair or dilute in an unfair manner, or take unfair advantage of, that reputation;

    (b) any other practice liable to mislead consumers as to the true origin, provenance or nature of the goods.

(2) *[Content of Protection in Respect of Certain Uses]* Paragraph (1)(a) shall also apply to use of the appellation of origin or geographical indication amounting to its imitation, even if the true origin of the goods is indicated, or if the appellation of origin or the geographical indication is used in translated form or is accompanied by terms such as 'style', 'kind', 'type', 'make', 'imitation', 'method', 'as produced in', 'like', 'similar' or the like.

(3) *[Use in a Trademark]* Without prejudice to Article 13(1), a Contracting Party shall, *ex officio* if its legislation so permits or at the request of an interested party, refuse or invalidate the registration of a later trademark if use of the trademark would result in one of the situations covered by paragraph (1).

Article 12 Protection Against Becoming Generic

Subject to the provisions of this Act, registered appellations of origin and registered geographical indications cannot be considered to have become generic in a Contracting Party.

Article 13 Safeguards in Respect of Other Rights

(1) *[Prior Trademark Rights]* The provisions of this Act shall not prejudice a prior trademark applied for or registered in good faith, or acquired through use in good faith, in a Contracting Party. Where the law of a Contracting Party provides a limited exception to the rights conferred by a trademark to the effect that such a prior trademark in certain circumstances may not entitle its owner to prevent a registered appellation of origin or geographical indication from being granted protection or used in that Contracting Party, protection of the registered appellation of origin or geographical indication shall not limit the rights conferred by that trademark in any other way.

(2) *[Personal Name Used in Business]* The provisions of this Act shall not prejudice the right of any person to use, in the course of trade, that person's name or the name of that person's predecessor in business, except where such name is used in such a manner as to mislead the public.

(3) *[Rights Based on a Plant Variety or Animal Breed Denomination]* The provisions of this Act shall not prejudice the right of any person to use a plant variety or animal breed denomination in the course of trade, except where such plant variety or animal breed denomination is used in such a manner as to mislead the public.

(4) *[Safeguards in the Case of Notification of Withdrawal of Refusal or a Grant of Protection]* Where a Contracting Party that has refused the effects of an international registration under Article 15 on the ground of use under a prior trademark or other right, as referred to in this Article, notifies the withdrawal of that refusal under Article 16 or a grant of protection under Article 18, the resulting protection of the appellation of origin or geographical indication shall not prejudice that right or its use, unless the protection was granted following the cancellation, non-renewal, revocation or invalidation of the right.

Article 14   Enforcement Procedures and Remedies

Each Contracting Party shall make available effective legal remedies for the protection of registered appellations of origin and registered geographical indications and provide that legal proceedings for ensuring their protection may be brought by a public authority or by any interested party, whether a natural person or a legal entity and whether public or private, depending on its legal system and practice.

Chapter IV   Refusal and Other Actions in Respect of International Registrations

Article 15   Refusal

(1) *[Refusal of Effects of International Registration]*
    (a) Within the time limit specified in the Regulations, the Competent Authority of a Contracting Party may notify the International Bureau of the refusal of the effects of an international registration in its territory. The notification of refusal may be made by the Competent Authority *ex officio*, if its legislation so permits, or at the request of an interested party.
    (b) The notification of refusal shall set out the grounds on which the refusal is based.

(2) *[Protection Under Other Instruments]* The notification of a refusal shall not be detrimental to any other protection that may be available, in accordance with Article 10(2), to the denomination or indication concerned in the Contracting Party to which the refusal relates.

(3) *[Obligation to Provide Opportunity for Interested Parties]* Each Contracting Party shall provide a reasonable opportunity, for anyone whose interests would be affected by an international registration, to request the Competent Authority to notify a refusal in respect of the international registration.

(4) *[Registration, Publication and Communication of Refusals]* The International Bureau shall record the refusal and the grounds for the refusal in the International Register. It shall publish the refusal and the grounds for the refusal and shall communicate the notification of refusal to the Competent Authority of the Contracting Party of Origin or, where the application has been filed directly in accordance with Article 5(3), the beneficiaries or the natural person or legal entity referred to in Article 5(2)(ii) as well as the Competent Authority of the Contracting Party of Origin.

(5) *[National Treatment]* Each Contracting Party shall make available to interested parties affected by a refusal the same judicial and administrative remedies that are available to its own nationals in respect of the refusal of protection for an appellation of origin or a geographical indication.

Article 16   Withdrawal of Refusal

A refusal may be withdrawn in accordance with the procedures specified in the Regulations. A withdrawal shall be recorded in the International Register.

Article 17   Transitional Period

(1) *[Option to Grant Transitional Period]* Without prejudice to Article 13, where a Contracting Party has not refused the effects of an international registration on the ground of prior use by a third party or has withdrawn such refusal or has notified a grant of protection, it may, if its legislation so permits, grant a defined period as specified in the Regulations, for terminating such use.

(2) *[Notification of a Transitional Period]* The Contracting Party shall notify the International Bureau of any such period, in accordance with the procedures specified in the Regulations.

Article 18   Notification of Grant of Protection

The Competent Authority of a Contracting Party may notify the International Bureau of the grant of protection to a registered appellation of origin or geographical indication. The International Bureau shall record any such notification in the International Register and publish it.

Article 19   Invalidation

(1) *[Opportunity to Defend Rights]* Invalidation of the effects, in part or in whole, of an international registration in the territory of a Contracting Party may be pronounced only after having given the beneficiaries an opportunity to defend their rights. Such opportunity shall also be given to the natural person or legal entity referred to in Article 5(2)(ii).

(2) *[Notification, Recordal and Publication]* The Contracting Party shall notify the invalidation of the effects of an international registration to the International Bureau, which shall record the invalidation in the International Register and publish it.

(3) *[Protection Under Other Instruments]* Invalidation shall not be detrimental to any other protection that may be available, in accordance with Article 10(2), to the denomination or indication concerned in the Contracting Party that invalidated the effects of the international registration.

Article 20   Modifications and Other Entries in the International Register

Procedures for the modification of international registrations and other entries in the International Register shall be specified in the Regulations.

Chapter V   Administrative Provisions

Article 21   Membership of the Lisbon Union

The Contracting Parties shall be members of the same Special Union as the States party to the Lisbon Agreement or the 1967 Act, whether or not they are party to the Lisbon Agreement or the 1967 Act.

. . .

Article 30   Prohibition of Reservations

No reservations to this Act are permitted.

Article 31   Application of the Lisbon Agreement and the 1967 Act

(1) *[Relations Between States Party to Both This Act and the Lisbon Agreement or the 1967 Act]* This Act alone shall be applicable as regards the mutual relations of States party to both this Act and the Lisbon Agreement or the 1967 Act. However, with regard to international registrations of appellations of origin effective under the Lisbon Agreement or the 1967 Act, the States shall accord no lower protection than is required by the Lisbon Agreement or the 1967 Act.

(2) *[Relations Between States Party to Both This Act and the Lisbon Agreement or the 1967 Act and States Party to the Lisbon Agreement or the 1967 Act Without Being Party to This Act]* Any State party to both this Act and the Lisbon Agreement or the 1967 Act shall continue to apply the Lisbon Agreement or the 1967 Act, as the case may be, in its relations with States party to the Lisbon Agreement or the 1967 Act that are not party to this Act.

. . .

Agreed Statement concerning Article 11(2)

For the purposes of this Act, it is understood that where certain elements of the denomination or indication constituting the appellation of origin or geographical indication have a generic character in the Contracting Party of Origin, their protection under this paragraph shall not be required in the other Contracting Parties. For greater certainty, a refusal or invalidation of a trademark, or a finding of infringement, in the Contracting Parties under the terms of Article 11 cannot be based on the component that has a generic character.

Agreed Statement concerning Article 12

For the purposes of this Act, it is understood that Article 12 is without prejudice to the application of the provisions of this Act concerning prior use, as, prior to international registration, the denomination or indication constituting the appellation of origin or geographical indication may already, in whole or in part, be generic in a Contracting Party other than the Contracting Party of Origin, for example, because the denomination or indication, or part of it, is identical with a term customary in common language as the common name of a good or service in such Contracting Party, or is identical with the customary name of a grape variety in such Contracting Party.

Uniform Domain Name Dispute Resolution Policy

as approved by ICANN on October 24, 1999

1. *Purpose.* This Uniform Domain Name Dispute Resolution Policy (the 'Policy') has been adopted by the Internet Corporation for Assigned Names and Numbers ('ICANN'), is incorporated by reference into your Registration Agreement, and sets forth the terms and conditions in connection with a dispute between you and any party other than us (the registrar) over the registration and use of an Internet domain name registered by you. Proceedings under *Paragraph 4* of this Policy will be conducted according to the Rules for Uniform Domain Name Dispute Resolution Policy (the 'Rules of Procedure'), which are available at https://www.icann.org/resources/pages/udrp-rules-2015-03-11-en, and the selected administrative-dispute-resolution service provider's supplemental rules.

2. *Your representations.* By applying to register a domain name, or by asking us to maintain or renew a domain name registration, you hereby represent and warrant to us that (a) the statements that you made in your Registration Agreement are complete and accurate; (b) to your knowledge, the registration of the domain name will not infringe upon or otherwise violate the rights of any third party; (c) you are not registering the domain name for an unlawful purpose; and (d) you will not knowingly use the domain name in violation of any applicable laws or regulations. It is your responsibility to determine whether your domain name registration infringes or violates someone else's rights.

3. *Cancellations, transfers, and changes.* We will cancel, transfer or otherwise make changes to domain name registrations under the following circumstances:

(a) subject to the provisions of *Paragraph 8,* our receipt of written or appropriate electronic instructions from you or your authorised agent to take such action;

(b) our receipt of an order from a court or arbitral tribunal, in each case of competent jurisdiction, requiring such action; and/or

(c) our receipt of a decision of an Administrative Panel requiring such action in any administrative proceeding to which you were a party and which was conducted under this Policy or a later version of this Policy adopted by ICANN. (See *Paragraph 4(i)* and *(k)* below.)

We may also cancel, transfer or otherwise make changes to a domain name registration in accordance with the terms of your Registration Agreement or other legal requirements.

4. *Mandatory administrative proceeding.*

This Paragraph sets forth the type of disputes for which you are required to submit to a mandatory administrative proceeding. These proceedings will be conducted before one of the administrative-dispute-resolution service providers listed at https://www.icann.org/en/dndr/udrp/approved-providers.htm (each, a 'Provider').

(a) *Applicable disputes.* You are required to submit to a mandatory administrative proceeding in the event that a third party (a 'complainant') asserts to the applicable Provider, in compliance with the Rules of Procedure, that

(i) your domain name is identical or confusingly similar to a trademark or service mark in which the complainant has rights; and

(ii) you have no rights or legitimate interests in respect of the domain name; and

(iii) your domain name has been registered and is being used in bad faith.

In the administrative proceeding, the complainant must prove that each of these three elements are present.

(b) *Evidence of registration and use in bad faith.* For the purposes of *Paragraph 4(a)(iii),* the following circumstances, in particular but without limitation, if found by the Panel to be present, shall be evidence of the registration and use of a domain name in bad faith:

(i) circumstances indicating that you have registered or you have acquired the domain name primarily for the purpose of selling, renting, or otherwise transferring the domain name registration to the complainant who is the owner of the trademark or service mark or to a competitor of that complainant, for valuable consideration in excess of your documented out-of-pocket costs directly related to the domain name; or

(ii) you have registered the domain name in order to prevent the owner of the trademark or service mark from reflecting the mark in a corresponding domain name, provided that you have engaged in a pattern of such conduct; or

(iii) you have registered the domain name primarily for the purpose of disrupting the business of a competitor; or

(iv) by using the domain name, you have intentionally attempted to attract, for commercial gain, Internet users to your web site or other on-line location, by creating a likelihood of confusion with the complainant's mark as to the source, sponsorship, affiliation, or endorsement of your web site or location or of a product or service on your web site or location.

(c) *How to demonstrate your rights to and legitimate interests in the domain name in responding to a complaint.* When you receive a complaint, you should refer to *Paragraph* 5 of the Rules of Procedure in determining how your response should be prepared. Any of the following circumstances, in particular but without limitation, if found by the Panel to be proved based on its evaluation of all evidence presented, shall demonstrate your rights or legitimate interests to the domain name for purposes of Paragraph 4(a)(ii):

(i) before any notice to you of the dispute, your use of, or demonstrable preparations to use, the domain name or a name corresponding to the domain name in connection with a bona fide offering of goods or services; or

(ii) you (as an individual, business, or other organisation) have been commonly known by the domain name, even if you have acquired no trademark or service mark rights; or

(iii) you are making a legitimate noncommercial or fair use of the domain name, without intent for commercial gain to misleadingly divert consumers or to tarnish the trademark or service mark at issue.

(d) *Selection of Provider.* The complainant shall select the Provider from among those approved by ICANN by submitting the complaint to that Provider. The selected Provider will administer the proceeding, except in cases of consolidation as described in *Paragraph 4(f)*.

(e) *Initiation of proceeding and process and appointment of Administrative Panel.* The Rules of Procedure state the process for initiating and conducting a proceeding and for appointing the panel that will decide the dispute (the 'Administrative Panel').

(f) *Consolidation.* In the event of multiple disputes between you and a complainant, either you or the complainant may petition to consolidate the disputes before a single Administrative Panel. This petition shall be made to the first Administrative Panel appointed to hear a pending dispute between the parties. This Administrative Panel may consolidate before it any or all such disputes in its sole discretion, provided that the disputes being consolidated are governed by this Policy or a later version of this Policy adopted by ICANN.

(g) *Fees.* All fees charged by a Provider in connection with any dispute before an Administrative Panel pursuant to this Policy shall be paid by the complainant, except in cases where you elect to expand the Administrative Panel from one to three panelists as provided in *Paragraph 5(b)(iv)* of the Rules of Procedure, in which case all fees will be split evenly by you and the complainant.

(h) *Our involvement in administrative proceedings.* We do not, and will not, participate in the administration or conduct of any proceeding before an Administrative Panel. In addition, we will not be liable as a result of any decisions rendered by the Administrative Panel.

(i) *Remedies.* The remedies available to a complainant pursuant to any proceeding before an Administrative Panel shall be limited to requiring the cancellation of your domain name or the transfer of your domain name registration to the complainant.

(j) *Notification and publication.* The Provider shall notify us of any decision made by an Administrative Panel with respect to a domain name you have registered with us. All decisions under this Policy will be published in full over the Internet, except when an Administrative Panel determines in an exceptional case to redact portions of its decision.

(k) *Availability of court proceedings.* The mandatory administrative proceeding requirements set forth in *Paragraph 4* shall not prevent either you or the complainant from submitting the dispute to a court of competent jurisdiction for independent resolution before such mandatory administrative proceeding is commenced or after such proceeding is concluded. If an Administrative Panel decides that your domain name registration should be cancelled or transferred, we will wait ten (10) business days (as observed in the location of our principal office) after we are informed by the applicable Provider of the Administrative Panel's decision before implementing that decision. We will then implement the decision unless we have received from you during that ten (10) business day period official documentation (such as a copy of a complaint, file-stamped by the clerk of the court) that you have commenced a lawsuit against the complainant in a jurisdiction to which the complainant has submitted under *Paragraph 3(b)(xiii)* of the Rules of Procedure. (In general, that jurisdiction is either the location of our principal office or of your address as shown in our Whois database. See *Paragraphs 1* and *3(b)(xiii)* of the Rules of Procedure for details.) If we receive such documentation within the ten (10) business day period, we will not implement the Administrative Panel's decision, and we will take no further action, until we receive (i) evidence satisfactory to us of a resolution between the parties; (ii) evidence satisfactory to us that your lawsuit has been dismissed or withdrawn; or (iii) a copy of an order from such court dismissing your lawsuit or ordering that you do not have the right to continue to use your domain name.

5. *All other disputes and litigation.* All other disputes between you and any party other than us regarding your domain name registration that are not brought pursuant to the mandatory administrative proceeding provisions of *Paragraph 4* shall be resolved between you and such other party through any court, arbitration or other proceeding that may be available.

6. *Our involvement in disputes.* We will not participate in any way in any dispute between you and any party other than us regarding the registration and use of your domain name. You shall not name us as a party or otherwise include us in any such proceeding. In the event that we are named as a party in any such proceeding, we reserve the right to raise any and all defenses deemed appropriate, and to take any other action necessary to defend ourselves.

7. *Maintaining the status quo.* We will not cancel, transfer, activate, deactivate, or otherwise change the status of any domain name registration under this Policy except as provided in *Paragraph 3* above.

8. *Transfers during a dispute.*

(a) *Transfers of a domain name to a new holder.* You may not transfer your domain name registration to another holder (i) during a pending administrative proceeding brought pursuant to *Paragraph 4* or for a period of fifteen (15) business days (as observed in the location of our principal place of business) after such proceeding is concluded; or (ii) during a pending court proceeding or arbitration commenced regarding your domain name unless the party to whom the domain name registration is being transferred agrees, in writing, to be bound by the decision of the court or arbitrator. We reserve the right to cancel any transfer of a domain name registration to another holder that is made in violation of this subparagraph.

(b) *Changing registrars.* You may not transfer your domain name registration to another registrar during a pending administrative proceeding brought pursuant to *Paragraph 4* or for a period of fifteen (15) business days (as observed in the location of our principal place of business) after such proceeding is concluded. You may transfer administration of your domain name registration to another registrar during a pending court action or arbitration, provided that the domain name you have registered with us shall continue to be subject to the proceedings commenced against you in accordance with the terms of this Policy. In the event that you transfer a domain name registration to us during the pendency of a court action or arbitration, such dispute shall remain subject to the domain name dispute policy of the registrar from which the domain name registration was transferred.

9. *Policy modifications.* We reserve the right to modify this Policy at any time with the permission of ICANN. We will post our revised Policy at least thirty (30) calendar days before it becomes effective. Unless this Policy has already been invoked by the submission of a complaint to a Provider, in which event the version of the Policy in effect at the time it was invoked will apply to you until the dispute is over, all such changes will be binding upon you with respect to any domain name registration dispute, whether the dispute arose before, on or after the effective date of our change. In the event that you object to a change in this Policy, your sole remedy is to cancel your domain name registration with us, provided that you will not be entitled to a refund of any fees you paid to us. The revised Policy will apply to you until you cancel your domain name registration.

Part C

Patents, Plant Varieties and Related Rights

C1. UNITED KINGDOM

Patents Act 1977*

(1977, c. 37)

An Act to establish a new law of patents applicable to future patents and applications of patents; to amend the law of patents applicable to existing patents and applications for patents; to give effect to certain international conventions on patents; and for connected purposes. [29 July 1977]

Arrangement of Sections

---

* **Editor's Note:** Contains amendments effected by *Competition (Amendment etc.) (EU Exit) (No. 2) Regulations 2019*. By virtue of the *European Union (Withdrawal Agreement) Act 2020*, these amendments take effect on 'IP completion day', which is defined to be 31 December 2020 at 11:00pm.

PART I   NEW DOMESTIC LAW

Patentability

1   Patentable inventions

(1) A patent may be granted only for an invention in respect of which the following conditions are satisfied, that is to say—

(a) the invention is new;

(b) it involves an inventive step;

(c) it is capable of industrial application;

(d) the grant of a patent for it is not excluded by subsections (2) and (3) or section 4A below;

and references in this Act to a patentable invention shall be construed accordingly.

(2) It is hereby declared that the following (among other things) are not inventions for the purposes of this Act, that is to say, anything which consists of—

(a) a discovery, scientific theory or mathematical method;

(b) a literary, dramatic, musical or artistic work or any other aesthetic creation whatsoever;

(c) a scheme, rule or method for performing a mental act, playing a game or doing business, or a program for a computer;

(d) the presentation of information;

but the foregoing provision shall prevent anything from being treated as an invention for the purposes of this Act only to the extent that a patent or application for a patent relates to that thing as such.

(3) A patent shall not be granted for an invention the commercial exploitation of which would be contrary to public policy or morality.

(4) For the purposes of subsection (3) above exploitation shall not be regarded as contrary to public policy or morality only because it is prohibited by any law in force in the United Kingdom or any part of it.

(5) The Secretary of State may by order vary the provisions of subsection (2) above for the purpose of maintaining them in conformity with developments in science and technology; and no such order shall be made unless a draft of the order has been laid before, and approved by resolution of, each House of Parliament.

2   Novelty

(1) An invention shall be taken to be new if it does not form part of the state of the art.

(2) The state of the art in the case of an invention shall be taken to comprise all matter (whether a product, a process, information about either, or anything else) which has at any time before the priority date of that invention been made available to the public (whether in the United Kingdom or elsewhere) by written or oral description, by use or in any other way.

(3) The state of the art in the case of an invention to which an application for a patent or a patent relates shall be taken also to comprise matter contained in an application for another patent which was published on or after the priority date of that invention, if the following conditions are satisfied, that is to say—

(a) that matter was contained in the application for that other patent both as filed and as published; and

(b) the priority date of that matter is earlier than that of the invention.

(4) For the purposes of this section the disclosure of matter constituting an invention shall be disregarded in the case of a patent or an application for a patent if occurring later than the beginning of the period of six months immediately preceding the date of filing the application for the patent and either—

    (a) the disclosure was due to, or made in consequence of, the matter having been obtained unlawfully or in breach of confidence by any person—

        (i) from the inventor or from any other person to whom the matter was made available in confidence by the inventor or who obtained it from the inventor because he or the inventor believed that he was entitled to obtain it; or

        (ii) from any other person to whom the matter was made available in confidence by any person mentioned in sub-paragraph (i) above or in this sub-paragraph or who obtained it from any person so mentioned because he or the person from whom he obtained it believed that he was entitled to obtain it;

    (b) the disclosure was made in breach of confidence by any person who obtained the matter in confidence from the inventor or from any other person to whom it was made available, or who obtained it, from the inventor; or

    (c) the disclosure was due to, or made in consequence of the inventor displaying the invention at an international exhibition and the applicant states, on filing the application, that the invention has been so displayed and also, within the prescribed period, files written evidence in support of the statement complying with any prescribed conditions.

(5) In this section references to the inventor include references to any proprietor of the invention for the time being.

   . . .

3 Inventive step

An invention shall be taken to involve an inventive step if it is not obvious to a person skilled in the art, having regard to any matter which forms part of the state of the art by virtue only of section 2(2) above (and disregarding section 2(3) above).

4 Industrial application

(1) An invention shall be taken to be capable of industrial application if it can be made or used in any kind of industry, including agriculture.

4A Methods of treatment or diagnosis

(1) A patent shall not be granted for the invention of—

    (a) a method of treatment of the human or animal body by surgery or therapy, or

    (b) a method of diagnosis practised on the human or animal body.

(2) Subsection (1) above does not apply to an invention consisting of a substance or composition for use in any such method.

(3) In the case of an invention consisting of a substance or composition for use in any such method, the fact that the substance or composition forms part of the state of the art shall not prevent the invention from being taken to be new if the use of the substance or composition in any such method does not form part of the state of the art.

(4) In the case of an invention consisting of a substance or composition for a specific use in any such method, the fact that the substance or composition forms part of the state of the art shall not prevent the invention from being taken to be new if that specific use does not form part of the state of the art.

5 Priority date

(1) For the purposes of this Act the priority date of an invention to which an application for a patent relates and also of any matter (whether or not the same as the invention) contained in any such application is, except as provided by the following provisions of this Act, the date of filing the application.

(2) If in or in connection with an application for a patent (the application in suit) a declaration is made, whether by the applicant or any predecessor in title of his, complying with the relevant requirements of rules and specifying one or more earlier relevant applications for the purposes of this section made by the applicant or a predecessor in title of his and the application in suit has a date of filing during the period allowed under subsection (2A)(a) or (b) below, then—

    (a) if an invention to which the application in suit relates is supported by matter disclosed in the earlier relevant application or applications, the priority date of that invention shall instead of being the date of filing the application in suit be the date of filing the relevant application in which that matter was disclosed or, if it was disclosed in more than one relevant application, the earliest of them;

    (b) the priority date of any matter contained in the application in suit which was also disclosed in the earlier relevant application or applications shall be the date of filing the relevant application in which that matter was disclosed or, if it was disclosed in more than one relevant application, the earliest of them.

(2A) The periods are—

    (a) the period of twelve months immediately following the date of filing of the earlier specified relevant application, or if there is more than one, of the earliest of them; and

    (b) where the comptroller has given permission under subsection (2B) below for a late declaration to be made under subsection (2) above, the period commencing immediately after the end of the period allowed under paragraph (a) above and ending at the end of the prescribed period.

(2B) The applicant may make a request to the comptroller for permission to make a late declaration under subsection (2) above.

(2C) The comptroller shall grant a request made under subsection (2B) above if, and only if—

    (a) the request complies with the relevant requirements of rules; and

    (b) the comptroller is satisfied that the applicant's failure to file the application in suit within the period allowed under subsection (2A)(a) above was unintentional.

(3) Where an invention or other matter contained in the application in suit was also disclosed in two earlier relevant applications filed by the same applicant as in the case of the application in suit or a predecessor in title of his and the second of those relevant applications was specified in or in connection with the application in suit, the second of those relevant applications shall, so far as concerns that invention or matter, be disregarded unless—

    (a) it was filed in or in respect of the same country as the first; and

    (b) not later than the date of filing the second, the first (whether or not so specified) was unconditionally withdrawn, or was abandoned or refused, without—

        (i) having been made available to the public (whether in the United Kingdom or elsewhere);

        (ii) leaving any rights outstanding; and

        (iii) having served to establish a priority date in relation to another application, wherever made.

(4) The foregoing provisions of this section shall apply for determining the priority date of an invention for which a patent has been granted as they apply for determining the priority date of an invention to which an application for that patent relates.

(5) In this section 'relevant application' means any of the following applications which has a date of filing, namely—

    (a) an application for a patent under this Act;

    (aa) an application in or for a country (other than the United Kingdom) which is a member of the World Trade Organisation for protection in respect of an invention which, in accordance with the law of that country or a treaty or international obligation to which it is a party, is equivalent to an application for a patent under this Act;

    (b) an application in or for a convention country (specified under section 90 below) for protection in respect of an invention or an application which, in accordance with the law of a convention country or a treaty or international convention to which a convention country is a party, is equivalent to an application for a patent under this Act.

6 Disclosure of matter, etc., between earlier and later applications

(1) It is hereby declared for the avoidance of doubt that where an application (the application in suit) is made for a patent and a declaration is made in accordance with section 5(2) above in or in connection with the application specifying an earlier relevant application, the application in suit and any patent granted in pursuance of it shall not be invalidated by reason only of relevant intervening acts.

(2) In this section—

'relevant application' has the same meaning as in section 5 above; and

'relevant intervening acts' means acts done in relation to matter disclosed in an earlier relevant application between the dates of the earlier relevant application and the application in suit, as for example, filing another application for the invention for which the earlier relevant application was made, making information available to the public about the invention or that matter or working that invention, but disregarding any application, or the disclosure to the public of matter contained in any application, which is itself to be disregarded for the purposes of section 5(3) above.

Right to apply for and obtain a patent and be mentioned as inventor

7 Right to apply for and obtain a patent

(1) Any person may make an application for a patent either alone or jointly with another.

(2) A patent for an invention may be granted—

(a) primarily to the inventor or joint inventors;

(b) in preference to the foregoing, to any person or persons who, by virtue of any enactment or rule of law, or any foreign law or treaty or international convention, or by virtue of an enforceable term of any agreement entered into with the inventor before the making of the invention, was or were at the time of the making of the invention entitled to the whole of the property in it (other than equitable interests) in the United Kingdom;

(c) in any event, to the successor or successors in title of any person or persons mentioned in paragraph (a) or (b) above or any person so mentioned and the successor or successors in title of another person so mentioned;

and to no other person.

(3) In this Act 'inventor' in relation to an invention means the actual deviser of the invention and 'joint inventor' shall be construed accordingly.

(4) Except so far as the contrary is established, a person who makes an application for a patent shall be taken to be the person who is entitled under subsection (2) above to be granted a patent and two or more persons who make such an application jointly shall be taken to be the persons so entitled.

8 Determination before grant of questions about entitlement to patents, etc.

(1) At any time before a patent has been granted for an invention (whether or not an application has been made for it)—

(a) any person may refer to the comptroller the question whether he is entitled to be granted (alone or with any other persons) a patent for the invention or has or would have any right in or under any patent so granted or any application for such a patent; or

(b) any of two or more co-proprietors of an application for a patent for that invention may so refer the question whether any right in or under the application should be transferred or granted to any other person;

and the comptroller shall determine the question and may make such order as he thinks fit to give effect to the determination.

. . .

9 Determination after grant of questions referred before grant

If a question with respect to a patent or application is referred by any person to the comptroller under section 8 above, whether before or after the making of an application for the patent, and is not determined before the time when the application is first in order for a grant of a patent in pursuance of the application, that fact shall not prevent the grant of a patent, but on its grant that person shall be treated as having referred to the comptroller under section 37 below any question mentioned in that section which the comptroller thinks appropriate.

10 Handling of application by joint applicants

If any dispute arises between joint applicants for a patent whether or in what manner the application should be proceeded with, the comptroller may, on a request made by any of the parties, give such directions as he thinks fit for enabling the application to proceed in the name of one or more of the parties alone or for regulating the manner in which it shall be proceeded with, or for both those purposes, according as the case may require.

. . .

12 Determination of questions about entitlement to foreign and convention patents, etc.

(1) At any time before a patent is granted for an invention in pursuance of an application made under the law of any country other than the United Kingdom or under any treaty or international convention (whether or not that application has been made)—

    (a) any person may refer to the comptroller the question whether he is entitled to be granted (alone or with any other persons) any such patent for that invention or has or would have any right in or under any such patent or an application for such a patent; or

    (b) any of two or more co-proprietors of an application for such a patent for that invention may so refer the question whether any right in or under the application should be transferred or granted to any other person;

and the comptroller shall determine the question so far as he is able to and may make such order as he thinks fit to give effect to the determination.

13 Mention of inventor

(1) The inventor or joint inventors of an invention shall have a right to be mentioned as such in any patent granted for the invention and shall also have a right to be so mentioned if possible in any published application for a patent for the invention and, if not so mentioned, a right to be so mentioned in accordance with rules in a prescribed document.

(2) Unless he has already given the Patent Office the information hereinafter mentioned, an applicant for a patent shall within the prescribed period file with the Patent Office a statement—

    (a) identifying the person or persons whom he believes to be the inventor or inventors; and

    (b) where the applicant is not the sole inventor or the applicants are not the joint inventors, indicating the derivation of his or their right to be granted the patent; and, if he fails to do so, the application shall be taken to be withdrawn.

(3) Where a person has been mentioned as sole or joint inventor in pursuance of this section, any other person who alleges that the former ought not to have been so mentioned may at any time apply to the comptroller for a certificate to that effect, and the comptroller may issue such a certificate; and if he does so, he shall accordingly rectify any undistributed copies of the patent and of any documents prescribed for the purposes of subsection (1) above.

Applications

14 Making of application

(1) Every application for a patent—

    (a) shall be made in the prescribed form and shall be filed at the Patent Office in the prescribed manner;

(1A) Where an application for a patent is made, the fee prescribed for the purposes of this subsection ('the application fee') shall be paid not later than the end of the period prescribed for the purposes of section 15(10)(c) below.

(2) Every application for a patent shall contain—

(a) a request for the grant of a patent;

(b) a specification containing a description of the invention, a claim or claims and any drawing referred to in the description or any claim; and

(c) an abstract;

but the foregoing provision shall not prevent an application being initiated by documents complying with section 15(1) below.

(3) The specification of an application shall disclose the invention in a manner which is clear enough and complete enough for the invention to be performed by a person skilled in the art.

(5) The claim or claims shall—

(a) define the matter for which the applicant seeks protection;

(b) be clear and concise;

(c) be supported by the description; and

(d) relate to one invention or to a group of inventions which are so linked as to form a single inventive concept.

(6) Without prejudice to the generality of subsection (5)(d) above, rules may provide for treating two or more inventions as being so linked as to form a single inventive concept for the purposes of this Act.

(7) The purpose of the abstract is to give technical information and on publication it shall not form part of the state of the art by virtue of section 2(3) above, and the comptroller may determine whether the abstract adequately fulfils its purpose and, if it does not, may reframe it so that it does.

(9) An application for a patent may be withdrawn at any time before the patent is granted and any withdrawal of such an application may not be revoked.

(10) Subsection (9) above does not affect the power of the comptroller under section 117(1) below to correct an error or mistake in a withdrawal of an application for a patent.

15 Date of filing application

(1) Subject to the following provisions of this Act, the date of filing an application for a patent shall be taken to be the earliest date on which documents filed at the Patent Office to initiate the application satisfy the following conditions—

(a) the documents indicate that a patent is sought;

(b) the documents identify the person applying for a patent or contain information sufficient to enable that person to be contacted by the Patent Office; and

(c) the documents contain either—

(i) something which is or appears to be a description of the invention for which a patent is sought; or

(ii) a reference, complying with the relevant requirements of rules, to an earlier relevant application made by the applicant or a predecessor in title of his.

(2) It is immaterial for the purposes of subsection (1)(c)(i) above—

(a) whether the thing is in, or is accompanied by a translation into, a language accepted by the Patent Office in accordance with rules;

(b) whether the thing otherwise complies with the other provisions of this Act and with any relevant rules.

. . .

(9) Where, after an application for a patent has been filed and before the patent is granted—

(a) a new application is filed by the original applicant or his successor in title in accordance with rules in respect of any part of the matter contained in the earlier application, and

(b) the conditions mentioned in subsection (1) above are satisfied in relation to the new application (without the new application contravening section 76 below), the new application shall be treated as having, as its date of filing, the date of filing the earlier application.

(10) Where an application has a date of filing by virtue of this section, the application shall be treated as having been withdrawn if any of the following applies—

  (a) the applicant fails to file at the Patent Office, before the end of the prescribed period, one or more claims and the abstract;

  (b) where a reference to an earlier relevant application has been filed as mentioned in subsection (1)(c)(ii) above—

    (i) the applicant fails to file at the Patent Office, before the end of the prescribed period, a description of the invention for which the patent is sought;

    (ii) the applicant fails to file at the Patent Office, before the end of the prescribed period, a copy of the application referred to, complying with the relevant requirements of rules;

  (c) the applicant fails to pay the application fee before the end of the prescribed period;

  (d) the applicant fails, before the end of the prescribed period, to make a request for a search under section 17 below and pay the search fee.

. . .

15A   Preliminary examination

(1) The comptroller shall refer an application for a patent to an examiner for a preliminary examination if—

  (a) the application has a date of filing;

  (b) the application has not been withdrawn or treated as withdrawn; and

  (c) the application fee has been paid.

(2) On a preliminary examination of an application the examiner shall—

  (a) determine whether the application complies with those requirements of this Act and the rules which are designated by the rules as formal requirements for the purposes of this Act; and

  (b) determine whether any requirements under section 13(2) or 15(10) above remain to be complied with.

. . .

16   Publication of application

(1) Subject to section 22 below and to any prescribed restrictions, where an application has a date of filing, as soon as possible after the end of the prescribed period, the comptroller shall, unless the application is withdrawn or refused before preparations for its publication have been completed by the Patent Office, publish it as filed (including not only the original claims but also any amendments of those claims and new claims subsisting immediately before the completion of those preparations) and he may, if so requested by the applicant, publish it as aforesaid during that period, and in either event shall advertise the fact and date of its publication in the journal.

(2) The comptroller may omit from the specification of a published application for a patent any matter—

  (a) which in his opinion disparages any person in a way likely to damage him, or

  (b) the publication or exploitation of which would in his opinion be generally expected to encourage offensive, immoral or anti-social behaviour.

Examination and search

17   Search

(1) The comptroller shall refer an application for a patent to an examiner for a search if, and only if—

  (a) the comptroller has referred the application to an examiner for a preliminary examination under section 15A(1) above;

  (b) the application has not been withdrawn or treated as withdrawn;

(c) before the end of the prescribed period—
   (i) the applicant makes a request to the Patent Office in the prescribed form for a search; and
   (ii) the fee prescribed for the search ('the search fee') is paid;
(d) the application includes—
   (i) a description of the invention for which a patent is sought; and
   (ii) one or more claims; and
(e) the description and each of the claims comply with the requirements of rules as to language.

18   Substantive examination and grant or refusal of patent

(1) Where the conditions imposed by section 17(1) above for the comptroller to refer an application to an examiner for a search are satisfied and at the time of the request under that subsection or within the prescribed period—
   (a) a request is made by the applicant to the Patent Office in the prescribed form for a substantive examination; and
   (b) the prescribed fee is paid for the examination; the comptroller shall refer the application to an examiner for a substantive examination; and if no such request is made or the prescribed fee is not paid within that period, the application shall be treated as having been withdrawn at the end of that period.
   . . .

(2) On a substantive examination of an application the examiner shall investigate, to such extent as he considers necessary in view of any examination carried out under section 15A above and search carried out under section 17 above, whether the application complies with the requirements of this Act and the rules and shall determine that question and report his determination to the comptroller.

(3) If the examiner reports that any of those requirements are not complied with, the comptroller shall give the applicant an opportunity within a specified period to make observations on the report and to amend the application so as to comply with those requirements (subject, however, to section 76 below), and if the applicant fails to satisfy the comptroller that those requirements are complied with, or to amend the application so as to comply with them, the comptroller may refuse the application.

(4) If the examiner reports that the application, whether as originally filed or as amended in pursuance of section 15A above, this section or section 19 below, complies with those requirements at any time before the end of the prescribed period, the comptroller shall notify the applicant of that fact and, subject to subsection (5) and sections 19 and 22 below and on payment within the prescribed period of any fee prescribed for the grant, grant him a patent.

(5) Where two or more applications for a patent for the same invention having the same priority date and filed by the same applicant or his successor in title, the comptroller may on that ground refuse to grant a patent in pursuance of more than one of the applications.

19   General power to amend application before grant

(1) At any time before a patent is granted in pursuance of an application the applicant may, in accordance with the prescribed conditions and subject to section 76 below, amend the application of his own volition.

(2) The comptroller may, without an application being made to him for the purpose, amend the specification and abstract contained in an application for a patent so as to acknowledge a registered trade mark.

20   Failure of application

(1) If it is not determined that an application for a patent complies before the end of the prescribed period with all the requirements of this Act and the rules, the application shall be treated as having been refused by the comptroller at the end of that period, and section 97 below shall apply accordingly.
   . . .

21 Observations by third party on patentability

(1) Where an application for a patent has been published but a patent has not been granted to the applicant, any other person may make observations in writing to the comptroller on the question whether the invention is a patentable invention, stating reasons for the observations, and the comptroller shall consider the observations in accordance with rules.

(2) It is hereby declared that a person does not become a party to any proceedings under this Act before the comptroller by reason only that he makes observations under this section.

Security and safety

22 Information prejudicial to national security or safety of public

(1) Where an application for a patent is filed in the Patent Office (whether under this Act or any treaty or international convention to which the United Kingdom is a party and whether before or after the appointed day) and it appears to the comptroller that the application contains information of a description notified to him by the Secretary of State as being information the publication of which might be prejudicial to national security, the comptroller may give directions prohibiting or restricting the publication of that information or its communication to any specified person or description of persons.

(2) If it appears to the comptroller that any application so filed contains information the publication of which might be prejudicial to the safety of the public, he may give directions prohibiting or restricting the publication of that information or its communication to any specified person or description of persons until the end of a period not exceeding three months from the end of the period prescribed for the purposes of section 16 above.

. . .

23 Restrictions on applications abroad by United Kingdom residents

(1) Subject to the following provisions of this section, no person resident in the United Kingdom shall, without written authority granted by the comptroller, file or cause to be filed outside the United Kingdom an application for a patent for an invention if subsection (1A) below applies to that application, unless—

    (a) an application for a patent for the same invention has been filed in the Patent Office (whether before, on or after the appointed day) not less than six weeks before the application outside the United Kingdom; and

    (b) either no directions have been given under section 22 above in relation to the application in the United Kingdom or all such directions have been revoked.

(1A) This subsection applies to an application if—

    (a) the application contains information which relates to military technology or for any other reason publication of the information might be prejudicial to national security; or

    (b) the application contains information the publication of which might be prejudicial to the safety of the public.

(2) Subsection (1) above does not apply to an application for a patent for an invention for which an application for a patent has first been filed (whether before or after the appointed day) in a country outside the United Kingdom by a person resident outside the United Kingdom.

. . .

Provisions as to patents after grant

24 Publication and certificate of grant

(1) As soon as practicable after a patent has been granted under this Act the comptroller shall publish in the journal a notice that it has been granted.

. . .

(3) The comptroller shall, at the same time as he publishes a notice under subsection (1) above in relation to a patent publish the specification of the patent, the names of the proprietor and (if different) the inventor and any other matters constituting or relating to the patent which in the comptroller's opinion it is desirable to publish.

(4) Subsection (3) above shall not require the comptroller to identify as inventor a person who has waived his right to be mentioned as inventor in any patent granted for the invention.

25 Term of patent

(1) A patent granted under this Act shall be treated for the purposes of the following provisions of this Act as having been granted, and shall take effect, on the date on which notice of its grant is published in the journal and, subject to subsection (3) below, shall continue in force until the end of the period of 20 years beginning with the date of filing the application for the patent or with such other date as may be prescribed.

. . .

26 Patent not to be impugned for lack of unity

No person may in any proceeding object to a patent or to an amendment of a specification of a patent on the ground that the claims contained in the specification of the patent, as they stand or, as the case may be, as proposed to be amended, relate—

    (a) to more than one invention, or

    (b) to a group of inventions which are not so linked as to form a single inventive concept.

27 General power to amend specification after grant

(1) Subject to the following provisions of this section and to section 76 below, the comptroller may, on an application made by the proprietor of a patent, allow the specification of the patent to be amended subject to such conditions, if any, as he thinks fit.

. . .

29 Surrender of patents

(1) The proprietor of a patent may at any time by notice given to the comptroller offer to surrender his patent.

. . .

Property in patents and applications, and registration

30 Nature of, and transactions in, patents and applications for patents

(1) Any patent or application for a patent is personal property (without being a thing in action), and any patent or any such application and rights in or under it may be transferred, created or granted in accordance with subsections (2) to (7) below.

(2) Subject to section 36(3) below, any patent or any such application, or any right in it, may be assigned or mortgaged.

(3) Any patent or any such application or right shall vest by operation of law in the same way as any other personal property and may be vested by an assent of personal representatives.

(4) Subject to section 36(3) below, a licence may be granted under any patent or any such application for working the invention which is the subject of the patent or the application; and—

    (a) to the extent that the licence so provides, a sub-licence may be granted under any such licence and any such licence or sub-licence may be assigned or mortgaged; and

    (b) any such licence or sub-licence shall vest by operation of law in the same way as any other personal property and may be vested by an assent of personal representatives.

(5) Subsections (2) to (4) above shall have effect subject to the following provisions of this Act.

(6) Any of the following transactions, that is to say—

    (a) any assignment or mortgage of a patent or any such application, or any right in a patent or any such application;

    (b) any assent relating to any patent or any such application or right;

shall be void unless it is in writing and is signed by or on behalf of the assignor or mortgagor (or, in the case of an assent or other transaction by a personal representative, by or on behalf of the personal representative).

. . .

(7) An assignment of a patent or any such application or a share in it, and an exclusive licence granted under any patent or any such application, may confer on the assignee or licensee the right of the assignor or licensor to bring proceedings by virtue of section 61 or 69 below for a previous infringement or to bring proceedings under section 58 below for a previous act.

31   Nature of, and transactions in, patents and applications for patents in Scotland

(1) Section 30 above shall not extend to Scotland, but instead the following provisions of this section shall apply there.

(2) Any patent or application for a patent, and any right in or under any patent or any such application, is incorporeal moveable property, and the provisions of the following subsections and of section 36(3) below shall apply to any grant of licences, assignations and securities in relation to such property.

(3) Any patent or any such application, or any right in it, may be assigned and security may be granted over a patent or any such application or right.

(4) A licence may be granted, under any patent or any application for a patent, for working the invention which is the subject of the patent or application.

(5) To the extent that any licence granted under subsection (4) above so provides, a sub-licence may be granted under any such licence and any such licence or sub-licence may be assigned and security granted over it.

(6) Any assignation or grant of security under this section may be carried out only by writing subscribed in accordance with the Requirements of Writing (Scotland) Act 1995.

(7) Any assignation of a patent or application for a patent or a share in it, and an exclusive licence granted under any patent or any such application, may confer on the assignee or licensee the right of the assignor or licensor to bring proceedings by virtue of section 61 or 69 below for a previous infringement or to bring proceedings under section 58 below for a previous act.

32   Register of patents, etc.

(1) The comptroller shall maintain the register of patents, which shall comply with rules made by virtue of this section and shall be kept in accordance with such rules.

(2) Without prejudice to any other provision of this Act or rules, rules may make provisions with respect to the following matters, including provision imposing requirements as to any of those matters—

    (a)   the registration of patents and of published applications for patents;

    (b)   the registration of transactions, instruments or events affecting rights in or under patents and applications;

    (ba) the entering on the register of notices concerning opinions issued, or to be issued, under section 74A below;

    (c)   the furnishing to the comptroller of any prescribed documents or description of documents in connection with any matter which is required to be registered;

    (d)   the correction of errors in the register and in any documents filed at the Patent Office in connection with registration; and

    (e)   the publication and advertisement of anything done under this Act or rules in relation to the register.

(3) Notwithstanding anything in subsection (2)(b) above, no notice of any trust, whether express, implied or constructive, shall be entered in the register and the comptroller shall not be affected by any such notice.

. . .

33   Effect of registration, etc., on rights in patents

(1) Any person who claims to have acquired the property in a patent or application for a patent by virtue of any transaction, instrument or event to which this section applies shall be entitled as against any other person who claims to have acquired that property by virtue of an earlier transaction,

instrument or event to which this section applies if, at the time of the later transaction, instrument or event—

    (a) the earlier transaction, instrument or event was not registered, or

    (b) in the case of any application which has not been published, notice of the earlier transaction, instrument or event had not been given to the comptroller, and

    (c) in any case, the person claiming under the later transaction, instrument or event, did not know of the earlier transaction, instrument or event.

    (2) Subsection (1) above shall apply equally to the case where any person claims to have acquired any right in or under a patent or application for a patent, by virtue of a transaction, instrument or event to which this section applies, and that right is incompatible with any such right acquired by virtue of an earlier transaction, instrument or event to which this section applies.

    (3) This section applies to the following transactions, instruments and events:—

    (a) the assignment or assignation of a patent or application for a patent, or a right in it;

    (b) the mortgage of a patent or application or the granting of security over it;

    (c) the grant, assignment or assignation of a licence or sub-licence, or mortgage of a licence or sub-licence, under a patent or application;

    (d) the death of the proprietor or one of the proprietors of any such patent or application or any person having a right in or under a patent or application and the vesting by an assent of personal representatives of a patent, application or any such right; and

    (e) any order or directions of a court or other competent authority—

       (i) transferring a patent or application or any right in or under it to any person; or

       (ii) that an application should proceed in the name of any person;

       and in either case the event by virtue of which the court or authority had power to make any such order or give any such directions.

    (4) Where an application for the registration of a transaction, instrument or event has been made, but the transaction, instrument or event has not been registered, then, for the purposes of subsection (1)(a) above, registration of the application shall be treated as registration of the transaction, instrument or event.

34 Rectification of register

    (1) The court may, on the application of any person aggrieved, order the register to be rectified by the making, or the variation or deletion, of any entry in it.

    . . .

36 Co-ownership of patents and applications for patents

    (1) Where a patent is granted to two or more persons, each of them shall, subject to any agreement to the contrary, be entitled to an equal undivided share in the patent.

    (2) Where two or more persons are proprietors of a patent, then, subject to the provisions of this section and subject to any agreement to the contrary—

    (a) each of them shall be entitled, by himself or his agents, to do in respect of the invention concerned, for his own benefit and without the consent of or the need to account to the other or others, any act which would apart from this subsection and section 55 below, amount to an infringement of the patent concerned; and

    (b) any such act shall not amount to an infringement of the patent concerned.

    (3) Subject to the provisions of sections 8 and 12 above and section 37 below and to any agreement for the time being in force, where two or more persons are proprietors of a patent one of them shall not without the consent of the other or others

    (a) amend the specification of the patent or apply for such an amendment to be allowed or for the patent to be revoked, or

    (b) grant a licence under the patent or assign or mortgage a share in the patent or in Scotland cause or permit security to be granted over it.

    (4) Subject to the provisions of those sections, where two or more persons are proprietors of a patent, anyone else may supply one of those persons with the means, relating to an essential element

of the invention, for putting the invention into effect, and the supply of those means by virtue of this subsection shall not amount to an infringement of the patent.

(5) Where a patented product is disposed of by any of two or more proprietors to any person, that person and any other person claiming through him shall be entitled to deal with the product in the same way as if it had been disposed of by a sole registered proprietor.

(6) Nothing in subsection (1) or (2) above shall affect the mutual rights or obligations of trustees or of the personal representatives of a deceased person, or their rights or obligations as such.

(7) The foregoing provisions of this section shall have effect in relation to an application for a patent which is filed as they have effect in relation to a patent and—

    (a) references to a patent and a patent being granted shall accordingly include references respectively to any such application and to the application being filed; and

    (b) the reference in subsection (5) above to a patented product shall be construed accordingly.

37 Determination of right to patent after grant

(1) After a patent has been granted for an invention any person having or claiming a proprietary interest in or under the patent may refer to the comptroller the question—

    (a) who is or are the true proprietor or proprietors of the patent,

    (b) whether the patent should have been granted to the person or persons to whom it was granted, or

    (c) whether any right in or under the patent should be transferred or granted to any other person or persons;

and the comptroller shall determine the question and make such order as he thinks fit to give effect to the determination.

. . .

(5) On any such reference no order shall be made under this section transferring the patent to which the reference relates on the ground that the patent was granted to a person not so entitled, and no order shall be made under subsection (4) above on that ground, if the reference was made after the end of the period of two years beginning with the date of the grant, unless it is shown that any person registered as a proprietor of the patent knew at the time of the grant or, as the case may be, of the transfer of the patent to him that he was not entitled to the patent.

(6) An order under this section shall not be so made as to affect the mutual rights or obligations of trustees or of the personal representatives of a deceased person, or their rights or obligations as such.

. . .

Employees' inventions

39 Right to employees' inventions

(1) Notwithstanding anything in any rule of law, an invention made by an employee shall, as between him and his employer, be taken to belong to his employer for the purposes of this Act and all other purposes if—

    (a) it was made in the course of the normal duties of the employee or in the course of duties falling outside his normal duties, but specifically assigned to him, and the circumstances in either case were such that an invention might reasonably be expected to result from the carrying out of his duties; or

    (b) the invention was made in the course of the duties of the employee and, at the time of making the invention, because of the nature of his duties and the particular responsibilities arising from the nature of his duties he had a special obligation to further the interests of the employer's undertaking.

(2) Any other invention made by an employee shall, as between him and his employer, be taken for those purposes to belong to the employee.

(3) Where by virtue of this section an invention belongs, as between him and his employer, to an employee, nothing done—

(a) by or on behalf of the employee or any person claiming under him for the purposes of pursuing an application for a patent, or

(b) by any person for the purpose of performing or working the invention, shall be taken to infringe any copyright or design right to which, as between him and his employer, his employer is entitled in any model or document relating to the invention.

40   Compensation of employees for certain inventions

(1) Where it appears to the court or the comptroller on an application made by an employee within the prescribed period that—

(a) the employee has made an invention belonging to the employer for which a patent has been granted,

(b) having regard among other things to the size and nature of the employer's undertaking, the invention or the patent for it (or the combination of both) is of outstanding benefit to the employer, and

(c) by reason of those facts it is just that the employee should be awarded compensation to be paid by the employer,

the court or the comptroller may award him such compensation of an amount determined under section 41 below.

(2) Where it appears to the court or the comptroller on an application made by an employee within the prescribed period that—

(a) a patent has been granted for an invention made by and belonging to the employee;

(b) his rights in the invention, or in any patent or application for a patent for the invention, have since the appointed day been assigned to the employer or an exclusive licence under the patent or application has since the appointed day been granted to the employer;

(c) the benefit derived by the employee from the contract of assignment, assignation or grant or any ancillary contract ('the relevant contract') is inadequate in relation to the benefit derived by the employer from the invention or the patent for it (or both); and

(d) by reason of those facts it is just that the employee should be awarded compensation to be paid by the employer in addition to the benefit derived from the relevant contract;

the court or the comptroller may award him such compensation of an amount determined under section 41 below.

(3) Subsections (1) and (2) above shall not apply to the invention of an employee where a relevant collective agreement provides for the payment of compensation in respect of inventions of the same description as that invention to employees of the same description as that employee.

(4) Subsection (2) above shall have effect notwithstanding anything in the relevant contract or any agreement applicable to the invention (other than any such collective agreement).

(5) If it appears to the comptroller on an application under this section that the application involves matters which would more properly be determined by the court, he may decline to deal with it.

(6) In this section—

'the prescribed period', in relation to proceedings before the court, means the period prescribed by rules of court, and

'relevant collective agreement' means a collective agreement within the meaning of the Trade Union and Labour Relations (Consolidation) Act 1992 made by or on behalf of a trade union to which the employee belongs, and by the employer or an employers' association to which the employer belongs which is in force at the time of the making of the invention.

(7) References in this section to an invention belonging to an employer or employee are references to it so belonging as between the employer and the employee.

41   Amount of compensation

(1) An award of compensation to an employee under section 40(1) or (2) above shall be such as will secure for the employee a fair share (having regard to all the circumstances) of the benefit which the employer has derived, or may reasonably be expected to derive, from any of the following—

    (a) the invention in question;

    (b) the patent for the invention;

    (c) the assignment, assignation or grant of—

        (i)   the property or any right in the invention, or

        (ii) the property in, or any right in or under, an application for the patent,

        to a person connected with the employer.

(2) For the purposes of subsection (1) above the amount of any benefit derived or expected to be derived by an employer from the assignment, assignation or grant of—

    (a) the property in, or any right in or under, a patent for the invention or an application for such a patent; or

    (b) the property or any right in the invention;

to a person connected with him shall be taken to be the amount which could reasonably be expected to be so derived by the employer if that person had not been connected with him.

(3) Where the Crown, United Kingdom Research and Innovation or a Research Council in its capacity as employer assigns or grants the property in, or any right in or under, an invention, patent or application for a patent to a body having among its functions that of developing or exploiting inventions resulting from public research and does so for no consideration or only a nominal consideration, any benefit derived from the invention, patent or application by that body shall be treated for the purposes of the foregoing provisions of this section as so derived by the Crown, United Kingdom Research and Innovation or the Research Council (as the case may be).

In this subsection 'Research Council' means a body which is a Research Council for the purposes of the Science and Technology Act 1965 or the Arts and Humanities Research Council (as defined by section 1 of the Higher Education Act 2004).

(4) In determining the fair share of the benefit to be secured for an employee in respect of an invention which has always belonged to an employer, the court or the comptroller shall, among other things, take the following matters into account, that is to say—

    (a) the nature of the employee's duties, his remuneration and the other advantages he derives or has derived from his employment or has derived in relation to the invention under this Act;

    (b) the effort and skill which the employee has devoted to making the invention;

    (c) the effort and skill which any other person has devoted to making the invention jointly with the employee concerned, and the advice and other assistance contributed by any other employee who is not a joint inventor of the invention; and

    (d) the contribution made by the employer to the making, developing and working of the invention by the provision of advice, facilities and other assistance, by the provision of opportunities and by his managerial and commercial skill and activities.

(5) In determining the fair share of the benefit to be secured for an employee in respect of an invention which originally belonged to him, the court or the comptroller shall, among other things, take the following matters into account, that is to say—

    (a) any conditions in a licence or licences granted under this Act or otherwise in respect of the invention or the patent for it;

    (b) the extent to which the invention was made jointly by the employee with any other person; and

    (c) the contribution made by the employer to the making, developing and working of the invention as mentioned in subsection (4)(d) above.

(6) Any order for the payment of compensation under section 40 above may be an order for the payment of a lump sum or for periodical payment, or both.

(7) Without prejudice to section 32 of the Interpretation Act 1889 (which provides that a statutory power may in general be exercised from time to time), the refusal of the court or the

comptroller to make any such order on an application made by an employee under section 40 above shall not prevent a further application being made under that section by him or any successor in title of his.

(8) Where the court or the comptroller has made any such order, the court or he may on the application of either the employer or the employee vary or discharge it or suspend any provision of the order and revive any provision so suspended, and section 40(5) above shall apply to the application as it applies to an application under that section.

. . .

42   Enforceability of contracts relating to employees' inventions

(1) This section applies to any contract (whenever made) relating to inventions made by an employee, being a contract entered into by him—

(a) with the employer (alone or with another); or

(b) with some other person at the request of the employer or in pursuance of the employee's contract of employment.

(2) Any term in a contract to which this section applies which diminishes the employee's rights in inventions of any description made by him after the appointed day and the date of the contract, or in or under patents for those inventions or applications for such patents, shall be unenforceable against him to the extent that it diminishes his rights in an invention of that description so made, or in or under a patent for such an invention or an application for any such patent.

(3) Subsection (2) above shall not be construed as derogating from any duty of confidentiality owed to his employer by an employee by virtue of any rule of law or otherwise.

(4) This section applies to any arrangement made with a Crown employee by or on behalf of the Crown as his employer as it applies to any contract made between an employee and an employer other than the Crown, and for the purposes of this section 'Crown employee' means a person employed under or for the purposes of a government department or any officer or body exercising on behalf of the Crown functions conferred by any enactment or a person serving in the naval, military or air forces of the Crown.

43   Supplementary

(1) Sections 39 to 42 above shall not apply to an invention made by an employee unless at the time he made the invention one of the following conditions was satisfied in his case, that is to say—

(a) he was mainly employed in the United Kingdom; or

(b) he was not mainly employed anywhere or his place of employment could not be determined, but his employer had a place of business in the United Kingdom to which the employee was attached, whether or not he was also attached elsewhere.

(3) In sections 39 to 42 above and this section, except so far as the context otherwise requires, references to the making of an invention by an employee are references to his making it alone or jointly with any other person, but do not include references to his merely contributing advice or other assistance in the making of an invention by another employee.

(4) Any references in sections 39 to 42 above to a patent and to a patent being granted are respectively references to a patent or other protection and to its being granted whether under the law of the United Kingdom or the law in force in any other country or under any treaty or international convention.

(5) For the purposes of sections 40 and 41 above the benefit derived or expected to be derived by an employer from an invention or patent shall, where he dies before any award is made under section 40 above in respect of it, include any benefit derived or expected to be derived from it by his personal representatives or by any person in whom it was vested by their assent.

(5A) For the purposes of sections 40 and 41 above the benefit derived or expected to be derived by an employer from an invention shall not include any benefit derived or expected to be derived from the invention after the patent for it has expired or has been surrendered or revoked.

(6) Where an employee dies before an award is made under section 40 above in respect of a patented invention made by him, his personal representatives or their successors in title may exercise

his right to make or proceed with an application for compensation under subsection (1) or (2) of that section.

(7) In sections 40 and 41 above and this section 'benefit' means benefit in money or money's worth.

(8) Section 533 of the Income and Corporation Taxes Act 1970 (definition of connected persons) shall apply for determining for the purposes of section 41(2) above whether one person is connected with another as it applies for determining that question for the purposes of the Tax Acts.

Licences of right and compulsory licences

46 Patentee's application for entry in register that licences are available as of right

(1) At any time after the grant of a patent its proprietor may apply to the comptroller for an entry to be made in the register to the effect that licences under the patent are to be available as of right.

(2) Where such an application is made, the comptroller shall give notice of the application to any person registered as having a right in or under the patent and, if satisfied that the proprietor of the patent is not precluded by contract from granting licences under the patent, shall make the entry.

(3) Where such an entry is made in respect of a patent—

    (a) any person shall, at any time after the entry is made, be entitled as of right to a licence under the patent on such terms as may be settled by agreement or, in default of agreement, by the comptroller on the application of the proprietor of the patent or the person requiring the licence;

    (b) the comptroller may, on the application of the holder of any licence granted under the patent before the entry was made, order the licence to be exchanged for a licence of right on terms so settled;

    (c) if in proceedings for infringement of the patent (otherwise than by the importation of any article from a country which is not a member State of the European Union) the defendant or defender undertakes to take a licence on such terms, no injunction or interdict shall be granted against him and the amount (if any) recoverable against him by way of damages shall not exceed double the amount which would have been payable by him as licensee if such a licence on those terms had been granted before the earliest infringement;

    (d) if the expiry date in relation to a renewal fee falls after the date of the entry, that fee shall be half the fee which would be payable had the entry not been made.

(3A) An undertaking under subsection (3)(c) above may be given at any time before final order in the proceedings, without any admission of liability.

(3B) For the purposes of subsection (3)(d) above the expiry date in relation to a renewal fee is the day at the end of which, by virtue of section 25(3) above, the patent in question ceases to have effect if that fee is not paid.

(4) The licensee under a licence of right may (unless, in the case of a licence the terms of which are settled by agreement, the licence otherwise expressly provides) request the proprietor of the patent to take proceedings to prevent any infringement of the patent; and if the proprietor refuses or neglects to do so within two months after being so requested, the licensee may institute proceedings for the infringement in his own name as if he were proprietor, making the proprietor a defendant or defender.

(5) A proprietor so added as defendant or defender shall not be liable for any costs or expenses unless he enters an appearance and takes part in the proceedings.

47 Cancellation of entry made under s. 46

(1) At any time after an entry has been made under section 46 above in respect of a patent, the proprietor of the patent may apply to the comptroller for cancellation of the entry.

. . .

48   Compulsory licences: general

(1) At any time after the expiration of three years, or of such other period as may be prescribed, from the date of the grant of a patent, any person may apply to the comptroller on one or more of the relevant grounds—

(a) for a licence under the patent;

(b) for an entry to be made in the register to the effect that licences under the patent are to be available as of right; or

(c) where the applicant is a government department, for the grant to any person specified in the application of a licence under the patent.

(2) Subject to sections 48A and 48B below, if he is satisfied that any of the relevant grounds are established, the comptroller may—

(a) where the application is under subsection (1)(a) above, order the grant of a licence to the applicant on such terms as the comptroller thinks fit;

(b) where the application is under subsection (1)(b) above, make such an entry as is there mentioned;

(c) where the application is under subsection (1)(c) above, order the grant of a licence to the person specified in the application on such terms as the comptroller thinks fit.

(3) An application may be made under this section in respect of a patent even though the applicant is already the holder of a licence under the patent; and no person shall be estopped or barred from alleging any of the matters specified in the relevant grounds by reason of any admission made by him, whether in such a licence or otherwise, or by reason of his having accepted a licence.

(4) In this section 'the relevant grounds' means—

(a) in the case of an application made in respect of a patent whose proprietor is a WTO proprietor, the grounds set out in section 48A(1) below;

(b) in any other case, the grounds set out in section 48B(1) below.

(5) A proprietor is a WTO proprietor for the purposes of this section and sections 48A, 48B, 50 and 52 below if—

(a) he is a national of, or is domiciled in, a country which is a member of the World Trade Organisation; or

(b) he has a real and effective industrial or commercial establishment in such a country.

(6) A rule prescribing any such other period under subsection (1) above shall not be made unless a draft of the rule has been laid before, and approved by resolution of, each House of Parliament.

48A   Compulsory licences: WTO proprietors

(1) In the case of an application made under section 48 above in respect of a patent whose proprietor is a WTO proprietor, the relevant grounds are—

(a) where the patented invention is a product, that a demand in the United Kingdom for that product is not being met on reasonable terms;

(b) that by reason of the refusal of the proprietor of the patent concerned to grant a licence or licences on reasonable terms—

(i)   the exploitation in the United Kingdom of any other patented invention which involves an important technical advance of considerable economic significance in relation to the invention for which the patent concerned was granted is prevented or hindered, or

(ii) the establishment or development of commercial or industrial activities in the United Kingdom is unfairly prejudiced;

(c) that by reason of conditions imposed by the proprietor of the patent concerned on the grant of licences under the patent, or on the disposal or use of the patented product or on the use of the patented process, the manufacture, use or disposal of materials not protected by the patent, or the establishment or development of commercial or industrial activities in the United Kingdom, is unfairly prejudiced.

(2) No order or entry shall be made under section 48 above in respect of a patent whose proprietor is a WTO proprietor unless—

(a) the applicant has made efforts to obtain a licence from the proprietor on reasonable commercial terms and conditions; and

(b) his efforts have not been successful within a reasonable period.

(3) No order or entry shall be so made if the patented invention is in the field of semiconductor technology.

(4) No order or entry shall be made under section 48 above in respect of a patent on the ground mentioned in subsection (1)(b)(i) above unless the comptroller is satisfied that the proprietor of the patent for the other invention is able and willing to grant the proprietor of the patent concerned and his licensees a licence under the patent for the other invention on reasonable terms.

(5) A licence granted in pursuance of an order or entry so made shall not be assigned except to a person to whom the patent for the other invention is also assigned.

(6) A licence granted in pursuance of an order or entry made under section 48 above in respect of a patent whose proprietor is a WTO proprietor—

(a) shall not be exclusive;

(b) shall not be assigned except to a person to whom there is also assigned the part of the enterprise that enjoys the use of the patented invention, or the part of the goodwill that belongs to that part;

(c) shall be predominantly for the supply of the market in the United Kingdom;

(d) shall include conditions entitling the proprietor of the patent concerned to remuneration adequate in the circumstances of the case, taking into account the economic value of the licence; and

(e) shall be limited in scope and in duration to the purpose for which the licence was granted.

48B   Compulsory licences: other cases

(1) In the case of an application made under section 48 above in respect of a patent whose proprietor is not a WTO proprietor, the relevant grounds are—

(a) where the patented invention is capable of being commercially worked in the United Kingdom, that it is not being so worked or is not being so worked to the fullest extent that is reasonably practicable;

(b) where the patented invention is a product, that a demand for the product in the United Kingdom—

(i)   is not being met on reasonable terms, or

(ii) is being met to a substantial extent by importation from a country which is not a member State;

(c) where the patented invention is capable of being commercially worked in the United Kingdom, that it is being prevented or hindered from being so worked—

(i)   where the invention is a product, by the importation of the product from a country which is not a member State,

(ii) where the invention is a process, by the importation from such a country of a product obtained directly by means of the process or to which the process has been applied;

(d) that by reason of the refusal of the proprietor of the patent to grant a licence or licences on reasonable terms—

(i)   a market for the export of any patented product made in the United Kingdom is not being supplied, or

(ii)   the working or efficient working in the United Kingdom of any other patented invention which makes a substantial contribution to the art is prevented or hindered, or

(iii) the establishment or development of commercial or industrial activities in the United Kingdom is unfairly prejudiced;

(e) that by reason of conditions imposed by the proprietor of the patent on the grant of licences under the patent, or on the disposal or use of the patented product or on the use of the patented process, the manufacture, use or disposal of materials not protected by the patent, or the establishment or development of commercial or industrial activities in the United Kingdom, is unfairly prejudiced.

(2) Where—

(a) an application is made on the ground that the patented invention is not being commercially worked in the United Kingdom or is not being so worked to the fullest extent that is reasonably practicable; and

(b) it appears to the comptroller that the time which has elapsed since the publication in the journal of a notice of the grant of the patent has for any reason been insufficient to enable the invention to be so worked,

he may by order adjourn the application for such period as will in his opinion give sufficient time for the invention to be so worked.

(3) No order or entry shall be made under section 48 above in respect of a patent on the ground mentioned in subsection (1)(a) above if—

(a) the patented invention is being commercially worked in a country which is a member State; and

(b) demand in the United Kingdom is being met by importation from that country.

(4) No entry shall be made in the register under section 48 above on the ground mentioned in subsection (1)(d)(i) above, and any licence granted under section 48 above on that ground shall contain such provisions as appear to the comptroller to be expedient for restricting the countries in which any product concerned may be disposed of or used by the licensee.

(5) No order or entry shall be made under section 48 above in respect of a patent on the ground mentioned in subsection (1)(d)(ii) above unless the comptroller is satisfied that the proprietor of the patent for the other invention is able and willing to grant to the proprietor of the patent concerned and his licensees a licence under the patent for the other invention on reasonable terms.

49 Provisions about licences under s. 48

(1) Where the comptroller is satisfied, on an application made under section 48 above in respect of a patent, that the manufacture, use or disposal of materials not protected by the patent is unfairly prejudiced by reason of conditions imposed by the proprietor of the patent on the grant of licences under the patent, or on the disposal or use of the patented product or the use of the patented process, he may (subject to the provisions of that section) order the grant of licences under the patent to such customers of the applicant as he thinks fit as well as to the applicant.

(2) Where an application under section 48 above is made in respect of a patent by a person who holds a licence under the patent, the comptroller—

(a) may, if he orders the grant of a licence to the applicant, order the existing licence to be cancelled, or

(b) may, instead of ordering the grant of a licence to the applicant, order the existing licence to be amended.

(3) (repealed)

(4) Section 46(4) and (5) above shall apply to a licence granted in pursuance of an order under section 48 above and to a licence granted by virtue of an entry under that section as it applies to a licence granted by virtue of an entry under section 46 above.

50 Exercise of powers on applications under s. 48

(1) The powers of the comptroller on an application under section 48 above in respect of a patent whose proprietor is not a WTO proprietor shall be exercised with a view to securing the following general purposes:—

(a) that inventions which can be worked on a commercial scale in the United Kingdom and which should in the public interest be so worked shall be worked there without undue delay and to the fullest extent that is reasonably practicable;

(b) that the inventor or other person beneficially entitled to a patent shall receive reasonable remuneration having regard to the nature of the invention;

(c) that the interests of any person for the time being working or developing an invention in the United Kingdom under the protection of a patent shall not be unfairly prejudiced.

(2) Subject to subsection (1) above, the comptroller shall, in determining whether to make an order or entry in pursuance of any application under section 48 above, take account of the following matters, that is to say—

(a) the nature of the invention, the time which has elapsed since the publication in the journal of a notice of the grant of the patent and the measures already taken by the proprietor of the patent or any licensee to make full use of the invention;

(b) the ability of any person to whom a licence would be granted under the order concerned to work the invention to the public advantage; and

(c) the risks to be undertaken by that person in providing capital and working the invention if the application for an order is granted,

but shall not be required to take account of matters subsequent to the making of the application.

50A Powers exercisable following merger and market investigations or in respect of retained EU merger commitments

(1) Subsection (2) below applies where—

(a) section 41(2), 55(2), 66(6), 75(2), 83(2), 84C(2), 138(2), 147(2), 147A(2) or 160(2) of, or paragraph 5(2) or 10(2) of Schedule 7 to, the Enterprise Act 2002 (powers to take remedial action following merger or market investigations, or in respect of retained EU merger commitments) applies;

(b) the Competition and Markets Authority or (as the case may be) the Secretary of State considers that it would be appropriate to make an application under this section for the purpose of remedying, mitigating or preventing a matter which cannot be dealt with under the enactment concerned; and

(c) the matter concerned involves—

(i) conditions in licences granted under a patent by its proprietor restricting the use of the invention by the licensee or the right of the proprietor to grant other licences; or

(ii) a refusal by the proprietor of a patent to grant licences on reasonable terms.

(2) The Competition and Markets Authority or (as the case may be) the Secretary of State may apply to the comptroller to take action under this section.

. . .

51 Powers exercisable in consequence of report of Competition and Markets Authority

(1) Where a report of the Competition and Markets Authority has been laid before Parliament containing conclusions to the effect—

(c) on a competition reference, that a person was engaged in an anti-competitive practice which operated or may be expected to operate against the public interest, or

(d) on a reference under section 11 of the Competition Act 1980 (reference of public bodies and certain other persons), that a person is pursuing a course of conduct which operates against the public interest,

the appropriate Minister or Ministers may apply to the comptroller to take action under this section.

. . .

52 Opposition, appeal and arbitration

(1) The proprietor of the patent concerned or any other person wishing to oppose an application under sections 48 to 51 above may, in accordance with rules, give to the comptroller notice of opposition; and the comptroller shall consider the opposition in deciding whether to grant the application.

. . .

53 Compulsory licences; supplementary provisions

. . .

(4) An entry made in the register under sections 48 to 51 above shall for all purposes have the same effect as an entry made under section 46 above.

(5) No order or entry shall be made in pursuance of an application under sections 48 to 51 above which would be at variance with any treaty or international convention to which the United Kingdom is a party.

. . .

Use of patented inventions for services of the Crown

55   Use of patented inventions for services of the Crown

(1) Notwithstanding anything in this Act, any government department and any person author-ised in writing by a government department may, for the services of the Crown and in accordance with this section, do any of the following acts in the United Kingdom in relation to a patented invention without the consent of the proprietor of the patent, that is to say—

   (a) where the invention is a product, may—

     (i)   make, use, import or keep the product, or sell or offer to sell it where to do so would be incidental or ancillary to making, using, importing or keeping it; or

     (ii) in any event, sell or offer to sell it for foreign defence purposes or for the production or supply of specified drugs and medicines, or dispose or offer to dispose of it (other-wise than by selling it) for any purpose whatever;

   (b) where the invention is a process, may use it or do in relation to any product obtained dir-ectly by means of the process anything mentioned in paragraph (a) above;

   (c) without prejudice to the foregoing, where the invention or any product obtained directly by means of the invention is a specified drug or medicine, may sell or offer to sell the drug or medicine;

   (d) may supply or offer to supply to any person any of the means, relating to an essential element of the invention, for putting the invention into effect;

   (e) may dispose or offer to dispose of anything which was made, used, imported or kept in the exercise of the powers conferred by this section and which is no longer required for the purpose for which it was made, used, imported or kept (as the case may be),

and anything done by virtue of this subsection shall not amount to an infringement of the patent concerned.

. . .

56   Interpretation, etc., of provisions about Crown use

(1) Any reference in section 55 above to a patented invention, in relation to any time, is a refer-ence to an invention for which a patent has before that time been, or is subsequently, granted.

(2) In this Act, except so far as the context otherwise requires, 'the services of the Crown' includes—

   (a) the supply of anything for foreign defence purposes;

   (b) the production or supply of specified drugs and medicines; and

   (c) such purposes relating to the production or use of atomic energy or research into matters connected therewith as the Secretary of State thinks necessary or expedient;

and 'use for the services of the Crown' shall be construed accordingly.

. . .

57   Rights of third parties in respect of Crown use

(1) In relation to—

   (a) any use made for the services of the Crown of an invention by a government department, or a person authorised by a government department, by virtue of section 55 above, or

   (b) anything done for the services of the Crown to the order of a government department by the proprietor of a patent in respect of a patented invention or by the proprietor of an ap-plication in respect of an invention for which an application for a patent has been filed and is still pending,

the provisions of any licence, assignment, assignation or agreement to which this subsection applies shall be of no effect so far as those provisions restrict or regulate the working of the invention, or the use of any model, document or information relating to it, or provide for the making of payments in respect of, or calculated by reference to, such working or use; and the reproduction or publication of any model or document in connection with the said working or use shall not be deemed to be an infringement of any copyright or design right subsisting in the model or document or of any topography right.

(2) Subsection (1) above applies to a licence, assignment, assignation or agreement which is made, whether before or after the appointed day, between (on the one hand) any person who is a proprietor of or an application for the patent, or anyone who derives title from any such person or from whom such person derives title, and (on the other hand) any person whatever other than a government department.

. . .

57A   Compensation for loss of profit

(1) Where use is made of an invention for the services of the Crown, the government department concerned shall pay—

(a) to the proprietor of the patent, or

(b) if there is an exclusive licence in force in respect of the patent, to the exclusive licensee,

compensation for any loss resulting from his not being awarded a contract to supply the patented product or, as the case may be, to perform the patented process or supply a thing made by means of the patented process.

. . .

(5) The amount payable shall, if not agreed between the proprietor or licensee and the government department concerned with the approval of the Treasury, be determined by the court on a reference under section 58, and is in addition to any amount payable under section 55 or 57.

. . .

58   References of disputes as to Crown use

(1) Any dispute as to—

(a) the exercise by a government department, or a person authorised by a government department, of the powers conferred by section 55 above,

(b) terms for the use of an invention for the services of the Crown under that section,

(c) the right of any person to receive any part of a payment made in pursuance of subsection (4) of that section, or

(d) the right of any person to receive a payment under section 57A,

may be referred to the court by either party to the dispute after a patent has been granted for the invention.

(2) If in such proceedings any question arises whether an invention has been recorded or tried as mentioned in section 55 above, and the disclosure of any document recording the invention, or of any evidence of the trial thereof, would in the opinion of the department be prejudicial to the public interest, the disclosure may be made confidentially to the other party's legal representative or to an independent expert mutually agreed upon.

. . .

Infringement

60   Meaning of infringement

(1) Subject to the provisions of this section, a person infringes a patent for an invention if, but only if, while the patent is in force, he does any of the following things in the United Kingdom in relation to the invention without the consent of the proprietor of the patent, that is to say—

(a) where the invention is a product, he makes, disposes of, offers to dispose of, uses or imports the product or keeps it whether for disposal or otherwise;

(b) where the invention is a process, he uses the process or he offers it for use in the United Kingdom when he knows, or it is obvious to a reasonable person in the circumstances, that its use there without the consent of the proprietor would be an infringement of the patent;

(c) where the invention is a process, he disposes of, offers to dispose of, uses or imports any product obtained directly by means of that process or keeps any such product whether for disposal or otherwise.

(2) Subject to the following provisions of this section, a person (other than the proprietor of the patent) also infringes a patent for an invention if, while the patent is in force and without the consent of the proprietor, he supplies or offers to supply in the United Kingdom a person other than a licensee or other person entitled to work the invention with any of the means, relating to an essential element of the invention, for putting the invention into effect when he knows, or it is obvious to a reasonable person in the circumstances, that those means are suitable for putting, and are intended to put, the invention into effect in the United Kingdom.

(3) Subsection (2) above shall not apply to the supply or offer of a staple commercial product unless the supply or the offer is made for the purpose of inducing the person supplied or, as the case may be, the person to whom the offer is made to do an act which constitutes an infringement of the patent by virtue of subsection (1) above.

. . .

(5) An act which, apart from this subsection, would constitute an infringement of a patent for an invention shall not do so if—

(a) it is done privately and for purposes which are not commercial;

(b) it is done for experimental purposes relating to the subject-matter of the invention;

(c) it consists of the extemporaneous preparation in a pharmacy of a medicine for an individual in accordance with a prescription given by a registered medical or dental practitioner or consists of dealing with a medicine so prepared;

(d) it consists of the use, exclusively for the needs of a relevant ship, of a product or process in the body of such a ship or in its machinery, tackle, apparatus or other accessories, in a case where the ship has temporarily or accidentally entered the internal or territorial waters of the United Kingdom;

(e) it consists of the use of a product or process in the body or operation of a relevant aircraft, hovercraft or vehicle which has temporarily or accidentally entered or is crossing the United Kingdom (including the air space above it and its territorial waters) or the use of accessories for such a relevant aircraft, hovercraft or vehicle;

(f) it consists of the use of an exempted aircraft which has lawfully entered or is lawfully crossing the United Kingdom as aforesaid or of the importation into the United Kingdom, or the use or storage there, of any part or accessory for such an aircraft;

(g) it consists of the use by a farmer of the product of his harvest for propagation or multiplication by him on his own holding, where there has been a sale of plant propagating material to the farmer by the proprietor of the patent or with his consent for agricultural use;

(h) it consists of the use of an animal or animal reproductive material by a farmer for an agricultural purpose following a sale to the farmer, by the proprietor of the patent or with his consent, of breeding stock or other animal reproductive material which constitutes or contains the patented invention,

(i) it consists of—

(i) an act done in conducting a study, test or trial which is necessary for and is conducted with a view to the application of paragraphs 1 to 5 of article 13 of Directive 2001/82/EC or paragraphs 1 to 4 of article 10 of Directive 2001/83/EC, or

(ii) any other act which is required for the purpose of the application of those paragraphs.

(6) For the purposes of subsection (2) above a person who does an act in relation to an invention which is prevented only by virtue of paragraph (a), (b) or (c) of subsection (5) above from constituting an infringement of a patent for the invention shall not be treated as a person entitled to work the invention, but—

(a) the reference in that subsection to a person entitled to work an invention includes a reference to a person so entitled by virtue of section 55 above, and

(b) a person who by virtue of section 20B(4) or (5) above or section 28A(4) or (5) above or section 64 below or section 117A(4) or (5) below is entitled to do an act in relation to the invention without it constituting such an infringement shall, so far as concerns that act, be treated as a person entitled to work the invention.

(6A) Schedule A1 contains—

(a) provisions restricting the circumstances in which subsection (5)(g) applies; and

(b) provisions which apply where an act would constitute an infringement of a patent but for subsection (5)(g).

(6B) For the purposes of subsection (5)(h), use for an agricultural purpose—

(a) includes making an animal or animal reproductive material available for the purposes of pursuing the farmer's agricultural activity; but

(b) does not include sale within the framework, or for the purposes, of a commercial reproduction activity.

(6C) In paragraphs (g) and (h) of subsection (5) 'sale' includes any other form of commercialisation.

(6D) For the purposes of subsection (5)(b), anything done in or for the purposes of a medicinal product assessment which would otherwise constitute an infringement of a patent for an invention is to be regarded as done for experimental purposes relating to the subject-matter of the invention.

(6E) In subsection (6D), 'medicinal product assessment' means any testing, course of testing or other activity undertaken with a view to providing data for any of the following purposes—

(a) obtaining or varying an authorisation to sell or supply, or offer to sell or supply, a medicinal product (whether in the United Kingdom or elsewhere);

(b) complying with any regulatory requirement imposed (whether in the United Kingdom or elsewhere) in relation to such an authorisation;

(c) enabling a government or public authority (whether in the United Kingdom or elsewhere), or a person (whether in the United Kingdom or elsewhere) with functions of—

(i) providing health care on behalf of such a government or public authority, or

(ii) providing advice to, or on behalf of, such a government or public authority about the provision of health care,

to carry out an assessment of suitability of a medicinal product for human use for the purpose of determining whether to use it, or recommend its use, in the provision of health care.

(6F) In subsection (6E) and this subsection—

'medicinal product' means a medicinal product for human use or a veterinary medicinal product;

'medicinal product for human use' has the meaning given by article 1 of Directive 2001/83/EC;

'veterinary medicinal product' has the meaning given by article 1 of Directive 2001/82/EC.

(6G) Nothing in subsections (6D) to (6F) is to be read as affecting the application of subsection (5)(b) in relation to any act of a kind not falling within subsection (6D).

(7) In this section—

'relevant ship' and 'relevant aircraft, hovercraft or vehicle' mean respectively a ship and an aircraft, hovercraft or vehicle registered in, or belonging to, any country, other than the United Kingdom, which is a party to the Convention for the Protection of Industrial Property signed at Paris on 20 March 1883 or which is a member of the World Trade Organisation; and

'exempted aircraft' means an aircraft to which section 89 of the Civil Aviation Act 1982 (aircraft exempted from seizure in respect of patent claims) applies;

'Directive 2001/82/EC' means Directive 2001/82/EC of the European Parliament and of the Council on the Community code relating to veterinary medicinal products as amended by Directive 2004/28/EC of the European Parliament and of the Council;

'Directive 2001/83/EC' means Directive 2001/83/EC of the European Parliament and of the Council of the Community code relating to medicinal products for human use, as amended by Directive 2002/98/EC of the European Parliament and of the Council, by Commission Directive 2003/63/EC and by Directives 2004/24/EC and 2004/27/EC of the European Parliament and of the Council.

61   Proceedings for infringement of patent

(1) Subject to the following provisions of this Part of this Act, civil proceedings may be brought in the court by the proprietor of a patent in respect of any act alleged to infringe the patent and (without prejudice to any other jurisdiction of the court) in those proceedings a claim may be made—

   (a) for an injunction or interdict restraining the defendant or defender from any apprehended act of infringement;

   (b) for an order for him to deliver up or destroy any patented product in relation to which the patent is infringed or any article in which that product is inextricably comprised;

   (c) for damages in respect of the infringement;

   (d) for an account of the profits derived by him from the infringement;

   (e) for a declaration or declarator that the patent is valid and has been infringed by him.

(2) The court shall not, in respect of the same infringement, both award the proprietor of a patent damages and order that he shall be given an account of the profits.

(3) The proprietor of a patent and any other person may by agreement with each other refer to the comptroller the question whether that other person has infringed the patent and on the reference the proprietor of the patent may make any claim mentioned in subsection (1)(c) or (e) above.

(4) Except so far as the context requires, in the following provisions of this Act—

   (a) any reference to proceedings for infringement and the bringing of such proceedings includes a reference to a reference under subsection (3) above and the making of such a reference;

   (b) any reference to a claimant or pursuer includes a reference to the proprietor of the patent; and

   (c) any reference to a defendant or defender includes a reference to any other party to the reference.

(5) If it appears to the comptroller on a reference under subsection (3) above that the question referred to him would more properly be determined by the court, he may decline to deal with it and the court shall have jurisdiction to determine the question as if the reference were proceedings brought in the court.

(6) Subject to the following provisions of this part of this Act, in determining whether or not to grant any kind of relief claimed under this section and the extent of the relief granted the court or the comptroller shall apply the principles applied by the court in relation to that kind of relief immediately before the appointed day.

(7) If the comptroller awards any sum by way of damages on a reference under subsection (3) above, then—

   (a) in England and Wales, the sum shall be recoverable, if the county court so orders, under section 85 of the County Courts Act 1984 or otherwise as if it were payable under an order of that court;

   (b) in Scotland, payment of the sum may be enforced in like manner as an extract registered decree arbitral bearing a warrant for execution issued by the sheriff court of any sheriffdom in Scotland;

   (c) in Northern Ireland, payment of the sum may be enforced as if it were a money judgment.

62   Restrictions on recovery of damages for infringement

(1) In proceedings for infringement of a patent damages shall not be awarded, and no order shall be made for an account of profits, against a defendant or defender who proves that at the date of the infringement he was not aware, and had no reasonable grounds for supposing, that the patent existed; and a person shall not be taken to have been so aware or to have had reasonable grounds for so supposing by reason only of the application to a product of the word 'patent' or 'patented', or any word or words expressing or implying that a patent has been obtained for the product, unless the number of the patent or a relevant internet link accompanied the word or words in question.

(1A) The reference in subsection (1) to a relevant internet link is a reference to an address of a posting on the internet—

   (a) which is accessible to the public free of charge, and

   (b) which clearly associates the product with the number of the patent.

(2) In proceedings for infringement of a patent the court or the comptroller may, if it or he thinks fit, refuse to award any damages or make any such order in respect of an infringement committed during the further period specified in section 25(4) above, but before the payment of the renewal fee and any additional fee prescribed for the purposes of that subsection.

(3) Where an amendment of the specification of a patent has been allowed under any of the provisions of this Act, the court or the comptroller shall, when awarding damages or making an order for an account of profits in proceedings for an infringement of the patent committed before the decision to allow the amendment, take into account the following—

(a) whether at the date of infringement the defendant or defender knew, or had reasonable grounds to know, that he was infringing the patent;

(b) whether the specification of the patent as published was framed in good faith and with reasonable skill and knowledge;

(c) whether the proceedings are brought in good faith.

63   Relief for infringement of partially valid patent

(1) If the validity of a patent is put in issue in proceedings for infringement of the patent and it is found that the patent is only partially valid, the court or the comptroller may, subject to subsection (2) below, grant relief in respect of that part of the patent which is found to be valid and infringed.

(2) Where in any such proceedings it is found that a patent is only partially valid, the court or the comptroller shall, when awarding damages, costs or expenses or making an order for an account of profits, take into account the following—

(a) whether at the date of the infringement the defendant or defender knew, or had reasonable grounds to know, that he was infringing the patent;

(b) whether the specification of the patent was framed in good faith and with reasonable skill and knowledge;

(c) whether the proceedings are brought in good faith;

and any relief granted shall be subject to the discretion of the court or the comptroller as to costs or expenses and as to the date from which the damages or an account should be reckoned.

(3) As a condition of relief under this section the court or the comptroller may direct that the specification of the patent shall be amended to its or his satisfaction upon an application made for the purpose under section 75 below, and an application may be so made accordingly, whether or not all other issues in the proceedings have been determined.

(4) The court or the comptroller may also grant relief under this section in the case of a European patent (UK) on condition that the claims of the patent are limited to its or his satisfaction by the European Patent Office at the request of the proprietor.

64   Right to continue use begun before priority date

(1) Where a patent is granted for an invention, a person who in the United Kingdom before the priority date of the invention—

(a) does in good faith an act which would constitute an infringement of the patent if it were in force, or

(b) makes in good faith effective and serious preparations to do such an act,

has the right to continue to do the act or, as the case may be, to do the act, notwithstanding the grant of the patent; but this right does not extend to granting a licence to another person to do the act.

(2) If the act was done, or the preparations were made, in the course of a business, the person entitled to the right conferred by subsection (1) may—

(a) authorise the doing of that act by any partners of his for the time being in that business, and

(b) assign that right, or transmit it on death (or in the case of a body corporate on its dissolution), to any person who acquires that part of the business in the course of which the act was done or the preparations were made.

(3) Where a product is disposed of to another in exercise of the rights conferred by subsection (1) or (2), that other and any person claiming through him may deal with the product in the same way as if it had been disposed of by the registered proprietor of the patent.

65 Certificate of contested validity of patent

(1) If in any proceedings before the court or the comptroller the validity of a patent to any extent is contested and that patent is found by the court or the comptroller to be wholly or partially valid, the court or the comptroller may certify the finding and the fact that the validity of the patent was so contested.

(2) Where a certificate is granted under this section, then, if in any subsequent proceedings before the court or the comptroller for infringement of the patent concerned or for revocation of the patent a final order or judgment or interlocutor is made or given in favour of the party relying on the validity of the patent as found in the earlier proceedings, that party shall, unless the court or the comptroller otherwise directs, be entitled to his costs or expenses as between solicitor and own client (other than the costs or expenses of any appeal in the subsequent proceedings).

66 Proceedings for infringement by a co-owner

(1) In the application of section 60 above to a patent of which there are two or more joint proprietors the reference to the proprietor shall be construed—

(a) in relation to any act, as a reference to that proprietor or those proprietors who, by virtue of section 36 above or any agreement referred to in that section, is or are entitled to do that act without its amounting to an infringement; and

(b) in relation to any consent, as a reference to that proprietor or those proprietors who, by virtue of section 36 above or any such agreement, is or are the proper person or persons to give the requisite consent.

(2) One of two or more joint proprietors of a patent may without the concurrence of the others bring proceedings in respect of an act alleged to infringe the patent, but shall not do so unless the others are made parties to the proceedings; but any of the others made a defendant or defender shall not be liable for any costs or expenses unless he enters an appearance and takes part in the proceedings.

67 Proceedings for infringement by exclusive licensee

(1) Subject to the provisions of this section, the holder of an exclusive licence under a patent shall have the same right as the proprietor of the patent to bring proceedings in respect of any infringement of the patent committed after the date of the licence; and references to the proprietor of the patent in the provisions of this Act relating to infringement shall be construed accordingly.

(2) In awarding damages or granting any other relief in any such proceedings the court or the comptroller shall take into consideration any loss suffered or likely to be suffered by the exclusive licensee as such as a result of the infringement, or, as the case may be, the profits derived from the infringement, so far as it constitutes an infringement of the rights of the exclusive licensee as such.

(3) In any proceedings taken by an exclusive licensee by virtue of this section the proprietor of the patent shall be made a party to the proceedings, but if made a defendant or defender shall not be liable for any costs or expenses unless he enters an appearance and takes part in the proceedings.

68 Effect of non-registration on infringement proceedings

Where by virtue of a transaction, instrument or event to which section 33 above applies a person becomes the proprietor or one of the proprietors or an exclusive licensee of a patent and the patent is subsequently infringed, in proceedings for such an infringement, the court or comptroller shall not award him costs or expenses before the transaction, instrument or event is registered unless—

(a) the transaction, instrument or event is registered within the period of six months beginning with its date; or

(b) the court or the comptroller is satisfied that it was not practicable to register the transaction, instrument or event before the end of that period and that it was registered as soon as practicable thereafter.

69 Infringement of rights conferred by publication of application

(1) Where an application for a patent for an invention is published, then, subject to subsections (2) and (3) below, the applicant shall have, as from the publication and until the grant of the patent, the same right as he would have had, if the patent had been granted on the date of the publication of

the application, to bring proceedings in the court or before the comptroller for damages in respect of any act which would have infringed the patent; and (subject to subsections (2) and (3) below) references in sections 60 to 62 and 66 to 68 above to a patent and the proprietor of a patent shall be respectively construed as including references to any such application and the applicant, and references to a patent being in force, being granted, being valid or existing shall be construed accordingly.

(2) The applicant shall be entitled to bring proceedings by virtue of this section in respect of any act only—

    (a) after the patent has been granted; and

    (b) if the act would, if the patent had been granted on the date of the publication of the application, have infringed not only the patent, but also the claims (as interpreted by the description and any drawings referred to in the description or claims) in the form in which they were contained in the application immediately before the preparations for its publication were completed by the Patent Office.

(3) Section 62(2) and (3) above shall not apply to an infringement of the rights conferred by this section, but in considering the amount of any damages for such an infringement, the court or the comptroller shall consider whether or not it would have been reasonable to expect, from a consideration of the application as published under section 16 above, that a patent would be granted conferring on the proprietor of the patent protection from an act of the same description as that found to infringe those rights, and if the court or the comptroller finds that it would not have been reasonable, it or he shall reduce the damages to such an amount as it or he thinks just.

Unjustified Threats

70 Threats of infringement proceedings

(1) A communication contains a 'threat of infringement proceedings' if a reasonable person in the position of a recipient would understand from the communication that—

    (a) a patent exists, and

    (b) a person intends to bring proceedings (whether in a court in the United Kingdom or elsewhere) against another person for infringement of the patent by—

        (i) an act done in the United Kingdom, or

        (ii) an act which, if done, would be done in the United Kingdom.

(2) References in this section and in section 70C to a 'recipient' include, in the case of a communication directed to the public or a section of the public, references to a person to whom the communication is directed.

70A Actionable threats

(1) Subject to subsections (2) to (5), a threat of infringement proceedings made by any person is actionable by any person aggrieved by the threat.

(2) A threat of infringement proceedings is not actionable if the infringement is alleged to consist of—

    (a) where the invention is a product, making a product for disposal or importing a product for disposal, or

    (b) where the invention is a process, using a process.

(3) A threat of infringement proceedings is not actionable if the infringement is alleged to consist of an act which, if done, would constitute an infringement of a kind mentioned in subsection (2)(a) or (b).

(4) A threat of infringement proceedings is not actionable if the threat—

    (a) is made to a person who has done, or intends to do, an act mentioned in subsection (2)(a) or (b) in relation to a product or process, and

    (b) is a threat of proceedings for an infringement alleged to consist of doing anything else in relation to that product or process.

(5) A threat of infringement proceedings which is not an express threat is not actionable if it is contained in a permitted communication.

(6) In sections 70C and 70D 'an actionable threat' means a threat of infringement proceedings that is actionable in accordance with this section.

70B   Permitted communications

(1) For the purposes of section 70A(5), a communication containing a threat of infringement proceedings is a 'permitted communication' if—

    (a) the communication, so far as it contains information that relates to the threat, is made for a permitted purpose;

    (b) all of the information that relates to the threat is information that—

        (i)   is necessary for that purpose (see subsection (5)(a) to (c) for some examples of necessary information), and

        (ii) the person making the communication reasonably believes is true.

(2) Each of the following is a 'permitted purpose'—

    (a) giving notice that a patent exists;

    (b) discovering whether, or by whom, a patent has been infringed by an act mentioned in section 70A(2)(a) or (b);

    (c) giving notice that a person has a right in or under a patent, where another person's awareness of the right is relevant to any proceedings that may be brought in respect of the patent.

(3) The court may, having regard to the nature of the purposes listed in subsection (2)(a) to (c), treat any other purpose as a 'permitted purpose' if it considers that it is in the interests of justice to do so.

(4) But the following may not be treated as a 'permitted purpose'—

    (a) requesting a person to cease doing, for commercial purposes, anything in relation to a product or process,

    (b) requesting a person to deliver up or destroy a product, or

    (c) requesting a person to give an undertaking relating to a product or process.

(5) If any of the following information is included in a communication made for a permitted purpose, it is information that is 'necessary for that purpose' (see subsection (1)(b)(i))—

    (a) a statement that a patent exists and is in force or that an application for a patent has been made;

    (b) details of the patent, or of a right in or under the patent, which—

        (i)   are accurate in all material respects, and

        (ii) are not misleading in any material respect; and

    (c) information enabling the identification of the products or processes in respect of which it is alleged that acts infringing the patent have been carried out.

70C   Remedies and defences

(1) Proceedings in respect of an actionable threat may be brought against the person who made the threat for—

    (a) a declaration that the threat is unjustified;

    (b) an injunction against the continuance of the threat;

    (c) damages in respect of any loss sustained by the aggrieved person by reason of the threat.

(2) In the application of subsection (1) to Scotland—

    (a) 'declaration' means 'declarator', and

    (b) 'injunction' means 'interdict'.

(3) It is a defence for the person who made the threat to show that the act in respect of which proceedings were threatened constitutes (or if done would constitute) an infringement of the patent.

(4) It is a defence for the person who made the threat to show—

    (a) that, despite having taken reasonable steps, the person has not identified anyone who has done an act mentioned in section 70A(2)(a) or (b) in relation to the product or the use of a process which is the subject of the threat, and

    (b) that the person notified the recipient, before or at the time of making the threat, of the steps taken.

70D   Professional advisers

(1) Proceedings in respect of an actionable threat may not be brought against a professional adviser (or any person vicariously liable for the actions of that professional adviser) if the conditions in subsection (3) are met.

(2) In this section 'professional adviser' means a person who, in relation to the making of the communication containing the threat—

    (a) is acting in a professional capacity in providing legal services or the services of a trade mark attorney or a patent attorney, and

    (b) is regulated in the provision of legal services, or the services of a trade mark attorney or a patent attorney, by one or more regulatory bodies (whether through membership of a regulatory body, the issue of a licence to practise or any other means).

(3) The conditions are that—

    (a) in making the communication the professional adviser is acting on the instructions of another person, and

    (b) when the communication is made the professional adviser identifies the person on whose instructions the adviser is acting.

(4) This section does not affect any liability of the person on whose instructions the professional adviser is acting.

(5) It is for a person asserting that subsection (1) applies to prove (if required) that at the material time—

    (a) the person concerned was acting as a professional adviser, and

    (b) the conditions in subsection (3) were met.

70E   Supplementary: pending registration

(1) In sections 70 and 70B references to a patent include references to an application for a patent that has been published under section 16.

(2) Where the threat of infringement proceedings is made after an application has been published (but before grant) the reference in section 70C(3) to 'the patent' is to be treated as a reference to the patent as granted in pursuance of that application.

70F   Supplementary: proceedings for delivery up etc.

In section 70(1)(b) the reference to proceedings for infringement of a patent includes a reference to proceedings for an order under section 61(1)(b) (order to deliver up or destroy patented products etc.) and proceedings in the Unified Patent Court for an order for delivery up made in accordance with articles 32(1)(c) and 62(3) of the Agreement on a Unified Patent Court.

Declaration or declarator as to non-infringement

71   Declaration or declarator as to non-infringement

(1) Without prejudice to the court's jurisdiction to make a declaration or declarator apart from this section, a declaration or declarator that an act does not, or a proposed act would not, constitute an infringement of a patent may be made by the court or the comptroller in proceedings between the person doing or proposing to do the act and the proprietor of the patent, notwithstanding that no assertion to the contrary has been made by the proprietor, if it is shown—

    (a) that that person has applied in writing to the proprietor for a written acknowledgment to the effect of the declaration or declarator claimed, and has furnished him with full particulars in writing of the act in question; and

    (b) that the proprietor has refused or failed to give any such acknowledgment.

(2) Subject to section 72(5) below, a declaration made by the comptroller under this section shall have the same effect as a declaration or declarator by the court.

Revocation of patents

72   Power to revoke patents on application

(1) Subject to the following provisions of this Act, the court or the comptroller may by order revoke a patent for an invention on the application of any person (including the proprietor of the patent) on (but only on) any of the following grounds, that is to say—

    (a) the invention is not a patentable invention;

(b) that the patent was granted to a person who was not entitled to be granted that patent;

(c) the specification of the patent does not disclose the invention clearly enough and completely enough for it to be performed by a person skilled in the art;

(d) the matter disclosed in the specification of the patent extends beyond that disclosed in the application for the patent, as filed, or, if the patent was granted on a new application filed under section 8(3), 12 or 37(4) above or as mentioned in section 15(9) above, in the earlier application, as filed;

(e) the protection conferred by the patent has been extended by an amendment which should not have been allowed.

(2) An application for the revocation of a patent on the ground mentioned in subsection (1)(b) above—

(a) may only be made by a person found by the court in an action for a declaration or declarator, or found by the court or the comptroller on a reference under section 37 above, to be entitled to be granted that patent or to be granted a patent for part of the matter comprised in the specification of the patent sought to be revoked; and

(b) may not be made if that action was commenced or that reference was made after the second anniversary of the date of the grant of the patent sought to be revoked, unless it is shown that any person registered as a proprietor of the patent knew at the time of the grant or of the transfer of the patent to him that he was not entitled to the patent.

...

(5) A decision of the comptroller or on appeal from the comptroller shall not estop any party to civil proceedings in which infringement of a patent is in issue from alleging invalidity of the patent on any of the grounds referred to in subsection (1) above, whether or not any of the issues involved were decided in the said decision.

...

73 Comptroller's power to revoke patents on his own initiative

(1) If it appears to the comptroller that an invention for which a patent has been granted formed part of the state of the art by virtue only of section 2(3) above, he may on his own initiative by order revoke the patent, but shall not do so without giving the proprietor of the patent an opportunity of making any observations and of amending the specification of the patent so as to exclude any matter which formed part of the state of the art as aforesaid without contravening section 76 below.

(1A) Where the comptroller issues an opinion under section 74A that section 1(1)(a) or (b) is not satisfied in relation to an invention for which there is a patent, the comptroller may revoke the patent.

(1B) The power under subsection (1A) may not be exercised before—

(a) the end of the period in which the proprietor of the patent may apply under the rules (by virtue of section 74B) for a review of the opinion, or

(b) if the proprietor applies for a review, the decision on the review is made (or, if there is an appeal against that decision, the appeal is determined).

(1C) The comptroller shall not exercise the power under subsection (1A) without giving the proprietor of the patent an opportunity to make any observations and to amend the specification of the patent without contravening section 76.

...

Putting validity in issue

74 Proceedings in which validity of patent may be put in issue

(1) Subject to the following provisions of this section, the validity of a patent may be put in issue—

(a) by way of defence, in proceedings for infringement of the patent under section 61 above or proceedings under section 69 above for infringement of rights conferred by the publication of an application;

(b) in proceedings in respect of an actionable threat under section 70A above;

(c) in proceedings in which a declaration in relation to the patent is sought under section 71 above;

(d) in proceedings before the court or the comptroller under section 72 above for the revocation of the patent;

(e) in proceedings under section 58 above.

(2) The validity of a patent may not be put in issue in any other proceedings and, in particular, no proceedings may be instituted (whether under this Act or otherwise) seeking only a declaration as to the validity or invalidity of a patent.

(3) The only grounds on which the validity of a patent may be put in issue (whether in proceedings for revocation under section 72 above or otherwise) are the grounds on which the patent may be revoked under that section.

(4) No determination shall be made in any proceedings mentioned in subsection (1) above on the validity of a patent which any person puts in issue on the ground mentioned in section 72(1)(b) above unless—

(a) it has been determined in entitlement proceedings commenced by that person or in the proceedings in which the validity of the patent is in issue that the patent should have been granted to him and not some other person; and

(b) except where it has been so determined in entitlement proceedings, the proceedings in which the validity of the patent is in issue are commenced on or before the second anniversary of the date of the grant of the patent or it is shown that any person registered as a proprietor of the patent knew at the time of the grant or of the transfer of the patent to him that he was not entitled to the patent.

(5) Where the validity of a patent is put in issue by way of defence or counterclaim the court or the comptroller shall, if it or he thinks it just to do so, give the defendant an opportunity to comply with the condition in subsection (4)(a) above.

(6) In subsection (4) above 'entitlement proceedings', in relation to a patent, means a reference under section 37(1) above on the ground that the patent was granted to a person not entitled to it or proceedings for a declaration or declarator that it was so granted.

(7) Where proceedings with respect to a patent are pending in the court under any provision of this Act mentioned in subsection (1) above, no proceedings may be instituted without the leave of the court before the comptroller with respect to that patent under section 61(3), 69, 71 or 72 above.

(8) It is hereby declared that for the purposes of this Act the validity of a patent is not put in issue merely because—

(a) the comptroller is considering its validity in order to decide whether to revoke it under section 73 above or

(b) its validity is being considered in connection with an opinion under section 74A below or a review of such an opinion.

Opinions by Patent Office

74A   Opinions on matters prescribed in the rules

(1) The proprietor of a patent or any other person may request the comptroller to issue an opinion on a prescribed matter in relation to the patent.

(2) Subsection (1) above applies even if the patent has expired or has been surrendered.

(3) The comptroller shall issue an opinion if requested to do so under subsection (1) above, but shall not do so—

(a) in such circumstances as may be prescribed, or

(b) if for any reason he considers it inappropriate in all the circumstances to do so.

(4) An opinion under this section shall not be binding for any purposes.

(5) An opinion under this section shall be prepared by an examiner.

(6) In relation to a decision of the comptroller whether to issue an opinion under this section—

(a) for the purposes of section 101 below, only the person making the request under subsection (1) above shall be regarded as a party to a proceeding before the comptroller; and

(b) no appeal shall lie at the instance of any other person.

74B Reviews of opinions under section 74A

(1) Rules may make provision for a review before the comptroller, on an application by the proprietor or an exclusive licensee of the patent in question, of an opinion under section 74A above.

(2) The rules may, in particular—

    (a) prescribe the circumstances in which, and the period within which, an application may be made;

    (b) provide that, in prescribed circumstances, proceedings for a review may not be brought or continued where other proceedings have been brought;

    (d) provide for there to be a right of appeal against a decision made on a review only in prescribed cases.

General provisions as to amendment of patents and applications

75 Amendment of patent in infringement or revocation proceedings

(1) In any proceedings before the court or the comptroller in which the validity of a patent may be put in issue the court or, as the case may be, the comptroller may, subject to section 76 below, allow the proprietor of the patent to amend the specification of the patent in such manner, and subject to such terms as to advertising the proposed amendment and as to costs, expenses or otherwise, as the court or comptroller thinks fit.

(2) A person may give notice to the court or the comptroller of his opposition to an amendment proposed by the proprietor of the patent under this section, and if he does so the court or the comptroller shall notify the proprietor and consider the opposition in deciding whether the amendment or any amendment should be allowed.

(3) An amendment of a specification of a patent under this section shall have effect and be deemed always to have had effect from the grant of the patent.

(4) Where an application for an order under this section is made to the court, the applicant shall notify the comptroller, who shall be entitled to appear and be heard and shall appear if so directed by the court.

(5) In considering whether or not to allow an amendment proposed under this section, the court or the comptroller shall have regard to any relevant principles applicable under the European Patent Convention.

76 Amendments of applications and patents not to include added matter

(1) An application for a patent which—

    (a) is made in respect of matter disclosed in an earlier application, or in the specification of a patent which has been granted, and

    (b) discloses additional matter, that is, matter extending beyond that disclosed in the earlier application, as filed, or the application for the patent, as filed,

may be filed under section 8(3), 12 or 37(4) above, or as mentioned in section 15(9) above, but shall not be allowed to proceed unless it is amended so as to exclude the additional matter.

(1A) Where, in relation to an application for a patent—

    (a) a reference to an earlier relevant application has been filed as mentioned in section 15(1)(c)(ii) above; and

    (b) the description filed under section 15(10)(b)(i) above discloses additional matter, that is, matter extending beyond that disclosed in the earlier relevant application,

the application shall not be allowed to proceed unless it is amended so as to exclude the additional matter.

(2) No amendment of an application for a patent shall be allowed under section 15A(6), 18(3) or 19(1) if it results in the application disclosing matter extending beyond that disclosed in the application as filed.

(3) No amendment of the specification of a patent shall be allowed under section 27(1), 73 or 75 if it—

    (a) results in the specification disclosing additional matter, or

    (b) extends the protection conferred by the patent.

(4) In subsection (1A) above 'relevant application' has the meaning given by section 5(5) above.

76A   Biotechnological inventions

(1) Any provision of, or made under, this Act is to have effect in relation to a patent or an application for a patent which concerns a biotechnological invention, subject to the provisions of Schedule A2.

(2) Nothing in this section or Schedule A2 is to be read as affecting the application of any provision in relation to any other kind of patent or application for a patent.

PART II   PROVISIONS ABOUT INTERNATIONAL CONVENTIONS

European patents and patent applications

77   Effect of European patent (UK)

(1) Subject to the provisions of this Act, a European patent (UK) shall, as from the publication of the mention of its grant in the European Patent Bulletin, be treated for the purposes of Parts I and III of this Act as if it were a patent under this Act granted in pursuance of an application made under this Act and as if notice of the grant of the patent had, on the date of that publication, been published under section 24 above in the journal; and—

   (a) the proprietor of a European patent (UK) shall accordingly as respects the United Kingdom have the same rights and remedies, subject to the same conditions, as the proprietor of a patent under this Act;

   (b) references in Parts I and III of this Act to a patent shall be construed accordingly; and

   (c) any statement made and any certificate filed for the purposes of the provision of the convention corresponding to section 2(4)(c) above shall be respectively treated as a statement made and written evidence filed for the purposes of the said paragraph (c).

   . . .

78   Effect of filing an application for a European patent (UK)

(1) Subject to the provisions of this Act, an application for a European patent (UK) having a date of filing under the European Patent Convention shall be treated for the purposes of the provisions of this Act to which this section applies as an application for a patent under this Act having that date as its date of filing and having the other incidents listed in subsection (3) below, but subject to the modifications mentioned in the following provisions of this section.

   . . .

79   Operation of s. 78 in relation to certain European patent applications

(1) Subject to the following provisions of this section, section 78 above, in its operation in relation to an international application for a patent (UK) which is treated by virtue of the European Patent Convention as an application for a European patent (UK), shall have effect as if any reference in that section to anything done in relation to the application under the European Patent Convention included a reference to the corresponding thing done under the Patent Co-operation Treaty.

   . . .

PART III   MISCELLANEOUS AND GENERAL

Legal proceedings

   . . .

100   Burden of proof in certain cases

(1) If the invention for which a patent is granted is a process for obtaining a new product, the same product produced by a person other than the proprietor of the patent or a licensee of

his shall, unless the contrary is proved, be taken in any proceedings to have been obtained by that process.

(2) In considering whether a party has discharged the burden imposed upon him by this section, the court shall not require him to disclose any manufacturing or commercial secrets if it appears to the court that it would be unreasonable to do so.

. . .

Offences

. . .

110   Unauthorised claim of patent rights

(1) If a person falsely represents that anything disposed of by him for value is a patented product he shall, subject to the following provisions of this section, be liable on summary conviction to a fine not exceeding level 3 on the standard scale.

(2) For the purposes of subsection (1) above a person who for value disposes of an article having stamped, engraved or impressed on it or otherwise applied to it the word 'patent' or 'patented' or anything expressing or implying that the article is a patented product, shall be taken to represent that the article is a patented product.

(3) Subsection (1) above does not apply where the representation is made in respect of a product after the patent for that product or, as the case may be, the process in question has expired or been revoked and before the end of a period which is reasonably sufficient to enable the accused to take steps to ensure that the representation is not made (or does not continue to be made).

(4) In proceedings for an offence under this section it shall be a defence for the accused to prove that he used due diligence to prevent the commission of the offence.

111   Unauthorised claim that patent has been applied for

(1) If a person represents that a patent has been applied for in respect of any particle disposed of for value by him and—

(a) no such application has been made, or

(b) any such application has been refused or withdrawn,

he shall, subject to the following provisions of this section, be liable on summary conviction to a fine not exceeding level 3 on the standard scale.

(2) Subsection (1)(b) above does not apply where the representation is made (or continues to be made) before the expiry of a period which commences with the refusal or withdrawal and which is reasonably sufficient to enable the accused to take steps to ensure that the representation is not made (or does not continue to be made).

(3) For the purposes of subsection (1) above a person who for value disposes of an article having stamped, engraved or impressed on it or otherwise applied to it the words 'patent applied for' or 'patent pending', or anything expressing or implying that a patent has been applied for in respect of the article, shall be taken to represent that a patent has been applied for in respect of it.

(4) In any proceedings for an offence under this section it shall be a defence for the accused to prove that he used due diligence to prevent the commission of such an offence.

. . .

Supplemental

. . .

125   Extent of invention

(1) For the purposes of this Act an invention for a patent for which an application has been made or for which a patent has been granted shall, unless the context otherwise requires, be taken to be that specified in a claim of the specification of the application or patent, as the case may be, as interpreted by the description and any drawings contained in that specification, and the extent of the protection conferred by a patent or application for a patent shall be determined accordingly.

(2) It is hereby declared for the avoidance of doubt that where more than one invention is specified in any such claim, each invention may have a different priority date under section 5 above.

(3) The Protocol on the Interpretation of Article 69 of the European Patent Convention (which Article contains a provision corresponding to subsection (1) above) shall, as for the time being in force, apply for the purposes of subsection (1) above as it applies for the purposes of that Article.

125A   Disclosure of invention by specification: availability of samples of biological material

(1) Provision may be made by rules prescribing the circumstances in which the specification of an application for a patent, or of a patent, for an invention which involves the use of or concerns biological material is to be treated as disclosing the invention in a manner which is clear enough and complete enough for the invention to be performed by a person skilled in the art.

(2) The rules may in particular require the applicant or patentee—

    (a) to take such steps as may be prescribed for the purposes of making available to the public samples of the biological material, and

    (b) not to impose or maintain restrictions on the uses to which such samples may be put, except as may be prescribed.

(3) The rules may provide that, in such cases as may be prescribed, samples need only be made available to such persons or descriptions of persons as may be prescribed; and the rules may identify a description of persons by reference to whether the comptroller has given his certificate as to any matter.

(4) An application for revocation of the patent under section 72(1)(c) above may be made if any of the requirements of the rules cease to be complied with.

. . .

129   Application of Act to Crown

This Act does not affect Her Majesty in her private capacity but, subject to that, it binds the Crown.

130   Interpretation

(1) In this Act, except so far as the context otherwise requires—

'application fee' means the fee prescribed for the purposes of section 14(1A) above;

'application for a European patent (UK)' and (subject to subsection (4A) below) 'international application for a patent (UK)' each mean an application of the relevant description which, on its date of filing, designates the United Kingdom;

'appointed day', in any provision of this Act, means the day appointed under section 132 below for the coming into operation of that provision;

'biological material' means any material containing genetic information and capable of reproducing itself or being reproduced in a biological system;

'biotechnological invention' means an invention which concerns a product consisting of or containing biological material or a process by means of which biological material is produced, processed or used;

'Community Patent Convention' means the Convention for the European Patent for the Common Market;

'comptroller' means the Comptroller-General of Patents, Designs and Trade Marks;

'Convention on International Exhibitions' means the Convention relating to International Exhibitions signed in Paris on 22 November 1928, as amended or supplemented by any protocol to that convention which is for the time being in force;

'court' means

    (a) as respects England and Wales, the High Court;

    (b) as respects Scotland, the Court of Session;

    (c) as respects Northern Ireland, the High Court in Northern Ireland;

'date of filing' means—

    (a) in relation to an application for a patent made under this Act, the date which is the date of filing that application by virtue of section 15 above; and

(b) in relation to any other application, the date which, under the law of the country where the application was made or in accordance with the terms of a treaty or convention to which that country is a party, is to be treated as the date of filing that application or is equivalent to the date of filing an application in that country (whatever the outcome of the application);

'designate' in relation to an application or a patent, means designate the country or countries (in pursuance of the European Patent Convention or the Patent Co-operation Treaty) in which protection is sought for the invention which is the subject of the application or patent and includes a reference to a country being treated as designated in pursuance of the convention or treaty;

...

'employee' means a person who works or (where the employment has ceased) worked under a contract of employment or in employment under or for the purposes of a government department or a person who serves (or served) in the naval, military or air forces of the Crown;

'employer', in relation to an employee, means the person by whom the employee is or was employed;

'European Patent Convention' means the Convention on the Grant of European Patents, 'European patent' means a patent granted under that convention, 'European patent (UK)' means a European patent designating the United Kingdom, 'European Patent Bulletin' means the bulletin of that name published under that convention, and 'European Patent Office' means the office of that name established by that convention;

'exclusive licence' means a licence from the proprietor of or applicant for a patent conferring on the licensee, or on him and persons authorised by him, to the exclusion of all other persons (including the proprietor or applicant), any right in respect of the invention to which the patent or application relates, and 'exclusive licensee' and 'non-exclusive licence' shall be construed accordingly;

'formal requirements' means those requirements designated as such by rules made for the purposes of section 15A above;

'international application for a patent' means an application made under the Patent Cooperation Treaty;

'International Bureau' means the secretariat of the World Intellectual Property Organisation established by a convention signed at Stockholm on 14 July 1967;

'international exhibition' means an official or officially recognised international exhibition falling within the terms of the Convention on International Exhibitions or falling within the terms of any subsequent treaty or convention replacing that convention;

'inventor' has the meaning assigned to it by section 7 above;

'journal' has the meaning assigned to it by section 123(6) above;

'mortgage', when used as a noun, includes a charge for securing money or money's worth and, when used as a verb, shall be construed accordingly;

'1949 Act' means the Patents Act 1949;

'patent' means a patent under this Act;

'Patent Co-operation Treaty' means the treaty of that name signed at Washington on 19 June 1970;

'patented invention' means an invention for which a patent is granted and

'patented process' shall be construed accordingly;

'patented product' means a product which is a patented invention or, in relation to a patented process, a product obtained directly by means of the process or to which the process has been applied;

'prescribed' and 'rules' have the meanings assigned to them by section 123 above;

'priority date' means the date determined as such under section 5 above;

'published' means made available to the public (whether in the United Kingdom or elsewhere) and a document shall be taken to be published under any provision of this Act if it can be inspected as of right at any place in the United Kingdom by members of the public, whether on payment of a fee or not; and 'republished' shall be construed accordingly;

'register' and cognate expressions have the meanings assigned to them by section 32 above;

'relevant convention court', in relation to any proceedings under the European Patent Convention or the Patent Co-operation Treaty, means that court or other body which under that convention or treaty has jurisdiction over those proceedings, including (where it has such jurisdiction) any department of the European Patent Office;

'right', in relation to any patent or application, includes an interest in the patent or application and, without prejudice to the foregoing, any reference to a right in a patent includes a reference to a share in the patent;

'search fee' means the fee prescribed for the purposes of section 17(1) above;

'services of the Crown' and 'use for the services of the Crown' have the meanings assigned to them by section 56(2) above, including, as respects any period of emergency within the meaning of section 59 above, the meanings assigned to them by the said section 59.

(2) Rules may provide for stating in the journal that an exhibition falls within the definition of international exhibition in subsection (1) above and any such statement shall be conclusive evidence that the exhibition falls within that definition.

(3) For the purposes of this Act matter shall be taken to have been disclosed in any relevant application within the meaning of section 5 above or in the specification of a patent if it was either claimed or disclosed (otherwise than by way of disclaimer or acknowledgment of prior art) in that application or specification.

(4) References in this Act to an application for a patent, as filed, are references to such an application in the state it was on the date of filing.

(4A) An international application for a patent is not, by reason of being treated by virtue of the European Patent Convention as an application for a European patent (UK), to be treated also as an international application for a patent (UK).

(5) References in this Act to an application for a patent being published are references to its being published under section 16 above.

(5A) References in this Act to the amendment of a patent or its specification (whether under this Act or by the European Patent Office) include, in particular, limitation of the claims (as interpreted by the description and any drawings referred to in the description or claims).

(6) References in this Act to any of the following conventions, that is to say—

(a) The European Patent Convention;

(b) The Community Patent Convention;

(c) The Patent Co-operation Treaty;

are references to that convention or any other international convention or agreement replacing it, as amended or supplemented by any convention or international agreement (including in either case any protocol or annex), or in accordance with the terms of any such convention or agreement, and include references to any instrument made under any such convention or agreement.

(7) Whereas by a resolution made on the signature of the Community Patent Convention the governments of the member states of the European Union resolved to adjust their laws relating to patents so as (among other things) to bring those laws into conformity with the corresponding provisions of the European Patent Convention, the Community Patent Convention and the Patent Co-operation Treaty, it is hereby declared that the following provisions of this Act, that is to say, sections 1(1) to (4), 2 to 6, 14(3), (5) and (6), 37(5), 54, 60, 69, 72(1) and (2), 74(4), 82, 83, 100 and 125, are so framed as to have, as nearly as practicable, the same effects in the United Kingdom as the corresponding provisions of the European Patent Convention, the Community Patent Convention and the Patent Co-operation Treaty have in the territories to which those Conventions apply.

(8) Nothing in any of sections 1 to 15 of and schedule 1 to the Arbitration (Scotland) Act 2010 or Part I of the Arbitration Act 1996 applies to any proceedings before the comptroller under this Act.

(9) Except so far as the context otherwise requires, any reference in this Act to any enactment shall be construed as a reference to that enactment as amended or extended by or under any other enactment, including this Act.

. . .

132 Short title, extent, commencement, consequential amendments and repeals

(1) This Act may be cited as the Patents Act 1977.

(2) This Act shall extent to the Isle of Man, subject to any modifications contained in an Order made by Her Majesty in Council, and accordingly, subject to any such order, references in this Act to the United Kingdom shall be construed as including references to the Isle of Man.

(3) For the purposes of this Act the territorial waters of the United Kingdom shall be treated as part of the United Kingdom.

(4) This Act applies to acts done in an area designated by order under section 1(7) of the Continental Shelf Act 1964, in connection with the exploration of the sea bed or subsoil or exploitation of their natural resources, as it applies to acts done in the United Kingdom.

...

SCHEDULE A2 BIOTECHNOLOGICAL INVENTIONS

1. An invention shall not be considered unpatentable solely on the ground that it concerns—
   (a) a product consisting of or containing biological material; or
   (b) a process by which biological material is produced, processed or used.

2. Biological material which is isolated from its natural environment or produced by means of a technical process may be the subject of an invention even if it previously occurred in nature.

3. The following are not patentable inventions—
   (a) the human body, at the various stages of its formation and development, and the simple discovery of one of its elements, including the sequence or partial sequence of a gene;
   (b) processes for cloning human beings;
   (c) processes for modifying the germ line genetic identity of human beings;
   (d) uses of human embryos for industrial or commercial purposes;
   (e) processes for modifying the genetic identity of animals which are likely to cause them suffering without any substantial medical benefit to man or animal, and also animals resulting from such processes;
   (f) any variety of animal or plant or any essentially biological process for the production of animals or plants, not being a micro-biological or other technical process or the product of such a process.

4. Inventions which concern plants or animals may be patentable if the technical feasibility of the invention is not confined to a particular plant or animal variety.

5. An element isolated from the human body or otherwise produced by means of a technical process, including the sequence or partial sequence of a gene, may constitute a patentable invention, even if the structure of that element is identical to that of a natural element.

6. The industrial application of a sequence or partial sequence of a gene must be disclosed in the patent application as filed.

7. The protection conferred by a patent on a biological material possessing specific characteristics as a result of the invention shall extend to any biological material derived from that biological material through propagation or multiplication in an identical or divergent form and possessing those same characteristics.

8. The protection conferred by a patent on a process that enables a biological material to be produced possessing specific characteristics as a result of the invention shall extend to biological material directly obtained through that process and to any other biological material derived from the directly obtained biological material through propagation or multiplication in an identical or divergent form and possessing those same characteristics.

9. The protection conferred by a patent on a product containing or consisting of genetic information shall extend to all material, save as provided for in paragraph 3 (a) above, in which the product is incorporated and in which the genetic information is contained and performs its function.

10. The protection referred to in paragraphs 7, 8 and 9 above shall not extend to biological material obtained from the propagation or multiplication of biological material placed on the market by the proprietor of the patent or with his consent, where the multiplication or propagation necessarily results from the application for which the biological material was marketed, provided that the material obtained is not subsequently used for other propagation or multiplication.

11. In this Schedule:

'essentially biological process' means a process for the production of animals and plants which consists entirely of natural phenomena such as crossing and selection;

'microbiological process' means any process involving or performed upon or resulting in microbiological material;

'plant variety' means a plant grouping within a single botanical taxon of the lowest known rank, which grouping can be:

    (a) defined by the expression of the characteristics that results from a given genotype or combination of genotypes; and

    (b) distinguished from any other plant grouping by the expression of at least one of the said characteristics; and

    (c) considered as a unit with regard to its suitability for being propagated unchanged.

Plant Varieties Act 1997*

(1997, c. 66)

An Act to make provision about rights in relation to plant varieties; to make provision about the Plant Varieties and Seeds Tribunal; to extend the time limit for institution of proceedings for contravention of seeds regulations; and for connected purposes.   [27 November 1997]

Arrangement of Sections

* **Editor's Note:** Contains amendments effected *by Plant Breeeders' Rights (Amendment etc.) (EU Exit) Regulations 2019*. By virtue of the *European Union (Withdrawal Agreement) Act 2020*, these amendments take effect on 'IP completion day', which is defined to be 31 December 2020 at 11:00pm.

PART I   PLANT VARIETIES

Preliminary

1   Plant breeders' rights

(1) Rights, to be known as plant breeders' rights, may be granted in accordance with this Part of this Act.

(2) Plant breeders' rights may subsist in varieties of all plant genera and species.

(3) For the purposes of this Act, 'variety' means a plant grouping within a single botanical taxon of the lowest known rank, which grouping, irrespective of whether the conditions for the grant of plant breeders' rights (which are laid down in section 4 below) are met, can be—

(a) defined by the expression of the characteristics resulting from a given genotype or combination of genotypes,

(b) distinguished from any other plant grouping by the expression of at least one of those characteristics, and

(c) considered as a unit with regard to its suitability for being propagated unchanged.

. . .

Grant of plant breeders' rights

3   Grant on application

(1) Subject to this Part of this Act, plant breeders' rights shall be granted to an applicant by the Controller on being satisfied that the conditions laid down in section 4 below are met.

. . .

4   Conditions for the grant of rights

(1) The conditions which must be met in relation to an application for the grant of plant breeders' rights are—

(a) that the variety to which the application relates is a qualifying variety, and

(b) that the person by whom the application is made is the person entitled to the grant of plant breeders' rights in respect of the variety to which it relates.

(2) For the purposes of subsection (1) above, a variety is a qualifying variety if it is—

(a) distinct,

(b) uniform,

(c) stable, and

(d) new;

and Part I of Schedule 2 to this Act has effect for the purpose of determining whether these criteria are met.

(3) Subject to subsections (4) and (5) below, the person entitled to the grant of plant breeders' rights in respect of a variety is the person who breeds it, or discovers and develops it, or his successor in title.

(4) If a person breeds a variety, or discovers and develops it, in the course of his employment, then, subject to agreement to the contrary, his employer, or his employer's successor in title, is the person entitled to the grant of plant breeders' rights in respect of it.

(5) Part II of Schedule 2 to this Act shall have effect as respects priorities between two or more persons who have independently bred, or discovered and developed, a variety.

(6) In this section and Schedule 2 to this Act, references to the discovery of a variety are to the discovery of a variety, whether growing in the wild or occurring as a genetic variant, whether artificially induced or not.

...

Scope of plant breeders' rights

6 Protected variety

(1) Plant breeders' rights shall have effect to entitle the holder to prevent anyone doing any of the following acts as respects the propagating material of the protected variety without his authority, namely—

(a) production or reproduction (multiplication),

(b) conditioning for the purpose of propagation,

(c) offering for sale,

(d) selling or other marketing,

(e) exporting,

(f) importing,

(g) stocking for any of the purposes mentioned in paragraphs (a) to (f) above, and

(h) any other act prescribed for the purposes of this provision.

(2) The holder of plant breeders' rights may give authority for the purposes of subsection (1) above with or without conditions or limitations.

(3) The rights conferred on the holder of plant breeders' rights by subsections (1) and (2) above shall also apply as respects harvested material obtained through the unauthorised use of propagating material of the protected variety, unless he has had a reasonable opportunity before the harvested material is obtained to exercise his rights in relation to the unauthorised use of the propagating material.

(4) In the case of a variety of a prescribed description, the rights conferred on the holder of plant breeders' rights by subsections (1) and (2) above shall also apply as respects any product which—

(a) is made directly from harvested material in relation to which subsection (3) above applies, and

(b) is of a prescribed description, unless subsection (5) below applies.

(5) This subsection applies if, before the product was made, any act mentioned in subsection (1) above was done as respects the harvested material from which the product was made and either—

(a) the act was done with the authority of the holder of the plant breeders' rights, or

(b) the holder of those rights had a reasonable opportunity to exercise them in relation to the doing of the act.

(6) In this section—

(a) 'prescribed' means prescribed by regulations made by the Ministers, and

(b) references to harvested material include entire plants and parts of plants.

7 Dependent varieties

(1) The holder of plant breeders' rights shall have, in relation to any variety which is dependent on the protected variety, the same rights as he has under section 6 above in relation to the protected variety.

(2) For the purposes of this section, one variety is dependent on another if—

(a) its nature is such that repeated production of the variety is not possible without repeated use of the other variety, or

(b) it is essentially derived from the other variety and the other variety is not itself essentially derived from a third variety.

(3) For the purposes of subsection (2) above, a variety shall be deemed to be essentially derived from another variety ('the initial variety') if—

(a) it is predominantly derived from—

(i) the initial variety, or

(ii) a variety that is itself predominantly derived from the initial variety,

while retaining the expression of the essential characteristics resulting from the genotype or combination or genotypes of the initial variety,

(b) it is clearly distinguishable from the initial variety by one or more characteristics which are capable of a precise description, and

(c) except for the differences which result from the act of derivation, it conforms to the initial variety in the expression of the essential characteristics that result from the genotype or combination of genotypes of the initial variety.

(4) For the purposes of subsection (3) above, derivation may, for example, be by—

(a) the selection of—

(i)   a natural or induced mutant,

(ii) a somaclonal variant, or

(iii) a variant individual from plants of the initial variety,

(b) backcrossing, or

(c) transformation by genetic engineering.

(5) Subsection (1) above shall not apply where the existence of the dependent variety was common knowledge immediately before the coming into force of this Act.

Exceptions

8 General exceptions

Plant breeders' rights shall not extend to any act done—

(a) for private and non-commercial purposes,

(b) for experimental purposes, or

(c) for the purpose of breeding another variety.

9 Farm saved seed

(1) Subject to subsection (2) below, plant breeders' rights shall not extend to the use by a farmer for propagating purposes in the field, on his own holding, of the product of the harvest which he has obtained by planting on his own holding propagating material of—

(a) the protected variety, or

(b) a variety which is essentially derived from the protected variety.

(2) Subsection (1) above only applies if the material is of a variety which is of a species or group specified for the purposes of this subsection by order made by the Ministers.

(3) If a farmer's use of material is excepted from plant breeders' rights by subsection (1) above, he shall, at the time of the use, become liable (subject to any contractual agreement entered into between the farmer and the holder of the plant breeders' rights) to pay the holder of the rights equitable remuneration, which shall be sensibly lower than the amount charged for the production of propagating material of the same variety in the same area with the holder's authority.

(4) Subsection (3) above shall not apply to a farmer who is a small farmer for the purposes of this section

(6) The Ministers may by order provide that, on such date after 30 June 2001 as may be specified in the order, subsection (5) above shall cease to have effect in relation to a variety so specified, or varieties of a species or group so specified.

(7) The Ministers may by regulations—

(a) make provision enabling—

(i)   holders of plant breeders' rights to require farmers or seed processors, and

(ii) farmers or seed processors to require holders of plant breeders' rights, to supply such information as may be specified in the regulations, being information the supply of which the Ministers consider necessary for the purposes of this section,

(b) make provision restricting the circumstances in which the product of a harvest of a variety which is subject to plant breeders' rights may be moved, for the purpose of being processed for planting, from the holding on which it was obtained, and

(c) make provision for the purpose of enabling the Ministers to monitor the operation of any provision of this section or regulations under this section.

(8) Regulations under subsection (7)(a) above may include provision imposing obligations of confidence in relation to information supplied by virtue of the regulations.

(9) Subsections (3) and (4) of section 7 above shall apply for the purposes of subsection (1)(b) above as they apply for the purposes of subsection (2) of that section.

(10) In this section, 'small farmer' means—

(a) in a case where the material referred to in subsection (3) is used for propagating potatoes, a farmer who grows potatoes in an area no bigger than that which would be needed to produce 185 tonnes of potatoes per harvest, and

(b) in a case where the material referred to in subsection (3) is used for propagating any other variety specified for the purpose of subsection (1), a farmer who grows that variety in an area no bigger than that which would be needed to produce 92 tonnes of cereals per harvest.

(11) In this section, references to a farmer's own holding are to any land which he actually exploits for plant growing, whether as his property or otherwise managed under his own responsibility and on his own account.

10   Exhaustion of rights

(1) Plant breeders' rights shall not extend to any act concerning material of a variety if the material—

(a) has been sold or otherwise marketed in the United Kingdom by, or with the consent of, the holder of the rights, or

(b) is derived from material which has been so sold or otherwise marketed.

(2) Subsection (1) above shall not apply where the act involves—

(a) further propagation of the variety, or

(b) the export of material which enables propagation of the variety to a non-qualifying country, otherwise than for the purposes of final consumption.

(3) For the purposes of subsection (2)(b) above, a non-qualifying country is one which does not provide for the protection of varieties of the genus or species to which the variety belongs.

(4) In this section, 'material', in relation to a variety, means—

(a) any kind of propagating material of the variety,

(b) harvested material of the variety, including entire plants and parts of plants, and

(c) any product made directly from material falling within paragraph (b) above.

Duration and transmission of plant breeders' rights

11   Duration

(1) A grant of plant breeders' rights shall have effect—

(a) in the case of potatoes, trees and vines, for 30 years from the date of the grant, and

(b) in other cases, for 25 years from that date.

(2) The Ministers may by regulations provide that, in relation to varieties of a species or group specified in the regulations, subsection (1) above shall have effect with the substitution in paragraph (a) or (b), as the case may be, of such longer period, not exceeding—

(a) in the case of paragraph (a), 35 years, and

(b) in the case of paragraph (b), 30 years, as may be so specified.

(3) The period for which a grant of plant breeders' rights has effect shall not be affected by the fact it becomes impossible to invoke the rights—

(b) because of suspension under section 23 below.

12   Transmission

Plant breeders' rights shall be assignable like other kinds of proprietary rights, but in any case rights under section 6 above and rights under section 7 above may not be assigned separately.

Remedies for infringement

13 Remedies for infringement

(1) Plant breeders' rights shall be actionable at the suit of the holder of the rights.

(2) In any proceedings for the infringement of plant breeders' rights, all such relief by way of damages, injunction, interdict, account or otherwise shall be available as is available in any corresponding proceedings in respect of infringements of other proprietary rights.

14 Presumptions in proceedings relating to harvested material

(1) This section applies to any proceedings for the infringement of plant breeders' rights as respects harvested material.

(2) If, in any proceedings to which this section applies, the holder of the plant breeders' rights proves, in relation to any of the material to which the proceedings relate—

(a) that it has been the subject of an information notice given to the defendant by or on behalf of the holder, and

(b) that the defendant has not, within the prescribed time after the service of the notice, supplied the holder with the information about it requested in the notice,

then, as regards the material in relation to which the holder proves that to be the case, the presumptions mentioned in subsection (3) below shall apply, unless the contrary is proved or the defendant shows that he had a reasonable excuse for not supplying the information.

(3) The presumptions are—

(a) that the material was obtained through unauthorised use of propagating material, and

(b) that the holder did not have a reasonable opportunity before the material was obtained to exercise his rights in relation to the unauthorised use of the propagating material.

(4) The reference in subsection (2) above to an information notice is to a notice which—

(a) is in the prescribed form,

(b) specifies the material to which it relates,

(c) contains, in relation to that material, a request for the supply of the prescribed, but no other, information, and

(d) contains such other particulars as may be prescribed.

(5) In this section, 'prescribed' means prescribed by regulations made by the Ministers.

15 Presumptions in proceedings relating to products made from harvested material

(1) This section applies to any proceedings for the infringement of plant breeders' rights as respects any product made directly from harvested material.

(2) If, in any proceedings to which this section applies, the holder of the plant breeders' rights proves, in relation to any product to which the proceedings relate—

(a) that it has been the subject of an information notice given to the defendant by or on behalf of the holder, and

(b) that the defendant has not, within the prescribed time after the service of the notice, supplied the holder with the information about it requested in the notice,

then, as regards the product in relation to which the holder proves that to be the case, the presumptions mentioned in subsection (3) below shall apply, unless the contrary is proved or the defendant shows that he had a reasonable excuse for not supplying the information.

(3) The presumptions are—

(a) that the harvested material from which the product was made was obtained through unauthorised use of propagating material,

(b) that the holder did not have a reasonable opportunity before the harvested material was obtained to exercise his rights in relation to the unauthorised use of the propagating material, and

(c) that no relevant act was done, before the product was made, as respects the harvested material from which it was made.

(4) An act is relevant for the purposes of subsection (3)(c) above if it is mentioned in section 6(1) above and is—

    (a) done with the authority of the holder, or

    (b) one in relation to the doing of which he has a reasonable opportunity to exercise his rights.

(5) The reference in subsection (2) above to an information notice is to a notice which—

    (a) is in the prescribed form,

    (b) specifies the product to which it relates,

    (c) contains, in relation to that product, a request for the supply of the prescribed, but no other, information, and

    (d) contains such other particulars as may be prescribed.

(6) In this section, 'prescribed' means prescribed by regulations made by the Ministers.

Duties of holders of plant breeders' rights

16   Maintenance of protected variety

(1) The holder of any plant breeders' rights shall ensure that, throughout the period for which the grant of the rights has effect, he is in a position to produce to the Controller propagating material which is capable of producing the protected variety.

. . .

17   Compulsory licences

(1) Subject to subsections (2) and (3) below, if the Controller is satisfied on application that the holder of any plant breeders' rights—

    (a) has unreasonably refused to grant a licence to the applicant, or

    (b) has imposed or put forward unreasonable terms in granting, or offering to grant, a licence to the applicant,

he may grant to the applicant in the form of a licence under this section any such rights as might have been granted by the holder.

(2) The Controller shall not grant an application for a licence under this section unless he is satisfied—

    (a) that it is necessary to do so for the purpose of securing that the variety to which the application relates—

      (i)   is available to the public at reasonable prices,

      (ii)   is widely distributed, or

      (iii) is maintained in quality,

    (b) that the applicant is financially and otherwise in a position to exploit in a competent and businesslike manner the rights to be conferred on him, and

    (c) that the applicant intends so to exploit those rights.

(3) A licence under this section shall not be an exclusive licence.

. . .

Naming of protected varieties

. . .

20   Improper use of registered name

(1) If any person uses the registered name of a protected variety in offering for sale, selling or otherwise marketing material of a different variety within the same class, the use of the name shall be a wrong actionable in proceedings by the holder of the rights.

(2) Subsection (1) above shall also apply to the use of a name so nearly resembling the registered name as to be likely to deceive or cause confusion.

(3) In any proceedings under this section, it shall be a defence to a claim for damages to prove that the defendant took all reasonable precautions against committing the wrong and had not, when using the name, any reason to suspect that it was wrongful.

(4) In this section—

'class' means a class prescribed for the purposes of regulations under section 18(1) above,

'registered name', in relation to a protected variety, means the name registered in respect of it under section 18 above.

Termination and suspension of plant breeders' rights

21 Nullity

(1) The Controller shall declare the grant of plant breeders' rights null and void if it is established—

- (a) that when the rights were granted the protected variety did not meet the criterion specified in paragraph (a) or (d) of section 4(2) above,
- (b) where the grant of the rights was essentially based upon information and documents furnished by the applicant, that when the rights were granted the protected variety did not meet the criterion specified in paragraph (b) or (c) of that provision, or
- (c) that the person to whom the rights were granted was not the person entitled to the grant of the rights and the rights have not subsequently been transferred to him, or his successor in title.

(2) If, because of paragraph 6 of Schedule 2 to this Act, priority is established for an application for the grant of plant breeders' rights after such rights have been granted in pursuance of an application against which priority is established, subsection (1)(c) above shall only apply to the grant if the Controller decides that the application for which priority is established should be granted.

(3) Where the grant of plant breeders' rights is declared null and void under this section, it shall be deemed never to have had effect.

22 Cancellation

(1) The Controller may terminate the period for which a grant of plant breeders' rights has effect if—

- (a) he is satisfied that the protected variety no longer meets the criterion specified in paragraph (b) or (c) of section 4(2) above,
- (b) it appears to him that the holder of the rights is no longer in a position to provide him with the propagating material mentioned in section 16(1) above,
- (c) he is satisfied that the holder of the rights has failed to comply with a request under section 16(2) above, or
- (d) on application by the holder of the rights, he is satisfied that the rights may properly be surrendered.

. . .

23 Suspension

(1) The Controller may suspend the exercise of any plant breeders' rights if, on application by the holder of a licence under section 17 above, he is satisfied that the holder of the rights is in breach of any obligation imposed on him by the licence.

. . .

Proceedings before the Controller

. . .

False information and representations as to rights

. . .

32 False representations as to rights

(1) If, in relation to any variety, a person falsely represents that he is entitled to exercise plant breeders' rights, or any rights derived from such rights, and he knows that the representation is false, or makes it recklessly, he shall be guilty of an offence and liable on summary conviction to a fine not exceeding level 3 on the standard scale.

(2) It is immaterial for the purposes of subsection (1) above whether or not the variety to which the representation relates is the subject of plant breeders' rights.

Miscellaneous

. . .

General

. . .

38   Interpretation of Part I

(1) In this Part of this Act—

'gazette' means the gazette published under section 34 of the Plant Varieties and Seeds Act 1964;

'name' includes any designation;

'protected variety', in relation to any plant breeders' rights, means the variety which was the basis of the application for the grant of the rights;

'variety' has the meaning given by section 1(3) above.

(2) In this Part of this Act references to an applicant for the grant of plant breeders' rights, or to the holder of plant breeders' rights, include, where the context allows, references to his predecessors in title or his successors in title.

(3) For the purposes of this Part of this Act, the existence of a variety shall be taken to be a matter of common knowledge if—

(a) it is, or has been, the subject of a plant variety right under any jurisdiction,

(b) it is, or has been, entered in an official register of plant varieties under any jurisdiction, or

(c) it is the subject of an application which subsequently leads to its falling within paragraph (a) or (b) above.

(4) Otherwise, common knowledge may be established for those purposes by reference, for example, to—

(a) plant varieties already in cultivation or exploited for commercial purposes,

(b) plant varieties included in a recognised commercial or botanical reference collection, or

(c) plant varieties of which there are precise descriptions in any publication.

. . .

Section 4   **SCHEDULE 2   CONDITIONS FOR THE GRANT OF PLANT BREEDERS' RIGHTS**

PART I   CRITERIA FOR GRANT OF RIGHTS

Distinctness

1. The variety shall be deemed to be distinct if it is clearly distinguishable by one or more characteristics which are capable of a precise description from any other variety whose existence is a matter of common knowledge at the time of the application.

Uniformity

2. The variety shall be deemed to be uniform if, subject to the variation that may be expected from the particular features of its propagation, it is sufficiently uniform in those characteristics which are included in the examination for distinctness.

Stability

3. The variety shall be deemed to be stable if those characteristics which are included in the examination for distinctness, as well as any others used for the variety description, remain unchanged after repeated propagation or, in the case of a particular cycle of propagation, at the end of each such cycle.

Novelty

4.—(1) The variety shall be deemed to be new if sub-paragraphs (2) and (3) below apply.

(2) This sub-paragraph applies if no sale or other disposal of propagating or harvested material of the variety for the purposes of exploiting the variety has, with the consent of the applicant, taken place in the United Kingdom earlier than one year before the date of the application.

(3) This sub-paragraph applies if no sale or other disposal of propagating or harvested material of the variety for the purposes of exploiting the variety has, with the consent of the applicant, taken place elsewhere than in the United Kingdom earlier than 4 years, or, in the case of trees or vines, 6 years, before the date of the application.

(4) For the purposes of sub-paragraphs (2) and (3) above, there shall be disregarded any sale or other disposal to which sub-paragraph (5), (6), (8) or (9) below applies.

(5) This sub-paragraph applies to any sale or other disposal of a stock of material of the variety to a person who at the time of the sale or other disposal is, or who subsequently becomes, the person entitled to the grant of plant breeders' rights in respect of the variety.

(6) This sub-paragraph applies to—

    (a) any sale or other disposal of propagating material of the variety to a person as part of qualifying arrangements, and

    (b) any sale or other disposal to the applicant, by a person who uses propagating material of the variety under any such arrangements, or the material produced directly or indirectly from the use.

(7) For the purposes of sub-paragraph (6) above, qualifying arrangements are arrangements under which—

    (a) a person uses propagating material of the variety under the applicant's control for the purpose of increasing the applicant's stock, or of carrying out tests or trials, and

    (b) the whole of the material produced, directly or indirectly, from the material becomes or remains the property of the applicant.

(8) This sub-paragraph applies to any sale or other disposal of material of the variety, other than propagating material, produced in the course of—

    (a) the breeding of the variety,

    (b) increasing the applicant's stock of material of the variety, or

    (c) carrying out tests or trials of the variety,

which does not involve identifying the variety from which the material is produced.

(9) This sub-paragraph applies to any disposal of material of the variety, otherwise than by way of sale, at an exhibition or for the purposes of display at an exhibition.

(10) For the purposes of sub-paragraphs (2) and (3) above, any sale or other disposal of propagating or harvested material of a variety for the purposes of exploiting the variety shall, if the variety is related to another variety, be treated as being also a sale or other disposal of propagating or harvested material of the other variety for the purposes of exploiting that variety.

(11) For the purposes of sub-paragraph (10) above, a variety is related to another if its nature is such that repeated production of the variety is not possible without repeated use of the other variety.

PART II PRIORITIES BETWEEN APPLICANTS FOR RIGHTS

5.—(1) If a variety is bred, or discovered and developed, by two or more persons independently, the first of those persons, and any successors in title of theirs, to apply for the grant of plant breeders' rights in respect of it shall be the person entitled to the grant.

. . .

Patents and Plant Variety Rights (Compulsory Licensing) Regulations 2002*

(SI 2002/247)

PART I   INTRODUCTORY

1   Citation, commencement and extent

(1) These Regulations may be cited as the Patents and Plant Variety Rights (Compulsory Licensing) Regulations 2002 and shall come into force on 1st March 2002.

(2) These Regulations extend to England, Wales, Scotland and Northern Ireland.

2   Interpretation

(1) In these Regulations—

'the 1977 Act' means the Patents Act 1977;

'the 1997 Act' means the Plant Varieties Act 1997;

'biotechnological invention' has the meaning given by section 130 of the 1977 Act;

'Breeders' regulations' means the Plant Breeders' Regulations as extended and applied by regulation 23, unless and until the Ministers exercise their powers under sections 24, 26(2)(a), 28, 29, 44 and 48(1) of the 1997 Act as extended by regulation 21, at which time 'Breeders' regulations' shall refer to the regulations so made and in force;

'Comptroller General of Patents' means the Comptroller-General of Patents, Designs and Trade Marks appointed under section 63(1) of the Patents and Designs Act 1907;

'compulsory patent licence' means a licence ordered to be granted by the controllers under regulation 6;

'compulsory plant variety licence' means a licence granted by the controllers under regulation 13;

'Controller of Plant Variety Rights' means the officer appointed under section 2(1) of the 1997 Act;

'controllers' means the Controller of Plant Variety Rights and the Comptroller General of Patents acting jointly in accordance with the provisions of these Regulations;

'court' means—

(a) in England, Wales and Northern Ireland, the Patents Court of the High Court,

(b) in Scotland, the Court of Session;

'Ministers' has the meaning given by section 49 of the 1997 Act;

'new plant variety' means the plant variety produced, or to be produced as the case may be, by using an invention protected by a patent;

'patent' has the meaning given by section 130 of the 1977 Act;

'Patents (Fees) Rules' means the Patents (Fees) Rules 2007;

'Patents Rules' means the Patents Rules 2007;

'plant breeders' fee' means the fee payable under the Plant Breeders' (Fees) Regulations as extended and applied by regulation 25, unless and until the Ministers exercise their powers to make regulations under sections 29 and 48(1) of the 1997 Act as extended by regulation 21 and prescribe a fee, at which time 'plant breeders' fee' shall mean that fee in respect of applications under these Regulations;

'Plant Breeders' (Fees) Regulations' mean the Plant Breeders' Rights (Fees) Regulations 1998 in force immediately before the coming into force of these Regulations;

'Plant Breeders' Regulations' means the Plant Breeders' Rights Regulations 1998 in force immediately before the coming into force of these Regulations;

'plant breeders' right' means—

---

* **Editor's Note:** Contains amendments effected by *Competition (Amendment etc.) (EU Exit) (No. 2) Regulations 2019.* By virtue of the *European Union (Withdrawal Agreement) Act 2020*, these amendments take effect on 'IP completion day', which is defined to be 31 December 2020 at 11:00pm.

    (a) any right granted under, or having effect as if granted under, section 3 of the 1997 Act (including existing rights as defined by section 40(4) of that Act); and

    (b) any right which by virtue of regulation 3 of the Plant Breeders' Rights (Amendment etc.) (EU Exit) Regulations 2019 is treated as if it were a plant breeders' right granted in accordance with the 1997 Act and as if the variety were registered in accordance with regulations under section 18(1)(c) of the 1997 Act;

'plant variety' has the meaning given by paragraph 11 of Schedule A2 to the 1977 Act;

'prescribed fee' means the fee payable under the Patents (Fees) Rules as extended and applied by regulation 24, unless and until the Secretary of State exercises her powers to make rules under section 123 of the 1977 Act as extended by regulation 20 and prescribes a fee, at which time 'prescribed fee' shall mean that fee in respect of applications under these Regulations;

'rules' means the Patents Rules as extended and applied by regulation 22, unless and until the Secretary of State exercises her powers under section 123 of the 1977 Act as extended by regulation 20, at which time 'rules' shall refer to the rules so made and in force;

'Tribunal' means the Plant Varieties and Seeds Tribunal referred to in section 42 of the 1997 Act; and

'UK' means England, Wales, Scotland and Northern Ireland.

    (2) Any reference to a numbered regulation is a reference to the regulation so numbered in these Regulations and any reference to a numbered paragraph is a reference to the paragraph so numbered in the regulation in which the reference occurs.

PART II   COMPULSORY PATENT LICENCES

3   Applications
    (1) Where a person cannot acquire or exploit plant breeders' rights in a new variety without infringing a prior patent, he may apply in accordance with rules to the Comptroller General of Patents for a licence under the patent and on such application shall pay the prescribed fee.

    . . .

6   Grant
Where, having considered the application made under regulation 3(1), the controllers are satisfied that—

    (a) the applicant cannot acquire or exploit plant breeders' rights without infringing a prior patent,

    (b) the applicant has applied unsuccessfully to the proprietor of the patent concerned for a licence to use the prior patent to acquire or exploit plant breeders' rights, and

    (c) the new plant variety, in which the applicant wishes to acquire or exploit the plant breeders' rights, constitutes significant technical progress of considerable economic interest in relation to the invention protected by the patent,

the controllers shall order the grant to the applicant (or, where the applicant is a government department, shall order the grant to any person specified in the application) of a licence to use the invention protected by the prior patent in so far as the licence is necessary for the exploitation of the new plant variety on the conditions set out in regulation 7 and on such other terms as the controllers think fit.

7   Conditions
    (1) A compulsory patent licence shall—

    (a) not be exclusive,

    (b) entitle the proprietor of the patent concerned to an appropriate royalty, and

    (c) entitle the proprietor of the patent concerned to a cross licence on reasonable terms to use the new plant variety.

    (2) Where the controllers order the grant of a compulsory patent licence to a person who has been granted plant breeders' rights in the new plant variety, the proprietor of the patent concerned may request, a cross licence on reasonable terms of the plant breeders' rights to use the new plant variety in respect of which the compulsory patent licence has been granted and, on such request, the controllers shall order the grant of such a cross licence to that proprietor (or, where the proprietor of the patent is a government department, to any person specified in the request).

    . . .

9 Revocation

(1) A party may, at any time, apply to the Comptroller General of Patents in accordance with rules to revoke an order for grant of—

(a) a compulsory patent licence, or

(b) cross licence under regulation 7(2) or 7(3),

if the circumstances which led to the order for grant have ceased to exist or are unlikely to recur.

(2) On receipt by the Comptroller General of Patents of an application under paragraph (1), the controllers shall consider and process the application in accordance with rules and if the controllers are satisfied that the circumstances which led to an order for grant of a—

(a) compulsory patent licence, or

(b) cross licence under regulation 7(2) or 7(3),

have ceased to exist or are unlikely to recur, the controllers may revoke the order and terminate the licence granted under the order, subject to such terms and conditions as they think necessary for the protection of the legitimate interests of the holder of the compulsory patent licence or the cross licence ordered to be granted under regulation 7(2) or 7(3).

10 In regulations 8 and 9, 'party' means the proprietor of the patent concerned or the applicant, as the case may be, in an application under regulation 3(1) or their respective successors in title.

PART III COMPULSORY PLANT VARIETY LICENCES

11 Applications

(1) Where a proprietor of a patent for a biotechnological invention cannot exploit a biotechnological invention protected by the patent without infringing prior plant breeders' rights, he may apply in accordance with Breeders' regulations to the Controller of Plant Variety Rights for a licence and on such application shall pay the plant breeders' fee.

. . .

13 Grant

Where, having considered the application under regulation 11(1), the controllers are satisfied that—

(a) the proprietor of a patent for a biotechnological invention cannot exploit the biotechnological invention protected by the patent without infringing prior plant breeders' rights,

(b) the proprietor of the patent has unsuccessfully applied to the holder of the prior plant breeders' rights for a licence, and

(c) the biotechnological invention protected by the patent constitutes significant technical progress of considerable economic interest in relation to the plant variety protected by the prior plant breeders' rights,

the controllers shall grant to the proprietor of the patent for the biotechnological invention (or, where the proprietor is a government department, to any person specified in the application) a licence to use the plant variety protected by prior plant breeders' rights on the conditions set out in regulation 14 and on such other terms as the controllers see fit.

14 Conditions

(1) A compulsory plant variety licence shall—

(a) not be exclusive,

(b) entitle the holder of the plant breeders' rights concerned to an appropriate royalty, and

(c) entitle the holder of the plant breeders' rights concerned to a cross licence on reasonable terms to use the biotechnological invention protected by the patent.

(2) Where the controllers grant a compulsory plant variety licence to a proprietor of a patent for a biotechnological invention, the holder of the plant breeders' rights concerned may request the grant of a cross licence on reasonable terms to use the biotechnological invention protected by the patent and, on such request, the controllers shall grant such cross licence to the holder of plant breeders' rights (or, where the holder is a government department, to any person specified in the request).

. . .

PART IV   APPEALS AND GENERAL PROVISIONS

17   Appeals

(1) An appeal lies from a decision of the controllers or Comptroller General of Patents under these Regulations.

(2) Where a decision of the controllers relates to a compulsory patent licence or cross licence ordered to be granted under regulation 7(2) or 7(3), an appeal may be made to the court.

(3) Where a decision of the controllers relates to a compulsory plant variety licence or cross licence of a patent for a biotechnological invention granted under regulation 14(2), an appeal may be brought to the Tribunal as if the decision of the controllers were one made by the Controller of Plant Variety Rights under section 17, and referred to in section 26(1)(c), of the 1997 Act and section 45 of the 1997 Act shall apply accordingly.

. . .

Trade Secrets (Enforcement, etc.) Regulations 2018

(SI 2018/597)

Citation, commencement and extent

1.—(1) These Regulations may be cited as the Trade Secrets (Enforcement, etc.) Regulations 2018 and come into force on 9th June 2018.

(2) These Regulations extend to England and Wales, Scotland and Northern Ireland.

Interpretation

2. For the purposes of these Regulations—

'court' means—

(a) in England and Wales, a County Court hearing centre where there is also a Chancery District Registry or the High Court (as provided for in rule 63.13 of the Civil Procedure Rules 1998),

(b) in Scotland, the sheriff or the Court of Session, and

(c) in Northern Ireland, a county court or the High Court;

'infringer' means a person who has unlawfully acquired, used or disclosed a trade secret;

'infringing goods' means goods, the design, functioning, production process, marketing or a characteristic of which significantly benefits from a trade secret unlawfully acquired, used or disclosed;

'trade secret' means information which—

(a) is secret in the sense that it is not, as a body or in the precise configuration and assembly of its components, generally known among, or readily accessible to, persons within the circles that normally deal with the kind of information in question,

(b) has commercial value because it is secret, and

(c) has been subject to reasonable steps under the circumstances, by the person lawfully in control of the information, to keep it secret;

'trade secret holder' means any person lawfully controlling a trade secret.

Wider protection

3.—(1) The acquisition, use or disclosure of a trade secret is unlawful where the acquisition, use or disclosure constitutes a breach of confidence in confidential information.

(2) A trade secret holder may apply for and a court may grant measures, procedures, and remedies available in an action for breach of confidence where the measures, procedures and remedies—

(a) provide wider protection to the trade secret holder than that provided under these Regulations in respect of the unlawful acquisition, use or disclosure of a trade secret, and

(b) comply with the safeguards referred to in Article 1 of Directive (EU) 2016/943 of the European Parliament and of the Council of 8 June 2016 on the protection of undisclosed know-how and business information (trade secrets) against their unlawful acquisition, use and disclosure.

(3) A trade secret holder may apply for and a court may grant the measures, procedures and remedies referred to in paragraph (2) in addition, or as an alternative, to the measures procedures and remedies provided for in these Regulations in respect of the unlawful acquisition, use or disclosure of a trade secret.

Time limits for bringing proceedings

4.—(1) Proceedings may not be brought before a court in respect of a claim for the unlawful acquisition, use or disclosure of a trade secret and for the application of measures, procedures and remedies provided for under these Regulations—

(a) in England and Wales and Northern Ireland, after the end of the limitation period for the claim, and

(b) in Scotland, after the end of the prescriptive period for the claim, except where the subsistence of the obligation in relation to which the claim is made was relevantly acknowledged before the end of that period.

(2) The limitation period referred to in paragraph 1(a) is to be determined in accordance with this regulation and regulations 5 to 7 and 9.

(3) Section 36 of the Limitation Act 1980 (equitable jurisdiction and remedies) does not apply in relation to proceedings in respect of a claim for the unlawful acquisition, use or disclosure of a trade secret.

(4) The prescriptive period referred to in paragraph 1(b)   is to be determined in accordance with this regulation and regulations 5, 6 and 8.

(5) Section 6 of the Prescription and Limitation (Scotland) Act 1973 (extinction of obligations by prescriptive periods of five years) does not apply in relation to an obligation arising from a claim for the unlawful acquisition, use or disclosure of a trade secret.

(6) The following provisions of the Prescription and Limitation (Scotland) Act 1973 apply for the purposes of, or in relation to, paragraph (1)(b)   as they apply for the purposes of, or in relation to, section 6 of that Act—

(a) section 10 (relevant acknowledgment);

(b) section 13 (prohibition of contracting out);

(c) section 14(1)(c)   and (d)   (computation of prescriptive periods).

Length of limitation or prescriptive period

5.—(1) The limitation period is six years.

(2) The prescriptive period is five years.

(3) The limitation or prescriptive period begins with the day specified in regulation 6.

Beginning of limitation or prescriptive period

6.—(1) The limitation or prescriptive period for a claim for the unlawful acquisition, use or disclosure of a trade secret against an infringer begins with the later of—

(a) the day on which the unlawful acquisition, use or disclosure that is the subject of the claim ceases, and

(b) the day of knowledge of the trade secret holder.

(2) In paragraph (1)(b), 'the day of knowledge of the trade secret holder' is the day on which the trade secret holder first knows or could reasonably be expected to know—

(a) of the infringer's activity,

(b) that the activity constitutes an unlawful acquisition, use or disclosure of a trade secret, and

(c) the identity of the infringer.

(3) The reference in paragraph (2) to the trade secret holder knowing something is to the trade secret holder having sufficient knowledge of it to bring a claim for the unlawful acquisition, use or disclosure of a trade secret.

(4) Where a person has acquired the liability of an infringer from another person (whether by operation of law or otherwise)—

(a) the reference to an infringer in paragraph (1) is to be read as a reference to the person who has acquired the liability, but

(b) the references to the infringer in paragraph (2) are to be read as references to the original infringer.

(5) This regulation has effect subject to—

(a) regulation 7 in relation to the limitation period, and

(b) regulation 8 in relation to the prescriptive period.

Effect of disability on limitation period

7.—(1) If, in relation to a claim in England and Wales and Northern Ireland for the unlawful acquisition, use or disclosure of a trade secret, the trade secret holder is under a disability during the whole or any part of the limitation period, the limitation period for the claim begins with the earlier of—

(a) the day on which the trade secret holder ceases to be under a disability, and

(b) the day on which the trade secret holder dies.

(2) In England and Wales, references in paragraph (1) to a person being 'under a disability' have the same meaning as in section 38(2) of the Limitation Act 1980 (interpretation).

(3) In Northern Ireland, references in paragraph (1) to a person being 'under a disability' have the same meaning as in article 47 of the Limitation (Northern Ireland) Order 1989 (persons under a disability).

Suspension of prescriptive period during period of disability

8.—(1) If, in relation to a claim in Scotland for the unlawful acquisition, use or disclosure of a trade secret, the trade secret holder is under legal disability for a period at any time, the period during which the trade secret holder is under legal disability—

(a) is not to be counted when calculating whether the prescriptive period for the claim has expired, and

(b) is not to be regarded as separating the time immediately before it from the time immediately after it.

(2) In paragraph (1), 'legal disability' has the same meaning as in section 15(1) of the Prescription and Limitation (Scotland) Act 1973 (interpretation).

New claims in pending actions: England and Wales and Northern Ireland

9. For the purposes of regulations 4 to 7—

(a) section 35 of the Limitation Act 1980 (new claims in pending action) applies in relation to a claim for the unlawful acquisition, use or disclosure of a trade secret that is a new claim and to proceedings for the unlawful acquisition, use or disclosure of a trade secret as it applies in relation to new claims and proceedings for the purposes of that Act; and

(b) Article 73 of the Limitation (Northern Ireland) Order 1989 (new claims in pending actions) applies in relation to a claim for the unlawful acquisition, use or disclosure of a trade secret that is a new claim and to proceedings for the unlawful acquisition, use or disclosure of a trade secret as it applies in relation to new claims and proceedings for the purposes of that Order.

Preservation of confidentiality of trade secrets in the course of proceedings

10.—(1) A participant, or a participant who has access to documents which form part of the proceedings, must not use or disclose any trade secret or alleged trade secret—

(a) which, on a duly reasoned application by an interested party or on a court's own initiative, a court by order identifies as confidential, and

(b) of which a participant has become aware as a result of participation in the proceedings or the access.

(2) The obligation referred to in paragraph (1) remains in force after the proceedings have ended, subject to paragraph (3).

(3) The obligation in paragraph (1) ceases to exist—

    (a) where a court, by final decision, finds that the alleged trade secret does not meet the requirements of a trade secret, or

    (b) where over time the information in question becomes generally known among, or readily accessible to, persons within the circles that normally deal with that kind of information.

(4) On a duly reasoned application by a party or on a court's own initiative, a court may order any of the measures set out in paragraph (5) as may be necessary to preserve the confidentiality of any trade secret or alleged trade secret used or referred to in the course of proceedings.

(5) A court may—

    (a) restrict access to any document containing a trade secret or alleged trade secret submitted by the parties or third parties, in whole or in part, to a limited number of persons,

    (b) restrict access to hearings, when trade secrets or alleged trade secrets may be disclosed, and to the record or transcript of those hearings to a limited number of persons, and

    (c) make available to a person, who is not one of the limited number of persons referred to in sub-paragraph (a)   or (b), a non-confidential version of any judicial decision, in which the passages containing trade secrets have been removed or redacted.

(6) The number of persons referred to in paragraph 5(a)   or (b)   must be no greater than necessary to ensure compliance with the right of the parties to the legal proceedings to an effective remedy and to a fair trial, and must include, at least, one individual from each party and the lawyers or other representatives of those parties to the proceedings.

(7) In deciding whether or not to grant the measures in paragraph (5) in accordance with paragraphs (4) and (6) and which of the measures to order and in assessing the proportionality of the measures, a court must take into account—

    (a) the need to ensure the right to an effective remedy and to a fair trial,

    (b) the legitimate interests of the parties, and

    (c) any potential harm for the parties.

(8) In this regulation—

'participant' means a party, a lawyer or other representative of a party, a court official, a witness, an expert or any other person participating in proceedings;

'parties', in paragraph (7), includes, where appropriate, third parties;

'proceedings' means legal proceedings relating to the unlawful acquisition, use or disclosure of a trade secret.

Interim measures

11.—(1) On the application of a trade secret holder, a court may order any of the following measures against the alleged infringer—

    (a) the cessation of, or (as the case may be) the prohibition of, the use or disclosure of the trade secret on a provisional basis;

    (b) the prohibition of the production, offering, placing on the market or use of infringing goods, or the importation, export or storage of infringing goods for those purposes;

    (c) the seizure or delivery up of the suspected infringing goods, including imported goods, so as to prevent the goods entering into, or circulating on, the market.

(2) A person to whom the suspected infringing goods are delivered up under paragraph (1)(c) must retain the infringing goods pending a decision to make or not to make an order under regulation 14(2).

(3) A court making an order under paragraph (1) may set a reasonable period within which a trade secret holder must bring proceedings for a decision on the merits of the case before a court.

(4) Where no period is set under paragraph (3), a trade secret holder must bring proceedings before a court within a period not exceeding 20 working days or 31 calendar days after the day on which the order under paragraph (1) has been made, whichever is the longer.

(5) For the purposes of paragraph (4)—

(a) if the period of 20 working days ends on a day other than a working day, the proceedings are in time if they are brought on the next working day, and

(b) 'working day' means any day except a Saturday or Sunday, Christmas Day, Good Friday or a day which is a bank holiday in any part of the United Kingdom under section 1 of the Banking and Financial Dealings Act 1971 (bank holidays).

(6) As an alternative to the measures referred to in paragraph (1), a court may make an order making the continuation of the alleged unlawful use conditional upon the lodging by the alleged infringer of guarantees intended to ensure the compensation of the trade secret holder.

(7) An order under paragraph (6) must not permit disclosure of a trade secret in return for the lodging of guarantees.

(8) A court may make an order under paragraph (1) or (6) conditional upon the lodging by the trade secret holder of adequate security or an equivalent assurance intended to ensure compensation for any prejudice suffered by the alleged infringer and, where appropriate, by any other person affected by the order.

Matters to be considered before making an order under regulation 11(1)

12.—(1) Before making an order under regulation 11(1), a court may require the trade secret holder to provide evidence that may reasonably be considered available to satisfy the court with a sufficient degree of certainty that—

(a) a trade secret exists,

(b) the trade secret holder is making the application, and

(c) the alleged infringer—

    (i)   has acquired the trade secret unlawfully,

    (ii) is unlawfully using or disclosing the trade secret, or

    (iii) is about to unlawfully use or disclose the trade secret.

(2) In considering whether to make an order under regulation 11(1) and in assessing the proportionality of such an order, a court must take into account the specific circumstances of the case, including where appropriate—

(a) the value and other specific features of the trade secret,

(b) the measures taken to protect the trade secret,

(c) the conduct of the alleged infringer in acquiring, using or disclosing the trade secret,

(d) the impact of the unlawful use or disclosure of the trade secret,

(e) the legitimate interests of the parties and the impact which the granting or rejection of the measures could have on the parties,

(f) the legitimate interests of third parties,

(g) the public interest, and

(h) the safeguard of fundamental rights.

Revocation of order under regulation 11(1)

13.—(1) Where a court makes an order under regulation 11(1), the court may, on the application of the alleged infringer, revoke the order—

(a) if the trade secret holder does not bring proceedings leading to a decision on the merits of the case before a court within the period set under regulation 11(3) or in regulation 11(4), or

(b) if the information in question is no longer a trade secret for reasons that cannot be attributed to the alleged infringer.

(2) A court may, on the application of the alleged infringer or an injured third party, order the trade secret holder to provide the alleged infringer, or the injured third party, appropriate compensation for any injury caused by a measure ordered under regulation 11(1)—

(a) where a court revokes an order under paragraph (1)(a),

(b) where the measure lapses due to any act or omission by the trade secret holder, or

(c) where it is subsequently found that there has been no unlawful acquisition, use or disclosure of a trade secret or threat of such conduct.

Injunctions or interdicts and corrective measures

14.—(1) Where a court finds on the merits of the case that there has been an unlawful acquisition, use or disclosure of a trade secret, the court may, on application by the trade secret holder, order one or more of the following measures against the infringer—

(a) the cessation of, or (as the case may be) the prohibition of, the use or disclosure of the trade secret;

(b) the prohibition of the production, offering, placing on the market or use of infringing goods, or the importation, export or storage of infringing goods for those purposes;

(c) the adoption of corrective measures with regard to the infringing goods, including where appropriate—

(i)   recall of the infringing goods from the market;

(ii) depriving the infringing goods of their infringing quality;

(iii) destruction of the infringing goods or their withdrawal from the market, provided that the withdrawal does not undermine the protection of the trade secret in question;

(d) the destruction of all or part of any document, object, material, substance or electronic file containing or embodying the trade secret, or where appropriate, the delivery up to the applicant of all or part of that document, object, material, substance or electronic file.

(2) Where a court orders that infringing goods be withdrawn from the market, the court may order, on the application of the trade secret holder, that the infringing goods be delivered up and forfeited to the trade secret holder together with all or part of any document, object, material, substance or electronic file containing or embodying the trade secret.

(3) Where a court makes an order for a measure under paragraph (1)(c)   or (d)   or   paragraph (2), the court must—

(a) order that the measure be carried out at the expense of the infringer, unless there are particular reasons for not doing so, and

(b) ensure the measure is without prejudice to any damages that may be due to the trade secret holder by reason of the unlawful acquisition, use or disclosure of the trade secret.

Matters to be considered when making an order under regulation 14

15.—(1) In considering an application for an order under regulation 14 and assessing the proportionality of such an order, the court must take into account the specific circumstances of the case, including where appropriate—

(a) the value or other specific features of the trade secret,

(b) the measures taken to protect the trade secret,

(c) the conduct of the infringer in acquiring, using or disclosing the trade secret,

(d) the impact of the unlawful use or disclosure of the trade secret,

(e) the legitimate interests of the parties and the impact which the granting or rejection of the measures could have on the parties,

(f) the legitimate interests of third parties,

(g) the public interest, and

(h) the safeguard of fundamental rights.

(2) Where a court makes an order limiting the duration of a measure ordered under regulation 14(1)(a) or (b), the duration must be sufficient to eliminate any commercial or economic advantage that the infringer could have derived from the unlawful acquisition, use or disclosure of the trade secret.

(3) On the application of the defendant, the court must revoke a measure ordered under regulation 14(1)(a) or (b) if the information in question no longer constitutes a trade secret for reasons that cannot be attributed directly or indirectly to the defendant.

(4) In the application of paragraph (3) to Scotland, 'defendant' means defender.

Compensation instead of order under regulation 14

16.—(1) A person liable to the imposition of an order under regulation 14 may apply for, and a court may make, an order for compensation to be paid to the injured party instead of an order under regulation 14—

(a) if at the time of use or disclosure the person neither knew nor ought, under the circumstances, to have known that the trade secret was obtained from another person who was using or disclosing the trade secret unlawfully,

(b) if the execution of the measures in question would cause disproportionate harm to the person liable to the measures, and

(c) if it appears reasonably satisfactory to pay compensation to the injured party.

(2) Where a court makes an order for the payment of compensation instead of an order under regulation 14(1)(a) or (b), the compensation must not exceed the amount of royalties or fees which would have been due, had that person obtained a licence to use the trade secret in question, for the period for which use of the trade secret could have been prohibited.

Assessment of damages

17.—(1) On the application of an injured party, a court must order an infringer, who knew or ought to have known that unlawful acquisition, use or disclosure of a trade secret was being engaged in, to pay the trade secret holder damages appropriate to the actual prejudice suffered as a result of the unlawful acquisition, use or disclosure of the trade secret.

(2) A court may award damages under paragraph (1) on the basis of either paragraph (3) or (4).

(3) When awarding damages under paragraph (1) on the basis of this paragraph, a court must take into account all appropriate factors, including in particular—

(i) the negative economic consequences, including any lost profits, which the trade secret holder has suffered, and any unfair profits made by the infringer, and

(ii) elements other than economic factors, including the moral prejudice caused to the trade secret holder by the unlawful acquisition, use or disclosure of the trade secret.

(4) When awarding damages under paragraph (1) on the basis of this paragraph, a court may, where appropriate, award damages on the basis of the royalties or fees which would have been due had the infringer obtained a licence to use the trade secret in question.

Publication of judicial decisions

18.—(1) In proceedings for the unlawful acquisition, use or disclosure of a trade secret, a court may order, on the application of the trade secret holder and at the expense of the infringer, appropriate measures for the dissemination of information concerning the judgment, including its publication in whole or in part.

(2) Any measure a court may order under paragraph (1) must preserve the confidentiality of trade secrets as provided for in regulation 10.

(3) In deciding whether to order a measure under paragraph (1) and when assessing whether such measure is proportionate, the court must take into account where appropriate—

(a) the value of the trade secret,

(b) the conduct of the infringer in acquiring, using or disclosing the trade secret,

(c) the impact of the unlawful use or disclosure of the trade secret,

(d) the likelihood of further unlawful use, or disclosure of the trade secret by the infringer, and

(e) whether the information on the infringer would be such as to allow an individual to be identified and, if so, whether publication of that information would be justified, in particular in the light of the possible harm that such measure may cause to the privacy and reputation of the infringer.

Proceedings to which these Regulations apply

19. These Regulations apply only to proceedings—

(a) brought before a court after the coming into force of these Regulations,

(b) in respect a claim for the unlawful acquisition, use or disclosure of a trade secret, and

(c) for the application of measures, procedures and remedies provided for under these Regulations.

C2. UNITED STATES

Patent Act of 1952

(United States Code Title 35 – Patents)

. . .

PART II – PATENTABILITY OF INVENTIONS AND GRANT OF PATENTS

Chapter 10 – Patentability of Inventions

§ 100. Definitions

When used in this title unless the context otherwise indicates—

(a) The term 'invention' means invention or discovery.

(b) The term 'process' means process, art or method, and includes a new use of a known process, machine, manufacture, composition of matter, or material.

(c) The terms 'United States' and 'this country' mean the United States of America, its territories and possessions.

(d) The word 'patentee' includes not only the patentee to whom the patent was issued but also the successors in title to the patentee.

. . .

(f) The term 'inventor' means the individual or, if a joint invention, the individuals collectively who invented or discovered the subject matter of the invention.

. . .

§ 101. Inventions patentable

Whoever invents or discovers any new and useful process, machine, manufacture, or composition of matter, or any new and useful improvement thereof, may obtain a patent therefor, subject to the conditions and requirements of this title.

§ 102. Conditions for patentability; novelty

(a) Novelty; Prior Art.—A person shall be entitled to a patent unless—

(1) the claimed invention was patented, described in a printed publication, or in public use, on sale, or otherwise available to the public before the effective filing date of the claimed invention; or

(2) the claimed invention was described in a patent issued under section 151, or in an application for patent published or deemed published under section 122(b), in which the patent or application, as the case may be, names another inventor and was effectively filed before the effective filing date of the claimed invention.

(b) Exceptions.—

    (1) Disclosures made 1 year or less before the effective filing date of the claimed invention.— A disclosure made 1 year or less before the effective filing date of a claimed invention shall not be prior art to the claimed invention under subsection (a)(1) if—

        (A) the disclosure was made by the inventor or joint inventor or by another who obtained the subject matter disclosed directly or indirectly from the inventor or a joint inventor; or

        (B) the subject matter disclosed had, before such disclosure, been publicly disclosed by the inventor or a joint inventor or another who obtained the subject matter disclosed directly or indirectly from the inventor or a joint inventor.

    (2) Disclosures appearing in applications and patents.—A disclosure shall not be prior art to a claimed invention under subsection (a)(2) if—

        (A) the subject matter disclosed was obtained directly or indirectly from the inventor or a joint inventor;

        (B) the subject matter disclosed had, before such subject matter was effectively filed under subsection (a)(2), been publicly disclosed by the inventor or a joint inventor or another who obtained the subject matter disclosed directly or indirectly from the inventor or a joint inventor; or

        (C) the subject matter disclosed and the claimed invention, not later than the effective filing date of the claimed invention, were owned by the same person or subject to an obligation of assignment to the same person.

. . .

§ 103. Conditions for patentability; non-obvious subject matter

A patent for a claimed invention may not be obtained, notwithstanding that the claimed invention is not identically disclosed as set forth in section 102, if the differences between the claimed invention and the prior art are such that the claimed invention as a whole would have been obvious before the effective filing date of the claimed invention to a person having ordinary skill in the art to which the claimed invention pertains. Patentability shall not be negated by the manner in which the invention was made.

. . .

Chapter 15 – Plant Patents

§ 161. Patents for plants

Whoever invents or discovers and asexually reproduces any distinct and new variety of plant, including cultivated sports, mutants, hybrids, and newly found seedlings, other than a tuber propagated plant or a plant found in an uncultivated state, may obtain a patent therefor, subject to the conditions and requirements of this title.

    The provisions of this title relating to patents for inventions shall apply to patents for plants, except as otherwise provided.

§ 162. Description, claim

No plant patent shall be declared invalid for noncompliance with section 112 if the description is as complete as is reasonably possible.

    The claim in the specification shall be in formal terms to the plant shown and described.

§ 163. Grant

In the case of a plant patent, the grant shall include the right to exclude others from asexually reproducing the plant, and from using, offering for sale, or selling the plant so reproduced, or any of its parts, throughout the United States, or from importing the plant so reproduced, or any parts thereof, into the United States.

. . .

Chapter 16 – Designs

§ 171. Patents for designs

Whoever invents any new, original and ornamental design for an article of manufacture may obtain a patent therefor, subject to the conditions and requirements of this title.

The provisions of this title relating to patents for inventions shall apply to patents for designs, except as otherwise provided.

§ 172.   Right of priority

The right of priority provided for by subsections (a) through (d) of section 119 shall be six months in the case of designs. The right of priority provided for by section 119(e) shall not apply to designs.

§ 173.   Term of design patent

Patents for designs shall be granted for the term of fourteen years from the date of grant.

. . .

PART III – PATENTS AND PROTECTION OF PATENT RIGHTS

. . .

Chapter 28 – Infringement of Patents

§ 271.   Infringement of patent

(a) Except as otherwise provided in this title, whoever without authority makes, uses, offers to sell, or sells any patented invention, within the United States or imports into the United States any patented invention during the term of the patent therefor, infringes the patent.

(b) Whoever actively induces infringement of a patent shall be liable as an infringer.

(c) Whoever offers to sell or sells within the United States or imports into the United States a component of a patented machine, manufacture, combination or composition, or a material or apparatus for use in practicing a patented process, constituting a material part of the invention, knowing the same to be especially made or especially adapted for use in an infringement of such patent, and not a staple article or commodity of commerce suitable for substantial noninfringing use, shall be liable as a contributory infringer.

. . .

    (e)

      (1) It shall not be an act of infringement to make, use, offer to sell, or sell within the United States or import into the United States a patented invention (other than a new animal drug or veterinary biological product (as those terms are used in the Federal Food, Drug, and Cosmetic Act and the Act of March 4, 1913) which is primarily manufactured using recombinant DNA, recombinant RNA, hybridoma technology, or other processes involving site specific genetic manipulation techniques) solely for uses reasonably related to the development and submission of information under a Federal law which regulates the manufacture, use, or sale of drugs or veterinary biological products.

      (2) It shall be an act of infringement to submit—

        (A) an application under section 505(j) of the Federal Food, Drug, and Cosmetic Act or described in section 505(b)(2) of such Act for a drug claimed in a patent or the use of which is claimed in a patent, . . .

if the purpose of such submission is to obtain approval under such Act to engage in the commercial manufacture, use, or sale of a drug, veterinary biological product, or biological product claimed in a patent or the use of which is claimed in a patent before the expiration of such patent.

(3) In any action for patent infringement brought under this section, no injunctive or other relief may be granted which would prohibit the making, using, offering to sell, or selling within the United States or importing into the United States of a patented invention under paragraph (1).

. . .

(f)

(1) Whoever without authority supplies or causes to be supplied in or from the United States all or a substantial portion of the components of a patented invention, where such components are uncombined in whole or in part, in such manner as to actively induce the combination of such components outside of the United States in a manner that would infringe the patent if such combination occurred within the United States, shall be liable as an infringer.

(2) Whoever without authority supplies or causes to be supplied in or from the United States any component of a patented invention that is especially made or especially adapted for use in the invention and not a staple article or commodity of commerce suitable for substantial noninfringing use, where such component is uncombined in whole or in part, knowing that such component is so made or adapted and intending that such component will be combined outside of the United States in a manner that would infringe the patent if such combination occurred within the United States, shall be liable as an infringer.

(g) Whoever without authority imports into the United States or offers to sell, sells, or uses within the United States a product which is made by a process patented in the United States shall be liable as an infringer, if the importation, offer to sell, sale, or use of the product occurs during the term of such process patent. In an action for infringement of a process patent, no remedy may be granted for infringement on account of the noncommercial use or retail sale of a product unless there is no adequate remedy under this title for infringement on account of the importation or other use, offer to sell, or sale of that product. A product which is made by a patented process will, for purposes of this title, not be considered to be so made after—

(1) it is materially changed by subsequent processes; or

(2) it becomes a trivial and nonessential component of another product.

(h) As used in this section, the term 'whoever' includes any State, any instrumentality of a State, and any officer or employee of a State or instrumentality of a State acting in his official capacity. Any State, and any such instrumentality, officer, or employee, shall be subject to the provisions of this title in the same manner and to the same extent as any nongovernmental entity.

(i) As used in this section, an 'offer for sale' or an 'offer to sell' by a person other than the patentee, or any designee of the patentee, is that in which the sale will occur before the expiration of the term of the patent.

. . .

§ 273. Defense to infringement based on earlier inventor

(a) In General.—A person shall be entitled to a defense under section 282(b) with respect to subject matter consisting of a process, or consisting of a machine, manufacture, or composition of matter used in a manufacturing or other commercial process, that would otherwise infringe a claimed invention being asserted against the person if—

(1) such person, acting in good faith, commercially used the subject matter in the United States, either in connection with an internal commercial use or an actual arm's length sale or other arm's length commercial transfer of a useful end result of such commercial use; and

(2) such commercial use occurred at least 1 year before the earlier of either—

(A) the effective filing date of the claimed invention; or

(B) the date on which the claimed invention was disclosed to the public in a manner that qualified for the exception from prior art under section 102(b).

(b) Burden of proof.—A person asserting a defense under this section shall have the burden of establishing the defense by clear and convincing evidence.

(c) Additional commercial uses.—

(1) Premarketing regulatory review.—Subject matter for which commercial marketing or use is subject to a premarketing regulatory review period during which the safety or efficacy of the subject matter is established, including any period specified in section 156(g), shall be deemed to be commercially used for purposes of subsection (a)(1) during such regulatory review period.

(2) Nonprofit laboratory use.—A use of subject matter by a nonprofit research laboratory or other nonprofit entity, such as a university or hospital, for which the public is the intended beneficiary, shall be deemed to be a commercial use for purposes of subsection (a)(1), except that a defense under this section may be asserted pursuant to this paragraph only for continued and noncommercial use by and in the laboratory or other nonprofit entity.

(d) Exhaustion of rights.—Notwithstanding subsection (e)(1), the sale or other disposition of a useful end result by a person entitled to assert a defense under this section in connection with a patent with respect to that useful end result shall exhaust the patent owner's rights under the patent to the extent that such rights would have been exhausted had such sale or other disposition been made by the patent owner.

(e) Limitations and exceptions.—

. . .

(5) University exception.—

(A) In general.—A person commercially using subject matter to which subsection (a) applies may not assert a defense under this section if the claimed invention with respect to which the defense is asserted was, at the time the invention was made, owned or subject to an obligation of assignment to either an institution of higher education (as defined in section 101(a) of the Higher Education Act of 1965 (20 U.S.C. 1001(a)), or a technology transfer organization whose primary purpose is to facilitate the commercialization of technologies developed by one or more such institutions of higher education.

(B) Exception.—Subparagraph (A) shall not apply if any of the activities required to reduce to practice the subject matter of the claimed invention could not have been undertaken using funds provided by the Federal Government.

. . .

Chapter 29 – Remedies for Infringement of Patent, and Other Actions

§ 281. Remedy for infringement of patent

A patentee shall have remedy by civil action for infringement of his patent.

§ 282. Presumption of validity; defenses

(a) In General.—A patent shall be presumed valid. Each claim of a patent (whether in independent, dependent, or multiple dependent form) shall be presumed valid independently of the validity of other claims; dependent or multiple dependent claims shall be presumed valid even though dependent upon an invalid claim. The burden of establishing invalidity of a patent or any claim thereof shall rest on the party asserting such invalidity.

(b) Defenses.—The following shall be defenses in any action involving the validity or infringement of a patent and shall be pleaded:

(1) Noninfringement, absence of liability for infringement or unenforceability,

(2) Invalidity of the patent or any claim in suit on any ground specified in part II as a condition for patentability,

(3) Invalidity of the patent or any claim in suit for failure to comply with—

    (A) any requirement of section 112, except that the failure to disclose the best mode shall not be a basis on which any claim of a patent may be canceled or held invalid or otherwise unenforceable; or

    (B) any requirement of section 251.

(4) Any other fact or act made a defense by this title.

. . .

§ 287. Limitation on damages and other remedies; marking and notice

(a) Patentees, and persons making, offering for sale, or selling within the United States any patented article for or under them, or importing any patented article into the United States, may give notice to the public that the same is patented, either by fixing thereon the word 'patent' or the abbreviation 'pat.', together with the number of the patent, or by fixing thereon the word 'patent' or the abbreviation 'pat.' together with an address of a posting on the Internet, accessible to the public without charge for accessing the address, that associates the patented article with the number of the patent, or when, from the character of the article, this can not be done, by fixing to it, or to the package wherein one or more of them is contained, a label containing a like notice. In the event of failure so to mark, no damages shall be recovered by the patentee in any action for infringement, except on proof that the infringer was notified of the infringement and continued to infringe thereafter, in which event damages may be recovered only for infringement occurring after such notice. Filing of an action for infringement shall constitute such notice.

. . .

(c)

(1) With respect to a medical practitioner's performance of a medical activity that constitutes an infringement under section 271(a) or (b), the provisions of sections 281, 283, 284, and 285 shall not apply against the medical practitioner or against a related health care entity with respect to such medical activity.

(2) For the purposes of this subsection:

    (A) the term 'medical activity' means the performance of a medical or surgical procedure on a body, but shall not include

        (i) the use of a patented machine, manufacture, or composition of matter in violation of such patent,

        (ii) the practice of a patented use of a composition of matter in violation of such patent, or

        (iii) the practice of a process in violation of a biotechnology patent.

    (B) the term 'medical practitioner' means any natural person who is licensed by a State to provide the medical activity described in subsection (c)(1) or who is acting under the direction of such person in the performance of the medical activity.

    (C) the term 'related health care entity' shall mean an entity with which a medical practitioner has a professional affiliation under which the medical practitioner performs the medical activity, including but not limited to a nursing home, hospital, university, medical school, health maintenance organization, group medical practice, or a medical clinic.

    (D) the term 'professional affiliation' shall mean staff privileges, medical staff membership, employment or contractual relationship, partnership or ownership interest, academic appointment, or other affiliation under which a medical practitioner provides the medical activity on behalf of, or in association with, the health care entity.

    (E) the term 'body' shall mean a human body, organ or cadaver, or a nonhuman animal used in medical research or instruction directly relating to the treatment of humans.

(F) the term 'patented use of a composition of matter' does not include a claim for a method of performing a medical or surgical procedure on a body that recites the use of a composition of matter where the use of that composition of matter does not directly contribute to achievement of the objective of the claimed method.

(G) the term 'State' shall mean any State or territory of the United States, the District of Columbia, and the Commonwealth of Puerto Rico.

. . .

§ 295.   Presumption: Product made by patented process

In actions alleging infringement of a process patent based on the importation, sale, offer for sale, or use of a product which is made from a process patented in the United States, if the court finds—

(1) that a substantial likelihood exists that the product was made by the patented process, and

(2) that the plaintiff has made a reasonable effort to determine the process actually used in the production of the product and was unable to so determine,

the product shall be presumed to have been so made, and the burden of establishing that the product was not made by the process shall be on the party asserting that it was not so made.

. . .

C3.   EUROPEAN UNION

Council Regulation (EC) No. 2100/94

of 27 July 1994 on Community plant variety rights

THE COUNCIL OF THE EUROPEAN UNION,

Having regard to the Treaty establishing the European Community, and in particular Article 235 thereof,

Having regard to the proposal from the Commission,

Having regard to the opinion of the European Parliament,

Having regard to the opinion of the Economic and Social Committee,

Whereas plant varieties pose specific problems as regards the industrial property regime which may be applicable;

Whereas industrial property regimes for plant varieties have not been harmonised at Community level and therefore continue to be regulated by the legislation of the Member States, the content of which is not uniform;

Whereas in such circumstances it is appropriate to create a Community regime which, although co-existing with national regimes, allows for the grant of industrial property rights valid throughout the Community;

Whereas it is appropriate that the implementation and application of this Community regime should not be carried out by the authorities of the Member States but by a Community Office with legal personality, the 'Community Plant Variety Office';

Whereas the system must also have regard to developments in plant breeding techniques including biotechnology; whereas in order to stimulate the breeding and development of new varieties, there should be improved protection compared with the present situation for all plant breeders without, however, unjustifiably impairing access to protection generally or in the case of certain breeding techniques;

Whereas varieties of all botanical genera and species should be protectable;

Whereas protectable varieties must comply with internationally recognised requirements, i.e., distinctness, uniformity, stability and novelty, and also be designated by a prescribed variety denomination;

Whereas it is important to provide for a definition of a plant variety, in order to ensure the proper functioning of the system;

Whereas this definition is not intended to alter definitions which may have been established in the field of intellectual property rights, especially the patent field, nor to interfere with or exclude from application laws governing the protectability of products, including plants and plant material, or processes under such other industrial property rights;

Whereas it is however highly desirable to have a common definition in both fields; whereas therefore appropriate efforts at international level should be supported to reach such a common definition;

Whereas for the grant of Community plant variety rights an assessment of important characteristics relating to the variety is necessary; whereas, however, these characteristics need not necessarily relate to their economic importance;

Whereas the system must also clarify to whom the right to Community plant variety protection pertains; whereas in some cases it would be to several persons in common, not just to one; whereas the formal entitlement to make applications must be regulated;

Whereas the system must also define the term 'holder' used in this Regulation; whereas that term 'holder' without further specification is used in this Regulation including in its Article 29(5), it is intended to be within the meaning of Article 13(1) thereof;

Whereas, since the effect of a Community plant variety right should be uniform throughout the Community, commercial transactions subject to the holder's agreement must be precisely delimited; whereas the scope of protection should be extended, compared with most national systems, to certain material of the variety to take account of trade via countries outside the Community without protection; whereas, however, the introduction of the principle of exhaustion of rights must ensure that the protection is not excessive;

Whereas in order to stimulate plant breeding, the system basically confirms the internationally accepted rule of free access to protected varieties for the development therefrom, and exploitation, of new varieties;

Whereas in certain cases where the new variety, although distinct, is essentially derived from the initial variety, a certain form of dependency from the holder of the latter one should be created;

Whereas, the exercise of Community plant variety rights must be subjected to restrictions laid down in provisions adopted in the public interest;

Whereas this includes safeguarding agricultural production; whereas that purpose requires an authorisation for farmers to use the product of the harvest for propagation under certain conditions;

Whereas it must be ensured that the conditions are laid down at Community level;

Whereas compulsory licensing should also be provided for under certain circumstances in the public interest, which may include the need to supply the market with material offering specified features, or to maintain the incentive for continued breeding of improved varieties;

Whereas the use of prescribed variety denominations should be made obligatory;

Whereas the Community plant variety right should in principle have a life of at least 25 years and in the case of vine and tree species, at least 30 years; whereas other grounds for termination must be specified;

Whereas a Community plant variety right is an object of the holder's property and its role in relation to the non-harmonised legal provisions of the Member States, particularly of civil law, must therefore be clarified; whereas this applies also to the settlement of infringements and the enforcement of entitlement to Community plant variety rights;

Whereas, it is necessary to ensure that the full application of the principles of the Community plant variety rights system is not impaired by the effects of other systems; whereas for this purpose certain rules, in conformity with Member States' existing international commitments, are required concerning the relationship to other industrial property rights;

Whereas it is indispensable to examine whether and to what extent the conditions for the protection accorded in other industrial property systems, such as patents, should be adapted or otherwise modified for consistency with the Community plant variety rights system; whereas this, where necessary, should be laid down in balanced rules by additional Community law;

Whereas the duties and powers of the Community Plant Variety Office, including its Boards of Appeal, relating to the grant, termination or verification of Community plant variety rights and publications are as far as possible to be modelled on rules developed for other systems, as are also the

Office's structure and Rules of Procedure, the collaboration with the Commission and Member States particularly through an Administrative Council, the involvement of Examination Offices in technical examination and moreover the necessary budgetary measures;

Whereas the Office should be advised and supervised by the aforementioned Administrative Council, composed of representatives of Member States and the Commission;

Whereas the Treaty does not provide, for the adoption of this Regulation, powers other than those of Article 235;

Whereas this Regulation takes into account existing international conventions such as the International Convention for the Protection of New Varieties of Plants (UPOV Convention), the Convention of the Grant of European Patents (European Patent Convention) or the Agreement on trade-related aspects of intellectual property rights, including trade in counterfeit goods; whereas it consequently implements the ban on patenting plant varieties only to the extent that the European Patent Convention so requires, i.e., to plant varieties as such;

Whereas this Regulation should be re-examined for amendment as necessary in the light of future developments in the aforementioned Conventions,

HAS ADOPTED THIS REGULATION:

PART ONE   GENERAL PROVISIONS

. . .

PART TWO   SUBSTANTIVE LAW

Chapter I   Conditions Governing the Grant of Community Plant Variety Rights

Article 5   Object of Community plant variety rights

1. Varieties of all botanical genera and species, including, *inter alia,* hybrids between genera or species, may form the object of Community plant variety rights.

2. For the purpose of this Regulation, 'variety' shall be taken to mean a plant grouping within a single botanical taxon of the lowest known rank, which grouping, irrespective of whether the conditions for the grant of a plant variety right are fully met, can be:

— defined by the expression of the characteristics that result from a given genotype or combination of genotypes,

— distinguished from any other plant grouping by the expression of at least one of the said characteristics, and

— considered as a unit with regard to its suitability for being propagated unchanged.

3. A plant grouping consists of entire plants or parts of plants as far as such parts are capable of producing entire plants, both referred to hereinafter as 'variety constituents'.

4. The expression of the characteristics referred to in paragraph 2, first indent, may be either invariable or variable between variety constituents of the same kind provided that also the level of variation results from the genotype or combination of genotypes.

Article 6   Protectable varieties

Community plant variety rights shall be granted for varieties that are:

(a) distinct;

(b) uniform;

(c) stable; and

(d) new.

Moreover, the variety must be designated by a denomination in accordance with the provisions of Article 63.

Article 7   Distinctness

1. A variety shall be deemed to be distinct if it is clearly distinguishable by reference to the expression of the characteristics that results from a particular genotype or combination of genotypes, from any other variety whose existence is a matter of common knowledge on the date of application determined pursuant to Article 51.

2. The existence of another variety shall in particular be deemed to be a matter of common knowledge if on the date of application determined pursuant to Article 51:

    (a) it was the object of a plant variety right or entered in an official register of plant varieties, in the Community or any State, or in any intergovernmental organisation with relevant competence;

    (b) an application for the granting of a plant variety right in its respect or for its entering in such an official register was filed, provided the application has led to the granting or entering in the meantime.

The implementing rules pursuant to Article 114 may specify further cases as examples which shall be deemed to be a matter of common knowledge.

Article 8   Uniformity

A variety shall be deemed to be uniform if, subject to the variation that may be expected from the particular features of its propagation, it is sufficiently uniform in the expression of those characteristics which are included in the examination for distinctness, as well as any other used for the variety description.

Article 9   Stability

A variety shall be deemed to be stable if the expression of the characteristics which are included in the examination for distinctness as well as any others used for the variety description, remain unchanged after repeated propagation or, in the case of a particular cycle of propagation, at the end of each such cycle.

Article 10   Novelty

1. A variety shall be deemed to be new if, at the date of application determined pursuant to Article 51, variety constituents or harvested material of the variety have not been sold or otherwise disposed of to others, by or with the consent of the breeder within the meaning of Article 11, for purposes of exploitation of the variety:

    (a) earlier than one year before the abovementioned date, within the territory of the Community;

    (b) earlier than four years or, in the case of trees or of vines, earlier than six years before the said date, outside the territory of the Community.

. . .

Chapter II   Persons Entitled

Article 11   Entitlement to Community plant variety rights

1. The person who bred, or discovered and developed the variety, or his successor in title, both—the person and his successor—referred to hereinafter as 'the breeder', shall be entitled to the Community plant variety right.

. . .

Article 12   Entitlement to file an application for a Community plant variety right

An application for a Community plant variety right may be filed by any natural or legal person, or any body ranking as a legal person under the law applicable to that body.

An application may be filed jointly by two or more such persons.

Chapter III   Effects of Community Plant Variety Rights

Article 13   Rights of the holder of a Community plant variety right and prohibited acts

1. A Community plant variety right shall have the effect that the holder or holders of the Community plant variety right, hereinafter referred to as 'the holder', shall be entitled to effect the acts set out in paragraph 2.

2. Without prejudice to the provisions of Articles 15 and 16, the following acts in respect of variety constituents, or harvested material of the protected variety, both referred to hereinafter as 'material', shall require the authorisation of the holder:

   (a) production or reproduction (multiplication);

   (b) conditioning for the purpose of propagation;

   (c) offering for sale;

   (d) selling or other marketing;

   (e) exporting from the Community;

   (f) importing to the Community;

   (g) stocking for any of the purposes mentioned in (a) to (f).

The holder may make his authorisation subject to conditions and limitations.

3. The provisions of paragraph 2 shall apply in respect of harvested material only if this was obtained through the unauthorised use of variety constituents of the protected variety, and unless the holder has had reasonable opportunity to exercise his right in relation to the said variety constituents.

4. In the implementing rules pursuant to Article 114, it may be provided that in specific cases the provisions of paragraph 2 of this Article shall also apply in respect of products obtained directly from material of the protected variety. They may apply only if such products were obtained through the unauthorised use of material of the protected variety, and unless the holder has had reasonable opportunity to exercise his right in relation to the said material. To the extent that the provisions of paragraph 2 apply to products directly obtained, they shall also be considered to be 'material'.

5. The provisions of paragraphs 1 to 4 shall also apply in relation to:

   (a) varieties which are essentially derived from the variety in respect of which the Community plant variety right has been granted, where this variety is not itself an essentially derived variety;

   (b) varieties which are not distinct in accordance with the provisions of Article 7 from the protected variety; and

   (c) varieties whose production requires the repeated use of the protected variety.

6. For the purposes of paragraph 5 (a), a variety shall be deemed to be essentially derived from another variety, referred to hereinafter as 'the initial variety' when:

   (a) it is predominantly derived from the initial variety, or from a variety that is itself predominantly derived from the initial variety;

   (b) it is distinct in accordance with the provisions of Article 7 from the initial variety; and

   (c) except for the differences which result from the act of derivation, it conforms essentially to the initial variety in the expression of the characteristics that results from the genotype or combination of genotypes of the initial variety.

7. The implementing rules pursuant to Article 114 may specify possible acts of derivation which come at least under the provisions of paragraph 6.

8. Without prejudice to Article 14 and 29, the exercise of the rights conferred by Community plant variety rights may not violate any provisions adopted on the grounds of public morality, public policy or public security, the protection of health and life of humans, animals or plants, the protection of the environment, the protection of industrial or commercial property, or the safeguarding of competition, of trade or of agricultural production.

Article 14   Derogation from Community plant variety right

1. Notwithstanding Article 13(2), and for the purposes of safeguarding agricultural production, farmers are authorised to use for propagating purposes in the field, on their own holding the product of the harvest which they have obtained by planting, on their own holding, propagating material of a variety other than a hybrid of synthetic variety, which is covered by a Community plant variety right.

2. The provisions of paragraph 1 shall only apply to agricultural plant species of:

(a) Fodder plants:

Cicer arietinum L.—Chickpea milkvetch

Lupinus luteus L.—Yellow lupin

Medicago sativa L.—Lucerne

Pisum sativum L. (partim)—Field pea

Trifolium alexandrinum L.—Berseem/Egyptian clover

Trifolium resupinatum L.—Persian clover

Vicia faba—Field bean

Vicia sativa L.—Common vetch

and in the case of Portugal, Lolium multiflorum lam—Italian rye-grass

(b) Cereals:

Avena sativa—Oats

Hordeum vulgare L.—Barley

Oryza sativa L.—Rice

Phalaris canariensis L.—Canary grass

Secale cereale L.—Rye

X Triticosecale Wittm.—Triticale

Triticium aestivum L. emend. Fiori et Paol.—Wheat

Triticum durum Desf.—Durum wheat

Triticum spelta L.—Spelt wheat

(c) Potatoes:

Solanum tuberosum—Potatoes

(d) Oil and fibre plants:

Brassica napus L. (partim)—Swede rape

Brassica rapa L. (partim)—Turnip rape

Linum usitatissimum—linseed with the exclusion of flax.

3. Conditions to give effect to the derogation provided for in paragraph 1 and to safeguard the legitimate interests of the breeder and of the farmer, shall be established, before the entry into force of this Regulation, in implementing rules pursuant to Article 114, on the basis of the following criteria:

— there shall be no quantitative restriction of the level of the farmer's holding to the extent necessary for the requirements of the holding,

— the product of the harvest may be processed for planting, either by the farmer himself or through services supplied to him, without prejudice to certain restrictions which Member States may establish regarding the organisation of the processing of the said product of the harvest, in particular in order to ensure identity of the product entered for processing with that resulting from processing,

— small farmers shall not be required to pay any remuneration to the holder, small farmers shall be considered to be:

— in the case of those of the plant species referred to in paragraph 2 of this Article to which Council Regulation (EEC) No 1765/92 of 30 June 1992 establishing a support system for producers of certain arable crops applies, farmers who do not grow plants on an area bigger than the area which would be needed to produce 92 tonnes of cereals; for the calculation of the area, Article 8(2) of the aforesaid Regulation shall apply,

— in the case of other plant species referred to in paragraph 2 of this Article, farmers who meet comparable appropriate criteria,

— other farmers shall be required to pay an equitable remuneration to the holder, which shall be sensibly lower than the amount charged for the licensed production of propagating material of the same variety in the same area; the actual level of this equitable remuneration may be subject to variation over time, taking into account the extent to which use will be made of the derogation provided for in paragraph 1 in respect of the variety concerned,

— monitoring compliance with the provisions of this Article or the provisions adopted pursuant to this Article shall be a matter of exclusive responsibility of holders; in organising that monitoring, they may not provide for assistance from official bodies,

— relevant information shall be provided to the holders on their request, by farmers and by suppliers of processing services; relevant information may equally be provided by official bodies involved in the monitoring of agricultural production, if such information has been obtained through ordinary performance of their tasks, without additional burden or costs. These provisions are without prejudice, in respect of personal data, to Community and national legislation on the protection of individuals with regard to the processing and free movement of personal data.

Article 15   Limitation of the effects of Community plant variety rights

The Community plant variety rights shall not extend to:

(a) acts done privately and for non-commercial purposes;

(b) acts done for experimental purposes;

(c) acts done for the purpose of breeding, or discovering and developing other varieties;

(d) acts referred to in Article 13(2) to (4), in respect of such other varieties, except where the provisions of Article 13(5) apply, or where the other variety or the material of this variety comes under the protection of a property right which does not contain a comparable provision; and

(e) acts whose prohibition would violate the provisions laid down in Articles 13(8), 14 or 29.

Article 16   Exhaustion of Community plant variety rights

The Community plant variety right shall not extend to acts concerning any material of the protected variety, or of a variety covered by the provisions of Article 13(5), which has been disposed of to others by the holder or with his consent, in any part of the Community, or any material derived from the said material, unless such acts:

(a) involve further propagation of the variety in question, except where such propagation was intended when the material was disposed of; or

(b) involve an export of variety constituents into a third country which does not protect varieties of the plant genus or species to which the variety belongs, except where the exported materials is for final consumption purposes.

Article 17   Use of variety denominations

1. Any person who, within the territory of the Community, offers or disposes of to others for commercial purposes variety constituents of a protected variety, or a variety covered by the provisions of Article 13(5), must use the variety denomination designated pursuant to Article 63; where it is used in writing, the variety denomination shall be readily distinguishable and clearly legible. If a trade mark, trade name or similar indication is associated with the designated denomination, this denomination must be easily recognisable as such.

2. Any person effecting such acts in respect of any other material of the variety, must inform of that denomination in accordance with other provisions in law or if a request is made by an authority, by the purchaser or by any other person having a legitimate interest.

3. Paragraphs 1 and 2 shall apply even after the termination of the Community plant variety right.

Article 18   Limitation of the use of variety denominations

1. The holder may not use any right granted in respect of a designation that is identical with the variety denomination to hamper the free use of that denomination in connection with the variety, even after the termination of the Community plant variety right.

2. A third party may use a right granted in respect of a designation that is identical with the variety denomination to hamper the free use of that denomination only if that right was granted before the variety denomination was designated pursuant to Article 63.

3. Where a variety is protected by a Community plant variety right or, in a Member State or in a Member of the International Union for the Protection of New Varieties of Plants by a national property right, neither its designated denomination or any designation which might be confused with it can be used, within the territory of the Community, in connection with another variety of the same botanical species or a species regarded as related pursuant to the publication made in accordance with Article 63(5), or for material of such variety.

Chapter IV   Duration and Termination of Community Plant Variety Rights

Article 19   Duration of Community plant variety rights

1. The term of the Community plant variety right shall run until the end of the 25th calendar year or, in the case of varieties of vine and tree species, until the end of the 30th calendar year, following the year of grant.

. . .

Article 20   Nullity of Community plant variety rights

1. The Office shall declare the Community plant variety right null and void if it is established:
   (a) that the conditions laid down in Articles 7 or 10 were not complied with at the time of the Community plant variety right; or
   (b) that where the grant of the Community plant variety right has been essentially based upon information and documents furnished by the applicant, the conditions laid down in Articles 8 and 9 were not complied with at the time of the grant of the right; or
   (c) that the right has been granted to a person who is not entitled to it, unless it is transferred to the person who is so entitled.

2. Where the Community plant variety right is declared null and void, it shall be deemed not to have had, as from the outset, the effects specified in this Regulation.

Article 21   Cancellation of Community plant variety rights

1. The Office shall cancel the Community plant variety right with effect in futurum if it is established that the conditions laid down in Article 8 or 9 are no longer complied with. If it is established that these conditions were already no longer complied with from a point in time prior to cancellation,

. . .

Chapter V   Community Plant Variety Rights as Objects of Property

Article 22   Assimilation with national laws

1. Save where otherwise provided in Articles 23 to 29, a Community plant variety right as an object of property shall be regarded in all respects, and for the entire territory of the Community, as a corresponding property right in the Member State in which:
   (a) according to the entry in the Register of Community Plant Variety Rights, the holder was domiciled or had his seat or an establishment on the relevant date; or
   (b) if the conditions laid down in subparagraph (a) are not fulfilled, the first-mentioned procedural representative of the holder, as indicated in the said Register, was domiciled or had his seat or an establishment on the date of registration.

2. Where the conditions laid down in paragraph 1 are not fulfilled, the Member State referred to in paragraph 1 shall be the Member State in which the seat of the Office is located.

. . .

Article 23   Transfer

1. A Community plant variety right may be the object of a transfer to one or more successors in title.

2. Transfer of a Community plant variety right by assignment can be made only to successors who comply with the conditions laid down in Article 12 and 82. It shall be made in writing and shall require the signature of the parties to the contract, except when it is a result of a judgment or of any other acts terminating court proceedings. Otherwise it shall be void.

3. Save as otherwise provided in Article 100, a transfer shall have no bearing on the rights acquired by third parties before the date of transfer.

4. A transfer shall not take effect for the Office and may not be cited *vis-a-vis* third parties unless documentary evidence thereof as provided for in the implementing rules is provided and until it has been entered in the Register of Community Plant Variety Rights. A transfer that has not yet been entered in the Register may, however, be cited *vis-a-vis* third parties who have acquired rights after the date of transfer but who knew of the transfer at the date on which they acquired those rights.

. . .

Article 29   Compulsory licensing

1. Compulsory licences shall be granted to one or more persons by the Office, on application by that person or those persons, but only on grounds of public interest and after consulting the Administrative Council referred to in Article 36.

. . .

7. Compulsory licences may not be granted by Member States in respect of a Community plant variety right.

. . .

PART FOUR   PROCEEDINGS BEFORE THE OFFICE

Chapter I   Applications

Article 49   Filing of applications

1. An application for a Community plant variety right shall be filed at the choice of the applicant:
   (a) at the Office directly; or
   (b) at one of the sub-offices or national agencies, established or entrusted, pursuant to Article 30(4), subject to the applicant forwarding an information on this filing to the Office directly within two weeks after filing.

. . .

Article 50   Conditions governing applications

1. The application for a Community plant variety right must contain at least the following:
   (a) a request for the grant of a Community plant variety right;
   (b) identification of the botanical taxon;
   (c) information identifying the applicant or, where appropriate, the joint applicants;
   (d) the name of the breeder and an assurance that, to the best of the applicants knowledge, no further persons have been involved in the breeding, or discovery and development, of the variety; if the applicant is not the breeder, or not the only breeder, he shall provide the relevant documentary evidence as to how the entitlement to the Community plant variety right came into his possession;
   (e) a provisional designation for the variety;
   (f) a technical description of the variety;
   (g) the geographic origin of the variety;
   (h) the credentials of any procedural representatives;
   (i) details of any previous commercialisation of the variety;
   (j) details of any other application made in respect of the variety.

. . .

3. An application shall propose a variety denomination which may accompany the application.

...

Chapter II   Examination

...

Article 54   Substantive examination

1. The Office shall examine whether the variety may be the object of a Community plant variety right pursuant to Article 5, whether the variety is new pursuant to Article 10, whether the applicant is entitled to file an application pursuant to Article 12 and whether the conditions laid down in Article 82 are complied with. The Office shall also examine whether the proposed variety denomination is suitable pursuant to Article 63. For such purposes, it may avail itself of the services of other bodies.

...

Article 55   Technical examination

1. Where the Office has not discovered any impediment to the grant of a Community plant variety right on the basis of the examination pursuant to Articles 53 and 54, it shall arrange for the technical examination relating to compliance with the conditions laid down in Articles 7, 8 and 9 to be carried out by the competent office or offices in at least one of the Member States entrusted with responsibility for the technical examination of varieties of the species concerned by the Administrative Council, hereafter referred to as the 'Examination Office or Offices'.

...

Article 59   Objections to grant of right

1. Any person may lodge with the Office a written objection to the grant of a Community plant variety right.

...

Chapter III   Decisions

...

Article 62   Grant

If the Office is of the opinion that the findings of the examination are sufficient to decide on the application and there are no impediments pursuant to Articles 59 and 61, it shall grant the Community plant variety right. The decision shall include an official description of the variety.

Article 63   Variety denomination

1. Where a Community plant variety right is granted, the Office shall approve, for the variety in question, the variety denomination proposed by the applicant pursuant to Article 50(3), if it considers, on the basis of the examination made pursuant to the second sentence of Article 54(1), that this denomination is suitable.

2. A variety denomination is suitable, if there is no impediment pursuant to paragraphs 3 or 4 of this Article.

3. There is an impediment for the designation of a variety denomination where:
   (a) its use in the territory of the Community is precluded by the prior right of a third party;
   (b) it may commonly cause its users difficulties as regards recognition of reproduction;
   (c) it is identical or may be confused with a variety denomination under which another variety of the same or of a closely related species is entered in an official register of plant varieties or under which material or another variety has been marketed in a Member State or in a Member of the International Unit for the Protection of New Varieties of Plants, unless the other variety no longer remains in existence and its denomination has acquired no special significance;
   (d) it is identical or may be confused with other designations which are commonly used for the marketing of goods or which have to be kept free under other legislation;

(e) it is liable to give offence in one of the Member States or is contrary to public policy;

(f) it is liable to mislead or to cause confusion concerning the characteristics, the value or the identity of the variety or the identity of the breeder or any other party to proceedings.

4. There is another impediment where, in the case of a variety which has already been entered:

(a) in one of the Member States; or

(b) in a Member of the International Union for the Protection of New Varieties of Plants; or

(c) in another State for which it has been established in a Community act that varieties are evaluated there under rules which are equivalent to those laid down in the Directives on common catalogues;

in an official register of plant varieties or material thereof and has been marketed there for commercial purposes, and the proposed variety denomination differs from that which has been registered or used there, unless the latter one is the object of an impediment pursuant to paragraph 3.

5. The Office shall publish the species which it considers 'closely related' within the meaning of paragraph 3(c).

Chapter IV   The Maintenance of Community Plant Variety Rights

. . .

PART FIVE   IMPACT ON OTHER LAWS

Article 92   Cumulative protection prohibited

1. Any variety which is the subject matter of a Community plant variety right shall not be the subject of a national plant variety right or any patent for that variety. Any rights granted contrary to the first sentence shall be ineffective.

2. Where the holder has been granted another right as referred to in paragraph 1 for the same variety prior to grant of the Community plant variety right, he shall be unable to invoke the rights conferred by such protection for the variety for as long as the Community plant variety right remains effective.

Article 93   Application of national law

Claims under Community plant variety rights shall be subject to limitations imposed by the law of the Member States only as expressly referred to in this Regulation.

PART SIX   CIVIL LAW CLAIMS, INFRINGEMENTS, JURISDICTION

. . .

Article 99   Obtaining identification of a variety

The holder of an initial variety and the breeder of a variety essentially derived from the initial variety shall be entitled to obtain an acknowledgement of the identification of the varieties concerned as initial and essentially derived.

. . .

Article 104   Entitlement to bring an action for infringement

1. Actions for infringement may be brought by the holder. Persons enjoying exploitation rights may bring such actions unless that has been expressly excluded by agreement with the holder in the case of an exclusive exploitation right or by the Office pursuant to Articles 2 or 100(2).

2. Any person enjoying exploitation rights shall, for the purpose of obtaining compensation for damage suffered by him, be entitled to intervene in an infringement action brought by the holder.

Article 105   Obligation of national courts or other bodies

A national court or other body hearing an action relating to a Community plant variety right shall treat the Community plant variety right as valid.

. . .

Article 107   Penalties for infringement of Community plant variety rights

Member States shall take all appropriate measures to ensure that the same provisions are made applicable to penalise infringements of Community plant variety rights as apply in the matter of infringements of corresponding national rights.

. . .

PART EIGHT   TRANSITIONAL AND FINAL PROVISIONS

. . .

Directive 98/44/EC of the European Parliament and of the Council

of 6 July 1998 on the legal protection of biotechnological inventions

THE EUROPEAN PARLIAMENT AND THE COUNCIL OF THE EUROPEAN UNION,

Having regard to the Treaty establishing the European Community, and in particular Article 100a thereof,

Having regard to the proposal from the Commission,

Having regard to the opinion of the Economic and Social Committee,

Acting in accordance with the procedure laid down in Article 189b of the Treaty,

(1) Whereas biotechnology and genetic engineering are playing an increasingly important role in a broad range of industries and the protection of biotechnological inventions will certainly be of fundamental importance for the Community's industrial development;

(2) Whereas, in particular in the field of genetic engineering, research and development require a considerable amount of high-risk investment and therefore only adequate legal protection can make them profitable;

(3) Whereas effective and harmonised protection throughout the Member States is essential in order to maintain and encourage investment in the field of biotechnology;

(4) Whereas following the European Parliament's rejection of the joint text, approved by the Conciliation Committee, for a European Parliament and Council Directive on the legal protection of biotechnological inventions, the European Parliament and the Council have determined that the legal protection of biotechnological inventions requires clarification;

(5) Whereas differences exist in the legal protection of biotechnological inventions offered by the laws and practices of the different Member States; whereas such differences could create barriers to trade and hence impede the proper functioning of the internal market;

(6) Whereas such differences could well become greater as Member States adopt new and different legislation and administrative practices, or whereas national case-law interpreting such legislation develops differently;

(7) Whereas uncoordinated development of national laws on the legal protection of biotechnological inventions in the Community could lead to further disincentives to trade, to the detriment of the industrial development of such inventions and of the smooth operation of the internal market;

(8) Whereas legal protection of biotechnological inventions does not necessitate the creation of a separate body of law in place of the rules of national patent law; whereas the rules of national patent law remain the essential basis for the legal protection of biotechnological inventions given that they must be adapted or added to in certain specific respects in order to take adequate account of technological developments involving biological material which also fulfil the requirements for patentability;

(9) Whereas in certain cases, such as the exclusion from patentability of plant and animal varieties and of essentially biological processes for the production of plants and animals, certain concepts in national laws based upon internal patent and plant variety conventions have created uncertainty regarding the protection of biotechnological and certain micro-biological inventions; whereas harmonisation is necessary to clarify the said uncertainty;

(10) Whereas regard should be had to the potential of the development of biotechnology for the environment and in particular the utility of this technology for the development of methods of cultivation which are less polluting and more economical in their use of ground; whereas the patent system should be used to encourage research into, and the application of, such processes;

(11) Whereas the development of biotechnology is important to developing countries, both in the field of health and combating major epidemics and endemic diseases and in that of combating hunger in the world; whereas the patent system should likewise be used to encourage research in these fields; whereas international procedures for the dissemination of such technology in the Third World and to the benefit of the population groups concerned should be promoted;

(12) Whereas the Agreement on Trade-Related Aspects of Intellectual Property Rights (TRIPs) signed by the European Community and the Member States, has entered into force and provides that patent protection must be guaranteed for products and processes in all areas of technology;

(13) Whereas the Community's legal framework for the protection of biotechnological inventions can be limited to laying down certain principles as they apply to the patentability of biological material as such, such principles being intended in particular to determine the difference between inventions and discoveries with regard to the patentability of certain elements of human origin, to the scope of protection conferred by a patent on a biotechnological invention, to the right to use a deposit mechanism in addition to written descriptions and lastly to the option of obtaining non-exclusive compulsory licences in respect of interdependence between plant varieties and inventions, and conversely;

(14) Whereas a patent for invention does not authorise the holder to implement that invention, but merely entitles him to prohibit third parties from exploiting it for industrial and commercial purposes; whereas, consequently, substantive patent law cannot serve to replace or render superfluous national, European or international law which may impose restrictions or prohibitions or which concerns the monitoring of research and of the use or commercialisation of its results, notably from the point of view of the requirements of public health, safety, environmental protection, animal welfare, the preservation of genetic diversity and compliance with certain ethical standards;

(15) Whereas no prohibition or exclusion exists in national or European patent law (Munich Convention) which precludes *a priori* the patentability of biological matter;

(16) Whereas patent law must be applied so as to respect the fundamental principles safeguarding the dignity and integrity of the person; whereas it is important to assert the principle that the human body, at any stage in its formation or development, including germ cells, and the simple discovery of one of its elements or one of its products, including the sequence or partial sequence of a human gene, cannot be patented; whereas these principles are in line with the criteria of patentability proper to patent law, whereby a mere discovery cannot be patented;

(17) Whereas significant progress in the treatment of diseases has already been made thanks to the existence of medicinal products derived from elements isolated from the human body and/or otherwise produced, such medicinal products resulting from technical processes aimed at obtaining elements similar in structure to those existing naturally in the human body and whereas, consequently, research aimed at obtaining and isolating such elements valuable to medicinal production should be encouraged by means of the patent system;

(18) Whereas, since the patent system provides insufficient incentive for encouraging research into the production of biotechnological medicines which are needed to combat rare or 'orphan' diseases, the Community and the Member States have a duty to respond adequately to this problem;

(19) Whereas account has been taken of Opinion No. 8 of the Group of Advisers on the Ethical Implications of Biotechnology to the European Commission;

(20) Whereas, therefore, it should be made clear that an invention based on an element isolated from the human body or otherwise produced by means of a technical process, which is susceptible of industrial application, is not excluded from patentability, even where the structure of that element is identical to that of a natural element, given that the rights conferred by the patent do not extend to the human body and its elements in their natural environment;

(21) Whereas such an element isolated from the human body or otherwise produced is not excluded from patentability since it is, for example, the result of technical processes used to identify, purify and classify it and to reproduce it outside the human body, techniques which human beings alone are capable of putting into practice and which nature is incapable of accomplishing by itself;

(22) Whereas the discussion on the patentability of sequences or partial sequences of genes is controversial; whereas, according to this Directive, the granting of a patent for inventions which concern such sequences or partial sequences should be subject to the same criteria of patentability as in all other areas of technology: novelty, inventive step and industrial application; whereas the industrial application of a sequence or partial sequence must be disclosed in the patent application as filed;

(23) Whereas a mere DNA sequence without indication of a function does not contain any technical information and is therefore not a patentable invention;

(24) Whereas, in order to comply with the industrial application criterion it is necessary in cases where a sequence or partial sequence of a gene is used to produce a protein or part of a protein, to specify which protein or part of a protein is produced or what function it performs;

(25) Whereas, for the purposes of interpreting rights conferred by a patent, when sequences overlap only in parts which are not essential to the invention, each sequence will be considered as an independent sequence in patent law terms;

(26) Whereas if an invention is based on biological material of human origin or if it uses such material, where a patent application is filed, the person from whose body the material is taken must have had an opportunity of expressing free and informed consent thereto, in accordance with national law;

(27) Whereas if an invention is based on biological material of plant or animal origin or if it uses such material, the patent application should, where appropriate, include information on the geographical origin of such material, if known; whereas this is without prejudice to the processing of patent applications or the validity of rights arising from granted patents;

(28) Whereas this Directive does not in any way affect the basis of current patent law, according to which a patent may be granted for any new application of a patented product;

(29) Whereas this Directive is without prejudice to the exclusion of plant and animal varieties from patentability; whereas on the other hand inventions which concern plants or animals are patentable provided that the application of the invention is not technically confined to a single plant or animal variety;

(30) Whereas the concept 'plant variety' is defined by the legislation protecting new varieties, pursuant to which a variety is defined by its whole genome and therefore possesses individuality and is clearly distinguishable from other varieties;

(31) Whereas a plant grouping which is characterised by a particular gene (and not its whole genome) is not covered by the protection of new varieties and is therefore not excluded from patentability even if it comprises new varieties of plants;

(32) Whereas, however, if an invention consists only in genetically modifying a particular plant variety, and if a new plant variety is bred, it will still be excluded from patentability even if the genetic modification is the result not of an essentially biological process but of a biotechnological process;

(33) Whereas it is necessary to define for the purposes of this Directive when a process for the breeding of plants and animals is essentially biological;

(34) Whereas this Directive shall be without prejudice to concepts of invention and discovery, as developed by national, European or international patent law;

(35) Whereas this Directive shall be without prejudice to the provisions of national patent law whereby processes for treatment of the human or animal body by surgery or therapy and diagnostic methods practised on the human or animal body are excluded from patentability;

(36) Whereas the TRIPS Agreement provides for the possibility that members of the World Trade Organisation may exclude from patentability inventions, the prevention within their territory of the commercial exploitation of which is necessary to protect *ordre public* or morality, including to protect human, animal or plant life or health or to avoid serious prejudice to the environment, provided that such exclusion is not made merely because the exploitation is prohibited by their law;

(37) Whereas the principle whereby inventions must be excluded from patentability where their commercial exploitation offends against *ordre public* or morality must also be stressed in this Directive;

(38) Whereas the operative part of this Directive should also include an illustrative list of inventions excluded from patentability so as to provide national courts and patent offices with a general guide to interpreting the reference to *ordre public* and morality; whereas this list obviously cannot presume to be exhaustive; whereas processes, the use of which offend against human dignity, such as processes to produce chimeras from germ cells or totipotent cells of humans and animals, are obviously also excluded from patentability;

(39) Whereas *ordre public* and morality correspond in particular to ethical or moral principles recognised in a Member State, respect for which is particularly important in the field of biotechnology in view of the potential scope of inventions in this field and their inherent relationship to living matter; whereas such ethical or moral principles supplement the standard legal examinations under patent law regardless of the technical field of the invention;

(40) Whereas there is a consensus within the Community that interventions in the human germ line and the cloning of human beings offends against *ordre public* and morality; whereas it is therefore important to exclude unequivocally from patentability processes for modifying the germ line genetic identity of human beings and processes for cloning human beings;

(41) Whereas a process for cloning human beings may be defined as any process, including techniques of embryo splitting, designed to create a human being with the same nuclear genetic information as another living or deceased human being;

(42) Whereas, moreover, uses of human embryos for industrial or commercial purposes must also be excluded from patentability; whereas in any case such exclusion does not affect inventions for therapeutic or diagnostic purposes which are applied to the human embryo and are useful to it;

(43) Whereas pursuant to Article F(2) of the Treaty on European Union, the Union is to respect fundamental rights, as guaranteed by the European Convention for the Protection of Human Rights and Fundamental Freedoms signed in Rome on 4 November 1950 and as they result from the constitutional traditions common to the Member States, as general principles of Community law;

(44) Whereas the Commission's European Group on Ethics in Science and New Technologies evaluates all ethical aspects of biotechnology; whereas it should be pointed out in this connection that that Group may be consulted only where biotechnology is to be evaluated at the level of basic ethical principles, including where it is consulted on patent law;

(45) Whereas processes for modifying the genetic identity of animals which are likely to cause them suffering without any substantial medical benefit in terms of research, prevention, diagnosis or therapy to man or animal, and also animals resulting from such processes, must be excluded from patentability;

(46) Whereas, in view of the fact that the function of a patent is to reward the inventor for his creative efforts by granting an exclusive but time-bound right, and thereby encourage inventive activities, the holder of the patent should be entitled to prohibit the use of patented self-reproducing material in situations analogous to those where it would be permitted to prohibit the use of patented, non-self-reproducing products, that is to say the production of the patented product itself;

(47) Whereas it is necessary to provide for a first derogation from the rights of the holder of the patent when the propagating material incorporating the protected invention is sold to a farmer for

farming purposes by the holder of the patent or with his consent; whereas that initial derogation must authorise the farmer to use the product of his harvest for further multiplication or propagation on his own farm; whereas the extent and the conditions of that derogation must be limited in accordance with the extent and conditions set out in Council Regulation (EC) No. 2100/94 of 27 July 1994 on Community plant variety rights;

(48) Whereas only the fee envisaged under Community law relating to plant variety rights as a condition for applying the derogation from Community plant variety rights can be required of the farmer;

(49) Whereas, however, the holder of the patent may defend his rights against a farmer abusing the derogation or against a breeder who has developed a plant variety incorporating the protected invention if the latter fails to adhere to his commitments;

(50) Whereas a second derogation from the rights of the holder of the patent must authorise the farmer to use protected livestock for agricultural purposes;

(51) Whereas the extent and the conditions of that second derogation must be determined by national laws, regulations and practices, since there is no Community legislation on animal variety rights;

(52) Whereas, in the field of exploitation of new plant characteristics resulting from genetic engineering, guaranteed access must, on payment of a fee, be granted in the form of a compulsory licence where, in relation to the genus or species concerned, the plant variety represents significant technical progress of considerable economic interest compared to the invention claimed in the patent;

(53) Whereas, in the field of the use of new plant characteristics resulting from new plant varieties in genetic engineering, guaranteed access must, on payment of a fee, be granted in the form of a compulsory licence where the invention represents significant technical progress of considerable economic interest;

(54) Whereas Article 34 of the TRIPS Agreement contains detailed provisions on the burden of proof which is binding on all Member States; whereas, therefore, a provision in this Directive is not necessary;

(55) Whereas following Decision 93/626/EEC the Community is party to the Convention on Biological Diversity of 5 June 1992; whereas, in this regard, Member States must give particular weight to Article 3 and Article 8(j), the second sentence of Article 16(2) and Article 16(5) of the Convention when bringing into force the laws, regulations and administrative provisions necessary to comply with this Directive;

(56) Whereas the Third Conference of the Parties to the Biodiversity Convention, which took place in November 1996, noted in Decision III/17 that 'further work is required to help develop a common appreciation of the relationship between intellectual property rights and the relevant provisions of the TRIPS Agreement and the Convention on Biological Diversity, in particular on issues relating to technology transfer and conservation and sustainable use of biological diversity and the fair and equitable sharing of benefits arising out of the use of genetic resources, including the protection of knowledge, innovations and practices of indigenous and local communities embodying traditional lifestyles relevant for the conservation and sustainable use of biological diversity',

HAVE ADOPTED THIS DIRECTIVE:

Chapter I   Patentability

Article 1

1. Member States shall protect biotechnological inventions under national patent law. They shall, if necessary, adjust their national patent law to take account of the provisions of this Directive.

2. This Directive shall be without prejudice to the obligations of the Member States pursuant to international agreements, and in particular the TRIPS Agreement and the Convention on Biological Diversity.

Article 2

1. For the purposes of this Directive,
   (a) 'biological material' means any material containing genetic information and capable of reproducing itself or being reproduced in a biological system;

    (b) 'microbiological process' means any process involving or performed upon or resulting in microbiological material.

    2. A process for the production of plants or animals is essentially biological if it consists entirely of natural phenomena such as crossing or selection.

    3. The concept of 'plant variety' is defined by Article 5 of Regulation (EC) No. 2100/94.

Article 3

    1. For the purposes of this Directive, inventions which are new, which involve an inventive step and which are susceptible of industrial application shall be patentable even if they concern a product consisting of or containing biological material or a process by means of which biological material is produced, processed or used.

    2. Biological material which is isolated from its natural environment or produced by means of a technical process may be the subject of an invention even if it previously occurred in nature.

Article 4

    1. The following shall not be patentable:
    (a) plant and animal varieties;
    (b) essentially biological processes for the production of plants or animals.

    2. Inventions which concern plants or animals shall be patentable if the technical feasibility of the invention is not confined to a particular plant or animal variety.

    3. Paragraph 1(b) shall be without prejudice to the patentability of inventions which concern a microbiological or other technical process or a product obtained by means of such a process.

Article 5

    1. The human body, at the various stages of its formation and development, and the simple discovery of one of its elements, including the sequence or partial sequence of a gene, cannot constitute patentable inventions.

    2. An element isolated from the human body or otherwise produced by means of a technical process, including the sequence or partial sequence of a gene, may constitute a patentable invention, even if the structure of that element is identical to that of a natural element.

    3. The industrial application of a sequence or a partial sequence of a gene must be disclosed in the patent application.

Article 6

    1. Inventions shall be considered unpatentable where their commercial exploitation would be contrary to *ordre public* or morality; however, exploitation shall not be deemed to be so contrary merely because it is prohibited by law or regulation.

    2. On the basis of paragraph 1, the following, in particular, shall be considered unpatentable:
    (a) processes for cloning human beings;
    (b) processes for modifying the germ line genetic identity of human beings;
    (c) uses of human embryos for industrial or commercial purposes;
    (d) processes for modifying the genetic identity of animals which are likely to cause them suffering without any substantial medical benefit to man or animal, and also animals resulting from such processes.

Article 7

The Commission's European Group on Ethics in Science and New Technologies evaluates all ethical aspects of biotechnology.

Chapter II   Scope of Protection

Article 8

    1. The protection conferred by a patent on a biological material possessing specific characteristics as a result of the invention shall extend to any biological material derived from that biological

material through propagation or multiplication in an identical or divergent form and possessing those same characteristics.

2. The protection conferred by a patent on a process that enables a biological material to be produced possessing specific characteristics as a result of the invention shall extend to biological material directly obtained through that process and to any other biological material derived from the directly obtained biological material through propagation or multiplication in an identical or divergent form and possessing those same characteristics.

Article 9

The protection conferred by a patent on a product containing or consisting of genetic information shall extend to all material, save as provided in Article 5(1), in which the product is incorporated and in which the genetic information is contained and performs its function.

Article 10

The protection referred to in Articles 8 and 9 shall not extend to biological material obtained from the propagation or multiplication of biological material placed on the market in the territory of a Member State by the holder of the patent or with his consent, where the multiplication or propagation necessarily results from the application for which the biological material was marketed, provided that the material obtained is not subsequently used for other propagation or multiplication.

Article 11

1. By way of derogation from Articles 8 and 9, the sale or other form of commercialisation of plant propagating material to a farmer by the holder of the patent or with his consent for agricultural use implies authorisation for the farmer to use the product of his harvest for propagation or multiplication by him on his own farm, the extent and conditions of this derogation corresponding to those under Article 14 of Regulation (EC) No. 2100/94.

2. By way of derogation from Articles 8 and 9, the sale or any other form of commercialisation of breeding stock or other animal reproductive material to a farmer by the holder of the patent or with his consent implies authorisation for the farmer to use the protected livestock for an agricultural purpose. This includes making the animal or other animal reproductive material available for the purposes of pursuing his agricultural activity but not sale within the framework or for the purpose of a commercial reproduction activity.

3. The extent and the conditions of the derogation provided for in paragraph 2 shall be determined by national laws, regulations and practices.

Chapter III   Compulsory Cross-Licensing

Article 12

1. Where a breeder cannot acquire or exploit a plant variety right without infringing a prior patent, he may apply for a compulsory licence for non-exclusive use of the invention protected by the patent inasmuch as the licence is necessary for the exploitation of the plant variety to be protected, subject to payment of an appropriate royalty. Member States shall provide that, where such a licence is granted, the holder of the patent will be entitled to a cross-licence on reasonable terms to use the protected variety.

2. Where the holder of a patent concerning a biotechnological invention cannot exploit it without infringing a prior plant variety right, he may apply for a compulsory licence for non-exclusive use of the plant variety protected by that right, subject to payment of an appropriate royalty. Member States shall provide that, where such a licence is granted, the holder of the variety right will be entitled to a cross-licence on reasonable terms to use the protected invention.

3. Applicants for the licences referred to in paragraphs 1 and 2 must demonstrate that:
   (a) they have applied unsuccessfully to the holder of the patent or of the plant variety right to obtain a contractual licence;

(b) the plant variety or the invention constitutes significant technical progress of considerable economic interest compared with the invention claimed in the patent or the protected plant variety.

4. Each Member State shall designate the authority or authorities responsible for granting the licence. Where a licence for a plant variety can be granted only by the Community Plant Variety Office, Article 29 of Regulation (EC) No. 2100/94 shall apply.

Chapter IV   Deposit, Access and Re-Deposit of a Biological Material

Article 13

1. Where an invention involves the use of or concerns biological material which is not available to the public and which cannot be described in a patent application in such a manner as to enable the invention to be reproduced by a person skilled in the art, the description shall be considered inadequate for the purposes of patent law unless:

(a) the biological material has been deposited no later than the date on which the patent application was filed with a recognised depositary institution. At least the international depositary authorities which acquired this status by virtue of Article 7 of the Budapest Treaty of 28 April 1977 on the international recognition of the deposit of micro-organisms for the purposes of patent procedure, hereinafter referred to as the 'Budapest Treaty', shall be recognised;

(b) the application as filed contains such relevant information as is available to the applicant on the characteristics of the biological material deposited;

(c) the patent application states the name of the depository institution and the accession number.

2. Access to the deposited biological material shall be provided through the supply of a sample:

(a) up to the first publication of the patent application, only to those persons who are authorised under national patent law;

(b) between the first publication of the application and the granting of the patent, to anyone requesting it or, if the applicant so requests, only to an independent expert;

(c) after the patent has been granted, and notwithstanding revocation or cancellation of the patent, to anyone requesting it.

3. The sample shall be supplied only if the person requesting it undertakes, for the term during which the patent is in force:

(a) not to make it or any material derived from it available to third parties; and

(b) not to use it or any material derived from it except for experimental purposes, unless the applicant for or proprietor of the patent, as applicable, expressly waives such an undertaking.

4. At the applicant's request, where an application is refused or withdrawn, access to the deposited material shall be limited to an independent expert for 20 years from the date on which the patent application was filed. In that case, paragraph 3 shall apply.

5. The applicant's requests referred to in point (b) of paragraph 2 and in paragraph 4 may only be made up to the date on which the technical preparations for publishing the patent application are deemed to have been completed.

Article 14

1. If the biological material deposited in accordance with Article 13 ceases to be available from the recognised depositary institution, a new deposit of the material shall be permitted on the same terms as those laid down in the Budapest Treaty.

2. Any new deposit shall be accompanied by a statement signed by the depositor certifying that the newly deposited biological material is the same as that originally deposited.

Chapter V   Final Provisions

Article 15

1. Member States shall bring into force the laws, regulations and administrative provisions necessary to comply with this Directive not later than 30 July 2000. They shall forthwith inform the Commission thereof.

When Member States adopt these measures, they shall contain a reference to this Directive or shall be accompanied by such reference on the occasion of their official publication. The methods of making such reference shall be laid down by Member States.

2. Member States shall communicate to the Commission the text of the provisions of national law which they adopt in the field covered by this Directive.

Article 16

The Commission shall send the European Parliament and the Council:

(a) every five years as from the date specified in Article 15(1) a report on any problems encountered with regard to the relationship between this Directive and international agreements on the protection of human rights to which the Member States have acceded;

(b) within two years of entry into force of this Directive, a report assessing the implications for basic genetic engineering research of failure to publish, or late publication of, papers on subjects which could be patentable;

(c) annually as from the date specified in Article 15(1), a report on the development and implications of patent law in the field of biotechnology and genetic engineering.

. . .

Directive (EU) 2016/943 of the European Parliament and of the Council

of 8 June 2016 on the protection of undisclosed know-how and business information (trade secrets) against their unlawful acquisition, use and disclosure (Text with EEA relevance)

THE EUROPEAN PARLIAMENT AND THE COUNCIL OF THE EUROPEAN UNION,

Having regard to the Treaty on the Functioning of the European Union, and in particular Article 114 thereof,

Having regard to the proposal from the European Commission,

After transmission of the draft legislative act to the national parliaments,

Having regard to the opinion of the European Economic and Social Committee,

Acting in accordance with the ordinary legislative procedure,

Whereas:

(1) Businesses and non-commercial research institutions invest in acquiring, developing and applying know-how and information which is the currency of the knowledge economy and provides a competitive advantage. This investment in generating and applying intellectual capital is a determining factor as regards their competitiveness and innovation-related performance in the market and therefore their returns on investment, which is the underlying motivation for business research and development. Businesses have recourse to different means to appropriate the results of their innovation-related activities when openness does not allow for the full exploitation of their investment in research and innovation. Use of intellectual property rights, such as patents, design rights or copyright, is one such means. Another means of appropriating the results of innovation is to protect access to, and exploit, knowledge that is valuable to the entity and not widely known. Such valuable know-how and business information, that is undisclosed and intended to remain confidential, is referred to as a trade secret.

(2) Businesses, irrespective of their size, value trade secrets as much as patents and other forms of intellectual property right. They use confidentiality as a business competitiveness and research

innovation management tool, and in relation to a diverse range of information that extends beyond technological knowledge to commercial data such as information on customers and suppliers, business plans, and market research and strategies. Small and medium-sized enterprises (SMEs) value and rely on trade secrets even more. By protecting such a wide range of know-how and business information, whether as a complement or as an alternative to intellectual property rights, trade secrets allow creators and innovators to derive profit from their creation or innovation and, therefore, are particularly important for business competitiveness as well as for research and development, and innovation-related performance.

(3) Open innovation is a catalyst for new ideas which meet the needs of consumers and tackle societal challenges, and allows those ideas to find their way to the market. Such innovation is an important lever for the creation of new knowledge, and underpins the emergence of new and innovative business models based on the use of co-created knowledge. Collaborative research, including cross-border cooperation, is particularly important in increasing the levels of business research and development within the internal market. The dissemination of knowledge and information should be considered as being essential for the purpose of ensuring dynamic, positive and equal business development opportunities, in particular for SMEs. In an internal market in which barriers to cross-border collaboration are minimised and cooperation is not distorted, intellectual creation and innovation should encourage investment in innovative processes, services and products. Such an environment conducive to intellectual creation and innovation, and in which employment mobility is not hindered, is also important for employment growth and for improving the competitiveness of the Union economy. Trade secrets have an important role in protecting the exchange of knowledge between businesses, including in particular SMEs, and research institutions both within and across the borders of the internal market, in the context of research and development, and innovation. Trade secrets are one of the most commonly used forms of protection of intellectual creation and innovative know-how by businesses, yet at the same time they are the least protected by the existing Union legal framework against their unlawful acquisition, use or disclosure by other parties.

(4) Innovative businesses are increasingly exposed to dishonest practices aimed at misappropriating trade secrets, such as theft, unauthorised copying, economic espionage or the breach of confidentiality requirements, whether from within or from outside of the Union. Recent developments, such as globalisation, increased outsourcing, longer supply chains, and the increased use of information and communication technology contribute to increasing the risk of those practices. The unlawful acquisition, use or disclosure of a trade secret compromises legitimate trade secret holders' ability to obtain first-mover returns from their innovation-related efforts. Without effective and comparable legal means for protecting trade secrets across the Union, incentives to engage in innovation-related cross-border activity within the internal market are undermined, and trade secrets are unable to fulfil their potential as drivers of economic growth and jobs. Thus, innovation and creativity are discouraged and investment diminishes, thereby affecting the smooth functioning of the internal market and undermining its growth-enhancing potential.

(5) International efforts made in the framework of the World Trade Organisation to address this problem led to the conclusion of the Agreement on Trade-related Aspects of Intellectual Property Rights (the TRIPS Agreement). The TRIPS Agreement contains, inter alia, provisions on the protection of trade secrets against their unlawful acquisition, use or disclosure by third parties, which are common international standards. All Member States, as well as the Union itself, are bound by this Agreement which was approved by Council Decision 94/800/EC.

(6) Notwithstanding the TRIPS Agreement, there are important differences in the Member States' legislation as regards the protection of trade secrets against their unlawful acquisition, use or disclosure by other persons. For example, not all Member States have adopted national definitions of a trade secret or the unlawful acquisition, use or disclosure of a trade secret, therefore knowledge on the scope of protection is not readily accessible and that scope differs across the Member States. Furthermore, there is no consistency as regards the civil law remedies available in the event of unlawful acquisition, use or disclosure of trade secrets, as cease and desist orders are not always available in all Member States against third parties who are not competitors of the legitimate trade secret holder. Divergences also exist across the Member States with respect to the treatment of a third party

who has acquired the trade secret in good faith but subsequently learns, at the time of use, that the acquisition derived from a previous unlawful acquisition by another party.

(7) National rules also differ as to whether legitimate trade secret holders are allowed to seek the destruction of files or materials containing or embodying the unlawfully acquired or used trade secret. Furthermore, applicable national rules on the calculation of damages do not always take account of the intangible nature of trade secrets, which makes it difficult to demonstrate the actual profits lost or the unjust enrichment of the infringer where no market value can be established for the information in question. Only a few Member States allow for the application of abstract rules on the calculation of damages based on the reasonable royalty or fee which could have been due had a licence for the use of the trade secret existed. Additionally, many national rules do not provide for appropriate protection of the confidentiality of a trade secret where the trade secret holder introduces a claim for alleged unlawful acquisition, use or disclosure of the trade secret by a third party, thereby reducing the attractiveness of the existing measures and remedies and weakening the protection offered.

(8) The differences in the legal protection of trade secrets provided for by the Member States imply that trade secrets do not enjoy an equivalent level of protection throughout the Union, thus leading to fragmentation of the internal market in this area and a weakening of the overall deterrent effect of the relevant rules. The internal market is affected in so far as such differences lower the incentives for businesses to undertake innovation-related cross-border economic activity, including research cooperation or production cooperation with partners, outsourcing or investment in other Member States, which depends on the use of information that enjoys protection as trade secrets. Cross-border network research and development, as well as innovation-related activities, including related production and subsequent cross-border trade, are rendered less attractive and more difficult within the Union, thus also resulting in Union-wide innovation-related inefficiencies.

(9) In addition, there is a higher risk for businesses in Member States with comparatively lower levels of protection, due to the fact that trade secrets may be stolen or otherwise unlawfully acquired more easily. This leads to inefficient allocation of capital to growth-enhancing innovation within the internal market because of the higher expenditure on protective measures to compensate for the insufficient legal protection in some Member States. It also favours the activity of unfair competitors who, subsequent to the unlawful acquisition of trade secrets, could spread goods resulting from such acquisition across the internal market. Differences in legislative regimes also facilitate the importation of goods from third countries into the Union through entry points with weaker protection, when the design, production or marketing of those goods rely on stolen or otherwise unlawfully acquired trade secrets. On the whole, such differences hinder the proper functioning of the internal market.

(10) It is appropriate to provide for rules at Union level to approximate the laws of the Member States so as to ensure that there is a sufficient and consistent level of civil redress in the internal market in the event of unlawful acquisition, use or disclosure of a trade secret. Those rules should be without prejudice to the possibility for Member States of providing for more far-reaching protection against the unlawful acquisition, use or disclosure of trade secrets, as long as the safeguards explicitly provided for in this Directive for protecting the interests of other parties are respected.

(11) This Directive should not affect the application of Union or national rules that require the disclosure of information, including trade secrets, to the public or to public authorities. Nor should it affect the application of rules that allow public authorities to collect information for the performance of their duties, or rules that allow or require any subsequent disclosure by those public authorities of relevant information to the public. Such rules include, in particular, rules on the disclosure by the Union's institutions and bodies or national public authorities of business-related information they hold pursuant to Regulation (EC) No 1049/2001 of the European Parliament and of the Council, Regulation (EC) No 1367/2006 of the European Parliament and of the Council and Directive 2003/4/EC of the European Parliament and of the Council, or pursuant to other rules on public access to documents or on the transparency obligations of national public authorities.

(12) This Directive should not affect the right of social partners to enter into collective agreements, where provided for under labour law, as regards any obligation not to disclose a trade secret or to limit its use, and the consequences of a breach of such an obligation by the party subject to it. This

should be on the condition that any such collective agreement does not restrict the exceptions laid down in this Directive when an application for measures, procedures or remedies provided for in this Directive for alleged acquisition, use or disclosure of a trade secret is to be dismissed.

(13) This Directive should not be understood as restricting the freedom of establishment, the free movement of workers or the mobility of workers as provided for in Union law. Nor is it intended to affect the possibility of concluding non-competition agreements between employers and employees, in accordance with applicable law.

(14) It is important to establish a homogenous definition of a trade secret without restricting the subject matter to be protected against misappropriation. Such definition should therefore be constructed so as to cover know-how, business information and technological information where there is both a legitimate interest in keeping them confidential and a legitimate expectation that such confidentiality will be preserved. Furthermore, such know-how or information should have a commercial value, whether actual or potential. Such know-how or information should be considered to have a commercial value, for example, where its unlawful acquisition, use or disclosure is likely to harm the interests of the person lawfully controlling it, in that it undermines that person's scientific and technical potential, business or financial interests, strategic positions or ability to compete. The definition of trade secret excludes trivial information and the experience and skills gained by employees in the normal course of their employment, and also excludes information which is generally known among, or is readily accessible to, persons within the circles that normally deal with the kind of information in question.

(15) It is also important to identify the circumstances in which legal protection of trade secrets is justified. For this reason, it is necessary to establish the conduct and practices which are to be regarded as unlawful acquisition, use or disclosure of a trade secret.

(16) In the interest of innovation and to foster competition, the provisions of this Directive should not create any exclusive right to know-how or information protected as trade secrets. Thus, the independent discovery of the same know-how or information should remain possible. Reverse engineering of a lawfully acquired product should be considered as a lawful means of acquiring information, except when otherwise contractually agreed. The freedom to enter into such contractual arrangements can, however, be limited by law.

(17) In some industry sectors, where creators and innovators cannot benefit from exclusive rights and where innovation has traditionally relied upon trade secrets, products can nowadays be easily reverse-engineered once in the market. In such cases, those creators and innovators can be victims of practices such as parasitic copying or slavish imitations that free-ride on their reputation and innovation efforts. Some national laws dealing with unfair competition address those practices. While this Directive does not aim to reform or harmonise the law on unfair competition in general, it would be appropriate that the Commission carefully examine the need for Union action in that area.

(18) Furthermore, the acquisition, use or disclosure of trade secrets, whenever imposed or permitted by law, should be treated as lawful for the purposes of this Directive. This concerns, in particular, the acquisition and disclosure of trade secrets in the context of the exercise of the rights of workers' representatives to information, consultation and participation in accordance with Union law and national laws and practices, and the collective defence of the interests of workers and employers, including co-determination, as well as the acquisition or disclosure of a trade secret in the context of statutory audits performed in accordance with Union or national law. However, such treatment of the acquisition of a trade secret as lawful should be without prejudice to any obligation of confidentiality as regards the trade secret or any limitation as to its use that Union or national law imposes on the recipient or acquirer of the information. In particular, this Directive should not release public authorities from the confidentiality obligations to which they are subject in respect of information passed on by trade secret holders, irrespective of whether those obligations are laid down in Union or national law. Such confidentiality obligations include, inter alia, the obligations in respect of information forwarded to contracting authorities in the context of procurement procedures, as laid down, for example, in Directive 2014/23/EU of the European Parliament and of the Council, Directive 2014/24/EU

of the European Parliament and of the Council and Directive 2014/25/EU of the European Parliament and of the Council.

(19) While this Directive provides for measures and remedies which can consist of preventing the disclosure of information in order to protect the confidentiality of trade secrets, it is essential that the exercise of the right to freedom of expression and information which encompasses media freedom and pluralism, as reflected in Article 11 of the Charter of Fundamental Rights of the European Union ('the Charter'), not be restricted, in particular with regard to investigative journalism and the protection of journalistic sources.

(20) The measures, procedures and remedies provided for in this Directive should not restrict whistleblowing activity. Therefore, the protection of trade secrets should not extend to cases in which disclosure of a trade secret serves the public interest, insofar as directly relevant misconduct, wrongdoing or illegal activity is revealed. This should not be seen as preventing the competent judicial authorities from allowing an exception to the application of measures, procedures and remedies in a case where the respondent had every reason to believe in good faith that his or her conduct satisfied the appropriate criteria set out in this Directive.

(21) In line with the principle of proportionality, measures, procedures and remedies intended to protect trade secrets should be tailored to meet the objective of a smooth-functioning internal market for research and innovation, in particular by deterring the unlawful acquisition, use and disclosure of a trade secret. Such tailoring of measures, procedures and remedies should not jeopardise or undermine fundamental rights and freedoms or the public interest, such as public safety, consumer protection, public health and environmental protection, and should be without prejudice to the mobility of workers. In this respect, the measures, procedures and remedies provided for in this Directive are aimed at ensuring that competent judicial authorities take into account factors such as the value of a trade secret, the seriousness of the conduct resulting in the unlawful acquisition, use or disclosure of the trade secret and the impact of such conduct. It should also be ensured that the competent judicial authorities have the discretion to weigh up the interests of the parties to the legal proceedings, as well as the interests of third parties including, where appropriate, consumers.

(22) The smooth-functioning of the internal market would be undermined if the measures, procedures and remedies provided for were used to pursue illegitimate intents incompatible with the objectives of this Directive. Therefore, it is important to empower judicial authorities to adopt appropriate measures with regard to applicants who act abusively or in bad faith and submit manifestly unfounded applications with, for example, the aim of unfairly delaying or restricting the respondent's access to the market or otherwise intimidating or harassing the respondent.

(23) In the interest of legal certainty, and considering that legitimate trade secret holders are expected to exercise a duty of care as regards the preservation of the confidentiality of their valuable trade secrets and the monitoring of their use, it is appropriate to restrict substantive claims or the possibility of initiating actions for the protection of trade secrets to a limited period. National law should also specify, in a clear and unambiguous manner, from when that period is to begin to run and under what circumstances that period is to be interrupted or suspended.

(24) The prospect of losing the confidentiality of a trade secret in the course of legal proceedings often deters legitimate trade secret holders from instituting legal proceedings to defend their trade secrets, thus jeopardising the effectiveness of the measures, procedures and remedies provided for. For this reason, it is necessary to establish, subject to appropriate safeguards ensuring the right to an effective remedy and to a fair trial, specific requirements aimed at protecting the confidentiality of the litigated trade secret in the course of legal proceedings instituted for its defence. Such protection should remain in force after the legal proceedings have ended and for as long as the information constituting the trade secret is not in the public domain.

(25) Such requirements should include, as a minimum, the possibility of restricting the circle of persons entitled to have access to evidence or hearings, bearing in mind that all such persons should be subject to the confidentiality requirements set out in this Directive, and of publishing only the non-confidential elements of judicial decisions. In this context, considering that assessing the nature of the information which is the subject of a dispute is one of the main purposes of legal proceedings, it

is particularly important to ensure both the effective protection of the confidentiality of trade secrets and respect for the right of the parties to those proceedings to an effective remedy and to a fair trial. The restricted circle of persons should therefore consist of at least one natural person from each of the parties as well as the respective lawyers of the parties and, where applicable, other representatives appropriately qualified in accordance with national law in order to defend, represent or serve the interests of a party in legal proceedings covered by this Directive, who should all have full access to such evidence or hearings. In the event that one of the parties is a legal person, that party should be able to propose a natural person or natural persons who ought to form part of that circle of persons so as to ensure proper representation of that legal person, subject to appropriate judicial control to prevent the objective of the restriction of access to evidence and hearings from being undermined. Such safeguards should not be understood as requiring the parties to be represented by a lawyer or another representative in the course of legal proceedings where such representation is not required by national law. Nor should they be understood as restricting the competence of the courts to decide, in conformity with the applicable rules and practices of the Member State concerned, whether and to what extent relevant court officials should also have full access to evidence and hearings for the exercise of their duties.

(26) The unlawful acquisition, use or disclosure of a trade secret by a third party could have devastating effects on the legitimate trade secret holder, as once publicly disclosed, it would be impossible for that holder to revert to the situation prior to the loss of the trade secret. As a result, it is essential to provide for fast, effective and accessible provisional measures for the immediate termination of the unlawful acquisition, use or disclosure of a trade secret, including where it is used for the provision of services. It is essential that such relief be available without having to await a decision on the merits of the case, while having due respect for the right of defence and the principle of proportionality, and having regard to the characteristics of the case. In certain instances, it should be possible to permit the alleged infringer, subject to the lodging of one or more guarantees, to continue to use the trade secret, in particular where there is little risk that it will enter the public domain. It should also be possible to require guarantees of a level sufficient to cover the costs and the injury caused to the respondent by an unjustified application, particularly where any delay would cause irreparable harm to the legitimate trade secret holder.

(27) For the same reasons, it is also important to provide for definitive measures to prevent unlawful use or disclosure of a trade secret, including where it is used for the provision of services. For such measures to be effective and proportionate, their duration, when circumstances require a limitation in time, should be sufficient to eliminate any commercial advantage which the third party could have derived from the unlawful acquisition, use or disclosure of the trade secret. In any event, no measure of this type should be enforceable if the information originally covered by the trade secret is in the public domain for reasons that cannot be attributed to the respondent.

(28) It is possible that a trade secret could be used unlawfully to design, produce or market goods, or components thereof, which could be spread across the internal market, thus affecting the commercial interests of the trade secret holder and the functioning of the internal market. In such cases, and when the trade secret in question has a significant impact on the quality, value or price of the goods resulting from that unlawful use or on reducing the cost of, facilitating or speeding up their production or marketing processes, it is important to empower judicial authorities to order effective and appropriate measures with a view to ensuring that those goods are not put on the market or are withdrawn from it. Considering the global nature of trade, it is also necessary that such measures include the prohibition of the importation of those goods into the Union or their storage for the purposes of offering or placing them on the market. Having regard to the principle of proportionality, corrective measures should not necessarily entail the destruction of the goods if other viable options are present, such as depriving the good of its infringing quality or the disposal of the goods outside the market, for example, by means of donations to charitable organisations.

(29) A person could have originally acquired a trade secret in good faith, but only become aware at a later stage, including upon notice served by the original trade secret holder, that that person's knowledge of the trade secret in question derived from sources using or disclosing the relevant trade

secret in an unlawful manner. In order to avoid, under those circumstances, the corrective measures or injunctions provided for causing disproportionate harm to that person, Member States should provide for the possibility, in appropriate cases, of pecuniary compensation being awarded to the injured party as an alternative measure. Such compensation should not, however, exceed the amount of royalties or fees which would have been due had that person obtained authorisation to use the trade secret in question, for the period of time for which use of the trade secret could have been prevented by the original trade secret holder. Nevertheless, where the unlawful use of the trade secret would constitute an infringement of law other than that provided for in this Directive or would be likely to harm consumers, such unlawful use should not be allowed.

(30) In order to avoid a person who knowingly, or with reasonable grounds for knowing, unlawfully acquires, uses or discloses a trade secret being able to benefit from such conduct, and to ensure that the injured trade secret holder, to the extent possible, is placed in the position in which he, she or it would have been had that conduct not taken place, it is necessary to provide for adequate compensation for the prejudice suffered as a result of that unlawful conduct. The amount of damages awarded to the injured trade secret holder should take account of all appropriate factors, such as loss of earnings incurred by the trade secret holder or unfair profits made by the infringer and, where appropriate, any moral prejudice caused to the trade secret holder. As an alternative, for example where, considering the intangible nature of trade secrets, it would be difficult to determine the amount of the actual prejudice suffered, the amount of the damages might be derived from elements such as the royalties or fees which would have been due had the infringer requested authorisation to use the trade secret in question. The aim of that alternative method is not to introduce an obligation to provide for punitive damages, but to ensure compensation based on an objective criterion while taking account of the expenses incurred by the trade secret holder, such as the costs of identification and research. This Directive should not prevent Member States from providing in their national law that the liability for damages of employees is restricted in cases where they have acted without intent.

(31) As a supplementary deterrent to future infringers and to contribute to the awareness of the public at large, it is useful to publicise decisions, including, where appropriate, through prominent advertising, in cases concerning the unlawful acquisition, use or disclosure of trade secrets, on the condition that such publication does not result in the disclosure of the trade secret or disproportionally affect the privacy and reputation of a natural person.

(32) The effectiveness of the measures, procedures and remedies available to trade secret holders could be undermined in the event of non-compliance with the relevant decisions adopted by the competent judicial authorities. For this reason, it is necessary to ensure that those authorities enjoy the appropriate powers of sanction.

(33) In order to facilitate the uniform application of the measures, procedures and remedies provided for in this Directive, it is appropriate to provide for systems of cooperation and the exchange of information as between Member States on the one hand, and between the Member States and the Commission on the other, in particular by creating a network of correspondents designated by Member States. In addition, in order to review whether those measures fulfil their intended objective, the Commission, assisted, as appropriate, by the European Union Intellectual Property Office, should examine the application of this Directive and the effectiveness of the national measures taken.

(34) This Directive respects the fundamental rights and observes the principles recognised in particular by the Charter, notably the right to respect for private and family life, the right to protection of personal data, the freedom of expression and information, the freedom to choose an occupation and right to engage in work, the freedom to conduct a business, the right to property, the right to good administration, and in particular the access to files, while respecting business secrecy, the right to an effective remedy and to a fair trial and the right of defence.

(35) It is important that the rights to respect for private and family life and to protection of personal data of any person whose personal data may be processed by the trade secret holder when taking steps to protect a trade secret, or of any person involved in legal proceedings concerning the unlawful acquisition, use or disclosure of trade secrets under this Directive, and whose personal data are processed, be respected. Directive 95/46/EC of the European Parliament and of the Council governs

the processing of personal data carried out in the Member States in the context of this Directive and under the supervision of the Member States' competent authorities, in particular the public independent authorities designated by the Member States. Thus, this Directive should not affect the rights and obligations laid down in Directive 95/46/EC, in particular the rights of the data subject to access his or her personal data being processed and to obtain the rectification, erasure or blocking of the data where it is incomplete or inaccurate and, where appropriate, the obligation to process sensitive data in accordance with Article 8(5) of Directive 95/46/EC.

(36) Since the objective of this Directive, namely to achieve a smooth-functioning internal market by means of the establishment of a sufficient and comparable level of redress across the internal market in the event of the unlawful acquisition, use or disclosure of a trade secret, cannot be sufficiently achieved by Member States but can rather, by reason of its scale and effects, be better achieved at Union level, the Union may adopt measures in accordance with the principle of subsidiarity as set out in Article 5 of the Treaty on European Union. In accordance with the principle of proportionality, as set out in that Article, this Directive does not go beyond what is necessary in order to achieve that objective.

(37) This Directive does not aim to establish harmonised rules for judicial cooperation, jurisdiction, the recognition and enforcement of judgments in civil and commercial matters, or deal with applicable law. Other Union instruments which govern such matters in general terms should, in principle, remain equally applicable to the field covered by this Directive.

(38) This Directive should not affect the application of competition law rules, in particular Articles 101 and 102 of the Treaty on the Functioning of the European Union ('TFEU'). The measures, procedures and remedies provided for in this Directive should not be used to restrict unduly competition in a manner contrary to the TFEU.

(39) This Directive should not affect the application of any other relevant law in other areas, including intellectual property rights and the law of contract. However, where the scope of application of Directive 2004/48/EC of the European Parliament and of the Council and the scope of this Directive overlap, this Directive takes precedence as *lex specialis*.

(40) The European Data Protection Supervisor was consulted in accordance with Article 28(2) of Regulation (EC) No 45/2001 of the European Parliament and of the Council and delivered an opinion on 12 March 2014,

HAVE ADOPTED THIS DIRECTIVE:

Chapter I   Subject matter and scope

Article 1   Subject matter and scope

1. This Directive lays down rules on the protection against the unlawful acquisition, use and disclosure of trade secrets.

Member States may, in compliance with the provisions of the TFEU, provide for more far-reaching protection against the unlawful acquisition, use or disclosure of trade secrets than that required by this Directive, provided that compliance with Articles 3, 5, 6, Article 7(1), Article 8, the second subparagraph of Article 9(1), Article 9(3) and (4), Article 10(2),
Articles 11, 13 and Article 15(3) is ensured.

2. This Directive shall not affect:

    (a) the exercise of the right to freedom of expression and information as set out in the Charter, including respect for the freedom and pluralism of the media;

    (b) the application of Union or national rules requiring trade secret holders to disclose, for reasons of public interest, information, including trade secrets, to the public or to administrative or judicial authorities for the performance of the duties of those authorities;

    (c) the application of Union or national rules requiring or allowing Union institutions and bodies or national public authorities to disclose information submitted by businesses which those institutions, bodies or authorities hold pursuant to, and in compliance with, the obligations and prerogatives set out in Union or national law;

(d) the autonomy of social partners and their right to enter into collective agreements, in accordance with Union law and national laws and practices.

3. Nothing in this Directive shall be understood to offer any ground for restricting the mobility of employees. In particular, in relation to the exercise of such mobility, this Directive shall not offer any ground for:

(a) limiting employees' use of information that does not constitute a trade secret as defined in point (1) of Article 2;

(b) limiting employees' use of experience and skills honestly acquired in the normal course of their employment;

(c) imposing any additional restrictions on employees in their employment contracts other than restrictions imposed in accordance with Union or national law.

Article 2 Definitions

For the purposes of this Directive, the following definitions apply:

(1) 'trade secret' means information which meets all of the following requirements:

(a) it is secret in the sense that it is not, as a body or in the precise configuration and assembly of its components, generally known among or readily accessible to persons within the circles that normally deal with the kind of information in question;

(b) it has commercial value because it is secret;

(c) it has been subject to reasonable steps under the circumstances, by the person lawfully in control of the information, to keep it secret;

(2) 'trade secret holder' means any natural or legal person lawfully controlling a trade secret;

(3) 'infringer' means any natural or legal person who has unlawfully acquired, used or disclosed a trade secret;

(4) 'infringing goods' means goods, the design, characteristics, functioning, production process or marketing of which significantly benefits from trade secrets unlawfully acquired, used or disclosed.

Chapter II Acquisition, use and disclosure of trade secrets

Article 3 Lawful acquisition, use and disclosure of trade secrets

1. The acquisition of a trade secret shall be considered lawful when the trade secret is obtained by any of the following means:

(a) independent discovery or creation;

(b) observation, study, disassembly or testing of a product or object that has been made available to the public or that is lawfully in the possession of the acquirer of the information who is free from any legally valid duty to limit the acquisition of the trade secret;

(c) exercise of the right of workers or workers' representatives to information and consultation in accordance with Union law and national laws and practices;

(d) any other practice which, under the circumstances, is in conformity with honest commercial practices.

2. The acquisition, use or disclosure of a trade secret shall be considered lawful to the extent that such acquisition, use or disclosure is required or allowed by Union or national law.

Article 4 Unlawful acquisition, use and disclosure of trade secrets

1. Member States shall ensure that trade secret holders are entitled to apply for the measures, procedures and remedies provided for in this Directive in order to prevent, or obtain redress for, the unlawful acquisition, use or disclosure of their trade secret.

2. The acquisition of a trade secret without the consent of the trade secret holder shall be considered unlawful, whenever carried out by:

(a) unauthorised access to, appropriation of, or copying of any documents, objects, materials, substances or electronic files, lawfully under the control of the trade secret holder, containing the trade secret or from which the trade secret can be deduced;

(b) any other conduct which, under the circumstances, is considered contrary to honest commercial practices.

3. The use or disclosure of a trade secret shall be considered unlawful whenever carried out, without the consent of the trade secret holder, by a person who is found to meet any of the following conditions:

(a) having acquired the trade secret unlawfully;

(b) being in breach of a confidentiality agreement or any other duty not to disclose the trade secret;

(c) being in breach of a contractual or any other duty to limit the use of the trade secret.

4. The acquisition, use or disclosure of a trade secret shall also be considered unlawful whenever a person, at the time of the acquisition, use or disclosure, knew or ought, under the circumstances, to have known that the trade secret had been obtained directly or indirectly from another person who was using or disclosing the trade secret unlawfully within the meaning of paragraph 3.

5. The production, offering or placing on the market of infringing goods, or the importation, export or storage of infringing goods for those purposes, shall also be considered an unlawful use of a trade secret where the person carrying out such activities knew, or ought, under the circumstances, to have known that the trade secret was used unlawfully within the meaning of paragraph 3.

Article 5   Exceptions

Member States shall ensure that an application for the measures, procedures and remedies provided for in this Directive is dismissed where the alleged acquisition, use or disclosure of the trade secret was carried out in any of the following cases:

(a) for exercising the right to freedom of expression and information as set out in the Charter, including respect for the freedom and pluralism of the media;

(b) for revealing misconduct, wrongdoing or illegal activity, provided that the respondent acted for the purpose of protecting the general public interest;

(c) disclosure by workers to their representatives as part of the legitimate exercise by those representatives of their functions in accordance with Union or national law, provided that such disclosure was necessary for that exercise;

(d) for the purpose of protecting a legitimate interest recognised by Union or national law.

Chapter III   Measures, procedures and remedies

Section 1   General provisions

Article 6   General obligation

1. Member States shall provide for the measures, procedures and remedies necessary to ensure the availability of civil redress against the unlawful acquisition, use and disclosure of trade secrets.

2. The measures, procedures and remedies referred to in paragraph 1 shall:

(a) be fair and equitable;

(b) not be unnecessarily complicated or costly, or entail unreasonable time-limits or unwarranted delays; and

(c) be effective and dissuasive.

Article 7   Proportionality and abuse of process

1. The measures, procedures and remedies provided for in this Directive shall be applied in a manner that:

(a) is proportionate;

(b) avoids the creation of barriers to legitimate trade in the internal market; and

(c) provides for safeguards against their abuse.

2. Member States shall ensure that competent judicial authorities may, upon the request of the respondent, apply appropriate measures as provided for in national law, where an application concerning the unlawful acquisition, use or disclosure of a trade secret is manifestly unfounded and the

applicant is found to have initiated the legal proceedings abusively or in bad faith. Such measures may, as appropriate, include awarding damages to the respondent, imposing sanctions on the applicant or ordering the dissemination of information concerning a decision as referred to in Article 15.

Member States may provide that measures as referred to in the first subparagraph are dealt with in separate legal proceedings.

Article 8 Limitation period

1. Member States shall, in accordance with this Article, lay down rules on the limitation periods applicable to substantive claims and actions for the application of the measures, procedures and remedies provided for in this Directive.

The rules referred to in the first subparagraph shall determine when the limitation period begins to run, the duration of the limitation period and the circumstances under which the limitation period is interrupted or suspended.

2. The duration of the limitation period shall not exceed 6 years.

Article 9 Preservation of confidentiality of trade secrets in the course of legal proceedings

1. Member States shall ensure that the parties, their lawyers or other representatives, court officials, witnesses, experts and any other person participating in legal proceedings relating to the unlawful acquisition, use or disclosure of a trade secret, or who has access to documents which form part of those legal proceedings, are not permitted to use or disclose any trade secret or alleged trade secret which the competent judicial authorities have, in response to a duly reasoned application by an interested party, identified as confidential and of which they have become aware as a result of such participation or access. In that regard, Member States may also allow competent judicial authorities to act on their own initiative.

The obligation referred to in the first subparagraph shall remain in force after the legal proceedings have ended. However, such obligation shall cease to exist in any of the following circumstances:

- (a) where the alleged trade secret is found, by a final decision, not to meet the requirements set out in point (1) of Article 2; or
- (b) where over time, the information in question becomes generally known among or readily accessible to persons within the circles that normally deal with that kind of information.

2. Member States shall also ensure that the competent judicial authorities may, on a duly reasoned application by a party, take specific measures necessary to preserve the confidentiality of any trade secret or alleged trade secret used or referred to in the course of legal proceedings relating to the unlawful acquisition, use or disclosure of a trade secret. Member States may also allow competent judicial authorities to take such measures on their own initiative.

The measures referred to in the first subparagraph shall at least include the possibility:

- (a) of restricting access to any document containing trade secrets or alleged trade secrets submitted by the parties or third parties, in whole or in part, to a limited number of persons;
- (b) of restricting access to hearings, when trade secrets or alleged trade secrets may be disclosed, and the corresponding record or transcript of those hearings to a limited number of persons;
- (c) of making available to any person other than those comprised in the limited number of persons referred to in points (a) and (b) a non-confidential version of any judicial decision, in which the passages containing trade secrets have been removed or redacted.

The number of persons referred to in points (a) and (b) of the second subparagraph shall be no greater than necessary in order to ensure compliance with the right of the parties to the legal proceedings to an effective remedy and to a fair trial, and shall include, at least, one natural person from each party and the respective lawyers or other representatives of those parties to the legal proceedings.

3. When deciding on the measures referred to in paragraph 2 and assessing their proportionality, the competent judicial authorities shall take into account the need to ensure the right to an effective remedy and to a fair trial, the legitimate interests of the parties and, where appropriate, of third parties, and any potential harm for either of the parties, and, where appropriate, for third parties, resulting from the granting or rejection of such measures.

4. Any processing of personal data pursuant to paragraphs 1, 2 or 3 shall be carried out in accordance with Directive 95/46/EC.

Section 2   Provisional and precautionary measures

Article 10   Provisional and precautionary measures

1. Member States shall ensure that the competent judicial authorities may, at the request of the trade secret holder, order any of the following provisional and precautionary measures against the alleged infringer:

  (a) the cessation of or, as the case may be, the prohibition of the use or disclosure of the trade secret on a provisional basis;

  (b) the prohibition of the production, offering, placing on the market or use of infringing goods, or the importation, export or storage of infringing goods for those purposes;

  (c) the seizure or delivery up of the suspected infringing goods, including imported goods, so as to prevent their entry into, or circulation on, the market.

2. Member States shall ensure that the judicial authorities may, as an alternative to the measures referred to in paragraph 1, make the continuation of the alleged unlawful use of a trade secret subject to the lodging of guarantees intended to ensure the compensation of the trade secret holder. Disclosure of a trade secret in return for the lodging of guarantees shall not be allowed.

Article 11   Conditions of application and safeguards

1. Member States shall ensure that the competent judicial authorities have, in respect of the measures referred to in Article 10, the authority to require the applicant to provide evidence that may reasonably be considered available in order to satisfy themselves with a sufficient degree of certainty that:

  (a) a trade secret exists;

  (b) the applicant is the trade secret holder; and

  (c) the trade secret has been acquired unlawfully, is being unlawfully used or disclosed, or unlawful acquisition, use or disclosure of the trade secret is imminent.

2. Member States shall ensure that in deciding on the granting or rejection of the application and assessing its proportionality, the competent judicial authorities shall be required to take into account the specific circumstances of the case, including, where appropriate:

  (a) the value and other specific features of the trade secret;

  (b) the measures taken to protect the trade secret;

  (c) the conduct of the respondent in acquiring, using or disclosing the trade secret;

  (d) the impact of the unlawful use or disclosure of the trade secret;

  (e) the legitimate interests of the parties and the impact which the granting or rejection of the measures could have on the parties;

  (f) the legitimate interests of third parties;

  (g) the public interest; and

  (h) the safeguard of fundamental rights.

3. Member States shall ensure that the measures referred to in Article 10 are revoked or otherwise cease to have effect, upon the request of the respondent, if:

  (a) the applicant does not institute legal proceedings leading to a decision on the merits of the case before the competent judicial authority, within a reasonable period determined by the judicial authority ordering the measures where the law of a Member State so permits or, in the absence of such determination, within a period not exceeding 20 working days or 31 calendar days, whichever is the longer; or

  (b) the information in question no longer meets the requirements of point (1) of Article 2, for reasons that cannot be attributed to the respondent.

4. Member States shall ensure that the competent judicial authorities may make the measures referred to in Article 10 subject to the lodging by the applicant of adequate security or an equivalent assurance intended to ensure compensation for any prejudice suffered by the respondent and, where appropriate, by any other person affected by the measures.

5. Where the measures referred to in Article 10 are revoked on the basis of point (a) of paragraph 3 of this Article, where they lapse due to any act or omission by the applicant, or where it is subsequently found that there has been no unlawful acquisition, use or disclosure of the trade secret or threat of such conduct, the competent judicial authorities shall have the authority to order the applicant, upon the request of the respondent or of an injured third party, to provide the respondent, or the injured third party, appropriate compensation for any injury caused by those measures.

Member States may provide that the request for compensation referred to in the first subparagraph is dealt with in separate legal proceedings.

Section 3   Measures resulting from a decision on the merits of the case

Article 12   Injunctions and corrective measures

1. Member States shall ensure that, where a judicial decision taken on the merits of the case finds that there has been unlawful acquisition, use or disclosure of a trade secret, the competent judicial authorities may, at the request of the applicant, order one or more of the following measures against the infringer:

   (a) the cessation of or, as the case may be, the prohibition of the use or disclosure of the trade secret;

   (b) the prohibition of the production, offering, placing on the market or use of infringing goods, or the importation, export or storage of infringing goods for those purposes;

   (c) the adoption of the appropriate corrective measures with regard to the infringing goods;

   (d) the destruction of all or part of any document, object, material, substance or electronic file containing or embodying the trade secret or, where appropriate, the delivery up to the applicant of all or part of those documents, objects, materials, substances or electronic files.

2. The corrective measures referred to in point (c) of paragraph 1 shall include:

   (a) recall of the infringing goods from the market;

   (b) depriving the infringing goods of their infringing quality;

   (c) destruction of the infringing goods or, where appropriate, their withdrawal from the market, provided that the withdrawal does not undermine the protection of the trade secret in question.

3. Member States may provide that, when ordering the withdrawal of the infringing goods from the market, their competent judicial authorities may order, at the request of the trade secret holder, that the goods be delivered up to the holder or to charitable organisations.

4. The competent judicial authorities shall order that the measures referred to in points (c) and (d) of paragraph 1 be carried out at the expense of the infringer, unless there are particular reasons for not doing so. Those measures shall be without prejudice to any damages that may be due to the trade secret holder by reason of the unlawful acquisition, use or disclosure of the trade secret.

Article 13   Conditions of application, safeguards and alternative measures

1. Member States shall ensure that, in considering an application for the adoption of the injunctions and corrective measures provided for in Article 12 and assessing their proportionality, the competent judicial authorities shall be required to take into account the specific circumstances of the case, including, where appropriate:

   (a) the value or other specific features of the trade secret;

   (b) the measures taken to protect the trade secret;

   (c) the conduct of the infringer in acquiring, using or disclosing the trade secret;

   (d) the impact of the unlawful use or disclosure of the trade secret;

   (e) the legitimate interests of the parties and the impact which the granting or rejection of the measures could have on the parties;

   (f) the legitimate interests of third parties;

   (g) the public interest; and

   (h) the safeguard of fundamental rights.

Where the competent judicial authorities limit the duration of the measures referred to in points (a) and (b) of Article 12(1), such duration shall be sufficient to eliminate any commercial or economic advantage that the infringer could have derived from the unlawful acquisition, use or disclosure of the trade secret.

2. Member States shall ensure that the measures referred to in points (a) and (b) of Article 12(1) are revoked or otherwise cease to have effect, upon the request of the respondent, if the information in question no longer meets the requirements of point (1) of Article 2 for reasons that cannot be attributed directly or indirectly to the respondent.

3. Member States shall provide that, at the request of the person liable to be subject to the measures provided for in Article 12, the competent judicial authority may order pecuniary compensation to be paid to the injured party instead of applying those measures if all the following conditions are met:

(a) the person concerned at the time of use or disclosure neither knew nor ought, under the circumstances, to have known that the trade secret was obtained from another person who was using or disclosing the trade secret unlawfully;

(b) execution of the measures in question would cause that person disproportionate harm; and

(c) pecuniary compensation to the injured party appears reasonably satisfactory.

Where pecuniary compensation is ordered instead of the measures referred to in points (a) and (b) of Article 12(1), it shall not exceed the amount of royalties or fees which would have been due, had that person requested authorisation to use the trade secret in question, for the period of time for which use of the trade secret could have been prohibited.

Article 14   Damages

1. Member States shall ensure that the competent judicial authorities, upon the request of the injured party, order an infringer who knew or ought to have known that he, she or it was engaging in unlawful acquisition, use or disclosure of a trade secret, to pay the trade secret holder damages appropriate to the actual prejudice suffered as a result of the unlawful acquisition, use or disclosure of the trade secret.

Member States may limit the liability for damages of employees towards their employers for the unlawful acquisition, use or disclosure of a trade secret of the employer where they act without intent.

2. When setting the damages referred to in paragraph 1, the competent judicial authorities shall take into account all appropriate factors, such as the negative economic consequences, including lost profits, which the injured party has suffered, any unfair profits made by the infringer and, in appropriate cases, elements other than economic factors, such as the moral prejudice caused to the trade secret holder by the unlawful acquisition, use or disclosure of the trade secret.

Alternatively, the competent judicial authorities may, in appropriate cases, set the damages as a lump sum on the basis of elements such as, at a minimum, the amount of royalties or fees which would have been due had the infringer requested authorisation to use the trade secret in question.

Article 15   Publication of judicial decisions

1. Member States shall ensure that, in legal proceedings instituted for the unlawful acquisition, use or disclosure of a trade secret, the competent judicial authorities may order, at the request of the applicant and at the expense of the infringer, appropriate measures for the dissemination of the information concerning the decision, including publishing it in full or in part.

2. Any measure referred to in paragraph 1 of this Article shall preserve the confidentiality of trade secrets as provided for in Article 9.

3. In deciding whether to order a measure referred to in paragraph 1 and when assessing its proportionality, the competent judicial authorities shall take into account, where appropriate, the value of the trade secret, the conduct of the infringer in acquiring, using or disclosing the trade secret, the impact of the unlawful use or disclosure of the trade secret, and the likelihood of further unlawful use or disclosure of the trade secret by the infringer.

The competent judicial authorities shall also take into account whether the information on the infringer would be such as to allow a natural person to be identified and, if so, whether publication of that information would be justified, in particular in the light of the possible harm that such measure may cause to the privacy and reputation of the infringer.

Chapter IV   Sanctions, reporting and final provisions

Article 16   Sanctions for non-compliance with this Directive

Member States shall ensure that the competent judicial authorities may impose sanctions on any person who fails or refuses to comply with any measure adopted pursuant to Articles 9, 10 and 12.

The sanctions provided for shall include the possibility of imposing recurring penalty payments in the event of non-compliance with a measure adopted pursuant to Articles 10 and 12.

The sanctions provided for shall be effective, proportionate and dissuasive.

. . .

C4.   INTERNATIONAL

International Convention for the Protection of New Varieties of Plants (UPOV Convention)

on 2 December 1961, as revised at Geneva on 10 November 1972, on 23 October 1978, and on 19 March 1991

Chapter I   Definitions

Article 1   Definitions

For the purpose of this Act:

- (i) 'this Convention' means the present (1991) Act of the International Convention for the Protection of New Varieties of Plants;
- (ii) 'Act of 1961/1972' means the International Convention for the Protection of New Varieties of Plants of 2 December 1961, as amended by the Additional Act of 10 November 1972;
- (iii) 'Act of 1978' means the Act of 23 October 1978, of the International Convention for the Protection of New Varieties of Plants;
- (iv) 'breeder' means
  - — the person who bred, or discovered and developed, a variety,
  - — the person who is the employer of the aforementioned person or who has commissioned the latter's work, where the laws of the relevant Contracting Party so provide, or
  - — the successor in title of the first or second aforementioned person, as the case may be;
- (v) 'breeder's right' means the right of the breeder provided for in this Convention;
- (vi) 'variety' means a plant grouping within a single botanical taxon of the lowest known rank, which grouping, irrespective of whether the conditions for the grant of a breeder's right are fully met, can be
  - — defined by the expression of the characteristics resulting from a given genotype or combination of genotypes,
  - — distinguished from any other plant grouping by the expression of at least one of the said characteristics and
  - — considered as a unit with regard to its suitability for being propagated unchanged;
- (vii) 'Contracting Party' means a State or an intergovernmental organisation party to this Convention;
- (viii) 'territory,' in relation to a Contracting Party, means, where the Contracting Party is a State, the territory of that State and, where the Contracting Party is an intergovernmental

organisation, the territory in which the constituting treaty of that intergovernmental organisation applies;

(ix) 'authority' means the authority referred to in Article 30(1)(ii);

(x) 'Union' means the Union for the Protection of New Varieties of Plants founded by the Act of 1961 and further mentioned in the Act of 1972, the Act of 1978 and in this Convention;

(xi) 'member of the Union' means a State party to the Act of 1961/1972 or the Act of 1978, or a Contracting Party.

Chapter II   General Obligations of the Contracting Parties

Article 2   Basic obligation of the Contracting Parties

Each Contracting Party shall grant and protect breeders' rights.

Article 3   Genera and species to be protected

(1) [*States already members of the Union*] Each Contracting Party which is bound by the Act of 1961/1972 or the Act of 1978 shall apply the provisions of this Convention,

(i) at the date on which it becomes bound by this Convention, to all plant genera and species to which it applies, on the said date, the provisions of the Act of 1961/1972 or the Act of 1978 and,

(ii) at the latest by the expiration of a period of five years after the said date, to all plant genera and species.

(2) [*New members of the Union*] Each Contracting Party which is not bound by the Act of 1961/1972 or the Act of 1978 shall apply the provisions of this Convention,

(i) at the date on which it becomes bound by the Convention, to at least 15 plant genera or species and,

(ii) at the latest by the expiration of a period of 10 years from the said date, to all plant genera and species.

Article 4   National treatment

(1) [*Treatment*] Without prejudice to the rights specified in this Convention, nationals of a Contracting Party as well as natural persons resident and legal entities having their registered offices within the territory of a Contracting Party shall, insofar as the grant and protection of breeders' rights are concerned, enjoy within the territory of each other Contracting Party the same treatment as is accorded or may hereafter be accorded by the laws of each such other Contracting Party to its own nationals, provided that the said nationals, natural persons or legal entities comply with the conditions and formalities imposed on the nationals of the said other Contracting Party.

(2) ['*Nationals*'] For the purposes of the preceding paragraph, 'nationals' means, where the Contracting Party is a State, the nationals of that State and, where the contracting Party is an intergovernmental organisation, the nationals of the States which are members of that organisation.

Chapter III   Conditions for the Grant of the Breeder's Right

Article 5   Conditions of protection

(1) [*Criteria to be satisfied*] The breeder's right shall be granted where the variety is

(i) new,

(ii) distinct,

(iii) uniform and

(iv) stable.

(2) [*Other conditions*] The grant of the breeder's right shall not be subject to any further or different conditions, provided that the variety is designated by a denomination in accordance with the provisions of Article 20, that the applicant complies with the formalities provided for by the law of the

Contracting Party with whose authority the application has been filed and that he pays the required fees.

Article 6   Novelty

(1) [*Criteria*] The variety shall be deemed to be new if, at the date of filing of the application for a breeder's right, propagating or harvested material of the variety has not been sold or otherwise disposed of to others, by or with the consent of the breeder, for purposes of exploitation of the variety

(i) in the territory of the Contracting Party in which the application has been filed earlier than one year before that date and

(ii) in a territory other than that of the Contracting Party in which the application has been filed earlier than four years or, in the case of trees or of vines, earlier than six years before the said date.

(2) [*Varieties of recent creation*] Where a Contracting Party applies this Convention to a plant genus or species to which it did not previously apply this Convention or an earlier Act, it may consider a variety of recent creation existing at the date of such extension of protection to satisfy the condition of novelty defined in paragraph (1) even where the sale or disposal to others described in that paragraph took place earlier than the time limits defined in that paragraph.

(3) [*'Territory' in certain cases*] For the purposes of paragraph (1), all the Contracting Parties which are member States of one and the same intergovernmental organisation may act jointly, where the regulations of that organisation so require, to assimilate acts done on the territories of the States members of that organisation to acts done on their own territories and, should they do so, shall notify the Secretary-General accordingly.

Article 7   Distinctness

The variety shall be deemed to be distinct if it is clearly distinguishable from any other variety whose existence is a matter of common knowledge at the time of the filing of the application. In particular, the filing of an application for the granting of a breeder's right or for the entering of another variety in an official register of varieties, in any country, shall be deemed to render that other variety a matter of common knowledge from the date of the application, provided that the application leads to the granting of a breeder's right or to the entering of the said other variety in the official register of varieties, as the case may be.

Article 8   Uniformity

The variety shall be deemed to be uniform if, subject to the variation that may be expected from the particular features of its propagation, it is sufficiently uniform in its relevant characteristics.

Article 9   Stability

The variety shall be deemed to be stable if its relevant characteristics remain unchanged after repeated propagation or, in the case of a particular cycle of propagation, at the end of each such cycle.

Chapter IV   Application for the Grant of the Breeder's Right

Article 10   Filing of applications

(1) [*Place of first application*] The breeder may choose the Contracting Party with whose authority he wishes to file his first application for a breeder's right.

(2) [*Time of subsequent applications*] The breeder may apply to the authorities of other Contracting Parties for the grant of breeders' rights without waiting for the grant to him of a breeder's right by the authority of the Contracting Party with which the first application was filed.

(3) [*Independence of protection*] No Contracting Party shall refuse to grant a breeder's right or limit its duration on the ground that protection for the same variety has not been applied for, has been refused or has expired in any other State or intergovernmental organisation.

Article 11   Right of priority

(1) [*The right; its period*] Any breeder who has duly filed an application for the protection of a variety in one of the Contracting Parties (the 'first application') shall, for the purpose of filing an application for the grant of a breeder's right for the same variety with the authority of any other Contracting Party (the 'subsequent application'), enjoy a right of priority for a period of 12 months. This period shall be computed from the date of filing of the first application. The day of filing shall not be included in the latter period.

...

(4) [*Events occurring during the period*] Events occurring within the period provided for in paragraph (1), such as the filing of another application or the publication or use of the variety that is the subject of the first application, shall not constitute a ground for rejecting the subsequent application. Such events shall also not give rise to any third-party right.

Article 12   Examination of the application

Any decision to grant a breeder's right shall require an examination for compliance with the conditions under Articles 5 to 9. In the course of the examination, the authority may grow the variety or carry out other necessary tests, cause the growing of the variety or the carrying out of other necessary tests, or take into account the results of growing tests or other trials which have already been carried out. For the purposes of examination, the authority may require the breeder to furnish all the necessary information, documents or material.

Article 13   Provisional protection

Each Contracting Party shall provide measures designed to safeguard the interest of the breeder during the period between the filing or the publication of the application for the grant of a breeder's right and the grant of that right. Such measures shall have the effect that the holder of a breeder's right shall at least be entitled to equitable remuneration from any person who, during the said period, has carried out acts which, once the right is granted, require the breeder's authorisation as provided in Article 14. A Contracting Party may provide that the said measures shall only take effect in relation to persons whom the breeder has notified of the filing of the application.

Chapter V   The Rights of the Breeder

Article 14   Scope of the breeder's right

(1) [*Act in respect of the propagating material*]

    (a) Subject to Articles 15 and 16, the following acts in respect of the propagating material of the protected variety shall require the authorisation of the breeder:

        (i)   production or reproduction (multiplication),

        (ii) conditioning for the purpose of propagation,

        (iii) offering for sale,

        (iv) selling or other marketing,

        (v)   exporting,

        (vi) importing,

        (vii) stocking for any of the purposes mentioned in (i) to (iv), above,

    (b) The breeder may make his authorisation subject to conditions and limitations.

(2) [*Acts in respect of the harvested material*] Subject to Articles 15 and 16, the acts referred to in items (i) to (vii) of paragraph (1)(a) in respect of harvested material, including entire plants and parts of plants, obtained through the unauthorised use of propagating material of the protected variety shall require the authorisation of the breeder, unless the breeder has had reasonable opportunity to exercise his right in relation to the said propagating material.

(3) [*Acts in respect of certain products*] Each Contracting Party may provide that, subject to Articles 15 and 16, the acts referred to in items (i) to (vii) of paragraph (1)(a) in respect of products made directly from harvested material of the protected variety falling within the provisions of paragraph (2) through the unauthorised use of the said harvested material shall require the authorisation

of the breeder, unless the breeder has had reasonable opportunity to exercise his right in relation to the said harvested material.

(4) [*Possible additional acts*] Each Contracting Party may provide that, subject to Articles 15 and 16, acts other than those referred to in items (i) to (vii) of paragraph (1)(a) shall also require the authorisation of the breeder.

(5) [*Essentially derived and certain other varieties*]

    (a) The provisions of paragraphs (1) to (4) shall also apply in relation to

        (i)   varieties which are essentially derived from the protected variety, where the protected variety is not itself an essentially derived variety,

        (ii) varieties which are not clearly distinguishable in accordance with Article 7 from the protected variety and

        (iii) varieties whose production requires the repeated use of the protected variety.

    (b) For the purposes of subparagraph (a)(i), a variety shall be deemed to be essentially derived from another variety ('the initial variety') when

        (i)   it is predominantly derived from the initial variety, or from a variety that is itself predominantly derived from the initial variety, while retaining the expression of the essential characteristics that result from the genotype or combination of genotypes of the initial variety,

        (ii) it is clearly distinguishable from the initial variety and

        (iii) except for the differences which result from the act of derivation, it conforms to the initial variety in the expression of the essential characteristics that result from the genotype or combination of genotypes of the initial variety.

    (c) Essentially derived varieties may be obtained for example by the selection of a natural or induced mutant, or of a somaclonal variant, the selection of a variant individual from plants of the initial variety, backcrossing, or transformation by genetic engineering.

Article 15   Exceptions to the breeder's right

(1) [*Compulsory exceptions*] The breeder's right shall not extend to

    (i)   acts done privately and for non-commercial purposes,

    (ii) acts done for experimental purposes and

    (iii) acts done for the purpose of breeding other varieties, and, except where the provisions of Article 14(5) apply, acts referred to in Article 14(1) to (4) in respect of such other varieties.

(2) [*Optional exception*] Notwithstanding Article 14, each Contracting Party may, within reasonable limits and subject to the safeguarding of the legitimate interests of the breeder, restrict the breeder's right in relation to any variety in order to permit farmers to use for propagating purposes, on their own holdings, the product of the harvest which they have obtained by planting, on their own holdings, the protected variety or a variety covered by Article 14(5)(a)(i) or (ii).

Article 16   Exhaustion of the breeder's right

(1) [*Exhaustion of right*] The breeder's right shall not extend to acts concerning any material of the protected variety, or of a variety covered by the provisions of Article 14(5), which has been sold or otherwise marketed by the breeder or with his consent in the territory of the Contracting Party concerned, or any material derived from the said material, unless such acts (i) involve further propagation of the variety in question or (ii) involve an export of material of the variety, which enables the propagation of the variety, into a country which does not protect varieties of the plant genus or species to which the variety belongs, except where the exported material is for final consumption purposes.

(2) [*Meaning of 'material'*] For the purposes of paragraph (1), 'material' means, in relation to a variety,

    (i)   propagating material of any kind,

    (ii) harvested material, including entire plants and parts of plants, and

(iii) any product made directly from the harvested material.

(3) [*'Territory' in certain cases*] For the purposes of paragraph (1), all the Contracting Parties which are member States of one and the same intergovernmental organisation may act jointly, where the regulations of that organisation so require, to assimilate acts done on the territories of the States members of that organisation to acts done on their own territories and, should they do so, shall notify the Secretary-General accordingly.

Article 17   Restrictions on the exercise of the breeder's right

(1) [*Public interest*] Except where expressly provided in this Convention, no Contracting Party may restrict the free exercise of a breeder's right for reasons other than of public interest.

(2) [*Equitable remuneration*] When any such restriction has the effect of authorising a third party to perform any act for which the breeder's authorisation is required, the Contracting Party concerned shall take all measures necessary to ensure that the breeder receives equitable remuneration.

Article 18   Measures regulating commerce

The breeder's right shall be independent of any measure taken by a Contracting Party to regulate within its territory the production, certification and marketing of material of varieties or the importing or exporting of such material. In any case, such measures shall not affect the application of the provisions of this Convention.

Article 19   Duration of the breeder's right

(1) [*Period of protection*] The breeder's right shall be granted for a fixed period.

(2) [*Minimum period*] The said period shall not be shorter than 20 years from the date of the grant of the breeder's right. For trees and vines, the said period shall not be shorter than 25 years from the said date.

Chapter VI   Variety Denomination

Article 20   Variety denomination

(1) [*Designation of varieties by denominations; use of the denomination*]

  (a) The variety shall be designated by a denomination which will be its generic designation.

  (b) Each Contracting Party shall ensure that, subject to paragraph (4), no rights in the designation registered as the denomination of the variety shall hamper the free use of the denomination in connection with the variety, even after the expiration of the breeder's right.

(2) [*Characteristics of the denomination*] The denomination must enable the variety to be identified. It may not consist solely of figures except where this is an established practice for designating varieties. It must not be liable to mislead or to cause confusion concerning the characteristics, value or identity of the variety or the identity of the breeder. In particular, it must be different from every denomination which designates, in the territory of any Contracting Party, an existing variety of the same plant species or of a closely related species.

(3) [*Registration of the denomination*] The denomination of the variety shall be submitted by the breeder to the authority. If it is found that the denomination does not satisfy the requirements of paragraph (2), the authority shall refuse to register it and shall require the breeder to propose another denomination within a prescribed period. The denomination shall be registered by the authority at the same time as the breeder's right is granted.

(4) [*Prior rights of third persons*] Prior rights of third persons shall not be affected. If, by reason of a prior right, the use of the denomination of a variety is forbidden to a person who, in accordance with the provisions of paragraph (7), is obliged to use it, the authority shall require the breeder to submit another denomination for the variety.

(5) [*Same denomination in all Contracting Parties*] A variety must be submitted to all Contracting Parties under the same denomination. The authority of each Contracting Party shall register the denomination so submitted, unless it considers the denomination unsuitable within its territory. In the latter case, it shall require the breeder to submit another denomination.

(6) [*Information among the authorities of Contracting Parties*] The authority of a Contracting Party shall ensure that the authorities of all the other Contracting Parties are informed of matters concerning variety denominations, in particular the submission, registration and cancellation of denominations. Any authority may address its observations, if any, on the registration of a denomination to the authority which communicated that denomination.

(7) [*Obligation to use the denomination*] Any person who, within the territory of one of the Contracting Parties, offers for sale or markets propagating material of a variety protected within the said territory shall be obliged to use the denomination of that variety, even after the expiration of the breeder's right in that variety, except where, in accordance with the provisions of paragraph (4), prior rights prevent such use.

(8) [*Indications used in association with denominations*] When a variety is offered for sale or marketed, it shall be permitted to associate a trademark, trade name or other similar indication with a registered variety denomination. If such an indication is so associated, the denomination must nevertheless be easily recognisable.

Chapter VII   Nullity and Cancellation of the Breeder's Right

Article 21   Nullity of the breeder's right

(1) [*Reasons of nullity*] Each Contracting Party shall declare a breeder's right granted by it null and void when it is established

   (i)   that the conditions laid down in Articles 6 or 7 were not complied with at the time of the grant of the breeder's right,

  (ii)   that, where the grant of the breeder's right has been essentially based upon information and documents furnished by the breeder, the conditions laid down in Articles 8 or 9 were not complied with at the time of the grant of the breeder's right, or

 (iii)   that the breeder's right has been granted to a person who is not entitled to it, unless it is transferred to the person who is so entitled.

(2) [*Exclusion of other reasons*] No breeder's right shall be declared null and void for reasons other than those referred to in paragraph (1).

Article 22   Cancellation of the breeder's right

(1) [*Reasons for cancellation*]

  (a) Each Contracting Party may cancel a breeder's right granted by it if it is established that the conditions laid down in Articles 8 or 9 are no longer fulfilled.

  (b) Furthermore, each Contracting Party may cancel a breeder's right granted by it if, after being requested to do so and within a prescribed period,

     (i)   the breeder does not provide the authority with the information, documents or material deemed necessary for verifying the maintenance of the variety,

    (ii)   the breeder fails to pay such fees as may be payable to keep his right in force, or

   (iii)   the breeder does not propose, where the denomination of the variety is cancelled after the grant of the right, another suitable denomination.

(2) [*Exclusion of other reasons*] No breeder's right shall be cancelled for reasons other than those referred to in paragraph (1).

. . .

European Convention on the Grant of European Patents (European Patent Convention)

of 5 October 1973 as revised by the Act revising Article 63 EPC of 17 December 1991 and the Act revising the EPC of 29 November 2000

Preamble

The Contracting States,

Desiring to strengthen co-operation between the States of Europe in respect of the protection of inventions,

Desiring that such protection may be obtained in those States by a single procedure for the grant of patents, and by the establishment of certain standard rules governing patents so granted,

Desiring, for this purpose, to conclude a Convention which establishes a European Patent Organisation and which constitutes a special agreement within the meaning of Article 19 of the Convention for the Protection of Industrial Property, signed in Paris on 20 March 1883 and last revised on 14 July 1967, and a regional patent treaty within the meaning of Article 45, paragraph 1, of the Patent Co-operation Treaty of 19 June 1970,

Have agreed on the following provisions:

PART I GENERAL AND INSTITUTIONAL PROVISIONS

Chapter I General Provisions

Article 1 European law for the grant of patents

A system of law, common to the Contracting States, for the grant of patents for invention is established by this Convention.

Article 2 European patent

(1) Patents granted under this Convention shall be called European patents.

(2) The European patent shall, in each of the Contracting States for which it is granted, have the effect of and be subject to the same conditions as a national patent granted by that State, unless this Convention provides otherwise.

Article 3 Territorial effect

The grant of a European patent may be requested for one or more of the Contracting States.

. . .

PART II SUBSTANTIVE PATENT LAW

Chapter I Patentability

Article 52 Patentable inventions

(1) European patents shall be granted for any inventions, in all fields of technology, provided that they are new, involve an inventive step and are susceptible of industrial application.

(2) The following in particular shall not be regarded as inventions within the meaning of paragraph 1:

    (a) discoveries, scientific theories and mathematical methods;

    (b) aesthetic creations;

    (c) schemes, rules and methods for performing mental acts, playing games or doing business, and programs for computers;

    (d) presentations of information.

(3) Paragraph 2 shall exclude the patentability of the subject-matter or activities referred to therein only to the extent to which a European patent application or European patent relates to such subject-matter or activities as such.

Article 53 Exceptions to patentability

European patents shall not be granted in respect of:

    (a) inventions the commercial exploitation of which would be contrary to '*ordre public*' or morality; such exploitation shall not be deemed to be so contrary merely because it is prohibited by law or regulation in some or all of the Contracting States;

(b) plant or animal varieties or essentially biological processes for the production of plants or animals; this provision shall not apply to microbiological processes or the products thereof;

(c) methods for treatment of the human or animal body by surgery or therapy and diagnostic methods practised on the human or animal body; this provision shall not apply to products, in particular substances or compositions, for use in any of these methods.

Article 54   Novelty

(1) An invention shall be considered to be new if it does not form part of the state of the art.

(2) The state of the art shall be held to comprise everything made available to the public by means of a written or oral description, by use, or in any other way, before the date of filing of the European patent application.

(3) Additionally, the content of European patent applications as filed, the dates of filing of which are prior to the date referred to in paragraph 2 and which were published on or after that date, shall be considered as comprised in the state of the art.

(4) Paragraphs 2 and 3 shall not exclude the patentability of any substance or composition, comprised in the state of the art, for use in a method referred to in Article 53(c), provided that its use for any such method is not comprised in the state of the art.

(5) Paragraphs 2 and 3 shall also not exclude the patentability of any substance or composition referred to in paragraph 4 for any specific use in a method referred to in Article 53(c), provided that such use is not comprised in the state of the art.

Article 55   Non-prejudicial disclosures

(1) For the application of Article 54, a disclosure of the invention shall not be taken into consideration if it occurred no earlier than six months preceding the filing of the European patent application and if it was due to, or in consequence of:

(a) an evident abuse in relation to the applicant or his legal predecessor, or

(b) the fact that the applicant or his legal predecessor has displayed the invention at an official, or officially recognised, international exhibition falling within the terms of the Convention on international exhibitions signed at Paris on 22 November 1928 and last revised on 30 November 1972.

(2) In the case of paragraph 1(b), paragraph 1 shall apply only if the applicant states, when filing the European patent application, that the invention has been so displayed and files a supporting certificate within the time limit and under the conditions laid down in the Implementing Regulations.

Article 56   Inventive step

An invention shall be considered as involving an inventive step if, having regard to the state of the art, it is not obvious to a person skilled in the art. If the state of the art also includes documents within the meaning of Article 54, paragraph 3, these documents shall not be considered in deciding whether there has been an inventive step.

Article 57   Industrial application

An invention shall be considered as susceptible of industrial application if it can be made or used in any kind of industry, including agriculture.

Chapter II   Persons Entitled to Apply for and Obtain European Patents—Mention of the Inventor

Article 58   Entitlement to file a European patent application

A European patent application may be filed by any natural or legal person, or any body equivalent to a legal person by virtue of the law governing it.

Article 59   Multiple applicants

A European patent application may also be filed either by joint applicants or by two or more applicants designating different Contracting States.

Article 60   Right to a European patent

(1) The right to a European patent shall belong to the inventor or his successor in title. If the inventor is an employee, the right to a European patent shall be determined in accordance with the law of the State in which the employee is mainly employed; if the State in which the employee is mainly employed cannot be determined, the law to be applied shall be that of the State in which the employer has the place of business to which the employee is attached.

(2) If two or more persons have made an invention independently of each other, the right to a European patent therefor shall belong to the person whose European patent application has the earliest date of filing, provided that this application has been published.

(3) In proceedings before the European Patent Office, the applicant shall be deemed to be entitled to exercise the right to a European patent.

. . .

Article 62   Right of the inventor to be mentioned

The inventor shall have the right, *vis-a-vis* the applicant for or proprietor of a European patent, to be mentioned as such before the European Patent Office.

Chapter III   Effects of the European Patent and the European Patent Application

Article 63   Term of the European patent

(1) The term of the European patent shall be 20 years from the date of filing of the application.

(2) Nothing in the preceding paragraph shall limit the right of a Contracting State to extend the term of a European patent, or to grant corresponding protection which follows immediately on expiry of the term of the patent, under the same conditions as those applying to national patents:

    (a) in order to take account of a state of war or similar emergency conditions affecting that State;

    (b) if the subject-matter of the European patent is a product or a process for manufacturing a product or a use of a product which has to undergo an administrative authorisation procedure required by law before it can be put on the market in that State.

(3) Paragraph 2 shall apply *mutatis mutandis* to European patents granted jointly for a group of Contracting States in accordance with Article 142.

(4) A Contracting State which makes provision for extension of the term or corresponding protection under paragraph 2(b) may, in accordance with an agreement concluded with the Organisation, entrust to the European Patent Office tasks associated with implementation of the relevant provisions.

Article 64   Rights conferred by a European patent

(1) A European patent shall, subject to the provisions of paragraph 2, confer on its proprietor from the date on which the mention of its grant is published in the European Patent Bulletin, in each Contracting State in respect of which it is granted, the same rights as would be conferred by a national patent granted in that State.

(2) If the subject-matter of the European patent is a process, the protection conferred by the patent shall extend to the products directly obtained by such process.

(3) Any infringement of a European patent shall be dealt with by national law.

. . .

Article 67   Rights conferred by a European patent application after publication

(1) A European patent application shall, from the date of its publication, provisionally confer upon the applicant the protection provided for by Article 64, in the Contracting States designated in the application.

(2) Any Contracting State may prescribe that a European patent application shall not confer such protection as is conferred by Article 64. However, the protection attached to the publication of the European patent application may not be less than that which the laws of the State concerned attach to the compulsory publication of unexamined national patent applications. In any event, each State shall ensure at least that, from the date of publication of a European patent application, the applicant can claim compensation reasonable in the circumstances from any person who has used the invention in that State in circumstances where that person would be liable under national law for infringement of a national patent.

. . .

(4) The European patent application shall be deemed never to have had the effects set out in paragraphs 1 and 2 when it has been withdrawn, deemed to be withdrawn or finally refused. The same shall apply in respect of the effects of the European patent application in a Contracting State the designation of which is withdrawn or deemed to be withdrawn.

Article 68   Effect of revocation of the European patent

The European patent application and the resulting European patent shall be deemed not to have had, from the outset, the effects specified in Articles 64 and 67, to the extent that the patent has been revoked or limited in opposition, limitation or revocation proceedings.

Article 69   Extent of protection

(1) The extent of the protection conferred by a European patent or a European patent application shall be determined by the claims. Nevertheless, the description and drawings shall be used to interpret the claims.

(2) For the period up to grant of the European patent, the extent of the protection conferred by the European patent application shall be determined by the claims contained in the application as published. However, the European patent as granted or as amended in opposition, limitation or revocation proceedings shall determine retroactively the protection conferred by the application, in so far as such protection is not thereby extended.

. . .

Chapter IV   The European Patent Application as an Object of Property

Article 71   Transfer and constitution of rights

A European patent application may be transferred or give rise to rights for one or more of the designated Contracting States.

Article 72   Assignment

An assignment of a European patent application shall be made in writing and shall require the signature of the parties to the contract.

Article 73   Contractual licensing

A European patent application may be licensed in whole or in part for the whole or part of the territories of the designated Contracting States.

Article 74   Law applicable

Unless this Convention provides otherwise, the European patent application as an object of property shall, in each designated Contracting State and with effect for such State, be subject to the law applicable in that State to national patent applications.

PART III   APPLICATION FOR EUROPEAN PATENTS

Chapter I   Filing and Requirements of the European Patent Application

Article 75   Filing of a European patent application

(1) A European patent application may be filed:

    (a) with the European Patent Office, or

    (b) if the law of the Contracting State so permits, and subject to Article 76, paragraph 1, with the central industrial property office or other competent authority of that State. An application filed in this way shall have the same effect as if it had been filed on the same date at the European Patent Office.

    . . .

Article 78   Requirements of a European patent application

(1) A European patent application shall contain:

    (a) a request for the grant of a European patent;

    (b) a description of the invention;

    (c) one or more claims;

    (d) any drawings referred to in the description or the claims;

    (e) an abstract,

and satisfy the requirements laid down in the Implementing Regulations.

    . . .

Article 79   Designation of contracting states

(1) All the Contracting States party to this Convention at the time of filing of the European patent application shall be deemed to be designated in the request for the grant of a European patent.

    . . .

Article 80   Date of filing

The date of filing of a European patent application shall be the date on which the requirements laid down in the Implementing Regulations are fulfilled.

Article 81   Designation of the inventor

The European patent application shall designate the inventor. If the applicant is not the inventor or is not the sole inventor, the designation shall contain a statement indicating the origin of the right to the European patent.

Article 82   Unity of invention

The European patent application shall relate to one invention only or to a group of inventions so linked as to form a single general inventive concept.

Article 83   Disclosure of the invention

The European patent application shall disclose the invention in a manner sufficiently clear and complete for it to be carried out by a person skilled in the art.

Article 84   Claims

The claims shall define the matter for which protection is sought. They shall be clear and concise and be supported by the description.

Article 85   Abstract

The abstract shall serve the purpose of technical information only; it may not be taken into account for any other purpose, in particular for interpreting the scope of the protection sought applying Article 54, paragraph 3.

    . . .

Chapter II   Priority

Article 87   Priority right

(1) Any person who has duly filed, in or for

(a) any State party to the Paris Convention for the Protection of Industrial Property or

(b) any Member of the World Trade Organisation,

an application for a patent, a utility model or a utility certificate, or his successor in title, shall enjoy, for the purpose of filing a European patent application in respect of the same invention, a right of priority during a period of twelve months from the date of filing of the first application.

. . .

Article 89   Effect of priority right

The right of priority shall have the effect that the date of priority shall count as the date of filing of the European patent application for the purposes of Article 54, paragraphs 2 and 3, and Articles 60, paragraph 2.

PART IV   PROCEDURE UP TO GRANT

Article 90   Examination on filing and examination as to formal requirements

. . .

(3) If the European patent application has been accorded a date of filing, the European Patent Office shall examine, in accordance with the Implementing Regulations, whether the requirements in Articles 14, 78 and 81, and, where applicable, Article 88, paragraph 1, and Article 133, paragraph 2, as well as any other requirement laid down in the Implementing Regulations, have been satisfied.

. . .

Article 92   Drawing up of the European search report

The European Patent Office shall, in accordance with the Implementing Regulations, draw up and publish a European search report of the European patent application on the basis of the claims, with due regard to the description and any drawings.

Article 93   Publication of the European patent application

(1) The European Patent Office shall publish the European patent application as soon as possible

(a) after the expiry of a period of eighteen months from the date of filing or, if priority has been claimed, from the date of priority, or

(b) at the request of the applicant, before the expiry of that period.

(2) The European patent application shall be published at the same time as the specification of the European patent when the decision to grant the patent becomes effective before the expiry of the period referred to in paragraph 1(a).

Article 94   Examination of the European patent application

(1) The European Patent Office shall, in accordance with the Implementing Regulations, examine on written request whether the European patent application and the invention to which it relates meet the requirements of this Convention. The request shall not be deemed to be filed until the examination fee has been paid.

. . .

Article 97   Grant or refusal

(1) If the Examining Division is of the opinion that the European patent application and the invention to which it relates meet the requirements of this Convention, it shall decide to grant a European patent, provided that the conditions laid down in the Implementing Regulations are fulfilled.

(2) If the Examining Division is of the opinion that the European patent application or the invention to which it relates does not meet the requirements of this Convention, it shall refuse the application unless the Convention provides for a different legal consequence.

(3) The decision to grant a European patent shall take effect on the date on which the mention of the grant is published in the European Patent Bulletin.

Article 98   Publication of the specification of the European patent

The European Patent Office shall publish the specification of the European patent as soon as possible after the mention of the grant of the European patent has been published in the European Patent Bulletin.

PART V   OPPOSITION AND LIMITATION PROCEDURE

Article 99   Opposition

(1) Within nine months of the publication of the mention of the grant of the European patent in the European Patent Bulletin, any person may give notice to the European Patent Office of opposition to that patent, in accordance with the Implementing Regulations. Notice of opposition shall not be deemed to have been filed until the opposition fee has been paid.

. . .

Article 100   Grounds for opposition

Opposition may only be filed on the grounds that:

(a) the subject-matter of the European patent is not patentable under Articles 52 to 57;

(b) the European patent does not disclose the invention in a manner sufficiently clear and complete for it to be carried out by a person skilled in the art;

(c) the subject-matter of the European patent extends beyond the content of the application as filed, or, if the patent was granted on a divisional application or on a new application filed under Article 61, beyond the content of the earlier application as filed.

Article 101   Examination of the opposition—Revocation or maintenance of the European patent

(1) If the opposition is admissible, the Opposition Division shall examine, in accordance with the Implementing Regulations, whether at least one ground for opposition under Article 100 prejudices the maintenance of the European patent. During this examination, the Opposition Division shall invite the parties, as often as necessary, to file observations on communications from another party or issued by itself.

(2) If the Opposition Division is of the opinion that at least one ground for opposition prejudices the maintenance of the European patent, it shall revoke the patent. Otherwise, it shall reject the opposition.

(3) If the Opposition Division is of the opinion that, taking into consideration the amendments made by the proprietor of the European patent during the opposition proceedings, the patent and the invention to which it relates

(a) meet the requirements of this Convention, it shall decide to maintain the patent as amended, provided that the conditions laid down in the Implementing Regulations are fulfilled;

(b) do not meet the requirements of this Convention, it shall revoke the patent.

. . .

PART VI   APPEALS PROCEDURE

Article 106   Decisions subject to appeal

(1) An appeal shall lie from decisions of the Receiving Section, Examining Divisions, Opposition Divisions and the Legal Division. It shall have suspensive effect.

Article 107   Persons entitled to appeal and to be parties to appeal proceedings

Any party to proceedings adversely affected by a decision may appeal. Any other parties to the proceedings shall be parties to the appeal proceedings as of right.

. . .

Article 111   Decision in respect of appeals

(1) Following the examination as to the allowability of the appeal, the Board of Appeal shall decide on the appeal. The Board of Appeal may either exercise any power within the competence of the department which was responsible for the decision appealed or remit the case to that department for further prosecution.

(2) If the Board of Appeal remits the case for further prosecution to the department whose decision was appealed, that department shall be bound by the ratio decidendi of the Board of Appeal, in so far as the facts are the same. If the decision under appeal was taken by the Receiving Section, the Examining Division shall also be bound by the ratio decidendi of the Board of Appeal.

Article 112   Decision or opinion of the Enlarged Board of Appeal

(1) In order to ensure uniform application of the law, or if a point of law of fundamental importance arises:

    (a) the Board of Appeal shall, during proceedings on a case and either of its own motion or following a request from a party to the appeal, refer any question to the Enlarged Board of Appeal if it considers that a decision is required for the above purposes. If the Board of Appeal rejects the request, it shall give the reasons in its final decision;

    (b) the President of the European Patent Office may refer a point of law to the Enlarged Board of Appeal where two Boards of Appeal have given different decisions on that question.

(2) In the cases referred to in paragraph 1(a) the parties to the appeal proceedings shall be parties to the proceedings before the Enlarged Board of Appeal.

(3) The decision of the Enlarged Board of Appeal referred to in paragraph 1(a) shall be binding on the Board of Appeal in respect of the appeal in question.

Article 112a   Petition for review by the Enlarged Board of Appeal

(1) Any party to appeal proceedings adversely affected by the decision of the Board of Appeal may file a petition for review of the decision by the Enlarged Board of Appeal.

(2) The petition may only be filed on the grounds that:

    (a) a member of the Board of Appeal took part in the decision in breach of Article 24, paragraph 1, or despite being excluded pursuant to a decision under Article 24, paragraph 4;

    (b) the Board of Appeal included a person not appointed as a member of the Boards of Appeal;

    (c) a fundamental violation of Article 113 occurred;

    (d) any other fundamental procedural defect defined in the Implementing Regulations occurred in the appeal proceedings; or

    (e) a criminal act established under the conditions laid down in the Implementing Regulations may have had an impact on the decision.

(3) The petition for review shall not have suspensive effect.

. . .

PART VII   COMMON PROVISIONS

Chapter I   Common Provisions Governing Procedure

Article 113   Right to be heard and basis of decisions

(1) The decisions of the European Patent Office may only be based on grounds or evidence on which the parties concerned have had an opportunity to present their comments.

(2) The European Patent Office shall examine and decide upon the European patent application or the European patent only in the text submitted to it, or agreed, by the applicant or the proprietor of the patent.

Article 114   Examination by the European Patent Office of its own motion

(1) In proceedings before it, the European Patent Office shall examine the facts of its own motion; it shall not be restricted in this examination to the facts, evidence and arguments provided by the parties and the relief sought.

(2) The European Patent Office may disregard facts or evidence which are not submitted in due time by the parties concerned.

Article 115 Observations by third parties

(1) In proceedings before the European Patent Office, following the publication of the European patent application, any third party may, in accordance with the Implementing Regulations, present observations concerning the patentability of the invention to which the application or patent relates. That person shall not be a party to the proceedings.

. . .

Article 123 Amendments

(1) The European patent application or European patent may be amended in proceedings before the European Patent Office, in accordance with the Implementing Regulations. In any event, the applicant shall be given at least one opportunity to amend the application of his own volition.

(2) The European patent application or European patent may not be amended in such a way that it contains subject-matter which extends beyond the content of the application as filed.

(3) The European patent may not be amended in such a way as to extend the protection it confers.

. . .

Article 125 Reference to general principles

In the absence of procedural provisions in this Convention, the European Patent Office shall take into account the principles of procedural law generally recognised in the Contracting States.

Chapter II Information to the Public or Official Authorities

Article 127 European Patent Register

The European Patent Office shall keep a European Patent Register, in which the particulars specified in the Implementing Regulations shall be recorded. No entry shall be made in the European Patent Register before the publication of the European patent application. The European Patent Register shall be open to public inspection.

. . .

PART VIII IMPACT ON NATIONAL LAW

Chapter I Conversion into a National Patent Application

Article 135 Request for conversion

(1) The central industrial property office of a designated Contracting State shall, at the request of the applicant for or proprietor of a European patent, apply the procedure for the grant of a national patent in the following circumstances:

(a) where the European patent application is deemed to be withdrawn under Article 77, paragraph 3;

(b) in such other cases as are provided for by the national law, in which the European patent application is refused or withdrawn or deemed to be withdrawn, or the European patent is revoked under this Convention.

(2) In the case referred to in paragraph 1(a), the request for conversion shall be filed with the central industrial property office with which the European patent application has been filed. That office shall, subject to the provisions governing national security, transmit the request directly to the central industrial property offices of the Contracting States specified therein.

(3) In the cases referred to in paragraph 1(b), the request for conversion shall be submitted to the European Patent Office in accordance with the Implementing Regulations. It shall not be deemed to

be filed until the conversion fee has been paid. The European Patent Office shall transmit the request to the central industrial property offices of the Contracting States specified therein.

(4) The effect of the European patent application referred to in Article 66 shall lapse if the request for conversion is not submitted in due time.

. . .

Chapter II   Revocation and Prior Rights

Article 138   Revocation of European patents

(1) Subject to Article 139, a European patent may be revoked with effect for a Contracting State only on the grounds that:

(a) the subject-matter of the European patent is not patentable under Articles 52 to 57;

(b) the European patent does not disclose the invention in a manner sufficiently clear and complete for it to be carried out by a person skilled in the art;

(c) the subject-matter of the European patent extends beyond the content of the application as filed or, if the patent was granted on a divisional application or on a new application filed under Article 61, beyond the content of the earlier application as filed;

(d) the protection conferred by the European patent has been extended;

(e) the proprietor of the European patent is not entitled under Article 60, paragraph 1.

(2) If the grounds for revocation affect the European patent only in part, the patent shall be limited by a corresponding amendment of the claims and revoked in part.

(3) In proceedings before the competent court or authority relating to the validity of the European patent, the proprietor of the patent shall have the right to limit the patent by amending the claims. The patent as thus limited shall form the basis for the proceedings.

Article 139   Prior rights and rights arising on the same date

(1) In any designated Contracting State a European patent application and a European patent shall have with regard to a national patent application and a national patent the same prior right effect as a national patent application and a national patent.

(2) A national patent application and a national patent in a Contracting State shall have with regard to a European patent designating that Contracting State the same prior right effect as if the European patent were a national patent.

(3) Any Contracting State may prescribe whether and on what terms an invention disclosed in both a European patent application or patent and a national application or patent having the same date of filing or, where priority is claimed, the same date of priority, may be protected simultaneously by both applications or patents.

. . .

Protocol on the Interpretation of Article 69 of the European Patent Convention

Article 1   General principles

Article 69 should not be interpreted as meaning that the extent of the protection conferred by a European patent is to be understood as that defined by the strict, literal meaning of the wording used in the claims, the description and drawings being employed only for the purpose of resolving an ambiguity found in the claims. Nor should it be taken to mean that the claims serve only as a guideline and that the actual protection conferred may extend to what, from a consideration of the description and drawings by a person skilled in the art, the patent proprietor has contemplated. On the contrary, it is to be interpreted as defining a position between these extremes which combines a fair protection for the patent proprietor with a reasonable degree of legal certainty for third parties.

Article 2   Equivalents

For the purpose of determining the extent of protection conferred by a European patent, due account shall be taken of any element which is equivalent to an element specified in the claims.

Convention on Biological Diversity (Rio Convention)

of 5 June 1992, Signed in Rio de Janeiro

Preamble

The Contracting Parties,

Conscious of the intrinsic value of biological diversity and of the ecological, genetic, social, economic, scientific, educational, cultural, recreational and aesthetic values of biological diversity and its components,

Conscious also of the importance of biological diversity for evolution and for maintaining life sustaining systems of the biosphere,

Affirming that the conservation of biological diversity is a common concern of humankind,

Reaffirming that States have sovereign rights over their own biological resources,

Reaffirming also that States are responsible for conserving their biological diversity and for using their biological resources in a sustainable manner,

Concerned that biological diversity is being significantly reduced by certain human activities,

Aware of the general lack of information and knowledge regarding biological diversity and of the urgent need to develop scientific, technical and institutional capacities to provide the basic understanding upon which to plan and implement appropriate measures,

Noting that it is vital to anticipate, prevent and attack the causes of significant reduction or loss of biological diversity at source,

Noting also that where there is a threat of significant reduction or loss of biological diversity, lack of full scientific certainty should not be used as a reason for postponing measures to avoid or minimise such a threat,

Noting further that the fundamental requirement for the conservation of biological diversity is the *in-situ* conservation of ecosystems and natural habitats and the maintenance and recovery of viable populations of species in their natural surroundings,

Noting further that *ex-situ* measures, preferably in the country of origin, also have an important role to play,

Recognising the close and traditional dependence of many indigenous and local communities embodying traditional lifestyles on biological resources, and the desirability of sharing equitably benefits arising from the use of traditional knowledge, innovations and practices relevant to the conservation of biological diversity and the sustainable use of its components,

Recognising also the vital role that women play in the conservation and sustainable use of biological diversity and affirming the need for the full participation of women at all levels of policy-making and implementation for biological diversity conservation,

Stressing the importance of, and the need to promote, international, regional and global cooperation among States and intergovernmental organisations and the non-governmental sector for the conservation of biological diversity and the sustainable use of its components,

Acknowledging that the provision of new and additional financial resources and appropriate access to relevant technologies can be expected to make a substantial difference in the world's ability to address the loss of biological diversity,

Acknowledging further that special provision is required to meet the needs of developing countries, including the provision of new and additional financial resources and appropriate access to relevant technologies,

Noting in this regard the special conditions of the least developed countries and small island States,

Acknowledging that substantial investments are required to conserve biological diversity and that there is the expectation of a broad range of environmental, economic and social benefits from those investments,

Recognising that economic and social development and poverty eradication are the first and over-riding priorities of developing countries,

Aware that conservation and sustainable use of biological diversity is of critical importance for meeting the food, health and other needs of the growing world population, for which purposes access to and sharing of both genetic resources and technologies are essential,

Noting that, ultimately, the conservation and sustainable use of biological diversity will strengthen friendly relations among States and contribute to peace for humankind,

Desiring to enhance and complement existing international arrangements for the conservation of biological diversity and sustainable use of its components, and

Determined to conserve and sustainably use biological diversity for the benefit of present and future generations,

Have agreed as follows:

Article 1   Objectives

The objectives of this Convention, to be pursued in accordance with its relevant provisions, are the conservation of biological diversity, the sustainable use of its components and the fair and equitable sharing of the benefits arising out of the utilisation of genetic resources, including by appropriate access to genetic resources and by appropriate transfer of relevant technologies, taking into account all rights over those resources and to technologies, and by appropriate funding.

Article 2   Use of terms

For the purposes of this Convention:

'Biological diversity' means the variability among living organisms from all sources including, *inter alia,* terrestrial, marine and other aquatic ecosystems and the ecological complexes of which they are part; this includes diversity within species, between species and of ecosystems.

'Biological resources' includes genetic resources, organisms or parts thereof, populations, or any other biotic component of ecosystems with actual or potential use or value for humanity.

'Biotechnology' means any technological application that uses biological systems, living organisms, or derivatives thereof, to make or modify products or processes for specific use.

'Country of origin of genetic resources' means the country which possesses those genetic resources in *in-situ* conditions.

'Country providing genetic resources' means the country supplying genetic resources collected from *in-situ* sources, including populations of both wild and domesticated species, or taken from *ex-situ* sources, which may or may not have originated in that country.

'Domesticated or cultivated species' means species in which the evolutionary process has been influenced by humans to meet their needs.

'Ecosystem' means a dynamic complex of plant, animal and micro-organism communities and their non-living environment interacting as a functional unit.

'*Ex-situ* conservation' means the conservation of components of biological diversity outside their natural habitats.

'Genetic material' means any material of plant, animal, microbial or other origin containing functional units of heredity.

'Genetic resources' means genetic material of actual or potential value.

'Habitat' means the place or type of site where an organism or population naturally occurs.

'*In-situ* conditions' means conditions where genetic resources exist within ecosystems and natural habitats, and, in the case of domesticated or cultivated species, in the surroundings where they have developed their distinctive properties.

'*In-situ* conservation' means the conservation of ecosystems and natural habitats and the maintenance and recovery of viable populations of species in their natural surroundings and, in the case of domesticated or cultivated species, in the surroundings where they have developed their distinctive properties.

'Protected area' means a geographically defined area which is designated or regulated and managed to achieve specific conservation objectives.

'Regional economic integration organisation' means an organisation constituted by sovereign States of a given region, to which its member States have transferred competence in respect of matters governed by this Convention and which has been duly authorised, in accordance with its internal procedures, to sign, ratify, accept, approve or accede to it.

'Sustainable use' means the use of components of biological diversity in a way and at a rate that does not lead to the long-term decline of biological diversity, thereby maintaining its potential to meet the needs and aspirations of present and future generations.

'Technology' includes biotechnology.

Article 3   Principle

States have, in accordance with the Charter of the United Nations and the principles of international law, the sovereign right to exploit their own resources pursuant to their own environmental policies, and the responsibility to ensure that activities within their jurisdiction or control do not cause damage to the environment of other States or of areas beyond the limits of national jurisdiction.

Article 4   Jurisdictional scope

Subject to the rights of other States, and except as otherwise expressly provided in this Convention, the provisions of this Convention apply, in relation to each Contracting Party:

    (a) In the case of components of biological diversity, in areas within the limits of its national jurisdiction; and

    (b) In the case of processes and activities, regardless of where their effects occur, carried out under its jurisdiction or control, within the area of its national jurisdiction or beyond the limits of national jurisdiction.

    ...

Article 8   *In-situ* conservation

Each Contracting Party shall, as far as possible and as appropriate:

    ...

    (j) Subject to its national legislation, respect, preserve and maintain knowledge, innovations and practices of indigenous and local communities embodying traditional lifestyles relevant for the conservation and sustainable use of biological diversity and promote their wider application with the approval and involvement of the holders of such knowledge, innovations and practices and encourage the equitable sharing of the benefits arising from the utilisation of such knowledge, innovations and practices;

    ...

Article 15   Access to genetic resources

1. Recognising the sovereign rights of States over their natural resources, the authority to determine access to genetic resources rests with the national governments and is subject to national legislation.

2. Each Contracting Party shall endeavour to create conditions to facilitate access to genetic resources for environmentally sound uses by other Contracting Parties and not to impose restrictions that run counter to the objectives of this Convention.

3. For the purpose of this Convention, the genetic resources being provided by a Contracting Party, as referred to in this Article and Articles 16 and 19, are only those that are provided by Contracting Parties that are countries of origin of such resources or by the Parties that have acquired the genetic resources in accordance with this Convention.

4. Access, where granted, shall be on mutually agreed terms and subject to the provisions of this Article.

5. Access to genetic resources shall be subject to prior informed consent of the Contracting Party providing such resources, unless otherwise determined by that Party.

6. Each Contracting Party shall endeavour to develop and carry out scientific research based on genetic resources provided by other Contracting Parties with the full participation of, and where possible in, such Contracting Parties.

7. Each Contracting Party shall take legislative, administrative or policy measures, as appropriate, and in accordance with Articles 16 and 19 and, where necessary, through the financial mechanism established by Articles 20 and 21 with the aim of sharing in a fair and equitable way the results of research and development and the benefits arising from the commercial and other utilisation of genetic resources with the Contracting Party providing such resources. Such sharing shall be upon mutually agreed terms.

Article 16   Access to and transfer of technology

1. Each Contracting Party, recognising that technology includes biotechnology, and that both access to and transfer of technology among Contracting Parties are essential elements for the attainment of the objectives of this Convention, undertakes subject to the provisions of this Article to provide

and/or facilitate access for and transfer to other Contracting Parties of technologies that are relevant to the conservation and sustainable use of biological diversity or make use of genetic resources and do not cause significant damage to the environment.

2. Access to and transfer of technology referred to in paragraph 1 above to developing countries shall be provided and/or facilitated under fair and most favourable terms, including on concessional and preferential terms where mutually agreed, and, where necessary, in accordance with the financial mechanism established by Articles 20 and 21. In the case of technology subject to patents and other intellectual property rights, such access and transfer shall be provided on terms which recognise and are consistent with the adequate and effective protection of intellectual property rights. The application of this paragraph shall be consistent with paragraphs 3, 4 and 5 below.

3. Each Contracting Party shall take legislative, administrative or policy measures, as appropriate, with the aim that Contracting Parties, in particular those that are developing countries, which provide genetic resources are provided access to and transfer of technology which makes use of those resources, on mutually agreed terms, including technology protected by patents and other intellectual property rights, where necessary, through the provisions of Articles 20 and 21 and in accordance with international law and consistent with paragraphs 4 and 5 below.

4. Each Contracting Party shall take legislative, administrative or policy measures, as appropriate, with the aim that the private sector facilitates access to, joint development and transfer of technology referred to in paragraph 1 above for the benefit of both governmental institutions and the private sector of developing countries and in this regard shall abide by the obligations included in paragraphs 1, 2 and 3 above.

5. The Contracting Parties, recognising that patents and other intellectual property rights may have an influence on the implementation of this Convention, shall cooperate in this regard subject to national legislation and international law in order to ensure that such rights are supportive of and do not run counter to its objectives.

Article 17　Exchange of information

1. The Contracting Parties shall facilitate the exchange of information, from all publicly available sources, relevant to the conservation and sustainable use of biological diversity, taking into account the special needs of developing countries.

2. Such exchange of information shall include exchange of results of technical, scientific and socio-economic research, as well as information on training and surveying programmes, specialised knowledge, indigenous and traditional knowledge as such and in combination with the technologies referred to in Article 16, paragraph 1. It shall also, where feasible, include repatriation of information.

Article 18　Technical and scientific cooperation

1. The Contracting Parties shall promote international technical and scientific cooperation in the field of conservation and sustainable use of biological diversity, where necessary, through the appropriate international and national institutions.

2. Each Contracting Party shall promote technical and scientific cooperation with other Contracting Parties, in particular developing countries, in implementing this Convention, *inter alia,* through the development and implementation of national policies. In promoting such cooperation, special attention should be given to the development and strengthening of national capabilities, by means of human resources development and institution building.

3. The Conference of the Parties, at its first meeting, shall determine how to establish a clearing-house mechanism to promote and facilitate technical and scientific cooperation.

4. The Contracting Parties shall, in accordance with national legislation and policies, encourage and develop methods of cooperation for the development and use of technologies, including indigenous and traditional technologies, in pursuance of the objectives of this Convention. For this purpose, the Contracting Parties shall also promote cooperation in the training of personnel and exchange of experts.

5. The Contracting Parties shall, subject to mutual agreement, promote the establishment of joint research programmes and joint ventures for the development of technologies relevant to the objectives of this Convention.

Article 19   Handling of biotechnology and distribution of its benefits

1. Each Contracting Party shall take legislative, administrative or policy measures, as appropriate, to provide for the effective participation in biotechnological research activities by those Contracting Parties, especially developing countries, which provide the genetic resources for such research, and where feasible in such Contracting Parties.

2. Each Contracting Party shall take all practicable measures to promote and advance priority access on a fair and equitable basis by Contracting Parties, especially developing countries, to the results and benefits arising from biotechnologies based upon genetic resources provided by those Contracting Parties. Such access shall be on mutually agreed terms.

3. The Parties shall consider the need for and modalities of a protocol setting out appropriate procedures, including, in particular, advance informed agreement, in the field of the safe transfer, handling and use of any living modified organism resulting from biotechnology that may have adverse effect on the conservation and sustainable use of biological diversity.

4. Each Contracting Party shall, directly or by requiring any natural or legal person under its jurisdiction providing the organisms referred to in paragraph 3 above, provide any available information about the use and safety regulations required by that Contracting Party in handling such organisms, as well as any available information on the potential adverse impact of the specific organisms concerned to the Contracting Party into which those organisms are to be introduced.

. . .

Article 22   Relationship with other International Conventions

1. The provisions of this Convention shall not affect the rights and obligations of any Contracting Party deriving from any existing international agreement, except where the exercise of those rights and obligations would cause a serious damage or threat to biological diversity.

2. Contracting Parties shall implement this Convention with respect to the marine environment consistently with the rights and obligations of States under the law of the sea.

. . .

Article 27   Settlement of disputes

1. In the event of a dispute between Contracting Parties concerning the interpretation or application of this Convention, the parties concerned shall seek solution by negotiation.

2. If the parties concerned cannot reach agreement by negotiation, they may jointly seek the good offices of, or request mediation by, a third party.

3. When ratifying, accepting, approving or acceding to this Convention, or at any time thereafter, a State or regional economic integration organisation may declare in writing to the Depositary that for a dispute not resolved in accordance with paragraph 1 or paragraph 2 above, it accepts one or both of the following means of dispute settlement as compulsory:

    (a) Arbitration in accordance with the procedure laid down in Part I of Annex II;

    (b) Submission of the dispute to the International Court of Justice.

4. If the parties to the dispute have not, in accordance with paragraph 3 above, accepted the same or any procedure, the dispute shall be submitted to conciliation in accordance with Part 2 of Annex II unless the parties otherwise agree.

5. The provisions of this Article shall apply with respect to any protocol except as otherwise provided in the protocol concerned.

. . .

Article 37   Reservations

No reservations may be made to this Convention.

. . .

Part D

Multi-Regime Measures

Human Rights Act 1998

(1998, c. 42)

An Act to give further effect to rights and freedoms guaranteed under the European Convention on Human Rights; to make provision with respect to holders of certain judicial offices who become judges of the European Court of Human Rights; and for connected purposes.   [9 November 1998]

Introduction

1   The Convention rights

(1) In this Act 'the Convention rights' means the rights and fundamental freedoms set out in—

(a) Articles 2 to 12 and 14 of the Convention,

(b) Articles 1 to 3 of the First Protocol, and

(c) Article 1 of the Thirteenth Protocol,

as read with Articles 16 to 18 of the Convention.

(2) Those Articles are to have effect for the purposes of this Act subject to any designated derogation or reservation (as to which see sections 14 and 15).

(3) The Articles are set out in Schedule 1.

(4) The Secretary of State may by order make such amendments to this Act as he considers appropriate to reflect the effect, in relation to the United Kingdom, of a protocol.

(5) In subsection (4) 'protocol' means a protocol to the Convention—

(a) which the United Kingdom has ratified; or

(b) which the United Kingdom has signed with a view to ratification.

(6) No amendment may be made by an order under subsection (4) so as to come into force before the protocol concerned is in force in relation to the United Kingdom.

2   Interpretation of Convention rights

(1) A court or tribunal determining a question which has arisen in connection with a Convention right must take into account any—

(a) judgment, decision, declaration or advisory opinion of the European Court of Human Rights,

(b) opinion of the Commission given in a report adopted under Article 31 of the Convention,

(c) decision of the Commission in connection with Article 26 or 27(2) of the Convention, or

(d) decision of the Committee of Ministers taken under Article 46 of the Convention,

whenever made or given, so far as, in the opinion of the court or tribunal, it is relevant to the proceedings in which that question has arisen.

(2) Evidence of any judgment, decision, declaration or opinion of which account may have to be taken under this section is to be given in proceedings before any court or tribunal in such manner as may be provided by rules.

(3) In this section 'rules' means rules of court or, in the case of proceedings before a tribunal, rules made for the purposes of this section—

 (a) by the Lord Chancellor or the Secretary of State, in relation to any proceedings outside Scotland;

 (b) by the Secretary of State, in relation to proceedings in Scotland; or

 (c) by a Northern Ireland department, in relation to proceedings before a tribunal in Northern Ireland—

  (i) which deals with transferred matters; and

  (ii) for which no rules made under paragraph (a) are in force.

Legislation

3   Interpretation of legislation

(1) So far as it is possible to do so, primary legislation and subordinate legislation must be read and given effect in a way which is compatible with the Convention rights.

(2) This section—

 (a) applies to primary legislation and subordinate legislation whenever enacted;

 (b) does not affect the validity, continuing operation or enforcement of any incompatible primary legislation; and

 (c) does not affect the validity, continuing operation or enforcement of any incompatible subordinate legislation if (disregarding any possibility of revocation) primary legislation prevents removal of the incompatibility.

4   Declaration of incompatibility

(1) Subsection (2) applies in any proceedings in which a court determines whether a provision of primary legislation is compatible with a Convention right.

(2) If the court is satisfied that the provision is incompatible with a Convention right, it may make a declaration of that incompatibility.

(3) Subsection (4) applies in any proceedings in which a court determines whether a provision of subordinate legislation, made in the exercise of a power conferred by primary legislation, is compatible with a Convention right.

(4) If the court is satisfied—

 (a) that the provision is incompatible with a Convention right, and

 (b) that (disregarding any possibility of revocation) the primary legislation concerned prevents removal of the incompatibility,

it may make a declaration of that incompatibility.

(5) In this section 'court' means—

 (a) the Supreme Court;

 (b) the Judicial Committee of the Privy Council;

 (c) the Court Martial Appeal Court;

 (d) in Scotland, the High Court of Justiciary sitting otherwise than as a trial court or the Court of Session;

 (e) in England and Wales or Northern Ireland, the High Court or the Court of Appeal;

 (f) the Court of Protection, in any matter being dealt with by the President of the Family Division, the Chancellor of the High Court or a puisne judge of the High Court.

(6) A declaration under this section ('a declaration of incompatibility')—

 (a) does not affect the validity, continuing operation or enforcement of the provision in respect of which it is given; and

 (b) is not binding on the parties to the proceedings in which it is made.

5 Right of Crown to intervene

(1) Where a court is considering whether to make a declaration of incompatibility, the Crown is entitled to notice in accordance with rules of court.

(2) In any case to which subsection (1) applies—

(a) a Minister of the Crown (or a person nominated by him),

(b) a member of the Scottish Executive,

(c) a Northern Ireland Minister,

(d) a Northern Ireland department,

is entitled, on giving notice in accordance with rules of court, to be joined as a party to the proceedings.

(3) Notice under subsection (2) may be given at any time during the proceedings.

(4) A person who has been made a party to criminal proceedings (other than in Scotland) as the result of a notice under subsection (2) may, with leave, appeal to the Supreme Court against any declaration of incompatibility made in the proceedings.

(5) In subsection (4)—

'criminal proceedings' includes all proceedings before the Court Martial Appeal Court; and

'leave' means leave granted by the court making the declaration of incompatibility or by the Supreme Court.

Public authorities

6 Acts of public authorities

(1) It is unlawful for a public authority to act in a way which is incompatible with a Convention right.

(2) Subsection (1) does not apply to an act if—

(a) as the result of one or more provisions of primary legislation, the authority could not have acted differently; or

(b) in the case of one or more provisions of, or made under, primary legislation which cannot be read or given effect in a way which is compatible with the Convention rights, the authority was acting so as to give effect to or enforce those provisions.

(3) In this section 'public authority' includes—

(a) a court or tribunal, and

(b) any person certain of whose functions are functions of a public nature,

but does not include either House of Parliament or a person exercising functions in connection with proceedings in Parliament.

(5) In relation to a particular act, a person is not a public authority by virtue only of subsection (3)(b) if the nature of the act is private.

(6) 'An act' includes a failure to act but does not include a failure to—

(a) introduce in, or lay before, Parliament a proposal for legislation; or

(b) make any primary legislation or remedial order.

7 Proceedings

(1) A person who claims that a public authority has acted (or proposes to act) in a way which is made unlawful by section 6(1) may—

(a) bring proceedings against the authority under this Act in the appropriate court or tribunal, or

(b) rely on the Convention right or rights concerned in any legal proceedings,

but only if he is (or would be) a victim of the unlawful act.

(2) In subsection (1)(a) 'appropriate court or tribunal' means such court or tribunal as may be determined in accordance with rules; and proceedings against an authority include a counterclaim or similar proceeding.

(3) If the proceedings are brought on an application for judicial review, the applicant is to be taken to have a sufficient interest in relation to the unlawful act only if he is, or would be, a victim of that act.

(4) If the proceedings are made by way of a petition for judicial review in Scotland, the applicant shall be taken to have title and interest to sue in relation to the unlawful act only if he is, or would be, a victim of that act.

(5) Proceedings under subsection (1)(a) must be brought before the end of—

    (a) the period of one year beginning with the date on which the act complained of took place; or

    (b) such longer period as the court or tribunal considers equitable having regard to all the circumstances,

but that is subject to any rule imposing a stricter time limit in relation to the procedure in question.

(6) In subsection (1)(b) 'legal proceedings' includes—

    (a) proceedings brought by or at the instigation of a public authority; and

    (b) an appeal against the decision of a court or tribunal.

(7) For the purposes of this section, a person is a victim of an unlawful act only if he would be a victim for the purposes of Article 34 of the Convention if proceedings were brought in the European Court of Human Rights in respect of that act.

(8) Nothing in this Act creates a criminal offence.

(9) In this section 'rules' means—

    (a) in relation to proceedings before a court or tribunal outside Scotland, rules made by the Lord Chancellor or the Secretary of State for the purposes of this section or rules of court,

    (b) in relation to proceedings before a court or tribunal in Scotland, rules made by the Secretary of State for those purposes,

    (c) in relation to proceedings before a tribunal in Northern Ireland—

        (i)   which deals with transferred matters; and

        (ii) for which no rules made under paragraph (a) are in force,

    rules made by a Northern Ireland department for those purposes,

and includes provision made by order under section 1 of the Courts and Legal Services Act 1990.

(10) In making rules, regard must be had to section 9.

(11) The Minister who has power to make rules in relation to a particular tribunal may, to the extent he considers it necessary to ensure that the tribunal can provide an appropriate remedy in relation to an act (or proposed act) of a public authority which is (or would be) unlawful as a result of section 6(1), by order add to—

    (a) the relief or remedies which the tribunal may grant; or

    (b) the grounds on which it may grant any of them.

(12) An order made under subsection (11) may contain such incidental, supplemental, consequential or transitional provision as the Minister making it considers appropriate.

(13) 'The Minister' includes the Northern Ireland department concerned.

. . .

8   Judicial remedies

(1) In relation to any act (or proposed act) of a public authority which the court finds is (or would be) unlawful, it may grant such relief or remedy, or make such order, within its powers as it considers just and appropriate.

(2) But damages may be awarded only by a court which has power to award damages, or to order the payment of compensation, in civil proceedings.

(3) No award of damages is to be made unless, taking account of all the circumstances of the case, including—

    (a) any other relief or remedy granted, or order made, in relation to the act in question (by that or any other court), and

    (b) the consequences of any decision (of that or any other court) in respect of that act,

the court is satisfied that the award is necessary to afford just satisfaction to the person in whose favour it is made.

(4) In determining—

(a) whether to award damages, or

(b) the amount of an award,

the court must take into account the principles applied by the European Court of Human Rights in relation to the award of compensation under Article 41 of the Convention.

(5) A public authority against which damages are awarded is to be treated—

(a) in Scotland, for the purposes of section 3 of the Law Reform (Miscellaneous Provisions) (Scotland) Act 1940 as if the award were made in an action of damages in which the authority has been found liable in respect of loss or damage to the person to whom the award is made;

(b) for the purposes of the Civil Liability (Contribution) Act 1978 as liable in respect of damage suffered by the person to whom the award is made.

(6) In this section—

'court' includes a tribunal;

'damages' means damages for an unlawful act of a public authority; and

'unlawful' means unlawful under section 6(1).

9 Judicial acts

(1) Proceedings under section 7(1)(a) in respect of a judicial act may be brought only—

(a) by exercising a right of appeal;

(b) on an application (in Scotland a petition) for judicial review; or

(c) in such other forum as may be prescribed by rules.

(2) That does not affect any rule of law which prevents a court from being the subject of judicial review.

(3) In proceedings under this Act in respect of a judicial act done in good faith, damages may not be awarded otherwise than—

(a) to compensate a person to the extent required by Article 5(5) of the Convention, or

(b) to compensate a person for a judicial act that is incompatible with Article 6 of the Convention in circumstances where the person is detained and, but for the incompatibility, the person would not have been detained or would not have been detained for so long.

(4) An award of damages permitted by subsection (3) is to be made against the Crown; but no award may be made unless the appropriate person, if not a party to the proceedings, is joined.

(5) In this section—

'appropriate person' means the Minister responsible for the court concerned, or a person or government department nominated by him;

'court' includes a tribunal;

'judge' includes a member of a tribunal, a justice of the peace (or, in Northern Ireland, a lay magistrate) and a clerk or other officer entitled to exercise the jurisdiction of a court;

'judicial act' means a judicial act of a court and includes an act done on the instructions, or on behalf, of a judge; and

'rules' has the same meaning as in section 7(9).

Remedial action

10 Power to take remedial action

(1) This section applies if—

(a) a provision of legislation has been declared under section 4 to be incompatible with a Convention right and, if an appeal lies—

(i) all persons who may appeal have stated in writing that they do not intend to do so;

(ii) the time for bringing an appeal has expired and no appeal has been brought within that time; or

(iii) an appeal brought within that time has been determined or abandoned; or

(b) it appears to a Minister of the Crown or Her Majesty in Council that, having regard to a finding of the European Court of Human Rights made after the coming into force of this section in proceedings against the United Kingdom, a provision of legislation is incompatible with an obligation of the United Kingdom arising from the Convention.

(2) If a Minister of the Crown considers that there are compelling reasons for proceeding under this section, he may by order make such amendments to the legislation as he considers necessary to remove the incompatibility.

(3) If, in the case of subordinate legislation, a Minister of the Crown considers—

(a) that it is necessary to amend the primary legislation under which the subordinate legislation in question was made, in order to enable the incompatibility to be removed, and

(b) that there are compelling reasons for proceeding under this section,

he may by order make such amendments to the primary legislation as he considers necessary.

(4) This section also applies where the provision in question is in subordinate legislation and has been quashed, or declared invalid, by reason of incompatibility with a Convention right and the Minister proposes to proceed under paragraph 2(b) of Schedule 2.

(5) If the legislation is an Order in Council, the power conferred by subsection (2) or (3) is exercisable by Her Majesty in Council.

(6) In this section 'legislation' does not include a Measure of the Church Assembly or of the General Synod of the Church of England.

(7) Schedule 2 makes further provision about remedial orders.

Other rights and proceedings

11   Safeguard for existing human rights

A person's reliance on a Convention right does not restrict—

(a) any other right or freedom conferred on him by or under any law having effect in any part of the United Kingdom; or

(b) his right to make any claim or bring any proceedings which he could make or bring apart from sections 7 to 9.

12   Freedom of expression

(1) This section applies if a court is considering whether to grant any relief which, if granted, might affect the exercise of the Convention right to freedom of expression.

(2) If the person against whom the application for relief is made ('the respondent') is neither present nor represented, no such relief is to be granted unless the court is satisfied—

(a) that the applicant has taken all practicable steps to notify the respondent; or

(b) that there are compelling reasons why the respondent should not be notified.

(3) No such relief is to be granted so as to restrain publication before trial unless the court is satisfied that the applicant is likely to establish that publication should not be allowed.

(4) The court must have particular regard to the importance of the Convention right to freedom of expression and, where the proceedings relate to material which the respondent claims, or which appears to the court, to be journalistic, literary or artistic material (or to conduct connected with such material), to—

(a) the extent to which—

(i)   the material has, or is about to, become available to the public; or

(ii) it is, or would be, in the public interest for the material to be published;

(b) any relevant privacy code.

(5) In this section—

'court' includes a tribunal; and

'relief' includes any remedy or order (other than in criminal proceedings).

13   Freedom of thought, conscience and religion

(1) If a court's determination of any question arising under this Act might affect the exercise by a religious organisation (itself or its members collectively) of the Convention right to freedom of thought, conscience and religion, it must have particular regard to the importance of that right.

(2) In this section 'court' includes a tribunal.

...

21   Interpretation, etc

(1) In this Act—

'amend' includes repeal and apply (with or without modifications);

'the appropriate Minister' means the Minister of the Crown having charge of the appropriate authorised government department (within the meaning of the Crown Proceedings Act 1947);

'the Commission' means the European Commission of Human Rights;

'the Convention' means the Convention for the Protection of Human Rights and Fundamental Freedoms, agreed by the Council of Europe at Rome on 4th November 1950 as it has effect for the time being in relation to the United Kingdom;

'declaration of incompatibility' means a declaration under section 4;

'Minister of the Crown' has the same meaning as in the Ministers of the Crown Act 1975;

'Northern Ireland Minister' includes the First Minister and the deputy First Minister in Northern Ireland;

'primary legislation' means any—

   (a) public general Act;
   (b) local and personal Act;
   (c) private Act;
   (d) Measure of the Church Assembly;
   (e) Measure of the General Synod of the Church of England;
   (f) Order in Council—
       (i)   made in exercise of Her Majesty's Royal Prerogative;
       (ii) made under section 38(1)(a) of the Northern Ireland Constitution Act 1973 or the corresponding provision of the Northern Ireland Act 1998; or
       (iii) amending an Act of a kind mentioned in paragraph (a), (b) or (c);

and includes an order or other instrument made under primary legislation (otherwise than by the Welsh Ministers, the First Minister for Wales, the Counsel General to the Welsh Assembly Government, a member of the Scottish Executive, a Northern Ireland Minister or a Northern Ireland department) to the extent to which it operates to bring one or more provisions of that legislation into force or amends any primary legislation;

'the First Protocol' means the protocol to the Convention agreed at Paris on 20th March 1952;

...

'the Eleventh Protocol' means the protocol to the Convention (restructuring the control machinery established by the Convention) agreed at Strasbourg on 11th May 1994;

'the Thirteenth Protocol' means the protocol to the Convention (concerning the abolition of the death penalty in all circumstances) agreed at Vilnius on 3rd May 2002;

'remedial order' means an order under section 10;

'subordinate legislation' means any—

   (a)   Order in Council other than one—
       (i)   made in exercise of Her Majesty's Royal Prerogative;
       (ii) made under section 38(1)(a) of the Northern Ireland Constitution Act 1973 or the corresponding provision of the Northern Ireland Act 1998; or
       (iii) amending an Act of a kind mentioned in the definition of primary legislation;
   (b)   Act of the Scottish Parliament;
   (ba) Measure of the National Assembly for Wales;
   (bb) Act of the National Assembly for Wales;
   (c)   Act of the Parliament of Northern Ireland;
   (d)   Measure of the Assembly established under section 1 of the Northern Ireland Assembly Act 1973;
   (e)   Act of the Northern Ireland Assembly;

(f) order, rules, regulations, scheme, warrant, byelaw or other instrument made under primary legislation (except to the extent to which it operates to bring one or more provisions of that legislation into force or amends any primary legislation);

(g) order, rules, regulations, scheme, warrant, byelaw or other instrument made under legislation mentioned in paragraph (b), (c), (d) or (e) or made under an Order in Council applying only to Northern Ireland;

(h) order, rules, regulations, scheme, warrant, byelaw or other instrument made by a member of the Scottish Executive, Welsh Ministers, the First Minister for Wales, the Counsel General to the Welsh Assembly Government, a Northern Ireland Minister or a Northern Ireland department in exercise of prerogative or other executive functions of Her Majesty which are exercisable by such a person on behalf of Her Majesty;

'transferred matters' has the same meaning as in the Northern Ireland Act 1998; and

'tribunal' means any tribunal in which legal proceedings may be brought.

(2) The references in paragraphs (b) and (c) of section 2(1) to Articles are to Articles of the Convention as they had effect immediately before the coming into force of the Eleventh Protocol.

(3) The reference in paragraph (d) of section 2(1) to Article 46 includes a reference to Articles 32 and 54 of the Convention as they had effect immediately before the coming into force of the Eleventh Protocol.

(4) The references in section 2(1) to a report or decision of the Commission or a decision of the Committee of Ministers include references to a report or decision made as provided by paragraphs 3, 4 and 6 of Article 5 of the Eleventh Protocol (transitional provisions).

22   Short title, commencement, application and extent

(1) This Act may be cited as the Human Rights Act 1998.

...

(5) This Act binds the Crown.

(6) This Act extends to Northern Ireland.

SCHEDULES

SCHEDULE 1   THE ARTICLES

PART I   THE CONVENTION

RIGHTS AND FREEDOMS

Article 2

...

Article 8

Right to Respect for Private and Family Life

1. Everyone has the right to respect for his private and family life, his home and his correspondence.

2. There shall be no interference by a public authority with the exercise of this right except such as is in accordance with the law and is necessary in a democratic society in the interests of national security, public safety or the economic well-being of the country, for the prevention of disorder or crime, for the protection of health or morals, or for the protection of the rights and freedoms of others.

Article 9

Freedom of Thought, Conscience and Religion

1. Everyone has the right to freedom of thought, conscience and religion; this right includes freedom to change his religion or belief and freedom, either alone or in community with others and in public or private, to manifest his religion or belief, in worship, teaching, practice and observance.

2. Freedom to manifest one's religion or beliefs shall be subject only to such limitations as are prescribed by law and are necessary in a democratic society in the interests of public safety, for the protection of public order, health or morals, or for the protection of the rights and freedoms of others.

Article 10

Freedom of Expression

1. Everyone has the right to freedom of expression. This right shall include freedom to hold opinions and to receive and impart information and ideas without interference by public authority and regardless of frontiers. This Article shall not prevent States from requiring the licensing of broadcasting, television or cinema enterprises.

2. The exercise of these freedoms, since it carries with it duties and responsibilities, may be subject to such formalities, conditions, restrictions or penalties as are prescribed by law and are necessary in a democratic society, in the interests of national security, territorial integrity or public safety, for the prevention of disorder or crime, for the protection of health or morals, for the protection of the reputation or rights of others, for preventing the disclosure of information received in confidence, or for maintaining the authority and impartiality of the judiciary.

. . .

Article 14

Prohibition of Discrimination

The enjoyment of the rights and freedoms set forth in this Convention shall be secured without discrimination on any ground such as sex, race, colour, language, religion, political or other opinion, national or social origin, association with a national minority, property, birth or other status.

Article 16

Restrictions on Political Activity of Aliens

Nothing in Articles 10, 11 and 14 shall be regarded as preventing the High Contracting Parties from imposing restrictions on the political activity of aliens.

Article 17

Prohibition of Abuse of Rights

Nothing in this Convention may be interpreted as implying for any State, group or person any right to engage in any activity or perform any act aimed at the destruction of any of the rights and freedoms set forth herein or at their limitation to a greater extent than is provided for in the Convention.

Article 18

Limitation on use of Restrictions on Rights

The restrictions permitted under this Convention to the said rights and freedoms shall not be applied for any purpose other than those for which they have been prescribed.

PART II   THE FIRST PROTOCOL

Article 1

Protection of Property

Every natural or legal person is entitled to the peaceful enjoyment of his possessions. No one shall be deprived of his possessions except in the public interest and subject to the conditions provided for by law and by the general principles of international law.

The preceding provisions shall not, however, in any way impair the right of a State to enforce such laws as it deems necessary to control the use of property in accordance with the general interest or to secure the payment of taxes or other contributions or penalties.

. . .

SCHEDULE 3   DEROGATION AND RESERVATION

. . .

PART II   RESERVATION

At the time of signing the present (First) Protocol, I declare that, in view of certain provisions of the Education Acts in the United Kingdom, the principle affirmed in the second sentence of Article 2 is accepted by the United Kingdom only so far as it is compatible with the provision of efficient instruction and training, and the avoidance of unreasonable public expenditure.

Dated 20 March 1952

Made by the United Kingdom Permanent Representative to the Council of Europe.

. . .

Intellectual Property (Enforcement, etc.) Regulations 2006

(SI 2006/1028)

1   Citation and commencement

These Regulations may be cited as the Intellectual Property (Enforcement, etc.) Regulations 2006 and shall come into force on 29th April 2006.

. . .

3   Assessment of damages

(1) Where in an action for infringement of an intellectual property right the defendant knew, or had reasonable grounds to know, that he engaged in infringing activity, the damages awarded to the claimant shall be appropriate to the actual prejudice he suffered as a result of the infringement.

(2) When awarding such damages—

(a) all appropriate aspects shall be taken into account, including in particular—

(i) the negative economic consequences, including any lost profits, which the claimant has suffered, and any unfair profits made by the defendant; and

(ii) elements other than economic factors, including the moral prejudice caused to the claimant by the infringement; or

(b) where appropriate, they may be awarded on the basis of the royalties or fees which would have been due had the defendant obtained a licence.

(3) This regulation does not affect the operation of any enactment or rule of law relating to remedies for the infringement of intellectual property rights except to the extent that it is inconsistent with the provisions of this regulation.

(4) In the application of this regulation to—

    (a) Scotland, 'claimant' includes pursuer; 'defendant' includes defender; and 'enactment' includes an enactment comprised in, or an instrument made under, an Act of the Scottish Parliament; and

    (b) Northern Ireland, 'claimant' includes plaintiff.

4 Order in Scotland for disclosure of information

(1) This regulation applies to proceedings in Scotland concerning an infringement of an intellectual property right.

(2) The pursuer may apply to the court for an order that information regarding the origin and distribution networks of goods or services which infringe an intellectual property right shall be disclosed to him by the relevant person.

(3) The court may only order the information to be disclosed where it considers it just and proportionate having regard to the rights and privileges of the relevant person and others; such an order may be subject to such conditions as the court thinks fit.

(4) The relevant person is—

    (a) the alleged infringer,

    (b) any person who—

        (i) was found in possession of the infringing goods on a commercial scale,

        (ii) was found to be using the infringing services on a commercial scale, or

        (iii) was found to be providing services on a commercial scale, which are used in activities which infringe an intellectual property right, or

    (c) any person who has been identified by a person specified in sub-paragraph (b) as being involved in—

        (i) the production, manufacture or distribution of the infringing goods, or

        (ii) the provision of the infringing services.

(5) For the purposes of paragraph (3), the court may order the disclosure of any of the following types of information—

    (a) the names and addresses of—

        (i) each producer, manufacturer, distributor or supplier of the infringing goods or services;

        (ii) any person who previously possessed the infringing goods; and

        (iii) the intended wholesaler and retailer of the infringing goods or services; and

    (b) information relating to—

        (i) the quantities of infringing goods or the amount of infringing services provided, produced, manufactured, delivered, received or ordered; and

        (ii) the price paid for the infringing goods or infringing services in question.

(6) Nothing in this regulation affects—

    (a) any right of the pursuer to receive information under any other enactment (including an enactment comprised in, or an instrument made under, an Act of the Scottish Parliament) or rule of law; and

    (b) any other power of the court.

(7) For the purposes of this regulation and regulation 5, 'court' means the Court of Session or the sheriff.

5 Order in Scotland for publication of judgments

In Scotland, where the court finds that an intellectual property right has been infringed, the court may, at the request of the pursuer, order appropriate measures for the dissemination and publication of the judgment to be taken at the defender's expense.

European Union (Withdrawal) Act 2018

(2018, c. 16)

An Act to repeal the European Communities Act 1972 and make other provision in connection with the withdrawal of the United Kingdom from the EU. [26th June 2018]

Be it enacted by the Queen's most Excellent Majesty, by and with the advice and consent of the Lords Spiritual and Temporal, and Commons, in this present Parliament assembled, and by the authority of the same, as follows:—

Repeal of the ECA

1 Repeal of the European Communities Act 1972

The European Communities Act 1972 is repealed on exit day.

Retention of existing EU law

2 Saving for EU-derived domestic legislation

(1) EU-derived domestic legislation, as it has effect in domestic law immediately before exit day, continues to have effect in domestic law on and after exit day.

(2) In this section 'EU-derived domestic legislation' means any enactment so far as—

    (a) made under section 2(2) of, or paragraph 1A of Schedule 2 to, the European Communities Act 1972,

    (b) passed or made, or operating, for a purpose mentioned in section 2(2)(a) or (b) of that Act,

    (c) relating to anything—

        (i) which falls within paragraph (a) or (b), or

        (ii) to which section 3(1) or 4(1) applies, or

    (d) relating otherwise to the EU or the EEA,

but does not include any enactment contained in the European Communities Act 1972.

(3) This section is subject to section 5 and Schedule 1 (exceptions to savings and incorporation).

3 Incorporation of direct EU legislation

(1) Direct EU legislation, so far as operative immediately before exit day, forms part of domestic law on and after exit day.

(2) In this Act 'direct EU legislation' means—

    (a) any EU regulation, EU decision or EU tertiary legislation, as it has effect in EU law immediately before exit day and so far as—

        (i) it is not an exempt EU instrument (for which see section 20(1) and Schedule 6),

        (ii) it is not an EU decision addressed only to a member State other than the United Kingdom, and

        (iii) its effect is not reproduced in an enactment to which section 2(1) applies,

    (b) any Annex to the EEA agreement, as it has effect in EU law immediately before exit day and so far as—

        (i) it refers to, or contains adaptations of, anything falling within paragraph (a), and

        (ii) its effect is not reproduced in an enactment to which section 2(1) applies, or

    (c) Protocol 1 to the EEA agreement (which contains horizontal adaptations that apply in relation to EU instruments referred to in the Annexes to that agreement), as it has effect in EU law immediately before exit day.

(3) For the purposes of this Act, any direct EU legislation is operative immediately before exit day if—

    (a) in the case of anything which comes into force at a particular time and is stated to apply from a later time, it is in force and applies immediately before exit day,

    (b) in the case of a decision which specifies to whom it is addressed, it has been notified to that person before exit day, and

    (c) in any other case, it is in force immediately before exit day.

(4) This section—

    (a) brings into domestic law any direct EU legislation only in the form of the English language version of that legislation, and

    (b) does not apply to any such legislation for which there is no such version,

but paragraph (a) does not affect the use of the other language versions of that legislation for the purposes of interpreting it.

(5) This section is subject to section 5 and Schedule 1 (exceptions to savings and incorporation).

4 Saving for rights etc. under section 2(1) of the ECA

(1) Any rights, powers, liabilities, obligations, restrictions, remedies and procedures which, immediately before exit day—

    (a) are recognised and available in domestic law by virtue of section 2(1) of the European Communities Act 1972, and

    (b) are enforced, allowed and followed accordingly,

continue on and after exit day to be recognised and available in domestic law (and to be enforced, allowed and followed accordingly).

(2) Subsection (1) does not apply to any rights, powers, liabilities, obligations, restrictions, remedies or procedures so far as they—

    (a) form part of domestic law by virtue of section 3, or

    (b) arise under an EU directive (including as applied by the EEA agreement) and are not of a kind recognised by the European Court or any court or tribunal in the United Kingdom in a case decided before exit day (whether or not as an essential part of the decision in the case).

(3) This section is subject to section 5 and Schedule 1 (exceptions to savings and incorporation).

5 Exceptions to savings and incorporation

(1) The principle of the supremacy of EU law does not apply to any enactment or rule of law passed or made on or after exit day.

(2) Accordingly, the principle of the supremacy of EU law continues to apply on or after exit day so far as relevant to the interpretation, disapplication or quashing of any enactment or rule of law passed or made before exit day.

(3) Subsection (1) does not prevent the principle of the supremacy of EU law from applying to a modification made on or after exit day of any enactment or rule of law passed or made before exit day if the application of the principle is consistent with the intention of the modification.

(4) The Charter of Fundamental Rights is not part of domestic law on or after exit day.

(5) Subsection (4) does not affect the retention in domestic law on or after exit day in accordance with this Act of any fundamental rights or principles which exist irrespective of the Charter (and references to the Charter in any case law are, so far as necessary for this purpose, to be read as if they were references to any corresponding retained fundamental rights or principles).

(6) Schedule 1 (which makes further provision about exceptions to savings and incorporation) has effect.

6 Interpretation of retained EU law

(1) A court or tribunal—

    (a) is not bound by any principles laid down, or any decisions made, on or after exit day by the European Court, and

    (b) cannot refer any matter to the European Court on or after exit day.

(2) Subject to this and subsections (3) to (6), a court or tribunal may have regard to anything done on or after exit day by the European Court, another EU entity or the EU so far as it is relevant to any matter before the court or tribunal.

(3) Any question as to the validity, meaning or effect of any retained EU law is to be decided, so far as that law is unmodified on or after exit day and so far as they are relevant to it—

    (a) in accordance with any retained case law and any retained general principles of EU law, and

    (b) having regard (among other things) to the limits, immediately before exit day, of EU competences.

(4) But—

 (a) the Supreme Court is not bound by any retained EU case law,

 (b) the High Court of Justiciary is not bound by any retained EU case law when—

  (i) sitting as a court of appeal otherwise than in relation to a compatibility issue (within the meaning given by section 288ZA(2) of the Criminal Procedure (Scotland) Act 1995) or a devolution issue (within the meaning given by paragraph 1 of Schedule 6 to the Scotland Act 1998), or

  (ii) sitting on a reference under section 123(1) of the Criminal Procedure (Scotland) Act 1995, and

 (c) no court or tribunal is bound by any retained domestic case law that it would not otherwise be bound by.

(5) In deciding whether to depart from any retained EU case law, the Supreme Court or the High Court of Justiciary must apply the same test as it would apply in deciding whether to depart from its own case law.

(6) Subsection (3) does not prevent the validity, meaning or effect of any retained EU law which has been modified on or after exit day from being decided as provided for in that subsection if doing so is consistent with the intention of the modifications.

(7) In this Act—

'retained case law' means—

 (a) retained domestic case law, and

 (b) retained EU case law;

'retained domestic case law' means any principles laid down by, and any decisions of, a court or tribunal in the United Kingdom, as they have effect immediately before exit day and so far as they—

 (a) relate to anything to which section 2, 3 or 4 applies, and

 (b) are not excluded by section 5 or Schedule 1,

(as those principles and decisions are modified by or under this Act or by other domestic law from time to time);

'retained EU case law' means any principles laid down by, and any decisions of, the European Court, as they have effect in EU law immediately before exit day and so far as they—

 (a) relate to anything to which section 2, 3 or 4 applies, and

 (b) are not excluded by section 5 or Schedule 1,

(as those principles and decisions are modified by or under this Act or by other domestic law from time to time);

'retained EU law' means anything which, on or after exit day, continues to be, or forms part of, domestic law by virtue of section 2, 3 or 4 or subsection (3) or (6) above (as that body of law is added to or otherwise modified by or under this Act or by other domestic law from time to time);

'retained general principles of EU law' means the general principles of EU law, as they have effect in EU law immediately before exit day and so far as they—

 (a) relate to anything to which section 2, 3 or 4 applies, and

 (b) are not excluded by section 5 or Schedule 1,

(as those principles are modified by or under this Act or by other domestic law from time to time).

7 Status of retained EU law

(1) Anything which—

 (a) was, immediately before exit day, primary legislation of a particular kind, subordinate legislation of a particular kind or another enactment of a particular kind, and

 (b) continues to be domestic law on and after exit day by virtue of section 2,

continues to be domestic law as an enactment of the same kind.

(2) Retained direct principal EU legislation cannot be modified by any primary or subordinate legislation other than—

 (a) an Act of Parliament,

 (b) any other primary legislation (so far as it has the power to make such a modification), or

 (c) any subordinate legislation so far as it is made under a power which permits such a modification by virtue of—

    (i)   paragraph 3, 5(3)(a) or (4)(a), 8(3), 10(3)(a) or (4)(a), 11(2)(a) or 12(3) of Schedule 8,

    (ii) any other provision made by or under this Act,

    (iii) any provision made by or under an Act of Parliament passed before, and in the same Session as, this Act, or

    (iv) any provision made on or after the passing of this Act by or under primary legislation.

  (3) Retained direct minor EU legislation cannot be modified by any primary or subordinate legislation other than—

    (a) an Act of Parliament,

    (b) any other primary legislation (so far as it has the power to make such a modification), or

    (c) any subordinate legislation so far as it is made under a power which permits such a modification by virtue of—

      (i)   paragraph 3, 5(2) or (4)(a), 8(3), 10(2) or (4)(a) or 12(3) of Schedule 8,

      (ii) any other provision made by or under this Act,

      (iii) any provision made by or under an Act of Parliament passed before, and in the same Session as, this Act, or

      (iv) any provision made on or after the passing of this Act by or under primary legislation.

  (4) Anything which is retained EU law by virtue of section 4 cannot be modified by any primary or subordinate legislation other than—

    (a) an Act of Parliament,

    (b) any other primary legislation (so far as it has the power to make such a modification), or

    (c) any subordinate legislation so far as it is made under a power which permits such a modification by virtue of—

      (i)   paragraph 3, 5(3)(b) or (4)(b), 8(3), 10(3)(b) or (4)(b), 11(2)(b) or 12(3) of Schedule 8,

      (ii) any other provision made by or under this Act,

      (iii) any provision made by or under an Act of Parliament passed before, and in the same Session as, this Act, or

      (iv) any provision made on or after the passing of this Act by or under primary legislation.

  (5) For other provisions about the status of retained EU law, see—

    (a) section 5(1) to (3) (status of retained EU law in relation to other enactments or rules of law),

    (b) section 6 (status of retained case law and retained general principles of EU law),

    (c) section 15(2) and Part 2 of Schedule 5 (status of retained EU law for the purposes of the rules of evidence),

    (d) paragraphs 13 to 16 of Schedule 8 (affirmative and enhanced scrutiny procedure for, and information about, instruments which amend or revoke subordinate legislation under section 2(2) of the European Communities Act 1972 including subordinate legislation implementing EU directives),

    (e) paragraphs 19 and 20 of that Schedule (status of certain retained direct EU legislation for the purposes of the Interpretation Act 1978), and

    (f) paragraph 30 of that Schedule (status of retained direct EU legislation for the purposes of the Human Rights Act 1998).

  (6) In this Act—

'retained direct minor EU legislation' means any retained direct EU legislation which is not retained direct principal EU legislation;

'retained direct principal EU legislation' means—

    (a) any EU regulation so far as it—

      (i)   forms part of domestic law on and after exit day by virtue of section 3, and

      (ii) was not EU tertiary legislation immediately before exit day, or

    (b) any Annex to the EEA agreement so far as it—

      (i)   forms part of domestic law on and after exit day by virtue of section 3, and

      (ii) refers to, or contains adaptations of, any EU regulation so far as it falls within paragraph (a),

(as modified by or under this Act or by other domestic law from time to time).

. . .

D2.   UNITED STATES

Constitution of the United States of America

. . .

Article I

. . .

Section 8

The Congress shall have power . . .

To promote the progress of science and useful arts, by securing for limited times to authors and inventors the exclusive right to their respective writings and discoveries;

. . .

D3.   EUROPEAN UNION

Directive 2004/48/EC of the European Parliament and of the Council

of 29 April 2004 on the enforcement of intellectual property rights

THE EUROPEAN PARLIAMENT AND THE COUNCIL OF THE EUROPEAN UNION,

Having regard to the Treaty establishing the European Community, and in particular Article 95 thereof,

Having regard to the proposal from the Commission,

Having regard to the Opinion of the European Economic and Social Committee,

After consulting the Committee of the Regions,

Acting in accordance with the procedure laid down in Article 251 of the Treaty,

Whereas:

(1) The achievement of the Internal Market entails eliminating restrictions on freedom of movement and distortions of competition, while creating an environment conducive to innovation and investment. In this context, the protection of intellectual property is an essential element for the success of the Internal Market. The protection of intellectual property is important not only for promoting innovation and creativity, but also for developing employment and improving competitiveness.

(2) The protection of intellectual property should allow the inventor or creator to derive a legitimate profit from his invention or creation. It should also allow the widest possible dissemination of works, ideas and new know-how. At the same time, it should not hamper freedom of expression, the free movement of information, or the protection of personal data, including on the Internet.

(3) However, without effective means of enforcing intellectual property rights, innovation and creativity are discouraged and investment diminished. It is therefore necessary to ensure that the substantive law on intellectual property, which is nowadays largely part of the *acquis communautaire*, is applied effectively in the Community. In this respect, the means of enforcing intellectual property rights are of paramount importance for the success of the Internal Market.

(4) At international level, all Member States, as well as the Community itself as regards matters within its competence, are bound by the Agreement on Trade-Related Aspects of Intellectual

Property (the 'TRIPS Agreement'), approved, as part of the multilateral negotiations of the Uruguay Round, by Council Decision 94/800/EC and concluded in the framework of the World Trade Organisation.

(5) The TRIPS Agreement contains, in particular, provisions on the means of enforcing intellectual property rights, which are common standards applicable at international level and implemented in all Member States. This Directive should not affect Member States' international obligations, including those under the TRIPS Agreement.

(6) There are also international conventions to which all Member States are parties and which also contain provisions on the means of enforcing intellectual property rights. These include, in particular, the Paris Convention for the Protection of Industrial Property, the Berne Convention for the Protection of Literary and Artistic Works, and the Rome Convention for the Protection of Performers, Producers of Phonograms and Broadcasting Organisations.

(7) It emerges from the consultations held by the Commission on this question that, in the Member States, and despite the TRIPS Agreement, there are still major disparities as regards the means of enforcing intellectual property rights. For instance, the arrangements for applying provisional measures, which are used in particular to preserve evidence, the calculation of damages, or the arrangements for applying injunctions, vary widely from one Member State to another. In some Member States, there are no measures, procedures and remedies such as the right of information and the recall, at the infringer's expense, of the infringing goods placed on the market.

(8) The disparities between the systems of the Member States as regards the means of enforcing intellectual property rights are prejudicial to the proper functioning of the Internal Market and make it impossible to ensure that intellectual property rights enjoy an equivalent level of protection throughout the Community. This situation does not promote free movement within the Internal Market or create an environment conducive to healthy competition.

(9) The current disparities also lead to a weakening of the substantive law on intellectual property and to a fragmentation of the Internal Market in this field. This causes a loss of confidence in the Internal Market in business circles, with a consequent reduction in investment in innovation and creation. Infringements of intellectual property rights appear to be increasingly linked to organised crime. Increasing use of the Internet enables pirated products to be distributed instantly around the globe. Effective enforcement of the substantive law on intellectual property should be ensured by specific action at Community level. Approximation of the legislation of the Member States in this field is therefore an essential prerequisite for the proper functioning of the Internal Market.

(10) The objective of this Directive is to approximate legislative systems so as to ensure a high, equivalent and homogeneous level of protection in the Internal Market.

(11) This Directive does not aim to establish harmonised rules for judicial cooperation, jurisdiction, the recognition and enforcement of decisions in civil and commercial matters, or deal with applicable law. There are Community instruments which govern such matters in general terms and are, in principle, equally applicable to intellectual property.

(12) This Directive should not affect the application of the rules of competition, and in particular Articles 81 and 82 of the Treaty. The measures provided for in this Directive should not be used to restrict unduly competition in a manner contrary to the Treaty.

(13) It is necessary to define the scope of this Directive as widely as possible in order to encompass all the intellectual property rights covered by Community provisions in this field and/or by the national law of the Member State concerned. Nevertheless, that requirement does not affect the possibility, on the part of those Member States which so wish, to extend, for internal purposes, the provisions of this Directive to include acts involving unfair competition, including parasitic copies, or similar activities.

(14) The measures provided for in Articles 6(2), 8(1) and 9(2) need to be applied only in respect of acts carried out on a commercial scale. This is without prejudice to the possibility for Member States to apply those measures also in respect of other acts. Acts carried out on a commercial scale are those carried out for direct or indirect economic or commercial advantage; this would normally exclude acts carried out by end-consumers acting in good faith.

(15) This Directive should not affect substantive law on intellectual property, Directive 95/46/EC of 24 October 1995 of the European Parliament and of the Council on the protection of individuals with regard to the processing of personal data and on the free movement of such data, Directive 1999/93/EC of the European Parliament and of the Council of 13 December 1999 on a Community framework for electronic signatures and Directive 2000/31/EC of the European Parliament and of the Council of 8 June 2000 on certain legal aspects of information society services, in particular electronic commerce, in the Internal Market.

(16) The provisions of this Directive should be without prejudice to the particular provisions for the enforcement of rights and on exceptions in the domain of copyright and related rights set out in Community instruments and notably those found in Council Directive 91/250/EEC of 14 May 1991 on the legal protection of computer programs or in Directive 2001/29/EC of the European Parliament and of the Council of 22 May 2001 on the harmonisation of certain aspects of copyright and related rights in the information society.

(17) The measures, procedures and remedies provided for in this Directive should be determined in each case in such a manner as to take due account of the specific characteristics of that case, including the specific features of each intellectual property right and, where appropriate, the intentional or unintentional character of the infringement.

(18) The persons entitled to request application of those measures, procedures and remedies should be not only the rightholders but also persons who have a direct interest and legal standing in so far as permitted by and in accordance with the applicable law, which may include professional organisations in charge of the management of those rights or for the defence of the collective and individual interests for which they are responsible.

(19) Since copyright exists from the creation of a work and does not require formal registration, it is appropriate to adopt the rule laid down in Article 15 of the Berne Convention, which establishes the presumption whereby the author of a literary or artistic work is regarded as such if his name appears on the work. A similar presumption should be applied to the owners of related rights since it is often the holder of a related right, such as a phonogram producer, who will seek to defend rights and engage in fighting acts of piracy.

(20) Given that evidence is an element of paramount importance for establishing the infringement of intellectual property rights, it is appropriate to ensure that effective means of presenting, obtaining and preserving evidence are available. The procedures should have regard to the rights of the defence and provide the necessary guarantees, including the protection of confidential information. For infringements committed on a commercial scale it is also important that the courts may order access, where appropriate, to banking, financial or commercial documents under the control of the alleged infringer.

(21) Other measures designed to ensure a high level of protection exist in certain Member States and should be made available in all the Member States. This is the case with the right of information, which allows precise information to be obtained on the origin of the infringing goods or services, the distribution channels and the identity of any third parties involved in the infringement.

(22) It is also essential to provide for provisional measures for the immediate termination of infringements, without awaiting a decision on the substance of the case, while observing the rights of the defence, ensuring the proportionality of the provisional measures as appropriate to the characteristics of the case in question and providing the guarantees needed to cover the costs and the injury caused to the defendant by an unjustified request. Such measures are particularly justified where any delay would cause irreparable harm to the holder of an intellectual property right.

(23) Without prejudice to any other measures, procedures and remedies available, right holders should have the possibility of applying for an injunction against an intermediary whose services are being used by a third party to infringe the rightholder's industrial property right. The conditions and procedures relating to such injunctions should be left to the national law of the Member States. As far as infringements of copyright and related rights are concerned, a comprehensive level of harmonisation is already provided for in Directive 2001/29/EC. Article 8(3) of Directive 2001/29/EC should therefore not be affected by this Directive.

(24) Depending on the particular case, and if justified by the circumstances, the measures, procedures and remedies to be provided for should include prohibitory measures aimed at preventing further infringements of intellectual property rights. Moreover there should be corrective measures, where appropriate at the expense of the infringer, such as the recall and definitive removal from the channels of commerce, or destruction, of the infringing goods and, in appropriate cases, of the materials and implements principally used in the creation or manufacture of these goods. These corrective measures should take account of the interests of third parties including, in particular, consumers and private parties acting in good faith.

(25) Where an infringement is committed unintentionally and without negligence and where the corrective measures or injunctions provided for by this Directive would be disproportionate, Member States should have the option of providing for the possibility, in appropriate cases, of pecuniary compensation being awarded to the injured party as an alternative measure. However, where the commercial use of counterfeit goods or the supply of services would constitute an infringement of law other than intellectual property law or would be likely to harm consumers, such use or supply should remain prohibited.

(26) With a view to compensating for the prejudice suffered as a result of an infringement committed by an infringer who engaged in an activity in the knowledge, or with reasonable grounds for knowing, that it would give rise to such an infringement, the amount of damages awarded to the rightholder should take account of all appropriate aspects, such as loss of earnings incurred by the rightholder, or unfair profits made by the infringer and, where appropriate, any moral prejudice caused to the rightholder. As an alternative, for example where it would be difficult to determine the amount of the actual prejudice suffered, the amount of the damages might be derived from elements such as the royalties or fees which would have been due if the infringer had requested authorisation to use the intellectual property right in question. The aim is not to introduce an obligation to provide for punitive damages but to allow for compensation based on an objective criterion while taking account of the expenses incurred by the rightholder, such as the costs of identification and research.

(27) To act as a supplementary deterrent to future infringers and to contribute to the awareness of the public at large, it is useful to publicise decisions in intellectual property infringement cases.

(28) In addition to the civil and administrative measures, procedures and remedies provided for under this Directive, criminal sanctions also constitute, in appropriate cases, a means of ensuring the enforcement of intellectual property rights.

(29) Industry should take an active part in the fight against piracy and counterfeiting. The development of codes of conduct in the circles directly affected is a supplementary means of bolstering the regulatory framework. The Member States, in collaboration with the Commission, should encourage the development of codes of conduct in general. Monitoring of the manufacture of optical discs, particularly by means of an identification code embedded in discs produced in the Community, helps to limit infringements of intellectual property rights in this sector, which suffers from piracy on a large scale. However, these technical protection measures should not be misused to protect markets and prevent parallel imports.

(30) In order to facilitate the uniform application of this Directive, it is appropriate to provide for systems of cooperation and the exchange of information between Member States, on the one hand, and between the Member States and the Commission on the other, in particular by creating a network of correspondents designated by the Member States and by providing regular reports assessing the application of this Directive and the effectiveness of the measures taken by the various national bodies.

(31) Since, for the reasons already described, the objective of this Directive can best be achieved at Community level, the Community may adopt measures, in accordance with the principle of subsidiarity as set out in Article 5 of the Treaty. In accordance with the principle of proportionality as set out in that Article, this Directive does not go beyond what is necessary in order to achieve that objective.

(32) This Directive respects the fundamental rights and observes the principles recognised in particular by the Charter of Fundamental Rights of the European Union. In particular, this Directive seeks to ensure full respect for intellectual property, in accordance with Article 17(2) of that Charter,

HAVE ADOPTED THIS DIRECTIVE:

Chapter I   Objective and Scope

Article 1   Subject-matter

This Directive concerns the measures, procedures and remedies necessary to ensure the enforcement of intellectual property rights. For the purposes of this Directive, the term 'intellectual property rights' includes industrial property rights.

Article 2   Scope

1. Without prejudice to the means which are or may be provided for in Community or national legislation, in so far as those means may be more favourable for rightholders, the measures, procedures and remedies provided for by this Directive shall apply, in accordance with Article 3, to any infringement of intellectual property rights as provided for by Community law and/or by the national law of the Member State concerned.

2. This Directive shall be without prejudice to the specific provisions on the enforcement of rights and on exceptions contained in Community legislation concerning copyright and rights related to copyright, notably those found in Directive 91/250/EEC and, in particular, Article 7 thereof or in Directive 2001/29/EC and, in particular, Articles 2 to 6 and Article 8 thereof.

3. This Directive shall not affect:

   (a) the Community provisions governing the substantive law on intellectual property, Directive 95/46/EC, Directive 1999/93/EC or Directive 2000/31/EC, in general, and Articles 12 to 15 of Directive 2000/31/EC in particular;

   (b) Member States' international obligations and notably the TRIPS Agreement, including those relating to criminal procedures and penalties;

   (c) any national provisions in Member States relating to criminal procedures or penalties in respect of infringement of intellectual property rights.

Chapter II   Measures, Procedures and Remedies

Section 1   General Provisions

Article 3   General obligation

1. Member States shall provide for the measures, procedures and remedies necessary to ensure the enforcement of the intellectual property rights covered by this Directive. Those measures, procedures and remedies shall be fair and equitable and shall not be unnecessarily complicated or costly, or entail unreasonable time-limits or unwarranted delays.

2. Those measures, procedures and remedies shall also be effective, proportionate and dissuasive and shall be applied in such a manner as to avoid the creation of barriers to legitimate trade and to provide for safeguards against their abuse.

Article 4   Persons entitled to apply for the application
of the measures, procedures and remedies

1. Member States shall recognise as persons entitled to seek application of the measures, procedures and remedies referred to in this Chapter:

   (a) the holders of intellectual property rights, in accordance with the provisions of the applicable law,

   (b) all other persons authorised to use those rights, in particular licensees, in so far as permitted by and in accordance with the provisions of the applicable law,

   (c) intellectual property collective rights management bodies which are regularly recognised as having a right to represent holders of intellectual property rights, in so far as permitted by and in accordance with the provisions of the applicable law,

(d) professional defence bodies which are regularly recognised as having a right to represent holders of intellectual property rights, in so far as permitted by and in accordance with the provisions of the applicable law.

Article 5   Presumption of authorship or ownership

For the purposes of applying the measures, procedures and remedies provided for in this Directive,

(a) for the author of a literary or artistic work, in the absence of proof to the contrary, to be regarded as such, and consequently to be entitled to institute infringement proceedings, it shall be sufficient for his name to appear on the work in the usual manner;

(b) the provision under (a) shall apply *mutatis mutandis* to the holders of rights related to copyright with regard to their protected subject matter.

Section 2   Evidence

Article 6   Evidence

1. Member States shall ensure that, on application by a party which has presented reasonably available evidence sufficient to support its claims, and has, in substantiating those claims, specified evidence which lies in the control of the opposing party, the competent judicial authorities may order that such evidence be presented by the opposing party, subject to the protection of confidential information. For the purposes of this paragraph, Member States may provide that a reasonable sample of a substantial number of copies of a work or any other protected object be considered by the competent judicial authorities to constitute reasonable evidence.

2. Under the same conditions, in the case of an infringement committed on a commercial scale Member States shall take such measures as are necessary to enable the competent judicial authorities to order, where appropriate, on application by a party, the communication of banking, financial or commercial documents under the control of the opposing party, subject to the protection of confidential information.

Article 7   Measures for preserving evidence

1. Member States shall ensure that, even before the commencement of proceedings on the merits of the case, the competent judicial authorities may, on application by a party who has presented reasonably available evidence to support his claims that his intellectual property right has been infringed or is about to be infringed, order prompt and effective provisional measures to preserve relevant evidence in respect of the alleged infringement, subject to the protection of confidential information. Such measures may include the detailed description, with or without the taking of samples, or the physical seizure of the infringing goods, and, in appropriate cases, the materials and implements used in the production and/or distribution of these goods and the documents relating thereto. Those measures shall be taken, if necessary without the other party having been heard, in particular where any delay is likely to cause irreparable harm to the rightholder or where there is a demonstrable risk of evidence being destroyed.

Where measures to preserve evidence are adopted without the other party having been heard, the parties affected shall be given notice, without delay after the execution of the measures at the latest. A review, including a right to be heard, shall take place upon request of the parties affected with a view to deciding, within a reasonable period after the notification of the measures, whether the measures shall be modified, revoked or confirmed.

2. Member States shall ensure that the measures to preserve evidence may be subject to the lodging by the applicant of adequate security or an equivalent assurance intended to ensure compensation for any prejudice suffered by the defendant as provided for in paragraph 4.

3. Member States shall ensure that the measures to preserve evidence are revoked or otherwise cease to have effect, upon request of the defendant, without prejudice to the damages which may be claimed, if the applicant does not institute, within a reasonable period, proceedings leading to a decision on the merits of the case before the competent judicial authority, the period to be determined

by the judicial authority ordering the measures where the law of a Member State so permits or, in the absence of such determination, within a period not exceeding 20 working days or 31 calendar days, whichever is the longer.

4. Where the measures to preserve evidence are revoked, or where they lapse due to any act or omission by the applicant, or where it is subsequently found that there has been no infringement or threat of infringement of an intellectual property right, the judicial authorities shall have the authority to order the applicant, upon request of the defendant, to provide the defendant appropriate compensation for any injury caused by those measures.

5. Member States may take measures to protect witnesses' identity.

Section 3   Right of Information

Article 8   Right of information

1. Member States shall ensure that, in the context of proceedings concerning an infringement of an intellectual property right and in response to a justified and proportionate request of the claimant, the competent judicial authorities may order that information on the origin and distribution networks of the goods or services which infringe an intellectual property right be provided by the infringer and/or any other person who:

(a) was found in possession of the infringing goods on a commercial scale;

(b) was found to be using the infringing services on a commercial scale;

(c) was found to be providing on a commercial scale services used in infringing activities; or

(d) was indicated by the person referred to in point (a), (b) or (c) as being involved in the production, manufacture or distribution of the goods or the provision of the services.

2. The information referred to in paragraph 1 shall, as appropriate, comprise:

(a) the names and addresses of the producers, manufacturers, distributors, suppliers and other previous holders of the goods or services, as well as the intended wholesalers and retailers;

(b) information on the quantities produced, manufactured, delivered, received or ordered, as well as the price obtained for the goods or services in question.

3. Paragraphs 1 and 2 shall apply without prejudice to other statutory provisions which:

(a) grant the rightholder rights to receive fuller information;

(b) govern the use in civil or criminal proceedings of the information communicated pursuant to this Article;

(c) govern responsibility for misuse of the right of information; or

(d) afford an opportunity for refusing to provide information which would force the person referred to in paragraph 1 to admit to his own participation or that of his close relatives in an infringement of an intellectual property right; or

(e) govern the protection of confidentiality of information sources or the processing of personal data.

Section 4   Provisional and Precautionary Measures

Article 9   Provisional and precautionary measures

1. Member States shall ensure that the judicial authorities may, at the request of the applicant:

(a) issue against the alleged infringer an interlocutory injunction intended to prevent any imminent infringement of an intellectual property right, or to forbid, on a provisional basis and subject, where appropriate, to a recurring penalty payment where provided for by national law, the continuation of the alleged infringements of that right, or to make such continuation subject to the lodging of guarantees intended to ensure the compensation of the rightholder; an interlocutory injunction may also be issued, under the same conditions, against an intermediary whose services are being used by a third party to infringe an intellectual property right; injunctions against intermediaries whose services are used by a third party to infringe a copyright or a related right are covered by Directive 2001/29/EC;

(b) order the seizure or delivery up of the goods suspected of infringing an intellectual property right so as to prevent their entry into or movement within the channels of commerce.

2. In the case of an infringement committed on a commercial scale, the Member States shall ensure that, if the injured party demonstrates circumstances likely to endanger the recovery of damages, the judicial authorities may order the precautionary seizure of the movable and immovable property of the alleged infringer, including the blocking of his bank accounts and other assets. To that end, the competent authorities may order the communication of bank, financial or commercial documents, or appropriate access to the relevant information.

3. The judicial authorities shall, in respect of the measures referred to in paragraphs 1 and 2, have the authority to require the applicant to provide any reasonably available evidence in order to satisfy themselves with a sufficient degree of certainty that the applicant is the right-holder and that the applicant's right is being infringed, or that such infringement is imminent.

4. Member States shall ensure that the provisional measures referred to in paragraphs 1 and 2 may, in appropriate cases, be taken without the defendant having been heard, in particular where any delay would cause irreparable harm to the rightholder. In that event, the parties shall be so informed without delay after the execution of the measures at the latest.

A review, including a right to be heard, shall take place upon request of the defendant with a view to deciding, within a reasonable time after notification of the measures, whether those measures shall be modified, revoked or confirmed.

5. Member States shall ensure that the provisional measures referred to in paragraphs 1 and 2 are revoked or otherwise cease to have effect, upon request of the defendant, if the applicant does not institute, within a reasonable period, proceedings leading to a decision on the merits of the case before the competent judicial authority, the period to be determined by the judicial authority ordering the measures where the law of a Member State so permits or, in the absence of such determination, within a period not exceeding 20 working days or 31 calendar days, whichever is the longer.

6. The competent judicial authorities may make the provisional measures referred to in paragraphs 1 and 2 subject to the lodging by the applicant of adequate security or an equivalent assurance intended to ensure compensation for any prejudice suffered by the defendant as provided for in paragraph 7.

7. Where the provisional measures are revoked or where they lapse due to any act or omission by the applicant, or where it is subsequently found that there has been no infringement or threat of infringement of an intellectual property right, the judicial authorities shall have the authority to order the applicant, upon request of the defendant, to provide the defendant appropriate compensation for any injury caused by those measures.

Section 5   Measures Resulting from a Decision on the Merits of the Case

Article 10   Corrective measures

1. Without prejudice to any damages due to the rightholder by reason of the infringement, and without compensation of any sort, Member States shall ensure that the competent judicial authorities may order, at the request of the applicant, that appropriate measures be taken with regard to goods that they have found to be infringing an intellectual property right and, in appropriate cases, with

regard to materials and implements principally used in the creation or manufacture of those goods. Such measures shall include:

    (a) recall from the channels of commerce,

    (b) definitive removal from the channels of commerce, or

    (c) destruction.

    2. The judicial authorities shall order that those measures be carried out at the expense of the infringer, unless particular reasons are invoked for not doing so.

    3. In considering a request for corrective measures, the need for proportionality between the seriousness of the infringement and the remedies ordered as well as the interests of third parties shall be taken into account.

Article 11   Injunctions

Member States shall ensure that, where a judicial decision is taken finding an infringement of an intellectual property right, the judicial authorities may issue against the infringer an injunction aimed at prohibiting the continuation of the infringement. Where provided for by national law, non-compliance with an injunction shall, where appropriate, be subject to a recurring penalty payment, with a view to ensuring compliance. Member States shall also ensure that rightholders are in a position to apply for an injunction against intermediaries whose services are used by a third party to infringe an intellectual property right, without prejudice to Article 8(3) of Directive 2001/29/EC.

Article 12   Alternative measures

Member States may provide that, in appropriate cases and at the request of the person liable to be subject to the measures provided for in this section, the competent judicial authorities may order pecuniary compensation to be paid to the injured party instead of applying the measures provided for in this section if that person acted unintentionally and without negligence, if execution of the measures in question would cause him disproportionate harm and if pecuniary compensation to the injured party appears reasonably satisfactory.

Section 6   Damages and Legal Costs

Article 13   Damages

    1. Member States shall ensure that the competent judicial authorities, on application of the injured party, order the infringer who knowingly, or with reasonable grounds to know, engaged in an infringing activity, to pay the rightholder damages appropriate to the actual prejudice suffered by him as a result of the infringement.

    When the judicial authorities set the damages:

    (a) they shall take into account all appropriate aspects, such as the negative economic consequences, including lost profits, which the injured party has suffered, any unfair profits made by the infringer and, in appropriate cases, elements other than economic factors, such as the moral prejudice caused to the rightholder by the infringement; or

    (b) as an alternative to (a), they may, in appropriate cases, set the damages as a lump sum on the basis of elements such as at least the amount of royalties or fees which would have been due if the infringer had requested authorisation to use the intellectual property right in question.

    2. Where the infringer did not knowingly, or with reasonable grounds to know, engage in infringing activity, Member States may lay down that the judicial authorities may order the recovery of profits or the payment of damages, which may be pre-established.

Article 14   Legal costs

Member States shall ensure that reasonable and proportionate legal costs and other expenses incurred by the successful party shall, as a general rule, be borne by the unsuccessful party, unless equity does not allow this.

Section 7   Publicity Measures

Article 15   Publication of judicial decisions

Member States shall ensure that, in legal proceedings instituted for infringement of an intellectual property right, the judicial authorities may order, at the request of the applicant and at the expense of the infringer, appropriate measures for the dissemination of the information concerning the decision, including displaying the decision and publishing it in full or in part. Member States may provide for other additional publicity measures which are appropriate to the particular circumstances, including prominent advertising.

Chapter III   Sanctions by Member States

Article 16   Sanctions by Member States

Without prejudice to the civil and administrative measures, procedures and remedies laid down by this Directive, Member States may apply other appropriate sanctions in cases where intellectual property rights have been infringed.

Chapter IV   Codes of Conduct and Administrative Cooperation

Article 17   Codes of conduct

Member States shall encourage:

  (a) the development by trade or professional associations or organisations of codes of conduct at Community level aimed at contributing towards the enforcement of the intellectual property rights, particularly by recommending the use on optical discs of a code enabling the identification of the origin of their manufacture;

  (b) the submission to the Commission of draft codes of conduct at national and Community level and of any evaluations of the application of these codes of conduct.

. . .

Statement by the Commission

concerning Article 2 of Directive 2004/48/EC of the European Parliament and of the Council on the enforcement of intellectual property rights (2005/295/EC)

Directive 2004/48/EC of the European Parliament and of the Council of 29 April 2004 on the enforcement of intellectual property rights states in Article 2(1) that the Directive applies to any infringement of intellectual property rights as provided for by Community law and/or by the national law of the Member State concerned.

The Commission considers that at least the following intellectual property rights are covered by the scope of the Directive:

  — copyright,
  — rights related to copyright,
  — *sui generis* right of a database maker,
  — rights of the creator of the topographies of a semiconductor product,
  — trademark rights,
  — design rights,
  — patent rights, including rights derived from supplementary protection certificates,
  — geographical indications,
  — utility model rights,
  — plant variety rights,
  — trade names, in so far as these are protected as exclusive property rights in the national law concerned.

Regulation (EU) 2022/2065 of the European Parliament and of the Council

of 19 October 2022 on a Single Market For Digital Services and amending Directive 2000/31/EC (Digital Services Act) (Text with EEA relevance)

THE EUROPEAN PARLIAMENT AND THE COUNCIL OF THE EUROPEAN UNION,

. . .

HAVE ADOPTED THIS REGULATION:

Chapter I   General provisions

Article 1   Subject matter

1. The aim of this Regulation is to contribute to the proper functioning of the internal market for intermediary services by setting out harmonised rules for a safe, predictable and trusted online environment that facilitates innovation and in which fundamental rights enshrined in the Charter, including the principle of consumer protection, are effectively protected.

2. This Regulation lays down harmonised rules on the provision of intermediary services in the internal market. In particular, it establishes:

    (a) a framework for the conditional exemption from liability of providers of intermediary services;

    (b) rules on specific due diligence obligations tailored to certain specific categories of providers of intermediary services;

    (c) rules on the implementation and enforcement of this Regulation, including as regards the cooperation of and coordination between the competent authorities.

Article 2   Scope

1. This Regulation shall apply to intermediary services offered to recipients of the service that have their place of establishment or are located in the Union, irrespective of where the providers of those intermediary services have their place of establishment.

2. This Regulation shall not apply to any service that is not an intermediary service or to any requirements imposed in respect of such a service, irrespective of whether the service is provided through the use of an intermediary service.

3. This Regulation shall not affect the application of Directive 2000/31/EC.

4. This Regulation is without prejudice to the rules laid down by other Union legal acts regulating other aspects of the provision of intermediary services in the internal market or specifying and complementing this Regulation, in particular, the following:

    (a) Directive 2010/13/EU;

    (b) Union law on copyright and related rights;

    (c) Regulation (EU) 2021/784;

    (d) Regulation (EU) 2019/1148;

    (e) Regulation (EU) 2019/1150;

    (f) Union law on consumer protection and product safety, including Regulations (EU) 2017/2394 and (EU) 2019/1020 and Directives 2001/95/EC and 2013/11/EU;

    (g) Union law on the protection of personal data, in particular Regulation (EU) 2016/679 and Directive 2002/58/EC;

    (h) Union law in the field of judicial cooperation in civil matters, in particular Regulation (EU) No 1215/2012 or any Union legal act laying down the rules on law applicable to contractual and non-contractual obligations;

    (i) Union law in the field of judicial cooperation in criminal matters, in particular a Regulation on European Production and Preservation Orders for electronic evidence in criminal matters;

    (j) a Directive laying down harmonised rules on the appointment of legal representatives for the purpose of gathering evidence in criminal proceedings.

Article 3   Definitions

For the purpose of this Regulation, the following definitions shall apply:

(a) 'information society service' means a 'service' as defined in Article 1(1), point (b), of Directive (EU) 2015/1535;

(b) 'recipient of the service' means any natural or legal person who uses an intermediary service, in particular for the purposes of seeking information or making it accessible;

(c) 'consumer' means any natural person who is acting for purposes which are outside his or her trade, business, craft, or profession;

(d) 'to offer services in the Union' means enabling natural or legal persons in one or more Member States to use the services of a provider of intermediary services that has a substantial connection to the Union;

(e) 'substantial connection to the Union' means a connection of a provider of intermediary services with the Union resulting either from its establishment in the Union or from specific factual criteria, such as:

— a significant number of recipients of the service in one or more Member States in relation to its or their population; or

— the targeting of activities towards one or more Member States;

(f) 'trader' means any natural person, or any legal person irrespective of whether it is privately or publicly owned, who is acting, including through any person acting in his or her name or on his or her behalf, for purposes relating to his or her trade, business, craft or profession;

(g) 'intermediary service' means one of the following information society services:

(i) a 'mere conduit' service, consisting of the transmission in a communication network of information provided by a recipient of the service, or the provision of access to a communication network;

(ii) a 'caching' service, consisting of the transmission in a communication network of information provided by a recipient of the service, involving the automatic, intermediate and temporary storage of that information, performed for the sole purpose of making more efficient the information's onward transmission to other recipients upon their request;

(iii) a 'hosting' service, consisting of the storage of information provided by, and at the request of, a recipient of the service;

(h) 'illegal content' means any information that, in itself or in relation to an activity, including the sale of products or the provision of services, is not in compliance with Union law or the law of any Member State which is in compliance with Union law, irrespective of the precise subject matter or nature of that law;

(i) 'online platform' means a hosting service that, at the request of a recipient of the service, stores and disseminates information to the public, unless that activity is a minor and purely ancillary feature of another service or a minor functionality of the principal service and, for objective and technical reasons, cannot be used without that other service, and the integration of the feature or functionality into the other service is not a means to circumvent the applicability of this Regulation;

(j) 'online search engine' means an intermediary service that allows users to input queries in order to perform searches of, in principle, all websites, or all websites in a particular language, on the basis of a query on any subject in the form of a keyword, voice request, phrase or other input, and returns results in any format in which information related to the requested content can be found;

(k) 'dissemination to the public' means making information available, at the request of the recipient of the service who provided the information, to a potentially unlimited number of third parties;

(l) 'distance contract' means 'distance contract' as defined in Article 2, point (7), of Directive 2011/83/EU;

(m) 'online interface' means any software, including a website or a part thereof, and applications, including mobile applications;

(n) 'Digital Services Coordinator of establishment' means the Digital Services Coordinator of the Member State where the main establishment of a provider of an intermediary service is located or its legal representative resides or is established;

(o) 'Digital Services Coordinator of destination' means the Digital Services Coordinator of a Member State where the intermediary service is provided;

(p) 'active recipient of an online platform' means a recipient of the service that has engaged with an online platform by either requesting the online platform to host information or being exposed to information hosted by the online platform and disseminated through its online interface;

(q) 'active recipient of an online search engine' means a recipient of the service that has submitted a query to an online search engine and been exposed to information indexed and presented on its online interface;

(r) 'advertisement' means information designed to promote the message of a legal or natural person, irrespective of whether to achieve commercial or non-commercial purposes, and presented by an online platform on its online interface against remuneration specifically for promoting that information;

(s) 'recommender system' means a fully or partially automated system used by an online platform to suggest in its online interface specific information to recipients of the service or prioritise that information, including as a result of a search initiated by the recipient of the service or otherwise determining the relative order or prominence of information displayed;

(t) 'content moderation' means the activities, whether automated or not, undertaken by providers of intermediary services, that are aimed, in particular, at detecting, identifying and addressing illegal content or information incompatible with their terms and conditions, provided by recipients of the service, including measures taken that affect the availability, visibility, and accessibility of that illegal content or that information, such as demotion, demonetisation, disabling of access to, or removal thereof, or that affect the ability of the recipients of the service to provide that information, such as the termination or suspension of a recipient's account;

(u) 'terms and conditions' means all clauses, irrespective of their name or form, which govern the contractual relationship between the provider of intermediary services and the recipients of the service;

(v) 'persons with disabilities' means 'persons with disabilities' as referred to in Article 3, point (1), of Directive (EU) 2019/882 of the European Parliament and of the Council;

(w) 'commercial communication' means 'commercial communication' as defined in Article 2, point (f), of Directive 2000/31/EC;

(x) 'turnover' means the amount derived by an undertaking within the meaning of Article 5(1) of Council Regulation (EC) No 139/2004.

Chapter II   Liability of providers of intermediary services

Article 4   'Mere conduit'

1. Where an information society service is provided that consists of the transmission in a communication network of information provided by a recipient of the service, or the provision of access to a communication network, the service provider shall not be liable for the information transmitted or accessed, on condition that the provider:

(a) does not initiate the transmission;

(b) does not select the receiver of the transmission; and

(c) does not select or modify the information contained in the transmission.

2. The acts of transmission and of provision of access referred to in paragraph 1 shall include the automatic, intermediate and transient storage of the information transmitted in so far as this takes place for the sole purpose of carrying out the transmission in the communication network, and provided that the information is not stored for any period longer than is reasonably necessary for the transmission.

3. This Article shall not affect the possibility for a judicial or administrative authority, in accordance with a Member State's legal system, to require the service provider to terminate or prevent an infringement.

Article 5   'Caching'

1. Where an information society service is provided that consists of the transmission in a communication network of information provided by a recipient of the service, the service provider shall not be liable for the automatic, intermediate and temporary storage of that information, performed for the sole purpose of making more efficient or more secure the information's onward transmission to other recipients of the service upon their request, on condition that the provider:

  (a) does not modify the information;
  (b) complies with conditions on access to the information;
  (c) complies with rules regarding the updating of the information, specified in a manner widely recognised and used by industry;
  (d) does not interfere with the lawful use of technology, widely recognised and used by industry, to obtain data on the use of the information; and
  (e) acts expeditiously to remove or to disable access to the information it has stored upon obtaining actual knowledge of the fact that the information at the initial source of the transmission has been removed from the network, or access to it has been disabled, or that a judicial or an administrative authority has ordered such removal or disablement.

2. This Article shall not affect the possibility for a judicial or administrative authority, in accordance with a Member State's legal system, to require the service provider to terminate or prevent an infringement.

Article 6   Hosting

1. Where an information society service is provided that consists of the storage of information provided by a recipient of the service, the service provider shall not be liable for the information stored at the request of a recipient of the service, on condition that the provider:

  (a) does not have actual knowledge of illegal activity or illegal content and, as regards claims for damages, is not aware of facts or circumstances from which the illegal activity or illegal content is apparent; or
  (b) upon obtaining such knowledge or awareness, acts expeditiously to remove or to disable access to the illegal content.

2. Paragraph 1 shall not apply where the recipient of the service is acting under the authority or the control of the provider.

3. Paragraph 1 shall not apply with respect to the liability under consumer protection law of online platforms that allow consumers to conclude distance contracts with traders, where such an online platform presents the specific item of information or otherwise enables the specific transaction at issue in a way that would lead an average consumer to believe that the information, or the product or service that is the object of the transaction, is provided either by the online platform itself or by a recipient of the service who is acting under its authority or control.

4. This Article shall not affect the possibility for a judicial or administrative authority, in accordance with a Member State's legal system, to require the service provider to terminate or prevent an infringement.

Article 7   Voluntary own-initiative investigations and legal compliance

Providers of intermediary services shall not be deemed ineligible for the exemptions from liability referred to in Articles 4, 5 and 6 solely because they, in good faith and in a diligent manner, carry out voluntary own-initiative investigations into, or take other measures aimed at detecting, identifying and removing, or disabling access to, illegal content, or take the necessary measures to comply with the requirements of Union law and national law in compliance with Union law, including the requirements set out in this Regulation.

Article 8   No general monitoring or active fact-finding obligations

No general obligation to monitor the information which providers of intermediary services transmit or store, nor actively to seek facts or circumstances indicating illegal activity shall be imposed on those providers.

Article 9 Orders to act against illegal content

1. Upon the receipt of an order to act against one or more specific items of illegal content, issued by the relevant national judicial or administrative authorities, on the basis of the applicable Union law or national law in compliance with Union law, providers of intermediary services shall inform the authority issuing the order, or any other authority specified in the order, of any effect given to the order without undue delay, specifying if and when effect was given to the order.

...

Article 10 Orders to provide information

1. Upon receipt of an order to provide specific information about one or more specific individual recipients of the service, issued by the relevant national judicial or administrative authorities on the basis of the applicable Union law or national law in compliance with Union law, providers of intermediary services shall, without undue delay inform the authority issuing the order, or any other authority specified in the order, of its receipt and of the effect given to the order, specifying if and when effect was given to the order.

...

Chapter III Due diligence obligations for a transparent and safe online environment

Section 1 Provisions applicable to all providers of intermediary services

Article 11 Points of contact for Member States' authorities, the Commission and the Board

1. Providers of intermediary services shall designate a single point of contact to enable them to communicate directly, by electronic means, with Member States' authorities, the Commission and the Board referred to in Article 61 for the application of this Regulation.

2. Providers of intermediary services shall make public the information necessary to easily identify and communicate with their single points of contact. That information shall be easily accessible, and shall be kept up to date.

3. Providers of intermediary services shall specify in the information referred to in paragraph 2 the official language or languages of the Member States which, in addition to a language broadly understood by the largest possible number of Union citizens, can be used to communicate with their points of contact, and which shall include at least one of the official languages of the Member State in which the provider of intermediary services has its main establishment or where its legal representative resides or is established.

Article 12 Points of contact for recipients of the service

1. Providers of intermediary services shall designate a single point of contact to enable recipients of the service to communicate directly and rapidly with them, by electronic means and in a user-friendly manner, including by allowing recipients of the service to choose the means of communication, which shall not solely rely on automated tools.

2. In addition to the obligations provided under Directive 2000/31/EC, providers of intermediary services shall make public the information necessary for the recipients of the service in order to easily identify and communicate with their single points of contact. That information shall be easily accessible, and shall be kept up to date.

Article 13 Legal representatives

1. Providers of intermediary services which do not have an establishment in the Union but which offer services in the Union shall designate, in writing, a legal or natural person to act as their legal representative in one of the Member States where the provider offers its services.

2. Providers of intermediary services shall mandate their legal representatives for the purpose of being addressed in addition to or instead of such providers, by the Member States' competent

authorities, the Commission and the Board, on all issues necessary for the receipt of, compliance with and enforcement of decisions issued in relation to this Regulation. Providers of intermediary services shall provide their legal representative with necessary powers and sufficient resources to guarantee their efficient and timely cooperation with the Member States' competent authorities, the Commission and the Board, and to comply with such decisions.

3. It shall be possible for the designated legal representative to be held liable for non-compliance with obligations under this Regulation, without prejudice to the liability and legal actions that could be initiated against the provider of intermediary services.

4. Providers of intermediary services shall notify the name, postal address, email address and telephone number of their legal representative to the Digital Services Coordinator in the Member State where that legal representative resides or is established. They shall ensure that that information is publicly available, easily accessible, accurate and kept up to date.

5. The designation of a legal representative within the Union pursuant to paragraph 1 shall not constitute an establishment in the Union.

Article 14   Terms and conditions

1. Providers of intermediary services shall include information on any restrictions that they impose in relation to the use of their service in respect of information provided by the recipients of the service, in their terms and conditions. That information shall include information on any policies, procedures, measures and tools used for the purpose of content moderation, including algorithmic decision-making and human review, as well as the rules of procedure of their internal complaint handling system. It shall be set out in clear, plain, intelligible, user-friendly and unambiguous language, and shall be publicly available in an easily accessible and machine-readable format.

2. Providers of intermediary services shall inform the recipients of the service of any significant change to the terms and conditions.

3. Where an intermediary service is primarily directed at minors or is predominantly used by them, the provider of that intermediary service shall explain the conditions for, and any restrictions on, the use of the service in a way that minors can understand.

4. Providers of intermediary services shall act in a diligent, objective and proportionate manner in applying and enforcing the restrictions referred to in paragraph 1, with due regard to the rights and legitimate interests of all parties involved, including the fundamental rights of the recipients of the service, such as the freedom of expression, freedom and pluralism of the media, and other fundamental rights and freedoms as enshrined in the Charter.

5. Providers of very large online platforms and of very large online search engines shall provide recipients of services with a concise, easily-accessible and machine-readable summary of the terms and conditions, including the available remedies and redress mechanisms, in clear and unambiguous language.

6. Very large online platforms and very large online search engines within the meaning of Article 33 shall publish their terms and conditions in the official languages of all the Member States in which they offer their services.

Article 15   Transparency reporting obligations for providers of intermediary services

1. Providers of intermediary services shall make publicly available, in a machine-readable format and in an easily accessible manner, at least once a year, clear, easily comprehensible reports on any content moderation that they engaged in during the relevant period. Those reports shall include, in particular, information on the following, as applicable:

    (a) for providers of intermediary services, the number of orders received from Member States' authorities including orders issued in accordance with Articles 9 and 10, categorised by the type of illegal content concerned, the Member State issuing the order, and the median time needed to inform the authority issuing the order, or any other authority specified in the order, of its receipt, and to give effect to the order;

    (b) for providers of hosting services, the number of notices submitted in accordance with Article 16, categorised by the type of alleged illegal content concerned, the number of notices submitted by trusted flaggers, any action taken pursuant to the notices by differentiating whether the action was taken on the basis of the law or the terms and conditions of the provider, the number of notices processed by using automated means and the median time needed for taking the action;

(c) for providers of intermediary services, meaningful and comprehensible information about the content moderation engaged in at the providers' own initiative, including the use of automated tools, the measures taken to provide training and assistance to persons in charge of content moderation, the number and type of measures taken that affect the availability, visibility and accessibility of information provided by the recipients of the service and the recipients' ability to provide information through the service, and other related restrictions of the service; the information reported shall be categorised by the type of illegal content or violation of the terms and conditions of the service provider, by the detection method and by the type of restriction applied;

(d) for providers of intermediary services, the number of complaints received through the internal complaint-handling systems in accordance with the provider's terms and conditions and additionally, for providers of online platforms, in accordance with Article 20, the basis for those complaints, decisions taken in respect of those complaints, the median time needed for taking those decisions and the number of instances where those decisions were reversed;

(e) any use made of automated means for the purpose of content moderation, including a qualitative description, a specification of the precise purposes, indicators of the accuracy and the possible rate of error of the automated means used in fulfilling those purposes, and any safeguards applied.

2. Paragraph 1 of this Article shall not apply to providers of intermediary services that qualify as micro or small enterprises as defined in Recommendation 2003/361/EC and which are not very large online platforms within the meaning of Article 33 of this Regulation.

3. The Commission may adopt implementing acts to lay down templates concerning the form, content and other details of reports pursuant to paragraph 1 of this Article, including harmonised reporting periods. Those implementing acts shall be adopted in accordance with the advisory procedure referred to in Article 88.

Section 2   Additional provisions applicable to providers of hosting services, including online platforms

Article 16   Notice and action mechanisms

1. Providers of hosting services shall put mechanisms in place to allow any individual or entity to notify them of the presence on their service of specific items of information that the individual or entity considers to be illegal content. Those mechanisms shall be easy to access and user-friendly, and shall allow for the submission of notices exclusively by electronic means.

2. The mechanisms referred to in paragraph 1 shall be such as to facilitate the submission of sufficiently precise and adequately substantiated notices. To that end, the providers of hosting services shall take the necessary measures to enable and to facilitate the submission of notices containing all of the following elements:

(a) a sufficiently substantiated explanation of the reasons why the individual or entity alleges the information in question to be illegal content;

(b) a clear indication of the exact electronic location of that information, such as the exact URL or URLs, and, where necessary, additional information enabling the identification of the illegal content adapted to the type of content and to the specific type of hosting service;

(c) the name and email address of the individual or entity submitting the notice, except in the case of information considered to involve one of the offences referred to in Articles 3 to 7 of Directive 2011/93/EU;

(d) a statement confirming the bona fide belief of the individual or entity submitting the notice that the information and allegations contained therein are accurate and complete.

3. Notices referred to in this Article shall be considered to give rise to actual knowledge or awareness for the purposes of Article 6 in respect of the specific item of information concerned where they

allow a diligent provider of hosting services to identify the illegality of the relevant activity or information without a detailed legal examination.

4. Where the notice contains the electronic contact information of the individual or entity that submitted it, the provider of hosting services shall, without undue delay, send a confirmation of receipt of the notice to that individual or entity.

5. The provider shall also, without undue delay, notify that individual or entity of its decision in respect of the information to which the notice relates, providing information on the possibilities for redress in respect of that decision.

6. Providers of hosting services shall process any notices that they receive under the mechanisms referred to in paragraph 1 and take their decisions in respect of the information to which the notices relate, in a timely, diligent, non-arbitrary and objective manner. Where they use automated means for that processing or decision-making, they shall include information on such use in the notification referred to in paragraph 5.

Article 17   Statement of reasons

1. Providers of hosting services shall provide a clear and specific statement of reasons to any affected recipients of the service for any of the following restrictions imposed on the ground that the information provided by the recipient of the service is illegal content or incompatible with their terms and conditions:

(a) any restrictions of the visibility of specific items of information provided by the recipient of the service, including removal of content, disabling access to content, or demoting content;

(b) suspension, termination or other restriction of monetary payments;

(c) suspension or termination of the provision of the service in whole or in part;

(d) suspension or termination of the recipient of the service's account.

2. Paragraph 1 shall only apply where the relevant electronic contact details are known to the provider. It shall apply at the latest from the date that the restriction is imposed, regardless of why or how it was imposed.

Paragraph 1 shall not apply where the information is deceptive high-volume commercial content.

3. The statement of reasons referred to in paragraph 1 shall at least contain the following information:

(a) information on whether the decision entails either the removal of, the disabling of access to, the demotion of or the restriction of the visibility of the information, or the suspension or termination of monetary payments related to that information, or imposes other measures referred to in paragraph 1 with regard to the information, and, where relevant, the territorial scope of the decision and its duration;

(b) the facts and circumstances relied on in taking the decision, including, where relevant, information on whether the decision was taken pursuant to a notice submitted in accordance with Article 16 or based on voluntary own-initiative investigations and, where strictly necessary, the identity of the notifier;

(c) where applicable, information on the use made of automated means in taking the decision, including information on whether the decision was taken in respect of content detected or identified using automated means;

(d) where the decision concerns allegedly illegal content, a reference to the legal ground relied on and explanations as to why the information is considered to be illegal content on that ground;

(e) where the decision is based on the alleged incompatibility of the information with the terms and conditions of the provider of hosting services, a reference to the contractual ground relied on and explanations as to why the information is considered to be incompatible with that ground;

(f) clear and user-friendly information on the possibilities for redress available to the recipient of the service in respect of the decision, in particular, where applicable through internal complaint-handling mechanisms, out-of-court dispute settlement and judicial redress.

4. The information provided by the providers of hosting services in accordance with this Article shall be clear and easily comprehensible and as precise and specific as reasonably possible under the given circumstances. The information shall, in particular, be such as to reasonably allow the

recipient of the service concerned to effectively exercise the possibilities for redress referred to in of paragraph 3, point (f).

5. This Article shall not apply to any orders referred to in Article 9.

Article 18   Notification of suspicions of criminal offences

1. Where a provider of hosting services becomes aware of any information giving rise to a suspicion that a criminal offence involving a threat to the life or safety of a person or persons has taken place, is taking place or is likely to take place, it shall promptly inform the law enforcement or judicial authorities of the Member State or Member States concerned of its suspicion and provide all relevant information available.

2. Where the provider of hosting services cannot identify with reasonable certainty the Member State concerned, it shall inform the law enforcement authorities of the Member State in which it is established or where its legal representative resides or is established or inform Europol, or both.

For the purpose of this Article, the Member State concerned shall be the Member State in which the offence is suspected to have taken place, to be taking place or to be likely to take place, or the Member State where the suspected offender resides or is located, or the Member State where the victim of the suspected offence resides or is located.

Section 3   Additional provisions applicable to providers of online platforms

Article 19   Exclusion for micro and small enterprises

1. This Section, with the exception of Article 24(3) thereof, shall not apply to providers of online platforms that qualify as micro or small enterprises as defined in Recommendation 2003/361/EC.

This Section, with the exception of Article 24(3) thereof, shall not apply to providers of online platforms that previously qualified for the status of a micro or small enterprise as defined in Recommendation 2003/361/EC during the 12 months following their loss of that status pursuant to Article 4(2) thereof, except when they are very large online platforms in accordance with Article 33.

2. By derogation from paragraph 1 of this Article, this Section shall apply to providers of online platforms that have been designated as very large online platforms in accordance with Article 33, irrespective of whether they qualify as micro or small enterprises.

Article 20   Internal complaint-handling system

1. Providers of online platforms shall provide recipients of the service, including individuals or entities that have submitted a notice, for a period of at least six months following the decision referred to in this paragraph, with access to an effective internal complaint-handling system that enables them to lodge complaints, electronically and free of charge, against the decision taken by the provider of the online platform upon the receipt of a notice or against the following decisions taken by the provider of the online platform on the grounds that the information provided by the recipients constitutes illegal content or is incompatible with its terms and conditions:

    (a) decisions whether or not to remove or disable access to or restrict visibility of the information;

    (b) decisions whether or not to suspend or terminate the provision of the service, in whole or in part, to the recipients;

    (c) decisions whether or not to suspend or terminate the recipients' account;

    (d) decisions whether or not to suspend, terminate or otherwise restrict the ability to monetise information provided by the recipients.

2. The period of at least six months referred to in paragraph 1 of this Article shall start on the day on which the recipient of the service is informed about the decision in accordance with Article 16(5) or Article 17.

3. Providers of online platforms shall ensure that their internal complaint-handling systems are easy to access, user-friendly and enable and facilitate the submission of sufficiently precise and adequately substantiated complaints.

4. Providers of online platforms shall handle complaints submitted through their internal complaint-handling system in a timely, non-discriminatory, diligent and non-arbitrary manner. Where a

complaint contains sufficient grounds for the provider of the online platform to consider that its decision not to act upon the notice is unfounded or that the information to which the complaint relates is not illegal and is not incompatible with its terms and conditions, or contains information indicating that the complainant's conduct does not warrant the measure taken, it shall reverse its decision referred to in paragraph 1 without undue delay.

5. Providers of online platforms shall inform complainants without undue delay of their reasoned decision in respect of the information to which the complaint relates and of the possibility of out-of-court dispute settlement provided for in Article 21 and other available possibilities for redress.

6. Providers of online platforms shall ensure that the decisions, referred to in paragraph 5, are taken under the supervision of appropriately qualified staff, and not solely on the basis of automated means.

Article 21   Out-of-court dispute settlement

1. Recipients of the service, including individuals or entities that have submitted notices, addressed by the decisions referred to in Article 20(1) shall be entitled to select any out-of-court dispute settlement body that has been certified in accordance with paragraph 3 of this Article in order to resolve disputes relating to those decisions, including complaints that have not been resolved by means of the internal complaint-handling system referred to in that Article.

Providers of online platforms shall ensure that information about the possibility for recipients of the service to have access to an out-of-court dispute settlement, as referred to in the first subparagraph, is easily accessible on their online interface, clear and user-friendly.

The first subparagraph is without prejudice to the right of the recipient of the service concerned to initiate, at any stage, proceedings to contest those decisions by the providers of online platforms before a court in accordance with the applicable law.

2. Both parties shall engage, in good faith, with the selected certified out-of-court dispute settlement body with a view to resolving the dispute.

Providers of online platforms may refuse to engage with such out-of-court dispute settlement body if a dispute has already been resolved concerning the same information and the same grounds of alleged illegality or incompatibility of content.

The certified out-of-court dispute settlement body shall not have the power to impose a binding settlement of the dispute on the parties.

. . .

5. If the out-of-court dispute settlement body decides the dispute in favour of the recipient of the service, including the individual or entity that has submitted a notice, the provider of the online platform shall bear all the fees charged by the out-of-court dispute settlement body, and shall reimburse that recipient, including the individual or entity, for any other reasonable expenses that it has paid in relation to the dispute settlement. If the out-of-court dispute settlement body decides the dispute in favour of the provider of the online platform, the recipient of the service, including the individual or entity, shall not be required to reimburse any fees or other expenses that the provider of the online platform paid or is to pay in relation to the dispute settlement, unless the out-of-court dispute settlement body finds that that recipient manifestly acted in bad faith.

. . .

Article 22   Trusted flaggers

1. Providers of online platforms shall take the necessary technical and organisational measures to ensure that notices submitted by trusted flaggers, acting within their designated area of expertise, through the mechanisms referred to in Article 16, are given priority and are processed and decided upon without undue delay.

2. The status of 'trusted flagger' under this Regulation shall be awarded, upon application by any entity, by the Digital Services Coordinator of the Member State in which the applicant is established, to an applicant that has demonstrated that it meets all of the following conditions:

(a) it has particular expertise and competence for the purposes of detecting, identifying and notifying illegal content;

(b) it is independent from any provider of online platforms;

(c) it carries out its activities for the purposes of submitting notices diligently, accurately and objectively.

3. Trusted flaggers shall publish, at least once a year easily comprehensible and detailed reports on notices submitted in accordance with Article 16 during the relevant period. The report shall list at least the number of notices categorised by:

    (a) the identity of the provider of hosting services,

    (b) the type of allegedly illegal content notified,

    (c) the action taken by the provider.

Those reports shall include an explanation of the procedures in place to ensure that the trusted flagger retains its independence.

Trusted flaggers shall send those reports to the awarding Digital Services Coordinator, and shall make them publicly available. The information in those reports shall not contain personal data.

. . .

Article 23   Measures and protection against misuse

1. Providers of online platforms shall suspend, for a reasonable period of time and after having issued a prior warning, the provision of their services to recipients of the service that frequently provide manifestly illegal content.

2. Providers of online platforms shall suspend, for a reasonable period of time and after having issued a prior warning, the processing of notices and complaints submitted through the notice and action mechanisms and internal complaints-handling systems referred to in Articles 16 and 20, respectively, by individuals or entities or by complainants that frequently submit notices or complaints that are manifestly unfounded.

3. When deciding on suspension, providers of online platforms shall assess, on a case-by-case basis and in a timely, diligent and objective manner, whether the recipient of the service, the individual, the entity or the complainant engages in the misuse referred to in paragraphs 1 and 2, taking into account all relevant facts and circumstances apparent from the information available to the provider of online platforms. Those circumstances shall include at least the following:

    (a) the absolute numbers of items of manifestly illegal content or manifestly unfounded notices or complaints, submitted within a given time frame;

    (b) the relative proportion thereof in relation to the total number of items of information provided or notices submitted within a given time frame;

    (c) the gravity of the misuses, including the nature of illegal content, and of its consequences;

    (d) where it is possible to identify it, the intention of the recipient of the service, the individual, the entity or the complainant.

4. Providers of online platforms shall set out, in a clear and detailed manner, in their terms and conditions their policy in respect of the misuse referred to in paragraphs 1 and 2, and shall give examples of the facts and circumstances that they take into account when assessing whether certain behaviour constitutes misuse and the duration of the suspension.

Article 24   Transparency reporting obligations for providers of online platforms

1. In addition to the information referred to in Article 15, providers of online platforms shall include in the reports referred to in that Article information on the following:

    (a) the number of disputes submitted to the out-of-court dispute settlement bodies referred to in Article 21, the outcomes of the dispute settlement, and the median time needed for completing the dispute settlement procedures, as well as the share of disputes where the provider of the online platform implemented the decisions of the body;

    (b) the number of suspensions imposed pursuant to Article 23, distinguishing between suspensions enacted for the provision of manifestly illegal content, the submission of manifestly unfounded notices and the submission of manifestly unfounded complaints.

. . .

Article 25   Online interface design and organisation

1. Providers of online platforms shall not design, organise or operate their online interfaces in a way that deceives or manipulates the recipients of their service or in a way that otherwise materially distorts or impairs the ability of the recipients of their service to make free and informed decisions.

. . .

Article 26   Advertising on online platforms

1. Providers of online platforms that present advertisements on their online interfaces shall ensure that, for each specific advertisement presented to each individual recipient, the recipients of the service are able to identify, in a clear, concise and unambiguous manner and in real time, the following:

   (a) that the information is an advertisement, including through prominent markings, which might follow standards pursuant to Article 44;

   (b) the natural or legal person on whose behalf the advertisement is presented;

   (c) the natural or legal person who paid for the advertisement if that person is different from the natural or legal person referred to in point (b);

   (d) meaningful information directly and easily accessible from the advertisement about the main parameters used to determine the recipient to whom the advertisement is presented and, where applicable, about how to change those parameters.

2. Providers of online platforms shall provide recipients of the service with a functionality to declare whether the content they provide is or contains commercial communications.

When the recipient of the service submits a declaration pursuant to this paragraph, the provider of online platforms shall ensure that other recipients of the service can identify in a clear and unambiguous manner and in real time, including through prominent markings, which might follow standards pursuant to Article 44, that the content provided by the recipient of the service is or contains commercial communications, as described in that declaration.

3. Providers of online platforms shall not present advertisements to recipients of the service based on profiling as defined in Article 4, point (4), of Regulation (EU) 2016/679 using special categories of personal data referred to in Article 9(1) of Regulation (EU) 2016/679.

Article 27   Recommender system transparency

1. Providers of online platforms that use recommender systems shall set out in their terms and conditions, in plain and intelligible language, the main parameters used in their recommender systems, as well as any options for the recipients of the service to modify or influence those main parameters.

2. The main parameters referred to in paragraph 1 shall explain why certain information is suggested to the recipient of the service. They shall include, at least:

   (a) the criteria which are most significant in determining the information suggested to the recipient of the service;

   (b) the reasons for the relative importance of those parameters.

3. Where several options are available pursuant to paragraph 1 for recommender systems that determine the relative order of information presented to recipients of the service, providers of online platforms shall also make available a functionality that allows the recipient of the service to select and to modify at any time their preferred option. That functionality shall be directly and easily accessible from the specific section of the online platform's online interface where the information is being prioritised.

. . .

Section 5   Additional obligations for providers of very large online platforms and of very large online search engines to manage systemic risks

Article 33   Very large online platforms and very large online search engines

1. This Section shall apply to online platforms and online search engines which have a number of average monthly active recipients of the service in the Union equal to or higher than 45 million, and which are designated as very large online platforms or very large online search engines pursuant to paragraph 4.

. . .

Article 36   Crisis response mechanism

1. Where a crisis occurs, the Commission, acting upon a recommendation of the Board may adopt a decision, requiring one or more providers of very large online platforms or of very large online search engines to take one or more of the following actions:

   (a) assess whether, and if so to what extent and how, the functioning and use of their services significantly contribute to a serious threat as referred to in paragraph 2, or are likely to do so;

(b) identify and apply specific, effective and proportionate measures, such as any of those provided for in Article 35(1) or Article 48(2), to prevent, eliminate or limit any such contribution to the serious threat identified pursuant to point (a) of this paragraph;

(c) report to the Commission by a certain date or at regular intervals specified in the decision, on the assessments referred to in point (a), on the precise content, implementation and qualitative and quantitative impact of the specific measures taken pursuant to point (b) and on any other issue related to those assessments or those measures, as specified in the decision.

When identifying and applying measures pursuant to point (b) of this paragraph, the service provider or providers shall take due account of the gravity of the serious threat referred to in paragraph 2, of the urgency of the measures and of the actual or potential implications for the rights and legitimate interests of all parties concerned, including the possible failure of the measures to respect the fundamental rights enshrined in the Charter.

2. For the purpose of this Article, a crisis shall be deemed to have occurred where extraordinary circumstances lead to a serious threat to public security or public health in the Union or in significant parts of it.

3. When taking the decision referred to in paragraph 1, the Commission shall ensure that all of the following requirements are met:

(a) the actions required by the decision are strictly necessary, justified and proportionate, having regard in particular to the gravity of the serious threat referred to in paragraph 2, the urgency of the measures and the actual or potential implications for the rights and legitimate interests of all parties concerned, including the possible failure of the measures to respect the fundamental rights enshrined in the Charter;

(b) the decision specifies a reasonable period within which specific measures referred to in paragraph 1, point (b), are to be taken, having regard, in particular, to the urgency of those measures and the time needed to prepare and implement them;

(c) the actions required by the decision are limited to a period not exceeding three months.

4. After adopting the decision referred to in paragraph 1, the Commission shall, without undue delay, take the following steps:

(a) notify the decision to the provider or providers to which the decision is addressed;

(b) make the decision publicly available; and

(c) inform the Board of the decision, invite it to submit its views thereon, and keep it informed of any subsequent developments relating to the decision.

5. The choice of specific measures to be taken pursuant to paragraph 1, point (b), and to paragraph 7, second subparagraph, shall remain with the provider or providers addressed by the Commission's decision.

. . .

Article 38   Recommender systems
In addition to the requirements set out in Article 27, providers of very large online platforms and of very large online search engines that use recommender systems shall provide at least one option for each of their recommender systems which is not based on profiling as defined in Article 4, point (4), of Regulation (EU) 2016/679.

Article 39   Additional online advertising transparency
1. Providers of very large online platforms or of very large online search engines that present advertisements on their online interfaces shall compile and make publicly available in a specific section of their online interface, through a searchable and reliable tool that allows multicriteria queries and through application programming interfaces, a repository containing the information referred to in paragraph 2, for the entire period during which they present an advertisement and until one year after the advertisement was presented for the last time on their online interfaces. They shall ensure that the repository does not contain any personal data of the recipients of the service to whom the advertisement was or could have been presented, and shall make reasonable efforts to ensure that the information is accurate and complete.

2. The repository shall include at least all of the following information:
   (a) the content of the advertisement, including the name of the product, service or brand and the subject matter of the advertisement;
   (b) the natural or legal person on whose behalf the advertisement is presented;
   (c) the natural or legal person who paid for the advertisement, if that person is different from the person referred to in point (b);
   (d) the period during which the advertisement was presented;
   (e) whether the advertisement was intended to be presented specifically to one or more particular groups of recipients of the service and if so, the main parameters used for that purpose including where applicable the main parameters used to exclude one or more of such particular groups;
   (f) the commercial communications published on the very large online platforms and identified pursuant to Article 26(2);
   (g) the total number of recipients of the service reached and, where applicable, aggregate numbers broken down by Member State for the group or groups of recipients that the advertisement specifically targeted.

3. As regards paragraph 2, points (a), (b) and (c), where a provider of very large online platform or of very large online search engine has removed or disabled access to a specific advertisement based on alleged illegality or incompatibility with its terms and conditions, the repository shall not include the information referred to in those points. In such case, the repository shall include, for the specific advertisement concerned, the information referred to in Article 17(3), points (a) to (e), or Article 9(2), point (a)(i), as applicable.

The Commission may, after consultation of the Board, the relevant vetted researchers referred to in Article 40 and the public, issue guidelines on the structure, organisation and functionalities of the repositories referred to in this Article.

. . .

Article 52   Penalties

1. Member States shall lay down the rules on penalties applicable to infringements of this Regulation by providers of intermediary services within their competence and shall take all the necessary measures to ensure that they are implemented in accordance with Article 51.

2. Penalties shall be effective, proportionate and dissuasive. Member States shall notify the Commission of those rules and of those measures and shall notify it, without delay, of any subsequent amendments affecting them.

. . .

Article 53   Right to lodge a complaint

Recipients of the service and any body, organisation or association mandated to exercise the rights conferred by this Regulation on their behalf shall have the right to lodge a complaint against providers of intermediary services alleging an infringement of this Regulation with the Digital Services Coordinator of the Member State where the recipient of the service is located or established. The Digital Services Coordinator shall assess the complaint and, where appropriate, transmit it to the Digital Services Coordinator of establishment, accompanied, where considered appropriate, by an opinion. Where the complaint falls under the responsibility of another competent authority in its Member State, the Digital Services Coordinator receiving the complaint shall transmit it to that authority. During these proceedings, both parties shall have the right to be heard and receive appropriate information about the status of the complaint, in accordance with national law.

Article 54   Compensation

Recipients of the service shall have the right to seek, in accordance with Union and national law, compensation from providers of intermediary services, in respect of any damage or loss suffered due to an infringement by those providers of their obligations under this Regulation.

. . .

D4. INTERNATIONAL

Paris Convention for the Protection of Industrial Property

of March 20, 1883, as revised at Brussels on December 14, 1900, at Washington on June 2, 1911, at The Hague on November 6, 1925, at London on June 2, 1934, at Lisbon on October 31, 1958, and at Stockholm on July 14, 1967, and as amended on September 28, 1979

Article 1   Establishment of the Union; scope of industrial property

(1) The countries to which this Convention applies constitute a Union for the protection of industrial property.

(2) The protection of industrial property has as its object patents, utility models, industrial designs, trademarks, service marks, trade names, indications of source or appellations of origin, and the repression of unfair competition.

(3) Industrial property shall be understood in the broadest sense and shall apply not only to industry and commerce proper, but likewise to agricultural and extractive industries and to all manufactured or natural products, for example, wines, grain, tobacco leaf, fruit, cattle, minerals, mineral waters, beer, flowers, and flour.

(4) Patents shall include the various kinds of industrial patents recognised by the laws of the countries of the Union, such as patents of importation, patents of improvement, patents and certificates of addition, etc.

Article 2   Treatment for nationals of countries of the Union

(1) Nationals of any country of the Union shall, as regards the protection of industrial property, enjoy in all the other countries of the Union the advantages that their respective laws now grant, or may hereafter grant, to nationals; all without prejudice to the rights specially provided for by this Convention. Consequently, they shall have the same protection as the latter, and the same legal remedy against any infringement of their rights, provided that the conditions and formalities imposed upon nationals are complied with.

(2) However, no requirement as to domicile or establishment in the country where protection is claimed may be imposed upon nationals of countries of the Union for the enjoyment of any industrial property rights.

(3) The provisions of the laws of each of the countries of the Union relating to judicial and administrative procedure and to jurisdiction, and to the designation of an address for service or the appointment of an agent, which may be required by the laws on industrial property are expressly reserved.

Article 3   Same treatment for certain categories of persons as for nationals of countries of the Union

Nationals of countries outside the Union who are domiciled or who have real and effective industrial or commercial establishments in the territory of one of the countries of the Union shall be treated in the same manner as nationals of the countries of the Union.

Article 4   A to I. Patents, utility models, industrial designs, marks, inventors' certificates: right of priority.—G. Patents: division of the application

A.—(1) Any person who has duly filed an application for a patent, or for the registration of a utility model, or of an industrial design, or of a trademark, in one of the countries of the Union, or his successor in title, shall enjoy, for the purpose of filing in the other countries, a right of priority during the periods hereinafter fixed.

(2) Any filing that is equivalent to a regular national filing under the domestic legislation of any country of the Union or under bilateral or multilateral treaties concluded between countries of the Union shall be recognised as giving rise to the right of priority.

(3) By a regular national filing is meant any filing that is adequate to establish the date on which the application was filed in the country concerned, whatever may be the subsequent fate of the application.

B.—Consequently, any subsequent filing in any of the other countries of the Union before the expiration of the periods referred to above shall not be invalidated by reason of any acts accomplished in the interval, in particular, another filing, the publication or exploitation of the invention, the putting on sale of copies of the design, or the use of the mark, and such acts cannot give rise to any third-party right or any right of personal possession. Rights acquired by third parties before the date of the first application that serves as the basis for the right of priority are reserved in accordance with the domestic legislation of each country of the Union.

C.—(1) The periods of priority referred to above shall be twelve months for patents and utility models, and six months for industrial designs and trademarks.

(2) These periods shall start from the date of filing of the first application; the day of filing shall not be included in the period.

(3) If the last day of the period is an official holiday, or a day when the Office is not open for the filing of applications in the country where protection is claimed, the period shall be extended until the first following working day.

(4) A subsequent application concerning the same subject as a previous first application within the meaning of paragraph (2), above, filed in the same country of the Union, shall be considered as the first application, of which the filing date shall be the starting point of the period of priority, if, at the time of filing the subsequent application, the said previous application has been withdrawn, abandoned, or refused, without having been laid open to public inspection and without leaving any rights outstanding, and if it has not yet served as a basis for claiming a right of priority. The previous application may not thereafter serve as a basis for claiming a right of priority.

D.—(1) Any person desiring to take advantage of the priority of a previous filing shall be required to make a declaration indicating the date of such filing and the country in which it was made. Each country shall determine the latest date on which such declaration must be made.

(2) These particulars shall be mentioned in the publications issued by the competent authority, and in particular in the patents and the specifications relating thereto.

(3) The countries of the Union may require any person making a declaration of priority to produce a copy of the application (description, drawings, etc.) previously filed. The copy, certified as correct by the authority which received such application, shall not require any authentication, and may in any case be filed, without fee, at any time within three months of the filing of the subsequent application. They may require it to be accompanied by a certificate from the same authority showing the date of filing, and by a translation.

(4) No other formalities may be required for the declaration of priority at the time of filing the application. Each country of the Union shall determine the consequences of failure to comply with the formalities prescribed by this Article, but such consequences shall in no case go beyond the loss of the right of priority.

(5) Subsequently, further proof may be required.

Any person who avails himself of the priority of a previous application shall be required to specify the number of that application; this number shall be published as provided for by paragraph (2), above.

E.—(1) Where an industrial design is filed in a country by virtue of a right of priority based on the filing of a utility model, the period of priority shall be the same as that fixed for industrial designs.

(2) Furthermore, it is permissible to file a utility model in a country by virtue of a right of priority based on the filing of a patent application, and vice versa.

F.—(1) No country of the Union may refuse a priority or a patent application on the ground that the applicant claims multiple priorities, even if they originate in different countries, or on the ground that an application claiming one or more priorities contains one or more elements that were not included in the application or applications whose priority is claimed, provided that, in both cases, there is unity of invention within the meaning of the law of the country.

With respect to the elements not included in the application or applications whose priority is claimed, the filing of the subsequent application shall give rise to a right of priority under ordinary conditions.

G.—(1) If the examination reveals that an application for a patent contains more than one invention, the applicant may divide the application into a certain number of divisional applications and preserve as the date of each the date of the initial application and the benefit of the right of priority, if any.

(2) The applicant may also, on his own initiative, divide a patent application and preserve as the date of each divisional application the date of the initial application and the benefit of the right of priority, if any. Each country of the Union shall have the right to determine the conditions under which such division shall be authorised.

H.—Priority may not be refused on the ground that certain elements of the invention for which priority is claimed do not appear among the claims formulated in the application in the country of origin, provided that the application documents as a whole specifically disclose such elements.

I.—(1) Applications for inventors' certificates filed in a country in which applicants have the right to apply at their own option either for a patent or for an inventor's certificate shall give rise to the right of priority provided for by this Article, under the same conditions and with the same effects as applications for patents.

(2) In a country in which applicants have the right to apply at their own option either for a patent or for an inventor's certificate, an applicant for an inventor's certificate shall, in accordance with the provisions of this Article relating to patent applications, enjoy a right of priority based on an application for a patent, a utility model, or an inventor's certificate.

Article 4*bis* Patents: independence of patents obtained for the same invention in different countries

(1) Patents applied for in the various countries of the Union by nationals of countries of the Union shall be independent of patents obtained for the same invention in other countries, whether members of the Union or not.

(2) The foregoing provision is to be understood in an unrestricted sense, in particular, in the sense that patents applied for during the period of priority are independent, both as regards the grounds for nullity and forfeiture, and as regards their normal duration.

(3) The provision shall apply to all patents existing at the time when it comes into effect.

(4) Similarly, it shall apply, in the case of the accession of new countries, to patents in existence on either side at the time of accession.

(5) Patents obtained with the benefit of priority shall, in the various countries of the Union, have a duration equal to that which they would have, had they been applied for or granted without the benefit of priority.

Article 4*ter* Patents: mention of the inventor in the patent

The inventor shall have the right to be mentioned as such in the patent.

Article 4*quater* Patents: patentability in case of restrictions of sale by law

The grant of a patent shall not be refused and a patent shall not be invalidated on the ground that the sale of the patented product or of a product obtained by means of a patented process is subject to restrictions or limitations resulting from the domestic law.

Article 5 A. Patents: importation of articles; failure to work or insufficient working; compulsory licences.—B. Industrial designs: failure to work; importation of articles.—C. Marks: failure to use; different forms; use by co-proprietors.—D. Patents, utility models, marks, industrial designs: marking

A.—(1) Importation by the patentee into the country where the patent has been granted of articles manufactured in any of the countries of the Union shall not entail forfeiture of the patent.

(2) Each country of the Union shall have the right to take legislative measures providing for the grant of compulsory licences to prevent the abuses which might result from the exercise of the exclusive rights conferred by the patent, for example, failure to work.

(3) Forfeiture of the patent shall not be provided for except in cases where the grant of compulsory licenses would not have been sufficient to prevent the said abuses. No proceedings for the forfeiture or revocation of a patent may be instituted before the expiration of two years from the grant of the first compulsory license.

(4) A compulsory license may not be applied for on the ground of failure to work or insufficient working before the expiration of a period of four years from the date of filing of the patent application or three years from the date of the grant of the patent, whichever period expires last; it shall be refused if the patentee justifies his inaction by legitimate reasons. Such a compulsory license shall be non-exclusive and shall not be transferable, even in the form of the grant of a sub-license, except with that part of the enterprise or goodwill which exploits such license.

(5) The foregoing provisions shall be applicable, *mutatis mutandis,* to utility models.

B.—The protection of industrial designs shall not, under any circumstance, be subject to any forfeiture, either by reason of failure to work or by reason of the importation of articles corresponding to those which are protected.

C.—(1) If, in any country, use of the registered mark is compulsory, the registration may be cancelled only after a reasonable period, and then only if the person concerned does not justify his inaction.

(2) Use of a trademark by the proprietor in a form differing in elements which do not alter the distinctive character of the mark in the form in which it was registered in one of the countries of the Union shall not entail invalidation of the registration and shall not diminish the protection granted to the mark.

(3) Concurrent use of the same mark on identical or similar goods by industrial or commercial establishments considered as co-proprietors of the mark according to the provisions of the domestic law of the country where protection is claimed shall not prevent registration or diminish in any way the protection granted to the said mark in any country of the Union, provided that such use does not result in misleading the public and is not contrary to the public interest.

D.—No indication or mention of the patent, of the utility model, of the registration of the trademark, or of the deposit of the industrial design, shall be required upon the goods as a condition of recognition of the right to protection.

Article 5bis All industrial property rights: period of grace for the payment of fees for the maintenance of rights; patents: restoration

(1) A period of grace of not less than six months shall be allowed for the payment of the fees prescribed for the maintenance of industrial property rights, subject, if the domestic legislation so provides, to the payment of a surcharge.

(2) The countries of the Union shall have the right to provide for the restoration of patents which have lapsed by reason of non-payment of fees.

Article 5ter Patents: patented devices forming part of vessels, aircraft or land vehicles

In any country of the Union the following shall not be considered as infringements of the rights of a patentee:

1. the use on board vessels of other countries of the Union of devices forming the subject of his patent in the body of the vessel, in the machinery, tackle, gear and other accessories, when such vessels temporarily or accidentally enter the waters of the said country, provided that such devices are used there exclusively for the needs of the vessel;

2. the use of devices forming the subject of the patent in the construction or operation of aircraft or land vehicles of other countries of the Union, or of accessories of such aircraft or land vehicles, when those aircraft or land vehicles temporarily or accidentally enter the said country.

Article 5^{quater} Patents: importation of products manufactured by a process patented in the importing country

When a product is imported into a country of the Union where there exists a patent protecting a process of manufacture of the said product, the patentee shall have all the rights, with regard to the imported product, that are accorded to him by the legislation of the country of importation, on the basis of the process patent, with respect to products manufactured in that country.

Article 5^{quinquies} Industrial designs

Industrial designs shall be protected in all the countries of the Union.

Article 6 Marks: conditions of registration; independence of protection of same mark in different countries

(1) The conditions for the filing and registration of trademarks shall be determined in each country of the Union by its domestic legislation.

(2) However, an application for the registration of a mark filed by a national of a country of the Union in any country of the Union may not be refused, nor may a registration be invalidated, on the ground that filing, registration, or renewal, has not been effected in the country of origin.

(3) A mark duly registered in a country of the Union shall be regarded as independent of marks registered in the other countries of the Union, including the country of origin.

Article 6bis Marks: well-known marks

(1) The countries of the Union undertake, *ex officio* if their legislation so permits, or at the request of an interested party, to refuse or to cancel the registration, and to prohibit the use, of a trademark which constitutes a reproduction, an imitation, or a translation, liable to create confusion, of a mark considered by the competent authority of the country of registration or use to be well known in that country as being already the mark of a person entitled to the benefits of this Convention and used for identical or similar goods. These provisions shall also apply when the essential part of the mark constitutes a reproduction of any such well-known mark or an imitation liable to create confusion therewith.

(2) A period of at least five years from the date of registration shall be allowed for requesting the cancellation of such a mark. The countries of the Union may provide for a period within which the prohibition of use must be requested.

(3) No time limit shall be fixed for requesting the cancellation or the prohibition of the use of marks registered or used in bad faith.

Article 6ter Marks: prohibitions concerning state emblems, official hallmarks, and emblems of intergovernmental organisations

(1)(a) The countries of the Union agree to refuse or to invalidate the registration, and to prohibit by appropriate measures the use, without authorisation by the competent authorities, either as trademarks or as elements of trademarks, of armorial bearings, flags, and other State emblems, of the countries of the Union, official signs and hallmarks indicating control and warranty adopted by them, and any imitation from a heraldic point of view.

(b) The provisions of subparagraph (a), above, shall apply equally to armorial bearings, flags, other emblems, abbreviations, and names, of international intergovernmental organisations of which one or more countries of the Union are members, with the exception of armorial bearings, flags, other emblems, abbreviations, and names, that are already the subject of international agreements in force, intended to ensure their protection.

(c) No country of the Union shall be required to apply the provisions of subparagraph (b) above, to the prejudice of the owners of rights acquired in good faith before the entry into force, in that country, of this Convention. The countries of the Union shall not be required to apply the said provisions when the use or registration referred to in subparagraph (a), above, is not of such a nature as to suggest to the public that a connection exists between the organisation concerned and the armorial bearings, flags, emblems, abbreviations, and names, or if such use or registration is probably not of such a nature as to mislead the public as to the existence of a connection between the user and the organisation.

(2) Prohibition of the use of official signs and hallmarks indicating control and warranty shall apply solely in cases where the marks in which they are incorporated are intended to be used on goods of the same or a similar kind.

(3)(a) For the application of these provisions, the countries of the Union agree to communicate reciprocally, through the intermediary of the International Bureau, the list of State emblems, and official signs and hallmarks indicating control and warranty, which they desire, or may hereafter desire, to place wholly or within certain limits under the protection of this Article, and all subsequent modifications of such list. Each country of the Union shall in due course make available to the public the lists so communicated. Nevertheless such communication is not obligatory in respect of flags of States.

(b) The provisions of subparagraph (b) of paragraph (1) of this Article shall apply only to such armorial bearings, flags, other emblems, abbreviations, and names, of international intergovernmental organisations as the latter have communicated to the countries of the Union through the intermediary of the International Bureau.

(4) Any country of the Union may, within a period of twelve months from the receipt of the notification, transmit its objections, if any, through the intermediary of the International Bureau, to the country or international intergovernmental organisation concerned.

(5) In the case of State flags, the measures prescribed by paragraph (1), above, shall apply solely to marks registered after 6 November 1925.

(6) In the case of State emblems other than flags, and of official signs and hallmarks of the countries of the Union, and in the case of armorial bearings, flags, other emblems, abbreviations, and names,

of international intergovernmental organisations, these provisions shall apply only to marks registered more than two months after receipt of the communication provided for in paragraph (3), above.

(7) In cases of bad faith, the countries shall have the right to cancel even those marks incorporating State emblems, signs, and hallmarks, which were registered before 6 November 1925.

(8) Nationals of any country who are authorised to make use of the State emblems, signs, and hallmarks, of their country may use them even if they are similar to those of another country.

(9) The countries of the Union undertake to prohibit the unauthorised use in trade of the State armorial bearings of the other countries of the Union, when the use is of such a nature as to be misleading as to the origin of the goods.

(10) The above provisions shall not prevent the countries from exercising the right given in paragraph (3) of Article 6*quinquies*, Section B, to refuse or to invalidate the registration of marks incorporating, without authorisation, armorial bearings, flags, other State emblems, or official signs and hallmarks adopted by a country of the Union, as well as the distinctive signs of international intergovernmental organisations referred to in paragraph (1), above.

Article 6*quater*   Marks: assignment of marks

(1) When, in accordance with the law of a country of the Union, the assignment of a mark is valid only if it takes place at the same time as the transfer of the business or goodwill to which the mark belongs, it shall suffice for the recognition of such validity that the portion of the business or goodwill located in that country be transferred to the assignee, together with the exclusive right to manufacture in the said country, or to sell therein, the goods bearing the mark assigned.

(2) The foregoing provision does not impose upon the countries of the Union any obligation to regard as valid the assignment of any mark the use of which by the assignee would, in fact, be of such a nature as to mislead the public, particularly as regards the origin, nature, or essential qualities, of the goods to which the mark is applied.

Article 6*quinquies* Marks: protection of marks registered in one country of the union in the other countries of the union

A.—(1) Every trademark duly registered in the country of origin shall be accepted for filing and protected as is in the other countries of the Union, subject to the reservations indicated in this Article. Such countries may, before proceeding to final registration, require the production of a certificate of registration in the country of origin, issued by the competent authority. No authentication shall be required for this certificate.

(2) Shall be considered the country of origin the country of the Union where the applicant has a real and effective industrial or commercial establishment, or, if he has no such establishment within the Union, the country of the Union where he has his domicile, or, if he has no domicile within the Union but is a national of a country of the Union, the country of which he is a national.

B.—Trademarks covered by this Article may be neither denied registration nor invalidated except in the following cases:

1. when they are of such a nature as to infringe rights acquired by third parties in the country where protection is claimed;

2. when they are devoid of any distinctive character, or consist exclusively of signs or indications which may serve, in trade, to designate the kind, quality, quantity, intended purpose, value, place of origin, of the goods, or the time of production, or have become customary in the current language or in the bona fide and established practices of the trade of the country where protection is claimed;

3. when they are contrary to morality or public order and, in particular, of such a nature as to deceive the public. It is understood that a mark may not be considered contrary to public order for the sole reason that it does not conform to a provision of the legislation on marks, except if such provision itself relates to public order.

This provision is subject, however, to the application of Article 10*bis*.

C.—(1) In determining whether a mark is eligible for protection, all the factual circumstances must be taken into consideration, particularly the length of time the mark has been in use.

(2) No trademark shall be refused in the other countries of the Union for the sole reason that it differs from the mark protected in the country of origin only in respect of elements that do not alter

its distinctive character and do not affect its identity in the form in which it has been registered in the said country of origin.

D.—No person may benefit from the provisions of this Article if the mark for which he claims protection is not registered in the country of origin.

E.—However, in no case shall the renewal of the registration of the mark in the country of origin involve an obligation to renew the registration in the other countries of the Union in which the mark has been registered.

F.—The benefit of priority shall remain unaffected for applications for the registration of marks filed within the period fixed by Article 4, even if registration in the country of origin is effected after the expiration of such period.

Article 6*sexies*   **Marks: service marks**
The countries of the Union undertake to protect service marks. They shall not be required to provide for the registration of such marks.

Article 6*septies*   **Marks: registration in the name of the agent or representative of the proprietor without the latter's authorisation**
(1) If the agent or representative of the person who is the proprietor of a mark in one of the countries of the Union applies, without such proprietor's authorisation, for the registration of the mark in his own name, in one or more countries of the Union, the proprietor shall be entitled to oppose the registration applied for or demand its cancellation or, if the law of the country so allows, the assignment in his favour of the said registration, unless such agent or representative justifies his action.

(2) The proprietor of the mark shall, subject to the provisions of paragraph (1), above, be entitled to oppose the use of his mark by his agent or representative if he has not authorised such use.

(3) Domestic legislation may provide an equitable time limit within which the proprietor of a mark must exercise the rights provided for in this Article.

Article 7   **Marks: nature of the goods to which the mark is applied**
The nature of the goods to which a trademark is to be applied shall in no case form an obstacle to the registration of the mark.

Article 7*bis*   **Marks: collective marks**
(1) The countries of the Union undertake to accept for filing and to protect collective marks belonging to associations the existence of which is not contrary to the law of the country of origin, even if such associations do not possess an industrial or commercial establishment.

(2) Each country shall be the judge of the particular conditions under which a collective mark shall be protected and may refuse protection if the mark is contrary to the public interest.

(3) Nevertheless, the protection of these marks shall not be refused to any association the existence of which is not contrary to the law of the country of origin, on the ground that such association is not established in the country where protection is sought or is not constituted according to the law of the latter country.

Article 8   **Trade names**
A trade name shall be protected in all the countries of the Union without the obligation of filing or registration, whether or not it forms part of a trademark.

Article 9   **Marks, trade names: seizure, on importation, etc., of goods unlawfully bearing a mark or trade name**
(1) All goods unlawfully bearing a trademark or trade name shall be seized on importation into those countries of the Union where such mark or trade name is entitled to legal protection.

(2) Seizure shall likewise be effected in the country where the unlawful affixation occurred or in the country into which the goods were imported.

(3) Seizure shall take place at the request of the public prosecutor, or any other competent authority, or any interested party, whether a natural person or a legal entity, in conformity with the domestic legislation of each country.

(4) The authorities shall not be bound to effect seizure of goods in transit.

(5) If the legislation of a country does not permit seizure on importation, seizure shall be replaced by prohibition of importation or by seizure inside the country.

(6) If the legislation of a country permits neither seizure on importation nor prohibition of importation nor seizure inside the country, then, until such time as the legislation is modified accordingly, these measures shall be replaced by the actions and remedies available in such cases to nationals under the law of such country.

Article 10   False indications: seizure, on importation, etc., of goods bearing false indications as to their source or the identity of the producer

(1) The provisions of the preceding Article shall apply in cases of direct or indirect use of a false indication of the source of the goods or the identity of the producer, manufacturer, or merchant.

(2) Any producer, manufacturer, or merchant, whether a natural person or a legal entity, engaged in the production or manufacture of or trade in such goods and established either in the locality falsely indicated as the source, or in the region where such locality is situated, or in the country falsely indicated, or in the country where the false indication of source is used, shall in any case be deemed an interested party.

Article 10*bis*   Unfair competition

(1) The countries of the Union are bound to assure to nationals of such countries effective protection against unfair competition.

(2) Any act of competition contrary to honest practices in industrial or commercial matters constitutes an act of unfair competition.

(3) The following in particular shall be prohibited:

1. all acts of such a nature as to create confusion by any means whatever with the establishment, the goods, or the industrial or commercial activities, of a competitor;

2. false allegations in the course of trade of such a nature as to discredit the establishment, the goods, or the industrial or commercial activities, of a competitor;

3. indications or allegations the use of which in the course of trade is liable to mislead the public as to the nature, the manufacturing process, the characteristics, the suitability for their purpose, or the quantity, of the goods.

Article 10*ter*   Marks, trade names, false indications, unfair competition: remedies, right to sue

(1) The countries of the Union undertake to assure to nationals of the other countries of the Union appropriate legal remedies effectively to repress all the acts referred to in Articles 9, 10, and 10*bis*.

(2) They undertake, further, to provide measures to permit federations and associations representing interested industrialists, producers, or merchants, provided that the existence of such federations and associations is not contrary to the laws of their countries, to take action in the courts or before the administrative authorities, with a view to the repression of the acts referred to in Articles 9, 10, and 10*bis*, in so far as the law of the country in which protection is claimed allows such action by federations and associations of that country.

Article 11   Inventions, utility models, industrial designs, marks: temporary protection at certain international exhibitions

(1) The countries of the Union shall, in conformity with their domestic legislation, grant temporary protection to patentable inventions, utility models, industrial designs, and trademarks, in respect of goods exhibited at official or officially recognised international exhibitions held in the territory of any of them.

(2) Such temporary protection shall not extend the periods provided by Article 4. If, later, the right of priority is invoked, the authorities of any country may provide that the period shall start from the date of introduction of the goods into the exhibition.

(3) Each country may require, as proof of the identity of the article exhibited and of the date of its introduction, such documentary evidence as it considers necessary.

Article 12   Special national industrial property services

(1) Each country of the Union undertakes to establish a special industrial property service and a central office for the communication to the public of patents, utility models, industrial designs, and trademarks.

(2) This service shall publish an official periodical journal. It shall publish regularly:

    (a) the names of the proprietors of patents granted, with a brief designation of the inventions patented;

    (b) the reproductions of registered trademarks.

...

Article 19   Special agreements
It is understood that the countries of the Union reserve the right to make separately between themselves special agreements for the protection of industrial property, in so far as these agreements do not contravene the provisions of this Convention.
...

Agreement on Trade-related Aspects of Intellectual Property Rights 1994 (TRIPS Agreement)

Members,

Desiring to reduce distortions and impediments to international trade, and taking into account the need to promote effective and adequate protection of intellectual property rights, and to ensure that measures and procedures to enforce intellectual property rights do not themselves become barriers to legitimate trade;

Recognising, to this end, the need for new rules and disciplines concerning:

    (a) the applicability of the basic principles of GATT 1994 and of relevant international intellectual property agreements or conventions;

    (b) the provision of adequate standards and principles concerning the availability, scope and use of trade-related intellectual property rights;

    (c) the provision of effective and appropriate means for the enforcement of trade-related intellectual property rights, taking into account differences in national legal systems;

    (d) the provision of effective and expeditious procedures for the multilateral prevention and settlement of disputes between governments; and

    (e) transitional arrangements aiming at the fullest participation in the results of the negotiations;

Recognising the need for a multilateral framework of principles, rules and disciplines dealing with international trade in counterfeit goods;

Recognising that intellectual property rights are private rights;

Recognising the underlying public policy objectives of national systems for the protection of intellectual property, including developmental and technological objectives;

Recognising also the special needs of the least-developed country Members in respect of maximum flexibility in the domestic implementation of laws and regulations in order to enable them to create a sound and viable technological base;

Emphasising the importance of reducing tensions by reaching strengthened commitments to resolve disputes on trade-related intellectual property issues through multilateral procedures;

Desiring to establish a mutually supportive relationship between the WTO and the World Intellectual Property Organisation (referred to in this Agreement as 'WIPO') as well as other relevant international organisations;

Hereby agree as follows:

PART I   GENERAL PROVISIONS AND
BASIC PRINCIPLES

Article 1   Nature and scope of obligations

1. Members shall give effect to the provisions of this Agreement. Members may, but shall not be obliged to, implement in their law more extensive protection than is required by this Agreement, provided that such protection does not contravene the provisions of this Agreement. Members shall be free to determine the appropriate method of implementing the provisions of this Agreement within their own legal system and practice.

2. For the purposes of this Agreement, the term 'intellectual property' refers to all categories of intellectual property that are the subject of Sections 1 through 7 of Part II.

3. Members shall accord the treatment provided for in this Agreement to the nationals of other Members.[1] In respect of the relevant intellectual property right, the nationals of other Members shall be understood as those natural or legal persons that would meet the criteria for eligibility for protection provided for in the Paris Convention (1967), the Berne Convention (1971), the Rome Convention and the Treaty on Intellectual Property in Respect of Integrated Circuits, were all Members of the WTO members of those conventions.[2] Any Member availing itself of the possibilities provided in

---

[1] When 'nationals' are referred to in this Agreement, they shall be deemed, in the case of a separate customs territory Member of the WTO, to mean persons, natural or legal, who are domiciled or who have a real and effective industrial or commercial establishment in that customs territory.

[2] In this Agreement, 'Paris Convention' refers to the Paris Convention for the Protection of Industrial Property; 'Paris Convention (1967)' refers to the Stockholm Act of this Convention of 14 July 1967. 'Berne Convention' refers to the Berne Convention for the Protection of Literary and Artistic Works; 'Berne Convention (1971)' refers to the Paris Act of this Convention of 24 July 1971. 'Rome Convention' refers to the International Convention for the Protection of Performers, Producers of Phonograms and Broadcasting Organisations, adopted at Rome on 26 October 1961. 'Treaty on Intellectual Property in Respect of Integrated Circuits' (IPIC Treaty) refers to the Treaty on Intellectual Property in Respect of Integrated Circuits, adopted at Washington on 26 May 1989. 'WTO Agreement' refers to the Agreement Establishing the WTO.

paragraph 3 of Article 5 or paragraph 2 of Article 6 of the Rome Convention shall make a notification as foreseen in those provisions to the Council for Trade-Related Aspects of Intellectual Property Rights (the 'Council for TRIPS').

Article 2   Intellectual property conventions

1. In respect of Parts II, III and IV of this Agreement, Members shall comply with Articles 1 through 12, and Article 19, of the Paris Convention (1967).

2. Nothing in Parts I to IV of this Agreement shall derogate from existing obligations that Members may have to each other under the Paris Convention, the Berne Convention, the Rome Convention and the Treaty on Intellectual Property in Respect of Integrated Circuits.

Article 3   National treatment

1. Each Member shall accord to the nationals of other Members treatment no less favourable than that it accords to its own nationals with regard to the protection[3] of intellectual property, subject to the exceptions already provided in, respectively, the Paris Convention (1967), the Berne Convention (1971), the Rome Convention or the Treaty on Intellectual Property in Respect of Integrated Circuits. In respect of performers, producers of phonograms and broadcasting organisations, this obligation only applies in respect of the rights provided under this Agreement. Any Member availing itself of the possibilities provided in Article 6 of the Berne Convention (1971) or paragraph 1(b) of Article 16 of the Rome Convention shall make a notification as foreseen in those provisions to the Council for TRIPS.

2. Members may avail themselves of the exceptions permitted under paragraph 1 in relation to judicial and administrative procedures, including the designation of an address for service or the appointment of an agent within the jurisdiction of a Member, only where such exceptions are necessary to secure compliance with laws and regulations which are not inconsistent with the provisions of this Agreement and where such practices are not applied in a manner which would constitute a disguised restriction on trade.

Article 4   Most-favoured-nation treatment

With regard to the protection of intellectual property, any advantage, favour, privilege or immunity granted by a Member to the nationals of any other country shall be accorded immediately and unconditionally to the nationals of all other Members. Exempted from this obligation are any advantage, favour, privilege or immunity accorded by a Member:

(a) deriving from international agreements on judicial assistance or law enforcement of a general nature and not particularly confined to the protection of intellectual property;

(b) granted in accordance with the provisions of the Berne Convention (1971) or the Rome Convention authorising that the treatment accorded be a function not of national treatment but of the treatment accorded in another country;

(c) in respect of the rights of performers, producers of phonograms and broadcasting organisations not provided under this Agreement;

(d) deriving from international agreements related to the protection of intellectual property which entered into force prior to the entry into force of the WTO Agreement, provided that such agreements are notified to the Council for TRIPS and do not constitute an arbitrary or unjustifiable discrimination against nationals of other Members.

Article 5   Multilateral agreements on acquisition or maintenance of protection

The obligations under Articles 3 and 4 do not apply to procedures provided in multilateral agreements concluded under the auspices of WIPO relating to the acquisition or maintenance of intellectual property rights.

---

[3] For the purposes of Articles 3 and 4, 'protection' shall include matters affecting the availability, acquisition, scope, maintenance and enforcement of intellectual property rights as well as those matters affecting the use of intellectual property rights specifically addressed in this Agreement.

Article 6   Exhaustion

For the purposes of dispute settlement under this Agreement, subject to the provisions of Articles 3 and 4 nothing in this Agreement shall be used to address the issue of the exhaustion of intellectual property rights.

Article 7   Objectives

The protection and enforcement of intellectual property rights should contribute to the promotion of technological innovation and to the transfer and dissemination of technology, to the mutual advantage of producers and users of technological knowledge and in a manner conducive to social and economic welfare, and to a balance of rights and obligations.

Article 8   Principles

1. Members may, in formulating or amending their laws and regulations, adopt measures necessary to protect public health and nutrition, and to promote the public interest in sectors of vital importance to their socio-economic and technological development, provided that such measures are consistent with the provisions of this Agreement.

2. Appropriate measures, provided that they are consistent with the provisions of this Agreement, may be needed to prevent the abuse of intellectual property rights by right holders or the resort to practices which unreasonably restrain trade or adversely affect the international transfer of technology.

PART II   STANDARDS CONCERNING THE AVAILABILITY, SCOPE AND USE OF INTELLECTUAL PROPERTY RIGHTS

Section 1   Copyright and Related Rights

Article 9   Relation to the Berne Convention

1. Members shall comply with Articles 1 through 21 of the Berne Convention (1971) and the Appendix thereto. However, Members shall not have rights or obligations under this Agreement in respect of the rights conferred under Article 6bis of that Convention or of the rights derived therefrom.

2. Copyright protection shall extend to expressions and not to ideas, procedures, methods of operation or mathematical concepts as such.

Article 10   Computer programs and compilations of data

1. Computer programs, whether in source or object code, shall be protected as literary works under the Berne Convention (1971).

2. Compilations of data or other material, whether in machine readable or other form, which by reason of the selection or arrangement of their contents constitute intellectual creations shall be protected as such. Such protection, which shall not extend to the data or material itself, shall be without prejudice to any copyright subsisting in the data or material itself.

Article 11   Rental rights

In respect of at least computer programs and cinematographic works, a Member shall provide authors and their successors in title the right to authorise or to prohibit the commercial rental to the public of originals or copies of their copyright works. A Member shall be excepted from this obligation in respect of cinematographic works unless such rental has led to widespread copying of such works which is materially impairing the exclusive right of reproduction conferred in that Member on authors and their successors in title. In respect of computer programs, this obligation does not apply to rentals where the program itself is not the essential object of the rental.

Article 12   Term of protection

Whenever the term of protection of a work, other than a photographic work or a work of applied art, is calculated on a basis other than the life of a natural person, such term shall be no less than 50 years from the end of the calendar year of authorised publication, or, failing such authorised publication within 50 years from the making of the work, 50 years from the end of the calendar year of making.

Article 13   Limitations and exceptions

Members shall confine limitations or exceptions to exclusive rights to certain special cases which do not conflict with a normal exploitation of the work and do not unreasonably prejudice the legitimate interests of the right holder.

Article 14   Protection of performers, producers of phonograms (sound recordings) and broadcasting organisations

1. In respect of a fixation of their performance on a phonogram, performers shall have the possibility of preventing the following acts when undertaken without their authorisation: the fixation of their unfixed performance and the reproduction of such fixation. Performers shall also have the possibility of preventing the following acts when undertaken without their authorisation: the broadcasting by wireless means and the communication to the public of their live performance.

2. Producers of phonograms shall enjoy the right to authorise or prohibit the direct or indirect reproduction of their phonograms.

3. Broadcasting organisations shall have the right to prohibit the following acts when undertaken without their authorisation: the fixation, the reproduction of fixations, and the rebroadcasting by wireless means of broadcasts, as well as the communication to the public of television broadcasts of the same. Where Members do not grant such rights to broadcasting organisations, they shall provide owners of copyright in the subject matter of broadcasts with the possibility of preventing the above acts, subject to the provisions of the Berne Convention (1971).

4. The provisions of Article 11 in respect of computer programs shall apply *mutatis mutandis* to producers of phonograms and any other right holders in phonograms as determined in a Member's law. If on 15 April 1994 a Member has in force a system of equitable remuneration of right holders in respect of the rental of phonograms, it may maintain such system provided that the commercial rental of phonograms is not giving rise to the material impairment of the exclusive rights of reproduction of right holders.

5. The term of the protection available under this Agreement to performers and producers of phonograms shall last at least until the end of a period of 50 years computed from the end of the calendar year in which the fixation was made or the performance took place. The term of protection granted pursuant to paragraph 3 shall last for at least 20 years from the end of the calendar year in which the broadcast took place.

6. Any Member may, in relation to the rights conferred under paragraphs 1, 2 and 3, provide for conditions, limitations, exceptions and reservations to the extent permitted by the Rome Convention. However, the provisions of Article 18 of the Berne Convention (1971) shall also apply, *mutatis mutandis,* to the rights of performers and producers of phonograms in phonograms.

Section 2   Trademarks

Article 15   Protectable subject matter

1. Any sign, or any combination of signs, capable of distinguishing the goods or services of one undertaking from those of other undertakings, shall be capable of constituting a trademark. Such signs, in particular words including personal names, letters, numerals, figurative elements and combinations of colours as well as any combination of such signs, shall be eligible for registration as trademarks. Where signs are not inherently capable of distinguishing the relevant goods or services, Members may make registrability depend on distinctiveness acquired through use. Members may require, as a condition of registration, that signs be visually perceptible.

2. Paragraph 1 shall not be understood to prevent a Member from denying registration of a trademark on other grounds, provided that they do not derogate from the provisions of the Paris Convention (1967).

3. Members may make registrability depend on use. However, actual use of a trademark shall not be a condition for filing an application for registration. An application shall not be refused solely on the ground that intended use has not taken place before the expiry of a period of three years from the date of application.

4. The nature of the goods or services to which a trademark is to be applied shall in no case form an obstacle to registration of the trademark.

5. Members shall publish each trademark either before it is registered or promptly after it is registered and shall afford a reasonable opportunity for petitions to cancel the registration. In addition, Members may afford an opportunity for the registration of a trademark to be opposed.

Article 16   Rights conferred

1. The owner of a registered trademark shall have the exclusive right to prevent all third parties not having the owner's consent from using in the course of trade identical or similar signs for goods or services which are identical or similar to those in respect of which the trademark is registered where such use would result in a likelihood of confusion. In case of the use of an identical sign for identical goods or services, a likelihood of confusion shall be presumed. The rights described above shall not prejudice any existing prior rights, nor shall they affect the possibility of Members making rights available on the basis of use.

2. Article 6*bis of* the Paris Convention (1967) shall apply, *mutatis mutandis,* to services. In determining whether a trademark is well-known, Members shall take account of the knowledge of the trademark in the relevant sector of the public, including knowledge in the Member concerned which has been obtained as a result of the promotion of the trademark.

3. Article 6*bis* of the Paris Convention (1967) shall apply, *mutatis mutandis,* to goods or services which are not similar to those in respect of which a trademark is registered, provided that use of that trademark in relation to those goods or services would indicate a connection between those goods or services and the owner of the registered trademark and provided that the interests of the owner of the registered trademark are likely to be damaged by such use.

Article 17   Exceptions

Members may provide limited exceptions to the rights conferred by a trademark, such as fair use of descriptive terms, provided that such exceptions take account of the legitimate interests of the owner of the trademark and of third parties.

Article 18   Term of protection

Initial registration, and each renewal of registration, of a trademark shall be for a term of no less than seven years. The registration of a trademark shall be renewable indefinitely.

Article 19   Requirement of use

1. If use is required to maintain a registration, the registration may be cancelled only after an uninterrupted period of at least three years of non-use, unless valid reasons based on the existence of obstacles to such use are shown by the trademark owner. Circumstances arising independently of the will of the owner of the trademark which constitute an obstacle to the use of the trademark, such as import restrictions on or other government requirements for goods or services protected by the trademark, shall be recognised as valid reasons for non-use.

2. When subject to the control of its owner, use of a trademark by another person shall be recognised as use of the trademark for the purpose of maintaining the registration.

Article 20   Other requirements

The use of a trademark in the course of trade shall not be unjustifiably encumbered by special requirements, such as use with another trademark, use in a special form or use in a manner detrimental to its capability to distinguish the goods or services of one undertaking from those of other undertakings. This will not preclude a requirement prescribing the use of the trademark identifying the undertaking producing the goods or services along with, but without linking it to, the trademark distinguishing the specific goods or services in question of that undertaking.

Article 21   Licensing and assignment

Members may determine conditions on the licensing and assignment of trademarks, it being understood that the compulsory licensing of trademarks shall not be permitted and that the owner of a registered trademark shall have the right to assign the trademark with or without the transfer of the business to which the trademark belongs.

Section 3   Geographical Indications

Article 22   Protection of geographical indications

1. Geographical indications are, for the purposes of this Agreement, indications which identify a good as originating in the territory of a Member, or a region or locality in that territory, where a given quality, reputation or other characteristic of the goods is essentially attributable to its geographical origin.

2. In respect of geographical indications, Members shall provide the legal means for interested parties to prevent:

(a) the use of any means in the designation or presentation of a good that indicates or suggests that the good in question originates in a geographical area other than the true place of origin in a manner which misleads the public as to the geographical origin of the good;

(b) any use which constitutes an act of unfair competition within the meaning of Article 10*bis* of the Paris Convention (1967).

3. A Member shall, *ex officio* if its legislation so permits or at the request of an interested party, refuse or invalidate the registration of a trade mark which contains or consists of a geographical indication with respect to goods not originating in the territory indicated, if use of the indication in the trademark for such goods in that Member is of such a nature as to mislead the public as to the true place of origin.

4. The protection under paragraphs 1, 2 and 3 shall be applicable against a geographical indication which, although literally true as to the territory, region or locality in which the goods originate, falsely represents to the public that the goods originate in another territory.

Article 23   Additional protection for geographical indications for wines and spirits

1. Each Member shall provide the legal means for interested parties to prevent use of a geographical indication identifying wines for wines not originating in the place indicated by the geographical indication in question or identifying spirits for spirits not originating in the place indicated by the geographical indication in question, even where the true origin of the goods is indicated or the geographical indication is used in translation or accompanied by expressions such as 'kind', 'types', 'style', 'imitation' or the like.[4]

2. The registration of a trademark for wines which contains or consists of a geographical indication identifying wines or for spirits which contains or consists of a geographical indication identifying spirits shall be refused or invalidated, *ex officio* if a Member's legislation so permits or at the request of an interested party, with respect to such wines or spirits not having this origin.

3. In the case of homonymous geographical indications for wines, protection shall be accorded to each indication, subject to the provisions of paragraph 4 of Article 22. Each Member shall determine the practical conditions under which the homonymous indications in question will be differentiated from each other, taking into account the need to ensure equitable treatment of the producers concerned and that consumers are not misled.

---

[4] Notwithstanding the first sentence of Article 42, Members may, with respect to these obligations, instead provide for enforcement by administrative action.

4. In order to facilitate the protection of geographical indications for wines, negotiations shall be undertaken in the Council for TRIPS concerning the establishment of a multilateral system of notification and registration of geographical indications for wines eligible for protection in those Members participating in the system.

Article 24   International negotiations; exceptions

1. Members agree to enter into negotiations aimed at increasing the protection of individual geographical indications under Article 23. The provisions of paragraphs 4 through 8 below shall not be used by a Member to refuse to conduct negotiations or to conclude bilateral or multilateral agreements. In the context of such negotiations, Members shall be willing to consider the continued applicability of these provisions to individual geographical indications whose use was the subject of such negotiations.

2. The Council for TRIPS shall keep under review the application of the provisions of this Section; the first such review shall take place within two years of the entry into force of the WTO Agreement. Any matter affecting the compliance with the obligations under these provisions may be drawn to the attention of the Council, which, at the request of a Member, shall consult with any Member or Members in respect of such matter in respect of which it has not been possible to find a satisfactory solution through bilateral or plurilateral consultations between the Members concerned. The Council shall take such action as may be agreed to facilitate the operation and further the objectives of this Section.

3. In implementing this Section, a Member shall not diminish the protection of geographical indications that existed in that Member immediately prior to the date of entry into force of the WTO Agreement.

4. Nothing in this Section shall require a Member to prevent continued and similar use of a particular geographical indication of another Member identifying wines or spirits in connection with goods or services by any of its nationals or domiciliaries who have used that geographical indication in a continuous manner with regard to the same or related goods or services in the territory of that Member either (a) for at least 10 years preceding 15 April 1994 or (b) in good faith preceding that date.

5. Where a trademark has been applied for or registered in good faith, or where rights to a trademark have been acquired through use in good faith either:

    (a) before the date of application of these provisions in that Member as defined in Part VI; or

    (b) before the geographical indication is protected in its country of origin; measures adopted to implement this Section shall not prejudice eligibility for or the validity of the registration of a trademark, or the right to use a trademark, on the basis that such a trademark is identical with, or similar to, a geographical indication.

6. Nothing in this Section shall require a Member to apply its provisions in respect of a geographical indication of any other Member with respect to goods or services for which the relevant indication is identical with the term customary in common language as the common name for such goods or services in the territory of that Member. Nothing in this Section shall require a Member to apply its provisions in respect of a geographical indication of any other Member with respect to products of the vine for which the relevant indication is identical with the customary name of a grape variety existing in the territory of that Member as of the date of entry into force of the WTO Agreement.

7. A Member may provide that any request made under this Section in connection with the use or registration of a trade mark must be presented within five years after the adverse use of the protected indication has become generally known in that Member or after the date of registration of the trademark in that Member provided that the trademark has been published by that date, if such date is earlier than the date on which the adverse use became generally known in that Member, provided that the geographical indication is not used or registered in bad faith.

8. The provisions of this Section shall in no way prejudice the right of any person to use, in the course of trade, that person's name or the name of that person's predecessor in business, except where such name is used in such a manner as to mislead the public.

9. There shall be no obligation under this Agreement to protect geographical indications which are not or cease to be protected in their country of origin, or which have fallen into disuse in that country.

Section 4   Industrial Designs

Article 25   Requirements for protection

1. Members shall provide for the protection of independently created industrial designs that are new or original. Members may provide that designs are not new or original if they do not significantly differ from known designs or combinations of known design features. Members may provide that such protection shall not extend to designs dictated essentially by technical or functional considerations.

2. Each Member shall ensure that requirements for securing protection for textile designs, in particular in regard to any cost, examination or publication, do not unreasonably impair the opportunity to seek and obtain such protection. Members shall be free to meet this obligation through industrial design law or through copyright law.

Article 26   Protection

1. The owner of a protected industrial design shall have the right to prevent third parties not having the owner's consent from making, selling or importing articles bearing or embodying a design which is a copy, or substantially a copy, of the protected design, when such acts are undertaken for commercial purposes.

2. Members may provide limited exceptions to the protection of industrial designs, provided that such exceptions do not unreasonably conflict with the normal exploitation of protected industrial designs and do not unreasonably prejudice the legitimate interests of the owner of the protected design, taking account of the legitimate interests of third parties.

3. The duration of protection available shall amount to at least 10 years.

Section 5   Patents

Article 27   Patentable subject matter

1. Subject to the provisions of paragraphs 2 and 3, patents shall be available for any inventions, whether products or processes, in all fields of technology, provided that they are new, involve an inventive step and are capable of industrial application.[5] Subject to paragraph 4 of Article 65, paragraph 8 of Article 70 and paragraph 3 of this Article, patents shall be available and patent rights enjoyable without discrimination as to the place of invention, the field of technology and whether products are imported or locally produced.

2. Members may exclude from patentability inventions, the prevention within their territory of the commercial exploitation of which is necessary to protect *ordre public* or morality, including to protect human, animal or plant life or health or to avoid serious prejudice to the environment, provided that such exclusion is not made merely because the exploitation is prohibited by their law.

3. Members may also exclude from patentability:
   (a) diagnostic, therapeutic and surgical methods for the treatment of humans or animals;
   (b) plants and animals other than micro-organisms, and essentially biological processes for the production of plants or animals other than non-biological and microbiological processes. However, Members shall provide for the protection of plant varieties either by patents or by an effective *sui generis* system or by any combination thereof. The provisions of this subparagraph shall be reviewed four years after the date of entry into force of the WTO Agreement.

Article 28   Rights conferred

1. A patent shall confer on its owner the following exclusive rights:
   (a) where the subject matter of a patent is a product, to prevent third parties not having the owner's consent from the acts of: making, using, offering for sale, selling, or importing[6] for these purposes that product;

---

[5] For the purposes of this Article, the terms 'inventive step' and 'capable of industrial application' may be deemed by a Member to be synonymous with the terms 'non-obvious' and 'useful' respectively.

[6] This right, like all other rights conferred under this Agreement in respect of the use, sale, importation or other distribution of goods, is subject to the provisions of Article 6.

(b) where the subject matter of a patent is a process, to prevent third parties not having the owner's consent from the act of using the process, and from the acts of: using, offering for sale, selling, or importing[6] for these purposes at least the product obtained directly by that process.

2. Patent owners shall also have the right to assign, or transfer by succession, the patent and to conclude licensing contracts.

Article 29   Conditions on patent applicants

1. Members shall require that an applicant for a patent shall disclose the invention in a manner sufficiently clear and complete for the invention to be carried out by a person skilled in the art and may require the applicant to indicate the best mode for carrying out the invention known to the inventor at the filing date or, where priority is claimed, at the priority date of the application.

2. Members may require an applicant for a patent to provide information concerning the applicant's corresponding foreign applications and grants.

Article 30   Exceptions to rights conferred

Members may provide limited exceptions to the exclusive rights conferred by a patent, provided that such exceptions do not unreasonably conflict with a normal exploitation of the patent and do not unreasonably prejudice the legitimate interests of the patent owner, taking account of the legitimate interests of third parties.

Article 31   Other use without authorisation of the right holder

Where the law of a Member allows for other use[7] of the subject matter of a patent without the authorisation of the right holder, including use by the government or third parties authorised by the government, the following provisions shall be respected:

  (a) authorisation of such use shall be considered on its individual merits;
  (b) such use may only be permitted if, prior to such use, the proposed user has made efforts to obtain authorisation from the right holder on reasonable commercial terms and conditions and that such efforts have not been successful within a reasonable period of time. This requirement may be waived by a Member in the case of a national emergency or other circumstances of extreme urgency or in cases of public non-commercial use. In situations of national emergency or other circumstances of extreme urgency, the right holder shall, nevertheless, be notified as soon as reasonably practicable. In the case of public non-commercial use, where the government or contractor, without making a patent search, knows or has demonstrable grounds to know that a valid patent is or will be used by or for the government, the right holder shall be informed promptly;
  (c) the scope and duration of such use shall be limited to the purpose for which it was authorised, and in the case of semi-conductor technology shall only be for public non-commercial use or to remedy a practice determined after judicial or administrative process to be anti-competitive;
  (d) such use shall be non-exclusive;
  (e) such use shall be non-assignable, except with that part of the enterprise or goodwill which enjoys such use;
  (f) any such use shall be authorised predominantly for the supply of the domestic market of the Member authorising such use;
  (g) authorisation for such use shall be liable, subject to adequate protection of the legitimate interests of the persons so authorised, to be terminated if and when the circumstances which led to it cease to exist and are unlikely to recur. The competent authority shall have the authority to review, upon motivated request, the continued existence of these circumstances;

---

[6] This right, like all other rights conferred under this Agreement in respect of the use, sale, importation or other distribution of goods, is subject to the provisions of Article 6.

[7] 'Other use' refers to use other than that allowed under Article 30.

    (h) the right holder shall be paid adequate remuneration in the circumstances of each case, taking into account the economic value of the authorisation;

    (i) the legal validity of any decision relating to the authorisation of such use shall be subject to judicial review or other independent review by a distinct higher authority in that Member;

    (j) any decision relating to the remuneration provided in respect of such use shall be subject to judicial review or other independent review by a distinct higher authority in that Member;

    (k) Members are not obliged to apply the conditions set forth in subparagraphs (b) and (f) where such use is permitted to remedy a practice determined after judicial or administrative process to be anti-competitive. The need to correct anticompetitive practices may be taken into account in determining the amount of remuneration in such cases. Competent authorities shall have the authority to refuse termination of authorisation if and when the conditions which led to such authorisation are likely to recur;

    (l) where such use is authorised to permit the exploitation of a patent ('the second patent') which cannot be exploited without infringing another patent ('the first patent'), the following additional conditions shall apply:

       (i) the invention claimed in the second patent shall involve an important technical advance of considerable economic significance in relation to the invention claimed in the first patent;

       (ii) the owner of the first patent shall be entitled to a cross-licence on reasonable terms to use the invention claimed in the second patent; and

       (iii) the use authorised in respect of the first patent shall be non-assignable except with the assignment of the second patent.

Article 31*bis*

1. The obligations of an exporting Member under Article 31(f) shall not apply with respect to the grant by it of a compulsory licence to the extent necessary for the purposes of production of a pharmaceutical product(s) and its export to an eligible importing Member(s) in accordance with the terms set out in paragraph 2 of the Annex to this Agreement.

2. Where a compulsory licence is granted by an exporting Member under the system set out in this Article and the Annex to this Agreement, adequate remuneration pursuant to Article 31(h) shall be paid in that Member taking into account the economic value to the importing Member of the use that has been authorized in the exporting Member. Where a compulsory licence is granted for the same products in the eligible importing Member, the obligation of that Member under Article 31(h) shall not apply in respect of those products for which remuneration in accordance with the first sentence of this paragraph is paid in the exporting Member.

3. With a view to harnessing economies of scale for the purposes of enhancing purchasing power for, and facilitating the local production of, pharmaceutical products: where a developing or least developed country WTO Member is a party to a regional trade agreement within the meaning of Article XXIV of the GATT 1994 and the Decision of 28 November 1979 on Differential and More Favourable Treatment Reciprocity and Fuller Participation of Developing Countries (L/4903), at least half of the current membership of which is made up of countries presently on the United Nations list of least developed countries, the obligation of that Member under Article 31(f) shall not apply to the extent necessary to enable a pharmaceutical product produced or imported under a compulsory licence in that Member to be exported to the markets of those other developing or least developed country parties to the regional trade agreement that share the health problem in question. It is understood that this will not prejudice the territorial nature of the patent rights in question.

4. Members shall not challenge any measures taken in conformity with the provisions of this Article and the Annex to this Agreement under subparagraphs 1(b) and 1(c) of Article XXIII of GATT 1994.

5. This Article and the Annex to this Agreement are without prejudice to the rights, obligations and flexibilities that Members have under the provisions of this Agreement other than paragraphs (f) and (h) of Article 31, including those reaffirmed by the Declaration on the TRIPS Agreement and Public Health (WT/MIN(01)/DEC/2), and to their interpretation. They are also without prejudice to the extent to which pharmaceutical products produced under a compulsory licence can be exported under the provisions of Article 31(f).

Article 32   Revocation/forfeiture

An opportunity for judicial review of any decision to revoke or forfeit a patent shall be available.

Article 33   Term of protection

The term of protection available shall not end before the expiration of a period of twenty years counted from the filing date.[8]

Article 34   Process patents: burden of proof

1. For the purposes of civil proceedings in respect of the infringement of the rights of the owner referred to in paragraph 1(b) of Article 28, if the subject matter of a patent is a process for obtaining a product, the judicial authorities shall have the authority to order the defendant to prove that the process to obtain an identical product is different from the patented process. Therefore, Members shall provide, in at least one of the following circumstances, that any identical product when produced without the consent of the patent owner shall, in the absence of proof to the contrary, be deemed to have been obtained by the patented process:

   (a) if the product obtained by the patented process is new;

   (b) if there is a substantial likelihood that the identical product was made by the process and the owner of the patent has been unable through reasonable efforts to determine the process actually used.

2. Any Member shall be free to provide that the burden of proof indicated in paragraph 1 shall be on the alleged infringer only if the condition referred to in subparagraph (a) is fulfilled or only if the condition referred to in subparagraph (b) is fulfilled.

3. In the adduction of proof to the contrary, the legitimate interests of defendants in protecting their manufacturing and business secrets shall be taken into account.

Section 6   Layout-Designs (Topographies)
of Integrated Circuits

Article 35   Relation to the IPIC Treaty

Members agree to provide protection to the layout-designs (topographies) of integrated circuits (referred to in this Agreement as 'layout-designs') in accordance with Articles 2 through 7 (other than paragraph 3 of Article 6), Article 12 and paragraph 3 of Article 16 of the Treaty on Intellectual Property in Respect of Integrated Circuits and, in addition, to comply with the following provisions.

Article 36   Scope of the protection

Subject to the provisions of paragraph 1 of Article 37, Members shall consider unlawful the following acts if performed without the authorisation of the right holder:[9] importing, selling, or otherwise distributing for commercial purposes a protected layout-design, an integrated circuit in which a protected layout-design is incorporated, or an article incorporating such an integrated circuit only in so far as it continues to contain an unlawfully reproduced layout-design.

Article 37   Acts not requiring the authorisation of the right holder

1. Notwithstanding Article 36, no Member shall consider unlawful the performance of any of the acts referred to in that Article in respect of an integrated circuit incorporating an unlawfully reproduced layout-design or any article incorporating such an integrated circuit where the person performing or ordering such acts did not know and had no reasonable ground to know, when acquiring the integrated circuit or article incorporating such an integrated circuit, that it incorporated an unlawfully reproduced layout-design. Members shall provide that, after the time that such person has received sufficient notice that the layout-design was unlawfully reproduced, that person may perform any of the acts with respect to the stock on hand or ordered before such time, but shall be liable to pay to the right holder a sum equivalent to a reasonable royalty such as would be payable under a freely negotiated licence in respect of such a layout-design.

---

[8] It is understood that those Members which do not have a system of original grant may provide that the term of protection shall be computed from the filing date in the system of original grant.

[9] The term 'right holder' in this Section shall be understood as having the same meaning as the term 'holder of the right' in the IPIC Treaty.

2. The conditions set out in subparagraphs (a) through (k) of Article 31 shall apply *mutatis mutandis* in the event of any non-voluntary licensing of a layout-design or of its use by or for the government without the authorisation of the right holder.

Article 38   Term of protection

1. In Members requiring registration as a condition of protection, the term of protection of layout-designs shall not end before the expiration of a period of 10 years counted from the date of filing an application for registration or from the first commercial exploitation wherever in the world it occurs.

2. In Members not requiring registration as a condition for protection, layout-designs shall be protected for a term of no less than 10 years from the date of the first commercial exploitation wherever in the world it occurs.

3. Notwithstanding paragraphs 1 and 2, a Member may provide that protection shall lapse 🖋 15 years after the creation of the layout-design.

Section 7   Protection of Undisclosed Information

Article 39

1. In the course of ensuring effective protection against unfair competition as provided in Article 10*bis* of the Paris Convention (1967), Members shall protect undisclosed information in accordance with paragraph 2 and data submitted to governments or governmental agencies in accordance with paragraph 3.

2. Natural and legal persons shall have the possibility of preventing information lawfully within their control from being disclosed to, acquired by, or used by others without their consent in a manner contrary to honest commercial practices[10] so long as such information:

    (a) is secret in the sense that it is not, as a body or in the precise configuration and assembly of its components, generally known among or readily accessible to persons within the circles that normally deal with the kind of information in question;

    (b) has commercial value because it is secret; and

    (c) has been subject to reasonable steps under the circumstances, by the person lawfully in control of the information, to keep it secret.

3. Members, when requiring, as a condition of approving the marketing of pharmaceutical or of agricultural chemical products which utilise new chemical entities, the submission of undisclosed test or other data, the origination of which involves a considerable effort, shall protect such data against unfair commercial use. In addition, Members shall protect such data against disclosure, except where necessary to protect the public, or unless steps are taken to ensure that the data are protected against unfair commercial use.

Section 8   Control of Anti-Competitive Practices in Contractual Licences

Article 40

1. Members agree that some licensing practices or conditions pertaining to intellectual property rights which restrain competition may have adverse effects on trade and may impede the transfer and dissemination of technology.

2. Nothing in this Agreement shall prevent Members from specifying in their legislation licensing practices or conditions that may in particular cases constitute an abuse of intellectual property rights having an adverse effect on competition in the relevant market. As provided above, a Member may adopt, consistently with the other provisions of this Agreement, appropriate measures to prevent or control such practices, which may include for example exclusive grantback conditions, conditions preventing challenges to validity and coercive package licensing, in the light of the relevant laws and regulations of that Member.

3. Each Member shall enter, upon request, into consultations with any other Member which has cause to believe that an intellectual property right owner that is a national or domiciliary of the

---

[10] For the purpose of this provision, 'a manner contrary to honest commercial practices' shall mean at least practices such as breach of contract, breach of confidence and inducement to breach, and includes the acquisition of undisclosed information by third parties who knew, or were grossly negligent in failing to know, that such practices were involved in the acquisition.

Member to which the request for consultations has been addressed is undertaking practices in violation of the requesting Member's laws and regulations on the subject matter of this Section, and which wishes to secure compliance with such legislation, without prejudice to any action under the law and to the full freedom of an ultimate decision of either Member. The Member addressed shall accord full and sympathetic consideration to, and shall afford adequate opportunity for, consultations with the requesting Member, and shall cooperate through supply of publicly available non-confidential information of relevance to the matter in question and of other information available to the Member, subject to domestic law and to the conclusion of mutually satisfactory agreements concerning the safeguarding of its confidentiality by the requesting Member.

4. A Member whose nationals or domiciliaries are subject to proceedings in another Member concerning alleged violation of that other Member's laws and regulations on the subject matter of this Section shall, upon request, be granted an opportunity for consultations by the other Member under the same conditions as those foreseen in paragraph 3.

PART III   ENFORCEMENT OF INTELLECTUAL PROPERTY RIGHTS

Section 1   General Obligations

Article 41

1. Members shall ensure that enforcement procedures as specified in this Part are available under their law so as to permit effective action against any act of infringement of intellectual property rights covered by this Agreement, including expeditious remedies to prevent infringements and remedies which constitute a deterrent to further infringements. These procedures shall be applied in such a manner as to avoid the creation of barriers to legitimate trade and to provide for safeguards against their abuse.

2. Procedures concerning the enforcement of intellectual property rights shall be fair and equitable. They shall not be unnecessarily complicated or costly, or entail unreasonable time-limits or unwarranted delays.

3. Decisions on the merits of a case shall preferably be in writing and reasoned. They shall be made available at least to the parties to the proceeding without undue delay. Decisions on the merits of a case shall be based only on evidence in respect of which parties were offered the opportunity to be heard.

4. Parties to a proceeding shall have an opportunity for review by a judicial authority of final administrative decisions and, subject to jurisdictional provisions in a Member's law concerning the importance of a case, of at least the legal aspects of initial judicial decisions on the merits of a case. However, there shall be no obligation to provide an opportunity for review of acquittals in criminal cases.

5. It is understood that this Part does not create any obligation to put in place a judicial system for the enforcement of intellectual property rights distinct from that for the enforcement of law in general, nor does it affect the capacity of Members to enforce their law in general. Nothing in this Part creates any obligation with respect to the distribution of resources as between enforcement of intellectual property rights and the enforcement of law in general.

Section 2   Civil and Administrative Procedures and Remedies

Article 42   Fair and equitable procedures

Members shall make available to right holders[11] civil judicial procedures concerning the enforcement of any intellectual property right covered by this Agreement. Defendants shall have the right to written notice which is timely and contains sufficient detail, including the basis of the claims. Parties shall be allowed to be represented by independent legal counsel, and procedures shall not impose overly burdensome requirements concerning mandatory personal appearances. All parties to such

---

[11] For the purpose of this Part, the term 'right holder' includes federations and associations having legal standing to assert such rights.

procedures shall be duly entitled to substantiate their claims and to present all relevant evidence. The procedure shall provide a means to identify and protect confidential information, unless this would be contrary to existing constitutional requirements.

Article 43   Evidence

1. The judicial authorities shall have the authority, where a party has presented reasonably available evidence sufficient to support its claims and has specified evidence relevant to substantiation of its claims which lies in the control of the opposing party, to order that this evidence be produced by the opposing party, subject in appropriate cases to conditions which ensure the protection of confidential information.

2. In cases in which a party to a proceeding voluntarily and without good reason refuses access to, or otherwise does not provide necessary information within a reasonable period, or significantly impedes a procedure relating to an enforcement action, a Member may accord judicial authorities the authority to make preliminary and final determinations, affirmative or negative, on the basis of the information presented to them, including the complaint or the allegation presented by the party adversely affected by the denial of access to information, subject to providing the parties an opportunity to be heard on the allegations or evidence.

Article 44   Injunctions

1. The judicial authorities shall have the authority to order a party to desist from an infringement, *inter alia* to prevent the entry into the channels of commerce in their jurisdiction of imported goods that involve the infringement of an intellectual property right, immediately after customs clearance of such goods. Members are not obliged to accord such authority in respect of protected subject matter acquired or ordered by a person prior to knowing or having reasonable grounds to know that dealing in such subject matter would entail the infringement of an intellectual property right.

2. Notwithstanding the other provisions of this Part and provided that the provisions of Part II specifically addressing use by governments, or by third parties authorised by a government, without the authorisation of the right holder are complied with, Members may limit the remedies available against such use to payment of remuneration in accordance with subparagraph (h) of Article 31. In other cases, the remedies under this Part shall apply or, where these remedies are inconsistent with a Member's law, declaratory judgments and adequate compensation shall be available.

Article 45   Damages

1. The judicial authorities shall have the authority to order the infringer to pay the right holder damages adequate to compensate for the injury the right holder has suffered because of an infringement of that person's intellectual property right by an infringer who knowingly, or with reasonable grounds to know, engaged in infringing activity.

2. The judicial authorities shall also have the authority to order the infringer to pay the right holder expenses, which may include appropriate attorney's fees. In appropriate cases, Members may authorise the judicial authorities to order recovery of profits and/or payment of pre-established damages even where the infringer did not knowingly, or with reasonable grounds to know, engage in infringing activity.

Article 46   Other remedies

In order to create an effective deterrent to infringement, the judicial authorities shall have the authority to order that goods that they have found to be infringing be, without compensation of any sort, disposed of outside the channels of commerce in such a manner as to avoid any harm caused to the right holder, or, unless this would be contrary to existing constitutional requirements, destroyed. The judicial authorities shall also have the authority to order that materials and implements the predominant use of which has been in the creation of the infringing goods be, without compensation of any sort, disposed of outside the channels of commerce in such a manner as to minimise the risks of further infringements. In considering such requests, the need for proportionality between the seriousness of the infringement and the remedies ordered as well as the interests of third parties shall be taken into account. In regard to counterfeit trademark goods, the simple removal of the trademark unlawfully affixed shall not be sufficient, other than in exceptional cases, to permit release of the goods into the channels of commerce.

Article 47   Right of information

Members may provide that the judicial authorities shall have the authority, unless this would be out of proportion to the seriousness of the infringement, to order the infringer to inform the right holder of the identity of third persons involved in the production and distribution of the infringing goods or services and of their channels of distribution.

Article 48   Indemnification of the defendant

1. The judicial authorities shall have the authority to order a party at whose request measures were taken and who has abused enforcement procedures to provide to a party wrongfully enjoined or restrained adequate compensation for the injury suffered because of such abuse. The judicial authorities shall also have the authority to order the applicant to pay the defendant expenses, which may include appropriate attorney's fees.

2. In respect of the administration of any law pertaining to the protection or enforcement of intellectual property rights, Members shall only exempt both public authorities and officials from liability to appropriate remedial measures where actions are taken or intended in good faith in the course of the administration of that law.

Article 49   Administrative procedures

To the extent that any civil remedy can be ordered as a result of administrative procedures on the merits of a case, such procedures shall conform to principles equivalent in substance to those set forth in this Section.

Section 3   Provisional Measures

Article 50

1. The judicial authorities shall have the authority to order prompt and effective provisional measures:

   (a) to prevent an infringement of any intellectual property right from occurring, and in particular to prevent the entry into the channels of commerce in their jurisdiction of goods, including imported goods immediately after customs clearance;

   (b) to preserve relevant evidence in regard to the alleged infringement.

2. The judicial authorities shall have the authority to adopt provisional measures *inaudita altera parte* where appropriate, in particular where any delay is likely to cause irreparable harm to the right holder, or where there is a demonstrable risk of evidence being destroyed.

3. The judicial authorities shall have the authority to require the applicant to provide any reasonably available evidence in order to satisfy themselves with a sufficient degree of certainty that the applicant is the right holder and that the applicant's right is being infringed or that such infringement is imminent, and to order the applicant to provide a security or equivalent assurance sufficient to protect the defendant and to prevent abuse.

4. Where provisional measures have been adopted *inaudita altera parte,* the parties affected shall be given notice, without delay after the execution of the measures at the latest. A review, including a right to be heard, shall take place upon request of the defendant with a view to deciding, within a reasonable period after the notification of the measures, whether these measures shall be modified, revoked or confirmed.

5. The applicant may be required to supply other information necessary for the identification of the goods concerned by the authority that will execute the provisional measures.

6. Without prejudice to paragraph 4, provisional measures taken on the basis of paragraphs 1 and 2 shall, upon request by the defendant, be revoked or otherwise cease to have effect, if proceedings leading to a decision on the merits of the case are not initiated within a reasonable period, to be determined by the judicial authority ordering the measures where a Member's law so permits or, in the absence of such a determination, not to exceed 20 working days or 31 calendar days, whichever is the longer.

7. Where the provisional measures are revoked or where they lapse due to any act or omission by the applicant, or where it is subsequently found that there has been no infringement or threat of infringement of an intellectual property right, the judicial authorities shall have the authority to order the applicant, upon request of the defendant, to provide the defendant appropriate compensation for any injury caused by these measures.

8. To the extent that any provisional measure can be ordered as a result of administrative procedures, such procedures shall conform to principles equivalent in substance to those set forth in this Section.

Section 4   Special Requirements
Related to Border Measures[12]

Article 51   Suspension of release by customs authorities

Members shall, in conformity with the provisions set out below, adopt procedures[13] to enable a right holder, who has valid grounds for suspecting that the importation of counterfeit trademark or pirated copyright goods[14] may take place, to lodge an application in writing with competent authorities, administrative or judicial, for the suspension by the customs authorities of the release into free circulation of such goods. Members may enable such an application to be made in respect of goods which involve other infringements of intellectual property rights, provided that the requirements of this Section are met. Members may also provide for corresponding procedures concerning the suspension by the customs authorities of the release of infringing goods destined for exportation from their territories.

Article 52   Application

Any right holder initiating the procedures under Article 51 shall be required to provide adequate evidence to satisfy the competent authorities that, under the laws of the country of importation, there is *prima facie* an infringement of the right holder's intellectual property right and to supply a sufficiently detailed description of the goods to make them readily recognisable by the customs authorities. The competent authorities shall inform the applicant within a reasonable period whether they have accepted the application and, where determined by the competent authorities, the period for which the customs authorities will take action.

Article 53   Security or equivalent assurance

1. The competent authorities shall have the authority to require an applicant to provide a security or equivalent assurance sufficient to protect the defendant and the competent authorities and to prevent abuse. Such security or equivalent assurance shall not unreasonably deter recourse to these procedures.

2. Where pursuant to an application under this Section the release of goods involving industrial designs, patents, layout-designs or undisclosed information into free circulation has been suspended by customs authorities on the basis of a decision other than by a judicial or other independent authority, and the period provided for in Article 55 has expired without the granting of provisional relief by the duly empowered authority, and provided that all other conditions for importation have been complied with, the owner, importer, or consignee of such goods shall be entitled to their release on the

---

[12] Where a Member has dismantled substantially all controls over movement of goods across its border with another Member with which it forms part of a customs union, it shall not be required to apply the provisions of this Section at that border.

[13] It is understood that there shall be no obligation to apply such procedures to imports of goods put on the market in another country by or with the consent of the right holder, or to goods in transit.

[14] For the purposes of this Agreement:

(a) 'counterfeit trademark goods' shall mean any goods, including packaging, bearing without authorization a trademark which is identical to the trademark validly registered in respect of such goods, or which cannot be distinguished in its essential aspects from such a trademark, and which thereby infringes the rights of the owner of the trademark in question under the law of the country of importation;

(b) 'pirated copyright goods' shall mean any goods which are copies made without the consent of the right holder or person duly authorized by the right holder in the country of production and which are made directly or indirectly from an article where the making of that copy would have constituted an infringement of a copyright or a related right under the law of the country of importation.

posting of a security in an amount sufficient to protect the right holder for any infringement. Payment of such security shall not prejudice any other remedy available to the right holder, it being understood that the security shall be released if the right holder fails to pursue the right of action within a reasonable period of time.

Article 54 Notice of suspension

The importer and the applicant shall be promptly notified of the suspension of the release of goods according to Article 51.

Article 55 Duration of suspension

If, within a period not exceeding 10 working days after the applicant has been served notice of the suspension, the customs authorities have not been informed that proceedings leading to a decision on the merits of the case have been initiated by a party other than the defendant, or that the duly empowered authority has taken provisional measures prolonging the suspension of the release of the goods, the goods shall be released, provided that all other conditions for importation or exportation have been complied with; in appropriate cases, this time-limit may be extended by another 10 working days. If proceedings leading to a decision on the merits of the case have been initiated, a review, including a right to be heard, shall take place upon request of the defendant with a view to deciding, within a reasonable period, whether these measures shall be modified, revoked or confirmed. Notwithstanding the above, where the suspension of the release of goods is carried out or continued in accordance with a provisional judicial measure, the provisions of paragraph 6 of Article 50 shall apply.

Article 56 Indemnification of the importer and of the owner of the goods

Relevant authorities shall have the authority to order the applicant to pay the importer, the consignee and the owner of the goods appropriate compensation for any injury caused to them through the wrongful detention of goods or through the detention of goods released pursuant to Article 55.

Article 57 Right of inspection and information

Without prejudice to the protection of confidential information, Members shall provide the competent authorities the authority to give the right holder sufficient opportunity to have any goods detained by the customs authorities inspected in order to substantiate the right holder's claims. The competent authorities shall also have authority to give the importer an equivalent opportunity to have any such goods inspected. Where a positive determination has been made on the merits of a case, Members may provide the competent authorities the authority to inform the right holder of the names and addresses of the consignor, the importer and the consignee and of the quantity of the goods in question.

Article 58 *Ex officio* action

Where Members require competent authorities to act upon their own initiative and to suspend the release of goods in respect of which they have acquired *prima facie* evidence that an intellectual property right is being infringed:

   (a) the competent authorities may at any time seek from the right holder any information that may assist them to exercise these powers;
   (b) the importer and the right holder shall be promptly notified of the suspension. Where the importer has lodged an appeal against the suspension with the competent authorities, the suspension shall be subject to the conditions, *mutatis mutandis,* set out at Article 55;
   (c) Members shall only exempt both public authorities and officials from liability to appropriate remedial measures where actions are taken or intended in good faith.

Article 59 Remedies

Without prejudice to other rights of action open to the right holder and subject to the right of the defendant to seek review by a judicial authority, competent authorities shall have the authority to order the destruction or disposal of infringing goods in accordance with the principles set out in Article 46. In regard to counterfeit trademark goods, the authorities shall not allow the re-exportation of the infringing goods in an unaltered state or subject them to a different customs procedure, other than in exceptional circumstances.

Article 60   *De minimis* imports

Members may exclude from the application of the above provisions small quantities of goods of a non-commercial nature contained in travellers' personal luggage or sent in small consignments.

Section 5   Criminal Procedures

Article 61

Members shall provide for criminal procedures and penalties to be applied at least in cases of wilful trademark counterfeiting or copyright piracy on a commercial scale. Remedies available shall include imprisonment and/or monetary fines sufficient to provide a deterrent, consistently with the level of penalties applied for crimes of a corresponding gravity. In appropriate cases, remedies available shall also include the seizure, forfeiture and destruction of the infringing goods and of any materials and implements the predominant use of which has been in the commission of the offence. Members may provide for criminal procedures and penalties to be applied in other cases of infringement of intellectual property rights, in particular where they are committed wilfully and on a commercial scale.

PART IV   ACQUISITION AND MAINTENANCE OF INTELLECTUAL PROPERTY RIGHTS AND RELATED INTER-PARTES PROCEDURES

Article 62

1. Members may require, as a condition of the acquisition or maintenance of the intellectual property rights provided for under Sections 2 through 6 of Part II, compliance with reasonable procedures and formalities. Such procedures and formalities shall be consistent with the provisions of this Agreement.

2. Where the acquisition of an intellectual property right is subject to the right being granted or registered, Members shall ensure that the procedures for grant or registration, subject to compliance with the substantive conditions for acquisition of the right, permit the granting or registration of the right within a reasonable period of time so as to avoid unwarranted curtailment of the period of protection.

3. Article 4 of the Paris Convention (1967) shall apply *mutatis mutandis* to service marks.

4. Procedures concerning the acquisition or maintenance of intellectual property rights and, where a Member's law provides for such procedures, administrative revocation and *inter partes* procedures such as opposition, revocation and cancellation, shall be governed by the general principles set out in paragraphs 2 and 3 of Article 41.

5. Final administrative decisions in any of the procedures referred to under paragraph 4 shall be subject to review by a judicial or quasi-judicial authority. However, there shall be no obligation to provide an opportunity for such review of decisions in cases of unsuccessful opposition or administrative revocation, provided that the grounds for such procedures can be the subject of invalidation procedures.

PART V   DISPUTE PREVENTION AND SETTLEMENT

Article 63   Transparency

1. Laws and regulations, and final judicial decisions and administrative rulings of general application, made effective by a Member pertaining to the subject matter of this Agreement (the availability, scope, acquisition, enforcement and prevention of the abuse of intellectual property rights) shall be published, or where such publication is not practicable made publicly available, in a national

language, in such a manner as to enable governments and right holders to become acquainted with them. Agreements concerning the subject matter of this Agreement which are in force between the government or a governmental agency of a Member and the government or governmental agency of another Member shall also be published.

2. Members shall notify the laws and regulations referred to in paragraph 1 to the Council for TRIPS in order to assist that Council in its review of the operation of this Agreement. The Council shall attempt to minimise the burden on Members in carrying out this obligation and may decide to waive the obligation to notify such laws and regulations directly to the Council if consultations with WIPO on the establishment of a common register containing these laws and regulations are successful. The Council shall also consider in this connection any action required regarding notifications pursuant to the obligations under this Agreement stemming from the provisions of Article 6ter of the Paris Convention (1967).

3. Each Member shall be prepared to supply, in response to a written request from another Member, information of the sort referred to in paragraph 1. A Member, having reason to believe that a specific judicial decision or administrative ruling or bilateral agreement in the area of intellectual property rights affects its rights under this Agreement, may also request in writing to be given access to or be informed in sufficient detail of such specific judicial decisions or administrative rulings or bilateral agreements.

4. Nothing in paragraphs 1, 2 and 3 shall require Members to disclose confidential information which would impede law enforcement or otherwise be contrary to the public interest or would prejudice the legitimate commercial interests of particular enterprises, public or private.

Article 64   Dispute settlement

1. The provisions of Articles XXII and XXIII of GATT 1994 as elaborated and applied by the Dispute Settlement Understanding shall apply to consultations and the settlement of disputes under this Agreement except as otherwise specifically provided herein.

2. Subparagraphs 1(b) and 1(c) of Article XXIII of GATT 1994 shall not apply to the settlement of disputes under this Agreement for a period of five years from the date of entry into force of the WTO Agreement.

3. During the time period referred to in paragraph 2, the Council for TRIPS shall examine the scope and modalities for complaints of the type provided for under subparagraphs 1(b) and 1(c) of Article XXIII of GATT 1994 made pursuant to this Agreement, and submit its recommendations to the Ministerial Conference for approval. Any decision of the Ministerial Conference to approve such recommendations or to extend the period in paragraph 2 shall be made only by consensus, and approved recommendations shall be effective for all Members without further formal acceptance process.

PART VI   TRANSITIONAL ARRANGEMENTS

Article 65   Transitional arrangements

1. Subject to the provisions of paragraphs 2, 3 and 4, no Member shall be obliged to apply the provisions of this Agreement before the expiry of a general period of one year following the date of entry into force of the WTO Agreement.

2. A developing country Member is entitled to delay for a further period of four years the date of application, as defined in paragraph 1, of the provisions of this Agreement other than Articles 3, 4 and 5.

3. Any other Member which is in the process of transformation from a centrally-planned into a market, free-enterprise economy and which is undertaking structural reform of its intellectual property system and facing special problems in the preparation and implementation of intellectual property laws and regulations, may also benefit from a period of delay as foreseen in paragraph 2.

4. To the extent that a developing country Member is obliged by this Agreement to extend product patent protection to areas of technology not so protectable in its territory on the general date of application of this Agreement for that Member, as defined in paragraph 2, it may delay the

application of the provisions on product patents of Section 5 of Part II to such areas of technology for an additional period of five years.

5. A Member availing itself of a transitional period under paragraphs 1, 2, 3 or 4 shall ensure that any changes in its laws, regulations and practice made during that period do not result in a lesser degree of consistency with the provisions of this Agreement.

Article 66   Least-developed country members

1. In view of the special needs and requirements of least-developed country Members, their economic, financial and administrative constraints, and their need for flexibility to create a viable technological base, such Members shall not be required to apply the provisions of this Agreement, other than Articles 3, 4 and 5, for a period of 10 years from the date of application as defined under paragraph 1 of Article 65. The Council for TRIPS shall, upon duly motivated request by a least-developed country Member, accord extensions of this period.

2. Developed country Members shall provide incentives to enterprises and institutions in their territories for the purpose of promoting and encouraging technology transfer to least-developed country Members in order to enable them to create a sound and viable technological base.

Article 67   Technical cooperation

In order to facilitate the implementation of this Agreement, developed country members shall provide, on request and on mutually agreed terms and conditions, technical and financial cooperation in favour of developing and least-developed country Members. Such cooperation shall include assistance in the preparation of laws and regulations on the protection and enforcement of intellectual property rights as well as on the prevention of their abuse, and shall include support regarding the establishment or reinforcement of domestic offices and agencies relevant to these matters, including the training of personnel.

PART VII   INSTITUTIONAL ARRANGEMENTS; FINAL PROVISIONS

Article 68   Council for Trade-Related aspects of Intellectual Property Rights

The Council for TRIPS shall monitor the operation of this Agreement and, in particular, Members' compliance with their obligations hereunder, and shall afford Members the opportunity of consulting on matters relating to the trade-related aspects of intellectual property rights. It shall carry out such other responsibilities as assigned to it by the Members, and it shall, in particular, provide any assistance requested by them in the context of dispute settlement procedures. In carrying out its functions, the Council for TRIPS may consult with and seek information from any source it deems appropriate. In consultation with WIPO, the Council shall seek to establish, within one year of its first meeting, appropriate arrangements for cooperation with bodies of that Organisation.

Article 69   International cooperation

Members agree to cooperate with each other with a view to eliminating international trade in goods infringing intellectual property rights. For this purpose, they shall establish and notify contact points in their administrations and be ready to exchange information on trade in infringing goods. They shall, in particular, promote the exchange of information and cooperation between customs authorities with regard to trade in counterfeit trademark goods and pirated copyright goods.

Article 70   Protection of existing subject matter

1. This Agreement does not give rise to obligations in respect of acts which occurred before the date of application of the Agreement for the Member in question.

2. Except as otherwise provided for in this Agreement, this Agreement gives rise to obligations in respect of all subject matter existing at the date of application of this Agreement for the Member in question, and which is protected in that Member on the said date, or which meets or comes subsequently to meet the criteria for protection under the terms of this Agreement. In respect of this

paragraph and paragraphs 3 and 4, copyright obligations with respect to existing works shall be solely determined under Article 18 of the Berne Convention (1971), and obligations with respect to the rights of producers of phonograms and performers in existing phonograms shall be determined solely under Article 18 of the Berne Convention (1971) as made applicable under paragraph 6 of Article 14 of this Agreement.

3. There shall be no obligation to restore protection to subject matter which on the date of application of this Agreement for the Member in question has fallen into the public domain.

4. In respect of any acts in respect of specific objects embodying protected subject matter which become infringing under the terms of legislation in conformity with this Agreement, and which were commenced, or in respect of which a significant investment was made, before the date of acceptance of the WTO Agreement by that Member, any Member may provide for a limitation of the remedies available to the right holder as to the continued performance of such acts after the date of application of this Agreement for that Member. In such cases the Member shall, however, at least provide for the payment of equitable remuneration.

5. A Member is not obliged to apply the provisions of Article 11 and of paragraph 4 of Article 14 with respect to originals or copies purchased prior to the date of application of this Agreement for that Member.

6. Members shall not be required to apply Article 31, or the requirement in paragraph 1 of Article 27 that patent rights shall be enjoyable without discrimination as to the field of technology, to use without the authorisation of the right holder where authorisation for such use was granted by the government before the date this Agreement became known.

7. In the case of intellectual property rights for which protection is conditional upon registration, applications for protection which are pending on the date of application of this Agreement for the Member in question shall be permitted to be amended to claim any enhanced protection provided under the provisions of this Agreement. Such amendments shall not include new matter.

8. Where a Member does not make available as of the date of entry into force of the WTO Agreement patent protection for pharmaceutical and agricultural chemical products commensurate with its obligations under Article 27, that Member shall:

(a) notwithstanding the provisions of Part VI, provide as from the date of entry into force of the WTO Agreement a means by which applications for patents for such inventions can be filed;

(b) apply to these applications, as of the date of application of this Agreement, the criteria for patentability as laid down in this Agreement as if those criteria were being applied on the date of filing in that Member or, where priority is available and claimed, the priority date of the application; and

(c) provide patent protection in accordance with this Agreement as from the grant of the patent and for the remainder of the patent term, counted from the filing date in accordance with Article 33 of this Agreement, for those of these applications that meet the criteria for protection referred to in subparagraph (b).

9. Where a product is the subject of a patent application in a Member in accordance with paragraph 8(a), exclusive marketing rights shall be granted, notwithstanding the provisions of Part VI, for a period of five years after obtaining marketing approval in that Member or until a product patent is granted or rejected in that Member, whichever period is shorter, provided that, subsequent to the entry into force of the WTO Agreement, a patent application has been filed and a patent granted for that product in another Member and marketing approval obtained in such other Member.

Article 71   Review and amendment

1. The Council for TRIPS shall review the implementation of this Agreement after the expiration of the transitional period referred to in paragraph 2 of Article 65. The Council shall, having regard to the experience gained in its implementation, review it two years after that date, and at identical intervals thereafter. The Council may also undertake reviews in the light of any relevant new developments which might warrant modification or amendment of this Agreement.

2. Amendments merely serving the purpose of adjusting to higher levels of protection of intellectual property rights achieved, and in force, in other multilateral agreements and accepted under those agreements by all Members of the WTO may be referred to the Ministerial Conference for action in accordance with paragraph 6 of Article X of the WTO Agreement on the basis of a consensus proposal from the Council for TRIPS.

Article 72   Reservations

Reservations may not be entered in respect of any of the provisions of this Agreement without the consent of the other Members.

Article 73   Security exceptions

Nothing in this Agreement shall be construed:

- (a) to require a Member to furnish any information the disclosure of which it considers contrary to its essential security interests; or
- (b) to prevent a Member from taking any action which it considers necessary for the protection of its essential security interests;
  - (i) relating to fissionable materials or the materials from which they are derived;
  - (ii) relating to the traffic in arms, ammunition and implements of war and to such traffic in other goods and materials as is carried on directly or indirectly for the purpose of supplying a military establishment;
  - (iii) taken in time of war or other emergency in international relations; or
- (c) to prevent a Member from taking any action in pursuance of its obligations under the United Nations Charter for the maintenance of international peace and security.

ANNEX TO THE TRIPS AGREEMENT

1. For the purposes of Article 31*bis* and this Annex:
   - (a) 'pharmaceutical product' means any patented product, or product manufactured through a patented process, of the pharmaceutical sector needed to address the public health problems as recognized in paragraph 1 of the Declaration on the TRIPS Agreement and Public Health (WT/MIN(01)/DEC/2). It is understood that active ingredients necessary for its manufacture and diagnostic kits needed for its use would be included[1];
   - (b) 'eligible importing Member' means any least-developed country Member, and any other Member that has made a notification[2] to the Council for TRIPS of its intention to use the system set out in Article 31*bis* and this Annex ('system') as an importer, it being understood that a Member may notify at any time that it will use the system in whole or in a limited way, for example only in the case of a national emergency or other circumstances of extreme urgency or in cases of public non-commercial use. It is noted that some Members will not use the system as importing Members[3] and that some other Members have stated that, if they use the system, it would be in no more than situations of national emergency or other circumstances of extreme urgency;
   - (c) 'exporting Member' means a Member using the system to produce pharmaceutical products for, and export them to, an eligible importing Member.
2. The terms referred to in paragraph 1 of Article 31*bis* are that:
   - (a) the eligible importing Member(s)[4] has made a notification[2] to the Council for TRIPS, that:

---

[1] This subparagraph is without prejudice to subparagraph 1(b).

[2] It is understood that this notification does not need to be approved by a WTO body in order to use the system.

[3] Australia, Canada, the European Communities with, for the purposes of Article 31*bis* and this Annex, its member States, Iceland, Japan, New Zealand, Norway, Switzerland, and the United States.

[4] Joint notifications providing the information required under this subparagraph may be made by the regional organizations referred to in paragraph 3 of Article 31*bis* on behalf of eligible importing Members using the system that are parties to them, with the agreement of those parties.

  (i) specifies the names and expected quantities of the product(s) needed[5];

  (ii) confirms that the eligible importing Member in question, other than a least developed country Member, has established that it has insufficient or no manufacturing capacities in the pharmaceutical sector for the product(s) in question in one of the ways set out in the Appendix to this Annex; and

  (iii) confirms that, where a pharmaceutical product is patented in its territory, it has granted or intends to grant a compulsory licence in accordance with Articles 31 and 31*bis* of this Agreement and the provisions of this Annex[6];

(b) the compulsory licence issued by the exporting Member under the system shall contain the following conditions:

  (i) only the amount necessary to meet the needs of the eligible importing Member(s) may be manufactured under the licence and the entirety of this production shall be exported to the Member(s) which has notified its needs to the Council for TRIPS;

  (ii) products produced under the licence shall be clearly identified as being produced under the system through specific labelling or marking. Suppliers should distinguish such products through special packaging and/or special colouring/shaping of the products themselves, provided that such distinction is feasible and does not have a significant impact on price; and

  (iii) before shipment begins, the licensee shall post on a website[7] the following information:

    – the quantities being supplied to each destination as referred to in indent (i) above; and

    – the distinguishing features of the product(s) referred to in indent (ii) above;

(c) the exporting Member shall notify[8] the Council for TRIPS of the grant of the licence, including the conditions attached to it.[9] The information provided shall include the name and address of the licensee, the product(s) for which the licence has been granted, the quantity(ies) for which it has been granted, the country(ies) to which the product(s) is (are) to be supplied and the duration of the licence. The notification shall also indicate the address of the website referred to in subparagraph (b)(iii) above.

3. In order to ensure that the products imported under the system are used for the public health purposes underlying their importation, eligible importing Members shall take reasonable measures within their means, proportionate to their administrative capacities and to the risk of trade diversion to prevent re-exportation of the products that have actually been imported into their territories under the system. In the event that an eligible importing Member that is a developing country Member or a least-developed country Member experiences difficulty in implementing this provision, developed country Members shall provide, on request and on mutually agreed terms and conditions, technical and financial cooperation in order to facilitate its implementation.

4. Members shall ensure the availability of effective legal means to prevent the importation into, and sale in, their territories of products produced under the system and diverted to their markets inconsistently with its provisions, using the means already required to be available under this Agreement. If any Member considers that such measures are proving insufficient for this purpose, the matter may be reviewed in the Council for TRIPS at the request of that Member.

5. With a view to harnessing economies of scale for the purposes of enhancing purchasing power for, and facilitating the local production of, pharmaceutical products, it is recognized that the development of systems providing for the grant of regional patents to be applicable in the Members described

---

[5] The notification will be made available publicly by the WTO Secretariat through a page on the WTO website dedicated to the system.

[6] This subparagraph is without prejudice to Article 66.1 of this Agreement.

[7] The licensee may use for this purpose its own website or, with the assistance of the WTO Secretariat, the page on the WTO website dedicated to the system.

[8] It is understood that this notification does not need to be approved by a WTO body in order to use the system.

[9] The notification will be made available publicly by the WTO Secretariat through a page on the WTO website dedicated to the system.

in paragraph 3 of Article 31*bis* should be promoted. To this end, developed country Members undertake to provide technical cooperation in accordance with Article 67 of this Agreement, including in conjunction with other relevant intergovernmental organizations.

6. Members recognize the desirability of promoting the transfer of technology and capacity building in the pharmaceutical sector in order to overcome the problem faced by Members with insufficient or no manufacturing capacities in the pharmaceutical sector. To this end, eligible importing Members and exporting Members are encouraged to use the system in a way which would promote this objective. Members undertake to cooperate in paying special attention to the transfer of technology and capacity building in the pharmaceutical sector in the work to be undertaken pursuant to Article 66.2 of this Agreement, paragraph 7 of the Declaration on the TRIPS Agreement and Public Health and any other relevant work of the Council for TRIPS.

7. The Council for TRIPS shall review annually the functioning of the system with a view to ensuring its effective operation and shall annually report on its operation to the General Council.

APPENDIX TO THE ANNEX TO THE TRIPS AGREEMENT

Assessment of Manufacturing Capacity in the Pharmaceutical Sector

Least-developed country Members are deemed to have insufficient or no manufacturing capacities in the pharmaceutical sector.

For other eligible importing Members insufficient or no manufacturing capacities for the product(s) in question may be established in either of the following ways:

(i)   the Member in question has established that it has no manufacturing capacity in the pharmaceutical sector; or

(ii) where the Member has some manufacturing capacity in this sector, it has examined this capacity and found that, excluding any capacity owned or controlled by the patent owner, it is currently insufficient for the purposes of meeting its needs. When it is established that such capacity has become sufficient to meet the Member's needs, the system shall no longer apply.

Doha Declaration on the TRIPS Agreement and Public Health

Adopted on 14 November 2001

1. We recognize the gravity of the public health problems afflicting many developing and least-developed countries, especially those resulting from HIV/AIDS, tuberculosis, malaria and other epidemics.

2. We stress the need for the WTO Agreement on Trade-Related Aspects of Intellectual Property Rights (TRIPS Agreement) to be part of the wider national and international action to address these problems.

3. We recognize that intellectual property protection is important for the development of new medicines. We also recognize the concerns about its effects on prices.

4. We agree that the TRIPS Agreement does not and should not prevent Members from taking measures to protect public health. Accordingly, while reiterating our commitment to the TRIPS Agreement, we affirm that the Agreement can and should be interpreted and implemented in a manner supportive of WTO Members' right to protect public health and, in particular, to promote access to medicines for all.

In this connection, we reaffirm the right of WTO Members to use, to the full, the provisions in the TRIPS Agreement, which provide flexibility for this purpose.

5. Accordingly and in the light of paragraph 4 above, while maintaining our commitments in the TRIPS Agreement, we recognize that these flexibilities include:

(a) In applying the customary rules of interpretation of public international law, each provision of the TRIPS Agreement shall be read in the light of the object and purpose of the Agreement as expressed, in particular, in its objectives and principles.

(b) Each Member has the right to grant compulsory licences and the freedom to determine the grounds upon which such licences are granted.

(c) Each Member has the right to determine what constitutes a national emergency or other circumstances of extreme urgency, it being understood that public health crises, including those relating to HIV/AIDS, tuberculosis, malaria and other epidemics, can represent a national emergency or other circumstances of extreme urgency.

(d) The effect of the provisions in the TRIPS Agreement that are relevant to the exhaustion of intellectual property rights is to leave each Member free to establish its own regime for such exhaustion without challenge, subject to the MFN and national treatment provisions of Articles 3 and 4.

6. We recognize that WTO Members with insufficient or no manufacturing capacities in the pharmaceutical sector could face difficulties in making effective use of compulsory licensing under the TRIPS Agreement. We instruct the Council for TRIPS to find an expeditious solution to this problem and to report to the General Council before the end of 2002.

7. We reaffirm the commitment of developed-country Members to provide incentives to their enterprises and institutions to promote and encourage technology transfer to least-developed country Members pursuant to Article 66.2. We also agree that the least-developed country Members will not be obliged, with respect to pharmaceutical products, to implement or apply Sections 5 and 7 of Part II of the TRIPS Agreement or to enforce rights provided for under these Sections until 1 January 2016, without prejudice to the right of least-developed country Members to seek other extensions of the transition periods as provided for in Article 66.1 of the TRIPS Agreement. We instruct the Council for TRIPS to take the necessary action to give effect to this pursuant to Article 66.1 of the TRIPS Agreement.

Convention for the Safeguarding of the Intangible Cultural Heritage 2003

The General Conference of the United Nations Educational, Scientific and Cultural Organization hereinafter referred to as UNESCO, meeting in Paris, from 29 September to 17 October 2003, at its 32nd session,

Referring to existing international human rights instruments, in particular to the Universal Declaration on Human Rights of 1948, the International Covenant on Economic, Social and Cultural Rights of 1966, and the International Covenant on Civil and Political Rights of 1966,

Considering the importance of the intangible cultural heritage as a mainspring of cultural diversity and a guarantee of sustainable development, as underscored in the UNESCO Recommendation on the Safeguarding of Traditional Culture and Folklore of 1989, in the UNESCO Universal Declaration on Cultural Diversity of 2001, and in the Istanbul Declaration of 2002 adopted by the Third Round Table of Ministers of Culture,

Considering the deep-seated interdependence between the intangible cultural heritage and the tangible cultural and natural heritage,

Recognizing that the processes of globalization and social transformation, alongside the conditions they create for renewed dialogue among communities, also give rise, as does the phenomenon of intolerance, to grave threats of deterioration, disappearance and destruction of the intangible cultural heritage, in particular owing to a lack of resources for safeguarding such heritage,

Being aware of the universal will and the common concern to safeguard the intangible cultural heritage of humanity,

Recognizing that communities, in particular indigenous communities, groups and, in some cases, individuals, play an important role in the production, safeguarding, maintenance and re-creation of the intangible cultural heritage, thus helping to enrich cultural diversity and human creativity,

Noting the far-reaching impact of the activities of UNESCO in establishing normative instruments for the protection of the cultural heritage, in particular the Convention for the Protection of the World Cultural and Natural Heritage of 1972,

Noting further that no binding multilateral instrument as yet exists for the safeguarding of the intangible cultural heritage,

Considering that existing international agreements, recommendations and resolutions concerning the cultural and natural heritage need to be effectively enriched and supplemented by means of new provisions relating to the intangible cultural heritage,

Considering the need to build greater awareness, especially among the younger generations, of the importance of the intangible cultural heritage and of its safeguarding,

Considering that the international community should contribute, together with the States Parties to this Convention, to the safeguarding of such heritage in a spirit of cooperation and mutual assistance,

Recalling UNESCO's programmes relating to the intangible cultural heritage, in particular the Proclamation of Masterpieces of the Oral and Intangible Heritage of Humanity,

Considering the invaluable role of the intangible cultural heritage as a factor in bringing human beings closer together and ensuring exchange and understanding among them,

Adopts this Convention on this seventeenth day of October 2003.

I.   GENERAL PROVISIONS

Article 1   Purposes of the Convention

The purposes of this Convention are:

(a) to safeguard the intangible cultural heritage;
(b) to ensure respect for the intangible cultural heritage of the communities, groups and individuals concerned;
(c) to raise awareness at the local, national and international levels of the importance of the intangible cultural heritage, and of ensuring mutual appreciation thereof;
(d) to provide for international cooperation and assistance.

Article 2   Definitions

For the purposes of this Convention,

1. The 'intangible cultural heritage' means the practices, representations, expressions, knowledge, skills—as well as the instruments, objects, artefacts and cultural spaces associated therewith—that communities, groups and, in some cases, individuals recognize as part of their cultural heritage. This intangible cultural heritage, transmitted from generation to generation, is constantly recreated by communities and groups in response to their environment, their interaction with nature and their history, and provides them with a sense of identity and continuity, thus promoting respect for cultural diversity and human creativity. For the purposes of this Convention, consideration will be given solely to such intangible cultural heritage as is compatible with existing international human rights instruments, as well as with the requirements of mutual respect among communities, groups and individuals, and of sustainable development.

2. The 'intangible cultural heritage', as defined in paragraph 1 above, is manifested inter alia in the following domains:

(a) oral traditions and expressions, including language as a vehicle of the intangible cultural heritage;
(b) performing arts;
(c) social practices, rituals and festive events;
(d) knowledge and practices concerning nature and the universe;
(e) traditional craftsmanship.

3. 'Safeguarding' means measures aimed at ensuring the viability of the intangible cultural heritage, including the identification, documentation, research, preservation, protection, promotion, enhancement, transmission, particularly through formal and non-formal education, as well as the revitalization of the various aspects of such heritage.

4. 'States Parties' means States which are bound by this Convention and among which this Convention is in force.

5. This Convention applies mutatis mutandis to the territories referred to in Article 33 which become Parties to this Convention in accordance with the conditions set out in that Article. To that extent the expression 'States Parties' also refers to such territories.

Article 3   Relationship to other international instruments

Nothing in this Convention may be interpreted as:

(a) altering the status or diminishing the level of protection under the 1972 Convention concerning the Protection of the World Cultural and Natural Heritage of World Heritage properties with which an item of the intangible cultural heritage is directly associated; or

(b) affecting the rights and obligations of States Parties deriving from any international instrument relating to intellectual property rights or to the use of biological and ecological resources to which they are parties.

II.   ORGANS OF THE CONVENTION

Article 4   General Assembly of States Parties

1. A General Assembly of the States Parties is hereby established, hereinafter referred to as 'the General Assembly'. The General Assembly is the sovereign body of this Convention.

...

Article 5   Intergovernmental Committee for the Safeguarding of the Intangible Cultural Heritage

1. An Intergovernmental Committee for the Safeguarding of the Intangible Cultural Heritage, hereinafter referred to as 'the Committee', is hereby established within UNESCO. It shall be composed of representatives of 18 States Parties, elected by the States Parties meeting in General Assembly, once this Convention enters into force in accordance with Article 34.

2. The number of States Members of the Committee shall be increased to 24 once the number of the States Parties to the Convention reaches 50.

...

Article 7   Functions of the Committee

Without prejudice to other prerogatives granted to it by this Convention, the functions of the Committee shall be to:

(a) promote the objectives of the Convention, and to encourage and monitor the implementation thereof;

(b) provide guidance on best practices and make recommendations on measures for the safeguarding of the intangible cultural heritage;

(c) prepare and submit to the General Assembly for approval a draft plan for the use of the resources of the Fund, in accordance with Article 25;

(d) seek means of increasing its resources, and to take the necessary measures to this end, in accordance with Article 25;

(e) prepare and submit to the General Assembly for approval operational directives for the implementation of this Convention;

(f) examine, in accordance with Article 29, the reports submitted by States Parties, and to summarize them for the General Assembly;

(g) examine requests submitted by States Parties, and to decide thereon, in accordance with objective selection criteria to be established by the Committee and approved by the General Assembly for:

(i)   inscription on the lists and proposals mentioned under Articles 16, 17 and 18;

(ii)   the granting of international assistance in accordance with Article 22.

...

III.   SAFEGUARDING OF THE INTANGIBLE CULTURAL HERITAGE AT THE NATIONAL LEVEL

Article 11   Role of States Parties

Each State Party shall:

(a) take the necessary measures to ensure the safeguarding of the intangible cultural heritage present in its territory;

(b) among the safeguarding measures referred to in Article 2, paragraph 3, identify and define the various elements of the intangible cultural heritage present in its territory, with the participation of communities, groups and relevant non-governmental organizations.

Article 12   Inventories

1. To ensure identification with a view to safeguarding, each State Party shall draw up, in a manner geared to its own situation, one or more inventories of the intangible cultural heritage present in its territory. These inventories shall be regularly updated.

2. When each State Party periodically submits its report to the Committee, in accordance with Article 29, it shall provide relevant information on such inventories.

Article 13   Other measures for safeguarding

To ensure the safeguarding, development and promotion of the intangible cultural heritage present in its territory, each State Party shall endeavour to:

(a) adopt a general policy aimed at promoting the function of the intangible cultural heritage in society, and at integrating the safeguarding of such heritage into planning programmes;

(b) designate or establish one or more competent bodies for the safeguarding of the intangible cultural heritage present in its territory;

(c) foster scientific, technical and artistic studies, as well as research methodologies, with a view to effective safeguarding of the intangible cultural heritage, in particular the intangible cultural heritage in danger;

(d) adopt appropriate legal, technical, administrative and financial measures aimed at:

(i) fostering the creation or strengthening of institutions for training in the management of the intangible cultural heritage and the transmission of such heritage through forums and spaces intended for the performance or expression thereof;

(ii) ensuring access to the intangible cultural heritage while respecting customary practices governing access to specific aspects of such heritage;

(iii) establishing documentation institutions for the intangible cultural heritage and facilitating access to them.

Article 14   Education, awareness-raising and capacity-building

Each State Party shall endeavour, by all appropriate means, to:

(a) ensure recognition of, respect for, and enhancement of the intangible cultural heritage in society, in particular through:

(i) educational, awareness-raising and information programmes, aimed at the general public, in particular young people;

(ii) specific educational and training programmes within the communities and groups concerned;

(iii) capacity-building activities for the safeguarding of the intangible cultural heritage, in particular management and scientific research; and

(iv) non-formal means of transmitting knowledge;

(b) keep the public informed of the dangers threatening such heritage, and of the activities carried out in pursuance of this Convention;

(c) promote education for the protection of natural spaces and places of memory whose existence is necessary for expressing the intangible cultural heritage.

Article 15   Participation of communities, groups and individuals

Within the framework of its safeguarding activities of the intangible cultural heritage, each State Party shall endeavour to ensure the widest possible participation of communities, groups and, where appropriate, individuals that create, maintain and transmit such heritage, and to involve them actively in its management.

IV. SAFEGUARDING OF THE INTANGIBLE CULTURAL HERITAGE AT THE INTERNATIONAL LEVEL

Article 16 Representative List of the Intangible Cultural Heritage of Humanity

1. In order to ensure better visibility of the intangible cultural heritage and awareness of its significance, and to encourage dialogue which respects cultural diversity, the Committee, upon the proposal of the States Parties concerned, shall establish, keep up to date and publish a Representative List of the Intangible Cultural Heritage of Humanity.

2. The Committee shall draw up and submit to the General Assembly for approval the criteria for the establishment, updating and publication of this Representative List.

Article 17 List of Intangible Cultural Heritage in Need of Urgent Safeguarding

1. With a view to taking appropriate safeguarding measures, the Committee shall establish, keep up to date and publish a List of Intangible Cultural Heritage in Need of Urgent Safeguarding, and shall inscribe such heritage on the List at the request of the State Party concerned.

2. The Committee shall draw up and submit to the General Assembly for approval the criteria for the establishment, updating and publication of this List.

3. In cases of extreme urgency—the objective criteria of which shall be approved by the General Assembly upon the proposal of the Committee—the Committee may inscribe an item of the heritage concerned on the List mentioned in paragraph 1, in consultation with the State Party concerned.

Article 18 Programmes, projects and activities for the safeguarding of the intangible cultural heritage

1. On the basis of proposals submitted by States Parties, and in accordance with criteria to be defined by the Committee and approved by the General Assembly, the Committee shall periodically select and promote national, subregional and regional programmes, projects and activities for the safeguarding of the heritage which it considers best reflect the principles and objectives of this Convention, taking into account the special needs of developing countries.

...

VII. REPORTS

Article 29 Reports by the States Parties

The States Parties shall submit to the Committee, observing the forms and periodicity to be defined by the Committee, reports on the legislative, regulatory and other measures taken for the implementation of this Convention.

Article 30 Reports by the Committee

1. On the basis of its activities and the reports by States Parties referred to in Article 29, the Committee shall submit a report to the General Assembly at each of its sessions.

2. The report shall be brought to the attention of the General Conference of UNESCO.

VIII. TRANSITIONAL CLAUSE

Article 31 Relationship to the Proclamation of Masterpieces of the Oral and Intangible Heritage of Humanity

1. The Committee shall incorporate in the Representative List of the Intangible Cultural Heritage of Humanity the items proclaimed "Masterpieces of the Oral and Intangible Heritage of Humanity" before the entry into force of this Convention.

2. The incorporation of these items in the Representative List of the Intangible Cultural Heritage of Humanity shall in no way prejudge the criteria for future inscriptions decided upon in accordance with Article 16, paragraph 2.

3. No further Proclamation will be made after the entry into force of this Convention.

...

AGREEMENT on the Withdrawal of the United Kingdom of Great Britain and Northern Ireland from the European Union and the European Atomic Energy Community

PREAMBLE

THE EUROPEAN UNION AND THE EUROPEAN ATOMIC ENERGY COMMUNITY

AND

THE UNITED KINGDOM OF GREAT BRITAIN AND NORTHERN IRELAND,

. . .

HAVE AGREED AS FOLLOWS:

. . .

Part Three   Separation Provisions

. . .

Title IV   Intellectual Property

Article 54   Continued protection in the United Kingdom of registered or granted rights

1. The holder of any of the following intellectual property rights which have been registered or granted before the end of the transition period shall, without any re-examination, become the holder of a comparable registered and enforceable intellectual property right in the United Kingdom under the law of the United Kingdom:

   (a) the holder of a European Union trade mark registered in accordance with Regulation (EU) 2017/1001 of the European Parliament and of the Council shall become the holder of a trade mark in the United Kingdom, consisting of the same sign, for the same goods or services;

   (b) the holder of a Community design registered and, where applicable, published following a deferral of publication in accordance with Council Regulation (EC) No 6/2002 shall become the holder of a registered design right in the United Kingdom for the same design;

   (c) the holder of a Community plant variety right granted pursuant to Council Regulation (EC) No 2100/94 shall become the holder of a plant variety right in the United Kingdom for the same plant variety.

2. Where a geographical indication, designation of origin or traditional speciality guaranteed within the meaning of Regulation (EU) No 1151/2012 of the European Parliament and of the Council, a geographical indication, designation of origin or traditional term for wine within the meaning of Regulation (EU) No 1308/2013 of the European Parliament and of the Council, a geographical indication within the meaning of Regulation (EC) No 110/2008 of the European Parliament and of the Council or a geographical indication within the meaning of Regulation (EU) No 251/2014 of the European Parliament and of the Council, is protected in the Union on the last day of the transition period by virtue of those Regulations, those persons who are entitled to use the geographical indication, the designation of origin, the traditional speciality guaranteed or the traditional term for wine concerned shall be entitled, as from the end of the transition period, without any re-examination, to use the geographical indication, the designation of origin, the traditional speciality guaranteed or the traditional term for wine concerned in the United Kingdom, which shall be granted at least the same level of protection under the law of the United Kingdom as under the following provisions of Union law:

   (a) points (i), (j) and (k) of Article 4(1) of Directive (EU) 2015/2436 of the European Parliament and of the Council; and

(b) in view of the geographical indication, designation of origin, traditional speciality guaranteed or traditional term for wine concerned, Article 13, Article 14(1), Article 24, Article 36(3), Articles 38 and 44 and point (b) of Article 45(1) of Regulation (EU) No 1151/2012; Article 90(1) of Regulation (EU) No 1306/2013 of the European Parliament and of the Council; Article 100(3), Article 102(1), Articles 103 and 113, and point (c)(x) of Article 157(1) of Regulation (EU) No 1308/2013; Article 62(3) and (4) of Commission Regulation (EC) No 607/2009; the first subparagraph of Article 15(3), Article 16 and Article 23(1) of Regulation (EC) No 110/2008 and, insofar as to the extent related to compliance with those provisions of that Regulation, Article 24(1) of that Regulation; or Article 19(1) and Article 20 of Regulation (EU) No 251/2014.

Where a geographical indication, designation of origin, traditional speciality guaranteed or traditional term for wine referred to in the first subparagraph ceases to be protected in the Union after the end of the transition period, the first subparagraph shall cease to apply in respect of that geographical indication, designation of origin, traditional speciality guaranteed or traditional term for wine.

The first subparagraph shall not apply where protection in the Union is derived from international agreements to which the Union is a party.

This paragraph shall apply unless and until an agreement as referred to in Article 184 that supersedes this paragraph enters into force or becomes applicable.

3. Notwithstanding paragraph 1, if an intellectual property right referred to in that paragraph is declared invalid or revoked, or, in the case of a Community plant variety right, is declared null and void or is cancelled, in the Union as the result of an administrative or judicial procedure which was ongoing on the last day of the transition period, the corresponding right in the United Kingdom shall also be declared invalid or revoked, or declared null and void, or be cancelled. The date of effect of the declaration or revocation or cancellation in the United Kingdom shall be the same as in the Union. By way of derogation from the first subparagraph, the United Kingdom shall not be obliged to declare invalid or to revoke the corresponding right in the United Kingdom where the grounds for the invalidity or revocation of the European Union trade mark or registered Community design do not apply in the United Kingdom.

4. A trade mark or registered design right which arises in the United Kingdom in accordance with point (a) or (b) of paragraph 1 shall have as its first renewal date the renewal date of the corresponding intellectual property right registered in accordance with Union law.

5. In respect of trade marks in the United Kingdom referred to in point (a) of paragraph 1 of this Article, the following shall apply:

(a) the trade mark shall enjoy the date of filing or the date of priority of the European Union trade mark and, where appropriate, the seniority of a trade mark of the United Kingdom claimed under Article 39 or 40 of Regulation (EU) 2017/1001;

(b) the trade mark shall not be liable to revocation on the ground that the corresponding European Union trade mark had not been put into genuine use in the territory of the United Kingdom before the end of the transition period;

(c) the owner of a European Union trade mark that has acquired a reputation in the Union shall be entitled to exercise in the United Kingdom rights equivalent to those provided for in point (c) of Article 9(2) of Regulation (EU) 2017/1001 and point (a) of Article 5(3) of Directive (EU) 2015/2436 in respect of the corresponding trade mark on the basis of the reputation acquired in the Union by the end of the transition period and thereafter the continuing reputation of that trade mark shall be based on the use of the mark in the United Kingdom.

6. In respect of registered design rights and plant variety rights in the United Kingdom referred to in points (b) and (c) of paragraph 1, the following shall apply:

(a) the term of protection under the law of the United Kingdom shall be at least equal to the remaining period of protection under Union law of the corresponding registered Community design or Community plant variety right;

(b) the date of filing or date of priority shall be that of the corresponding registered Community design or Community plant variety right.

...

Article 56   Continued protection in the United Kingdom of international registrations designating the Union

The United Kingdom shall take measures to ensure that natural or legal persons who have obtained protection before the end of the transition period for internationally registered trade marks or designs designating the Union pursuant to the Madrid system for the international registration of marks, or pursuant to the Hague system for the international deposit of industrial designs, enjoy protection in the United Kingdom for their trade marks or industrial designs in respect of those international registrations.

Article 57   Continued protection in the United Kingdom of unregistered Community designs

The holder of a right in relation to an unregistered Community design which arose before the end of the transition period in accordance with Regulation (EC) No 6/2002 shall in relation to that unregistered Community design *ipso iure* become the holder of an enforceable intellectual property right in the United Kingdom, under the law of the United Kingdom, that affords the same level of protection as that provided for in Regulation (EC) No 6/2002. The term of protection of that right under the law of the United Kingdom shall be at least equal to the remaining period of protection of the corresponding unregistered Community design under Article 11(1) of that Regulation.

Article 58   Continued protection of databases

1. The holder of a right in relation to a database in respect of the United Kingdom in accordance with Article 7 of Directive 96/9/EC of the European Parliament and of the Council which arose before the end of the transition period shall, in relation to that database, maintain an enforceable intellectual property right in the United Kingdom, under the law of the United Kingdom, that affords the same level of protection as that provided for in Directive 96/9/EC, provided that the holder of that right continues to comply with the requirements of Article 11 of that Directive. The term of protection of that right under the law of the United Kingdom shall be at least equal to the remaining period of protection under Article 10 of Directive 96/9/EC.

2. The following persons and undertakings shall be deemed to comply with the requirements of Article 11 of Directive 96/9/EC:

(a) United Kingdom nationals;

(b) natural persons with a habitual residence in the United Kingdom;

(c) undertakings established in the United Kingdom, provided that where such an undertaking has only its registered office in the United Kingdom, its operations are genuinely linked on an ongoing basis with the economy of the United Kingdom or of a Member State.

Article 59   Right of priority with respect to pending applications for European Union trade marks, Community designs and Community plant variety rights

1. Where a person has filed an application for a European Union trade mark or a Community design in accordance with Union law before the end of the transition period and where that application was accorded a date of filing, that person shall have, for the same trade mark in respect of goods or services which are identical with or contained within those for which the application has been filed in the Union or for the same design, the right to file an application in the United Kingdom within 9 months from the end of the transition period. An application made pursuant to this Article shall be deemed to have the same filing date and date of priority as the corresponding application filed in the Union and, where appropriate, the seniority of a trade mark of the United Kingdom claimed under Article 39 or 40 of Regulation (EU) 2017/1001.

2. Where a person has filed an application for a Community plant variety right in accordance with Union law before the end of the transition period, that person shall have, for the purpose of filing

an application for the same plant variety right in the United Kingdom, an ad hoc right of priority in the United Kingdom during a period of 6 months from the end of the transition period. The right of priority shall cause the date of priority of the application for the Community plant variety right to be deemed to be the date of application for a plant variety right in the United Kingdom for the purpose of determining distinctness, novelty and entitlement to the right.

Article 60   Pending applications for supplementary protection certificates in the United Kingdom

1. Regulations (EC) No 1610/96 and No 469/2009 of the European Parliament and of the Council, respectively, shall apply in respect of applications for supplementary protection certificates for plant protection products and for medicinal products, as well as to applications for the extension of the duration of such certificates, where such applications were submitted to an authority in the United Kingdom before the end of the transition period in cases where the administrative procedure for the grant of the certificate concerned or of the extension of its duration was ongoing at the end of the transition period.

2. Any certificate granted pursuant to paragraph 1 shall provide for the same level of protection as that provided for in Regulation (EC) No 1610/96 or Regulation (EC) No 469/2009.

Article 61   Exhaustion of rights

Intellectual property rights which were exhausted both in the Union and in the United Kingdom before the end of the transition period under the conditions provided for by Union law shall remain exhausted both in the Union and in the United Kingdom.

. . .

Political Declaration setting out the framework for the future relationship between the European Union and the United Kingdom

19 October 2019

. . .

Part I   Initial Provisions

. . .

VII. Intellectual Property

42. The Parties should provide for the protection and enforcement of intellectual property rights to stimulate innovation, creativity and economic activity, going beyond the standards of the WTO Agreement on Trade-Related Aspects of Intellectual Property Rights and the World Intellectual Property Organisation conventions where relevant.

43. This should preserve the Parties' current high levels of protection, inter alia, of certain rights under copyright law, such as the sui generis right on databases and the artists' resale right. Noting the protection afforded to existing geographical indications in the Withdrawal Agreement, the Parties should seek to put in place arrangements to provide appropriate protection for their geographical indications.

44. The Parties should maintain the freedom to establish their own regimes for the exhaustion of intellectual property rights.

45. The Parties should establish a mechanism for cooperation and exchange of information on intellectual property issues of mutual interest, such as respective approaches and processes regarding trademarks, designs and patents.

. . .

List of useful IP websites

IP Legislation

legislation.gov.uk	UK legislation
eur-lex.europa.eu/homepage.html	EU legislation
wipolex.wipo.int/en/main/legislation	Treaties and national laws of WIPO, WTO and UN Members
wto.org/english/tratop_e/trips_e/trips_e.htm	Materials related to the TRIPS Agreement
en.unesco.org	Materials related to Intangible Cultural Heritage
cbd.int	Materials related to Biological Diversity
upov.int/portal/	Materials related to the Protection of New Varieties of Plants

General IP Information

gov.uk/government/organisations/intellectual-property-office	UK Intellectual Property Office (trade marks, patents, copyright, designs)
euipo.europa.eu/	European Union Intellectual Property Office (trade marks, designs)
epo.org	European Patent Office
uspto.gov	US Patent and Trademark Office
wipo.int	World Intellectual Property Organization

Index